The complete book of baby names

The Most Names, Most Lists, Most Help to Find the Best Name

* More Names *AND* Richer Definitions
* The Most (600+) Creative Lists to Inspire You
* The Most Idea-Sparking Celebrity Baby Names
* The Most Popular—and Unique—Names
* The Newest Trends, Including What Makes the Perfect Name!

Lesley Bolton

SOURCEBOOKS, INC.®
NAPERVILLE, ILLINOIS

Cover and internal design © 2006, 2009 by Sourcebooks, Inc.
Cover Design by Dawn Pope
Cover photo © ivanchenko/istockphoto.com

Sourcebooks and the colophon are registered trademarks of Sourcebooks, Inc.

Published by Sourcebooks, Inc.
P.O. Box 4410, Naperville, Illinois 60567-4410
(630) 961-3900
Fax: (630) 961-2168
www.sourcebooks.com

Library of Congress Cataloging-in-Publication Data

Bolton, Lesley.
  Complete book of baby names / Lesley Bolton.
      p. cm.
  1. Names, Personal--Dictionaries. 2. Names, Personal--United States--Dictionaries. I. Title.

CS2377.B653 2006
929.4'403--dc22

2006014064

Printed and bound in the United States of America.
DR 10 9 8 7

Contents

Introduction

One of the first questions you will be asked by those who learn of your pregnancy is "Have you picked out a name?"—second only to "Are you having a boy or girl?" While this may be endearing at first, and somewhat annoying later, it only goes to show that there is an importance placed on names. As if preparing for the arrival of a baby isn't stressful enough, you are now under the added pressure of giving your child a name that he or she will have to live with for the rest of his or her life—or at least until he or she is old enough to legally change it. Add to that the never-ending suggestions from well-meaning family and friends—and possibly a few arguments with your partner—and baby-naming can become quite the daunting task! But it doesn't have to be. Believe it or not, you can actually have fun with the baby-naming process.

Yes, names influence first impressions. Yes, names sometimes spawn not-so-flattering nicknames that can follow a person all the way through retirement. Yes, names affect children's self-esteem. Yes, names are often obligatory ties to family. And yes, there are thousands to choose from. But what you must keep in mind is that this decision is yours. Not society's. Not your family's. Not your friends'. And certainly not strangers'. If you choose a name you take great pride in, your child will be proud of his or her name as well.

One of the biggest stressors surrounding the baby-naming process is the input you are guaranteed to receive from family members. Everyone from parents to aunts to good friends of the family will have an opinion that they're not afraid to share. And while you might want to honor your family by using one of their names (either as a first name, middle name, or both), there are a few factors you should think about before doing so, which will be outlined in this book. And you thought naming the baby would be the easy part!

If you want the advice of others—terrific. You are certainly going to get it. If, however, you don't want the added pressure of having to defend a name you choose or finding polite excuses not to name your daughter after Great Aunt Gertie, then keep your thoughts to yourself. Since more and more couples want to know the baby's sex beforehand these days, the element of surprise has been taken away from family and friends. Instead, many couples choose to keep their baby's name a secret, which is a good way to work the surprise back into the event. Another plus is that it allows you to avoid negative feedback from others. Once Grandma gazes upon those newbie eyes for the first time, she won't even remember she disapproved of the name you chose, let alone why. However, even if you do choose to keep the name a secret, open your mind to suggestions from others. Someone just might throw that perfect name your way.

Some of the most important decisions you make for your child take place before birth, including choosing a name. While it might seem intimidating at first, once you begin to think of it as a creative process, you'll be able to let your imagination go and have fun.

Of course, choosing a name requires some forethought—and therefore work—on your part. Even if you've had a name picked out since you were six years old, it is still a good idea to look around. Your child might not be all too appreciative of the fact that ten baby dolls (and possibly several pets) before her carried the same name. Besides, tastes change. Just as the thought of eating broccoli turned your stomach when you were a child and now it's your favorite vegetable, that name you had chosen so long ago may now leave a bad taste in your mouth.

Parents find several different ways to begin the baby-naming process. To some, it is important to incorporate a family name, so this becomes their starting point. To others, religion is a major factor in choosing a name. Some prefer to seek out a meaning or virtue, while others simply want a name that sounds good. What it all boils down to is what is important to you. So, before you begin scouring these pages, making endless lists, and seeking the advice of others, be sure to determine what it is that you want from a name.

The following chapters offer advice, tips, and suggestions to help you maneuver the baby-naming maze, and hopefully have a little fun along the way. Choosing a name is an important and serious task, but it doesn't have to be a sour and dreaded experience. Make up games to accompany the decision-making process, such as trying out a new name each week. If you already have some favorites in mind, there's no reason why you have to go about your daily tasks referring to your unborn child as It, Baby, or Fetus. Try out those you are considering and see if any stick. (Of course, if you have decided to keep the name a secret, be careful not to try out the names in public; reserve this as an at-home game only.) Follow a few simple guidelines, keep your mind open, save your humorous and cutesy titles for your pets, and your baby will have a name he or she is proud to hear, say, and write.

Above all, remember that the decision is yours.

Chapter 1

baby-naming history

The origin of baby-naming is not known. However, oral history (before even written history) records the use of names to identify individuals, so we can guess that it dates back quite a while. Many parents are moving beyond the sound of a name to find out its meaning and background. Delving into the history of a name is a good way to embrace it on an intimate level. Plus, as your child grows older, you can relate the stories and history behind the name, letting your son or daughter know how special of a gift you have bestowed upon him or her. Some parents are interested in researching specific ethnicities or cultures, tracing their own families back to the roots and choosing names that had meaning for their ancestors. This is a great way to tie in the tradition of the family and give your child a meaningful name.

Names themselves have historically been most influenced by religion and/or myth and legend. For instance, the rise in Christianity brought about the rise in popularity of biblical names, and as Christianity spread throughout the world, so too did those names. Many Norse names are based on their mythology, such as Thorald, which means follower of Thor. Speaking of the Norse, conquering countries spread their uses of names to those places they invaded. For instance, with the Norse invasion and Cromwellian colonization came the emergence of Anglo names such as Robert into Ireland. Of course, we could delve into each country's history of baby names but as we are in America, it might interest you most to learn the history of American baby names.

Early Beginnings

America is rightly called the melting pot, as we have a variety of cultures and ethnicities mixed into our history. With these different cultures and ethnicities came different names for children, adding flavor to the stock of Anglo-Saxon names already established. But let's start at the beginning.

The earliest settlers brought names such as John, William, Richard, Edward, Thomas, Elizabeth, Sarah, and Mary. These, of course, are the traditional boys' and girls' names we all know and love. They are also still popular, proving that we aren't as far removed from these early settlers as we think—at least not in the way of baby names, anyway.

Religion was an important part of these settlers' lives, and therefore, biblical names became the most popular source for baby names. Just as today, many parents were concerned about the associations tagged onto their children's names, and choosing names from the Bible of those who were portrayed as estimable was a way to ensure, hopefully, their children grew to be good and God-fearing adults. The Puritans also chose redeeming qualities they wanted their children to uphold and used these for names. For instance, there were several instances of Thankful, Hopewell, Remember, and Experience showing up in the birth records. And of course we have the virtue names to thank the Puritans for: Honor, Charity, Purity, Faith, and Reverence, for example.

The homeland was also important to the settlers, and many kept and passed along their British names. The same held true with the flood of European immigrants to America. This brought variety and spice to the traditional British, biblical, and Puritan names. Suddenly we had Patricks, Andrews, Alexanders, Patricias, and Veronicas running around.

Following the Revolutionary War, surnames emerged as the newest baby-naming popularity trend for boys. (Sound like a familiar trend?) Thus, names such as Grant, Otis, Franklin, and Winthrop were added to the mix. For girls, the newest thing was using nicknames as the standard first name. For instance, Abby replaced Abigail, and Betsy/Betty replaced Elizabeth.

From the Nineteenth to the Twentieth Century

In the nineteenth century, parents began looking to literature for their inspiration. Classic novels, poems, and legends, from Homer to Shakespeare, were ripe for giving birth to new and exciting baby names. Suddenly names had romantic, adventurous, or heroic stories behind them. Girls moved from Elizabeth and Mary to Rosalind and Gwendolyn. Boys moved from William and John to Douglas and Roland. These names were much more elegant and elaborate, and because there were so many of them, this became the most colorful variety of names in the pool so far. But wait, there's more to come.

Oh yes, we can't forget the nature names that also emerged during this time. The beauty of nature became inspiration in itself. Everything from flowers to trees to stones to gems was fair game. Thus, the Opals, Roses, Myrtles, and Violets of the world were born.

In the early twentieth century, more and more parents were deciding that while traditional names were nice, so also were the distinguishing names that would set their children apart from the others. The top ten lists of girls' names began to welcome newcomers (though Mary would still reign), such as Mildred, Betty, Frances, and Nancy. Also popular were variations of the traditional names. For instance, Marie and Maria were becoming just as popular as Mary (well, almost). The boys' names were a little slower on the take, however. John, William, James, George, and Robert hadn't yet learned to let go of their top spots.

Following World War II, America was home to numerous celebrations and good feeling—and don't forget the baby boom. With so many new additions to families arriving on the scene, it only made sense that more and more names would be added to the favored lists for boys and girls.

With the popularity of television in the 1950s also came the trend of naming children for celebrities and television characters. This would help the standard boys' names list shake things up a bit and add a little more variety. Though the names added were historically sound, such as Joshua, they had been sitting on the bench for quite some time.

The most drastic shaking of the boys' names list though came during the 1960s. Men and women were rebelling against the traditional ways and names were no exception. The concept of inventing names suddenly found favor with parents; and for those who weren't quite ready to move entirely to the wild side, spelling variations of traditional names seemed to suit their desires. Unisex names also made their mark during this period of free love. Speaking of free love, we must give kudos to the hippies who brought nature names back to the spotlight.

The seventies, in comparison, seemed to settle down a bit and looked to tradition for names. Again, we visited the Bible and the early settlers for inspiration. But we were also visiting foreign names for inspiration, such as French and Irish. Also during this time, the girls' names were split into categories with frilly and lacy names on one end of the spectrum and unisex names on the other end. The eighties followed closely with the roots-reaching ideals.

Family was important at the end of the century. Parents were searching family trees and distant relatives for names. The use of surnames was regurgitated, and parents dove into different ethnicities to give their children different but historically sound names.

The Twenty-First Century and Beyond

This takes us to the here and now. And we all know what is hip: everything. Just look at some of the names celebrities are giving their children—and they get away with it! We are in the day of anything goes. Parents these days have a plethora of names to choose from. Feeling nostalgic? Choose a traditional name. Feeling worldly? Choose a foreign name. Feeling outdoorsy? Choose a nature name. Feeling ambiguous? Choose a unisex name. In the next chapter, we will focus on some of the popular baby-naming trends of today.

African American Names

African Americans' baby-naming trends and traditions are distinct from white Americans'. In all of America, it is this group that can stand tall and claim uniqueness. African American parents are much more creative with their children's names than are white Americans, and they tend to be prolific with inventing names. Let's take a look at a brief history of African American baby-naming.

When the first Africans came to America as slaves, their owners typically made them shed their African names and adopt new names. Let's face it, the white slave owners were afraid of the African culture, and renaming their slaves made them feel more comfortable. These names came from a variety of sources, and it was unusual to have many slaves on the same plantation with the same name. One popular source for names was mythology. Names such as Sappho, Dido, Hercules, and Titus were given to the slaves. These names were far enough removed from the white culture that there was little worry over a slave and a white having the same name. Some slave owners handed out place names or days of the week, and some even allowed the slaves to keep their African names, though this was but a small percentage.

As time went on and generations had been established within slave families, slaves were allowed to name their own children. As was custom in Africa, many parents chose to name their children for other members of the family, though more so for grandparents than parents. Also during this time, many slaves began converting to Christianity, which gave birth to the popularity of biblical and virtue names among the slaves. This created an overlap with white names, and for quite some time, both blacks and whites held the same or similar names, with one exception: one trend among the slaves' names was to take the nickname version of those names the whites were using. This not only set them slightly apart but also gave them a position of subordination, taking on names that children would adopt.

Once the slaves were freed, most would drop any name that had a connection with slavery and instead adopt a new name of their choice, again mostly biblical names. Baby-naming trends for blacks and whites seemed to go hand in hand until the individualism movement of the 1960s. During this time, parents looked to their roots in Africa and chose many native names for their children. They also began a new trend of inventing names, using the root of an African name and putting their own spin on it. Instead of dying off and then later re-emerging as do most trends, this trend held strong and flourished even more, making its way into the baby-naming world of today.

African Americans are known for the unique names they give their children. Whereas white Americans will sometimes invent names but typically stay on the conservative end, African Americans use all of their creative skills to come up with names that embody style, meaning, tradition, and beauty. The following is but a small sample of some African American names.

Girls		Boys	
Alondra	Kalinda	Antwon	Jamel
Camika	Keisha	Ashante	Juwan
Chantal	Lateisha	Darnell	Keshawn
Cherise	Markeesha	Dashawn	Malik
Dashay	Nakari	Denzel	Montel
Desiree	Raisha	Germaine	Nile
Imani	Rashanda	Gervaise	Rashaun
Jada	Samisha	Imari	Shaquille
Jaleesa	Shaniqua	Jahan	Tariq
Jameeka	Tamika	Jaleel	Tyrell
Jayla	Zeleka	Jamar	Tyrone

Jewish Names

Jewish parents are no exception in following the trend of looking to one's roots for inspiration in choosing a baby name. Many Jewish parents are now searching the Old Testament and researching names given in Israel. But it has been a large circle to come back to this.

While many Jews who immigrated to America preserved their own names, they opted to give their children Anglo names to help them better fit in with mainstream society. In holding to a vein of the tradition of naming a child for a relative, parents would use the first initial of the chosen relative as the first initial of their new child's Anglo name.

Some parents of today choose to give their children two names, one a Jewish name and the other a secular name. Each of these names will begin with the same letter. For instance, a child's Jewish name might be Barak, and his secular name Blake. Thus, the child would go by his secular name in the secular world and his Jewish name for religious purposes and legal documents.

In Jewish tradition, the naming of a child is a very important affair. Whereas many parents will name their child based on sound alone, Jewish parents look to the meaning as top priority. They believe that the child's name will directly impact his or her future and soul. In other words, if you decide to give your child a Jewish name, it would be best to do your research, not just close your eyes and pick a name from the Old Testament—you could ultimately bring shame to your child. Keep in mind though that although the actual meaning of the name is important, so are the character traits of the relative the child may be named for.

Baby-naming is a joyous and celebrated affair for Jewish parents and children. The naming ceremony for a boy is typically made part of the circumcision rite. Because girls obviously do not have this occasion to celebrate, parents often hold their own naming ceremony. This is a time not only to celebrate the child's birth and name but also to reflect upon ancestors and to share any stories and accolades of character of the namesake if the child is named for a relative.

As stated previously, many parents turn to the Old Testament to find names; therefore many mainstream names are also popular for Jewish children. The following lists are a few of the more unusual names not found often in mainstream America.

Girls		*Boys*	
Adaya	Mahalah	Abiel	Maluch
Avivah	Miryam	Amit	Noam
Bithia	Nediva	Asael	Oran
Chaya	Nissa	Boaz	Raviv
Dorit	Ophira	Chaim	Selig
Elula	Penina	Dovev	Shaviv
Gitel	Rivka	Elazar	Talmai
Idra	Shifra	Gaal	Uziah
Keturah	Tavora	Gilead	Yamin
Lilit	Yafa	Idan	Yosha
Livya	Zemorah	Itzak	Zebedee

Muslim Names

Islam is another prevalent religion in the United States. Particularly among African Americans, this religion is rapidly spreading. As evidenced by the spread of Christianity and the subsequent spread of names favored by that religion, the spread of Islam is likely to also increase the spread of Muslim or Arabic names. As the prophet Muhammad is a central figure of Islam, many parents choose one of hundreds of variants of his name in honor of him. Also becoming popular are several invented names using the Arabic root name. The following is a short list of Muslim/Arabic names.

Girls		*Boys*	
Aisha	Raja	Abdul	Jamal
Amina	Saba	Ahmad	Kadar
Aziza	Saliha	Akbar	Karim
Fatima	Samira	Aziz	Mehmet
Hamida	Shadiya	Farid	Omar
Iamar	Tabina	Hakeem	Rashid
Jamila	Tamasha	Hamal	Sadik
Kamilah	Ulima	Hanif	Tahir
Nabila	Yamina	Husain	Yazid
Oma	Zahira	Jafar	

Your Child Will Create History

As you can see, names have a vast history, full of meaning, tradition, and creativity. Because names provide a sense of identity as well as a source of pride, naming your child isn't a task to be taken lightly. If names didn't mean anything to our society, we would just go around addressing each other with a grunt. A name can be one of the greatest gifts you will ever give your child—aside from life itself, that is.

You will find that while you choose the name for your son or daughter, he or she will grow into it and become it. No longer will the name simply embody the meaning its root has; it will instead take on a greater meaning and bigger associations, reflecting all the character traits your child will have. Your daughter Bridget may very well be a "strong and protective woman," but she may also be the most beautiful and caring woman you have ever known. In which case, the original meaning will expand and encompass all that is your daughter.

Are you ready to take the baby-naming journey?

Chapter 2

in vogue: modern naming trends

Each generation has a few names that seem to be wildly popular. Some of these names fall out of fashion in the next generation, only to re-emerge a generation or two later as a retro, trendy name. Some of these names seem to be permanent classics. The list of sources for baby names is endless. People draw inspiration from everything and everyone in their environment—family, history, books, television, nature, mythology, and maps, to name a few. Certain sources seem to be more fertile ground for picking names at certain times, though.

Let's look at some of the most popular names in past generations, according to the Social Security Administration. In the 1940s, the five most popular boys' names were James, Robert, John, William, and Richard; for girls, the list was comprised of Mary, Linda, Barbara, Patricia, and Carol. By the 1960s, for boys, the most popular names were Michael, David, John, James, and Robert; for girls, Lisa, Mary, Karen, Susan, and Kimberly. The 1980s had Michael, Christopher, Matthew, Joshua, and David for boys, and Jessica, Jennifer, Amanda, Ashley, and Sarah for girls. The year 2000 saw Jacob, Michael, Matthew, Joshua, and Christopher claim the honors for boys, and Emily, Hannah, Madison, Ashley, and Sarah for girls. The most popular names for 2009 were Jacob, Ethan, Michael, Alexander, and William for boys, and Isabella, Emma, Olivia, Sophie, and Ava for girls.

As you can see, in the past, boys' names were far less susceptible to drastic changes in trends than girls' names. However, it appears that now boys' names are catching up to girls in terms of trendiness.

What influences trends in naming? As with almost every aspect of life in the information age, people are exposed to countless sources every day. A unique aspect of the modern age is the exposure to names and cultures from all over the world. Popular culture, through the media of Internet, television, music, movies, and books, influences the popularity of certain names at certain times. For example, prior to the movie *Splash*, with Darryl Hannah, the name Madison was virtually nonexistent as a girl's first name. After this movie, Madison started gracing birth certificates of American female babies, and rose in popularity from there, reaching the number-three spot in popularity in 2000. Even more recently, the show *Friends* popularized the name Emma, which made it to number two in 2004. People now watch to see what names celebrities will give their offspring, leaving us to wonder if Gwyneth Paltrow's Apple or Gwen Stefani's Zuma will catch on. Names such as Lexus, Armani, and Destiny are also starting to show up more and more.

Since a name is so integral to a person's identity, and is a badge one will be stuck with for life, people put a lot of thought into naming their children. They want the name to convey something about themselves, whether it is their creativity, their trendiness, or their pride in their family honor. People want their children to have unique and interesting names. After all, this is a new member of and ambassador for the family. So where are modern parents going for inspiration? What types of names are modern American babies touting? In the remainder of this chapter, we will look at the most popular trends in naming babies in America.

Family History

One of the most common places expecting parents look to find names is within their own family history. They want to instill in their children a sense of the family's past and the pride of belonging. Often, a maternal ancestor's family name (for example, the baby's own mother, or the father's mother) is incorporated into the child's given name, either first or middle. This trend first arose within the aristocracy and eventually spread to all classes. At first, the practice of including the mother's name was primarily used with male children. However, by the 1900s the practice was beginning to spread to females as well. With the rise of the women's movement in recent times, more attention is being given to the mother's family history than ever before. And the fact that many famous people carry their mother's name as a first or second name only serves to help this trend.

The trend to use traditional last names as first names has expanded. Now, many people use popular surnames as given names when there is little or no connection to the family by that name. Figures in history often provide first names for children generations later, such as presidents Washington, Jefferson, and Kennedy, and religious reformers Nelson, Luther, and Wesley.

Furthermore, a trend in which English last names derived from trade occupations are used as first names has grown in the United States; some of the more popular ones are Taylor, Tyler, Hunter, Spencer, Tanner, Sawyer, Walker, and Carter. Most of these names today are used for either male or female children. Another popular source is surnames derived from English place names. During the development of the first name/last name system, people often acquired their surname from their place of origin; for example, Thomas of Ainsley would become Thomas Ainsley. Many of these place names have become common as first names, such as Ainsley, Ashley, Lesley, Bailey, and Hadley. These names are used more often for female children, perhaps because the *ey* sound at the end sounds more like a traditional female name to English speakers.

Surnames of different ethnic groups, particularly Celtic, are also becoming increasingly popular. Examples from Ireland include Dillon, Kelly, Ryan, and Shannon. From Wales, the name Rhys and its variations are making their way into mainstream American names. Scottish family names have long been popular as first names; for example, Grant, Mackenzie, Mckinley, Cameron, and surnames derived from place names such as Logan, Douglas, and Blair. Today, many of these names could be for either girls or boys, although the Scottish names have traditionally been more masculine.

Many surnames were originally patronymics—derived from the father's first name. In English, this usually manifests as something-son. For example,

Leif Eriksson was the son of Erik. Many names of patronymic origin are becoming popular as first names, whether or not the child's family has any connection; examples include Jackson, Dawson, Addison, and Emerson. They can be used for either sex, although certain ones are more popular for males than females, and vice versa.

Unisex Names

The rise in popularity of using traditional surnames as first names has aided in the erosion of the line of demarcation between male and female names and given rise to the trend of unisex names. There have always been a few names that could be either for male or female children; however, in recent times, this number has greatly increased both through the addition of new names and the desexing of certain common names. As previously mentioned, many names derived from surnames could be either masculine or feminine (Taylor, Ashley, Bailey, Kelly). Many traditional first names also have a unisex nature and are being increasingly used for boys and girls; for example, Jordan, Morgan, and Riley. Many of the unisex names tend to be more recent first-name innovations. Traditional masculine and feminine names often are highly resistant to such change. Names such as John, Matthew, Robert, and William are not likely to surface with female children, nor are Sarah, Amanda, Mary, Barbara, etc., likely to appear on a male child's birth certificate. However, there are names that have traditionally been used both for male and female children such as Francis, Robin, Terry, Tracy, and Sydney, although these are often distinguished by different spellings. Several unisex names have been increasing in popularity, for example Adrian, Ashton, Evan, Mallory, Peyton, Reagan, Reese, Rory, Sage, Tory, and Zane. Reasons cited for choosing a unisex name, apart from personal preference for a certain name or family reasons, are to avoid having to come up with male and female choices, and the belief that it aids in preventing sexual stereotyping. However, some experts warn that it is often more acceptable for a girl to have a masculine-sounding name than for a boy to have a feminine-sounding name. Hence, unisex names in practice are more often given to girls than to boys.

The Classics

Some names seem to be perennial favorites. Trends in boys' names in particular tend to favor classic names. Michael, James, Robert, and David are names that seem to retain their popularity across generations. However, the girls' names category has its staples as well; Elizabeth, Mary (and its variants), and Sarah can often be found consistently near the top ten of the popular-names list. These are names that do not seem to take on the dated quality many popular names do. One cannot look at the name Elizabeth and be able to guess with assurance at which generation the woman belongs to, unlike a Bertha or a Madison. This is even more often true of boys' names. Some researchers suggest the common practice of naming boys after their fathers slows the rate of change in boys' names. Although recently, newer, trendier names have been working their way onto the boys' names charts; for example, Logan and Jayden were in a recent top twenty. Researchers also cite the greater acceptance of trendiness in naming girls. The classics seem to withstand the pressure to change.

While the classics maintain their hold on the boys' names charts, they are also making a comeback for girls. Instead of just maintaining a respectable position in the top twenty or fifty consistently, some of the names have started to climb the charts. In 2008, Emma made it to number one; Ella and Grace also made the list. Note that according to the Social Security Administration, in 1880, Emma was number three, Grace number nineteen, and Ella number thirteen. For boys, in 1880, John, William, and James comprised the top three. All three names are still in the top thirty.

Many parents opt for classic names out of fear of giving their child a name that will not stand the test of time, a name that might sound "silly" for an adult or on a diploma, or simply to avoid trendiness. Some parents indicate that the name sounds more prestigious or serious. Often a classic name has significance within the family.

Parents need not fear: choosing a classic name need not force them to abandon all creativity and individuality. Many parents are resorting to unusual spellings or non-English variants of classic names; for example, Mattias (Swedish version of Matthew), Alain (French for Allen), Phillippe, etc., for boys, and for girls Emilie, Nathalie, Laure, and Anni.

The Generation Gap

Quite often, names that are popular in one generation fall out of fashion in the next. For example, in the 1930s, names like Betty, Dorothy, and Dolores were very popular for girls, and Harold, Walter, and Frank were popular for boys. By the next generation, these names were not anywhere near the top of the popular lists. Unlike classic names, they do not maintain their position but fall out altogether, at least for a while. It's often been noted that fashions come back, often after skipping a generation. The same trend appears to hold for baby names. Parents shun trendy names from their parents' generation (Donna, Cynthia, Roger, and Kevin are out) but gravitate toward their grandparents' generation (Edith, Agnes, Charles, and Edward are in). Some researchers suggest this has to do with people associating names of their parents' generation with being "old" and thus unsuitable for a baby. Names from the generations preceding their parents' are not as closely connected to age for them. Because these names are from the past and have fallen out of fashion, to many parents they have a unique ring to them. They have the benefit of being established names (important for people who have a phobia of giving their child a "trendy" but fleetingly fashionable name) but a sort of retro newness as well, so that their child will not be one of five little Ediths or Edwards in their classes. Also, the resurgence in popularity of these names allows many parents to name their children after beloved or admired older relatives and friends without fear of their child having such an unusual name that he or she becomes a target for ridicule.

Some of the more popular old-fashioned names making a comeback for girls are Ada, Alice, Amelia, Beatrice, Evelyn, Evie, Greta, Lena, Lillian, and Nora; for boys, Albert, Arthur, Edgar, Ernest, Oscar, Reginald, Stanley, and Winston.

Ethnic Names

In this era of globalization, baby-names trends are not immune to worldwide influence. Many parents are selecting names that were previously deemed "ethnic," meaning non-mainstream. While many parents choose to honor their roots by selecting a name from their own ethnic background, it appears that having a familial connection to an ethnicity is not a prerequisite for choosing a name from that ethnicity. This is actually not a brand-new trend; it has happened before that one ethnicity's names take on a mainstream popularity for a period of time. For instance, names of Hispanic origin became popular in the sixties, leading to the rise in popularity of names like Juanita among non-Hispanics. However, never before has the average American parent had access to such a wide variety of names. Since there are so many different cultures and ethnicities, it would be impossible in a chapter to discuss all of them, so we will just focus on a few sources which appear to be currently contributing the most names to the baby-name pool. As with most trends, in the future, it may shift and a new source will take precedence.

Celtic Names

Americans have long held a fascination with Celtic culture. Recently, this interest has grown in magnitude and strength, helped along by the rising popularity of Celtic literature, music, and dance, and the fact that so many Americans trace their roots back to the Celtic strongholds of Wales, England, Ireland, and Scotland. Many of these names have grown in popularity so much that they have lost the slightly odd, new feeling many names from other countries have. Many new Celtic names have been increasingly breaking into the ranks of common American baby names.

From Ireland, some of the more popular girls' names are Aisling, Briana, Ciara, Caoimhe, Fiona, Moira, Niamh, Shannon, and Siobhan; for the boys, Aidan, Colin, Connor, Kyan, Murray, Quinn, and Teagan.

Scotland has contributed many names from last names, but Scottish first names are also popular choices for American parents. Scottish boys' names include Alasdair, Blair, Calum, Fraser, Euan, Hamish, Lauchlan, and

Malcolm. Scottish girls' names include Amie, Abbie, Isla, Sconaid, Tam, Morag, Lorna, Aileen, and Edme.

Wales is also a prominent source for Celtic names today. Some increasingly popular Welsh names are Ioan, Rhys, Dafydd (David), Dewey, Gareth, Quinn, and Maddock for boys, and Meredith, Guinevere, Rhonwen, Rhiannon, Catrin, Bryn, Freya, Phoebe, and Carys for girls.

Other Celtic peoples, such as the Bretons and Cornish, also contribute to the Celtic naming trend but not yet on the scale that the others do.

British Names

One can argue that Britain and United States draw from a nearly similar name pool. However, certain names are used in each country that are rarely used in the other. With the success of many British authors, notably J.K. Rowling (*Harry Potter*) and Helen Fielding (*Bridget Jones*), and British films and television programs in the United States, some of these uniquely British names have been working their way into American popular consciousness and thus into baby-naming trends as well. This is true particularly for girls, with names like Poppy, Gemma, Nicola, Maisie, Pippa, and Tamzin appearing in the United States. Names for boys that are considered traditionally British like Ian, Winston, Cedric, Nigel, and Clive are also beginning to appear.

African Names

Obviously, Africa is a continent of many nations and peoples and accordingly a source of great variety of names and naming customs. In recent times, many Americans of African descent have looked to Africa for names that represent their history and culture and represent their pride therein. However, African names have also been shown to appeal to a broader spectrum of the public. There is a wide variety of sources for traditional African names, including information about the origin and meanings. Since there are so many distinct cultures and peoples in Africa, we will just list a few of the more well-known names in America: for boys, Abdul, Farid, Maalik, Tahir, and Tan; for girls, Baina, Kali, Malia, Radhi, and Zaina.

Uniquely American

Americans are a creative people, not bound by tradition and rules. These qualities are expressed in naming as well. Early Americans happily used adjectives describing desired qualities for their children, including Patience, Temperance, Makepeace, and Prudence. Many of these names are making a comeback, along with Hope, Faith, Joy, and Peace. Many popular American names come from American Indian names, words, and tribes (Cheyenne, Dakota, Cherokee). However, parents seeking to name their children one of these names should do their research. There is a lot of folklore surrounding names that is inaccurate, and some names may have special status for American Indians, and naming a child with that name may be disrespectful.

Other World Sources

Since the American people are composed of people from many different countries, we can expect a wide variety of names to appear on the landscape, many of which will have broad appeal. Names from countries like France (Yves and Etienne for boys; Pascale and Amelie for girls), Germany, and Italy have also increased in popularity. Middle Eastern, Indian, Chinese, Japanese, and other countries and cultures are contributing names on an ever-increasing basis due to the "shrinking globe." Hispanic names, some of which are already quite common, are also increasing in frequency of use. Russian names such as Natasha, Sasha, Ludmila, and Nadia are being used. The names Misha and Nikita are being given as names for female children, even though in Russian they are traditionally male names (Misha being a diminutive for Mikhail).

For parents who are looking into ethnic names, there are numerous websites and books that cover each country or region and give meanings and origins of the names as well. It is particularly important for parents who have little or no background with a certain country or group to look into the meanings and associations with certain names.

For example, the name Tristan (popularized by Brad Pitt in *Legends of the Fall*) actually comes from the French word *triste* meaning "sad," and Mallory means "unlucky." Many parents would not wish to have their children stuck with names with such dubious meanings.

Place Names

Maps have long provided inspiration in the naming of children, whether because the locale had a particular significance to the parents, or just because they liked the way it sounded. Many children share their names with cities, states, countries, and regions.

Celebrities appear to be spearheading the revival of this trend; Madonna named her daughter Lourdes; David Beckham named his son Brooklyn; and then there is Paris Hilton. Names like China and India have been around for a while. Some state names have become quite common, like Virginia, Georgia, and Carolina. Other states are now starting to appear on birth certificates, like Dakota, Indiana, and Montana. Cities are also inspiring parents: Savannah, Austin, Houston, Atlanta, and Phoenix. Even ancient lands and cities, such as Troy and Atlantis, are popular names. Country names often used include Israel, Cuba, Kenya, and Jordan. Many of these names are considered unisex; some are primarily one or the other depending on whether the sound of the name is more feminine or masculine to the parents.

Biblical Names

The Bible is and always has been perhaps the most prolific source for baby names in the United States. This is particularly true of boys' names. Many staples of American naming are taken directly from the Bible (Matthew, Mark, Luke, John, Peter, James, Mary, Deborah, Anne, Rachel, Rebecca, and Sarah, to name a few). However, a recent trend in American naming is to find less well-known or even obscure names from the Bible, names like Ezra, Elijah, Amos, Havilah, Naomi, and Dinah. Some of these names have been popular in the past and then dropped out of fashion. The Bible has a wealth of names. These names appeal particularly to parents who wish to convey a message with a name; for example, Hosea means savior or safety, and Neri means my light.

Many names from the Bible are so commonly used people do not really think of them as from the Bible. However, many of the more obscure names may sound quite foreign. If a child is given such a name, they may often be asked the meaning of the name and how to spell it.

Given that the Bible is well-known throughout much of the world, biblical names have been adapted into many languages. As a result, for many of these names there are countless variations and spellings. Parents looking for a unique name often find one amongst them.

Mythological Names

Mythology has always been a source of names for children in America. This is particularly true of Greek and Roman mythological figures and places. These names are associated with certain characteristics; for example, Athena/Minerva was the goddess of wisdom. Other popular names from Greek and Roman mythology that are becoming popular are Apollo, Evander, Odysseus, Hector, Callista, Delia, and Medea.

Recent trends have also seen a rise in names from other world mythologies, including Norse, Indian, German, and Celtic. Parents again are cautioned to do their research. Some of the stories surrounding these mythological characters are less than pleasant (for example, Medea kills her own children to punish Jason).

Mother Nature

Always a source of inspiration, Mother Nature contributes many names to children around the world. Recent trends have shown an increase in popularity of these names. Popular girls' names from flowers and plants include Ivy, Lily, Rose (and variations), and Willow (also sometimes used as a boys' name). Studies show that parents want girls' names to confirm femininity while reflecting individuality whereas boys' names tend to be chosen to express tones of individuality and strength. Popular boys' names include River, Stone, and Lake. Seasons such as spring and summer were used for girls' names in the seventies, but now Winters and Autumns are beginning to appear.

Once a very common source of girls' names, precious stones and minerals are making a comeback as well, sometimes even for boys' names, like Jade and Diamond. Names like Opal, Pearl, and Ruby may sound old-fashioned, but as previously discussed, these trends tend to move in cycles. The heavens are not exempt from this trend; names like Stella, meaning "star," are also beginning to reappear.

Hyphenated First Names

Many people do not have a distinct first and middle name but two first names. The trend of hyphenating two first names, particularly for girls, actually caught on in the eighties but not to a great extent (Tracy-Anne, Mary-Elizabeth). Now, this trend is re-emerging on the American naming scene, thanks in part to the popularity of such Hollywood stars as Mary-Kate Olsen.

There are many reasons parents choose to hyphenate a first name. By hyphenating, parents do not have to choose between two names which perhaps have special significance, or it can be a compromise between two favored names (one child, two favorite aunts or uncles). Either way, the hyphenated first name is a way of assuring the names are said together, not the first given prominence and actual usage and the second being relegated to formal use. Children with hyphenated first names may or may not also have a middle name, depending on parental preference.

Created Names

Do-it-yourself is a huge industry in America today. This trend also appears to influence naming. Many people are now creating their own names. Perhaps they fear their child's name will lack originality if they go the traditional route of naming, or maybe they just like the way a particular sound combination sounds. Sometimes parents combine two traditional names by taking parts from each. This is a creative way to come up with a unique name. However, parents are again cautioned to do their research. This sound combination may be a word in another language and may carry a meaning the new parents do not necessarily wish to have attached to their child. Also, bear in mind the child will have this name for a lifetime (well, in theory, anyway). What sounds cute for a newborn or toddler may not sound quite so distinguished at a college graduation ceremony.

Spelling Variation

One of the hottest trends in naming is to create unique spellings. This is often done by changing *y* to *i* or *ee* (Amy, Amee, Ami) or doubling a consonant or even slightly changing the sound (Zara to Zarai) or with many names ending in *a*, adding an *h* (Zara to Zarah). While changing the spelling often creates a name that is unique-looking and maybe even pretty to look at, parents must remember that the child will probably have to spend the rest of his or her life spelling out his or her name. Some children may like this aspect of their given name, whereas others may find it a bit of a hassle.

Whether you want your child's name to be in keeping with the latest fashion or you want your child's name to be anti-trendy, it is important to know what the latest trends in naming are. There are many websites and books that discuss trends in naming. One of the best places to look for naming trends in the United States from the past (1879 to the present) is the Social Security Administration's website, http://www.ssa.gov/OACT/babynames.

Chapter 3

war of the
sexes

One of the biggest decisions couples face when expecting a child is whether or not to learn the sex of the baby before birth. If the parents are in agreement, it's easy sailing. However, one parent may want to know the sex, whereas the other may not. This can create tension in the household, especially if each feel strongly about the matter. A compromise could be that one parent does in fact find out the sex and the other simply doesn't. But will the one be able to keep such a secret from the other? It's advised that the couple sit down and weigh the advantages and disadvantages of each option. Remember, once you make the decision to know the baby's sex, there's no taking it back. So make sure you are certain of your decision.

Advanced technology has made preparing for baby easier than ever. You can now know the sex well ahead of time and start stocking up on boys' or girls' accessories, choosing a specific name, and educating yourself on specific gender needs. You will no longer have to call the child such generic names as It or Baby but can instead use the more intimate Son or Daughter. You won't have to worry about returning gifts that are inappropriate for your child's sex. You won't have to stick with gender-neutral colors but can instead decorate in the colors that are traditional for your baby's sex. You can also decorate the nursery with gender-specific baby accessories. All this is great, but are you willing to give up the surprise to gain it?

Being surprised, for a lot of parents, is one of the biggest rewards received after delivery—second, of course, to the child itself. Who doesn't love a bit of anticipation? Couples can have a blast during the pregnancy dreaming of the different futures their child will have if a boy or a girl and creating separate baby-names lists for each. And who cares about traditional colors? Green is a favorite anyway, and that can work for either sex. The thrill of discovering the sex after nine long months compounds on that of giving birth to a healthy baby. It is the ultimate surprise.

Of course, if you want to keep the element of surprise and still know the sex of the baby beforehand, you can always simply keep the sex to yourself. Don't allow your family or friends to be in on the information. Keep them in suspense and hide your secret. You will be able to experience the surprise secondhand, which isn't quite as good, but better than not at all. Plus, it might have the added bonus of bringing you and your significant other closer together. Sharing such an important secret will create a fun and lasting bond.

Whether or not you decide to find out the baby's sex before birth, you will need to give some special considerations to each gender's sex when composing baby-naming lists. There is also the rising popularity of unisex names to consider. The following sections will help you to determine the gender implications of names and decide whether a unisex name is right for your baby.

Girls' Names

It has been said that females are the more complex of the sexes, and if the number of baby names to choose from is any indication, then females have hit an entirely new scale of complexity, leaving the males far behind. For your daughter, you will have several different types of names to choose from: the traditional feminine names, the feminine names with flair, the straight-cut feminine names, the feminine names derived from masculine names, unisex names, and even masculine names. The choices seem endless. However, each category comes with its own set of implications and guidelines, so please be aware of this fine print before settling on your daughter's name.

Let's conquer the largest group first: the traditional feminine names. Traditionally, girls' names are a bit more elaborate than boys' names. On average, they have more syllables and are much more decorative than boys' names. They sound and look prettier. They are dressed-up in a sense—but not overly so. Consider them the cocktail dresses of girls' names. They have a simplistic and soft elegance but are still comfortable at the same time. You will find most of the classic and popular girls' names in this category. They are the middle ground for parents who don't want their daughter to seem either overly flirtatious or rooted so firmly to the ground she never moves. These names are decidedly feminine without the curls and lace.

The biggest advantage to this category of names is that these names are familiar as being feminine. A daughter can easily embrace her name and feel good about being a girl. No one will question your child; there will be no need for the pink bow taped to the head. There are no limits, and, for the most part, these names do not come with expectations or assumptions. The most popular names will fall into this category, as many of these names have already stood the test of time and many more will accomplish the feat. The following is a brief list of traditional female names.

Abigail	Katherine
Angela	Lauren
Bridget	Lily
Christina	Michelle
Daphne	Naomi
Deborah	Olivia
Elaine	Penelope
Elizabeth	Rebecca
Flora	Rosemary
Gwendolyn	Ruby
Helena	Selena
Iris	Sophia
Jennifer	Valerie
Jessica	Vivian

The next category is the feminine names with flair. These names are the girliest of the girly. They are considered to be frilly names with lots of soft sounds, dripping with femininity. These names will never be mistaken for anything other than feminine; they are the embodiment of all that is girl. Consider them the evening gowns of girls' names. They are all dolled-up, straight from the salon, showing off the curves, and ready to turn the boys' heads.

One of the advantages to these names is that your daughter will feel girly; she will embrace her femininity and likely use it to her advantage in every aspect of her life. She will be the woman every man wants and every woman envies. Her name will carry with it associations of beauty, gentleness, cheerfulness, and yes, sex appeal. Many women debate the power these names hold. Some women say that there is nothing better for the feminist movement (in terms of name bias) than for a woman with an ultra-girly name to make her mark with strength, power, and femininity in this world. Others argue that women with such names are already pigeonholed as being beautiful but dumb and therefore never given the opportunity to hold positions of power. Regardless of your stance, there's no denying the femininity of these names. The following are a few examples.

Adriana	Juliana
Aurora	Luciana
Barbie	Monique
Chrissie	Priscilla
Crystal	Sabrina
Dolly	Scarlett
Emmaline	Tatiana
Felicia	Tiffany
Heather	Vanessa
Isabella	Venus

The next category of feminine names includes the straight-cut names. These are feminine names without the frill. There's no denying that they are girls' names, but they lack the extra dose of girlishness of the traditional feminine names, and they are certainly a far cry from the ultra-girlishness of the feminine names with flair. Consider them to be the business casual wear of girls' names. And just like the feminine names with flair, there are associations and assumptions tagged onto these names. Because they are typically shorter and choppier, they bring to mind straightforwardness. They are no-nonsense names. Women with these names will get right down to business and are firmly grounded.

An advantage to giving your daughter a straight-cut feminine name is that she will still have the outwardly identifiable feminine name but she might be taken a little more seriously than girls with more girly names. These names seem to embody the mother figure: loving but strict, womanly but restrained, and hardworking and calloused but gentle. Because these names have a more serious and businesslike feel to them, women so named may have more of an advantage in the business world. The following are a few examples of straight-cut feminine names.

Adele	Jane
Anne	Leigh
Beth	Mary
Claire	Mildred
Doris	Nora
Ellen	Rachel
Eve	Ruth
Gail	Susan
Grace	Trudy
Helen	Wanda
Irene	

The next category encompasses those names taken from masculine names and transformed into feminine names. These names, again, are decidedly feminine; there will be no confusion over whether you have a son or daughter. Consider these names to be the business suit of girls' names. There is a lot of flexibility with these names. Though they have masculine qualities, they are feminine through and through. If passing down paternal names is an important tradition to you, you can easily honor the namesake and feminize that masculine name at the same time.

An advantage to these names is that they carry associations of intelligence and strength while still maintaining the loveliness and goodness that is tagged onto girls' names. If you are concerned with your daughter making her mark in a man's world, giving her a name from this category may help. Some parents believe that giving their daughter a name that is derived from a masculine name will cause those who have a bias towards men, such as in the workforce, to favor their daughter over other women who have more of a girly name. The following are a few examples of such names.

Alberta	Ivana
Alexandra	Jacoba
Antonia	Josephine
Arthurine	Kevina
Bernadine	Leopolda
Calvina	Michaela
Danielle	Odessa
Edwina	Philippa
Frederica	Roberta
Gerardine	Thomasine

More and more parents are choosing to give their daughters boys' names. There may be many reasons for this. Perhaps the parents wish to strip their child of all negative associations of girly names. Perhaps they believe giving their daughter a masculine name will give her a better chance of climbing the ladder of success within the workforce. Perhaps they wish to honor a male member of their family by bestowing his name on their child. Or perhaps they simply do it because they can. Girls have the freedom to take names from the boys' list—a freedom that is not reversed.

Of course, there are some traditionally masculine names that aren't likely to cross over into mainstream girls' names use, such as William, Henry, or Robert, but several others have crossed over so successfully that they are now considered to be more of a girl's name than a boy's name—even though they have their roots in the masculine line. Once girls have taken over such names completely, there is no going back. For instance, not many parents these days name their sons Ashley, Leslie, or Courtney because these names have become too feminine. There are still those names that stand strong on masculine ground, however, such as Jamie, Jordan, and Taylor, even though the girls have been encroaching on their territory for several years now—of course, these names have fallen into the unisex-name pit, so perhaps they aren't as far from the girls' names list as we think.

Speaking of unisex, this is the last category of names parents expecting a daughter can choose from. But because it is so special and incorporates both boys and girls, it has its own section at the end of this chapter.

Many parents are also concerned about the meaning of their daughters' names. For this reason, you might also want to consider the fact that most names that fall within the traditional feminine names, feminine names with flair, and straight-cut feminine names categories revolve around themes of beauty, goodness, mothering, nature (such as flowers, water, and sky), and sincerity—traits that are traditionally female. Names within the feminine derived from masculine names, unisex names, and masculine names categories have meanings that focus more on traditionally male traits such as strength, power, rule, energy, wealth, and intelligence. There are exceptions, of course, but this is the general rule. If you want an ultra-feminine name but a meaning that conveys strength and power, you might want to consider choosing a name from one of the latter categories for a middle name. This compromise works well in that your daughter's name can embody both strength and beauty, goodness and rule, power and sincerity.

Boys' Names

Unfortunately, you have fewer choices for your son's name—or perhaps this will help to ease your baby-naming process. Even though there are historically more male names than female, the girls' names are slowly swallowing the boys' names one by one. In addition, most parents typically don't go out on a limb and invent boys' name or even get very creative with them. Of course, there are the exceptions, but most tend to stick with the traditional, tried-and-true, strong masculine names. Perhaps tradition itself plays a role in this. More boys are named for family members than girls. For as long as names have existed, boys have been viewed as the pillars of the family, the ones to carry on the name and the line. Though we've come a long, long way from the sexist attitudes of our forefathers, it seems as though a tiny bit of the idea that the boys uphold family tradition more so than girls has found its way into our egalitarian subconscious. Fathers especially seem to be in favor of giving their sons family names, and mothers don't really put up much of an argument. We see names such as Michael, James, John, and William being recycled over and over in the top ten lists over the decades.

Of course, there is absolutely nothing wrong with giving your son one of these traditional names. In fact, it can benefit him. These names carry a certain prestige and positive connotation that more unconventional names have not yet earned. The traditional names represent strength, intelligence, valor, and power. We associate these names with upstanding young men, with good providers, with family men, with those who are firmly grounded and as solid as a rock. After all, isn't this what we want our sons to grow to be? We have high hopes for them, and if giving them traditional names will help to move them ahead in the world and at the same time instill family pride, why not?

Maybe you'd rather not have your son be one of several Michaels in his class, but still want to provide him with a name that embodies all the masculine qualities and that he can wear with pride. Not to fear: there are plenty of names that have all of this and a little bit of variety as well. Names such as Christopher, Zachary, Daniel, Justin, and Alexander have grown to be a more stylistic take on the traditional names. These are still grounded in history, so they are full of powerful associations, but they also deviate from the ever-common Johns. Of course, these names are widely popular for this very reason and often are within the top twenty names year after year. Even so, there are more to choose from, and they don't waver in their masculinity.

If you are feeling a bit more ambitious in your choice, you can always look into foreign variants of these names and still maintain the tradition, pride, and masculinity of each. More and more foreign names are becoming popular in the United States. Even so, you might want to reign yourself in a bit and not delve into unrecognizable spellings and pronunciations—you might have others asking where he came from. Remember to name your child with his future in mind. If you give him a foreign name, he will likely have to spell it for everyone, and he might have to help others repeatedly with its pronunciation. However, there are several names that are easily recognizable that might fit well with your goal. For instance, Kristof might be a better choice than Krzysztof. It is still an unusual variant of Christopher, but not so unfamiliar that it will cause problems for your son.

You might also consider using shortened versions or changing the spelling to create variants of well-known masculine names. You will be able to maintain the traits of the original name, but add a little creativity to it so as to make it less common than its parent name. For example, you might choose to name your son Xander or Alex instead of the traditional Alexander. Or, if you'd rather have the full name but change the spelling, you might choose Aleksander, Alexandro, or Alisander. But keep in mind, the further you deviate from the original spelling, the more often your child will have to repeat its spelling throughout his life.

Another good source for masculine boys' names is the Bible. There are tons of names to choose from, and each and every one is steeped in history and tradition. Some are rather well-known, such as Elijah, Noah, and Samuel. Others are more obscure, such as Ephraim, Joachim, and Amos. If meanings are important to you, it would be a good idea to learn the story and meaning of each of the names you choose from the Bible. For instance, you might rethink your choice of Judas once you have discovered the story behind the name.

A trend that has gained popularity recently is that of choosing surnames as boys' first names. This would be a good way to pay tribute to your family. Dig up the family tree and see if anything catches your eye. Of course, the surname doesn't have to come from your own family. You could also scan the telephone book for ideas. This opens up a new door to a plethora of boys' names.

As girls are stealing more and more boys' names to add to their list, some parents are concerned that their son's name is going to become too feminine. It's true that there are several names that began as boys' names and have become almost entirely girls' names. For instance, you don't see many little boy Shannons or Danas on the playground much anymore. But there are still plenty that are holding their ground, and unisex names are more popular than ever.

Unisex Names

A unisex name is one that can be used for either gender. Most unisex names began as boys' names but for one reason or another appealed to parents of girls. Once it becomes common for girls to take on these names, they become unisex. As the movement progresses, those names that straddle the line between the sexes may eventually work their way over to the girls' side. Names such as Lindsay and Florence are true unisex names, as they have their roots in masculinity, but they have been so predominantly used for girls that they are considered to be part of the girls' names list and are no longer seen as an option for boys. As more and more girls are given a particular name, that name becomes associated with femininity and thus becomes too feminine for a boy. However, this evolution takes time, so the fear that your son's name will cross over to the girls' list by the time he reaches sixth grade shouldn't hold you back from choosing a unisex name. But his name may not be a candidate for passing down the male line in the future. The following is a list of the top unisex names—names that appear in both the boys' and girls' top 1000 names as compiled by the Social Security Administration.

The Top 67 Unisex Names

Addison	Harper
Alexis	Hayden
Amari	Jaden
Angel	Jadyn
Ariel	Jaiden
Armani	Jaidyn
Avery	Jamie
Bailey	Jayden
Cameron	Jaylen
Camryn	Jaylin
Casey	Jessie
Charlie	Jordan
Dakota	Jordyn
Devyn	Justice
Dylan	Kamari
Eden	Kamryn
Emerson	Kasey
Emery	Kayden
Finley	Kendall
Harley	Logan

London	River
Lyric	Rory
Marley	Rowan
Micah	Ryan
Morgan	Rylan
Parker	Rylee
Payton	Sage
Peyton	Sidney
Phoenix	Skylar
Quinn	Skyler
Reagan	Taylor
Reece	Teagan
Reese	Zion
Riley	

Unisex names have been around for ages, but they are just now pushing their way to the forefront of popularity. This could be due to the fact that there are more parents who want to strip their children of gender restraints. For instance, when the resume of Jordan Smith crosses the HR director's desk, there will be no way for him or her to tell whether Jordan is a man or woman, and therefore all gender bias has been erased. Jordan will have to secure that interview on merit alone. On the other hand, some parents choose unisex names because of the associations they carry. For instance, parents may want their daughter's name to embody strength and power; after all, she's going to be a beauty already, so why would she need a feminine name to reiterate that? Choosing a more masculine name may accomplish this. Parents expecting a son may decide that they want to give him a name that veers away from the power and aggression of traditional boys' names and veers toward a more sensitive side. In today's world, men no longer have to be the pillar of the family, the macho breadwinner, the stern and unwavering man. Instead, they can be loving, creative, and sincere and show emotion—traits that are typically associated with women—without giving up their manhood.

Another factor of the rising popularity of unisex names may be the influence celebrities have on baby-naming. Celebrities such as Ashton Kutcher, Cameron Diaz, Daryl Hannah, Reese Witherspoon, and Drew Barrymore have brought unisex names to the spotlight. Just as celebrities' names in themselves influence parents' decisions, so too do the celebrities' choices for their own children. Garth Brooks named his daughters August and Taylor. Tracey Gold named her son Sage. Teri Hatcher named her daughter Emerson, and Mason was the name Kelsey Grammer chose for his daughter. And let's not forget the place names that are widely popular and can be used for either a boy or girl. Dakota Fanning, Paris Hilton, and Olympia Dukakis wear their place names with pride. These are but a few examples of unisex names making their way into the Hollywood scene.

Some parents want to give their children names that are a bit unusual, those that will set their children apart in the sea of Michaels and Marys. The unisex names break away from the traditional feminine and masculine names, adding to the pot a variety of choices that will make the classroom roster a bit more colorful. There is also a wide variety of meanings to choose from. Whether you are looking for a name from nature, a place name, a name meaning "strength," a name meaning "beauty," or a name meaning "benevolence," you can find it in the list of unisex names available today.

Or maybe you'd prefer to bring a name to the unisex list. If you are expecting a daughter, you might want to browse the boys' names and see if there is one that sounds as though it has an ounce of femininity to it. Names that end in an *ie*, *ee*, or *ey* typically have a feminine sound to them. Maybe the feminine sound isn't at all important, and you'd rather name your daughter Robert. The choice is entirely yours; there are no rules when it comes to baby-naming. However, you will likely want to take into consideration the consequences of the name you choose.

Unisex names may have a long-reaching appeal, but they are not exempt from being problematic. Some children may not readily pat you on the back for your choice of name. A little girl with the name Dale may feel awkward surrounded by classmates with names such as Priscilla and Emma. And she may grow to feel as though since she has a boy's name, she should act more tomboyish. Though girls may struggle with the fear they are not as girly as they should be during childhood, they typically grow to approve of and appreciate their unisex names when it becomes important to distinguish themselves from their peers. Boys, on the other hand, may struggle a lot longer with unisex names. During childhood, a boy may find it humiliating to be in the same class with a girl of the same name. His classmates may very well tease him about it, and he may grow up thinking he isn't as "tough" as his classmates who have traditionally male names. In adulthood, others may consider him to be more sensitive and therefore not as assertive as the Williams and Johns of the world. The upside to all of this is that unisex names are becoming quite popular, so your child isn't likely to be alone while growing up with a unisex name. And some children have the personalities that readily embrace being different; they prefer to be set apart from others and may enjoy the attention it brings them.

One final note on the hazards of unisex names: if you have both a daughter and a son, please be sure to give the son a more masculine name than the daughter. In other words, don't name your daughter Daryl and your son Casey. To do so would be to invite teasing, tears, and identity crises.

Chapter 4

the attributes of a perfect name

So you've decided to name your baby something other than Zygote. That's good. But there are a few things to consider before bestowing an equally undesirable name on your son or daughter. In fact, when you go through the naming process, it's not a bad idea to compare the names you choose to Zygote to see how they measure up. After all, the last thing you want for your baby is a name that causes him or her to cringe every time someone says it.

Often the most challenging aspect of choosing a name is knowing where to begin. Let's face it: your kid has to live with the name you choose *forever*. (Or at least until he's old enough to legally change it himself, which is usually because his inner rock star got the best of him and Dan Green just isn't as cool as Stratus Phere.) To get going on your list, write down names you have always liked. Was there someone in school whose name you secretly wished you had? Did your favorite soap opera or sitcom have a character with a cool, trendy name? Browse the names chapters of this book and jot down any that stand out. Perhaps you are already receiving suggestions from friends and family. Are there any that appealed to you? List all the names you can think of that have caught your attention (in a good way) and list any family names you'd consider using.

Once you have a few (or maybe a few sheets' worth), consider the following attributes and see how each measures up.

Sound Advice

Think about how the name sounds in a variety of situations. You'll whisper it, sing it, call it, yell it, and use it in conversation repeatedly. Your child's teachers will say it out loud in front of his or her friends, and it'll be announced during special ceremonies, such as graduation. How the name might sound to the child and to others is also important.

Listen for rhythm—variations in sound using syllables and letter combinations—to determine if the name is compatible or harmonious with the middle and last names. Think of names as parts of a song that either complement or throw off other parts of the song. In a sense, you're not just *choosing* a name for your child, you're composing one. To hear what the name sounds like, say it out loud and have it said to you out loud. Say it alone, with the middle name you've chosen, with the last name, and with both the middle name and last name. Say it with your name, your significant other's name, and your other children's names. Is there balance and contrast? Do the names flow together beautifully? Do they sound choppy and disconnected? Do you love the names but not the sounds of them together? How important is it to you to have rhythm in a name?

The legendary singer Madonna certainly knows how to live up to a name. She also understands rhythm. Consider the name of her daughter, Lourdes Maria Ciccone Leon. It's pronounced LORD-ess Ma-RI-a Chick-OWN-nee Lee-ON. The name rolls right off your tongue, mainly because the consonants and vowels balance and harmonize with each other, creating a melodic, pleasant name. Now consider this name: John Dan Ted White. Because each name carries only one syllable, there is no variation in rhythm. The names don't sound like they relate to each other. To change the rhythm, consider using full names, as in Jonathan Daniel Theodore White. The difference you hear is the variation of syllables. Conversely, if a name sounds too long to you, shorten it by using the one- or two-syllable version.

Whether you choose to compose a name redolent of symphonic notes or one that represents a cheerful ditty, it's best to avoid composing the perfect rhyming poem. As imaginative as kids can be, they can also be harsh on another child's self-esteem. Dee Lee, Betty Petty, Manny Tanny, Rudy Ludy, and Zygote Bygote are all ammunition for other kids' insults. If you'd like the names to rhyme subtly, use slant rhymes (aka partial or off rhymes). A slant rhyme is created using consonance (consonants within words are similar, as in *think* and *sank*) or assonance (vowels within words are similar, as in *sink* or *tilt*). Dylan Aidan is an example of consonance, while Kayla Jayne is an example of assonance.

Vowels are tricky if they're used too closely together. For example, say Horatio Oro or Elena Albert out loud and notice how difficult it is to keep the two names separate. Your mouth almost comes to a complete stop before saying the second name to avoid sounding like you're chewing on Oreos while saying the full name. Think about using a vowel before a consonant, as in Isabella Rose, to create an uninterrupted flow of sounds. However, be aware of the pitfalls here, too. Christa Lee sounds like Crystal E if you say it too fast.

Some parents love to make connections between their names and their children's names, often using the same first letters of their first names. For instance, Mary and Mark have three children named Margaret, Michael, and Monique. While this provides cohesiveness, the alliteration can cause you to become tongue-tied if you need to call, say, five children's names all beginning with the letter M.

Original Works of Art

A unique name is one that's a little different and unexpected, but not so different that your child is afraid to use it and people are afraid to pronounce it. It's a name that makes a person stand apart from the crowd and feel a little special. However, if the name is too bizarre, the person can feel like a freak. Instead of imagining how your child's name will look in lights or on the big screen, imagine how it will look on his resume. To a prospective employer looking for someone to represent his or her company, Zygote Bygote might be difficult to take seriously. Also, think about the first impression the name will make on people. Is it something your child will be embarrassed by on first dates?

Let's say you're in love with a classic name, like Emily. Is it so bad to have a name that many people have? Not at all. In fact, one of the best things about it is that everyone knows how to say it and spell it. Your child might also have an easier time at school with a common name. What if you love the name Emily but still want your child's name to be a little different? That dilemma can be solved by simply playing around with spelling and/or using the middle name to offset it. Instead of the more traditional spelling, try Emilie, Emilee, or Emiley. If your last name is long and contains many different consonants, keep the first name simple but spell it differently. For example, Anah Schlotowitcz versus Sajaza Schlotowitcz.

As mentioned previously, middle names are great backup when your creativity is in jeopardy. If your last name is common or easy to pronounce, like Brown, and you're adamant about using your father's first name, Joseph, liven the ensemble up with a few jazzy middle names. Joseph Oren Astor Brown offers a cool, sophisticated sound to what could have potentially been a plain name.

There are other creative ways to design an original name. Think about the places that are important to you and your family members. Place names, like Georgia, Houston, Austin, Dakota, and Sonoma, fit the criteria of being different and special but not too out there. Also, put together a list of seasons, colors, and holidays that are significant to you and your family and try to come up with names from that list. April, Summer, Holly, and Rose are some examples.

Make anagrams by rearranging all the letters in a name or a combination of names to create new possibilities. Anagram servers are abundant on the Web, and they're easily found by typing in "anagram" in the search field. For example, Aden and Dena and Brian and Brina are anagrams. You can also use the anagram servers to discover names within names. Contained within June Anne are the names Jeanne, Jean, Juan, Jane, and Jan. If your husband's name is Charles and your name is Lynne, combine the two to create Charlynne and use it as either a first name or middle name.

Originality is especially important if you're having twins. While you don't want to ignore the fact that there is a special connection between twins, it's important to let them be individuals. You can help them feel special in their own right by giving them totally unrelated names. And this works for both same-sex and opposite-sex twins. Sean and Dawn look and sound cute when the kids are young, but it gets embarrassing at about age seven. Instead, try to make the connection in a subtle way. Here are some examples.

- Mia and Cara: Mia means "my" and Cara means "beloved." Together, they're "my Beloved."
- Erica and Heather: Erica means "heather" in Latin.
- Leon and Noel: each name spells the other backward.
- Nathaniel and Theodore: both mean "gift of God." The former is Hebrew and the latter is Greek.
- Brendan and Sarah: Brendan is Irish for "prince" and Sarah is Hebrew for "princess."

For other ways to name your twins, see chapter seven.

Whether you choose the traditional, more recognizable route or the different, slightly funky route when naming your baby, remember that all names are subjective because their appeal is contingent on the listener. Everyone has an opinion, and as long as the child's best interests are considered, no one is wrong.

Popularity: Past, Present, and Future

Every year yields a new crop of trendy names that makes last year's list, well, outdated. While these fresh, fun names are fabulous and exciting, they also face the threat of being "so five minutes ago." Of course, there are those names that have always been and always will be popular; they're classic and chic, and they always make top-ten lists. They're the names that are trendy one minute, but still sound good thirty years from now. The key to giving your child a popular name that he or she can be proud of is to avoid trend traps altogether, such as soap-opera names or sitcom-character names that have a popularity shelf life of about six months. Often, a child named after a memorable television personality will always be linked with that person's TV character or personality traits.

One factor that makes a name popular is variation of spelling on a familiar or common name. While the new look might be pleasing to the eye, it might become a nuisance when you (and eventually your child) have to constantly correct others, telling them that Denice is spelled with a *c*, not an *s*. Similarly, if you're looking for an exceptionally rare name, you'll constantly be correcting both the spelling and the pronunciation.

At best, name trends give your child individualism. At worst, they ostracize him or her from a society of "regular" names. However, more and more parents are creating their own names or choosing from a more eclectic list of foreign names, vintage names, surnames, and, as mentioned previously, place names or names that have positive connotations. And since the unique-name pool is rapidly growing, chances are that your child's classmates will have unique names, too.

The increasing popularity of foreign names allows parents to honor their families' cultures and give their children a sense of heritage. One of the most popular boy names of 2007, Aidan, is an Irish name that, spelled backward, is the girl's name Nadia, of Russian descent. Irish, Scottish, and Welsh names are on the rise, while Celtic boys' names for girls (Brynn, for example) have become popular. Greek, Russian, and Italian names have more presence than they did years ago, as the names Nikos, Logan, Giovanni, Kaitlyn, and Tatiana become more visible.

A nineteenth-century revival of names like Abigail, Emma, Anna, Thomas, Levi, and Elijah gives you a new perspective on old favorites. While these names might seem classic or old-fashioned to us now, most of them were the trendy names of their time that broke from the traditional pattern of settler and biblical names. During a period when a respectful tip of the hat was greeted by a graceful curtsy, these names reflected the chivalry and ladylike charm that made up society back then.

The use of surnames is another trend that seems to appear in cycles. Names like Madison, Palmer, Kennedy, Mackenzie, Taylor, Jackson, and Spencer can be used for both girls and boys. What's more, surnames can prove to be a convenient alternative to using the first name of a family member you'd like to honor. One point to note: if the baby's last name can also be used as a first name, avoid giving him or her a surname for a first name because the construction can read more like a business name. If you want to use a surname for your daughter but are afraid that it sounds too masculine, spell it in full on her birth certificate and legal documents, but shorten it for everyday use. For example, if you love the name Jackson and want to use it to honor your great uncle, call your child Jackie for short.

Gender Boundaries

If the appeal of a name is subjective, unisex names are even more so. Some people firmly believe that girl and boy names should reflect gender rather than confuse it, while others like to increase their options by stripping names of sex altogether. After all, who's to say that Montana or Lucky belong to one gender or the other? Then there's the question of where the line is drawn. Truth is, it's strictly up to you to decide. While some people view feminine names as beautiful, others see them as weak. And while some people shun unisex names altogether, others perceive them as cutting-edge, fresh, and modern.

The most important thing to keep in mind is that your child will have to live with the name, not you. If you can handle the potential hardships your son Nancy will endure throughout his formative years because he has a traditional girl's name, then don't hold back. But if it pains you to imagine your daughter Richard losing the love of her life because he can no longer kiss a girl with a traditional boy's name, then nix the idea.

If you're considering a unisex name, there are some pros and cons to weigh before making your decision. First, the pros. If you don't want to know the baby's sex but want to put together a concise list of names, unisex names allow you to do just that. It's also a little less time-consuming because you only have to make one list for both genders instead of one list per gender. A unisex name doesn't typecast a child into one role or the other. For example, a prospective employer looking at a resume is less inclined to make judgments based on the name alone. Since women are the minority in the workforce, a unisex name gives your daughter a little more of an edge when trying to land an interview. Unisex names come in handy when you want to honor a family member by their surname instead of their first name, or if you want to honor your late father by using his first name as your daughter's middle name.

You can't deny the fact that some names are simply feminine or simply masculine. The disadvantage of a unisex name is that it often causes distress for the child, especially during his or her younger years. You don't want your child to develop a complex because the kids on the playground were bent on teasing and making fun of him or her. Put yourself in your child's situation. If her name is David, and there are two other male Davids in her class, the environment can be very uncomfortable for her. Another downside to giving your child a unisex name is that you run the risk of taking a little piece of her identity away. Let your child know that it's fabulous to be a girl or that it's fun to be a boy by giving them a name that allows them to feel as such.

True unisex names aren't specifically feminine or masculine. However, sometimes a name will become popular because it's associated with someone famous. Dakota Fanning, the young actress who costarred in the films *I Am Sam* and *War of the Worlds*, among others, is someone whose name we'll be seeing in lights for many years. And although Dakota is a name that can be applied to either a girl or a boy, Fanning's fame has made it more popular as a girl's name. Usually, once a girl gets a boy's name, she takes it over completely, replacing any masculine qualities the name had. Ashley, Kelly, Shannon, Cameron, Shawn, Courtney, Blair, Jade, and Cassidy used to be boys' names—that is, before the girls took over.

Various studies show that girls aren't as frustrated by being confused with the opposite sex because of their names as boys are. To make life a little easier for your child, stick with names that don't have obvious genders attached to them.

Meaning

A fun, creative, and often unique way to choose your child's name is to look for positive associations that come with the name. It also makes the naming process intentional and more special. If one of your favorite places is a wooded area where your family vacations once a year, look for names that have "trees" or "earthy" in their meanings. You can also look for names that reflect your favorite color, time of year, season, animal, art, character trait, and flower. If your favorite relative loves to visit Ireland every year, and you wish to honor him or her, choose an Irish name for your baby and use your relative's name for the middle name.

It's a good idea to look up the meaning of the names you've put on your list because the last thing you want is to frighten your child if she finds out her name means "unlucky in life." A name should evoke good feelings, positive thoughts, and pride. It should also be significant to you and your partner. Meanings are a way for your child to feel connected to you, to your family, and to life. Of course, if you like a name just because, that's okay too.

Family Names

Using family names to create your child's name is a wonderful way to pay tribute to loved ones. Additionally, if after five hours you're still staring at a blank piece of paper, jot down all the names of your family members, including grandparents, aunts, uncles, close cousins, or even close friends of the family.

What do you do if your late grandfather's name, Burt, just isn't appealing to you, but you still want to include his name in your child's name? The way around that is to use the name Albert instead, for either your baby's first or middle name. The intent is still there, the name is more appealing, and the family is happy. Another alternative is to use your grandfather's middle or last name somewhere in your baby's name. You could also use other techniques, like anagrams or meanings to connect your child's name to your grandfather's name. For example, Burton is the surname of an African explorer, so you could look up "explorers" to find other names that have the same meaning.

If the first, middle, and last names are the same as the grandfather's, then "II" is added on at the end of your son's name. If your son has the exact same name as his father and grandfather, then "III" is added at the end. The Roman numerals are also added if your son shares a name with a great-uncle. The titles Senior and Junior are used to distinguish between fathers and sons with the same names, and the father must be living in order to do so. These titles aren't used if a girl is named after her mother and/or grandmother. However, you could be the pioneer of a new trend if you decide to use them with your daughter's name.

Origin/Ancestry

Perhaps you want your child's name to indicate his or her heritage. After all, it's an important part of his or her identity, and connecting with it only adds to the richness of your child's character. Similarly, if you come from a particular religious background, you might want to explore that group of names, too. If your family has been following a tradition for many generations, such as naming firstborn children after saints, but you have a different name in mind, consider moving the traditional name to the middle. You'll make your family happy and still get to use the name you want.

If you and your partner come from different backgrounds, selecting one name from each to create the first and middle names is a great way to compromise. If you're still having issues over whose name goes first, make them both part of the first name and use a hyphen. As for whose name goes before the hyphen, pick one out of a hat and be done with it. Julie-Ana is a combination of French and Spanish names, and in this case, the hyphen can be removed to spell Juliana. The name Nino Anani is a combination of an Italian name and a biblical name, and it also uses consonance (repetition of the *n* sound) to create rhythm.

A family tree and history can be helpful resources when linking your baby's name with your heritage. For example, if your grandparents' ancestors come from a village in France where they operated a cheese business that had been passed on from generation to generation, the name Monterey would be fitting. Or, if there were many carpenters in the family, Cedar would be appropriate for both boys and girls.

Spelling and Pronunciation

While creative spellings and pronunciations of traditional names make a name unique, some parents get out of control with it. The more difficult you make your child's name to spell and/or pronounce, the more annoying it becomes for them to constantly correct people.

Even if the name is as clear as Robin, but spelled Robbynn, your child will still have to spell it out every time someone writes it down because they will undoubtedly spell it traditionally. The following list provides examples of how a small change can have big impact on a name.

- Replace *i* or *e* with *y*. Bryttany, Mysty, Maryssa, Krysten, Kym, Nicholys, Eryka, Tymothy, Karyn, Lauryn, Nathyn.
- Add an extra letter (*h* or silent *e*). Annah, Lisah, Mariah, Donnah, Alissah, Taylore, Shaye, Roberte, Ronalde.
- Replace *s* with *z*. Izabelle, Suzan, Jazmin, Roze, Alexzander, Alexzandrea, Louize, Izadore, Izaiah.
- Add to or take away from double consonants. Jesica, Coleen, Britany, Mathew, Marilynne, Sarrah, Jenifer, Nanncy, Sheri, Robbert, Antthony.
- Add a capital letter in the middle. JulieAna, DaKota, McKenzie, MaryAnne, AnnaBelle, LoraLai, MoNique.

Stick to one change per name. Too many different styles make the name look like the parents were trying too hard to be different. Once you narrow your list of names down to the top contenders, play around with different spellings to see how each one looks on paper. Then, try the variants out on friends to see if they can easily recognize and pronounce the names.

Nicknames

As you narrow your search, anticipate any nicknames that could arise from both the name on its own as well as the first name and the last name together. It's inevitable that your child will receive several nicknames throughout his or her life (and some will have nothing to do with his or her name), so try to think of the ones that could have a negative effect. But don't let this scare you out of using the name you've fallen in love with. Unless they're obvious, most of the drawback names will probably never come up on the playground.

If you like a nickname and not its full name, consider using the nickname as the full name: Abbey instead of Abigail, Kate instead of Katherine, Tony instead of Anthony, and Jon instead of Jonathan. You might consider using the full version of the name anyway to give your child the option of using it in a professional manner for resumes, interviews, and in titles like Dr. Robert Green instead of Dr. Bobby Green. Full names are formal and sound more professional. For that reason, people tend to enlist the services of professionals with more sophisticated names. See if you can tell the difference in the following sentence: *After having my taxes done by Robert, I played baseball with Bobby*. That's not to say that Bobby wouldn't have prepared your taxes as accurately as Robert would, or that Robert wouldn't be fun to play baseball with. However, the names create different images in our minds because one is casual and the other is formal. How seriously would you be able to take someone named Zygote?

Full names tend to demand more respect and are more influential, whereas casual nicknames are associated with fun, relaxation, and lightheartedness. When Mom calls Bobby by his full name, it usually means one thing—trouble. And when she calls him by his full first name and his middle name, he quickly learns that she means business!

Stereotypes

Whether fictional or not, certain names are forever embedded in our psyche as having very specific character traits or legacies. You'll need to keep these associations in mind when creating the name that your child will live with for the rest of his or her life. Like it or not, Elvis, Oprah, Barack, Madonna, Aretha, Adolph, Saddam, Judas, and Jesus will always bring to mind the personalities they're most often associated with. Unless you're ready to face the consequences that come with these names and are willing to subject your child to them, you should remove them from your list. Ask yourself why you were drawn to the name in the first place. Can it be substituted with something similar?

The names of hurricanes and typhoons that have recently caused record-breaking damage and loss of life should be avoided. In 2005, the costliest hurricane—and one of the five most deadly storms—made landfall on New Orleans, Louisiana, and no one will ever forget it. As a category-3 hurricane, Katrina caused this vulnerable city a lot of destitution. If Katrina is on the top of your list, think about how your child might feel if every time someone meets her, they mention the hurricane and all the destruction and death it caused. Since the storm will be fresh in people's minds for a while, consider saving the name for a second child, when people might not be so quick to make the relevant connection. Like 1992's hurricane Andrew, the name could take some time to regain its positive qualities (Katrina dropped 200 places on the SSA's list in just two years).

Back to the Drawing Board

Has your list been torn to shreds? Are you back to that blank page staring you in the face? Have you become so confused and frustrated that Zygote is actually starting to sound good? Don't fret. These are just guidelines to use. They are in no way rules that you must follow to achieve the "perfect" name. They will, however, help you to think and to analyze the names on your list, hopefully narrowing them down.

Chapter 5

what not to name your baby

Okay, so you've been given tons of advice and suggestions, and read numerous books and articles, and now you have a pretty good idea of how to go about choosing a first name. There's just one more thing you need to take into consideration: what not to name your baby. The decision is still entirely yours, of course, but for the sake of your baby's childhood years, and possibly even adulthood years, please include the following points in your decision-making process.

The Age-Old Junior

Whether or not to name a child after his father is a debated issue. Some people want to follow family tradition or start a new one of their own by honoring the father and giving his name to his son, thus bringing forth a junior. Others feel that a child should have his own identity and make his own way through the world and therefore should have his own name. Giving Baby the junior title has its own set of advantages and disadvantages. But most parents of today seem to be in agreement that the disadvantages outweigh the advantages. Just to be fair, we'll take a look at the advantages first.

Naming the son for the father is a long-standing tradition. It brings honor, title, and in some cases influence to your son. Some sons take great pride in bearing their fathers' names and will want to carry forth the tradition with their own sons. Also, we can't discount the bond that is created through a shared name. The child naturally bonds with the mother; after all, he was a part of her for nine months. As the father doesn't have this benefit, some view junior-naming to be a way for Dad to give a part of himself to his son. If the name is well-known or well-respected, this will give Junior an added bonus as he grows; he will be automatically awarded that prestige without having to work for it.

But possibly the number-one advantage of Junior is that it is easy. You don't have to go through list after endless list searching for that perfect name with the perfect meaning with the perfect sound. It's already decided for you. All you have to do is write it on the birth certificate. No arguments, no guesswork, and no stress. And, of course, who can debate your naming your son for his father? Some may not like it, but will family and friends really risk insulting the dad to give their opinion on the baby's name? Some of you may be thinking that this advantage alone is worth it, but let's take a look at the disadvantages before you jump on the junior bandwagon.

First of all, the name is the father's, not the son's. Many people choose names to give their children a sense of identity, something they can call their own and shape through their own means. In this case, Junior's name belongs to the father. The father has already shaped that name, and Junior must live within that creation. In a sense, he will be living in a shadow. By carrying that name, he must live up to (or overcome) his father's deeds. The title of Junior forever reminds him that he is number two, and this can create low self-esteem.

Another obstacle to overcome when giving your son his father's name is deciding what to call him. Are you going to go with simply Junior? This may be cute when he is a child, but as he grows older, the name becomes a hindrance. To be branded with a title, and not an identifiable name, can dehumanize your son. If you stick with the first name, let's say John, then mass confusion is created. When you call for John, will both father and son come running (or worse, ignore you, assuming you are calling for the other)? What about when someone phones? Are you ready to constantly ask the callers if they are wishing to speak with Big John or Little John? And let's face it, moms, will you ever again feel comfortable saying your husband's name during lovemaking when it happens to also be your son's? The confusion doesn't end in the household. Bank accounts, credit cards, mail, etc., can be easily mixed up.

As a way around the confusion, many parents call Junior by his middle name at home. In this case, John Garrett Dorsey Jr. becomes Garrett. Problem solved, right? Not necessarily. Is this how he will be introduced, or will he maintain his first name everywhere outside of the home? Will he have to ask the teacher to call him by his middle name each year? Will he carry this middle name all through adulthood? If so, will he then disassociate with his given first name, thus losing the pride and tradition you wanted to instill? Perhaps he chooses to go back to his first name when becoming an adult. Does he then lose the sense of identity that was associated with his childhood? To avoid these questions, some parents choose to use a nickname for the child. In this case, John becomes Johnny. This is great... until he reaches adulthood (some even balk at the nicknames in high school). Is that how he's going to establish himself in the world, with a child's name? He can try to change his name to John, but again, will he disassociate with this? Plus, it's unlikely that anyone he knew when he was younger will ever call him anything other than Johnny. All of this begs the question: if you are going to refer to your son as something other than his first name, why then give him that first name?

As you can see, there are more disadvantages to Junior than advantages, and any rational person weighs the pros and cons of each important decision. Still not convinced? Okay, then, Junior it is, but you've been warned.

Clever but Cruel

Some parents like to exercise their comedic abilities by creating puns that they consider to be a clever play on words but that just might send their kid under his or her desk when the teacher calls it in front of the class. Remember, your child's name is going to be spoken aloud several times throughout his or her life, and most often during introductions. So the name you give your child will directly influence others' first impression of him or her. This is not only important during the formative years when your child will be learning to socialize and make his or her mark in school, but also during adulthood when he or she is competing in the workplace. A child named Ben Dover, for example, will not only be mercilessly teased during school but just might be passed over for an interview as the name becomes a joke in the HR department.

Of course, Ben Dover is an extreme example and you might be thinking you would never do such a thing to your precious child. However, other less-offensive puns could have the same impact. How would you feel if your parents stuck you with Justin Time, Lily Pad, or Grace Land for the rest of your life? While these may seem to be innocent plays on words, they each open up avenues for teasing. We all know kids can be cruel and that nicknames often become the weapon of choice. By making a pun of your child's name, you are handing over the ammunition on a silver platter, ultimately inviting the ridicule.

Some children might be able to embrace such a name and stand up tall, taking the hits and becoming all the stronger for it. This could very well help the child develop into a self-confident and outgoing adult. But the flip side is that the child might shy away from others, develop a submissive personality, and grow to become a passive adult. Is it worth the risk?

Growing up is hard enough without having a name that is easy to ridicule or make a joke of, so anything you can do to instill pride and self-confidence in your child will be greatly appreciated. Nicknames are inevitable, but if children are going to be cruel, at least make them work for it. Force them to create a teasing name for your child; don't just hand it over. So, before signing a name to the birth certificate, reconsider your choice of Ima Hooker or Yora Belcher or Harry Butts. Your child will thank you later for staying away from these, ahem, *clever* names.

Avoid Negative Connotations

Certain names evoke certain feelings in people. Whether the connotation is positive or negative depends on that individual's experience with the name. Several things can be blamed for arousing particular feelings toward a name (and by extension, a person, to a degree). For example, perhaps Great-Aunt Sue is dedicated to watching a particular soap opera where a character named Rhonda is an evil, manipulative, two-faced witch (we know she's a witch because she's died seven times already and just keeps coming back). Now, when you tell Great-Aunt Sue that you've picked out Rhonda as your baby girl's name, she cringes and gives you a string of reasons why Rhonda is the worst possible name you could ever choose. Now, does her argument have validity? Not likely. Her dislike of the name (and subsequent begging of you to change it) is influenced by the soap-opera character. In her mind, your daughter is going to embody all of soap-star Rhonda's qualities. This is just an example, and in no way are we saying you need to receive the approval of everyone who will ever come in contact with your child before giving her the name Rhonda. But you do need to be aware of your own feelings toward certain names, and to an extent the overall feelings of society with particular names.

Let's say you've always adored the name Zachary and insisted that all your Ken dolls were actually Zachary dolls. You even named a puppy and few of your hamsters Zachary. So you considered yourself quite lucky when you met and fell in love with a Zachary in high school. Ah, the memories. He was your first love, had the perfect name, and you were destined to live happily ever after. But it didn't quite work out that way. Zachary had a bit of a cheating problem and even his marvelous name couldn't make up for that. Zachary was thrown to the curb along with your dreams of cooing, "Zachary," with love in your voice every day...that is, until you found out you were having a son. Suddenly thoughts of resurrecting that oh-so-perfect name fill your head. Your husband's not so keen on the idea, knowing the history behind the name. But you are sure that all thoughts of that other Zachary (what other Zachary?) will immediately vanish and be replaced by thoughts of and adoration for your brand-new Zachary. This one is all yours and there's no fear of ever losing the name again. You may very well put up such an argument that you actually convince yourself of this. Think again.

Regardless of your resolve, you still have those memories of cheating Zachary. And those memories will resurface from time to time as you look at your son or call his name. Though you may have the very best intentions, you may even find yourself resenting him in small ways. And do you really want to throw your first love's name in your husband's face? He will be reminded over and over again that there were men before him. He might also wonder if there is any hidden meaning behind your choosing that name even though you insist it is simply for the sake of the name.

Whether it is a past love, grade-school bully, or former best friend, refrain from using names that are going to conjure negative emotions—regardless of how much you like the name itself.

Though you shouldn't let society dictate your name choice, you do need to take into consideration the feelings aroused by certain well-known names. For instance, naming your son Adolf might cause some people to recoil and wonder just what type of a person you are. It is advised if your surname is Manson not to name your son Charles. There are just some names that should remain unique. Other names to stay away from include names of natural disasters, such as Katrina, immediately following the occurrence, while it is fresh in people's minds. Diseases are also no-nos, such as Malaria. As a general rule, it's a good idea to keep away from names of things or people that harm others.

Cavity Causers

Some names are just so sweet that they are sickeningly so. You might be gushing over your newborn child, full of excitement, joy, and so much love that you can't contain it. Don't let all those emotions spill over into the naming of your child. Names such as Sugar, Cookie, or Snookums should be thought through and cleared with others before being set in stone, or on paper. Keep in mind that your hormones are running rampant, and they might get the better of you. While cutesy-utesy names might be fun during the child's younger years, he or she will likely be sick of it by the time kindergarten begins, if not sooner. Not to mention, these names have major teasing potential.

Think about the impact your child's name will have on him or her as an adult. Imagine yourself walking into an interview and introducing yourself as Snickerdoodle Smith. Now, really, do you expect to be taken seriously? Even beyond the workforce, how will other adults handle introductions? How will your son or daughter deal with the response of a giggle and "No, really, what is your first name?" over and over again throughout his or her life? Will this create a social barrier in both childhood and adulthood?

It's a good rule of thumb to save the super-sweet names for pet names used around the house—or even *for* your pets.

Red Rover, Red Rover, Send Rover on Over

Speaking of pets, have you ever met a Fifi or Rover? Not dogs; people. Believe it or not, they are out there. Please, please, please think twice about naming your child something that is typically reserved for a pet's name. Names should instill pride and encourage your child. Having a name such as Rover might serve only to encourage your child to hide during recess in fear of having to play the game Red Rover. What if Rover (the puppy, that is) makes an appearance during Show and Tell in your Rover's class? How many years will it take for children to forget that?

Like it or not, names influence others' first impressions. Fifi is likely to bring to mind a hyper lapdog or poodle. By extension, could your Fifi ever grow up to be anything other than a cheerleader? Of course, but others might not think so. You might feel that Fifi embodies your daughter's cuteness, and that may very well be true. But you will hope she outgrows that cuteness to be replaced with beauty. Does she then need to change her name?

Also, please do not name your child for past beloved pets, regardless of what the name may be. If you absolutely adore a name, refrain from giving it to your pet. The name itself may be one that is commonly used for people, but you don't want to later tell Cody that he was named after a dog, even if that dog was your best friend during elementary school. Not only will your child think that you hold him no higher than a dog, but he might also think that he resembles the dog in some ways.

As a parent, you will want to give your child every advantage you can before releasing him or her into the world; giving him or her a pet's name is only going to hinder that. He or she will have to work even harder to prove him- or herself. It's not fair, but that's the way it is—people are pigeonholed with names. Maybe you want to instill that fighting spirit in your child, to make him or her stronger. But there are plenty of other ways to do that. Don't make your child suffer a teasing childhood only to enter adulthood where he or she is judged by a name that is often used for an animal.

The Rhyming Game

Along the lines of the cutesy-utesy names are the rhyming names. The sound of a name and the way it flows from the first to middle to last is a common consideration of parents during the baby-naming process. It is important that the name flows well, but please stay away from rhyming. Rhyming is often a tool used by children to come up with nicknames for other children. Do you really want to mimic mocking children? Giving your child a first name that rhymes with his or her surname is just setting him or her up for the teasing of malicious children on the playground and snickers of good-natured kids in the classroom. How would you feel if a giggle accompanied each mention of your name aloud?

No good can come of names such as Mary Carrey, Kermit Dermit, Gordan Jordan, or Kelson Nelson. Do you remember the tragedy of Zowie Bowie? Enough said.

Hand in hand with rhyming names are identical first and last names. Yes, there is an African tribe that upholds the tradition of using the surname as the firstborn son's first name. But please don't follow suit. There is absolutely no reason for it. In this day and age of originality and creativity, why take the lazy route and deprive your child of his very own first name?

Tempting Fate

There are certain names that will hold your child to a high standard. As you know, names influence others' first impressions, but they also influence others' expectations. The virtue names, among others, have certain connotations that a child may either feel the need to live up to or rebel against. The names themselves are perfectly fine; it's the psychological impact that makes them baby-naming no-nos. Names such as Chastity, Charity, Justice, True, and Purity conjure particular values and ideals. For instance, Chastity and Purity bring to mind thoughts of one who is abstinent and goody-two-shoes. Some will automatically think a child named Justice or Truth is going to be an upstanding, honest boy.

This might be the reason you choose the name in the first place. Perhaps you want to give your child standards to live up to and influence others to think well of him or her with the first impression. There is nothing wrong with this. You should have standards for your child. The problem arises when the standards are set too high or the expectations of others are too great. If the child feels pressured psychologically to meet or exceed these standards, he or she might just give up and rebel against them. Imagine having a daughter named Chastity who runs around with a different guy every night. Imagine having a son named True who is known around town as a liar. Your child isn't destined to be a rebellious son or daughter if given a virtue name, but the possibility is there, opening a venue for additional teasing and ridicule.

Some names have associations already built in due to their use in literature, entertainment, or media. For instance, a boy named Romeo is going to be associated with romance. What if he never has a date in high school? The name Harley may inspire thoughts of a biker gang or a tough guy. What if he is reserved and a bookworm? A daughter named Aphrodite may be expected to be a beauty, but what if she turns out to be homely? The names Madonna and Prince will be burdened with associations with the singers. The list could go on and on. The point is, you don't want your child to go through life as an oxymoron or feeling as though he or she must live up to a particular expectation of society. This guideline can be rather lax and doesn't have nearly the repercussions as other baby-naming no-nos, but please do think twice about names that have high expectations or defined associations.

Other Considerations

In addition to these guidelines, there are a few other points to take into consideration.

- Unusual spellings: changing the spellings of names has become a popular way to add a bit of flavor and originality to an ordinarily common name. There's nothing wrong with this, and it is often applauded in most baby-naming circles. However, your child will likely have to correct people over and over, as most people will simply assume the traditional spelling is used. This can also create problems for official documents.
- Place names: naming a child for a place that you are fond of or that recalls good memories has become popular. Some parents even name their child for the place in which he or she was conceived, such as Hilton for a Hilton Hotel. However, in such a case as this, what are you going to tell your child when he or she asks for the story behind the name? If you tell the truth, do you want your child saddled with the thought of your lovemaking each time he or she thinks of his or her name?
- Fashion influences: there are several names that are inspired by fashion designers or labels. For instance, Armani has become a popular boy's name. However, because fashions come and go with the drop of a hat, if your child has such a name, he or she runs the risk of becoming a fashion faux pas in the future.
- Initials: as you are putting together first and middle names with the surname, please take into consideration any words the initials of the names may spell. For instance, don't burden your daughter with the name Penelope Ida Gunderson because it will eventually be revealed that her initials spell PIG. Also beware of acronyms that are created. For instance, Kenneth Karson Key has the unfortunate initials of KKK.

Chapter 6

adding a middle name or two

The definition of a middle name is "a name that occurs between a person's first name and surname." Sadly enough, the middle name does not just occur; you have to pick it, which adds to many parents' baby-naming stress. But it doesn't have to be painful. It's all about attitude. What is your feeling about middle names? Some people give the middle name just as much, if not more, consideration as the first name. Then there are others who refer to the middle name as a filler name or a throw-away name. And many people in today's world do not even have middle names. Well, others' opinions really don't matter. The truth is, the only thing that matters is how important *you* think the middle name of your child will be.

So, really, how important is a middle name? Some people will only ever use their child's middle name when disciplining them. Something about the addition of that middle name really puts some oomph into your scolding, right? So we definitely need to choose a middle name that flows well. "Brooke Ashley" rolls much easier off the tongue than "Brooke Annamaria!"

Middle names are very often abbreviated. Many forms today such as passport applications, drivers' licenses, and standardized-testing applications will only have "MI" (middle initial) written under the blank, leaving those people with the embarrassing middle names sighing in relief.

However, the middle name still counts, and the middle initial can still be a problem-causer. You must remember that a baby will not have this cute and cuddly eight-pound, wrinkled form for the rest of her or his life. Your baby will be a playground peer, a college student, a parent, and a grandparent someday, and his or her name should be able to follow him or her through life with dignity. Keep in mind that children are very vicious at times, and your child will carry the name through these playground years. He or she should always be proud of his or her name and the meaning behind it or the way it sounds. Sometimes people will only give their children a middle initial to write down in blanks. If the middle name is never used, why not just make sure your child can fill out that SAT form like all the other middle-name kids? You don't have to worry about making the whole middle name go well with the first and last; you only need to worry about one letter. It's something to think about if there is nothing else. (The Amish have been known to use the first letter of the mother's maiden name as a middle "name" for their children. There is no period behind the first letter of the middle name because that would suggest an abbreviation. For example, a child of Samantha Smith will be named Sara S Something-or-other. The "S" is Sara's middle name; it stands for nothing.)

Many people have middle names that are embarrassing or ridiculous and will only reveal them under the direst circumstances. Do you really want to do this to your child? Probably not—well, let's hope not—so there is a definite thought process along with giving your child any name, whether first, middle, or last.

Fret not! Just go by what your heart tells you. If you have a name in mind that most of your family has sneered at when you reveal it, perhaps rethink, but if that name feels right deep down, your child will pick up your pride in his or her name (or you can at least tell him or her why you chose it) so that he or she will be proud also. If your child grows up with a complex because of your choice of name, let's face it, there is always the possibility of legal name changes, and the middle name does certainly play a lesser role than the first and last names in a person's life.

Some parents choose to forego the middle name altogether. This is a popular route to take if you decide to give your child two first names, such as Ana Maria. But keep in mind that he or she might have to correct others who will assume the second first name is the middle name. Of course, there is no rule stating you must give your child a middle name. However, if you decide not to give your child a middle name, please keep in mind that problems may arise in the future if he or she has a common first and last name or if the name is passed down through the family. The middle name often acts as a distinguishing element.

If you would like for your child to have more than one middle name, keep in mind that the child will be using computer database systems more and more in the future to fill out government and educational forms. Many of these databases do not allow for a second or third middle name, so a decision will need to be made as to which middle name or initial the child wants to use when filling out these forms. Most commonly, the first middle name given to a child is the one used on such forms. Some controversy has arisen in modern times, claiming that the government's allowing only one blank for a middle name or initial is discriminating against those people who have more than one, particularly for religious or cultural reasons. Either way, the role of only one middle name is quite subdued; the role of a second, third, or fourth middle name will be almost nonexistent aside from the stories behind them.

History and Trends of Middle Names

But where did the middle name come from? The use of the term *middle name* was not recorded in the West until 1835, but existed for a long time before this. The popularity of using middle names grew very rapidly, and in the early twentieth century, the middle name was used to acknowledge remarkable attributes of a person, adding personality to a name. From the beginning of the middle name, biblical names were a very popular choice. Names such as John, Mark, Matthew, and James are all very common middle names for male children. Note: the biblical names mentioned are those that stand the test of time. Giving your child the middle name of Moses will most likely conjure up images of the great man who parted the Red Sea in the minds of both your child and other people. If the religious names that seem archaic are important to you, then by all means, use them! In the United States and the United

Kingdom, a trend was set giving male children a middle name that was the same as the father's first name. This, of course, still occurs, but has petered out and is no longer the common ground for naming male children. Children who grow up in the South in the United States are sometimes referred to by both first and middle names, like Mary Sue, or Billy Bob, which has created a somewhat infamous place in jokes about the South and Southerners.

The middle name has been established as the place to give respect to the families of parents. Of course, the first and last names can also be used, but we all know it is difficult to take your mother's strange maiden name and make your child suffer through life with that as his first name. Middle names are the perfect place to maintain the remembrance of a relative and also free up yourself and your child from making a difficult decision on how to go about life with a name that is extraordinary. Most common is using the maternal grandparents' last name as a middle name for your child, since the last name will not live on with the grandchildren. The paternal grandchildren have the last name, so give Mom's parents some publicity! Frequently, middle names also carry on from generation. Every girl in a certain family might have the middle name Pearl regardless of first name, or every boy might have Lee. Names like this are nostalgic and important, but do, in a sense, control the rest of the naming process since you have to work around them.

The multiple middle names are often used in the upper classes in the United Kingdom, particularly amongst royalty. Multiple middle names allow for such families to admire and pay respect to other family members if faced with the debacle of having only one child, particularly only one boy. Of course, multiple middle names are common in other countries, but typically popular in these situations. Most royal family members in the United Kingdom have three middle names for good measure.

In historical Catholic communities, particularly in Bavaria but also in France, Italy, and Spain, the middle name of many females was Maria, Mary, or some version of the Holy Mother's name. It came as almost a given, a norm amongst the believers, a tribute to the lady who gave birth to the Son of God. The French tended toward hyphenating Marie with other feminine first names; the Spanish also sometimes used the middle name Jose as often as Maria. Jose, although a male name, would be used as a middle name for females to give the child the protection of both male (the Trinity: Jesus, God, and the Holy Ghost) and the female (the Virgin Mary). Also in some Catholic communities, it is common to take another name when receiving Confirmation, which is added as a second middle name for the child.

The Guidelines and Suggestions

Now for some popular guidelines regarding giving your child a middle name. Keep in mind, no matter what is mentioned in this section, or any previous sections, it all comes down to your own decision. First and foremost, you must decide if you want you child to have a middle name. Is this something that is important to you, or are you doing it because everyone else is? The job of naming a child is not usually only up to the mother, but the last thing that everyone needs with a baby on the way is a complete meltdown about the middle name. Make naming your child a fun experience. You really don't want it to end in a heated argument, do you? Are you better off just disregarding tradition and leaving your child middle-nameless? Do you prefer the Amish fashion and want to give your child just a letter or initial as a middle name, like Harry S Truman? If you do choose just the middle initial or letter, then make sure that the letter flows with the first and last name of the child.

People generally look to a few things before picking a name for their baby. First, look to the meanings. Second, it might concern you to see how popular the name is. Do you want your child to be a Megan S. or a Sarah T. in school to distinguish her? Third, you must decide whether or not you want to honor a person in your family, or uphold a tradition by giving your child a name that has been in the family. Fourth, does the name flow well as a whole? Fifth, some people like to wait to see the child before they bestow a name. You could have the possibilities chosen beforehand, but use the inspiration of seeing your child for the first time to see which name fits the baby. The baby will obviously change quite drastically from what he or she looks like when he or she is born, but this still seems pretty popular amongst new parents today.

After you have decided to give your child one or more middle names, you must consider many things. First of all, make sure you have the first (and if need be, the last) name in place for the child before choosing the middle name. This might be somewhat obvious, but it is extremely difficult—and somewhat nonsensical—to work around a middle name, especially if you will not be using the middle name of the child as the primary name. Establish choices of first names that go well with the surname of the child. Once you are set with these choices, *then* begin the process of choosing a middle name for your child. The middle name acts as a bridge between the first and last name. They should all flow well together, and the name as a whole should be strong. Remember, once again, the full name will affect the baby's self-esteem, career, and schooling (or it will at least be mentioned and noted). Many people suggest avoiding using a middle name that has the same amount of syllables (and the same stressed syllables) as the first name. It makes the full name sound too singsongy, which might be good for a baby, but when the child grows up, it won't be so cute anymore. It is also suggested to avoid using middle names that begin or end with the same letter or sound as the first name: for example, Sara Sue or Mary Carry. Once again, the singsongy sound of these names will make the child an easy target for ridicule as an adult. Above all, avoid rhyming! It might flow all right, but your child is not living in a nursery rhyme.

When choosing a middle name for your child, you might want to keep meanings in mind. It might sound obvious, but many people do not pay attention to the meaning of names they have chosen. You don't want your child to grow up and realize her name means "death" or "accident." Your baby deserves a name that has a nice meaning, whether it is according to etymology or according to you (like a name of someone you know, or a character of a book). Make sure to pick names that evoke a good feeling in you. Again, it sounds obvious, but do not name your child after your childhood bully or your significant other's ex-girlfriend. You may like the name, but you may not outgrow the associations you have already established with it.

Consider your child when you choose any name for him or her. Your child will grow with the name, and the name should grow with your child. It should be able to stand the test of time. Remember, your child will have to learn how to spell the names you pick out. And please, please, please consider the initials the child will have when you have decided on a full name. Avoid combinations that lead to bad associations like Peter Edward Emerson (PEE) or Felicia Ann Thompson (FAT). It's hard enough growing up; don't make your child have to deal with your mistakes as well. Remember, there *will* be monogrammed baby gifts, too!

Try to stay away from puns when naming your child: for example, Mary Christmas. Your child's identity will be wrapped up in the pun that is their name. People will giggle when mentioning him or her to others. It's not really all that fair to do this to your child.

If you go by standard naming guidelines, the rules are pretty much the same for the first and middle names. However, you have a little more liberty with the middle name. You may use a song as inspiration. The title or lyrics might move you and contain a name that you think is beautiful. It could be quite nostalgic to have a copy of this song or the lyrics to give your child when he or she is older. It is common to use a character or title from a favorite book to look for names for your child as well. Just make sure the character is respectable and won't leave your child questioning why you named her after a vampire or something. You might use a character that inspires the thought of how you feel your child will grow up or who has the same qualities that you hope your child has when he or she grows into an adult. You may also choose a middle name that reflects something really personally important to you like your religion or ethnicity. Your pride will pass down through your child via naming and will have an interesting story behind it.

If you choose an exceptionally normal or traditional first name, you can use the middle name to spice things up a bit, especially if your child is going to be named after someone in the family. The child, as we discussed, will not be using his or her middle name all too often, so feel free to be creative. Parents tend to give male children middle names that are popular at the time, but female children tend to get the older names like Ann or Elizabeth, which are still popular, but somewhat archaic.

Upholding Family Traditions

You might have to make the difficult decision as to whether or not to name your child after a member of your own family or your spouse's. Middle names are a great place to uphold these family traditions while having the liberty to use whatever first name you would like for your child. You avoid hurting anyone's feelings and can call your child what you want. If you are having a difficult time with your spouse trying to come up with a name that you agree on, you can each choose a name; one person can choose the first name and the other chooses the middle. (I root for the mother choosing the first name; after all, she had to give birth.)

Many people claim that it is wrong to use your child's middle name to uphold family traditions, especially if the middle name weakens the first name or full name. In this case, you might work around the traditional family name, and still allow yourself to choose a name that you love.

If you absolutely hate the name that is to be passed down as tradition, you might compromise. Perhaps have the person who cannot stand the family name add a variation of spelling. For example, if the name is Jenny, your spouse might like the name spelled Ginny, and therefore everyone is happy. Also, if your family has a very traditional name that you would like passed down, like Maria, the person who is adamantly opposed to this name might choose a variant of Maria like Mia, Maribel, Mariah, or Maree. Play around with the names. There will always be a compromise somewhere if everyone is open to it.

In today's world, it is fairly common for women, especially those who have established themselves in the business or academic world before marriage, to take their maiden name as their middle name and accept the husband's last name. This way the woman is still known as who she established herself as but allows for the union of her marriage to be known as well.

If you are in a family that traditionally chooses the same name for father and son or mother and daughter, you can definitely play around with middle names. At times, people go by their middle names or will abbreviate the first name and write the middle name out fully: F. Scott Fitzgerald, for example. If you absolutely cannot handle using the same name for father and son in the household, use the middle name as the primary name for the child.

If you are having difficulty naming your child without help, there is a new field called nameology coming about in today's world. You can schedule an appointment with a nameologist after having decided on a few names that you would like to name your new baby. The nameologist will meet with you and discuss the repercussions of the names, the rhythm and flow, and the meanings behind the names. You can walk away with a better sense of knowledge about the names you have chosen for your child.

The best advice for parents who have chosen a few names or who have that perfect one in mind is to run it by people you know and love. Most likely they will give you their honest opinion since it will be their niece, granddaughter, or nephew that you are going to be giving that name to. Say the whole name aloud to yourself many, many times. Does it flow well? Do you like the way it sounds? Is it singsongy? Is it a pun? Also, you can let the name sit to the side for a while. Do not even think about it. Come back to the name with enough time in between to judge it as an outsider. Do you still love it? Or is it just okay?

Famous Middle Names

Many parents are influenced by celebrities while going through the baby-naming process. For those of you who turn to the names in lights for inspiration, here are a few middle-name ideas to help jump-start your thinking.

The Abbreviators

George H. W. Bush

Booker T. Washington

J. R. R. Tolkien

C. S. Lewis

George C. Scott

e. e. Cummings

Hunter S. Thompson

Went by Middle Names

Rudyard Kipling (Joseph Rudyard Kipling)

Ashton Kutcher (Christopher Ashton Kutcher)

Reese Witherspoon (Laura Jean Reese Witherspoon)

Alexis Bledel (Kimberly Alexis Bledel)

Brad Pitt (William Bradley Pitt)

Garth Brooks (Troyal Garth Brooks)

Kelsey Grammer (Allen Kelsey Grammer)

Multiple Middle Names

Kiefer William Frederick Dempsey George Rufus Sutherland

Elizabeth Alexandra Mary Windsor

Madonna Louise Veronica Ciccone

Hugh John Mungo Grant

Margaret Mary Emily Anne Hyra (Meg Ryan)

Brooke Christa Camille Shields

Liliane Rudabet Gloria Elsveta Sobieski (Leelee Sobieski)

Chapter 7

sibling rivalry

Maybe you are an experienced parent and you have lived through the whole baby-naming process once, and now it's time to do it again. Hopefully you can learn from your previous decisions, processes, and possibly mistakes and make a good decision for you and your family. Or maybe you haven't been through this at all and are expecting a multiple birth. Then you have the hardest job of all, naming more than one baby.

Choosing your child's name is not always an easy task; however, choosing the names for siblings can become even more difficult. Being responsible for deciding how a person will be referred to for a lifetime can cause parents to feel overwhelmed and frustrated. Forget the idea that the more often you do this the easier it gets. Quite the contrary. The more kids you have, the harder it can get. These names will be said together and associated with one another for the rest of their lives. But don't worry; this chapter will give you some helpful tips that can make this joyful but difficult experience a little easier and more fun.

Choose a Theme

Oftentimes people like to stick with a theme, whether it is using the same meaning, letters, origins, or celebrity or family names.

More than one name can have the same or similar meanings. One of the most popular reasons for choosing a name is because of its meaning. So some may want to stick with the same meaning for more than one child. The following are some examples.

Names	Meaning
Indira and Jamilah	A beautiful woman
Adara and Kasen	One who is pure, chaste
Doris and Matthew	A gift from God
Daire and Edmund	One who is wealthy
Bredon and Saxon	A swordsman

Family names are often a tradition in families and expected to be carried on. Many families have traditions when naming children such as choosing names from both sides of the family or carrying on one name in particular. These traditions may have been passed on for centuries. This can be either a help or a hindrance to the expecting parents, depending on your feelings toward family names. If you know that it is expected of you to use a particular name, and are okay with that name, then you don't have to worry about choosing; the job is done for you. However, if you don't like the name or any version of it, and want something different, this can cause strong negative feelings in the family. As a compromise, many families choose to continue the tradition of using a name that has been carried down, but make changes to it. Such changes can be the spelling, choosing a variant of the name, or using it for a different gender. For instance, James Harley Smith may be the name to be carried on, but the parents make changes to it to suit their tastes and to accommodate the gender, creating Harley Jo Smith for the daughter. If you are feeling pressured by the family to keep tradition, keep in mind that you have to say this name every day, several thousand times for years to come; this may help you come to a decision you are happy with.

Deciding on the initials to use is another way that people go about choosing a name. Some parents want the siblings to have the same initials or want to carry on the initials of someone else in the family, and still yet others like the initials to spell something. Using initials is a good way to honor a family member without having to use the actual name. It is also a good way to bring cohesiveness to siblings' names without making them sound too similar. However, be aware that giving your children the same initials may cause confusion (and possibly lead to arguments) over monogrammed articles. You will also need to be sure that the names are distinct. Lora and Lauren are too closely related and will create a lot of confusion. However, Lora and Lesley are distinct enough to get away with using the same initial.

Nicknames play a big part in naming a baby as well. It is very important to parents to have the baby called what they would like him or her to be called. Keeping this in mind, they will try many different versions of nicknames stemming from the original to make sure that they will be able to come up with the name they would like. This is especially true for newborns who have siblings, as they are usually the ones who come up with the nicknames. This can also go hand in hand with giving the baby a shortened version of another name, such as naming the baby Tom instead of Thomas.

Using names from the Bible is always popular, and oftentimes families carry this tradition through to all of their children, giving them the extra common bond of all having biblical names. Be careful with these names, however, as not all the names in the Bible are associated with good people, and not all the names have good meanings. Research the meanings and the people associated with the names before using them.

One strategy for naming multiple children that has become popular over the past several years is naming them after cities, states, towns, countries, or even streets that mean a lot to the parents. Madison, Dakota, Paris, and India are all examples of this practice.

Other themes might include using color words, gems, fruits, celebrity names, and in general what's in style that year. If you already have a child, make a list of the different themes you can create with his or her name. This might help you to create a list for the second child.

A Family Affair

Letting your older child help pick out the new baby's name is sometimes a good thing, but remember to give him or her guidelines and not to make promises of letting him or her name the baby whatever he or she wants. Letting the child be involved with the naming is way of letting the child know he or she is an important part of both the family and the new baby's life.

Children react differently to having a new baby in the house. Some are excited and can hardly wait for lil' sis or lil' bro. Others resent the fact that he or she will no longer be the baby. You can help to alleviate their concerns by including them in the baby-naming process.

Also be sure to include your partner in the baby-naming process. Sometimes it is taken for granted that the partner would not want to be involved a lot in this process, but this is not true. Your partner needs to be included even if you have different ideas about names. Compromise and come up with something that you will both be happy with.

18 Essentials for Finding and Choosing Names

The following are a few suggestions to help make the decision a little easier on you and your entire family.

Say the Names Out Loud

Often we think we like something, but then once we say it out loud, we realize it just isn't what we are looking for. This also works in the opposite way; you think you don't like a name until you say it out loud, and then realize it was exactly what you were looking for. Think of calling loudly for your children on the playground or to come in from playing outside for dinner. If you cringe when doing this, that name probably is not what you were looking for. You need to make sure you say all of your children's names together to see if they flow well. They shouldn't be overly similar or drastically dissimilar. Instead, find names that are harmonious without being singsongy.

Avoid Negative Namesakes

When choosing a name, steer clear of names that remind you of people you do not care for or that remind you of an ex-love. These names can only cause you problems in the future. If you happened to name one child for a negative namesake and not the other, you may subconsciously play favorites.

Don't Rush

It is always a good idea to have two names of each gender settled on. Make sure that even if you know the sex of your child that you choose a name of the opposite sex, just in case—we all know people who have had everything picked out according to the ultrasound, especially the name, and then found out they had to come up with something else at the last minute.

Say All Names Together

Say the name with not only the middle name, but with just the last name. We don't always use our children's middle names, but always use the last name, and if they don't sound right together or come out smoothly together, you need to keep looking.

Test Nicknames

Can your child's name hold up to the playground test? Are there ways that kids can turn the name into something awful that would crush your child's self-esteem and possibly brand him or her for life? Remember, kids can be cruel, especially siblings. Also make sure that your children won't have the same nicknames. This can happen if the names are too similar or if you use a feminine form of a masculine name for a girl and the masculine name itself for a boy.

Make It Meaningful

Your child's name should be something that makes you feel good. It should reflect qualities that you hope your child will someday possess. Be sure that every child's name is meaningful, not just one. For instance, little Claudia might become resentful if she finds out her name means "one who is lame" while her sister Keisha's name means "the favorite child."

Keep in Mind Spelling and Pronunciations

Names that are difficult to spell and pronounce will be misspelled and mispronounced throughout the child's entire life. Also, keep in mind that using lengthy first names, middle names, and last names all together can be very difficult for a young child to learn to spell and say. An example would be Joshua Zachariah Karkowski. The poor child would have to learn almost the entire alphabet to spell his name.

Consider Gender Sensitivity

This is especially true in the case of boys' names; it will be important to the child as he gets older. It is not so much of a problem for a girl to have a name that is traditionally for a boy, but when you turn it around and use a girl's name for a boy, this can cause some major problems for him. For instance, the name Mary would not be suitable for a boy, but the name Dakota is okay for a girl. If you use a unisex name for your daughter, make sure you use a masculine name for your son. You certainly don't want your daughter's name to sound more masculine than your son's.

Be Creative

Try spelling names of things backwards; many unique names can be discovered by doing this. For instance, the name Heaven produces the name Nevaeh. Also play around with dropping letters from established names to create new and unique names that you maybe hadn't thought of. For instance, Mackenzie can become Kenzie, and Jasmine can become Jamine. Or, instead of giving Baby names of family members, such as Junior, try using a variation of the name. For instance, if the name is John, try Jonah.

Use Maiden Names

A popular way of creating a baby name is by using the mother's maiden name or the maiden name of family members. Mackenzie and Carter are good examples. This is also very popular for middle names as well.

Combine the Parents' Names

Another popular way of coming up with a baby name is by combining parts of the mother's and father's names. Jack and Anna might become Jana, or Henry and Sue might become Hugh. This is done for both the first and middle names. However, if you do this, make sure you can also create a combined name for another child. Don't play favorites with names; it will affect the self-esteem of and relationship between siblings.

Try Out Different Spellings

You might like a name, but not care for the spelling, thinking it is perhaps too drab or too common. In being creative, anything goes. Stephanie might become Stefani; Lee Ann might become Leighann; Nicholas might become Nikolas. But keep in mind that a child who has an unusual spelling will likely have to correct others over and over during his or her life.

Explore Genealogy

Another good way to find names is by exploring your family's genealogy. Do a family tree on both the baby's mother's side of the family and the baby's father's side, going back as far as you can. You might need some help from family members with this. Be sure to get the first, middle, and last names of everyone. Then go through these and look for names that stand out to you as something you would like to use. However, when doing this, keep in mind that some people are considered the black sheep of the family. If you settle on a name, be sure to get some background info on this person. You wouldn't want to name your baby something that reminds your mother of the person she most despises. This not only gives you some different names to choose from, but, if you keep it, would be a good gift for your children to have later.

Kids love to hear about their ancestors. Again, be sure to choose a name from your family tree for each child, not just one.

Ask for Suggestions

Talk to co-workers, neighbors, relatives, and friends. You don't have to use their opinions, but you will receive a ton of suggestions. Also ask them about people who have recently had babies and what those people named their children. This will not only give you name ideas, but will also tell you the names that are being used the most often.

Scour the Media

Consider names from books, television shows, movies, and celebrities. This can be a lot of fun, if you let it.

Consider the Classics

As a general rule of thumb, if your last name is unusual, it's a good idea to choose a more traditional first name. And if you have a common last name, choose a more distinctive first name. James Rothberry and Cleora Miller are some examples.

Look to Old-Fashioned Names

These names are making a comeback. They can be good choices because they have the ability to be both distinct and common. Names such as Hazel and Mabel are both easily pronounced and spelled, but are not so common that there would be several in the same classroom.

Maintain Language Families

Don't mix ethnic names among your children. For instance, if you have chosen a French name for your firstborn daughter, don't choose a Russian name for your second-born. Not only will this create confusion and a few odd looks, but the names will not be harmonious.

Many families spend countless hours making lists, reading books, playing games, talking with family members, and sometimes even visiting psychics to determine names that will both suit their baby and go along with the sibling's name.

Avoiding the Pitfalls of Naming

There are some things to keep in mind that may keep you from making baby-naming choices that you (and your child) will grow to regret.

Naming multiple children in the old-fashioned rhyming way is not a good idea. This does not allow the children to feel that they are individuals; it might set them up to feel they can only be a set. However, giving the babies separate names that begin with the same letter is okay, like Jim and John or Lila and Lindsey. With multiples, you have more work to do. You may find one or two names you like, but then find that when you say them together, the way you would if talking to both children, they do not go together well. Make sure that both names roll off the tongue together—and don't make you tongue-tied.

Often, multiple children are named in alphabetical order beginning with the oldest. But, keep in mind that with siblings this can be a constant reminder of who is the oldest and can cause rivalry. Such an example is Anna, Blake, Carol, and David.

Even though you may have a couple of names you are sure you will use, be sure that you hold your baby and look at him or her first. You may find that the names you have chosen do not suit your baby after all. This is why it is a good idea to have a few backups, just in case.

Using names that start out the same or sound similar when said aloud can cause much confusion. For example, Amy and Jamie sound so much alike, you might not always get a response from the right daughter—if you get a response at all. Also, having five children with names that all begin with a particular letter may cause you to become tongue-tied when calling for them—or even worse, to mix up the names and address a child with the wrong name.

Be careful of naming your baby after people who are dead. The circumstances around their death should be taken into consideration. This could be devastating to a child. It could also dredge up bad memories that others in the family are not ready to deal with.

Resist the urge to live in your favorite celebrity's shadow. Names that are popular for celebrities now will not be in ten years, and it will seem as if you are lacking imagination.

Special Considerations for Twins, Triplets, and Beyond

If you are expecting a multiple birth, you are quite likely under a lot of stress. Preparing for one baby is hard enough without having to think exponentially! Sorry to say, the baby-naming process doesn't get easier with multiple children, but there are a few guidelines that will help you to narrow the list down and possibly come up with that perfect combination.

First of all, get the thought of rhyming names out of your head. It may seem cute now, but it gets old fast, and both you and your children will come to regret it. Because it is important to give twins their own separate identities, you need to achieve this with their names as well. By naming your boys Harry and Barry, you are literally bonding them to one *arry* sound. This will not make them closer; it will only serve to drive them further apart, as they seek out ways in which to make them distinct. If they can't have that distinction with their names, they will find it in other ways such as behavior, dress, or rebellion. If you still aren't convinced, think about how many times you will have to use their names together. Because there is no variation, you are going to tire of the *arry* sound, and so will others. Not to mention the fact that because the names are so similar, you run the risk of calling a child by the wrong name. If they didn't have identity problems already, you will have just given them a reason to develop those issues.

Along the same lines of rhyming names comes alliteration. This guideline is rather lenient, as parents can successfully name children with the same first letter. The trick is to make sure the names are distinctive enough not to create same-name confusion. Naming your twins Mary and Maria isn't going to work. However, you could get away with Melissa and Monica. Do you see the difference? The first two names are just too closely related.

Be sure to respect the gender lines. If you have a boy and a girl, the boy's name needs to be more masculine than the girl's. There are some boys' names that sound a bit more on the girlish side (such as Carbry or Mischa), and girls, well, girls can pretty much take their pick—they can very easily be given boys' names. If you want to give your daughter a unisex name, please be sure to give your son a traditionally masculine name.

In addition, try to keep names within the same class. For instance, if you have two girls, give them both feminine names. If you were to give one a feminine name and the other a unisex name (or even more so, a boy's name), they might grow up with a few identity issues. The first may think she needs to be a girly girl whereas the second may feel she needs to be tomboyish. Other people are going to treat them this way as well. It's best to keep things on an even playing field. The same goes for boys. You don't want one to sense he is the lesser masculine of the two. For instance, if you were to name one boy Ashley and the other William, which do you think might have a few inferiority issues?

Succinctly, avoid cutesy-utesy pairings and try to keep things even for your children.

Have Fun with It!

If you try to have fun and keep the task of choosing a name light, it will go much more smoothly. Making games out of the task is an easier way that can take some of the stress off. Here are some game ideas that can be played with just a few people in the privacy of your home, or can be used at a baby shower to get guests to help with the process.

Put several boy names that you like into a hat, and then several girl names into a separate hat, and then both Mom and Dad get to take one piece of paper from each hat. This will end up giving you two names for each sex. Try these names out for a while; if one doesn't sit well with you, throw it out and choose another from the hat.

Find a piece of cardboard; it can even be an old cereal box opened up and laid out flat, plain-side up. Make a game board similar to Monopoly or Candy Land, using baby names in the squares. You can use different coins or anything you choose for markers. Use a die and take turns rolling it to move around the board. Whoever gets to the end first gets to choose a name from the board to use. Play it four times, choosing a girl name twice and a boy name twice, and you will have two names for each gender.

Play Scrabble using the rule that you can only make baby names from the letters.

Take a piece of paper, and down one side put the letters of the alphabet A–Z. Photocopy enough for each guest. Set a time limit and tell everyone to come up with a different or unique name for each letter. At the end, have guests read off the names they have, and any that match should be crossed off. The guest with the most names left wins a prize. The couple gets to keep these pages at the end to give them name ideas to choose from.

Take ten baby names; scramble the letters onto a piece of paper. Photocopy enough for each guest. Set a time limit and see who can come up with the most names using these letters. The couple keeps this at the end to refer to.

Write down the first and last name of the mother and father. Photocopy enough for each guest. Set a time limit and have each guest make names that begin with each letter of their names. Have the guests mark off any that match and see who has the most left at the end. The couple keeps this at the end to give them ideas.

Write down the first and last names of the mother and father. Photocopy enough for each guest. Set a time limit and see who can make the most names out of their names. Whoever has the most at the end wins. The couple also gets to keep these in the end to use for ideas.

Although this may seem like a long and extremely difficult task, keeping the spotlight on this joyous occasion will help. Try not to put so much pressure on yourself to have that exact and perfect name before the birth. This is not a task that should cause turmoil in the family, but joy.

Whatever method you and your partner choose, remember that ultimately you are the ones that must be happy with your decisions. Don't worry about what others think and say. You know the old saying is true: "You can't please all the people all the time, so just please yourself." However, it would help if you had a couple of level-headed confidantes to discuss ideas with. They may see some problems that you missed that might arise from the names. Placing emphasis on what others like and dislike should not determine the baby's name, but the ways that these names might be critiqued should be taken into account. Remember that naming your child is something that has been entrusted to you, by your baby.

Chapter 8

more than
600
fantastic lists

Popular Names in Australia

Boys	Girls
Jack	Emily
James	Lily
Lachlan	Sophie
Benjamin	Chloe
Joshua	Grace
Ryan	Jessica
John	Charlotte
Patrick	Emma
Samuel	Georgia
William	Mia

Popular Names in Finland

Boys	Girls
Juhani	Maria
Johannes	Emilia
Mikael	Sofia
Matias	Olivia
Oskari	Julia
Olavi	Johanna
Aleksi	Aino
Elias	Katariina
Valtteri	Aurora
Kristian	Amanda

Popular Names in Austria

Boys	Girls
Lukas	Anna
Florian	Sarah
Tobias	Leonie
David	Julia
Alexander	Lena
Fabian	Laura
Julian	Lisa
Simon	Katharina
Michael	Hannah
Sebastian	Sophie

Popular Names in Germany

Boys	Girls
Alexander	Marie
Maximilian	Sophie
Lukas	Anna
Leon	Leonie
Luca	Maria
Paul	Lena
Felix	Emily
Jonas	Lea
David	Laura
Tim	Julia

Popular Names in England and Wales

Boys	Girls
Jack	Emily
Joshua	Jessica
James	Olivia
Samuel	Sophie
Daniel	Chloe
Thomas	Ellie
Oliver	Lucy
William	Charlotte
Joseph	Katie
Harry	Grace

Popular Names in Ireland

Boys	Girls
Sean	Emma
Jack	Katie
Conor	Sarah
Adam	Amy
James	Aoife
Daniel	Ciara
Cian	Sophie
Luke	Chloe
Michael	Leah
Aaron	Niamh

Popular Names in New Zealand

Boys	Girls
Joshua	Emma
Jack	Sophie
Benjamin	Ella
Samuel	Emily
Daniel	Jessica
Jacob	Hannah
Ethan	Olivia
James	Grace
Thomas	Charlotte
Matthew	Georgia

Popular Names in Northern Ireland

Boys	Girls
Jack	Katie
Matthew	Emma
James	Ellie
Adam	Sophie
Daniel	Amy
Ben	Sarah
Ryan	Chloe
Dylan	Niamh
Conor	Aimee
Jamie	Rachel

Popular Names in Norway

Boys	Girls
Mathias	Emma
Martin	Julie
Andreas	Ida
Jonas	Thea
Tobias	Nora
Daniel	Emilie
Sander	Maria
Magnus	Ingrid
Andrian	Malin
Henrik	Tuva

Popular Names in Scotland

Boys	Girls
Lewis	Sophie
Jack	Emma
Callum	Ellie
James	Amy
Ryan	Erin
Cameron	Lucy
Kyle	Katie
Jamie	Chloe
Daniel	Rebecca
Matthew	Emily

Popular Names in Spain

Boys	Girls
Alejandro	Lucia
David	Maria
Daniel	Paula
Pablo	Laura
Adrian	Marta
Alvaro	Alba
Javier	Andrea
Sergio	Claudia
Carlos	Sara
Marcos	Nerea

Popular Names in Sweden

Boys	Girls
William	Emma
Filip	Maja
Oscar	Ida
Lucas	Elin
Erik	Julia
Emil	Linnea
Isak	Hanna
Alexander	Alva
Viktor	Wilma
Anton	Klara

Popular Names in Belgium

Boys	Girls
Thomas	Emma
Lucas	Laura
Noah	Marie
Nathan	Julie
Maxime	Sarah
Hugo	Manon
Louis	Lea
Arthur	Luna
Robbe	Lisa
Nicolas	Charlotte

Popular Names in British Columbia

Boys	Girls
Ethan	Emma
Jacob	Emily
Matthew	Hannah
Ryan	Olivia
Joshua	Madison
Nathan	Sarah
Benjamin	Jessica
Alexander	Ella
Nicholas	Grace
Owen	Sophia

Popular Names in Hungary

Boys	Girls
Bence	Anna
Máté	Viktória
Dávid	Vivien
Dániel	Fanni
Péter	Réka
Bálint	Zsófia
Tamás	Boglárka
Balázs	Petra
Levente	Eszter
Ádám	Laura

Popular Names in Slovenia

Boys	Girls
Luka	Nika
Nejc	Eva
Jan	Ana
Žan	Lara
Nik	Sara
Aljaž	Lana
Žiga	Nina
Matic	Zala
Jaka	Ema
Rok	Maja

Popular Names in Catalonia

Boys	Girls
Marc	Paula
Alex	Maria
Pau	Carla
David	Laura
Pol	Laia
Daniel	Julia
Arnau	Alba
Gerard	Marta
Joel	Claudia
Eric	Andrea

Popular Names in France

Boys	Girls
Enzo	Emma
Hugo	Clara
Lucas	Manon
Théo	Anais
Mathéo	Léa
Thomas	Chloé
Baptiste	Lucie
Léo	Camille
Clément	Marie
Louis	Jade

Popular Names in Alberta

Boys	Girls
Ethan	Emma
Joshua	Emily
Jacob	Hannah
Matthew	Madison
Logan	Ava
Carter	Grace
Liam	Sarah
Nathan	Olivia
Noah	Chloe
Alexander	Hailey

Popular Names in Chile

Boys	Girls
Benjamin	Catalina
Matias	Valentina
Sebastian	Constanza
Diego	Javiera
Vicente	Fernanda
Martin	Maria
Nicolas	Antonia
Joaquin	Francisca
Jose	Sofia
Cristobal	Martina

Popular Names in the Czech Republic

Boys	Girls
Jakub	Tereza
Jan	Katerina
Tomas	Natalie
Martin	Adela
David	Nikola
Lukas	Anna
Ondrej	Veronika
Daniel	Eliska
Filip	Michaela
Adam	Kristyna

Popular Names in Denmark

Boys	Girls
Mikkel	Emma
Frederik	Rolla
Mathias	Mathilde
Mads	Sofia
Rasmus	Laura
Emil	Caroline
Oliver	Cecilie
Christian	Ida
Magnus	Sarah
Lucas	Freja

Popular Names in Iceland

Boys	Girls
Sigurður	Guðrún
Guðmundur	Sigríður
Jón	Kristín
Gunnar	Margrét
Ólafur	Ingibjörg
Magnús	Sigrún
Einar	Helga
Kristján	Jóhanna
Björn	Anna
Bjarni	Ragnheiður

Popular Names in Japan

Boys	Girls
Shun	Misaki
Takumi	Aoi
Shō	Nanami
Ren	Miu
Shōta	Riko
Sōta	Miyu
Kaito	Moe
Kenta	Mitsuki
Daiki	Yūka
Yū	Rin

Popular Names in the Netherlands

Boys	Girls
Daan	Sanne
Sem	Emma
Thomas	Anna
Tim	Iris
Lucas	Anouk
Lars	Lisa
Thijs	Eva
Milan	Julia
Jesse	Lotte
Bram	Isa

Popular Names in Poland

Boys	Girls
Jan	Anna
Andrzej	Maria
Piotr	Katarzyna
Krzysztof	Małgorzata
Stanisław	Agnieszka
Tomasz	Krystyna
Paweł	Barbara
Józef	Ewa
Marcin	El bieta
Marek	Zofia

Popular Names in Portugal

Boys	Girls
Miguel	Catarina
João	Maria
Pedro	Joana
Tiago	Inês
Filipe	Ana
José	Cátia
Gonçalo	Filipa
Marco	Mafalda
Daniel	Vanessa
Carlos	Carolina

Popular Names in Basque Country

Boys	Girls
Iker	Ana
Unai	Irati
Jon	Leire
Mikel	Izaro
Ander	Naroa
Asier	Maria
Aitor	Nerea
Eneko	June
Julen	Paula
Aimar	Nahia

Popular Names in Italy

Boys	Girls
Matteo	Giulia
Lorenzo	Alessia
Andrea	Chiara
Alessandro	Martina
Francesco	Sara
Carlo	Carlotta
Vito	Sophia
Angelo	Gina
Enrico	Isabella
Guido	Maria

Spiritual Names

Boys	Girls
Justice	Faith
Fortune	Harmony
Guardian	Grace
Trust	Angel
Spirit	Serenity
Mystery	Peace
Guide	Promise
Truth	Hope
Eden	Eternity
Chance	Divinity

Southern Names

Boys	Girls
Jackson	Emmaline
Davis	Savannah
Logan	Peyton
Gareth	Georgia
Rhett	Chloe
Jasper	Violet
Blake	Aurora
Macon	Camelia
Sawyer	Atlanta
Brett	Scarlett

Polish Names

Boys	Girls
Pawel	Krystyna
Andrzej	Walcria
Czeslaw	Iwona
Walenty	Lucja
Marek	Mirka
Jozef	Roksana
Karol	Gizela
Aleksander	Otylia
Ryszard	Monika
Krzysztof	Honorata

Northeastern Names

Boys	Girls
Jeremiah	Emily
Spencer	Abigail
Calvin	Grace
Emerson	Clara
Quincy	Matilda
Caleb	Priscilla
Winston	Winifred
Hugh	Eliza
Nathaniel	Verity
Zacharias	Maude

Irish Names

Boys	Girls
Aidan	Briana
Colin	Ciara
Connor	Fiona
Kyan	Moira
Murray	Niamh
Quinn	Shannon
Teagan	Siobhan
Killian	Aoife
Shay	Riona
Devin	Ethnea

Asian Names

Boys	Girls
Shen	Li
Yen	Tam
An	Zi
Chang	Fang
Quon	Bao
Tan	Mai
Zhong	Ming
Liang	Nu
Hiro	Pang
Jin	Min

Scottish Names

Boys	Girls
Alasdair	Seonaid
Blair	Tam
Calum	Morag
Euan	Lorna
Hamish	Aileen
Lauchlan	Edme
Malcolm	Lexine
Kieran	Maisie
Gregor	Rowena
Angus	Nora

Welsh Names

Boys	Girls
Ioan	Meredith
Rhys	Guinevere
Dafydd	Rhonwen
Dewey	Rhiannon
Gareth	Catrin
Maddock	Bryn
Liam	Carys
Collum	Aelwyn
Morgan	Iola
Sion	Tegan

Dutch Names

Boys	Girls
Caspar	Sofie
Pieter	Katryn
Willem	Femke
Anton	Elisabeth
Klaas	Beatrix
Joren	Saskia
Bram	Gerda
Otto	Lotte
Hendrik	Romy
Jakob	Marieke

Arabic Names

Boys	Girls
Muhammad	Aisha
Ali	Fatima
Hassan	Kalila
Jamal	Salima
Omar	Alaia
Mustapha	Yamina
Yousef	Khadija
Karim	Hatima
Rashid	Raja
Yasir	Safia

African Names

Boys	Girls
Barack	Ashaki
Obasi	Salama
Rafiki	Kanika
Azizi	Zuwena
Kwami	Abina
Simba	Daura
Zuri	Lishan
Tano	Afya
Manu	Neema
Ebo	Oni

Greek Names

Boys	Girls
Matthias	Koren
Alexandros	Anatola
Stavros	Nerissa
Constantine	Delia
Leander	Phoebe
Gregorios	Xanthe
Loukas	Penelope
Ionnes	Calista
Andreas	Lydia
Claudios	Cassia

Spanish Names

Boys	Girls
Emilio	Ana
Alonzo	Isabela
Carlos	Luisa
Jose	Maribel
Filipe	Carlota
Eduardo	Valeria
Miguel	Yolanda
Pedro	Clio
Tomas	Esmeralda
Pasqual	Leticia

Italian Names

Boys	Girls
Rocco	Lucia
Arturo	Amalia
Raoul	Rosaria
Giorgio	Violetta
Guido	Flavia
Vito	Alessia
Carlo	Liliana
Lorenzo	Nicoletta
Mario	Emiliana
Matteo	Arianna

German Names

Boys	Girls
Rainer	Käthe
Dieter	Minna
Hans	Franka
Josef	Gertraud
Heinrich	Brigitte
Georg	Bianca
Arno	Heidi
Caspar	Natja
Stefan	Katja
Reinhold	Meike

Scandinavian Names

Boys	Girls
Anders	Marta
Roald	Annika
Kristoffer	Else
Johan	Malena
Benedikt	Amma
Greger	Sonja
Sven	Valeska
Viggo	Hedda
Henrik	Rakel
Mikkel	Elisabet

French Names

Boys	Girls
Marc	Dominique
Yves	Josie
Michele	Hélene
Pierre	Amélie
Jean	Lise
Luc	Genvieve
Tomas	Simone
Jacques	Yvonne
Gaston	Colette
Didier	Gabrielle

Russian Names

Boys	Girls
Ivan	Nina
Vladimir	Olga
Vadim	Tatiana
Yuri	Alexandra
Nikita	Ekaterina
Alexei	Anastasia
Nikolai	Nadia
Mikhail	Raisa
Sergei	Natasha
Fyodor	Daria

Astronauts

Boys	Girls
Neil	Kathryn
Buzz	Sally
John	Christa
James	Eileen
Alan	Ellen
Andrew	Judith
Charles	Valentina
Philip	Svetlana
Richard	Bonnie
Robert	Mae

Hockey Stars

Alex
Grant
Cam
Valeri
Paul
Shawn
Kimmo
Clark
Duncan

Baseball Stars

Ken
Grady
Mariano
Derek
Miguel
Ryan
Nolan
Albert
David
Cliff

Football Stars

Troy
Harry
John
Warren
Reggie
Eric
Joe
Dan
Marcus
Steve

Heisman Trophy–Winners

Reggie
Matt
Jason
Carson
Eric
Chris
Ron
Ricky
Troy
Tim

Basketball Stars

Boys	Girls
Drazen	Sheryl
LeBron	Lisa
Maurice	Cynthia
Steve	Teresa
Dino	Michele
Robert	Rebecca
James	Kim
Earvin	Tamika
Moses	Sue
Isiah	Kelly

Track and Field Stars

Boys	Girls
Usain	Evie
Jack	Jackie
Otis	Joan
Stan	Mary
Michael	Gwen
Gerry	Chandra
John	Maren
Larry	Francine
Earl	Evelyn
Steve	Valerie

Less-Than-Flattering Names

Boys	Girls
Mortimer	Hortense
Wilbur	Eunice
Elmer	Gertrude
Herbert	Hildegard
Hyman	Thelma
Oswald	Beulah
Wilfred	Irma
Mervyn	Wilma
Adolph	Mildred
Lester	Ethel

Lawyers

Boys	Girls
Clarence	Pamela
Gerry	Lynne
William	Gladys
Johnnie	Clara
Robert	Carmel
Mark	Emma
Simon	Katherine
Dwight	Wilena
Edmund	Margery
Hugo	Janet

Disney Names

Boys	Girls
Aladdin	Ariel
Eric	Lilo
Peter	Wendy
Nemo	Esmeralda
Robin	Belle
Timon	Ursula
Sebastian	Anastasia
Gaston	Dory
Oliver	Aurora
Tod	Marian

Yuppie Names

Boys	Girls
Francis	Chloe
Christian	Buffy
Alexander	Olivia
William	Grace
Malcolm	Elle
Zachary	Elena
Walker	Zoe
Biff	Virginia
Cooper	Isabella
Tru	Victoria

Nobel Prize–Winners

Boys	Girls
Theodor	Wangari
John	Shirin
Roy	Elfriede
Yves	Toni
Richard	Nadine
Robert	Linda
Harold	Christiane
Mohamed	Jody
Barry	Rigoberta
Finn	Aung

Mob Names

Boys	Girls
John	Moxie
Tony	Connie
Chaz	Kay
Jackie	Sophia
Freddy	Apollonia
Lorenz	Lucy
Vito	Sandra
Carlo	Theresa
Fredo	Maria
Luca	Yolanda

Biblical Names

Boys	Girls
Aaron	Eve
Darius	Sarah
Ezekiel	Deborah
Caleb	Anne
John	Mary
Elijah	Rachel
Zion	Naomi
Samuel	Rebecca
Levi	Dinah
Isaiah	Delilah

Biker Names

Boys	Girls
Rip	Angel
Duff	Sheila
Deuce	Dyna
Clyde	Aileen
Harley	Rochelle
Rocco	Breezy
Dino	Faith
Cy	Savannah
Dezi	Sunny
Rocky	Daytona

Exotic Names

Boys	Girls
Raines	Amelie
Armel	Angelique
Markum	Giovanna
Aurelio	Deadrana
Dominique	Esme
Lorenzo	Danica
Cloudy	Adriana
Diego	Xanthia
Orlando	Zoe
Adonis	Zenobia

Hippie Names

Boys	Girls
Trip	Stormy
Sage	Sunflower
Forest	Turquoise
Sky	Rainbow
Stone	Sunshine
Leaf	Petal
Tree	Iris
Incense	Lilac
Moon	Meadow
Dusty	Dandelion

Auto-Racing Names

Boys	Girls
Kenny	Danica
Dale	Melanie
Richard	Tammy
Tony	Lyn
Jeff	Shawna
John	Janet
Chase	Angie
A.J.	Erica
Rusty	Patty

Boxers

Boys	Girls
Muhammad	Michele
Leonard	Jackie
Mac	Yvonne
George	Shannah
Clay	Regina
Evander	Kelsey
Riddick	Bianca
Shane	Viktoria
Izzy	Molly
Rocky	Wendy

Zodiac Signs

Aries
Taurus
Gemini
Leo
Virgo
Scorpio
Libra
Capricorn
Aquarius
Pisces

Native American Tribal Names

Cheyenne
Dakota
Apache
Navajo
Seminole
Comanche
Seneca
Shawnee
Shoshone
Cherokee

Constellations

Boys	Girls
Orion	Andromeda
Draco	Ursa
Corvus	Lyra
Phoenix	Vela
Centaurus	Aquila
Sculptor	Hydra
Crux	Carina
Dorado	Antlia
Canis	Norma
Pavo	Sagitta

Bowlers

Boys	Girls
Ollie	Brenda
Patrick	Karen
Rick	Connie
Bill	Kathy
Eddie	Leanne
Tim	Sharon
Duane	Michelle
Michael	Theresa
Tom	Lisa
Roger	Nikki

Golfers

Boys	Girls
Phil	Michelle
Todd	Meena
Mike	Natalie
Jim	Lorena
Ben	Annika
Tiger	Karri
Rich	Alison
Ernie	Marlene
Vijay	Laura
Zach	Kelly

Bull Riders

Boys	Girls
Adriano	Dedee
Mike	Tavia
Guilherme	Vanessa
Chris	Kyane
Travis	Sherri
Sean	Mandy
Jody	Billi
Ross	Mary
Brian	Joe
Justin	Candy

International Spies

Boys	Girls
James	Selia
Lorenzo	Nina
Bennett	Nikita
Waldo	Tatiana
Isak	Leah
Markus	Eva
Winston	Ursula
Nicholas	Erika
Ivan	Lexine
Austin	Fiona

Redneck Names

Boys	Girls
Jeff	Raylene
Buddy	Merit
Larry	Peaches
Jethro	Georgia
Jerry	Lake
Ron	Savanne
Hunter	Donna
Forest	Star
Jebediah	Arlene
Amos	Tonya

Influential Names

Boys	Girls
Winston	Amelia
Albert	Madonna
Franklin	Betty
Bill	Margaret
Warren	Isabella
Ronald	Josephine
Elvis	Harriet
Jonas	Frances
Nelson	Ruth
Walt	Sarah

Police Officers

Boys	Girls
Roscoe	Sarah
Brian	Jodi
Andy	Rebecca
Law	Marissa
Rod	Liberty
Leon	Justice
Donnie	Loretta
Gomer	Edith
Ajay	Sheila
Barney	Aundrea

Editors

Boys	Girls
Eric	Anna
Mike	Kate
Peter	Tara
Todd	Samantha
Gary	Rachel
Scott	Rebecca
Ed	Michelle
Steve	Lesley
Al	Laura
Joe	Courtney

Wild-Child Names

Boys	Girls
Reese	Briana
Brandon	Kayla
Clint	Bethany
Justin	Dee
Dewey	Lindsay
Harley	Renee
Carl	Carrie
Tanner	Paris
Malcolm	Kelly
Bruce	Nicole

Jockeys

Boys	Girls
Eddie	Lisa
Aaron	Mary
David	Rolanda
Shawn	Jennifer
Gary	Emma
Chris	Zoe
Jerry	Shannon
Pat	Raina
Jorge	Kelly
Victor	Stacey

Grey's Anatomy Names

Boys	Girls
Mark	Miranda
Derek	Meredith
Alex	Cristina
Richard	Izzie
Preston	Lexie
George	Erica
Tucker	Callie

CEOs

Boys	Girls
Donald	Vivian
Warren	Catherine
Rick	Muriel
Jim	Mary Kay
Denis	Judith
Terence	Marjorie
Paul	Shelly
Daniel	Meg
Nolan	Andrea
Ralph	Dominique

Overachievers

Boys	Girls
Steve	Teresa
Nolan	Janese
Gordon	Ann
Alejandro	Sylvia
Howard	Barbara
Al	Joyce
Suhas	Julie
Paul	Ruth
Carl	Coco
Wolfgang	Gert

Grocery Clerks

Boys	Girls
Steve	Jennifer
Tom	Priscilla
Bobby	May
Scott	Dolores
Timothy	Georgia
Jeffrey	Pam
Raymond	Liz
Kip	Dawn
Joe	Megan
Ralph	Anne

Designers

Boys	Girls
Gianni	Kate
Isaac	Stella
Marc	Carolina
Oscar	Jill
Sergio	Lulu
Charles	Diane
Jean Paul	Betsey
Calvin	Anne
Bob	Liz
Kenneth	Laura

FBI Agents

Boys	Girls
Mulder	Dana
Randy	Dayle
Rodney	Clarice
Fred	Angie
Fox	Jill
Edgar	Sabrina
Elliot	Kelly
Gordon	Chris
Dick	Tiffany
Victor	Natalie

Unisex Names

Emery	Taylor
Devyn	Skyler
Riley	Rowan
Jayden	Payton
Kamryn	Spencer
Harper	Harley
Logan	Reese
Teagan	Justice
Avery	Quinn
Dylan	London

Powerful Names

Boys	Girls
Corbin	Corianna
Demetri	Gail
Raines	Delores
Gregor	Nadia
Keith	Melinda
Hunter	Marissa
Emerson	Natasha
Roderick	Elena
Harvey	Alexandra
Hamilton	Leah

Presidential Names

Boys	Girls
Franklin	Laura
George	Barbara
James	Nancy
Reagan	Eleanor
Calvin	Hillary
Benjamin	Martha
Barack	Jane
Andrew	Mamie
Abraham	Michelle
Dwight	Mary

Painters

Boys	Girls
Leonardo	Berthe
Michelangelo	Dorothea
Vincent	Sofonisba
Pablo	Mary
Salvador	Giovanna
Henri	Artemisia
Claude	Lavinia
Rembrandt	Marie
Gustav	Georgia
Francisco	Frida

Sculptors

Boys	Girls
David	Emma
Antoine	Harriet
Henry	Edmonia
Georges	Anna
Auguste	Elizabeth
Kent	Barbara
Torcuato	Maya
Eduardo	Louise
Gunter	Malvina
Vinnie	Jean

Lighthearted Names

Boys	Girls
Corky	Coco
Dusty	Mimi
Rodeo	Bambi
Champ	Peach
Boots	Honey
Sonny	Tweedie
Benji	Fifi
Rusty	Daphne
Galaxy	Buffy
Skip	Kitty

Eccentric Names

Boys	Girls
Arailia	Xanthia
Boaz	Rainie
Lorenzo	Porsche
Guinness	Liberty
Byrd	Allegra
Math	Aquanetta
Aluf	Aceline
Cicero	Borghild
Elmo	Fontenot
Iggy	Hildegarde

Skydivers

Boys	Girls
Mario	Alysia
Patt	Cassandra
Russ	Cheryl
Ray	Elisa
Mick	Martha
Tom	Elizabeth
DJ	Wendy
Tamsin	Carolyn
Jacques	Clare
BJ	Carol

Brand Names

Boys	Girls
Nike	Porsche
Klein	Lee
Killian	Jaclyn
Miller	Lotus
Levi	Victoria
Mack	Claire
Harley	Zima
Dell	Lucky
Jimmy John	Seven
Patron	Macy

Humorous People

Boys	Girls
Gene	Lily
Will	Goldie
Adam	Kristie
Mike	Rosie
Richard	Brett
Steve	Jane
Woody	Molly
Rocco	Tracey
Jerry	Rita
Chris	Julia

Nicknames as Names

Boys	Girls
Greg	Betty
Dick	Liz
Harry	Sue
Larry	Sasha
Bill	Bobbie
Bob	Carrie
Mike	Dee
Will	Allie
Matt	Abby
Jake	Sandy

Activists

Boys	Girls
Arthur	Abbie
Martin	Barbara
Ralph	Rosa
Muhammad	Ingrid
Saul	Maggie
Jeremy	Ethel
William	Simone
Edward	Gloria
Christopher	Emily
Paul	Fannie

Country Singers

Boys	Girls
Marty	Naomi
Johnny	Emmylou
Troy	Linda
Trace	Carrie
Chesney	Gretchen
Buck	Taylor
Joe Don	Roseanne
Brad	June
Keith	Deana
Sammy	Miranda

Chefs

Boys	Girls
Mario	Julia
Emeril	Nathalie
Wolfgang	Susan
Jacques	Mollie
Paolo	Maryann
Sam	Caprial
Nick	Sara
Martin	Rachael
Tom	Sandra
Jamie	Robin

Superheroes

Boys	Girls
Clark	Diana
Peter	Jean
Bruce	Selina
Logan	Jaime
Bruce	Linda
Hal	Susan
Steve	Ororo
Al	Barbara
Frank	May
Scott	Jessica

Olympians

Boys	Girls
Muhammad	Shawn
Jesse	Nastia
Carl	Jackie
Mark	Wilma
John	Kristi
Eric	Shannon
Dan	Evelyn
Bob	Natalie
Larry	Janet
Michael	Bonnie

Game-Show Hosts

Boys	Girls
Bob	Anne
Pat	Pat
Alex	Meredith
Guy	Brooke
Alan	Caroline
Chuck	Vanna
Eugene	Paula
Regis	Whoopi
Richard	Nancy
Gene	Kennedy

Senators

Boys	Girls
Robert	Mary
Richard	Barbara
John	Lisa
Thomas	Hillary
Lincoln	Susan
Michael	Elizabeth
William	Dianne
Russell	Blanche
James	Olympia
Edward	Debbie

Representatives

Boys	Girls
Neil	Tammy
Gary	Shelley
Rodney	Melissa
Spencer	Judy
Roscoe	Marsha
Xavier	Madeleine
Marion	Corrine
Sanford	Virginia
Earl	Lois
Sherrod	Donna

Old-West Names

Boys	Girls
Gus	Kitty
July	Jane
Bill	Annie
Cody	Clementine
Roscoe	Susannah
Duke	Dinah
Custer	Clara
Ned	Trixie
Ranger	Lorena
Amos	Juanita

State Names

Boys	Girls
Dakota	Virginia
Indiana	Georgia
Montana	Carolina
Kentucky	Florida
Tennessee	Alabama
Texas	Kansas
Washington	Nebraska
Idaho	Iowa
Michigan	Missouri
Delaware	Mississippi

Names Abroad

Boys	Girls
Paris	Paris
Troy	Orly
Cuba	Ankara
Kobe	Sydney
Berlin	Lourdes
Frankfurt	Adelaide
Seymour	Madras
Dublin	Florence
London	Cairo
Athens	Andorra

Royalty

Boys	Girls
Edward	Elizabeth
George	Mary
Charles	Victoria
William	Alexandra
Frederick	Christina
Henry	Catherine
Alexander	Isabella
Louis	Cleopatra
Rainier	Diana
James	Anne

Drama Queens

Boys	Girls
Rupaul	Jackie
Al	Mariah
Michael	Paris
Joel	Nicole
Dennis	Britney
Cato	Valerie
Andy	Carrie
Dick	Whitney
Elton	Liza
Julian	Anna Nicole

Saint Names

Boys	Girls
George	Catherine
Francis	Anne
Patrick	Mary
David	Theresa
Stephen	Bridget
Peter	Cecilia
Thomas	Elizabeth
Paul	Agnes
John	Joan
Anthony	Agatha

Colors

Boys	Girls
Brown	Violet
Blue	Hazel
Kelly	Mauve
Roan	Pink
Sage	Auburn
Sky	Olive
Russet	Magenta
Azul	Carmesi
Morado	Shell
Royal	Lemon

Car Names

Boys	Girls
Lexus	Porsche
Bentley	Lexus
Austin	Mercedes
Healy	Sierra
Dolorian	Cheyenne
Mack	Carrera
Willy	Audi
Ford	Chevrolet
Humvee	Hemi
Cadillac	Impala

Last Names First

Boys	Girls
Taylor	Addison
Wesley	Kelly
Tanner	Mackenzie
Murray	Alison
Grant	Ainsley
Ryan	Blair
Dillon	Shannon
Rhys	Bailey
Jackson	Hadley
Douglas	Ashley

Shakespearean Names

Boys	Girls
Romeo	Juliette
Hector	Ophelia
Henry	Helena
Richard	Hero
Othello	Beatrice
Hamlet	Olivia
Iago	Titania
Mercutio	Miranda
Claudio	Hermia
Horatio	Cordelia

Occupations

Hunter
Taylor
Carter
Tanner
Law
Jack
Fabio
Farmer
Sawyer
Spence

Gods and Goddesses

Boys	Girls
Zeus	Hera
Aries	Athena
Apollo	Minverva
Poseidon	Aphrodite
Hermes	Juno
Pluto	Demeter
Jupiter	Hestia
Bacchus	Persephone
Neptune	Diana
Sol	Venus

Mythological Characters

Boys	Girls
Adonis	Medea
Achilles	Helen
Hercules	Andromeda
Perseus	Cassandra
Theseus	Clytemnestra
Jason	Cleo
Odysseus	Dido
Romulus	Eos
Remus	Aurora
Aeneus	Psyche

Mother-Nature Names

Boys	Girls
Stone	Rain
Storm	Brooke
River	Lily
Cloudy	Petunia
Lake	Rainbow
Brook	Star
Sunny	Clover
Leaf	Oceana
Glen	Rose
Dale	Skye

Virtue Names

Temperance
Patience
Prudence
Charity
Chastity
Honor
Faith
Grace
Hope
Makepeace

Heroes and Heroines from American Literature

Boys	Girls
Ichabod	Annabelle
Rip	Sula
Nemo	Hester
Billy	Antonia
Huck	Jo
Tom	Cora
Rhett	Alexandra
Horton	Eliza
Holden	Brett
Lenny	Isabelle

Names That Mean Wise

Boys	Girls
Akili	Athena
Bathasar	Avery
Conaire	Dara
Conroy	Keyla
Drew	Landra
Eldrick	Medora
Hakim	Monique
Raymond	Rayna
Sarat	Sage
Shanahan	Sennet

U.S. Authors

Boys	Girls
Edgar	Emily
Mark	Anne
Ernest	Patricia
Aldus	Willa
Ambrose	Gertrude
Stephen	Margaret
Emerson	Kate
Henry	Madeline
Nathaniel	Laura
James	Marguerite

Celebrity Names

Boys	Girls
Keanu	Angelina
Ben	Calista
Vince	Beyonce
Tom	Paris
Michael	Britney
Douglas	Janet
Jake	Teri
Kevin	Eva
Justin	Ellen
Orlando	Katharine

Poets

Boys	Girls
Shel	Emily
John	Maya
Alfred	Joy
Ralph	Anna
James	Maria
Riley	Angela
Samuel	Elizabeth
Estlin	Mary
Oscar	Hilary
Ted	Sara

Roman Names

Boys	Girls
Claudius	Claudia
Marcus	Clara
Maximus	Maxima
Julius	Flora
Lucius	Julia
Cicero	Lucretia
Magnus	Antonia
Constantius	Flavia
Septus	Minerva
Augustus	Augusta

Icons

Boys	Girls
Martin	Rosa
Fonzi	Oprah
Clark	Martha
Donald	Madonna
James	Jackie
Michael	Betty
Charlie	Dolly
Hank	Tina
Willie	Katherine
Johnny	Audrey

Children's Lit

Boys	Girls
Harry	Charlotte
Peter	Mary
Edmund	Lucy
Colin	Matilda
Klaus	Sunny
Henry	Violet
Ronald	Hermione
Tom	Heidi
Nigel	Rebecca
James	Susan

Wines

Chardonnay
Syrah
Merlot
Chablis
Bordeaux
Beaujolais
Chianti
Rosé
Sherry
Claret

Bird Names

Robin
Eagle
Sparrow
Raven
Hawk
Jay
Phoenix
Birdie
Wren
Oriole

Democrats

Boys	Girls
John	Hillary
William	Jacqueline
Carter	Eleanor
James	Ruth
Evan	Madeleine
Barack	Gloria
Franklin	Janet
Robert	Dianne
Joe	Nancy
Daley	Chelsea

Republicans

Boys	Girls
George	Laura
Herbert	Ann
Rick	Elizabeth
Michael	Harriet
John	Marilyn
Dick	Maureen
Clarence	Karin
Karl	Sarah
Donald	Kay
Teddy	Rachel

Sports Legends

Boys	Girls
Mason	Serena
Jim	Desiree
Peyton	Sidney
Warren	Mariam
Marvin	Venus
Reggie	Miranda
Kobe	Athena
Jason	Vivica
Miller	Annika
Ricky	Claire

Presidential Last Names

Lincoln	Washington
Jefferson	Madison
Reagan	Jackson
Clinton	Hayes
Harrison	Pierce
McKinley	Roosevelt
Grant	Cleveland
Monroe	Wilson
Truman	Ford
Kennedy	Carter

Travelers

Boys	Girls
Orlando	Georgia
Amarillo	Kenya
Bexley	Savannah
Cuba	Paris
Elam	Asia
Rainier	Ireland
Cyprus	China
Dodge	Dayton
Arizona	Dallas
Austin	Biloxi

Names That Make an Impression

Boys	Girls
Jagger	Olivia
Jovan	Roxanne
Bucky	Fiona
Ryder	Vivica
Rodeo	Xanthia
Happy	Harley
Jazz	Pixie
Tru	Bliss
Preston	Charlie
Chaz	Tawny

Doctors

Boys	Girls
Hiroyuki	Annette
Tanner	Laura
Preston	Lillian
Ruben	Janelle
Alonzo	Angie
Mario	Inez
Alex	Izzy
Derek	Bailey
Noah	Cristina
Clooney	Addison

Soap-Opera Names

Boys	Girls
Gill	Haley
Randall	Angelica
Caleb	Cassidy
Reno	Rusty
Lucas	Dallas
Zach	Liv
Arizona	Drew
Wyatt	Renee
Curtis	Elena
Keenan	Coletta

First Children

Boys	Girls
George	Chelsea
Jeb	Barbara
Neil	Jenna
Marvin	Sasha
Ronald	Malia
Michael	Pauline
Jack	Dorothy
Jeff	Patricia
Chip	Christine
Patrick	Maureen

Class Clowns

Boys	Girls
Darby	Willow
Michael	Tashiani
Jesse	Kelly
Anthony	Carrie
Brandon	Kyla
Larry	Ashland
Dusty	Ashley
Eric	Chrissy
Harvey	Sam
Justin	Jenny

Inventors

Boys	Girls
Baldwin	Adiva
Blakely	Josey
Cassius	Kornelia
Clyde	Navina
Dalton	Ailsa
Dewitt	Nerissa
Hashum	Marilyn
Basye	Klarissa
Andreas	Maitlin
Agustin	Gwen

Mechanics

Boys	Girls
Buck	Johna
Jeb	Jena
Roc	Adra
Jesse	Amera
Chevy	Josee
Baley	Jovi
Boz	Kris
Casper	Marley
Clete	Klara
Dex	Symone

Architects

Boys	Girls
Adrian	Alysia
Brock	Kristalee
Carson	Adline
Coby	Sawyer
Brice	Nevada
Detliff	Marissa
Beck	Amoretta
Carnell	Marlycia
Beamer	Kyria
Andy	Haelee

Forensic Scientists

Boys	Girls
Bryant	Brooke
Dale	Chelsea
Joshua	April
Max	Ava
Casper	Bree
Craig	Drew
Keith	Sara
Bram	Rebecca
Kyle	Claudia

Sailors

Boys	Girls
Graham	Melanie
Thomas	Charlotte
Simon	Margaret
Christopher	Eleanor
Duncan	Breezy
Mariner	Courtney
Aaron	Fay
Burt	Keneitha
Daan	Cait

Interior Decorators

Boys	Girls
Darnell	Zora
Imari	Yasmin
Kyan	Tanisha
Malik	Kiana
Jarad	Danica
Dante	Alexia
Zander	Angel
Sebastian	Taisha
Lukas	Charisma
Robin	Niara

Home-Makeover Hosts

Boys	Girls
Darius	Tia
Ty	Kendra
Marcus	Keshia
Dirk	Tyra
Ruben	Raven
Crispin	Letitia
Baird	Vanessa
Cameron	Hope
Colin	Chloe
Cornelius	Flora

American Idols

Boys	Girls
Clay	Carrie
David	Diana
Elliott	Jordin
Constantine	Brooke
Blake	Melinda
Bo	Carly
Ruben	Fantasia
Taylor	Syesha
Justin	Ramiele
Jason	Kelly

Names That Are Candidates for Nicknames

Boys	Girls
Christopher	Abigail
Alexander	Elizabeth
Richard	Gwendolyn
Timothy	Katharine
Gregory	Deborah
Nicholas	Susannah
Franklin	Jacqueline
Michael	Joanne
Matthew	Amanda
Thomas	Samantha

Couch Potatoes

Boys	Girls
Homer	Roberta
Barney	Jethra
Ernie	Erlene
Mack	Randy-Jo
Tubby	Noreen
Jose	Carla
Larry	Doris
Bob	Bertha
George	Mabel
Earl	Bobbi-Claire

Names That Command Respect

Boys	Girls
William	Elizabeth
Edward	Alexandra
Graham	Jacqueline
Truman	Magdalena
Jackson	Katherine
Jefferson	Isabella
Augustus	Mary
Albert	Josephine
Caesar	Cleopatra
Phillip	Anne

Reality-TV Names

Boys	Girls
Bill	Kristin
Richard	LC
Brady	Omarosa
Andrew	Adrienne
Phil	Trista
Ryan	Sue
Rupert	Tyra
Jeff	Trishelle
Donald	Carolyn
Gervais	Katharine

Talk-Show Hosts

Boys	Girls
David	Oprah
Jay	Ellen
Jimmy	Rosie
Bill	Barbara
Carson	Star
Tony	Joy
Larry	Elisabeth
Regis	Kelly
Conan	Tyra
Anderson	Jenny

Disco Names

Boys	Girls
Stu	Darlene
Eddie	Donna
Tony	Carla
Ricky	Peggy
Bobby	Sharon
Sonny	Linda
Gerry	Janet
Danny	Chrissy
Larry	Rita
Rob	Rhonda

Dorks

Boys	Girls
Gabe	Bernice
Norm	Imogene
Cliff	Rhea
Ralph	Pansy
Dilbert	Edna
Roscoe	Gladys
Nermal	Hildie
Milhouse	Hortense
Urkel	Jute
PJ	Madge

Austen Fans

Boys	Girls
Fitzwilliam	Jane
Henry	Elizabeth
John	Elinor
Edward	Marianne
Brandon	Cassandra
Willoughby	Lucy
George	Jane
Charles	Katherine
William	Lydia
Bennet	Darcy

Risk-Takers

Boys	Girls
Chance	Chauncey
Chase	Rocket
Hector	Amelia
Colombo	Christa
Beau	Lucky
Racer	Dicey
Harry	Victoria
Geronimo	Boadicea
Rodeo	Sacagawea
Charles	Cleopatra

Names with Great Expectations

Boys	Girls
Romeo	Chastity
Justice	Honor
Alexander	Sunny
Truth	Felicity
Junior	Prudence
Victor	Belle
King	Queen
Arthur	Regina
Jesus	Joy
Beau	Charity

Literary Villains

Boys	Girls
Erik	Medea
Simon	Medusa
Iago	Rebecca
Saruman	Danny
Draco	Jadis
Brutus	Lucy
Don John	Catherine
Arturo	Lilith
Pavel	Morgan
Olaf	Rose

Pro Wrestlers

Boys	Girls
Ray	Torri
Jesse	Trish
Bret	Victoria
Hunter	Stacy
Vince	Melina
Hogan	Maria
Eddie	Kristal
John	Sharmell
Shelton	Candice
Chavo	Lita

Gymnasts

Boys	Girls
David	Larissa
Jonathan	Vera
Brett	Nadia
Michael	Olga
Justin	Mary Lou
Kevin	Shannon
Todd	Chellsie
Yewki	Nastia
Alexander	Alicia
Guillermo	Shawn

Sesame Street Characters

Boys	Girls
Barkley	Polly
Oscar	Dawn
Elmo	Merryl
Bruno	Gladys
Grover	Gina
Ernie	Alice
Bert	Elizabeth
Sully	Linda
Alan	Gabriella
Wally	Olivia

Muppets Characters

Boys	Girls
Kermit	Camilla
Gonzo	Gladys
Rizzo	Annie Sue
Zoot	Janice
Wayne	Wanda
Louis	Virginia
Robin	Mildred
Statler	Hilda
Bunson	Betsy
Beaker	Skeeter

Hurricane Names

Boys	Girls
Charley	Isabel
Frances	Jeanne
Ivan	Katrina
Fabian	Lili
Juan	Isidore
Keith	Allison
Floyd	Iris
Lenny	Michelle
Mitch	Opal
Georges	Marilyn

Famous Generals

Sherman
Thomas
Robert
George
Patton
Nathan
Mark
Lee
Ulysses
Joshua

MTV Names

Boys	Girls
Damien	Vanessa
Quddus	Susie
Carson	La La
Matt	Madison
Tim	Jessica
Nick	Ashlee
Johnny	Sharon
Andy	Kelly
Tom	Daria
Beavis	Ashton

British Authors

Boys	Girls
William	Angela
Clive	Helen
Thomas	Agatha
Henry	Jane
Charles	Elizabeth
Rudyard	Daphne
Graham	Edith
Walter	Diana
Andrew	Phillippa
Robert	Alice

Classic Names

Boys	Girls
John	Emily
Charles	Ann
George	Elizabeth
Alexander	Mary
Michael	Sarah
Richard	Jane
William	Katherine
Thomas	Margaret
David	Helen
Edward	Christine

Flavorful Names

Boys	Girls
Sage	Cinnamon
Oregano	Rosemary
Cilantro	Paprika
Cayenne	Parsley
Thyme	Ginger
Basil	Marjoram
Tarragon	Saffron
Curry	Poppy
Herb	Vanilla
Coriander	Pepper

Names on the Rise

Boys	Girls
Jacoby	Khloe
Kane	Harper
Beckett	Marely
Paxton	Audrina
Kale	Marley
August	Danna
Braylon	Jaslene
Ryker	Lilah
Kingston	Paisley
Kolton	Miley

Psychologists

Boys	Girls
Sigmund	Estelle
Alfred	Helen
Carl	Lily
Edward	Victoria
John	Esther
Jakob	Honora
Kinsey	Emma
Ivan	Ellen
Jean	May
Martin	Isabelle

Nouns as Names

Cat
Stone
Rush
Reed
Rice
River
Flint
Buck
Faith
Hope

Philosophers

Boys	Girls
Plato	Estelle
Socrates	Helen
William	Lily
Rene	Victoria
Edmund	Esther
Edward	Honora
John	Emma
Adam	Ellen
Carl	May
Isaiah	Isabelle

Fairy-Tale Names

Boys	Girls
Hansel	Gretel
Tom	Thumbelina
Roland	Katrinelje
Joseph	Hildebrand
John	Maleen
Hans	Cinderella
Lawrence	Rapunzel
Harry	Hulda
Joringel	Jorinda
Ferdinand	Else

Models

Boys	Girls
Travis	Tyra
Kevin	Elle
Hunter	Cindy
Maurice	Twiggy
Tab	Farrah
Tyson	Kate
Alex	Elizabeth
Michael	Heidi
Philip	Claudia
Derek	Daniela

Explorers

Boys	Girls
Leif	Meriweather
Christopher	Amelia
John	Sacagawea
Henry	Mary
Ferdinand	Isabella
Jacques	Roberta
Giovanni	Edith
Amerigo	Phyllis
William	Victoria
Juan	Ada

The In-Crowd Names

Boys	Girls
Trent	Danica
Trevor	Melissa
Troy	Tara
Brent	Trish
Brandon	Tiffany
Kevin	Amelia
Keith	Emily
Kyle	Heather
Josh	Stacey
Phil	Kristi

Plant Names

Rose
Ivy
Myrtle
Lily
Violet
Magnolia
Fern
Hyacinth
Daisy
Marigold

Tree Names

Hawthorn
Oak
Maple
Pine
Cherry
Mahogany
Cyprus
Spruce
Buckeye
Willow

Movie Directors/Producers

Boys	Girls
Ron	Kathleen
Alfred	Penny
Steven	Susana
Peter	Kathryn
Ang	Sofia
Frances	Martha
Clint	Claire
Quentin	Jodie
Frank	Amy
Stanley	Diane

Ballet Dancers

Boys	Girls
Sergei	Pierina
Mikhail	Mathilde
Billy	Galina
Fernando	Maya
Leonid	Simone
Vladimir	Nadia
Julio	Irina
Ross	Sylvia
Wayne	Cecilia
Will	Yvette

Names That Mean Beautiful

Arabella
Bella
Alaina
Bonnie
Calista
Ayanna
Caiomhe
Hermosa
Memphis
Belinda

Patriotic Names

Boys	Girls
Lincoln	Free
Washington	Liberty
Norman	Justice
Columbus	Librada
Knox	Spirit
Crane	Starr
William	Americus
Alamo	Peace
Bragg	Independence
Leavenworth	Eagle

Farmers

Boys	Girls
Harvey	Kassidy
Kendall	Brooke
George	Marylou
Jimbo	Butter
Jethro	Brody
Gideon	Chloe
Elson	River
Dixon	Breezy
Thurmond	June
Country	Felicia

Popular-Song Names

Boys	Girls
Arnold	Cecelia
Danny	Roxanne
John	Athena
Tom	Gloria
Ziggy	Dawn
Tony	Michelle
Sean	Jenny
Stan	Wendy
Jeremiah	Julie
Neil	Diane

Carpenters

Boys	Girls
Jacob	Gunun
Coye	Gay
Cowell	Hyde
Haynes	Idra
Harkin	Farrah
Lennox	Dusty
Leroy	Edie
Obard	Dylan
Moses	Makita
Porter	Carissa

Comic-Strip Characters

Boys	Girls
Mungo	Nancy
Satchel	Cathy
Bucky	Lois
Rob	Lucy
Garfield	Sally
Dilbert	Patty
Charlie	Betty
Dennis	Annie
Hagar	Blondie
Bailey	Dolly

Famous for Being Famous

Boys	Girls
Brandon	Paris
Kato	Nicole
Charles	Nicky
Stavros	Courtney
Kevin	Tara
Bobby	Angelyne
Jack	Jordan
Farnsworth	Susan
Nick	Anna Nicole
John	Tori

Clowns

Boys	Girls
Charlie	Annie
Don	Nola
Red	Peggy
Groucho	Frankie
Harpo	Mathurine
Chico	Tammy
Lou	Jackie
Otto	Lucy
Felix	Karen
Avner	Lily

Amish Names

Boys	Girls
Amos	Katie
Samuel	Annie
John	Mary
Daniel	Rebecca
David	Sarah
Moses	Rachel
Solomon	Deborah
Isaac	Leah
Jonathan	Susannah
Aaron	Eve

Pilots

Boys	Girls
Charles	Amelia
Wilbur	Blanche
Orville	Bessie
Eugene	Jackie
James	Laura
Frank	Amy
Harry	Maud
Gabriel	Polly
Steve	Harriet
Clyde	Ruth

Names That Mean Strong

Boys	Girls
Arthur	Andrea
Cale	Bridget
Everett	Charla
Magglio	Jerica
Nardo	Karla
Pierce	Mirit
Quinlan	Petronelle
Steele	Sela
Terrian	Sloane
Valerian	Trudy

College Football Stadiums

Kinnick

Neyland

Randall

Autzen

Kenan

Owen

Bryant

Williams

Brice

Michie

Chess Players

Boys	Girls
Alexander	Vera
Mikhail	Judit
Jose	Alexandra
Max	Sonja
Robert	Nona
Anatoly	Alisa
Garry	Maia
Emanuel	Elizaveta
Vasily	Nana
Boris	Elena

Gardeners

Boys	Girls
Isaac	Emma
Joshua	Wilma
Keith	Elena
Bradley	Evelea
Corbin	Cleora
Joseph	Delores
Curtis	Ivory
Dalton	Jordan
Ezzie	Marla
Hershell	Joy

Stunt Performers

Boys	Girls
David	Michelle
Evel	Spice
Ken	Eunice
Robbie	Jeannie
Dave	Alisa
Colin	Lee
Zelijko	Abbi
Bubba	Sophia
Thomas	Chrissy
Sam	Mary

Firefighters

Boys	Girls
Blaze	Sisteen
Smokey	Faith
Rocky	Angelle
Uland	Lansing
Sly	Marie
Chase	Naomi
Roscoe	Sean
Nat	Poe
Royce	Scout
Merv	Jacey

Names That Were Invented

Boys	Girls
Bandy	Jacey
Keontay	Chailyn
Fleada	Halzey
Phex	Larby
Cathan	Nevaeh
Reith	Olaide
Dobber	Hender
Melvis	Talisa
Dalgus	Xannon
Efton	Camassia

Urban Names

Boys	Girls
Jabari	Juanita
Juwon	Dashawn
Keshoh	Quanisha
Shaquille	Shaldona
Jarvis	Dasmine
Shawnell	Dawntelle
Tyree	Latasha
Tre	Tamika
Damarcus	Tearah
Devonte	Shawanna

Horticulturists

Boys	Girls
Lionel	Neva
Hector	Skyler
Max	Zora
Zeb	Morgan
Ian	Lanee
Horatio	Mona
Stony	Laurel
Izzy	Tammy
Fernando	Sheyn
Cal	Belle

Triathletes

Boys	Girls
Elliott	Flora
Peter	Jill
Will	Liz
Chris	Heather
Alan	Catriona
Tim	Kate
Gavin	Helen
Marc	Emma
Simon	Felicity
Hamish	Julie

Swimmers

Boys	Girls
Aaron	Katie
Brendan	Jessica
Ian	Kaitlin
Lewis	Natalie
Matt	Whitney
Johnny	Tracy
Mark	Amanda
Nate	Lindsay
Michael	Haley
Scott	Kristen

Surfers

Boys	Girls
Jason	Lisa
Micah	Jen
Cole	Malia
Ryan	Elizabeth
Eric	Keren
Lian	Kelea
Kelly	Linda
Bruce	Megan
Carwyn	Margo
Joel	Anne

Composers

Boys	Girls
Johann	Maria Teresa
Ludwig	Keiko
Frederic	Maryanne
Edward	Amalia
George	Anna
Gustav	Beth
Jacob	Ruth
Wolfgang	Katarina
Franz	Agatha
Sergei	Tekla

Geniuses

Boys	Girls
Plato	Hypatia
John	Sofia
Leonardo	Maria
Albert	Simone
Stephen	Maya
Srinivasa	Marilyn
William	Anna
Gottfried	Aurore
Immanuel	Laura
Johann	Natasha

Country Names

Boys	Girls
Cletus	Maryann
Ichabod	Esther
Randy	Harlee
Rusty	Ruby
Wendell	Daisy
Emmett	Dakota
Dustin	Bella
Wyatt	Dixie
Maverick	Abilene
Amos	Ira

Teachers

Boys	Girls
Hurley	Renee
Drake	Twilla
Ira	Johna
Jarvis	Venus
Keenan	Traci
Davis	Hazel
Linton	Carmen
Paxon	Reagan
Loren	Charlotte
Read	Ivy

Stylists

Boys	Girls
Laree	Story
Trevi	Fancy
Wesley	Evonne
Stacey	Cyprus
Lamont	Diana
Whitley	Daisha
Ripley	Yvette
Larkin	Daleah
Spencer	Estella
Ladden	Frannie

EMTs

Boys	Girls
Judd	Cydell
Frost	Sam
Damon	Jovi
Julius	Santana
Chevalle	Angel
Chase	Cylee
Flip	Brady
Jin	Joshi
Chaney	Sandra
Darian	Breena

Barflies

Boys	Girls
Norm	Ali
Cliff	Carla
Woody	Robin
Sam	Christi
Frazier	Arlette
Ted	Delia
Larry	Melissa
Jace	Asia
Barney	Delicia
Homer	Bridget

African American Names

Boys	Girls
Antwon	Keisha
Malik	Jameeka
Jaleel	Cherise
Tyrell	Tamika
Denzel	Raisha
Keshawn	Jada
Tyrone	Desiree
Rashaun	Camika
Shaquille	Alondra
Darnell	Jada

Bodybuilders

Boys	Girls
Cosner	Nakia
Arnold	Lucy
Lou	Katchen
Guy	Natashia
Hagen	Lizibeth
Blair	Jules
Alanson	Kashmir
Gregor	Naomi
Bettis	Lisarae
Cotton	Gunilla

Colleges

Drake
Emerson
Purdue
Murray
Smith
Austin
Duke
Boston
Yale
Hulman

Guitarists

Boys	Girls
Eddie	Sheryl
Eric	Brody
Stevie	Chanyee
Jimi	Ariella
B.B.	Karma
Paige	Boston
Van	Asysa
Sammy	Chaney
Ray	Arizona
Cantrell	Katchi

Soccer Players

Boys	Girls
Ronaldo	Mia
Diego	Brandi
Hristo	Carla
Zinedine	Julie
David	Michelle
Trifon	Alexi
Pele	Tiffany
Pavel	Katie
Raul	Meagan
Landon	Mackenzie

Names That Mean Gift

Boys	Girls
Cathan	Amariah
Jesse	Chipo
Mathias	Adia
Nathaniel	Dori
Niaz	Daryn
Seanan	Emsley
Shai	Grace
Ted	Makalo
Tesher	Theodora
Zani	Matea

Big-City Names

Boys	Girls
Austin	Alexandria
Boston	Atlanta
Chandler	Aurora
Dallas	Campbell
Dayton	Charlotte
Denver	Cheyenne
Houston	Memphis
Orlando	Savannah
Easton	Brooklyn
Kingston	Helena

A Names

Boys	Girls
Abel	Abby
Abraham	Adeline
Alan	Aileen
Alec	Ainsley
Amari	Ada
Amir	Agatha
Anderson	Agnes
Asher	Alice
Axel	Alejandra
Andres	America

B Names

Boys	Girls
Beau	Bella
Bennett	Bethany
Bradley	Belinda
Braxton	Bianca
Braylon	Breanna
Brennan	Bridget
Brett	Brielle
Brock	Brynn
Bryant	Bronwen
Bryce	Beth

C Names

Boys	Girls
Cade	Cadence
Calvin	Callie
Carl	Camila
Cash	Camryn
Cesar	Carly
Chad	Cassidy
Chance	Cecilia
Chandler	Clara
Charlie	Claudia
Clayton	Cora

D Names

Boys	Girls
Dallas	Daisy
Dalton	Dakota
Dane	Dana
Dante	Danica
Darius	Daniela
Davis	Dayanara
Dawson	Delaney
Dean	Delilah
Declan	Dominique
Dorian	Diamond

E Names

Boys	Girls
Easton	Eden
Eddie	Elaina
Edgar	Eleanor
Eduardo	Elise
Eli	Elle
Elias	Emerson
Emanuel	Erica
Enrique	Erin
Everett	Esther
Ezekiel	Estrella

F Names

Boys	Girls
Fabian	Fara
Felipe	Felicity
Felix	Fernanda
Fernando	Fiona
Finn	Francesca
Foster	Frances
Francisco	Fersia
Francois	Fallon
Franklin	Franka
Frisco	Frankie

G Names

Boys	Girls
Gage	Galina
Garrett	Genesis
Garrick	Genevieve
Grayson	Genoveva
George	Georgia
Giovanni	Giselle
Grady	Gerri
Grant	Gloria
Griffin	Guadalupe
Gustavo	Gwendolyn

H Names

Boys	Girls
Hanson	Hadley
Harry	Hanna
Harrison	Harley
Hector	Harlow
Hendrick	Harmony
Heinrich	Harper
Holden	Hayden
Horatio	Hazel
Hudson	Heather
Hugo	Heaven

I Names

Boys	Girls
Ivan	Isabelle
Ike	Isadora
Ian	Imogen
Isaac	India
Isaiah	Indra
Ishmael	Ivy
Israel	Isis
Itzak	Iris
Ivo	Iseult
Irving	Ingrid

J Names

Boys	Girls
Jace	Jacqueline
Jaime	Jada
Jake	Jaelyn
Jamari	Jane
Jameson	Janelle
Jared	Jenna
Jasper	Jillian
Jeremy	Jordana
Johan	Josie
Justice	Julissa

K Names

Boys	Girls
Kai	Kadence
Keaton	Kara
Keegan	Kate
Keith	Kathryn
Kellen	Keely
Kelvin	Kiera
Kenneth	Kendall
Khalil	Kenzie
Kingston	Kimora
Kyler	Kirsten

L Names

Boys	Girls
Lance	Lacey
Landon	Laura
Lane	Lila
Leland	Lindsay
Leif	Logan
Leo	Lola
Leon	London
Lincoln	Lucia
Luca	Luna
Luther	Lydia

M Names

Boys	Girls
Maddox	Macy
Malachi	Maggie
Malik	Malia
Manuel	Mallory
Marcos	Mariana
Mario	Marisol
Marshall	Miley
Mitchell	Miracle
Moises	Melissa
Myles	Monica

N Names

Boys	Girls
Nasir	Nadia
Neal	Nancy
Nehemiah	Naomi
Nelson	Natasha
Newton	Nayeli
Nigel	Nelia
Nicholson	Nevis
Noam	Nia
Noe	Nora
Nolan	Nyla

O Names

Boys	Girls
Oakley	Olivia
Olaf	Olimpia
Oliver	Orla
Olan	Olive
Oscar	Ozara
Otis	Ormanda
Orlando	Opa
Oslo	Olya
Owen	Omie
Otto	Odessa

P Names

Boys	Girls
Pablo	Paola
Parker	Paris
Patrick	Patricia
Paul	Paulina
Peter	Presley
Peyton	Penelope
Philip	Phoebe
Pierce	Piper
Porter	Poppy
Preston	Priscilla

Q Names

Boys	Girls
Quinn	Quinn
Quincy	Quincey
Quentin	Queen
Quirin	Qadira
Quon	Quinta
Quigley	Quintessa
Quimby	Quita
Qasim	Quinella
Quenby	Quimby
Quintus	Quisha

R Names

Boys	Girls
Raymond	Ramona
Reed	Raquel
Reese	Rebecca
Ricardo	Rhonwen
Rocco	Rhea
Rodney	Riana
Roman	Rosa
Rowan	Rowan
Ruben	Ruby
Ryder	Ruth

S Names

Boys	Girls
Salvador	Sabrina
Santiago	Sadie
Saul	Sage
Sawyer	Sasha
Scott	Scarlett
Sergio	Selena
Seth	Serenity
Silas	Shelby
Skyler	Sierra
Solomon	Stella

V Names

Boys	Girls
Victor	Valerie
Vincent	Victoria
Valeri	Viviane
Vadim	Vera
Valentino	Veronica
Vasily	Violet
Vance	Veda
Vigo	Vashti
Virgil	Verna
Vanya	Verity

T Names

Boys	Girls
Talon	Talia
Tate	Tamra
Terrance	Tara
Theodore	Taryn
Tobias	Tatiana
Trent	Tatum
Trey	Tessa
Theo	Tori
Tucker	Tonya
Tyson	Tracy

W Names

Boys	Girls
William	Willow
Warren	Whitney
Walker	Wanda
Washington	Whitley
Walter	Wynne
Willis	Winona
Wyatt	Wyoming
Weston	Wyss
Wilson	Wren
Wesley	Wallis

U Names

Boys	Girls
Udo	Uma
Udall	Udele
Ulan	Urbana
Ulrich	Una
Ulysses	Ulani
Uriah	Unice
Utah	Utica
Umberto	Uria
Ulriah	Uzona
Umi	Urania

X Names

Boys	Girls
Xavier	Xenia
Xander	Xanadu
Xenophon	Xanthe
Xerxes	Xylia
Xyle	Xavia
Xenik	Xylene
Xanthus	Ximena
Xylon	Xandra
Xerarch	Xana
Xen	Xara

Y Names

Boys	Girls
Yancy	Yvonne
Yale	Yael
Yeats	Yaki
Yves	Yakira
Yuri	Yolanda
Yule	Yasmine
Yardley	Yardley
Yasir	Ysabella
Yvonn	Yuliana
Yuan	Yori

Z Names

Boys	Girls
Zack	Zara
Zander	Zaza
Zed	Zelda
Zeke	Zelie
Zane	Zuri
Zyke	Zora
Zan	Zoe
Zent	Zuzanna
Zeb	Zosa
Zephariah	Zulie

Under the Radar Names

Boys		Girls	
Oscar	Darian	Bianca	Tia
Gage	Barrett	Alicia	Kinsley
Malachi	Nash	Jillian	Phoebe
Trent	Cullen	Vivian	Maran
Asher	Josiah	Elise	Anabel
Dante	Maverick	Piper	Clementine
Colby	Dexter	Lila	Ellery
Lane	Simeon	Cecilia	Bronwyn
Cash	Heath	Bethany	Josefina
Silas	Winston	Georgia	Darcy
Declan	Rex	Ivy	Lydia
Dean	Houston	Iris	Memphis
Philip	Rhys	Tatum	Greer
Holden	Madden	Brynn	Kenya
Finn	Finch	Bridget	Tuesday
Tate	Dallas	Natasha	Dorian
Judah	Victor	Sylvie	Penelope
Tobias	Lennon	Arely	Briony
Johan	Rafferty	Eve	Clara
Kellen	Easton	Laney	Georgia
Kendrick	Sullivan	Ansley	Bel
Jase	Trace	Adelaide	Orly

Most Popular in Alabama

Boys	Girls
William	Emma
James	Madison
Jacob	Isabella
Jackson	Ava
John	Anna
Joshua	Addison
Jayden	Olivia
Christopher	Chloe
Michael	Abigail
Ethan	Emily

Most Popular in Arkansas

Boys	Girls
William	Emma
Jacob	Madison
Ethan	Addison
Joshua	Isabella
Jayden	Ava
Noah	Alexis
Christopher	Emily
Jackson	Abigail
Landon	Olivia
Aiden	Chloe

Most Popular in Alaska

Boys	Girls
Michael	Isabella
Ethan	Sophia
Logan	Olivia
Samuel	Abigail
Elijah	Ava
James	Emma
Joseph	Madison
William	Chloe
David	Emily
Gabriel	Elizabeth

Most Popular in California

Boys	Girls
Daniel	Isabella
Anthony	Sophia
Angel	Emily
Jacob	Mia
Alexander	Samantha
Ethan	Natalie
David	Emma
Andrew	Ashley
Matthew	Abigail
Joshua	Olivia

Most Popular in Arizona

Boys	Girls
Jacob	Isabella
Alexander	Sophia
Daniel	Emma
Angel	Mia
Anthony	Emily
Ethan	Olivia
David	Madison
Michael	Abigail
Aiden	Ava
Jose	Samantha

Most Popular in Colorado

Boys	Girls
Alexander	Isabella
Jacob	Olivia
Noah	Sophia
William	Abigail
Benjamin	Emma
Ethan	Ava
Logan	Emily
Daniel	Addison
David	Elizabeth
Jackson	Madison

Most Popular in Connecticut

Boys	Girls
Michael	Isabella
Ryan	Olivia
Alexander	Sophia
Matthew	Ava
Jayden	Emma
Ethan	Madison
William	Abigail
Anthony	Mia
Joshua	Samantha
Christopher	Emily

Most Popular in Delaware

Boys	Girls
Alexander	Isabella
Michael	Olivia
James	Sophia
Jayden	Abigail
Ethan	Ava
Matthew	Emma
William	Madison
Logan	Samantha
Aiden	Emily
Chase	Elizabeth

Most Popular in District of Columbia

Boys	Girls
William	Ashley
John	Sophia
Christopher	Katherine
Michael	Elizabeth
Anthony	Caroline
Alexander	Kayla
Daniel	Madison
Kevin	Olivia
Andrew	Isabella
Noah	Abigail

Most Popular in Florida

Boys	Girls
Jayden	Isabella
Michael	Sophia
Joshua	Emma
Jacob	Emily
Anthony	Olivia
Christopher	Madison
Ethan	Ava
Daniel	Mia
Alexander	Abigail
Noah	Chloe

Most Popular in Georgia

Boys	Girls
William	Madison
Christopher	Isabella
Joshua	Emma
James	Olivia
Jayden	Ava
Jacob	Abigail
Michael	Emily
Christian	Chloe
Ethan	Elizabeth
Noah	Addison

Most Popular in Hawaii

Boys	Girls
Ethan	Isabella
Noah	Sophia
Jayden	Mia
Joshua	Ava
Elijah	Chloe
Caleb	Madison
Jacob	Olivia
Aiden	Taylor
Gabriel	Emma
Isaiah	Faith

Most Popular in Idaho

Boys	Girls
Logan	Olivia
Jacob	Emma
Ethan	Isabella
William	Sophia
Wyatt	Addison
Jackson	Abigail
Noah	Elizabeth
Aiden	Emily
Mason	Ava
Alexander	Madison

Most Popular in Iowa

Boys	Girls
Jacob	Ava
Ethan	Olivia
Carter	Emma
Noah	Isabella
William	Addison
Owen	Ella
Jackson	Sophia
Gavin	Chloe
Logan	Grace
Mason	Natalie

Most Popular in Illinois

Boys	Girls
Alexander	Isabella
Daniel	Olivia
Jacob	Sophia
Michael	Emma
Anthony	Emily
Ethan	Ava
Joshua	Abigail
William	Mia
Nathan	Madison
Aiden	Ella

Most Popular in Kansas

Boys	Girls
Ethan	Emma
William	Isabella
Jacob	Ava
Alexander	Olivia
Noah	Abigail
Aiden	Addison
Jackson	Madison
Gabriel	Sophia
Logan	Chloe
Joshua	Emily

Most Popular in Indiana

Boys	Girls
JEthan	Emma
Noah	Olivia
Jacob	Isabella
Logan	Ava
Elijah	Addison
Aiden	Sophia
Alexander	Abigail
William	Madison
Jackson	Chloe
Gavin	Lillian

Most Popular in Kentucky

Boys	Girls
Jacob	Emma
William	Isabella
James	Madison
Ethan	Olivia
Noah	Abigail
Landon	Alexis
Aiden	Addison
Brayden	Ava
Elijah	Chloe
Jackson	Emily

Most Popular in Louisiana

Boys	Girls
Jayden	Ava
Ethan	Emma
Landon	Isabella
Joshua	Madison
Noah	Olivia
William	Chloe
Michael	Addison
Aiden	Abigail
John	Emily
Christopher	Sophia

Most Popular in Maine

Boys	Girls
Noah	Emma
Logan	Olivia
Jacob	Isabella
Owen	Abigail
Aiden	Madison
Landon	Ava
William	Lily
Michael	Chloe
Carter	Sophia
Wyatt	Addison

Most Popular in Maryland

Boys	Girls
Michael	Madison
Jayden	Olivia
Joshua	Ava
Ethan	Isabella
William	Emma
Alexander	Sophia
Jacob	Abigail
Matthew	Chloe
Noah	Emily
Ryan	Taylor

Most Popular in Massachusetts

Boys	Girls
Ryan	Olivia
Jacob	Isabella
William	Sophia
Michael	Ava
Matthew	Emma
Benjamin	Abigail
John	Emily
Anthony	Grace
Alexander	Madison
Jack	Mia

Most Popular in Michigan

Boys	Girls
Jacob	Olivia
Ethan	Isabella
Logan	Ava
Noah	Emma
Aiden	Madison
Michael	Sophia
Alexander	Abigail
Joshua	Chloe
Andrew	Addison
William	Ella

Most Popular in Minnesota

Boys	Girls
Logan	Olivia
Benjamin	Ava
William	Emma
Ethan	Sophia
Jacob	Isabella
Alexander	Ella
Owen	Grace
Carter	Abigail
Samuel	Addison
Noah	Chloe

Most Popular in Mississippi

Boys	Girls
William	Madison
Jayden	Emma
James	Addison
Christopher	Ava
Joshua	Anna
John	Isabella
Michael	Chloe
Ethan	Olivia
Landon	Makayla
Jacob	Alyssa

Most Popular in Missouri

Boys	Girls
Jacob	Emma
Ethan	Olivia
William	Isabella
Jackson	Ava
Logan	Madison
Aiden	Sophia
Noah	Abigail
Michael	Chloe
Landon	Addison
Gavin	Elizabeth

Most Popular in Montana

Boys	Girls
Ethan	Emma
Wyatt	Isabella
Logan	Olivia
Landon	Ava
James	Madison
William	Sophia
Jacob	Hailey
Liam	Addison
Benjamin	Taylor
Isaac	Chloe

Most Popular in Nebraska

Boys	Girls
Alexander	Addison
Carter	Isabella
Noah	Ava
William	Olivia
Jacob	Emma
Ethan	Sophia
Logan	Ella
Samuel	Emily
Landon	Grace
Gavin	Alexis

Most Popular in Nevada

Boys	Girls
Anthony	Isabella
Jacob	Sophia
Daniel	Emma
Michael	Olivia
Alexander	Emily
Ethan	Ava
Jayden	Madison
Angel	Mia
David	Abigail
Aiden	Samantha

Most Popular in New Hampshire

Boys	Girls
Logan	Olivia
Jacob	Isabella
Liam	Ava
Aiden	Emma
Ryan	Abigail
Ethan	Alexis
Matthew	Madison
Benjamin	Sophia
Gavin	Lily
William	Emily

Most Popular in New Jersey

Boys	Girls
Michael	Isabella
Matthew	Olivia
Anthony	Sophia
Jayden	Ava
Ryan	Emily
Daniel	Mia
Joseph	Emma
Christopher	Madison
Alexander	Samantha
Nicholas	Abigail

Most Popular in North Carolina

Boys	Girls
William	Emma
Jacob	Madison
Christopher	Isabella
Noah	Ava
Joshua	Abigail
Ethan	Olivia
Michael	Emily
Alexander	Addison
Elijah	Chloe
James	Sophia

Most Popular in New Mexico

Boys	Girls
Aiden	Isabella
Noah	Olivia
Joshua	Mia
Jacob	Nevaeh
Gabriel	Sophia
Michael	Ava
Isaiah	Emily
Daniel	Alyssa
Elijah	Madison
Josiah	Emma

Most Popular in North Dakota

Boys	Girls
Ethan	Olivia
Logan	Ava
Jack	Emma
Carter	Ella
Jacob	Isabella
Mason	Chloe
Brayden	Taylor
Gavin	Abigail
Aiden	Lily
Jackson	Addison

Most Popular in New York

Boys	Girls
Michael	Isabella
Jayden	Sophia
Matthew	Olivia
Ethan	Emma
Daniel	Emily
Ryan	Madison
Anthony	Ava
Joseph	Mia
Jacob	Abigail
Christopher	Sarah

Most Popular in Ohio

Boys	Girls
Jacob	Isabella
Noah	Emma
Ethan	Olivia
Logan	Ava
William	Madison
Aiden	Sophia
Michael	Addison
Andrew	Abigail
Alexander	Chloe
James	Ella

Most Popular in Oklahoma

Boys	Girls
Ethan	Isabella
Jacob	Emma
Noah	Addison
William	Madison
Joshua	Abigail
Aiden	Chloe
James	Olivia
Michael	Emily
Gabriel	Ava
Logan	Alexis

Most Popular in Oregon

Boys	Girls
Alexander	Emma
Logan	Isabella
Jacob	Olivia
Daniel	Emily
Ethan	Sophia
Gabriel	Madison
Noah	Abigail
Elijah	Ava
William	Elizabeth
Benjamin	Ella

Most Popular in Pennsylvania

Boys	Girls
Michael	Isabella
Jacob	Olivia
Ethan	Ava
Logan	Emma
Matthew	Sophia
Ryan	Madison
Alexander	Emily
Chase	Abigail
Joseph	Ella
Aiden	Grace

Most Popular in Rhode Island

Boys	Girls
Anthony	Isabella
Jayden	Olivia
Logan	Sophia
Jacob	Ava
Michael	Emma
Aiden	Abigail
Joseph	Madison
Joshua	Mia
Matthew	Emily
Benjamin	Gabriella

Most Popular in South Carolina

Boys	Girls
William	Emma
Jayden	Madison
Christopher	Isabella
James	Olivia
Jacob	Abigail
Joshua	Ava
Michael	Elizabeth
Jackson	Addison
Noah	Emily
Caleb	Chloe

Most Popular in South Dakota

Boys	Girls
Ethan	Emma
Noah	Ava
Gavin	Isabella
Logan	Sophia
Jackson	Alexis
Aiden	Elizabeth
Jacob	Addison
Mason	Olivia
Wyatt	Madison
Carter	Brooklyn

Most Popular in Tennessee

Boys	Girls
William	Emma
Jacob	Madison
Joshua	Isabella
Noah	Olivia
Ethan	Abigail
James	Addison
Elijah	Ava
Jackson	Chloe
Michael	Emily
Aiden	Elizabeth

Most Popular in Vermont

Boys	Girls
Noah	Emma
William	Ava
Owen	Isabella
Logan	Madison
Aiden	Sophia
Hunter	Olivia
Jackson	Abigail
Jacob	Lily
Carter	Addison
Wyatt	Grace

Most Popular in Texas

Boys	Girls
JJose	Isabella
Daniel	Emily
Jacob	Mia
Angel	Emma
Christopher	Sophia
David	Abigail
Ethan	Madison
Joshua	Ava
Jayden	Natalie
Alexander	Olivia

Most Popular in Virginia

Boys	Girls
William	Isabella
Jacob	Madison
Michael	Emma
Noah	Olivia
Ethan	Abigail
Christopher	Sophia
Joshua	Ava
Alexander	Emily
James	Elizabeth
Jayden	Chloe

Most Popular in Utah

Boys	Girls
Ethan	Olivia
William	Emma
Jacob	Abigail
Isaac	Brooklyn
James	Lily
Mason	Isabella
Benjamin	Elizabeth
Samuel	Ava
Joshua	Sophia
Logan	Chloe

Most Popular in Washington

Boys	Girls
Alexander	Isabella
Jacob	Olivia
Ethan	Sophia
William	Emma
Daniel	Abigail
Logan	Emily
Benjamin	Ava
Aiden	Elizabeth
Samuel	Chloe
David	Madison

Most Popular in West Virginia

Boys	Girls
JJacob	Madison
Hunter	Isabella
Ethan	Emma
Noah	Alexis
Aiden	Emily
Brayden	Olivia
Logan	Abigail
Landon	Chloe
Elijah	Ava
James	Kaylee

Most Popular in Wisconsin

Boys	Girls
Ethan	Olivia
Jacob	Isabella
Noah	Emma
Logan	Ava
Mason	Sophia
Alexander	Addison
Aiden	Ella
Owen	Abigail
Carter	Elizabeth
Jackson	Grace

Most Popular in Wyoming

Boys	Girls
Wyatt	Isabella
William	Madison
Aiden	Ava
Jacob	Emma
Mason	Alexis
Noah	Elizabeth
Hunter	Addison
Logan	Olivia
James	Abigail
Brayden	Taylor

Most Popular of the 1910s

Boys	Girls
John	Mary
William	Helen
James	Dorothy
Robert	Margaret
Joseph	Ruth
George	Mildred
Charles	Anna
Edward	Elizabeth
Frank	Frances
Thomas	Virginia

Most Popular of the 1920s

Boys	Girls
Robert	Mary
John	Dorothy
James	Helen
William	Betty
Charles	Margaret
George	Ruth
Joseph	Virginia
Richard	Doris
Edward	Mildred
Donald	Frances

Most Popular of the 1930s

Boys	Girls
Robert	Mary
James	Betty
John	Barbara
William	Shirley
Richard	Patricia
Charles	Dorothy
Donald	Joan
George	Margaret
Thomas	Nancy
Joseph	Helen

Most Popular of the 1940s

Boys	Girls
James	Mary
Robert	Linda
John	Barbara
William	Patricia
Richard	Carol
David	Sandra
Charles	Nancy
Thomas	Sharon
Michael	Judith
Ronald	Susan

Most Popular of the 1950s

Boys	Girls
James	Mary
Michael	Linda
Robert	Patricia
John	Susan
David	Deborah
William	Barbara
Richard	Debra
Thomas	Karen
Mark	Nancy
Charles	Donna

Most Popular of the 1960s

Boys	Girls
Michael	Lisa
David	Mary
John	Susan
James	Karen
Robert	Kimberly
Mark	Patricia
William	Linda
Richard	Donna
Thomas	Michelle
Jeffrey	Cynthia

Most Popular of the 1970s

Boys	Girls
Michael	Jennifer
Christopher	Amy
Jason	Melissa
David	Michelle
James	Kimberly
John	Lisa
Robert	Angela
Brian	Heather
William	Stephanie
Matthew	Nicole

Most Popular of the 1980s

Boys	Girls
Michael	Jessica
Christopher	Jennifer
Matthew	Amanda
Joshua	Ashley
David	Sarah
James	Stephanie
Daniel	Melissa
Robert	Nicole
John	Elizabeth
Joseph	Heather

Most Popular of the 1990s

Boys	Girls
Michael	Jessica
Christopher	Ashley
Matthew	Emily
Joshua	Samantha
Jacob	Sarah
Nicholas	Amanda
Andrew	Brittany
Daniel	Elizabeth
Tyler	Taylor
Joseph	Megan

Most Popular of 2000

Boys	Girls
Jacob	Emily
Michael	Hannah
Matthew	Madison
Joshua	Ashley
Christopher	Sarah
Nicholas	Alexis
Andrew	Samantha
Joseph	Jessica
Daniel	Taylor
Tyler	Elizabeth

Most Popular of 2001

Boys	Girls
Jacob	Emily
Michael	Madison
Matthew	Hannah
Joshua	Ashley
Christopher	Alexis
Nicholas	Sarah
Andrew	Samantha
Joseph	Abigail
Daniel	Elizabeth
William	Olivia

Most Popular of 2002

Boys	Girls
Jacob	Emily
Michael	Madison
Joshua	Hannah
Matthew	Emma
Ethan	Alexis
Andrew	Ashley
Joseph	Abigail
Christopher	Sarah
Nicholas	Samantha
Daniel	Olivia

Most Popular of 2003

Boys	Girls
Jacob	Emily
Michael	Emma
Joshua	Madison
Matthew	Hannah
Andrew	Olivia
Ethan	Abigail
Joseph	Alexis
Daniel	Ashley
Christopher	Elizabeth
Anthony	Samantha

Most Popular of 2004

Boys	Girls
Jacob	Emily
Michael	Emma
Joshua	Madison
Matthew	Olivia
Ethan	Hannah
Andrew	Abigail
Daniel	Isabella
William	Ashley
Joseph	Samantha
Christopher	Elizabeth

Most Popular of 2005

Boys	Girls
Jacob	Emily
Michael	Emma
Joshua	Madison
Matthew	Abigail
Ethan	Olivia
Andrew	Isabella
Daniel	Hannah
Anthony	Samantha
Christopher	Ava
Joseph	Ashley

Most Popular of 2006

Boys	Girls
Jacob	Emily
Michael	Emma
Joshua	Madison
Ethan	Isabella
Matthew	Ava
Daniel	Abigail
Christopher	Olivia
Andrew	Hannah
Anthony	Sophia
William	Samantha

Most Popular of 2007

Boys	Girls
Jacob	Emily
Michael	Isabella
Ethan	Emma
Joshua	Ava
Daniel	Madison
Christopher	Sophia
Anthony	Olivia
William	Abigail
Matthew	Hannah
Andrew	Elizabeth

Most Popular of 2008

Boys	Girls
Jacob	Emma
Michael	Isabella
Ethan	Emily
Joshua	Madison
Daniel	Ava
Alexander	Olivia
Anthony	Sophia
William	Abigail
Christopher	Elizabeth
Matthew	Chloe

Most Popular Names of 2009

A ✪ in the text indicates one of the 100 Most Popular Names of 2009

Most Popular Boys' Names

Jacob	Mason
Ethan	Evan
Michael	Landon
Alexander	Angel
William	Brandon
Joshua	Lucas
Daniel	Isaac
Jayden	Isaiah
Noah	Jack
Anthony	Jose
Christopher	Kevin
Aiden	Jordan
Matthew	Justin
David	Brayden
Andrew	Luke
Joseph	Liam
Logan	Carter
James	Owen
Ryan	Connor
Benjamin	Zachary
Elijah	Aaron
Gabriel	Robert
Christian	Hunter
Nathan	Thomas
Jackson	Adrian
John	Cameron
Samuel	Wyatt
Tyler	Chase
Dylan	Julian
Jonathan	Austin
Caleb	Charles
Nicholas	Jeremiah
Gavin	Jason

Juan	Cooper	Brooklyn	Alexandra
Xavier	Ayden	Riley	Jocelyn
Luis	Carson	Evelyn	Maria
Sebastian	Josiah	Savannah	Valeria
Henry	Levi	Aubrey	Andrea
Aidan	Blake	Alexa	Trinity
Ian	Eli	Peyton	Zoey
Adam	Hayden	Makayla	Gianna
Diego	Bryan	Layla	Mackenzie
Nathaniel	Colton	Lauren	Jessica
Brody	Brian	Zoe	Camila
Jesus	Eric	Sydney	Faith
Carlos	Parker	Audrey	Autumn
Tristan	Sean	Julia	Ariana
Dominic	Oliver	Jasmine	Genesis
Cole	Miguel	Arianna	Payton
Alex	Kyle	Claire	Bailey
		Brooke	Angelina

Most Popular Girls' Names

		Amelia	Caroline
Isabella	Alyssa	Morgan	Mariah
Emma	Ashley	Destiny	Katelyn
Olivia	Sarah	Bella	Rachel
Sophia	Taylor	Madelyn	Vanessa
Ava	Hannah	Katherine	Molly
Emily	Brianna	Kylie	Melanie
Madison	Hailey	Maya	Serenity
Abigail	Kaylee	Aaliyah	Khloe
Chloe	Lillian	Madeline	Gabrielle
Mia	Leah	Sophie	Paige
Elizabeth	Anna	Kimberly	Mya
Addison	Allison	Kaitlyn	Eva
Alexis	Victoria	Charlotte	Isabelle
Ella	Avery		
Samantha	Gabriella		
Natalie	Nevaeh		
Grace	Kayla		
Lily	Sofia		

Just Missed the Top 100

Boys	Girls
Jaden	Lucy
Kaden	Mary
Caden	Natalia
Max	Michelle
Antonio	Megan
Steven	Sara
Riley	Naomi
Kaleb	Ruby
Brady	Jennifer
Timothy	Isabel
Bryce	Sadie
Colin	Stephanie
Jesse	Jada
Richard	Kennedy
Joel	Gracie
Ashton	Rylee
Victor	Lilly
Micah	Lydia
Vincent	Nicole
Preston	Liliana

Top Twin Names of 2009

A ❶ in the text indicates one of the
Top Twin Names of 2009

Female Twins

Isabella, Sophia
Faith, Hope
Olivia, Sophia
Ella, Emma
Hailey, Hannah
Ava, Emma
Heaven, Nevaeh
Madison, Morgan
Mackenzie, Madison
Ava, Olivia

Isabella, Olivia
Makayla, Makenzie
Ava, Ella
Faith, Grace
Gabriella, Isabella
Abigail, Olivia
Emma, Sophia
London, Paris
Elizabeth, Emily
Valeria, Vanessa
Emily, Emma
Emma, Grace
Gabriella, Isabella
Abigail, Allison
Abigail, Emma
Addison, Ava
Anna, Emma
Ava, Mia
Ava, Sophia
Abigail, Emily
Addison, Emma
Chloe, Sophie
Grace, Hope
Natalie, Nicole
Savannah, Sierra
Allison, Ashley
Ella, Lily
Emily, Natalie
Emily, Olivia

Female and Male Twins

Madison, Mason
Taylor, Tyler
Addison, Aiden
Emily, Ethan
Emma, Evan

Ella, Ethan

Emma, Ethan

Jayda, Jayden

Jada, Jaden

Aidan, Nadia

Aiden, Ava

Emma, William

Madison, Matthew

Anna, William

Emily, Evan

Emma, Jacob

Emma, Noah

Isabella, Isaiah

Madison, Michael

Addison, Andrew

Chloe, Connor

Emma, Jack

Nicholas, Sophia

Noah, Sophia

Olivia, Owen

Zachary, Zoe

Zachary, Zoey

Brian, Brianna

Caleb, Chloe

Ethan, Isabella

Grace, John

Isabella, Michael

Jacob, Jillian

Jada, Jayden

James, Julia

Landon, London

Lily, Luke

Olivia, William

Male Twins

Jacob, Joshua

Matthew, Michael

Daniel, David

Jayden, Jordan

Jayden, Jaylen

Elijah, Isaiah

Isaac, Isaiah

Ethan, Evan

Logan, Lucas

Logan, Luke

Caleb, Joshua

Landon, Logan

Andrew, Matthew

Nathan, Nicholas

Brandon, Bryan

Alexander, Benjamin

Hayden, Hunter

Alexander, Nicholas

Gabriel, Michael

Christian, Christopher

Jordan, Justin

Benjamin, Samuel

James, John

Jeremiah, Joshua

John, Joseph

Joseph, Joshua

Jeremiah, Josiah

Aiden, Ethan

Jacob, Noah

Alexander, Anthony

Caleb, Jacob

Ethan, Noah

Jacob, Joseph

James, William

Andrew, Anthony

Jacob, Zachary

Nathan, Noah

Aiden, Ashton

Celebrity Baby Names A–Z

Our society is fascinated with the names celebrities choose for their children. Any new celebrity birth instantly makes headlines. So, whether you're looking for inspiration or you're just curious, here's an alphabetical listing of baby names and the celebrities who chose them.

Ace Shane
Casey Daigle and Jennie Finch

Adelaide Rose
Rachel Griffiths and Andrew Taylor

Agnes Charles
Elisabeth Shue and Davis Guggenheim

Aidan McIntosh
Scott Hamilton and Tracie Hamilton

Alabama Gypsy Rose
Drea de Matteo and Shooter Jennings

Alabama Luella
Travis Barker and Shanna Moakler

Alastair Wallace
Rod Stewart and Penny Lancaster

Alchamy
Lance Henriksen and Mary Jane Henriksen

Alexander Pete
Naomi Watts and Liev Schreiber

Alexander Wolfgang
Wolfgang Puck and Gelila Assefa

Alfie
Gary Oldman and Lesley Manville

Alia
Stephen Baldwin and Kennya Baldwin

Alice Ann
Tom Cavanagh and Maureen Grise

Alizeh Keshvar
Geena Davis and Dr. Reza Jarrahy

Allegra Sky
John Leguizamo and Justine Maurer

Amandine
John Malkovich and Nicoletta Peyran

Amber Rose Tamara
Simon Le Bon and Yasmin Le Bon

Amedeo
John Turturro and Katherine Borowitz

Anniston Kae
Chyler Leigh and Nathan West

Apple Blythe Alison
Gwyneth Paltrow and Chris Martin

Aquinnah Kathleen
Michael J. Fox and Tracy Pollan

Archibald William Emerson
Amy Poehler and Will Arnett

Arpad Flynn Alexander
Elle MacPherson and Arpad Busson

Ash Edward
Chris Jericho and Jessica Lockhart

Ashby Grace
Nancy O'Dell and Keith Zubchevitch

Assisi Lola
Jade Jagger and Piers Jackson

Astrella Celeste
Donovan Leitch and Linda Lawrence

Atherton Grace
Don Johnson and Kelley Phleger

Atlas
Anne Heche and James Tupper

Atticus
Isabella Hoffman and Daniel Baldwin

Auden
Noah Wyle and Tracy Warbin

Audrey Mae
Greg Kinnear and Helen Labdon

August Miklos Friedrich
Mariska Hargitay and Peter Hermann

Ava Elizabeth
Reese Witherspoon and Ryan Phillippe

Avery Grace
Angie Harmon and Jason Sehorn

Aviana Olea
Amy Adams and Darren Legallo

Axel
Will Farrell and Viveca Paulin

Bandit Lee
Gerard Way and LynZ Way

Banjo Patrick
Rachel Griffiths and Andrew Taylor

Bardot Vita
David Boreanaz and Jaime Bergman

Beatrice Elizabeth Mary
Sarah Ferguson and Prince Andrew

Beau Grayson
Tanya Tucker and Ben Reed

Beckett Robert Lee
Stella McCartney and Alasdhair Willis

Billie Beatrice
Eric Dane and Rebecca Gayheart

Birdie Leigh
Busy Phillips and Marc Silverstein

Blaise Ray
Amanda Beard and Sacha Brown

Bluebell Madonna
Geri Halliwell and Sacha Gervasi

Bogart Che Peyote
David "Puck" Rainey and Betty Rainey

Braison Chance
Billy Ray and Leticia Cyrus

Braedon Cooper
Kevin Sorbo and Sam Jenkins

BreAzia Ranee
Olympia Scott-Richardson and Al Richardson

Brendan Joseph
Mark Wahlberg and Rhea Durham

Brighton Rose
Jon Favreau and Joya Tillem

Brody Jo
Gabrielle Reece and Laird Hamilton

Bronx Mowgli
Ashlee Simpson-Wentz and Pete Wentz

Bronwyn Golden
Angela Bassett and Courtney B. Vance

Brooklyn Joseph
Victoria and David Beckham

Bryce Maximus
LeBron James and Savannah Brinson

Buster Timothy
Jonny Lee Miller and Michele
Hicks

Caledonia Jean-Marie
Shawn Colvin and Mario Erwin

Calico
Alice and Sheryl Cooper

Callum Lyon
Kyle McLachlan and Desire Gruber

Camera
Arthur Ashe and Jeanne
Moutoussamy-Ashe

Camille Harley
Brody Dalle and Josh Homme

Cannon Edward
Larry King and Shawn Southwick

Caroline
Katie Couric and Jay Monahan

Carys Zeta
Catherine Zeta-Jones and
Michael Douglas

Cash Alexander
Annabeth Gish and Wade Allen

Cashel Blake
Daniel Day-Lewis and Rebecca
Miller

Caspar Matthew
Claudia Schiffer and Matthew
Vaughn

Cayden Wyatt
Kevin and Christine Costner

Chance Armstrong
Larry King and Shawn Southwick

Charlene Riva
Roger and Mirka Federer

Charlie Axel
Tiger Woods and Elin Nordegren

Charlotte Grace
Sarah Michelle Prinze and
Freddie Prinze, Jr.

Chloe Ava
Byron Allen and Jennifer Lucas

Cicely Yasin
Sandra Bernhard

Clementine Jane
Ethan Hawke and Ryan Shawhughes

Coco Riley
Courteney Cox Arquette and
David Arquette

Cole Cameron
Matt Leinart and Brynn Cameron

Colette
Dylan McDermott and Shiva
Afshar Rose

Colin Michael
Paul Stanley and Erin Sutton

Connor Anthony
Nicole Kidman and Tom Cruise

Cosima Violet
Claudia Schiffer and Matthew
Vaughn

Crumpet
Lisa Vidal and Jay Cohen

Cruz
Lleyton Hewitt and Bec
Cartwright Hewitt

Curtis Mohammed
Laila Ali and Curtis Conway

Damian Charles
Elizabeth Hurley

Daisy True
Meg Ryan

Dannielynn Hope
Anna Nicole Smith and Larry
Birkhead

Darby Galen
Patrick Dempsey and Jillian Dempsey

David
Madonna

Deacon Reese
Reese Witherspoon and Ryan Phillippe

Delaney Katherine
Martina and John McBride

Delilah Belle
Harry Hamlin and Lisa Rinna

Denim Cole
Toni Braxton and Keri Lewis

Destry Allyn
Steven Spielberg and Kate Capshaw

Devin Christian
Vanessa Williams and Ramon Hervey

Devon Rose
Johnny Damon and Michelle Mangan

Dexter Dean
Diane Keaton

Dezi James
Jaime Pressly and Eric Cubiche

Diezel Ky
Toni Braxton and Keri Lewis

D'Lila Star
Kim Porter and Sean Combs

Donovan Rory
Noel Gallagher and Sara McDonald

Duncan Zowie
Heywood Jones David Bowie and Angela Bowie

Dusti Raine
Robert Van Winkle and Laura Giarritta

Dylan Jagger
Pamela Anderson and Tommy Lee

Dylan John
Joan Cusack and Richard Burke

Dylan Paul
Nadia Comaneci and Bart Conner

Dylan Thomas
Pierce Brosnan and Keely Shaye Smith

Eden
Marcia Cross and Tom Mahoney

Eila Rose
Anna Gunn and Alastair Duncan

Elettra-Ingrid
Isabella Rossellini and Jonathan Wiedemann

Elijah Blue
Cher and Gregg Allman

Elijah Bob Patricus Guggi Q
Bono and Ali Hewson

Elinor Tully
Katie Couric and Jay Monahan

Ella Bleu
John Travolta and Kelly Preston

Elliot
Robert De Niro and Grace Hightower

Emerson Rose
Teri Hatcher and Jon Tenney

Emery Hope
Angie Harmon and Jason Sehorn

Emme Maribel
Jennifer Lopez and Marc Anthony

Enzo Edward
Annabeth Gish and Wade Allen

Enzo Luciano
Patricia Arquette and Paul Rossi

Esme Louise
Katey Sagal and Kurt Sutter

Ethan Page
Edward Furlong and Rachael Bella

Eugenie Victoria Helena
Sarah Ferguson and Prince Andrew

Eulala Grace
Marcia Gay Harden and Thaddaeus Scheel

Evan Jane
Jon Heder and Kirstin Heder

Evan Samuel
Phil and Amy Mickelson

Eve Julia
Jeffrey Tambor and Kasia Ostlun

Ever Gabo
Mila Jovovich and Paul Anderson

Everly Bear
Anthony Kiedis and Heather Christie

Felix
Gillian Anderson and Mark Griffiths

Fifi Trixibelle
Bob Geldof and Paula Yates

Finley
Sadie Frost and Gary Kemp

Finley
Lisa Marie Presley and Michael Lockwood

Finley Faith
Angie Harmon and Jason Sehorn

Finn
Christy Turlington and Ed Burns

Fiona Eve
Jennie Garth and Peter Facinelli

Frances Bean
Kurt Cobain and Courtney Love

Frances Pen
Amanda Peet and David Benioff

Francesca Nora
Jason Bateman and Amanda Anka

Francesca Ruth
Clint Eastwood and Frances Fisher

Free
Barbara Hershey and David Carradine

Freedom
Ving Rhames and Deborah Reed

Fuchsia Katherine
Sting and Frances Tomelty

Gable Ness
Susan Yeagley and Kevin Nealon

Gaia Romilly
Emma Thompson and Greg Wise

Galen Grier
Dennis Hopper and Victoria Duffy

Garrett
Bo Jackson and Linda Jackson

Georgia Tatum
Harry Connick Junior and Jill Goodacre

Georgie John
John Terry and Toni Poole

Gia Zavala
Matt Damon and Luciana Barroso

Gianna Maria-Onore
Kobe Bryant and Vanessa Laine Bryant

Gideon Robert Nesta
Ziggy Marley and Orly Agai Marley

Giselle Lynne
Jeri Ryan and Christopher Eme

Giulia Isabel
Debi Mazar and Gabriele Corcos

Goldie Priya
Ben Lee and Ione Skye

Greer Kandace
Kelsey Grammer and Barrie
Buckner

Grier Hammond
Brooke Shields and Chris
Henchy

Griffin Thomas
Joey McIntyre

Gulliver Flynn
Gary Oldman and Donya
Fiorentino

Harlow Olivia Calliope
Patricia Arquette and Thomas
Jane

Harlow Winter Kate
Nicole Richie and Joel Madden

Harper Renn
Tiffani Thiessen

Harper Willow
Dave Grohl and Jordyn Blum

Hartley Grace
Mark McGrath and Carin
Kingsland

Hayes Logan
Kevin Costner and Christine
Baumgartner

Hazel Patricia
Julia Roberts and Daniel Moder

Heaven Rain
Brooke Burke and David Charvet

Heavenly Hiraani Tiger Lily
Michael Hutchence and Paula
Yates

Henry Chance
Rachel Weisz and Darren
Aronofsky

Holden Fletcher
Brendan Fraser and Afton Smith

Homer James Jigme
Richard Gere and Carey Lowell

Honor Marie
Jessica Alba and Cash Warren

Hopper Jack
Robin Wright Penn and Sean Penn

Hud
John Cougar Mellencamp and
Elaine Irwin

Hudson Harden
Marcia Gay Harden and
Thaddaeus Scheel

Ignatius Martin
Cate Blanchett and Andrew Upton

Indiana August
Casey Affleck and Summer
Phoenix

Indio
Robert Downey Jr. and Deborah
Falconer

Ione Skye
Donovan Leitch and Enid Karl

Iris
Jude Law and Sadie Frost

Isabel Ann
Julie Foudy and Ian Sawyer

Isabella
Matt Damon and Luciana Barroso

Isabella Jane
Nicole Kidman and Tom Cruise

Isadora
Bjork and Matthew Barney

Isaiah Akin
Isaiah Washington and Jenisa
Marie Washington

Isla
Paula Radcliffe and Gary Lough

Italia
LL Cool J and Simone Johnson

Jaden
Will Smith and Jada Pinkett Smith

James Michael
Michael Owen and Louise Bonsall

James Wilkie
Sarah Jessica Parker and Matthew Broderick

Jamison Leon
William Baldwin and Chynna Phillips

Jagger Donovan
Joe Don Rooney and Tiffany Fallon

Jagger Jonathan
Lindsay Davenport and Jonathan Leach

Jagger Joseph Blue
Soleil Moon Frye and Jason Goldberg

Jasper Warren
Brad and Kimberly Paisley

Jayden James
Britney Spears and Kevin Federline

Jaz Elle
Steffi Graf and Andre Agassi

Jennifer Katharine
Bill Gates and Melinda Gates

Jessie James
Kim Porter and Sean Combs

Jett
John Travolta and Kelly Preston

Jillian Kristin
Vanessa Williams and Ramon Hervey

Joaquin Antonio
Kelly Ripa and Mark Consuelos

Johan Riley Fyodor Taiwo
Seal and Heidi Klum

John Abraham
Bono and Ali Hewson

John Edward Thomas
Tom Brady and Bridget Moynahan

Johnnie Rose
Melissa Etheridge and Tammy Lynn Michaels

Jonas Rocket
Tom DeLonge and Jennifer DeLonge

Jordan
Bono and Ali Hewson

Joscelyn Skye
A.J. Langer and Charles Courtenay

Josselyn Sydney
Samantha Harris and Michael Hess

Julian Fuego
Robin Thicke and Paula Patton

Julian Kal
Jessica and Jerry Seinfeld

Julitta Dee
Marcia Gay Harden and Thaddaeus Scheel

Juno
Will and Marianne Champion

Justice
John Cougar Mellencamp and Vicky Granucci

Justin
Andie MacDowell and Paul Qualley

Kadence Clover
Tony Hawk and Lhotse Merriam

Kaia Jordan
Cindy Crawford and Rande Gerber

Kaiis Steven
Geena Davis and Dr. Reza Jarrahy

Kal-el Coppola
Nicholas Cage and Alice Kim Cage

Keelee Breeze
Robert Van Winkle and Laura Giarritta

Keen
Mark Ruffalo and Sunrise Coigney

Kian William
Geena Davis and Dr. Reza Jarrahy

Kieran Lindsay
Julianna Margulies and Keith Lieberthal

Kimber Lynn
Clint Eastwood and Roxanne Tunis

Kingston James McGregor
Gwen Stefani and Gavin Rossdale

Knox Leon
Angelina Jolie and Brad Pitt

Kyd Miller
David Duchovny and Tea Leoni

Laird Vonne
Sharon Stone

Langley Fox
Mariel Hemingway and Steven Douglas Crisman

Laymen Lamar
Tracy McGrady and Clarenda Harris

Levi Alves
Matthew McConaughey and Camila Alves

Liam Aaron
Tori Spelling and Dean McDermott

Liam McAllister
Rachel Hunter and Rod Stewart

Liberty Irene
Casey and Jean Kasem

Lila Grace
Kate Moss and Jefferson Hack

Lily Aerin
Fred Savage and Jennifer Stone

Liv Helen
Julianne Moore and Bart Freundlich

Lola Simone
Chris Rock and Malaak Compton-Rock

Lorraine Broussard
Rebecca Broussard and Jack Nicholson

Lotus
Rain Pryor

Lou Solula
Heidi Klum and Seal

Louis Bardo
Sandra Bullock

Lourdes Maria Ciccone
Madonna and Carlos Leon

Luca Bella
Jennie Garth and Peter Facinelli

Lucian
Steve Buscemi and Jo Andreas

Luka Bodhi
Tom Colicchio and Lori Silverbush

Lydon Edward
Mark Mcgrath and Carin Kingsland

Lyla Rose
Lisa Loeb and Roey Hershkovitz

Lyric
Ashley Parker Angel and Tiffany Lynn

Mabel Ray
Dermot Mulroney and Tharita Catulle

Maddie Briann
Jamie Lynn Spears and Casey Aldridge

Maddox Chivan Thornton
Angelina Jolie and Brad Pitt

Madelaine West
David Duchovny and Tea Leoni

Maggie Rose
Jon Stewart and Tracey McShane

Makani Ravello
Woody Harrelson and Laura Louie

Makena'lei Gordon
Helen Hunt and Matthew Carnahan

Margaret Heather
Kellie Martin and Keith Christian

Marion Loretta Elwell
Matthew Broderick and Sarah Jessica Parker

Marlon
Dennis Miller and Carolyn Epsley

Mason Dash
Kourtney Kardashian and Scott Disick

Mason Olivia
Kelsey Grammer and Camille Donatucci

Mason Walter
Melissa Joan Hart and Mark Wilkerson

Mateo Braverly
Benjamin Bratt and Talisa Soto

Mathilda Plum
Moon Unit Zappa and Paul Doucette

Matilda Rose
Michelle Williams and Heath Ledger

Matteo
Ricky Martin

Mattias
Will Ferrell and Viveca Paulin

Max
Lance Armstrong and Anna Hansen

Maximilian David
Jennifer Lopez and Marc Anthony

Me'arah Sanaa
Shaquille O'Neal and Shaunie Nelson

Memphis Eve
Bono and Ali Hewson

Michaela Andrea
Kerry Kennedy and Andrew Cuomo

Milan Hayat
Scott Stapp and Jaclyn Nesheiwat

Miley Ray
Billy Ray and Leticia Cyrus

Miller Steven
Melissa Etheridge and Tammy Lynn Michaels

Milo William
Liv Tyler and Royston Langdon

Moses Bruce Anthony
Gwyneth Paltrow and Chris Martin

Moxie Crimefighter
Penn Jillette and Emily Jillette

Myla Rose
Roger and Mirka Federer

Myles Mitchell
Eddie Murphy and Nicole Mitchell

Nana Kwadjo
Isaac Hayes and Adjowa Hayes

Natalia Diamante
Kobe Bryant and Vanessa Laine Bryant

Nathan Thomas
Jon Stewart and Tracey McShane

Naviyd Ely
Usher and Tameka Foster

Nayib
Gloria Estefan and Emilio Estefan

Nell
Helena Bonham Carter and Tim Burton

Nevis
Nelly Furtado and Jasper Gahunia

Nahla Ariela
Halle Berry and Gabriel Aubry

Natashya Lorien
Tori Amos and Mark Hawley

Ocean Alexander
Forest Whitaker and Raye Dowell

Odette
Mark Ruffalo and Sunrise Coigney

Olive
Isla Fisher and Sacha Baron Cohen

Oliver Philip
Fred Savage and Jennifer Stone

Olivia Luna
Joely Fisher and Christopher Duddy

Oriole Nebula
Donovan Leitch and Linda Lawrence

Orion Christopher
Chris Noth and Tara Wilson

Oscar
Gillian Anderson and Mark Griffiths

Otis Tobias
Tobey Maguire and Jennifer Meyer

Paris Michael Katherine
Michael Jackson and Debbie Rowe

Parker Foster
Clay Aiken and Jaymes Foster

Pax Thien
Angelina Jolie and Brad Pitt

Petal Blossom Rainbow
Jamie Oliver and Jools Oliver

Phinnaeus Walter
Julia Roberts and Daniel Moder

Pilot Inspektor
Jason Lee and Beth Riesgraf

Piper Maru
Gillian Anderson and Clyde Klotz

Poet Sienna Rose
Soleil Moon Frye and Jason Goldberg

Poppy Honey
Jamie Oliver and Jools Oliver

Presley Walker
Cindy Crawford and Rande Gerber

Prince Michael
Michael Jackson and Debbie Rowe

Ptolemy John
Gretchen Mol and Kip Williams

Puma Rose
Erykah Badu and Tracy Curry

Quinn Kelly
Sharon Stone

Racer Maximilliano
Robert Rodriguez and Elizabeth Avellan

Rafferty
Jude Law and Sadie Frost

Raine
Tawny Kitaen and Chuck Finley

Ramona
Maggie Gyllenhaal and Peter Sarsgaard

Rebel Antonio
Robert Rodriguez and Elizabeth Avellan

Reignbeau
Ving Rhames and Deborah Reed

Rene-Charles
Celine Dion and Rene Angelil

Rhiannon
Robert Rodriguez and Elizabeth Avellan

Ridley Banfield
Ashleigh Banfield and Howard Gould

River Russell
Keri Russell and Shane Deary

River Samuel
Taylor Hanson and Natalie Bryant

Roan Joseph
Sharon Stone and Phil Bronstein

Rocco
Madonna and Guy Ritchie

Roman Walker
Debra Messing and Daniel Zelman

Romeo James
Victoria and David Beckham

Romy
Sofia Coppola and Thomas Mars

Ronan Cal
Daniel Day-Lewis and Rebecca Miller

Rowan Francis
Brooke Shields and Chris Henchy

Ruby Sweetheart
Tobey Maguire and Jennifer Meyer

Rudy
Jude Law and Sadie Frost

Rumer Glenn
Demi Moore and Bruce Willis

Ryder Lee
John Leguizamo and Justine Maurer

Ryder Russell
Kate Hudson and Chris Robinson

Rylan Jaxson
Eric Mabius and Ivy Sherman

Sadie Madison
Adam Sandler and Jackie Titone

Saffron Sahara
Simon Le Bon and Yasmin Parvaneh

Sage Florence
Toni Collette and David Galafassi

Sage Moonblood
Sylvester Stallone and Sasha Czack

Sailor Lee
Christie Brinkley and Peter Cook

Sam Alexis
Tiger Woods and Elin Nordegren

Samuel Kai
Naomi Watts and Liev Schreiber

Samuel Wyatt
Marc Cohn and Elizabeth Vargas

Santino
Adam Carolla and Lynette Paradise

Sascha
Jerry and Jessica Seinfeld

Savannah
Marcia Cross and Tom Mahoney

Scarlet Rose
Sylvester Stallone and Jennifer Flavin

Schuyler
Michael J. Fox and Tracy Pollan

Scout LaRue
Demi Moore and Bruce Willis

Sean Preston
Britney Spears and Kevin Federline

Seargeoh
Sylvester Stallone and Sasha Czack

Seraphina Rose Elizabeth
Ben Affleck and Jennifer Garner

Seven Sirius
Erykah Badu and Andre Benjamin

Shepherd Kellen
Jerry and Jessica Seinfeld

Shiloh Nouvel
Angelina Jolie and Brad Pitt

Sistine Rose
Sylvester Stallone and Jennifer Flavin

Slater Josiah
Angela Bassett and Courtney B. Vance

Sloane Sullivan
Rob and Sandry Corddry

Sonora Rose
Alice and Sheryl Cooper

Sophia Rose
Sylvester Stallone and Jennifer Flavin

Sosie Ruth
Kyra Sedgwick and Kevin Bacon

Sparrow James Midnight
Joel Madden and Nicole Ritchie

Speck Wildhorse
John Cougar Mellencamp and Elaine Irwin

Stella Doreen
Tori Spelling and Dean McDermott

Stella Luna
Ellen Pompeo and Chris Ivery

Stellan
Jennifer Connelly and Paul Bettany

Story Elias
Jenna and Bodhi Elfman

Sullivan Patrick
Patrick Dempsey and Jillian Dempsey

Sundance Thomas
Kerri Walsh and Casey Jennings

Sunday Rose
Nicole Kidman and Keith Urban

Sunny Madeline
Adam Sandler and Jackie Titone

Suri
Tom Cruise and Katie Holmes

Tabitha Hodge
Matthew Broderick and Sarah Jessica Parker

Tallulah Belle
Demi Moore and Bruce Willis

Tallulah Pine
Simon Le Bon and Yasmin Parvaneh

Tennyson Spencer
Russell Crowe and Danielle Spencer

Thijs
Matt Lauer and Annette Roque

Thyme
Isaiah Washington and Jenisa Marie Washington

Thomas Boone
Dennis and Kimberly Quaid

Travis Sedg
Kyra Sedgwick and Kevin Bacon

True Harlow
Joely Fisher and Christopher
Duddy

True Isabella Summer
Forest Whitaker and Keisha Nash

Truman Theodore
Tom Hanks and Rita Wilson

Tu Simone
Rob Morrow and Debbon Ayer

Valentina Paloma
Salma Hayek and Francois-Henri
Pinault

Valentino
Ricky Martin

Vida
Matthew McConaughey and
Camila Alves

Violet Anne
Jennifer Garner and Ben Affleck

Violet Maye
Dave Grohl and Jordyn Blum

Vivienne Marcheline
Angelina Jolie and Brad Pitt

Walker Nathaniel
Taye Diggs and Idina Menzel

Wilder Brooks
Oliver Hudson and Erinn Bartlett

Willa
Phillip Seymour Hoffman and
Mimi O'Donnell

William Huckleberry
Brad Paisley and Kimberly
Williams-Paisley

Willow Camille Reign
Will Smith and Jada Pinkett
Smith

Wynter
Tawny Kitaen and Chuck Finley

Zahara Marley
Angelina Jolie and Brad Pitt

Zahra Savannah
Chris Rock and Malaak
Compton-Rock

Zander Ryan
Mindy McCready and Billy
McKnight

Zephyr
Robby Benson and Karla DeVito

Zev Isaac
Marisa Jaret Winokur and Judah
Miller

Zion Malachi Airamis
Dwyane Wade and Siohvaughn
Wade

Zoe Grace
Dennis and Kimberly Quaid

Zolten Penn
Penn Jillette and Emily Jillette

Zuma Nesta Rock
Gwen Stefani and Gavin
Rossdale

Chapter 9

girls' names

a

Aadi (Hindi) Child of the beginning
*Aadie, Aady, Aadey, Aadee, Aadea, Aadeah,
Aadye*

● **Aaliyah** (Arabic) Form of Aliyah, meaning
"an ascender, one having the highest social
standing"
Aaleyah, Aaliya

Aaralyn (American) Woman with song
*Aaralynn, Aaralyn, Aaralynn, Aaralin,
Aaralinn, Aaralinne, Aralyn, Aralynn,
Aralynne, Aralin, Aralinn, Aralinne, Aralen,
Aralenn, Aralenne*

Aase (Norse) From the tree-covered mountain

Aba (African) Born on a Thursday
Abah, Abba, Abbah

Abarrane (Hebrew) Feminine form of
Abraham; mother of a multitude; mother
of nations
*Abarrayne, Abarraine, Abarane, Abarayne,
Abaraine, Abame, Abrahana*

Abdera (Greek) Woman of the city of
Abdera
*Abderah, Abderra, Abderrah, Abderia,
Abderiah*

Abeba (African) Woman who is delicate and
flowerlike
*Abedah, Abeeda, Abeida, Abyda, Abeedah,
Abeidah, Abydah, Abieda, Abiedah, Abeada,
Abeadah*

Abebe (African) Child who is asked for
*Abebi, Abebie, Abeby, Abebey, Abebye, Abebee,
Abebeah, Abebea*

Abedabun (Native American) Sight of day;
dawn's child

Abela (French) A breath or sigh; source of
life
*Abelah, Abella, Abelia, Abelya, Abellah,
Abeliah, Abelyah*

Abellone (Greek) Woman who is manly
*Abellona, Abellonia, Abellonea, Abelone,
Abelona*

Abena (African) Born on a Tuesday
*Abenah, Abeenu, Abynu, Abina, Abeenah,
Abynah, Abinah*

Abeni (African) A girl child who was prayed
for
*Abenie, Abeny, Abeney, Abenye, Abenea,
Abeneah, Abenee*

Abeque (Native American) Woman who
stays at home

Aberdeen (Scottish) A woman from a city
in northeast Scotland
*Aberdeene, Aberdeena, Aberdeenah,
Aberdeenia, Aberdeane, Aberdean, Aberdeana,
Aberdyne, Aberdyn, Aberdyna*

Aberfa (Welsh) From the mouth of the river
Aberfah, Aberpha, Aberphah

Abertha (Welsh) One who is sacrificed
Aberthah

Abha (Indian) One who shines; a lustrous
beauty
Abhah

Abhilasha (Hindi) One who is desired
Abhilashah, Abhylasha, Abhylashah

Abia (Arabic) One who is great
Abiah

Abiba (African) First child born after the
grandmother has died
*Abibah, Abeeba, Abyba, Abeebah, Abybah,
Abeiba, Abeibah, Abieba, Abiebah, Abeaba,
Abeabah*

Abida (Arabic / Hebrew) She who worships
or adores / having knowledge
*Abidah, Abeeda, Abyda, Abeedah, Abydah,
Abeida, Abeidah, Abieda, Abiedah, Abeada,
Abeadah*

Abiela (Hebrew) My father is Lord
*Abielah, Abiella, Abiellah, Abyela, Abyelah,
Abyella, Abyellah*

● **Abigail** (Hebrew) The source of a father's joy
○ *Abbigail, Abigael, Abigale, Abbygail, Abygail,
Abygayle, Abbygayle, Abbegale, Abigayle,
Abagail, Abaigael, Abaigeal, Abbey, Abbie,
Abbigail, Abie, Abby, Abegayle, Abey, Abhy,
Abiageal, Abichail, Avagail, Avigail, Avagale,
Avigale, Avagayle, Avichayil, Abbye*

Abijah (Hebrew) My father is Lord
Abija, Abisha, Abishah, Abiah, Abia, Aviah, Avia

Abila (Spanish) One who is beautiful
Abilah, Abyla, Abylah

Abilene (American / Hebrew) From a town in Texas / resembling grass
Abalene, Abalina, Abilena, Abiline, Abileene, Abileen, Abileena, Abilyn, Abilyne, Abilyna, Abilean, Abileane, Abileana

Abiona (Yoruban) Born during a journey
Abionah, Abionia, Abioniah

Abir (Arabic) Having a fragrant scent
Abeer, Abyr, Abire, Abeere, Abbir, Abhir

Abira (Hebrew) A source of strength; one who is strong
Abera, Abyra, Abyrah, Abirah, Abbira, Abeerah, Abhira

Abital (Hebrew) My father is the dew; in the Bible, the fifth wife of David
Avital, Abitall, Avitall

Ablah (Arabic) One who is perfectly formed; full-figured woman
Abla

Abra (Hebrew / Arabic) Feminine form of Abraham; mother of a multitude; mother of nations / lesson; example
Abri, Abrah, Abree, Abria, Abbra, Abrah, Abbrah

Abrianna (Italian) Feminine form of Abraham; mother of a multitude; mother of nations
Abriana, Abreana, Abryana, Abryann, Abreanne, Abrielle, Abrienne, Abriell, Abriele

Abrihet (African) Woman who emanates light

Acacia (Greek) Thorny tree; one who is naïve
Akacia, Acacya, Acaciah, Acatia, Acasha, Acacyah, Asasia, Akaciah

Academia (Latin) From a community of higher learning
Akademia, Academiah, Akademiah

Acadia (Canadian) From the land of plenty
Acadiah, Acadya, Akadia, Akadiah, Akadya

Acantha (Greek) Thorny; in mythology, a nymph who was loved by Apollo
Akantha, Ackantha, Acanthah, Akanthah, Ackanthah

Acarnania (Latin) Woman from western Greece

Accalia (Latin) In mythology, the foster mother of Romulus and Remus
Accaliah, Acalia, Accalya, Acalya, Acca, Ackaliah, Ackalia

Aceline (French) Born into nobility; high-born woman
Acelin, Asceline, Ascelin

Achaana (Navajo) One who is the protector

Achall (Celtic) In mythology, a loving sister who died of grief when her brother died
Achalle, Achal, Achale

Achlys (Greek) In mythology, the personification of sadness and misery

Achsah (Hebrew) Bracelet for the ankle
Achsa

Acima (Hebrew) Feminine form of Acim; God will judge
Acimah, Achima, Achimah

Acrasia (Greek) One who overindulges
Acrasiah, Akrasia, Acrasy, Acrasey, Acrasi, Acrasie, Acrasee, Acrasea, Acraseah, Acrasye

Adah (Hebrew) Ornament; beautiful addition to the family
Adda, Adaya, Ada

Adair (Scottish) From the oak-tree ford
Adaire, Adaira, Adairia, Athdara, Athdare, Athdaria, Athdair, Athdaire, Athdairia, Athdaira

Adalgisa (Italian / German) One who is noble / a highly valued promise
Adalgise, Adelgise, Adelvice, Adalgysa, Adalgyse

Adalwolfa (German) A noble she-wolf

Adama (African) A beautiful child; regal and majestic
Adamah, Adamma, Adammah

Adamina (Hebrew) Feminine form of Adam; of the earth
Adamia, Adamiah, Adaminah, Adamynah, Adameena, Adamine, Adaminna, Addie, Adameenah, Adamiena, Adamienah, Adameina, Adameinah, Adameana, Adameanah

Adanna (African) Her father's daughter; a father's pride
Adana, Adanah, Adannah, Adanya, Adanyah

Adanne (African) Her mother's daughter; a mother's pride
Adane, Adayne, Adaine, Adayn, Adain, Adaen, Adaene

Adaoma (Ibo) A good woman

Adara (Greek / Arabic) Beautiful girl / chaste one; virgin
Adair, Adare, Adaire, Adayre, Adarah, Adarra, Adaora, Adar, Adra, Athdara

Addiena (Welsh) Woman of beauty
Addien, Addienne, Adiena, Adiene, Adien, Adienna, Addienna

Addin (Hebrew) One who is adorned; voluptuous
Addine, Addyn, Addyne

● **Addison** (English) Daughter of Adam
Ⓣ *Addeson, Addyson, Adison, Adisson, Adyson*

Addula (Teutonic) One of noble cheer
Adula, Adulla, Addulla, Adulah, Addullah

Adeen (Irish) Little fire shining brightly
Adeene, Adean, Adeane, Adein, Adeine, Adeyn, Adeyne

Adela (German) Of the nobility; serene; of good humor
Adele, Adelia, Adella, Adelle, Adalene, Adelie, Adelina, Adali, Adalheida, Adilene, Adelaide, Adalaide, Adalaid, Adalayde, Adelaid, Adelayde, Adelade, Ada, Adelajda, Adelicia, Adelinda, Adeline, Adelheid, Adelheide, Adelisa, Adelise, Adelita, Adelynn, Adelyte, Adalicia, Ady, Adalina, Adaline, Adaliz, Adalyn, Addie

Adelpha (Greek) Beloved sister
Adelfa, Adelphe, Adelphie

Adeola (African) One who wears a crown of honor
Adeolah, Adeolla, Adeollah

Aderes (Hebrew) One who protects her loved ones

Aderyn (Welsh) Birdlike child
Aderyne, Aderin, Aderine

Adesina (Yoruban) The passage is open; acceptance
Adesinah, Adesine, Adeseena, Adesyna, Adeseenah, Adesynah, Adesiena, Adesienah, Adeseina, Adeseinah, Adeseana, Adeseanah

Adetoun (African) Princess; child of royalty
Adetouna

Adhama (Swahili) A child of glory
Adhamah, Adhamma, Adhammah

Adhara (Arabic) Maiden; the name of the second-brightest star in the constellation Canis Major
Adharah, Adharra, Adharrah

Adhelle (Teutonic) Lovely and happy woman
Adhella, Adhell, Adhele, Adhela

Adhiambo (African) Daughter born after sunset

Adhita (Hindi) A learned woman
Adhitta, Adhittah, Adhitah, Adhyta, Adhytah, Adhytta, Adhyttah

Adia (Swahili / English) Gift from God / wealthy; prosperous
Adea, Adiah, Addia, Adya, Adeah

Adiana (American) The night's falling reveals the angels' beauty
Adyana, Adianna, Adianah, Adyanna

Adianca (Native American) One who brings peace
Adianka, Adyanca, Adyanka

Adiba (Arabic) One who is polite, cultured, and refined
Adibah, Adeeba, Adyba, Adeebah, Adeaba, Adeabah, Adiebah, Adieba, Adeibah, Adeiba, Adeaba, Adeabah, Adybah

Adie (Hebrew / German) Jeweled ornament / noble and kind
Adi, Ady, Adey, Adye, Adee, Adea, Adeah

Adiella (Hebrew) An adornment of God
Adiela, Adielle, Adiell, Adiel, Adiele, Adyella, Adyela, Adyell, Adyel, Adyele

Adila (African / Arabic) One who is just and fair / equal
Adilah, Adeala, Adileh, Adilia, Adyla, Adeela, Adilla, Adillah

Adima (Teutonic) One who is renowned; noble
Adimah, Adimma, Adimmah, Adyma, Adymah, Adymma, Adymmah

Adina (Hebrew) One who is slender and delicate
Adinah, Adine, Adena, Adene, Adin, Adinam, Adyna, Adynah

Adira (Hebrew / Arabic) Powerful, noble woman / having great strength
Adirah, Adeera, Adyra, Adeerah, Adyrah, Adeira, Adeirah, Adiera, Adierah, Adeara, Adearah

Adishree (Hindi) One who is exalted
Adishrey, Adishry, Adishri, Adishrie, Adishrea, Adishreah, Adyshree, Adyshrea, Adyshreah, Adyshri, Adyshrie, Adyshry, Adyshrey

Aditi (Hindi) Unbound; limitless; in Hinduism, the goddess of consciousness, the sky, and fertility
Aditie, Adity, Aditee, Adithi, Adytee, Adytie, Adytey, Aditea, Aditeah, Aditye

Adiva (Arabic) One who is gentle and pleasant
Adivah, Addeva, Adeeva, Adyva, Adeevah, Adyvah, Adieva, Adievah, Adeiva, Adeivah, Adeava, Adeavah

Adjoa (African) Daughter born on a Monday; peaceful
Adwoa, Adjoah, Adwoah

Adlai (Hebrew) The Lord is just; an ornament
Adlay, Adlae, Adlaye

Admete (Greek) In mythology, a maiden who ordered one of Hercules's twelve labors
Admeta

Admina (Hebrew) Daughter of the red earth
Adminah, Admeena, Admyna, Admeenah, Admynah, Admeina, Admeinah, Admiena, Admienah, Admeana, Admeanah

Adoette (Native American) Of the large tree
Adoett, Adoet, Adoete, Adoetta, Adoeta

Adolpha (German) Feminine form of Adolph; noble she-wolf
Adolfa, Adolphina, Adolfina, Adolphine, Adolfine, Adoqhina

Adonia (Spanish / Greek) Beautiful / feminine form of Adonis; lady
Adonna, Adonya, Adoniah, Adonyah, Adonica, Adoncia

Adora (Latin) One who is beloved
Adore, Adorah, Adoria, Adoreh, Adorya, Adoriah, Adorlee, Adoree, Audora

Adorabella (Latin) Beautiful woman who is adored
Adorabelle, Adorabela, Adorabell, Adorabele, Adorabel

Adoración (Spanish) Having the adoration of all

Adowa (African) One who is noble

Adra (Arabic) One who is chaste; a virgin
Adrah

Adrasteia (Greek) One who will not run away; in mythology, another name for Nemesis, the goddess of vengeance

❶ **Adria** (Greek) Feminine form of Adrian; from the Adriatic Sea region; woman with dark features
*Adriah, Adrea, Adreana, Adreanna, Adreanah, Adrienna, Adriane, Adriene, Adrie, Adrienne, **Adriana**, Adrianna, Adrianne, Adriel, Adrielle*

Adrina (Italian) Having great happiness
Adrinna, Adreena, Adrinah, Adryna, Adreenah, Adrynah

Adrita (Sanskrit) A respected woman
Adritah, Adryta, Adrytah, Adreeta, Adreetah, Adrieta, Adrietah, Adreita, Adreitah, Adreata, Adreatah

Aduna (Wolof) Woman of the world
Adunah, Adunna, Adunnah

Adya (Indian) Born on a Sunday

Aedon (Greek) In mythology, the queen of Thebes who killed her son and was turned into a nightingale

Aefentid (Anglo-Saxon) Born in the evening

Aegea (Latin / Greek) From the Aegean Sea / in mythology, a daughter of the sun who was known for her beauty

Aegina (Greek) In mythology, a sea nymph
Aeginae, Aegyna, Aegynah

Aelan (Hawaiian) Delicate and flowerlike

Aelfthryth (English) Having an elf's strength
Aelfthrith

Aelfwine (English) A friend of the elves
Aelfwyne, Aethelwine, Aethelwyne

Aello (Greek) In mythology, an Amazon woman, name meaning "whirlwind"; also in mythology, a Harpy, name meaning "swift storm"
Aelo

Aelwen (Welsh) Woman with a fair brow
Aelwenn, Aelwenne, Aelwin, Aelwinn, Aelwinne, Aelwyn, Aelwynn, Aelwynne

Aelwyd (Welsh) From the hearth

Aerona (Welsh) Berry; from the river
Aeronna, Aeronnah, Aeronah

Aerwyna (English) A friend of the ocean

Aethelreda (English) A maiden born into nobility

Aethra (Greek) In mythology, mother of Theseus

Aetna (Greek) In mythology, the goddess of volcanoes

Afaf (Arabic) A virtuous woman; pure; chaste
Afaaf, Afifah

Afafa (African) The firstborn daughter of a second husband
Afafah, Afaffa, Afaffah

Afia (African) Born on a Friday
Afi, Affi, Affia

Afkica (Gaelic) One who is pleasant and agreeable
Afkicah, Afkika, Afkikah

Afra (Hebrew / Arabic) Young doe / white; an earth color
Affra, Affrah, Afrah, Afrya, Afryah, Afria, Affery, Affrie, Affrey, Aphra, Affera, Affrye

Afraima (Arabic) Woman who is fertile
Afraimah, Afrayma, Afraymah, Afraema, Afraemah

Afreda (English / Arabic) Elf counselor / one who is created
Afredah, Afreeda, Aafreeda, Afrida, Afridah, Aelfraed, Afreedah, Afryda, Afrydah

Africa (English) One who is pleasant; from Africa
Afrika, Affreeca, Affrica, Africah, Afrycka, Afrycah, Afric, Affryka, Afrikah, Afryka, Afrykah

Afrodille (French) Daffodil; showy and vivid
Afrodill, Afrodil, Afrodile, Afrodilla, Afrodila

Afroze (Arabic) One who is enlightening and shines brightly

Afton (English) From the Afton river

Afua (African) Born on a Friday
Afuah, Afooa, Afooah

Afya (African) One in good health

Agapi (Greek) One who loves; affectionate
Agape, Agappe, Agapie, Agapy, Agapey, Agapee, Agapea, Agapeah

Agate (Greek) Refers to the translucent semiprecious stone
Agait, Agaite, Agayt, Agayte, Agaet, Agaete

Agatha (Greek) Good and kind; St. Agatha is the patron saint of bell-founders
Agathe, Agathie, Agathy, Agathi, Agata, Agotha, Agota, Agytha, Agathyah, Agatah, Agathia, Agacia, Agafia, Agaue, Aggie, Agi, Agoti, Agueda

Agave (Greek) In mythology, a queen of Thebes

Agbenyaga (African) Life is precious and dear

Aghamora (Irish) From the vast meadow
Aghamore, Aghamorra, Aghamoria, Aghamorea

Aghanashini (Indian) One who destroys sins

Aghaveagh (Irish) From the field of ancient trees
Aghavilla, Aghaville, Aghavila, Aghavile

Aglaia (Greek) Having splendor, beauty, and glory; in mythology, one of the three Graces
Aglaiah, Aglaye, Aglaya, Aglayah, Aglae, Agalaia, Agalia

Aglauros (Greek) In mythology, a woman who was turned into stone by Hermes

Agnes (Greek) One who is pure; chaste
Agneis, Agnese, Agness, Agnies, Agnus, Agna, Agne, Agnesa, Agnesca, Agnessa, Agneta, Agnete, Agneti, Agnetis, Agnetta, Aghna, Agnek, Agnella, Aigneis, Anezka, Anis, Annice, Annis

Agraciana (Spanish) One who forgives
Agracianna, Agracyanna, Agracyana, Agraciann, Agraciane, Agracyann, Agracyane, Agracianne, Agracyanne

Agrafina (Latin) Girl child born feetfirst
Agrafine, Agrafyna, Agrafynah, Agrafeena, Agrafeenah, Agrafiena, Agrafienah, Agrafeina, Agrafeinah, Agrafeana, Agrafeanah

Agrippa (Greek) One who is born feetfirst
Agripa, Agryppa, Agrypa

Agrippina (Latin) A colonist; the name of several highborn women of ancient Rome
Agrippinae, Agrippinna, Agripinna

Agrona (Celtic) In mythology, the goddess of war and death
Agronna, Agronia, Agrone

Agurtzane (Basque) Refers to the Virgin Mary; chaste; pure
Aitziber

Ahalya (Hindi) In Hinduism, a woman who was turned to stone by her husband

Ahana (Irish) From the little ford
Ahanah, Ahanna, Ahannah

Ahava (Hebrew) Dearly loved, cherished; the name of a river
Ahavah, Ahuva, Ahuvah, Ahivia, Ahuda, Ahave

Ahelia (Hebrew) Breath; a source of life
Ahelie, Ahelya, Aheli, Ahelee, Aheleigh, Ahelea, Aheleah, Ahely, Aheley, Ahelye

Ahellona (Greek) Woman who has masculine qualities
Ahelona, Ahellonna, Ahelonna

Ahimsa (Hindi) One who avoids inflicting harm; nonviolent
Ahisma, Ahymsa, Aheemsa, Aheimsa, Ahiemsa, Aheamsa

Ahinoam (Hebrew) In the Bible, one of David's wives

Ahladita (Indian) One who is in a cheerful mood
Ahladit, Ahladtya, Ahladida, Ahladyda

Ahlam (Arabic) Witty; imaginative; one who has pleasant dreams
Ahlaam, Ahlama, Ahlamah

Ahuva (Hebrew) One who is dearly loved
Ahuvah, Ahuda, Ahudah

Ai (Japanese) One who loves and is loved; indigo blue

Aiandama (Estonian) Woman who gardens

Aibhilin (Gaelic) Of the shining light
Aibhlin

Aida (English / French / Arabic) One who is wealthy; prosperous / one who is helpful / a returning visitor
Ayda, Aydah, Aidah, Aidee, Aidia, Aieeda, Aaida

Aidan (Gaelic) One who is fiery; little fire
Aiden, Adeen, Aden, Aideen, Adan, Aithne, Aithnea, Ajthne, Aedan, Aeden

Aife (Celtic) In mythology, a great warrior woman; also a woman who turned her stepchildren into swans
Aoife

Aifric (Irish) One who is pleasant and agreeable

Aiglentine (French) Resembling the sweetbrier rose
Aiglentina

Aikaterine (Greek) One who is pure

Aiken (English) Of the oak tree

Aiko (Japanese) Little one who is dearly loved

Aila (Finnish / Scottish) One who bears light / from a protected place
Ailia, Aili, Ailie

Ailani (Hawaiian) Woman who holds rank as high chief
Aelani, Aelaney, Ailana, Ailanah, Ailanie, Ailany, Ailaney, Ailanea, Ailaneah

Ailbhe (Irish) Of noble character; one who is bright

Aileen (Irish / Scottish) Light-bearer / from the green meadow
Ailean, Ailein, Ailene, Ailin, Aillen, Ailyn, Alean, Aleane, Ayleen, Aylean, Ayleyn, Aylin, Aylein, Aylyn, Aileana, Aileene, Ailey

Ailing (Mandarin) A clever love
Ailyng

Ailis (Irish) One who is noble and kind
Ailish, Ailyse, Ailesh, Ailisa, Ailise

Aille (Gaelic) One of great beauty

Ailna (German) One who is sweet and pleasant; of the nobility
Ailne

Ailsa (Gaelic / Hebrew) From the island of elves / consecrated to God
Ailsah, Ailse, Ailsie, Ailsia

Aim (American) To direct toward a target

Aimatia (Latin) From the garden of flowers
Aimatiah, Aimatea, Aimateah, Aymatia, Aymatiah, Aymatea, Aymateah

Aimiliana (Teutonic) A hardworking woman
Aimilianah, Aimilianna, Aimilionia

Ain (Irish / Arabic) In mythology, a woman who wrote laws to protect the rights of women / precious eye

Aina (African) Child born of a complicated delivery

Aine (Celtic) One who brings brightness and joy

Aingeal (Irish) Heaven's messenger; angel
Aingealag

Ainhoa (Basque) Refers to the Virgin Mary; chaste
Ainhoah, Aenhoa, Aenhoah

Aini (Arabic) Resembling a spring flower
Ainie, Ainy, Ainey, Ainee, Ainea, Aineah, Ainye

Ainia (Greek) One who is swift
Ainiah, Ainea, Aineah, Aynia, Ayniah, Aynea, Ayneah

Ainsley (Scottish) One's own meadow
Ainslie, Ainslea, Ainslee, Ainsleigh, Ainsly, Ainslei, Aynslie, Aynslea, Aynslee, Aynsleigh, Aynsley, Aynslie, Aynsly, Ainsleah, Aynsleah, Ainslye

Aintza (Basque) One who holds the glory
Aintzane

Aionia (Greek) Everlasting life
Aioniah, Aionea, Aioneah, Ayonia, Ayoniah, Ayonea, Ayoneah

Aira (American) Of the wind
Aera

Airic (Celtic) One who is pleasant and agreeable
Airick, Airik, Aeric, Aerick, Aerik

Airla (Greek) Of the celestial spheres; ethereal
Airlia, Aerla, Aerlia

Airleas (Irish) A promise; an oath

Airmed (Celtic) In mythology, the goddess of herbalism
Airmeda, Aermed, Aermeda

Aisha (Arabic) Lively; womanly; the name of the prophet Muhammad's favorite wife
Aiesha, Aishia, Aesha, Aeshia, Aaisha, Aieysha, Aheesha, Aischa, Aisa, Aiysha, Ayse, Aysa, Aysha, Aysia, Aeesha, Aeeshah, Aeshah, Aishah, Aisia, Aisiah, Asha, Ashah, Ashia, Ashiah, Ayeesa, Ayeesah, Ayeesha, Ayeeshah, Ayeisa, Ayeisah, Ayeisha, Ayeishah, Ayisa, Ayisah, Ayisha, Ayishah, Ayesha, Ayska

Aisley (English) From the ash-tree meadow
Aisly, Aisli, Aislie, Aislee, Aisleigh, Aislye, Aysley, Aysli, Ayslie, Aysly, Ayslye, Ayslee, Aysleigh, Aislea, Ayslea, Aisleah, Aysleah

Aisling (Irish) A dream or vision; an inspiration
Aislin, Ayslin, Ayslinn, Ayslyn, Ayslynn, Aislyn, Aisylnn, Aislinn

Aissa (African) One who is thankful
Aisa

Aitama (Estonian) One who is helpful
Aitamah, Aytama, Aytamah

Aitana (Portuguese) The glorious one
Aitanah, Aitanna, Aitanne, Aitann, Aitannah

Aitheria (Greek) Of the wind
Aitheriah, Aitherea, Aithereah, Aytheria, Aytheriah, Aytherea, Aythereah

Aiya (Hebrew) One who is birdlike
Aiyah

Aiyana (Native American) An eternal bloom; forever beautiful
Aiyanna, Ayana, Ayanna, Aiyanah, Aiyonna, Aiyunna, Aianna, Ayiana, Ayianna

Aiza (Spanish) One who has honor
Aizza, Aizah, Aizzah

Aja (Yoruban) In mythology, a patroness of the forest, animals, and healers
Ajah, Ajaa, Ajae

Ajaya (Hindi) One who is invincible; having the power of a god
Ajay

Ajua (Ghanaian) Born on a Monday
Adwowa, Ajo, Aju, Ajuah

Aka (Maori / Turkish) Affectionate one / in mythology, a mother goddess
Akah, Akka, Akkah

Akakia (Greek) One who is naïve

Akako (Japanese) A red child

Akanke (African) She is loved by all who know her

Akasma (Turkish) A white climbing rose

Akela (Hawaiian) One who is noble
Akeyla, Akeylah, Akeelah, Akelah, Akelia, Akeliah, Akeya, Akella, Akellah

Akenehi (Maori) Woman who is pure; chaste
Akenehie, Akenehea, Akeneheah, Akenehy, Akenehey, Akenehee

Aki (Japanese) Born in autumn
Akey, Akie, Akee, Aky, Akea, Akeah, Akye

Akia (African) The firstborn child
Akiah, Akya, Akyah

Akiko (Japanese) Emanating a bright light

Akilah (Arabic) One who is intelligent, wise, and logical
Akila, Akeela, Akeila, Akiela, Akyla, Akillah, Akilia, Akeelah, Akeilah, Akielah, Akylah, Akeala, Akealah

Akili (Tanzanian) Having great wisdom
Akilea, Akilee, Akilie, Akylee, Akylie, Akyli, Akileah

Akilina (Latin) Resembling an eagle
Akilinah, Akileena, Akilyna, Akilinna, Ackilina, Acilina, Akylina, Akylyna

Akina (Japanese) Resembling a spring flower

Akira (Scottish) One who acts as an anchor
Akera, Akerra, Akiera, Akirah, Akiria, Akyra, Akirrah, Akeri, Akeira, Akeara

Akiva (Hebrew) One who protects and shelters
Akibe, Akiha

Akona (Maori) One who excites and enthuses
Akonah, Akonna, Akonnah

Akosua (African) Born on a Sunday

Akpenamawu (African) Thanks be to God
Akpena

Aksana (Russian) Form of Oksana, meaning "one who gives glory to God"
Aksanna, Aksanah, Aksannah

Akua (African) Born on a Wednesday

Akuti (Indian) A princess; born to royalty
Akutie, Akuteu, Akuty, Akutey, Akutee, Akutye

Alabama (Native American) From a tribal town; from the state of Alabama

Alaia (Arabic / Basque) One who is majestic, of high worth / joy

Alaina (French) Beautiful and fair woman; dear child
Alayna, Alaine, Allaine, Alayne, Alainah, Aleine, Alenne, Allayne, Alleine, Alenne, Aleyne, Alaana, Alanae, Alanea, Alawna, Alane, Aleine, Alanah, Alanna, Alana, Alanis, Alannis, Allayna, Allena, Allene, Alonna, Alyn, Alyna, Alaena, Alaenah

Alair (French) One who has a cheerful disposition
Alaire, Allaire, Allair, Aulaire, Alayr, Alayre, Alaer, Alaere

Alake (Yoruban) One who is adored

Alala (Hawaiian) Resembling an endangered crow
Alalla, Alalah, Alallah

Alamea (Hawaiian) Precious as a child

Alameda (Native American / Spanish) From the cottonwood grove / from the poplar tree
Alamida, Alamyda, Alameeda, Alameida, Alamieda, Alameada

Alani (Hawaiian) From the orange tree
Alanee, Alanie, Alaney, Alannie, Alany, Alaini, Alanea

Alanza (Spanish) Feminine form of Alonzo; noble and ready for battle

Alaqua (Native American) Resembling the sweet gum tree

Alarice (German) Feminine form of Alaric; ruler of all
Alarise, Allaryce, Alarica, Alarisa, Alaricia, Alrica, Alryca, Alryque

Alaska (Native American) From the great land; from the state of Alaska

Alastrina (Scottish) Form of Alexandra, meaning "helper and defender of mankind"
Alastriane, Alastriana, Alastrinah, Alastryan, Alastrine, Alastryana, Alastryn, Alastryne, Alastrynia, Alastrynah, Alastriona

Alaula (Hawaiian) The light of dawn

Alaura (Latin) Form of Laura, meaning "crowned with laurel; from the laurel tree"
Alauri, Alaurie, Alauree, Alaurea, Alaureah, Alaury, Alaurey, Alaurye

Alavda (French) Resembling a lark

Alazne (Basque) A miracle child

Alba (Latin) From the highlands
Albia, Alby, Albina, Albah, Allba, Allbah

Albany (Latin) From the white hill; white-skinned
Albaney, Albani, Albanie, Albanee, Albanye, Albin, Alban, Albhda, Albinia, Albinka, Albiona, Aubine, Aubina, Albanea, Albaneah

Alberga (Latin / German) Of noble character / a white-skinned woman
Alberge, Albergah, Albergia, Albergiah, Albergea, Albergeah

Alberta (German) Feminine form of Albert; noble and bright
Alburta, Albyrta, Albirta, Albertina, Albertine, Albrette, Alberte, Alberteen, Albertyna, Alhertina, Alhertine, Auberta

Albina (Etruscan) In mythology, the goddess of the dawn
Albinah, Albyna, Albynah, Albeena, Albeenah, Albiena, Albienah, Albeina, Albeinah, Albeana, Albeanah

Albreda (English) One who receives counsel from the elves

Alcestis (Greek) In mythology, a woman who died in place of her husband and was later rescued from Hades by Hercules

Alcimede (Greek) Having great cunning; in mythology, the mother of Jason

Alcina (Greek) One who is strong-willed and opinionated
Alceena, Alcyna, Alsina, Alsyna, Alzina, Alcine, Alcinia, Alcyne, Alsine, Alsyn, Alzine, Alcinah, Alcee, Alceenah, Alcynah, Alcienah, Alciena, Alceina, Alceinah, Alceana, Alceanah

Alcippe (Greek) A mighty horse; in mythology, the daughter of Ares
Alkippe

Alcmene (Greek) In mythology, the mother of Hercules
Alcmena, Alcemyne, Alcamene, Alcumena

Alcyone (Greek) A kingfisher; the name of the brightest star in the constellation Taurus; in mythology, a sea nymph
Alcieone, Alcione

Alda (German / Spanish) Long-lived, old; wise; an elder
Aldah, Aldine, Aldina, Aldinah, Aldene, Aldona, Aldeana, Allda, Alldah

Aldea (Teutonic) One who is wealthy and prosperous
Aldeah, Aldya, Aldiya, Aldyah, Aldiyah

Aldercy (English) Woman who holds the rank of chief
Aldercey, Alderci, Aldercie, Aldercee, Aldercye, Aldercea, Alderceah

Aldis (English) From the ancient house
Aldys, Aldiss, Aldisse, Aldyss, Aldysse

Aldonsa (Spanish) One who is kind and gracious
Aldonza, Aldonsia, Aldonzia

Aldora (English) One who is noble and superior
Aldorah, Aldorra, Aldorrah

Aldreda (English) Feminine form of Aldred; one who provides wise counsel

Alecto (Greek) In mythology, one of the Furies
Alecta, Alekto, Alekto

Aleda (Latin) Small and winged
Aletta, Alida, Alita, Allete, Alleta, Alleda, Allida, Aluld, Alyda

Aledwen (Welsh) Feminine form of Aled; offspring
Aledwenn, Aledwenne, Aledwyn, Aledwynn, Aledwynne, Aledwena, Aledwyna, Aledwynna, Aledwenna, Aledwin, Aledwinn, Aledwinne, Aledwina, Aledwinna

Aleen (Celtic) Form of Helen, meaning "the shining light"
Aleena, Aleenia, Alene, Alyne, Alena, Alenka, Alynah, Aleine, Aleina, Aleine, Aleina, Aleane, Aleana

Aleeza (Hebrew) One who is joyful
Aleezah, Alieza, Aliezah, Aliza, Alizah, Alitza, Aliz, Aleeze, Alizia, Alize, Aleiza, Aleizah, Aleaza, Aleazah

Alegria (Spanish) One who is cheerful and brings happiness to others
Alegra, Aleggra, Allegra, Alleffra, Allecra

Alera (Latin) Resembling an eagle
Alerra, Aleria, Alerya, Alerah, Alerrah

Aleshanee (Native American) Girl who is always playful

Aleshanie, Aleshany, Aleshani, Aleshaney, Aleshanea, Aleshaneah, Aleshanye

Alesta (Scottish) Form of Alexandra, meaning "helper and defender of mankind"
Alestah

Alethea (Greek) One who is truthful
Aletheia, Alethia, Aletha, Aletea, Althaia, Alithea, Alathea, Aletia, Alithia, Althaea

✪ **Alexa** (Greek) Form of Alexandra, meaning "helper and defender of mankind"
Aleka, Alexia

✪ **Alexandra** (Greek) Feminine form of
❶ Alexander; helper and defender of mankind
Alexandria, Alexandrea, Alixandra, Alessandra, Alondra, Aleksandra, Alejandra, Alexsandra, Alexandrina, Alandra, Alejandra, Alejandrina, Alesundese, Alewndra, Alewndrina, Alexandina, Alexandriana, Alexandrine, Alexandtea, Alexavia, Alexi, Alexina, Alexine, Alix, Alyssandra, Alyx, Axelia

✪ **Alexis** (Greek) Form of Alexandra, meaning
❶ "helper and defender of mankind"
Aleksys, Alexus, Alexys

Alfonsa (Spanish) Feminine form of Alfonso; noble and ready for battle
Alfonsine, Alfonsia, Alonsa, Alonza, Alphonsa, Alphonza

Alfreda (German) Feminine form of Alfred; one who counsels the elves
Alfreeda, Alfrida, Alfrieda, Alfryda, Alfreida, Alfreada

Algoma (Native American) From the valley of flowers
Algomma, Algomia, Algomea, Algomiya, Algomya

Alhena (Arabic) A star in the constellation Gemini
Alhenah, Alhenna, Alhennah

Alice (German) Woman of the nobility; truthful; having high moral character
Alyce, Alicia, Alecia, Alesia, Aleece, Aleecia, Aleesha, Alesha, Alessa, Ali, Alicea, Alise, Aleasha, Aleashia, Aleasia, Aleassa, Alisea, Alishah, Alishay, Aleeshya, Aleeshia, Alishia, Alisse, Alisz, Alli, Allie, Allis, Alliss, Ally, Allyce, Allys, Allyse, Alycia, Alys, Alyse, Alysha, Alysia, Alyss

Alika (Hawaiian) One who is honest
Alicku, Alicca, Alyka, Alycka, Alycca

Alike (Nigerian) Girl who drives away other women
Alyke

Alima (Arabic) Sea maiden; one who is learned in music and dance
Alimah, Alyma, Alymah, Aleema, Aleemah, Aliema, Aliemah, Aleima, Aleimah, Aleama, Aleamah

Alina (Arabic / Polish) One who is noble / one who is beautiful and bright
Aline

Alitash (African) May you always be found
Alytash, Alitasha, Alytasha, Alitashe, Alytashe

Alivette (English) Form of Olivetta, meaning "of the olive tree; one who is peaceful"
Alivet, Alivett, Alivetta, Alivete, Aliveta

Aliyah (Arabic) An ascender; one having the highest social standing
Aliya, Alliyah, Alieya, Aliyiah, Alliyia, Aleeya, Alee, Aleiya, Alea, Aleah, Alia, Aliah, Aliye, Aliyyah, Aleya, Aleyah, Alya

Alka (Indian) Young girl with long curly hair
Alkah

✿ **Allison** (English) Form of Alice, meaning "woman of the nobility, truthful; having high moral character"
Alisanne, Alison, Alicen, Alisen, Alisyn, Allyson, Alyson

Allona (Hebrew) Feminine form of Allon; one who is as strong as an oak
Allonia, Alona, Alonia, Atonia, Atona

Allsun (Irish) One who is honest

Allyriane (French) Resembling the lyre, a stringed instrument

Alma (Latin / Italian) One who is nurturing and kind / refers to the soul
Almah

Almarine (German) Refers to a work ruler
Almerin, Almerine, Almarin, Almaryne, Almaryn, Almeryn, Almeryne

Almas (Arabic) Resembling a diamond
Almaas

Almeta (Latin / Danish) One who is ambitious / resembling a pearl
Almeda

Almira (English) A princess; daughter born to royalty
Almeera, Almeira, Almiera, Almyra, Almirah, Almeerah, Almeirah, Almierah, Almyrah, Almeara, Almearah

Almodine (Latin) A highly prized stone
Almondyne, Almondeene, Almondeane, Almondeine, Almondiene

Almond (English) Resembling the almond nut
Almandina, Almandine

Almunda (Spanish) Refers to the Virgin Mary
Almundena, Almundina

Alodia (Spanish) Form of Elodia, meaning "a wealthy foreigner"
Alodiah, Alodya, Alodie, Alodi, Alody, Alodey, Alodee, Alodea, Alodeah, Alodye

Aloe (English) Resembling the aloe plant

Aloha (Hawaiian) One showing love, compassion, and affection

Alohilani (Hawaiian) From the bright sky
Alohilanie, Alohilany, Alohilaney, Alohilane, Alohilanea, Alohilaneah, Alohilanye

Aloise (Spanish) Feminine form of Aloysius; famous warrior
Aloisa, Aloisia, Aloysia

Aloma (Spanish) Form of Paloma, meaning "dovelike"
Alomah, Alomma, Alommah

Alonsa (French) Feminine form of Alonso; one who is ready for battle
Alonza

Alouette (French) Resembling a lark
Allouette, Alouetta, Alowette, Alouett, Alouet, Alouete, Aloueta

Alpa (Indian) A petite girl

Alpana (Indian) A beautiful decoration
Alpanah, Alpannah, Alpanna

Alpha (Greek) The firstborn child; the first letter of the Greek alphabet

Alphonsine (French) Feminine form of Alphonse; one who is ready for battle
Alphonsina, Alphonsyne, Alphonsyna, Alphonseene, Alphonseena, Alphonseane, Alphonseana, Alphonsiene, Alphonsiena, Alphonseine, Alphonseina

Alpina (Scottish) Feminine form of Alpin; blonde; white-skinned
Alpinah, Alpena, Alpeena, Alpyna, Alpeenah, Alpynah, Alpeina, Alpeinah, Alpiena, Alpienah, Alpeana, Alpeanah

Alsatia (English) Woman of the region Alsace

Alsoomse (Native American) One who is independent

Altagracia (Spanish) The high grace of the Virgin Mary
Alta

Altair (Arabic) Resembling the flying eagle; a bright star in the constellation Aquila
Altaire, Altaira, Altayr, Altayre, Altaer, Altaere, Altayra, Altaera

Althea (Greek) Possessing the power to heal; wholesome
Althia, Althaea, Altha, Altheda, Althya

Aludra (Arabic) A maiden; the name of a star in the constellation Canis Major
Aloodra

Alufa (Hebrew) One who is a leader
Alufah

Alula (Latin) As delicate and light as a feather

Aluma (Hebrew) A young maiden; chaste
Alumah, Alumit

Alumina (Latin) Surrounded by light
Allumina, Alumyna, Allumyna, Alumeena, Allumeena, Alumeana, Allumeana

Alura (English) A divine counselor
Allura, Alurea, Alhraed

Alva (Latin) One who has a fair complexion
Alvah

Alvar (German) Of the army of elves
Alvara, Alvaria, Alvarie, Alvare, Alvarr

Alvera (Spanish) Feminine form of Alvaro; guardian of all; speaker of the truth
Alveria, Alvara, Alverna, Alvernia, Alvira, Alvyra, Alvarita, Alverra

Alverdine (English) Feminine form of Alfred; one who counsels the elves
Alverdina, Alverdeene, Alverdeena, Alverdeane, Alverdeana, Alverdiene, Alverdiena, Alverdeine, Alverdeina

Alvina (English) Feminine form of Alvin; friend of the elves
Alvine, Alvinia, Alveena, Alvyna, Alvie, Alvy, Alvey, Alvee, Alvea, Alveah, Alvye

Alvita (Latin) One who has been anointed
Alvitah, Alveta, Alvyta, Alveeta, Alvytah, Alveetah, Alvieta, Alvietah, Alveita, Alveitah, Alveata, Alveatah

○ **Alyssa** (German) Form of Alice, meaning "woman of the nobility, truthful; having high moral character"
Alisa, Alissya, Alyssaya, Alishya, Alisia, Alissa, Allisa, Allyssa, Alysa, Alysse, Alyssia

Alzena (Arabic) A lovely woman
Alzenah, Alzina, Alzan, Alzene

Ama (African) Born on a Saturday
Amah, Amma, Ammah

Amabel (Latin) One who is lovable
Amabell, Amabelle, Amabella, Amabela, Amabilis, Amable, Amabele

Amachi (African) The child is a gift of God
Amachie, Amachy, Amachey, Amachee, Amachye, Amachea, Amacheah

Amada (Spanish) One who is loved by all
Amadia, Amadea, Amadita, Amadah

Amadahy (Native American) Of the forest's water
Amadahey, Amadahi, Amadahie, Amadahee, Amadahea, Amadaheah, Amadahye

Amadea (Latin) Feminine form of Amedeo; loved by God
Amadya, Amadia, Amadine, Amadina, Amadika, Amadis

Amadi (African) One who rejoices
Amadie, Amady, Amadey, Amadye, Amadee, Amadea, Amadeah

Amadore (Italian) One who has the gift of love
Amadora, Amadorah, Amadorra, Amadorrah

Amal (Arabic) One with dreams and aspirations
A'mal, Amala, Aamaal

Amalfi (Italian) From an Italian town overlooking the Gulf of Salerno
Amalfey, Amalfy, Amalfie, Amalfee, Amalfea, Amalfeah

Amalia (German) One who is industrious and hardworking
Amalea, Amalya, Amalie, Amalasanda, Amalasande, Amalasand, Amalasandia, Amalasandra, Amalija, Amaliji, Amalle, Amalda, Ameliya, Amilia, Amyleah, Amylya, Amella, Aimil, Amaline, Amalin, Amelinda, Amialiona

Amalthea (Greek) One who soothes; in mythology, the foster mother of Zeus
Amaltheah, Amalthia, Amalthya

Amalur (Spanish) From the homeland
Amalure, Amalura, Amaluria

Aman (African) A trustworthy woman
Amana

Amanda (Latin) One who is much loved
Amandi, Amandah, Amandea, Amandee, Amandey, Amande, Amandie, Amandy, Amandya, Amandalee, Amandalyn, Amandia, Amandina, Amandine

Amandeep (Indian) Emanating the light of peace
Amanpreet, Amanjot

Amandla (African) A powerful woman

Amani (African / Arabic) One who is peaceful / one with wishes and dreams
Amanie, Amany, Amaney, Amanee, Amanye, Amanea, Amaneah

Amapola (Arabic) Resembling a poppy
Amapolah, Amapolla, Amapollah, Amapolia

Amara (Greek) One who will be forever beautiful
Amarah, Amarya, Amaira, Amaria, Amar, Amari, Amaree, Amarie, Amarri, Amarra

Amaranta (Latin) A flower that never fades
Amarante, Amarantha, Amantha, Amaranda, Amaranthe, Amaranth, Amare

Amariah (Hebrew) A gift of God

Amarina (Australian) Brought with the rain
Amarinah, Amarine, Amaryn, Amarin, Amarynah, Amaryne, Amareena, Amareenah, Amariena, Amarienah, Amareina, Amareinah, Amareana, Amareanah

Amaris (Hebrew) Fulfilling God's promise
Amariss, Amarys, Amaryss, Amarisa, Amarissa, Amarysa, Amaryssa, Amarise

Amaryllis (Greek) As fresh as a flower; sparkling
Amarilis, Amarillis, Amarylis, Amaryl, Amaryla, Amarylla

Amata (Latin / Spanish) In mythology, a queen who committed suicide / one who is dearly loved
Amatah

Amaya (Japanese) Of the night rain
Amayah, Amaia, Amaiah

Amber (French) Resembling the jewel; a warm honey color
Ambur, Ambar, Amberly, Amberlyn, Amberli, Amberlee, Ambyr, Ambyre, Ambra, Ambria, Ambrea, Ahmber, Amberia, Amberise, Amberjill, Amberlynn, Ambre

Ambika (Hindi) In Hinduism, one of the wives of Vichitravirya
Ambikah, Ambyka, Ambykah

Ambrosia (Greek) Immortal; in mythology, the food of the gods
Ambrosa, Ambrosiah, Ambrosyna, Ambrosina, Ambrosyn, Ambrosine, Ambrozin, Ambrozyn, Ambrozyna, Ambrozyne, Ambrozine, Ambrose, Ambrotosa, Ambruslne, Amhrosine

Amedee (French) One who loves God
Amedi, Amedie, Amedy, Amedey, Amedea, Amedeah, Amedye

✪ **Amelia** (German) Form of Amalia or (Latin) form of Emily, meaning "one who is industrious and hardworking"
Amelie, Amelita, Amylia, Amely

America (Latin) A powerful ruler
Americus, Amerika, Amerikus

Amethyst (Greek) Resembling the purple gemstone; wine; in history, was used to prevent intoxication
Amathyste, Amethist, Amathist, Amethyste, Amathista, Amathysta, Amethista, Amethistia, Amethysta, Amethystia

Amhuinn (Gaelic) From the alder-tree river

Amica (Latin) One who is a beloved friend
Amicah, Amice, Amika, Amikah, Amyca, Amycah, Amyka, Amykah

Amina (Arabic) Honest; trustworthy; faithful; the mother of the prophet Muhammad
Aminah, Aamena, Aamina, Aminta, Aminda, Ameena, Ameenah, Amena, Amineh, Aminia, Amiena, Amienah, Ameina, Ameinah, Ameana, Ameanah

Amira (Arabic) A princess; one who commands
Amirah, Ameera, Amyra, Ameerah, Amyrah, Ameira, Ameirah, Amiera, Amierah, Ameara, Amearah

Amissa (Hebrew) One who is honest; a friend
Amisa, Amise, Amisia, Amiza, Amysa, Amysia, Amysya, Amyza

Amita (Indian) Feminine form of Amit; without limits; unmeasurable
Amitah, Ameeta, Amyta, Amitha, Ameetah, Amytah, Amieta, Amietah, Ameita, Ameitah, Ameata, Ameata

Amitola (Native American) Of the rainbow
Amitolah, Amytola, Amytolah, Amitolla, Amytolla, Amitollah, Amytollah

Amity (Latin) A dear friendship
Amitey, Amitee, Amiti, Amitie, Amytee, Amyti, Amytie, Amytey, Amyty, Amite, Amitee, Amitea, Amytea, Amiteah, Amyteah

Amlika (Indian) A nurturing woman; a mother
Amlikah, Amlyka, Amlykah

Amoke (Yoruban) One who is petted

Amoldina (Teutonic) Having the strength of an eagle
Amoldinah, Amoldeena, Amoldyna, Amoldena, Amoldine

Amorette (Latin) One who is beloved and loving
Amorete, Amorett, Amorit, Amoritt, Amoritte, Amoryt, Amortye, Amorytte, Amoreta, Amoretta, Amorita, Amoryta, Amor, Amora, Amorie, Amorina, Amory

Amorica (English) Woman of Britain
Amoricah, Amorika, Amoricka, Amoryca, Amoryka, Amorycka

Amparo (Spanish) One who offers shelter; a protector

Amphitrite (Greek) In mythology, a sea goddess and wife of Poseidon
Amfitrite

Amrita (Hindi) Having immortality; full of ambrosia
Amritah, Amritta, Amryta, Amrytta, Amrytte, Amritte, Amryte, Amreeta, Amreetah, Amrieta, Amrietah, Amreita, Amreitah, Amreata, Amreatah

Amritha (Indian) One who is precious
Amrytha

Amser (Welsh) A period of time

Amtullah (Arabic) A servant of Allah
Amtulla, Amtula, Amtulah

Amunet (Egyptian) In mythology, a fertility and mother goddess

Amy (Latin) Dearly loved
Aimee, Aimie, Aimi, Aimy, Aimya, Aimey, Amice, Amicia, Amie, Amye

Amymone (Greek) The blameless one; in mythology, a princess of Argos who bore a son to Poseidon

Amynta (Latin) Protector and defender of her loved ones
Amyntah, Amyntas, Aminta, Ameenta, Amenta

An (Chinese) One who is peaceful

Anaba (Native American) A woman returning from battle
Anabah, Annaba, Annabah

Anabal (Gaelic) One who is joyful
Anaball, Annabal, Annaball

Anafa (Hebrew) Resembling the heron
Anafah, Anapha, Anaphah

Anahid (Armenian) In mythology, the goddess of water and fertility

Anahita (Persian) The immaculate one; in mythology, a water goddess
Anahit, Anahyta, Anahyt

Anan (African) The fourth-born child
Anana

Ananda (Hindi) Feminine form of Anand; one who brings happiness
Anandah

Anani (Hawaiian) From the orange tree
Ananie, Ananee, Ananea, Ananeah, Anany, Ananey, Ananye

Anarosa (Spanish) A graceful rose
Annarosa, Anarose, Annarose

Anastasia (Greek) One who shall rise again
Anastase, Anastascia, Anastasha, Anastasie, Anastassia, Anastasya, Anastatia, Anestasia, Annastaysia, Anstace, Anstice, Anastazia, Anastazya, Anastacia, Anastashia, Anastazja, Anasztaizia, Annastasia, Anstey

Anasuya (Indian) One who is charitable
Anasuyah, Annasuya

Anat (Hebrew / Arabian) One who sings / in mythology, the goddess of fertility, war, and hunting
Anate, Anata, Anatie, Anati, Anaty, Anatey, Anatee, Anatea, Anateah

Anathema (Latin) One who is cursed and shunned
Anathemah, Annathema

Anatola (Greek) Woman from the East
Anatolah, Anatolya, Annatola, Anatolia, Annatolia, Annatolya, Anatole

Anaxarete (Greek) In mythology, an unfeeling woman who was turned to stone
Anawrete

Anaya (African) One who looks up to God
Anayah, Annaya

Anbar (Arabic) A fragrant or perfumed woman
Anbarre, Anbarr

Ancelin (French) A handmaiden
Anceline, Ancelina, Ancelyn, Ancelynn, Ancelynne

Ancelote (French) Feminine form of Lancelot; an attendant

Anchoret (Welsh / Latin) One who is loved / a hermit
Anachoret, Annchoret

Ancina (Latin) Form of Ann, meaning "a woman graced with God's favor"
Ancyna, Anncina, Anncyna, Anceina, Annceina, Anciena, Annciena, Anceena, Annceena, Anceana, Annceana

Andeana (Spanish) One who is leaving
Andeanna, Andeane, Andiana, Andianna, Andyana, Andyanna

Andes (Latin) Woman from the Andes

Andraste (Celtic) One who is invincible; in mythology, the goddess of victory
Andrasta, Andrastia

❂ **Andrea** (Greek / Latin) Courageous and
❶ strong / feminine form of Andrew; womanly
Andria, Andrianna, Andreia, Andreina, Andreya, Andriana, Andreana, Andera, Andraia, Andreja, Andrya, Andris, Andrette, Aindrea, Anda, Andee, Andena, Andere, Andra, Andralyn, Andi, Andie, Andranetta, Andraya, Andreanna, Andree, Andras, Andrena, Andrienne, Andrianne, Andrina, Andren, Andrya, Anndrea, Anndria, Aundrea

Andromache (Greek) In mythology, a Trojan princess and the wife of Hector
Andromacha

Andromeda (Greek) A northern constellation; in mythology, the wife of Perseus
Andromyda, Andromida

Andsware (Anglo-Saxon) An answer; a gift
Andswaru, Andswara

Aneira (Welsh) The golden woman
Aneera, Anyra, Aneirah, Aneerah, Anyrah, Aniera, Anierah, Aneara, Anearah

Aneko (Japanese) An older sister
Aniko, Anyko

Anela (Hawaiian) A messenger of heaven; an angel
Anelah, Anella, Anellah, Anel, Anelle

Anemone (Greek) Resembling a windflower; breath

Anevay (Native American) One who is superior
Anevaye, Anavai, Anavae

Angela (Greek) A heavenly messenger; an angel
Angelica, Angelique, Anjela, Anjelika, Angella, Angelita, Angelia, Ange, Anga, Angel, Angele, Angelee, Angeles, Angeletta, Angelette, Angeli, Angelika, Angeliki, Angilia, Angelisa, Angelita, Angell, Angelle, Angelynn, Angie, Angyalka, Anielka, Anjelica, Anjelita

○ **Angelina** (Greek) Form of Angela, meaning "a heavenly messenger; an angel"
Angeline, Angelyn, Angelene, Angelin, Angelena

Angeni (Native American) A spirit angel
Angeni, Angenie, Angenee, Angeny, Anjenee, Anjeney, Anjenie, Anjeny, Anjeenie, Anjeeny, Angenia, Angenea, Angeneah, Anjenea, Anjeneah

Angerona (Latin) In mythology, the goddess of winter, anguish, solstice, death, and silence
Angrona

Angevin (French) An angel of wine
Angevyn, Angeven

Angharad (Welsh) In mythology, the love of Peredur; one who is greatly loved
Anghard, Angharat

Angita (Latin) In mythology, goddess of healing and magic
Angyta, Angeeta, Angeta, Angeata, Angeita, Angieta

Anglides (English) In Arthurian legend, the mother of Alisander

Angrboda (Norse) In mythology, a giantess
Angerboda, Angerbotha

Angusina (Gaelic) Feminine form of Angus; of one choice
Angusinah, Angusyna, Angusynah, Angusiena, Angusienah, Anguseina, Anguseinah, Anguseena, Anguseenah, Anguseana, Anguseanah

Angwusnasomtaqa (Native American) A crow mother spirit

Anh (Vietnamese) One who offers safety and peace

Ani (Hawaiian) One who is very beautiful
Aneesa, Aney, Anie, Any, Aany, Aanye, Anea, Aneah, Anye

Aniceta (French) One who is unconquerable
Anicetta, Anniceta, Annicetta

Anila (Hindi) Child of the wind
Anilla, Anyla, Anylla, Anilah, Anylah, Anyllah

Anippe (Egyptian) A daughter of the Nile

Anisa (Arabic) One who is affectionate and friendly
Aneesa, Aneesah, Aneecia, Annisa, Annissa, Anyssa, Annyssa, Annysa, Anysa, Anysha, Anissa, Anisah, Aneisa, Aneisah, Aniesa, Aneisa, Aneasa, Aneasah

Anise (English) Resembling the herb
Aneese, Aneise, Anyse, Aniese, Anease

Anisha (Hindi) Born at the end of the night; form of Anna, meaning "a woman graced with God's favor"; form of Agnes, meaning "one who is pure; chaste"
Anicia, Aneisha, Annisha, Aanisha, Aeniesha, Aneasha, Anysha

Anjali (Indian) One who offers with both hands
Anjalie, Anjaley, Anjaly, Anjalee, Anjaleigh, Anjalea, Anjaleah, Anjalye

Anjanette (American) A gift of God's favor
Annjeanette, Anjeanette, Anjanique, Anjana

Ankareeda (Arabic) Resembling a night star; shining and graceful
Ankaryda, Ankareda, Ankarida, Ankareeta, Ankaryta, Ankareta, Ankarita

Ankine (Armenian) One who is valuable

Ankti (Native American) To repeat the dance
Anktie, Ankty, Anktey, Anktee, Anktea, Ankteah, Anktye

Anlicnes (Anglo-Saxon) One who has a good self-image
Anlienisse

○
❶ **Anna** (Latin) A woman graced with God's favor
Annah, Ana, Ann, Anne, Anya, Ane, Annze, Anouche, Annchen, Anais, Anaise, Anaiss, Anays, Anayss, Ance, Anechka, Aneisha, Anessa, Aneta, Anetta, Anka, Anki, Anku,

Anke, Ania, Anica, Anice, Anichka, Annaka, Anacka, Anikee, Anika, Aniki, Aniko, Anita, Anitchka, Anitia, Anitra, Aniya, Aniyah, Anja, Annette, Annora, Annorah, Anora, Antje, Asenka, Anyuta, Asenke, Anneke, Annas, Anni, Annick, Annie, Annika, Annike, Annikka, Annikke, Annikki, Anina, Annyna, Anyna, Anninah, Aninah, Annynah, Anynah, Annina, Annissa, Anny, Annys, Anouska, Ayn, Anyssa

Anna Christina (Latin) A graceful Christian
Anna Christina, Anna Kristina, Anna Chrystina, Anna Christeena, Anna Christyna, Anna Chrystyna, Ana Christina, Ana Kristina, Anna Christine, Anne Christine, Ana Christine, Anna Christie, Ana Christi

Anna Perenna (Latin) In mythology, a goddess who was the personification of the perennial year

Annabel (Italian) Graceful and beautiful woman
Annabelle, Annabell, Annabella, Annabele, Anabel, Anabell, Anabelle, Anabella, Anabela, Annabla, Anahella

Annabeth (English) Graced with God's bounty
Anabeth, Annabethe, Annebeth, Anebeth, Anabethe

Annakiya (African) Girl with a sweet face
Anakiya, Annakiyah, Anakiyah

Annalee (English) From the graceful meadow
Annali, Annalie, Annaleigh, Analee, Analeigh, Anali, Analie, Annalina, Anneli

Annalisa (Latin) Graced with God's bounty
Analisa, Analissa, Annelisa, Annelise, Analicia, Analiese, Analise, Analisia, Analyssa, Annalise, Annalissa, Annaliese, Anneliese

Annalynn (English) From the graceful lake
Analynn, Annalyn, Annaline, Annalin, Annalinn, Analyn, Analine, Analin, Analinn, Annalinda, Analinda, Annalynda, Analynda

Annapurna (Hindi) In Hinduism, the goddess of plenty

Annmarie (English) Filled with bitter grace
Annemarie, Annmaria, Annemaria, Annamarie, Annamaria, Anamarie, Anamaria, Anamari, Annemie

Annora (Latin) Having great honor
Anora, Annorah, Anorah, Anoria, Annore, Annorya, Anorya, Annoria

Annot (Hebrew) One who emanates light

Annunciata (Latin) Named for the Annunciation
Anunciata, Annuziata, Anuziata, Annunciatta, Annuziatta, Anunciacion

Annwn (Welsh) In mythology, the name of the Otherworld
Annwfn, Annwyn, Annwyfn, Annwfyn

Annwyl (Welsh) One who is loved

Anona (English) Resembling a pineapple
Anonah, Annona, Annoniah, Annonya, Annonia

Anonna (Latin) In mythology, a goddess of the harvest, food, and supplies
Annonna

Anouhea (Hawaiian) Having a soft, cool fragrance

Anoush (Armenian) Having a sweet disposition
Anousha, Anoushia

Anouska (French) One who is gracious
Annouska, Annushka, Anusha, Anyoushka

Ansa (Latin / Finnish) One who is constant / a virtuous woman
Anse

Anselma (German) Feminine form of Anselm; having divine protection
Anselmah, Anzelma, Anzelmah

Ansley (English) From the noble's pastureland
Ansly, Anslie, Ansli, Anslee, Ansleigh, Anslea, Ansleah, Anslye

Ansonia (German) Feminine form of Anson; child of the divine
Annesonia, Annsonia, Annsonya, Ansonya, Ansonea, Annsonea, Annsoniya, Ansoniya

Antalya (Russian) Born with the morning's first light
Antaliya, Antalyah, Antaliyah, Antalia, Antaliah

Antandra (Latin) An Amazon warrior

Antea (Greek) In mythology, a woman who was scorned and committed suicide
Anteia, Anteah

Anthea (Greek) Lady of the flowers
Anthia, Antheah, Anthya, Antha, Anthe

Anthemia (Greek) Resembling a flower in bloom
Antheemia, Anthemya, Anthymia, Anthemea, Anthemeah

Anticlea (Greek) In mythology, the mother of Odysseus
Antiklea, Antiklia

Antigone (Greek) In mythology, the daughter of Oedipus
Antigoni, Antigonie, Antigony, Antigoney, Antigonea, Antygone, Antygoni, Antygonie, Antygonee

Antiope (Greek) In mythology, a queen of the Amazons

Antje (German) A graceful woman

Antonia (Latin) Feminine form of Anthony; priceless and highly praiseworthy; a flourishing flower
Antoinette, Antoneta, Antonella, Antonette, Antonisha, Antonina, Antoinetta, Antonetta, Antonie, Antonietta, Antonique

Anulika (African) One who recognizes that happiness is best
Anulicka, Anulica, Anulyka, Anuleka, Anuleeka

Anumati (Hindi) In Hinduism, moon goddess of prosperity, intellect, children, and spirituality
Anumatie, Anumatey, Anumatee, Anumatia, Anumatea, Anumateah, Anumatye

Anuradha (Hindi) In Hinduism, goddess of good fortune
Anurada

Anusree (Indian) A pretty woman
Anusry, Anusrey, Anusri, Anusrie, Anusrea, Anusreah, Anusrye

Anwen (Welsh) A famed beauty
Anwin, Anwenne, Anwinne, Anwyn, Anwynn, Anwynne, Anwenn, Anwinn

Anyango (African) One who is a good friend

Aoibheann (Irish) Woman with a beautiful sheen; a name borne by several princesses
Aoibheane, Aoibheanne

Aoife (Irish) A beautiful woman; in mythology, a warrior princess
Aoiffe, Aoif, Aoiff

Aolani (Hawaiian) Cloud from heaven
Aolaney, Aolanee, Aolaniah, Aolanie, Aolany, Aolanya, Aolania, Aolanea, Aolanea

Apala (African) One who creates religious music
Apalla, Appalla, Appala, Apalah, Apallah, Appallah, Appalah

Apara (Yoruban) One who doesn't remain in one place
Aparra, Apparra, Appara, Aparah, Aparrah, Apparrah, Apparah

Aphrah (Hebrew) From the house of dust
Aphra

Aphria (Celtic) One who is pleasant and agreeable
Aphriah

Aphrodite (Greek) Love; in mythology, the goddess of love and beauty
Afrodite, Afrodita, Aphrodita, Aphrodyte, Aphhrodyta, Aphrodytah

Apirka (Gaelic) One who is pleasant and agreeable

Apollonia (Greek) A gift from the god Apollo
Apollina, Apolline, Apollonis, Apollinaris, Appolina, Appoline

Aponi (Native American) Resembling a butterfly
Aponni, Apponni, Apponi

Apphia (Hebrew) One who is productive
Apphiah

Apple (American) Sweet fruit; one who is cherished
Appel, Aple, Apel

Apria (Latin) Resembling an apricot
Aprea, Apriah, Aprya, Apreah, Apryah

April (English) Opening buds of spring; born in the month of April
Avril, Averel, Averill, Avrill, Apryl, Apryle, Aprylle, Aprel, Aprele, Aprila, Aprile, Aprili, Aprilla, Aprille, Aprielle, Aprial, Abril, Abrielle, Abrial, Aperira, Avrielle, Avrial, Abrienda, Avriel, Averyl, Averil, Avryl, Apryll

Apsaras (Indian) In mythology, nature spirits or water nymphs

Aqua (Greek) Of the water
Aquanetta, Aquanet, Aquaneta, Aquanett, Aquanette

Aquarius (Latin) The water-bearer; a constellation

Aquene (Native American) One who is peaceful
Aqueena, Aqueene, Aqueen

Aquila (Latin) Resembling an eagle; a constellation
Aquilla, Aquil, Aquileo, Aquill, Aquyl, Aquyll, Aquilas, Acquilla, Aquilino, Aquilina, Aquiline, Aquileene, Aquileena

Ar (Anglo-Saxon) A merciful woman

Ara (Arabic) An opinionated woman
Aira, Arah, Arae, Ahraya, Aaraa

Arabella (Latin) An answered prayer; beautiful altar
Arabel, Arabela, Arabelle, Arabele, Arabell

Araceli (Spanish) From the altar of heaven
Aricela, Arcilla, Aracelia, Arcelia, Aracely, Araseli, Arasely, Arceli, Aracelli, Aracele, Aracelea

Arachne (Greek) In mythology, a young woman who was changed into a spider by Athena
Arachnie, Arachni, Arachny, Arachney, Arackne, Aracknie, Arackni, Arackny, Arackney, Arachnee, Aracknee, Arakne, Araknie, Arakni, Arakny, Arakney, Araknee, Arachnea, Araknea, Arachneah, Arakneah

Aradia (Greek) In mythology, the goddess of witches; the daughter of Diana and Lucifer
Aradiah, Aradea, Aradeah

Arama (Spanish) Refers to the Virgin Mary
Aramah, Aramma, Arammah

Araminta (Hebrew) One who is lofty and exalted
Aramintah, Aramynta, Araminte

Aranka (Hungarian) The golden child

Aranrhod (Welsh) A large silver wheel; in mythology, the mother of a sea creature and a blob
Arianrhod, Arianrod

Arantxa (Basque) Resembling a thornbush

Ararinda (German) One who is tenacious
Ararindah, Ararynda, Araryndah

Arashel (Hebrew) From the strong and protected hill
Arashell, Arashelle, Arashele, Arashela, Arashella

Arava (Hebrew) Resembling a willow; of an arid land
Aravah, Aravva, Aravvah

Araxie (Armenian) From the river of inspiration
Araxi, Araxy, Araxey, Araxee, Araxea, Araxeah, Araxye

Arcadia (Greek / Spanish) Feminine form of Arkadios; woman from Arcadia / one who is adventurous
Arcadiah, Arkadia, Arcadya, Arkadya, Arckadia, Arckadya

Arcangela (Greek) Angel of high rank
Arcangel, Archangela, Archangelia, Archangelica

Arda (English) One who is warm and friendly
Ardi, Ardie, Ardy, Ardey, Ardee, Ardine, Ardea, Ardeah, Ardye

Ardala (Irish) Woman of high honor
Ardalla, Ardalle, Ardalia, Ardalah, Ardallah, Ardaliah

Ardara (Gaelic) From the stronghold on the hill
Ardarah, Ardarra, Ardaria, Ardarrah, Ardariah

Ardea (Greek) A fiery woman
Ardeah

Ardel (Latin) Feminine form of Ardos;
industrious and eager
*Ardelle, Ardella, Ardele, Ardelia, Ardelis,
Ardela, Ardell*

Arden (Latin / English) One who is passion-
ate and enthusiastic / from the valley of the
eagles
*Ardin, Ardeen, Ardena, Ardene, Ardan,
Ardean, Ardine, Ardun, Ardyn, Ardyne,
Ardana, Ardeana, Ardenia, Ardeene*

Ardith (Hebrew) From the field of flowers
*Ardyth, Ardythe, Ardath, Ardice, Ardise,
Ardisa, Ardyce, Ardyse, Ardyssa, Ardathe,
Ardathia, Aridatha*

Ardra (Celtic / Hindi) One who is noble /
the goddess of bad luck and misfortune
Ardrah

Areebah (Arabic) One who is smart and witty
*Areeba, Aribah, Ariba, Arybah, Aryba,
Arieba, Ariebah, Areaba, Areabah, Areiba,
Areibah*

Arella (Hebrew) A messenger from heaven;
an angel
*Arela, Arelah, Arellah, Arelle, Areli, Arelie,
Arely*

Arete (Greek) In mythology, the queen of
the Phaeacians

Aretha (Greek) One who is virtuous; excellent
*Areta, Aretta, Arette, Areata, Areatha,
Areathia, Areeta, Areetha, Arethea, Arethia,
Aretina, Arita, Aritha, Arytha, Arythya, Aret*

Arethusa (Greek) In mythology, a wood
nymph

Argea (Greek) In mythology, the wife of
Polynices
Argeia

Argel (Welsh) One who provides refuge
Argell, Argelle, Argele, Argella, Argela

Argenta (Latin) Resembling silver
Argentia, Argentina, Argene, Arjean

Arglwyddes (Welsh) A distinguished lady

Argoel (Welsh) A prophetic sign
Argoell, Argoele, Argoelle, Argoela, Argoella

Argraff (Welsh) One who makes an
impression
Argraffe, Argrafe

Aria (English) A beautiful melody
Ariah

Ariadne (Greek) Holy and chaste; in
mythology, the woman who helped
Theseus escape from the labyrinth
*Ariadna, Aryadnah, Ariette, Aryadna,
Ariadnah*

❍ **Ariana** (Welsh / Greek) Resembling silver /
one who is holy
*Ariane, Arian, **Arianna**, Arianne, Aerian,
Aerion, Arianie, Arieon, Aeriana, Ahriana,
Ariena, Arianell, Arriana*

Arianwen (Welsh) Resembling silver; one
who is holy or fair
*Arianwyn, Arianwenn, Arianwenne,
Arianwynn, Arianwynne, Arianwin,
Arianwinn, Arianwinne*

Aricia (Greek) In mythology, a niece of
Aegeus rumored to be a black witch

Ariel (Hebrew) A lioness of God
*Arielle, Ariele, Ariell, Arriel, Ahriel, Airial,
Arieal, Ariela, Ariella, Aryela, Aryella, Arial,
Areille, Ariellel, Ari*

Aries (Latin) Resembling a ram; the first
sign of the zodiac; a constellation

Arietta (Italian) A short but beautiful
melody
*Arieta, Ariete, Ariet, Ariett, Aryet, Aryeta,
Aryetta, Aryette, Ariette*

Arilda (Teutonic) A maiden of the hearth
Arilde, Arildha, Arildhe

Arin (English) Form of Erin, meaning
"woman from Ireland"
Aryn

Arisje (Danish) Feminine form of Aris; one
who is superior

Arissa (Greek) Feminine form of Aris; one
who is superior
Arisa, Aris, Aryssa, Arysa, Arys

Arista (Latin) A harvester of corn
Aristana, Aristen

Arizona (Native American) From the little
spring; from the state of Arizona

Arkansas (Native American) Of the down-river people; from the state of Arkansas

Arlais (Welsh) From the temple
Arlays, Arlaes, Arlaise, Arlayse, Arlaese

Arleigh (English) From the meadow of the hare
Arlee, Arlie, Arli, Arly, Arley, Arlea, Arleah, Arlye

Arlene (Irish) An oath; a pledge
Arleen, Arline, Arlena, Arlein, Arlen, Arleyne, Arlette, Arleta, ArIyne, Arlana, Arlenna, Arleene, Airleas, Arlane, Arleana, Arlet, Arletta, Arlina, Arlinda, Arly, Arlyn

Arliss (Irish) From the high fortress
Arlissa, Arlise, Arlyss, Arlyssa, Arlyse, Arlys, Arlis

Armanda (Spanish) Feminine form of Armando; battlemaiden

Armani (Persian) One who is desired; a goal
Armanee, Armanii, Armahni, Arman, Armanie, Armany, Armaney, Armanea, Armaneah

Armelle (French) A princess; born to royalty
Armell, Armele, Armel, Armella, Armela

Armenouhie (Armenian) A woman from Armenia

Armes (Welsh) One who foretells the future

Armide (Latin) An armed battlemaiden
Armid, Armidee, Armidea, Armydea, Armydee, Armydya, Armidia, Armydia, Armida, Armilda, Armilde

Armilla (Latin) A decorative bracelet
Armillah, Armila, Armilah, Armylla, Armyllah, Armyla, Armylah

Armine (Latin / German) Born into the nobility / a battlemaiden
Arminee, Arminey, Armini, Arminie, Armyn, Armyne, Armina, Arminel

Armona (Hebrew) A chestnut color of brown
Armonit, Armonah

Arnalda (German) One who is an eagle ruler
Arnolda, Arnaldia, Arnaldea, Arnoldia, Arnoldea

Arnelle (American) Feminine form of Arnold; the eagle rules
Arnel, Arnela, Arnessa, Arnisha, Arnell, Arnella

Arnette (English) A little eagle
Arnett, Arnetta, Arnete, Arneta, Arnet

Arnia (American) As strong as an eagle
Arniah, Arnea, Arnya, Arneah, Arnyah

Arnina (Hebrew) An enlightened one
Arninah, Arnyna, Arnynah, Aarnina, Arnine, Arnona

Arnon (Hebrew) From the river

Aroha (Maori) One who loves and is loved

Arona (Maori) One who is colorful and vivacious
Aronah, Aronnah, Aronna

Aronui (Maori) One who is greatly desired

Arrate (Basque) Refers to the Virgin Mary

Arrosa (Basque) Sprinkled with dew from heaven; resembling a rose
Arrose

Arseni (Russian) Feminine form of Arsenios; womanly
Arsenie, Arseny, Arsene, Arcene, Arceni, Arcenee, Arsenee, Arsenia, Arsenya, Arsenea, Arcenea, Arseneah, Arceneah

Artaith (Welsh) One who is tormented
Artaithe, Artayth, Artaythe, Artaeth, Artaethe

Artemis (Greek) Virgin huntress; in mythology, goddess of the hunt and the moon
Artemisa, Artemise, Artemys, Artema, Artemisia, Artemysia, Artemysya, Artemia, Artemus

Artha (Hindi) One who is prosperous; wealthy
Arthah, Arthi, Arthea

Arthurine (English) Feminine form of Arthur; as strong as a she-bear
Arthurina, Arthuretta, Arthuryne, Arthes, Arthene

Artis (Irish / English / Icelandic) Lofty hill; noble / rock / follower of Thor
Artisa, Artise, Artys, Artysa, Artyse, Artiss, Arti, Artina, Artine, Artice

Artois (French) Woman of the Netherlands

Arub (Arabic) A woman who loves her husband
Aruba, Arubah

Arundhati (Indian) One who is not restrained; the name of a star
Arundhatie, Arundhaty, Arundhatey, Arundhatee, Arundhatea, Arundhateah

Arusi (African) A girl born during the time of a wedding
Arusie, Arusy, Arusey, Arusee, Arusea, Aruseah, Arusye

Arva (Latin) From the sea; one who is fertile
Arvah, Arvia, Arvya

Arvida (English) Feminine form of Arvid; from the eagle tree
Arvidah, Arvidia, Arvada, Arvinda, Arvyda, Arvydah

Arwa (Arabic) A female mountain goat

Arwydd (Welsh) A prophetic sign

Arya (Indian) One who is noble and honored
Aryah, Aryana, Aryanna, Aryia

Arza (Hebrew) Cedar panels
Ariza, Arzice, Arzit

Arziki (African) One who is prosperous
Arzikie, Arzikee, Arzyki, Arzykie, Arzikea, Arzykea, Arziky, Arzikey, Arzyky, Arzykey

Asa (Japanese) Born in the morning
Asah

Asabi (African) Girl of select birth
Asabie, Asaby, Asabee, Asabey, Asabea, Asabeah, Asabye

Ascención (Spanish) Refers to the Ascension

Asdis (Scandinavian) A divine spirit; a goddess
Asdiss, Asdisse, Asdise, Asdys, Asdyss, Asdysse

Asela (Spanish) The foal of a donkey
Asella, Aselah, Asellah

Aselma (Gaelic) One who is fair-skinned
Aselmah

Asena (Turkish) In mythology, a she-wolf
Asenah, Asenna, Asennah

Asenath (Egyptian) A father's daughter; in the Bible, Joseph's Egyptian wife
Acenath, Asenathe, Acenathe

Asenka (Hebrew) Woman with grace
Asenkia, Asenke, Asenki, Asenkie, Asenkye

Asfoureh (Arabic) A birdlike woman

Asgre (Welsh) Having a noble heart

Asha (Sanskrit / African) Hope; in mythology, the wife of a Hindu demigod / one who is lively
Ashia, Ashah, Ashiah

Ashaki (African) A beautiful woman
Ashakie, Ashaky, Ashakey, Ashakee, Ashakea, Ashakeah, Ashakye

Ashanti (African) From a tribe in West Africa
Ashantee, Ashaunti, Ashaunte, Ashanta, Ashonti, Asante, Achante, Ashauntia, Ashaunty, Ashunti, Ashauntea, Ashantea, Ashanteah, Ashaunteah

Ashby (English) Home of the ash tree
Ashhea, Ashbie, Ashbeah, Ashbey, Ashbi, Ashbee

Asherat (Syrian) In mythology, goddess of the sea

Ashilde (Norse) One who fights for God
Ashilda, Ashild

Ashima (Hebrew) In the Bible, a deity worshipped at Hamath
Ashimuh, Ashyma, Asheema, Ashimia, Ashymah, Asheemah, Asheima, Asheimah, Ashiema, Ashiemuh, Asheuma, Asheamah

Ashira (Hebrew) One who is wealthy; prosperous
Ashyra, Ashyrah, Ashirah, Asheera, Asheerah, Ashiera, Ashierah, Asheira, Asheirah, Asheara, Ashearah

⚤ **Ashley** (English) From the meadow of ash trees
Ashlie, Ashlee, Ashleigh, Ashly, Ashleye, Ashlya, Ashala, Ashleay, Ash, Ashby, Ashely, Ashla, Ashlan, Ashlea, Ashleah, Ashleen, Ashleena, Ashlen, Ashli, Ashlin, Ashling, Ashlinn, Ashlyn, Ashlynn, Ashleene, Ashlynne, Ashlyne, Ashlene, Ashtyn, Ashten, Ashtin, Ashtine, Ashtynne, Ashton

Ashra (Hebrew) One who is fortunate
Asheera, Ashirah, Ashrah, Ashira, Asheeruh, Asheara, Ashearah, Ashyra, Ashyrah

Asia (Greek / English) Resurrection / the rising sun; a woman from the East; in the Koran, the woman who raised Moses
Aysia, Asya, Asyah, Azia, Asianne

Asima (Arabic) One who offers protection
Asimah, Aseema, Azima, Aseemah, Asyma, Asymah, Asiema, Asiemah, Aseima, Aseimah, Aseama, Aseamah

Asis (African) Of the sun
Asiss, Assis, Assiss

Asiya (Arabic) One who tends to the weak; healer
Asiyah

Aslaug (Norse) One who is devoted to God; in mythology, a queen

Asli (Turkish) One who is genuine and original
Aslie, Asly, Asley, Aslee, Asleigh, Aslea, Asleah, Alsye

Asma (Arabic) One having great prestige, one of high status
Asmah

Aspasia (Greek) One who is welcomed; in mythology, a lover of Pericles
Aspasiah, Aspasya, Aspasea

Aspen (English) From the aspen tree
Aspin, Aspine, Aspina, Aspyn, Aspyna, Aspyne

Asphodel (Greek) Resembling a lily
Asfodel, Asfodelle, Asphodelle, Asphodela, Asphodella, Asfodela, Asfodella

Assaggi (African) A woman with strength
Assaggie, Assaggey, Assaggy, Assaggea, Assaggeah, Assaggee, Asagi, Asagie, Asagy, Asagey, Asagee, Asagea, Asageah

Assana (Irish) From the waterfall
Assane, Assania, Assanna, Asanna, Asana

Assunta (Latin) One who is raised up
Assuntah, Asunta, Asuntah

Astarte (Egyptian) In mythology, a goddess of war and love

Asthore (Irish) One who is dearly loved
Asthora, Asthoria, Asthorea, Asthoreah, Asthor

Astra (Latin) Of the stars; as bright as a star
Astera, Astrea, Asteria, Astrey, Astara, Astraea, Astrah, Astree, Astria, Astrya, Asta, Aasta, Aster, Astah, Astin

Astrid (Scandinavian) One with divine strength
Astread, Astreed, Astrad, Astri, Astrod, Astrud, Astryd, Astrida, Astrik, Astred, Astlyr, Astlyrd

Asunción (Spanish) Refers to the Virgin Mary's assumption into heaven

Asura (African) Daughter born during the month of Ashur

Asvoria (Teutonic) One having divine wisdom
Asvora, Asvorea, Asvorya, Asvore, Asvor, Asvoriah, Asvoreah

Atalanta (Greek) Mighty huntress; in mythology, a huntress who would only marry a man who could beat her in a foot-race
Atalantah, Atlanta, Atlante, Atlantia, Atlantya, Atalaya, Atlee, Atalante

Atalaya (Spanish) From the watchtower

Atalia (Hebrew) God is just; God is great
Atalie, Atali, Ataly, Ataley, Atalee, Atalissa, Atalena, Atalina, Ataleena, Atalyna, Atalea, Ataleah

Atara (Hebrew) Wearing a crown; one who is blessed
Atarah, Atarya, Ataree, Ateara, Atera, Aterah, Atarra, Ataret, Atarrah

Ate (Greek) In mythology, goddess of irrationality and consequent punishment

Atgas (Welsh) One who is hateful

Athalia (Hebrew) The Lord is exalted
Athalie, Athalee, Athalea, Athaleah, Athaliah, Athalei, Athaleigh, Athaley, Athali, Athaly, Athalya, Athaleyah, Athalyah, Athaleya

Athanasia (Greek) One having immortality

Athena (Greek) Wise; in mythology, the goddess of war and wisdom
Athina, Atheena, Athene

Athilda (English) From the elder tree
Athilde, Athild, Atilda, Atilde, Atild, Attheaeldre, Atheaeldre

Atia (Arabic) Of an ancient line

Atifa (Arabic) One who shows affection and sympathy
Ateefa, Aatifa, Atipha, Ateepha, Aatipha, Atufa, Atupha, Atufah, Atiefa, Ateifa, Atyfa, Ateafa

Atira (Hebrew) One who bows in prayer
Atirah, Atyra, Atyrah, Ateera, Ateerah, Atiera, Atierah, Ateira, Ateirah, Ateara, Ateurah

Atiya (Arabic) A gift from God
Atiyah, Atiyya, Atiyaa, Atiyyaa

Atmaja (Hindi) A precious daughter

Atropos (Greek) In mythology, one of the three Fates
Atropes, Atropas, Antropas

Atsuko (Japanese) One of profound emotions

Atsukpi (African) A female twin
Atsukpie, Atsukpy, Atsukpey, Atsukpee, Atsukpea, Atsukpeah

Atthis (Greek) A woman from Attica; in mythology, the daughter of Cranaus who gave her name to Attica

Attracta (Irish) A virtuous woman; a saint
Athracht, Athrachta

Atun (Arabic) One who teaches; an educator
Atunn, Aatoon, Aatun, Atunne, Atune

❂ **Aubrey** (English) One who rules with elf-wisdom
Aubree, Aubrie, Aubry, Aubri, Aubriana, Aubrianne, Aubrianna, Aubrea, Aurbreah

Auburn (Latin) Having a reddish-brown color
Aubirn, Auburne, Aubyrn, Abern, Abirn, Aburn, Abyrn, Aubern

Audhilda (Norse) A wealthy woman warrior
Audhild, Audhilde

Audi (African) The last daughter born
Audie, Audy, Audey, Audee, Audlin, Audney, Audlin, Audea, Audeah

❂ **Audrey** (English) Woman with noble strength
Audree, Audry, Audra, Audrea, Adrey, Audre, Audray, Audrin, Audriya, Audrie, Audri, Audria, Audriana, Audrianna, Audrielle, Audrina, Audreana, Audreanna, Aude, Auda, Audelia, Audene, Aud, Audreah

Audris (German) One who is fortunate and wealthy; a form of Audrey, meaning "woman with noble strength"
Audrys, Audrisa, Audrysa, Audrissa, Audryssa, Audriz, Audriza, Audrisia, Audrisya, Audfis

Audumla (Norse) In mythology, a giant cow from which Ymir nursed
Audhumla, Audhumbla

Auduna (Norse) One who has been deserted

Augusta (Latin) Feminine form of Augustus; venerable; majestic
Augustina, Agustina, Augustine, Agostina, Agostine, Augusteen, Augustyna, Agusta, Augustia, Austina, Austen, Austin, Austine

Aulani (Hawaiian) The king's messenger
Aulaney, Aulanee, Aulanie, Aulany, Aulania, Aulanya, Aulanea, Aulaneah, Aulanye

Aulis (Greek) In mythology, a princess of Attica
Auliss, Aulisse, Aulys, Aulyss, Aulysse

Aura (Greek) Gentle breeze; in mythology, the goddess of breezes
Auria, Auriel, Auriana, Aurah, Aurea, Auri, Aurya, Aure

Aurear (English) One who plays gentle music
Aureare, Auriar, Auriare, Auryare

Aurelia (Latin) Feminine form of Aurelius; golden-haired woman
Aurelie, Aurielle, Arela, Arell, Arelie, Arella, Arely, Aurene, Aureli, Aurele, Aurek, Aureliana, Aurelianna, Aureline, Aurenne, Aurilia, Auriol, Aurlel, Aurnia, Aurum, Aurelea

Aurkene (Basque) One who has a favorable presence
Aurkena, Aurkenia, Aurkenne

Aurora (Latin) Morning's first light; in mythology, the goddess of the dawn
Aurore, Aurea, Aurorette

Auryon (American) A great huntress

Auset (Egyptian) In mythology, another name for Isis, the goddess of fertility
Ausett, Ausette, Auseta, Ausetta, Ausete

Austine (French) Feminine form of Austin; one who is respected
Austina, Austyn, Austyna, Austeene, Austeena, Austeine, Austeina, Austiene, Austiena, Austeane, Austeana

Autonoe (Greek) In mythology, a woman who was driven mad by Dionysus

❂ **Autumn** (English) Born in the fall
Autum

❂ **Ava** (German / Iranian) A birdlike woman / from the water
Avah, Avalee, Avaleigh, Avali, Avalie, Avaley, Avelaine, Avelina, Aveline, Avelyn, Avia, Avian, Aviana, Aviance, Avianna, Avis, Aves, Avice, Avais, Aveis, Avise, Avyce, Avyse, Avlynn

Avalbane (Gaelic) From the white orchard
Avalbayne, Availbaine, Avalbain, Avalbanne

Avalon (Latin / English) From the island paradise / in Arthurian legend, Arthur's burial place
Avallon, Avaloni, Avalona, Avalonia, Avalonie, Avalony, Avalonya, Avaron, Avarona, Avilon

Avani (Indian) From the earth
Avanie, Avany, Avaney, Avanee, Avanea, Avanye

Avari (American) From the heavens
Avarie, Avary, Avarey, Avaree, Avarea, Avarye

Avariella (American) A woman of great strength
Avarielle, Avariell, Avariel, Avariela

Avasa (Indian) One who is independent
Avasah, Avassa, Avasia, Avassah, Avasiah, Avasea, Avaseah

Avatara (Hindi) The incarnation of gods; descending
Avatarra, Avatarah, Avatari, Avatarie, Avatary, Avatarey, Avatarea, Avatareah, Avataree, Avatarrah

Ave (Latin) One to whom all bow

Avena (English) From the oat field
Avenah, Aviena, Avyna, Avina, Avinah, Avynah, Avienah, Aveinah, Aveina

Aveolela (Samoan) Resembling the rays of the sun

Avera (Hebrew) One who transgresses
Averah, Avyra, Avira

Averna (Latin) In mythology, the queen of the underworld
Avernah, Avirna

❂ **Avery** (English) One who is a wise ruler; of the nobility
Avrie, Averey, Averie, Averi, Averee, Averea, Avereah

Aveta (Celtic) In mythology, the goddess of childbirth and midwives
Avetah, Avetta, Avettah

Avi (Hebrew) The Lord is my father
Avie, Avy, Avey, Avee, Aveah, Avea

Aviana (Latin) Blessed with a gracious life
Avianah, Avianna, Aviannah, Aviane, Avianne, Avyana, Avyanna, Avyane, Avyanne

Avichayil (Hebrew) Our Lord is strong
Abichall, Avigail, Avigayil

Aviva (Hebrew) One who is innocent and joyful; resembling springtime
Avivi, Avivah, Aviv, Avivie, Avivice, Avni, Avri, Avyva, Avivit

Avonaco (Native American) One who is lean and bearlike

Avonmora (Irish) From the great river
Avonmoria, Avonmore, Avonmorra, Avon, Avonmorea

Awel (Welsh) One who is as refreshing as a breeze
Awell, Awele, Awela, Awella

Awen (Welsh) A fluid essence; a muse; a flowing spirit
Awenn, Awenne, Awin, Awinn, Awinne, Awyn, Awynn, Awynne

Awena (Welsh) One who can foretell the future
Awenna, Awyna, Awynna, Awina, Awinna

Awenasa (Native American) One's home

Awendela (Native American) Of the morning
Awendele, Awendell, Awendel, Awendella

Awenita (Native American) Resembling a fawn
Awenyta, Awenieta, Awentia, Awinita, Awinyta, Awintia

Awhina (Maori) One who helps; a supporter
Awhyna, Awheina, Awhiena, Awheana, Awheena

Axelle (German / Latin / Hebrew) Source of life; small oak / axe / peace
Axella, Axell, Axele, Axl, Axela, Axelia, Axellia

Aya (Hebrew / Japanese) Birdlike woman; ability to fly swiftly / woven silk
Ayah, Aiya, Aia, Aiah, Aiyah

Ayala (Hebrew) Resembling a gazelle
Ayalah, Ayalla, Ayallah

Ayame (Japanese) Resembling an iris
Ayami, Ayamie, Ayamee, Ayamey, Ayamy, Ayamea, Ayameah

Ayan (African) One who is bright

Ayanna (Hindi / African) One who is innocent / resembling a beautiful flower
Ayana, Ayania, Ahyana, Ayna, Ayaniah, Ayannah

Ayasha (Native American) Dear little child
Ayashe

Ayita (Native American) First in the dance; hardworking
Aitah, Aiyta

Ayla (Hebrew) From the oak tree
Aylah, Aylana, Aylanna, Aylee, Aylea, Aylene, Ayleena, Aylena, Aylie, Aylin

Aylin (Turkish) Having a moonlit halo

Ayo (African) One who brings joy to others
Ayoka

Aysel (Turkish) Resembling the moonlight
Aysell, Aysele, Aysela, Aysella

Ayushmati (Hindi) A long-lived woman
Ayushi, Ayushie, Ayushy, Ayushee, Ayushea, Ayushea, Ayushey, Ayushmatie, Ayushmatey, Ayushmaty, Ayushmatea, Ayushmateah, Ayushmatee

Aza (Arabic / African) One who provides comfort / powerful
Azia, Aiza, Aizia, Aizha

Azadeh (Persian) Of the dry earth; free of material things

Azalea (Latin / Hebrew) Of the dry earth; resembling the flower / one who is spared by God
Azalia, Azaleah, Azaley, Azalee, Azaleigh, Azalie, Azalei, Azali, Azaly, Azelia, Azalya, Azelya, Azelea, Azelie, Aziel, Azhar, Azhara

Azana (African) One who is superior
Azanah, Azunna, Azannah

Azania (Hebrew) One who is heard by God
Azaniah, Azanea, Azaneah, Azuniya, Azaniyah

Azar (Persian) One who is fiery; scarlet
Azara, Azaria, Azarah, Azarra, Azarrah, Azarr

Azinza (African) A seamaiden; a mermaid
Azinzah, Azynzah, Azynza

Aziza (Arabic) One who is beloved and precious
Azizi, Azizah, Azize, Azzeza, Azeeza, Azeezah

Azmera (African) A great harvester
Azmerah, Azmerra, Azmerrah

Aznii (Chechen) A famed beauty
Azni, Aznie, Azny, Azney, Aznee, Aznea, Azneah

Azra (Hebrew) One who is pure; chaste
Azrah, Azraa

Azriel (Hebrew) God is my helper
Azrael, Azriell, Azrielle, Azriela, Azriella, Azraela

Azuba (Hebrew) One who assists others
Azubah

Azuka (African) One who celebrates past glory
Azuca, Azucka, Azukah

Azure (French / Persian) Sky blue / resembling a blue semiprecious stone
Azura, Azuree, Azurine, Azora, Azurah, Azurina, Azuryn, Azuryne

Azusena (Arabic) Resembling the lily
Azucena, Asucena, Azusa

Azzah (Arabic) A young female gazelle
Azza

Baako (African) The firstborn child
Bako, Bakko, Baakko

Baara (Hebrew) In the Bible, the wife of Shaharaim
Bara, Barah, Barra, Barrah

Bab (Arabic) From the gate

Baba (African) Born on a Thursday
Babah, Babba, Babbah, Baaba

Babette (French) Form of Barbara, meaning "a traveler from a foreign land; a stranger"; form of Elizabeth, meaning "my God is bountiful"
Babett, Babete, Babet, Babbet, Babbett, Babbette, Babbete, Babita, Babitta, Babbitta, Babs

Baby (English) A beloved child; a spoiled daughter
Babi, Babie, Babey, Babe, Bebe, Babea, Babeah

Baca (English) From the valley of tears
Bacah, Bacca, Baka, Bakah, Backa, Backah, Baccah

Bach Yen (Vietnamese) A white-skinned woman

Badia (Arabic) An elegant lady; one who is unique
Badiah, Badi'a, Badiya, Badea, Badya, Badeah

Badu (African) The tenth-born child
Badoo

Bahar (Arabic) Born during the spring
Bahaar, Baharr, Baharre, Bahara, Baharah, Baharra, Baharrah

Bahati (African) One with good fortune
Bahatie, Bahaty, Bahatii, Bahatee, Bahiti, Bahyti, Bahyty, Bakht, Bahatea, Bahateah, Bahatey

Bahija (Arabic) A cheerful woman
Bahijah, Bahiga, Bahigah, Bahyja, Bahyjah, Bahyga, Bahygah

Bahira (Arabic) One who is sparkling; brilliant
Bahirah, Baheera, Bahyra, Bahiera, Baheira, Bahiya, Bahiyah, Baheerah, Bahyrah, Baheirah, Bahierah, Baheara, Bahearah

Balbina (Latin) A very strong woman
Balbinah, Balbinna, Balbyna, Balbeena, Balbara, Balbine, Balbyne, Balera, Balere, Balbeenah, Balbynah, Balbeina, Balbeinah, Balbienah, Balbiena, Balbeana, Balbeanah

Baila (Spanish) One who dances
Byla, Bayla, Baela

❂ **Bailey** (English) From the courtyard within castle walls; a public official
Bailee, Bayley, Baylee, Baylie, Baili, Bailie, Baileigh, Bayleigh, Baileah, Bailea, Baylea, Bayleah, Baylee, Bayli

Baina (African) A sparkling woman
Bayna, Baana, Baena, Bainah, Baenah

Baja (Spanish) From the lower region

Baka (Indian) Resembling a crane
Bakah, Bakka, Backa, Bacca

Bakarne (Basque) One who dwells in solitude

Bakura (Hebrew) Resembling ripened fruit
Bakurah

Baldhart (German) A bold woman having great strength
Balhart, Baldhard, Balhard, Ballard, Balard, Balarde

Baligha (Arabic) One who is forever eloquent
Balighah, Baleegha, Balygha, Baliegha, Baleagha, Baleigha

Ballade (English) A poetic woman
Ballad, Ballaid, Ballaed, Ballayd

Ballari (Indian) One who walks softly
*Balari, Ballarie, Balarie, Ballary, Balary,
Ballarey, Balarey, Ballaree, Balaree, Ballarea,
Balarea, Ballareah, Balareah*

Bambina (Italian) A young daughter; a baby
girl
*Bambyna, Bambinna, Bambie, Bambi,
Bambey, Bambee, Bamhi, Bambea, Bambeah*

Banan (Arabic) Having delicate fingertips

Banba (Irish) In mythology, a patron goddess

Bandana (Spanish) A brightly colored head-
wrap
Bandanah, Bandanna, Bandannah

Bandele (African) Child who is born away
from home
Bandel, Bandelle, Bandell, Bandela, Bandella

Banji (African) The second-born of twins
*Banjie, Banjey, Banjy, Banjee, Banjea,
Banjeah*

Banner (American) A decorative symbol
*Baner, Bannyr, Banyr, Bannor, Bannar,
Bannir*

Bano (Arabic) A princess; a distinguished
lady
Banow, Baano, Banoe, Banowe

Banon (Welsh) A woman sovereign

Bansuri (Indian) One who is musical
*Bansurie, Bansari, Banseri, Bansurri,
Bansury, Bansurey, Bansuree, Bansurea,
Bansureah*

Baptista (Greek) Feminine form of
Baptiste; the baptizer
*Baptistah, Baptistya, Baptistiya, Baptistia,
Baptistina, Baptysta, Bapteesta, Baptiesta,
Battista, Batista, Batysta, Bautista, Bautysta*

Bara (Hebrew) One who is chosen
Barah, Barra, Barrah

Baraka (Arabic) A white-skinned woman;
fair; having God's favor
Barakka, Baracka, Baracca, Barakah

Barbara (Latin) A traveler from a foreign
land; a stranger
*Barbra, Barbarella, Barbarita, Baibin, Baibre,
Bairbre, Barbary, Barb, Barbi, Barbie, Barby,
Barbey, Bobbie, Barbro, Barabal, Barabell,
Basha, Basham, Baubie, Bobbi, Bobby, Bora,
Borbala, Borhala, Borka, Boriska, Borsca,
Borska, Borsala, Brosca, Broska*

Barcelona (Spanish) Woman from the city
in Spain

Barika (African) A flourishing woman; one
who is successful
*Barikah, Baryka, Barikka, Barykka, Baricka,
Burycka, Baricca, Barycca*

Barkarna (Basque) One who is lonely
*Barkarne, Barkurniu, Barkarniah,
Barkarnya, Barkarniya, Barkarn*

Barr (English) A lawyer
Barre, Bar

Barran (Irish) From the little mountain's
top
*Barrane, Baran, Barane, Barrayne, Barayne,
Baranne, Barann, Barrann*

Barras (English) From among the trees

Barrett (German / English) Having the
strength of a bear / an argumentative
person
*Barett, Barrette, Barette, Barrete, Barete,
Barretta, Baretta, Barreta, Bareta*

Barrie (Irish) A markswoman
*Barea, Baree, Barey, Barri, Barria, Barriah,
Barrya, Barryah, Barya, Baryah*

Basanti (Indian) Born during the spring
*Basantie, Basanty, Basantii, Basantey,
Basantee, Basantea, Basanteah*

Bashirah (Arabic) One who is joyful; a
bringer of good tidings
*Bashira, Basheera, Bashyra, Bashiera,
Basheira, Basheyra, Bashiga, Bashyga,
Bushra, Basheerah, Bashyrah, Bashierah,
Basheirah, Basheyrah, Basheara, Bashearah*

Basilia (Greek) Feminine form of Basil; of
the royal line; queenly; one who is valiant
*Basiliya, Basilya, Basilie, Basilea, Basylia,
Basylya, Basili, Basylie, Basyli, Basileah*

Basimah (Arabic) One who smiles a lot
Basima, Basimma, Basymu, Buseema,
Basiema, Basmah, Basma, Basymah,
Baseemah, Basiemah, Baseima, Baseimah,
Baseama, Basemah

Bastet (Egyptian) A fiery woman; in mythology, goddess of fertility and the sun
Bastett, Bastette, Basteta, Bastetta

Bathild (German) Heroine of a bold battle
Bathilde, Bathilda

Bathsheba (Hebrew) The daughter of the oath, in the Bible, a wife of King David and mother of Solomon
Bathshebah, Bathsheeba, Bathshyba,
Bathshieba, Bethsheba, Bethshebah

Bathshira (Arabic) The seventh daughter
Bathshirah, Bathsheera, Bathsheerah,
Bathshiera, Bathshierah, Bathsheira,
Bathsheirah, Bathsheara, Bathshearah,
Bathshyra, Bathshyrah

Battseeyon (Hebrew) A daughter of Zion
Batseyon, Batseyonne, Battzion, Batzion

Batul (Arabic) Woman who is chaste; a virgin
Batulle, Batoole, Batool, Batula, Batulah,
Betul, Betool, Betulle, Betula, Betoole

Batya (Hebrew) A daughter of God
Batyah, Batiya, Bitya, Bitiya, Bityah

Baucis (Greek) In mythology, the wife of Philemon

Bay (French) Resembling a berry
Baye, Bai, Bae

Bayo (Nigerian) One who finds joy

Beadu (English) A warrior woman

Beagan (Gaelic) A petite woman

Beatha (Celtic) One who gives life
Betha, Beathah, Bethah

Beathag (Hebrew) One who serves God

Beathas (Scottish) Having great wisdom

Beatrice (Latin) One who blesses others
Beatrix, Beatriz, Beatriss, Beatrisse, Bea,
Beatrize, Beatricia, Beatrisa, Beate, Beata,
Beat, Bee, Beitris, Betrys, Bettrys, Bice

Bebba (Hebrew) One who is pledged to God
Bebbah

Bebhinn (Irish) An accomplished singer
Bebhin, Bebhynn, Bebhyn, Bevin, Bevinne,
Bevinn, Bevyn

Bechira (Hebrew) One who is chosen
Bechirah, Bechyra, Bechyrah, Becheara,
Bechearah, Becheera, Becheerah

Beckett (English) From the small brook
Becket, Bekett, Beckette, Bekette, Beket

Becky (English) Form of Rebecca, meaning "one who is bound to God"
Beckey, Becki, Beckie, Becca, Becka, Bekka,
Beckee, Beckea, Beckeah

Beda (German) A goddess; warrior woman
Bedah, Bedda, Beddah

Bedegrayne (English) From the castle
Bedegraine, Bedegrain, Bedegrane,
Bedegraene, Bedegrayn, Bedegraen

Bedelia (French) Woman of great strength
Bedelea, Bedeleah, Bedeliah

Befle (Latin) A beautiful and loving woman
Beffle, Befel, Beffel

Begonia (English) Resembling the flower
Begoniah, Begonea, Begoneah, Begoniya,
Begoniyah

Begum (Arabic) A woman of rank
Bagum, Baegum, Baigum, Baygum

Behula (Indian) The perfect wife
Behulah, Behulla, Behulia, Behoola,
Behullah, Behuliah, Behoolah, Behulea,
Behuleah

Beige (French) Of the beige color

Bel (Indian) From the sacred wood

Belakane (English) An African queen
Bellakane, Belakayne, Bellakayne, Belakaine,
Bellakaine, Belacane, Bellacane, Belacayne,
Bellacayne, Belacaine, Bellacaine

Belda (French) A fair maiden
Beldah, Bellda, Belldah

Belen (Spanish) Woman from Bethlehem

Belicia (Spanish) A woman dedicated to God
Beliciah, Beliciya, Belicya, Beleecia, Belycia, Belishia, Belisha, Belyshia, Beliecia, Belieciah, Beleicia, Beleiciah, Beleacia, Beleaciah

Belinda (English) A beautiful and tender woman
Belindah, Belynda, Balinda, Balynda, Belienda, Beliendah, Balyndah, Belyndah, Beleinda, Beleindah

Belisama (Celtic) In mythology, a goddess of rivers and lakes
Belisamah, Belisamma, Belysama, Belisma, Belysma, Belesama

❷ **Bella** (Italian) A woman famed for her beauty
Belle, Bela, Bell, Belita, Bellissa, Belva, Belladonna, Belia, Bellanca, Bellance, Bellini

Bellona (Latin) In mythology, the goddess of war
Bellonah, Belona, Bellonna, Belonna, Bellonia, Belonia

Bem (African) A peaceful woman
Berne

Bena (Native American) Resembling a pheasant
Benah, Benna, Bennah

Benedicta (Latin) Feminine form of Benedict; one who is blessed
Benedikta, Benedetta, Benetta, Benecia, Benicia, Benita, Bennett, Bente

Benigna (Spanish) Feminine form of Benigno; one who is kind; friendly

Benjamina (Hebrew) Feminine form of Benjamin; child of my right hand
Benjameena, Benyamina, Benyameena, Benjameana, Benyameana, Benjamyna, Benyamyna

Bennu (Egyptian) Resembling an eagle

Bentlee (English) Feminine form of Bentley; from the clearing
Bentleigh, Bently, Bentli, Bentlie, Bentley, Bentlea, Bentleah

Beomia (Anglo-Saxon) Battlemaid
Beomiya, Bemia, Beorhthilde, Beorhthild, Beorhthilda, Beomea, Beomeah

Bera (Teutonic) Resembling a bear

Berangari (English) A warrior woman bearing a spear
Berangarie, Berangary, Berangarey, Berangarri, Berangaree, Berangaria, Berangariya, Berengari, Berenguria

Bergdis (Norse) Having divine protection
Bergdiss, Bergdisse, Bergdys, Bergdyss, Bergdysse

Berhane (African) My child is my light
Berhayne, Berhaine, Berhayn, Berhain, Berhaen, Berhaene

Berit (German) A glorious woman
Beret, Bereta, Berete, Berett, Beretta, Berette, Biret, Bireta, Birete, Birett, Biretta, Birette, Byret, Byreta, Byrete, Byrett, Byretta, Byrette

Bernadine (English) Feminine form of Bernard; one who has bearlike strength and courage
Bernadina, Bernadette, Bernadetta, Berdina, Berdine, Berdyne, Berdyna, Berangër, Bernadea, Bernarda, Bernetta, Bernette, Bernita, Bernelle, Berna, Berneen, Bernardina, Bernardine, Berne, Bern

Bernice (Greek) One who brings victory
Berenisa, Berenise, Berenice, Bernicia, Bernisha, Berniss, Bernyce, Bernys, Beryss

Beronica (English) Form of Veronica, meaning "displaying her true image"
Beronicah, Beronic, Beronicca, Beronicka, Beronika, Beronicha, Beronique, Beranique, Beroniqua, Beronnica, Beronice, Baronica, Baronika, Berhonica, Berinica, Berohnica, Bironica, Bironiqua, Bironika, Bironique, Beronka, Beronkia, Beronne, Byronica, Bronica, Bronika, Broniqua, Bronique, Byroniqua, Byronique, Byronika, Beruka, Beruszhka

Berry (English) Feminine form of Barry; fair-haired woman; resembling a berry fruit
Berrey, Berri, Berrie, Berree, Beri, Berie, Bery, Beree, Berey, Berrea, Berea, Berreah, Bereah

Bertha (German) One who is famously bright and beautiful
Berta, Berthe, Berth, Bertina, Bertyna, Bertine, Bertyne, Birte, Birtha, Birthe

Berthog (Welsh) A wealthy woman; one who is prosperous

Bertilda (English) A luminous battlemaiden
Bertilde, Bertild

Bertille (French) A heroine
Bertill, Bertile, Bertil, Bertylle, Bertyll, Bertyle, Bertyl

Bertrade (English) An intelligent advisor
Bertraide, Bertrayde, Bertraed, Beortbtraed, Bertraid, Bertrayd, Bertraede

Beruriah (Hebrew) Woman selected by God
Beruria, Beruriya, Berurea, Berurya, Berureah

Beryl (English) Resembling the pale-green precious stone
Beryll, Berylle, Beril, Berill, Berille

Bess (English) Form of Elizabeth, meaning "my God is bountiful"
Besse, Bessi, Bessie, Bessy, Bessey, Bessee, Bessea, Besseah

Bestla (Norse) In mythology, a frost giant-ess and mother of Odin

Beth (English) Form of Elizabeth, meaning "my God is bountiful"
Bethe

Bethabara (Hebrew) From the house of confidence
Bethebara, Bethabarra, Bethebarra, Bethbara, Bethbarra

Bethany (Hebrew) From the house of figs
Bethan, Bethani, Bethanie, Bethanee, Bethaney, Bethane, Bethann, Bethanne, Bethanea, Bethaneah

Bethea (Hebrew) A maidservant of God
Bethia, Betheah, Bethiya, Bethya, Betia, Betje, Bethiyah, Bethyah

Bethel (Hebrew) Of the house of God
Bethell, Bethele, Bethelle, Bethelia, Betheliya, Betheli, Bethelie, Bethely, Bethelee, Bethiar, Betheley, Betheleigh, Bethelea, Betheleah

Bethesda (Hebrew) From the house of mercy
Bethseda, Bethsaida

Betty (English) Form of Elizabeth, meaning "my God is bountiful"
Betti, Bettie, Bettey, Bettee, Bette, Betsy, Betsey, Betsi, Betsie, Betsee, Bettina, Bettine, Bettyne, Bettyna, Betje, Bettea, Betteah, Betsea, Betseah

Beulah (Hebrew) Woman who is claimed as a wife
Beula, Beulla, Bulah, Bula, Beullah

Beverly (English) From the beaver's stream
Beverlee, Beverley, Beverlie, Beverli, Beverlee, Beverleigh, Beverlea, Beverleah

Bevin (Welsh) Daughter of Evan
Bevan, Bevann, Bevanne, Bevina, Bevine, Bevinnah, Bevyn, Bevyna, Bevyne

Beyla (Norse) In mythology, an elf and minor goddess
Beylah, Bayla, Baylah

Beyonce (American) One who surpasses others
Beyoncay, Beyonsay, Beyonsai, Beyonsae, Beyonci, Beyoncie, Beyoncee, Beyoncea, Beyonceah

Bha (Indian) Having a starlike quality

Bharati (Hindi) In Hinduism, goddess of sacrifice
Bharatie, Bharaty, Bharatey, Bharatee, Bharatea, Bharateah, Barati, Baratie, Baraty, Baratey, Baratee, Baratea, Barateah

Bhavani (Indian) A giver of life
Bhavanie, Bhavany, Bhavaney, Bhavanee, Bhavanea, Bhavaneah, Bavani, Bavanie, Bavany, Bavaney, Bavanee, Bavanea, Bavaneah

Bhumidevi (Hindi) In Hinduism, goddess of the earth
Bhumi, Bhoomi, Bhu, Bhudevi

Bian (Vietnamese) A secretive woman

Bianca (Italian) A shining, fair-skinned woman
Bianka, Byanca, Blanca, Blanche, Biana, Bianna, Biankeh, Byanka, Blanch, Blanka

Bibi (African) A king's daughter; a lady
Bibsbebe, Beebee, Byby, Beabea

Bibiana (Italian) Form of Vivian, meaning "one who is full of life; vibrant"
Bibiane, Bibianna, Bibianne, Bibiann, Bibine

Bienvenida (Spanish) A welcome daughter
Bienvenidah, Bienvenyda, Bienvenita, Bienvenyta

Bifrost (Scandinavian) From the bridge
Bifroste, Byfrost, Byfroste

Bijou (French) As precious as a jewel

Bikita (African) Resembling an anteater
Bikitah, Bikyta, Bykita, Bykyta, Bikeyta, Bikeita, Bikieta, Bikeata

Bilhah (Hebrew) One who is bashful; in the Bible, a concubine of Jacob
Bilha, Baalah, Balah, Bala, Bilhan, Billha, Billhah

Billie (English) Feminine form of William; having a desire to protect
Billi, Billy, Billey, Billee, Billeigh, Billea, Billeah

Bilqis (Arabic) The queen of Sheba
Bilqys, Bilqees, Bilquis

Bimala (Indian) One who is pure
Bimalla, Bymala, Bimalah, Bemala, Bemalla, Bymala

Binah (Hebrew) Having intelligence and understanding
Bina, Bynah, Byna

Binga (German) From the hollow
Bingah, Bynga, Binge, Bynge, Bingeh, Byngeh

Binta (African) With God
Binte, Bint, Binti, Binty, Bintie, Bintee, Bintea, Binteah

Birdena (American) Resembling a little bird
Birdine, Byrdene, Byrdena, Birdina, Byrdina, Byrdine, Birdeena, Birdeene, Byrdeena, Byrdeene, Birdyna, Birdyne, Byrdyna, Byrdyne, Birdie, Birdi, Birdy, Birdey, Birdee, Burdette

Birkita (Celtic) Woman of great strength
Birkitah, Birkyta, Byrkita, Byrkyta, Birkeyta, Birkeita, Birkeata, Birkieta

Bisa (African) A daughter who is greatly loved
Bisah, Bissa, Bissah, Bysa, Bysah, Byssa, Byssah

Bisgu (Anglo-Saxon) A compassionate woman
Bisgue, Bysgu, Bysgue

Bithron (Hebrew) A child of song

Bixenta (Basque) A victorious woman

Bjork (Scandinavian) Of the birch tree
Bjorke, Björk

Blaine (Scottish / Irish) A saint's servant / a thin woman
Blayne, Blane, Blain, Blayn, Blaen, Blaene

Blair (Scottish) From the field of battle
Blaire, Blare, Blayre, Blaer, Blaere, Blayr

Blaise (French) One with a lisp or a stammer
Blayse, Blaze, Blaize, Blas, Blasa, Blase, Blasia, Blaese, Blaeze, Blayze

Blake (English) A dark beauty
Blayk, Blayke, Blaik, Blaike, Blaek, Blaeke

Blanchefleur (French) Resembling a white flower
Blancheflor, Blancheflour, Blancheflora

Blanda (Latin / Spanish) A mild-tempered woman / a flattering woman
Blandah, Blandina, Blandine, Blandyna, Blandyne

Blathnaid (Irish) As delicate as a flower
Blathnaide, Blathnade, Blathnayde, Blathnayd, Blathnaed, Blathnaede

Blenda (Latin) Dazzling
Blendah, Blinda, Blynda, Blindah, Blyndah

Bletsung (English) One who is blessed by God
Blerung, Blessing

Blimah (Hebrew) One resembling a blossom
Blima, Blime, Blyma, Blymah

Bliss (English) Filled with extreme joy
Blyss, Blysse, Blisse, Blix, Blyx

Blodwedd (Welsh) The face of a flower

Blodwen (Welsh) Resembling a white flower
Blodwenne, Blodwyn, Blodwynne, Blodwin, Blodwinne, Blodwenn, Blodwynn, Blodwinn

Blondell (French) A fair-haired woman
Blondelle, Blondele, Blondene, Blondel, Blondela, Blondella

Blossom (English) A woman who is lovely, fresh, and flowerlike
Blosom, Blossum, Blosum

Blue (American) A woman with bright-blue eyes
Blu

Bluebell (English) Resembling the blue flower
Bluebelle, Blubell, Blubelle, Bluebella, Blubella

Bluinse (Irish) A white-skinned woman
Bluince, Bluynse, Bluynce

Bluma (Hebrew) Resembling a flower's bloom
Blumah, Blumma, Blummah, Blooma, Bloomah

Bly (Native American) A tall child

Blyana (Irish) Woman of great strength
Blyanna, Bliana, Blianna, Blyann, Blyane, Blyanne, Bliane, Bliann, Blianne

Blythe (English) Filled with happiness
Blyth, Blithe, Blith

Bo (Chinese / Swedish) A precious daughter / a lively woman

Boadicea (English) A heroic queen

Bo-bae (Korean) A treasured child

Bodgana (Polish) A gift of God
Bodganah, Bodganna, Bodgane, Bodgann, Bodganne, Bogna, Bohdana, Bohdanna, Bohdane, Bohdann, Bohdanne, Bohgana, Bohganna, Bohgane, Bohgann, Bohganne

Bodil (Norse) A fighting woman
Bodile, Bodille, Bodila, Bodilla

Bolade (Nigerian) Honor comes

Bolanile (Nigerian) From the house of riches

Bolbe (Latin) From the town near the lake
Bolbi, Bolbie, Bolbee, Bolbea, Bolbeah, Bolby, Bolbey

Bona Dea (Latin) In mythology, an ancient fertility goddess

Bonamy (French) A very good friend
Bonamey, Bonami, Bonamie, Bonamee, Bonamei, Bonamea, Bonameah

Bonfilia (Italian) A good daughter
Bonfiliah, Bonfilea, Bonfileah, Bonfiliya, Bonfiliyah

Bonie (English) A well-behaved young woman
Boni, Bona, Bonea, Boneah, Bonee

Bonnie (Scottish) A pretty and charming girl
Bonny, Bonni, Bonita, Bonnibel, Bonnibelle, Bonnibele, Bonnibell, Bonney, Bonnee, Bonnea, Bonneah

Borbala (Hungarian) From a foreign land
Bora, Boriska, Borka, Borsala, Borsca, Borah, Borballa

Borghild (Norse) Strong in battle; in mythology, the wife of Sigmund
Borghilde, Borghilda

Borgny (Norwegian) One who offers help
Borgney, Borgni, Borgnie, Borgnee, Borgnea, Borgneah

Botan (Japanese) As fresh as a blossom
Botann, Botane, Botanne, Botana, Botanna

Botilda (Norse) A commanding heroine
Botild, Botilde

Boudicca (Celtic) A victorious queen
Boudicea, Bodiccea, Bodicea, Bodicia

Bozica (Slavic) Born at Christmastime
Bozicah, Bozicca, Bozika, Bozicka, Bozyca, Bozyka, Bozycka, Bozi

Bracha (Hebrew) One who is blessed
Brachah, Bracca, Braca, Bracka, Braka, Brakka

Bracken (English) Resembling a large, coarse fern
Braken, Braccan

Bradana (Scottish) Resembling the salmon
*Bradanah, Bradanna, Bradan, Bradane,
Bradann, Bradanne, Braydan, Braydana,
Braydanne*

Bradley (English) From the broad field
*Bradlea, Bradleah, Bradlee, Bradlei,
Bradleigh, Bradli, Bradlia, Bradliah, Bradlie,
Bradly, Bradlya*

Brady (Irish) A large-chested woman
*Bradey, Bradee, Bradi, Bradie, Bradea,
Bradeah*

Braima (African) Mother of multitudes
*Braimah, Brayma, Braema, Braymah,
Braemah*

Braith (Welsh) A freckled young woman
Braithe, Brayth, Braythe, Braeth, Braethe

Brandy (English) A woman wielding a
sword; an alcoholic drink
*Brandey, Brandi, Brandie, Brandee, Branda,
Brande, Brandelyn, Brandilyn, Brandyn,
Brandice, Brandyce, Brendy, Brendi, Brendi,
Brendee, Brandea, Brandeah*

Branice (English) God is gracious
Branyce, Branise, Branyse

Branka (Slowenian) Feminine form of
Branislav; a glorious protector
*Brankah, Brancka, Branckah, Brancca,
Branccah*

Brann (Welsh) A ravenlike woman
Branne, Bran

Branwen (Welsh) A dark beauty; in mythol-
ogy, goddess of love and beauty
*Branwenn, Branwenne, Branwyn, Branwynn,
Branwynne, Brangwen, Brangwy, Bronwen,
Bronwenn, Bronwenne, Bronwyn, Bronwynn,
Bronwynne*

Brasen (American) Woman filled with self-
assurance
Brazen

Braulia (Spanish) One who is glowing
*Brauliah, Braulea, Brauleah, Brauliya,
Brauliyah*

Brazil (Spanish) Of the ancient tree
*Brasil, Brazile, Brazille, Brasille, Bresil,
Brezil, Bresille, Brezille*

Breck (Irish) A freckled girl
Brek, Brecken, Breckin, Breckan

Breena (Irish) From the fairy palace
*Brina, Bryna, Breen, Brenee, Breene, Breina,
Briena, Breyna*

Breezy (English) An animated and light-
hearted woman
*Breezey, Breezi, Breezie, Breezee, Breezea,
Breezeah*

Bregus (Welsh) A frail woman

Brencis (Slavic) Crowned with laurel

Brenda (Irish) Feminine form of Brendan;
a princess; wielding a sword
*Brynda, Brinda, Breandan, Brendalynn,
Brendolyn, Brend, Brienda*

Brenna (Welsh) A ravenlike woman
*Brinna, Brenn, Bren, Brennah, Brina, Brena,
Brenah*

Brennan (English) Resembling a little raven
Brennea, Brennen, Brennon, Brennyn

Brett (English) Woman of Britain or Brittany
*Bret, Bretta, Breta, Brette, Brit, Brita, Britta,
Brite*

Briallan (Welsh) Resembling a primrose
*Briallen, Brialan, Brialen, Breeallan,
Breeallen, Bryallan, Bryalan, Bryallen,
Bryalen*

❷ **Brianna** (Irish) Feminine form of Brian;
❶ from the high hill; one who ascends
*Breanna, Breanne, Breana, Breann, Breeana,
Breeanna, Breona, Breonna, Briana, Brianne,
Briann, Briannah, Brienna, Brienne, Bryana,
Bryann, Bryanna, Bryanne, Brina, Bryna,
Briannon, Brianda, Bria, Bree, Brie, Brea,
Brielle, Bryn, Bren, Brynn, Brenne, Brynne,
Brynna, Brynnan, Brynelle*

Briar (English) Resembling a thorny plant
Brier, Bryar, Bryer

Brice (Welsh) One who is alert; ambitious
Bryce

Bridget (Irish) A strong and protective woman; in mythology, goddess of fire, wisdom, and poetry
Bridgett, Bridgette, Briget, Brigette, Bridgit, Bridgitte, Birgit, Birgitte, Birgitta, Berget, Bergitte, Bergit, Berit, Biddy, Bridie, Bride, Brid, Brigetta, Bridgetta, Brighid, Bidelia, Bidina, Breeda, Brigid, Brigida, Brigidia, Brigit, Brigitta, Brigitte, Brietta, Briette, Brigantia, Bryga, Brygida, Brygid

Brilliant (American) A dazzling and sparkling woman

Brimlad (Anglo-Saxon) From the seaway
Brymlad, Brimlod, Brymlod

Briseis (Greek) In mythology, the Trojan widow abducted by Achilles
Brisys, Brisa, Brisia, Brisha, Brissa, Briza, Bryssa, Brysa

Brisingamen (Norse) In mythology, Freya's charmed necklace

Brites (Portuguese) One who has power

Brittany (English) A woman from Great Britain
Britany, Brittanie, Brittaney, Brittani, Brittanee, Britney, Britnee, Britny, Britni, Britnie, Brittania, Brittnee, Brittni, Brittnie, Brittney, Brittny, Brettany, Brettani, Brettanie, Brettaney, Brettanee, Britaine, Britaina, Britani, Britania, Brittanya

Brona (Irish) A sorrowful woman
Bronah, Bronna, Bronnah

❂ **Brooke** (English) From the running stream
Brook, *Brookie*

❂ **Brooklyn** (American) Borough of New York City
Brooklin, Brooklynn, Brooklynne

Brucie (French) Feminine form of Bruce; from the brushwood thicket
Brucina, Brucine, Brucy, Brucey, Brucea, Bruceah, Brucee, Bruci

Bruna (German) A dark-haired woman
Brune, Brunella, Brunelle, Brunela, Brunele, Brunetta

Brunhild (German / Norse) A dark and noble battlemaiden / in mythology, queen of the Valkyries
Brunhilde, Brunhilda, Brunnehild, Brunnehilde, Brunnehilda, Brynhild, Brynhilde, Brynhilda

Bryony (English) Of the healing vine
Briony, Brione, Brioni, Brionna, Brionne, Brionee, Bryonee, Bryoni, Bryone, Bryonie, Brionie, Bryani, Bryanie, Bryanee, Brionea, Bryonea, Brioneah, Bryoneah

Buena (Spanish) A good woman
Buen, Buan

Buffy (English) Form of Elizabeth, meaning "my God is bountiful"
Buffi, Buffie, Buffey, Buffee, Buffea, Buffeah

Bulbul (Arabic) Resembling the nightingale

Bunny (American) Resembling a little rabbit
Bunni, Bunnie, Bunney, Bunnee, Bunnea, Bunneah

Bupe (African) A hospitable woman

Burgundy (French) Woman from a region of France known for its Burgundy wine
Burgandee, Burgandey, Burgandi, Burgandie, Burgandy, Burgunde, Burgundee, Burgundey, Burgundi, Burgundie, Burgandea, Burgundea

Burnett (French) Referring to the color of brown
Burnet, Burnette, Burnetta, Burneta, Burnete

Bushra (Arabic) A good omen
Bushrah

Butch (American) A manly woman

Buthaynah (Arabic) From the soft sand; having soft skin
Buthayna, Buthainah, Buthaina, Buthana, Buthanah

Butterfly (American) Resembling a beautiful and colorful winged insect

Bysen (Anglo-Saxon) A unique young lady
Bysan, Byson

C

Cable (American) Resembling a heavy rope; having great strength
Cabel

Cabot (French) A fresh-faced beauty

Cabrina (American) Form of Sabrina, meaning "a legendary princess"
Cabrinah, Cabrinna, Cabreena, Cabriena, Cabreina, Cabryna, Cabrine, Cabryne, Cabreene, Cabrynna

Cabriole (French) An adorable girl
Cabriolle, Cabrioll, Cabriol, Cabryole, Cabryolle, Cabryoll, Cabryol, Cabriola, Cabriolla, Cabryola, Cabryolla

Caca (Latin) In mythology, the sister of a giant and the original goddess of the hearth

Cacalia (Latin) Resembling the flowering plant
Cacaliah, Cacalea, Cacaleah

Cachet (French) Marked with distinction; a prestigious woman
Cachette, Cache, Cashlin, Cashet, Cachee, Cachey, Cachay, Cachai, Cachae

Cacia (Greek) Form of Acacia, meaning "thorny tree; one who is naïve"; form of Casey, meaning "a vigilant woman"
Caciah, Cacea, Caceah

Cactus (American) Resembling the spiny plant
Caktus

Caddy (American) An alluring woman
Caddi, Caddie, Caddey, Caddee, Caddea, Caddeah

Cade (American) A precocious young woman
Caid, Caide, Cayd, Cayde, Caed, Caede

Caden (English) A battlemaiden
Cadan, Cadin, Cadon

Cadence (Latin) Rhythmic and melodious; a musical woman
Cadena, Cadenza, Cadian, Cadienne, Cadianne, Cadiene, Caydence, Cadencia

Cadha (Scottish) From the steep mountain
Cadhah

Cadhla (Irish) A beautiful woman
Cadhlah

Cadis (Greek) A sparkling young girl
Cadiss, Cadisse, Cadys, Cadyss, Cadysse

Cadwyn (Welsh) A bright, strong chain
Cadwynn, Cadwynne, Cadwin, Cadwinne, Cadwinn, Cadwen, Cadwenn, Cadwenne

Cady (American) One who is pure; finding happiness in simplicity
Cade, Cadee, Cadey, Cadi, Cadie, Cadye, Caidie, Cadyna, Cadea, Cadeah

Cael (Celtic) Of the victorious people
Caele, Caell, Caelle

Caeneus (Greek) In mythology, a woman who became a man
Caenis, Caenius

Caesaria (Greek) Feminine form of Caesar; an empress
Caesariah, Caesarea, Caesareah, Caezaria, Caezariah, Caezarea, Caezareah, Cesaria, Cesariah, Cesarea, Cesareah, Cesarina, Cesariena, Cesaryna, Cesareina, Cesareana, Cesareena, Cesarie, Cesari, Cesary, Cesarey, Cesaree, Cesareah, Cesarea

Caethes (Welsh) A slave girl

Cafell (Welsh) A priestess who is an oracle
Cafelle, Cafele, Cafel, Caffel

Caffaria (Irish) One who is helmeted
Caffarea, Caffara, Caffariah, Caffarea, Caffareah

Cahira (Irish) Feminine form of Cahir; a woman warrior
Cahirah, Caheera, Cahyra, Caheira, Cahiera, Caheerah, Cahyrah, Caheirah, Cahierah, Caheara, Cahearah

Caia (Latin) One who rejoices
Cai, Cais

Caieta (Latin) In mythology, the woman who nursed Aeneas

Cailin (Gaelic) A young woman; a lass
Caelan, Caelyn, Caileen, Cailyn, Caylin, Cailean, Caolan, Caelin

Cailleach (Scottish) An old woman; in mythology, the mother of all
Caillic

Cain (Hebrew) A spear huntress; in the Bible, murdered his brother Abel
Caine, Cayn, Cayne, Caen, Caene

Cainell (Welsh) A beautiful young girl
Cainelle, Cainele, Cainel, Caynell, Caynelle, Caynele, Caynel, Caenell, Caenel

Cainwen (Welsh) A beautiful treasure
Cainwenn, Cainwenne, Cainwin, Cainwinn, Cainwinne, Cainwyn, Cainwynn, Cainwynne, Caynwen, Caynwenn, Caynwenne, Caynwin, Caynwinne, Caynwinn, Caynwyn, Caynwynn, Caywynne

Cairo (African) From the city in Egypt

Cakusola (African) One who has the heart of a lion
Cakusolah, Cakusolla, Cakusollah

Cala (Arabic) From the castle
Calah

Calais (French) From the city in France

Calandra (Greek) Resembling a songbird; a lark
Calendre, Calynda, Calinda, Calandria, Callyr, Calynda

Calantha (Greek) Resembling a lovely flower
Calanthe, Calanthia, Calanthiah, Calantheah, Calanthea

Calatea (Greek) A flowering woman
Calateah, Calatia, Calatiah, Calatee, Calati, Calatie, Calaty, Calatey

Caldwell (English) Of the cold well
Caldwelle, Caldwele, Caldwel

Cale (Latin) A respected woman
Cayl, Cayle, Cael, Caele, Cail, Caile

Caledonia (Latin) Woman of Scotland
Caledoniah, Caledoniya, Caledona, Caledonya, Calydona

Calia (American) A known beauty
Caliah, Calea, Caleah

Calida (Spanish) A woman who is warm and loving
Calidah, Calyda, Caleeda, Caleida, Calieda, Caleda, Calydah, Caleedah, Caleidah, Caliedah, Caledah, Caleada, Caleadah

California (Spanish) From paradise; from the state of California
Califia

Calise (Greek) A gorgeous woman
Calyse, Calice, Calyce

Calista (Greek) Form of Kallisto, meaning "the most beautiful"
Calissa, Calisto, Callista, Calyssa, Calysta, Calixte, Colista, Collista, Colisto, Caliesta, Caleista, Caleasta, Caleesta

Calla (Greek) Resembling a lily; a beautiful woman
Callah

Callan (Gaelic / German) One who is powerful in battle / a talkative woman
Callen, Callon, Callyn, Calynn, Calan

Callida (Latin) A fiery young girl
Callidah, Callyda, Calleeda, Calleida, Callieda, Calleda, Callydah, Calleedah, Calleidah, Calliedah, Calledah, Calleada, Calleadah

Callidora (Greek) A beautiful gift
Callidorah, Calidora, Callydora, Calydora, Callidorra

Calligenia (Greek) Daughter born with beauty
Caligenia, Calligeniah, Caligeniah, Callygenia, Calygenia, Calligenea, Caligenea

Calliope (Greek) Form of Kalliope, meaning "having a beautiful voice"; in mythology, the muse of epic poetry
Calliopee, Calliopy, Calliopi, Calliopie, Caliope, Caliopi, Caliopie, Caliopy, Calliopea, Calliopeah, Caliopea, Caliopeah, Caliopa

Callisto (Greek) Form of Kallisto, meaning "the most beautiful"; in mythology, a nymph who was changed into a she-bear
Callista, Calisto, Calista, Calysta, Calysto, Callysto, Callysta, Calliste, Calleesto, Calleisto, Calleisto, Calleasto

Calluna (Latin) Resembling heather
Callunah, Caluna, Calunna

Calpurnia (Latin) A woman of power
Calpurniah, Calpurnea, Capurneah, Calpernia, Calpernea, Calperniah, Calperneah

Caltha (Latin) Resembling a yellow flower
Calthah, Calthia, Calthiah, Caltheah, Calthea

Calumina (Scottish) A calm and peaceful woman
Caluminah, Calumeena, Calumeenah, Calumeina, Calumeinah, Calumiena, Calumienah, Calumyna, Calumynah, Calumeana, Calumeanah

Calvina (Spanish) Feminine form of Calvino; one who is bald
Calvinah, Calvyna, Calveena, Calviena, Calvena, Calvine, Calveene, Calvinna, Calveina, Calviena, Calveana, Calvean, Calvien, Calvein

Calybe (Greek) In mythology, a nymph who was the wife of Laomedon

Calypso (Greek) A woman with secrets; in mythology, a nymph who captivated Odysseus for seven years

Camassia (American) One who is aloof
Camassiah, Camasia, Camasiah, Camassea, Camasseah, Camasea, Camaseah

Cambay (English) From the town in India
Cambaye, Cambai, Cambae

Camber (American) Form of Amber, meaning "resembling the jewel"
Cambur, Cambar, Camberly, Camberlyn, Camberli, Camberlee, Cambyr, Cambyre, Cambra, Cahmber, Camberia, Camberise, Camberlynn, Cambre

Cambria (Latin) A woman of Wales
Cambriah, Cambrea, Cambree, Cambre, Cambry, Cambrey, Cambri, Cambrie, Cymreiges, Cambreah

Camdyn (English) Of the enclosed valley
Camden, Camdan, Camdon, Camdin

Cameka (American) Form of Tameka, meaning "a twin"
Camekah, Cameeka, Camieka, Cameika, Camecka, Cemeka, Cymeka, Comeka, Cameca, Cameeca, Camekia, Camecia

Camelot (English) Of the king's court; in Arthurian legend, King's Arthur's castle
Camalot, Camolot, Camylot

Cameo (English) A small, perfect child
Cammeo

Cameron (Scottish) Having a crooked nose
Cameryn, Camryn, Camerin, Camren, Camrin, Camron

❶ **Camilla** (Italian) Feminine form of Camillus; a ceremonial attendant; a noble virgin
*Camile, Camille, **Camila**, Camillia, Caimile, Camillei, Cam, Camelai, Camelia, Camella, Camellia, Camela, Cammi*

Campbell (Scottish) Having a crooked mouth
Campbel, Campbelle, Campbele

Cana (Turkish) A beloved daughter
Canan

Canace (Greek) Born of the wind

Candace (Ethiopian / Greek) A queen / one who is white and glowing
Candice, Candiss, Candyce, Candance, Candys, Candyss

Candelara (Spanish) A spiritual woman
Candelora, Candelaria, Candelariah, Candelarea, Candelareah

Candida (Latin) A white-skinned woman
Candide

Candra (Latin) One who is glowing

Candy (English) A sweet girl; form of Candida, meaning "a white-skinned woman"; form of Candace, meaning "a queen / one who is white and glowing"
Candey, Candi, Candie, Candee, Candea, Candeah

Caneadea (Native American) From the horizon
Caneadeah, Caneadia, Caneadiah

Canei (Greek) One who is pure

Canens (Latin) The personification of song; in mythology, a nymph
Caniad, Cannia, Canta, Cantilena, Cantrix

Canika (American) A woman shining with grace
Canikah, Caneeka, Canicka, Canyka, Canycka, Caneekah, Canickah, Canykah, Canyckah, Caneika, Caneikah, Canieka, Caniekah, Caneaka, Caneakah

Canisa (Greek) One who is very much loved
Canisah, Canissa, Canysa, Caneesa, Canyssa

Cannelita (Italian) From the beautiful garden
Cannelitah, Canelita, Cannelyta, Canelyta, Canneleeta, Caneleeta, Canneleata, Caneleata, Canneleita, Caneleita, Cannelieta, Canelieta

Cannenta (Latin) A woman possessing healing powers

Cannes (French) A woman from Cannes

Cantabria (Latin) From the mountains
Cantabriah, Cantebria, Cantabrea, Cantebrea

Cantara (Arabic) From the small bridge
Cantarah, Cantarra, Cantera, Canterah, Canterra, Cantarrah, Canterrah

Caoilfhinn (Celtic) A slender and attractive woman

Caoimhe (Irish) One who is charming and beautiful

Capeka (Slavic) Resembling a young stork
Capekah, Capecca, Capeccah

Capelta (American) A fanciful woman

Capita (Latin) An intelligent and superior woman
Capitah, Capyta, Capeta, Capeeta, Capieta, Capeita, Capta, Capytah, Capetah, Capeetah, Capietah, Capeitah, Capeata, Capeatah

Caplice (American) One who is spontaneous
Caplise, Capleece, Capleese, Capliece, Capliese, Capleice, Capleise, Capleace, Caplease

Capote (Spanish) One who is protected; wearing a cloak

Caprice (Italian) One who is impulsive and unpredictable
Capri, Capricia, Capriana, Caprina, Capryce, Caprise, Capryse

Capricorn (Latin) The tenth sign of the zodiac; the goat

Caprina (Italian) Woman of the island Capri
Caprinah, Caprinna, Capryna, Capreena, Caprena, Capreenah, Carpynah, Capriena, Caprienah, Capreina, Capreinah, Capreana, Capreanah

Capucina (French) Resembling the watercress
Capucine, Capucinia, Capucinea

Cara (Italian / Gaelic) One who is dearly loved / a good friend
Carah, Caralee, Caralie, Caralyn, Caralynn, Carrah, Carra, Chara, Cahra, Caradoc, Caraf, Caraid, Carajean, Caralea, Caralisa, Carita, Carella, Carilla, Caraleigh, Caraleah

Cardea (Latin) In mythology, the goddess of thresholds
Cardeah, Cardia, Cardiah

Caresse (French) A woman with a tender touch
Caress, Caressa, Carressa

Carew (Latin) One who rides a chariot
Carewe, Crewe, Crew

Carina (Latin) Little darling
Carena, Carinna, Carrina, Cariana, Carin, Carine, Caren, Carinen, Caron, Carren, Carron, Carrin, Caryn, Caryna, Carynn, Careena, Cariena, Careina, Careana

Carinthia (English) From the city in Austria
Carinthiah, Carinthea, Carintheah, Carynthia, Carynthiah, Carynthea, Caryntheah

Carissa (Greek) A woman of grace
Carisa, Carrisa, Carrissa, Carissima

Carla (Latin) Feminine form of Carl; a free woman
Carlah, Carlana, Carlee, Carleen, Carleigh, Carlena, Carlene, Carletta, Carlette, Carley, Carli, Carlia, Carlie, Carlina, Carlisa, Carlita, Carlla, Carly, Carlyn, Carlen, Carlin, Carling, Carlea, Carleah

Carlanda (American) Our darling daughter
Carland, Carlande, Carlandia, Carlandiah, Carlandea, Carlandeah

Carlessa (American) One who is restless
Carlessah, Carlesa, Carlesah

Carlisa (Italian) A friendly woman
Carlisah, Carlissa, Carlissah, Carlysa, Carlysah, Carlyssa, Carlyssah

Carlisle (English) From the fort at Luguvalium
Carlysle, Carlyle, Carlile

Carmel (Hebrew) Of the fruitful orchard
Carmela, Carmella, Carmila, Carmilla, Carmel, Carmelle, Carmelita, Carmelina, Carmeline, Carmelia

Carmen (Latin) A beautiful song
Carma, Carmelita, Carmencita, Carmia, Carmie, Carmina, Carmine, Carmita, Carmyna, Carmyta, Carmea, Carman, Carmin, Carminda, Carmya

Carmensita (Spanish) One who is dear
Carmensyta, Carmensitah, Carmensytah, Carmens, Carmense

Carmenta (Latin) In mythology, the goddess of childbirth
Carminta, Carmynta

Carna (Latin) In mythology, a goddess who ruled the heart

Carnation (Latin) Resembling the flower; becoming flesh

Carnelian (Latin) Resembling the deep-red gem
Carnelyan, Carneliann, Carnelianne, Carnela, Carnelia

Carni (Latin) One who is vocal
Carnie, Carny, Carney, Carnee, Carnea, Carneah, Carnia, Carniah, Carnea, Carneah, Carniya, Carniyah, Carnielle, Carniele, Carniell, Carniella, Carniela

Carody (American) A humorous woman
Carodi, Carodey, Carodie, Carodee, Carodea, Carodeah

Carol (English) Form of Caroline, meaning "a joyous song; a small, strong woman"
Carola, Carole, Carolle, Carolla, Caroly, Caroli, Carolie, Carolee, Caroleigh, Carel, Caral, Caril, Carroll, Caryl

○ **Caroline** (Latin) Feminine form of Charles; a joyous song; a small, strong woman
Carolina, Carolan, Carolann, Carolanne, Carolena, Carolene, Carolena, Caroliana, Carolyn, Carolyne, Carolynn, Carrie, Carri, Carry, Caro, Carrey, Carree, Caree, Carrieann, Carilyn, Carilynne, Cary

Carrelle (American) A lively woman
Carrell, Carrel, Carrele, Carrella, Carrela

Carrington (English) A beautiful woman; a woman of Carrington
Carington, Carryngton, Caryngton

Carson (Scottish) From the swamp
Carsan, Carsen, Carsin

Carter (English) A transporter of merchandise
Cartar, Cartrell, Cartier

Cartimandua (Anglo-Saxon) A powerful queen

Caryatis (Greek) In mythology, goddess of the walnut tree
Carya, Cariatis, Caryatiss, Cariatiss, Caryatys, Cariatys, Caryatyss, Cariatyss

Carys (Welsh) One who loves and is loved
Caryss, Carysse, Caris, Cariss, Carisse, Cerys, Ceryss, Cerysse, Ceris, Ceriss, Cerisse

Cascadia (Latin) Woman of the waterfall
Cascadiya, Cascadea, Cascata

Casey (Irish) A vigilant woman
Casee, Casi, Casie, Casy, Cacey, Cacee, Cacy, Caci, Cacie, Caycee, Caycie, Caysie, Caysey, Casea, Caysea

Cashonya (American) A wealthy woman
Cashonyah, Cashona, Cashonah, Cashonia, Cashoniah, Cashonea, Cashoneah

Casilda (Latin / Spanish) Of the home / a warrior woman
Casildah, Cassilda, Casylda, Cassylda

Casilda (Latin) Of the home
Casildah, Casild, Casilde, Casylda, Casyldah, Casyld, Casylde

Cason (Greek) A seer
Cayson, Caison, Caeson

Cassandra (Greek) An unheeded prophetess; in mythology, she foretold the fall of Troy
Casandra, Cassandrea, Cassaundra, Cassondra, Cass, Cassy, Cassey, Cassi, Cassie, Cassara

Cassia (Greek / Latin) Of the spice tree / feminine form of Cassius; one who is hollow; empty
Cassea, Cassiah, Casseah

Cassidy (Irish) Curly-haired girl
Cassady, Cassidey, Cassidi, Cassidie, Cassidee, Cassadi, Cassadie, Cassadee, Casidhe, Cassidea, Cassadea

Cassielle (Latin) Feminine form of Cassiel, an archangel
Cassiell, Cassiel, Cassiele, Cassiella, Cassiela

Cassiopeia (Greek) In mythology, the mother of Andromeda who was changed into a constellation after she died
Cassiopia, Cassiopiya, Cassiopea

Casta (Spanish) One who is pure; chaste
Castah, Castalina, Castaleena, Castaleina, Castaliena, Castaleana, Castalyna, Castara, Castarah, Castarra, Castarrah

Castalia (Greek) In mythology, a nymph transformed into a sacred spring
Castalea, Casta, Castaliann, Castalianne, Castaliana, Castaliah, Castaleah

Catava (Greek) One who is uncorrupted
Catavah

Catherine (English) One who is pure; virginal
Catharine, Cathrine, Cathryn, Catherin, Catheryn, Catheryna, Cathi, Cathia, Cathicen, Cathie, CathIyn, Cathleen, Cathlin, Cathy, Catia, Catlee, Catlin, Catline, Catlyn, Cait, Caitie, Caitlin, Caitlan, Caitir, Cattee, Cat, Caitilin, CaitIyn, Caitlan, Caitland, Caitlinn, Caitlynn, Caitrin, Caitriona, Caitryn, Catalin, Catalina, Catalyn, Catalyna, Catarina, Catarine, Cate, Cateline, Catelyn, Catelyna, Caterina, Cath, Catharina, Catrin, Catrina, Catriona, Catylyn

Cathresha (American) One who is pure
Cathreshah, Cathreshia, Cathreshiah, Cathreshea, Cathresheah, Cathrisha, Cathrishah, Cathrysha, Cathryshah

Catima (Greek) One who is innocent
Catimah, Catyma, Catymah, Catiema, Catiemah, Cateima, Cateimah, Cateema, Cateemah, Cateama, Cateamah

Catrice (Greek) A wholesome woman
Catrise, Catryce, Catryse, Catreece, Catreese, Catriece, Catriese, Catreice, Catreise, Catreace, Catrease

Cavana (Irish) Feminine form of Cavan; from the hollow
Cavanna, Cavanah, Cavania, Cavaniya, Cavanea, Cavannah

Cavender (American) An emotional woman
Cavendar

Cayenne (French) Resembling the hot and spicy pepper

Caykee (American) A lively woman
Cayke, Cayki, Caykie, Caykey, Cayky, Caykea, Caikee, Caike, Caikey, Caiky, Caiki, Caikie, Caikea, Caekee, Caekey, Caeky, Caeki, Caekie, Caekea

Cayla (Hebrew / Gaelic) Crowned with laurel / one who is slender
Caela, Caila, Caileigh, Cailey, Cailie, Caleigh, Caley, Callie, Caylee, Cayleen, Cayleigh, Cayley, Caylia, Caylie, Cailley, Cali, Callee, Calli, Callia

Cayman (English) From the islands
Cayeman, Caman, Caiman, Caeman, Caymanne, Caimanne, Caemanne, Camanne

Ceallach (Gaelic) A bright-headed woman

Cecilia (Latin) Feminine form of Cecil; one who is blind; patron saint of music
Cecelia, Cecile, Cecilee, Cicely, Cecily, Cecille, Cecilie, Cicilia, Cicily, Cecia, Cece, Ceil, Cele, Celia, Celicia, Celie, Cili, Cilla, Ciss, Cissie, Cissi, Cissy

Cedrica (American) Feminine form of Cedric; one who is kind and loved
Cedricca, Cedrika, Cedricka, Cedra, Cedrina, Cedryna, Cedreena, Cedriana, Cedrianna, Cedrianne

Ceinwen (Welsh) A girl blessed with beauty
Ceinwenn, Ceinwenne, Ceinwin, Ceinwinn, Ceinwinne, Ceinwyn, Ceinwynn, Ceinwynne

Ceiteag (Scottish) A pure woman

Celaeno (Greek) In mythology, one of the Pleiades
Celeeno, Celeino, Celieno, Celeano, Celeyno

Celand (Latin) One who is meant for heaven
Celanda, Celande, Celandia, Celandea

Celandine (English) Resembling a swallow
Celandyne, Celandina, Celandyna, Celandeena, Celandena, Celandia, Celandea

Celery (American) Refers to the refreshing and healthy food
Celerey, Celeri, Celerie, Celerea, Celereah, Celeree

Celeste (Latin) A heavenly daughter
Celesta, Celestia, Celesse, Celestiel, Celisse, Celestina, Celestyna, Celestine, Celestyne, Celestielle, Celestyn, Ciel

Celina (Latin) In mythology, one of the daughters of Atlas who was turned into a star of the Pleiades constellation; feminine form of Celino; of the heavens; form of Selena, meaning "of the moon"
Celena, Celinna, Celene, Celenia, Celenne, Celicia, Celinda, Calina, Celine

Celisha (Greek) A passionate woman
Celishah, Celysha, Celyshah, Celiesha, Celieshah, Celeisha, Celeishah, Celeesha, Celeeshah, Celeasha, Celeashah

Celka (Latin) A celestial being
Celkah, Celki, Celkie, Celkee, Celkey, Celky, Celkea, Celkeah

Celosia (Greek) A fiery woman; burning; aflame
Celosiah, Celosea, Celoseah

Cenobia (Spanish) Form of Zenobia, meaning "sign or symbol"
Cenobiah, Cenobya, Cenobe, Cenobie, Cenobey, Cenovia, Cenobea, Cenobeah

Cera (French) A colorful woman
Cerah, Cerrah, Cerra

Cerea (Greek) A thriving woman
Cereah, Ceria, Ceriah

Ceres (Latin) Of the spring; in mythology, the goddess of agriculture and fertility
Ceress, Ceresse, Cerela, Cerelia, Cerealia

Ceridwen (Celtic) Beautiful poetry; in mythology, the goddess of poetry
Cerydwen, Ceridwyn, Ceridwin, Cerdwin, Ceridwenn, Ceridwenne, Ceridwynn, Ceridwynne, Ceridwinn, Ceridwinne

Cerina (Latin) Form of Serena, meaning "having a peaceful disposition"
Cerinah, Ceryna, Cerynah, Cerena, Cerenah, Ceriena, Cerienah, Cereina, Cereinah, Cereena, Cereenah, Cereana, Cereanah

Cerise (French) Resembling the cherry
Cerisa

Cesia (Spanish) A celestial being
Cesiah, Cesea, Ceseah

Chaba (Hebrew) Form of Hava, meaning "a lively woman; giver of life"
Chabah, Chaya, Chayka, Chaka, Chava, Chavah

Chablis (French) Resembling the dry white wine
Chabley, Chablie, Chabli, Chably, Chablea, Chableah, Chabliss, Chablisse, Chablys, Chablyss, Chablysse

Chadee (French) A divine woman; a goddess
Chadea, Chadeah, Chady, Chadey, Chadi, Chadie

Chaela (English) Form of Michaela, meaning "who is like God?"
Chaeli, Chaelie, Chaely, Chaeley, Chaelea, Chaeleah

Chahna (Hindi) One who brings light to the world
Chahnah

Chai (Hebrew) One who gives life
Chae, Chaili, Chailie, Chailee, Chaileigh, Chaily, Chailey, Chailea, Chaileah, Chaeli, Chaelie, Chaely, Chaeley, Chaelee, Chaelea, Chaeleah, Chaeleigh

Chailyn (American) Resembling a waterfall
Chailynn, Chailynne, Chaelyn, Chaelynn, Chaelynne, Chaylyn, Chaylynn, Chaylynne

Chaitali (Indian) Surrounded by light
Chaitalie, Chaitale, Chaitaly, Chaitaley, Chaitalee, Chaitalea, Chaitaleah, Chaitaleigh, Chaetali, Chaetalie, Chaetaly, Chaetaley, Chaetalee, Chaetalea, Chaetaleah, Chaetaleigh

Chaitra (Hindi) Born during the first month of the Hindi calendar
Chaetra, Chaitrah, Chaetrah, Chaytra, Chaytrah

Chakra (Arabic) A center of spiritual energy

Chala (American) An exuberant woman
Chalah, Challa, Challah

Chalciope (Greek) In mythology, a princess who was the sister of Medea

Chalette (American) Having good taste
Chalett, Chalet, Chalete, Chaletta, Chaleta

Chalice (French) Resembling a goblet
Chalyce, Chalise, Chalyse, Chalese

Chalina (Spanish) Form of Rosalina, meaning "resembling the beautiful and meaningful flower"
Chalinah, Chalyna, Chaleena, Chalena, Charo, Chaliena, Chaleina, Chaleana

Chalissa (American) One who is optimistic
Chalisa, Chalyssa, Chalysa

Challie (American) A charismatic woman
*Challi, Challey, Chally, Challee, Challea,
Challeah, Challeigh*

Chalondra (African) An intelligent woman

Chalsey (American) Form of Chelsea,
meaning "from the landing place for chalk"
*Chalsy, Chalsi, Chalsie, Chalsee, Chalsea,
Chalseah*

Chamania (Hebrew) Resembling a sun-
flower
*Chamaniah, Chamanea, Chamaneah,
Chamaniya, Chamaniyah, Chamaran,
Chamarann, Chamarana, Chamaranna*

Chambray (French) Resembling the light-
weight fabric
*Chambraye, Chambrai, Chambrae,
Chambree, Chambri, Chambrie, Chambry,
Chambrey, Chambrea, Chambreah*

Chameli (Hindi) Resembling jasmine
*Chamelie, Chamely, Chameley, Chamelee,
Chamelea, Chameleah, Chameleigh*

Chamomile (American) Resembling the
aromatic herb; one who is peaceful
Chamomyle, Camomile, Camomyle

Champagne (French) Resembling the sparkling wine

Chamunda (Hindi) In Hinduism, an aspect
of the mother goddess
Camunda

Chan (Sanskrit) A shining woman

Chana (Hebrew) Form of Hannah, mean-
ing "having favor and grace"
*Chanah, Channa, Chaanach, Chaanah,
Chanach, Channah*

Chanal (American) A moonlike woman
Chanall, Chanalle

Chance (American) One who takes risks
*Chanci, Chancie, Chancee, Chancea,
Chanceah, Chancy, Chancey*

Chanda (Sanskrit) An enemy of evil
*Chandy, Chaand, Chand, Chandey, Chandee,
Chandi, Chandie, Chandea, Chandeah*

Chandani (Hindi) Born with the moonbeams
*Chandunie, Chandany, Chandaney,
Chandanee, Chandanea, Chandaneah*

Chandelle (French) Resembling a candle
*Chandel, Chantelle, Chantel, Chandell,
Chantell*

Chandler (English) A candlemaker
Chandlar, Chandlor

Chandra (Hindi) Of the moon; another
name for the goddess Devi
*Chandara, Chandria, Chaundra, Chandrea,
Chandreah*

Chanel (French) From the canal; a channel
*Chanell, Chanelle, Channelle, Chenelle,
Chenel, Chenell*

Changla (Indian) An active woman

Chania (Hebrew) Blessed with grace from
God
*Chaniah, Chaneah, Chanea, Chaniya,
Chaniyah*

Chanicka (American) One who is dearly
loved
*Chanickah, Chanika, Chanikah, Chaniecka,
Chaneicka, Chaneecka, Chanycka,
Chaneacka, Chaneeka, Chaneika, Chanieka,
Chanyka, Chaneaka*

Chanina (Hebrew) The Lord is gracious
*Chaninah, Chaneena, Chaneenah, Chanyna,
Chanynah, Chaneana, Chaneanah,
Chaniena, Chanienah, Chaneina, Chaneinah*

Chanise (American) One who is adored
Chanyse, Chanice, Chanyce

Chanit (Hebrew) One who is ready for battle
Chanyt, Chanita, Chanyta

Channary (Cambodian) Of the full moon
*Channarie, Channari, Channarey,
Channaree, Chantrea, Chantria*

Channing (English) An official of the
church; resembling a young wolf
*Channon, Channer, Channery, Channerie,
Channerey, Channeree, Channeri, Channe*

Chansanique (American) A singing girl
*Chansaneek, Chansanik, Chansanike,
Chansanyk, Chansani, Chansanie,
Chansanee, Chansanea, Chansaneah,
Chansany, Chansaney*

Chantal (French) From a stony place; a beautiful singer
Chantalle, Chantel, Chantele, Chantell, Chantelle, Chantrell, Chauntel, Chantay, Chante, Chantae, Chaunte, Chanton, Chauntelle

Chantee (American) A talented singer
Chantey, Chanty, Chanti, Chuntie, Chantea, Chanteah

Chanterelle (French) A prized singer
Chanterell, Chanterel, Chanterele, Chanterella, Chanterela

Chantilly (French) Resembling the beautiful lace
Chantilley, Chantilli, Chantillie, Chantillee, Chantilleigh, Chantillea, Chantilleah

Chantou (French) One who sings

Chantoya (American) A renowned singer

Chantrice (French) A singer
Chantryce, Chantrise, Chantryse

Chanya (Hebrew) Blessed with God's love
Chanyah

Chao (Chinese) One who surpasses others

Chapa (Native American) A superior woman
Chapah, Chappah, Chappa

Chapawee (Native American) Resembling a beaver
Chapawi, Chapawie, Chapawy, Chapawey, Chapawea, Chapaweah

Chaquanne (American) A sassy young woman
Chaquane, Chaquann, Chaquan, Chaquanna, Chaquana

Charbonnet (French) A giving and loving woman
Charbonay, Charbonaye, Charbonae, Charbonai, Charbonnay, Charbonnae, Charbonnai

Chardonnay (French) Resembling the wine
Chardonnaye, Chardonay, Chardonaye, Chardonnae, Chardonae, Chardonnai, Chardonai, Charde, Charday, Charday, Chardae, Chardai

Charille (French) A delightful woman; womanly
Charill, Charile, Charil, Charilla, Charila, Charylle, Charyll, Charyle, Charylla, Charyla

Charis (English) Having grace and kindness
Charisa, Charise, Charissa, Charisse, Chariss, Charys, Charyss, Charysse

Charish (American) A cherished woman
Charisha, Cherish, Cherysh, Charysh, Chareesh

Charisma (Greek) Blessed with charm
Charismah, Charizma, Charizmuh, Charysma, Charyzma

Charity (Latin) A woman of generous love
Charitey, Chariti, Charitie, Charitee, Charyty, Charyti, Charytey, Charytie, Charytee, Charita, Charitea, Chariteah, Charytea, Charyteah

Charla (English) Feminine form of Charles; a small, strong woman
Charlee, Charlene, Charli, Charlie, Charly, Charlyn, Charlynn, Charlaine, Charlayne, Charleen, Churleena, Charleigh, Charlena, Charlette, Charline, Charlisa, Charlita, Charlize, Charlot, Charlotta, Charlotte, Carlita, Carlota, Carlotta, Chatlie, Cattie, Charlea

Charlesetta (German) Feminine form of Charles; a small, strong woman
Charleseta, Charlesett, Charleset, Charlesette, Charlesete, Charlsetta, Charlseta

Charlesia (American) Feminine form of Charles; a small, strong woman
Churlesiah, Charlesea, Charleseah, Charlsie, Charlsi, Charlsy, Charlsey, Charlsee, Charlsea, Charlseah

Charlianne (American) A small, strong, and graceful woman
Charliann, Charliane, Charlianna, Charliana, Charliean, Charlieanne, Charlieann, Charlieana, Charlieanna

❍ Charlotte (French) Form of Charles, meaning "a small, strong woman"
Charlize, Charlot, Charlotta

Charmaine (English) Charming and delightful woman
Charmain, Charmane, Charmayne, Charmian, Charmine, Charmion, Charmyan, Charmyn, Charmaen, Charmaen, Charm

Charminique (American) One who is dashing; charming
Charminik, Charminick, Charmynik, Charmynyk, Charmineek, Charmineyk, Charmonique, Charmonik, Charmonyk, Charmonick

Charnee (American) Filled with joy
Charny, Charney, Charnea, Charneah, Charni, Charnie

Charneeka (American) One who is obsessive
Charneekah, Charnykah, Charnieka, Charniekah, Charneika, Charneikah, Charneaka, Charneakah, Charnyka, Charnykah

Charnelle (American) One who sparkles
Charnell, Charnel, Charnele, Charnella, Charnela

Charnesa (American) One who gets attention
Charnesah, Charnessa, Charnessah

Charsetta (American) An emotional woman
Charsett, Charsette, Charset, Charsete, Charseta

Chartra (American) A classy lady
Chartrah

Chartres (French) One who plans
Chartrys

Charu (Hindi) One who is gorgeous
Charoo, Charou

Charumat (Hindi) An intelligent and beautiful woman
Charoomat, Charoumat

Chashmona (Hebrew) Born to royalty; a princess

Chasia (Hebrew) One who is protected; sheltered
Chasiah, Chasea, Chaseah, Chasya, Chasyah

Chasidah (Hebrew) A religious woman; pious
Chasida, Chasyda, Chasydah

Chasina (Aramaic) Having strength of character
Chasinah, Chasyna, Chasynah, Chasiena, Chasienah, Chaseina, Chaseinah, Chaseena, Chaseenah, Chaseana, Chaseanah, Chau

Chastity (Latin) Having purity; a woman of innocence
Chasity, Chasta, Chastina, Chastine, Chasida, Chassidy, Chastitey, Chastitie, Chastiti, Chastitee, Chastitea, Chastiteah

Chasya (Hebrew) One who offers shelter
Chasye

Chateria (Vietnamese) Born beneath the moonlight
Chateriah, Chaterea, Chatereah, Chateriya, Chateriyah

Chaucer (English) A demure woman
Chauser, Chawcer, Chawser

Chavela (Spanish) Form of Isabel, meaning "my God is bountiful"
Chavella, Chavelle, Chavele, Chavel, Chavell

Chavi (Egyptian) A precious daughter
Chavie, Chavy, Chavey, Chavee, Chavea, Chaveah

Chaviva (Hebrew) One who is dearly loved
Chavyva, Chavive, Chavyve, Chaveeva, Chaveevah, Chavieva, Chavievah, Chaveiva, Chaveivah, Chaveava, Chaveavah

Chavon (Hebrew) A giver of life
Chavonne, Chavonn, Chavona, Chavonna

Chazmin (American) Form of Jasmine, meaning "resembling the climbing plant with fragrant flowers"
Chaslyn, Chaslynn, Chasmeen, Chasmin, Chasmina, Chasminda, Chasmyn, Chasmyne, Chassamayn, Chazan, Chazmin, Chasmine, Chazmon, Chazmyn, Chazmyne, Chazzmin, Chazzmine, Chazzmon, Chazzmyn, Chazzmynn, Chasmyna, Chessamine, Chessamy, Chessamyn, Chasmeena, Chessimine, Chessimine

Chazona (Hebrew) A prophetess
Chazonah, Chazonna, Chazonnah

Chea (American) A witty woman
Cheah, Cheea, Cheeah

Cheche (African) A small woman

Chedra (Hebrew) Filled with happiness
Chedrah

Chedva (Hebrew) One who is joyous

Cheer (American) Filled with joy
Cheere

Cheifa (Hebrew) From a safe harbor
Cheifah, Cheiffa, Cheiffah

Chekia (American) A saucy woman
Cheekie, Checki, Checkie, Checky, Checkey, Checkee, Checkea, Checkeah

Cheletha (American) One who smiles a lot
Chelethah, Chelethe, Cheleth

Chelone (English) Resembling a flowering plant

Chelsea (English) From the landing place for chalk
Chelcie, Chelsa, Chelsee, Chelseigh, Chelsey, Chelsi, Chelsie, Chelsy, Chelsia

Chemarin (French) A dark beauty
Chemarine, Chemaryn, Chemareen, Chemarein, Chemarien

Chemash (Hebrew) A servant of God
Chemashe, Chemasha, Chemosh, Chemoshe, Chemosha, Chemesh, Chemeshe, Chemesha

Chemda (Hebrew) A charismatic woman
Chemdah

Chemdia (Hebrew) One who loves God
Chemdiah, Chemdea, Chemdeah, Chemdiya, Chemdiyah

Chen (Hebrew / Chinese) Having grace or favor / of the dawn

Chenia (Hebrew) One who lives within the grace of God
Cheniah, Chenea, Cheneah, Cheniya, Cheniyah

Chenille (American) A soft-skinned woman
Chenill, Chenil, Chenile, Chenilla, Chenila

Chenoa (Native American) Resembling a white dove; peaceful

Chephzibah (Hebrew) Her father's delight

Chepi (Native American) In mythology, a fairy spirit of the dead
Cheppi, Chepie, Cheppie, Chepy, Cheppy, Chepey, Cheppey, Chepea, Cheppea, Chepeah, Cheppeah, Chepee, Cheppee

Cher (French) One who is greatly loved; a darling
Chere, Cherée, Cherey, Cheri, Cherice, Cherie, Cherise, Cherish, Cherina, Cherisse, Chery, Cherye, Cherylee, Cherylie, Chereen, Cherell, Cherelle, Cherese, Cheresse, Charee, Cheree, Cherisa, Cherita, Cherree, Cherea, Charea

Cherika (French) One who is dear
Chericka, Cheryka, Cherycka, Cherieka, Cheriecka, Chereika, Chereicka, Cheryka, Cherycka, Chereaka, Chereacka

Cherlyn (American) One who is dearly loved
Cherlynn, Cherlynne, Cherlin, Cherlinn, Cherlinne

Chermona (Hebrew) From the sacred mountain
Chermonah, Chermonnah, Chermonna

Cherokee (Native American) A tribal name
Cheroki, Cherokie, Cherokey, Cheroky, Cherokeigh, Cherokea, Cherokeah

Cherron (American) A graceful dancer
Cherronn, Cherronne

Cherry (English) Resembling a fruit-bearing tree
Cherrie, Cherri, Cherrey, Cherree, Cherrea, Cherreah

Cheryl (English) One who is greatly loved; a darling
Cheryll, Charil, Charyl, Cheriann, Cherianne, Cherilyn, Cherilynn, Cherrell, Cherrill, Cherryl, Cheryll, Cherylle, Chyril, Chyrill, Cherlin, Cherrelle

Chesley (English) From the meadow
Chesli, Cheslie, Chesly, Chesleigh, Cheslea, Chesleah, Cheslee

Chesna (Slavic) One who is calm; bringer of peace
Chessa, Chessie, Chessy

Chesney (English) One who promotes peace
Chesny, Chesni, Chesnie, Chesnea, Chesneah, Chesnee

Chessteen (American) One who is needed
Chesstyn, Chessteene, Chesstyne, Chesstien, Chesstiene, Chesstein, Chessteine, Chesstean, Chessteane

Chestnut (American) Resembling the nut

Chet (American) A vivacious woman
Chett, Chette

Chevona (Irish) One who loves God
Chevonah, Chevonna, Chevonnah

Cheyenne (Native American) Unintelligible speaker
Cheyanna, Cheyenna, Cheyanne, Chiana, Chianna, Chayan, Chayanne

Cheyne (French) An oak-hearted woman
Cheney, Chane, Chayne, Chaney

Chhaya (Hebrew) One who loves life
Chhayah

Chi (African) Surrounded by light

Chiante (Italian) Resembling the wine
Chianti, Chiantie, Chiantee, Chianty, Chiantey, Chiantea

Chiara (Italian) Daughter of the light
Chiarah, Chiarra, Chiarrah

Chiba (Hebrew) One who loves and is loved
Chibah, Cheeba, Cheebah, Cheiba, Cheibah, Chieba, Chiebah, Cheaba, Cheabah, Chyba, Chybah

Chica (Spanish) A little girl
Chicah, Chicca, Chicka, Chika

Chick (American) A fun-loving girl
Chicki, Chickie, Chickee, Chicky, Chickey, Chickea

Chickoa (Native American) Born at daybreak
Chickoah, Chikoa, Chikoah

Chidi (Spanish) One who is cheerful
Chidie, Chidy, Chidey, Chidee, Chidea, Chideah

Chidori (Japanese) Resembling a shorebird
Chidorie, Chidory, Chidorey, Chidorea, Chidoreah, Chidoree

Chika (Japanese) A woman with great wisdom

Chikira (Spanish) A talented dancer
Chikirah, Chikiera, Chikierah, Chikeira, Chikeirah, Chikeera, Chikeerah, Chikyra, Chikyrah, Chikeara, Chikearah

Chiku (African) A talkative girl

Chilali (Native American) Resembling a snowbird
Chilalie, Chilalee, Chylali, Chylaly, Chilam, Chylam, Chilaleigh, Chilaly, Chilaley, Chilalea, Chilaleah

Childers (English) From a dignified family
Chylders, Chelders

Chimalis (Native American) Resembling a bluebird
Chymalis, Chimalys, Chymalys

Chimene (French) One who is ambitious
Chymene, Chimean, Chymean, Chimein, Chymein, Chimien, Chymien, Chimeen, Chymeen

China (Chinese) Woman from China
Chynna, Chyna, Chinah

Chinaka (African) God has chosen
Chinakah, Chynaka, Chinacka, Chinacca

Chinara (African) God receives
Chinarah, Chinarra, Chinarrah

Chinue (African) God's own blessing
Chinoo, Chynue, Chynoo

Chione (Egyptian) Daughter of the Nile

Chipo (African) A gift from God
Chippo, Chypo, Chyppo

Chiquita (Spanish) Little precious girl
Chyquita, Chiqueeta, Chiquyta, Chikita, Chykita, Chikeeta

Chiriga (African) One who is triumphant
Chyriga, Chyryga, Chiryga

Chirley (American) Form of Shirley, meaning "from the bright clearing"
Chirly, Chirli, Chirlie, Chirleigh, Chirlee, Chirlea, Chirleah

Chislaine (French) A faithful woman
Chislain, Chislayn, Chislayne, Chislaen, Chislaene, Chyslaine, Chyslain, Chyslayn, Chyslayne, Chyslaen, Chyslaene

Chitra (Hindi) In Hinduism, the goddess of misfortune
Chitrah, Chytra, Chytrah

Chitsa (Native American) One who is fair
Chitsah, Chytsa, Chytsah

Chivonne (American) Filled with happiness
Chivonn, Chivone, Chivon, Chivonna, Chivona, Chevonn, Chevonne, Chevon, Chevone, Chivaughn, Chevaughn

Chiyena (Hebrew) Blessed with the Lord's grace
Chiyenah

Chiyo (Japanese) Of a thousand years; eternal

Chizoba (African) One who is well-protected
Chizobah, Chyzoba, Chyzobah

Chizuko (Japanese) A bountiful woman
Chizu

⚲⊕ **Chloe** (Greek) A flourishing woman; blooming
Chloë, Clo, Cloe, Cloey

Chloris (Greek) In mythology, goddess of vegetation and spring
Chlorys, Chloriss, Chloryss

Cho (Japanese) Resembling a butterfly

Chofa (Polish) An able-bodied woman
Chofah, Choffa, Choffah

Cholena (Native American) A birdlike woman
Cholenah, Cholyna, Choleena, Cholynah, Choleenah

Chosovi (Native American) Resembling a bluebird
Chosovie, Chosovy, Chosovey, Chosovee, Chosposi, Chosposie, Chosovea, Chosposy, Chosposey, Chosposee, Chosposea

Christina (English) Follower of Christ
Christinah, Cairistiona, Christine, Christin, Christian, Christiana, Christiane, Christianna, Christi, Christie, Christen, Christena, Christene, Christy, Christyn, Christan, Christana, Christanne, Christeen, Christeena, Chrissa, Chrissie, Chrissy, Christa, Chrysta, Crista, Crysta, Chryssa, Christabel, Christabell, Christabella, Cristabel, Cristabell, Christahel, Christahella, Crissi, Crissa, Crissy, Crissie, Cristen, Cristie, Cristin, Cristina, Cristine, Cristiona, Cristy, Cristyn, Chrystina, Chrystine, Chrystie, Chryssa, Chrina, Chris, Cris, Carsten, Ciorstan

Christmas (English) Born during the festival of Christ

Chrysantha (Greek) Defender of the people
Chrisanna, Chrisanne, Chrysandra, Crisanna, Chrysann, Crisanne, Crisann

Chryseis (Latin) The golden daughter; in mythology, a woman captured by Agamemnon
Chrysilla

Chuki (African) Born during an unpleasant time
Chukie, Chuky, Chukey, Chukee, Chukea, Chukeah

Chula (Native American) Resembling a colorful flower
Chulah, Chulla, Chullah

Chulda (Hebrew) One who can tell fortunes
Chuldah

Chulisa (American) A clever woman
Chulisah, Chulissa, Chulissah, Chulysa, Chulysah, Chulyssa, Chulyssah

Chuma (Hebrew) A warmhearted woman
Chumah, Chumma, Chummah, Chumi, Chumie, Chumee, Chumy, Chumey, Chumea, Chumeah, Chumina, Chumyna, Chumeena, Chumeina, Chumiena, Chumeana, Chumyna

Chumana (Native American) Covered with dew
Chumanah, Chumanna, Chumannah

Chumani (Native American) Resembling a dewdrop
Chumanie, Chumany, Chumaney, Chumanee, Chumanea, Chumaneah

Chun (Chinese) Born during spring

Chyou (Chinese) Born during autumn

Ciana (Italian) Feminine form of John; God is gracious
Cianna, Ciannait, Ceana, Ceanna, Cyana, Cyanna

Ciandra (Italian) Surrounded by light
Ciandrah, Cyandra, Cyandrah

Ciara (Irish) A dark beauty
Ceara, Ciaran, Ciarra, Ciera, Cierra, Ciere, Ciar, Ciarda, Cyara, Cyarra

Cicada (Latin) Resembling the high-pitched insect
Cicayda, Cicaida, Cicala, Cicaeda, Cikada, Cikayda, Cikaida, Cikaeda

Cidrah (American) One who is unlike others
Cidra, Cydrah, Cydra

Cierra (Irish) A clear-eyed woman
Cierrah, Cyerra, Cyerrah

Cinderella (French) Beautiful girl of the ashes
Cendrillon, Cenerentola, Cinderelle, Cinderela, Cinderele, Cinderell

Cinnamon (American) Resembling the reddish-brown spice
Cinnia, Cinnie

Cinta (Spanish) From the good mountain
Cintah, Cynta, Cyntah

Cinxia (Latin) In mythology, the goddess of marriage

Ciona (American) One who is steadfast
Cionah, Cyona, Cyonah

Cipporah (Hebrew) Form of Zipporah, meaning "a beauty; little bird"
Cippora, Ciporah, Cipora, Cypora, Cyppora, Ciproh, Cipporia, Cepora, Ceporrah, Ceppora, Cepporah

Ciqala (Native American) Our little one
Cyqala, Ciqalla, Cyqalla

Circe (Greek) In mythology, a sorceress who changed Odysseus's men into swine
Circee, Curce, Cyrce, Curcee, Cyrcee, Circie, Circi, Circea, Circy, Circey, Circeah

Citare (Greek) A musically talented woman
Citarr, Citar, Citara, Ciatarra, Cita

Citlali (Native American) A starlike child
Citlalli, Citlalie, Citlallie, Citlaly, Citlaley, Citlalee, Citlaleigh, Citlalea, Citlaleah

Claennis (Anglo-Saxon) One who is pure
Claenis, Claennys, Claenys, Claynnis, Claynnys, Claynys, Claynyss

Claiborne (Old English) Born of the earth's clay
Claiborn, Claibourn, Claibourne, Clayborn, Clayborne, Claybourn, Claybourne, Claeborn, Claeborne, Claebourn, Claebourne

❍ **Claire** (French) Form of Clara, meaning "famously bright"
Clare, Clair

Clancey (American) A lighthearted woman
Clancy, Clanci, Clancie, Clancee, Clancea, Clanceah

Clara (Latin) Famously bright
Clarinda, Clarine, Clarita, Claritza, Clarrie, Clarry, Clarabelle, Claretha, Claribel, Clarice, Clarahelle, Claral, Clarette, Clarinde, Claribelle, Claretta, Clareta, Clorinda, Chlorinda

Clarice (French) A famous woman; a form of Clara, meaning "famously bright"
Claressa, Claris, Clarisa, Clarise, Clarisse, Claryce, Clerissa, Clerisse, Cleryce, Clerysse, Claresta, Clariss, Clarissa, Clarrisa, Clariee, Claryssa, Clarysa

Clarimond (German) A shining protectress
Clarimonda, Clarimonde, Clarimunde, Clarimunda, Clarimund, Claramond, Claramonda, Claramonde

Clarity (American) One who is clear-minded
Claritey, Claritee, Claritea, Clariteah, Clariti, Claritie, Claryty, Clarytey, Clarytee, Clarytea, Claryteah, Claryti, Clarytie

Clasina (Latin) An illuminated woman
Clasinah, Clasyna, Clasiena, Claseina, Claseena, Claseana, Clasynah, Clasienah, Claseinah, Claseenah, Claseanah

Claudia (Latin) Feminine form of Claud; one who is lame
Clauda, Claudella, Claudelle, Claudetta, Claudette, Claudey, Claudie, Claudina, Claudine, Claudy, Clodia, Clady, Clodagh

Clava (Spanish) A sincere woman
Clavah, Clavva, Clavvah

Clelia (Latin) A glorious woman
Cloelia, Cleliah, Clelea, Cleleah, Cloeliah, Cloelea, Cloeleah

Clematis (Greek) Resembling the flowering vine
Clematia, Clematice, Clematiss, Clematys, Clematyss

Clemence (Latin) An easygoing woman
Clemense

Clementine (French) Feminine form of Clement; one who is merciful
Clem, Clemence, Clemency, Clementia, Clementina, Clementya, Clementyna, Clementyn, Clemmie, Clemmy, Clementyne

Cleodal (Latin) A glorious woman
Cleodall, Cleodale, Cleodel, Cleodell, Cleodelle

Cleopatra (Greek) A father's glory; of the royal family
Clea, Cleo, Cleona, Cleone, Cleonie, Cleora, Cleta, Cleoni, Cleopetra, Cleonie, Cleony, Cleoney, Cleonee, Cleonea, Cleoneah

Cleva (English) Feminine form of Clive; woman of the cliffs

Clever (American) One who is quick-witted and smart

Cliantha (Greek) A flower of glory
Clianthe, Cleantha, Cleanthe, Clyantha, Clyanthe

Clio (Greek) Glory; in mythology, the muse of history

Cliodhna (Irish) A dark beauty

Cliona (Greek) One who has a good memory
Clionah, Clionna, Clionnah

Clodovea (Spanish) Feminine form of Clodoveo; a renowned warrior
Clodovia, Clodovya, Clodoviya

Cloreen (American) Filled with happiness
Cloreene, Clorien, Cloriene, Clorein, Cloreine, Clorean, Cloreane, Cloryn, Cloryne, Cloreena, Cloriena, Cloreina, Cloreana, Cloryna

Cloris (Greek) A flourishing woman; in mythology, the goddess of flowers
Clores, Clorys, Cloriss, Clorisse, Cloryss, Clorysse

Clory (Spanish) One who smiles often
Clorey, Clori, Clorie, Cloree, Clorea, Cloreah

Closetta (Spanish) A secretive woman
Closett, Closet, Closete, Closeta, Closette

Clotho (Greek) In mythology, one of the three Fates

Clotilde (German) A woman famous in battle
Clotild, Clotilda

Cloud (American) A lighthearted woman
Cloude, Cloudy, Cloudey, Cloudee, Cloudea, Cloudeah, Cloudi, Cloudie

Clove (French) Resembling the spice; a nail

Clover (English) Resembling the meadow flower
Claefer

Clydette (American) Feminine form of Clyde; from the river
Clydett, Clydet, Clydete, Clydetta, Clydeta

Clymene (Greek) In mythology, the mother of Atlas and Prometheus
Clymena, Clymyne, Clymyn, Clymyna, Clymeena, Clymeina, Clymiena, Clymeana, Clymeene, Clymeine, Clymiene, Clymeane

Clytemnestra (Greek) In mythology, the wife and murderer of Agamemnon

Clytie (Greek) The lovely one; in mythology, a nymph who was changed into a sunflower
Clyti, Clytee, Clyty, Clytey, Clyte, Clytea, Clyteah

Co (American) A jovial woman
Coe

Coahoma (Native American) Resembling a panther

Coby (Hebrew) Feminine form of Jacob; the supplanter
Cobey, Cobi, Cobie, Cobee, Cobea, Cobeah

Cochava (Hebrew) Having a starlike quality
Cochavah, Cochavia, Cochavea, Cochaviah, Cochaveah

Cocheta (Italian) One who is pure
Cochetah, Cochetta, Cochettah

Cochiti (Spanish) The forgotten child
Cochitie, Cochyty, Cochitee, Cochitea, Cochiteah

Coco (Spanish) Form of Socorro, meaning "one who offers help and relief"

Cody (Irish / English) One who is helpful; a wealthy woman / acting as a cushion
Codi, Codie, Codey, Codee, Codia, Codea, Codier, Codyr, Codeah, Codiah

Coffey (American) A lovely woman
Coffy, Coffe, Coffee, Coffea, Coffeah, Coffi, Coffie

Coira (Scottish) Of the churning waters
Coirah, Coyra, Coyrah

Coiya (American) One who is coquettish

Cokey (American) An intelligent woman
Coky, Coki, Cokie, Cokee, Cokea, Cokeah

Colanda (American) Form of Yolanda, meaning "resembling the violet flower; modest"
Colande, Coland, Colana, Colain, Colaine, Colane, Colanna, Corlanda, Calanda, Calando, Calonda, Colantha, Colanthe, Culanda, Culonda, Coulanda, Colonda

Colby (English) From the coal town
Colbey, Colbi, Colbie, Colbee, Collby, Coalby, Colbea, Colbeah, Coalbee, Coalbie, Coalbi, Coalbey, Coalbea, Coalbeah

Cole (English) A swarthy woman; having coal-black hair
Col, Coal, Coale, Coli, Colie, Coly, Coley, Colee, Colea, Coleah, Coleigh

Colemand (American) An adventurer
Colmand, Colemyan, Colemyand, Colmyan, Colmyand

Colette (French) Of the victorious people
Collette, Coleta, Coletta, Colletta, Colet, Colete

Coligny (French) Woman from Cologne
Coligney, Colignie, Coligni, Colignee, Colignea, Coligneah

Colina (Scottish) Feminine form of Colin; of the victorious people
Coline, Colyna, Colyne, Colene, Colena

Colisa (English) A delightful young woman
Colisah, Colissa, Colissah, Colysa, Colysah, Colyssa, Colyssah

Colleen (Gaelic) A young peasant girl
Coleen, Colley, Collena, Collene, Collie, Colline, Colly, Collice, Collyne, Collyna

Colmcilla (Irish) Woman of the church; a dove
Colmcillah, Colmcila, Colmcylla, Colmcyla

Colola (American) A victorious woman
Colo, Cola

Coloma (Spanish) One who is calm and peaceful
Colom, Colomia, Colomiah, Colomea, Colomeah

Colorado (Spanish) From the red river; from the state of Colorado

Columba (Latin) Resembling a dove
Columbia, Columbina, Columbine, Colomba, Colombia, Colombina, Colombe, Columbe

Colwyn (Welsh) From the river
Colwynne, Colwynn, Colwin, Colwinn, Colwinne, Colwen, Colwenn, Colwenne

Comfort (English) One who strengthens or soothes others
Comforte, Comfortyne, Comfortyna, Comforteene, Comforteena, Comfortene, Comfortena, Comfortiene, Comfortiena, Comforteine, Comforteina, Comforteane, Comforteana

Comyna (Irish) A shrewd woman
Comynah, Comina, Comeena, Comena, Comeina, Comiena, Comeana

Conary (Gaelic) A wise woman
Conarey, Conarie, Conari, Conaree, Conarea, Conareah

Concepción (Spanish) Refers to the Immaculate Conception
Concepta, Concetta, Conchetta, Conshita

Conchobarre (Irish) Feminine form of Connor; a wolf-lover; one who is strong-willed
Conchobarra, Conchobara, Conchobare

Concordia (Latin) Peace and harmony; in mythology, goddess of peace
Concordiah, Concordea, Concord, Concorde, Concordeah

Condoleezza (American) An intelligent and sweet woman
Condoleeza, Condoliza, Condolizza, Condolyzza, Condolyza, Condoleesa, Condoleessa, Condolyssa, Condolysa, Condolisa, Condolissa

Coneisha (American) A giving woman
Coneishah, Coniesha, Conieshah, Conysha, Conyshah, Coneesha, Coneeshah, Coneasha, Coneashah

Cong (Chinese) A clever girl

Connecticut (Native American) From the place beside the long river; from the state of Connecticut

Conradina (German) Feminine form of Conrad; a bold counselor
Conradine, Conradyna, Conradyne, Conrada, Conradia, Conrade, Conradeena, Conradiena, Conradeina, Conradeana

Conroe (American) From the town in Texas
Conrow, Conro, Conrowe

Conroy (English) A stately woman
Conroi, Conroye

Conseja (Spanish) One who advises others

Constance (Latin) One who is steadfast; constant
Constantia, Constancia, Constanza, Constantina, Congalie, Connal, Connie, Constancy, Constanci, Constancie, Constansie, Constansy, Constanze, Constanzie

Constanza (American) One who is constant; steadfast
Constanzia, Constanzeu

Consuela (Spanish) One who provides consolation
Consuelia, Consolata, Consolacion, Chela, Conswela, Conswelia, Conswelea, Consuella, Conswella

Content (American) One who is satisfied; happy

Contessa (Italian) A titled woman; a countess
Countess, Contesse, Countessa, Countesa, Contesa

Cookie (American) One who is cute
Cooki, Cooky, Cookey, Cookee, Cookea

Cooper (English) One who makes barrels
Couper

Copeland (English) One who is good at coping
Copelan, Copelyn, Copelynn

Copper (American) A red-headed woman
Coper, Coppar, Copar

Coppola (Italian) A theatrical woman
Copola, Copolla, Coppolla, Coppo, Copla

Cora (English) A young maiden; in mythology, another name for the goddess of the underworld
Corabel, Corabella, Corabelle, Corabellita, Coraima, Coralette, Coraletta, Coralete, Coralet, Corra, Corah

Coral (English) Resembling the semiprecious sea growth; from the reef
Coralee, Coralena, Coralie, Coraline, Corallina, Coralline, Coraly, Coralyn, Coralyne, Coralia, Coralin, Coralina, Coralea, Coraleah

Corazon (Spanish) Of the heart
Corazón, Corazana, Corazone, Corazona

Corbin (Latin) Resembling a crow; as dark as a raven
Corben, Corbet, Corbett, Corbie, Corbit, Corbitt, Corby, Corbyn, Corvin, Corbi

Corday (English) One who is well-prepared
Cordaye, Cordai, Cordae

Cordelia (Latin) A good-hearted woman; a woman of honesty
Cordella, Cordelea, Cordilia, Cordilea, Cordy, Cordie, Cordi, Cordee, Cordey, Cordelle

Cordula (Latin / German) From the heart / resembling a jewel
Cordulah, Cordulla, Cordullah, Cordoola, Cordoolah, Cordoolla, Cordoollah

Corey (Irish) From the hollow; of the churning waters
Cory, Cori, Coriann, Corianne, Corie, Corri, Corrianna, Corrie, Corry, Corre, Coree, Corella, Coretta, Corilla, Corisa, Corissa, Corita, Corlene, Corrella, Correlle, Corrissa, Coryssa, Corentine, Corette, Corrianne, Corea, Coreah, Correa, Correah

Corgie (American) A humorous woman
Corgy, Corgey, Corgi, Corgee, Corgea, Corgeah

Coriander (Greek) A romantic woman;
resembling the spice
Coryander, Coriender, Coryender

Corina (Latin) A spear-wielding woman
*Corinna, Coreen, Coreene, Coren, Corena,
Corine, Correen, Correena, Corrin, Corrina,
Corrine, Corenne, Corin, Corinda, Corinn,
Corinne, Correna, Corrianne, Corrienne,
Corrinda, Corrinn, Corrinna, Corryn, Coryn,
Corynn, Corynne, Correnda, Corynna,
Coreana, Correana*

Corinthia (Greek) A woman of Corinth
*Corinthiah, Corinthe, Corinthea, Corintheah,
Corynthia, Corynthea, Corynthe*

Coris (Greek) A beautiful singer
Corys, Corris, Corrys

Corky (American) An energetic young
woman
*Corki, Corkey, Corkie, Corkee, Corkea,
Corkeah*

Corliss (English) A carefree and cheerful
woman
*Corlisse, Corless, Corley, Corly, Corli, Corlie,
Corlea, Corleah, Corlee, Corleigh*

Cormella (Italian) A fiery woman
*Cormellah, Cormela, Cormelah, Cormellia,
Cormelia, Cormellea, Cormelea, Cormy,
Cormey, Cormi, Cormie, Cormee, Cormea,
Cormeah*

Cornelia (Latin) Feminine form of
Cornelius; referring to a horn
*Cornalia, Corneelija, Cornela, Cornelija,
Cornelya, Cornella, Cornelle, Cornie*

Cornesha (American) A talkative woman
*Corneshah, Corneisha, Corneishah,
Corniesha, Cornieshah, Corneesha,
Corneeshah, Corneasha, Corneashah,
Cornysha, Corynshah*

Corona (Spanish) A crowned woman
*Coronna, Coronetta, Coronette, Carona,
Coronete, Coronet, Coroneta*

Coronis (Greek) In mythology, Apollo's
lover who was killed by Artemis
*Coronys, Coroniss, Coronisse, Coronyss,
Coronysse*

Corsen (Welsh) Resembling a reed

Cosette (French) Of the victorious people;
little pet
*Cosetta, Cozette, Cozetta, Coset, Cosete,
Cozet, Cozete, Coseta, Cozeta*

Cosima (Greek) Of the universe; a harmo-
nious woman
*Cosyma, Cosema, Coseema, Cosma, Cosimia,
Cosimea, Cozma, Cozima, Cozimia,
Coseama, Cosiema, Coseima, Cozeema,
Coziema, Cozeima, Cozeama*

Costner (American) One who is embraced
by all
Cosner, Costnar, Cosnar, Costnor, Cosnor

Cota (Spanish) A lively woman
Cotah, Cotta, Cottah

Cotcha (American) A stylish woman
Cotchah, Catcha, Catchah

Cotia (Spanish) Full of life
Cotiah, Cotea, Coteah

Cotrena (American) One who is pure;
chaste
*Cotrina, Cotriena, Cotreina, Cotryna,
Cotreena, Cotreana, Contrenah, Cotrinah,
Cotrienah, Cotreinah, Cotrynah, Cotreenah,
Cotreanah*

Cotton (American) Resembling the com-
fortable fabric
*Cotti, Cottie, Cotty, Cottey, Cottee, Cottea,
Cotteah*

Coty (French) From the riverbank
Cotey, Coti, Cotie, Cotee, Cotea, Coteah

Courtney (English) A courteous woman;
courtly
*Cordney, Cordni, Cortenay, Corteney,
Cortland, Cortnee, Cortneigh, Cortney,
Cortnie, Cortny, Courtenay, Courteneigh,
Courteney, Courtland, Courtlyn, Courtnay,
Courtnee, Courtnie, Courtny, Courtnea,
Cortnea*

Coventina (Anglo-Saxon) In mythology, the
goddess of wells and springs
*Coventinah, Coventyna, Coventeena,
Coventena, Covintina, Covinteena, Covintyna,
Covintena, Coventeana, Coventeina,
Coventiena, Covinteana, Covintiena,
Covinteina*

Covin (American) An unpredictable woman
Covan, Coven, Covyn, Covon

Coy (English) From the woods, the quiet place
Coye, Coi

Cramer (American) Filled with joy
Cramir, Cramar, Cramor, Cramur

Crecia (Latin) Form of Lucretia, meaning "a bringer of light; a successful woman"
Crete, Crecea, Creciah, Creceah

Creda (English) A woman of faith
Credah, Cryda, Creida, Creyda, Crieda, Creada, Creeda, Crydah, Creidah, Creydah, Criedah, Creadah, Creedah

Cree (Native American) A tribal name
Crei, Crey, Crea, Creigh

Creiddylad (Welsh) Daughter of the sea; in mythology, the daughter of Llyr

Creirwy (Welsh) One who is lucky

Creola (American) Daughter of American birth but European heritage
Creole, Creolla, Criole, Criola, Criolla, Cryola, Cryolla

Crescent (French) One who creates; increasing; growing
Creissant, Crescence, Crescenta, Crescentia, Cressant, Cressent, Cressentia, Cressentya

Cressida (Greek) The golden girl; in mythology, a woman of Troy
Cressa, Criseyde, Cressyda, Crissyda

Creston (American) One who is worthy
Crestan, Cresten, Crestun, Crestin, Crest, Creste, Cresti, Crestie, Cresty, Crestey, Crestee, Crestea

Cresusa (English) One who is fickle
Cresusah, Cresussa, Cresussah

Creusa (Greek) In mythology, the wife of Aeneas

Cricket (American) Resembling a chirping insect of the night
Crycket, Criket, Cryket

Crimson (American) As rich and deep as the color
Crymson, Cremson, Crimsen, Crymsen, Crimsun, Crymsun

Criselda (American) Form of Griselda, meaning "a gray-haired battlemaid; one who fights the dark battle"
Cricelda, Cricely, Crisel, Criseldis, Crisella, Criselle, Criselly, Crishelda, Crishilde, Crissel, Crizel, Crizelda, Cryselde, Cryzelde, Criselde, Crizela, Crizzel, Cryselda

Crishona (American) A beautiful woman
Crishonah, Cryshona, Cryshonah, Crishonna, Crishonnah, Cryshonna, Cryshonnah

Crisiant (Welsh) As clear as a crystal
Crisiante, Crisianta, Crysiant, Crysyant, Crysianta, Crysiante, Crysyanta, Crysyante

Crispina (Latin) Feminine form of Crispin; a curly-haired girl
Crispyna, Crispeena, Crispena, Crispeina, Crispiena, Cripeana

Cristos (Greek) A dedicated and faithful woman
Crystos, Christos, Chrystos

Cruella (American) An evil, cruel woman
Cruelle, Cruell, Cruele, Cruel, Cruela

Crystal (Greek) Resembling clear, sparkling, brilliant glass
Cristal, Christal, Christel, Chrystal, Crystall, Crystell, Crystle, Crystalyn, Crystalynn, Crystalynne, Cristabelle, Crystabelle, Cristalena, Cristalyn, Chrystalline, Cristelle

Crystilis (Spanish) One who is focused
Crystilys, Crystylys, Cristilis, Cristilys

Csilla (Hungarian) One who provides defenses
Csillah, Csila, Csilah, Csylla, Csyllah, Csyla, Csylah

Cuba (Spanish) From the island
Cubah

Cullen (Irish) An attractive lady
Cullan, Cullun, Cullie, Cully, Culli, Culley, Cullea, Culleah, Cullee

Cullodina (Scottish) From the mossy ground
Cullodena, Culodina, Culodena, Cullodyna, Culodyna

Cumale (American) One with an open heart
Cumali, Cumalie, Cumaly, Cumaley,
Cumalee, Cumaleigh, Cumahli, Cumahle,
Cumahlee, Cumahleigh, Cumahlie,
Cumahlea, Cumahleah, Cumahly, Cumahley

Cumthia (American) One with an open mind
Cumthiah, Cumthea, Cumtheah, Cumthiya,
Cumthiyah

Cunina (Latin) In mythology, the protector
of infants
Cuninah, Cunyna, Cuneena, Cuniena,
Cuneina, Cuneana

Cupid (American) A romantic woman
Cupide, Cupyd, Cupyde

Curine (American) A good-looking woman
Curina, Curyna, Curyne, Curiena, Curiene,
Cureina, Cureine, Cureena, Cureene,
Cureana, Cureane, Curyna, Curyne

Curry (American) Resembling the spice
Currey, Curri, Currie, Curree, Currea, Curreah

Cursten (American) Form of Kirsten, mean-
ing "follower of Christ"
Cirsten, Cerstin, Cirsten, Cirstie, Cirstin,
Cirsty, Cirstyn, Cirstey, Cirstee, Cirsti, Cirstea

Cushaun (American) An elegant lady
Cushawn, Cusean, Cushauna, Cushawna,
Cuseana, Cooshaun, Cooshauna, Cooshawn,
Cooshawna, Coosean, Cooseana

Custelle (Latin) A majestic lady
Custele, Custell, Custella, Custela, Custel

Cwen (English) A royal woman; queenly
Cwene, Cwenn, Cwenne, Cwyn, Cwynn,
Cwynne, Cwin, Cwinn, Cwinne

Cyan (English) Having blue-green eyes
Cyann, Cyanne, Cyana, Cyanna, Cyanea,
Cyaneah, Cyania, Cyaniah

Cybele (Latin) A goddess of fertility and
nature
Cybely, Cybeley, Cybelee, Cybeli, Cybelie,
Cybelea, Cybeleah, Cybeleigh

Cybil (Greek) Form of Sybil, meaning "a
prophetess; a seer"
Cibyla, Cybella, Cibil, Cibella, Cibilla, Cibley,
Cibylla, Cybyla, Cybilla, Cybill, Cybille

Cydell (American) A girl from the country
Cydel, Cydelle, Cydele, Cydella, Cydela

Cydney (English) Form of Sydney, meaning
"of the wide meadow"
Cydny, Cydni, Cydnie, Cydnee, Cidney,
Cidnee, Cidnie, Cidni, Cidny, Cyd, Cydnea,
Cydneah, Cidnea, Cidneah

Cylee (American) A darling daughter
Cyleigh, Cyli, Cylie, Cylea, Cyleah, Cyly, Cyley

Cylene (American) A melodious woman
Cyleen, Cylean, Cylein, Cylien, Cylyn,
Cyleene, Cyleane, Cyleine, Cyliene, Cylyne

Cyllene (American) A sweetheart
Cylleen, Cyllean, Cyllein, Cyllien, Cyllyn,
Cylleene, Cylleane, Cylleine, Cylliene, Cyllyne

Cyma (Greek) A flourishing woman
Cymah, Cymma, Cymmah

Cynara (Greek) Resembling a thistly plant
Cynarah, Cynarra, Cynaria, Cynarea,
Cynarrah, Cynariah, Cynareah

Cyneburhleah (English) From the royal
meadow
Cynburleigh, Cimburleigh, Cymberleigh,
Cinberleigh, Cinburleigh, Cynberleigh,
Cynburleigh, Cimberleigh, Cymburhleah,
Cynberleah, Cymburleah, Cymberleah,
Cymberly, Cymberley, Cymberlee, Cymberlie,
Cymberli

Cynthia (Greek) Woman of Mount Kynthos;
in mythology, another name for the moon
goddess
Cinda, Cindee, Cindi, Cindie, Cindy, Cinnie,
Cinny, Cinthia, Cintia, Cinzia, Cyn, Cynda,
Cyndee, Cyndia, Cyndie, Cyndra, Cyndy,
Cynnie, Cynthea, Cynthie, Cynthya, Cyntia,
Cytia, Cynzia, Cindey, Cindia, Cindel,
Cyndea, Cindea, Cinthea

Cyntrille (American) A gossipy woman
Cyntrill, Cyntril, Cyntrile, Cyntrilla, Cyntrila,
Cyntrell, Cyntrelle, Cyntrella, Cyntrela,
Cyntrele, Cyntrel

Cypris (Greek) From the island of Cyprus
Cyprien, Cyprienne, Cyprianne, Cipriana,
Cypriane, Ciprienne, Cyprys, Cypryss, Cypriss

Cyrah (Persian) One who is enthroned; of the sun; feminine form of Cyrus; a lady
Cyra, Cira, Cirah

Cyrene (Greek) In mythology, a maiden-huntress loved by Apollo
Cyrina, Cyrena, Cyrine, Cyreane, Cyreana, Cyreene, Cyreena

Cyriece (American) One who is artistic
Cyreece, Cyreice, Cyreace, Cyryce

Cyrilla (Greek) Feminine form of Cyril; a noble lady
Ciri, Cerelia, Cerella, Cirilla, Cyrille, Cyrillia, Ciril, Cirila, Cirilia

Cytheria (Latin) In mythology, another name for the goddess of love and beauty
Cythera, Cytherea

Czarina (Russian) An empress; a female caesar
Czarinah, Czarinna, Czaryna, Czareena, Czarena, Cyzarine, Chezarina, Czarynah, Czareenah, Czarenah, Czareana, Czareanah, Czariena, Czarienah, Czareina, Czareinah

Czigany (Hungarian) A gypsy girl; one who moves from place to place
Cziganey, Czigani, Cziganie, Cziganee, Cziganea, Cziganeah

d

Dabney (French) One who is from Aubigny
Dabnie, Dabny, Dabni, Dabnee, Dabnea, Dabneah

Dabria (Latin) A heavenly messenger; an angel
Dabriah, Dabrea, Dabrya, Dabriya, Dabreah, Dabryah, Dabriyah

Dacey (Irish) Woman from the South
Daicey, Dacee, Dacia, Dacie, Dacy, Daicee, Daicy, Daci, Daici, Dacea, Daceah

Dada (African) A curly-haired young girl
Dadah, Dadda, Daddah

Daeshawna (American) The Lord is gracious
Daeshan, Daeshaun, Daeshauna, Daeshavon, Daeshawn, Daeshawntia, Daeshon, Daeshona, Daiseana, Daiseanah, Daishaughn, Daishaughna, Daishaughnah, Daishaun, Daishauna, Daishaunah, Daishawn, Daishawna, Daishawnah, Daysean, Dayseana, Dayseanah, Dayshaughna, Dayshaughnah, Dayshaun, Dayshauna, Dayshaunah, Dayshawn, Dayshawna

Daffodil (French) Resembling the yellow flower
Daffodill, Daffodille, Dafodil, Dafodill, Dafodille, Daff, Daffodyl, Dafodyl, Dafodyll, Daffi, Daffie, Daffey, Daffee, Daffea, Daffeah

Daganya (Hebrew) Feminine form of Dagan; grain of the earth
Daganyah, Dagania, Dagana, Daganna, Daganiya, Dagian, Dagonya, Dagonia, Dagoniya, Dagona

Dagmar (Scandinavian) Born on a glorious day
Dagmara, Dagmaria, Dagmarie, Dagomor, Dagomara, Dagomar, Dagomaria, Dagmarr, Dagomarr

Dagny (Norse) Born on a bright new day
Dagney, Dagni, Dagnie, Dagnee, Dagna, Dagnia, Dagne, Dagnea, Dagneah

Dahab (Arabic) The golden child
Dhahab, Dahabe, Dahabia, Dahabea, Dahabiah, Dahabeah

Dahlia (Swedish) From the valley; resembling the flower
Dahlea, Dahl, Dahiana, Dayha, Daleia

Dai (Japanese) The great one

Daira (Greek) One who is well-informed
Daeira, Danira, Dayeera

Daisy (English) Of the day's eye; resembling a flower
Daisee, Daisey, Daisi, Daisie, Dasie, Daizy, Daysi, Deysi, Deyzi, Daizie, Daizi, Daisha, Daesgesage, Daisea, Daiseah, Daizee, Dazea, Dazeah

Dakini (Sanskrit) The sky dancer
Dakinie, Dakyny, Dukyni, Dukynie, Dukiny, Dakiney, Dakin, Dakiny, Dakinee, Dakinea, Dakineah, Dakyney, Dakynee, Dakynea, Dakyneah

Dakota (Native American) A friend to all
Dakotah, Dakotta, Dakoda, Dakodah

Dalal (Arabic) A flirtatious woman
Dalall, Dalale, Dalalle

Dale (English) From the small valley
Dayle, Dael, Daelyn, Dail, Daile, Dalena, Dalene, Dalenna, Dalina, Dalla, Dayla, Daele, Dayl

Dalia (Arabic / Hebrew) One who is gentle / resembling a slender tree branch
Daliah, Dalit, Dalila, Daliya, Daliyah, Dalya, Dalyah, Dalis, Daliyah, Dalea, Daleah

Dallas (Scottish) From the valley meadow
Dallis, Dalles, Dallin, Dallon, Dallys

Dalmace (Latin) Women from Dalmatia, a region of Italy
Dalma, Dalmassa, Dalmatia, Dalmase, Dalmatea

Dalmar (African) A versatile woman
Dalmarr, Dalmare, Dalmarre

Daly (Irish) Of the assembly
Daley, Dalee, Daleigh, Dali, Dalie, Dailey, Daily, Dawley

Damali (Arabic) A beautiful vision
Damalie, Damaly, Damaley, Damalee, Damaleigh, Damalea, Damaleah

Damani (American) Of a bright tomorrow
Damanie, Damany, Damaney, Damanee, Damanea, Damaneah

Damaris (Latin) A gentle woman
Damara, Damaress, Damariss, Damariz, Dameris, Damerys, Dameryss, Damiris, Damris, Demaras, Demaris, Demarys, Damalas, Damalis, Damalit, Damalla

Damayanti (Indian) One who subdues others; in Hinduism, the name of a princess
Damayantie, Damayanty, Damayantey, Damayantee, Damayantea, Damayanteah

Dame (English) A female knight
Daim, Daime, Daym, Dayme, Daem, Daeme

Damhnait (Irish) Fawn
Devent, Downeti, Devnet, Downett

Damia (Greek) In mythology, a goddess of nature
Damea, Damiya, Dimaia, Damiah, Dameah, Damiyah

Damian (Greek) One who tames or subdues others
Damiane, Daimen, Daimon, Daman, Damen, Dameon, Damiana, Damianna, Damianus, Damien, Damion, Damon, Damyan, Damyen, Damyon, Dayman, Daymian, Daymon, Demyan, Damina

Damisi (African) A cheerful daughter
Damysi, Damisie, Damysie, Damisee, Damysee, Damisea, Damysea, Damiseah, Damyseah, Damisy, Damysy, Damisey, Damysey

Damita (Spanish) The little princess
Damitah, Damyta, Dameeta, Damieta, Damitta, Dameita, Dameata, Damytah, Dameetah, Damietah, Damittah, Dameitah, Dameatah

Dana (English) Woman from Denmark
Daena, Daina, Danaca, Danah, Dane, Danet, Daney, Dania, Danica, Danna, Danya, Dayna, Dayne

Danae (Greek) In mythology, the mother of Perseus
Danay, Danaye, Danea, Danee, Dee, Denae, Denay, Dene, Dinae, Dinay

Dangelis (Italian) Form of Angela, meaning "a heavenly messenger; an angel"
Dangela, Deangellis, Deangelis, Diangelis

Danica (Slavic) Of the morning star
Danaca, Danika, Dannica, Dannika, Donika, Donnica, Danyca, Danyka

Danielle (Hebrew) Feminine form of Daniel; God is my judge
Daanelle, Danee, Danele, Danella, Danelle, Danelley, Danette, Daney, Dani, Dania, Danice, Danie, Daniela, Daniele, Daniella, Danijela, Danila, Danit, Danita, Danitza, Danna, Dannette, Danney, Danni, Danniella, Dannielle, Danny, Dannyce, Dany, Danya, Danyell, Danyella, Danyelle, Dhanielle, Danise, Dannah, Dannalee, Dannaleigh, Dannell, Dannee, Dannelle, Dannia, Dannon, Danuta, Danylynn

Dante (Latin) An enduring woman; everlasting
Dantae, Dantay, Dantel, Daunte, Dontae, Dontay, Donte, Dontae, Dawnte, Dauntay, Dawntay, Dauntae, Dawntae

Daphne (Greek) Of the laurel tree; in mythology, a virtuous woman transformed into a laurel tree to protect her from Apollo
Daphna, Daphney, Daphni, Daphnie, Daffi, Daffie, Daffy, Dafna, Dafne, Dafnee, Dafneigh, Dafnie, Danfy, Daphnah, Daph, Daveney, Davne, Daphnea, Daphneah, Dafnea, Dafneah

Dara (Hebrew / Gaelic) A wise woman / from the oak tree
Darah, Darda, Dareen, Daria, Darian, Darissa, Darra, Darragh, Durruh, Darya, Daracha, Daralis

Darby (English) Of the deer park
Darb, Darbee, Darbey, Darbie, Darrbey, Darrbie, Darrby, Derby, Derbie, Derbey, Derbee, Darbea, Darbeah

Darcie (English) A dark beauty
D'Arcy, Darcee, Darcel, Darcell, Darceigh, Darcelle, Darcey, Darchelle, Darci, Darcia, Darcy, Darice, Darsee, Darseigh, Darsey, Darsie, Darcelle, Daray, Dorcey, Dorcy, Dorci, Dorcie, Dorcee, Dorsey, Dorsy, Dorsi, Dorsie, Dorsee, Darcea, Darceah, Dorcea, Dorceah

Daria (Greek) Feminine form of Darius; possessing good fortune; wealthy
Dari, Darian, Dariane, Darianna, Dariele, Darielle, Darien, Darienne, Darina, Darion, Darrelle, Darrian, Darya, Dhariana, Dorian, Dariana, Darinka, Darena, Dariya

Darice (Greek) Feminine form of Darius; possessing good fortune; wealthy
Dareece, Daryce, Dareese, Daryse, Darise

Daring (American) One who takes risks; a bold woman
Daryng, Derring, Dering, Deryng

Darlene (English) Our little darling
Dareen, Darla, Darleane, Darleen, Darleena, Darlena, Darlenny, Darlina, Darline, Darlinn, Darlyn, Darlyne, Darryleen, Darrylene, Darryline, Darlita, Darelene

Darnell (English) A secretive woman
Darnelle, Darnella, Darnae, Darnetta, Darnisha, Darnel, Darnele, Darnela, Darnette, Darnete, Darneta, Darnysha

Daron (Irish / English) The great one / from a small rocky hill
Darona, Daronah, Darron

Darva (Slavic) Resembling a honeybee
Darvah

Daryl (English) One who is greatly loved
Darel, Darille, Darolyn, Darrel, Darrell, Darrelle, Darrellyn, Darrill, Darrille, Darryl, Darrylene, Darrylin, Darryline, Darryll, Darrylyn, Darrylynn, Darylene, Darylin, Daryline, Daryll, Darylyn, Darylyne, Derrill, Darelle

Daryn (Greek) Feminine form of Darin; a gift of God
Darynn, Darynne, Darinne, Daren, Darenn, Darene

Datya (Hebrew) One who believes in God
Datia, Datiah, Datyah, Dateah, Datea

Davina (Scottish) Feminine form of David; the beloved one
Daveen, Davia, Daviana, Daviane, Davianna, Davida, Davidina, Davine, Davinia, Davita, Davy, Davynn, Davinah, Davite, Davyte, Davynu, Davyta, Davonna, Davi, Daveigh, Davan, Davin, Dava

Daw (Thai) Of the stars
Dawe

Dawn (English) Born at daybreak; of the day's first light
Dawna, Dawne, Dawnelle, Dawnetta, Dawnette, Dawnielle, Dawnika, Dawnita, Dawnyelle, Dawnysia, Dowan, Duwan, Dwan

Day (American) A father's hope for tomorrow
Daye, Dai, Dae

Daya (Hebrew) Resembling a bird of prey
Dayah, Dayana, Dayanara, Dayania, Dayaniah, Dayanea, Dayaneah

Dayo (African) Our joy has arrived

Dayton (English) From the sunny town
Dayten, Daytan

Dea (Greek) Resembling a goddess

Dea Roma (Latin) A goddess of Rome

Debonnaire (French) One who is suave; nonchalant
Debonair, Debonaire, Debonnayre, Debonayre, Debonaere, Debonnaere

Deborah (Hebrew) Resembling a bee; in the Bible, a prophetess
Debbera, Debbey, Debbi, Debbie, Debbra, Debby, Debee, Debera, Deberah, Debi, Debor, Debora, Debra, Debrah, Debralee, Debreanna, Debriana, Debs, Devora, Devorah, Deb, Debb, Debbee, Dobra, Devoria, Debira, Debiria, Devorit, Devra, Devri

December (American) Winter's child; born in December
Decimber, Decymber, Decembar, Decimbar, Decymbar

Dechtere (Celtic) In mythology, a virgin mother
Dechtire, Dechtyre

Decima (Latin) The tenth-born child
Decimah, Decema, Decyma, Decia, Decemah, Decymah

Deianira (Greek) In mythology, the wife of Heracles
Deianeira, Deianiera, Deianyra, Deianeera, Deianeara

Deidamea (Greek) In mythology, the mother of Achilles' only son
Deidameia, Deidamia, Deidameah, Deidameiah, Deidamiah

Deidre (Gaelic) A brokenhearted or raging woman
Deadra, Dede, Dedra, Deedra, Deedre, Deidra, Deirdre, Deidrie, Deirdra, Derdre, Didi, Diedra, Diedre, Diedrey, Dierdre, Deardriu, Dierdra

Deiene (Spanish) Born on a religious holiday
Deiena, Deine, Deina, Deikun

Deifilia (Latin) Daughter of God
Deifiliah, Deifilea, Deifileah

Deiondre (American) From the lush valley
Deiondra, Deiondria, Deiondrea, Deiondriya

Deja (French) One of remembrance
Daejah, Daejia, Daija, Daijah, Daijaah, Daijea, Daijha, Daijhah, Dayja, Dajah, Deija, Deijah, Dejah, Dejanae, Dejanee, Dejanique, Dejanira, Deyanira

Deka (African) A pleasing woman
Decca, Decka, Dekah, Deccah, Deckah

Dekla (Latvian) In mythology, a trinity goddess
Decla, Deckla, Deklah, Decklah, Declah

Delana (German) One who is a noble protector
Dalaina, Dalainah, Dalaine, Dalanah, Dalanna, Dalannah, Dalayna, Dalaynah, Delanah, Dalinah, Dalinda, Dalinna, Delania, Delanna, Delannah, Delanya, Deleina, Deleinah, Delena, Delenya, Deleyna, Deleynah, Dellaina

Delancey (French) Named for a street in New York City
Delancie, Delancy, Delanci, Delancea, Delanceah, Delancee

Delaney (Irish / French) The dark challenger / from the elder-tree grove
Delaina, Delaine, Delainey, Delainy, Delane, Delanie, Delany, Delayna, Delayne, Delani, Delainie, Delanea, Delainea, Delaeny, Delaeni, Delaenie, Delaenee, Delaenea

Delaware (English) From the state of Delaware
Delawair, Delaweir, Delwayr, Delawayre, Delawaire, Delawaer, Delawaere

Delbine (Greek) Resembling a flower
Delbina, Delbin, Delbyne, Delbyn, Delbyna, Delbeene, Delbeena, Delbeina, Delbeine, Delbiena, Delbiene, Delbeana, Delbeane

Delia (Latin) Woman from Delos; form of Cordelia, meaning "a good-hearted woman; a woman of honesty"
Delya, Deliya, Delea, Deelia, Deelea, Deelya, Deliah, Deleah, Deliyah, Delyah

Delicia (Latin) One who gives pleasure
Delice, Delisa, Delisha, Delissa, Deliza, Delyssa, Delicea, Deliciae, Delight, Delite, Delit, Deliz, Deliciah, Deliceah

Delilah (Hebrew) A seductive woman; in the Bible, the woman who discovered the source of Samson's strength
Dalila, Delila, Delyla, Dalyla, Dalilah, Delylah, Dalylah

Della (German) Born of the nobility
Delle, Dell, Dellene, Delline, Dellah, Dela, Delah

Delling (Scandinavian) One who is sparkling and witty
Dellyng, Delleng

Delma (German) A noble protector
Delmi, Delmy, Delmira, Delmah

Delmara (English) Feminine form of Delmar; woman of the sea
Delmaria, Delmare, Delma, Delmia, Delmarra, Dellmara, Dellmarra

Delphina (Greek) Woman from Delphi; resembling a dolphin
Delphine, Delphinea, Delphinia, Delfa, Delfin, Delfine, Delfyne, Delpha, Delfina, Delphia

Delta (Greek) From the mouth of the river; the fourth letter of the Greek alphabet
Dellta, Deltah, Delltah

Delu (African) The sole daughter
Delue, Deloo

Delyth (Welsh) A pretty young woman
Delythe, Delith, Delithe

Demelza (English) From the hill's fortress
Demelzah, Demelzia, Demelziah, Demelzea, Demelzeah

Demeter (Greek) In mythology, the goddess of the harvest
Demetra, Demitra, Demitras, Dimetria, Demetre, Demetria, Dimitra, Dimitre, Dimitria, Dimiter, Detria, Deetra, Deitra

Demi (Greek) A petite woman; half
Demie, Demee, Demy, Demey, Demye, Demia, Demiana, Demiane, Demianne, Demianna, Demiann, Demea, Demeah

Demos (Greek) Of the common people

Denali (Indian) A superior woman
Denalie, Denaly, Denally, Denalli, Denaley, Denalee, Denallee, Denallie, Denalley, Denalea, Denallea

Dendara (Egyptian) From the town on the river
Dendera, Dendaria, Denderia, Dendarra

Denim (American) Made of a strong cloth
Denym, Denem, Denam

Denise (French) Feminine form of Denis; follower of Dionysus
Deneigh, Denese, Dennet, Dennette, Deney, Deni, Denice, Deniece, Denisa, Denissa, Denisse, Denize, Denni, Dennie, Denisse, Dennise, Denny, Denyce, Denys, Denyse, Dinnie, Dinni, Dinny, Denisha

Denver (English) From the green valley

Deoch (Celtic) In mythology, a princess of Munster

Deolinda (Portuguese) God is beautiful
Deolynda, Deolenda

Deora (American) From a small town in Colorado

Dep (Vietnamese) A beautiful lady
Depp

Derica (American) Feminine form of Derek; a gifted ruler
Dereka, Dericka, Derrica, Derika, Derecka, Derecca, Deryca, Deryka, Derycca, Derycka

Dericia (American) An athletic and active woman
Dericiah, Derisea, Dericea, Derisia, Derycia, Derysia, Dericeah, Dericiyah, Dericiya

Derinda (English) Ruler of the people
Darinda, Derynda, Darynda, Derenda, Darenda

Derine (German) Feminine form of Derek; a gifted ruler
Deryne, Derina, Deryna, Deriena, Deriene, Dereina, Dereine, Dereena, Dereene, Dereana, Dereane

Derora (Hebrew) As free as a bird
Derorah, Derorra, Derorit, Drora, Drorah, Drorit, Drorlya, Derorice

Derry (Irish) From the oak grove
Derrey, Derri, Derrie, Derree, Derrea, Derreah

Derval (Irish) One's true desire; a poet's daughter
Dervala, Dervilia, Dervalia, Dervla, Dearbhail

Dervorgilla (Irish) A servant girl
Dervorgila, Derforgal, Derforgala

Deryn (Welsh) A birdlike woman
Derran, Deren, Derhyn, Deron, Derrin, Derrine, Derron, Derrynne, Derynne

Desdemona (Greek) An ill-fated woman
Dezdemona, Desmona, Dezmona

Desiree (French) One who is desired
*Desaree, Desirae, Desarae, Desire, Desyre,
Dezirae, Deziree, Desirat, Desideria, Desirata,
Des, Desi, Dezi, Dezie, Dezy, Dezey, Dezee,
Dezea, Desirai, Dezirai*

Desma (Greek) Of the binding oath
*Desme, Dezma, Dezme, Desmiah, Desmia,
Desmea, Desmeah*

Despina (Greek) The mistress; in mythol-
ogy, the daughter of Demeter and Poseidon
*Despoina, Despinna, Despyna, Despena,
Despona, Despeina, Despiena, Despeena,
Despeana*

Dessa (Greek) Feminine form of Odysseus;
one who wanders; an angry woman
Dessah

Desta (German) Hardworking woman
Destah

✿ **Destiny** (English) Recognizing one's certain
fortune; fate
*Destanee, Destinee, Destiney, Destini,
Destinie, Destine, Destina, Destyni, Destany,
Destinea, Destanea, Destynea*

Detta (Latin) Form of Benedetta, meaning
"one who is blessed"
Dette, Dete, Deta, Dett

Deva (Hindi) A divine being
Devi, Daeva

Devamatar (Indian) Mother of the gods

Devana (Hindi) One who is in love
Devanah, Devanna, Devannah

Devany (Irish) A dark-haired beauty
*Devaney, Devanie, Devinee, Devony, Devenny,
Devani, Devanee, Devanea, Devaneah*

Devera (Latin) In mythology, goddess of
brooms
Deverah

Deverell (Welsh) Woman from the river-
bank
*Deverelle, Deverele, Deverel, Deverella,
Deverela*

Deverra (Latin) In mythology, goddess of
midwives
Deverrah

Devika (Indian) The little goddess
Devicka, Devica, Devyka, Devycka, Devyca

Devon (English) From the beautiful farm-
land; of the divine
*Devan, Deven, Devenne, Devin, Devona,
Devondra, Devonna, Devonne, Devvon,
Devyn, Devynn, Deheune, Devina, Devyna*

Devota (Latin) A faithful woman

Dextra (Latin) Feminine form of Dexter;
one who is skillful
Dex

Deyanira (Spanish) One who is capable of
great destruction
Daianira, Dayanira, Dellanira, Diyanira

Dhana (Sanskrit) A wealthy woman; prosperous
Dhanna

Dharani (Hindi) A minor goddess
*Dharanie, Darani, Daranie, Dharanee,
Daranee, Dharany, Darany, Dharaney,
Daraney, Dharanea, Daranea*

Dharma (Hindi) The universal law of order
Darma

Dhisana (Hindi) In Hinduism, goddess of
prosperity
*Dhisanna, Disana, Disanna, Dhysana,
Dhysanna*

Dhyana (Hindi) One who meditates

Diamanta (French) Woman of high value;
resembling a diamond
*Diamanda, Diamonda, Diamantina,
Diamantia, Diamantea, Diamante,
Diamond, Diamonde, Diamonique,
Diamontina*

Diane (Latin) Of the divine; in mythology,
goddess of the moon and the hunt
*Danne, Dayann, Dayanna, Dayanne, Deana,
Deane, Deandra, Deann, Deanna, Dede,
Dee, DeeDee, Deeana, Deeane, Dianna, Di,
Diahann, Diahanne, Diahna, Dian, Diandra,
Diana, Diann, Deandria, Diannah, Dianne,
Didi, Dyan, Dyana, Dyane, Dyann, Dyanna,
Dyannah, Deon, Deona, Deondra, Deonna,
Deonne, Deandrea, Deeandra, Deanda,
Deanne, Deeanna, Deeanne, Deena, Dyanne*

Dianthe (Greek) The flower of the gods
Diantha, Diandra, Diandre, Dyanthe,
Dyantha, Dyandre, Dyandra

Diata (African) Resembling a lioness
Diatah, Dyata, Diatta, Dyatah, Dyatta,
Diattah, Dyattah

Dice (American) One who likes to gamble
Dyce

Didina (French) One who is desired
Dideena, Dideina, Didiena, Dideana, Didyna

Dido (Latin) In mythology, the queen of
Carthage who committed suicide
Dydo

Didrika (German) Feminine form of
Dietrich; the ruler of the people
Diedericka, Diedricka, Diedrika, Dydrika,
Didricka

Diega (Spanish) Feminine form of Diego;
the supplanter

Dielle (Latin) One who worships God
Diele, Diell, Diella, Diela, Diel

Digna (Latin) She who is worthy
Digne, Deenya, Dinya, Dygna

Dike (Greek) In mythology, the goddess of
justice

Dilys (Welsh) A perfect woman; one who is
reliable
Dillys, Dylis, Dyllis, Dil, Dill, Dilly

Dimity (English) Resembling a sheer cotton
fabric
Dimitee, Dimitey, Dimitie, Dimitea,
Dimiteah, Dimiti

Dimona (Hebrew) Woman from the South
Dimonah, Dymona, Demona, Demonah,
Dymonah

Dinah (Hebrew) One who is judged and
vindicated; in the Bible, Jacob's only daughter
Dina, Dinora, Dinorah, Dyna, Dynah, Dena,
Denna, Dene, Deneen, Denia, Denica

Dionne (English) Of the sacred spring
Dionna, Deiondra, Deon, Deonne, Dion,
Diona, Diondra, Dione, Dionetta, Dionis,
Deona, Deondra, Deonna

Dionysia (Greek) A gift from Dionysus, god
of wine
Dionysea, Dionisa, Dionysa, Dionis, Dionysie,
Dionyza, Dionyzia

Dior (French) The golden one
D'Or, Diorr, Diorre, Dyor, Deor, Dyorre,
Deorre

Dipali (Indian) A row of lights
Deepali, Dypali, Dipalie, Deepalie, Dypalie,
Dipaly, Deepaly, Dypaly, Dipalee, Deepalee,
Dypalee, Dipalea, Deepalea, Dypalea,
Dipaleigh, Deepaleigh, Dypaleigh

Dirce (Greek) In mythology, the wife of
Lycus
Dyrce

Disa (English) Resembling an orchid

Discordia (Latin) In mythology, goddess of
strife
Dyscordia, Diskordia, Dyskordia

Diti (Hindi) In Hinduism, an earth goddess
Dyti, Ditie, Dytie, Dity, Dyty, Ditey, Dytey,
Ditee, Dytee, Ditea, Dytea

Ditza (Hebrew) One who brings joy
Ditzah, Diza, Dizah, Dytza, Dytzah, Dyza,
Dyzah

Divina (Latin) One who is godlike
Devina, Divinah, Divone, Divya, Dyvina,
Dyvyna

Divsha (Hebrew) As sweet as honey
Divshah, Dyvsha, Dyvshah

Dixie (English) Woman from the South; the
tenth-born child
Dixi, Dixy, Dixey, Dixee, Dixea, Dixeah

Docilla (Latin) One who is calm and peaceful
Docila, Docylla, Docyla

Dohtor (Anglo-Saxon) Her father's daughter

Dolores (Spanish) Woman of sorrow; refers
to the Virgin Mary
Dalores, Delora, Delores, Deloria, Deloris,
Dolorcita, Dolorcitas, Dolorita, Doloritas,
Deloras, Delora, Deloros

Domela (Latin) The lady of the house
Domella, Domele, Domelle, Domell,
Domhnulla, Domel

Domiduca (Latin) In mythology, a goddess who protects children on their way home

Domina (Latin) An elegant lady
Dominah, Domyna, Domynah

Dominique (French) Feminine form of Dominic; born on the Lord's day
Domaneke, Domanique, Domenica, Domeniga, Domenique, Dominee, Domineek, Domineke, Dominga, Domini, Dominica, Dominie, Dominika, Dominizia, Domino, Dominica, Domitia, Domorique, Dominy, Domonique

Domitiana (Latin) Feminine form of Domitian; one who has been tamed
Domitianna, Domitiane, Domitianne, Domitiann, Domitilla

Donna (Italian) A titled woman; feminine form of Donald; ruler of the world
Dahna, Dahnya, Dona, Donalie, Donella, Donelle, Donetta, Donia, Donica, Donielle, Donisha, Donita, Donnalee, Donnalyn, Donna-Marie, Donnell, Donnella, Donnelle, Donni, Donnica, Donnie, Donnisse, Donny, Donya, Donatella, Donalda, Donaldina, Donata, Doneen

Dorcas (Greek) Resembling a gazelle
Dorkas, Dorckas

Doreen (French / Gaelic) The golden one / a brooding woman
Dorene, Doreyn, Dorine, Dorreen, Doryne, Doreena, Dore, Doirean, Doireann, Doireanne, Doireana, Doireanna

Doris (Greek) A gift from God; in mythology, a daughter of Oceanus
Doree, Dori, Doria, Dorian, Dorice, Dorie, Dorisa, Dorita, Dorri, Dorrie, Dorris, Dorry, Dorrys, Dory, Dorys, Doryse, Dorianne, Dorianna, Doriana, Dorrian, Dorelia, Dorea, Doralis, Doralie, Doralice, Doralia

Dorma (Latin) One who is sleeping
Dorrma, Dorrmah, Dormah

Dorona (Hebrew) A gift from God
Doran, Dorran

Dorothy (Greek) A gift of God
Dasha, Dasya, Dodie, Dody, Doe, Doll, Dolley, Dolli, Dollie, Dolly, Doortje, Dora, Doretta, Dori, Dorika, Dorinda, Dorit, Dorita, Doritha, Dorlisa, Doro, Doronit, Dorota, Dorotea, Dorotha, Dorothea, Dorothee, Dortha, Dorothée, Dorrit, Dorthea, Dorthy, Dory, Dosha, Dosya, Dot, Dottey, Dottie, Dotty, Dorottya, Dorri, Doroata, Dorote, Doroteia, Doroteya, Diorbhall, Doanna, Dorette, Dordei, Dordie, Doda

Douce (French) One who is sweet

Dove (American) Resembling a bird of peace
Duv

Doveva (Hebrew) A graceful woman

Draupnir (Norse) In mythology, an arm ring that was a source of endless wealth
Draupnyr, Draupneer

Drea (Greek) Form of Andrea, meaning "courageous and strong / womanly"
Dria, Dreah, Driah, Driya, Driyah

Dreama (English) A beautiful dream; one who produces joyous music
Dreema, Driema, Dreima, Dryma

Drew (English) Feminine form of Andrew; brave and womanly
Dru, Drue, Droo

Drina (Spanish) Form of Alexandra, meaning "helper and defender of mankind"
Drinah, Dreena, Dreenah, Driena, Drienah, Dryna, Drynah, Dreana, Dreanah, Dreina, Dreinah

Drisana (Indian) Daughter of the sun
Dhrisana, Drisanna, Drysana, Drysanna, Dhrysana, Dhrisanna, Dhrysanna

Drury (French) One who is greatly loved
Drurey, Druri, Drurie, Druree, Drurea, Drureah

Drusilla (Latin) Feminine form of Drusus; a mighty woman
Drewsila, Dru, Drucella, Drucie, Drucilla, Drucy, Drue, Druesilla, Druscilla, Drusella, Drisy, Drisi, Drusi, Drusie, Drusila

Dryope (Greek) In mythology, a woman who was turned into a black poplar tree
Driope

Duaa (Arabic) One who prays to God

Duana (Irish) Feminine form of Dwayne; little, dark one
Duane, Duayna, Duna, Dwana, Dwayna, Dubhain, Dubheasa

Duena (Spanish) One who acts as a chaperone

Duha (Arabic) Born in the morning
Dhuha, Duhr

Dulce (Latin) A very sweet woman
Delcina, Delcine, Delsine, Dulcee, Dulcea, Dulci, Dulcia, Dulciana, Dulcie, Dulcibella, Dulcibelle, Dulcina, Dulcine, Dulcinea, Dulcy, Dulsea, Dulsia, Dulsiana, Dulsibell, Dulsibelle, Dulsine, Dulsee, Dulcinia, Duka, Dukie, Dukine, Dukinea, Dulda, Duldne, Duldnia

Dumia (Hebrew) One who is silent
Dumiya, Dumiah, Dumiyah, Dumea, Dumeah

Durdana (Arabic) Resembling a pearl
Durandana, Durindana, Durdaana, Durriya

Durga (Hindi) One who is unattainable; in Hinduism, a wife of Shiva
Doorga

Duscha (Russian) One who brings happiness
Duschenka, Duschinka, Dusica, Dusa

Dusty (English) Feminine form of Dustin; a brave fighter; from a dusty place
Dustey, Dustee, Dusti, Dustie, Dustye, Dustine, Dustina, Dustyne, Dustyna, Dustyn, Dustan, Dustea, Dusteah

Duvessa (Irish) A dark beauty
Duvessah, Duvesa, Dubheasa, Duvesah

Duyen (Vietnamese) A charming and graceful woman

Dyani (Native American) Having the grace of a deer
Dyanie, Dyany, Dyaney, Dyanee, Dyanye, Dyanea, Dyaneah

Dylan (Welsh) Daughter of the waves
Dylana, Dylane, Dyllan, Dyllana, Dillon, Dillan, Dillen, Dillian

Dympna (Irish) Form of Damhnait, meaning "fawn"; the patron saint of the insane
Dymphna, Dimpna, Dimphna

Dyre (Scandinavian) One who is dear to the heart

Dysis (Greek) Born at sunset
Dysiss, Dysisse, Dysys, Dysyss, Dysysse

Eacnung (Anglo-Saxon) A fertile woman; one who bears children

Eada (English) One who is prosperous; wealthy
Eadah, Eadia, Eadea, Eadiah, Eadeah, Eadda, Eaddah

Eadaion (German) A joyous friend

Eadburga (Anglo-Saxon) From the rich fortress
Eadburgah, Edburga, Eadburgia, Eadburgea, Edburgia, Edburgea

Eadignes (Anglo-Saxon) One who is blissful
Eadignys, Eadygnys, Edignes, Edygnes, Edygnys

Eadlin (Anglo-Saxon) Born into royalty
Eadlinn, Eadlinne, Eadline, Eadlyn, Eadlynn, Eadlynne, Eadlina, Eadlyna, Eadlen, Eadlenn, Eadlenne

Eadrianne (American) One who stands out
Eadrian, Eadriann, Edriane, Edriana, Edrianna

Ealasaid (Gaelic) One who is devoted to God
Ealasayd, Ealasaida, Ealasayda

Ealga (Irish) Born into the nobility
Ealgah, Ealgia, Ealgea, Ealgiah, Ealgeah

Eara (Scottish) Woman from the East
Earah, Earra, Earrah, Earia, Earea, Earie, Eari, Earee, Eary, Earey

Earla (English) A great leader
Earlah

Earline (English) Feminine form of Earl; a noble woman; a great leader
Earlena, Earlene, Earlina, Earlyne, Earlyna, Earleene, Earleena, Earleane, Earleana, Earleine, Earleina, Earliene, Earliena

Early (American) Daughter born prematurely
Earli, Earlie, Earley, Earlee, Earleigh, Earlea, Earleah

Earna (English) Resembling an eagle
Earnah, Earnia, Earnea, Earniah, Earneah

Earric (English) A powerful young woman
Earrick, Earrik, Earrica, Earrika, Earricka

Eartha (German) Woman of the earth
Ertha, Earthe, Erthe

Easter (American) Born during the religious holiday
Eastere, Eastre, Eastir, Eastar, Eastor, Eastera, Easteria, Easterea

Easton (American) A wholesome woman
Eastan, Easten, Eastun, Eastyn

Eathelin (English) Noble woman of the waterfall
Eathelyn, Eathelinn, Eathelynn, Eathelina, Eathelyna, Ethelin, Ethelyn, Eathelen, Eathelena

Eathellreda (English) A noble young woman
Eathelreda, Eathellredia, Eathellredea, Eathelredia, Eathelredea, Ethelreda, Ethellreda

Ebba (English) Having the strength of the tide
Ebbah, Ebby, Ebbie, Ebbee, Ebbi, Ebbey, Ebbe, Ebb, Ebbea, Ebbeah

Ebban (American) A pretty woman
Ebann, Ebanne, Ebbann, Ebbanne

Ebed-melech (Hebrew) A servant in the king's house

Ebenezer (Hebrew) The stone of aid

Eber (Hebrew) One who moves beyond

Ebere (African) One who shows mercy
Eberre, Ebera, Eberia, Eberea, Eberria, Eberrea, Ebiere, Ebierre

Eberta (English) Feminine form of Ebert; wielding the shining sword
Ebertha, Ebertah, Ebyrta, Ebyrtha, Ebirta, Ebirtha

Ebony (Egyptian) A dark beauty
Eboni, Ebonee, Ebonie, Ebonique, Eboney, Ebonea, Eboneah

Ebrel (Cornish) Born during the month of April
Ebrell, Ebrele, Ebrelle, Ebriel, Ebriell, Ebriele, Ebrielle

Ebrill (Welsh) Born in April
Ebrille, Ebril, Evril, Evrill, Evrille

Ebronah (Hebrew) One who secures passage
Ebrona, Ebronna, Ebronnah, Ebronia, Ebronea, Ebroniah, Ebroneah

Ecaterina (Greek) Form of Catherine, meaning "one who is pure; virginal"
Ecaterinah, Ecateryna, Ecatereena, Ekaterina, Ekateryna, Ekatereena, Ecterine, Ecterina, Ecteryne, Ecteryna

Echidna (Greek) In mythology, a monster with the head of a nymph and the body of a serpent
Echidnia, Echidnea, Ekidna, Eckidna, Ekidnea, Eckidnea

Echo (Greek) Sound returned; in mythology, a nymph who pined away to nothing, leaving only the sound of her voice
Ekko, Ekho, Eko, Ecco, Ekow, Ecko

Ecstasy (American) Filled with extreme happiness
Ekstasy, Ecstacey, Ekstacey, Ecstacee, Ecstacea, Ekstacea, Ecstaci, Ekstaci, Ecstacie, Ekstacie

Edalene (Gaelic) A queenly woman; one who is noble
Edaleen, Edaleene, Edalena, Edaleena, Edalyne, Edalyna, Edaline, Edalina, Ediline, Edilyne, Edilina, Edilyna, Edaleana, Edaleane

Edana (Irish) Feminine form of Aidan; one who is fiery; little fire
Edanah, Edanna, Ena, Ethna, Eithna, Etney, Eideann, Eidana, Eidanna, Eithne, Edaena, Edayna

Edda (German) Form of Hedwig, meaning "suffering strife during war"
Eddah, Edwige, Edwig, Edwiga

Edeen (Scottish) Woman from Edinburgh
Edeene, Edeena, Edeenia, Edeenea, Edine, Edina, Edean, Edeana, Edyne, Edyna

Edel (German) A clever woman
Edell, Edele, Edelle

Eden (Hebrew) Place of pleasure; in the Bible, the first home of Adam and Eve
Edenia, Edan, Edin, Edon

Edith (English) The spoils of war; one who is joyous; a treasure
Edythe, Edytha, Eda, Edee, Edie, Edita, Edelina, Eadgyth, Ede, Edeline, Edelyne, Edelyna, Edit, Editta, Edyt, Edytta, Edyta, Edyte, Edyth, Eydie

Edjo (Egyptian) In mythology, another name for Wadjet, a snake goddess

Edlyn (English) A woman of the nobility
Edlynn, Edlynne, Edlyne, Edlin, Edlinn, Edlen, Edlenne, Edla

Edmunda (English) Feminine form of Edmund; a wealthy protector
Edmonda, Eadmunda, Eadmonda, Edmundia, Edmundea, Edmundiya, Edmanda, Eadmanda, Edmee, Edmi, Edmie, Edmy, Edmey

Edna (Hebrew) One who brings pleasure; a delight
Ednah, Edena, Edenah

Edolia (Teutonic) A woman of good humor
Edoliah, Edolea, Edoleah, Edoli, Edolie, Edoly, Edoley, Edolee, Edoleigh

Edra (English) A powerful and mighty woman
Edrah, Edrea, Edreah, Edria, Edriah

Edreanna (American) A joyful woman
Edreana, Edreann, Edreanne, Edreane, Edrean

Edrei (Hebrew) A woman of great strength

Edrina (American) An old-fashioned woman
Edrinah, Edryna, Edrynah, Edreena, Edreenah

Edris (Anglo-Saxon) A prosperous ruler
Edriss, Edrisse, Edrys, Edryss, Edrysse

Edsel (American) One who is plain
Edsell, Edsele, Esdelle, Edzel, Edzell, Edzelle, Edzele

Edshone (American) A wealthy woman
Edshun

Eduarda (Portugese) Feminine form of Edward; a wealthy protector
Eduardia, Eduardea, Edwarda, Edwardia, Edwardea, Eduardina, Eduardyna, Edwardina, Edwardyna

Edurne (Basque) Feminine form of Edur; woman of the snow
Edurna, Edurnia, Edurnea, Edurniya

Edusa (Latin) In mythology, the protector goddess of children
Edussa, Educa, Edulica, Edulisa

Edwina (English) Feminine form of Edwin; one who is wealthy in friendship
Edwinna, Edwyna, Edwynna, Eadwina, Eadwyna, Edwena, Edwenna, Eddie, Eddy, Eddey, Eddee, Eddea, Eddi

Eferhild (English) A warrior who is as strong as a bear
Eferhilde, Eferhilda

Effemy (Greek) A talented songstress
Effemey, Effemi, Effemie, Effemee, Effemea

Efia (African) Born on a Friday
Efiah, Efea, Efeah, Effia, Effea

Efrat (Hebrew) My God is bountiful
Efrata, Efratia, Efratea

Efterpi (Greek) A maiden with a pretty face
Efterpie, Efterpy, Efterpey, Efterpee, Efterpea, Efterpeah

Egan (American) A wholesome woman
Egann, Egen, Egun, Egon

Egberta (English) Feminine form of Egbert; wielding the shining sword
Egbertha, Egbertina, Egbertyna, Egberteena, Egbertyne, Egberteene, Egbertine

Egeria (Latin) A wise counselor; in mythology, a water nymph
Egeriah, Egerea, Egereah, Egeriya, Egeriyah

Eglah (Hebrew) Resembling a heifer
Egla, Eglon, Eglona, Eglia, Egliah, Eglea, Egleah

Eglaim (Hebrew) Of the two ponds
Eglaima, Eglaimia, Eglaimea, Eglayma, Eglaymia, Eglaymea, Eglaem, Eglaema, Eglaemia, Eglaemea

Eglantine (English) Resembling the sweet-brier flower
Eglantyne, Eglanteene, Eglantina, Eglantyna, Eglanteena, Eglanteane, Eglanteana, Eglantiene, Eglantiena, Eglanteina, Eglanteine

Eguskine (Basque) Of the sunshine
Eguskyne, Eguskeene, Eguskina, Eguskyna, Eguskeena, Eguskeane, Eguskeana, Eguskiene, Eguskiena, Eguskeine, Eguskeina

Egypt (Hebrew) From the land of pyramids and the Nile
Egipt

Egzanth (American) A yellow-haired woman
Egzanthe, Egzantha, Egzanthia, Egzanthea, Egzanthiya, Egzanthya

Eibhlhin (Gaelic) Form of Evelyn, meaning "a birdlike woman"
Eibhlin, Eihhlin

Eidothea (Greek) In mythology, a sea nymph
Eidotheah, Eidothia, Eidothiah

Eileen (Gaelic) Form of Evelyn, meaning "a birdlike woman"
Eila, Eileene, Eilena, Eilene, Eilin, Eilleen, Eily, Eilean, Eileane, Eileine, Eilein, Eilien, Eiliene, Eilyn, Eilyne

Eileithyia (Greek) In mythology, goddess of childbirth
Eileithyea, Eilithia, Eileithia, Eileithiya

Eiluned (Welsh) Feminine form of Eluned; an idol worshipper
Elined, Eiluneda, Elineda, Eluned, Eluneda

Eilwen (Welsh) One with a fair brow
Eilwenne, Eilwin, Eilwinne, Eilwyn, Eilwynne

Eirene (Greek) Form of Irene, meaning "a peaceful woman"
Eireen, Eireene, Eiren, Eir, Eireine, Eirein, Eirien, Eiriene, Eirean, Eireane, Eiryn, Eiryne

Eires (Greek) A peaceful woman
Eiress, Eiris, Eiriss, Eirys, Eiryss

Eirian (Welsh) One who is bright and beautiful
Eiriann, Eiriane, Eiriana, Eirianne, Eirianna

Eirny (Scandinavian) Born of new healing
Eirney, Eirni, Eirnie, Eirnee, Eirnea, Eirneah

Ekanta (Indian) A devoted woman
Ekantah, Eckanta, Ecanta, Eckantah, Ecantah

Ekron (Hebrew) One who is firmly rooted
Eckron, Ecron

Elain (Welsh) Resembling a fawn
Elayn, Elaen

Elaine (French) Form of Helen, meaning "the shining light"
Ellaine, Ellayne, Elaina, Elayna, Elayne, Elaene, Elaena, Ellaina

Elama (Hebrew) Feminine form of Elam; a secretive woman
Elamah, Elamma, Elamia, Elamea, Elamiah, Elameah

Elana (Hebrew) From the oak tree
Elanna, Elanah, Elanie, Elani, Elany, Elaney, Elanee, Elan, Elanea, Elaneah

Elata (Latin) A high-spirited woman
Elatah, Elatta, Elattah, Elatia, Elatea, Elatiah, Elateah

Elath (Hebrew) From the grove of trees
Elathe, Elatha, Elathia, Elathea

Elberta (English) Form of Alberta, meaning "noble and bright"
Elburta, Elbyrta, Elbirta, Elbertina, Elbertine, Elbrette, Elberte, Elberteen, Elbertyna, Elbertyne

Elda (Italian) Form of Hilda, meaning "a battlemaiden; a protector"
Elde, Eldi, Eldie, Eldee, Eldy, Eldey, Eldea, Eldeah

Eldora (Greek) A gift of the sun
Eleadora, Eldorah, Eldorra, Eldoria, Eldorea

Eldoris (Greek) Woman of the sea
Eldorise, Eldoriss, Eldorisse, Eldorys, Eldoryss, Eldorysse

Eldreda (English) Feminine form of Eldred; one who provides wise counsel
Eldredah, Eldrida, Eldridah, Eldryda, Eldrydah, Eldride, Eldrede, Eldreada, Eldreadah

Eleacie (American) One who is forthright
Eleaci, Eleacy, Eleacey, Eleacee, Eleacea

Eleanor (Greek) Form of Helen, meaning "the shining light"
Eleanora, Eleni, Eleonora, Eleonore, Elinor, Elnora, Eleanore, Elinora, Elenora, Elenore, Eilidh, Eilinora, Eilinore, Eilionoir, Eilionoira, Elie, Elienor, Elienora, Eleinor, Eleinora, Elinore, Ellinor, Ellnora, Ellinora, Ellenor, Ellenora, Ellie, Elly, Elli, Ellee

Eleftheria (Greek) An independent woman; one who is free
Eleftheriah, Eleftherea, Elefthereah, Elefteria, Elefteriah, Eleflerea, Eleflereah, Elepheteria, Elephteria

Elegy (American) A lasting beauty
Elegey, Elegi, Elegie, Elegee, Elegea

Elek (American) Resembling a star
Elec, Eleck

Elektra (Greek) Of the fiery sun; in mythology, the daughter of Agamemnon
Electra, Elecktra

Elena (Spanish) Form of Helen, meaning "the shining light"
Elenah, Eleena, Eleenah, Elyna, Elynah, Elina, Elinah, Eleni, Elenie, Elene, Eleene, Elenitsa, Eleyn, Elenea, Eleneah

Eleora (Hebrew) God is my light
Eleorah, Eleoria, Eleorea, Eliora, Elioria, Eliorea, Elora, Eloria, Elorea

Eleri (Welsh) Having smooth skin
Elerie, Elery, Elerey, Eleree, Elerea

Elethea (English) One who heals others
Eletheah, Elethia, Elethiah, Elethiya, Elethiyah, Eletheya, Eletheyah, Elthia, Elthea

Elettra (Latin) A shining woman
Elettrah, Eletra, Eletrah

Elexis (English) Form of Alexis, meaning "helper and defender of mankind"
Elexi, Elexia, Elexina, Elexine, Elexus, Elexys, Elix, Elexa, Elexea, Elexeah, Elexie, Elexy, Elexey, Elexee

Elfin (American) A small girl; resembling an elf
Elfyn, Elfan, Elfun, Elfee, Elfy, Elfey, Elfea, Elfie, Elfi, Elfe

Elfrida (Greek) A peaceful ruler; a good advisor
Elfridah, Elfreda, Elfredah, Elfryda, Elfrydah, Elfrieda, Elfriedah, Elfreida, Elfreidah, Elfreada, Elfreadah

Elga (Anglo-Saxon) Wielding an elf's spear
Elgan, Elgana, Elgania, Elganea

Eliana (Hebrew) The Lord answers our prayers
Eleana, Eli, Elia, Eliane, Elianna, Elianne, Eliann, Elyana, Elyanna, Elyann, Elyan, Elyanne, Elyane

Elica (German) One who is noble
Elicah, Elicka, Elika, Elyca, Elycka, Elyka, Elsha, Elsje

Elida (English) Resembling a winged creature
Elidah, Elyda, Eleeda, Eleda, Elieda, Eleida, Eleada

Elidad (Hebrew) Loved by God
Elidada, Elidade, Elydad, Elydada, Elydade

Elika (Hebrew) God will judge
Elikah, Elyka, Elicka, Elycka, Elica, Elyca

Eliphal (Hebrew) Delivered by God
Eliphala, Eliphall, Eliphalla, Eliphelet, Elipheleta

Elisa (English) Form of Elizabeth, meaning "my God is bountiful"
Elicia, Elisamarie, Elise, Elisha, Elishia, Elissa, Elisia, Elisse, Elysa, Elyse, Elysha, Elysia, Elyssa, Elysse

Elishaphat (Hebrew) God has judged
Elishafat, Elyshaphat, Elyshafat

Elisheba (Hebrew) God's promise; in the Bible, the wife of Aaron
Elishebah, Elishyba, Elisheeba, Elysheba, Elysheeba, Elyshyba

Eliska (Slavic) An honest woman; one who is truthful
Elishka, Elyska, Elyshka

Elita (Latin) The chosen one
Elitah, Elyta, Elytah, Eleta, Eletah, Elitia, Elitea, Electa, Elekta

Elite (Latin) A superior woman

❂
❂ **Elizabeth** (Hebrew) My God is bountiful
Elisabet, Elisabeth, Elisabetta, Elissa, Eliza, Elizabel, Elizabet, Elsa, Elspeth, Elyza, Elsbeth, Else, Elsie, Elsy, Elza, Elizabetta, Elizaveta, Elizavet, Elisamarie, Elisavet, Elisaveta, Eilis, Elisheva, Elishia, Ellisif, Els, Elzbieta, Erzebet, Erzsebet, Elzira, Erihapeti, Erssike, Erzsi, Erzsok

Elke (German) A noble and kind woman
Elka, Elkie, Elki, Elkee, Elkey, Elkea, Elkeah

❂
❂ **Ella** (German) From a foreign land
Elle, Ellee, Ellesse, Elli, Ellia, Ellie, Elly, Ela, Ellea, Elleah

Ellan (American) A coy woman
Ellane, Ellann

Ellema (African) A dairy farmer
Ellemah, Elema, Elemma, Ellemma, Elemah

Ellen (English) Form of Helen, meaning "the shining light"
Elin, Elleen, Ellena, Ellene, Ellyn, Elynn, Elen, Ellin

Ellender (American) One who is decisive
Elender, Ellandar, Elandar

Ellenweorc (Anglo-Saxon) A woman known for her courage

Ellery (English) Form of Hilary, meaning "a cheerful woman; bringer of joy"
Ellerey, Elleri, Ellerie, Elleree, Ellerea, Ellereah

Elletra (Greek) A shining woman
Elletrah, Eletra, Eletrah

Ellette (English) Resembling a little elf
Ellett, Ellete, Elette, Elete, Elletta, Elleta, Eleta, Ellet, Elet

Ellora (Indian) From the cave temples

Ellyanne (American) A shining and gracious woman
Ellianne, Ellyanna, Ellianna, Ellyann, Elliann, Ellyan, Ellian

Ellyce (English) Feminine form of Elijah; the Lord is my God
Ellecia, Ellice, Ellisha, Ellison, Elyce, Ellesse, Ellis

Elma (German) Having God's protection
Elmah

Elmas (Armenian) Resembling a diamond
Elmaz, Elmes, Elmis, Elmez, Elmiz

Elmina (Teutonic) One who is widely known
Elminah, Elmeena, Elmeenah, Elmyna, Elmynah, Elmine, Elmyne, Elmeene, Elmeina, Elmeinah, Elmiena, Elmienah, Elmeana, Elmeanah

Elmira (English) Form of Almira, meaning "a princess; daughter born to royalty"
Elmirah, Elmyra, Elmeera, Elmiera, Elmeira, Elmeara, Elmyrah, Elmeerah, Elmierah, Elmeirah, Elmearah

Elodia (Spanish) A wealthy foreigner
Elodiah, Elodea, Elodeah, Elodie, Elodi, Elodee, Elody, Elodey

Eloina (Latin) One who is trustworthy
Eloinia, Eloinea, Eloine, Eloyna, Eloyne, Eloynea

Eloisa (Latin) Form of Louise, meaning "a famous warrior"
Eloise, Eloiza, Eloisee, Eloize, Eloizee

Elon (African) Loved by God
Elona, Elonna, Elonia, Elonea, Eloniah, Eloneah

Elpida (Greek) Feminine form of Elpidius; filled with hope
Elpidah, Elpyda, Elpeeda, Elpieda, Elpeida, Elpeada, Espe, Elpydah, Elpeedah, Elpiedah, Elpeidah, Elpeadah

Elpidia (Spanish) A shining woman
Elpidiah, Elpidea, Elpideah, Elpie, Elpee, Elpea, Elpi, Elpy, Elpey, Elpidiya, Elpidiyah

Elrica (German) A great ruler
Elricah, Elrika, Elrikah, Elryca, Elrycah, Elryka, Elrykah, Elrick, Elryck

Elswyth (Anglo-Saxon) Of the willow tree
Elswith, Elswythe, Elswithe

Eltekeh (Hebrew) A God-fearing woman
Elteke, Elteckeh, Eltecke

Elton (American) A spontaneous woman
Elten, Eltan, Eltin, Eltyn, Eltun

Elu (Native American) A woman full of grace
Elue, Eloo

Elvia (Irish) A friend of the elves
Elva, Elvie, Elvina, Elvinia, Elviah, Elvea, Elveah, Elvyna, Elvyne, Elvin, Elveen, Elvine, Elfie, Elfi, Elvena, Elvene, Elvan, Elivina, Elwina, Elweena, Elwnya, Elwin, Elwinne, Elwyn, Elwynne

Elvira (Latin) A truthful woman; one who can be trusted
Elvera, Elvita, Elvyra, Elvirah, Elvyrah, Elwira

Elysia (Latin) One who is blissful; in mythology, refers to the land of the dead
Elysiah, Elysea, Elyseah

Ema (Polynesian / German) One who is greatly loved / a serious woman

Ember (English) A low-burning fire
Embar, Embir, Embyr

Emberatriz (Spanish) A respected lady
Emberatrise, Emberatreece, Emberatreese, Emberatryce, Emberatryse, Emberatrice

Emberli (American) A pretty young woman
Emberlie, Emberlee, Emberleigh, Emberly, Emberley, Emberlea

Emberlynn (American) As precious as a beautiful jewel
Emberlyn, Emberlyne, Emberlynne, Emberline, Emberlin, Emberlinn, Emberlinne, Emberlen, Emberlenn, Emberlenne

Embla (Norse) From the elm tree; in mythology, the first woman

Eme (German / Hawaiian) Having great strength / one who is dearly loved

Emelle (American) A kind and caring woman
Emell, Emel, Emele, Emella, Emela

Emena (Latin) Born into a wealthy family
Emene, Emina, Emine, Emeena, Emeene

Emer (Irish) One who is swift; in mythology, the woman who possessed the six gifts of womanhood
Emyr, Emir

Emiko (Japanese) A child blessed with beauty
Emyko

⊕ **Emily** (Latin) An industrious and hardworking woman
Emilee, Emilie, Emilia, Emelia, Emileigh, Emeleigh, Emeli, Emelie, Emelee, Emiley, Emalei, Emilei, Emalee, Emalia, Emely, Emelye, Emele, Emere, Emera, Emmly, Emilea, Emileah

Emims (Hebrew) Of a terrifying people

⊕ **Emma** (German) One who is complete; a universal woman
Emmy, Emmajean, Emmalee, Emmi, Emmie, Emmaline, Emelina, Emeline, Emaline, Emmalyn, Emmeline, Em, Emiline, Emelyn, Emelin, Emlyn

Emmanuela (Hebrew) Feminine form of Emmanuel; God is with us
Emmanuella, Emmanuele, Emmanuelle, Emunah, Emanuela, Emanuele, Emanuelle, Emanuella, Eman, Emman, Emmuna, Emann

Emmaus (Hebrew) From the place of hot baths
Emmaws, Emmas

Emme (German) One who is womanly

Emmylou (American) A universal ruler
Emmilou, Emmielou, Emylou, Emilou, Emielou

Emsley (English) A gift from God
Emsly, Emsli, Emslie, Emslee, Emsleigh, Emslea, Emsleah

Emylinda (American) One who is happy and beautiful
Emmylinda, Emylynda, Emmilinda, Emmilynda, Emilinda, Emilynda

Ena (Irish) A fiery and passionate woman
Enah, Enat, Eny, Enya

Encarnacion (Spanish) Refers to the Incarnation festival

Endah (Irish) A flighty woman
Endeh, Ende, Enda

Endia (American) A magical woman
Endiah, Endea, Endeah, Endie, Endi, Endee, Endy, Endey

Endora (Hebrew) From the fountain
Endorah, Endoria, Endorea, Endor, Endore, Endoriah, Endoreah, Endorra, Endorrah

Enedina (Spanish) One who is praised
Enedinah, Enedeena, Enedeenah, Enedeana, Enedeanah, Enedyna, Enedynah

En-eglaim (Hebrew) From the fountain of calves

En-gannim (Hebrew) From the fountain of gardens

Engedi (Hebrew) From the fountain of goats
Engedie, Engedy, Engedey, Engedea, Engedeah, Engedee

Engela (German) Feminine form of Engel; a heavenly messenger; an angel
Engelia, Engelea, Engelina, Engelyna, Engeleena, Engeleana, Engella

Engelbertha (German) A luminous angel
Engelberta, Engelberthe, Engelberte, Engelbertine, Engelbertina, Engelberteena, Engelberteen, Engelbertyna, Engelbertyne

Engracia (Spanish) A graceful woman
Engraciah, Engracea, Engraceah

En-hakkore (Hebrew) From the fountain of the crier

Enid (Welsh) One who gives life
Enide, Enit, Enite, Enyd, Enyde

Ennea (Greek) The ninth-born child
Enneah, Ennia, Enniah

Ennis (Irish) From the market town
Enniss, Ennisse, Ennys, Ennyss, Ennysse

Enore (English) One who is careful

Enrica (Spanish) Feminine form of Henry; ruler of the house
Enrika, Enricka, Enryca, Enryka, Enrichetta, Enrichette, Enriqua, Enriqueta, Enriquetta

Enslie (American) An emotional woman
Ensli, Ensley, Ensly, Enslee, Enslea, Ensleigh

Enye (Hebrew) Filled with grace

Enyo (Greek) In mythology, a war goddess

Eolande (Gaelic) Resembling the violet flower
Eoland, Eolanda, Eolandia, Eolandea

Eos (Greek) In mythology, goddess of the dawn
Eostre, Eosta, Eostia, Eostea, Eostria, Eostrea

Epaphras (Hebrew) A lovely and fair woman
Epaphroditus

Ephah (Hebrew) Woman of sorrow
Epha, Ephia, Ephea, Ephiah, Epheah

Ephes-dammim (Hebrew) Bound by blood

Ephesus (Hebrew) From the desired place

Ephphatha (Hebrew) An open-minded woman

Ephratah (Hebrew) One who is fruitful
Ephrata, Ephratia, Ephratea, Ephrath, Ephratha, Ephrathia, Ephrathea

Epicurean (Hebrew) Follower of Epicurus
Epicureana, Epicureane

Epifania (Spanish) Proof of our love
Epifaniah, Epifanea, Epifaneah, Epifaina, Epifainah, Epifayna, Epifaynah

Epione (Greek) In mythology, the wife of
Asclepius
Epyone

Epona (Celtic) In mythology, goddess of
horses
*Eponah, Eponna, Eponia, Eponea, Eponnah,
Eponiah, Eponeah*

Eppy (Greek) One who is lively
Eppey, Eppi, Eppie, Eppee, Eppea

Equoia (American) The great equalizer
*Equoiah, Ekoia, Ekoiah, Equowya, Equowyah,
Ekowya, Ekowyah*

Eramana (German) An honorable woman
*Eramanna, Eramanah, Eramane, Eramann,
Eramanne*

Eranthe (Greek) As delicate as a spring
flower
Erantha, Eranth, Eranthia, Eranthea

Erasema (Spanish) Filled with happiness
*Eraseme, Erasyma, Erasyme, Erasima,
Erasime*

Erasma (Greek) A friendly young woman
Erasmah, Erasmia, Erasmea

Erasta (African) A peaceful woman

Erato (Greek) In mythology, the muse of
lyric poetry

Ercilia (American) One who is frank
*Erciliah, Ercilea, Ercileah, Ercilya, Ercilyah,
Erciliya, Erciliyah*

Erelah (Hebrew) A heavenly messenger; an
angel
Erela, Erelia, Erelea, Ereliah, Ereleah

Erendira (Spanish) Daughter born into roy-
alty
*Erendirah, Erendiria, Erendirea, Erendyra,
Erendyria, Erendyrea, Erendeera, Erendiera,
Erendeira, Erendeara*

Eres (Welsh) An admirable woman

Eriantha (Greek) A sweet and kind woman
Erianthe, Erianthia, Erianthea

Erica (Scandinavian / Latin) Feminine form
of Eric; ever the ruler / resembling heather
*Erika, Ericka, Erikka, Eryka, Erike, Ericca,
Erics, Eiric, Eirica*

Eriko (Japanese) A child with a collar
Eryko

Erimentha (Greek) A devoted protector
Erimenthe, Erimenthia, Erimenthea

Erin (Gaelic) Woman from Ireland
*Erienne, Erina, Erinn, Erinna, Erinne, Eryn,
Eryna, Erynn, Erea, Erie, Errin*

Erinyes (Greek) In mythology, the Furies

Eriphyle (Greek) In mythology, the mother
of Alcmaeon
Eriphile, Erifyle, Erifile

Eris (Greek) In mythology, goddess of dis-
cord
Eriss, Erisse, Erys, Eryss, Erysse

Erith (Hebrew) Resembling a flower
Erithe, Eritha, Erithia, Erithea

Erla (Irish) A playful young woman
Erlah

Erlina (Spanish) Form of Hermelinda,
meaning "bearing a powerful shield"
*Erline, Erleena, Erleene, Erlyne, Erlyna,
Erlene, Erlena, Erleana, Erleane, Erleina,
Erleine, Erliena, Erliene*

Erlind (Hebrew) An angelic woman
Erlinde, Erlynd, Erlynde, Erlinda, Erlynda

Erma (German) One who is complete; uni-
versal
*Ermah, Ermelinda, Ermalinda, Ermelinde,
Ermalinde, Ermintrude, Ermyntrude*

Ermine (Latin) A wealthy woman
*Ermeen, Ermeena, Ermina, Ermyne, Ermyna,
Ermeane, Ermeana, Ermie, Ermee, Ermi,
Ermea, Ermy, Ermey*

Ernestina (German) Feminine form of
Ernest; one who is determined; serious
*Ernesta, Ernestine, Ernesha, Erna, Ernestyne,
Ernestyna, Ernesztina, Earnestyna,
Earnestina, Earnesteena, Emesta, Emestina,
Emestine, Emesteena, Emestyna, Emesteene,
Emestyne, Enerstina, Enerstine, Enerstyne,
Enerstyna, Enersteen, Enersteena,
Earnesteana, Ernesteana, Enersteana*

Erskina (Scottish) Feminine form of
Erskine; from the highest point
*Erskinah, Erskyna, Erskeena, Erskeana,
Erskena, Erskeina, Erskiena*

Erwina (English) Feminine form of Erwin; friend of the boar
Erwinna, Erwinah, Erwyne, Erwyna, Erwnynna, Earwina, Earwine, Earwyn, Earwyna, Earwinna, Earwynna, Erwena, Erwenna, Erwene

Erytheia (Greek) In mythology, one of the Hesperides
Erythia, Erythea, Eritheia, Erithia, Erithea

Esbelda (Spanish) A black-haired beauty
Esbellda, Ezbelda, Ezbellda, Esbilda, Ezbilda

Esdey (American) A warm and caring woman
Essdey, Esdee, Esdea, Esdy, Esdey, Esdi, Esdie, Esday, Esdai, Esdae, Esdaye

Esek (Hebrew) A quarrelsome woman
Eseka, Esekia, Esekea

Esen (Turkish) Of the wind

Eshah (African) An exuberant woman
Esha

Eshana (Indian) One who searches for the truth
Eshanah, Eshanna, Eshania, Eshanea, Eshannah, Eshaniah, Eshaneah

Eshcol (Hebrew) From the valley of grapes
Eshcole, Eshcola, Eshcoll, Eshcolle, Eshcolla

Eshe (African) Giver of life
Eshey, Eshay, Esh, Eshae, Eshai

Eshey (American) One who is full of life
Eshay, Eshaye, Eshae, Eshai, Eshe

Eshtaol (Hebrew) From the narrow pass
Eshtaole, Eshtaola

Eshtemoa (Hebrew) An obedient child
Eshtemoah, Eshtemo

Esi (African) Born on a Sunday
Esie, Esy, Esey, Esee, Esea, Eseah

Esiankiki (African) One who is pure; a maiden
Esiankikie, Esiankiky, Esiankyky, Esiankikey, Esiankykey, Esiankikee, Esiankikea, Esiankikeah

Esinam (African) God has heard
Esiname, Esynam, Esinama, Esynama, Esinamia, Esinamea

Eskama (Spanish) One who shows mercy
Eskamah, Eskamia, Eskamea, Eskame, Eskam

Esme (French) One who is esteemed
Esmai, Esmae, Esmay, Esmaye, Esmee

Esmeralda (Spanish) Resembling a prized emerald
Esmerald, Esmeralde, Ezmeralda, Ezmerald, Ezmeralde, Emerald, Esmeraude, Ezmeraude, Esmerelda, Ezmerelda, Emeralda, Emeraude, Emelda, Esma

Esne (English) Filled with happiness
Esnee, Esney, Esnea, Esni, Esnie, Esny

Esperanza (Spanish) Filled with hope
Esperanzah, Esperanzia, Esperanze, Esperanzea, Esperansa, Esperansah, Esperansia, Esperanse, Esperansea

Essence (American) A perfumed woman
Essince, Esense, Esince, Essynce, Esynce

Essien (African) A child of the people
Essienne, Esien, Esienne

Esta (Italian) Woman from the East
Estah, Easta, Estia, Estea, Eastia, Eastea

Estefana (Spanish) Feminine form of Stephen; crowned with laurel
Estefani, Estefania, Estefanie, Estefany, Estefaney, Estefanee, Estebana, Estebania, Estephanie, Estephani, Estephany, Estephaney, Estephanee, Esteva

Estella (Latin) Resembling a star
Estela, Estelle, Estelita, Estrella, Estrellita, Estee, Essie, Estralita, Estrela, Eustella

Estevina (Spanish) One who is adorned
Estevinah, Esteveena, Esteveenah, Estevyna, Estevynah, Esteveana, Esteveanah, Estevana, Estevanah

Esthelia (Spanish) A shining woman
Estheliah, Esthelea, Estheleah, Esthelya, Esthelyah, Estheliya, Estheliyah

Esther (Persian) Resembling the myrtle leaf
Ester, Eszter, Eistir, Eszti

Estherita (Spanish) A bright woman
Estherida, Estheryta, Estheryda

Estime (French) An esteemed woman

Estrid (Norse) Form of Astrid, meaning "one with divine strength"
Estread, Estreed, Estrad, Estri, Estrod, Estrud, Estryd, Estrida, Estrik, Estred

Esyllt (Welsh) Form of Isolda, meaning "a woman known for her beauty"
Eseult, Eseut, Esold, Esolda, Esolt, Esolte, Esota, Esotta, Esotte, Esoud, Esoude, Eyslk

Etain (Irish) In mythology, a sun goddess
Eteen, Eteyn, Etine, Etaina, Eteena, Eteyna, Etina, Etaine, Etayn, Etayne, Etaen, Etaene

Etana (Hebrew) A strong and dedicated woman
Etanah, Etanna, Etannah, Etania, Etanea, Ethana, Ethanah, Ethania, Ethanea, Ethanna

Etaney (Hebrew) One who is focused
Etany, Etanie, Etani, Etanee, Etanea

Etenia (Native American) One who is wealthy; prosperous
Eteniah, Etenea, Eteneah, Eteniya, Eteniyah

Eternity (American) Lasting forever
Eternitie, Eterniti, Eternitey, Eternitee, Eternyty, Eternyti, Eternytie, Eternytee, Eternytea, Eternitea

Etham (Hebrew) Of the fortress
Ethama, Ethame, Ethamia, Ethamea

Ethel (German) A noble woman
Etel, Etilka, Eth, Ethelda, Ethelde, Etheld, Ethelinde, Ethelind, Ethelinda

Etheswitha (Anglo-Saxon) Daughter born into royalty
Etheswithe, Etheswith, Etheswytha, Etheswyth, Etheswythe

Ethna (Irish) A graceful woman
Ethnah, Eithne, Ethne, Eithna, Eithnah

Ethnea (Irish) A puzzle piece
Ethneah, Ethnia, Ethniah

Etoile (French) Resembling a star

Etsuko (Japanese) A delightful child

Etta (American) Ruler of the house
Ettah, Etti, Ettie, Etty, Ettey, Ettee, Ettea, Etteah

Eudlina (Slavic) A generous woman
Eudlinah, Eudleena, Eudleenah, Eudleana, Eudleanah, Eudlyna, Eudlynah

Eudocia (Greek) One who is esteemed
Eudociah, Eudocea, Eudoceah, Eudokia, Eudokea, Eudosia, Eudosea, Eudoxia, Eudoxea

Eudora (Greek) A good gift
Eudorah, Eudoria, Eudorea, Eudoriah, Eudoreah

Eugenia (Greek) Feminine form of Eugene; a wellborn woman
Eugena, Eugenie, Eugina, Eugyna, Eugynia, Eugynie, Eugeni, Evgenia, Eugenea, Eugeny, Eugeney, Eugenee

Eulalie (Greek) Well-spoken
Eulalia, Eulia, Eula, Eulah, Eulallia, Eulalea, Eulaleah, Eulalee, Eulaleigh, Eulaly, Eulaley, Eulali

Eulanda (American) A fair woman
Eulande, Euland, Eulandia, Eulandea

Eulee (Greek) The wolf ruler; ruler of all
Euleigh, Eule, Eulie, Euli, Euly, Euley

Eunice (Greek) One who conquers
Eunise, Eunyce, Eunis, Euniss, Eunyss, Eunysse

Eunomia (Greek) In mythology, goddess of order
Eunomiah, Eunomea, Eunomeah, Eunoma, Eunomah

Euodias (Hebrew) A traveling woman
Euodia, Euodeas, Euodea

Euphemia (Greek) One who speaks well
Euphemiah, Euphemea, Euphemeah, Euphemie, Euphemi, Euphemy, Euphemey, Euphemee, Effie, Effi, Effy, Effey, Effee, Ephie, Ephi, Ephy, Ephey, Ephee, Eppie

Euphrates (Hebrew) From the great river
Euphratees, Eufrates, Eufratees

Euphrosyne (Greek) Woman of good cheer; in mythology, one of the three Graces
Euphrosyna, Euphrosine, Euphrosina, Euphroseen, Euphroseena, Euphroseane, Euphroseana

Eurayle (Greek) In mythology, a Gorgon
Euryle, Euraile, Eurale, Eurael, Euraele

Europa (Greek) In mythology, the mother of Minos

Eurybia (Greek) In mythology, a sea goddess and mother of Pallas, Perses, and Astraios
Eurybiah, Eurybea, Eurybeah, Euryba, Eurybah

Eurydice (Greek) In mythology, wife of Orpheus
Euridice, Eurydyce, Euridyce

Eurynome (Greek) In mythology, the mother of the Graces
Eurynomie, Eurynomi, Eurynomey, Eurynomee, Eurynomy, Eurynomea, Eurynomeah

Eustacia (Greek) Feminine form of Eustace; having an abundance of grapes
Eustaciah, Eustacea, Eustaceah, Eustatia, Eustatiah

Eustada (Latin) A calm and tranquil child

Euterpe (Greek) In mythology, muse of lyric poetry

Euvenia (American) A hardworking woman
Eveniah, Evenea, Eveneah, Eveniya, Eveniyah

Euzebia (Polish) One who is pious
Euzebiah, Euzebea, Euzebeah, Euzeba, Euzebiya, Euzebiyah

❀ **Eva** (Hebrew) Giver of life; a lively woman
Eve, Evetta, Evette, Evia, Eviana, Evie, Evita, Eeva, Evika, Evike, Evacska, Ewa, Evacsa, Efa, Evelia, Evelien, Evea, Eveah

Eva Marie (American) A gracious giver of life
Eva Maria, Eva Mary, Eva Mariah

Evadne (Greek) In mythology, daughter of Poseidon and mother of Iamus
Evadine, Evadna, Euadne, Euadna, Euadine

Evalouise (American) A famous giver of life
Evaluise, Evalouisa, Eva Louise

Evana (English) Feminine form of Evan; God is gracious
Evanah, Evanna, Evannah, Evania, Evanea, Evaniya, Evanee, Evani, Evanie, Evany, Evaney, Evin, Evyn, Evina, Evyna, Evinna, Evynna, Eavan, Eavana, Eavani, Eavanie, Eavanee, Evaneah

Evangelina (Greek) A bringer of good news
Evangela, Evangeline, Evangelyn, Evangelia, Evangelyna, Evangelea, Evangeleena, Evangeleina, Evangeliena, Evangeleana

Evanth (Greek) Resembling a flower
Evanthe, Evantha, Evanthia, Evanthea, Evanthie, Evanthi, Evanthy, Evanthey, Evanthee

❀ **Evelyn** (German) A birdlike woman
Evaleen, Evalina, Evaline, Evalyn, Evelin, Evelina, Eveline, Evelyne, Evelynn, Evelynne, Evie, Evlynn, Ewelina

Everilde (American) A great huntress
Everild, Everilda, Everhilde, Everhild, Everhilda

Evline (French) One who loves nature
Evleen, Evleene, Evlean, Evleane, Evlene, Evlyn, Evlyne

Evonne (French) Form of Yvonne, meaning "a young archer"
Evon, Evonna, Evony, Evonie, Evoney, Evonee, Evoni, Evonea, Evoneah

Exaltacion (Spanish) One who is lifted up

Exodus (Hebrew) Of the great deliverance
Exodis, Exodas, Exodos, Exodys

Eyota (Native American) A superior woman
Eyotah, Eyotta, Eyottah

Eyote (Native American) One who is great
Eyotee, Eyoti, Eyotie, Eyotea, Eyoty, Eyotey

Ezra (Hebrew) One who is helpful
Ezrah, Ezruh

Ezza (American) A healthy woman
Ezzah, Ezzia, Ezziah, Ezzea, Ezzeah

f

Fabia (Latin) Feminine form of Fabius; one who grows beans
Fabiah, Fabeea, Fabiya, Fabea, Fabeah, Fabiana, Fabianna, Fabiann, Fabianne, Fabienne, Fabiene, Fabiola, Fabra, Fabria, Fabrea, Favianna, Faviola, Faba, Fabah

Fabrizia (Italian) A laborer
Fabriziah, Fabrizea, Fabrizeah, Fabritzia, Fabritziah, Fabritzea, Fabritzeah

Fadhiler (Arabic) A virtuous woman
Fadhyler, Fadheler, Fadheeler, Fadilah, Fadila, Fadillah, Fadyla, Fadylla, Fadheela, Fadhila, Fadhealer, Fadheiler, Fadhieler

Fadwa (Arabic) A self-sacrificing woman
Fadwah

Faghira (Arabic) Resembling the jasmine flower
Faghirah, Fagira, Fagirah, Faghyra, Fagheera, Faaghira, Fagheara, Fagheiru, Faghiera

Fahimah (Arabic) Form of Fatima, meaning "the perfect woman"
Fahima, Fahyma, Fahymah, Fahiema, Fahiemah, Faheima, Faheimah, Faheema, Faheemah, Faheama, Faheamah

Faida (Arabic) One who is bountiful
Faide, Fayda, Fayde, Faeda, Faede

Faiga (Germanic) A birdlike woman
Fayga, Faga, Faega

Faillace (French) A delicate and beautiful woman
Faillase, Faillaise, Falace, Falase, Fallase, Fallace

Faina (Anglo-Saxon) One who is joyful
Fainah, Fainia, Fayna, Faena, Fana, Faine, Faene, Fayne

Fainche (Irish) One who is free; independent

Fair (Latin) A beautiful woman; one who is light-skinned
Faire, Fayr, Fayre, Fare

Fairly (English) From the far meadow
Fairley, Fairlee, Fairleigh, Fairli, Fairlie, Faerly, Faerli, Faerlie, Faerley, Fayrly, Fayrley, Fayrleigh, Fayrlee, Fayrli, Fayrlie, Fayrlea

Fairoza (Arabic) Resembling turquoise; a precious stone
Fairozah, Faroza, Faeroza, Fairozia, Farozia, Faerozia, Fairuza, Fayroza, Fayrozia, Farozea, Fairozea, Faerozea, Fayrozea

Fairy (English) A tiny mystical being possessing magical powers
Fairie, Faerie, Faery, Fairi, Faeri, Fairee, Fairey, Faerey, Faeree, Fayry, Fayrey, Fayri, Fayrie, Fayree

⊕❶ **Faith** (English) Having a belief and trust in God
Faythe, Faithe, Faithful, Fayana, Fayanna, Fayanne, Fayane, Fayth, Fe, Fealty

Faizah (African) A victorious woman
Faiza, Fayza, Faza, Faeza, Feyza, Fathia, Fathea, Fathiya, Fauzia, Fawzia, Fawziya, Fawziyyah, Fee'iza

Fakhira (Arabic) A magnificent woman
Fakhirah, Fakhyra, Fakhyrah, Fakheera, Fakira, Fakirah, Fakeera, Fakyra, Faakhira, Fakhriyya, Fakheara, Fakeara

Fala (Native American) Resembling a crow
Falah, Falla, Fallah

Falak (Arabic) Resembling a star
Falack, Falac

Falesyia (Spanish) An exotic woman
Falesyiah, Falesiya, Falesiyah

Fall (American) Born during the autumn season
Falle

Fallon (Irish) A commanding woman
Fallyn, Faline, Falinne, Faleen, Faleene, Falynne, Falyn, Falina, Faleena, Falyna, Falon, Fallan, Falline

Falsette (American) A fanciful woman
Falsett, Falset, Falsete, Falsetta, Falseta

Fama (Latin) In mythology, the personification of fame
Famah, Famma, Fammah

Fana (African) One who provides light
Fanah, Fanna, Fannah

Fancy (English) A decorated and sparkling woman
Fancey, Fanci, Fancie, Fansy, Fansie, Fansi, Fancee, Fancea, Fansey, Fansee, Fansea

Fanetta (French) One who is crowned with laurels
Faneta, Fanette, Fanett, Fanete, Fanet

Fanfara (American) One who is excited
Fanfarah, Fanfarra, Fanfarrah

Fang (Chinese) Pleasantly fragrant

Fanta (African) Born on a beautiful day
Fantah, Fantia, Fantiah, Fantea, Fanteah

Fantasia (Latin) From the fantasy land
Fantasiah, Fantasea, Fantasiya, Fantazia, Fantazea, Fantaziya

Fantina (French) One who is playful and childlike
Fantinah, Fanteena, Fantyna, Fantine, Fanteen, Fanteene, Fantyn, Fantyne, Fanteana, Fanteina, Fantiena, Fanteane, Fanteine, Fantiene

Faoiltiama (Irish) A wolflike lady
Faoiltiarna

Faqueza (Spanish) A weakness

Fara (English) A traveling woman; a wanderer

Farah (Arabic) One who is joyful; a bringer of happiness
Farhana, Farhanna, Farhane, Farhanne, Farhayne, Farhaine, Farhayna, Farhaina, Farihah, Fariha, Fareeha, Faryha, Farieha, Farhaen, Farhaena

Farfalla (Italian) Resembling a butterfly
Farfallah, Farfala, Farfalle, Farfale, Farfailini, Farfallone, Farfalah

Farica (German) A peaceful sovereign
Faricah, Farika, Faricka, Faryca, Faryka, Farycka

Faridah (Arabic) A unique woman
Farida, Faryda, Farydah, Fareeda, Fareedah, Farideh, Fareada, Fareadah, Farieda, Fariedah, Fareida, Fareidah

Faris (American) A forgiving woman
Fariss, Farisse, Farys, Faryss, Farysse, Farris, Farrys

Farkhande (Arabic) One who is blessed and happy
Farkhand, Farkhanda, Farkhandia, Farkhandea

Farley (English) From the fern clearing
Farly, Farli, Farlie, Farlee, Farleigh, Farlea, Farleah

Farrah (English / Arabic) Fair-haired woman / one who bears the burden
Farra

Farren (English) One who is adventurous; an explorer
Faren, Farin, Faryn, Farran, Farrin, Farron, Farryn, Ferran, Ferryn, Faran, Faron, Farina, Farinna, Farena, Farana

Farrow (American) A narrow-minded woman
Farow, Farro, Faro

Farsiris (Persian) A princess; born to royalty
Farsiriss, Farsirisse, Farsirys, Farsiryss, Farsirysse, Farsyris, Farsyrys

Faryl (American) One who inspires others
Farel, Farelle, Farylle, Faril, Farille

Farzana (Arabic) Having great wisdom and intelligence
Farzanah, Farzanna, Farzann, Farzanne, Farzane, Farzaana, Farzania, Farzanea

Fascienne (Latin) A dark beauty
Fuscienne, Fasciene, Fusciene

Fashion (American) A stylish woman
Fashyun, Fashyn, Fashon, Fashi, Fashie, Fashy, Fashea, Fasheah, Fashee

Fasiha (Arabic) One who is eloquent and literary
Fasihah, Fasyha, Faseeha, Fasieha, Faseaha

Fate (Greek) One's destiny
Fayte, Faite, Faete, Faet, Fait, Fayt

Fatima (Arabic) The perfect woman; in the Koran, a daughter of Muhammad
Fatimah, Fateema, Fatyma, Fateama, Fatime, Fatyme, Fateem, Fateam, Fatuma, Fatiema, Fateima

Fatinah (Arabic) A captivating woman
Fatina, Fateena, Fateenah, Fatyna, Fatynah,
Fatin, Fatine, Faatinah, Fateana, Fateanah,
Fatiena, Fatienah, Fateina, Fateinah

Faulk (American) A respected woman
Falk, Fawlk, Faulke, Falke, Fawlke

Fauna (Greek) In mythology, a goddess of
nature and fertility
Fawna, Faun, Fawn, Faunia, Fawnia,
Faunea, Fawnea, Fawne, Faune

Faunee (Latin) One who loves nature
Fauny, Fauni, Faunie, Fauney

Fausta (Italian) A lucky lady; one who is
fortunate
Fawsta, Faustina, Faustine, Faustyna,
Faustyne, Fausteena, Fausteene, Fawstina,
Fawstine, Fawstyna, Fawstyne, Fawsteena,
Fawsteene

Fauve (French) An uninhibited and
untamed woman

Favor (English) One who grants her
approval
Fuver, Favar, Favorre

Fay (English) From the fairy kingdom; a
fairy or an elf
Faye, Fai, Faie, Fae, Fayette, Faylinn, Faylyn,
Faylynn, Faylinne, Faylynne

Fayina (Russian) An independent woman
Fayinah, Fayena, Fayeena, Fayeana, Fayiena,
Fayeina

Fayme (French) A renowned woman who is
held in high esteem
Faime, Faym, Faim, Fame

Fayola (African) One who walks with honor
Fayolah, Fayolla, Fayollah

Fearchara (Scottish) One who is dearly
loved
Fearcharah, Fearcharra, Fearcharia,
Fearcharea

Feather (American) A lighthearted woman
Fether, Fhether, Feathyr

Febe (Polish) A bright woman
Febee, Febea, Febeah, Febi, Febie, Feby, Febey

February (American) Born in the month of
February
Februari, Februarie, Februarey, Februaree,
Februarea

Feechi (African) A woman who worships
God
Feechie, Feechy, Feechey, Feechee, Fychi,
Fychie, Fychey, Fychy, Feechea, Fychee,
Fychea

Feeidha (Arabic) A generous woman

Feenat (Irish) Resembling a deer
Feynat, Finat, Fianait

Felder (English) One who is bright
Felde, Feldy, Feldea, Feldeah, Feldey, Feldee,
Feldi, Feldie

Felicia (Latin) Feminine form of Felix; one
who is lucky and successful
Falisha, Felisha, Felice, Felisa, Feliciona,
Felecia, Feleta, Felcia, Fela, Felicienne, Filicia,
Felicity, Feliciona, Felicita, Felicitas, Felicite,
Felidtas, Felisberta, Felise, Felita, Felka, Felici,
Felicie, Felicy, Felicey, Felicee, Felicea

Felina (Latin) A catlike woman
Felinah, Felyna, Feleena, Feline, Felynna,
Feliena, Feleyna, Feleana, Feleina

Fellah (Arabic) An agricultural worker
Fella, Felah, Fela, Fellahin, Fellaheen,
Fellahyn, Felahin, Felaheen, Felahyn

Femay (American) A classy lady
Femaye, Femae, Femai

Femi (African) God loves me
Femmi, Femie, Femy, Femey, Femee, Femea,
Femeah

Femise (American) One who desires love
Femeese, Femease, Femice, Femeece, Femeace,
Femmis, Femmys

Fenia (Scandinavian) A gold worker
Feniah, Fenea, Feneah, Feniya, Feniyah,
Fenya, Fenyah, Fenja, Fenjah

Fenn (American) An intelligent woman
Fen

Feo (Greek) A gift from God
Feeo

Feodora (Russian) Form of Theodora, meaning "gift of God"
Feodorah, Feodorra, Feodore, Feodore, Fedorah, Fedora, Fedoria, Fedoriya, Fedorea, Fedosia, Fedorra

Fern (English) Resembling a green shade-loving plant
Ferne, Fyrn, Fyrne, Furn, Furne

Fernanda (Spanish) Feminine form of Fernando; an adventurous woman
Fernande, Fernand

Fernilia (American) A successful woman
Ferniliah, Fernilea, Fernileah, Fernilya, Fernilyah

Fernley (English) From the meadow of ferns
Fernly, Fernleigh, Fernlea, Fernleah, Fernlee, Fernli, Fernlie

Feronia (Latin) In mythology, a fertility goddess
Feroniah, Feronea, Feroniya, Feroneah, Feroniyah

Feryal (Arabic) Possessing the beauty of light
Feryall, Feryale, Feryalle

Feven (American) One who is shy
Fevun, Fevon, Fevan, Fevin

Ffion (Irish) Having a pale face

Fia (Portuguese / Italian / Scottish) A weaver / from the flickering fire / arising from the dark of peace
Fiah, Fea, Feah, Fya, Fiya, Fyah, Fiyah

Fiamma (Italian) A fiery lady
Fiammah, Fyamma, Fyammah, Fiama, Fiamah, Fyama, Fyamah

Fianna (Irish) A warrior huntress
Fiannah, Fiana, Fianne, Fiane, Fiann, Fian

Fiby (Spanish) A bright woman
Fibey, Fibee, Fibea, Fibeah, Fibi, Fibie

Fidelia (Latin) Feminine form of Fidel; a faithful woman
Fidelina, Fidessa, Fidelma, Fidella, Fidessa, Fedella, Fidelity, Fides, Fidelitey, Fidelitee, Fideliti, Fidelitie, Fidelitea

Fielda (English) From the field
Fieldah, Felda, Feldah

Fife (American) Having dancing eyes
Fyfe, Fifer, Fify, Fifey, Fifee, Fifea, Fifi, Fifie

Fifia (African) Born on a Friday
Fifiah, Fifea, Fifeah, Fifeea, Fifeeah

Filberta (English) Feminine form of Filibert; one who is dearly loved
Filiberta, Filbertha, Filibertha, Felabeorht, Felberta, Feliberta, Felbertha, Felibertha, Fulberta, Fulbertha, Fuliberta, Fulibertha

Filia (Greek) A beloved friend
Filiah, Fillia, Filiya, Filea, Fileah

Filipa (Spanish) Feminine form of Philip; a friend of horses
Filipah, Filipina, Filipeena, Filipyna, Filippa, Fillipa, Fillippa

Filma (Greek) One who is much loved
Fylma, Filmah, Fylmah

Filomena (Italian) Form of Philomena, meaning "a friend of strength"
Filomina, Filomeena, Filomyna, Filomenia, Filominia, Filomeenia, Filomynia, Filomeana, Filomeania, Filomenea

Fina (English) Feminine form of Joseph; God will add
Finah, Feena, Fyna, Fifine, Fifna, Fifne, Fini, Feana, Fiena, Feina

Finch (English) Resembling the bird
Fench, Finche, Fenche, Fynch, Fynche

Findabair (Celtic) Having fair eyebrows; in mythology, the daughter of Medb
Findabaire, Finnabair, Finnabaire, Findabhair, Findabhaire, Findabayr, Findabayre, Findabare, Findabaer, Findabaere

Fineen (Irish) A beautiful daughter
Fineena, Fineene, Fyneen, Fyneene, Fyneena, Finean, Fineane, Fineana, Fynean, Fyneane, Fyneana

Finesse (American) One who is smooth
Finese, Finess, Fines

Finn (Irish) One who is cool
Fin, Fyn, Fynn

Finnea (Gaelic) From the stream of the wood
Finneah, Finnia, Fynnea, Finniah, Fynnia

Fiona (Gaelic) One who is fair; a white-shouldered woman
Fionna, Fione, Fionn, Finna, Fionavar, Fionnghuala, Fionnuala, Fynballa, Fionnula, Finola, Fenella, Fennella, Finella, Finelle

Firdaus (Arabic) From the garden in paradise
Firdaws, Firdoos

Fire (American) A feisty and passionate woman
Fyre, Firey, Firy, Firi, Firie, Firee, Firea

Firmina (French) Feminine form of Firmin; a firm and strong woman
Firminah, Firmeena, Firmyna, Fermina, Ferminah, Fermeena, Fermyna, Firmeana, Fermeana

Firtha (Scottish) Woman of the sea
Fertha, Fyrtha, Firthe, Fyrthe, Ferthe

Fisseha (African) A bringer of happiness
Fissehah, Fiseha, Fisehah, Fysseha, Fyseha

Fjorgyn (Norse) In mythology, goddess of the earth and mother of Thor

Flair (English) An elegant woman of natural talent
Flaire, Flare, Flayr, Flayre, Flaer, Flaere

Flame (American) A passionate and fiery woman
Flaym, Flayme, Flaime, Flaim, Flaem, Flaeme

Flamina (Latin) A pious woman
Flaminah, Flamyna, Flamynah, Flamiena, Flamienah, Flameina, Flameinah, Flameena, Flameenah, Flameana, Flameanah

Flanders (English) Woman from Belgium
Flander, Flandars, Flandar, Flande, Fland

Flann (Irish) A red-haired woman
Flan, Flanna, Flana, Flynn, Flanne

Flannery (Gaelic) From the flatlands
Flanneri, Flannerie, Flannerey, Flannaree, Flannerea, Flannereah

Flash (American) Emanating bright light
Flashe, Flasha, Flashia, Flashea

Flavia (Latin) Feminine form of Flavius; a yellow-haired woman
Flaviah, Flavea, Flaviya, Fulvia, Fulvea, Fulviya, Flaveah, Flaviyah, Fulviah, Fulveah, Fulviyah, Fulvie, Fulvi, Fulvy, Fulvey, Fulvee

Flax (Latin) Resembling the plant with blue flowers
Flaxx, Fluxe, Flaxxe, Flacks, Flaks

Fleming (English) Woman from Belgium
Flemyng, Flemming, Flemmyng

Flemmi (Italian) A pretty young woman
Flemmie, Flemmy, Flemmey, Flemmea, Flemmeah, Flemmee

Fleta (English) One who is swift
Fletah, Flete, Fleda, Flita, Flyta

Flicky (American) A vivacious young woman
Flicki, Flickie, Flickea, Flickeah, Flickee, Flycki, Flyckie, Flyckee, Flyckea, Flyckeah, Flycky, Flyckey, Flicka

Flirt (American) A playfully romantic woman
Flyrt, Flirti, Flirtie, Flirty, Flirtey, Flirtea, Flirteah, Flirtee

Flis (Polish) A well-behaved girl
Fliss, Flisse, Flys, Flyss, Flysse

Flora (Latin) Resembling a flower; in mythology, the goddess of flowers
Fleur, Flor, Flori, Floria, Floressa, Floretta, Floriana, Florida, Florinda, Florita, Florrie, Florella, Floramaria, Flordelis, Flo, Florette, Florian, Floriane, Floriann, Florianna, Florice, Florku, Florinia, Flower, Fleurette, Fiorella, Fiorenza, Firenze, Floris, Flos, Floss, Flossie, Floy, Fjola, Forenza

Flordeperla (Spanish) A blooming pearl
Flordeperla, Flordeperle, Flordepearle, Flordeperl, Flordepearl

Florence (Latin) A flourishing woman; a blooming flower
Florencia, Florentina, Florenza, Florentine, Florentyna, Florenteena, Florenteene, Florentyne, Florenteane, Florenteana

Florizel (English) A young woman in bloom
Florizell, Florizelle, Florizele, Florizel, Florizella, Florizela, Florazel, Florazell, Florazelle, Florazele, Florazel, Florazella, Florazela

Fluffy (American) A fun-loving young woman
Fluffey, Fluffi, Fluffea, Fluffeah, Fluffee, Fluffie

Fog (American) A dreamer
Fogg, Foggy, Foggey, Foggi, Foggie, Foggea, Foggeah, Foggee

Fola (African) Woman of honor
Folah, Folla, Follah

Fonda (Spanish) Grounded to the earth
Fondah, Fondiah, Fondia, Fondea, Fondeah

Fondice (American) A friendly woman
Fondyce, Fondeece, Fondeace, Fondise, Fondyse, Fondeese, Fondease

Fontana (Italian) From the fountain
Fontanah, Fontanna, Fontane, Fontann, Fontanne, Fontaine, Fontayne, Fotina, Fountain, Fontaina, Fontaene, Fontayna, Fontaena

Fontenot (French) One who is special

Forba (Scottish) A headstrong young girl
Forbah, Forbia, Forbea, Forbiya, Forbiah, Forbeah, Forbiyah

Ford (English) From the water
Forde

Forest (English) A woodland dweller
Forrest

Forever (American) Everlasting

Forsythia (Latin) Resembling the flower
Forsythiah, Forsythea, Forsytheah, Forsithia, Forsithiah, Forsithea, Forsitheah

Fortney (Latin) Having great strength
Fortny, Fortni, Fortnie, Fortnea, Fortneah, Fortnee, Fourtney, Fourtny, Fourtni, Fourtnie, Fourtnea, Fourtneah, Fourtnee

Fortuna (Latin) A fortunate woman; in mythology, the goddess of fortune and chance
Fortunah, Fortuin, Fortuyn, Fortunata, Fortunatus

Fowler (English) One who traps birds
Fowlar, Fowlir, Fowla, Fowlia, Fowlea

Frances (Latin) Feminine form of Francis; woman from France; one who is free
Francesca, Francine, Francene, Francina, Francille, Francena, Franceska, Francisca, France, Francia, Fanceen, Fanchon, Franchesca, Francheska, Franci, Francie, Francique, Franciska, Franciszka, Franca, Fran, Francoise, Frangag, Franki, Frankie, Frannie, Franni, Franny, Frantiska, Franze, Franziska, Fanchone, Fani, Fania, Fannia, Fanny, Fannie, Fanni, Fanya, Fereng, Ferika, Ferike, French, Frenchie, Frenchi, Frenchy, Frenchey, Frenchee, Frenchea

Franchelle (French) A woman from France
Franchell, Franchel, Franchele, Franchella, Franchela

Franisbel (Spanish) A beautiful woman from France
Franisbell, Franisbelle, Franisbele, Franisbela, Franisbella, Fransabel, Fransabell, Fransabelle, Fransabele, Fransabela, Fransabella

Frayda (Scandinavian) A fertile woman
Frayde, Freyda, Freyde, Fraida, Fraide, Fraeda, Fraede

Frea (Scandinavian) A noble woman

Fredella (American) Feminine form of Frederick; a peaceful ruler
Fredela, Fredelle, Fredell, Fredele, Fredel

Frederica (German) Feminine form of Frederick; a peaceful ruler
Frederika, Fredrika, Fredrica, Fredericka, Fredricka, Frederyca, Federikke, Freda, Frida, Fryda, Fredda, Fridda, Freddi, Freddie, Frieda, Freida, Frici, Frideborg, Friede, Friedegard, Friedegarde, Friederika, Friederike, Frikka, Fritzi, Fritzie

Freedom (American) An independent woman
Free

Freesia (Latin) Resembling the flower
Freesiah, Freasia, Freasiah, Freesea, Freeseah, Freasea, Freaseah, Freezia, Freazia, Freeziah, Freaziah

Freira (Spanish) A sister
Freirah, Freyira, Freyirah

Freya (Norse) A lady; in mythology, the goddess of love, beauty, and fertility
Freyah, Freyja, Freja

Freydis (Norse) Woman born into the nobility
Freydiss, Freydisse, Freydys, Fredyss, Fraidis, Fradis, Fraydis, Fraedis, Fraidys, Fradys, Fraedys

Friedelinde (German) A gentle young woman
Friedelynde, Friedelind, Friedelynd, Friedelinda, Friedelynda

Frigg (Norse) In mythology, the mother goddess of the heavens, love, and the household
Frigga, Frig, Friga, Frygg, Frygga, Fryg, Fryga

Frodina (Teutonic) A wise and beloved friend
Frodinah, Frodyna, Frodeena, Frodine, Frodyne, Frodeen, Frodeene, Frodeana, Frodeane

Fronda (Latin) Resembling a leafy branch
Fronde, Frondah, Frondia, Frondiah, Frondea, Frondeah, Frondiya, Frondiyah, Frond

Fronia (Latin) A wise woman
Froniah, Fronea, Froniya, Froneah, Froniyah

Frosty (American) One who is cool and crisp
Frostey, Frostee, Frostea, Frosteah, Frosti, Frostie

Fructuose (Latin) One who is bountiful
Fructuosa, Fructuosia, Fructuosea, Fruta, Frue, Fru

Frula (German) A hardworking woman
Frulah, Frulla, Frullah

Fruma (Hebrew) One who is religious; pious
Frumma, Frumah, Frummah

Frythe (English) One who is calm and tranquil
Fryth, Frytha, Frith, Frithe, Fritha

Fuchsia (Latin) Resembling the flower
Fusha, Fushia, Fushea, Fewsha, Fewshia, Fewshea

Fudge (American) One who is stubborn; resembling the candy
Fudgi, Fudgey, Fudgy, Fudgie, Fudgea, Fudgeah

Fuensanta (Spanish) From the sacred fountain
Fuensantah, Fuensantia, Fuensantea, Fuensantiya, Fuenta

Fukayna (Egyptian) One who is intelligent
Fukaena, Fukaina, Fukunu

Fulgencia (Latin) A glowing woman
Fulgenciah, Fulgencea, Fulgenceah

Fulla (Norse) In mythology, one of Frigga's handmaidens
Fullah, Fula, Fylla, Fyllah, Fyla

Furina (Latin) In mythology, the patroness of thieves
Furinah, Furyna, Fureena, Furrina, Furryna, Furreena, Fureana, Furreana

Fury (Greek) An enraged woman; in mythology, a winged goddess who punished wrongdoers
Furey, Furi, Furie, Furee, Furea, Fureah

Fushy (American) An animated woman
Fushey, Fushi, Fushee, Fushea, Fusheah, Fushie

Fyllis (Greek) Form of Phyllis, meaning "of the foliage"
Fylis, Fillis, Filis, Fylys, Fyllida, Fylida, Fillida, Filida, Fyllina, Fylina, Fyliss

g

Gaal (Hebrew) One who is filled with loathing
Gaale

Gaash (Hebrew) A trembling woman

Gabbatha (Hebrew) From the temple mound
Gabbathah, Gabbathe, Gabatha, Gabbathia, Gabbathea, Gabathia, Gabathea

❷ **Gabriella** (Italian / Spanish) Feminine form of Gabriel, meaning "heroine of God"
Gabriela, Gabriellia, Gabrila, Gabryela, Gabryella

❂ **Gabrielle** (Hebrew) Feminine form of
Gabriel; heroine of God
*Gabriel, Gabriele, Gabriell, Gabriellen,
Gabryel, Gabryelle, Gaby, Gabysia, Gavi,
Gavra, Gavraila, Gavriella, Gavrielle,
Gavrila, Gavrilla, Gavrina, Gabbe, Gabbi,
Gabbie, Gabi, Gabby*

Gada (Hebrew) One who is lucky; fortunate
Gadah

Gadara (Armenian) From the mountain's
peak
*Gadarah, Gadarra, Gadarine, Gadaryne,
Gadarina, Gadaryna, Gadarrah, Gadareana,
Gadariena, Gadareina*

Gaea (Greek) Of the earth; in mythology,
the mother of the Titans and the goddess of
the earth
Gaia, Gaiana, Gaiea

Gael (Gaelic) Woman from Ireland
Gaela, Gaele

Gaelle (German) From a foreign land; a
stranger

Gaetana (Italian) Woman from Gaeta
*Gaetanah, Gaetanna, Gaetannah, Gaetane,
Gaetanne*

Gafna (Hebrew) Of the vine
Gafnah, Gaphna, Gaphnah, Gefen, Gephen

Gaho (Native American) A motherly woman

Gail (Hebrew) Form of Abigail, meaning
"the source of a father's joy"
*Gahl, Gaila, Gaile, Gaill, Gal, Gale, Galia,
Gayel, Gayelle, Gayla, Gayle, Gayleen,
Gaylene, Gayline, Gayll, Gaylla, Gaylle, Gaille*

Gaira (Scottish) A petite woman
Gayra, Gara, Gairia, Gairea, Gaera

Gala (French / Scandinavian / Latin) A mer-
rymaker; of the festive party / a singer /
woman from Gaul
*Galah, Galla, Gallah, Galia, Gallia, Gayla,
Galea*

Galatea (Greek) One with a milky-white
complexion; in mythology, a statue brought
to life
Galateah, Galatée, Galathea, Galatheah

Galeed (Hebrew) The mark of friendship
*Galeeda, Galyde, Galyda, Galeid, Galeida,
Galied, Galieda, Galead, Galeada*

Galena (Greek) Feminine form of Galen;
one who is calm and peaceful
Galene, Galenah, Galenia, Galenea

Gali (Hebrew) From the fountain
*Galie, Galice, Galit, Galy, Galey, Galee,
Galeigh, Galea, Galeah*

Galiana (Arabic) The name of a Moorish
princess
*Galianah, Galianna, Galianne, Galiane,
Galian, Galyana, Galyanna, Galyann,
Galyane, Galyanne*

Galiena (German) A haughty woman; one
who is highborn
*Galliena, Galiene, Galienne, Galyena,
Galyene, Galyenne*

Galila (Hebrew) From the rolling hills
*Galilah, Gelila, Gelilah, Gelilia, Gelilya,
Glila, Glilah, Galyla, Gelyla*

Galilahi (Native American) An attractive
young woman
*Galilahie, Galilahy, Galilahey, Galilahee,
Galilahea, Galilheah*

Galilee (Hebrew) From the sacred sea
Galileigh, Galilea, Galiley, Galily, Galili, Galilie

Galina (Russian) Form of Helen, meaning
"the shining light"
*Galinah, Galyna, Galynah, Galeena,
Galeenah, Galine, Galyne, Galeene, Galeane,
Galeana*

Galya (Hebrew) God has redeemed
Galyah, Galochka, Galenka, Geulah, Geula

Gamada (African) One who is pleased,
pleasing
Gamadia, Gamadea, Gamadiya

Gambhira (Hindi) Born into the nobility;
having great dignity
*Gambhiri, Gambhirie, Gambhiria,
Gambhirea, Gambheera, Gambheira,
Gambhiera, Gambheara*

Gamila (Arabic) Form of Jamilah, meaning
"a beautiful and elegant lady"
*Gameela, Gamela, Gamelia, Gamilah,
Gameelah, Gamilia, Gamilla, Gamille,
Gamelia, Gemila, Gemilla, Gemeela, Gemyla,
Gameala, Gemeala*

Gamma (Greek) The third letter of the
Greek alphabet
Gammah

Gammadim (Hebrew) Of the daring and valorous people
Gammadym, Gammadeem, Gammadeam

Gana (Hebrew) Lady of the gardens
Ganah, Ganna, Gannah, Ganit, Ganet, Gunice, Ganya

Gandhari (Indian) In mythology, a princess who blindfolded herself when she married a blind man
Gandharie, Gandhary, Gandharey, Gandharee, Gandharea, Gandhareah

Ganieda (English) In Arthurian legend, Merlin's sister
Ganeida, Ganeyda, Ganeeda, Ganeada

Garaitz (Basque) A victorious woman
Garaytz, Garaetz, Garatz

Garan (Welsh) Resembling a stork

Garbi (Basque) One who is pure; clean
Garbie, Garby, Garbey, Garbee, Garbea, Garbeah

Garbina (Spanish) Refers to the ceremonial purification
Garbinah, Garbyna, Garbeena, Garbine, Garbyne, Garbeene, Garabina, Garabine

Gardenia (English) Resembling the sweet-smelling flower
Gardeniah, Gardenea, Gardeneah, Gardeniya, Gardynia, Gardynea, Gardena, Gardyna, Gardeena

Gardner (English) One who works the earth
Gardener, Gardie, Gardi, Gardiner, Gardea, Gardeah, Gardy, Gardey

Garima (Indian) A woman of importance
Garimah, Garyma, Gareema, Garymah, Gareemah, Gareama, Gareamah, Gariema, Gariemah, Gareima, Gareimah

Garland (French) Decorated with a wreath of flowers
Garlande, Garlanda, Garldina, Garldyna, Garldena

Garnet (English) Resembling the dark-red gem
Garnette, Granata, Grenata, Grenatta

Garron (French) One who protects others
Garan, Garen, Garin, Garion, Garon, Garran, Garren, Garrin, Geron

Gasha (Russian) One who is well-behaved
Gashah, Gashia, Gashea, Gashiah, Gasheah

Gaspara (Spanish) One who is treasured
Gasparah, Gasparra, Gasparrah

Gath-rimmon (Hebrew) Refers to the pomegranate press

Gauri (Indian) A fair-skinned woman
Gaurie, Gaury, Gaurey, Gauree, Gaura, Gaurea, Gaureah

Gavina (Latin) Feminine form of Gavin; resembling the white falcon; woman from Gabio
Gavinah, Gaveena, Gaveenah, Gavyna, Gavynah, Gavenia, Gavenea, Gaveana, Gaveanah, Gaviena, Gavienah, Gaveina, Gaveinah

Gay (French) A lighthearted and happy woman
Gaye, Gae, Gai

Gaynell (American) A bright woman full of joy
Gaynelle, Gaynel, Gaynele, Gaynellu, Gaynela

Gaynor (Welsh) One with smooth and fair skin
Gaynora, Gaenor, Gaynoria, Gaenora, Gayner

Gayora (Hebrew) From the valley of sun
Gayoria, Gayorea

Gaza (Hebrew) Having great strength
Gazah, Gazza, Gazzuh

Gazella (Latin) As graceful as a gazelle
Gazellah, Gazela, Gazelah, Gazelle, Gazele

Gazit (Hebrew) Of the cut stone
Giza, Gizah, Gisa, Gisah

Geba (Hebrew) From the hill
Gebah, Gebba, Gebbah

Gebal (Hebrew) Of the natural boundary
Gebale, Geball, Gebala, Geballa

Geder (Hebrew) From the fortress
Gederah, Gedera, Gederoth, Gederothee, Gederotha

Gefjun (Norse) In mythology, a goddess and prophetess
Gefjon, Gefyon, Gefn

Gehazi (Hebrew) From the valley of visions
Gehazie, Gehazy, Gehazey, Gehazee, Gehazea, Gehazeah

Geila (Hebrew) One who brings joy to others
Geela, Geelah, Geelan, Geilah, Geiliya, Geiliyah, Gelisa, Gellah, Gella

Gelasia (Greek) One who is always joking and laughing
Gelasiah, Gelasea, Gelaseah, Gelazia, Gelaziah, Gelazea, Gelazeah

Gelsomina (Italian) Resembling the jasmine flower
Gelsominah, Gelsomeena, Gelsomyna, Gelsomeana, Gelsey, Gelsi, Gelsy, Gelsie, Gelsee, Gelsea, Gelseah

Gemini (Latin) The twins; the third sign of the zodiac
Gemineye, Gemyni, Gemella, Gemelle, Gemina, Gemyna, Gemeena

Gemma (Latin) As precious as a jewel
Gemmalyn, Gemmalynn, Gem, Gema, Gemmaline

Gen (Japanese) Born during the spring

Gene (English) Form of Eugenia, meaning "a wellborn woman"; form of Jean, meaning "God is gracious"
Genia, Genie, Geni, Geny, Geney, Genee, Genea, Geneah

Generosa (Spanish) One who is giving, generous
Generosah, Generose, Generosia, Generosea, Genera

⦾ **Genesis** (Hebrew) Of the beginning; the first book of the Bible
Genesies, Genesiss, Genessa, Genisa, Genisia, Genisis, Gennesis, Gennesiss

Genet (African) From the garden of paradise
Genete, Geneta, Genette, Genett, Genetta

Geneva (French) Of the juniper tree
Genever, Genevia, Genevra, Genevre, Genovefa, Genoveffa, Genoveva, Ginebra, Gena, Ginevre

Genevieve (French) Of the race of women; the white wave
Genavieve, Geneve, Geneveeve, Genevie, Genivee, Genivieve, Gennie, Genny, Genovera, Genoveva, Genica, Genna, Genae, Genaya, Genowefa, Ginerva, Ginebra, Ginessa, Ginevra

Genista (Latin) Resembling the broom plant
Genistah, Geneesta, Ginista, Genysta, Ginysta, Gynysta, Geneasta, Geneista, Geniesta

Genji (Japanese) Of the ruling clan
Genji, Genjy, Genjey, Genjee, Genjea

Gennesaret (Hebrew) From the garden of riches

Gentry (English) Woman with a high social standing
Gentri, Gentrey, Gentrie, Gentree, Gentrea, Gentreah

Georgia (Greek) From the state of Georgia; feminine form of George; one who works the earth; a farmer
Georgeann, Georgeanne, Georgina, Georgena, Georgene, Georgetta, Georgette, Georgiana, Georgianna, Georgianne, Georgie, Georgienne, Georginah, Georgine, Georgyann, Georgyanne, Georgyana, Giorgia, Giorgina, Giorgyna, Georgitte, Georgeina, Georgejean, Georjette, Gigi, Geegee

Geraldine (German) Feminine form of Gerald; one who rules with the spear
Geralda, Geraldeen, Geraldene, Geraldina, Geralyn, Geralynn, Geralynne, Gerdene, Gerdine, Geri, Gerianna, Gerianne, Gerilynn, Gerri, Gerrilyn, Gerroldine, Gerry, Giralda, Gerica, Gericka, Gerika, Girelda, Geraldeane, Geraldeana

Geranium (Latin) Resembling the flower; a crane
Geranyum, Geranum

Gerardine (English) Feminine form of Gerard; one who is mighty with a spear
Gerarda, Gerardina, Gerardyne, Gererdina, Gerardyna, Gerrardene, Gerhardina, Gerhardine, Gerhardyna, Gerhardyne, Gerwalt, Gerwalta, Gerardeane, Gerardeana

Gerd (Scandinavian) One who is guarded; protected
Gerde, Gerda, Gerdie, Gerdi, Gerdy, Gerdey, Gerdee, Garda, Geerda, Gjerta, Gerdea, Gerdeah

Gerizim (Hebrew) From the mountains
Gerizima, Gerizime, Gerizimia, Gerizimea, Gerizym, Gerizyme, Gerizyma, Gerizymea, Gerizymia

Germaine (Latin) Feminine form of Germain; one who is sisterly; woman from Germany
Germana, Germane, Germayn, Germayne, Germanna, Germaina, Germayna, Germaene, Germaena

Gersemi (Scandinavian) As precious as a jewel
Gersemie, Gersemy, Gersemey, Gersemee, Gersemea, Gersemeah

Gertrude (German) One who is strong with a spear
Geertruide, Geltruda, Geltrudis, Gert, Gerta, Gerte, Gertie, Gertina, Gertraud, Gertrud, Gertruda, Gertrudis, Gerty, Gertraude, Gertmda, Gertrudes, Gertrut, Gertea, Gerteah

Gerusha (Hebrew) Form of Jerusha, meaning "a faithful wife"
Gerushah, Geruscha, Garusha, Garuscha

Geshur (Hebrew) From the bridge
Geshura, Geshure, Geshuria, Geshurea, Geshuri, Geshurie, Geshuree, Geshurea, Geshureah, Geshury, Geshurey

Gessica (English) Form of Jessica, meaning "the Lord sees all"
Gess, Gessa, Gessaca, Gessaka, Gessalin, Gessalyn, Gesse, Gesseca, Gessey, Gessie, Gessika, Gesirae, Geslyn, Gessika, Gessicka, Geziree, Gessalynn, Gessamae, Gessana, Gessandra, Gesselyn, Gezeree, Gessi, Gessilyn, Gessina, Gesslyn, Gesslynn, Gessy, Gessye, Gesimae

Gethsemane (Hebrew) Worker of the oil press
Gethsemanie, Gethsemana, Gethsemani, Gethsemaney, Gethsemany, Gethsemanee, Gethsemanea

Geva (Hebrew) From the farm
Gevah, Gevia, Gevea, Geviah, Geveah

Gevira (Hebrew) A highborn daughter
Gevirah, Gevyra, Gevyrah, Geveera, Geveerah, Geviera, Gevierah, Geveira, Geveirah, Geveara, Gevearah

Gezana (Spanish) Refers to the doctrine of Incarnation
Gezanah, Gezanna, Gezania, Gezanea, Gezune, Gizana, Gizane, Gizania, Gizanea

Gezer (Hebrew) From the cliffs
Gezera, Gezeria, Gezerea, Gezerah, Gezere

Ghada (Arabic) A beautiful young girl
Ghadah, Ghadda, Ghaddah, Ghayda, Ghaydah

Ghaliya (Arabic) One who smells sweet
Ghaliyah, Ghaleeya, Ghaleeyah, Ghaleya, Ghaleyah, Ghaleaya, Ghaleayah

Ghalyela (African) One who is precious
Ghalyelah, Ghalyella, Ghalyele, Ghalyelle

Ghazala (Arabic) As graceful as a gazelle
Ghazalah, Ghazalla, Ghazaala, Ghazalia, Ghazalea, Ghazallah, Ghazaliah, Ghazaleah

Ghislaine (French) Born of the sweet oath
Ghislayne, Ghislane, Ghislaina, Ghislayna, Ghislana, Gislaine, Gislayne, Gislane, Guilaine, Guiliaine

Ghita (Italian) Resembling a pearl
Ghitah, Gheeta, Ghyta, Gheata, Gheita, Ghieta

Ghusun (Arabic) Of the trees' branches
Ghusune, Ghusoon, Ghusoone

Giacinta (Italian) Resembling the hyacinth
Giacynta, Giacenta, Gacenta, Gacynta, Gacinta, Giacintha, Giacyntha, Giancinta, Giancinte, Gyacinta, Gyacenta, Gyacynta

⊙ **Gianna** (Italian) Feminine form of John; God is gracious
Geonna, Gia, Giana, Ginara, Gianina, Gianella, Giannina, Gionna, Gianetta, Giannine, Ginetta, Ginette, Ginnette, Gianara, Geona, Geovana

Gibbethon (Hebrew) From the high house
Gibbethona, Gibbethonia, Gibbethonea, Gibbethone

Gibeah (Hebrew) From the hill town
Gibea, Gibia, Gibiah, Gibeon, Gibeona, Gibeonea, Gibeonia, Gibeoneah, Gibiya, Gibiyah

Gihon (Hebrew) Of the stream or river
Gihona, Gihonah, Gihonia, Gihonea, Gihoniah, Gihoneah

Gila (Hebrew) One who is forever joyous
Gilah, Gilia, Gili, Gilala, Gilal, Gilana, Gilat, Gilit, Geela, Geelah, Gilla, Gillah

Gilberta (German) Feminine form of Gilbert; of the bright pledge; a hostage
Gilbertha, Gilberthe, Gilbertina, Gilbertine, Gill, Gillie, Gilly, Gilberte, Gilbertyna, Gilbertyne, Gilberteena, Gilberteene, Gilbarta, Gilbarte, Gilen, Gijs

Gilboa (Hebrew) From the boiling springs
Gilboah, Gylboa, Gylboah

Gilda (English) The golden child
Gildah, Gilde, Gildie, Gildy, Gildi, Gildey, Gildee, Gildan, Gildana, Gildane, Gylda, Gyldan, Gildea, Gildeah

Gildas (Celtic) A woman in the service of the Lord
Gildes, Gildys

Gilead (Hebrew) From the mountain of testimony

Gillian (Latin) One who is youthful
Ghilian, Ghiliane, Ghillian, Gilian, Giliana, Gillan, Gillianna, Gillianne, Gillyanne, Gillien, Gillienne, Gillot

Gimbya (African) Daughter born to royalty; a princess
Gimbyah, Gimbiya, Gimbeya, Gimbaya, Gimbiyah, Gimbayah, Gimbeyah

Gimle (Norse) From the most beautiful place on earth
Gimli, Gimlie, Gimly, Gimley, Gimlee, Gimleigh, Gimlea, Gimleah, Gymle, Gymli, Gymlie, Gymleigh, Gymley, Gymly, Gymlee, Gymlea

Gimzo (Hebrew) From the valley of sycamores

Gina (Italian / English) A silvery woman / form of Eugenia, meaning "a wellborn woman"; form of Jean, meaning "God is gracious"
Geana, Geanndra, Geena, Geina, Gena, Genalyn, Geneene, Genelle, Genette, Ginamaria, Gineen, Ginelle, Ginette, Gin

Ginata (Italian) As delicate as a flower
Ginatah, Ginatta, Ginatia, Ginatea, Ginatiah, Ginateah

Ginger (English) A lively woman; resembling the spice
Gingee, Gingie, Ginjer, Gingea, Gingy, Gingey, Gingi

Ginnungagap (Norse) In mythology, the abyss that gave birth to all living things

Ginny (English) Form of Virginia, meaning "one who is chaste; virginal"
Ginnee, Ginnelle, Ginnette, Ginnie, Ginnilee, Ginna, Ginney, Ginni, Ginnea

Gioconda (Italian) A delightful daughter
Gyoconda, Geoconda

Gioia (Italian) One who brings joy
Gioya

Giona (Italian) Resembling the bird of peace
Gionah, Gionna, Gyona, Gyonna, Gionnah, Gyonah, Gyonnah

Giordana (Italian) Feminine form of Jordan; of the down-flowing river
Giordanah, Giordanna, Giordannah

Giovanna (Italian) Feminine form of John; God is gracious
Geovana, Geovanna, Giavanna, Giovana, Giovani, Giovanni, Giovanie, Giovanee, Giovaney, Giovany, Giovanea

Giselle (French) Of God's promise; a hostage
Ghisele, Ghisella, Gisela, Giselda, Gisele, Gisella, Giza, Gizela, Gizella, Gizelle, Gisel, Gisilberhta, Gisselle, Gisli, Gizi, Gizike, Gizus

Gita (Hindi / Hebrew) A beautiful song / a good woman
Gitah, Geeta, Geetah, Gitika, Gatha, Gayatri, Gitel, Gittel, Gutka

Gitana (Spanish) A gypsy woman
Gitanah, Gitanna, Gitannah, Gitane

Gitanjali (Indian) An offering of songs
*Gitanjalie, Gytanjaly, Gitanjalee, Gytanjalee,
Gitanjaly, Gytanjaly, Gitanjaley, Gytanjaley,
Gitunjalea, Gytanjalea*

Githa (Anglo-Saxon) A gift from God
Githah

Gitta (Gaelic) From of Bridgette, meaning
"a strong and protective woman"
Gittah, Gitte, Gitteh

Gittaim (Hebrew) One who works the wine
press
*Gitaim, Gittaima, Gittaym, Gittayma,
Gitaym, Gittaem, Gittaema, Gitaem*

Giuditta (Italian) Form of Judith, meaning
"woman from Judea"
Giudytta, Guidita, Guidyta, Guiditta

Giulia (Italian) Form of Julia, meaning "one
who is youthful; daughter of the sky"
*Giula, Giuliana, Giulietta, Giullia, Guilia,
Guilie*

Giustinia (Italian) Feminine form of Justin;
one who is just and fair
*Giustina, Giustyna, Giustinea, Giusteena,
Giustiniah, Giustineah*

Gizem (Turkish) A mysterious woman
*Gizim, Gizam, Gizym, Gizema, Gizima,
Gizyma, Gizama*

Gjalp (Norse) In mythology, a frost giantess

Glade (English) From the meadow in the
woods
Glayd, Glayde, Glaid, Glaide, Glaed, Glaede

Gladys (Welsh) Form of Claudia, meaning
"one who is lame"
*Gladdis, Gladdys, Gladi, Gladis, Gladyss,
Gwladys, Gwyladyss, Gleda, Glad, Gladdie,
Gladdy, Gladdi, Gladdey, Gladdea, Gladdee*

Glain (Welsh) As precious as jewel
*Glaine, Glaina, Glayne, Glayna, Glaen,
Glayn, Glaene, Glaena*

Glan (Welsh) From the seashore
Glann

Glauce (Greek) In mythology, a woman
murdered by Medea

Glenda (Welsh) One who is good and fair
Glinda, Glynda, Glennda, Glynae

Glenna (Gaelic) From the valley between
the hills
*Gleana, Gleneen, Glenene, Glenine, Glen,
Glenn, Glenne, Glennene, Glennette, Glennie,
Glyn, Glynn, Glynna, Ghleanna*

Glenys (Welsh) A holy woman
Glenice, Glenis, Glennice, Glennis, Glennys

Gloria (Latin) A renowned and highly
praised woman
*Glaura, Glaurea, Glora, Glorea, Gloree,
Glorey, Gloreya, Glori, Gloriana, Gloriane,
Glorianna, Glorianne, Gloribel, Gloribell,
Glorie, Glorra, Glorria, Glory, Glorya,
Gloryan, Gloryanna, Gloryanne, Gloriann,
Gloriosa*

Glynis (Welsh) From the narrow valley
*Glennis, Glinnis, Glinyce, Glinyss,
Glynae, Glynice, Glynnis, Glynnes*

Gna (Norse) In mythology, one of Frigg's
handmaidens

Gobinet (Irish) Form of Abigail, meaning
"the source of a father's joy"
*Gobnait, Gobnat, Gubnat, Gobnayt, Gobnate,
Gobynet, Gobinette, Gobynette*

Godfreya (German) Feminine form of
Godfrey; having the peace of God
Godfredya, Gotfreya, Godafrid, Godafryd

Godiva (English) Gift from God
Godivah, Godgifu, Godyva, Godyvah

Golan (Hebrew) One who has been exiled
Golana, Golanah, Golane, Golanne

Golda (English) Resembling the precious
metal
*Goldarina, Goldarine, Goldee, Goldi, Goldie,
Goldina, Goldy, Goldia, Goldea, Golds*

Goleuddydd (Welsh) Born on a bright day
Goleudydd, Goleu, Gwenddydd

Gorane (Slavic) Feminine form of Goran;
woman from the mountain
*Gorayne, Goraine, Gorain, Gorayn, Gorana,
Goranna, Gorania, Goranea, Goraen,
Goraene, Goraena*

Gorawen (Welsh) One who brings joy to others
Gorawenne, Gorawin, Gorawyn, Gorawinne, Gorawynne, Gorawenn, Gorawinn, Gorawynn

Gordana (Serbian / Scottish) A proud woman / one who is heroic
Gordanah, Gordanna, Gordania, Gordaniya, Gordanea, Gordannah, Gordaniah, Gordaniyah, Gordaneah

Gormghlaith (Irish) Woman of sorrow
Gormghlaithe, Gormley, Gormly, Gormlie, Gormli, Gormlee, Gormleigh

Gota (Swedish) Having great strength
Gotah, Gote, Goteh, Gotilda, Gotilde, Gotild

Gotzone (Basque) Feminine form of Gotzon; a messenger of God; an angel
Gotzonie, Gotzoni, Gotzona, Gotzonia, Gotzonea, Gotzonee, Gotzony, Gotzoney

✿ **Grace** (Latin) Having God's favor; in mythology, the Graces were the personification of beauty, charm, and grace
Gracee, Gracella, Gracelynn, Gracelynne, Gracey, Gracia, Graciana, Gracie, Graciela, Graciella, Gracielle, Gracija, Gracina, Gracious, Grata, Gratia, Gratiana, Gratiela, Gratiella, Grayce, Grazia, Graziella, Grazina, Graziosa, Grazyna, Graca, Graciene, Gracinha, Gradana, Gechina, Gratiane, Grazinia, Gricie, Graci, Graece

Gracie (Latin) Form of Grace, meaning "having God's favor"
Gracee, Gracey, Graci

Graeae (Greek) In mythology, the personification of old age
Graiae

Grainne (Irish) One who loves and is loved
Graine, Grainnia, Grania, Graynne, Grayne, Graynia, Graenne, Graene, Graenia

Granada (Spanish) From the Moorish kingdom
Granadda, Grenada, Grenadda

Greer (Scottish) Feminine form of Gregory; one who is alert and watchful
Grear, Grier, Gryer

Gregoria (Latin) Feminine form of Gregory; one who is alert and watchful
Gregoriana, Gregorijana, Gregorina, Gregorine, Gregorya, Gregoryna, Gregorea, Gregoriya

Greip (Norse) In mythology, a frost giantess

Greta (German) Resembling a pearl
Greeta, Gretal, Grete, Gretel, Gretha, Grethe, Grethel, Gretna, Gretta, Grette, Grietje, Gryta, Gretchen, Gredel

Grid (Norse) One who is peaceful; in mythology, a frost giantess
Gryd

Grimhild (Norse) In mythology, a witch
Grimhilde, Grimhilda, Grimild, Grimilda, Grimilde

Griselda (German) A gray-haired battle-maid; one who fights the dark battle
Gricelda, Gricely, Grisel, Griseldis, Grisella, Griselle, Griselly, Grishelda, Grishilde, Grissel, Grizel, Grizelda, Gryselde, Gryzelde, Griselde, Grisjahilde, Giorsal, Gnishilda, Grizela, Grizzel, Gryselda

Griswalda (German) Woman from the gray woodland
Griswalde, Grizwalda, Grizwalde, Griswald, Grizwald

Gro (Norwegian) One who works the earth
Groa, Grow, Growe

Gryphon (Greek) In mythology, a beast representing strength, protection, and vigilance
Gryfon, Griffin, Griffon, Gryffin

Guadalupe (Spanish) From the valley of wolves
Godalupe, Gwadalupe

Gudny (Swedish) One who is unspoiled
Gudney, Gudni, Gudnie, Gudne, Gudnee, Gudnea, Gudneah

Gudrun (Scandinavian) A battlemaiden
Gudren, Gudrid, Gudrin, Gudrinn, Gudruna, Gudrunn, Gudrunne, Guthrun, Guthrunn, Guthrunne

Guida (Italian) One who acts as a guide
Geeda, Geida, Gieda, Geada, Gwyda, Gwida

Guinevak (English) In Arthurian legend, Guinevere's sister
Gwenhwyfach, Gwenhwyvach

Guinevere (Welsh) One who is fair; of the white wave; in mythology, King Arthur's queen
Guenever, Guenevere, Gueniver, Guenna, Guennola, Guinever, Guinna, Gwen, Gwenevere, Gweniver, Gwenn, Gwennie, Gwennola, Gwennora, Gwennore, Gwenny, Gwenora, Gwenore, Gwyn, Gwynn, Gwynna, Gwynne, Guanhamara, Guanhumora, Gvenour, Gwenhwyfar, Gwenhwyvar, Gwenhyvar, Gwenifer, Gwennor, Gwenyver

Guiseppina (Italian) Feminine form of Guiseppe; the Lord will add
Giuseppyna, Giuseppa, Giuseppia, Giuseppea, Guiseppie, Giuseppia, Giuseppa, Giuseppina

Gula (Babylonian) In mythology, a goddess
Gulah, Gulla, Gullah

Gulab (Arabic) Resembling the rose
Gulaab, Gul

Gulielma (German) Feminine form of Wilhelm; determined protector
Guglielma, Guillelmina, Guillielma, Gulielmina, Guillermina

Gulinar (Arabic) Resembling the pomegranate
Gulinare, Gulinear, Gulineir, Gulinara, Gulinaria, Gulinarea

Gullveig (Norse) In mythology, a dark goddess
Gullveiga, Gullveige, Gulveig, Gulveiga, Gulveige

Gulzar (Arabic) From the gardens
Gulzare, Gulzaar, Gulzara, Gulzaria, Gulzarea, Gulshan, Gulshana, Gulshania, Gulshanea

Gunhilda (Norse) A battlemaiden
Gunhilde, Gunilda, Gunilla, Gunna, Gunnel, Gunnhilda, Gunda, Gunnef, Gunnhild, Gunnhildr

Gunnlod (Norse) In mythology, the daughter of Suttung

Guri (Hebrew) Resembling a young lioness
Gurie, Guriele, Gurielle, Gurice, Gurit, Gury, Gurey, Guree, Gureah, Gurea

Gussie (English) Form of Augusta, meaning "venerable; majestic"
Gussi, Gussy, Gussey, Gussee, Gustela, Gustella, Gustel, Gustele, Gustelle, Gusty, Gussea, Gusseah

Gustava (Swedish) Feminine form of Gustave; from the staff of the gods
Gustavah, Gustha, Guusa, Gustaafa, Gusta, Gust

Gwanwyn (Welsh) Born during the spring
Gwanwynn, Gwanwynne, Gwanwin, Gwanwinn, Gwanwinne, Gwanwen, Gwanwenn, Gwanwenne

Gwawr (Welsh) Born with the morning light

Gwendolyn (Welsh) One who is fair; of the white ring
Guendolen, Guendolin, Guendolinn, Guendolynn, Guenna, Gwen, Gwenda, Gwendaline, Gwendalyn, Gwendolen, Gwendolene, Gwendolin, Gwendoline, Gwendolynn, Gwendolynne, Gwenna, Gwenette, Gwenndolen, Gwenni, Gwennie, Gwenny, Gwyn, Gwyndolyn, Gwynn, Gwynna, Gwynne, Gwenn, Gwynda, Gwendoloena, Gwendelyn, Gwendi, Guennola, Gwener, Gwenllian, Gwylan, Gwyndolen, Gwyndolin

Gwyneth (Welsh) One who is blessed with happiness
Gweneth, Gwenith, Gwenyth, Gwineth, Gwinneth, Gwinyth, Gwynith, Gwynna, Gwynne, Gwynneth, Gwenneth, Gwynedd, Gwennan

Gypsy (English) A wanderer; a nomad
Gipsee, Gipsey, Gipsy, Gypsi, Gypsie, Gypsey, Gypsee, Gipsi, Gipsie, Gipsea, Gypsea

Gytha (English) One who is treasured
Gythah

Gzifa (African) One who is at peace
Gzifah, Gzyfa, Gzyfah, Gziffa, Gziffah, Gzyffa, Gzyffah

h

Ha (Vietnamese) One who is kissed by the sunshine

Haafizah (Arabic) One who loves literature
Hafizah, Hafiza, Hafyzah, Hafeeza, Hafeezah, Hafeazah, Hafeaza

Haarisah (Hindi) Daughter of the sun
*Harisah, Haarysah, Harisa, Harysah,
Harysa, Haaresah, Haresah, Haresa*

Haarithah (Arabic) A heavenly messenger
Harithah, Haarithe, Haaritheh, Harithe

Habbai (Arabic) One who is much loved
Habbae, Habbay, Habbaye

Habiba (Arabic) Feminine form of Habib;
one who is dearly loved; sweetheart
*Habibah, Habeeba, Habyba, Habieba,
Habeiba, Habika, Habyka, Habicka,
Habycka, Habeabah, Habeaba, Habeebah,
Habybah, Habiebah, Habeibah*

Hachi (Native American / Japanese) From
the river / having good fortune
*Hachie, Hachee, Hachiko, Hachiyo, Hachy,
Hachey, Hachikka*

Hachilah (Hebrew) From the dark hill
*Hachila, Hachyla, Hachylah, Hacheela,
Hacheelah, Hachiela, Hachielah, Hacheilah,
Hacheila, Hacheala, Hachealah*

Hada (African) From the salty place
Hadah, Hadda, Haddah

Hadara (Hebrew) A spectacular ornament;
adorned with beauty
*Hadarah, Hadarit, Haduraq, Hadarra,
Hadarrah*

Hadassah (Hebrew) From the myrtle tree
Hadassa, Hadasah, Hadasa

Hadeel (Arabic) Resembling a dove
Hadil, Hadyl, Hadeil, Hadiel, Hadeal

Hadenna (English) From the meadow of
flowers
*Hadennah, Hadena, Hadynna, Hadinna,
Hadyna, Hadina*

Hadiya (Arabic) A gift from God; a righ-
teous woman
*Hadiyah, Hadiyyah, Haadiyah, Haadiya,
Hadeeya, Hadeeyah, Hadieya, Hadieyah,
Hadeiya, Hadeiyah, Hadeaya, Hadeayah*

Hadlai (Hebrew) In a resting state; one who
hinders
Hadlae, Hadlay, Hadlaye

Hadley (English) From the field of heather
*Hadlea, Hadleigh, Hadly, Hedlea, Hedleigh,
Hedley, Hedlie, Hadlee, Hadlie, Hadli, Hedly,
Hedlee, Hedleah, Hedli*

Hadria (Latin) From the town in northern
Italy
*Hadrea, Hadriana, Hadriane, Hadrianna,
Hadrien, Hadrienne, Hadriah, Hadreah*

Hady (Greek) One who is soulful
Hadey, Hadi, Hadie, Hadee, Hadea

Hadya (Arabic) Feminine form of Hadi;
serving as a religious guide
Hadyah, Hadiya, Hadiyah

Hafsa (Arabic) Resembling a young lioness;
a wife of Muhammad
Hafza, Hafsah, Hafzah, Haphsa, Haphza

Hafthah (Arabic) One who is protected by
God
Haftha

Hafwen (Welsh) Possessing the beauty of
summer
*Hafwenne, Hafwin, Hafwyn, Hafwinne,
Hafwynne, Hafwenn, Hafwinn, Hafwynn*

Hagab (Hebrew) Resembling a grasshopper
Hagabah, Hagaba, Hagabe

Hagai (Hebrew) One who has been aban-
doned
*Hagae, Hagay, Hagaye, Haggai, Haggae,
Hagie, Haggie, Hagi, Haggi, Hagee, Haggee,
Hagea, Haggea, Hagy, Haggy, Hagey,
Haggey*

Hagar (Hebrew) One who is forsaken; taking flight; a stranger
Haggar, Hagir, Hajar, Hagyr, Hagarr

Hagen (Irish) A youthful woman
Hagan, Haggen, Haggan

Haggith (Hebrew) One who rejoices; the
dancer
*Haggithe, Haggyth, Haggythe, Hagith,
Hagithe, Hagyth, Hagythe*

Hagne (Greek) One who is pure; chaste
*Hagna, Hagni, Hagnie, Hagnee, Hagnea,
Hagneah, Hagny, Hagney*

Haiba (African) A charming woman
Hayba, Haibah, Haybah, Haeba, Haebah

Haidee (Greek) A modest woman; one who is well-behaved
Hadee, Haydee, Haydy, Haidi, Haidie, Haydi, Haydie, Haidy, Haedee, Haedi, Haedie, Haedy, Haedey, Haedea, Haidea, Haydea

Haimati (Indian) A queen of the snow-covered mountains
Haimatie, Haimaty, Haimatey, Haimatee, Haymati, Haymatie, Haymatee, Haimatea, Haymatea

Haimi (Hawaiian) One who searches for the truth
Haimie, Haimy, Haimey, Haimee, Haymi, Haymie, Haymee, Haimea, Haymea

Haiwee (Native American) Resembling the dove; bird of peace
Haiwea, Haiwie, Haiwi, Haiwy, Haiwey

Hajna (Hungarian) Form of Ann, meaning "a woman graced with God's favor"
Hajne

Hajnal (Hungarian) Born with the morning's first light
Hajnale, Hujnula, Hajnalla, Hajnalka

Hakana (Turkish) Feminine form of Hakan; ruler of the people; an empress
Hakanah, Hakanna, Hakane, Hakann, Hakanne

Hakidonmuya (Native American) Born during a period of expectation

Hakkoz (Hebrew) One who has the qualities of a thorn
Hakoz, Hakkoze, Hakoze, Hakkoza, Hakoza

Hala (Arabic) Possessing a lunar halo
Halah, Haala, Hila, Hilah

Halag (German) A religious woman; one who is pious

Halak (Hebrew) One who is bald; smooth

Halcyone (Greek) Resembling a kingfisher; born during a time of peace and calm
Halcyon, Halcyona, Halcyonia, Halcyonea

Halda (Scandinavian) One who is half Danish
Haldah, Haldane, Haldayn, Haldayne, Haldain, Haldaine, Haldaen, Haldaene, Haldana, Haldania, Haldanea, Halden, Haldin, Haldyn, Haldi, Haldie, Haldee, Haldea, Haldey, Haldy, Haldis

Haldana (Norse) One who is half Danish
Haldanah, Haldanna, Haldane, Haldayne, Haldaine, Haldaene

Haldis (Teutonic / Greek) A stone spirit / a reliable helper
Haldisa, Haldys, Haldiss, Haldisse, Haldyss, Haldysse, Halldis, Halldiss, Halldisse, Halldys, Halldyss, Halldysse

Haldora (Norse) Feminine form of Haldor; Thor's rock
Haldorah, Haldoria, Haldorea, Haldorra, Halldora, Halldorra, Halldoria, Halldorea

Hale (English) From the hall of light; a heroine
Hayle, Haile, Haylan, Haylen, Hael, Haele, Hayl

Haleigha (Hawaiian) Born with the rising sun
Haleea, Haleya, Halya

Halene (Russian) A steadfast woman
Haleen, Haleene, Halein, Haleine, Halien, Haliene

Haletta (Greek) A little girl from the meadow
Halett, Halet, Haleta, Halette, Halete

❶ Haley (English) From the field of hay
❶ *Hailey, Hayle, Hailee, Haylee, Haylie, Haleigh, Hayley, Haeleigh, Haeli, Haili, Haily, Halea, Hayleigh, Hayli, Hailea, Haile, Hailie, Halie, Hali, Halee, Haelee*

Halfrida (German) A peaceful woman
Halfryda, Halfrieda, Halfreida, Halfreeda, Halfreada

Halhul (Hebrew) One who is hollow inside; full of grief

Halia (Hawaiian) The remembrance of one who was loved

Halima (Arabic) A mild-mannered woman; one who is gentle
Halimah, Haleema, Haleemah, Haleima, Halyma, Helima, Helimah, Helyma, Heleema, Heleemah, Haleama, Haleamah, Heleama, Heleamah

Halimeda (Greek) Woman from the sea
Halameda, Halymeda, Halimyda, Halymyda, Halamyda, Halimida, Halamida

Halina (Greek / Polish) Born of the light / one who is calm
Halinah, Haleena, Haleenah, Halyna, Halynah, Haleina, Haleinah, Haleana, Haleanah, Haliena, Halienah, Halena, Halenah

Hall (American) One who is distinguished
Haul

Halla (African) An unexpected gift
Hallah

Hallam (English) From the valley
Hallem, Halam, Halem

Hallan (English) From the manor's hall
Hallen, Halan, Halen

Hallei (Hebrew) One who is much praised

Hallela (Hebrew) One who is praiseworthy
Hallella, Halleli, Hallelie, Hallely, Halleley, Hallelee, Hallelea

Hallelujah (Hebrew) Praise the Lord our God
Halleluja

Hallie (Scandinavian / Greek / English) From the hall / woman of the sea / from the field of hay
Halley, Hallie, Halle, Hallee, Hally, Halleigh, Hallea, Halleah

Halo (Latin) Having a blessed aura
Haylo, Haelo, Hailo

Haloke (Native American) Resembling a salmon
Haloka, Halokia, Halokea

Halona (Native American) Woman of good fortune
Halonna, Halonah, Halonia, Halonea

Halsey (American) A playful woman
Halsy, Halsee, Halsea, Halsi, Halsie, Halcie, Halcy, Halcey, Halcea, Halcee, Halci

Halston (American) A stylish woman
Halsten, Halstin, Halstun, Halstan, Halstyn

Halyn (American) A unique young woman
Halynn, Halynne, Halin, Halinn, Halinne

Halzey (American) A great leader
Halzy, Halzee, Halzea, Halzi, Halzie

Hama (Arabic) From the city on the river
Hamah, Hamma, Hammah

Hamath (Hebrew) From the mighty fortress
Hamathe, Hamoth, Hamothe, Hamatha, Hamotha

Hamida (Arabic) One who gives thanks
Hamidah, Hamyda, Hameeda, Hameida, Hamieda, Hameada, Hamydah, Hameedah, Hameidah, Hamiedah, Hameadah

Hamilton (American) A dreamer; one who is wishful
Hamylton, Hamilten, Hamylten, Hamiltyn, Hamyltyn

Hammon (Hebrew) Of the warm springs

Hamony (Latin) Form of Harmony, meaning "unity; musically in tune"
Hamoney, Hamoni, Hamonie, Hamonee, Hamonea

Hamula (Hebrew) Feminine form of Hamul; spared by God
Hamulah, Hamulla, Hamullah

Hamutal (Hebrew) Of the morning dew
Hamutala, Hamutalle, Hamutalla

Hana (Japanese / Arabic) Resembling a flower blossom / a blissful woman
Hanah, Hanako

Hanameel (Hebrew) A gift from God
Hanameela, Hannameel, Hanamele, Hanamelle, Hanamella, Hananeel, Hananeela, Hanameal, Hanameala, Hananeal, Hananeala

Hanan (Arabic) One who shows mercy and compassion

Hananna (Hebrew) Feminine form of Hanan; one who is gracious
Hanannah, Hanana, Hananah

Hande (Turkish) A woman with an infectious smile

Ha-neul (Korean) Of the sky

Hang (Vietnamese) Of the moon

Hanh (Vietnamese) From the apricot tree

Hanifa (Arabic) Feminine form of Hanif; a true believer; one who is upright
Hanifah, Haneefa, Haneefah, Hanyfa, Hanyfah, Haneifa, Haneifah, Haniefa, Haniefah, Haneafa, Haneafah

Hanika (Hebrew) A graceful woman
Hanikah, Haneeka, Haneekah, Hanyka, Hanykah, Haneika, Haneikah, Hanieka, Haniekah, Haneaka, Haneakah

Hanima (Indian) Of the waves
Hanimah, Hanyma, Haneema, Hanymah, Haneemah, Haneima, Haneimah, Haniema, Haniemah, Haneama, Haneamah

Hanita (Indian) Favored with divine grace
Hanitah, Hanyta, Haneeta, Hanytah, Haneetah, Haneita, Haneitah, Hanieta, Hanietah, Huneata, Haneatah

Haniyah (Arabic) One who is pleased; happy
Haniya, Haniyyah, Haniyya, Hani, Hanie, Hanee, Hany, Haney, Hanea, Haneah

Hannabel (German) Favored with grace and beauty
Hannabelle, Hannabell, Hannabele, Hannabela, Hannabella

❷❶ **Hannah** (Hebrew) Having favor and grace; in the Bible, mother of Samuel
Hanalee, Hanalise, Hanna, Hanne, Hannele, Hannelore, Hannie, Hanny, Honna, Hannalee, Hendel, Hannaleigh, Honna, Hannea, Hanneka, Hannika, Hannela, Hannella, Hannalea

Hannette (American) One who is graceful
Hannett, Hannet, Hannete, Hannetta, Hanneta

Hansa (Indian) As graceful as a swan
Hansika, Hansini, Hansinie, Hansia, Hansea

Hansine (Hebrew) Feminine form of John; God is gracious
Hansyne, Hanseen, Hansinah, Hansina, Hansyna, Hannes, Hanseane, Hanseana, Hanseena

Hanya (Aboriginal) As solid as a stone

Hanzila (African) Traveling a road or path
Hanzilah, Hanzilla, Hanzillah, Hanzyla, Hanzylla, Hanzylah, Hanzyllah

Hao (Vietnamese) One who is perfectly behaved

Happy (American) A joyful woman
Happey, Happi, Happie, Happee, Happea

Haqikah (Egyptian) A truthful woman; one who is honest
Haqika, Haquikah, Haquika, Haqyka

Hara (Hebrew) From the mountainous land
Harah, Harra, Harrah

Haracha (African) Resembling a frog

Haradah (Hebrew) One who is filled with fear
Harada

Haralda (Norse) Feminine form of Harold; the ruler of an army
Haraldene, Haraldina, Harolda, Haroldene, Haroldina, Haraldia, Harelda, Hareldina, Hareldene, Harelde, Harolde, Haraldyna, Haroldyna, Hareldyna, Haraldyne, Haroldyne, Hareldyne

Harana (Hebrew) Feminine form of Haran; a great moutaineer; one who is parched
Haranah, Haranna, Haranne, Harane, Harann

Harhur (Hebrew) Possessing a burning heat
Harhure, Harhurr, Harhura, Harhurra

Harika (Turkish) A superior woman
Harikah, Haryka, Hareeka, Harykah, Hareekah, Hareaka, Hareakah

Harimanna (German) A warrior maiden
Harimanne, Harimana, Harimane

Harimanti (Indian) Born during the spring
Harimantie, Harymanti, Harimanty, Harymanty, Harymantie, Harimantea, Harymantea

Harinakshi (Indian) A doe-eyed young woman
Harinakshie, Harynakshi, Harinakshy, Harynakshy, Harinakshea, Harynakshea, Harynakshie

Harini (Indian) Resembling a deer
Harinie, Harinee, Hariny, Haryni, Harynie, Haryny, Harinea, Harynea, Harynee

Hariti (Indian) In mythology, the goddess for the protection of children
Haritie, Haryti, Harytie, Haritee, Harytee, Haritea, Harytea

Harla (English) From the fields
Harlah

Harlan (English) An athletic woman
Harlen, Harlon, Harlun, Harlyn

Harlequine (American) A romantic woman
Harlequin, Harlequen, Harlequene, Harlequinne, Harlequinn

Harley (English) From the meadow of the hares
Harlea, Harlee, Harleen, Harleigh, Harlene, Harlie, Harli, Harly

Harlow (American) An impetuous woman
Harlowe, Harlo, Harloe

Harmony (English / Latin) Unity; musically in tune / in mythology, Harmonia was the daughter of Ares and Aphrodite; a beautiful blending
Harmonie, Harmoni, Harmonee, Harmonia, Harmoney, Harmonea

Harper (English) One who plays or makes harps
Harpur, Harpar, Harpir, Harpyr

Harrell (American) A great leader
Harel, Harell, Harrel, Harelle, Harrelle

Harriet (German) Feminine form of Henry; ruler of the house
Harriett, Hanriette, Hanrietta, Harriette, Harrietta, Harrette, Harriot, Harriotte, Harriotte, Harriotta, Heirierte, Heirrierte

Harsha (Hebrew / Indian) An enchantress; a hardworking woman / a bringer of happiness
Harshada, Harshah, Harshini, Harshinie, Harshyni, Harshynie, Harshita, Harshitah, Harshinea

Hartley (American) A warmhearted woman
Hartly, Hartlee, Hartlea, Hartleigh, Hartlie, Hartli

Haru (Japanese) Daughter born in the spring
Haruko, Haruo, Haruki, Harue

Haruma (Hebrew) Feminine form of Harum; one who is elevated

Haruphite (Hebrew) Born of autumn's rain
Harupha, Haruphyte, Haruphita, Haruphitia

Harva (English) A warrior of the army

Hasibah (Arabic) Feminine form of Hasib; one who is noble and respected
Hasiba, Hasyba, Hasybah, Haseeba, Haseebah, Haseiba, Haseibah, Hasieba, Hasiebah, Haseaba, Haseabah

Hasina (African) One who is good and beautiful
Hasinah, Hasyna, Hasynah, Haseena, Haseenah, Hasiena, Hasienah, Haseina, Haseinah, Haseana, Haseanah

Hasita (Indian) A bringer of happiness
Hasumati

Hasna (Arabic) A beautiful woman
Hasnah, Hasnaa, Husinya, Husniyah, Husna, Husn

Hassaanah (African) The first daughter
Hassanah, Hassana, Hassaana

Hasuna (Arabic) One who is well-behaved; good
Hasunah

Hateya (Native American) Leaving footprints in the sand

Hathor (Egyptian) In mythology, goddess of love
Hathora, Hathoria, Hathorea, Hathore

Hatita (Hebrew) A traveling woman; an explorer
Hatitah, Hatyta, Hatytah, Hateetah, Hateeta, Hateata, Hateatah

Hatshepsut (Egyptian) A successful ruler; a female pharoah
Hatchepsut

Hatsu (Japanese) The firstborn daughter

Haukea (Hawaiian) Of the white snow
Haukia, Haukeah, Haukiah, Haukiya, Haukiyah

Haunani (Hawaiian) Of the heavenly dew
Haunanie, Haunany, Haunaney, Haunanee, Haunanea

Haurana (Hebrew) Feminine form of Hauran; woman from the caves
Hauranna, Hauranah, Haurann, Hauranne, Haurane

Hausis (Native American) A wise old woman
Hausisse, Hausiss, Hausys, Hausyss, Hausysse

Haut (French) A stylish woman
Haute, Hauti, Hautie, Hautey, Hauty, Hautee, Hautea

Hava (Hebrew) A lively woman; giver of life
Havah, Haya, Hayat, Havaa

Havana (Spanish) From the capital city of Cuba
Havanah, Havanna, Havannah, Havane, Havann, Havanne

Haven (English) One who provides a safe place
Hayven, Havan, Hayvan, Havon, Hayvon, Havin, Hayvin, Havyn, Hayvyn, Haeven, Haevin, Haevan

Havilah (Hebrew) From the stretch of sand
Havila, Havillah, Havilla, Havily, Havili, Havilli, Havilie, Havillie, Havilea, Havillea

Haviland (American) A lively woman
Havyland, Havilande, Havylande, Havilanda, Havylanda

Havva (Turkish) A giver of the breath of life
Havvah, Havvia, Havviah

Hawa (African) One who is desired
Hawah

Hawadah (Arabic) A pleasant woman
Hawada

Hawaii (Hawaiian) From the homeland; from the state of Hawaii

Hawazin (Arabic) A tribal name

Hawke (American) Resembling the bird
Hawki, Hawkie, Hawky, Hawkey, Hawkee, Hawkea

Hawkins (American) A cunning woman
Haukins, Hawkens, Haukens, Hawkuns, Haukuns

Hawlee (American) One who negotiates
Hawleigh, Hawli, Hawlie, Hawlea, Hawly, Hawley

Hawwa (Arabic) A lively woman; a giver of life
Hawaa, Hawwah, Hawwaa

Haya (Japanese / Hebrew) One who is quick and light / form of Havva, meaning "a giver of the breath of life"
Hayah

Hayam (Arabic) One who is madly in love
Hayaam

Haydee (American) A capable woman
Haydi, Haydea, Haydie, Haydie, Haydy, Haydey

Hayden (English) From the hedged valley
Haden, Haydan, Haydn, Haydon, Hayes, Haeden, Haedyn, Hadyn

Hayfa (Arabic) A slender and delicate woman
Hayfah, Haifa, Haifah, Haefa, Haefah

Hayud (Arabic) From the mountain
Hayuda, Hayudah, Hayood, Hayooda

Hazan (Turkish) Born during autumn
Hazann, Hazanne, Hazana, Hazanna, Hazane

Hazar (Arabic) Resembling a nightingale
Hazare, Hazara, Hazarra, Hazarre, Hazarr

Hazarenan (Hebrew) From the town of fountains
Hazara, Hazarah, Hazarenanna, Hazarena, Hazaryna

Hazargaddah (Hebrew) From the town of fortune
Hazargadda, Hazargada, Hazargadah

Haze (American) One who is spontaneous
Haize, Haise, Hase, Hayze, Hayse, Haeze, Haese, Hazi, Hazie, Hazy, Hazey, Hazee, Hazea

Hazel (English) From the hazel tree
Hazell, Hazelle, Haesel, Hazle, Hazal,
Hayzel, Haezel, Haizel

Hazelelponi (Hebrew) A shadowed woman
Hazelelponie, Hazelelpony, Hazelelponey,
Hazelelponee, Hazelelponea

Hazina (African) One who is treasured
Hazinah, Hazyna, Hazeena, Hazena,
Hazeana, Hazynah, Hazeenah, Hazenah,
Hazeanah

Hazor (Hebrew) From the stronghold
Hazora, Hazoria, Hazorea, Hazorya,
Hazorra, Hazorah

Heart (American) One who is romantic
Hearte, Hart, Harte

Heartha (Teutonic) A gift from Mother
Earth

Heather (English) Resembling the evergreen flowering plant
Hether, Heatha, Heath, Heathe

❂ **Heaven** (American) From paradise; from
the sky
Heavely, Heavenly, Hevean, Hevan,
Heavynne, Heavenli, Heavenlie, Heavenleigh,
Heavenlee, Heavenley, Heavenlea, Heavyn

Hebe (Greek) A youthful woman; in
mythology, goddess of youth and spring
and cupbearer to the gods
Heebee, Hebee, Heebe

Hebron (Hebrew) Born of the community;
a good friend
Hebrona, Hebronah, Hebrone, Hebrun

Hecate (Greek) In mythology, a goddess of
fertility and witchcraft
Hekate

Hecuba (Greek) In mythology, the mother
of Paris, Hector, and Cassandra
Hekuba

Hedasaa (Hebrew) Resembling a star
Hedasa, Hedassa, Hedassaa

Hedia (Hebrew) Voice of the Lord
Hedya, Hediah, Hedyah, Hediya, Hediyah

Hedieh (Turkish) A gift from God

Hedva (Hebrew) A bringer of joy
Hedvah

Hedwig (German) Suffering strife during
war
Hadvig, Hadwig, Hedvig, Hedviga, Hedvige,
Hedwiga, Hedwige, Hedda, Heda, Heddi,
Heddie, Hedi, Hedy, Haduwig, Hadu

Hedy (Greek) One who is pleasing; delightful; a sweetheart
Hedea, Hedeah, Hedyla, Hedylah

Heeni (Maori) Form of Jane, meaning "God
is gracious"
Heenie, Heeny, Heeney, Heenee, Heenea,
Heani, Heanie, Heany, Heaney, Heanee,
Heanea

Heera (Indian) As precious as a diamond

Heget (Egyptian) In mythology, a frog goddess who symbolized fertility
Heqet, Heket, Hehet

Hehewuti (Native American) The warrior
mother spirit
Hehewutie, Hehewute, Hehewuty, Hehewutey,
Hehewutee, Hehewutea

Heidi (German) Form of Adelaide, meaning
"of the nobility; serene; of good humor"
Heide, Heid, Heidie, Heidy, Heida, Haidee,
Heidey, Hydi, Hydie, Hydey, Hydee, Hydy

Heidrun (Norse) In mythology, the goat
who provided the gods with mead

Heilwig (German) Born of a safe war
Heilwyg

Heirnine (Greek) Form of Helen, meaning
"the shining light"
Heirnyne, Heirneine, Heirniene, Heirneene,
Heirneane

Hekaterine (Greek) Form of Catherine,
meaning "one who is pure; virginal"
Hekateros, Hekateryn, Hekateryne,
Hekaterina, Hekateryna, Hekaterin

Hel (Norse) In mythology, the goddess of
the dead
Hela, Helah

Helam (Hebrew) From the wealthy village
Helama, Helamah, Helamma, Helame

Helbah (Hebrew) A healthy woman; one who is fertile
Helbon, Helba, Helbia, Helbona, Helbea

Held (Welsh) Surrounded by light

Heledd (Welsh) One who is highborn; a princess
Heled, Helede

Helen (Greek) The shining light; in mythology, Helen was the most beautiful woman in the world
Helene, Halina, Helaine, Helana, Heleena, Helena, Helenna, Hellen, Helaina, Helenka, Heleana, Heley, Helina, Heleanor, Helenore, Helenann, HélÊne, Hellena, Hellene, Hellenor, Hellia, Heli, Helli, Helie, Hella, Helle

Helga (German) A holy woman; one who is successful

Helia (Greek) Daughter of the sun
Heliah, Helea, Heleah, Heliya, Heliyah, Heller, Hellar

Helice (Greek) Form of Helen, meaning "the shining light"
Helyce, Heleece, Heliece, Heleace

Helike (Greek) In mythology, a willow nymph who nurtured Zeus
Helica, Helyke, Helika, Helyka, Helyca

Helki (Native American) A sensuous woman
Helkie, Helky, Helkey, Helkee, Helkea

Helle (Greek) In mythology, the daughter of Athamas who escaped sacrifice on the back of a golden ram

Helma (German) Form of Wilhelmina, meaning "determined protector"
Helmah, Helmia, Helmea, Helmina, Helmyna, Helmeena, Helmine, Helmyne, Helmeen, Helmeene

Heloise (French) One who is famous in battle
Helois, Heloisa, Helewidis

Helsa (Danish) Form of Elizabeth, meaning "my God is bountiful"
Helsah, Helisa, Helise, Helissa, Helisse

Hemangini (Indian) The golden child; one who shines
Hemangi, Hemangie, Hema, Hemlata, Hem

Hemanti (Indian) Born during the early winter
Hemantie, Hemanty, Hemantey, Hemantee, Hemantea

Hemera (Greek) Born during daylight; in mythology, the goddess of the day
Hemerah, Hemerra, Hemyra, Hemira

Hen (English) Resembling the mothering bird

Hender (American) One who is embraced by all
Hendere

Heng (Chinese) An eternal beauty

Henley (American) A social butterfly
Henleigh, Henlee, Henly, Henlea, Henli, Henlie

Henrietta (German) Feminine form of Henry; ruler of the house
Henretta, Henrieta, Henriette, Henrika, Henryetta, Hetta, Hette, Hettie, Henrieeta, Hatsie, Hatsy, Hattie, Hatty, Hendrika, Henia, Henie, Henka, Hennie, Henrie, Henny, Henni, Henriqua, Henuite, Henuita, Hanrietta, Hanriette, Hanretta, Hanriet

Hensley (American) One who is ambitious
Hensly, Henslee, Hensleigh, Henslea, Hensli, Henslie

Hephzibah (Hebrew) She is my delight
Hepsiba, Hepzibeth, Hepsey, Hepsie, Hepsy, Hepzibah, Hepsee, Hepsea

Hera (Greek) The chosen heroine; in mythology, the wife of Zeus, and the goddess of marriage and childbirth
Here, Herah

Herdis (Scandinavian) A battlemaiden
Herdiss, Herdisse, Herdys, Herdyss, Herdysse

Herendira (American) A tender woman
Herendyra, Herendeera, Herendeara, Herendiera, Herendeira

Herise (American) A warmhearted woman
Heryse, Hereese, Heriese, Hereise, Herease

Herleen (American) A quiet and peaceful woman
Herleene, Herlean, Herleane, Herlein, Herleine, Herlien, Herliene, Herlyn, Herlyne

Hermandina (Greek) A wellborn woman
*Hermandine, Hermandyna, Hermandeenu,
Hermandena, Hermandyne, Hermandeene,
Hermandeane, Hermandeana*

Hermelinda (Spanish) Bearing a powerful
shield
*Hermelynda, Hermalinda, Hermalynda,
Hermelenda, Hermalenda*

Hermia (Greek) Feminine form of Hermes;
a messenger of the gods
*Hermiah, Hermea, Hermila, Hermilla,
Hermilda, Herminia, Hermenia, Herma,
Hermina, Hermine, Hermione*

Hermippe (Greek) In mythology, the
mother of Orchomenus
Hermipe, Hermip, Hermipp

Hermona (Hebrew) From the mountain
peak
Hermonah, Hermonna, Hermonnah

Hermosa (Spanish) A beautiful young
woman
*Hermossa, Hermosah, Hermoza, Hermosia,
Hermozia, Hermosea, Hermozea*

Hernanda (Spanish) One who is daring
Hernandia, Hernandea, Hernandiya

Hero (Greek) The brave defender; a heroine; in mythology, the lover of Leander
who killed herself when she discovered his
death
Heroe

Herodias (Greek) One who watches over
others; in the Bible, the mother of Salome

Herra (Greek) Daughter of the earth
Herrah

Hersala (Spanish) A lovely woman
*Hersalah, Hersalla, Hersallah, Hersalia,
Hersaliah, Hersalea, Hersaleah*

Herschelle (Hebrew) Feminine form of
Hirsh; resembling a deer
*Herschele, Herschell, Hershelle, Hershele,
Hershell*

Hersilia (Latin) In mythology, the wife of
Romulus
*Hersiliah, Hersilea, Hersileah, Hersylia,
Hersylea, Hersyleah, Hersiliya, Hersiliyah*

Hertha (English) Of the earth
Herthe, Herta, Herte

Hertnia (English) Of the earth
*Hertniah, Hertnea, Hertneah, Hertniya,
Hertniyah*

Hervie (English) A battle-ready woman war-
rior
*Hervi, Hervy, Hervey, Hervee, Hervea,
Herveah*

Heshbon (Hebrew) An industrious woman;
one with great intelligence

Hesiena (African) The firstborn of twins
*Hesienna, Hesienah, Heseina, Hasana,
Hasanah, Hasanna, Hasane*

Hesione (Greek) In mythology, a Trojan
princess saved by Hercules from a sea
monster

Hesper (Greek) Born under the evening
star
*Hespera, Hesperie, Hesperi, Hespery,
Hesperey, Hesperee, Hesperea*

Hesperia (Greek) In mythology, one of the
Hesperides
Hesperiah, Hesperea, Hespereah

Hester (Greek) A starlike woman
Hestere, Hesther, Hesta, Hestar

Hestia (Greek) In mythology, goddess of
the hearth
Hestiah, Hestea, Hesteah, Hestya, Hestyah

Hetal (Hindi) A friendly young girl
*Hetall, Hetale, Hetalia, Hetalea, Hetala,
Hetalla, Hetalle*

Heulwen (Welsh) As bright as the light
from the sun
*Heulwenn, Heulwenne, Heulwin, Heulwinn,
Heulwinne, Heulwyn, Heulwynn, Heulwynne*

Heven (American) A pretty young woman
*Hevin, Hevon, Hevun, Hevven, Hevvin,
Hevvon, Hevvun*

Heyzell (American) Form of Hazel, meaning "from the hazel tree"
Heyzel, Heyzelle, Heyzill, Heyzille, Heyzil

Hezer (Hebrew) A woman of great strength
Hezir, Hezyr, Hezire, Hezyre, Hezere

Hiah (Korean) A bright woman
Heija, Heijah, Hia

Hiawatha (Native American) She who makes rivers
Hiawathah, Hyawatha, Hiwatha, Hywatha

Hiba (Arabic) A gift from God
Hibah, Heba, Hebah

Hibernia (Latin) Woman from Ireland
Hiberniah, Hibernea, Hybernia, Hybernea, Hibernya, Hybernya

Hibiscus (Latin) Resembling the showy flower
Hibiskus, Hibyscus, Hibyskus, Hybiscus, Hybiskus, Hybyscus, Hybyskus

Hicks (American) A saucy woman
Hiks, Hycks, Hyks, Hicksi, Hicksie, Hicksee, Hicksy, Hicksey, Hicksea

Hidayah (Arabic) One who provides guidance for others
Hidaya, Hydayah, Hydaya

Hidde (German) An honorable woman
Hiddee, Hiddy, Hiddey, Hidda, Hiddea

Hide (Japanese) A superior woman
Hideyo

Hideko (Japanese) A superior woman
Hydeko

Hidi (African) One who is rooted to the earth
Hidie, Hidy, Hidey, Hidee, Hidea

Hien (Vietnamese) A meek and gentle woman

Hierapolis (Hebrew) From the sacred city

Higgaion (Hebrew) One who meditates; a pause for reflection

Hija (African) Her father's daughter

Hijrah (Arabic) Refers to the migration of Muhammad
Hijra

Hikmah (Arabic) Having great wisdom
Hikmat, Hikma

Hilan (Greek) Filled with happines
Hylan, Hilane, Hilann, Hilanne, Hylane, Hylann, Hylanne

Hilary (Greek) A cheerful woman; bringer of joy
Hillary, Hilaree, Hilarie, Hilarey, Hilari, Hillari, Hillarie, Hillaree, Hillarey, Hillory, Hilaire, Hilaria, Hilery, Hillery, Hiliary, Hiliarie, Hylary, Hylarie, Hylari, Hylarey, Hylaree, Hyllari, Hyllary, Hilaeira, Hiolair, Hillarea, Hylarea, Hyllarea, Hilarea

Hildar (Scandinavian) A feisty woman
Hildarr, Hildare, Hildayr, Hildaer, Hyldar, Hyldarr, Hyldare, Hyldayr, Hyldaer, Hildair, Hyldair

Hildebrand (German) Having great strength
Hildibrund, Hildebrande, Hildibrande, Hyldebrand, Hyldibrand

Hildegard (German) A battlemaiden; a protector; in mythology, a Valkyrie
Hildegarde, Hildagarde, Hildagard, Hilda, Hilde, Hulda, Hylda, Hildred, Hildee, Hildi, Hildie, Hildey, Hildy, Hildia, Hildea, Hyldi, Hylda, Hylde, Hyldy, Hyldegard, Hyldegarde, Hyldagard, Hyldagarde, Hild, Hildegunn, Hildigunn, Holda, Hyldea

Hildemare (German) A glorious woman; famous in battle
Hildemara, Hildimar, Hildimara, Hildemar, Hyldemare, Hyldemar, Hyldemara

Hildireth (German) An advisor during war time
Hildreth

Hildur (Icelandic) A battlemaiden
Hildurr, Hyldur, Hyldurr, Hildura, Hyldura

Hilina (Hawaiian) Resembling a celestial body
Hilinah, Hileena, Hileenah, Hilyna, Hilynah, Hileana, Hileanah, Hiliena, Hilienah, Hileina, Hileinah

Hilliard (English / German) From the hill / a guardian during battle
Hiller, Hillierd, Hillyard, Hillyer, Hillyerd

Hilma (German) One who is protected
Hilmah, Hylma, Hylmah

Hilton (American) A wealthy woman
Hylton, Hiltan, Hyltan, Hiltun, Hyltun, Hillton, Hiltin, Hyltin

Himalaya (American) Woman from the mountains
Hymalaya

Hina (Polynesian) In mythology, a dual goddess symbolizing day and night
Hinna, Henna, Hinaa, Hinah, Heena, Hena

Hind (Arabic) Owning a group of camels; a wife of Muhammad
Hynd, Hinde, Hynde

Hinda (Hebrew) Resembling a doe
Hindah, Hindy, Hindey, Hindee, Hindi, Hindie, Hynda, Hyndy, Hyndey, Hyndee, Hyndi, Hyndie, Hindea, Hyndea, Hindal

Hine (Polynesian) One who is chaste; a maiden

Hinnom (Hebrew) From the deep ravine

Hinto (Native American) Having deep-blue eyes

Hinton (American) A wealthy woman
Hynton, Hintan, Hyntan, Hintun, Hyntun

Hippodamia (Greek) A tamer of horses; in mythology, a bride who was nearly kidnapped by centaurs
Hippodamea, Hippodameia, Hipodamia, Hipodamea, Hipodameia

Hippolyte (Greek) Feminine form of Hippolytus; one who frees the horses; in mythology, the queen of the Amazons
Hippolyta, Hippolite, Hippothoe

Hiral (Indian) A lustrous woman

Hiriwa (Polynesian) A silvery woman

Hirkani (Indian) Resembling a small diamond
Hirkanie, Hirkany, Hirkaney, Hirkanee, Hirkanea

Hiroko (Japanese) One who is noble and generous
Hiriko, Hyroko, Hyriko, Hyryko

Hisa (Japanese) A long-lived woman
Hisah, Hysa, Hisako, Hisayo, Hisano

Hisaye (Japanese) An everlasting beauty
Hisay, Hysaye, Hysay, Hisai, Hysai, Hisae, Hysae

Hisolda (Irish) Form of Isolda, meaning "a woman known for her beauty"
Hiseult, Hiseut, Hisold, Hisolde, Hisolt, Hisolte, Hisota, Hisotta, Hisotte, Hisoud, Hisoude

Hitomi (Japanese) One who has beautiful eyes
Hitomie, Hitomee, Hitomea, Hitomy, Hitomey

Hiya (Indian) Of the heart

Hoa (Vietnamese) One who is peaceful; resembling a flower
Hoah, Hoai

Hodaiah (Hebrew) One who praises God
Hodaviah, Hodiah, Hodijah, Hoda

Hodel (Hebrew) From the flowering myrtle tree
Hodell, Hodele, Hodelle, Hodela, Hodella

Hodesh (Hebrew) Born during the new moon
Hodesha, Hodeshah, Hodeshia, Hodeshea

Hodge (American) One who is confident
Hoge

Hoku (Polynesian) One who shines as bright as a star
Hokulani, Hokulanie, Hokulanee, Hokulanea, Hokulany, Hokulaney

Holbrook (English) From the brook on the hillside
Holebrook, Holbrooke, Holebrooke

Holda (German) A secretive woman; one who is hidden
Holde

Holden (English) One who is willing and eager
Holdin, Holdyn, Holdan

Holder (English) One who has a beautiful voice
Holdar, Holdir, Holdyr, Holdur

Holiday (American) Born on a festive day
Holliday, Holidaye, Hollidaye, Holidai, Hollidai, Holidae, Hollidae

Holine (American) A special woman
Holyne, Holeene, Holeane, Holeine, Holene

Holla (German) A secretive woman
Hollah

Hollander (Dutch) A woman from Holland
Hollynder, Hollender, Holander, Holynder, Holender, Hollande, Hollanda

Hollis (English) Near the valley of the holly bushes
Hollace, Holisa, Hollisa, Holise, Holyse, Hollice, Hollissa, Holyce, Hollyse, Hollisse, Holisse, Hollysa

Hollisha (English) A genius
Holleesha, Holleisha, Holliesha, Holleasha, Hollysha

Holly (English) Of the holly tree
Holli, Hollie, Hollee, Holley, Hollye, Hollyanne, Holle, Hollea, Hollei, Holleigh, Hollianne, Holleah, Hollyn, Holeena

Holsey (American) An easygoing woman
Holsy, Holsi, Holsie, Holsee, Holsea

Holton (American) One who is whimsical
Holten, Holtan, Holtin, Holtyn, Holtun

Holy (American) One who is pious or sacred
Holey, Holee, Holeigh, Holi, Holie, Holye, Holea, Holeah

Holyn (American) A fresh-faced woman
Holen, Holan, Holun, Holin

Homer (American) A tomboyish woman
Homar, Homir, Homyr, Homur, Homor

Honesty (American) One who is truthful and trustworthy
Honestey, Honesti, Honestie, Honestee, Honestea

Honey (American) A very sweet woman
Hony, Honie, Honi, Honee, Honye, Hunig, Honbria, Honbrie, Honbree, Honea

Hong (Vietnamese) A young girl with a rosy complexion

Honora (Latin) Having a good name and integrity; an honorable woman
Honour, Honoria, Honor, Honorata, Honoratas, Honnor, Honorina, Honorine, Honore, Honoree, Honori, Honorie, Honory, Honouri, Honourie, Honoury, Honoura, Honouria, Honoure, Honorea, Honourea

Honovi (Native American) As strong as a deer
Honovie, Honovee, Honovy, Honovey, Honovea

Hop (Vietnamese) One who is consistent

⊕ **Hope** (English) One who has expectations through faith

Hopkins (American) One who is perky
Hopkens, Hopkans, Hopkin, Hopkyns

Hor (Hebrew) Woman from the mountains

Horatia (English) Feminine form of Horace; the keeper of time
Horacia, Horacya, Horatya, Horatiah, Hora, Horada, Horae

Horem (Hebrew) One who is dedicated to God
Horema, Horemah, Horym, Horyma

Horiya (Japanese) Woman of the gardens
Horiyah, Horya, Horyah

Horonaim (Hebrew) Of the two caverns
Horonaima, Horonama, Horonayma, Horonayme, Horonaem, Horonaema

Hortensia (Latin) Woman of the garden
Hartencia, Hartinsia, Hortencia, Hortense, Hortenspa, Hortenxia, Hortinzia, Hortendana, Hortendanna, Hortendane

Hosah (Hebrew) One who provides refuge
Hosa

Hosanna (Latin) Raising one's voice in praise of God
Hosannah, Hosann, Hosane, Hosanne, Hosana, Hosanah

Hoshi (Japanese) One who shines as brightly as a star
Hoshiko, Hoshie, Hoshee, Hoshy, Hoshey, Hoshiyo, Hoshea

Hotaru (Japanese) Resembling a firefly

Hourig (Slavic) A small, fiery woman

Houston (American) From the city in Texas
Hewston, Huston

Hova (African) Born into the middle class

Howardena (German) Feminine form of
Howard; guardian of the home
*Howardina, Howardyna, Howardeena,
Howardiena, Howardeina, Howardeana*

Hristina (Slavic) Form of Christina, mean-
ing "follower of Christ"
*Hristinah, Hristeena, Hristyna, Hristiena,
Hristeina, Hristine, Hristyne, Hristeen,
Hristeene*

Hrothbeorhta (English) A famously bright
woman
Hrothberta, Hrothbertina, Hrothnerta

Hua (Chinese) Resembling a flower

Huang (Chinese) Yellow

Hubab (Arabic) An ambitious and focused
woman

Huda (Arabic) One who provides the right
guidance
Hooda, Hudah, Hoodah, Houda, Houdah

Hudel (Scandinavian) One who is lovable
Hudell, Hudele, Hudelle, Hudela, Hudella

Hudes (Hebrew) Form of Judith, meaning
"woman from Judea"

Hudi (Arabic) One who chooses the right
path
Hudie, Hudy, Hudey, Hudee, Hudea

Hudson (English) One who is adventurous;
an explorer
Hudsen, Hudsan, Hudsun, Hudsyn, Hudsin

Hudun (Arabic) One who is peaceful; quiet

Hue (Vietnamese) Resembling the lily
flower

Hueline (German) An intelligent woman
*Huelene, Huelyne, Hueleine, Hueliene,
Hueleene, Huleane*

Huette (German) Feminine form of Hugh;
having a bright mind; an intelligent woman
*Huguetta, Hugette, Huetts, Hughetta,
Hughette, Hugiet, Huberta, Huberte,
Hubertine, Hubertina, Huet, Hueta, Huetta,
Huitta, Huitte, Hugetta, Hughette, Huyet,
Huyete, Huyette, Huyett, Huyetta, Hughet,
Hugiherahta, Huela, Huella*

Huhana (Maori) Form of Susan, meaning
"resembling a graceful white lily"
*Huhanah, Huhanna, Huhanne, Huhann,
Huhane*

Huldah (Hebrew) Resembling a weasel; in
the Bible, the name of a prophetess
Hulda

Hulde (German) One who is dearly loved

Huma (Arabic) A bird who brings good
fortune
Humah, Humma, Humaa, Hummaa

Humairaa (Asian) A generous woman
*Humaira, Humayraa, Humayra, Humaeraa,
Humaera*

Humita (Native American) One who shells
corn
*Humitah, Humyta, Humeeta, Humieta,
Humeita, Humeata, Humytah, Humeetah,
Humietah, Humeitah, Humeatah*

Hunter (English) A great huntress and provider

Huong (Vietnamese) Having a delicate
scent of a flower

Hur (Arabic) An untouched woman; a virgin

Huraira (Arabic) A red-haired woman
*Hureaira, Hurairah, Hurayra, Hurayrah,
Huraera, Huraerah*

Huraiva (Arabic) A catlike woman
Huraivah, Hurayva, Hurava, Huraeva

Hurit (Native American) A beauty

Huriyah (Arabic) An independent woman;
freedom
*Huriya, Huriyyah, Hooriya, Huriyya,
Hooriyah*

Hurley (English) A healthy woman
*Hurly, Hurli, Hurlie, Hurlee, Hurlea,
Hurleigh*

Hushai (Hebrew) A quick-witted woman
Hushae, Hushay, Husha, Hushaye

Hutena (Hurrian) In mythology, the goddess of fate
Hutenah, Hutenna, Hutyna, Hutina

Hutton (English) One who is knowledgeable
Huttan, Hutten, Huttun, Hullyn, Huttin

Huwaidah (Arabic) One who is gentle
Huwaydah, Huwaida, Huwayda, Huwaeda, Huwaedah

Huxlee (American) One who is creative
Huxleigh, Huxly, Huxley, Huxli, Huxlie, Huxlea

Huyana (Native American) Daughter of the rain
Huyanna, Huyane, Huyann, Huyanne

Huyen (Vietnamese) A woman with jet-black hair

Hvergelmir (Norse) In mythology, the well-spring of cold waters
Hvergelmire, Hvergelmira, Hvergelmeer, Hvergelmeera

Hyacinth (Greek) Resembling the colorful fragrant flower
Hyacintha, Hyacinthe, Hycinth, Hycynth, Hyacinthia, Hyacinthea, Hyacinthie, Hyacynth, Hyacyntha

Hyades (Greek) A cluster of stars in the constellation Taurus; in mythology, daughters of the ocean

Hyatt (English) From the high gate
Hyat, Hyate, Hyatte, Hiatt, Hiat, Hiate, Hiatte

Hydeira (Greek) Woman of the water
Hydira, Hydyra, Hydeyra, Hydeera, Hydeara, Hydiera

Hydra (Greek) A constellation; in mythology, a monster killed by Hercules

Hye (Korean) A graceful woman
Hea, Hei

Hygeia (Greek) In mythology, the goddess of health
Hygia, Hygeiah, Hygea

Hyndla (Norse) In mythology, a priestess

Hypatia (Greek) An intellectually superior woman
Hypasia, Hypacia, Hypate

Hypermnestra (Greek) In mythology, the mother of Amphiareos

Hypsipyle (Greek) In mythology, the queen of Lemnos
Hypsypyle, Hipsipyle, Hipsipile, Hypsipile, Hypsypile

Hyrrokkin (Norse) In mythology, a giantess
Hyrokin, Hyrrokin, Hyrokkin

Hyun (Korean) Having great wisdom

■

I

Iamar (Arabic) Of the moon
Iumarah, Iamaria, Iamarea, Iamarra, Iamariah, Iamareah, Iamarrah

Ianeke (Hawaiian) God is gracious
Ianeki, Ianekie, Ianeky, Ianekey, Ianekea, Ianekee

Ianna (Gaelic) Feminine form of Ian; God is gracious
Iannah, Iana, Ianah, Ionna, Iona

Ianthe (Greek) Resembling the violet flower; in mythology, a sea nymph and a daughter of Oceanus
Iantha, Ianthia, Ianthina, Ianthyna, Ianthea, Ianthiya, Ianthya

Iara (Brazilian) In mythology, a water queen
Iarah, Iarra, Iarrah

Ibernia (Irish) Woman of Ireland
Iberniah, Ibernea, Iberneah, Iberniya, Iberniyah, Ibernya, Ibernyah

Ibolya (Hungarian) Violet; resembling a flower
Ibollya, Ibolyah, Ibolia, Iboliya

Ibtesam (Arabic) One who smiles often
Ibtisam, Ibtysam

Ibtihaj (Arabic) A delight; bringer of joy
Ibtehaj, Ibtyhaj

Ida (Greek) One who is diligent; hardworking; in mythology, the nymph who cared for Zeus on Mount Ida
Idania, Idaea, Idalee, Idaia, Idania, Idalia, Idalie, Idana, Idaline, Idalina, Idette, Idetta, Idett, Idet, Ideta, Idete

Idaa (Hindi) Woman of the earth

Idahlia (Greek) One with a sweet disposition
Idahliah, Idahlea, Idahleah, Idahliya, Idahliyah, Idahlya, Idahlyah

Idalika (Arabic) A queen; born to royalty
Idalikah, Idalicca, Idalica, Idalicka, Idalyka, Idalykah

Idarah (American) A social butterfly
Idara, Idarra, Idarrah

Idasia (English) Filled with joy
Idasiah, Idasea, Idaseah

Ide (Irish) One who is thirsty; also the name of a saint
Ideh

Idelle (Welsh) One who is happy; bountiful
Idelisa, Idella, Idelissa, Idele, Idela

Idil (Latin) A pleasant woman
Idyl, Idill, Idyll

Idoia (Spanish) Refers to the Virgin Mary
Idoea, Idurre, Iratze, Izazkun

Idola (German) A hardworking woman
Idolah, Idolla, Idollah, Idolina, Idolyna, Idoleena, Idoleana, Idoleina, Idoliena

Idona (Scandinavian) A fresh-faced woman
Idonah, Idonna, Idonnah, Idonia, Idoniah, Idonea, Idoneah, Idonya, Idonyah

Idony (Scandinavian) One who has been reborn
Idoney, Idonee, Idonea, Idoni, Idonie

Idowu (African) Daughter born after twins

Idra (Aramaic) A flourishing woman
Idrah

Idriya (Hebrew) A wealthy woman
Idriyah, Idria, Idriah

Idun (Norse) In mythology, goddess of youth, fertility, and death
Iduna, Idunna, Idunn, Idunnor

Iduvina (Spanish) A dedicated woman
Iduvinuh, Iduveena, Iduveenah, Iduviena, Iduvienah, Iduveina, Iduveinah, Iduveana, Iduveanah

Ierne (Irish) Woman from Ireland

Iesha (English) Form of Aisha, meaning "lively; womanly"
Ieshia, Ieshea, Ieesha, Ieasha, Ieashia, Ieashiah, Ieeshah, Ieeshia

Ifama (African) One's well-being
Ifamah, Ifamma, Ifammah

Ife (African) One who loves and is loved
Ifeh, Iffe

Ifeoma (African) A beautiful woman; a good thing
Ifeomah, Ifyoma, Ifyomah

Ignatia (Latin) A fiery woman; burning brightly
Igantiah, Ignacia, Ignazia, Iniga

Igone (Basque) Feminine form of Igon; ascension
Igona, Igoneh, Igonia, Igonea

Igraine (English) In Arthurian legend, Arthur's mother
Igrayne, Igrain, Igerne, Igrayn, Igraen, Igraene

Ihab (Arabic) A gift from God

Iheoma (Hawaiian) Lifted up by God

Ihsan (Arabic) Goodwill toward others
Ihsane, Ihsann, Ihsana, Ihsanna, Ihsanne

Ijada (Spanish) As beautiful as jade

Ikabela (Hawaiian) Form of Isabel, meaning "my God is bountiful"
Ikabell, Ikabelle, Ikabel, Ikabele, Ikabella

Ikea (Scandinavian) Having smooth skin
Ikeah, Ikiya, Ikiyah, Ikia, Ikiah

Ikeida (American) A spontaneous woman
Ikeidah, Ikeyda, Ikeydah, Ikeda, Ikedah, Ikieda, Ikiedah, Ikeeda, Ikeedah, Ikeada, Ikeadah

Iku (Japanese) A nurturing woman

Ila (Indian / French) Of the earth / from the island
Ilanis, Ilanys, Ilsa

Ilamay (French) From the island
Ilamaye, Ilamai, Ilamae

Ilana (Hebrew) Feminine form of Ilan; from the trees
Ilane, Ilania, Ilanit

Ilandere (American) Moon woman
Ilander, Ilanderre, Ilandera, Ilanderra

Ilaria (Italian) Form of Hilary, meaning "a cheerful woman; bringer of joy"
Illaire, Ilareu, Illaria, Ilaire, Ilariya, Illariya

Ildiko (Hungarian) Form of Hilda, meaning "a battlemaiden; a protector"
Ildyko, Ildicko, Ildycko, Ilda, Ildah

Ilena (English) Form of Aileen, meaning "the light-bearer; from the green meadow"
Ilene, Ilean, Ileen, Ileene, Ileena, Ilenna, Ileana

Ilepsie (Hebrew) Form of Hephzibah, meaning "she is my delight"
Ilepsi, Ilepsy, Ilepsey, Ilepsee, Ilepsea

Ilesha (Hindi) Of the earth
Ileshah, Ileesha, Ileeshah, Ileasha, Ileashah, Ilysha, Ilyshah

Ilham (Arabic) The heart's inspiration

Ilia (Greek) From the ancient city
Iliah, Ilea, Ileah, Iliya, Iliyah, Ilya, Ilyah

Iliana (Greek) Form of Helen, meaning "the shining light"
Ileana, Ileane, Ileanna, Ileanne, Illeanna, Illia, Illiana, Illianna, Illionya, Ilona, Ilonna, Iliona, Ilone, Ilonka, Illonna, Ilon

Ilima (Hebrew) The flower of Oahu
Ilimah, Illima, Ilyma, Ilymah, Iliema, Iliemah, Ileima, Ileimah, Ileema, Ileemah, Ileama, Ileamah

Ilisapesi (Tonga) The blessed child
Ilisapesie, Ilysapesi, Ilysapesie, Ilisapesy, Ilisapesea, Ilysupesie, Ilysapesea

Ilithyia (Greek) In mythology, goddess of childbirth
Ilithya, Ilithiya, Ilithyiah

Ilka (Slavic) A hardworking woman
Ilkah, Ilke, Ilkeh

Illinois (Native American) From the tribe of warriors; from the state of Illinois

Ilma (German) Form of Wilhelmina, meaning "determined protector"
Ilmah, Illma, Illmah

Ilori (African) A special child; one who is treasured
Illori, Ilorie, Illorie, Ilory, Illory, Ilorey, Illorey, Iloree, Illoree, Ilorea, Illorea

Ilse (German) Form of Elizabeth, meaning "my God is bountiful"
Ilseh, Ilsa, Ilsah, Ilisa, Illsa, Ilsae, Ilsaie, Ilyssa, Ilysa, Ilsea

Ilta (Finnish) Born at night
Iltah, Illta

Iluminada (Spanish) One who shines brightly
Iluminata, Ilumynada, Ilumynata, Iluska, Ilu

Ilyse (German / Greek) Born into the nobility / form of Elyse, meaning "my God is bountiful"
Ilysea, Ilysia, Ilysse, Ilysea

Ima (German) Form of Emma, meaning "one who is complete; a universal woman"
Imah, Imma, Immah

Imala (Native American) One who disciplines others
Imalah, Imalla, Imallah, Immala, Immalla

Iman (Arabic) Having great faith
Imani, Imanie, Imania, Imaan, Imany, Imaney, Imanee, Imanea, Imain, Imaine, Imaen, Imaene, Imayn, Imayne

Imanuela (Spanish) A faithful woman
Imanuella, Imanuel, Imanuele, Imanuell

Imara (Hungarian) A great ruler
Imarah, Imarra, Imarrah

Imari (Japanese) Daughter of today
Imarie, Imaree, Imarea, Imary, Imarey

Imelda (Italian) Warrior in the universal battle
Imeldah, Imalda, Imaldah

Imena (African) A dream
Imenah, Imenna, Imina, Imyna

Immaculata (Latin) Refers to the Immaculate Conception
Immaculatta, Immaculatah, Immaculada

Imogen (Gaelic / Latin) A maiden / one who is innocent and pure
Imogene, Imogenia, Imogine, Imojean, Imojeen, Imogenea, Immy, Immi, Immie

Imperia (Latin) A majestic woman
Imperiah, Imperea, Impereah, Imperial, Imperiel, Imperielle, Imperialle

Imtithal (Arabic) One who is polite and obedient
Imtithala, Imtithaal, Imtithalia, Imtithalea

Ina (Polynesian) In mythology, a moon goddess
Inah, Inna, Innah

Inaki (Asian) Having a generous nature
Inakie, Inaky, Inakey, Inakea, Inakee

In'am (Arabic) One who bestows kindness

Inanna (Sumerian) A lady of the sky; in mythology, goddess of love, fertility, war, and the earth
Inannah, Inana, Inanah, Inann, Inanne, Inane

Inara (Arabic) A heaven-sent daughter; one who shines with light
Inarah, Innara, Inarra, Innarra

Inari (Finnish / Japanese) Woman from the lake / one who is successful
Inarie, Inaree, Inary, Inarey, Inarea, Inareah

Inas (Arabic) One who is friendly and sociable
Inass, Inasse, Inasa, Inassa

Inaya (Arabic) One who cares for the well-being of others
Inayah, Inayat

Inca (Indian) An adventurer
Incah, Inka, Inkah, Incka, Inckah

Independence (American) One who has freedom
Independance, Indepindence, Indipindince, Indypyndynce

India (English) From the river; woman from India
Indea, Indiah, Indeah, Indya, Indiya, Indee, Inda, Indy, Indi

Indiana (English) From the land of the Indians; from the state of Indiana
Indianna, Indyana, Indyanna

Indiece (American) A capable woman
Indeice, Indeace, Indeece, Indiese, Indeise, Indeese, Indease

Indigo (English) Resembling the plant; a purplish-blue dye
Indygo, Indeego

Indira (Hindi) A beautiful woman; in Hinduism, another name for Lakshmi
Indirah, Indyra, Indiera, Indeera, Indeira, Indeara, Indyrah, Indierah, Indeerah, Indeirah, Indearah

Indra (Hindi) One who possesses the rain; in Hinduism, a deity of thunder and rain
Indrah, Indrani, Indranie, Indranee, Indrina

Indray (American) One who is outspoken
Indraye, Indrae, Indrai, Indree

Indre (Hindi) Woman of splendor

Indu (Hindi) Woman of the moon
Indukala, Induma

Indumati (Hindi) Born beneath the full moon
Indumatie, Indumaty, Indumatey, Indumatee, Indumatea

Ineesha (American) A sparkling woman
Ineeshah, Ineisha, Ineishah, Iniesha, Inieshah, Ineasha, Ineashah, Ineysha, Ineyshah

Ineke (Japanese) One who nurtures

Ines (Spanish) Form of Agnes, meaning "one who is pure; chaste"
Inez, Inesa, Inesita, Inessa, Inetta, Ineta

Infinity (American) A woman unbounded by space or time
Infinitey, Infiniti, Infinitie, Infinitee, Infinitye, Infinitea

Ingalill (Scandinavian) A fertile woman
Ingulyll, Ingalil, Ingalyl, Ingalille, Ingalylle

Ingalls (American) A peaceful woman

Ingeborg (Scandinavian) Protected by the god Ing
Ingaberg, Ingaborg, Inge, Ingegerg, Inngeborg, Ingibjorg, Inga, Ingunn, Ingunna, Injerd

Ingegard (Scandinavian) Of the god Ing's kingdom
Ingagard, Ingegerd, Ingagerd, Ingigard, Ingigerd

Ingelise (Danish) Having the grace of the god Ing
Ingelisse, Ingeliss, Ingelyse, Ingelisa, Ingelissa, Ingelysa, Ingelyssa

Inghean (Scottish) Her father's daughter
Ingheane, Inghinn, Ingheene, Ingheen, Inghynn

Ingrid (Scandinavian) Having the beauty of the god Ing
Ingred, Ingrad, Inga, Inge, Inger, Ingmar, Ingrida, Ingria, Ingrit, Inkeri

Iniguez (Spanish) A good woman

Iniko (African) Daughter born during hardship
Inicko, Inicco, Inico, Inyko, Inycko, Inycco, Inyco

Inis (Irish) Woman from Ennis
Iniss, Inisse, Innis, Inys, Innys, Inyss, Inysse

Ino (Greek) In mythology, the daughter of Cadmus

Inocencia (Spanish) One who is pure and innocent
Innocencia, Innocenta, Inocenta, Inocentia, Inoceneia, Innoceneia, Innocentia, Innocence

Inoke (Hawaiian) A faithful woman

Integra (Latin) A woman of importance

Integrity (American) One who is truthful; of good character
Integritey, Integritee, Integritea, Integriti, Integritie

Intisar (Arabic) One who is victorious; triumphant
Intisara, Intisarah, Intizar, Intizara, Intizarah, Intisarr, Intysarr, Intysar

Invidia (Latin) An envious woman
Invidiah, Invidea, Invideah, Invydia, Invydea, Invidiya, Invidiyah

Io (Greek) In mythology, a woman who was turned into a cow to elude Zeus

Iokina (Hawaiian) God will develop
Iokinah, Iokyna, Iokeena, Iokine, Iokyne, Iokeen, Iokeane, Iokeana

Iola (Greek) Of the violet-colored dawn
Iolah, Iolla, Iollah, Iole, Iolle, Inola, Inolah, Inolla, Inollah

Iolana (Hawaiian) Soaring like a hawk
Iolanah, Iolanna, Iolann, Iolanne, Iolane, Iolani, Iolanie, Iolanee, Iolany, Iolaney

Iolanthe (Greek) Resembling a violet flower
Iolanda, Iolanta, Iolantha, Iolante, Iolande, Iolanthia, Iolanthea

Iona (Greek) Woman from the island
Ionna, Ioane, Ioann, Ioanne

Ionanna (Hebrew) Filled with grace
Ionannah, Ionana, Ionann, Ionane, Ionanne

Ione (Greek) Resembling the violet flower
Ionie, Ioni, Ionee, Ioney, Iony

Ionia (Greek) Of the sea and islands
Ionya, Ionija, Ioniah, Ionea, Ionessa, Ioneah, Ioniya

Iora (Greek) A birdlike woman
Iorra, Ioria, Iorea, Iore, Iorie, Iori, Iory, Iorey, Ioree

Iorwen (Welsh) A beautiful woman
Iorwenn, Iorwenne, Iorwin, Iorwinn, Iorwinne, Iorwyn, Iorwynn, Iorwynne

Iosepine (Hawaiian) Form of Josephine, meaning "God will add"
Iosephine, Iosefa, Iosefena, Iosefene, Iosefina, Iosefine, Iosepha, Iosephe, Iosephene, Iosephina, Iosephyna, Iosephyna, Iosephyne, Iosepyne, Iosapine, Iosapyne, Iosepeen, Iosapeen

Iowa (Native American) Of the Iowa tribe; from the state of Iowa

Iphedeiah (Hebrew) One who is saved by the Lord
Iphedeia, Iphedia, Iphedea, Iphidea, Iphidia, Iphideia

Iphigenia (Greek) One who is born strong; in mythology, daughter of Agamemnon
Iphigeneia, Iphigenie, Iphagenia, Iphegenia, Iphegenie, Iphegeneia, Ifigenia, Ifegenia, Ifagenia

Iphimedeia (Greek) In mythology, the wife of Poseidon
Iphimedea, Iphimedea, Ifimedeia, Ifimedea, Ifimedia

Ipo (Hawaiian) A sweet woman; a darling

Ipsa (Indian) One who is desired
Ipsita, Ipsyta, Ipseeta, Ipseata, Ipsah

Ira (Hebrew / Indian) One who is watchful / of the earth
Irah, Irra, Irrah

Iratze (Basque) Refers to the Virgin Mary
Iratza, Iratzia, Iratzea, Iratzi, Iratzie, Iratzy, Iratzey, Iratzee

Irem (Turkish) From the heavenly gardens
Irema, Ireme, Iremia, Iremea

Irene (Greek) A peaceful woman; in mythology, the goddess of peace
Ira, Irayna, Ireen, Iren, Irena, Irenea, Irenee, Irenka, Iriana, Irina, Irine, Iryna, Irenke, Iryne, Irini, Irinia, Irynia

Ireta (Greek) One who is serene
Iretah, Iretta, Irettah, Irete, Iret, Irett, Ireta

Iris (Greek) Of the rainbow; a flower; in mythology, a messenger goddess
Irida, Iridiana, Iridianny, Irisa, Irisha, Irita, Iria, Irea, Iridian, Iridiane, Iridianna, Iriss, Irys, Iryss

Irish (American) Woman from Ireland
Irysh, Irisha, Irysha

Irma (German) A universal woman
Irmina, Irmine, Irmgard, Irmgarde, Irmagard, Irmagarde, Irmeena, Irmyna, Irmuska

Irodell (American) A peaceful woman
Irodelle, Irodel, Irodele, Irodella, Irodela

Irta (Greek) Resembling a pearl
Irtah

Irune (Basque) Refers to the Holy Trinity
Iroon, Iroone, Iroun, Iroune

Irvette (English) Friend of the sea
Irvetta, Irvett, Irvete, Irvet, Irveta, Irvina, Irvinna, Irvena

Isabel (Spanish) Consecrated to God
*Isabeau, Isabele, Isabell, **Isabelle**, Ishbel, Isobel, Isobell, Isobelle, Issie, Issy, Izabel, Izabelle, Izzie, Izzy, Ibby, Ib, Ibbi, Ibbie, Isa, Isibeal, Isibelle, Isibel, Isibell, Isahel, Isahelle, Iseabal, Isobail, Isobael, Isohel*

☺ **Isabella** (Italian / Spanish) Form of Isabel, meaning "consecrated to God"
Isabela, Isabelita, Isobella, Izabella, Isibella, Isibela, Isahella

Isabis (African) A beautiful child
Isabys, Isabiss, Isabisse, Isabyss, Isabysse

Isadore (Greek) A gift from the goddess Isis
Isadora, Isador, Isadoria, Isidor, Isidoro, Isidorus, Isidro, Isidora, Isidoria, Isidore, Izidore, Izadore, Izidora, Izadora, Izidoria, Izadoria

Isairis (Spanish) A lively woman
Isairys, Isaeris, Isaerys, Isaire, Isaere, Isair

Isamu (Japanese) One who has a lot of energy

Isana (German) A strong-willed woman
Isanah, Isanna, Isane, Isann, Isanne, Isan

Isaura (Greek) Of the soft breeze
Isaure, Isauria, Isaurea

Isela (American) A giving woman
Iselah, Isella, Isellah

Isha (Indian / Hebrew) The protector / a lively woman
Ishah

Ishana (Indian) A wealthy lady
Ishanah, Ishanna, Ishannah, Ishann, Ishanne, Ishane, Ishani, Ishanie, Ishany, Ishaney, Ishanee, Ishara, Isharah, Isharra

Ishi (Japanese) As solid as a rock
Ishie, Ishy, Ishey, Ishee, Ishea, Isheah, Ishiko

Ishtar (Persian) In mythology, a mother goddess of love and fertility
Ishtarr, Ishtarre, Ishtara, Ishtarah, Ishtarra, Ishtarrah

Isi (Native American) Resembling a deer
Isie, Isee, Isey, Isy, Isea, Ise

Isis (Egyptian) In mythology, the most powerful of all goddess

Isla (Gaelic) From the island
Islay, Islae, Islai, Isleta, Isletta, Islyta

Isleen (Gaelic) Form of Aislinn, meaning "a dream or vision; an inspiration"
Isleene, Islyne, Islyn, Isline, Isleine, Isliene, Islene, Isleyne, Isleane

Ismaela (Spanish) Feminine form of Ismael; God will listen
Ismaelah, Ismaila, Ismala, Ismalia, Ismalea, Ismayla

Ismat (Arabic) One who safeguards others
Ismate, Ismatte, Ismata, Ismatta, Ismatah

Ismay (French) Form of Esme, meaning "one who is esteemed"
Isme, Ismai, Ismae, Ismaa, Ismaye

Ismene (Greek) In mythology, the daughter of Oedipus and Jocasta
Ismeen, Ismeene, Ismyn, Ismyne, Ismine, Ismey, Ismenia, Ismenea, Ismi, Ismie, Ismini, Ismean, Ismeane, Ismea

Ismitta (African) Daughter of the mountains
Ismittah, Ismita, Ismytta, Ismyta

Isoke (African) A gift from God
Isoka, Isokah

Isolde (Celtic) A woman known for her beauty; in mythology, the lover of Tristan
Iseult, Iseut, Isold, Isolda, Isolt, Isolte, Isota, Isotta, Isotte, Isoud, Isoude, Izett

Isra (Arabic) One who travels in the evening
Israh, Isria, Isrea, Israt

Istas (Native American) A snow queen
Istass, Istasse, Istasa, Istassa, Isatas, Isatass

Ita (Irish) One who is thirsty
Itah, Itta, Ittah, Iti, Itie, Ity, Itey, Itee, Itea, Itka

Italia (Italian) Woman from Italy
Italiah, Italea, Italeah, Itala, Italla, Itali, Italie, Italy, Italey, Italee, Italeigh

Itiah (Hebrew) One who is comforted by God
Itia, Iteah, Itea, Itiyah, Itiya, Ityah, Itya

Itica (Spanish) One who is eloquent
Iticah, Itika, Itikah, Iticka, Itickah, Ityca, Itycah, Ityka, Itykah, Itycka, Ityckah

Itidal (Arabic) One who is cautious
Itidalle, Itidall, Itidale

Itinsa (Hawaiian) From the waterfall
Itinsah, Itynsa, Itynsah

Ito (Japanese) A delicate woman

Itsaso (Basque) Woman of the ocean
Itasasso, Itassaso, Itassasso

Ituha (Native American) As sturdy as an oak
Ituhah, Itooha, Itoohah, Itouha, Itouhah

Itxaro (Basque) One who has hope
Itxarro

Itzel (Spanish) Form of Isabel, meaning "my God is bountiful"
Itzell, Itzele, Itzelle, Itzela, Itzella

Itzy (American) A lively woman
Itzey, Itzi, Itzie, Itzea, Itzee

Iuana (Welsh) God is gracious
Iuanah, Iuanna, Iuannah, Iuanne, Iuan, Iuann, Iuane

Iudita (Hawaiian) An affectionate woman
Iuditah, Iudyta, Iudytah, Iudeta, Iudetah

Iuginia (Hawaiian) Form of Eugenia, meaning "a wellborn woman"
Iuginiah, Iuginea, Iugineah, Iugynia, Iugyniah, Iugynea, Iugyneah, Iugenia, Iugeniah, Iugenea, Iugeneah

Iulaua (Hawaiian) One who is eloquent

Iulia (Latin) Form of Julia, meaning "one who is youthful; daughter of the sky"
Iuliah, Iulea, Iulea, Iulie, Iuli, Iuly, Iuley, Iulee, Iuleigh, Iulius, Iuliet, Iuliette

Iusitina (Hawaiian) Form of Justine, meaning "one who is just and upright"
Iusitinah, Iusiteena, Iusiteenah, Iusityna, Iusitynah, Iusiteana, Iusiteanah

Ivana (Slavice) Feminine form of Ivan; God is gracious
Iva, Ivah, Ivania, Ivanka, Ivanna, Ivanya, Ivanea, Ivane, Ivanne

Iverem (African) One who is favored by God

Iviana (American) One who is adorned
Ivianah, Ivianna, Iviannah, Ivianne, Iviane, Ivian, Ivyana, Ivyanna, Ivyanne, Ivyane, Ivyann

Ivisse (American) A graceful woman
Iviss, Ivise, Iviese, Ivysse, Ivyss, Ivyse, Ivease, Iveese

Ivonne (French) Form of Yvonne, meaning "a young archer"
Ivonn, Ivon, Ivone, Ivona, Ivonna, Ivette, Ivett, Ivet, Ivete, Ivetta, Iveta

Ivory (English) Having a creamy-white complexion; as precious as elephant tusks
Ivorie, Ivorine, Ivoreen, Ivorey, Ivoree, Ivori, Ivoryne, Ivorea, Ivoreah, Ivoreane

Ivria (Hebrew) From the opposite side of the river
Ivriah, Ivrea, Ivreah, Ivriya, Ivriyah

Ivy (English) Resembling the evergreen vining plant
Ivee, Ivey, Ivie, Ivalyn, Ivyanne, Ivi, Ivyane, Ivea, Iveah

Iwa (Japanese) Of strong character
Iwah

Iwalani (Hawaiian) Resembling a seagull in the sky
Iwalanie, Iwalany, Iwalaney, Iwalanee, Iwalanea

Iwilla (American) She shall rise
Iwillah, Iwilah, Iwila, Iwylla, Iwyllah, Iwyla, Iwylah

Iwona (Polish) Form of Yvonne, meaning "a young archer"
Iwonah, Iwonne, Iwone, Iwonna, Iwonn, Iwon

Ixchel (Mayan) The rainbow lady; in mythology, the goddess of the earth, moon, and healing
Ixchell, Ixchelle, Ixchela, Ixchella, Ixchal, Ixchall, Ixchalle, Ixchala, Ixchalla

Iyabo (African) The mother is home

Iyana (Hebrew) A sincere woman
Iyanah, Iyanna, Iyannah, Iyanne, Iyane, Iyan

Izanne (American) One who calms others
Izann, Izane, Izana, Izan, Izanna

Izar (Spanish) A starlike woman
Izare, Izarre, Izarr, Izarra, Izara, Izaria, Izarea

Izdihar (Arabic) A flourishing woman; blooming
Izdihare, Izdihara, Izdiharia, Izdiharea, Izdiharra, Izdiharre

Izebe (African) One who supports others
Izeby, Izebey, Izebee, Izebea, Izebi, Izebie

Izefia (African) A childless woman
Izefiah, Izefya, Izefiya, Izephia, Izefa, Izepha, Izefea, Izephea

Izegbe (African) One who was asked for
Izegby, Izegbey, Izegbee, Izegbea, Izegbi, Izegbie

Izellah (American) A princess; a devoted woman
Izella, Izela, Izelah

Izolde (Greek) One who is philosophical
Izold, Izolda

Izso (Hebrew) One who is saved by God
Izsa, Izsah, Isso, Issa

Izusa (Native American) Resembling the white stone
Izusah, Izussa, Izuza, Izuzza

Izzy (American) A fun-loving woman
Izzey, Izzi, Izzie, Izzee, Izzea

j

Jaakkina (Finnish) Feminine form of Jukka; God is gracious
Jakkina, Jaakkinah, Jaakina, Jakina, Jakyna, Jakeena, Jadeana

Jaala (Hebrew) Resembling a she-goat of the wild
Jaalah

Jaantje (Hebrew) A gift from heaven
Jantje

Jaasau (Hebrew) One who makes goods; a fabricator

Jabmen (Arabic) Woman with a high forehead
Jabmin, Jabman, Jabmon, Jabmun

Jacaranda (Latin) Resembling the tree with purple flowers
Jacarannda, Jacarranda, Jacarandah, Jacarandia, Jacurandea, Jakaranda, Jackaranda

Jacey (American) Form of Jacinda, meaning "resembling the hyacinth"
Jacee, Jacelyn, Jaci, Jacine, Jacy, Jaicee, Jaycee, Jacie, Jaycey, Jaycie, Jayci, J.C., Jacea, Jaycea

Jachan (Hebrew) Woman of sorrow; one who mourns
Jachane, Jachana, Jachanne, Jachann, Jachanna

Jacinda (Spanish) Resembling the hyacinth
Jacenda, Jacenia, Jacenta, Jacindia, Jacinna, Jacinta, Jacinth, Jacintha, Jacinthe, Jacinthia, Jacynth, Jacyntha, Jacynthe, Jacynthia, Jakinda, Jakinta, Jaikinda, Jaekinda

Jacoba (Hebrew) Feminine form of Jacob; she who supplants
Jacobetta, Jacobette, Jacobine, Jacobyna, Jakobina, Jakoba, Jakobetta, Jakobette, Jakobine, Jakobyna, Jacobyne, Jackoba, Jackobine, Jackobina, Jackobyne, Jackobyna, Jakobe, Jakobie

Jacqueline (French) Feminine form of Jacques; the supplanter
Jacalin, Jacalyn, Jacalynn, Jackalin, Jackalinne, Jackelyn, Jacketta, Jackette, Jacki, Jackie, Jacklin, Jacklyn, Jacklynne, Jackqueline, Jacky, Jaclin, Jaclyn, Jacolyn, Jacqi, Jacqlyn, Jacqualine, Jacqualyn, Jacquel, Jacquelean, Jacqueleen, Jacquelin, Jacquelina, Jacquella, Jacquelle, Jacquelyn, Jacquelyne, Jacquelynn, Jacquelynne, Jacquenetta, Jacquenette, Jacquetta, Jacquette, Jacqui, Jacquine, Jaculine, Jakleen, Jaklyn, Jaquelin, Jaqueline, Jaquelyn, Jaquelynn, Jaquith, Jaquenetta, Jaquetta

Jaddua (Hebrew) One who is well-known
Jadduah, Jadua, Jaduah

❶ **Jade** (Spanish) Resembling the green gemstone
Jada, *Jadeana, Jadee, Jadine, Jadira, Jadrian, Jadrienne, Jady, Jaeda, Jaida, Jaide, **Jayda**, Jayde, Jaydee, Jadea, Jaydea*

❶ **Jaden** (Hebrew / English) One who is thankful to God / form of Jade, meaning "resembling the green gemstone"
*Jadine, Jadyn, Jadon, **Jayden**, Jadyne, Jaydyn, Jaydon, Jaydine, Jadin, Jaydin, Jaidyn, Jaedan, Jaeden, Jaedin, Jaedon, Jaedyn, Jaidan, Jaidin, Jaidon, Jaidyn, Jaydan*

Jadwige (Polish) One who is protected in battle
Jadwyge, Jadwig, Jadwyg, Jadwiga, Jadwyga, Jadriga, Jadryga, Jadreega

Jadzia (Polish) A princess; born into royalty
Jadziah, Jadzea, Jadzeah, Judziya, Jadziyah, Jadzya, Jadzyah

Jae (English) Feminine form of Jay; resembling a jaybird
Jai, Jaelana, Jaeleah, Jaeleen, Jaelyn, Jaenette, Jaya, Jaylee, Jayleen, Jaylene, Jaylynn, Jaye, Jay, Jaylea

Jael (Hebrew) Resembling a mountain goat
Jaella, Jaelle, Jayel, Jaela, Jaele, Jayil

Jaen (Hebrew) Resembling an ostrich
Jaena, Jaenia, Jaenea, Jaenne

Jaffa (Hebrew) A beautiful woman
Jaffah, Jafit, Jafita

Jaganmatri (Indian) Mother of nations
Jaganmatrie, Jaganmatree, Jaganmata,
Jaganmatria, Jaganmatrea

Jagrati (Indian) Of the awakening
Jagratie, Jagraty, Jagratey, Jagratee, Jagratea

Jaha (African) One who has dignity
Jahah

Jahana (Iranian) Feminine form of Jahan; a
woman of the world
Jahane, Jahania, Jahanea, Jahanna, Jahanne

Jahath (Hebrew) Recognizing the importance of a union
Jahathe, Jahatha

Jahaziah (Hebrew) The Lord's vision
Jahaziel, Jahazia, Jahazea, Jahazeah,
Jahaziell, Jahazielle

Jahia (African) One who is widely known
Jahiah, Jahea, Jaheah, Jahiya, Jahiyah

Jahnavi (Indian) Woman from the river
Jahnavie, Janavi, Janavie, Jahnavee, Janavee,
Jahnavea, Janavea, Jahnavy, Janavy,
Jahnavey, Janavey

Jahzara (African) One who is blessed with
power and wealth
Jahzarah, Jazara, Jazarra, Jazarah

Jaione (Basque) Refers to the Nativity

Jaira (Hebrew) Feminine form of Jairus; she
who shines
Jaera, Jayra, Jairia, Jairea

Jairdan (American) One who educates others
Jardan, Jayrdan, Jaerdan

Jakayla (Native American) One who is
crowned with laurel
Jakaela, Jakaila

Jakim (Hebrew) One who brings others
together; the establisher
Jakima, Jakimah, Jakime, Jakyma, Jakeema,
Jakeima, Jakiema, Jakeama

Jala (Arabic) Woman of clarity
Jalah, Jalla, Jallah

Jaleh (Persian) Born of the rain

Ⓣ Jalen (American) One who is calm; a healer
Jaelan, Jaelin, Jaelon, Jailin, Jaillen, Jaillin,
*Jailon, Jalan, Jalin, Jalon, Jayelan, **Jaylen**,*
Jayelen, Jaylan, Jaylon, Jaylonn, Jalena,
Jalina, Jalona, Jalana, Jailene, Jailyn, Jalene,
Jalynn, Jalyn

Jalia (American) A noble woman
Jaliah, Jalea, Jaleah

Jalila (Arabic) An important woman; one
who is exalted
Jalilah, Jalyla, Jalylah, Jaleela, Jaleelah, Jalil,
Jaleala, Jalealah

Jaliyah (English) A gift of God
Jaliya, Jaleeya, Jaleeyah, Jalieya, Jaleyah,
Jalieyah, Jaleya, Jaleaya

Jam (American) One who is sweet

Jamaica (American) From the island of
springs
Jamaeca, Jamaika, Jemaica, Jamika,
Jamieka, Jameika, Jamyka, Jemayka,
Jamaeka, Jemaeka

Jamari (French) A woman warrior
Jamarie, Jamary, Jamarey, Jamaree, Jamarea

Jameelah (Arabic) A beautiful and elegant
lady
Jameela, Jamela, Jamelia, Jamilah, Jamila,
Jamilia, Jamilla, Jamille, Jamelia, Jemila,
Jemilla, Jemeela, Jemyla, Jameala, Jemeala

Jamie (Hebrew) Feminine form of James;
she who supplants
Jaima, Jaime, Jaimee, Jaimelynn, Jaimey,
Jaimi, Jaimie, Jaimy, Jama, Jamee, Jamei,
Jamese, Jamey, Jami, Jamia, Jamielee,
Jamilyn, Jammie, Jayme, Jaymee, Jaymie,
Jaymi, Jamesina, Jameson, Jamison, Jamese,
Jaimica, Jame, Jamea, Jaimea

Jamuna (Indian) From the sacred river
Jamoona, Jamunah, Jamoonah, Jamouna,
Jamounah

Janae (Hebrew) God has answered our
prayers
Janai, Janais, Janay, Janaya, Janaye, Janea,
Jannae, Jeanae, Jeanay, Jeanay, Jenae, Jenai,
Jenay, Jenee, Jennae, Jennay, Jinae, Jinnea

Janan (Arabic) Of the heart and soul

Jane (Hebrew) Feminine form of John; God is gracious
Jaina, Jaine, Jainee, Janey, Jana, Janae, Janaye, Jandy, Janeczka, Janeen, Janel, Janela, Janelba, Janella, Janelle, Janean, Janeane, Janee, Janene, Janerita, Janessa, Jayney, Jania, Janicu, Janie, Janina, Janine, Janique, Janka, Janna, Jannel, Jannelle, Janney, Janny, Jany, Jayna, Jayne, Jaynell, Jayni, Jaynie, Jenda, Jenella, Jenelle, Jenica, Jeniece, Jeni, Jenie, Jensina, Jensine, Jess, Jinna, Jonella, Jonelle, Joni, Jonie, Jeena, Jiana, Jianna, Janecska, Jenina, Jenine, Jensen, Jaen, Jaena

Janeeva (American) Resembling the juniper
Janeevah, Janyva, Janyvah, Janeava, Janeavah, Janeva, Janevah

Janet (Scottish) Feminine form of John; God is gracious
Janeta, Janeth, Janett, Janetta, Janette, Janit, Jannet, Janneth, Janetta, Jannette, Janot, Jenetta, Jenette, Jennet, Jennette, Jinnet, Jinnett

Janis (English) Feminine form of John; God is gracious
Janice, Juneece, Janess, Janessa, Janesse, Janessia, Janicia, Janiece, Janique, Janise, Janiss, Jannice, Jannis, Janyce, Jency, Jenice, Jeniece, Jenise, Jennice, Janisa, Janys, Jannys

Jannat (Arabic) From the garden of heaven
Jannate, Jannata, Jannatia, Jannatea, Jennet, Jenneta, Jennetia, Jennetea

Janoah (Hebrew) A quiet and calm child
Janoa, Jonoah, Jonoa, Janowa, Janowah

January (Latin) A winter child; born during the month of January
Januarie, Januari, Januarey, Januaree, Januarea

Janya (Indian) A lively woman; one who gives life
Janyah, Janiya, Janiyah

Japera (African) One who gives thanks to God
Japerah, Japerra, Japiera, Japeira, Japyra

Jara (Slavic) Daughter born in spring

Jarah (Hebrew) A sweet and kind woman

Jardena (Spanish / Hebrew) From the garden / form of Jordan; of the down-flowing river
Jardina, Jardenah, Jardinah, Jardeena, Jardyna, Jardeina, Jardiena, Jardeana, Jardeenah, Jardynah, Jardeinah, Jardienah, Jardeanah

Jarina (Greek) One who works the earth; a farmer
Jarine, Jarinah, Jarineh, Jaryne, Jaryna, Jaryn, Jareena, Jareene

Jarita (Indian) A birdlike woman
Jaritah, Jareeta, Jareetah, Jaryta, Jarytah, Jarieta, Jarietah, Jareita, Jareitah, Jareata, Jareatah

Jarnsaxa (Norse) In mythology, the mother of Magni by Thor
Jarnsax, Jarnsaxe, Jarnsaxia, Jarnsaxea

Jarvia (German) Having great intelligence
Jarvinia, Jarviah, Jarvea, Jarveah, Jarviya, Jarvinea, Jarvina

Jasher (Hebrew) One who is righteous; upright
Jashiere, Jasheria, Jasherea, Jashera, Jashiera

☘ **Jasmine** (Persian) Resembling the climbing plant with fragrant flowers
Jaslyn, Jaslynn, Jasmeen, Jasmin, Jasmina, Jasminda, Jasmyn, Jasmyne, Jassamayn, Jazan, Jazmin, Jazmine, Jazmon, Jazmyn, Jazmyne, Jazzmin, Jazzmine, Jazzmon, Jazzmyn, Jazzmynn, Jasmyna, Jessamine, Jessamy, Jessamyn, Jasmeena, Jessimine, Jessimine

Jauhera (Arabic) As precious as a jewel
Jauherah, Jawahar, Jawahara, Jawaahar, Jawahare, Johari, Johara, Joharra, Joharie, Joharee

Jaunie (American) A brave and courteous woman
Jauni, Jaunee, Jauny, Jauney, Jaunea

Javana (Hebrew) Feminine form of Javan; woman from Greece
Javane, Javanna, Javanne, Javann

Javiera (Spanish) Feminine form of Xavier; owner of a new house; one who is bright
Javierah, Javyera, Javyerah, Javeira, Javeirah

Jaxine (American) Form of Jacinda, meaning "resembling the hyacinth"
Jaxin, Jaxyne, Jaxeen, Jaxyn, Jaxeene, Jax, Jaxi, Jaxie, Jaxee, Jaxea

Jaya (Hindi) A victorious woman; in Hinduism, one of the names of the wife of Shiva
Jayah

Jayanti (Indian) Feminine form of Jayant; a victorious woman
Jayantie, Jayantee, Jayanty, Jayantey, Jayantea

Jaydra (Arabic) Filled with goodness
Jaydrah, Jadra, Jadrah, Jaidra, Jaedra

Jayla (Arabic) One who is charitable
Jaylah, Jaila, Jaela

Jazzelle (American) One who is promised; influenced by the style of music
Jazelle, Jazzele, Jazzell, Jazele, Jazell, Jazzlyn, Jazette, Jazlyn, Jazlynn, Jazzalyn, Jazzy, Jazz, Jaslynn

Jean (Hebrew) Feminine form of John; God is gracious
Jeanae, Jeanay, Jeane, Jeanee, Jeanelle, Jeanetta, Jeanette, Jeanice, Jeanie, Jeanna, Jehane, Jeanne, Jeana, Jeanine, Jeannine, Jeanea

Jearim (Hebrew) Woman from the woodland
Jearym, Jeareem, Jeaream

Jearl (American) Form of Pearl, meaning "a precious gem of the sea"
Jearla, Jearle, Jearlie, Jearly, Jearline, Jearlina, Jearlea, Jearli, Jearley, Jearlee, Jearleigh

Jecoliah (Hebrew) All things are possible through the Lord
Jecolia, Jecolea, Jecoleah, Jecholia, Jekolia, Jecoliya, Jekoliya, Jekolea

Jedida (Hebrew) One who is greatly loved
Jedidah, Jedyda, Jedydah, Jedeeda, Jedeedah, Jeddida, Jedieda, Jediedah, Jedeida, Jedeidah, Jedeada, Jedeadah

Jehaleleel (Hebrew) One who praises God
Jehalelel, Jahaleleil, Jehaleliel, Jehalelyl, Jehaleleal

Jehan (Arabic) Resembling a beautiful flower; woman of the world
Jihan, Jyhan

Jehonadab (Hebrew) The Lord gives liberally
Jonadab

Jehosheba (Hebrew) An oath of the Lord
Jehoshebah, Jehoshyba, Jehosheeba, Jehosheiba, Jehoshieba, Jehosheaba

Jehucal (Hebrew) An able-bodied woman
Jehucale, Jucal, Jehucala

Jela (Swahili) Born of the suffering father
Jelah, Jella, Jellah

Jelena (Russian) Form of Helen, meaning "the shining light"
Jalaina, Jalaine, Jalayna, Jalena, Jelina, Jelka, Jelaena

Jemima (Hebrew) Our little dove; in the Bible, the eldest of Job's daughters
Jemimah, Jamina, Jeminah, Jemmimah, Jemmie, Jemmy, Jem, Jemmi, Jemmey, Jemmee, Jemmea

Jemina (Hebrew) One who is listened to
Jeminah, Jemyna, Jemynah, Jemeena, Jemeenah, Jemeina, Jemeinah, Jemiena, Jemienah, Jemeana, Jemeanah

Jemma (English) Form of Gemma, meaning "precious jewel"
Jemmah, Jema, Jemah, Jemmalyn, Jemalyn, Jemmalynn, Jemalynn

Jena (Arabic) Our little bird
Jenah

Jenavieve (English) Form of Genevieve, meaning "of the race of women; the white wave"
Jenevieve, Jennavieve, Jeneva, Jenneva

Jendayi (Egyptian) One who is thankful
Jendayie, Jendayey, Jendayee, Jendaya, Jendayia, Jendayea

Jendyose (Ugandan) An accomplishment of the mother
Jendyosa, Jendyosia, Jendyosea, Jendyosi, Jendyosie

Jeneil (American) A champion
Jeneile, Jeneel, Jeneele, Jeneal, Jeneale

Jenis (Hebrew) Form of Genesis, meaning "of the beginning"
Jenesis, Jennis, Jenesys

Jennifer (Welsh) One who is fair; a beautiful girl
Jenefer, Jeni, Jenifer, Jeniffer, Jenn, Jennee, Jenni, Jennica, Jennie, Jenniver, Jenny, Jen, Jenalee, Jenalynn, Jenarae, Jeneen, Jenene, Jenetta, Jeni, Jenica, Jenice, Jeniece, Jenika, Jenise, Jenita, Jenna, Jennessa, Jenni, Jennie, Jennika, Jennilee, Jennilyn, Jennis, Jennita, Jennyann, Jennylee, Jinni, Jinny, Jenai, Jenae, Jenay, Jenalyn, Jenaya, Jenara, Jenibelle, Jennelle

Jenski (English) One who comes home
Jenskie, Jensky, Jenskey, Jenskee, Jenskea

Jeorjia (American) Form of Georgia, meaning "one who works the earth; a farmer"
Jeorgia, Jeorja, Jorja, Jorjette, Jorgette, Jorjeta, Jorjetta, Jorgete, Jorjete, Jorgeta, Jorgetta

Jera (American) A religious woman
Jerah, Jerra, Jerrah

Jeraldine (English) Form of Geraldine, meaning "one who rules with the spear"
Jeraldeen, Jeraldene, Jeraldine, Jeralee, Jere, Jeri, Jerilene, Jerrie, Jerrileen, Jerroldeen, Jerry, Jeralyn, Jenralyn, Jerelyn, Jerilynn, Jerilyn, Jerrilyn, Jerrica

Jeremia (Hebrew) Feminine form of Jeremiah; the Lord is exalted
Jeremea, Jerimia, Jerimea, Jeree, Jeremee, Jeremie, Jeremiya

Jereni (Slavic) One who is peaceful
Jerenie, Jereny, Jereney, Jerenee

Jerica (American) One who is strong; a talented ruler
Jerika, Jerrica, Jerrika, Jericka, Jericha, Jerricka, Jerricha

Jeriel (Hebrew) God has witnessed
Jeriele, Jeriela, Jerielle, Jeriell, Jeriella

Jermaine (French) Woman from Germany
Jermainaa, Jermane, Jermayne, Jermina, Jermana, Jermayna, Jermaen, Jermaena

Jersey (English) From one of the Channel Islands
Jersy, Jersee, Jersi, Jersie, Jerzey, Jerzy, Jerzee, Jerzi, Jerzie, Jersea, Jerzea

Jerusha (Hebrew) A faithful wife
Jerushah, Jeruscha, Jarusha, Jaruscha

Jessenia (Arabic) As delicate as a flower
Jesseniah, Jasenia, Jesenia, Jesenya, Jessenya, Jassenia, Jasenya, Jassenya

❷ ❶ Jessica (Hebrew) The Lord sees all
Jess, Jessa, Jessaca, Jessuka, Jessalin, Jessalyn, Jesse, Jesseca, Jessey, Jessie, Jessika, Jesirae, Jeslyn, Jessika, Jessicka, Jeziree, Jessalynn, Jessamae, Jessana, Jessandra, Jesselyn, Jezeree, Jessi, Jessilyn, Jessina, Jesslyn, Jesslynn, Jessy, Jessye, Jesimae

Jestina (Welsh) Feminine form of Justin; one who is just and upright
Jesstina, Jestine, Jestyna, Jesstyna, Jestyne, Jesstyne, Jesteena, Jessteena, Jesteene, Jessteene

Jesusa (Spanish) Refers to the Virgin Mary
Jesusah, Josune

Jethetha (Hebrew) Feminine form of Jetheth; a princess
Jethethia, Jethethea, Jethethiya

Jethra (Hebrew) Feminine form of Jethro; the Lord's excellence; one who has plenty; abudance
Jethrah, Jethria, Jethrea, Jethriya, Jeth, Jethe

Jetje (Teutonic) Ruler of the house

Jetta (Danish) Resembling the jet-black lustrous gemstone
Jette, Jett, Jeta, Jete, Jettie, Jetty, Jetti, Jettey, Jettee, Jettea

Jewel (French) One who is playful; resembling a precious gem
Jewell, Jewelle, Jewelyn, Jewelene, Jewelisa, Jule, Jewella, Juelline

Jezebel (Hebrew) One who is not exalted; in the Bible, the queen of Israel punished by God
Jessabell, Jetzabel, Jezabel, Jezabella, Jezebelle, Jezibel, Jezibelle, Jezybell, Jezabella

Jezreel (Hebrew) The Lord provides
Jesreel, Jezreele, Jesreele, Jezreal, Jezreale, Jesreal, Jesreale

Jia Li (Chinese) One who is beautiful and kind

Jie (Chinese) One who is pure; chaste

Jiera (Lithuanian) A lively woman
Jierah, Jyera, Jyerah, Jierra, Jyerra

Jifunza (African) A self-learner
Jifunzah, Jifoonza, Jifoonzah, Jifounza, Jifounzah

Jigisha (Indian) One who wants to learn
Jigishah, Jigysha, Jigyshah

Jiles (American) Resembling a young goat
Jyles

Jill (English) Form of Jillian, meaning "one who is youthful"
Jillet, Jil, Jilli, Jillie, Jilly, Jillyan, Jyl, Jyll, Jyllina, Jylina

Jillian (English) Form of Gillian, meaning "one who is youthful"
Jilian, Jiliana, Jillaine, Jillan, Jillana, Jillane, Jillanne, Jillayne, Jillene, Jillesa, Jilliana, Jilliane, Jilliann, Jillianna, Jillianne, Jillyan, Jillyanna, Jillyanne, Jyllina

Jimena (Spanish) One who is heard
Jimenah, Jymena, Jimeena, Jimyna, Jymeena, Jymyna

Jimmi (English) Feminine form of Jimmy; she who supplants
Jimi, Jimmie, Jimie, Jimmy, Jimmey, Jimmee, Jimmea, Jimy, Jimey, Jimee, Jimea

Jin (Japanese / Chinese) A superior woman / a golden child; one who is elegant

Jina (Swahili) The named one
Jinah

Jinelle (Welsh) Form of Genevieve, meaning "of the race of women; the white wave"
Jinell, Jinele, Jinel, Jynelle, Jynell, Jynele, Jynel

Jinx (Latin) One who performs charms or spells
Jynx, Jinxx, Jynxx

Jiselle (American) Form of Giselle, meaning "of God's promise; a hostage"
Jisell, Jisele, Jisela, Jizelle, Joselle, Jisella, Jizella, Jozelle, Josella, Jozella

Jiva (Hindi) In Hinduism, one's immortal essence
Jivah, Jyva, Jyvah

Jivanta (Indian) One who gives life
Jivantah, Jevanta, Javanta, Jevantah, Javantah

Jo (English) Feminine form of Joseph; God will add
Jobelle, Jobeth, Jodean, Jodelle, Joetta, Joette, Jolinda, Jolisa, Jolise, Jolissa, Jo-Marie, Jonetia, Joniece, Jonique, Jonisa, Joquise, Jorene, Josanna, Josanne, Jovelle

Joakima (Hebrew) Feminine form of Joachim; God will judge
Joachima, Joaquina, Joaquine, Joaquima

Joan (Hebrew) Feminine form of John; God is gracious
Joane, Joanie, Joannue, Jone, Jonee, Joni, Jonie, Jo, Joann, Jo-Ann, Joanne, Jo-Anne, Joeanne, Joeann, Joeanna, Joeanne, Johanna, Joanna, Johannah

Jobey (Hebrew) One who is persecuted
Joby, Jobie, Jobi, Jobee, Jobina, Jobyna, Jobeena, Jobea

Jocasta (Greek) In mythology, the queen of Thebes who married her son
Jocastah, Jokasta, Jokastah, Jockasta, Joccasta

❂ **Jocelyn** (German / Latin) From the tribe of Gauts / one who is cheerful, happy
Jocelin, Jocelina, Jocelinda, Joceline, Jocelyne, Jocelynn, Jocelynne, Josalind, Josaline, Josalyn, Josalynn, Joscelin, Josceline, Joscelyn, Joselina, Joseline, Joselyn, Joselyne, Josiline, Josilyn, Joslin, Josline, Joslyn, Jossline, Josselyn, Josslyn, Jozlyn, Joss

Jochebed (Hebrew) God is her glory
Jochebedaa, Jochebedia, Jochebedea

Jocosa (Latin) One who is gleeful and always joking
Jocose, Jocosia, Jocosea

Joda (Hebrew) An ancestor of Christ

Jody (English) Form of Judith, meaning "woman from Judea"
Jodey, Jodi, Jodie, Jodee, Jodea

Joelle (Hebrew) Feminine form of Joel; Jehovah is God; God is willing
Joela, Joelin, Joell, Joella, Joellen, Joelliane, Joellin, Joelly, Joellyn, Joely, Joelynn, Joetta, Jowella, Jowelle

Johnna (English) Feminine form of John; God is gracious
Johna, Johnelle, Johnetta, Johnette, Johnna, Johnnie, Johnda, Johyna, Jonalyn, Jonalynn, Jonay, Jonell, Jonetta, Jonette, Jonita, Jonna, Jonni, Jonnah, Jonnie, Jonnelle

Jokim (Hebrew) Blessed by God
Jokima, Jokym, Jokyme, Jokeem, Jokimia, Jokimea, Joka, Jokeam, Jokeame

Jokmeam (Hebrew) From the gathering of people
Jokmime, Jokmym, Jokmeem

Jolan (Greek) Resembling a violet flower
Jola, Jolaine, Jolande, Jolanne, Jolanta, Jolantha, Jolandi, Jolanka, Jolanna, Jolana

Jolene (English) Feminine form of Joseph; God will add
Joeline, Joeleen, Joeline, Jolaine, Jolean, Joleen, Jolena, Jolina, Joline, Jolleen, Jollene, Jolyn, Jolyna, Jolyne, Jolynn

Jolie (French) A pretty young woman
Joly, Joely, Jolee, Joleigh, Joley, Joli, Joliet, Jolietta, Joliette, Jolea

Jones (English) From the family of John
Jonesy, Jonesi, Jonesie, Jonesee, Jonesey, Jonesea

Jonina (Israeli) Resembling a little dove
Joninah, Jonyna, Jonynah, Joneenah, Jonine, Jonyne, Joneene, Jonati, Jonatie, Jonatee, Jonatey, Jonaty, Joneana, Joneanah

Jonquil (English) Resembling the flower
Jonquill, Jonquille, Jonquile, Jonquila, Jonquilla

Joo-eun (Korean) Resembling a silver pearl

Jorah (Hebrew) Resembling an autumn rose
Jora

Jord (Norse) In mythology, goddess of the earth
Jorde

● **Jordan** (Hebrew) Of the down-flowing river; in the Bible, the river where Jesus was baptized
Jardena, Johrdan, Jordain, Jordaine, Jordana, Jordane, Jordanka, Jordann, Jordanna, Jordanne, Jorden, Jordena, Jordenn, Jordie, Jordin, Jordyn, Jordynn, Jorey, Jori, Jorie, Jorrdan, Jorry, Jourdan, Jourdain

Jorgina (English) Form of Georgina, meaning "one who works the earth; a farmer"
Jorgeanne, Jorgelina, Jorjana, Jorjina, Jorjanna, Jorcina, Jorcyna, Jorceena, Jorciena, Jorceina, Jory

Jorryn (American) Loved by God
Jorran, Jorren, Jorron, Jorrun

Jorunn (Norse) One who loves horses

Josephine (Hebrew) Feminine form of Joseph; God will add
Josefa, Josefena, Josefene, Josefina, Josefine, Josepha, Josephe, Josephene, Josephina, Josephyna, Josephyna, Josephyne, Josette, Josetta, Joxepa, Josebe, Jose, Josie, Josee, Jozsa, Josina

Journey (American) One who likes to travel
Journy, Journi, Journie, Journee, Journye, Journea

Jovana (Spanish) Feminine form of Jovian; daughter of the sky
Jeovana, Jeovanna, Jovanna, Jovena, Jovianne, Jovina, Jovita, Joviana

Joy (Latin) A delight; one who brings pleasure to others
Jioia, Jioya, Joi, Joia, Joie, Joya, Joyann, Joyanna, Joyanne, Joye, Joyelle, Joyela, Joyella, Joyous, Joylyn

Joyce (English) One who brings joy to others
Joice, Joyceanne, Joycelyn, Joycelynn, Joyse, Joyceta

Jozachar (Hebrew) God has remembered
Jozachare, Jozachara, Jozacharia, Jozacharea

Juana (Spanish) Feminine form of Juan; God is gracious
Juanita, Janita, Juanetta, Juanisha, Juniata, Junita, Juwaneeta, Juwanita, Juandalynn

Juba (African) Born on a Monday
Jubah, Jubba, Jubia, Jubea

Jubilee (Hebrew) One who rejoices; a ram's horn
Jubileigh, Jubilie, Jubili, Jubily, Jubiley, Jubalee, Jubaleigh, Jubaley, Jubaly, Jubali, Jubalie, Jubalea, Jubilea

Juci (Hebrew) One who is praised
Jucika, Jucie, Jucee, Jucye, Jutka, Jucea, Jucey, Jucy

Juda (Arabic) Filled with goodness
Judah

Judith (Hebrew) Woman from Judea
Judithe, Juditha, Judeena, Judeana, Judyth, Judit, Judytha, Judita, Judite, Jutka, Jucika, Jutta, Judythe

Judy (Hebrew) Form of Judith, meaning "woman from Judea"
Judee, Judey, Judi, Judie, Judye, Judea

Juhi (Indian) Resembling a fragrant flower
Jui

Juin (French) Born during the month of June

Juji (African) One who is greatly loved
Jujie, Jujy, Jujey, Jujee, Jujea

♦ **Julia** (Latin) One who is youthful; daughter of the sky
Jiulia, Joleta, Joletta, Jolette, Julaine, Julayna, Julee, Juleen, Julena, Juley, Juli, Juliaeta, Juliaetta, Juliana, Juliane, Juliann, Julianne, Julie, Julienne, Juliet, Julieta, Julietta, Juliette, Julina, Juline, Julinka, Juliska, Julissa, Julita, Julitta, Julyana, Julyanna, Julyet, Julyetta, Julyette, Julyne, Jooley, Joolie, Julisa, Julisha, Julyssa, Jolyon, Julcsa, Julene, Jules

July (Latin) Form of Julia, meaning "one who is youthful; daughter of the sky"; born during the month of July
Julye

Jumanah (Arabic) Resembling a silver pearl
Jumana, Jumanna, Jumannah

Jumoke (African) A child who is loved by all

June (Latin) One who is youthful; born during the month of June
Junae, Junel, Junelle, Junette, Junita, Junia

Juniper (Latin) Resembling the evergreen shrub with berries
Junyper, Junipyre, Junypyre

Juno (Latin) In mythology, queen of the heavens and goddess of marriage and women
Junot, Juneau, Juneaux

Justice (English) One who upholds moral rightness and fairness
Justyce, Justiss, Justyss, Justis, Justus, Justise

Justine (Latin) Feminine form of Justin; one who is just and upright
Justa, Justeen, Justeene, Justene, Justie, Justina, Justinn, Justy, Justyna, Justyne, Justeena, Justyna, Justea

Juturna (Latin) In mythology, goddess of fountains and springs
Jutorna, Jutourna

Juventas (Latin) In mythology, goddess of youth

Jwahir (African) The golden woman
Jwahyr, Jwaheer, Jwahear

Jyoti (Indian) Born of the light
Jyotika, Jyotis, Jyotie, Jyoty, Jyotey, Jyotee, Jyotea

Jyotsna (Indian) Woman of the moonlight

k

Kabibe (African) A petite woman
Kabybe

Kabira (African) One who is powerful
Kabirah, Kabyra, Kabyrah, Kabeera, Kabeerah, Kabeira, Kabeirah, Kabiera, Kabierah, Kabeara, Kabearah

Kacela (African) A great huntress
Kacelah, Kacella, Kacellah

Kachina (Native American) A spiritual dancer
Kachine, Kachinah, Kachineh, Kachyna, Kacheena, Kachynah, Kacheenah, Kacheana, Kacheanah

Kacondra (American) One who is bold
Kacondrah, Kacondria, Kacondriah, Kacondrea, Kacondreah, Kaecondra, Kaycondra, Kakondra, Kaekondra, Kaykondra

Kadence (American) Rhythmic and melodious; a musical woman
Kadian, Kadienne, Kadianne, Kadiene, Kaydence, Kaedence, Kadense, Kaydense, Kaedense

Kadin (Arabic) A beloved companion
Kadyn, Kadan, Kaden, Kadon, Kudun, Kaedin, Kaeden, Kaydin, Kayden

Kadisha (Hebrew) A holy woman; one who is religious
Kadishah, Kadysha, Kadeesha, Kadiesha, Kadeasha, Kadyshah, Kadeeshah, Kadieshah, Kadeashah

Kaede (Japanese) Resembling a maple leaf
Kaide, Kayde

Kaelyn (English) A beautiful girl from the meadow
Kaelynn, Kaelynne, Kaelin, Kailyn, Kaylyn, Kaelinn, Kaelinne

Kafi (African) A quiet child; one who is well-behaved
Kaffi, Kafie, Kafy, Kafey, Kafee, Kaffy, Kaffie, Kaffey, Kaffee, Kafea, Kaffea

Kagami (Japanese) Displaying one's true image
Kagamie, Kagamy, Kagamey, Kagamee, Kagamea

Kai (Hawaiian) Woman of the sea
Kaia

Kaida (Japanese) Resembling a small dragon
Kaidah, Kaeda, Kayda, Kada, Kaedah, Kaydah, Kadah

Kaila (Hebrew) Crowned with laurel
Kailah, Kailan, Kaela, Kaelah, Kailene, Kailyn, Kailynne, Kailin, Kalea

Kailani (Hawaiian) Of the sky and sea
Kailanie, Kaylani, Kaylanie, Kuelani, Kaelanie, Kailany, Kaylany, Kailaney, Kaylaney, Kailanee, Kaylanee, Kailanea, Kaylanea, Kaelany, Kaelaney, Kaelanee, Kaelanea

Kailasa (Indian) From the silver mountain
Kailasah, Kailassa, Kaylasa, Kaelasa, Kailas, Kailase

Kaimi (Polynesian) The seeker; one who searches
Kaimie, Kaimy, Kaimey, Kaimee, Kaimea

Kainda (African) The daughter of a great hunter
Kaindah, Kaynda, Kaenda, Kayndah, Kaendah

Kairos (Greek) Woman of opportunity
Kayros, Kaeros

● **Kaitlyn** (Greek) Form of Katherine, meaning "one who is pure, virginal"
*Kaitlin, Kaitlan, Kaitleen, Kaitlynn, Katalin, Katalina, Katalyn, Katelin, Kateline, Katelinn, **Katelyn**, Katelynn, Katilyn, Katlin*

Kaiya (Japanese) A forgiving woman
Kaiyo, Kaeya, Kaeyo

Kajal (Indian) A woman with appealing eyes

Kakawangwa (Native American) A bitter woman

Kakra (Egyptian) The younger of twins
Kakrah

Kala (Arabic / Hawaiian) A moment in time / form of Sarah, meaning "princess; lady"
Kalah, Kalla, Kallah

Kalama (Hawaiian) Resembling a flaming torch
Kalamah, Kalamia, Kalamiah, Kalamea, Kalameah

Kalani (Hawaiian) From the heavens
Kalanie, Kalany, Kalaney, Kalanee, Kaloni, Kalonie, Kalonee, Kalony, Kaloney, Keilana, Keilani, Kalanea, Kalonea

Kalanit (Hebrew) Resembling a flower

Kaleen (Slavic) Resembling a delicate flower
Kaleena, Kaline, Kalynne, Kalyne, Kalina, Kalyna, Kaleene, Kalene, Kalena, Kaleane, Kaleana

Kalet (French) Having beautiful energy
Kalett, Kalete, Kalette, Kalay, Kalaye

Kali (Hindi) The dark one; in Hinduism, a destructive force

Kalidas (Greek) The most beautiful woman
Kalydas, Kaleedas, Kaleidas, Kaliedas, Kaleadas

Kalifa (Somali) A chaste and holy woman
Kalifah, Kalyfa, Kalyfah, Kaleefa, Kaleefah, Kalipha, Kalypha, Kaleepha, Kaleafa, Kaleafah, Kaleapha

Kalika (Greek / Arabic) Resembling a rosebud; one who is dearly loved
Kalikah, Kalyka, Kalykah, Kaleeka, Kaleekah, Kalica, Kalicca, Kalyca, Kaleeca, Kaleaka, Kaleakah

Kalilah (Arabic) A darling girl; sweetheart
Kalila, Kaleila, Kaleyla, Kaleela, Kaleilah, Kaleylah, Kaleelah, Kaliyah, Kaliya, Kaleala, Kalealah

Kalima (Arabic) An eloquent speaker
Kalimah, Kalyma, Kaleema, Kallima, Kalleema, Kallyma, Kaleama, Kalleama

Kalinda (Indian) Of the sun
Kalindah, Kalynda, Kalinde, Kalindeh, Kalindi, Kalindie, Kalyndi, Kalyndie, Kalindee, Kalyndee

Kalisha (American) A beautiful and caring woman
Kalishah, Kalysha, Kalyshah, Kaliesha, Kalieshah, Kaleisha, Kaleishah, Kaleesha, Kaleeshah, Kaleasha, Kaleashah

Kallan (Scandinavian / Gaelic) Of the flowing water / powerful in battle

Kallie (English) A beautiful girl
Kalli, Kallita, Kally, Kalley, Kallee, Kalleigh, Kallea, Kalleah

Kalliope (Greek) Having a beautiful voice; in mythology, the muse of epic poetry
Kalliopee, Kalliopy, Kalliopi, Kalliopie, Kaliope, Kaliopi, Kaliopie, Kaliopy, Kaliopee, Kalliopea, Kalipea

Kallisto (Greek) The most beautiful; in mythology, a nymph who was changed into a she-bear
Kallista, Kalisto, Kalista, Kalysta, Kalysto, Kallysto, Kallysta

Kalma (Finnish) In mythology, goddess of the dead

Kalonice (Greek) A victorious beauty
Kalonyce, Kaloneece, Kaloneace, Kaloniece, Kaloneice

Kalpana (Indian) Having a great imagination
Kalpanah, Kalpanna, Kalpannah

Kalwa (Finnish) A heroine

Kalyan (Indian) A beautiful and auspicious woman
Kalyane, Kalyanne, Kalyann, Kayluna, Kaylanna, Kalliyan, Kaliyan, Kaliyane, Kaliyanne, Kalliyane

Kama (Indian) One who loves and is loved
Kamah, Kamma, Kammah

Kamala (Arabic) A woman of perfection
Kamalah, Kammala, Kamalla

Kamali (Rhodesian) Having divine protection
Kamalie, Kamalli, Kamaly, Kamaley, Kamalee, Kamaleigh, Kamalea, Kamaleah

Kamana (Indian) One who is desired
Kamanah, Kammana, Kamanna, Kamna

Kamaria (African) Of the moon
Kamariah, Kamarea, Kamareah, Kamariya, Kamariyah

Kambiri (African) Newest addition to the family
Kambirie, Kambiry, Kambyry, Kambiree, Kambirea, Kambyree, Kambyrea, Kambyri

Kambo (African) A hardworking woman

Kambria (English) A woman of Wales
Kambriah, Kambreea, Kambrea, Kambriya

Kamea (Hawaiian) The one and only; precious one
Kameo

Kameko (Japanese) A turtle child; having a long life
Kamyko, Kamiko

Kameron (English) Form of Cameron, meaning "having a crooked nose"
Kamerin, Kameryn, Kamrin, Kamron, Kamryn, Kamren, Kameren, Kamran, Kameran

Kamilah (Arabic / Italian) The perfect one / form of Camilla, meaning "ceremonial attendant; a noble virgin"
Kamila, Kamilla, Kamillia, Kamille, Kamelia, Kamelea, Kamilia, Kamilea, Kami, Kamili, Kamlyn, Kammi, Kammie, Kamiila, Kamillra, Kamikla, Kamela, Kamella

Kamin (Indian) A joyful child
Kamen, Kamon, Kaman

Kamyra (American) Surrounded by light
Kamira, Kamera, Kamiera, Kameira, Kameera, Kameara

Kana (Japanese) A powerful woman

Kanan (Indian) From the garden

Kanani (Hawaiian) The beautiful girl
Kananie, Kanany, Kananey, Kananni, Kananee, Kananea, Kananeah

Kanara (Hebrew) Resembling a small bird
Kanarah, Kanarra, Kanarrah

Kanda (Native American) A magical woman
Kandah

Kandace (English) Form of Candace, meaning "a queen / one who is white and glowing"
Kandee, Kandi, Kandice, Kandis, Kandiss, Kandy, Kandyce, Kandys, Kandyss, Kandake, Kandie, Kandey, Kandea

Kande (African) The firstborn daughter

Kandra (American) A shining woman
Kandrah

Kane (Irish) A warrior woman ready for battle
Kaine, Kayne, Kaene, Kain, Kayn, Kaen

Kaneesha (American) A dark-skinned beauty
Kaneisha, Kaniesha, Kaneasha, Kanesha, Kanisha, Kanysha

Kanga (Native American) Resembling a raven

Kanika (African) A dark, beautiful woman
Kanikah, Kanyka, Kanicka, Kanycka, Kaneeka, Kaneecka, Kaneaka, Kaneacka

Kaniz (Arabic) A servant girl
Kaneez, Kanyz

Kannitha (Vietnamese) An angelic woman
Kannytha, Kanitha, Kanytha

Kanoni (African) Resembling a little bird
Kanonni, Kanonie, Kanony, Kanoney, Kanonee, Kanonea

Kansas (Native American) Of the south wind people; from the state of Kansas

Kantha (Indian) A delicate woman
Kanthah, Kanthe, Kantheh, Kanthia, Kanthia, Kanthea, Kantheah, Kanthiya, Kanthiyah, Kanthya, Kanthyah

Kanti (Native American) One who sings beautifully
Kantie, Kanty, Kantey, Kantee, Kantea

Kanya (Thai) A young girl; a virgin

Kaoru (Japanese) A fragrant girl
Kaori

Kaprice (English) Form of Caprice, meaning "one who is impulsive and unpredictable"
Kapricia, Kaprisha, Kapryce, Kaprycia, Kaprysha, Kapri, Kaprie, Kapry, Kaprey, Kapree, Kaprea, Kaprise, Kapryse, Kaprece, Kaprese, Kapreese, Kapreece, Kapreace, Kaprease

Kapuki (African) The firstborn daughter
Kapukie, Kapuky, Kapukey, Kapukee, Kapukea

Kara (Greek / Italian / Gaelic) One who is pure / dearly loved / a good friend
Karah, Karalee, Karalie, Karalyn, Karalynn, Karrah, Karra, Khara, Kahra

Karasi (African) Full of wisdom and life
Karasie, Karasy, Karasey, Karasee, Karasea

Karbie (American) An energetic woman
Karbi, Karby, Karbey, Karbee, Karbea

Karcsi (French) A joyful singer
Karcsie, Karcsy, Karcsey, Karcsee, Karcsea

Karen (Greek) Form of Katherine, meaning "one who is pure; virginal"
Karan, Karena, Kariana, Kariann, Karianna, Karianne, Karin, Karina, Karine, Karon, Karren, Karrin, Karyn, Karna, Keran, Keren, Keryn, Kerin, Kerryn, Kerrin

Karida (Arabic) A virgin; an untouched woman
Karidah, Karyda, Kareeda, Kareyda, Karieda, Kareada

Karima (Arabic) Feminine form of Karim; one who is generous and noble
Karimah, Kareema, Karyma, Kareama

Karina (Scandinavian, Russian) One who is dear and pure
Karinah, Kareena, Karyna, Kareana, Kariena, Kareina

Karisma (English) Form of Charisma, meaning "blessed with charm"
Kharisma, Karizma, Kharizma

Karissa (Greek) Filled with grace and kindess; very dear
Karisa, Karyssa, Karysa, Karessa, Karesa, Karis, Karise

Karla (German) Feminine form of Karl; a small, strong woman
Karly, Karli, Karlie, Karleigh, Karlee, Karley, Karlin, Karlyn, Karlina, Karline, Karleen, Karlen, Karlene, Karlesha, Karlysha, Karlea

Karma (Indian) One's actions determine one's destiny
Karmah

Karmel (Latin) Form of Carmel, meaning "of the fruitful orchard"
Karmelle, Karmell, Karmele, Karmela, Karmella

Karmelit (Hebrew) Of God's vineyard
Karmelita, Kannelite, Karmelitah, Karmelyte, Karmelyta, Karmelite, Karmit

Karmen (Latin) Form of Carmen, meaning "a beautiful song"
Karman, Karmin, Karmon, Karmine, Karmia, Karmina, Karmita, Karmyn

Karmiti (Native American) From the trees
Karmitie, Karmity, Karmitey, Karmitee, Karmyty, Karmyti, Karmytie, Karmytee, Karmitea, Karmytea

Karnesha (American) A feisty woman
Karneshah, Karnisha, Karnishah, Karnysha, Karnyshah

Karol (English) Form of Carol, meaning "a joyous song; a small, strong woman"
Karola, Karole, Karolle, Karolla, Karoly, Karoli, Karolie, Karolee, Karoleigh, Karel, Karal, Karil

Karoline (English) Form of Caroline, meaning "a joyous song; a small, strong woman"
Karolina, Karolinah, Karolyne, Karrie, Karie, Karri, Kari, Karry, Kary, Karlotta, Karee, Karielle

Karrington (English) One who is admired
Karington, Karryngton, Karyngton

Karsen (American) Feminine form of Carson; from the swamp
Karson, Karsin, Karsan, Karsyn

Karsten (Greek) The anointed one
Karstin, Karstine, Karstyn, Karston, Karstan, Kiersten, Keirsten

Karuna (Indian) A compassionate woman
Karunah, Karoona, Karoonah, Karouna, Karounah

Karyan (Armenian) The dark one

Kasen (Scandinavian) One who is pure; chaste
Kasin, Kasyn, Kasan, Kason, Kasienka

Kasey (Irish) Form of Casey, meaning "a vigilant woman"
Kacie, Kaci, Kacy, KC, Kacee, Kacey, Kasie, Kasi, Kasy, Kasee, Kacia, Kacea, Kayce, Kayci, Kaycie, Kaycee, Kaesha, Kasia, Kasea, Kaycea

Kashawna (American) One who enjoys debate
Kashawn, Kaseana, Kasean, Kashaun, Kashauna, Kashona, Kashonna

Kashmir (Sanskrit) From the state in India
Kashmira, Kasha, Kashmeer, Kazmir, Kazmira, Kazmeer, Kazhmir

Kashonda (American) A dramatic woman
Kashondah, Kashaunda, Kashaundah, Kashawnda, Kashawndah, Kashanda, Kashandah

Kashondra (American) A bright woman
Kashawndra, Kaseandra, Kashaundra, Kashandra, Kashondre, Kachaundra, Kachondra

Kasi (Indian) From the holy city; shining

Kasinda (African) Daughter born to a family with twins
Kasindah, Kasynda, Kasenda

Kasmira (Slavice) A peacemaker
Kasmirah, Kasmeera, Kasmeerah, Kasmyra, Kasmyrah, Kazmira, Kazmirah, Kazmyrah, Kazmyra, Kazmeera, Kazmeerah

Kassandra (English) Form of Cassandra, meaning "an unheeded prophetess"
Kassandrah, Kasandra, Kasaundra, Kassondra, Kassi, Kassia, Kassie, Kassy

Kassidy (English) Form of Cassidy, meaning "curly-haired girl"
Kassidey, Kassidi, Kassidie, Kassidee, Kasidy, Kasidey, Kasidi, Kasidie, Kasidee, Kassidea, Kasidea

Kasumi (Japanese) From the mist
*Kasumie, Kasume, Kasumy, Kasumey,
Kasumee, Kasumea*

Kataniya (Hebrew) A young girl
Kataniyah, Katanya, Katanyah

Katchi (American) A sassy woman
Katchie, Katchy, Katchey, Katchee, Katchea

Katera (American) One who celebrates
*Katerah, Katerra, Katerrah, Katura, Katurah,
Katurra, Katurrah*

❷ **Katherine** (Greek) Form of Catherine,
meaning "one who is pure; virginal"
*Katharine, Katharyn, Kathy, Kathleen,
Katheryn, Kathie, Kathrine, Kathryn,
Kathryne, Kaythrynn, Kady, Kadie, Kaethe,
Kaira, Kaisa, Kaska, Kat, Katherina, Kata,
Katakin, Katanyna, Katarina, Katarin,
Katarzyna, Katchen, Kate, Katen, Katerina,
Kath, Kathe, Kathelyn, Kathleena, Kathlene,
Kathlynn, Kathrina, Kati, Katia, Katica, Katie,
Katine, Katinka, Katiya, Katja, Katle, Katina,
Katoka, Katri, Katria, Katriane, Katriana,
Katrien, Katrikki, Katrin, Katrina, Katrine,
Katrya, Katy, Katya, Katyenka, Katyuska,
Kayiyn, Kaysa, Kolina, Koline, Kolena, Kolene,
Koleyna, Kethryn, Kiska, Kitlyn*

Kathlaya (American) A stylish woman

Katima (American) A daughter with power
*Katimah, Kateema, Katyma, Katiema,
Kateima, Kateama*

Katrice (American) A graceful woman
*Katryce, Katriece, Katreice, Katreace, Katrise,
Katryse, Katriese, Katreise, Katrease*

Katriel (Hebrew) Crowned by God
Katriele, Katrielle, Katriell, Katriela, Katriella

Kauket (Egyptian) In mythology, an ancient
goddess
Keket

Kaula (Polynesian) Child of the heavens

Kaulana (Hawaiian) A well-known young
woman
*Kaulanah, Kaulanna, Kaulannah, Kaulanne,
Kaulane*

Kaveri (Indian) From the sacred river
*Kaverie, Kauveri, Kauverie, Kavery, Kaverey,
Kaveree, Kaverea, Kauvery, Kauverey,
Kauveree, Kauverea*

Kavi (Indian) A great poetess
*Kavita, Kavindra, Kavie, Kavy, Kavey, Kavee,
Kavea*

Kavinli (American) One who is eager
*Kavinlie, Kavinly, Kavinley, Kavinlee,
Kavinlea, Kavinleigh*

Kawthar (Arabic) From the river in paradise
Kawthare, Kawthara, Kawtharr

Kay (English / Greek) The keeper of the
keys / form of Katherine, meaning "one
who is pure; virginal"
*Kaye, Kae, Kai, Kaie, Kaya, Kayana, Kayane,
Kayanna, Kayann*

Kayin (African) A long-awaited daughter
Kayen, Kayan, Kayon

❷ **Kayla** (Arabic / Hebrew) Form of Kaila,
meaning "crowned with laurel"
*Kaylah, Kalan, Kalen, Kalin, Kalynn,
Kaylan, Kaylana, Kaylin, Kaylen, Kaylynn,
Kaylyn, Kayle*

❷❶ **Kaylee** (American) Form of Kaila, meaning
"crowned with laurel"
*Kaleigh, Kaley, Kalie, Kaelee, Kaeleigh,
Kaeley, Kaelene, Kaeli, Kaelie, Kailee, Kailey,
Kaili, Kalee, Kahli, Kalei, Kalia, Kaleah,
Kayleah, Kaylea, Kayleigh, Kayley, Kayli,
Kaylie, Kayleen, Kaylei*

Keahi (Hawaiian) A fiery woman
Keahie, Keahy, Keahey, Keahee, Keahea

Keana (Irish) Feminine form of Keane; of
an ancient family
*Keanna, Kiana, Kianna, Kyana, Kyanna,
Keene, Keen, Kean, Keena, Keenat, Keiana,
Keana, Kinnat*

Keanu (Hawaiian) Resembling a cool
mountain breeze

Kearney (Irish) The winner
Kearny, Kearni, Kearnie, Kearnee, Kearnea

Keaton (English) From a shed town
Keatan, Keatyn, Keatin, Keatun

Keavy (Irish) A lovely and graceful girl
Keavey, Keavi, Keavie, Keavee, Keavea

Kedma (Hebrew) Woman of the East

Keegan (Gaelic) Small and fiery woman
Keygan, Keigan, Kiegan, Kegan, Keagan

Keegsquaw (Native American) One who is chaste; a virgin

Keelan (Irish) A slender and beautiful woman
Keylan, Keilan, Kielan, Kelan, Kealan, Keelia

Keenan (Irish) A small woman
Keanan, Keynan, Keinan, Kienan

Keeya (African) Resembling a flower
Keeyah, Kieya, Keiya, Keyya

Kefira (Hebrew) Resembling a young lioness
Kefirah, Kefiera, Kefeira, Kefeera, Kefyra, Kephira, Kepheera, Kepheira, Kephiera, Kephyra, Kepheara, Kefeara

Kehinde (African) The second-born of twins
Kehindeh, Kehynde, Kehyndeh

Keidra (American) One who is alert; aware
Keidrah, Kiedra, Kiedrah, Keadra, Keadrah, Keydra, Keydrah, Keedra, Keedrah

Keiki (Hawaiian) A precious baby; resembling an orchid
Kiki, Kyki, Keeki, Keki, Keyki, Kaki, Kaeki, Kayki, Kaiki

Keiko (Japanese) A respectful and well-behaved child
Kiko, Kyko, Keeko, Kako, Kayko, Kaeko, Kaiko

Keisha (American) The favorite child; form of Kezia, meaning "of the spice tree"
Keishla, Keishah, Kecia, Kesha, Keysha, Keesha, Kiesha, Keshia, Keishia, Keasha, Keashia

Keitha (Scottish) Feminine form of Keith; woman of the wood
Keetha, Keytha, Kietha, Keita, Kieta, Keeltie, Keelti, Keeltey, Keeltee, Keelty, Keeltea

Kekona (Hawaiian) The second-born child

Kelby (Gaelic) From the waters
Kelbey, Kelbi, Kelbie, Kelbee, Kelda, Keldah, Kelbea

Kelilah (Hebrew) A victorious woman
Kelila, Kelula, Kelulah, Kelyla, Kelylah

Kelis (American) A beautiful and talented woman
Keliss, Kelisse, Kelys, Kelyss, Kelysse

Kellen (Gaelic) A slender, beautiful, and powerful woman
Kellan, Kellyn, Kellin, Kellon, Kellun

Keller (Irish) One who is daring
Kellers, Kellar, Kellir, Kellyr

Kelly (Irish) A lively and bright-headed woman
Kelley, Kelli, Kellie, Kellee, Kelleigh, Kellye, Keely, Keelie, Keeley, Keelyn, Keilah, Keila, Keelia, Keelin, Keelyn, Kellyanne, Kella, Keelea, Keeleigh, Keelee, Kellea

Kelsey (English) From the island of ships; of the ship's victory
Kelsie, Kelcey, Kelcie, Kelcy, Kellsie, Kelsa, Kelsea, Kelsee, Kelsi, Kelsy, Kellsey, Kelcea, Kelcee

Kember (American) A fun-loving woman

Kemella (American) One who is self-assured
Kemela, Kemell, Kemele, Kemel, Kemelle

Kemena (Spanish) Having great strength
Kemina, Kemeena, Kemyna

Kempley (English) From the meadow
Kemply, Kempli, Kemplie, Kemplee, Kempleigh, Kemplea, Kempleah

Kenae (Irish) A good-looking woman
Kenai, Kenay, Kenaye, Kennae, Kennai, Kennay, Kennaye

Kendall (Welsh) From the royal valley
Kendal, Kendyl, Kendahl, Kindall, Kyndal, Kyndall, Kenda

Kendi (African) One who is dearly loved
Kendie, Kendee, Kendy, Kendey, Kendea

Kendis (American) A pure woman; one who is chaste
Kendiss, Kendisse, Kendys, Kendyss, Kendysse

Kendra (English) Feminine form of Kendrick; having royal power; from the high hill
Kendrah, Kendria, Kendrea, Kindra, Kindria

Kenley (English) From the royal meadow
Kenlie, Kenli, Kenly, Kenlee, Kenleigh, Kenlea

Kenna (Celtic) Feminine form of Kenneth; a beauty; born of fire

Kennedy (Gaelic) A helmeted chief
Kennedi, Kennedie, Kennedey, Kennedee, Kenadia, Kenadie, Kenadi, Kenady, Kenadey, Kenadee, Kennedea, Kenadea

Kennice (English) A beautiful and gracious woman
Kennis, Kenice, Keniss, Kenys, Kennita, Kenita, Kenneece, Keneece, Kenyce, Kenneeta, Keneeta, Kennocha, Kenisha, Keniesha, Keneesha, Kenysha, Keneisha

Kensington (English) A brash lady
Kensyngton, Kensingtyn, Kinsington, Kinsyngton, Kinsingtyn

Kentucky (Native American) From the land of tomorrow; from the state of Kentucky
Kentucki, Kentuckie, Kentuckey, Kentuckee, Kentuckea

Kenwei (Arabic) Resembling a water lily

Kenya (African) An innocent; from the country of Kenya
Kenyatta, Kenia, Keniya, Kennya

Kenyangi (Ugandan) Resembling the white egret
Kenyangie, Kenyangy, Kenyangey, Kenyangee, Kenyangea

Kenzie (English) Form of Mackenzie, meaning "daughter of a wise leader; a fiery woman; one who is fair"
Kenzi, Kenzy, Kenzey, Kenzee, Kenzea

Keoshawn (American) One who is clever
Keoshawna, Keosean, Keoseana, Keoshaun, Keoshauna

Kepa (Basque) As solid as a stone
Kepah, Keppa, Keppah

Kerdonna (American) One who is loquacious
Kerdonnah, Kerdona, Kerdonah, Kerdonia, Kerdoniah, Kerdonea, Kerdoneah, Kirdonna, Kirdona, Kyrdonna, Kyrdona

Kerensa (Cornish) One who loves and is loved
Kerinsa, Keransa, Kerensia, Kerensea, Kerensya, Kerenz, Kerenza, Keranz, Keranza

Keres (Greek) In mythology, vengeful spirits of death and doom

Kermeilde (English) A gilded woman
Kermilda, Kermilla, Kermillie

Kerr (Scottish) From the marshland

Kerry (English) Form of Kiera, meaning "little dark-haired one"
Kerri, Kerrie, Kerrey, Kerree, Keri, Kerie, Kery, Keree, Keriana, Kerianna, Keriane, Kerianne, Kerilyn, Keriam, Kerilynne, Kern, Kerrianne, Kerrea, Kerea

Kerta (Teutonic) A brave woman warrior
Kertta, Kertu, Kerttu

Kerthia (American) A giving woman
Kerthiah, Kerthea, Kertheah, Kerthiya, Kerthiyah, Kerthie, Kerthi, Kerthee, Kerthea, Kerthy, Kerthey

Kesara (English) A girl with a beautiful head of hair
Kesare, Kesarah, Kesarra, Kesarre, Kesaria, Kesarea, Kesava, Kesave, Kesavia, Kesavea

Keshon (American) Filled with happiness
Keyshon, Keshawn, Keyshawn, Kesean, Keysean, Keshaun, Keyshaun, Keshonna, Keyshonna, Keshawna, Keyshawna, Keseana, Keyseana, Keshauna, Keyshauna

Keshondra (American) Form of Keshon, meaning "filled with happiness"
Keshondrah, Keshawndra, Keshawndrah, Keshaundra, Keshaundrah, Keshondriah, Keshondria, Keshondrea, Keshondreah

Ketaki (Indian) The golden daughter
Ketakie, Ketaky, Ketakey, Ketakee, Ketakea

Ketifa (Arabic) A flourishing woman; flowering
Ketifah, Ketyfa, Keteefa, Ketipha, Keteepha, Ketypha, Keteafa, Keteapha

Ketura (Hebrew) Resembling incense
Keturah, Keturra

Kevina (Gaelic) Feminine form of Kevin; a beautiful and beloved child
Kevinah, Keva, Kevia, Kevinne, Kevyn, Kevynn, Kevynne, Keveena, Keveene, Kevinna, Kevine, Kevlyn, Kevlynne, Kevan, Kevay, Keveana, Keveane

Keydy (American) A knowledgeable woman
Keydey, Keydi, Keydie, Keydee, Keydea

Keyla (English) A wise daughter

Keyonna (American) An energetic woman
Keyonnah, Keyona, Keyonah

Kezia (Hebrew) Of the spice tree
Keziah, Kesia, Kesiah, Kesi, Kessie, Ketzia

Khadija (Arabic / African) The prophet Muhammad's first wife; a perfect woman / a child born prematurely
Khadeeja, Khadijah, Khadyja, Kadija, Kadijah, Kadeeja, Kadyja, Khadeaja, Kadeaja

Khai (American) Unlike the others; unusual
Khae, Khay, Khaye

Khaki (American) Full of personality
Khakie, Khaky, Khakey, Khakee, Khakea

Khali (American) A lively woman
Khalie, Khaly, Khaley, Khalee, Khaleigh, Khalea

Khalida (Arabic) Feminine form of Khalid; an immortal woman
Khalidah, Khaleeda, Khalyda, Khaalida, Khulud, Khulood, Khaleada

Khalilah (Arabic) Feminine form of Khalil; a beloved friend
Khalila, Khalyla, Khalylah, Kahlilia, Khaleela, Khaleala

Khaliqa (Arabic) Feminine form of Khaliq; a creator; one who is well-behaved
Khaliqah, Khalyqa, Khaleeqa, Kaliqua, Kaleequa, Kalyqua, Khaleaqa, Kaleaqua

Khanh (Vietnamese) Resembling a precious stone
Khann, Khan

Khasa (Arabic) Of an ancient people
Khasah, Khassa, Kahsa, Kahsah

Khatiba (Arabic) Feminine form of Khatib; one who leads the prayers; an orator
Khateeba, Khatyba, Khateba, Khatibah, Khateaba

Khatiti (African) A petite woman
Khatitie, Khatyty, Katiti, Katitie, Khatitee, Khatitey, Khatitea, Katitee, Katitea, Katity, Katitey

Khatun (Arabic) A daughter born to nobility; a lady
Khatune, Khatoon, Khaatoon, Khanom, Kanom, Khanam, Khaanam, Khatoun, Khatoune

Khawala (Arabic) A dancing servant girl
Khawalah, Khawalla, Kawala, Kawalah

Khayriyyah (Arabic) A charitable woman
Khayriyah, Khariyyah, Khariya, Khareeya

Khepri (Egyptian) Born of the morning sun
Kheprie, Kepri, Keprie, Khepry, Kepry, Khepree, Kepree, Kheprea, Keprea, Kheprey, Keprey

Khiana (American) One who is different
Khianna, Khiane, Khianne, Khian, Khyana, Khyanna, Kheana, Kheanna

❂ **Khloe** (Greek) A flourishing woman; blooming

Khuyen (Vietnamese) An advisor

Ki (Korean) One who is reborn

Kiana (Hawaiian / Irish) Of the mountains / feminine form of Kian; of an ancient family
Kianna, Kiahna, Keanna, Keiana, Keona, Keonna, Kia, Kiah, Kiahna, Kiani, Kianni, Kiauna, Kiona, Kionah, Kioni, Kionna, Kiandra, Keyanna, Keyah, Keya

Kianga (African) Of the sunshine
Kyanga, Keanga

Kiaria (Japanese) Having great fortune

Kibibi (African) The little lady
Kibibe, Kibebe

Kichi (Japanese) The fortunate one
Kichie, Kichy, Kichey, Kichee, Kichea

Kiden (African) Daughter born after sons

Kidre (American) A loyal woman
Kidrea, Kidreah, Kidria, Kidriah, Kidri, Kidrie, Kidry, Kidrey, Kidree

Kiele (Hawaiian) Resembling the gardenia
Kielle, Kiel, Kiell, Kiela, Kiella

Kienalle (American) Surrounded by light
Kienall, Kienale, Kienalla, Kienala, Kienal

Kienna (American) A brash woman
Kiennah, Kiena, Kienah, Kyenna, Kyennah, Kyena, Kyenah, Kienne, Kyenne

Kiera (Irish) Feminine form of Kieran; little dark-haired one
Kierra, Kyera, Kyerra, Keaira, Keira, Kieranne, Kierane, Kierana, Kiara, Keara,

Keeran, Keera, Keir, Kyra, Kyria, Kyrie, Kyrene, Kira, Kiarra, Kera, Kerra, Kiora, Kiri, Kirra, Kiriana, Kiran

Kieu (Vietnamese) One who is beloved

Kiho (African) From the fog

Kijana (African) A youthful woman
Kijanna, Kijann, Kijan, Kijane, Kijanne

Kikka (German) The mistress of all
Kika, Kykka, Kyka

Kiku (Japanese) Resembling a mum

Kilenya (Native American) Resembling the coughing fish
Kilenyah, Kileniya, Kileniyah

Killian (Irish) A warrior woman; of the church
Kilian, Killiane, Killiana, Kiliane, Kiliana

Kimama (Native American) Resembling a butterfly
Kimimela

Kimana (American) Girl from the meadow
Kimanah, Kimanna, Kimannah, Kymana, Kymanah, Kymanna, Kymannah

Kimatra (Indian) A seductive woman

○ **Kimball** (English) Chief of the warriors; possessing royal boldness
Kimbal, Kimbell, Kimbel, Kymball, Kymbal

Kimberly (English) Of the royal fortress
Kimberley, Kimberli, Kimberlee, Kimberleigh, Kimberlin, Kimberlyn, Kymberlie, Kymberly, Kymberlee, Kim, Kimmy, Kimmie, Kimmi, Kym, Kimber, Kymber, Kimberlie, Kimbra, Kimbro, Kimbrough, Kinborough, Kimberlea, Kimberleah, Kymberlea, Kymberleah

Kimbrell (American) One who smiles a lot
Kimbrelle, Kimbrel, Kimbrele, Kimbrella, Kimbrela, Kymbrell, Kymbrelle, Kymbrel, Kymbrele, Kymbrella, Kymbrela

Kimeo (American) Filled with happiness
Kimeyo

Kimetha (American) Filled with joy
Kimethah, Kymetha, Kymethah, Kimethia, Kymethia, Kimethea, Kymethea

Kimiko (Japanese) A noble child; without equal

Kimone (American) A darling daughter
Kymone

Kin (Japanese) The golden child

Kina (Hawaiian) Woman of China

Kindle (American) To set fire; to arouse
Kindel, Kyndle, Kyndel

Kineks (Native American) Resembling a rosebud

Kineta (Greek) One who is active; full of energy
Kinetikos

Kinipela (Hawaiian) One who is fair; white wave

Kinsey (English) The king's victory
Kinnsee, Kinnsey, Kinnsie, Kinsee, Kinsie, Kinzee, Kinzie, Kinzey, Kinnsea, Kinsea

Kinsley (English) From the king's meadow
Kinsly, Kinslee, Kinsleigh, Kinslea, Kinsli, Kinslie, Kingsley, Kingsly, Kingslee, Kingsleigh, Kingslea, Kingsli, Kingslie

Kintra (American) A joyous woman
Kintrah, Kentra, Kentrah, Kintria, Kentria, Kintrea, Kentrea, Kintrey, Kintry, Kintri, Kintrie, Kintree, Kintrea

Kinza (American) A kinswoman
Kinzah, Kynza, Kynzah

Kioko (Japanese) A daughter born with happiness

Kipp (English) From the small pointed hill
Kip, Kipling, Kippling, Kypp, Kyp

Kirabo (African) A gift from God

Kirati (Indian) From the mountain
Kiratie, Kiraty, Kiratey, Kiratee, Kiratea

Kirby (English) From the church town
Kirbey, Kirbi, Kirbie, Kirbee, Kirbea, Kirbeah

Kiri (Indian) Resembling the amaranth flower
Kirie, Kiry, Kirey, Kiree, Kirea

Kirima (Eskimo) From the hill
Kirimah, Kiryma, Kirymah, Kirema, Kiremah, Kireema, Kireemah, Kireama, Kireamah

Kirit (Indian) One who is crowned
Kitra

Kisha (Russian) A genius
Kishah, Kysha, Kyshah

Kishi (African) From the hills
Kishie, Kishy, Kishey, Kishee, Kishea

Kismet (English) One's destiny; fate
Kizmet

Kiss (American) A caring and compassionate woman
Kyss, Kissi, Kyssi, Kissie, Kyssie, Kissy, Kyssy, Kissey, Kyssey, Kissee, Kyssee, Kissea, Kyssea

Kissa (African) Daughter born after twins
Kissah, Kyssa, Kyssah

Kit (American) Having great strength
Kitt, Kyt, Kytt

Kita (Japanese) Woman from the north

Kitoko (African) A beautiful woman

Kitty (English) Resembling a young cat;
form of Katherine, meaning "one who is
pure; virginal"
Kitti, Kittie, Kity, Kiti, Kitie, Kitee, Kittee, Kittea, Kitea

Kiva (Hebrew) Protected by God
Kivah, Kivi, Kiba

Kiwa (African) A lively woman
Kiwah, Kywa, Kywah, Kiewa, Kiewah, Keiwa, Keiwah, Keewa, Keewah, Keawa, Keawah

Kiwidinok (Native American) Woman of the
wind

Kiya (Australian) Form of Kylie, meaning
"from the narrow channel"
Kiyah, Kya, Kyah

Kiyoshi (Japanese) A quiet child; one who
is pure
Kiyoshie, Kiyoshy, Kiyoshey, Kiyoshee, Kiyoshea

Kizzy (African) An energetic woman
Kizzey, Kizzi, Kizzie, Kizzee, Kizzea

Klara (Scandinavian) Form of Clara, meaning "famously bright"
Klarah, Klaire, Klariss, Klarissa, Klari, Klarika, Kalara, Kalate, Klarisza, Klarysa

Klaribel (Polish) A beautiful woman
Klarybel, Klaribell, Klarybell, Klaribelle, Klarybelle, Klaribela, Klarybela, Klaribella, Klarybella

Klaudia (English) Form of Claudia, meaning "one who is lame"
Klaudiah, Klaudine, Klaudeene, Klaudyne, Klaudette, Klaudett, Klaudete, Klaudeta, Klaudina, Klaudeena, Klaudyna, Klaudelle, Klaudele, Klaudell, Klauda, Klavdia

Klementine (Polish) Form of Clementine,
meaning "one who is merciful"
Klem, Klemence, Klemency, Klementia, Klementina, Klementya, Klementyna, Klementyn, Klemmie, Klemmy, Klementyne

Kleopatra (English) Form of Cleopatra,
meaning "a father's glory; of the royal family"
Klea, Kleo, Kleona, Kleone, Kleonie, Kleora, Kleta, Kleoni, Kleopetra, Kleonie, Kleony, Kleoney, Kleonee, Kleonea, Kleoneah

Klotild (Hungarian) A well-known lady
Klotilde, Klotilda, Klothild, Klothilde, Klothilda

Kobi (American) Woman from California
Kobie, Koby, Kobee, Kobey, Kobea

Kochava (Hebrew) Resembling a star

Kodi (English) Form of Cody, meaning "one
who is helpful; a wealthy woman / acting
as a cushion"
Kody, Kodie, Kodee, Kodey, Kodea, Kodia

Koemi (Japanese) Having a small smile
Koemie, Koemy, Koemey, Koemee, Koemea

Koffi (African) Born on a Friday
Koffie, Koffee, Koffea, Koffy, Koffey, Koffe

Kogan (English) A self-assured woman
Kogann, Kogen, Kogon, Kogin, Kogie, Kogi, Kogy, Kogey, Kogee, Kogea

Kohana (Japanese) Resembling a fragile
flower
Kohanah, Kohanna, Kohannah

Koko (Japanese) The stork has come

Kolby (English) Form of Colby, meaning
"from the coal town"
Kolbey, Kolbi, Kolbie, Kolbee, Kolbea

Koldobika (Teutonic) A renowned warrior
Koldobike

Kolette (English) Form of Colette, meaning "of the victorious people"
Kolete, Kolett, Koleta, Koletta, Kolet

Kolinka (Danish) Born to the victors
Kolinka, Koleenka, Kolynka, Kolenka

Komala (Indian) A delicate and tender woman
Komalah, Komalla, Komal, Komali, Komalie, Komalee, Komaleigh, Komalea

Kona (Hawaiian) A girly woman
Konah, Konia, Koniah, Konea, Koneah, Koni, Konie, Koney, Kony, Konee

Konane (Hawaiian) Daughter of the moonlight

Konstanza (English) Form of Constanza, meaning "one who is constant; steadfast"
Konstanze, Konstanzia, Konstanzea

Kora (Greek) A maiden; in mythology, another name for the goddess Persephone
Korah, Korra, Kore, Koren, Kori, Korie, Koree, Kory, Korey

Koral (American) Form of Coral, meaning "resembling the semiprecious sea growth"
Korale, Korall, Koralle

Kordell (English) Form of Cordelle, meaning "a good-hearted woman; a woman of honesty"
Kordel, Kordelle, Kordele, Kordela, Kordella

Korina (Latin) Form of Corina, meaning "a spear-wielding woman"
Korinna, Koreen, Koreene, Koren, Korena, Korine, Korreen, Korreena, Korrin, Korrina, Korrine, Korenne, Korin, Korinda, Korinn, Korinne, Korrena, Korrianne, Korrienne, Korrinda, Korrinn, Korrinna, Korryn, Koryn, Korynn, Korynne, Korrenda, Korynna, Koreana, Korreana

Kornelia (Polish) Form of Cornelia, meaning "referring to a horn"
Korneliah, Kornelie, Korneli, Kornela, Kornella, Kornelea, Korneliya, Korneleah

Koshatta (Native American) One who is diligent
Koshata, Koshatte, Koshate, Koshat, Koushatta, Koushata, Koushatte, Koushate, Koushat

Kosmo (Greek) A universal woman
Kosma, Kosmah, Kozmo, Kozma, Kasma, Kasmah, Kasmo, Kazma, Kazmo

Kosta (Latin) A steadfast woman
Kostia, Kostiah, Kostya, Kostya, Kostea, Kosteah, Kostusha

Kostya (Slavic) One who is faithful

Koto (Japanese) A harp player

Kourtney (American) Form of Courtney, meaning "a courteous woman; courtly"
Kourtny, Kordney, Kortney, Kortni, Kourtenay, Kourtneigh, Kourtni, Kourtnee, Kourtnie, Kortnie, Kortnea, Kourtnea

Kozue (Japanese) Of the trees
Kozu, Kozoo, Kozou

Krasna (Slavic) A beautiful daughter
Krasava

Kreeli (American) A charming and kind girl
Kreelie, Krieli, Krielie, Kryli, Krylie, Kreely, Kriely, Kryly, Kreelee, Krielee, Krylee, Kreelea, Krielea, Krylea

Krenie (American) A capable woman
Kreni, Kreny, Kreney, Krenee, Krenea

Kriemhild (Norse) In mythology, the wife of Siegfried
Kriemhilda, Kriemhilde

Krishen (American) A talkative woman
Kryshen, Krishon, Kryshon, Krishan, Kryshan, Krishin, Kryshin

Krissy (American) One who is friendly
Krissey, Krissi, Krissie, Krissee, Krissea

Kristina (English) Form of Christina, meaning "follower of Christ"
Kristena, Kristine, Kristyne, Kristyna, Krystina, Krystine, Kristjana, Krisalyn, Kris, Kristy, Kristi, Kristie, Kriszta, Krisztina, Karasi, Kristin, Kristen, Kristyn, Krysten, Krystin, Krystyn, Kristian, Kristiana, Kristiane, Kristianna, Kristianne, Kristel, Kristell, Kristeena, Kristeene, Krista, Krysta, Krystka, Kriska, Krystianna, Krystiana, Krystynka, Krystyna, Krysia, Khristeen, Khristen, Khristin, Khristina, Khristine, Khristyana, Khristyna, Khrystina, Khrystyn, Khrystyna, Khrystyne, Khrustina, Kerstin, Kirsten, Kirstie, Kirstin, Kirsty, Kirstyn, Kirsi

Kriti (Indian) An exquisite work of art
Kritie, Krity, Kritey, Kritee, Kryti, Kryty, Krytie, Krytee, Kritea, Krytea

Krupali (Indian) A forgiving woman
Krupalie, Krupaly, Krupaley, Krupalee, Krupaleigh, Krupalea, Krupaleah, Krupalia

Krystal (English) Form of Crystal, meaning "resembling clear, sparkling, brilliant glass"
Kristal, Krystle, Krystalyn, Krystalynn, Krystalynne, Kristabelle, Krystabelle, Kristalena, Kristalyn, Khrystalline

Ksana (Russian) Praise be to God
Ksanochka, Ksena, Ksanna, Ksann, Ksane, Ksanne

Kubria (Arabic) A wise elder
Kubrea, Kubriah, Kubriya, Kubreah, Kubriyah

Kuma (Japanese) Resembling a bear
Kumah, Kooma, Koomah

Kumani (African) Fulfilling one's destiny
Kumanie, Kumany, Kumaney, Kumanee, Kumanea

Kumari (Indian) Feminine form of Kumar; a princess; another name for the goddess Durga
Kumarie, Kumaria, Kumara, Kumary, Kumarey, Kumaree, Kumarea

Kumi (Japanese) An everlasting beauty
Kumie, Kumy, Kumey, Kumee, Kumea

Kumiko (Japanese) A child who is forever beautiful
Kumeeko, Kumyko

Kumuda (Indian) Resembling a flower
Kumud, Kumudia, Kumudea

Kumudavati (Indian) A woman among lotuses

Kunigunde (German) Brave during time of war
Kundegunde, Kunigunda, Kundegunda, Kunegunda, Kunegunde, Kunegundy, Kunigundy, Kundegundy

Kuniko (Japanese) From the country estate
Kuneeko, Kunyko

Kunti (Hindi) In Hinduism, the mother of the Pandavas
Kuntie, Kunty, Kuntey, Kuntea, Koonti, Koontie, Koonty, Koontey, Koontee, Koontea

Kuonrada (German) One who provides bold counsel

Kura (Turkish) Of the river
Kurah

Kuron (African) One who gives thanks

Kurrsten (Scandinavian) Form of Kirsten, meaning "follower of Christ"
Kursten, Kurrstin, Kurstin, Kursti, Kurstie, Kursty, Kurstee, Kurstea

Kwanita (Native American) God is gracious
Kwanitah, Kwaneeta, Kwanyta, Kwaneata

Kwesi (African) Born on a Saturday
Kwesie, Kwesy, Kwesey, Kwesee, Kwesea

Kyla (English) Feminine form of Kyle; from the narrow channel
Kylah, Kylar, Kyle, Kylia, Kylianne, Kylin, Kya, Kylea

○ **Kylie** (Australian) A boomerang
Kylee, Kyleigh, Kyley, Kyli, Kyleen, Kyleen, Kyler, Kiley, Kily, Kileigh, Kilee, Kilie, Kili, Kilea, Kylea

Kynthia (Greek) In mythology, another name for the moon goddess
Kynthiah, Kynthea, Kinthia, Kinthea, Kynthiya, Kinthiya

Kyoko (Japanese) One who sees her true image

Kyrielle (French) A poetess
Kyriell, Kyriele, Kyriel, Kyriella, Kyriela

I

Laadan (Hebrew) A distinguished woman;
fair-skinned
Laden

Laasya (Indian) A graceful dancer
Laasyah, Lasya, Lasyah

Labana (Hebrew) Feminine form of Labon;
white; fair-skinned
*Labanah, Labanna, Labania, Labanea,
Labaniya, Labannah, Lubaniah, Labaneah,
Labaniyah*

Labe (American) One who moves slowly
Labie, Labi, Laby, Labey, Labee, Labea

Labhaoise (Irish) A mighty battlemaiden;
crowned with laurel
Laoise, Laoiseach, Laobhaoise

Labiba (Arabic) Having great wisdom; one
who is intelligent
*Labibah, Labeeba, Labeebah, Labyba,
Labybah, Labieba, Labiebah, Labeiba,
Labeibah, Labeaba, Labeabah*

Labonita (Spanish) The beautiful one
*Labonitah, Laboneeta, Labonyta, Labonieta,
Laboneita, Laboneata*

Lacey (French) Woman from Normandy; as
delicate as lace
*Lace, Lacee, Lacene, Laci, Laciann, Lacie,
Lacina, Lacy, Lacyann, Laicee, Laicey, Laisey,
Laycie, Layci, Laycee, Lacea, Laycea, Laicea*

Lachelle (American) A sweet woman
Lachell, Lachel, Lachele, Lachela, Lachella

Lachesis (Greek) In mythology, one of the
three Fates
Lachesiss, Lachesisse, Lachesys, Lacheses

Lachlan (Gaelic) From the land of the lochs
*Lochlan, Lachlana, Lochlana, Lachina,
Lachyna, Locke, Loche, Lacklan, Locklan*

Lacole (American) A sly woman
Lakole, Lucole, Lukole

Lacreta (Spanish) Form of Lucretia, meaning
"a bringer of light; a successful woman"
Lacrete, Lacrita, Lacrite, Lacryta, Lacryte

Lada (Slavic) In mythology, goddess of love,
harmony, and fertility
Ladah, Ladda, Laddah

LaDawn (American) As beautiful as the
sunrise
*Ladawn, LaDaun, Ladaun, LeDawn, Ledawn,
LeDaun, Ledaun*

Ladislava (Slavic) Feminine form of
Vladislav; a glorious ruler
*Ladislavah, Ladislavia, Ladislavea, Ladyslava,
Ladyslavia, Ladyslavea*

Ladonna (American) Form of Donna,
meaning "ruler of the world"
*Ladona, Ladonnah, Ladonah, Ledonna,
Ledona*

Ladrenda (American) One who is guarded
*Ladrendah, Ladrynda, Ladryndah, Ladrinda,
Ladrindah*

Lady (English) One who kneads bread; the
head of the house
*Lady, Ladee, Ladi, Ladie, Laidy, Laydy, Laydi,
Laydie, Laidi, Laidie, Laydee, Laidee, Ladea,
Laydea, Laidea*

Lael (Hebrew) One who belongs to God
Laele, Laelle

Laelia (Latin) Feminine form of Laelius;
resembling the orchid
*Laeliah, Laeliya, Laelea, Laeleah, Lueliyah,
Laelya, Laelyah*

Lafonde (American) One who is affectionate

Lage (Swedish) Woman from the ocean

Laguna (American) From the beach
*Lagoona, Lagunah, Lagoonah, Lagouna,
Lagounah*

Lahela (Hawaiian) As innocent as a lamb
Lahelah, Lahella, Lahellah

Lahja (Finnish) Gift from God

Laila (Arabic) A beauty of the night; born at
nightfall
*Laela, Laliah, Lailie, Laily, Lailie, Laili,
Lailaa, Leila, Leela, Leelah, Leilah, Lela,
Lelah, Lelia, Leyla, Loelia*

Laima (Latvian) One who is fortunate; in mythology, goddess of luck
Layma, Laema

Lainil (American) A softhearted woman
Lainill, Lainyl, Lainyll, Laenil, Laenill, Laenyl, Laenyll, Laynil, Laynill, Laynyl, Laynyll

Laire (Scottish) Resembling a mare
Lair, Laira, Lairia, Lairea, Layr, Layre, Laer, Laere

Lais (Greek) A legendary courtesan
Laise, Lays, Layse, Laisa, Laes, Laese

Laish (Hebrew) Resembling a lioness
Laisha, Lashia, Lashea, Laysh, Laishe, Layshe, Laysha, Laesh, Laeshe, Laesha

Lajean (French) A soothing woman
Lajeane, LaJean, LaJeane, Lajeanne, L'Jean

Lajila (Indian) One who is modest; shy
Lajyla, Lajeela, Lajeala

Lajita (Indian) A truthful woman
Lajyta, Lajeeta, Lajeata

Laka (Polynesian) In mythology, the patron goddess of dancers
Lakah

Lake (American) From the still waters
Laken, Laiken, Layken, Layk, Layke, Laik, Laike, Laeken, Laek, Laeke

Lakeisha (American / African) A lively and healthy woman / the favorite
Lakeesha, Lakecia, Lakesha, Lakeshia, Laketia, Lakeysha, Lakicia, Lakiesha, Lakisha, Lakitia, Laquisha, Lekeesha, Lekeisha, Lekisha, Laquiesha, Lakeasha, Lekeasha

Lakela (Hawaiian) A girly woman
Lakelah, Lakella, Lakellah

Lakia (Arabic) One who is treasured
Lakiah, Lakeea, Lakeah, Lakeya, Lakea, Lakiyah, Lakiya, Lakeyah

Laksha (Indian) As beautiful as a white rose
Lakshah, Lakshia, Lakshiya, Lakshea, Lakshya

Lakshmi (Hindi) A good omen; in Hinduism, the goddess of wealth, light, and beauty
Lakshmie, Lakshmy, Laxmi, Laxmie, Laxmy, Lakshmey, Laxmey, Lakshmee, Laxmee, Lakshmea, Laxmea

Lakya (Indian) Born on a Thursday

Lala (Slavic) Resembling a tulip
Lalah, Lalla, Lallah, Laleh

Lalage (Greek) One who often prattles
Lallie, Lally, Lalli, Lalley, Lallea, Lalleah

Lalaine (American) A hardworking woman
Lalain, Lalaina, Lalayn, Lalayne, Lalayna, Lalaen, Lalaene, Lalaena

Lalasa (Indian) Resembling a dove; one who is peaceful and promotes love
Lalasah, Lalassa, Lallassa, Lallasa

Laleema (Spanish) A devoted woman
Laleemah, Laleima, Laleimah, Laliema, Laliemah, Lalyma, Lalymah, Laleama, Laleamah

Lalia (Greek) One who is well-spoken
Lali, Lallia, Lalya, Lalea, Lalie, Lalee, Laly, Laley

Lalika (Indian) A lovely young woman
Lalica, Lalicka, Lalyka, Lalycka, Lalyca, Lalikah

Lalita (Indian) A playful and charming woman
Lalitah, Laleeta, Laleetah, Lalyta, Lalytah, Laleita, Laleitah, Lalieta, Lalietah, Laleata, Laleatah

Lamaara (Slavic) A girl from the mountains
Lamaarah, Lamara, Lamarah, Laamarra, Lamarra

Lamarian (American) One who is conflicted
Lamariane, Lamarean, Lamareane

Lamia (Greek) In mythology, a female vampire
Lamiah, Lamiya, Lamiyah, Lamea, Lameah

Lamika (American) One who is calm and peaceful
Lamikah, Lamyka, Lamykah, Lameeka, Lameekah, Lameika, Lameikah, Lamieka, Lamiekah, Lameaka, Lameakah

Lamis (Arabic) A soft-skinned woman
Lamiss, Lamisse, Lamys, Lamyss, Lamysse, Lamees, Lameese

L'Amour (French) One who loves and is loved
Lamour, Lamoure, L'Amoure, Lamore, Lamoura

Lamya (Arabic) Having lovely dark lips
Lamyah, Lamyia, Lama

Lan (Chinese) Resembling an orchid

Lana (German / Greek) Form of Alana, meaning "beautiful and fair woman; dear child" / form of Helen, meaning "the shining light"
Lanae, Lanette, Lanna, Lanny, Lannice, Lanice

Lanai (Hawaiian) A veranda; from the island
Lenai

Lanassa (Russian) A lighthearted woman; cheerful
Lanasa, Lanassia, Lanasia, Lanassiya, Lanasiya

Land (American) Of the earth
Lande, Landy, Landey, Landee, Landea, Landi, Landie

Landa (Spanish) Refers to the Virgin Mary

Landen (English) From the grassy meadow
Landin, Landyn

Landon (English) From the long hill
Landan, Lanton, Lantan

Landra (Latin) A wise counselor
Landrada, Landria, Landrea, Landradah

Landry (English) Of the rough terrain
Landrey, Landri, Landrie, Landree, Landrea, Landreah

Lane (English) One who takes the narrow path
Laine, Lainey, Laney, Lanie, Layne, Laina, Layna, Lainie, Laen, Laene, Laena, Laeni, Laenie, Lanee, Laynee, Laenee

Lanelle (American) One who takes the narrow path
Lanell, Lanele, Lanella, Lanela, Lanel

Lang (Scandinavian) Woman of great height

Langley (English) From the long meadow
Langly, Langli, Langlie, Langlee, Langleigh, Langlea

Lani (Hawaiian) From the sky; one who is heavenly
Lanikai

Lanka (Hindi) From the island fortress
Lankah, Lankia, Lankiah, Lankea, Lankeah

Lansing (English) Filled with hope
Lanseng, Lansyng

Lantana (English) Resembling the flower with orange or purple blossoms
Lantunah, Lantanna, Lantania, Lantanea, Lantaniya, Lantanya

Lanza (Italian) One who is noble and willing
Lanzah, Lanzia, Lanziah, Lanzea, Lanzeah

Laodamia (Greek) In mythology, daughter of Bellerophon
Laodamiah, Laodamea, Laodameah

Laoidheach (Gaelic) From the meadowland

Lapis (Egyptian) Resembling the dark-blue gemstone
Lapiss, Lapisse, Lapys, Lapyss, Lapysse

Laquanna (American) An outspoken woman
Laquana, Laquann, Laquane, Laquan

Laqueta (American) A quiet and well-behaved child
Laquetta, Laquita, Laquitta

Laquinta (American) The fifth-born child

Lara (Latin) One who is protected; a cheerful woman
Larra, Laralaine, Laramae, Larina, Larinda, Larita, Larya

Laramie (French) Shedding tears of love
Larami, Laramy, Laramey, Laramee, Laramea

Larby (American) Form of Darby, meaning "of the deer park"
Larbey, Larbi, Larbie, Larbee, Larbea

Larch (American) One who is full of life
Larche

Lareina (Spanish) The queen; one born to royalty
Laraene, Larayne, Lareine, Larena, Larrayna, Larreina, Laranya, Laraena, Larayna

Larenta (Latin) In mythology, an earth goddess
Larentia, Larentea, Larynta

Larhonda (American) A flashy woman
Larhondah, Larhondia, Larhondiah, Larhondea, Larhondeah, Laranda

Larissa (Latin) A lighthearted woman
Lari, Larisa, Laryssa, Lerissa, Lorissa, Lyssa, Larisse, Laryssa, Larysse, Laurissa

Lark (English) Resembling the songbird
Larke

Larkin (American) A pretty young woman
Larkyn, Larkine, Larkyne, Larken, Larkene, Larkun, Larkune

Larkspur (English) Resembling the blue flower
Larkspurr, Larkspurre

Larrie (American) A tomboyish woman
Larri, Larry, Larrey, Larree, Larrea

Larsen (Scandinavian) Daughter of Lars
Larson, Larssen, Larsson

Larue (American) Form of Rue, meaning "from the medicinal herb"
LaRue, Laroo, Larou

Lasha (Spanish) One who is forlorn
Lashah, Lashe

Lashanda (American) A brassy woman
Lashonda, Lashounda, Lashunda

Lashawna (American) Filled with happiness
Lashauna, Laseana, Lashona, Lashawn, Lasean, Lashone, Lashaun

Lassie (Scottish) A young girl; one who is pure
Lassi, Lassey, Lassy, Lassee, Lass, Lasseu

Lata (Indian) Of the lovely vine
Latah

Latanya (American) Daughter of the fairy queen
Latanyah, Latonya, Latania, Latanja, Latonia, Latanea

Latasha (American) Form of Natasha, meaning "born on Christmas Day"
Latashah, Latascha, Latashia, Latasia, Latashea, Latashiya

LaTeasa (Spanish) A flirtatious woman
Lateasa, Lateaza

Lathenia (American) A talkative woman
Latheniah, Lathena, Lathenah, Lathenea, Latheneah

Latifah (Arabic) One who is gentle and kind
Latifa, Lateefa, Lateefah, Lateifa, Lateiffa, Latiffa, Latyfa, Latiefa, Lateifah, Latiefah, Lateafa, Lateafah, Latyfah

Latika (Indian) An elegant and majestic lady
Latikah, Laticka, Latica, Lateeka, Latieka, Lateaka, Latyka, Lateika

Latisehsha (American) A happy woman

Latona (Latin) In mythology, the Roman equivalent of Leto, the mother of Artemis and Apollo
Latonah, Latonia, Latonea, Lantoniah, Latoneah

Latosha (American) Filled with happiness
Latoshia, Latoshah, Latoshiah, Latoshea, Latosheah

Latoya (Spanish) One who is victorious
Letoya, Latoia, Latoria, Latorya, Latoyah, Latoyla, Latoiya

Latrelle (American) One who laughs a lot
Latrell, Latrel, Latrele, Latrella, Latrela

Latrice (English) Born into the nobility
Latrecia, Latreece, Latreese, Latreshia, Latricia, Leetriss, Letrice, Leatrice, Letreece

Latrisha (American) One who is high maintenance
Latrishah, Latrysha, Latryshah, Latriesha, Latrieshah, Latreisha, Latreishah, Latreesha, Latreeshah, Latreasha, Latreashah

Lauda (Latin) One who is praised

Laudine (English) Lady of the fountain; in Arthurian legend, the wife of Yvain
Laudene, Laudyne, Laudina, Laudena, Laudyna, Laudeen, Laudean, Laudeena, Laudeana

Laudonia (Italian) Praises the house
Laudonea, Laudoniya, Laudomia, Laudomea, Laudomiya

Laufeia (Norse) From the wooded island
Laufia, Laufea, Laufeiya, Laufeya

Laura (Latin) Crowned with laurel; from the laurel tree
Lauraine, Lauralee, Laralyn, Laranca, Larea, Lari, Lauralee, Laurana, Laure, Laurel, Laurella, Laurence, Laurentia, Laurentine, Laurestine, Lauretha, Lauretta, Laurette, Lauri, Lauriane, Laurianne, Laurice, Lauricia, Laurie, Laurina, Laurinda, Laurine, Lauritu, Laurnea, Lavra, Lawra, Lollie, Lolly, Laural, Lauralle, Laurell, Laurelle, Lauriel, Lauralyn, Lauene, Lauica, Laurencia, Lawrencia, Lonyn, Loura, Larunda, Lawena, Laria

❂ **Lauren** (French) Form of Laura, meaning "crowned with laurel; from the laurel tree"
Laren, Larentia, Larentina, Larenzina, Larren, Laryn, Larryn, Larrynn, Larsina, Larsine, Laurenne, Laurin, Lauryn, Laurynn, Laurena, Laurene, Laureen, Lareen

Laurent (French) A graceful woman
Laurente, Lorent, Lorente

Lavada (American) One who is creative; muscially talented
Lavadah, Lavadia, Lavadea, Lavadiya

Lavanya (Indian) One who is filled with grace
Lavania, Lavani, Lavanie, Lavany, Lavaney, Lavanee, Lavanea, Lavaneah, Lavaniya

Lave (Latin) One who is washed clean

Laveda (Latin) One who is innocent; cleansed
Lavedah, Lavella, Lavelle, Laveta, Lavetta, Lavette

Lavender (English) Resembling the purple flowering plant
Lavinder, Lavandar, Lavander, Lavindar, Lavynder, Lavyndar

Laverne (Latin) Born in the spring; in mythology, Laverna was the goddess of thieves
Laverine, Lavern, Laverna, Laverrne, Leverne, Loverna, Lavyrne, Lavyrna, Lavernia, La Verne, La Vergne, Lativerna, Levema

Lavinia (Latin) In mythology, the daughter of Latinus and wife of Aeneas
Lavena, Lavenia, Lavina, Lavinie, Levenia, Levinia, Livinia, Louvenia, Louvinia, Lovina, Lovinia, Luvena, Luvenia, Luvina, Luvinia

Lavita (American) A charming woman
Lavitah, Laveeta, Laveetah, Laveata, Laveatah, Lavieta, Lavietah, Laveita, Laveitah, Lavyta, Lavytah

Lavonne (French) Form of Yvonne, meaning "a young archer"
Lavonda, Lavonna, Lahvonne, Levonne, Levonda, Lavonn

Lawanda (American) Form of Wanda, meaning "a wanderer"
Lawandah, Lawannda, Lawahnda, Lawonda, Lawonnda, Lawohnda, Lawande, Lawandis

❂ **Layla** (Arabic) form of Laila, meaning "a beauty of the night; born at nightfall"
Laylah, Laylie, Layli

Le (Chinese) One who brings joy to others

Lea (English) From the meadow
Lee, Leigh, Ley

Leaf (American) Woman of the forest
Leafi, Leafie, Leafy, Leafey, Leafee, Leafea

❂ **Leah** (Hebrew) One who is weary; in the Bible, Jacob's first wife
Leia, Leigha, Lia, Liah, Leeya

Leala (French) One who is faithful; loyal
Leola, Lealia, Lealie, Leal, Liealia

Leandra (Greek) Feminine form of Leander; resembling a lioness
Leandre, Leandria, Leanza, Leanda, Leiandra, Leodora, Leoine, Leoline, Leonelle

Leanna (Gaelic) Form of Helen, meaning "the shining light"
Leana, Leann, Leanne, Lee-Ann, Leeann, Leeanne, Leianne, Leyanne, Leigh-Anne, Leighanna, Leeahnne, Leane, Leianna, Leighanne, Leighna, Leena, Leauna

Leatrice (American) Form of Beatrix, meaning "one who blesses others"
Leatrix, Leatriz, Leatriss, Leatrisse, Leatrize, Leatricia, Leatrisa, Leate, Leata, Leat, Leitris, Letrys, Lettrys

Leba (Hebrew) One who is dearly loved
Lebah, Lebba, Lebbah

Lebonah (Hebrew) Refers to frankincense
Lebona, Lebonna, Lebonia, Lebonea, Leboniya, Levona, Levonia, Levonah, Levonea, Levonna

Lechsinska (Polish) A beautiful maiden of the forest

Lecia (English) Form of Alice, meaning "woman of the nobility; truthful; having high moral character"
Licia, Lecea, Licea, Lisha, Lysha, Lesha

Ledell (Greek) One who is queenly
Ledelle, Ledele, Ledella, Ledela, Ledel

Leela (Indian) An accomplished actress

Legarre (Spanish) Refers to the Virgin Mary
Legare, Legarra, Legara, Lera, Leira

Legend (American) One who is memorable
Legende, Legund, Legunde

Legia (Spanish) A bright woman
Legiah, Legea, Legeah, Legiya, Legiyah, Legya, Legyah

Lehava (Hebrew) A fiery woman; the little flame
Lehavah, Lehavia, Lehavea, Lehavit, Lehaviya

Lei (Hawaiian) Adorned with flowers

Leiko (Hawaiian) Resembling a small flower
Leeko, Lyko, Liko, Lieko

Leilani (Hawaiian) Child of heaven; adorned with heavenly flowers
Leia, Lalani, Leilanie, Leilanee, Leilaney, Leilany, Lalanie, Lalaney, Lalanee, Lalany, Leilanea, Lalanea

Leitha (Greek) One who is forgetful; in mythology, Lethe was the river of forgetfulness
Leith, Leithe, Lethe, Letha, Lethia, Lethea

Lejoi (French) Filled with happiness
Lejoy, Lejoye

Lemuela (Hebrew) Feminine form of Lemuel; devoted to God
Lemuelah, Lemuella, Lemuellah, Lemuel, Lemuele, Lemuelle

Lena (German) Form of Helen, meaning "the shining light"
Lina, Leena, Leyna, Leina, Lyna, Lenci, Lencie, Lency, Lencey, Lencee, Lenka, Lencea

Lenesha (American) One who smiles a lot
Lenesha, Leneesha, Leneeshah, Leniesha, Lenieshah, Leneisha, Leneishah, Leneasha, Leneashah, Lenysha, Lenyshah

Lenis (Latin) One who has soft and silky skin
Lene, Leneta, Lenice, Lenita, Lennice, Lenos, Lenys, Lenisse, Lenysse, Lenyce, Lenet

Lenmana (Native American) Talented with the flute
Lenmanna, Linmana, Linmanna, Lynmana, Lynmanna

Lennon (English) Daughter of love
Lennan, Lennin, Lenon, Lenan, Lenin

Lenore (Greek) Form of Eleanor, meaning "the shining light"
Lenor, Lenora, Lenorah, Lenorr, Lenorra, Lenorre, Leonora, Leonore, Lanora, Leanor, Leanora, Leanore, Leora, Leorah, Leeora, Liora, Leeor, Lior, Liorit, Leonor, Linore, Linor, Linora, Lenoa

Lenusy (Russian) As delicate as a flower
Lenusey, Lenusi, Lenusie, Lenusee, Lenusea

Leoda (German) Daughter of the people
Leota, Leodah, Leotah, Luete, Lueta

Leona (Latin) Feminine form of Leon; having the strength of a lion
Leeona, Leeowna, Leoine, Leola, Leone, Leonelle, Leonia, Leonie, Leontine, Leontina, Leontyne, Leontyna, Leowna, Leoma, Leonda, Leondra, Leondrea, Leonline, Leonela, Leoni, Leonine, Leonita, Leonlina, Leontin, Liona, Lione, Lyonene, Lyonet, Lyonette, Lyoneta, Lyonetta, Leonee, Leonea

Leonarda (French) Feminine form of Leonard; having the strength of a lion
Lenarda, Leonda, Lennarda, Leonarde, Lenna, Leondra, Leodora, Leoarrie

Leonsio (Spanish) One who is fierce
Leonsa, Leonsiu, Leonsea, Leonsi, Leonsie, Leonsy, Leonsey, Leonsee

Leopolda (German) Feminine form of Leopold; a bold ruler of the people
Leopoldia, Leopoldea, Leopoldina, Leopoldyna, Leopoldeena, Leopoldeana, Leopoldena, Leopoldine, Leopoldyne, Leopoldeen

Leotie (Native American) Resembling a wildflower
Leoti, Leotee, Leoty, Leotey, Leotea

Lequoia (Native American) Form of Sequoia, meaning "of the giant redwood tree"
Lequoya, Lequoiya, Lekoya, Lekoia

Lerola (Latin) Resembling a blackbird
Lerolla, Lerolah, Lerolia, Lerolea

Lesham (Hebrew) Our precious child
Leshama, Leshamah, Leshamia, Leshamea, Leshamiya, Leshmya

Leslie (Gaelic) From the holly garden; of the gray fortress
Leslea, Leslee, Lesleigh, Lesley, Lesli, Lesly, Lezlee, Lezley, Lezlie, Lezleigh, Lezli, Lioslaith, Lezlea

Leta (Latin) One who is glad; joyful; loved by all
Leeta, Lita, Lida, Leeda, Leita, Leida, Leyta, Lyta, Leyda, Lyda, Loida, Loyda, Leda, Luda, Ledaea, Ledah

Letichel (American) Filled with happiness
Letichell, Letichele, Letichelle, Letichela, Letichella, Letishel, Letishell, Letishele, Letishelle, Letishela, Letishella

Letitia (Latin) One who brings joy to others
Laetitia, Laetizia, Latashia, Latia, Latisha, Letice, Leticia, Leticja, Letisha, Letizia, Letta, Lettice, Lettie, Lettitia, Letty, Letycja, Lateisha, Latesha, Laticia, Latitia

Leto (Greek) In mythology, mother of Apollo and Artemis

Letsey (American) Form of Letitia, meaning "one who brings joy to others"
Letsy, Letsee, Letsea, Letsi, Letsie

Leucippe (Greek) In mythology, a nymph
Lucippe, Leucipe, Lucipe

Leucothea (Greek) In mythology, a sea nymph
Leucothia, Leucothiah, Leucotheah

Levana (Latin) One who is raised up; in mythology, goddess and protector of newborns
Livana, Livaun, Levanah, Levanna, Levania, Levanea, Livanna, Livania, Livanea

Levane (Irish) Of the great elm
Levayne, Levaine, Levayn, Levain, Levaen, Levaene

Levia (Hebrew) One who joins forces with others
Leviah, Leviya, Leviyah, Levya, Levyah, Levea, Leveah

Levina (Latin) Resembling a lightning bolt
Levyna, Levena, Leveena, Leviena, Leveina, Leveana

Levitt (American) One who is straightforward
Levit, Levitte, Levytt, Levyt, Levytte

Levity (American) A lighthearted woman
Leviti, Levitie, Levitee, Levitea, Levitey

Levora (American) A homebody
Levorah, Levorra, Levorrah, Levoria, Levoriah, Levorea, Levoreah, Levorya, Levoryah

Lewa (African) A very beautiful woman
Lewah

Lewana (Hebrew) Of the white moon
Lewanah, Lewanna, Lewannah

Lexie (Greek) Form of Alexandra, meaning "helper and defender of mankind"
Lexa, Lexandra, Lexann, Lexi, Lexia, Lexina, Lexine, Lexus, Lexya, Lexea, Lex, Lexis, Lexiss, Lexy, Lexy, Lexee

Leya (Spanish) One who upholds the law
Leyah

Lezena (American) One who smiles often
Lezenah, Lezina, Lezinuh, Lezyna, Lezynah, Lezene, Lyzena

Lhasa (Indian) From the sacred city
Lhasah, Lasa, Lassa, Laasa

Li (Chinese) Having great strength; one who is sharp

Liadan (Irish) An older woman; the gray lady
Leadan, Lyadan

Liana (French / English) Of the jungle vine; bound / form of Eliana, meaning "the Lord answers our prayers"
Liann, Lianna, Lianne, Liahna, Liahne, Liane, Liani, Lianie, Lianee, Liany, Lianey, Lyanne, Lyane, Lyana, Lyanna, Lianea

Libby (English) Form of Elizabeth, meaning "my God is bountiful"
Libba, Libbee, Libbey, Libbie, Libet, Liby, Lilibet, Lilibeth, Lilibet, Lillibet, Lilybet, Lilybeth, Lilybell, Lib, Libbea, Libea

Liberty (English) An independent woman; having freedom
Libertey, Libertee, Libertea, Liberti, Libertie, Libertas, Libera, Liber, Libyr

Libitina (Latin) In mythology, goddess of death
Lybitina, Lybytyna, Libitena, Libityna, Libiteena, Libiteana, Libitiena, Libiteina

Libni (Hebrew) A distinguished woman; fair-skinned
Libnie, Libney, Libny, Libnee, Libnea

Libra (Latin) One who is balanced; the seventh sign of the zodiac
Leebra, Leibra, Liebra, Leabra, Leighbra, Lybra

Librada (Spanish) One who is free
Libradah, Lybrada, Lybradah

Licia (Latin / English) Woman from Lycia / form of Alicia, meaning "woman of the nobility; truthful; having high moral character"
Liciah, Leecea, Leecia, Leesha, Lesia, Lisia, Lycia

Lidwina (Scandinavian) A friend to all
Lidwyna, Lidweena, Lidwiena, Lidweina, Lidweana

Lien (Vietnamese) Resembling the lotus
Lian

Lieselette (American) Form of Liesl, meaning "my God is bountiful"
Lieselet, Lieselete, Lieselett, Lieseleta, Lieseletta

Liesl (German) Form of Elizabeth, meaning "my God is bountiful"
Liezl, Liesa, Liese, Liesel, Liezel, Liesei, Liesheth, Liesi, Liesie

Lieu (Vietnamese) Of the willow tree

Light (American) A lighthearted woman
Lite, Lyte

Ligia (Greek) One who is musically talented
Ligiah, Ligya, Ligiya, Lygia, Ligea, Lygea, Lygya, Lygiya

Liguria (Greek) One who loves music
Liguriah, Lyguria, Lyguriah, Ligurea, Ligureah, Lygurea, Lygureah

Lila (Arabic / Greek) Born at night / resembling a lily
Lilah, Lyla, Lylah

Lilac (Latin) Resembling the bluish-purple flower
Lilack, Lilak, Lylac, Lylack, Lylak, Lilach

Lileah (Latin) Resembling a lily
Lilea, Lyleah, Lylea, Lilya, Lilyah, Lylya, Lylyah

Lilette (Latin) Resembling a budding lily
Lilett, Lilete, Lilet, Lileta, Liletta, Lylette, Lylett, Lylete, Lylet, Lyletta, Lyleta

Liliash (Spanish) Resembling a lily
Liliashe, Lilyash, Lilyashe

Liliha (Hawaiian) One who holds rank as chief

Lilith (Babylonian) Woman of the night
Lilyth, Lillith, Lillyth, Lylith, Lyllith, Lylyth, Lyllyth, Lilithe, Lylithe, Lilythe

❂ **Lillian** (Latin) Resembling the lily
Lilian, Liliana, Liliane, Lilianne, Lilias, Lilas, Lillas, Lillias, Lilianna, Lilliana, Lilliane, Lilliann, Lillianna, Lillianne, Lillyan, Lillyanne, Lilyan, Lilyann, Lillis, Lilis

Lilo (Hawaiian) One who is generous
Lylo, Leelo, Lealo, Leylo, Lielo, Leilo

Liluye (Native American) Resembling the soaring hawk

⚥ **Lily** (English) Resembling the flower; one who is innocent and beautiful
Leelee, Lil, Lili, Lilie, Lilla, Lilley, Lilli, Lillie, Lillika, Lillita, Lilly, Lilybel, Lilybell, Lilybella, Lilybelle, Lillah, Lilia, Lilch, Lilika, Lilike

Limber (African) One who is joyful
Lymber, Lember

Limor (Hebrew) Refers to myrrh
Limora, Limoria, Limorea, Leemor, Leemora, Leemoria, Leemorea

Lin (Chinese) Resembling jade; from the woodland

Lina (Arabic) Of the palm tree
Leena, Leina, Leyna, Lena, Lyna, Leana

Linda (Spanish) One who is soft and beautiful
Lindalee, Lindee, Lindey, Lindi, Lindie, Lindira, Lindka, Lindy, Lynda, Lynde, Lyndy, Lyndi, Lyndall, Lyndee, Lynnda, Lynndie, Lueinda, Lindea, Lyndea

Linden (English) From the hill of lime trees
Lindenn, Lindon, Lindynn, Lynden, Lyndon, Lyndyn, Lyndin, Lindin

Lindiwe (African) The daughter we have waited for

Lindley (English) From the pastureland
Lindly, Lindlee, Lindleigh, Lindli, Lindlie, Leland, Lindlea

Lindsay (English) From the island of linden trees; from Lincoln's wetland
Lind, Lindsea, Lindsee, Lindseigh, Lindsey, Lindsy, Linsay, Linsey, Linsie, Linzi, Linzee, Linzy, Lyndsay, Lyndsey, Lyndsie, Lynnsey, Lynnzey, Lynsey, Lynzey, Lynzi, Lynzy, Lynzee, Lynzie, Lindse

Ling (Chinese) As sweet as the tinkling of a bell
Lyng

Linn (Scottish) Resembling the cascade of a waterfall
Linne

Linnea (Scandinavian) Resembling a small mountain flower; of the lime tree
Lenae, Linea, Linna, Linnae, Linnaea, Lynae, Lynea, Lynnae, Lynnea

Liriene (French) One who enjoys reading aloud
Lirienne, Liriena, Lirienna, Lirien, Lirienn

Liriope (Greek) In mythology, a nymph and the mother of Narcissus
Leiriope, Leirioessa

Lirit (Hebrew) One who is musically talented
Lirita, Liritia, Liritea, Leerit

Lisa (English) Form of Elizabeth, meaning "my God is bountiful"
Leesa, Liesa, Lisebet, Lise, Liseta, Lisette, Liszka, Lisebeth, Lisabet, Lisabeth, Lisabette, Lisbet, Lisbeth, Lisavet, Lissa, Lissette, Lyssa, Lysa, Lesa, Liesbet, Liisa, Lis, Leysa, Leisa, Leasa

Lishan (African) One who is awarded a medal
Lishana, Lishanna, Lyshan, Lyshana, Lyshanna

Lissie (American) Resembling a flower
Lissi, Lissy, Lissey, Lissee, Lissea

Liv (Scandinavian / Latin) One who protects others / from the olive tree
Livia, Livea, Liviya, Livija, Livvy, Livy, Livya, Lyvia, Livi, Livie, Livee

Livonah (Hebrew) A vibrant woman; full of life
Livona, Lyvonah, Lyvona, Levona, Levonah

Liya (Hebrew) The Lord's daughter
Liyah, Leeya, Leeyah, Leaya, Leayah

Liza (English) Form of Elizabeth, meaning "my God is bountiful"
Lyza, Leeza, Litsea, Litzea, Liz, Lizzie, Lizabeth, Lizandra, Lizann, Lizbet, Lizbeth, Lizeth, Lizette, Lizina, Lizzy, Lyzbeth, Lyzbet, Lyzabeth, Lyzz, Lizz, Lyz, Leyza, Liiza, Leza

Llamrei (English) In Arthurian legend, Arthur's steed

Llesenia (Spanish) Form of Yesenia, meaning "resembling a flower"
Lleseniah, Llesinia, Llesenya, Llecenia, Llasenya, Llesnia, Llessenia, Llessena, Llessenya, Llissenia, Llesenea, Lleseneah, Llesinea

Lleucu (Welsh) The treasured light
Lleyke

Lo (American) A feisty woman
Loe, Low, Lowe

Loanna (American) A gracious and loving woman
Loana, Loann, Loane, Loanne

Lodema (English) One who provides guidance
Lodemah, Lodima, Lodimah, Lodyma, Lodymah, Lodeema, Lodeemah

Lofn (Norse) In mythology, one of the principal goddesses

Logan (Gaelic) From the hollow
Logann, Logane, Loganne

Logestilla (French) Daughter of a legend
Logistilla, Logestila, Logistila, Logestylla, Logistylla, Logestile, Logestille, Logistile, Logistille

Loicy (American) A delightful woman
Loicey, Loicee, Loicea, Loici, Loicie, Loyce, Loice, Loyci, Loycie, Loycee, Loycea, Loycy, Loycey

Loire (French) From the river in France
Loir

Lois (Greek) A superior woman
Loes

Lojean (American) A bravehearted woman
Lojeane, Lojeanne

Lokelani (Hawaiian) Resembling a small red rose
Lokelanie, Lokelany, Lokelaney, Lokelanee, Lokelanea

Loki (Norse) In mythology, a trickster god
Lokie, Lokee, Lokey, Loky, Lokea, Lokeah, Lokia, Lokiah

Lola (Spanish) Form of Dolores, meaning "woman of sorrow"
Lolah, Lolla, Loela, Lolita, Lolitta, Loleta, Loletta, Lo, Loe

Loleen (American) Filled with joy
Loleena, Lolene, Lolena, Loliene, Loliena, Loleine, Loleina, Loleana, Loleane, Lolyne, Lolyna

Lomahongva (Native American) Of the pretty clouds

Lomasi (Native American) Resembling a beautiful flower
Lomasie, Lomasee, Lomasy, Lomasey, Lomasea

Lomita (Spanish) A good woman
Lomitah, Lomeeta, Lomeetah, Lomieta, Lomietah, Lomeita, Lomeitah, Lomeata, Lomeatah, Lomyta, Lomytah

Londa (American) One who is shy
Londah, Londe, Londeh, Londy, Londey, Londee, Londea, Londi, Londie

❂ **London** (English) From the captial of England

Loni (English) Form of Leona, meaning "having the strength of a lion"
Lona, Lonee, Lonie, Lonna, Lonni, Lonnie, Lonee, Lony, Loney, Lonea, Lonnea, Lonnee, Lonny, Lonney

Lora (Latin) Form of Laura, meaning "crowned with laurel; from the laurel tree"
Lorabelle, Lorah, Loranna, Loreanna, Loree, Lorenna, Lorey, Lori, Loribelle, Lorinda, Lorita, Lorra, Lorrae, Lorree, Lorrie, Lory, Lowra, Lorna, Loria, Lorian, Loriane, Loriana, Loriann, Lorianne, Lorianna, Lorie, Lorilla, Loriel, Lorilynn, Lorrella, Loralle, Lorel, Lorelle, Lowrelle, Lorand, Lorant, Loris, Lowri, Lowrie

Loranden (American) A genius
Lorandena, Lorandyn, Lorandyna, Luranden, Lurandena, Lurandyna, Lurandyne

Lordyn (American) An enchanting woman
Lordynn, Lordynne, Lordin, Lordinn, Lordinne, Lordyne, Lordine

Lore (Basque / English) Resembling a flower / form of Lora, meaning "crowned with laurel; from the laurel tree"
Lorea

Lorelei (German) From the rocky cliff; in mythology, a siren who lured sailors to their deaths
Laurelei, Laurelie, Loralee, Loralei, Loralie, Loralyn, Lorilee, Lorilyn, Lura, Lurette, Lurleen, Lurlene, Lurline, Lurlyne, Lorali, Loreli, Laureli

Loren (English) Form of Laura, meaning "crowned with laurel; from the laurel tree"
Lorin, Lorren, Lorrin, Lorryn, Loryn, Lorena, Loreen, Loreene, Lorene, Lorenia, Lorenna, Lorine, Larena, Lorrina, Lourana

Loretta (Italian) Form of Laura, meaning "crowned with laurel; from the laurel tree"
Laretta, Larretta, Lauretta, Laurette, Leretta, Loreta, Lorette, Lorretta, Lowretta, Larette, Larrette

Lorraine (French) From the kingdom of Lothair
Laraine, Larayne, Laurraine, Leraine, Lerayne, Lorain, Loraina, Loraine, Lorayne, Lorraina, Lorrayne, Laraene, Laruyne, Lareine, Larina, Larine, Larraine, Lorenza, Lourine

Lo-ruhamah (Hebrew) One who does not receive mercy

Lottie (French) Form of Charlotte, meaning "a small, strong woman"
Lotti, Lotty, Lotte, Lottey, Lottee, Lotta, Loti, Lotie, Lotye, Letya, Letje, Lottea, Lotea

Lotus (Greek) Resembling the water lily
Lotas, Lotuss, Lotis, Lotiss, Lotass

Louise (German) Feminine form of Louis; a famous warrior
Loise, Louella, Louisa, Louisetta, Louisette, Louisina, Louisiana, Louisiane, Louisine, Louiza, Lovisa, Lowise, Loyise, Lu, Ludovica, Ludovika, Ludwiga, Luella, Luisa, Luise, Lujza, Lujzika, Luiza, Loyce, Ludkhannah, Luijzika, Likla, Ludka, Lilka, Luell, Luelle, Luigina, Loring, Lodoiska

Lourdes (French) From the place of healing and miracles
Lurdes, Lourdecita, Lourdetta, Lourdette, Louredes, Loordes, Lorda

Louvain (English) From the city in Belgium
Leuven, Loovain

Love (English) One who is full of affection
Lovey, Loveday, Lovette, Lovi, Lovie, Lov, Luv, Luvey, Luvee, Luvi, Luvie, Lovee, Lovea, Luvea, Luvy

Loveada (Spanish) A loving woman
Loveadah, Loviada, Loviadah, Lovyada, Lovyadah, Lovada

Loveanna (American) A gracious and loving woman
Loveann, Lovean, Loveane, Loveanne, Lovanna, Lovana, Lovann, Lovane, Lovanne

Lovejoy (American) Filled with love and joy
Lovjoy, Lovejoye, Lovjoi, Lovejoi, Luvjoi, Luvjoy, Luvjoye

Lovella (Native American) Having a soft spirit
Lovell, Lovela, Lovele, Lovelle, Lovel

Lovely (American) An attractive and pleasant woman
Loveli, Loveley, Lovelie, Lovelee, Loveleigh, Lovelea

Lowena (American) Form of Louise, meaning "a famous warrior"
Lowenna, Lowenah, Lowennah, Loweniah, Lowenia, Lowenea, Loweneah

Loyal (English) One who is faithful and true
Loyalty, Loyalti, Loyaltie, Loyaltee, Loyaltea, Loyaltey

Luana (Hawaiian) One who is content and enjoys life
Lewanna, Lou-Ann, Louann, Louanna, Louanne, Luanda, Luane, Luann, Luanna, Luannah, Luanne, Luannie, Luwanna, Luwana, Lujuana

Luba (Hebrew) One who is dearly loved
Liba, Lubah, Libena, Lyuba, Lyubah

Lubaba (Arabic) A soulful woman
Lubabah, Lubabia, Lubaby, Lubabie, Lubabey, Lubabee, Lubabea, Lubabi

Luberda (Spanish) Surrounded by light
Luberdah, Luberdia, Luberdiah, Luberdea, Luberdeah, Luberdiya, Luberdiyah

Lubomira (Slavic) One who yearns for peace
Lubomirah, Lubomiria, Lubomirea, Lubomyra, Lubomyrah, Lubomeera, Lubomeira, Lubomiera

Lucasta (English) Feminine form of Lucas; woman from Lucanus
Luca, Lucania, Lucanea, Lukasta, Luka, Lukina

Lucerne (Latin) One who is surrounded by light
Lucerna, Luceria, Lucena, Lucenia, Lucenea, Lucernia, Lucernea, Lucero

Lucille (French) Form of Lucy, meaning "one who is illuminated"
Lusile, Loucille, Luciela, Lucila, Lucile, Lucilia, Lucilla, Lucyle, Luseele, Lucja, Lucyna, Lucylle, Luceil

Lucja (Polish) Lady of the light
Luscia

Lucky (American) One who is fortunate
Lucki, Luckie, Luckey, Luckee, Luckea, Luckette, Lucket, Lucketta, Luckete, Lucketa

Lucretia (Latin) A bringer of light; a successful woman; in mythology, a maiden who was raped by the prince of Rome
Lacretia, Loucrecia, Loucresha, Loucretia, Loucrezia, Lucrece, Lucrecia, Lucreecia, Lucreesha, Lucreisha, Lucresha, Lucrezia, Luighseach

Lucy (Latin) Feminine form of Lucius; one who is illuminated
Luce, Lucetta, Lucette, Luci, Lucia, Luciana, Lucianna, Lucida, Lucie, Lucienne, Lucina, Lucinda, Lucine, Lucita, Lucyna, Lucyja, Lucza, Lusita, Luz, Luzija, Lucinna, Liusaidh, Lucee, Lucea

Lucylynn (American) A lighthearted woman
Lucylyn, Lucylynne, Lucilynn, Lucilyn, Lucilynne

Ludivina (Slavic) One who is greatly loved
Ludivinah, Ludivyna, Ludivynah, Ludiveena, Ludiveenah, Ludiviena, Ludivienah, Ludiveina, Ludiveinah, Ludiveana, Ludiveanah

Ludmila (Slavic) Having the favor of the people
Ludmilah, Ludmilla, Ludmillah, Ludmyla, Ludmylla, Lyubochka, Lyudmila, Lyuha, Lubmilla, Lubmila, Ljudmila, Ljudumilu

Luenetter (American) A self-centered woman
Luenette, Luenett, Luenete, Luenet, Luenetta, Lueneta

Lulani (Polynesian) Sent from heaven
Lulanie, Lulaney, Lulany, Lulanee, Lulanea

Lully (American) One who soothes others
Lulli, Lullie, Lullee, Lulleigh, Lullea

Lulu (Hawaiian / African) A calm, peaceful woman / as precious as a pearl
Lu'lu, Luloah, Lula, Lo'loo, Looloo

Lulubell (American) A well-known beauty
Lulubelle, Lulubele, Lulubel, Lulubela, Lulubella

Lumina (Latin) Surrounded by a brilliant light
Luminah, Lumeena, Lumeenah, Lumyna, Lumynah, Luminosa

Luna (Latin) Of the moon; in mythology, the goddess of the moon
Lunah, Luneth, Lunetta, Lunette, Lunneta, Lunethe, Lunetha

Lundy (French / Gaelic) Born on a Monday / from the marshland
Lundey, Lundi, Lundie, Lundee, Lundea, Lunde, Lund

Lundyn (American) One who is unlike others
Lundynn, Lundynne, Lundan, Lundann, Lunden, Lundon

Luned (Welsh) Form of Eiluned, meaning "an idol worshipper"
Luneda, Lunedia, Lunedea

Lunet (English) Of the crescent moon
Lunett, Lunette, Luneta, Lunete, Lunetta

Lupita (Spanish) Form of Guadalupe, meaning "from the valley of wolves"
Lupe, Lupyta, Lupelina, Lupeeta, Lupieta, Lupeita, Lupeata

Luquitha (American) An affectionate woman
Luquithah, Luquithia, Luquithiah, Luquithea, Luquitheah, Luquithe, Luquetha

Lur (Spanish) Of the earth

Lurissa (American) A beguiling woman
Lurisa, Luryssa, Lurysa, Luressa, Luresa

Luvelle (American) Surrounded by light
Luvell, Luvel, Luvele, Luvela, Luvella

Luvina (English) Little one who is dearly loved
Luvinah, Luvena, Luvyna, Luveena, Luveina, Luviena, Luveana

Lux (Latin) Lady of the light
Luxe, Luxi, Luxie, Luxee, Luxea, Luxy, Luxey

Luyu (Native American) Resembling the dove

Luz (Spanish / Armenian) Refers to the Virgin Mary, Our Lady of Light / of the moon
Luzelena, Luzette, Luziana, Luzetta, Luzianna, Luzianne, Luzian, Luziane

Luzille (Spanish) A shining woman
Luzill, Luzil, Luzile, Luzila, Luzilla

Lyawonda (American) A beloved friend
Lyawanda, Lyawunda, Lywonda, Lywanda, Lywunda

Lycoris (Greek) Born at twilight
Lycoriss, Lycorisse, Lycorys, Lycorysse, Lycoryss

Lydia (Greek) A beautiful woman from Lydia
Lidia, Lidie, Lidija, Lyda, Lydie, Lydea, Liddy, Lidiy, Lidochka

Lykaios (Greek) Resembling a she-wolf

Lyle (English) From the island
Lisle, Lysle, Lile

Lymekia (Greek) Woman of royalty
Lymekiah, Lymekea, Lymekeah, Lymekiya, Lymekiyah, Lymekya, Lymekyah

Lynette (Welsh) A beautiful maiden; resembling a songbird
Lanette, Linett, Linette, Linnet, Lynet, Lynessa, Lynett, Lynetta, Lynnet, Lynnette, Lenette, Linet, Linetta, Linnette, Linnetta, Lonette, Linytte, Lynete, Lynley, Lyneth

Lynn (English) Woman of the lake; form of Linda, meaning "one who is soft and beautiful"
Linell, Linnell, Lyn, Lynae, Lyndel, Lyndell, Lynell, Lynelle, Lynlee, Lynley, Lynna, Lynne, Lynnelle, Lynnea

Lynton (English) From the town of lime trees
Lynten, Lyntan, Linton, Linten, Lintan

Lyonesse (English) From the lost land
Lyoness, Lyonness, Lyonnesse, Lyones

Lyra (Greek) One who plays the lyre
Lyria, Lyris, Lyrea, Lyre

Lyric (French) Of the lyre; the words of a song
Lyrica, Lyricia, Lyrik, Lyrick, Lyrika, Lyricka

Lysandra (Greek) Form of Alexandra, meaning "helper and defender of mankind"
Lisandra, Lissandra, Lizandra, Lisandrina, Lisandrine, Lissandrina, Lissandrine, Lyssandra, Lyssa, Lyaksandra

Lysett (American) A pretty young girl
Lysette, Lyset, Lysete, Lysetta, Lyseta

Lysimache (Greek) Feminine form of Lysimachus; released from battle
Lysimachie, Lysimachi, Lysimachee, Lysimacha, Lysimachia, Lysimachea

Lyssan (Greek) Form of Alexandra, meaning "helper and defender of mankind"
Lyssana, Lyssann, Lyssane, Lyssanne, Lysan, Lysann, Lysane, Lysanne, Lysana, Lysanna

Lytanisha (American) A scintillating woman
Lytanesha, Lytaniesha, Lytaneisha, Lytanysha, Lytaneesha, Lytaneasha

m

Maachah (Hebrew) One who has been oppressed; in the Bible, one of David's wives
Maacha

Maarath (Hebrew) From the desolate land
Maaratha, Marath, Marathe, Maratha, Maarathe

Maarii (German) Resembling a dragonfly

Maasiai (Hebrew) One who does God's work
Masiai, Maasai, Masai

Maat (Egyptian) In mythology, the goddess of truth, order, and justice

Maata (Australian) A highborn lady

Maath (Hebrew) A petite woman; small
Maathe, Maatha

Mab (Gaelic) One who is filled with joy

Mabel (English) One who is lovable
*Mabelle, Mable, Maible, Maybel, Maybell,
Maybelle, Mayble, Mablean, Mabelean,
Mabeleen, Moibeal*

Mabina (Celtic) One who is nimble
*Mabbina, Mabene, Mabine, Mabena,
Mabyna, Mabinah, Maeveen, Maevina,
Maeveena, Maevine, Mabeana, Mabeena*

Mabli (Welsh) The beautiful one
*Mablie, Mably, Mabley, Mablee, Mableigh,
Mablea*

Mabyn (Welsh) One who is forever young
Mabyne, Mabin, Maben, Maban, Mabon

Macanta (Gaelic) A kind and gentle woman
Macan, Macantia, Macantea, Macantah

Macaria (Spanish) One who is blessed
*Macarisa, Macarria, Maccaria, Makaria,
Makarria, Macarea, Macareah*

Macha (Native American / Irish / Scottish)
Aurora / goddess of war / woman from the
plains
Machara, Macharia, Macharea

Machi (Taiwanese) A good friend
Machie, Machy, Machey, Machee, Machea

Machiko (Japanese) A beautiful child; one
who is taught the truth
Machika, Machyko, Machyka

Machpelah (Hebrew) From the double
caves
Machpela, Machpellah, Machpella

Mackenna (Gaelic) Daughter of the hand-
some man
*Mackendra, Mackennah, McKenna,
McKendra, Makenna, Makennah*

❂
❂ **Mackenzie** (Gaelic) Daughter of a wise
leader; a fiery woman; one who is fair
*Mackenzey, Makensie, **Makenzie**, M'Kenzie,
McKenzie, Meckenzie, Mackenzee, Mackenzy,
Mackenzi, Mackenzea*

Macy (French) One who wields a weapon
*Macee, Macey, Maci, Macie, Maicey, Maicy,
Macea, Maicea, Maecy, Maeccy, Maeci,
Maecie, Maecee, Maecea, Maici, Maicie,
Maicee*

Mada (Arabic) One who has reached the
end of the path
Madah

Madana (Ethiopian) One who heals others
*Madayna, Madaina, Madania, Madaynia,
Madainia*

Maddox (English) Born into wealth and
prosperity
Madox, Madoxx, Maddoxx

Madeira (Spanish) From the place of sweet
wine
*Madiera, Madera, Madira, Madyra, Madeera,
Madeara*

Madelhari (German) A counselor to the
troops
*Madelharie, Madelhary, Madelharey,
Madelharee, Madelharea*

❂ **Madeline** (Hebrew) Woman from Magdala
*Mada, Madalaina, Madaleine, Madalena,
Madalene, Madalyn, Madalynn, Maddelena,
Maddie, Maddy, Madel, Madelaine,
Madelayne, Madeleine, Madelena, Madelene,
Madelina, Madella, Madelle, Madelon,
Madelyn, Madelyne, Madelynn, Madelynne,
Madena, Madilyn, Madina, Madlen,
Madlin, Madlyn, Mady, Madzia, Magda,
Magdala, Magdalen, Magdalena, Magdalene,
Magdalina, Magdaline, Magdalini,
Magdeleine, Magdelina, Magdolna, Maidel,
Maighdlin, Madalen, Madelia, Magdiel,
Maialen, Makda, Malena, Malene, Malin,
Matxalen, Modlen*

Madge (English) Form of Margaret, meaning "resembling a pearl / the child of light"

Madhavi (Indian) Feminine form of
Madhav; born in the springtime
*Madhavie, Madhavee, Madhavey, Madhavy,
Madhavea*

Madhu (Indian) As sweet as honey
*Madhul, Madhula, Madhulika, Madhulia,
Madhulea*

Madhur (Indian) One who is gentle and kind
*Madhuri, Madhurie, Madhura, Madhuria,
Madhurea*

Madihah (Arabic) One who is praiseworthy
Madeeha, Madiha, Madyha, Madyhah, Madeehah, Madeaha, Madieha, Madeiha

Madini (Swahili) As precious as a gemstone
Madinie, Madiny, Madiney, Madinee, Madyny, Madyni, Madinea, Madynie, Madyney, Madynee, Madynea

♀
♂ **Madison** (English) Daughter of a mighty warrior
Maddison, Madisen, Madisson, Madisyn, Madyson

Madoline (English) One who is accomplished with the stringed instrument
Mandalin, Mandalyn, Mandalynn, Mandelin, Mandellin, Mandellyn, Mandolin, Mandolyn, Mandolynne

Madonna (Italian) My lady; refers to the Virgin Mary
Madonnah, Madona, Madonah

Madora (Greek) A great ruler
Madorah, Madorra, Madorrah

Madra (Spanish) One who is motherly
Madre, Madrina, Madrena, Madrona, Madryna

Madri (Indian) In mythology, the second wife of Pandu
Madrie, Madry, Madrey, Madree, Madrea

Maeko (Japanese) A truthful child
Maekiko, Maekiyo, Masako, Maseko

Maemi (Japanese) Having a truthful smile
Maemie, Maemee, Maemy, Maemey, Maemea

Maera (Greek) In mythology, the daughter of Atlas

Maertisa (English) One who is well-known

Maeve (Irish) An intoxicating woman
Mave, Meave, Medb, Meabh

Mafuane (Egyptian) Daughter of the earth
Mafuann, Mafuanne, Mafuana, Mafuanna

Magali (English) Form of Margaret, meaning "resembling a pearl / the child of light"
Magaley, Magalie, Maggali, Magaly, Magalee, Magaleigh, Maggalie, Maggalee, Magalea, Maggalea

Magara (Rhodesian) A child who cries often
Magarah, Magarra, Magaria

Magena (Native American, Hebrew) One who is protected

Magic (American) One who is full of wonder and surprise
Majic, Magyc, Magik, Magick, Majik, Majick

Magna (Latin) Having great strength

Magnhilda (German) A strong battle-maiden
Magnild, Magnilda, Magnilde, Magnhild, Magnhilde, Maganhildi, Maganhildie, Maganhilde, Maganhilda

Magnolia (French) Resembling the flowering tree
Magnoliya, Magnoliah, Magnolea, Magnoleah, Magnoliyah, Magnolya, Magnolyah

Maha (African) A woman with beautiful eyes
Mahah

Mahadevi (Hindi) In Hinduism, a mother goddess
Mahadevie, Mahadevy, Mahadevey, Mahadevee, Mahadevea

Mahal (Native American) A tender and loving woman
Mahall, Mahale, Mahalle

Mahala (Arabic) One who is powerful yet gentle
Mahalia, Mahalah, Mahlah, Mahla, Mahalea, Mahaliah, Mahalcah

Mahalaleel (Hebrew) One who praises God
Maleleel, Malaleel, Mahaleel, Maheleel

Mahalia (Hebrew) One who is tender
Mahala, Mahalah, Mahalath, Mahali, Mahalee, Mahaliah, Mahalla, Mahelia, Mahaleigh, Mahalie, Mehalia, Mahalea

Mahanaim (Hebrew) Of the place of two camps
Mahanaime, Mahanaima, Mahanayme, Mahanaym, Mahanayma, Mahanaem, Mahanaema

Mahari (African) One who offers forgiveness
Maharie, Mahary, Maharey, Maharee, Maharai, Maharae, Maharea

Mahath (Hebrew) The act of grasping
Mahathe, Mahatha, Mahathia

Mahbubi (Arabic) One who is dearly loved;
a sweetheart
Mabubi, Mahbubee, Mahbubie, Mabubie,
Mabubee, Mahbubey, Mabubey

Mahdi (African) The expected daughter
Mahdie, Mahdy, Mahdey, Mahdee, Mahdea

Mahdis (Persian) A moonlike woman
Mahdiss, Mahdise, Mahdisse, Mahdys,
Mahdyss, Mahdysse

Mahendra (Sanskrit) From the mountains
Mahindra, Mahendria, Mahindria,
Mahendrea, Mahindrea, Mahyndra,
Mahyndria, Mahyndrea

Maheona (Native American) A medicine
woman
Maheo, Maheonia, Maheonea

Mahesa (Indian) A powerful and great lady
Maheshvari

Mahina (Hawaiian) Daughter of the moon-
light
Maheena, Mahyna, Maheana, Maheyna,
Mahiena, Maheina

Mahira (Arabic) A clever and adroit woman
Mahirah, Mahir, Mahire, Mahiria, Mahirea,
Maheera, Mahyra, Mahiera, Maheira,
Maheara

Mahjabin (Arabic) Having a high forehead
Maahjahbeen, Mahjabeen, Mahjabine,
Mahjabyne, Maahjabyne

Mahlah (Hebrew) A diseased woman; one
to be pitied
Mahli, Mahlon

Mahmoode (Arabic) One who is given
praise
Mahmude, Mahmudee, Mahmoude,
Mamoudee

Mahogany (English) Resembling the rich,
dark wood
Mahogani, Mahoganey, Mahoganie,
Mahogane, Mahogonee, Mahogonea

Mahola (Hebrew) One who enjoys dancing
Maholah, Maholla, Mahollah

Mahsa (Persian) Resembling the moon
Mahsah

Mahteab (Arabic) Born beneath the moon

Mahtowa (Sioux) A sacred she-bear
Mahtowah, Matowa

Maia (Latin / Maori) The great one; in
mythology, the goddess of spring / a brave
warrior
Maaja, Maiah, Maja, Moia, Moja, Moya

Maibe (Egyptian) A dignified and serious
lady

Maida (English) A maiden; a virgin
Maidel, Maidie, Mayda, Maydena, Maydey,
Mady, Maegth, Magd, Maidel, Maeda

Maiki (Japanese) Resembling the dancing
flower
Maikie, Maikei, Maikki, Maikee

Maile (Hawaian) From the sweet-smelling
vine

Maille (Gaelic) Form of Molly, meaning
"star of the sea / from the sea of bitterness"
Mailsi, Mailsea, Mailsie, Mailsy, Mailsey,
Mailsee

Maimun (Arabic) One who is lucky; fortunate
Maimoon, Maimoun

Maimuna (Arabic) One who is trustworthy
Maimoona, Maimouna

Maina (Indian) Resembling a bird

Maine (French) From the mainland; from
the state of Maine

Maiolaine (French) As delicate as a flower
Maiolainie, Maiolani, Maiolaney, Maiolany,
Maiolanee, Maiolayne, Maiolanea

Mairwen (Welsh) One who is fair; form of
Mary, meaning "star of the sea / from the
sea of bitterness"
Mairwenn, Mairwenne, Mairwyn, Mairwynn,
Mairwynne, Mairwin, Mairwinn, Mairwinne

Maisara (Arabic) One who lives an effort-
less life
Maisarah, Maisarra, Maisarrah

Maise (Gaelic) An adorned beauty
Mayse, Maisa, Maysa, Maese, Maesa

Maisha (African) Giver of life
Maysha, Maishah, Mayshah, Maesha, Maeshah

Maisie (Scottish) Form of Margaret, meaning "resembling a pearl / the child of light"
Maisee, Maisey, Maisy, Maizie, Mazey, Mazie, Maisi, Maizi, Maizee, Maizea, Maisea

Maitane (English) One who is dearly loved
Maite, Maitena, Maitayne, Maitaine, Maitana, Maita, Maitea, Maitaene

Maitland (English) From the meadow
Maitlanda, Maytland, Maetland, Maytlanda, Maetlanda, Maitlande, Maytlande, Maetlande

Maitra (Sanskrit) A beloved friend
Maitri, Maitrie, Maitry, Maitrey, Maitree, Maitria, Maitrea

Maitraka (Sanskrit) The little loving one
Maitrakah, Maitracka, Maytraka, Maytracka, Maetraka, Maetracka

Maitreya (Sanskrit) One who offers love to all
Maitreyah, Muetreya, Maitraya, Maetruya

Maitrya (Sanskrit) A benevolent woman
Matriya, Mitravan, Maitryi, Maitryie

Maiya (Japanese) Of the rice valley
Maiyah

Maizah (African) One who has good judgment and keen insight
Maiza, Mayzah, Mayzah, Maeza, Maezah

Majaliwa (Swahili) Filled with God's grace
Majaliwuh, Majalewa, Majalywa, Majalewah, Majalywah

Majaya (Indian) A victorious woman
Majayah

Majda (Arabic) A glorious woman
Majdah

Majesta (Latin) One who has a royal bearing
Majestas, Majesty, Majesti, Majestie, Majestee, Majestey, Majestea, Majestic

Majida (Arabic) Feminine form of Majid; noble glory
Majeeda, Majeedah, Majidah, Maji, Maajida

Majime (Japanese) An earnest woman

Makaio (Hawaiian) A gift from God

Makala (Hawaiian) Resembling myrtle
Makalah, Makalla, Makallah

Makani (Hawaiian) Of the wind
Makanie, Makaney, Mukany, Makanee, Makanea

Makara (Australian) The seven stars that make up the Pleiades
Makarah, Makarra, Makarrah

Makareta (Maori) Form of Margaret, meaning "resembling a pearl / the child of light"
Makaretah, Makarita, Makaryta

Makarim (Arabic) An honorable woman
Makarime, Makarym, Makaryme, Makarima, Makaryma

Makato (Native American) Of the blue earth
Maka, Makata

⚥ **Makayla** (Celtic / Hebrew / English) Form of Michaela, meaning "who is like God?"
Macaela, MacKayla, Mak, Mechaela, Meeskaela, Mekea, Mekelle

Makea (Finnish) One who is sweet
Makeah, Makia, Makiah

Makeda (African) A queenly woman; greatness
Makedah

Makelina (Hawaiian) Form of Madeline, meaning "woman from Magdala"
Makelinah, Makeleena, Mukelyna, Makeleana, Makeline, Makelyne, Makeleane, Makeleene

Makena (African) One who is filled with happiness
Makenah, Makeena, Makeenah, Makeana, Makeanah, Makyna, Makynah, Mackena, Mackenah

Makheloth (Hebrew) Woman of the congregation
Makhelothe, Makhelotha, Makhelothia

Makin (Arabic) An able-bodied woman
Makina, Makine, Makinya

Makiyo (Japanese) From the tree of truth
Makiko

Makkedah (Hebrew) From the herdsman's camp
Makkeda, Makedah, Makeda

Makoto (Japanese) A thankful woman

Makya (Native American) A huntress of eagles
Makyah, Makiya, Makiyah

Malak (Arabic) A heavenly messenger; an angel
Malaka, Malaika, Malayka, Malaeka, Malake, Malayk, Malaek, Malakia

Malana (Hawaiian) A lighthearted woman
Malanah, Malanna, Malannah

Malann (Hebrew) A great ruler
Malanne, Mallann, Mallanne

Malati (Indian) Resembling a fragrant flower
Malatie, Malaty, Malatey, Malatee, Malatea

Malaya (Spanish) An independent woman; one who is free
Malayah

Malcomina (Scottish) Feminine form of Malcolm; devotee of St. Columba
Malcomeena, Malcomyna, Malcominia, Malcominea, Malcomena, Malcomeina, Malcomiena, Malcomeana

Malcsi (Hungarian) An industrious woman
Malcsie, Malcsee, Malcsey, Malcsy, Malksi, Malksie, Malksy, Malksee, Malksey, Malcsea, Malksea

Maleda (Ethiopian) Born with the rising sun
Maledah

Mali (Thai / Welsh) Resembling a flower / form of Molly, meaning "star of the sea / from the sea of bitterness"
Malie, Malee, Maleigh, Maly, Maley

Malia (Hawaiian) Form of Mary, meaning "star of the sea / from the sea of bitterness"
Maliah, Malea, Maleah, Maleia, Maliyah, Maliya, Malya, Malyah

Maliha (Indian) A beautiful woman of great strength
Malihah, Malyha, Maleeha, Maleiha, Maleaha

Malika (Arabic) Destined to be queen
Mulikah, Malyka, Maleeka, Maleika, Malieka, Maliika, Maleaka

Malila (Native American) Resembling the salmon
Malilah, Maleela, Maleila, Maliela, Malyla, Maleala

Malina (Hawaiian) A peaceful woman
Malinah, Maleena, Maleenah, Malyna, Malynah, Maleina, Maliena, Maleana

Malini (Indian) A gardener
Malinie, Maliny, Malinee, Maliney, Malinea

Malinka (Russian) As sweet as a little berry
Malinkah, Malynka, Maleenka, Malienka, Maleinka, Maleanka

Malise (Gaelic) A dark beauty
Malyse, Malese, Melusina

Maliza (Swahili) An accomplished woman
Malizah, Maleeza, Malyza, Malieza, Maleaza

Malka (Hebrew) A queenly woman
Malcah, Malkah, Malke, Malkia, Malkie, Milcah, Milka, Milke, Milca, Malha, Malhah

Mallika (Indian) Resembling jasmine
Mallikah, Malleeka, Malleika, Mallieka, Mallyka, Malleaka

Mallory (French) An unlucky young woman; ill-fated
Mallary, Mallerey, Mallery, Malloreigh, Mallorey, Mallori, Mallorie, Malorey, Malori, Malorie, Malory, Malloren, Mallorea, Malorea, Maloree

Mallow (Gaelic) Woman from the river; resembling the flowering plant
Mallowe, Mallo, Malloe, Malow, Malowe, Maloe

Malmuira (Scottish) A dark-skinned beauty
Malmurie, Malmuria, Malmura, Malmuri

Malone (Lithuanian) By the grace of God
Malona, Malonne, Maloni, Malonie, Malonia, Malony, Maloney, Malonee, Malonea

Malu (Hawaiian) A peaceful woman

Maluna (Hawaiian) One who rises above
Maloona, Malunia, Malunai, Maloonia, Maloonai, Malouna, Malounia, Malounai

Malva (Greek) One who is soft and slender
Malvah, Malvia, Malvea

Malvina (English) Having a smooth brow
Malvinah, Malveena, Malveenah, Malviena, Malveina, Malveana, Malvyna, Malvine, Malvyne

Malvinia (Latin) A beloved friend
Malvenia, Malvinea, Malvenea, Malvynia, Malvynea, Malviniya

Mamaki (Sanskrit) Darling little mother
Mamakie, Mamaky, Mamakey, Mamakee, Mamakea

Mamani (Incan) Resembling a falcon
Mamanie, Mamanee, Mamaney, Mamany, Mamanea

Mamie (English) Form of Mary, meaning "star of the sea / from the sea of bitterness"; form of Margaret, meaning "resembling a pearl / the child of light"
Maime, Mame, Maymie, Mayme, Maimie, Mamia, Mamee, Mamea, Mami

Mamiko (Japanese) Daughter of the sea
Mameeko, Mamyko

Mana (Polynesian) A charismatic and prestigious woman
Manah

Manal (Arabic) An accomplished woman
Manala, Manall, Manalle, Manalla, Manali

Manami (Japanese) Having a love of the ocean
Manamie, Manamy, Manamey, Manamee, Manamea

Manar (Arabic) Woman of the light
Manara, Manaria, Manarr, Manarre, Manarra, Manari, Manarri, Mannara, Mannarra

Manasa (Indian) Having great strength of mind
Maanasa, Manassa, Manasah

Mandana (Persian) Beauty everlasting
Mandanah, Mandanna, Mandannah

Mandeep (Indian) Having a bright mind
Mandeepe, Mandyp, Mandype, Mandeepa, Mandypa

Mandisa (African) A sweet woman
Mandisah, Mandysa, Mandysah

Mandraya (Sanskrit) An honorable woman
Mandray, Mandrayia, Mandraye

Mandy (English) Form of Amanda, meaning "one who is much loved"
Mandi, Mandie, Mandee, Mandey, Manda, Mandalyn, Mandalynn, Mandelina, Mandeline, Mandalyna, Mandea

Mangena (Hebrew) As sweet as a melody
Mangenah, Mangenna, Mangennah

Manhattan (English) From the whiskey town
Manhatton, Manhatan, Manhaton

Mania (Greek) In mythology, the personification of insanity
Maniah, Mainia, Maynia, Maniya

Manika (Sanskrit) Her mind is a jewel
Maanika, Manicka, Manyka, Manycka, Manicca, Manica, Maniya, Manikya, Maneka

Manina (Polish) A warring woman
Maninah, Maneena, Maneina, Manyna, Maneana, Maniena

Manisa (Native American) One who travels on foot
Manisah, Manysa, Manysah

Manisha (Indian) Having great intelligence; a genius
Maneesha, Manishah, Manysha, Maniesha, Maneisha, Maneasha

Manjari (Indian) Of the sacred blossom
Manjarie, Manjary, Manjarey, Manjaree, Manjarea

Manjula (Indian) A sweet young woman
Manjulah, Manjulia, Manjulie, Manjule, Manjuli

Manjusha (Sanskrit) As treasured as a box of gems
Manjushah, Manjushia, Manjousha, Manjoushia

Manning (English) Daughter of Man
Maning, Mannyng, Manyng

Manoush (Persian) Born under the sweet sun
Manoushe, Manousha, Manoushai, Manoushia, Manoushea

Mansa (African) The third-born child
Mansah, Mansia

Mansi (Native American) Resembling a picked flower
Mansie, Mansy, Mansey, Mansee, Mansea, Mausi, Mausie, Mausee, Mausy, Mausey, Mausea

Manto (Greek) A prophetess; in mythology, mother of Mopsus
Mantia, Mantika, Manteia, Mantea, Mantai, Mantae

Mantrana (Sanskrit) One who counsels others
Mantrini, Mantrania, Mantranna, Mantrani, Mantrinie, Mantranie

Mantreh (Persian) One who is pure; chaste
Mantre

Manuela (Spanish) Feminine form of Emmanuel; God is with us
Manuella, Manuelita, Manuelyta, Manueleeta, Manoela, Manuel, Manuelle, Manuele

Manulani (Hawaiian) Resembling a bird in the heavens
Manulanie, Manulane, Manulaney, Manulanee, Manulanea

Manyara (African) A humble woman
Manyarah

Maola (Irish) A handmaiden
Maoli, Maole, Maolie, Maolia, Maoly, Maoley, Maolee, Maolea

Maolmin (Gaelic) A woman holding rank as chief
Maolmine, Maolmina, Maolminia, Maolmyn, Maolmyna, Maolmyne

Maon (Hebrew) Woman of the home

Mapenzi (African) One who is dearly loved
Mpenzi, Mapenzie, Mapenze, Mapenzy, Mapenzee, Mapenzea

Mara (Hebrew) A grieving woman; one who is sorrowful
Marra, Mahra, Marah, Maralina, Maralinda, Maraline

Maralah (Hebrew) Born during the earth's trembling
Marala, Marallah, Maralla

Maram (Arabic) One who is wished for
Marame, Marama, Marami, Maramie, Maramee, Maramy, Maramey, Maramea

Maravilla (Spanish) One who is marveled at; a miracle child
Marivella, Marivilla, Marevilla, Marevella, Maravella, Maraville, Marivel, Marivelle

Marcail (Scottish) Form of Margaret, meaning "resembling a pearl / the child of light"
Marcaila, Marcaile, Marcayl, Marcayle, Marcayla, Marcael, Marcaele, Marcaela

Marcella (Latin) Feminine form of Marcellus; dedicated to Mars, the god of war
Marcela, Marcele, Marcelina, Marcelinda, Marceline, Marcelle, Marcellina, Marcelline, Marcelyn, Marchella, Marchelle, Marcile, Marcilee, Marcille, Marquita, Marsalina, Marsella, Marselle, Marsellonia, Marshella, Marsiella, Marcila, Marsil, Marsille, Marsilla, Marsila, Marsali

March (Latin) Born during the month of March
Marche

Marcia (Latin) Feminine form of Marcus; dedicated to Mars, the god of war
Marcena, Marcene, Marchita, Marciana, Marciane, Marcianne, Marcilyn, Marcilynn, Marcina, Marcine, Marcita, Marseea, Marsia, Martia, Marsha, Marek, Marcsa

Marcy (Latin) Form of Marcella or Marcia, meaning "dedicated to Mars, the god of war"
Marcey, Marci, Marcie, Marcee, Marsee, Marsey, Marsy, Marsie, Marsi, Marcea, Marsea

Marde (Latin) A woman warrior
Mardane, Mardayne

Mardea (African) The last-born child
Mardeah

Mardi (French) Born on a Tuesday
Mardie, Mardy, Mardey, Mardee, Mardea

Marelda (German) A famous woman warrior
*Marelde, Mareldah, Marrelda, Marilda,
Marilde, Mareld, Marild*

Marenda (Latin) An admirable woman
Marendah

Margana (Sanskrit) One who seeks the truth
Marganah, Marganna, Margannuh

Margaret (Greek / Persian) Resembling a pearl / the child of light
*Maighread, Mairead, Mag, Maggi, Maggie,
Maggy, Maiga, Malgorzata, Marcheta,
Marchieta, Marga, Margalit, Margalo,
Margareta, Margarete, Margarethe,
Margarettu, Margarette, Margarida,
Margarit, Margarita, Margarite, Margaruite,
Marge, Marged, Margeen, Margeret,
Margeretta, Margerie, Margerita, Marget,
Margette, Margey, Marghanita, Margharita,
Margherita, Marghretta, Margies, Margisia,
Margit, Margita, Margize, Margred,
Margret, Margrete, Margreth, Margrett,
Margrit, Margrid, Marguarette, Marguarita,
Marguerita, Marguerite, Marguita, Maarit,
Marjeta, Margosha, Marjeta, Marared,
Margaid, Marenka, Maret, Mererid*

Marged (Welsh) Form of Margaret, meaning "resembling a pearl / the child of light"
Margred, Margeda, Margreda

Margo (French) Form of Margaret, meaning "resembling a pearl / the child of light"
Margeaux, Margaux, Margolo, Margot

Marhilda (German) A famous battlemaiden
*Marhildi, Marhilde, Marhild, Marhildie,
Marhildy, Marhildey, Marhildee, Marildi,
Marildie*

Mari (Hebrew) A wished-for daughter

❂ **Maria** (Spanish) Form of Mary, meaning "star of the sea / from the sea of bitterness"
*Marialena, Marialinda, Marialisa, Maaria,
Mayria, Maeria, Mariabella, Mariabelle,
Mariabell, Mariasha, Marea*

❂ **Mariah** (Latin) Form of Mary, meaning "star of the sea"

Mariama (African) A gift from God
Mariamah, Mariamma, Mariame

Mariamne (Hebrew) A rebellious woman
Mamre, Meria

Mariane (French) A combination of Mary and Ann, meaning "star of the sea / from the sea of bitterness" and "a woman graced with God's favor"
*Mariam, Mariana, Marian, Marion,
Maryann, Maryanne, Maryanna, Maryane,
Maryanu, Marianne, Marianna, Mariann,
Maryam, Marianda, Marien*

Mariatu (African) One who is pure; innocent

Maribel (Spanish) Form of Mary, meaning "star of the sea / from the sea of bitterness"; the beautiful Mary
*Maribell, Maribelle, Maribella, Maribele,
Maribela, Marahel, Marabelle, Marabelu,
Marabella, Marybel, Marybell, Marybella,
Marybelle, Marybele, Marybela*

Marica (Latin) In mythology, a nymph and mother of Latinus

Maricela (Spanish) Form of Marcella, meaning "dedicated to Mars, the god of war"
*Maricel, Maricella, Marisela, Maresella,
Marisella, Maryzela, Marecela, Marecella*

Maridhia (Swahili) One who is content
*Maridha, Maridhea, Maridhe, Marydhia,
Marydhiya*

Marie (French) Form of Mary, meaning "star of the sea / from the sea of bitterness"
Maree, Marea

Mariel (Danish) Form of Mary, meaning "star of the sea / from the sea of bitterness"
*Mariela, Mariele, Mariellu, Marielle, Mariell,
Mariola*

Marietta (French) Form of Mary, meaning "star of the sea / from the sea of bitterness"
*Mariette, Maretta, Mariet, Maryetta,
Maryette, Marieta*

Marifa (Arabic) Having great knowledge
*Marifah, Maryfa, Maryfah, Maripha,
Marypha*

Marigold (English) Resembling the golden flower
*Marrigold, Maragold, Maregold, Marygold,
Marigolde*

Marika (Danish) Form of Mary, meaning "star of the sea / from the sea of bitterness"
Marieke, Marijke, Marike, Maryk, Maryka

Mariko (Japanese) Daughter of Mari; a ball or sphere
Maryko, Mareeko, Marieko, Mareiko

Marilla (English) Of the shining sea
Marillah, Marila, Marillis, Marilis, Marella, Marela, Marelle

Marilyn (English) Form of Mary, meaning "star of the sea / from the sea of bitterness"
Maralin, Maralyn, Maralynn, Marelyn, Marilee, Marilin, Marillyn, Marilynn, Marilynne, Marlyn, Marralynn, Marrilin, Marrilyn, Marylin, Marylyn, Marylynn, Marilena, Mariline

Marina (Latin) Woman of the sea
Mareen, Mareena, Mareina, Marena, Marine, Marinda, Marinell, Marinella, Marinelle, Marinna, Maryn, Marin, Marinochka

Mariposa (Spanish) Resembling a butterfly
Maryposa, Marriposa, Marryposa, Mareposa, Maraposa

Mariska (Slavic) Form of Mary, meaning "star of the sea / from the sea of bitterness"
Maryska, Mariske, Maryske, Maruska, Maruske, Martuska

Marissa (Latin) Woman of the sea
Maressa, Maricia, Marisabel, Marisha, Marisse, Maritza, Mariza, Marrissa, Maryssa, Meris, Merissa, Meryssa, Marisa, Mareesa, Mareisa, Marysa, Marysia, Maris, Marris, Marys, Maryse, Marisol, Merise

Marjah (Sanskrit) One who is hopeful

Marjam (Slavic) One who is merry
Marjama, Marjamah, Marjami, Marjamie, Marjamy, Marjamey, Marjamee, Marjamea

Marjan (Polish) Form of Mary, meaning "star of the sea / from the sea of bitterness"
Marjann, Marjanne, Marjana, Marjanna, Marjon, Marjonn, Marjonne

Marjani (African) Of the coral reef
Marjanie, Marjany, Marjaney, Marjanee, Marjean, Marjeani, Marjeanie, Marijani, Marijanie

Marjolaina (French) Resembling the sweet flower
Marjolaine, Marjolayn, Marjolayne, Marjolayna, Marjolaene, Marjolaen, Marjolaena

Marjorie (English) Form of Margaret, meaning "resembling a pearl / the child of light"
Marcharie, Marge, Margeree, Margery, Margerie, Margery, Margey, Margi, Margie, Margy, Marja, Marje, Marjerie, Marjery, Marji, Marjie, Marjorey, Marjory, Marjy, Majori, Majorie, Majory, Majorey, Majoree, Marjo

Marka (African) Born during a steady rain
Markah

Markeisha (American) Form of Keisha, meaning "the favorite child"
Markeishla, Markeishah, Markecia, Markesha, Markeysha, Markeesha, Markiesha, Markeshia, Markeishia, Markeasha

Marketa (Slavic) Form of Margaret, meaning "resembling a pearl / the child of light"
Markeda, Markee, Markeeta, Markia, Markie, Markita, Marqueta, Marquetta

Markku (Scandinavian) A rebellious woman

Marlee (English) Of the marshy meadow
Marley, Marleigh, Marli, Marlie, Marly, Marlea

Marlene (German) A combination of Mary and Magdalene, meaning "star of the sea / from the sea of bitterness" and "woman from Magdala"
Marlaina, Marlana, Marlane, Marlayna, Marlayne, Marleen, Marleena, Marleene, Marleina, Marlen, Marlena, Marleni, Marna, Marlin, Marlina, Marline, Marlyn, Marlynne, Marla, Marlette

Marlis (German) Form of Mary, meaning "star of the sea / from the sea of bitterness"
Marlisa, Marliss, Marlise, Marlisse, Marlissa, Marlys, Marlyss, Marlysa, Marlyssa, Marlysse

Marlo (English) One who resembles driftwood
Marloe, Marlow, Marlowe, Marlon

Marmara (Greek) From the sparkling sea
Marmarra, Marmarah, Marmarrah

Marmarin (Arabic) Resembling marble
Marmareen, Marmarine, Marmareene,
Marmarina, Marmareena

Marni (American) Form of Marina, mean-
ing "woman of the sea"
Marna, Marne, Marnee, Marnell, Murney,
Marnie, Marnina, Marnisha, Marnja,
Marnya, Marnette, Marnetta, Marnia,
Marnea

Maroth (Hebrew) Woman of sorrow; per-
fect grief
Marothe, Marotha, Marothia, Marothea,
Marothiya

Marpessa (Greek) In mythology, the grand-
daughter of Ares
Marpesa, Marpessah, Marpesah, Marpe,
Marpes

Marquise (French) Feminine form of the
title marquis; born to royalty
Marchesa, Marchessa, Markaisa, Markessa,
Marquesa, Marquessa, Marqui, Marquisa,
Marquisha

Marsala (Italian) From the place of sweet
wine
Marsalah, Marsalla, Marsallah

Martha (Aramaic) Mistress of the house; in
the Bible, the sister of Lazarus and Mary
Maarva, Marfa, Marhta, Mariet, Marit,
Mart, Marta, Marte, Martella, Martelle,
Marth, Marthe, Marthena, Marthine,
Marthini, Marthy, Marti, Martie, Martita,
Martje, Martta, Marty, Mata, Matha, Matti,
Mattie, Mirtha, Marva

Martina (English) Feminine form of
Martin; dedicated to Mars, the god of war
Martynne, Martyne, Marteene, Marteena,
Martyna, Martine, Martinne, Martynna,
Marteen, Marteane, Martean, Marteana

Marvell (Latin) An extraordinary woman
Marve, Marvel, Marvela, Marvele, Marvella,
Marvelle, Marvelyn, Marveille

Marvina (English) Feminine form of
Marvin; friend of the sea
Marvinah, Marveena, Marveene, Marvyna,
Marvyne, Marvadene, Marvene, Marvena,
Marva

Marwarid (Arabic) Form of Margaret, mean-
ing "resembling a pearl / the child of light"
Marwaareed, Marwareed, Marwaryd,
Marwaryde, Marwaride

Mary (Latin / Hebrew) Star of the sea /
from the sea of bitterness
Mair, Mal, Mallie, Manette, Manon, Manya,
Mare, Maren, Maretta, Marette, Marice,
Maridel, Mariquilla, Mariquita, Marita,
Maritsa, Marya, Maribeth, Marybeth,
Maryjo, Marylee, Marylou, Marylu, Masha,
Mayra, Meiriona, Maryon, Maeron, Maeryn,
Maija, Maiju, Maili, Maira, Maire, Mairi,
Mairia, Mairona, Mallaidh, Marusya, Masia,
Marynia, Marira, Marquilla, Maricruz,
Marilu, Miren, Murron, Mura, Mearr, Mere,
Mele

Maryland (English) Honoring Queen Mary;
from the state of Maryland
Mariland, Maralynd, Marylind, Marilind

Maryweld (English) Mary of the woods
Marywelde, Marywelda, Mariweld, Mariwelde,
Mariwelda

Marzhan (Slavic) From the coral reef
Marzhane, Marzhann, Marzhanne,
Marzhana, Marzhanna

Masako (Japanese) Child of justice

Masalda (Hebrew) One who offers support;
a good foundation
Masada, Masalde, Masaldia, Masaldea

Masami (African / Japanese) A command-
ing woman / one who is truthful
Masamie, Masamee, Masamy, Masamey,
Masamea

Masara (African) A magical woman; a sorceress
Masaramusi, Masarra

Mashaka (African) A troublemaker; a mis-
chievous woman
Mashakah, Mashakia, Mashake, Mashaki,
Mashakie, Mashaky, Mashakey, Mashakee,
Mashakea

Masika (Egyptian) Born during a rainstorm
Masikah, Masyka, Maseeka, Masieka,
Maseika, Maseaka

Ma'sma (Arabic) One who is innocent
Maa'sma

Mason (English) A stoneworker
Maison, Mayson, Maisen, Masen, Maysen, Maeson, Maesen

Mas'ouda (Arabic) One who is fortunate; lucky
Maas'ouda

Masrekah (Hebrew) From the vineyard
Masreka, Masrecka, Masrekia, Masrekiah

Massachusetts (Native American) From the big hill; from the state of Massachusetts
Massachusets, Massachusette, Massachusetta, Massa, Massachute, Massachusta

Massah (Hebrew) One who tempts others
Massa

Massarra (Arabic) Filled with happiness

Massassi (African) In mythology, the first woman of earth
Massassie, Masasi, Masasie, Massasi, Masassi, Massassy, Masasy, Massassee, Masasee

Massima (Italian) A superior woman; the greatest

Mastura (Arabic) One who is pure; chaste
Mastoora, Masturah, Masturia, Masturiya, Mastooria, Mastoura, Mastrouria

Matana (Hebrew) A gift from God
Matanah, Matanna, Matannah, Matai

Matangi (Hindi) In Hinduism, the patron of inner thought
Matangy, Matangie, Matangee, Matangey, Matangea

Matea (Hebrew) Feminine form of Matthew; a gift from God
Mattea, Matthea, Matthia, Mathea, Mathia, Mateja, Matia, Mathia, Matthan, Matthanias

Matilda (German) One who is mighty in battle
Maitilde, Maltilda, Maltilde, Mat, Matelda, Mathilda, Mathilde, Matilde, Matti, Mattie, Matty, Mahault, Maitilda, Maiti, Matia, Mathild, Matyidy

Matisoon (Native American) Giver of life
Mati, Matisun, Matisune, Matisoone, Matisoun, Matisoune

Matriona (Latin) Lady of the house; a matron
Matrena, Matresha, Matrina, Matryna, Motreina

Matsuko (Japanese) Child of the pine tree

Mattox (English) A gift from God
Matox, Mattoxx, Matoxx, Mattoxa, Mattoxi, Mattoxia

Matuta (Latin) In mythology, goddess of childbirth
Matutah

Maud (German) Form of Matilda, meaning "one who is mighty in battle"
Maude, Maudie, Maudi, Maudy, Maudee, Maudey, Maudea

Maureen (Irish) Form of Mary, meaning "star of the sea / from the sea of bitterness"
Maura, Maurene, Maurianne, Maurine, Maurya, Mavra, Maure, Mo, Maurean, Maureane

Maurissa (Latin) Feminine form of Maurice; a dark-skinned beauty
Maurisa, Maurelle, Maurell, Maurella, Maurita, Mauryta, Maurizia, Mauriza, Maurise, Maurisse

Mauve (French) Of the mallow plant
Mawve

Mave (Gaelic) One who brings joy to others
Mava

Mavelle (Celtic) Resembling a songbird
Mavell, Mavele, Mavella, Mavela, Mavel, Mavie

Maven (English) Having great knowledge
Mavin, Mavyn

Maverick (American) One who is wild and free
Maverik, Maveryck, Maveryk, Mavarick, Mavarik

Mavis (French) Resembling a songbird
Mavise, Maviss, Mavisse, Mavys, Mavyss, Mavysse

Mavonde (African) Of the abundant harvest
Mavonda, Mavondia, Mavondea

Mawiyah (Arabic) Possessing the essence of life
Mawiya

Mawunyaga (African) God is great

Maxine (English) Feminine form of Max; the greatest
Maxeen, Maxena, Maxence, Maxene, Maxi, Maxie, Maxime, Maximina, Maxina, Maxy, Maxanda, Maxima, Maxea

May (Latin) Born during the month of May; form of Mary, meaning "star of the sea / from the sea of bitterness"
Mae, Mai, Maelynn, Maelee, Maj, Mala, Mayana, Maye, Mayleen, Maylene, Mei

❍ **Maya** (Indian / Hebrew) An illusion; a dream / woman of the water
Mayah, Mya

Mayes (English) From the meadow

Maylea (Hawaiian) Resembling a wild-flower
Maylee, Mayli, Maylie, Mayley, Mayly, Mayleigh

Maylin (American) Of the wondrous water-fall
Mayleh, Maylan

Maymunah (Arabic) One who is blessed
Maymuna, Maymoona, Maymoonah, Maymouna, Maymounah

Maysa (Arabic) One who is graceful
Maysah

Maysun (Arabic) A woman with a beautiful face
Maysoon, Maysuna, Maysoona, Maysoun, Maysouna

Mayumi (Japanese) One who embodies truth, wisdom, and beauty
Mayumie, Mayumee, Mayumy, Mayumey, Mayumea

Mayuri (Indian) Resembling a peahen
Mayurie, Mayuree, Mayurey, Mayury, Mayurea

Mazarine (French) Having deep-blue eyes
Mazareen, Mazareene, Mazaryn, Mazaryne, Mazine, Mazyne, Mazeene

Mazel (Hebrew) One who is lucky
Mazell, Mazele, Mazelle, Mazela, Mazella

Mazhira (Hebrew) A shining woman
Mazhirah, Mazheera, Mazhyra, Mazheira, Mazhiera, Mazheara

Mazzaroth (Hebrew) A seer; refers to the twelve signs of the zodiac
Mazzarothe, Mazzarotha, Mazaroth, Mazarothe, Mazarotha

McKayla (Gaelic) A fiery woman
McKale, McKaylee, McKaleigh, McKay, McKaye, McKaela

Mead (English) From the meadow
Meade, Meed, Meede

Meadghbh (Celtic) One who is nimble

Meadow (American) From the beautiful field
Meadowe, Meado, Meadoe, Medow, Medowe, Medoe

Meahpaara (Arabic) Slice of the moon
Meahparah, Meahparra, Meapara

Meantuna (Arabic) One who is trustworthy
Meantoona, Meantouna

Meara (Gaelic) One who is filled with happiness
Mearah

Meciria (African) A kind and thoughtful woman
Meciriah, Mecyria, Mecyriah

Meda (Native American) A prophetess

Meddela (Swedish) A well-spoken woman
Medela, Meddella, Medella

Medea (Greek) A cunning ruler; in mythology, a sorceress
Madora, Medeia, Media, Medeah, Mediah, Mediya, Mediyah

Medeba (Hebrew) From the quiet waters
Medebah

Medina (Arabic) From the city of the prophet
Medinah, Medyna, Medynah, Medeena, Medeenah, Mediena, Medeina, Medeana, Mdina

Medini (Indian) Daughter of the earth
Medinie, Mediny, Mediney, Medinee,
Medinea

Meditrina (Latin) The healer; in mythology,
goddess of health and wine
Meditreena, Meditryna, Meditriena

Medora (Greek) A wise ruler
Medoria, Medorah, Medorra, Medorea

Medusa (Greek) In mythology, a Gorgon
with snakes for hair
Medoosa, Medusah, Medoosah, Medousa,
Medousah

Meena (Hindi) Resembling a fish; in
Hinduism, the daughter of the goddess
Usha
Meenah, Meana, Meanah

Meenakshi (Indian) Having beautiful eyes

Meera (Israeli) A saintly woman; woman of
the light
Meerah, Meira, Meirah, Meir

Megaera (Greek) In mythology, a Fury
Magaere, Magaera, Megaere

Megan (Welsh) Form of Margaret, meaning
"resembling a pearl / the child of light"
Maegan, Meg, Magan, Magen, Megin,
Maygan, Meagan, Meaghan, Meagin,
Meeghan, Meegan, Meghan, Megdn, Meggen,
Megen, Meggan, Meggie, Meggy, Meganira,
Meighan

Megha (Indian) Resembling a cloud
Meghana, Meghah

Megiddo (Hebrew) From the army's camp
Megiddon

Mehadi (Indian) Resembling a flower
Mehadie, Mehady, Mehadey, Mehadee,
Mehadea

Mehalah (Hebrew) Filled with tenderness
Mehala, Mehalla, Mehallah

Mehalia (Hebrew) An affectionate woman
Mehaliah, Mehalea, Mehaleah, Mehaliya,
Mehaliyah

Mehana (Hawaiian) A warm and friendly
woman
Mehanah, Mehannah, Mehanna

Mehetabel (Hebrew) God makes one joy-
ous
Mehitabelle, Mettabel, Meheytabel, Mehitabel,
Mehitahelle

Mehuman (Hebrew) One who is faithful
Mehumann, Mehumane, Mehumana,
Mehumanna

Mei (Latin / Hawaiian) The great one / May
Meiying

Meishan (Chinese) One who is virtuous
and beautiful
Meishana, Meishawn, Meishaun, Meishon

Meiwei (Chinese) One who is forever
enchanting

Mejarkon (Hebrew) From the clear waters
Mejarkona, Mejarkonia, Mejarkone

Meki (Croatian) A tender woman
Mekie, Mekee, Mekey, Meky, Mekea

Mekonah (Hebrew) A source of strength; a
solid foundation
Mekona, Mekonia, Mekoniah, Mekonna

Melanctha (Greek) Resembling the black
flower
Melancthia, Melancthea

Melangell (Welsh) A sweet messenger from
heaven
Melangelle, Melangela, Melangella, Melangele,
Melangel

❀ **Melanie** (Greek) A dark-skinned beauty
Malaney, Malanie, Mel, Mela, Melaina,
Melaine, Melainey, Melana, Melanee,
Melaney, Melani, Melania, Melanney,
Melannie, Melany, Mella, Mellanie, Melli,
Mellie, Melloney, Melly, Meloni, Melonie,
Melonnie, Melony, Melaena, Melanea,
Malanea, Melonea

Melantha (Greek) Resembling a dark-violet
flower
Melanthe, Melanthia, Melanthea, Malantha,
Mallantha, Mellantha

Melba (Australian) From the city of
Melbourne
Melbah, Mellba, Mellbah

Melcia (Teutonic) One who is ambitious and hardworking
Melciah

Melek (Arabic) A heavenly messenger; an angel
Melak

Melete (Greek) In mythology, the muse of medication
Meleet, Meelete, Meleat, Meleate

Meli (Native American) One who is bitter
Melie, Melee, Melea, Meleigh, Mely, Meley

Melia (Hawaiian / Greek) Resembling the plumeria / of the ash tree; in mythology, a nymph
Melidice, Melitine, Meliah, Meelia, Melya

Melika (Turkish) A great beauty
Melikah, Melicka, Melicca, Melyka, Melycka, Meleeka, Meleaka

Melina (Greek) As sweet as honey
Mellina, Meleana, Meleena, Melene, Melibella, Melibelle, Meline, Melyne, Melyna, Mellea, Melleta, Mellona, Meleda, Meleta

Melinda (Latin) One who is sweet and gentle
Melynda, Malinda, Malinde, Mallie, Mally, Malynda, Melinde, Mellinda, Mallee, Mallea

Meliora (Latin) One who is better than others
Melyora, Meliorah, Melyorah, Meleeora

Melisande (French) Having the strength of an animal
Malisande, Malissande, Malyssandre, Melesande, Melisandra, Melisandre, Melissande, Melissandre, Mellisande, Melysande, Melyssandre

Melisha (American) Form of Alisha, meaning "woman of the nobility; truthful; having high moral character"
Mellisha, Malicia, Malisha, Malitia, Melicia, Melitia, Mellicia, Melicia, Melysha

Melissa (Greek) Resembling a honeybee; in mythology, a nymph
Malissa, Mallissa, Mel, Melesa, Melessa, Melisa, Melise, Melisse, Melitta, Meliza, Mellie, Mellisa, Melly, Melosa, Milisa

Melita (Greek) As sweet as honey
Malita, Malitta, Melida, Melitta, Melyta, Malyta, Meleeta, Meleata, Melieta, Meleita

Melka (Polish) A dark-skinned beauty
Melkah

Melody (Greek) A beautiful song
Melodee, Melodey, Melodi, Melodia, Melodie, Melodea

Melora (Greek) Resembling the golden apple
Melorah, Melorra, Melorrah

Melpomene (Greek) In mythology, the muse of tragedy

Melva (Celtic) One who holds the rank of chief
Melvina, Mevah, Melvena, Melveena, Melvyna

Memphis (Greek) Established and beautiful

Menachema (Hebrew) One who offers consolation
Menachemah

Menahem (Hebrew) One who comforts others
Menahema, Menaheme, Menahemia, Menahemai

Menaka (Indian) A heavenly maiden
Menacka, Menakah, Menakia

Mendi (Spanish) Refers to the Virgin Mary
Mendia, Mendie, Mendy, Mendey, Mendee, Mendea

Mene (Hebrew) One whose deeds have been weighed

Menefer (Egyptian) From the city of beauty
Meneferr, Meneferre, Menefere

Menora (Hebrew) Resembling the candelabra
Menorah

Menula (Lithuanian) Born beneath the moon
Menulah, Menoola, Menoolah, Menoula, Menoulah

Meonenim (Hebrew) A soothsayer; one who foretells events
Meonenime, Meonenima, Meonenimia

Meoquanee (Native American) Lady in red
Meoquani, Meoquaney, Meoquanie, Meoquany, Meoquanea

Mephaath (Hebrew) A lustrous woman
Mephath, Mephatha, Mephaatha

Meralda (Latin) Form of Esmeralda, meaning "resembling a prized emerald"
Meraldah, Meraldia, Maralda, Maraldia

Merana (American) Woman of the waters
Meranah, Meranna, Merannah

Mercedes (Spanish) Lady of mercies; refers to the Virgin Mary
Mercedez, Mersadize, Merced, Mercede, Mercedeez

Mercer (English) A prosperous merchant

Mercurius (Hebrew) An orator; a messenger

Mercy (English) One who shows compassion and pity
Mercey, Merci, Mercie, Mercilla, Mercina, Mercena, Mersey, Mircea, Mercea, Mircy, Mircie, Mersy, Mersie, Mersi

Merdeka (Indonesian) An independent woman; one who is free
Merdekah, Merdecka, Merdecca

Meredith (Welsh) A great ruler; protector of the sea
Maredud, Meridel, Meredithe, Meredyth, Meridith, Merridie, Meradith, Meredydd

Meribah (Hebrew) A quarrelsome woman
Meriba

Mericia (Spanish) Woman of great merit
Mericiah, Mericea, Mericeah

Merle (French) Resembling a blackbird
Merl, Merla, Merlina, Merline, Merola, Murle, Myrle, Myrleen, Myrlene, Myrline, Maryl, Maryla

Merom (Hebrew) One who is elevated
Meroma, Meromia, Meromai, Merome, Meromea

Merona (Hebrew) Resembling a sheep
Meronah, Merrona, Meroona, Meronna

Merope (Greek) In mythology, one of the Pleiades
Meropi, Meropie, Meropy, Meropey, Meropee, Meropea

Meroz (Hebrew) From the cursed plains
Meroza, Merozia, Meroze

Merrick (English) A great and powerful ruler
Merrik, Merryck, Merryk, Meryk, Meryck

Merry (English) One who is lighthearted and joyful
Merree, Merri, Merrie, Merrielle, Merrile, Merrilee, Merrili, Merrily, Merryn, Merrilie, Meri, Merrea, Merie

Mert (Egyptian) One who loves silence
Mertekert

Mertice (English) A well-known lady
Mertise, Mertyce, Mertyse, Mertysa, Mertisa, Mertiece, Merteace

Merton (English) From the village near the pond
Mertan, Mertin, Mertun

Meryl (English) Form of Muriel, meaning "of the shining sea"; form of Merle, meaning "resembling a blackbird"
Maryl, Meral, Merel, Merla, Merlyn, Merryl, Meryle, Meryll, Mirla, Myrla, Merula, Merolla

Mesa (Spanish) From the flat-topped hill
Mesah, Messa, Messah

Mesi (Egyptian) Woman of the waters
Mesie, Mesy, Mesey, Mesee, Mesea

Meskhenet (Egyptian) A fated woman

Mesopotamia (Hebrew) From the land between two rivers
Mesopotama, Mesopotamea

Messina (Arabic) The middle child
Messinah, Massina, Mussina, Messena, Messinia

Meta (German / Latin) Form of Margaret, meaning "resembling a pearl / the child of light" / one who is ambitious
Metah, Metta, Mettah

Metea (Greek) A gentle woman
Meteah, Metia, Metiah

Metin (Greek) A wise counselor
Metine, Metyn, Metyne

Metis (Greek) One who is industrious
Metiss, Metisse, Metys, Metyss, Metysse

Metsa (Finnish) Woman of the forest
Metsah

Mettabel (Hebrew) Favored by God
Mettabell, Mettabele, Mettabelle, Mettabela, Mettabella

Mettalise (Danish) As graceful as a pearl
Metalise, Mettalisse, Mettalisa, Mettalissa

Meunim (Hebrew) Of the dwelling place
Mehunim

Mhina (African) A delightful lady
Mhinah, Mhinna, Mhena, Mhenah

❂ **Mia** (Israeli / Latin) Feminine form of
Michael; who is like God? / form of Mary,
meaning "star of the sea / from the sea of
bitterness"
Miah, Mea, Meah, Meya

Miakoda (Native American) Possessing the
power of the moon
Myakoda, Miacoda, Myacoda

Mianda (Spanish) Of my journey
Miandah, Myanda, Miandia, Meanda

Mibzar (Hebrew) From the fortress
Mibzarr, Mibzara, Mibzare, Mibzarre, Mibzarra

Micah (Hebrew) Feminine form of Michael;
who is like God?
Micaiah, Mica, Meeca, Meica, Mika, Myka, Mykah, Mikah

Michaela (Celtic / Hebrew / English)
Feminine form of Michael; who is like
God?
Micaela, Michal, Michael, Michaelina, Michaeline, Michaila, Michalin, Mickee, Mickie, Miguela, Miguelina, Miguelita, Mahalya, Mihaila, Mihalia, Mihaliya, Mikaela, Mikayla, Mikella, Mikelle, Mikhaila, Mikhayla, Miskaela, Mychaela, Makaila, Micole, Mika, Mikkel

Michelle (French) Feminine form of
Michael; who is like God?
Machelle, Mashelle, M'chelle, Mechelle, Meechelle, Me'Shell, Meshella, Michaella, Michela, Michele, Michelina, Micheline, Michell, Michella, Mishaila, Midge, Mischaela, Misha, Mishaelle, Mishelle, M'shell, Mychele, Mychelle, Myshell, Myshella, Michon, Miesha

Michewa (Tibetan) Sent from heaven
Michewah

Michigan (Native American) From the great
waters; from the state of Michigan
Mishigan, Michegen, Mishegen

Michiko (Japanese) Child of beautiful wisdom
Michi, Michyko, Meecheeko, Mecheeko, Meechiko, Michee

Michima (Japanese) Possessing beautiful
wisdom

Michmethah (Hebrew) A secretive woman;
from the hiding place

Michri (Hebrew) Gift from God
Michrie, Michry, Michrey, Michree, Michrea

Michtam (Hebrew) One who has been
given the gift of writing
Michtame, Michtaam, Michtami, Michtama

Mickey (American) Feminine form of
Michael; who is like God?
Micki, Micky, Mickie, Mickee, Mickea

Middin (Hebrew) One who has been measured

Mide (Irish) One who is thirsty
Meeda, Mida

Midori (Japanese) Having green eyes
Midorie, Midory, Midorey, Midoree, Midorea

Mieko (Japanese) Born into wealth
Meeko, Meako

Mielikki (Finnish) A pleasant woman
Mieliki, Mielikkie, Mielikie

Miette (French) A petite, sweet young
woman
Miett, Miet, Miete, Mieta, Mietta

Migdalia (Hebrew) Feminine form of Migdal; of the high tower
Migdala, Migdalla, Migdalea, Migdaliah, Migdaleah, Migdalgad, Migdaliya, Migdaliyah

Migdana (Hebrew) A gift from God
Migdanah, Migdanna, Migdania, Migdanea

Migina (Native American) Born beneath the returning moon
Migyna, Migena, Mygina, Mygyna

Migisi (Native American) Resembling an eagle
Migisie, Migysi, Mygisi, Migisy, Migisea

Mignon (French) One who is cute and petite
Mignonette, Mignonne, Mingnon, Minyonne, Minyonette

Migron (Hebrew) Woman of the cliffs
Migrona, Migrone, Migronai, Migronya

Mikaia (American) Of God's green earth

Mikaili (African) A godly woman
Mikailie, Mikayli, Mikali, Mikaylie, Mikalie

Miki (Japanese / Hawaiian) Of the beautiful tree / one who is nimble
Mikki, Mikko, Mika, Mikil

Mila (Slavic) One who is industrious and hardworking
Milaia, Milaka, Milla, Milia

Milada (Slavic) My daughter is my love
Miladah, Miladda, Millada

Milagros (Spanish) Lady of miracles; refers to the Virgin Mary
Milagritos, Milagrosa, Miligrosa, Miligritos

Milan (Latin) From the city in Italy; one who is gracious
Milaana

Milanka (Croatian) A sweet young woman
Milankaa, Milankai, Milanke, Milankia, Mylanka, Mylanke

Mildred (English) Woman of gentle strength
Mildri, Mildrid, Mildryd, Mildrie, Mildree, Mildraed, Millie, Milly, Milley, Milli, Millee, Millea, Mildrea

Milena (Slavic) The favored one
Mileena, Milana, Miladena, Milanka, Mlada, Mladena

Miletum (Hebrew) From the seaport town

Mili (Hebrew) A virtuous woman
Milie, Mily, Miley, Milee, Milea, Mileigh

Miliana (Latin) Feminine form of Emeliano; one who is eager and willing
Milianah, Milianna, Miliane, Miliann, Milianne

Miliani (Hawaiian) Of the gentle caress
Milianie, Milianee, Miliany, Milianey, Milianea

Milima (Swahili) Woman from the mountains
Milimah, Mileema, Milyma

Miller (English) One who works at a mill
Millar, Millir, Mills

Millicent (French) A woman with great strength and determination
Melicent, Mellicent, Mellie, Mellisent, Melly, Milicent, Milisent, Millisent, Milzie, Milicente

Millo (Hebrew) Defender of the sacred city
Milloh, Millowe, Milloe

Miloslava (Russian) Feminine form of Miloslav; having the favor and glory of the people
Miloslavah, Miloslavia, Miloslavea

Mima (Hebrew) Form of Jemima, meaning "our little dove"
Mimah, Mymah, Myma

Mimala (Native American) A holy woman
Mimalah, Mimalla, Mimallah

Mina (Japanese / German) Woman from the South / one who is greatly loved
Minah, Min, Minette, Minnette, Minna

Minako (Japanese) A beautiful child

Minal (Native American) As sweet as fruit
Minall, Minalle, Minala, Minalla

Minau (Persian) Child of heaven

Minda (Native American, Hindi) Having great knowledge
Mindah, Mynda, Myndah, Menda, Mendah

Mindel (Hebrew) Form of Mary, meaning "star of the sea / from the sea of bitterness"
Mindell, Mindelle, Mindele, Mindela, Mindella

Mindy (English) Form of Melinda, meaning "one who is sweet and gentle"
Minda, Mindee, Mindi, Mindie, Mindey, Mindea

Minerva (Latin) Having strength of mind; in mythology, the goddess of wisdom
Minervah, Menerva, Minirva, Menirva

Minetta (French) Form of Wilhelmina, meaning "determined protector"
Minette, Mineta, Minete, Minett, Minet, Mine

Ming Yue (Chinese) Born beneath the bright moon

Mingmei (Chinese) A bright and beautiful girl

Miniya (African) She is expected to do great things
Miniyah

Minjonet (French) Resembling the small blue flower
Minjonett, Minjonete, Minjonette, Minjoneta, Minjonetta

Minka (Teutonic) One who is resolute; having great strength
Minkah, Mynka, Mynkah, Minna, Minne

Minnesota (Native American) From the sky-tinted waters
Minesota, Minnesoda, Minesoda, Minisota, Minisoda

Minnie (English) Form of Wilhelmina, meaning "determined protector"
Minny, Minni, Minney, Minnee, Minnea

Minor (American) A young woman; a lass

Minowa (Native American) One who has a moving voice
Minowah, Mynowa, Mynowah

Minta (Greek) Form of Amynta, meaning "protector and defender of her loved ones"
Mintha, Mintah, Minty, Minti, Mintie, Mintee, Mintey, Mintea

Minuit (French) Born at midnight
Minueet

Minya (Native American) The older sister
Miniya, Minyah, Miniyah

Mio (Japanese) Having great strength

Mira (Indian / Slavic / Latin) One who is prosperous / a peaceful woman / one who is wonderful
Mirah, Mirana, Mireille, Mirella, Mirelle, Miri, Miriana, Mirielle, Mirilla, Mirka, Mirra, Myrella, MyrÈne, Myrilla, Mir, Mirko, Mirke

Mirabel (Latin / French) One who is wonderful / a rare beauty
Meribel, Meribelle, Mirabell, Mirabella, Mirabelle

Miracle (American) An act of God's hand
Mirakle, Mirakel, Myracle, Myrakle

Mirage (French) An illusion or fantasy

Mirai (Basque) A miracle child
Miraya, Mirari, Mirarie, Miraree, Mirae

Miranda (Latin) One who is worthy of admiration
Maranda, Meranda, Miran, Mirandah, Mirranda, Myranda

Mirani (Spanish) An attractive lady
Miranie, Mirany, Miraney, Miranee, Miranea

Mireille (French) One who is greatly admired
Mirella, Mireile, Mireilla, Mireila, Mireio, Mirei

Mirella (Hebrew) God has spoken
Mirela, Mirelah, Mirellah, Mirelle, Mirell, Mirele, Mirel, Mirielle

Miremba (Ugandan) A promoter of peace
Mirembe, Mirem, Mirembah, Mirembeh, Mirema

Mireya (Spanish) Form of Miranda, meaning "one who is worthy of admiration"
Miraya, Maraya, Mareya, Myrelle, Myrella

Miriam (Hebrew) Form of Mary, meaning "star of the sea / from the sea of bitterness"
Mariam, Maryam, Meriam, Meryam, Mirham, Mirjam, Mirjana, Mirriam, Miryam, Miyana, Miyanna, Myriam, Marrim, Mijam

Mirias (Greek) Woman of plenty
Miriass, Miriasse, Miriase, Miriasa, Miryas, Miryase, Miryasa

Mirinesse (English) Filled with joy
Miriness, Mirinese, Mirines, Mirinessa, Mirinesa

Mirit (Hebrew) One who is strong-willed

Miriuia (Latin) A marvelous lady

Miroslava (Slavic) Feminine form of Miroslav; one who basks in peaceful glory
Miroslavia, Miroslavea, Myroslava, Myroslavia, Myroslavea

Mirta (Spanish) Crowned with thorns
Mirtah, Meerta, Meertha, Mirtha

Misae (Native American) Born beneath the white sun
Mysae, Misay, Misaye, Mysay, Mysaye, Misai, Mysai

Mischa (Russian) Form of Michelle, meaning "who is like God?"
Misha

Misrak (African) Woman from the East
Misrake, Misraka, Misrakia

Mississippi (Native American) Of the great river; from the state of Mississippi
Misisipi, Missisippi, Mississipi, Misissippi, Misisippi

Missouri (Native American) From the town of large canoes
Missourie, Mizouri, Mizourie, Missoury, Mizoury, Missuri, Mizuri, Mizury, Missury

Missy (English) Form of Melissa, meaning "resembling a honeybee"
Missey, Misse, Missee, Missie, Missi, Missea

Mistico (Italian) A mystical woman
Mistica, Mystico, Mystica, Mistiko, Mystiko

Misty (American) Covered with dew; of the mists
Mistie, Misti, Mistey, Mistee, Mystee, Mysti, Mystie, Mysty, Mystey, Mystea, Mistea

Misu (Native American) Of the rippling waters
Misoo, Misou, Mysu, Mysoo, Mysou

Misumi (Japanese) A pure, beautiful woman
Misumie, Misumee, Misumy, Misumey, Misumea

Mitali (Indian) A friendly and sweet woman
Mitalie, Mitalee, Mitaleigh, Mitaly, Mitaley, Meeta, Mitalea

Mitena (Native American) Born beneath the new moon
Mitenah, Mytena, Mitenna, Mytenna

Mitexi (Native American) Born beneath the sacred moon
Mitexie, Mitexee, Mitexy, Mitexey, Mitexa, Mitexea

Mithcah (Hebrew) A sweet and pleasant woman
Mithca, Mithcah, Mitheca

Mitra (Persian) A heavenly messenger; an angel
Mitran, Mitrania, Mitrane, Mitrana

Mitsu (Japanese) Lady of light
Mitsuko

Mitylene (Hebrew) From the island city
Mityleen, Mitylean, Mityleene, Mityleane, Mitylen, Mitylein

Mitzi (German) Form of Mary, meaning "star of the sea / from the sea of bitterness"
Mitzie, Mitzy, Mitzey, Mitzee, Mitzea

Miya (Japenese) From the sacred temple
Miyah

Miyanda (African) One who is grounded
Miyandah, Myanda, Meyanda

Miyo (Japanese) A beautiful daughter
Miyoko

Mizar (Hebrew) A little woman; petite
Mizarr, Mizarre, Mizare, Mizara, Mizaria, Mizarra

Mizpah (Hebrew) From the watchtower
Mizpeh, Mizpa

Mliss (Cambodian) Resembling a flower
Mlissa, Mlisse, Mlyss, Mlysse, Mlyssa

Mnason (Hebrew) One who has a good memory

Mnemosyne (Greek) In mythology, goddess of memory

Moana (Hawaiian) Woman of the ocean
Moanna, Moanah, Moannah, Moane, Moaenne

Moani (Hawaiian) A fragrance on the gentle breeze
Moanie, Moany, Moaney, Moanee, Moanea

Mocha (Arabic) As sweet as chocolate
Mochah

Modesty (Latin) One who is without conceit
Modesti, Modestie, Modestee, Modestus, Modestey, Modesta, Modestia, Modestina, Modestine, Modestea

Modron (Welsh) In mythology, the divine mother

Moesha (American) Drawn from the water
Moisha, Moysha, Moeesha, Moeasha, Moeysha

Mohala (Hawaiian) Resembling the unfolding of a flower
Mohalah, Mohalla, Mohallah

Mohan (Indian) An attractive woman
Mohani, Mohana, Mohanie, Mohanee, Mohania, Mohanea

Mohini (Indian) The most beautiful
Mohinie, Mohinee, Mohiny, Mohiney, Mohinea

Moina (Celtic) A mild-mannered lady
Moyna, Moinah, Moynah

Moira (English) Form of Mary, meaning "star of the sea / from the sea of bitterness"
Moyra, Moire, Moyre, Moreen, Morene, Morine

Moirae (Greek) In mythology, the Fates
Moirai, Moerae, Moyrae, Moyrai

Moireach (Scottish) A respected lady

Moja (African) One who is content with life
Mojah

Moke (Hawaiian) Feminine form of Moses; savior
Mokie, Mokei, Moky, Mokey, Mokee, Mokea

Moladah (Hebrew) A giver of life
Molada

Molara (Spanish) Refers to the Virgin Mary
Molarah, Molarra, Molaria, Molarea

⊙ **Molly** (Irish) Form of Mary, meaning "star of the sea / from the sea of bitterness"
Moll, Mollee, Molley, Molli, Mollie, Molle, Mollea

Molpe (Greek) In mythology, a siren
Molpie, Molpi, Molpa, Molpy, Molpey, Molpee, Molpea

Momo (Japanese) Resembling a peach
Momoko

Mona (Gaelic) One who is born into the nobility
Moina, Monah, Monalisa, Monalissa, Monna, Moyna, Monalysa, Monalyssa

Monahana (Gaelic) A religious woman
Monahanah, Monahanna, Monahannah

Monca (Irish) Having great wisdom
Moncah

Moncha (Irish) A solitary woman
Monchah

Monet (French) Form of Monica, meaning "a solitary woman / one who advises others"
Monay, Mone, Monai, Monae, Monee

Monica (Greek / Latin) A solitary woman / one who advises others
Monnica, Monca, Monicka, Monika, Monike

Monifa (Egyptian) One who is lucky
Monifah, Monipha, Moniphah, Moneefa, Moneifa, Moniefa, Moneafa

Monique (French) One who provides wise counsel
Moniqua, Moneeque, Moneequa, Moneeke, Moeneek, Moneaque, Moneaqua, Moneake

Monisha (Hindi) Having great intelligence
Monishah, Monesha, Moneisha, Moniesha, Moneysha, Moneasha

Monita (Spanish) A noble woman
Monitah, Moneeta, Monyta, Moneita, Monieta, Moneata

Monroe (Gaelic) Woman from the river
Monrow, Monrowe, Monro

Monserrat (Latin) From the jagged mountain
Montserrat

Montague (French) Of the steep mountain
Montahue

Montana (Latin) Woman of the mountains; from the state of Montana
Montanna, Montina, Monteene, Montese

Montsho (African) A dark-skinned beauty
Montshow, Montshowe, Montshoe

Mor (Celtic / Irish) An exceptional woman
More

Mora (Spanish) Resembling a blueberry
Morah, Morra, Morrah

Morag (Gaelic) One who embraces the sun

Moraika (Incan) A heavenly messenger; an angel
Moraikah, Morayka, Moraykah, Moraeka, Moraekah

Morcan (Welsh) Of the bright sea
Morcane, Morcana, Morcania, Morcanea

Moreh (Hebrew) A great archer; a teacher

Morela (Polish) Resembling an apricot
Morella, Morelah, Morellah, Morele, Morelle

Morena (Spanish) A brown-haired woman

✿
❶ **Morgan** (Welsh) Circling the bright sea; a sea dweller
Morgaine, Morgana, Morgance, Morgane, Morganica, Morgann, Morganne, Morgayne, Morgen, Morgin, Morgaen, Morgaene, Morgaena

Morguase (English) In Arthurian legend, the mother of Gawain
Marguase, Margawse, Morgawse, Morgause, Margause

Moriah (Hebrew) God is my teacher; of the hill country
Moraia, Moraiah, Moria, Morit, Moriel, Morice, Morise, Moriya

Morina (Japanese) From the woodland town
Morinah, Moreena, Moryna, Moriena, Moreina, Moreana

Morisa (Spanish) Feminine form of Maurice; a dark-skinned beauty
Morissa, Morrisa, Morrissa

Morley (English) Woman from the moor
Morly, Morli, Morlie, Morlee, Morleigh, Morlea

Morna (Irish) One who is affectionate; beloved
Mornah

Morrigan (Celtic) In mythology, a war goddess
Morrigane, Morigan, Morigane

Morrin (Irish) A long-haired woman
Morrina, Morrine, Morren, Morrene, Morrena

Morwenna (Welsh) Maiden of the white seas
Morwena, Morwina, Morwinna, Morwyn, Morwynna, Morwyna, Morwen, Morwenne

Moselle (Hebrew) Feminine form of Moses; savior
Mosell, Mosele, Mosel, Mosella, Mosela, Mosette, Moiselle, Moisella

Moserah (Hebrew) Disciplined in learning
Moseroth, Moserothe

Mosi (Egyptian) The firstborn child
Mosie, Mosee, Mosy, Mosey, Mosea

Mostyn (Welsh) Of the meadow's fortress
Mostynn, Mostynne, Mosteen, Mosteene, Mostine, Mostean, Mosteane

Motayma (Native American) A wise leader
Motaymah, Motaima, Motama, Motaema

Mouna (Arabic) One who is desired
Mounia, Muna, Munia

Mounira (Arabic) An illuminated woman
Mourneera, Mounyra, Mounera, Mouneara

Mridula (Indian) One who is soft to the touch
Mridulah, Mridulla, Mridullah

Mrinal (Hindi) Resembling a lotus blossom
Mrinalini, Mrinali, Mrinalie, Mrinalina, Mrinala

Muadhnait (Gaelic) A young noblewoman

Mu'azzama (Arabic) One who is respected

Mubarika (Arabic) One who is blessed
Mubaarika, Mubaricka, Mubaryka, Mubaricca, Mubarycca

Mubina (Arabic) One who displays her true image
Mubeena, Mubinah, Mubyna, Mubeana, Mubiena

Mudan (Mandarin) Daughter of a harmonious family
Mudane, Mudana, Mudayne, Mudaine, Mudann, Mudaen, Mudaena

Mudiwa (African) One who is greatly loved
Mudiwah, Mudywa, Mudywah

Mudraya (Russian) One with great wisdom and reason
Mudrayah, Mudraia

Mufidah (Arabic) One who is helpful to others
Mufeeda, Mufeyda, Mufyda, Mufeida, Mufieda, Mufeada

Mugain (Irish) In mythology, the wife of the king of Ulster
Mugayne, Mugaine, Mugane, Mugayn, Mugaen, Mugaene, Mugaina, Mugayna, Mugaena

Muhjah (Arabic) Our heart's blood
Muhju

Muhsana (Arabic) One who is well-protected
Muhsanah, Muhsanan, Muhsanna

Muicl (Irish) Woman of the sea
Muiell, Muielle, Muiele, Muireann, Murieall, Muirgheal

Muira (Scottish) Woman from the moor
Muire

Muirne (Irish) One who is dearly loved
Muirna

Mujahida (Arabic) A crusader
Mujaahida, Mujahyda, Mujaheeda, Mujaheada

Mujia (Chinese) A healer; medicine woman

Mujiba (Arabic) One who provides the answers
Mujeeha, Mujibah, Mujeebah, Mujeaba, Mujeabah

Mukantagara (Egyptian) Born during a time of war

Mukarramma (Egyptian) One who is honored and respected
Mukarama, Mukaramma, Mukkarama

Mulan (Chinese) Resembling a magnolia blossom
Mulana, Mulania, Mulane, Mulann, Mulanna, Mulanne

Muminah (Arabic) A pious woman
Mumina, Mumeena, Mumyna, Mumeina, Mumiena, Mumeana

Muna (Arabic) God is with me
Moona, Munah, Moonah

Munay (African) One who loves and is loved
Manay, Munaye, Munae, Munai

Munaya (African) The rainmaker
Munayah

Munazza (Arabic) An independent woman; one who is free
Munazzah, Munaza, Munazah

Muncel (American) A strong-willed woman
Muncele, Muncelle, Muncell, Muncela, Muncella

Munin (Scandinavian) One with a good memory
Munine, Munyn, Munyne, Munina, Munyna

Munira (Arabic) A lustrous and brilliant woman
Muneera, Munirah, Muneira, Muniera, Munyra, Munawwara, Munawara, Muneara

Muniya (Indian) Resembling a small bird
Muniyah

Muqaddasa (Arabic) One who is sacred

Murata (African) A beloved friend
Muraty, Muratia, Murati, Muratie, Muratee, Muratea

Muriel (Irish) Of the shining sea
Merial, Meriel, Merrill, Miureall, Murial, Muriella, Murielle, Merill, Merral, Merrall, Merril, Meriol, Murel

Murphy (Celtic) Daughter of a great sea warrior
Murphi, Murphie, Murphey, Murphee, Murfi, Murfy, Murfie, Murphea, Murfea

Musetta (French) Little muse; a joyful song
Musette, Musett, Muset, Musete, Museta

Mushana (African) Born with the morning's light
Mushanah, Mushania, Mushanna, Mushane

Musharrifa (Arabic) An exalted woman
Musharifa, Musharrifah, Musharifah, Musharyfa

Mushira (Arabic) A wise counselor
Mushirah, Musheera, Musheira, Mushiera, Musheara

Musidora (Greek) Gift of the Muses
Musadora, Musedora, Musidoria, Musadoria, Musedoria

Muslimah (Arabic) A devout believer
Muslima, Muslyma, Muslymah, Muslema, Muslemah

Musoke (African) Having the beauty of a rainbow

Mut (Egyptian) In mythology, the creator goddess

Muta (Latin) In mythology, the personification of silence
Mute, Mutah, Muteh

Mutehhara (Arabic) One who is pure; chaste
Mutehara, Mutehharah, Muteharra, Muteharah

Mutia (African) An honored woman; respected
Mutiah, Mutiya, Mutiyah, Mutea, Muteah, Mutya, Mutyah

❂ **Mya** (Indian / Hebrew) An illusion; a dream / woman of the water

Mychau (Vietnamese) Known for her greatness

My-duyen (Vietnamese) A beautiful woman

Myfanawy (Welsh) A sweet and rare woman
Myfanawi, Myfanawie, Myfanawee, Myfanawea, Myfanawey

Myisha (Arabic) Form of Aisha, meaning "lively; womanly"
Myesha, Myeisha, Myeshia, Myiesha, Myeasha

Myka (Hebrew) Feminine of Micah, meaning "Who is like God?"

Myla (English) Feminine form of Myles; one who is merciful
Mylene, Myleen, Mylah, Myleene, Mylyne, Mylas, Mylean, Myleane, Mayla

Myma (Irish) One who is greatly loved
Mymah

Myra (Greek) Form of Myrrh, meaning "resembling the fragrant oil"
Myrah, Myree, Myriah

Myrina (Latin) In mythology, an Amazon
Myrinah, Myreena, Myreina, Myriena, Myreana

Myrna (Gaelic) One who is much loved
Meirna, Merna, Mirna, Moina, Moyna, Muirna, Murna

Myrrh (Egyptian) Resembling the fragrant oil

Myrta (Greek) Resembling the evergreen shrub myrtle
Myrtia, Myrtice, Mytra, Merta, Merte, Merteh

Myrtle (Latin) Of the sacred evergreen shrub
Myrtilla, Myrtisa, Myrtis, Mertice, Mertis, Mertle, Mirtie, Myrta, Myrtia, Myrtice, Myrtie, Myrtiece, Myrteace, Myrtee

Mystery (American) A lady of the unknown
Mysteri, Mysterie, Mysterey, Mysteree, Mistery, Misteri, Misterie, Misteree, Misterey, Mysterea, Misterea

Mystique (French) Woman with an air of mystery
Mystica, Mistique, Mysteek, Misteek, Mystiek, Mistiek, Mysteeque, Misteeque

Mythri (Indian) One who values friendship
Mythrie, Mithri, Mithrie, Mithree, Mythree, Mithry, Mithrey, Mythry, Mythrey, Mithrea, Mythrea

n

Naama (Hebrew) Feminine form of Noam; an attractive woman; good-looking
Naamah

Naarah (Hebrew) A young woman; a girl; in the Bible, one of Ashur's wives
Naarai, Naarae

Naava (Hebrew) A lovely and pleasant woman
Naavah, Nava, Navah, Navit

Nabiha (Arabic) One who is intelligent
Nabeeha, Nabyha, Nabihah, Nabeehah, Nabyhah, Nabeaha, Nabeahah

Nabila (Arabic) Daughter born into nobility; a highborn daughter
Nabilah, Nabeela, Nabyla, Nabeelah, Nabylah, Nabeala, Nabealah

Nabirye (Egyptian) One who gives birth to twins
Naberye

Nachine (Spanish) A fiery young woman
Nacheene, Nachyne, Nachina, Nachinah, Nachynu, Nacheena, Nacheane, Nacheana

Nadda (Arabic) A very generous woman
Naddah, Nada, Nadah

Nadetta (French) Form of Bernadette, meaning "one who has bearlike strength and courage"
Nadette, Nadett, Nadet, Nadete, Nadeta

Nadhira (Arabic) A flourishing woman; one who is precious
Nadhirah, Naadhira, Nadheera, Nadhyra, Nadhiera, Nadheira, Nadhera, Naadhirah, Nadheerah, Nadhyrah, Nadhierah, Nadheirah, Nadherah, Nadheara

⊕ Nadia (Slavic) One who is full of hope
Nadja, Nadya, Naadiya, Nadine, Nadie, Nadiyah, Nadea, Nadija, Nadka, Nadenka, Nadezhda, Nadusha, Nadiah, Nadeen, Nadeene, Nadean, Nadyne, Nadien, Nadin, Nadene, Nadina, Nadena, Nadyna, Nadyn, Nadeana, Nadeane, Nadeena, Naydene, Naydeen, Naydin, Naydyn, Naidene, Naidine, Naidyne, Naideen, Naydine, Nadezda, Nadiya, Nadjae, Nadjah, Nads, Nadyenka, Nadyuiska, Nadzia, Naiya, Naia, Naiyana, Naya, Nadege, Natia

Nadifa (African) One who is born between the seasons
Nadifah, Nadeefa, Nadyfa, Nadeefah, Nadyfah, Nadeafa, Nadeafah

Nadirah (Arabic) One who is precious; rare
Nadira, Nadyra, Nadyrah, Nadeera, Nadeerah, Nadra, Nadrah

Nadwah (Arabic) One who gives wise counsel
Nadwa

Naeemah (Egyptian) A kind and benevolent woman
Nayma, Nayima, Nayema

Naenia (Latin) In mythology, the goddess of funerals
Naenie, Naeni, Naeny, Naeney, Naenee, Naenea, Naeniah

Naeva (French) Born in the evening
Naevah, Naevia, Naevea, Nayva, Nayvah, Nayvia, Nayvea

Nafisa (Arabic) As precious as a gem
Nafeesa, Nafeeza, Nafisah, Nafeesah, Nafeezah, Nafysa, Nafysah, Nafeasa, Nafeasah

Nafuna (African) A child who is delivered feetfirst
Nafunah, Nafunna, Nafoona, Nafoonah, Naphuna, Naphunah, Naphoona, Naphoonah, Nafouna, Naphouna

Nagesa (African) Born during the time of harvest
Nagesah, Nagessa, Nagessah

Nagge (Hebrew) A radiant woman

Nagida (Hebrew) A wealthy woman
Nagidah, Nagyda, Nugydah, Negida,
Negidah, Negyda, Negydah, Nageeda,
Nageedah, Negeeda, Negeedah, Nageada,
Nageadah

Nagina (Arabic) As precious as a pearl
Nageena, Naginah, Nageenah, Nagyna,
Nagynah, Nageana, Nageanah

Nahia (Basque) One who is greatly desired
Nahiah, Nahea, Naheah, Nahiya, Nahiyah

Nahid (Persian) One who is elevated; in
mythology, the goddess of love
Naaheed, Naheed, Naheede, Nahyde, Nahyd,
Nahead, Naheade

Naida (Greek) A water nymph
Naiadia, Naidah, Nyad, Nayad, Naiad,
Nyada, Nayada, Niadah, Naeda, Naedah

Nailah (Arabic) Feminine form of Nail; a
successful woman; the acquirer
Na'ila, Na'ilah, Naa'ilah, Naila, Nayla,
Naylah, Naela, Naelah

Naima (African / Arabic) A contented
woman / one who brings comfort and
peace
Na'ima, Na'imah, Naimah, Nayma,
Naymah, Naeema, Naeemah, Naema,
Naemah

Naira (Native American) A woman with big
eyes
Nairah, Nayra, Nayrah, Naera, Naerah

Nairi (Armenian) From the mountainous
land
Nairie, Nairy, Nairey, Nairee, Nairea

Nairna (Scottish) From the alder-tree river
Naime, Nairnia, Nairnea, Naerna, Nayrna

Nairobi (African) Woman from the capital
of Kenya
Nairobie, Nairoby, Nairobey, Nairobee,
Nayrobi, Nayrobie, Nayroby, Nayrobey,
Nayrobee, Nairobea, Nayrobea

Najam (Arabic) A starlike woman
Naja, Najah, Najama, Najma

Najia (Arabic) An independent woman; one
who is free
Naajia

Najiba (Arabic) An intellectually superior
woman; born into the nobility
Najibah, Najeeba, Najeebah, Najyba,
Najybah, Najeaba, Najeabah

Najila (Arabic) A woman with shining eyes
Najilah, Najyla, Najylah, Najla, Najlah,
Nagla, Naglah, Najeela, Najeelah, Najeala,
Najealah

Najja (African) The second-born child
Najjah

Najjiyya (Arabic) One who is beneficial to
others
Najjiyyah, Najiyah, Najiya

Najwa (Arabic) A secretve woman
Nagwa, Najwah, Nagwah

Najya (Arabic) A victorious woman
Najyah

Nakeisha (American) Form of Keisha,
meaning "the favorite child"
Nakeesha, Nakysha, Nakeasha, Nakiesha,
Nakeysha, Narkeasha

Naki (African) The firstborn daughter
Nakie, Naky, Nakey, Nakee, Nakye

Nakia (Arabic) One who is pure; chaste
Nakiah, Nakea, Nakeah, Nakya, Nakyah,
Nakiya, Nakiyah, Nakeya, Nakeyah,
Nakiaya, Nakiea, Nakeyia

Nala (African / Latin) A successful woman /
of the olive tree
Nalah, Nalla, Nallah, Nalia, Nalea

Nalani (Hawaiian) A calmness of the skies;
heaven's calm
Nalanie, Nalany, Nalaney, Nalany, Nalanee,
Nalaneigh, Nalanea, Nalania, Nalanya,
Nallely

Naliaka (African) A future wife
Naliakah, Nalyaka, Naliacca, Naliacka,
Nalyacka

Nalin (Indian) Resembling the lotus flower
Naline, Naleen, Nalyne, Nalyn, Nalen

Nalini (Sanskrit) A beautiful and lovely
woman
Nalinie, Naliny, Naliney, Nalinee, Nalyni,
Nalynie, Nalynee, Nalinea

Nalo (African) A lovable daughter

Nami (Japanese) Woman of the waves
Namie, Namee, Namy, Namey, Namika, Namiko, Namea

Namid (Native American) A star dancer
Namide, Namyd, Namyde

Namita (Papuan) In mythology, a mother goddess
Namitah, Nameeta, Namyta, Nameetah, Namytah, Nameata, Nameatah

Nana (Hawaiian / English) Born during the spring; a star / a grandmother or one who watches over children

Nancy (English) Form of Ann, meaning "a woman graced with God's favor"
Nainsey, Nainsi, Nance, Nancee, Nancey, Nanci, Nancie, Nancsi, Nanice, Nann, Nanncey, Nanncy, Nannie, Nanny, Nansee, Nansey, Ninacska, Nin, Ninockha, Nancea, Nansea

Nanda (Indian) One who is full of joy
Nandah, Nandia, Nandea

Nandalia (Australian) A fiery woman
Nandaliah, Nandalea, Nandaleah, Nandali, Nandalie, Nandalei, Nandalee, Nandaleigh, Nandaly, Nandaley, Nandalya

Nandini (Hindi) In Hinduism, a divine cow who can grant wishes
Nandinie, Nandiny, Nandiney, Nandinee, Nandinea

Nandita (Indian) A delightful daughter
Nanditah, Nanditia, Nanditea

Nanette (French) Form of Anna, meaning "a woman graced with God's favor"
Nanine, Nannette, Nettie, Netty, Nanetta, Nanete, Naneta, Nanelia, Nanna, Nette, Ninette, Nynette

Nangila (African) Born during travel
Nangilah, Nangyla, Nangeela, Nangylah, Nangeelah

Nani (Greek / Hawaiian) A charming woman / one who is beautiful
Nanie, Nanee, Naney, Nany, Nania, Nanya, Naniya, Nanea, Naniah, Naneah, Naniyah

Nanon (French) Form of Ann, meaning "a woman graced with God's favor"
Nanone, Nanona, Nanonia, Nanonea, Nanonya, Ninon, Ninone, Ninona, Ninonia, Ninonea, Ninonya, Ninan

Naoko (Japanese) An obediant daughter

Naomi (Hebrew / Japanese) One who is pleasant / a beauty above all others
Naoma, Naomia, Naomie, Nayomi, Naomee, Neoma, Neomi, Noami, Noémi, Noémie, Noemi, Noemie, Nohemi, Naomy, Naomey, Naomea

Napua (Hawaiian) Young woman of the flowers

Naqiba (Arabic) A strong leader
Naqeeba, Naqyba, Naqibah, Naqeebah, Naqybah

Nara (English) A contented woman
Narah, Narra, Narrah, Nareen, Nareene, Nareena, Nareane, Nareana

Narcissa (Greek) Resembling a daffodil; self-love; in mythology, a youth who fell in love with his reflection
Narcisa, Narcisse, Narkissa, Narcissah, Narcisah, Narcessa, Narcissus, Narcyssa, Narcysa, Nargis, Nargiss, Nargys, Naryss, Nargisse, Nargysse

Narda (Latin) One who is fragrantly anointed
Nardah, Nardia, Nardea, Nardiya, Nardya

Narella (Greek) A bright woman; intelligent
Narellah, Narela, Narelah, Narelle, Narell, Narele

Nariko (Japanese) A gentle child
Nari

Narmada (Indian) Woman of the river
Narmadah, Narmadia, Narmadea

Nascha (Native American) Resembling an owl

Nascio (Latin) In mythology, goddess of childbirth

Nasha (African) Born during the season of rain
Nashaly, Nashalee, Nashaley, Nashalia, Nashalea, Nashaleigh, Nashalie, Nashali

Nashita (Arabic) A lively woman; one who is energetic
Nashitah, Nashyta, Nasheeta, Nasheata, Nashieta, Nasheita

Nashota (Native American) The second-born of twins
Nashotah, Nashotta, Nashottah

Nashwa (Arabic) One who provides a feeling of ecstasy
Nashwah

Nasiba (Arabic) Feminine form of Nasib; one who is noble
Naseeba, Nasyba, Nasibah, Nasybah, Naseebah, Naseaba, Naseabah

Nasiha (Arabic) One who gives good advice
Naasiha, Nasihah, Naseeha, Naseehah, Nasyha, Nasyhah, Naseaha, Naseahah

Nasima (Arabic) As gentle as a breeze
Naasima, Nasimah, Naseema, Naseemah, Nasyma, Nasymah, Naseama, Naseamah

Nasira (Arabic) One who is victorious; a helper
Naasira, Nasirah, Naseera, Naseerah, Nasyra, Nasyrah, Naseara, Nasearah

Nasnan (Native American) Filled with music
Nasnane, Nasnana, Nasnann, Nasnanne, Nasnanna

Nastasia (Greek) Form of Anastasia, meaning "one who shall rise again"
Nastassia, Nastassija, Nastassja, Nastassiya, Nastassya, Nastasiya, Nastunye, Nastya

Nasya (Hebrew) A miracle child of God
Nasyah, Nasiya, Nasiyah, Nasia, Nasiah, Naysa

Nata (Latin) A strong swimmer

✪ **Natalie** (Latin) Born on Christmas Day;
❶ refers to Christ's birthday
Natala, Natalee, Natalene, Natalia, Natalja, Natalina, Nataline, Nataly, Nataliya, Natalya, Natelie, Nately, Nathalee, Nathalia, Nathalie, Nathaliely, Nathalija, Nathaly, Natilie, Natividad, Nattilie, Nattie, Nettie, Nat, Natuche, Nadalia, Nadalie, Nasia, Natille, Natica, Natalea, Nathalea

Natana (Hebrew) Feminine form of Nathan; a gift from God
Natanuh, Natania, Natanna, Nataniela, Nataniella, Natanielle, Nataniele, Nataniya, Natanya, Natanyah, Nathaniella, Nathanielle, Netanela, Netanella, Netania, Netanya, Nethania, Nathania

Natane (Native American) Her father's daughter
Natanne

Natasha (Russian) Form of Natalie, meaning "born on Christmas Day"
Nastaliya, Nastalya, Natacha, Natascha, Natashenka, Natashia, Natasia, Natosha, Natucha, Natyashenka, Natasa, Nathacha, Nitca

Nathifa (Arabic) One who is pure; clean
Nathifah, Nathipha, Nathiphah, Nathyfa, Nathyfah, Nathypha, Nathyphah, Nadhifa, Nadhyfa, Natifa, Natifah, Natyfa

Natividad (Spanish) Refers to the Nativity
Natividade, Natividada, Natyvydad, Nativydad, Natyvidad

Natsuko (Japanese) Child born during the summer
Natsu, Natsumi

Natura (Spanish) Woman of the outdoors
Naturah, Naturia, Naturea, Nature

Naunet (Egyptian) In mythology, goddess of the watery abyss
Nunet

Nausicaa (Greek) In mythology, a princess who is kind to Odysseus
Nausikaa, Nausica, Nausika

Nautica (English) Woman of the sea
Nautika, Nautia, Nautea, Nautyca, Nautyka

Naveen (Gaelic / Indian) A pleasant, lovely woman / one who is strong-willed
Naveena, Navine, Navyne, Navina, Navyna, Navean, Naveana

Navida (Iranian) Feminine form of Navid; bringer of good news
Navyda, Navidah, Navyda, Naveeda, Naveedah, Naveada, Naveadah

Navya (Indian) One who is youthful
Navyah, Naviya, Nuviyah

Nawal (Arabic) A gift of God
Nawall, Nawalle, Nawala, Nawalla

Nawar (Arabic) Resembling a flower
Nawaar

Nayan (Indian) Having beautiful eyes
Nayana, Nayann, Nayane, Nayanne

Nayeli (Native American) One who loves and is loved
Nayelie, Nayely, Nayeley, Nayeli, Nayelee, Nayeleigh, Nayelea

Nazahah (Arabic) One who is pure and honest
Nazaha, Nazihah, Naziha

Nazakat (Arabic) A delicate woman
Nazaakat

Nazima (Arabic) One who is motherly
Naazima, Nazimah, Nazeema, Nazyma, Nazeama, Naziema, Nazeima

Nazira (Arabic) A spectator
Naazira, Nazirah, Nazyra, Nazeera, Nazeara

Nazneen (Farsi) A charming and beautiful woman
Nazneene, Naznine, Nazyne, Naazneen, Naznin, Naznean, Nazneane

Ndila (African) Resembling a goat
Ndyla, Ndilah, Ndylah

Nea (Swedish) Form of Linnea, meaning "resembling a small mountain flower; of the lime tree"
Neah

Neala (Gaelic) Feminine form of Neal; a champion
Neale, Nealla, Neila, Neile, Neilla, Neille, Neely, Neelie, Nealina, Neilina, Neelle, Neela, Nealie, Neali, Nelia, Nelea, Niall, Niala, Nialla, Niela, Nielsine

Nebraska (Native American) From the flat water land; from the state of Nebraska

Nebula (Latin) Woman of the mists
Nebulah, Nebulla, Nebulia, Nebulea

Nechama (Hebrew) One who provides comfort
Nehama, Nehamah, Nachmanit, Nachuma, Nechamah, Nechamit

Neci (Latin) A passionate woman; one who is fiery
Necia, Necie, Necee, Necy, Necey, Necea

Neda (Slavic) Born on a Sunday
Nedda, Nedah, Nedi, Nedie, Neddi, Neddie, Nedaa

Nediva (Hebrew) A giving and noble woman
Nedivah, Nedeeva, Nedyva, Nedeevah, Nedyvuh, Nedeava, Nedeavah

Nedra (English) Woman of the underground
Nedrah, Neddra, Needra, Needrah

Neeharika (Indian) Of the morning dew
Neharika, Neeharyka, Neharyka

Neeja (Indian) Resembling a water lily
Neejah, Nyja, Neerja, Neerjah, Nyrja, Neaja, Neajah, Nearja

Neelam (Indian) As precious as a sapphire
Nelam, Nylam, Nealam, Neylam

Neema (African) Born into prosperity
Neemah, Neama, Neamah, Neyma, Neymah

Neena (Hindi) A woman who has beautiful eyes
Neenah, Neanah, Neana, Neyna, Neynah

Nefertiti (Egyptian) A queenly woman
Nefertari, Nefertyty, Nefertity, Nefertitie, Nefertitee, Nefertytie, Nefertitea

Negeen (Persian) As precious as a gem
Negeene, Negyne, Negyn, Negine, Negean, Negeane

Neginoth (Hebrew) An accomplished musician
Neginothe, Negynoth, Negynothe, Neginotha, Negynotha

Neha (Indian) One who loves and is loved
Nehah, Nyha, Nyhah

Nehama (Hebrew) One who provides comfort
Nehamah, Nehamma, Nehammah, Nehamia, Nehamea, Nehamiya

Nehanda (African) Our beautiful daughter has come to us
Nehandah, Nehandia, Nehandea, Nehandiya

Nehara (Hebrew) Born of the light
Neharah, Neharra, Nehira, Nehirah, Nehura, Nehurah, Nehora, Nehorah, Nahara, Naharah

Nehelamite (Hebrew) A dreamer
Nehelamitte, Nehelamit, Nehelamyte, Nehelamytte, Nehelamyt

Nehushta (Hebrew) Resembling copper
Nehushtah

Neith (Egyptian) In mythology, goddess of war and hunting
Neitha, Neytha, Neyth, Neit, Neita, Neitia, Neitea, Neithe, Neythe

Nekana (Spanish) Woman of sorrow
Nekane, Nekania, Nekanea

Nekhbet (Egyptian) In mythology, a goddess depicted as a vulture
Nechbet, Nekbet, Nekhebit

Nelly (English) Form of Helen, meaning "the shining light"
Nel, Nelida, Nell, Nella, Nellene, Nellie, Nellwen, Nellwin, Nelle, Nelley, Nelli, Nellee, Nellis, Nelma, Nellwinne, Nellwenne, Nellwyn, Nellwynne, Nelwina, Nelwena, Nellwina, Nellwena, Nelda, Nelleke

Nelsey (English) Form of Kelsey, meaning "from the island of ships; of the ship's victory"
Nellsea, Nellseigh, Nellsey, Nellsie, Nelsea, Nelseigh, Nelsie, Nelsy, Nelsee, Nellsee, Nellsy, Nellsi

Nemera (Hebrew) Resembling a leopard
Nemerah, Nemerra, Nemeria, Nemerea, Nemerya, Nemra

Nemesis (Greek) In mythology, goddess of vengeance
Nemisiss, Nemisys, Nemisyss, Nemysis, Nemysiss, Nemysys, Nemysyss

Neneca (Spanish) Form of Amelia, meaning "one who is industrious and hardworking"
Nenecah, Nenica, Nenneca, Nennica

Neo (African) A gift from God

Neola (Greek) One who is youthful
Neolla, Neolah, Neollah

Neoma (Greek) Born under the new moon
Neomea, Neomenia, Neomia, Neomenea, Neomah, Neona, Neonea, Neonia, Neonah

Nephele (Greek) In mythology, a nymph created from a cloud
Nephelle, Nephel, Nephell, Nephelia, Nephelea

Nephthys (Egyptian) In mythology, one of the nine most important deities; the lady of the house

Neptunine (Latin) Feminine form of Neptune, the god of the sea
Neptuna, Neptunia, Neptunea, Neptunina, Neptuninia, Neptuninea

Nera (Hebrew) Resembling a flickering candle; born during Hannukah
Nerah, Neriya, Nerit

Nerea (Basque) Daughter of mine
Nereah, Neria, Neriah

Nereida (Greek) A sea nymph; in mythology, the Nereids were mermaids
Nereyda, Nerida, Nireida, Nerine, Narine, Nerida, Nerina, Neried, Nerin, Ninfa

Nerio (Latin) In mythology, the wife of the god of war

Nerissa (Italian / Greek) A black-haired beauty / form of Nereida, meaning "a sea nymph"
Narissa, Naryssa, Nericcia, Neryssa, Narice, Nerice, Neris

Nerita (Greek) Woman from the sea
Neritah, Nereeta, Nereetah, Neryta, Nerytah, Nirita, Nireta, Nyrita, Nyreta, Nereata, Nereatah

Nerola (Italian) Resembling the orange flower
Nerolia, Nerolie, Nerolea, Neroli, Neroley, Neroly, Nerolee, Neroleigh

Nerthus (German) In mythology, goddess of fertility
Nerthos, Nerthous

Nerys (Welsh) A daughter born into nobility
Neris, Neriss, Neryss, Nerisse, Nerysse

Nessa (Hebrew / Greek) A miracle child / form of Agnes, meaning "one who is pure; chaste"
Nesha, Nessah, Nessia, Nessya, Nesta, Neta, Netia, Nessie, Nessy, Nessi, Nessey, Nessee, Nest, Nestia, Nesy, Netta, Netah, Nettah, Neysa, Nicsha

Nethinim (Hebrew) Those who are set apart; given
Nethinima, Nethynima, Nethynym, Nethynyma, Nethinimia, Nethinimea

Netis (Native American) One who is trustworthy
Netiss, Netisse, Netys, Netyss, Netysse

Neva (Latin) From the place covered with snow
Nevah, Neve, Nevara, Nevarra, Nevaria, Nevarea, Nieve, Neiva, Nieva, Neive

Nevada (Latin) From the state of Nevada; form of Neva, meaning "from the place covered with snow"

● **Nevaeh** (American) Child from heaven
●

Neveah (Slavic) Resembling a butterfly
Nevea, Neviah, Neviya, Nevia, Neviyah

Nevina (Scottish) Feminine form of Nevin; daughter of a saint
Nevinah, Neveena, Nevyna, Nevinne, Nevynne, Neveene, Neveana, Neveane

Newlyn (Gaelic) Born during the spring
Newlynn, Newlynne, Newlin, Newlinn, Newlinne, Newlen, Newlenn, Newlenne

Neylan (Turkish) The child of our desire
Neylana, Neylanna, Neylann, Neylanne, Neylane

Neziah (Hebrew) One who is pure; a victorious woman
Nezia, Nezea, Nezeah, Neza, Nezah, Neziya, Neziyah

Ngaio (Maori) From the trees; a clever woman

Ngaire (Maori) A yellow-haired woman
Ngare, Ngair, Ngayre, Ngaira, Ngara, Nyree, Nyri, Nyrie, Nyrea, Ngaer, Ngaera

Ngoc (Vietnamese) As precious as jade

Nguyet (Vietnamese) Woman of the moon

Nhi (Vietnamese) Our little one
Nhie, Nhee, Nhea, Nhy, Nhey

Nhung (Vietnamese) Resembling velvet

Nia (Welsh / African) A lustrous woman / one with a purpose
Niah, Nya, Nyah, Niya, Niyah

Niabi (Native American) Resembling a fawn
Niabie, Niabee, Niabey, Niaby, Nyabi, Nyabie, Niabea, Nyabea, Nyaby, Nyabey, Nyabee

Niagara (English) From the famous waterfall
Niagarah, Niagurra, Niagarrah, Nyagara, Nyagarra

Niamh (Irish) A bright woman; in mythology, daughter of the sea god

Nibelung (Norse) In mythology, a follower of Siegfried
Nabelung, Nebelung, Nybelung

Nicanor (Hebrew / Spanish) A conqueror / of the victorious army
Nicanora, Nicanorre, Nicanorra, Nicanore

Nichelle (American) A victorious young woman
Nachell, Nichele, Nishell, Nishelle, Nishele, Nychelle, Nychele, Nyshelle, Nyshele

Nicia (English) Form of Berenice, meaning "one who brings victory"
Niciah, Neecia, Nicija, Nicci, Nicea

● **Nicole** (Greek) Feminine form of Nicholas; of the victorious people
Necole, Niccole, Nichol, Nichole, Nicholle, Nickol, Nickole, Nicol, Nicola, Nikita, Nikki, Nikkole, Nikky, Niko, Nikol, Nikola, Nikole, Nikoleta, Nikoletta, Nikole, Nikolia, Niquole, Niquolle, Nychole, Nycholl, Nykia, Nycole, Nykole, Nykolia, Nyquole, Nyquolle, Nicoletta, Nicolette, Nicoleta, Nicolete, Nickie, Nicki, Nicky, Nickey, Nickee, Nichola, Nicolleta, Nicollet, Nakeeta, Nakita, Nickita, Nikeeta, Niquita, Nikolaevna, Nijole

Nicosia (English) Woman from the capital of Cyprus
Nicosiah, Nicosea, Nicoseah, Nicotia, Nicotea

Nida (Native American / Arabic) An elflike woman
Needah, Nidah, Needa, Nyda, Nydah, Neada, Neadah

Nidia (Spanish) One who is gracious
Nydia, Nidiah, Nydiah, Nidea, Nideah, Nibia, Nibiah, Nibea, Nibeah, Nydia, Nydea, Nybia, Nybea

Nigelia (Arabic) Feminine form of Nigel; a champion
Nigeliah, Nigela, Nigella, Nigelea

Nigesa (African) Daughter of the harvest
Nigessa, Nigese, Nigesse, Nygesa, Nygessa

Nighean (Scottish) A young woman; a maiden
Nighinn, Nigheen

Night (American) Born in the evening; child of the darkness
Nite, Nyt, Nyte, Nyght

Nika (Russian) Form of Veronica, meaning "displaying her true image"
Nyka, Nicka, Nicca, Nica

Nike (Greek) One who brings victory; in mythology, goddess of victory
Nikee, Nikey, Nykee, Nyke

Nikhila (Indian) Feminine form of Nikhil; one who is complete
Nikhilah, Nikhilla, Nykhila, Nykhyla

Nilam (Arabic) Resembling a precious blue stone
Neelam, Nylam, Nilima, Nilyma, Nylyma, Nylima, Nealam, Nealama

Nilda (Italian) Form of Brunhilda, meaning "a dark and noble battlemaiden"
Nilda, Nild, Nilde, Nillda, Nillde, Nilld

Nile (Egyptian) From the Nile river
Nilea, Nilia, Nila, Nyla, Naila

Nilofar (Arabic) Resembling the water lily
Neelofar, Nylofar, Nealofar

Niloufer (Indian) Of the heavens

Nilsine (Scandinavian) Feminine form of Neil; a champion
Nilsina, Nilsyne, Nilsyna, Nylsine, Nylsyna, Nylsina, Nylsyne, Nilsa

Nimah (Arabic) Blessed by God
Ni'mah, Nima, Nymah, Nyma, Nimat, Nymat

Nimeesha (African) A princess; daughter born to royalty
Nimeeshah, Nimiesha, Nimisha, Nimysha, Nymeesha, Nymisha, Nymysha, Nimeasha, Nymeasha

Nina (Spanish / Native American) A little girl / a fiery woman
Ninah, Nyna, Neena, Neenah, Nena, Neneh, Neina, Nenna, Ninacska, Nineta, Ninete, Ninetta, Ninette, Ninnette, Ninon, Ninochka, Ninoska, Ninotchka

Nini (African) As solid as a stone
Ninie, Niny, Niney, Ninee, Ninea

Niobe (Greek) Resembling a fern; in mythology, a weeping queen who turned to stone
Niobee, Niobeh, Nyobe, Nyobee, Niobey, Nyobey, Niobea, Nyobea, Niobi, Nyobi, Niobie, Nyobie

Nipa (Indian) From the brook
Nipah, Nypa, Nypah

Nira (Hebrew) Of the plowed field
Niria, Nirea, Niran, Nirela, Nirit

Nirit (Hebrew) Resembling a flowering plant
Nurit, Nurita, Nureet, Nirita, Nureeta

Nirvana (English) In a state of ultimate bliss
Nirvanah, Nervana, Nirvanna, Nervanna, Nyrvana, Nyrvanna, Narvana, Narvanna

Nisa (Arabic) A lady
Neesaa, Nisaa, Neesa, Neasa

Nisha (Indian) Born at night
Neesha, Niesha, Neisha, Nysha, Neasha

Nishan (African) One who wins awards
Nishann, Nishanne, Nishana, Nishanna, Nyshan, Nyshana

Nishi (Japanese) Woman from the West
Nishie, Nishee, Nishey, Nishy, Nishea

Nishtha (Indian) A woman of faith
Nishthia, Nishthea

Nissa (Scandinavian / Hebrew) A friendly elf / one who tests others
Nisse, Nissah, Nissnana, Nissanit, Nyssa, Nysa, Nysse

Nita (Native American / Spanish / Hebrew) Resembling a bear / God is giving / having grace
Nitah, Neeta, Nyta, Neetah, Nytah, Neata, Neatah

Nitara (Indian) One who is deeply rooted
Nitarah, Nitarra, Nitarrah, Nytara, Nytarra

Nitika (Native American) As precious as a gem
Nitikah, Nityka, Nytika, Nytyka

Nitsa (German) Form of Irene, meaning "a peaceful woman"
Nitsah, Nytsa, Nytsah

Nituna (Native American) My daughter
Nitunah, Nytuna, Nytunah, Nitunna, Nitoona, Nytoona, Nitouna, Nytouna

Nitya (Indian) An eternal beauty
Nithya, Nithyah, Nityah

Nitza (Hebrew) A budding young woman; a blossom
Nitzah, Nitzana, Nitzanna, Nitzaniya, Nytza, Nytzana, Nytzaniya, Nizana

Niu (Chinese) A young girl

Nivedita (Indian) One who is dedicated to helping others
Niveditah, Nivedeeta, Nivedyta, Nyvedita, Nyvedyta, Nivedeata, Nyvedeata

Nixie (German) A beautiful water sprite
Nixi, Nixy, Nixey, Nixee, Nixea

Niyati (Hindi) Realizing one's destiny; fate
Niyatie, Niyatee, Niyatey, Niyaty, Niyatea

Nizhoni (Native American) A beautiful woman
Nizhonie, Nyzhoni, Nyzhonie, Nizhony, Nizhoney, Nizhonea, Nyzhony, Nyzhoney, Nyzhonea, Nizhonee, Nyzhonee

Njemile (African) An upstanding woman
Njemille, Njemyle, Njemylle

Nkechi (African) One who is loyal
Nkechie, Nkechy, Nkechey, Nkechee, Nkechea

Noa (Hebrew) An active woman; movement
Noah, Nowa, Nowah

Nobah (Hebrew) A howling woman
Noba, Nobia, Nobiah, Nobea, Nobeah

Noel (French) Born at Christmastime
Noelle, Noela, Noele, Noeleen, Noelene, Noeline, Noeliz, Noell, Noella, Noelleen, Noelynn, Nowel, Noweleen, Nowell, Noe, Noelia, Nohely

Noelani (Hawaiian) Born of the mist of heaven
Noelanie, Noelany, Noelaney, Noelanee, Nohealani, Nohealanie, Nohealanee, Noelanea, Nohealanea

Nogah (Hebrew) A bright woman; one who is lustrous
Noga

Nokomis (Native American) A daughter of the moon
Nokomiss, Nokomisse, Nokomys, Nokomyss, Nokomysse

Nola (Irish) Form of Finola, meaning "one who is fair; a white-shouldered woman"
Nolah, Nolla, Nollah, Nowla, Nuala, Nualla, Nula, Nulla, Noola, Noolla, Nuallan

Nolan (Irish) A champion of the people
Nollan, Nolana, Noland, Nolanda, Nolen, Nolene, Nolin, Nolynn

Nolcha (Native American) Of the sun
Nolchia, Nolchea

Noma (Hawaiian / African) One who sets an example / a farmer
Nomah, Nomma, Nommah

Nomusa (African) One who is merciful
Nomusah, Nomusha, Nomusia, Nomusea, Nomushia, Nomushea

Nona (Latin) The ninth-born child
Nonah, Noni, Nonie, Nonna, Nonnah, Nonnie, Nonni, Nuna, Nunna

Nora (English) Form of Eleanor, meaning "the shining light"; form of Honora, meaning "having a good name and integrity; an honorable woman"
Norah, Noora, Norella, Norelle, Norissa, Norri, Norrie, Norry, Noreen, Noreena, Norene, Norine, Norena, Norina, Norma, Normina, Normie, Normee, Normi, Neorah, Noirin, Norabel

Norberta (German) Feminine form of Norbert; a bright heroine from the North
Norberte, Norbertha, Norberaht, Norberthe

Nordica (German) Woman from the North
Nordika, Nordicka, Nordyca, Nordyka, Nordycka, Norda, Norell, Norelle, Norella, Norele, Norela

Noriko (Japanese) One who upholds the law
Nori

Normandie (French) Woman from Normandy
Normandi, Normandee, Normandy, Normandey, Normandea

Norna (Scandinavian) In mythology, goddess of fate
Nornah, Norne, Norn

Nortia (Etruscan) In mythology, goddess of chance
Nortiah

Nosiwe (African) Mother of the homeland

Noura (Arabic) Having an inner light
Nureh, Nourah, Nure

Nourbese (Egyptian) A superior woman
Nurbese, Nourbeze, Nurbeze

Nousha (Iranian) A sweet woman; one who is pleasant
Noushah, Noushia, Noushiah, Noushea, Nousheah

Nova (Latin / Native American) New; a bright star / a butterfly chaser
Novah, Novia, Novea, Novelle, Novele, Novella, Novela, Novy, Novey, Novee, Novie, Novi

November (American) Born in the month of November
Novimber, Novymber

Novia (Spanish) A girlfriend
Noviah, Novea, Noveah

Nox (Latin) In mythology, the personification of night
Noxi, Noxia, Noxea, Noxy, Noxey, Noxie, Noxee

Noya (Arabic) One who is beautifully ornamented
Noyah, Noy, Noye

Nozomi (Japanese) One who brings hope to others
Nozomie, Nozomy, Nozomey, Nozomee, Nozomea

Nsia (African) The sixth-born child

Nsonowa (African) The seventh-born child

Nthanan (African) A starlike woman

Nubia (Egyptian) A woman from Nubia; resembling a cloud
Nubea, Nubiah, Nubeah, Nubiane, Nubiann, Nubianna, Nubiana, Nubianne

Nudar (Arabic) The golden daughter
Nudhar, Nudara, Nudaria, Nudarea

Nuha (Arabic) Having great wisdom
Nuhah

Nuka (Native American) The younger daughter
Nukah, Nucka, Nucca

Nunzia (Italian) One who makes announcements; a messenger
Nunziah, Nunzea, Nunzeah, Nunciata, Nuncia, Nuncea, Nunziata, Nunziatina, Nunziateena, Nunziatyna

Nuo (Chinese) A graceful woman

Nura (Arabic) Woman of the light
Noor, Nour, Noura, Nur, Nureen, Nurine, Nuru

Nuray (Turkish) Born under the bright moon
Nuraye, Nurai, Nurae

Nuria (Catalan) Refers to the Virgin Mary
Nuriah, Nurea, Nureah, Nuriya, Nuriyah

Nurin (Arabic) A luminous woman
Nurine, Nurina, Nuryne, Nureen, Nureene, Nuryna, Nureena

Nuru (African) Born during the daylight

Nusa (Hungarian) Woman of grace
Nusah, Nussa, Nussah, Nusi, Nusie, Nusia, Nusea

Nut (Egyptian) In mythology, a goddess of the sky

Nuttah (Native American) Child of my heart
Nutta

Nya (African) A tenacious woman
Nyah

Nyala (African) Resembling an antelope
Nyalah, Nyalla, Nyallah

Nyarai (African) One who is humble
Nyarae, Nyara, Nyaria, Nyarea

Nydia (English) Of the nest
Nydiah

Nyfain (Welsh) A pious woman
Nefyn, Nyfaine, Nyfayne, Nyfayn, Nefayn, Nefain, Nyfaen, Nefaen

Nympha (Greek) In mythology, a beautiful minor deity
Nymph, Nymphe

Nyneve (English) In Arthurian legend, another name for the lady of the lake
Nineve, Niniane, Ninyane, Nyniane, Ninieve, Niniveve

Nyoka (African) A snakelike woman
Nyokah, Nioka, Niokah

Nyura (Ukrainian) A graceful woman
Nyrurah, Nyrurra, Niura, Neura

Nyx (Greek) Born at night; in mythology, the goddess of night
Nyxi, Nyxie, Nyxee, Nyxe, Nyxea

O

Oadira (Arabic) A powerful woman
Oadirah, Oadyra, Oadyrah, Oadeera, Oadeerah, Oadeara, Oadearah

Oaisara (Arabic) A great ruler; an empress
Oaisarah, Oaisarra, Oaisarrah

Oakley (American) From the field of oak trees
Oakly, Oaklee, Oakleigh, Oakli, Oaklie, Oakes, Oake, Oaklea

Oamra (Arabic) Daughter of the moon
Oamrah, Oamira, Oamyra, Oameera

Oanez (Breton) Form of Agnes, meaning "one who is pure; chaste"
Ownah, Ownu, Oaneza, Oanezia, Oanezea

Oba (African) In mythology, the goddess of rivers
Obah, Obba, Obbah

Obala (African) A river goddess
Obalah, Oballa, Oballah, Obalia, Obaliah, Obalea, Obaleah, Obla, Oblah

Obax (African) As delicate and beautiful as a flower
Obaxx, Obaxe, Obaxa, Obaxia, Obaxea

Obedience (American) A well-behaved and complying child
Obeedience, Obediance, Obedienne, Obedianne, Obey, Obeye, Obede, Obedi, Obedie, Obedy, Obedey, Obedee, Obedea

Obelia (Greek) One who acts as a pillar of strength
Obeliah, Obeliya, Obelea, Obelie, Obeli, Obeley, Obely, Obeleah

Obioma (African) A kind and caring woman
Obiomah, Obeoma, Obeomah, Obyoma, Obyomah

Oceana (Greek) Feminine form of Oceanus, father of the rivers; from the ocean
Oceania, Ocean, Oceanea, Oceane

Octavia (Latin) Feminine form of Octavius; the eighth-born child
Octaviana, Octavianne, Octavie, Octiana, Octoviana, Ottavia, Octavi, Octavy, Octavey, Octavee, Octavea

October (American) Born during autumn; born in the month of October
Oktober, Octobar, Oktobar

Ocypete (Greek) In mythology, a Harpy

Oda (German) Wielding a spear of the elves
Odah, Odiana, Odiane, Odianna, Odianne, Odiann, Ordalf, Ordalph

Odahingum (Native American) Of the rippling waters

Odanda (Spanish) From the well-known land
Odandah, Odandia, Odandea, Odande

Oddfrid (Norse) As sharp as the point of a sword
Oddfride, Oddfrida, Oddfreid, Oddfreide, Oddfreida, Odd, Oddfryd, Oddfryda

Oddnaug (Norse) A pointed woman
Oddnauge, Oddnauga, Oddvieg, Oddviege, Oddviega, Oddny, Oddni, Oddney, Oddnie, Oddnee, Oddnea

Oddrun (Scandinavian) Our secret love

Oddveig (Scandinavian) One who wields a spear

Ode (Egyptian / Greek) Traveler of the road / a lyric poem
Odea

Odeda (Hebrew) Having great strength
Odedia, Odedah, Odede

Odele (Greek / German) A sweet melody / one who is wealthy
Odela, Odelet, Odelette, Odelina, Odeline, Odell, Odella, Odelle, Odeletta, Odelyn, Odelyna

Odelia (Hebrew) One who praises God
Oda, Odeelia, Odelinda, Odellia, Odilia, Odelea, Odellea

Odelita (Spanish) One who sings
Odelitah, Odelyta, Odelytah, Odeleeta, Odeleetah, Odeleata, Odeleatah, Odeleta, Odeletah

Odera (Hebrew) One who plows the earth
Oderah, Oderra, Oderrah, Oderia, Oderria, Oderea, Oderrea

Odessa (Greek) Feminine form of Odysseus; one who wanders; an angry woman
Odissa, Odyssa, Odessia, Odissia, Odyssia, Odysseia

Odetta (French) A wealthy woman; one who is prosperous
Odette, Odeta, Odete, Odett

Odharnait (Gaelic) A pale-skinned woman
Omat

Odila (French) Form of Otthild, meaning "one who is prosperous in battle; the fortunate heroine"
Odile, Odilia, Odolia, Odilea, Odola, Odalis, Odalys

Odina (Latin / Scandinavian) From the mountain / feminine form of Odin, the highest of the gods
Odinah, Odeena, Odeene, Odeen, Odyna, Odyne, Odynn, Odeana, Odeane

Odiya (Hebrew) Song of the Lord
Odiyah, Odya, Odyah

Oenone (Greek) In mythology, a nymph who acted as a healer
Oenonie, Oenonee

Ofa (Polynesian) One who loves and is loved
Ofah, Offa, Offah, Opha, Ophah

Ogenya (Hebrew) God provides assistance
Ogenyah, Ogeniya, Ogeniyah

Ogin (Native American) Resembling the wild rose

Ohanna (Armenian) A gift from God
Ohannah, Ohana, Ohanah, Ohanny, Ohanney, Ohanni, Ohannie, Ohannea, Ohannee

Ohara (Japanese) One who meditates
Oharah, Oharra, Oharrah

Ohela (Hebrew) One who lives in a tent
Ohelah

Oheo (Native American) A beautiful woman

Ohio (Native American) Of the good river; from the state of Ohio

Oighrig (Gaelic) A freckled child

Oihane (Spanish) From the woodland
Oihanne, Oihana, Oihanna, Oihann, Oihaine, Oihain, Oihayn, Oihayne, Oihaen, Oihaene

Oilell (Celtic) In mythology, a queen
Oilelle, Oilel, Oilele, Oilella, Oilela

Oira (Latin) One who prays to God
Oyra, Oirah, Oyrah

Oisin (Irish) Resembling a young deer
Oisine, Oisina, Oisinia, Oisinea, Oisinn, Oisinne, Oisinna

Ojal (Indian) A dream or vision
Ojall, Ojale, Ojala, Ojalle, Ojalla

Ojufemi (Egyptian) Loved by the gods
Ojufemie, Ojufemy, Ojufemey, Ojufemee, Olufemi, Olufemie, Olufemee, Olufemy, Olufemey, Ojufemea, Olufemea

Okalani (Hawaiian) Form of Kalani, meaning "from the heavens"
Okalanie, Okalany, Okalaney, Okalanee, Okaloni, Okalonie, Okalonee, Okalony, Okaloney, Okeilana, Okelani, Okelani, Okelanie, Okelany, Okelaney, Okelanee, Okalanea, Okalonea, Okelanea

Okei (Japanese) Woman of the ocean

Oki (Japanese) From the center of the ocean
Okie, Oky, Okey, Okee, Okea

Oklahoma (Native American) Of the red people; from the state of Oklahoma

Okoth (African) Born during rainfall
Okothe, Okotha, Okothia, Okothea, Okothiya

Oksana (Russian) One who gives glory to God
Oksanah, Oksanna, Oksania, Oksanea, Oksaniya, Oksanochka

Ola (Nigerian / Hawaiian / Norse) One who is precious / giver of life; well-being / a relic of one's ancestors
Olah, Olla, Ollah

Olabisi (Egyptian) One who brings joy to others
Olabisie, Olabisy, Olabisey, Olabisee, Olabisea

Olaide (American) A thoughtful woman
Olaid, Olaida, Olayd, Olayde, Olayda, Olaed, Olaede, Olaeda

Olathe (Native American) A lovely young woman

Olaug (Scandinavian) A loyal woman

Olayinka (Yoruban) Surrounded by wealth and honor
Olayenka, Olayanka

Oldriska (Czech) A noble ruler
Oldryska, Oldri, Oldrie, Oldry, Oldrey, Oldree, Oldrea

Oldwin (English) A special and beloved friend
Oldwinn, Oldwinne, Oldwina, Oldwinna, Oldwyn, Oldwynn, Oldwynne, Oldwyna, Oldwynna, Oldwen, Oldwenn, Oldwenne, Oldwenna

Oleda (English) Resembling a winged creature
Oldedah, Oleta, Olita, Olida, Oletah, Olitah, Olidah

Oleia (Greek) One who is smooth

Oleisa (Greek) Form of Elizabeth, meaning "my God is bountiful"
Oleisia, Oleisah, Oleisia, Oleesa, Oleasa, Oleysa

Olena (Russian) Form of Helen, meaning "the shining light"
Olenah, Olenia, Olenya, Olinija, Olinia

Olesia (Polish) Form of Alexandra, meaning "helper and defender of mankind"
Olesiah, Olexa, Olexia, Olexea, Olex

Olethea (Latin) Form of Alethea, meaning "one who is truthful"
Oletheia, Olethia, Oletha, Oletea, Olthaia, Olithea, Olathea, Oletia, Olithia, Olthaea, Oleta

Olga (Scandinavian) One who is blessed and successful
Olgah, Olenka, Olia, Oliah, Olya

Oliana (Hawaiian) Resembling the oleander
Olianah, Olianna, Oleana, Oleanna, Oliane, Oliann, Oleane, Oleann, Oleanne

Olidie (Spanish) Surrounded by light
Olidi, Olidy, Olidey, Olidee, Olidea, Olydie, Olydi, Olydie, Olydy, Olydey, Olydee, Olydea

Olina (Hawaiian) One who is joyous
Oline, Oleen, Oleene, Olyne, Oleena, Olyna, Olin

Olinda (German) Resembling a wild fig; a protector of the land
Olindah, Olynda, Olynda, Olenda, Olendah

Olisa (Native American) Devoted to God
Olisah, Olissa, Olissah, Olysa, Olyssa

Olivia (Latin) Feminine form of Oliver; of the olive tree; one who is peaceful
Oliviah, Oliva, Olive, Oliveea, Olivet, Olivetta, Olivette, Olivija, Olivine, Olivya, Ollie, Olva, Olia, Oliff, Oliffe, Olivie, Olivi, Olivey, Olivee, Olivy, Oliveria, Oleta, Olida, Oilbhe

Olubayo (African) A dazzling woman
Olubaya, Oloubayo, Oloubaya

Olvyen (Welsh) Form of Olwen, meaning "one who leaves a white footprint"
Olvyin

Olwen (Welsh) One who leaves a white footprint
Olwenn, Olwin, Olwyn, Olwynne, Olwynn, Olwenne, Olwinn, Olwinne, Olwena, Olwenna, Olwina, Olwinna, Olwyna, Olwynna

Olympia (Greek) From Mount Olympus; a goddess
Olympiah, Olimpe, Olimpia, Olimpiada, Olimpiana, Olypme, Olympie, Olympi, Olympy, Olympey, Olimpi, Olimpie, Olympas

Oma (Arabic) A great leader; one who is commanding
Omma

Omah (Hebrew) From the cedar tree
Omette, Omett, Omete, Ometta, Ometa, Ornetta, Ornette

Omana (Indian) A lovely woman
Omanah, Omanna, Omannah

Omanie (American) An exuberant woman
Omani, Omany, Omaney, Omanee, Omanea

Omayra (Latin / Spanish) Having a pleasant fragrance / one who is dearly loved
Omayrah, Omaira, Omairah, Omaera, Omaerah

Omega (Greek) The last great one; the last letter of the Greek alphabet
Omegah, Omegia, Omegiah

Omemee (Native American) Resembling a dove
Omemea, Omemi, Omemie, Omemey, Omemy

Omesha (American) A spendid woman
Omeshah, Omeesha, Omeeshah, Omeashu, Omeashah, Omeisha, Omeishah, Omiesha, Omieshah, Omysha, Omyshah

Omie (Italian) A homebody
Omi, Omee, Omea, Omy, Omey

Ominotago (Native American) Having a beautiful voice

Omolara (African) A welcomed daughter
Omolarah, Omolarra, Omolarrah

Omorose (Egyptian) One who is beautiful
Omorosa, Omorosia, Omorosie, Omorosi, Omorosee, Omorosea, Omorosey, Omorosy

Omphale (Greek) In mythology, a queen of Lydia
Omphaile, Omphayle, Omfale, Omfaile, Omfayle, Omphael, Omphaele, Omphaela

Omri (Arabic) A red-haired woman
Omrie, Omree, Omrea, Omry, Omrey

Omusa (African) One who is adored
Omusah, Omousa, Omousah

Omusupe (African) One who is precious
Omusuppe, Omusepe, Omuseppe

Omyra (English) Form of Myra, meaning "resembling the fragrant oil"
Omeira, Omira, Omeera, Omiera, Omeara, Omera

Ona (Hebrew) Filled with grace
Onit, Onat, Onah

Onaedo (African) The golden child
Onaydo, Onaido

Onaona (Hawaiian) Having a sweet fragrance
Onanonah

Onatah (Native American) Daughter of the earth
Onata, Onatia, Onatiah, Onatea, Onateah

Onawa (Native American) One who is wide-awake
Onawah

Ondine (Latin) Resembling a small wave
Ondina, Ondyne, Ondinia, Ondyna

Ondrea (Slavic) Form of Andrea, meaning "courageous and strong / womanly"
Ondria, Ondrianna, Ondreia, Ondreina, Ondreya, Ondriana, Ondreana, Ondera, Ondraia, Ondreja, Ondrya, Ondris, Ondrette, Oindrea, Onda, Ondee, Ondena, Ondere, Ondra, Ondralyn, Ondi, Ondie, Ondranetta, Ondraya, Ondreanna, Ondree, Ondreah, Ondras, Ondrena, Ondrienne, Ondrianne, Ondrina, Ondren, Ondrya, Onndrea, Onndria, Odra

Oneida (Native American) Our long-awaited daughter
Onieda, Oneyda, Onida, Onyda

Onella (Greek) Lady of light
Onela, Onellia, Onellea, Onelia, Onelea

Onesha (American) A patient woman
Oneshah, Oneisha, Oneishah, Oniesha, Onieshah, Oneesha, Oneeshah, Oneasha, Oneashah, Onysha, Onyshah, Oneshia, Oneshiah, Oneshea, Onesheah

Onesiphorus (Hebrew) One who brings in profit

Ongela (English) Form of Angela, meaning "a heavenly messenger; an angel"
Ongelica, Ongelina, Ongelique, Onjela, Onjelika, Ongella, Ongelita, Ongeline, Ongelyn, Ongelene, Ongelin, Ongelia, Onge, Onga, Ongel, Ongele, Ongelee, Ongelena, Ongeles, Ongeletta, Ongelette, Ongeli, Ongelika, Ongeliki, Ongilia, Ongelisa, Ongelita, Ongell, Ongelle, Ongelynn, Ongie, Ongyalka, Onielka, Onjelica, Onjelita, Onnjel, Onjella

Oni (Native American) Born on sacred ground
Onie, Ony, Oney, Onee, Onea

Onia (Latin) Our one and only
Oniah, Onya, Onyah, Oniya, Oniyah

Onida (Native American) The one who has been expected
Onidah, Onyda, Onydah

Onora (Irish) Form of Honora, meaning "having a good name and integrity; an honorable woman"
Onour, Onoria, Onor, Onorata, Onoratas, Onnor, Onorina, Onorine, Onore, Onoree, Onori, Onorie, Onory, Onouri, Onourie, Onoury, Onoura, Onouria, Onoure, Ohnicio, Omora, Omorra

Ontibile (African) Protected by God
Ontibyle, Ontybile, Ontybyle

Ontina (American) An open-minded woman
Ontinah, Onteena, Ontcenah, Onteanu, Onteanah, Ontiena, Ontienah, Onteina, Onteinah, Ontyna, Ontynah

Onyx (Latin) As precious as the stone
Onix, Onyks, Oniks, Onycks, Onicks

Oona (Gaelic) Form of Agnes, meaning "one who is pure; chaste"
Oonaugh, Oonagh, Oonah, Ouna, Ounah, Ounagh, Ounaugh

Oota dabun (Native American) Born beneath the daystar

Opa (Native American) As wise as an owl
Opah, Oppa, Oppah

Opal (Sanskrit) A treasured jewel; resembling the iridescent gemstone
Opall, Opalle, Opale, Opalla, Opala, Opalina, Opaline, Opaleena, Opaleene, Opalyna, Opalyne, Opel

Ophel (Hebrew) From the temple hill
Ophela, Ophie, Ophi, Ophy, Ophey, Ophee, Ophea

Ophelia (Greek) One who offers help to others
Ofelia, Ofilia, Ophélie, Ophelya, Ophilia, Ovalia, Ovelia, Opheliah, Ofeliah, Ophelie

Ophira (Hebrew) Feminine form of Ophir; from a place of wealth; golden
Ophirah, Opheera, Ophyra, Ophiera, Opheira, Ofira, Ofeera, Ofeira, Ofiera, Ofyra, Opheura, Ofeara

Ophrah (Hebrew) Resembling a fawn; from the place of dust
Ofra, Ofrit, Ophra, Oprah, Orpa, Orpah, Ofrat, Ofrah

Opportina (Latin) One who seizes opportunity
Oportina, Opportyna, Oportyna, Opporteena, Oporteena, Opporteana, Oporteana, Opportine, Opportyne, Opporteen, Opportean

Ops (Latin) In mythology, the goddess of harvests

Ora (Latin) One who prays to God
Orah, Orra, Orrah, Orit, Orya

Oralee (Hebrew) The Lord is my light
Oralie, Orali, Oraleigh, Oraly, Oraley, Oralit, Orlee, Orli, Orlie, Orly, Orley, Orleigh, Oralea, Orlea

Oraleyda (Spanish) Born with the light of dawn
Oraleydah, Oraleida, Oraleidah, Oralida, Oralidah, Oralyda, Oralydah, Oraleda, Oraledah, Oralieda, Oraliedah

Oralia (Latin) Form of Aurelia, meaning "golden-haired woman"
Orelia, Oraliah, Oriel, Orielle, Oriell, Oriele, Oriella, Oriela, Orlena, Orlene, Orielda, Orial, Oriall, Orialle, Oriala, Orialla

Orane (French) Born at sunrise
Oraine, Orayne, Oriane, Orania, Oraen, Oraene

Orange (Latin) Resembling the sweet fruit
Orangetta, Orangia, Orangina, Orangea

Orbelina (American) One who brings excitement
Orbelinah, Orbeleena, Orbeleenah, Orbeleana, Orbeleanah, Orbelyna, Orbelynah, Orbie, Orbi, Orby, Orbey, Orbee, Orbea

Orbona (Latin) In mythology, goddess who provided children to those without
Orbonah, Orbonna, Orbonnah

Ordell (Latin) Of the beginning
Ordelle, Ordele, Ordel, Ordella, Ordela, Orde

Orea (Greek) From the mountains
Oreah

Oreille (Latin) A golden woman
Oreile, Oreill, Oreilla, Oreila

Orela (Latin) Announcement from the gods
Orelah, Orella, Orellah, Orila, Orilla, Orelda, Oracle, Oracula

Orenda (Iroquois) A woman with magical powers

Orene (French) A nurturing woman
Oreene, Oreen, Oreane, Orean, Orena, Oreena, Oreana

Orfea (Greek) Feminine form of Orpheus; having a beautiful voice
Orfeah, Orfeya, Orfia, Orphea, Orpheya, Orphia

Orfelinda (Spanish) Having the beauty of the dawn
Orfelynda, Orphelinda, Orphelynda, Orfelenda, Orphelenda

Orguelleuse (English) One who is arrogant

Oria (Latin) Woman from the Orient
Oriah, Orien, Orienne, Oriena, Orienna

Oriana (Latin) Born at sunrise
Oreana, Orianna, Oriane, Oriann, Orianne

Oribel (Latin) A beautiful golden child
Orabel, Orabelle, Orabell, Orabela, Orabella, Oribell, Oribelle, Oribele, Oribela, Oribella, Orinda, Orynda

Orin (Irish) A dark-haired beauty
Orine, Orina, Oryna, Oryn, Oryne

Orino (Japanese) One who works outside the home
Oryno, Oreno

Orinthia (Hebrew / Gaelic) Of the pine tree / a fair lady
Orrinthia, Orenthia, Orna, Ornina, Orinthea, Orenthea, Orynthia, Orynthea

Oriole (Latin) Resembling the gold-speckled bird
Oreolle, Oriolle, Oreole, Oriola, Oriolla, Oriol, Oreola, Oreolla

Orion (Greek) The huntress; a constellation

Oritha (Greek) One who is motherly
Orithe, Orith, Orytha, Oryth, Orythe, Orithia, Orithea, Orythia, Orythea

Orithna (Greek) One who is natural
Orithne, Orythna, Orythne, Orithnia, Orythnia, Orithnea, Orythnea, Orithniya, Orythniya

Orla (Gaelic) The golden queen
Orlah, Orrla, Orrlah, Orlagh, Orlaith, Orlaithe, Orghlaith, Orghlaithe

Orlain (French) One who is famous
Orlaine, Orlaina, Orlaen, Orlaene, Orlaena, Orlayn, Orlayne, Orlayna

Orlanda (Latin) Feminine form of Orlando; from the renowned land
Orlandia, Orlandea, Orlantha, Orlande, Orlanthe, Orlanthia, Orlanthea

Orlenda (Russian) Resembling an eagle
Orlinda, Orlynda

Orlina (French) The golden child
*Orlinah, Orlyna, Orlynah, Orlean, Orleane,
Orleana, Orleans, Orleene, Orleena*

Orma (African) An independent woman;
one who is free
Ormah

Ormanda (German) Woman of the sea
*Ormandy, Ormandey, Ormadee, Ormandi,
Ormandie, Ormandea*

Orna (Irish / Hebrew) One who is pale-
skinned / of the cedar tree
*Ornah, Ornette, Ornetta, Ornete, Orneta,
Obharnait, Ornat*

Ornella (Italian) Of the flowering ash tree
Ornelle, Ornell, Ornela, Ornele, Ornel

Ornice (Irish) A pale-skinned woman
*Ornyce, Ornise, Orynse, Orneice, Orneise,
Orniece, Orniese, Orneece, Orneese, Orneace,
Ornease*

Orphne (Greek) In mythology, a nymph
and mother of Ascalaphus
*Orphnie, Orphny, Orphney, Orphnee,
Orphnea*

Orquidea (Spanish) Resembling the orchid
*Orquideah, Orquidia, Orquida, Orquidana,
Orquidiya*

Orsa (Latin) Form of Ursula, meaning
"resembling a little bear"
*Orsah, Orsalina, Orsaline, Orsel, Orselina,
Orseline, Orsola, Orssa*

Orszebet (Hungarian) Form of Elizabeth,
meaning "my God is bountiful"
*Orsebet, Orszebeth, Orsebeth, Orzebet,
Orzebeth, Orzsebet, Orzsebeth*

Ortensia (Latin) From the garden
*Ortensiah, Ortensea, Ortenseah, Ortense,
Ortenze, Ortenzia, Ortenzea, Ortensiana,
Ortensie, Ortensi, Ortensy, Ortensey, Ortensee,
Ortenzi, Ortenzie, Ortenzee*

Orthia (Greek) One who takes the straight
path
Orthiah, Orthea, Ortheah, Orthiya, Orthiyah

Ortruda (Teutonic) Resembling a serpent
*Ortrud, Ortrude, Ortrouda, Ortroude,
Ortroud*

Ortygia (Greek) In mythology, an island
where Artemis and Apollo were born
Ortegia, Ortigia

Orva (Anglo-Saxon / French) A courageous
friend / as precious as gold
Orvah

Orynko (Ukrainian) A peaceful woman
Orinko, Orynka, Orinka

Orzora (Hebrew) Having the strength of
God
*Orzorah, Orzorra, Orzorrah, Orzoria,
Orzorea*

Osaka (Japanese) From the city of industry
*Osaki, Osakie, Osakee, Osaky, Osakey,
Osakea*

Osanna (English) Form of Hosanna, mean-
ing "raising one's voice in praise of God"
*Osannah, Osann, Osane, Osanne, Osana,
Osanah*

Osarma (American) One who is sleek
Osarmah

Osberga (Anglo-Saxon) A queenly woman
Osburga, Ozberga, Ozburga

Oseye (Egyptian) One who is filled with
happiness

Osithe (Italian) Woman from Italy
Osith, Osyth, Osythe, Ositha, Osytha

Osma (English) Feminine form of Osmond;
protected by God
Osmah, Ozma, Ozmah

Ostia (Italian) From the ancient city
Ostiah, Ostea, Osteah, Ostiya, Ostiyah

Osyka (Native American) One who is eagle-
eyed
Osykah, Osika, Osikah, Oseka, Osekah

Otamisia (Greek) The perfect one
Otameesia, Ottamisia, Ottmeesia

Otha (Anglo-Saxon) The little rich child
*Othili, Othilie, Othily, Othiley, Othilee,
Othia, Othea, Othilea, Othileigh*

Otina (American) A fortunate woman
Otinah, Otyna, Otynah, Oteena, Oteenah,
Oteana, Oteanah, Otiena, Otienah, Oteina,
Oteinah

Otrera (Greek) In mythology, the mother of
the Amazons
Otreria, Otrerea, Otrere

Otthild (German) One who is prosperous in
battle; the fortunate heroine
Otthilda, Ottila, Ottilia, Ottalia, Ottilie,
Ottolie, Ottiline, Ottoline, Otthilde, Otylia,
Ottillia, Otilie, Otka

Otzara (Hebrew) Possessing great wealth
and treasure
Otzarah, Otzarra, Otzarrah, Ozara, Ozarra

Oudsiyya (Arabic) One who is pious
Oudsiya, Oudsiyyah, Oudsiyah

Ouida (English) Form of Louise, meaning
"a famous warrior"

Ourania (Greek) A heavenly woman
Ouraniah, Ouranea, Ouraneah, Ouraniya,
Ouraniyah

Ova (Latin) Giver of life; egg
Ovah, Ovia, Ovea, Ove

Overton (English) From the upper side of
town
Overtown

Ovida (Hebrew) One who worships God
Ovidah, Ovyda, Ovydah, Oveda, Ovedah,
Ovieda, Oviedah, Oveida, Oveidah, Oveeda,
Oveedah, Oveada, Oveadah

Ovyena (Spanish) One who helps others
Ovyenah, Oviena, Ovienah, Oviyena,
Oviyenah

Owena (Welsh) A highborn woman
Owenah, Owenna, Owennah, Owenia,
Owenea

Oya (Native American) One who has been
called for
Oyah

Oyama (African) One who has been called
Oyamah, Oyamma, Oyammah, Oyamia,
Oyamea, Oyamiah, Oyameah

Oz (Hebrew) Having great strength
Oza, Ozia, Ozz, Ozzi, Ozzie, Ozzy, Ozzey,
Ozzee, Ozzea

Ozera (Hebrew) Woman of merit
Ozerah, Ozerru, Ozerrah, Ozeria, Ozeriah,
Ozerea, Ozereah

Ozioma (American) Having strength of
character
Oziomah, Ozeoma, Ozeomah, Ozyoma,
Ozyomah

Ozora (Hebrew) One who is wealthy
Ozorah, Ozorra, Ozorrah

Paavna (Hindi) One who is pure; chaste
Pavna, Paavnah, Pavnah, Paavani, Pavani,
Pavany, Pavaney, Pavanie, Pavanee, Pavanea

Pabiola (Spanish) A little girl
Pabiolla, Pabiolah, Pabiollah, Pabyola,
Pabeola, Pabeolla, Pabyolla

Paca (Spanish) One who is free

Pace (American) A charismatic young woman
Paice, Payce, Paece, Pase, Paise, Payse, Paese

Pacifica (Spanish) A peaceful woman
Pacifika, Pacyfyca, Pacyfyka, Pacifyca,
Pacifyka, Pacyfica, Pacyfika

Packard (German) From the brook; a
peddler's pack
Packarde, Pakard, Pakarde, Pacard, Pacarde

Pacquita (Latin) One who is unbounded;
free; independent
Pacquitah, Pacquyta, Pacqueta, Paquita,
Paqueta, Pakita, Packita

Padgett (French) One who strives to better
herself
Padget, Padgette, Padgete, Padgeta, Padgetta,
Padge

Padma (Hindi) Resembling the lotus
flower; in Hinduism, another name for the
goddess Lakshmi
Padmah, Padmia, Padmini, Padminia,
Padmea, Padminea

Pageant (American) A dramatic woman
Pagent, Padgeant, Padgent

Pahana (Native American) A lost white-skinned sibling
Pahanah, Pahanna, Pahann, Pahanne, Pahane, Pahan

❂ **Paige** (English) A young assistant
Page, Payge, Paege

Paisley (English) Woman of the church
Paisly, Paisli, Paislie, Paislee, Paysley, Paysly, Paysli, Payslie, Payslee, Pasley, Pasly, Pasli, Paslie, Paslee, Paizley, Payzley, Pazley, Paislea, Paizlea, Paslea, Payslea

Paiva (Finnish) Born during daylight
Paeva, Payva

Paka (African) A catlike woman
Pakah, Pakka, Packa, Pacca

Paki (African) A witness of God
Pakki, Packi, Pacci, Pakie, Pakkie, Paky, Pakky, Pakey, Pakkey, Pakee, Pakkee, Pakea, Pakkea

Pakuna (Native American) Resembling a deer running through the hills
Pakunah, Pukvuna, Packuna, Pacuna, Pakouna, Pacouna

Pakwa (Native American) Resembling a frog
Pakwah

Pala (Native American) Woman of the water
Palah

Palakika (Hawaiian) One who is dearly loved
Palakyka, Palakeka, Palakeeka, Palakieka, Pulakeika, Palakeaka

Palani (Hawaiian) An independent woman
Pallani, Palanie, Palany, Palaney, Palanee, Pallanee, Palanea, Pallanea, Pallanie, Pallany, Pallaney

Palba (Spanish) A fair-haired woman

Palemon (Spanish) A kindhearted woman
Palemond, Palemona, Palemonda

Pales (Latin) In mythology, goddess of shepherds and flocks
Paless, Palesse, Palus, Palles, Pallus

Palesa (African) Resembling a flower
Palessa, Palesah, Palysa, Palisa, Paleesa

Palila (Hawaiian) A birdlike woman
Palilla, Palilah, Pallila, Pallilla, Palyla, Palylla

Paliuli (Polynesian) Woman from the paradise garden
Paliulie, Paliuly, Paliuley, Paliulee, Paliulea

Pallas (Greek) Full of wisdom and understanding; a maiden; in mythology, a friend of Athena
Palla

Pallavi (Indian) Resembling new leaves
Palavi, Pallavie, Palavie, Pallavy, Palavy, Pallavey, Palavey, Pullavee, Palavee, Pallavea, Palavea

Palmira (Spanish / Latin) Feminine form of Palmiro; a pilgrim / from the city of palm trees
Palmyra, Palmera, Palmeira, Palmiera, Palmer, Palmyr, Palma, Pameera, Palmeara

Paloma (Spanish) Dovelike
Palomah, Palloma, Palomina, Palomyna, Palomeena, Poloma, Palomeana, Palomeina, Palomiena

Palti (Hebrew) My escape; deliverance
Paltie, Palty, Paltee, Paltey, Paltea

Pamba (African) In mythology, the mother of the people

Pamela (English) A woman who is as sweet as honey
Pamelah, Pamella, Pammeli, Pammelie, Pameli, Pamelie, Pamelia, Pamelea, Pamelee, Pameleigh, Pamelina, Pameleena, Pamelyna

Pamuy (Native American) Born during the water moon

Pana (Native American) Resembling a partridge
Panah

Panagiota (Greek) Feminine form of Panagiotis; a holy woman

Panchali (Indian) A princess; a highborn woman
Panchalie, Panchaly, Panchalli, Panchaley, Panchalee, Panchalea, Panchaleigh

Panda (English) Resembling the bamboo-eating animal
Pandah

Pandara (Indian) A good wife
Pandarah, Pandarra, Pandaria, Pandarea

Pandia (Greek) In mythology, the personification of brightness
Pandiah, Pandea, Pandiya, Pandya, Pandeah, Pandiyah, Pandyah

Pandita (Indian) A studious woman
Panditah, Pandyta, Pandeta, Pandeyta, Pandeeta, Pandeata

Pandora (Greek) A gifted, talented woman; in mythology, the first mortal woman, who unleashed evil upon the world
Pandorah, Pandorra, Pandoria, Pandorea, Pandoriya

Pang (Chinese) One who is innovative

Pangiota (Greek) One who is sacred
Pangyota, Pangeota

Pani (Polynesian) In mythology, goddess of plants and fertility
Panni, Panie, Pany, Paney, Pannie, Panee, Panea

Paniz (Persian) A girl who is as sweet as sugar
Panize, Panyz, Panez, Panizia, Panizea

Pankita (Indian) A young girl; one who is liberal
Pankitah, Pankyta, Panketa, Pankeeta, Pankieta, Pankeita, Pankeata

Panna (Hindi) Resembling an emerald
Pannah

Panola (Greek) One who is all-knowing
Panolah, Panolla, Panollah, Panolia, Panoliah, Panolea, Panoleah, Panoliya, Panoliyah

Panphila (Greek) Daughter who is loved by all
Panphilah, Panphilla, Panfila, Panfilah, Panfilla

Pansy (English) As delicate as a flower; a thoughtful girl
Pansey, Pansi, Pansie, Pansee, Panzi, Panzy, Panzie, Panzee, Pansea, Panzea

Panthea (Greek) Of the gods and goddesses
Pantheah, Panthia, Panthiya, Pantheia, Panthya

Panther (American) Resembling the wild animal
Panthar, Panthur, Panthir, Panthyr

Pantxike (Latin) A woman who is free
Pantxikey, Pantxikye, Pantxeke, Pantxyke

Panya (Slavic / Latin) An enthroned woman; crowned with laurel / a small child; mousy
Panyah, Panyin, Panyen

Papina (Native American) Resembling ivy
Papinah, Papyna, Papena, Papeena, Papiena, Papeina, Papeana

Papina (African) Of the vine
Papyna, Papeena, Papiena, Papeina, Papeana

Paprika (English) Resembling the spice; a lively woman
Paprikah, Papryka, Papreka, Papricka, Paprycka, Paprecka, Papreeka, Papreaka, Papreika, Paprieka

Para (Finnish) In mythology, household spirits

Paraaha (Russian) Born on Good Friday
Paraha, Parashy, Parashie, Parashi, Parashey, Parashee, Parashea

Paradise (English) From the perfect place
Paradice, Paradyse, Paradyce

Paras (Indian) A woman against whom others are measured

Parcae (Latin) In mythology, a name that refers to the Fates
Parca, Parcia, Parcee, Parsae, Parsee, Parsia, Parcea

Pari (Persian) A fairylike young girl
Parie, Pary, Parey, Paree, Parisa, Parihan, Parehan, Paryhan, Parea

⊙ Paris (English) Woman of the city in France
Pariss, Parisse, Parys, Paryss, Parysse

Park (Chinese) Of the cypress tree
Parke, Parka

Parker (English) The keeper of the park

Parley (English) One who negotiates
Parly, Parli, Parlie, Parlee, Parleigh, Parlea

Parmida (Persian) Daughter born to royalty
Parmidah, Parmyda, Parmeda, Parmeeda, Parmita, Parmyta, Parmeta, Parmeeta, Parmeada, Parmeata

Parminder (Hindi) An attractive lady
Parmender, Parmynder, Parmindar, Parmendar, Parmyndar

Parnika (Indian) A successful woman
Parnikah, Parnikka, Parnicka, Parnyka, Parneka, Parnita, Parneta, Parnyta

Parrish (Latin) Woman of the church
Parish, Parrishe, Parishe, Parrysh, Parysh, Paryshe

Parry (Welsh) Daughter of Harry
Parri, Parrie, Purrey, Parree, Parrea

Parsley (American) Resembling the garnish
Parslee, Parsleigh, Parsly, Parsli, Parslie, Parslea

Parson (English) A member of the clergy
Parsan, Parsun, Parsin, Parsyn

Parthenia (Greek) One who is chaste; a virgin
Parthenie, Parthenea, Partheniya, Partheniah, Partheni, Partheny, Partheney, Parthenee, Parthenea

Parthenope (Greek) In mythology, a siren

Parvaneh (Persian) Resembling a butterfly
Parveneh, Parvane, Parvene

Parvani (Indian) Born during a full moon
Parvanie, Parvany, Parvaney, Parvanee, Parvanea

Parvati (Hindi) Daughter of the mountain; in Hinduism, a name for the wife of Shiva
Parvatie, Parvaty, Parvatey, Parvatee, Pauravi, Parvatea, Pauravie, Pauravy, Pauravee, Pauravea

Parvin (Persian) Cluster of stars in the constellation Taurus
Parvine, Parveen, Parveene, Parvyn, Parvynne, Parvean, Parveane

Pascale (French) Feminine form of Pascal; born on Easter
Pascaleh, Pascala, Pascaline, Pasclina, Pascalla, Pascalia, Pascha

Pascasia (French) Born on Easter
Paschasia, Pasua

Paschel (African) A spiritual woman
Paschell, Paschele, Paschelle, Paschela, Paschella

Pash (French) A clever woman
Pashe, Pasch, Pasche

Pasha (Greek) Woman of the sea
Pashah, Passha, Passhah

Pasiphae (Greek) In mythology, the wife of Minos and mother of the Minotaur
Pasiphay, Pasiphai

Pasithea (Greek) In mythology, the oldest of the Graces
Pasitheah, Pasithia, Pasithiya, Pasithee, Pasithi, Pasithie

Passion (American) A sensual woman
Pashon, Pashun, Pasyun, Passyun

Pastora (Spanish) A shepherdess
Pastore, Pastoria, Pastorea, Pastoriya

Paterekia (Hawaiian) An upper-class woman
Paterekea, Pakelekia, Pakelekea

Pati (African) One who fishes
Patie, Paty, Patey, Patee, Patea

Patia (Latin) An open-minded woman

Patia (Greek) One who is intellectually superior

Patience (English) One who is patient; an enduring woman
Patiencia, Paciencia, Pacencia, Pacyncia, Pacincia, Pacienca

Patrice (French) Form of Patricia, meaning "of noble descent"
Patriece, Patreece, Patreace, Patreice, Patryce

Patricia (English) Feminine form of Patrick; of noble descent
Patrisha, Patrycia, Patrisia, Patsy, Patti, Patty, Patrizia, Pattie, Padraigin, Pat

Patrina (American) Born into the nobility
Patreena, Patriena, Patreina, Patryna, Patreana

Paula (English) Feminine form of Paul; a petite woman
Paulina, Pauline, Paulette, Paola, Pauleta, Pauletta, Pauli, Paulete, Pabla, Paulita, Pavlina, Pavleena, Pavlyna, Pavliena, Pavla

Pausha (Hindi) Resembling the moon
Paushah

Pavan (Indian / Latin) Resembling a fresh breeze / a dancer of the court
Pavane, Pavania, Pavana, Pavanea

Pavati (Native American) From the clear waters
Pavatie, Pavaty, Pavatey, Pavatee, Pavatea

Pax (Latin) One who is peaceful; in mythology, the goddess of peace
Paxi, Paxie, Paxton, Paxten, Paxtan, Paxy, Paxey, Paxee, Paxea

❂ **Payton** (English) From the warrior's village
Paton, Paeton, Paiton, Payten, Paiten

Paz (Arabic) The golden one
Paza, Pazia, Pazice, Pazit, Pazz, Pazzy, Pazzi, Pazzie, Pazzee, Pazzea, Pazzey

Peace (American) A harmonious woman

Peaches (American) As sweet as the fruit
Peeches, Peachy, Peachey, Peachee, Peachea, Peachi, Peachie

Peakalika (Hawaiian) Filled with happiness

Pearl (Latin) A precious gem of the sea
Pearla, Pearle, Pearlie, Pearly, Pearline, Pearlina, Pearli, Pearley, Pearlee, Pearlea, Pearleigh, Pearleah

Pebbles (American) Resembling a small rock

Pecola (American) A brazen woman
Pecolah, Pekola, Pekolah

Pedzi (American) A golden woman
Pedzie, Pedzy, Pedzey, Pedzee, Pedzea

Peggy (English) Form of Margaret, meaning "resembling a pearl / the child of light"
Peggi, Peggie, Pegeen, Peg, Peigi, Peggee, Peggea, Peggey

Pegma (Greek) Filled with happiness
Pegmah, Pegmia, Pegmiah, Pegmea, Pegmeah

Peke (Hawaiian) A giving woman

Pela (Polish) Woman of the sea
Pelah, Pella, Pellah

Pelagia (Greek) Feminine form of Pelagius; woman of the sea
Pelagiah, Pelagea, Pelagiya, Pelageah, Pelagla, Pelaglah, Pelagie, Pelagy, Pelagi, Pelagey, Pelagee, Pelagias, Pelaga

Pele (Hawaiian) From the volcano

Peleka (Hawaiian) Having great strength
Pelekah, Pelika, Pelikah, Pelyka, Pelykah

Pelham (English) One who is thoughtful
Pellam, Pelhim, Pellham, Pelim

Pelia (Hebrew) A marvelous woman
Peliah, Peliya, Peliyah, Pelea, Peleah

Pelicia (Greek) A weaving woman
Peliciah, Pelicea, Peliciya, Pelycia, Pelycea

Pelipa (African) One who loves horses
Pelypa, Peliepa, Peleipa, Peleepa, Peleapa

Pellikita (Latin) A bringer of happiness
Pellikitah, Pelikita, Pellkita, Pelkita

Pellonia (Latin) A defender against enemies
Pelloniah, Pelonia, Pellonea, Pelonea

Pelopia (Greek) In mythology, the wife of Thyestes and mother of Aegisthus
Pelopiah, Pelopea, Pelopeah, Pelopiya

Pelulio (Hawaiian) A treasure from the sea
Pelulia, Peluliyo, Peluliya

Pemba (African) A powerful woman
Pembah, Pembia, Pembiah, Pembea, Pembeah

Pembroke (English) From the broken hill
Pembrook, Pembrok, Pembrooke

Pemphredo (Greek) An alarm; in mythology, one of the three Graces

Penarddun (Celtic) In mythology, the wife of Llyr

Penda (African) One who loves and is loved
Pendah, Penha, Penhah

Pendant (French) A decorated woman
Pendent, Pendante, Pendente

Penelope (Greek) Resembling a duck; in mythology, the faithful wife of Odysseus
Peneloppe, Penelopy, Penelopey, Penelopi, Penelopie, Penelopee, Penella, Penelia, Pen, Penn, Penne, Penny, Pennie, Penni, Penney, Peni, Pennea, Penelopea

Penia (Greek) In mythology, the personification of poverty
Peniah, Penea, Peniya, Peneah, Peniyah

Penninah (Hebrew) Resembling a precious stone
Penina, Peninah, Peninna, Penyna, Pennyna, Penine, Penyne

Pennsylvania (English) The land of Penn; from the state of Pennsylvania

Pensee (French) A thoughtful woman
Pense, Pensi, Pensie, Pensy, Pensey, Pensea

Penthea (Greek) The fifth-born child
Penthia, Pentheah, Penthiah, Penthiya, Penthiyah

Penthesilea (Greek) In mythology, a queen of the Amazons

Peony (Greek) Resembling the flower
Peoney, Peoni, Peonie, Peonee, Peonea

Pepin (French) An awe-inspiring woman
Peppin, Pepine, Peppine, Pipin, Pippin, Pepen, Pepan, Peppen

Pepita (Spanish) Feminine form of Joseph; God will add
Pepitah, Pepitta, Pepitia, Pepitina

Pepper (American) Resembling the pepper plant; flavorful
Peper

Peppy (American) A cheerful woman
Peppey, Peppi, Peppie, Peppee, Peppea

Perach (Hebrew) A flourishing woman
Pericha, Percha, Pircha, Perchiya, Pirchiya

Perahta (German) A glorious woman
Perata, Perchta, Perchte

Perdita (Latin) A lost woman
Perditah, Perditta, Perdy, Perdie, Perdi, Perdee, Perdea, Perdeeta, Perdeata

Perdix (Latin) Resembling a partridge
Perdixx, Perdyx, Perdyxx

Peregrina (Latin) A traveler; a wanderer
Peregrine, Peregrinna, Peregrinia, Peregrinea, Perrin

Perel (Latin) One who has been tested
Perell, Perelle, Perela, Perele, Perella

Perfecta (Spanish) One who is flawless
Perfecte, Perfectia, Perfectea, Perfect, Perfection

Peri (Persian / English) In mythology, a fairy / from the pear tree
Perry, Perri, Perie, Perrie, Pery, Perrey, Perey, Peree, Perree, Perrea, Perea

Peridot (Arabic) One who is treasured

Periwinkle (English) Resembling the flower
Perriwinkle, Perywinkle, Perrywinkle

Perla (Latin) An important woman
Perlah

Perlace (Spanish) Resembling a small pearl
Perlase, Perlaice, Perlaise, Perlayce, Perlayse

Perlette (French) Resembling a small pearl
Perlett, Perlet, Perlete, Perleta, Perletta

Perlie (Latin) Resembling a pearl
Perli, Perly, Perley, Perlee, Perlea, Perleigh

Perlina (American) Resembling a small pearl
Perlinah, Perlyna, Perlynah, Perleena, Perleenah, Perleana, Perleanah, Perliena, Perlienah, Perleina, Perleinah

Pernella (Scandinavian) As solid as a rock
Pernell, Pernela, Pernele, Pernel, Pernelle

Peron (Latin) One who travels

Perouze (Armenian) Resembling the turquoise gem
Perooze, Perouse, Peroose, Perouza, Perousa

Perpetua (Latin) One who is constant; steadfast

Perse (Greek) From the water; in mythology, one of the Oceanids
Persa, Perseis

Persephone (Greek) In mythology, the daughter of Demeter and Zeus who was abducted to the underworld
Persephoni, Persephonie, Persephony, Persephoney, Persephonee, Persefone, Persefoni, Persefonie, Persefony, Persefoney, Persefonee

Pershella (American) A generous woman
Pershela, Pershel, Pershell, Pershele, Pershelle

Persis (Greek) Woman of Persia
Persiss, Persisse, Persys, Persyss, Persysse

Perzsi (Hebrew) A woman devoted to God
Perzsie, Perzsy, Perzsee, Perzsike, Perke, Perzsey, Perzsea

Pesha (Hebrew) A flourishing woman
Peshah, Peshia, Peshiah, Peshea, Pesheah, Peshe

Petronela (Latin) Feminine form of Peter; as solid and strong as a rock
Petronella, Petronelle, Petronia, Petronilla, Petronille, Petrona, Petronia, Petronel, Petronele, Pernila, Pernilla, Parnella, Pedra, Petra, Petrine, Pedrine, Perrine, Peirene, Peronel, Peronelle, Peta, Pier, Piera, Pierra, Pierce, Pierette, Pietra, Pita

Petula (Latin) An impatient woman
Petulah, Petulla, Petoola, Petoula

Petunia (English) Resembling the flower
Petuniah, Petuniya, Petunea, Petoonia, Petounia

❂ **Peyton** (English) From the warrior's village
Peyten

Phaedra (Greek) A bright woman; in mythology, the wife of Theseus
Phadra, Phaidra, Phedra, Phaydra, Phedre, Phaedre

Phan (Asian) One who shares with others

Phashestha (American) One who is decorated
Phashesthea, Phashesthia, Phashesthiya

Pheakkley (Vietnamese) A faithful woman
Pheakkly, Pheakkli, Pheakklie, Pheakklee, Pheakkleigh, Pheakklea

Pheba (Greek) One who smiles a lot
Phebah, Phiba, Phibah

Pheme (Greek) In mythology, the personification of fame
Phemie, Phemia, Phemi, Phemy, Phemey, Phemee, Phemea

Phenice (American) One who enjoys life
Phenyce, Phenise, Phenyse, Phenicia, Phenicea

Phenyo (African) A victorious woman

Pheodora (Greek) A supreme gift
Pheodorah, Phedora, Phedorah

Phernita (American) A well-spoken woman
Pherneeta, Phernyta, Phernieta, Pherneita, Pherneata

Phia (Italian) A saintly woman
Phiah, Phea, Pheah

Philadelphia (Greek) One who offers sisterly love
Philly, Phillie, Philli, Philley, Phillee, Phillea

Philana (Greek) One who adores mankind
Philena, Philanna, Philanne, Philenne, Philenna, Philene, Phileane, Phileene

Philantha (Greek) A woman who loves flowers
Philanthia, Philanthea, Philanthiya

Philberta (English) Feminine form of Philibert; one who is dearly loved
Philiberta, Philbertha, Philibertha, Philberte, Philiberte, Philiberthe, Philberthe

Phile (Greek) Feminine form of Philo; one who loves and is loved
Phila

Philippa (English) Feminine form of Philip; a friend of horses
Phillippa, Philipa, Phillipa, Philipinna, Philippine, Phillipina, Phillipine, Pilis, Pippa

Philise (Greek) A loving woman
Phileese, Philease, Phileise, Philiese, Philyse, Philese

Philomel (Greek) Resembling a nightingale
Philomela, Philomele, Philomell, Philomelle, Philomella

Philomena (English) A friend of strength
Philomina, Philomeena, Philomyna, Philomenia, Philominia, Philomeenia, Philomynia, Phiomeana

Philyra (Greek) A woman who loves music
Philyre, Philyria, Philyrea

Phiona (Scottish) Form of Fiona, meaning "one who is fair; a white-shouldered woman"
Phionna, Phyona, Phyonna, Phione, Phionne, Phyone, Phyonne

Phira (Greek) One who loves music
*Phirah, Pheera, Pheerah, Phiera, Phierah,
Pheira, Pheirah, Pheara, Phearah*

Phoebe (Greek) A bright, shining woman;
in mythology, another name for the goddess of the moon
*Phebe, Phoebi, Phebi, Phoebie, Phebie,
Pheobe, Phoebee, Phoebea, Phebee, Phebea*

Phoena (Greek) Resembling a mystical bird
Phoenah, Phoenna, Phena, Phenna

Phoenix (Greek) A dark-red color; in
mythology, an immortal bird
Phuong, Phoenyx

Phonsa (American) Filled with joy
*Phonsah, Phonsia, Phonsiah, Phonsea,
Phonseah, Phonza, Phonzia, Phonzea*

Photina (American) A stylish woman
*Photeena, Photeana, Photiena, Photeina,
Photyna*

Phylicia (Greek) One who is fortunate
*Phyliciah, Phylicea, Phyliceah, Phylecia,
Phylecea, Phyleciah, Phyleceah*

Phyllis (Greek) Of the foliage; in mythology,
a girl who was turned into an almond tree
*Phylis, Phillis, Philis, Phylys, Phyllida,
Phylida, Phillida, Philida, Phyllina, Phylina,
Phyliss*

Phyre (Armenian) One who burns brightly
Phyra, Phyria, Phyrea

Pia (Italian / Polynesian) One who is pious /
from the land of ice

Piedad (Spanish) A devout woman
Piedade, Piedadd, Pyedad

Pierina (Greek) One who is dependable
*Pierinah, Piereena, Piereenah, Piereana,
Piereanah, Pieryna, Pierynah*

Pilar (Spanish) Resembling a pillar; having
great strength
Pilarre, Pylar, Pylarre

Pili (Egyptian) The second-born child
Pilie, Pily, Piley, Pilee, Pilea, Pileigh

Pilialoha (Hawaiian) One who is dearly
loved

Pililani (Hawaiian) Having great strength
*Pililanie, Pililany, Pililaney, Pililanee,
Pililanea*

Pilisi (Hawaiian) Living the simple life
Pilisie, Pilisy, Pilisey, Pilisee, Pilisea

Piluki (Hawaiian) Resembling a small leaf
Pilukie, Piluky, Pilukey, Pilukee, Pilukea

Pilvi (Italian) A cheerful woman
Pilvie, Pilvee, Pilvea, Pilvy, Pilvey

Pineki (Hawaiian) Resembling a peanut
Pinekie, Pineky, Pinekey, Pinekee, Pinekea

Ping (Chinese) One who is peaceful
Pyng

Pinga (Inuit) In mythology, goddess of the
hunt, fertility, and healing
Pingah, Pyngah, Pyngah

Pingjarje (Native American) Resembling a
young doe
*Pingjarji, Pingjarjie, Pingjarjy, Pingjarjey,
Pingjarjee, Pingjarjea*

Pink (American) One who is healthy
*Pinke, Pinka, Pinki, Pinkie, Pinky, Pinkey,
Pinkee, Pinkea*

Pinquana (Native American) Having a
pleasant fragrance
*Pinquan, Pinquann, Pinquanne, Pinquanna,
Pinquane*

Piper (English) One who plays the flute
*Pipere, Piperel, Piperell, Piperele, Piperelle,
Piperela, Piperella, Pyper, Pypere, Pyperelle,
Pyperella*

Pippi (French / English) A friend of horses /
a blushing young woman
Pippie, Pippy, Pippey, Pippee, Pippea

Pirene (Greek) Of the sacred well
*Pireen, Pireene, Piryne, Pirynne, Pireane,
Pireane, Pyrene, Pyreen, Pyrean*

Pirouette (French) A ballet dancer
*Piroette, Pirouett, Piroett, Piroueta, Piroeta,
Pirouetta, Piroetta, Pirouet, Piroet*

Pisces (Latin) The twelfth sign of the
zodiac; the fishes
Pysces, Piscees, Pyscees, Piscez, Pisceez

Pitana (American) One who is adorned
Pitanna, Pytana, Pytanna, Pitania, Pytania, Pitanea, Pytanea

Pitarra (American) An intriguing woman
Pitarrah, Pitara, Pitarah

Pithasthana (Hindi) In Hinduism, a name for the wife of Shiva

Pity (American) A sorrowful woman
Piti, Pitie, Pitey, Pitee, Pitea

Pixie (Celtic) A playful sprite; a fairy or elfin creature
Pixi, Pixy, Pixey, Pixee, Pixea

Placida (Italian) Feminine form of Placido; one who is calm; tranquil
Placidah, Placyda, Placeda, Placeyda, Placidia, Placidea, Placeeda, Placeada

Platinum (English) As precious as the metal
Platynum, Platnum, Platie, Plati, Platee, Platy, Platey, Platea

Platona (Spanish) A beloved friend
Platonia, Platonea, Platonya, Platoniya

Platt (French) From the plains
Platte

Pleasance (French) One who is agreeable
Plaisance, Playsance, Plasance, Plesance

Pleshette (American) An extravagent woman
Pleshett, Pleshet, Pleshete, Plesheta, Pleshetta

Pleun (American) One who is good with words
Pleune

Plum (American) Resembling the fruit

Po (Italian) A lively woman

Pocahontas (Native American) Filled with joy
Pokahontas, Pocohontas, Pokohontas, Pocahantas, Pokahantas

Podarge (Greek) In mythology, one of the Harpies

Poe (English) A mysterious woman

Poetry (American) A romantic woman
Poetrey, Poetri, Poetrie, Poetree, Poetrea

Polete (Hawaiian) A kind young woman
Polet, Polett, Polette, Poleta, Poletta

Polina (Russian) A small woman
Polinah, Poleena, Poleenah, Poleana, Poleanah, Poliena, Polienah, Poleina, Poleinah, Polyna, Polynah

Polly (English) Form of Mary, meaning "star of the sea / from the sea of bitterness"
Polley, Polli, Pollie, Pall, Paili, Paley, Paliki, Poll, Pollyanna, Pollyana, Pollee, Pollea

Polyhymnia (Greek) In mythology, the muse of sacred songs and dance
Polyhymniah, Polymnia, Polymniah

Polyxena (Greek) In mythology, a daughter of Priam who was loved by Achilles
Polyxenah, Polyxenia, Polyxenna, Polyxene, Polyxenea

Pomona (Latin) In mythology, goddess of fruit trees
Pomonah, Pomonia, Pomonea, Pamona, Pamonia, Pamonea

Pompa (American) An arrogant woman
Pompah, Pompy, Pompey, Pompee, Pompea, Pompi, Pompie

Pompeya (Latin) Feminine form of Pompey; fifth-born child; woman from Pompeii
Pompaya, Pompaiya, Pompaeya

Poni (African) The second-born daughter
Ponni, Ponie, Ponnie, Pony, Ponny, Poney, Ponney, Ponee, Ponnee, Ponea, Ponnea

Poodle (American) Resembling the dog; one with curly hair
Poudle, Poodel, Poudel

Pooky (American) A cute and cuddly girl
Pookey, Pooki, Pookie, Pookee, Pookea

Poonam (Hindi) A kind and caring woman
Pounam

Poppy (English) Resembling the red flower
Poppey, Poppi, Poppie, Poppee, Popi, Popie, Popy, Poppea, Popee, Popey, Popea

Pora (Hebrew) A fertile woman
Porah, Porrah, Porra, Poria, Poriah, Porea, Poreah

Porter (Latin) The doorkeeper

Portia (Latin) Piglike woman; an offering
Portiah, Porsha, Porscha

Posala (Native American) Born at the end of spring
Posalah, Posalla, Posallah

Posh (American) A fancy young woman
Poshe, Posha

Posy (English) Resembling a bouquet of flowers; form of Josephine, meaning "God will add"
Posey, Posi, Posie, Posee, Pozy, Pozey, Pozi, Pozie, Pozee, Posea, Pozea

Potina (Latin) In mythology, goddess of children's food and drink
Potinah, Potyna, Potena, Poteena, Potiena, Poteina, Poteana

Pounamu (Maori) A treasured gift

Powder (American) A lighthearted woman
Powdar, Powdir, Powdur, Powdor, Powdi, Powdie, Powdy, Powdey, Powdee, Powdea

Prabhu (Indian) A mighty woman

Pradeepta (Indian) Feminine form of Pradeep; one who provides light
Pradypta, Pradeapta, Pradeypta

Pragyata (Hindi) One who is knowledgeable

Prairie (American) From the flatlands
Prairi, Prairy, Prairey, Prairee, Prairea

Praise (Latin) One who expresses admiration
Prayse, Praize, Prayze, Praze, Praese, Praeze

Pramada (Indian) One who is indifferent

Pramlocha (Hindi) In Hinduism, a celestial nymph

Prarthana (Hindi) One who prays

Pratibha (Hindi) An understanding woman
Pratibhah, Pratybha, Pratybhah

Pratima (Indian) An image or icon
Pratimah, Pratema, Pratyma, Prateema, Prateima, Pratiema, Prateama

Precia (Latin) An important lady
Preciah, Presha, Preshah, Pretia, Pretiah

Precious (American) One who is treasured
Preshis, Preshys

Preeti (Indian) One who loves and is loved
Priti, Preetie, Pritie, Pritika, Priya, Preati

Prema (Hindi) One who is dearly loved
Premah, Premma, Premmah

Premlata (Hindi) A loving woman
Premlatah, Premlatta, Premlatia, Premlatea

Prentice (English) A student; an apprentice
Prentyce, Prentise, Prentyse

Prescilian (Spanish) A fashionable woman
Presciliann, Prescilianne

Presencia (Spanish) One who presents herself well
Presenciah, Presencea, Presenceah, Presenciya, Presenciyah

Presley (English) Of the priest's town
Presly, Presle, Presli, Preslie, Preslee, Presleigh, Preslea, Prezley, Prezly, Prezli, Prezlie, Prezlee, Prezleigh, Prezlea

Pribislava (Polish) One who is glorified
Pribislavia, Pribislavea, Pribislawa, Pribka, Pribuska

Prima (Latin) The firstborn child
Primalia, Primma, Pryma, Primia, Primea, Preema, Preama

Primavera (Spanish) Born during spring

Primola (Latin) Resembling a primrose
Primolah, Primolia, Primoliah, Primolea, Primoleah

Primrose (Latin) The first rose; resembling the flower
Prymrose, Primula, Primulia, Primrosa, Prymrosa

Princess (English) A highborn daughter; born to royalty
Princessa, Princesa, Princie, Princi, Princy, Princee, Princey, Princea, Prinsess, Prinscella, Prinscelle, Princella, Princelle, Prinscilla

Prisca (Latin) From an ancient family
Priscah, Priska, Priscca, Priscka, Piroska, Pirosca, Piroscka, Piri

Priscilla (Latin) Form of Prisca, meaning "from an ancient family"
Priscella, Precilla, Presilla, Prescilla, Prisilla, Prisella, Prissy, Prissi, Prissie, Prissey, Prissee, Prissea, Prisy, Pris, Priss

Prisisima (Spanish) Having great wisdom
Prisima

Prisma (Hindi) One who is cherished
Prismah, Prizma, Prizmah

Pristina (Latin) One who is unspoiled
Prystina, Pristeena, Prysteena, Pristeana, Prysteana, Pristyna, Prystyna, Pristiena, Prystiena, Pristeina, Prysteina

Prochora (Latin) One who guides others
Prochorah, Prochoria, Prochoriah, Prochorea, Prochoreah

Procne (Greek) In mythology, an Athenian princess

Promise (American) A faithful woman
Promice, Promyse, Promyce, Promis, Promiss, Promys, Promyss

Proserpina (Latin) In mythology, goddess of the underworld
Proserpinah, Proserpyna, Proserpeena, Proserpiena, Proserpeana

Prospera (Latin) One who is fortunate
Prosperia, Prosper, Prosperea, Prosperous

Protima (Hindi) One who dances
Protimah, Proteema, Proteemah, Proteima, Proteimah, Protiema, Protiemah, Proteama, Proteamah, Protyma, Protymah

Prova (French) Woman of the province
Provah, Provva, Provvah, Provia, Proviah, Provea, Proveah

Prudence (English) One who is cautious and exercises good judgment
Prudencia, Prudensa, Prudensia, Prudentia, Predencia, Predentia, Prue, Pru

Prunella (Latin) Resembling a little plum
Prunellah, Prunela, Prunellia, Prunelia, Prunelle, Prunele, Prunell, Prunel

Pryce (American / Welsh) One who is very dear / an enthusiastic child
Price, Prise, Pryse

Pryor (American) A wealthy woman; prosperous
Pryar, Pryer, Pryier

Psyche (Greek) Of the soul; in mythology, a maiden loved by Eros

Pua (Hawaiian) Resembling a flower

Puck (English) A mischievous fairy

Puja (Hindi) In Hinduism, a religious ritual
Pujah, Pooja, Pouja

Pulcheria (Italian) A chubby baby
Pulcheriah, Pulcherea, Pulchereah, Pulcherya, Pulcheryah, Pulcheriya, Pulcheriyah

Pules (Native American) Resembling a pigeon

Pulika (African) An obedient and well-behaved girl
Pulikah, Pulicca, Pulicka, Pulyka, Puleeka, Puleaka

Puma (Latin) Resembling the mountain lion
Pumah, Pumma, Pooma, Poomah, Pouma

Purity (English) One who is chaste; clean
Puritey, Puritee, Puriti, Puritie, Pura, Pureza, Purisima, Pure, Puritea

Purnima (Hindi) Born beneath the full moon
Purnyma, Purnema, Purneima, Purniema, Purneema, Purneama

Pyera (Italian) Formidable woman
Pyerah, Pyerra, Pyerrah, Pyira, Pyirra, Pyirah, Pyirrah

Pyllyon (English) An enthusiastic woman
Pylyon

Pyrena (Greek) A fiery woman
Pyrenah, Pyrina, Pyrinah, Pyryna, Pyrynah, Pyreena, Pyreenah, Pyriena, Pyrienah, Pyreina, Pyreinah, Pyreana, Pyreanah

Pyria (American) One who is cherished
Pyriah, Pyrea, Pyreah, Pyriya, Pyriyah, Pyra, Pyrah

Pyrrha (Greek) In mythology, Pandora's daughter

Pythia (Greek) A prophetess; in mythology, a priestess of Apollo
Pythiah, Pythea, Pytheah, Pythiya, Pythiyah

q

Qadesh (Syrian) In mythology, goddess of love and sensuality
Quedesh, Qadesha, Quedesha, Qadeshia, Quedeshiya

Qadira (Arabic) Feminine form of Qadir; powerful; capable
Qadirah, Qadyra, Qadyrah, Qadiria, Qadirra, Quadira, Quadyra, Qadeera, Qadeira, Qadeara

Qamra (Arabic) Of the moon
Qamrah, Qamar, Qamara, Qamrra, Qamaria, Qamrea, Qamria

Qeturah (Hebrew) Form of Keturah, meaning "resembling incense"
Qetura, Qeturra, Qeturia, Qeturiya, Qeterea

Qi (Chinese) A life force

Qiana (American) One who is gracious
Qianah, Qiania, Qyana, Qianna, Qiannia, Qyanna, Qianne, Qiann, Qianiya

Qiao (Chinese) One who is beautiful; attractive

Qimat (Indian) A valuable woman
Qimate, Qimatte, Qimata, Qimatta

Qing Yuan (Chinese) From the clear spring

Qitarah (Arabic) Having a nice fragrance
Qitara, Qytaruh, Qytara, Qitaria, Qitarra, Qitarria, Qytarra, Qytarria, Qitaria, Qytaria, Qitariya, Qitarriya

Qoqa (Chechen) Resembling a dove

Quan (Chinese) A compassionate woman

Quana (Native American) One who is aromatic; sweet-smelling
Quanah, Quanna, Quannah, Quaniu, Quaniya, Quanniya, Quannia, Quanea

Quanda (American) A beloved companion; friend
Quandah, Quannda, Quandia, Quandiah, Quandea, Quandeah

Quaneisha (American) A royal hawk
Quanesha, Quanisha, Quaniesha, Quaynisha, Quanishia, Quynisha, Quynishia, Queenisha, Qynisha, Qynysha, Quaneesha, Quaneasha, Quanecia, Quaneasa, Qynisha, Qynecia, Qwanisha, Quanessa, Quannezia, Queisha, Queshya, Queshia, Qeysha

Quanella (American) A sparkling woman
Quanell, Quanel, Quanela, Quanelle, Quanele

Quanika (American) Form of Nika, meaning "displaying her true image"
Quanikah, Quanica, Quanicka, Quanyka, Quanikka, Quaniqua, Quanykka, Quanique, Queenika, Quaniki, Quanyki, Quaneeka, Quaneaka

Quantina (American) A courageous queen
Quantinah, Quanteena, Quanteenah, Quantyna, Quantynah, Quantiena, Quantienah, Quanteina, Quanteinah, Quanteana, Quanteanah

Quartilla (Latin) The fourth-born child
Quartillah, Quartila, Quartylla, Quartyla, Quartille, Quartylle, Quartilc, Quartyle

Qubilah (Arabic) One who is agreeable; pleasing
Qubila, Quibilah, Quabila, Quabyla, Qubyla, Qubilla, Qubylla

Queen (English) A woman sovereign
Queene, Queenie, Queeni, Queena, Queeny, Quenna, Queenika, Queenique, Queenya, Queenia, Queenette, Queeney, Queeneta, Queaney, Queany, Queani, Queunie, Queania, Queanya, Queanee, Quean

Quella (English) One who pacifies; quiet
Quell, Quelle, Quellah, Quela, Quele, Quelia, Quellia

Quenby (Scandinavian) Womanly; feminine
Quenbey, Quenbi, Quenbie, Quenbye, Quenbee, Queenby, Queenbey, Queenbi, Queenbie, Queenbee, Quenbea, Quenbee

Quennell (French) From the small oak tree
Quennel, Quenell, Quennelle, Quynnell, Quynell, Quynele, Quynnel, Quynnelle

Querida (Spanish) One who is dearly loved; beloved
Queridah, Queryda, Querydah, Querrida, Queridda, Querridda, Quereeda, Quereada

Questa (Latin) One who searches; a seeker
Questah, Queste, Quest, Quystu, Quyste, Quessta, Questia, Questea

Queta (Spanish) Head of the household
Quetah, Quetta, Quettah

Quiana (American) Living with grace; heavenly
Quianah, Quianna, Quiane, Quian, Quianne, Quianda, Quiani, Quianita, Quyanna, Quyana, Quyann, Quyanne, Quionna

Quies (Latin) A peaceful woman; bringer of tranquility
Quiese, Queise, Queis, Quiesse, Quiess

Quilla (Incan / English) In mythology, goddess of the moon / a quill
Quillah, Quila, Quilah, Quille, Quyla, Quylla, Quylle, Quyle

Quinby (Scandinavian) From the queen's estate
Quinbey, Quinbi, Quinbie, Quinbee, Quinbea, Quynby, Quynbey, Quynbi, Quynbie, Quynbee, Quynbea

Quincy (English) The fifth-born child
Quincey, Quinci, Quincie, Quincee, Quincia, Quinncy, Quinnci, Quyncy, Quyncey, Quynci, Quyncie, Quyncee, Quynncy

Quincylla (American) The fifth-born child
Quincilla, Quincyla, Quincila

Quinevere (English) Form of Guinevere, meaning "one who is fair; of the white wave"
Quineviere, Quineverre, Quynevere, Quineveire

Quinlan (Gaelic) One who is slender and very strong
Quinnlan, Quynlan, Qwinlan, Quinlane, Quinlania, Quinlanna, Quinlann, Quinlanne

Quinn (German) Woman who is queenly
Quin, Quinne, Quina, Quynn, Qwin, Quiyn, Quyn, Quinna, Qwinn, Qwinne

Quintana (Latin / English) The fifth girl / queen's lawn
Quintanah, Quinella, Quinta, Quintina, Quintanna, Quintann, Quintara, Quintona, Quintonice, Quyntana, Quyntanna, Quyntara, Quinela, Quynella, Quynela, Quinetta, Quinita, Quintia, Quyntina, Quyntilla, Quyntila

Quintessa (Latin) Of the essence
Quintessah, Quintesa, Quintesha, Quintisha, Quintessia, Quyntessa, Quintoshu, Quinticia, Quintesse, Quintice, Quyntesse

Quinyette (American) The fifth-born child
Quinyett, Quinyet, Quinyeta, Quinyette, Quinyete

Quirina (Latin) One who is contentious
Quirinah, Quiryna, Quirynah, Quireena, Quireenah, Quireina, Quireinah, Quiriena, Quirienah, Quireana, Quireanah

Quirita (Latin) A loyal citizen
Quiritah, Quiritta, Quiryta, Quirytta, Quyryta, Quyrytta, Quiritte, Quirytte, Quyrytte

Quiritis (Latin) In mythology, goddess of motherhood
Quiritiss, Quiritisse, Quirytis, Quirytys, Quiritys, Quirityss

Quisha (American) Having a beautiful mind
Quishah

Quiterie (French) One who is peaceful; tranquil
Quiteri, Quitery, Quiterey, Quiteree, Quiterye, Quyterie, Quyteri, Quyteree, Quytery, Quyterey, Quyterye, Quiteria, Quyteria, Quita

Quorra (Italian) From the heart
Quorrah, Quora, Quorah, Quoria, Quorria, Quoriya, Quorriya

r

Ra (English) Resembling a doe

Raananah (Hebrew) An unspoiled child
Rananah, Ranana, Raanana, Rananna, Raananna

Rabab (Arabic) Resembling a pale cloud
Raabab

Rabah (Hebrew) The fourth-born child
Raba, Rabba, Rabbah

Rabea (German) Resembling a raven
Rabeah

Rabiah (Egyptian / Arabic) Born in the springtime / of the gentle wind
Rabia, Raabia, Rabi'ah, Rabi

Raca (Hebrew) A vain or empty woman
Racah, Racca, Raccah

Rachana (Hindi) Born of the creation
Rachanna, Rashana, Rashanda, Rachna

⊘ **Rachel** (Hebrew) The innocent lamb; in the Bible, Jacob's wife
Ruchael, Racheal, Rachelanne, Rachelce, Rachele, Racheli, Ruchell, Rachelle, Rachil, Raechel, Raechell, Raychel, Raychelle, Rashell, Rashelle, Raychel, Rechell, Rakel

Radcliffe (English) Of the red cliffs
Radcleff, Radclef, Radclif, Radclife, Radclyffe, Radclyf, Radcliphe, Radclyphe

Radella (English) An elfin counselor
Radell, Radel, Radele, Radella, Radela, Raedself, Radself, Raidself

Radeyah (Arabic) One who is content; satisfied
Radeya, Radhiya, Radhiyah, Radhia, Radhiah, Radhea, Radheah

Radha (Hindi) A successful woman; in Hinduism, one of Krishna's consorts
Radhah, Radhika, Radhikah, Radheeka, Radhyka, Radheaka

Radmilla (Slavic) Hardworking for the people
Radilla, Radinka, Radmila, Redmilla, Radilu

Radwa (Arabic) From the mountain in Medina
Radwah, Radhwa, Radhwah

Rae (English) Form of Rachel, meaning "the innocent lamb"
Raedell, Raedine, Raelaine, Raelani, Raelee, Raeleen, Raelena, Raelene, Raelina, Raella, Raelyn, Raelynn, Raelynne, Raenisha, Ray, Raye, Rayette, Raylene, Raylina, Rayma, Raynelle, Rayona, Rayla, Raynesha, Raynisha, Raylyn, Raylynn, Raelin

Raeka (Spanish) A beautiful and unique woman
Raekah, Rayka, Raika, Raykah, Raikah

Rafa (Arabic) One who is happy and prosperous
Rafah, Raafa, Raffa, Raffah

Rafela (Hebrew) Form of Raphaela, meaning "the divine healer"
Rafelah, Rafellah, Rafella, Rafele, Rafelle

Rafferty (Gaelic) A prosperous lady; wealthy
Raffertey, Rafferti, Raffertie, Raffertee, Raffertea

Rafi'a (Arabic) An exalted woman
Rafia, Rafi'ah, Rafee'a, Rafeea, Rafeeah, Rafiya, Rafiyah

Rafiga (Arabic) A pleasant companion; a sweetheart
Rafigah, Rafeega, Rafeegah, Rafyga, Rafygah

Rafiki (African) A beloved friend
Rafikie, Rafiky, Rafikey, Rafikee, Rafikea, Raficki, Rafickie, Raficci

Raghd (Arabic) A pleasant young woman

Ragnall (English) In Arthurian legend, Gawain's wife
Rugnal, Ragnalle, Ragnalla, Ragnale, Ragnala, Ragnallia, Ragnallea

Ragnara (Swedish) Feminine form of Ragnar; one who provides counsel to the army
Ragnarah, Ragnarra, Ragnaria, Ragnarea, Ragnari, Ragnarie, Ragnary, Ragnarey, Ragnaree

Ragnfrid (Norse) One who gives beautiful advice
Ragnfride, Ragnfrida, Ragna, Ragnfryd, Ragnfryde, Ragnfryda, Ragni, Ragnie, Ragny, Ragney, Ragnee, Ragnea

Ragnhild (Norse / Teutonic) One who provides counsel in battle / an all-knowing being
Ragnild, Ragnhilda, Ragnhilde, Ragnilda, Ranilllda, Renild, Renilda, Renilde, Reynilda, Reynilde, Ragnilde

Rahab (Hebrew) A trustworthy and helpful woman
Rahabe, Rahabb, Rahaba, Rahabah

Rahi (Arabic) Born during the springtime
Rahii, Rahy, Rahey, Rahee, Rahea, Rahie

Rahil (Hebrew) Form of Rachel, meaning "the innocent lamb"
Rahill, Raaheel, Rahille, Rahila, Rahilla, Raheela, Rahel, Rahelle

Rahimah (Arabic) A compassionate woman; one who is merciful
Rahima, Raheema, Raheemah, Raheima, Rahiema, Rahyma, Rahymah, Raheama, Raheamah

Rahimateh (Arabic) Filled with grace
Rahimate, Rahimata, Rahimatia, Rahymateh, Rahymata

Rai (Japanese) One who is trustworthy

Ra'idah (Arabic) A great leader
Raidah, Raida, Ra'ida, Raa'idah

Raina (Polish) Form of Regina, meaning "a queenly woman"
Raenah, Raene, Rainah, Raine, Rainee, Rainey, Rainelle, Rainy, Reina, Reinella, Reinelle, Reinette, Reyna, Reynalda, Reynelle, Reyney, Reine, Ranee, Reia

Rainbow (American) As colorful as the rainbow; symbolizing promise
Rainbowe, Raynbow, Raynebow, Raynebowe, Reinbow, Reinbowe

Raisa (Hebrew / Greek) As beautiful as the rose / one who is carefree
Raisabel, Raisse, Raiza, Raizel, Rayzel, Ra'isa, Raisie, Raizie, Raisi, Raizi, Rayzi, Rayzie, Ra'eesa

Raissa (French) A great thinker
Raisa, Raissah, Rayssa, Raysa, Raison, Rayson, Raeson, Raessa

Raja (Arabic) One who is filled with hope
Rajah

Rajani (Hindi) Born at night; in Hinduism, another name for the goddess Kali
Rajanie, Rajany, Rajaney, Rajanee, Rajanae, Rajni, Rajnie, Rajny, Rajney, Rajnee, Rajnea, Rajanea

Rakhshanda (Arabic) A lustrous woman
Rakshanda, Rakhshonda, Rakshonda, Rakshona, Rakhsha, Raksha

Rakkath (Hebrew) From the shore town
Rakkathe, Rakkatha, Rakath, Rakathe, Rakatha, Rakkon, Rakon, Rakkona, Rakona

Raleigh (English) From the clearing of roe deer
Raileigh, Railey, Raley, Rawleigh, Rawley, Raly, Rali, Ralie, Ralee, Rawli, Rawlie, Rawlee, Rawly

Ralphina (English) Feminine form of Ralph; wolf counsel
Raphine, Ralpheene, Ralpheyne, Ralfina, Ralfeene, Ralfine

Rama (Hebrew) One who is exalted
Ramah, Ramath, Ramatha, Ramathe

Ramira (Spanish) A sensible and thoughtful woman
Ramirah, Rameera, Rameerah, Rameira, Ramiera, Ramyrah, Ramyra, Rameirah, Ramierah, Rameara, Ramearah

Ramla (African) A prophetess
Ramlah, Ramli, Ramlie, Ramly, Ramley, Ramleigh, Ramlee, Ramlea

Ramona (Spanish) Feminine form of Ramon; one who offers wise protection
Ramee, Ramie, Ramoena, Ramohna, Ramonda, Ramonde, Ramonita, Ramonna, Ramowna, Remona, Remonna, Romona, Romonda, Romonde, Romonia, Raimunda, Raimonda, Raimona

Ramsey (English) From the raven island; from the island of wild garlic
Ramsay, Ramsie, Ramsi, Ramsee, Ramsy, Ramsea

Ramya (Hindi) An elegant and beautiful woman
Ramyah, Ramiya, Ramiyah, Ramia, Ramiah

Rana (Arabic) An eye-catching woman; to gaze upon
Ranah, Ra'naa, Rand, Raniyah, Ranarauna, Ranaraunaa, Raunaa

Ranait (Irish) A charming woman; one who is prosperous
Ranalt, Rathnait, Ranaite, Rathnaite, Ranalta

Randi (English) Feminine form of Randall; shielded by wolves; form of Miranda, meaning "one who is worthy of admiration"
Randa, Randee, Randelle, Randene, Randie, Randy, Randey, Randilyn, Randilynn, Randilynne

Rani (Hebrew) A lovely singer; a queenly woman
Rania, Ranice, Ranique, Ranit, Ranica, Ranita, Ranite, Ranith, Ranitta, Raanee, Rane, Ranie

Ranielle (American) Form of Danielle, meaning "God is my judge"
Ranele, Ranelle, Raniele, Raniela, Raniella, Raniel

Ranjita (Indian) Feminine form of Ranjit; a charming and delightful woman
Ranjitah, Ranjyta, Ranjytah, Ranjeeta, Ranjeetah

Ranveig (Norse) A house woman
Rannveig, Ranveiga, Ranveige, Ronnaug, Ronaug

Raonaid (Gaelic) Form of Rachel, meaning "the innocent lamb"
Raonaide, Raonaida, Raonayd, Raonayde, Raonaild, Raonailde, Raonailda, Raoghnailt

Raoule (French) Feminine form of Raoul; wolf counsel
Raoula, Raula

Raphaela (Hebrew) Feminine form of Raphael; the divine healer
Rafuela, Rafaelia, Raffaella, Raffaela, Raffaele, Raffaella, Rafella, Rafelle, Raphaella, Raphaelle, Raphayella, Raphella, Refaella, Refella, Rephaela, Rephayelle

Raphah (Hebrew) A tall, looming woman
Rapha, Raphae, Raphia, Raphiah, Raphea, Rapheah

Raphu (Hebrew) One who has been healed by God
Raphoo, Raphou

Raquel (Spanish) Form of Rachel, meaning "the innocent lamb"
Racquel, Racquell, Rayuela, Raquelle, Roquel, Roquela, Rakel, Rakell

Rasha (Arabic) Resembling a young gazelle
Rashah, Raisha, Raysha, Rashia, Raesha

Rashida (Arabic) Feminine form of Rashid; a righteous woman; one who is guided in the right direction
Rasheda, Rasheeda, Rasheedah, Rasheida, Rashidah, Rashyda, Rachida, Raashida, Raashidah

Rashmika (Indian) A sweet woman
Rashmikah, Rashmyka, Rashmeeka, Rashmeika

Ratana (Thai) Resembling a crystal
Ratanah, Ratanna, Ratannah, Rathana, Rathanna

Rati (Hindi) In Hinduism, goddess of passion and lust
Ratie, Ratea, Ratee, Raty, Ratey

Ratna (Indian) As precious as a jewel
Ratnah, Ratnia, Ratnea

Ratri (Indian) Born in the evening
Ratrie, Ratry, Ratrey, Ratree, Ratrea

Raven (English) Resembling the black bird; a dark and mysterious beauty
Ravina, Rayvenne, Rayven, Rayvinn, Ravyn, Raevin, Raeven, Ravenne

Rawdah (Arabic) One who works the earth; a gardener
Rawda, Rawdha, Rawdhah

Rawiyah (Arabic) One who recites ancient poetry
Rawiya, Rawiyya, Rawiyyah

Rawnie (English) An elegant lady
Rawni, Rawny, Rawney, Rawnee, Rawnea

Raya (Israeli) A beloved friend
Rayah

Rayann (English) An innocent woman full of grace
Raeann, Raeanna, Raeanne, Rayana, Rayanna, Rayanne, Rayane, Raeane, Raeana, Raiann, Raiane, Raianne, Raianna, Raiana

Raymonde (German) Feminine form of Raymond; one who offers wise protection
Raymondi, Raymondie, Raymondee, Raymondea, Raymonda, Raymunde, Raymunda

Rayna (Hebrew / Scandinavian) One who is pure / one who provides wise counsel
Raynah, Raynee, Rayni, Rayne, Raynea, Raynie

Rayya (Arabic) One who's thirst has been quenched
Rayyah

Raziah (Hebrew) God's secret; a mysterious woman
Razia, Razi, Raziela, Raziella, Razili, Raziella, Raziel, Raziele, Razie, Razee

Raziya (Swahili) A good-natured woman; one who is agreeable
Raziyah

Reanna (Irish) Form of Rhiannon, meaning "the great and sacred queen"
Reannah, Reanne, Reannon, Reanon, Reann, Reana, Reeanne, Reanan, Reannan

Reba (Hebrew) Form of Rebecca, meaning "one who is bound to God"
Rebah, Reeba, Rheba, Rebba, Ree, Reyba, Reaba

Rebecca (Hebrew) One who is bound to God; in the Bible, the wife of Isaac
Rebakah, Rebbeca, Rebbecca, Rebbecka, Rebbie, Rebeca, Rebeccah, Rebeccea, Rebeccka, Rebecha, Rebecka, Rebeckah, Rebeckia, Rebecky, Rebeha, Rebeka, Rebekah, Rebekha, Rebekka, Rebekkah, Rebekke, Rebeque, Reveka, Revekah, Revekka, Ribecca, Rebi, Rimca

Redell (English) From the red meadow
Redel, Redelle, Redele, Redella, Redela

Redmonde (American) Feminine form of Redmond; one who offers wise protection
Redmondi, Redmondie, Redmondee, Redmondea, Redmonda, Redmunde, Redmunda

Reed (English) A red-haired lady
Read, Reade, Reid, Reida

Refugia (Spanish) Feminine form of Refugio; one who is sheltered; protected
Refugiah, Refugiya, Refugiyah, Refugea, Refugeah

Regan (Gaelic) Born into royalty; the little ruler
Raegan, Ragan, Raygan, Reganne, Regann, Regane, Reghan, Reagan, Reaghan, Reegan

Regina (Latin) A queenly woman
Regeena, Regena, Reggi, Reggie, Régine, Regine, Reginette, Reginia, Reginna, Rejine, Reginy

Rehan (Armenian) Resembling a flower
Rehane, Rehann, Rehanne, Rehana, Rehanna, Rehanan, Rehannan, Rehania, Rehanea, Rehaniya

Rehema (African) A compassionate woman
Rehemah, Rehemma, Rehemia, Rehemiya, Rehemea

Rehoboth (Hebrew) From the city by the river
Rehobothe, Rehobotha, Rehobothia

Reiko (Japanese) One who is thankful
Rei

Reinheld (Teutonic) A wise and strong ruler
Reinhelde, Reinhelda, Reinhold, Reinholde, Reinholda

Rekha (Indian) One who walks a straight line
Rekhah, Reka, Rekah

Rella (English) Form of Ella, meaning "from a foreign land"
Rellah, Rela, Relah

Remedios (Spanish) Feminine form of Remedio; assisted by God
Remedy, Remedi, Remedie, Remedee, Remedey, Remedea

Remphan (Hebrew) Follower of the false god
Remphana, Remphane, Remphaine, Remphayn, Remphena, Remphaen, Remphaina, Remphayna, Remphaena

Remy (French) Woman from the town of Rheims
Remi, Remie, Remmy, Remmi, Remmie, Remy, Remmey, Remey, Rhemy, Rhemmy, Remee, Remmee

Ren (Japanese) Resembling a water lily

Rena (Hebrew) One who sings a joyous song
Reena, Reene, Rina, Rinah, Rinna, Rinnah, Renna, Rennah

Renée (French) One who has been reborn
Ranae, Ranay, Ranée, Renae, Renata, Renay, Renaye, René, Rene, Reneisha, Renell, Renelle, Renie, Renisha, Renne, Rennie, Renny, Rhianaye, Rrenae, Renee, Rennay, Renate

Renenet (Egyptian) In mythology, the personification of fortune

Reneta (Latin) A dignified woman
Renetah, Renetta, Renettah

Renita (Latin) One who stands firm; resistant
Reneeta, Renyta, Reneata, Renieta, Reneita

Renuka (Indian) Resembling fine grains of sand
Renukah, Renooka, Renookah, Renouka, Renoukah

Rephidim (Hebrew) One who offers support
Rephidima, Rephydim, Rephydima, Rephidem, Rephydem, Rephedem

Reseda (Latin) Resembling the mignonette flower
Resedah, Reselda, Resedia, Reseldia

Resen (Hebrew) From the head of the stream; refers to a bridle

Reshma (Arabic) Having silky skin
Reshmah, Reshman, Reshmane, Reshmann, Reshmanne, Reshmana, Reshmanna, Reshmaan, Reshmia, Reshmea

Reuela (Hebrew) A feminine form of Reuel; a friend of God
Reuelah, Reuella, Reuellah, Reuelia, Reuelea, Reueliah, Reueleah

Reumah (Hebrew) One who has been exalted
Reuma, Reumia, Ruemiah, Ruema, Ruemah

Reveka (Hebrew) A captivating woman
Revekah, Revecka, Reveckah

Rexanne (Latin) A queen full of grace
Rexalla, Rexana, Rexanna, Rexane, Rexella, Rexetta, Rexina, Rexine

Reya (Spanish) A queenly woman
Reyah, Reyeh, Reye, Reyia, Reyiah, Reyea, Reyeah

Reyhan (Arabic) One who is favored by God
Reyhann, Reyhane, Reyhanne, Reyhana, Reyhanna, Reyhanah, Reyhannah

Reza (Hungarian) Form of Theresa, meaning "a harvester"
Rezah, Rezia, Reziah, Rezi, Rezie, Rezy, Rezee, Resi, Resee, Resie, Resea, Resy, Resey, Rezea, Resea

Rezeph (Hebrew) As solid as a stone
Rezepha, Rezephe, Rezephia, Rezephah, Rezephiah

Rhan (Welsh) One's destiny
Rhane, Rhanne, Rhann, Rhanna, Rhana

Rhawn (Welsh) A woman with long and coarse hair
Rhawne, Rhaun, Rhaune, Rhawna, Rhauna

Rhaxma (African) A sweet-tempered woman
Rhaxmah, Rhaxima, Rhaxmia, Rhaxmana, Rhaxmae, Rhaxmai

Rhea (Greek) Of the flowing stream; in mythology, the wife of Cronus and mother of gods and goddesses
Rea, Rhae, Rhaya, Rhia, Rhiah, Rhiya, Rheya

Rhea Silvia (Latin) In mythology, a Vestal virgin and mother of Remus and Romulus
Rhea Silva, Rea Silvia, Rea Silva

Rheda (Anglo-Saxon) A divine woman; a goddess
Rhedah

Rhedyn (Welsh) Resembling a fern
Rhedynn, Rhedyne, Rhedynne, Rhedin, Rheden

Rhesa (Hebrew) An affectionate woman
Rhesah, Rhesia, Rhesiah, Rheza, Rhezah, Rhezia, Rheziah

Rheta (Latin) Feminine form of Rhett; a well-spoken woman
Rhetah, Retta, Rhetta

Rhiamon (Welsh) A magical woman; a witch
Rhiamone, Rhiamona, Rhiamonia, Rhiamonea, Rhyamon, Rhyamone, Rhyamona, Rhyamonia, Rhyamonea

Rhiannon (Welsh) The great and sacred queen
Rheanna, Rheanne, Rhiana, Rhiann, Rhianna, Rhiannan, Rhianon, Rhyan, Riannon, Rianon, Rheann, Rhian, Rhiain, Rhyanon, Rhyannon

Rhianwen (Welsh) A comely young woman
Rhianwenn, Rhianwenne, Rhianwyn, Rhianwynn, Rhianwynne, Rhianwin, Rhianwinn, Rhianwinne, Rhyanwen, Rhyanwin, Rhyanwyn

Rhoda (Greek) Resembling a rose; a woman from Rhodes
Rhodeia, Rhodia, Rhodie, Rhody, Roda, Rodi, Rodie, Rodina, Rodyna, Rodine, Rhodyna, Rhodine, Rhodina, Rhodee, Rhodea

Rhodantha (Greek) From the rosebush
Rhodanthe, Rhodanta, Rhodante, Rodantha, Rodanthe, Rodanta, Rodante

Rhode (Greek) In mythology, the oldest daughter of Oceanus and wife of Helios
Rhodus

Rhodes (Greek) From the Greek island

Rhonda (Welsh) Wielding a good spear
Rhondelle, Rhondene, Rhondiesha, Rhonette, Rhonnda, Ronda, Rondel, Rondelle, Rondi, Ronnda, Rhondah, Rhondia, Rhondea

Rhys (Welsh) Having great enthusiasm for life
Rhyss, Rhysse, Reece, Reese, Reice, Reise, Reace, Rease, Riece, Riese

Ria (Spanish) From the river's mouth
Riah

Riane (Gaelic) Feminine form of Ryan; little ruler
Riana, Rianna, Rianne, Ryann, Ryanne, Ryana, Ryanna, Riann, Riayn, Ryane, Rye, Ryen, Ryenne, Ryette, Ryetta, Rynn

Riblah (Hebrew) A fruitful woman; giver of life
Ribla, Ryblah, Rybla, Riblia, Rybliah, Ribliah, Ribliya, Ribliyah

Rica (English) Form of Frederica, meaning "peaceful ruler"; form of Erica, meaning "ever the ruler / resembling heather"
Rhica, Ricca, Ricah, Rieca, Riecka, Rieka, Riqua, Ryca, Rycca, Ryka, Rika, Rikka

Ricarda (German) Feminine form of Richard; a brave and strong ruler
Richanda, Richarda, Richardella, Richardene, Richardette, Richardina, Richardyne, Richenda, Richenza, Richette, Richia, Richilene, Richina, Richmal, Richmalle, Ricadonna, Ricadona

Richael (Irish) A saintly woman
Raichael

Richelle (American) Combination of Ricarda and Rachel, meaning "a brave and strong ruler" and "the innocent lamb"
Richel, Richela, Richele, Richella, Richell, Rychelle, Rychell, Rychele, Rychella, Rychela

Rickie (English) Form of Frederica, meaning "peaceful ruler"; form of Erica, meaning "ever the ruler / resembling heather"
Ricki, Ricky, Ricquie, Riki, Rikki, Rikky, Ryckie, Ricci, Rikie, Rickee, Rikee, Rickena, Rike

Rida (Arabic) One who is favored by God
Ridah, Reda, Reeda, Redah, Reedah, Ryda, Rydah

Riddhi (Indian) A prosperous woman
Riddhie, Riddhy, Riddhey, Riddhee, Riddhea

Ridhwana (Arabic) A pleasant woman
Ridhwanah, Ridhwanna, Ridwana, Ridwanna, Ridhwaana, Ridwaana, Ridhaa, Ridha, Ridhah

Rigg (English) Woman from the ridge
Rigge, Rigga, Riggi, Riggie, Riggee, Riggia, Riggea, Rygg, Rygge, Rygga

Rigmor (Swedish) A queenly woman
Rigmore, Rigmorr, Rigmorre, Rigmora, Rigmorra, Rigmoria, Rigmorea

Rihana (Arabic) Resembling sweet basil
Rihanah, Rihanna, Rihannah, Ryhana, Ryhanna, Raihana, Raihaana, Raihanna, Raihanah

⦿ **Riley** (Gaelic) From the rye clearing; a courageous woman
Reilley, Reilly, Rilee, Rileigh, Ryley, Rylee, Ryleigh, Rylie, Rilie, Rili, Reileigh, Rilea, Rylea, Ryson, Rysen, Ryesen, Ryelana

Rilla (German) From the small brook
Rillah, Rilletta, Rillette, Rille, Rillia, Rillie, Rillea, Rilly, Rilley

Rima (Arabic) Resembling the white antelope
Rimah, Reema, Reemah, Ryma, Rymah, Rim, Reem, Reama, Reamah

Rimona (Arabic) Resembling the pomegranate
Rimonah, Rimonia, Rimonna, Rimonea, Rymona, Rymonia, Rymonea

Rin (Japanese) A pleasant companion
Rinako

Rind (Norse) In mythology, a giantess
Rinda, Rindia, Rindea, Rindi, Rindie, Rindee, Rindy, Rindey

Rini (Japanese) Resembling a young rabbit
Rinie, Rinee, Rinea, Riny, Riney

Rio (Spanish) Woman of the river
Rhio

Riona (Irish) A queenly woman
Rionah, Rionach, Rionagh, Rionna, Rionnagh, Rionnah, Rioghnach

Risa (Latin) One who laughs often
Risah, Reesa, Riesa, Rise, Rysa, Rysah, Riseh, Risako

Rishona (Hebrew) The firstborn child
Rishonah, Ryshona, Rishonna, Ryshonna

Rissah (Hebrew) Covered with dew
Rissa, Ryssa, Ryssah

Rita (Spanish) Form of Margarita, meaning "resembling a pearl / the child of light"
Ritta, Reeta, Reita, Rheeta, Riet, Rieta, Ritah, Reta, Reit, Reata

Rithmah (Hebrew) From the valley of broom bushes
Rithma, Rythmah, Rythma, Rithmia, Rithmiah

Ritsa (Greek) Form of Alexandra, meaning "helper and defender of mankind"
Ritsah, Ritza, Ritzah, Ritsia, Ritsea, Ritzia, Ritzea

Riva (Hebrew / French) Form of Rebecca, meaning "one who is bound to God" / from the shore
Reeva, Reevabel, Reva, Rifka, Rivalee, Rivi, Rivka, Rivke, Rivkah, Rivy, Rivie, Rivah, Rivekka, Rive, Reava

Rizpah (Greek) One who is filled with hope
Rizpa, Ritzpa, Ritzpah, Rhizpa, Rhizpah

Roana (Spanish) A woman with reddish-brown skin
Roane, Roann, Roanne, Roanna, Roan, Rhoan, Rhoane, Rhoana

Roberta (English) Feminine form of Robert; one who is bright with fame
Reberta, Roba, Robbee, Robbey, Robbi, Robbie, Robby, Robeena, Robella, Robelle, Robena, Robenia, Robertena, Robertene, Robertha, Robertina, Robetta, Robette, Robettina, Ruperta, Rupetta, Robertia, Rupette

Robin (English) Form of Roberta, meaning "one who is bright with fame"; resembling the red-breasted songbird
Robbin, Robee, Robena, Robene, Robenia, Robi, Robina, Robine, Robinet, Robinett, Robinette, Robinia, Robyn, Robyna, Robynette, Robynn, Robynne, Robinetta, Robynetta, Rohine, Rohina

Roch (German) A glorious woman
Roche, Rocha

Rochelle (French) From the little rock
Rochel, Rochele, Rochell, Rochella, Rochette, Roschella, Roschelle, Roshelle

Rocio (Spanish) Covered with dewdrops
Roceo, Rociyo

Roderica (German) Feminine form of Roderick; a famous ruler
Roddie, Rodericka, Roderiga, Roderika, Roderqua, Roderique, Roderiga, Roderyca, Roderyka

Rohana (Indian) Resembling sandalwood
Rohanah, Rohannah, Rohanna, Rohane, Rohann, Rohan, Rohanne

Rohini (Indian) A beautiful woman
Rohinie, Rohiny, Rohiney, Rohinee, Rohinea

Roja (Spanish) A red-haired lady
Rojah

Rolanda (German) Feminine form of Roland; well-known throughout the land
Rolandah, Rolandia, Roldandea, Rolande, Rolando, Rollanda, Rollande

Roline (English) Form of Caroline, meaning "a joyous song; a small, strong woman"
Roelene, Roeline, Rolene, Rollene, Rolleen, Rollina, Rolline, Rolyne, Roleine, Roliene

Roma (Italian) Woman from Rome
Romah, Romma, Romalda, Romana,
Romelia, Romelle, Romilda, Romina,
Romaana, Romaine, Romayne, Romaina,
Romayna, Roman, Romane, Romania,
Romeine, Romene, Romea, Romala, Romella,
Romelle, Rommola, Romolla, Romola,
Romula, Romy, Romi, Romie, Romia

Romhilda (German) A glorious battle-
maiden
Romhilde, Romhild, Romeld, Romelde,
Romelda, Romilda, Romild, Romilde,
Ruomhildi, Ruomhild, Ruomhilde,
Ruomhilda

Romney (Welsh) Of the winding river
Romny, Romni, Romnie, Romnee, Romnea

Rona (Scottish) From the rough island
Rhona, Ronah, Rhonah, Ronella, Ronelle,
Ronna, Ronalee, Ronaleigh

Ronalda (English) Feminine form of
Ronald; the ruler's counsel
Ronalde, Ronaldia, Ronaldiya, Ronaldea

Ronat (Gaelic) Resembling a seal
Ronan, Ronana, Ronann, Ronane, Ronana,
Ronanna

Rong (Chinese) A glorious woman
Ronga, Rongia, Rongiya, Rongea

Ronli (Hebrew) My joy is the Lord
Ronlie, Ronlee, Ronleigh, Ronly, Ronley,
Ronlea, Ronia, Roniya, Roniah

Ronni (English) Form of Veronica, meaning
"displaying her true image"
Ronae, Ronay, Ronee, Ronelle, Ronette, Roni,
Ronica, Ronika, Ronisha, Ronna, Ronnee,
Ronnelle, Ronnella, Ronnette, Ronney,
Ronnie, Ronny

Rory (Gaelic) The red queen
Rorie, Rorey, Roree, Rorea, Rori

Rosabel (English) Resembling the beautiful
rose
Rosabell, Rosabele, Rosabelle, Rosabela,
Rosabella, Rozabel, Rozabell, Rozabele,
Rozabelle, Rozabela, Rozabella

Rosalba (Latin) Resembling the white rose
Rosalbah, Rosalbia, Rosalbea, Rhoswen,
Rhoswenn, Rhoswyn, Rhoswynn

Rosalie (Italian) Of the rose garden
Rosalee, Rosaley, Rosalia, Roselia, Rosella,
Roselle, Rozalia, Rozalie, Rozele, Rozelie,
Rozely, Rozella, Rozelle, Rozellia, Rosel,
Rozali, Rosali, Rosalea, Rosaleigh

Rosalind (German / English) Resembling a
gentle horse / form of Rose, meaning "resem-
bling the beautiful and meaningful flower"
Ros, Rosaleen, Rosalen, Rosalin, Rosalina,
Rosalinda, Rosalinde, Rosaline, Rosalinn,
Rosalyn, Rosalynd, Rosalynda, Rosalynn,
Rosanie, Roselin, Roselina, Roselind,
Roselinda, Roselinde, Roseline, Roselinn,
Roselyn, Roselynda, Roselynde, Roslyn,
Roslynn, Roslynne, Roz, Rozalin, Rozalind,
Rozalinda, Rozalynn, Rozalynne, Rozelin,
Rozelind, Rozelinda, Rozelyn, Rozelynda,
Rhoslyn, Rhozlyn, Roslin, Rozlin

Rosamond (German) Protector of horses;
the rose of the world
Rosamonde, Rosamund, Rosamunda,
Rosemond, Rosemonda, Rosmund, Rosmunda,
Rozamond, Rozamund, Rosamunde,
Rozmonda, Rozmond, Rozmund, Rozmunda

Rosario (Spanish) Refers to the rosary and
Our Lady of the Rosary
Rosaria, Rasario, Rasaria, Rosareo, Rasareo

Rose (Greek) Resembling the beautiful and
meaningful flower
Rasia, Rasine, Rasja, Rasya, Rosa, Rosella,
Roselle, Rosena, Rosenah, Rosene, Rosetta,
Rosette, Rosey, Rosheen, Rosie, Rosina, Rosine,
Rosio, Rosita, Rosy, Roza, Roze, Rozele,
Rozella, Rozene, Rozina, Rozsa, Rozsi,
Rozsika, Rozy, Ruza, Ruzena, Ruzenka,
Ruzha, Ruzsa, Rosai, Rosay, Rosee, Rosae,
Roesia, Rohais, Rhosyn, Rois, Roisin, Ros,
Russu, Ruusu, Rozeena, Rozyuka, Rhodia

Roseanne (English) Resembling the grace-
ful rose
Ranna, Rosana, Rosanagh, Rosanna,
Rosannah, Rosanne, Roseann, Roseanna,
Rosehannah, Rossana, Rossanna, Rozanna,
Rozanne, Rozeanna, Rosanie

Roselani (Hawaiian) Resembling a heavenly
rose
Roselanie, Roselany, Roselaney, Roselanee,
Rosalanea

Rosemary (Latin / English) The dew of the
sea / resembling a bitter rose
Rosemaree, Rosemarey, Rosemaria, Rosemarie,
Rosmarie, Rozmary, Rosamaria, Rosamarie

Roshan (Indian) The shining light
Roshana, Roshandra, Roshaundra, Roshawn,
Roshawna, Roshni, Roshnie, Roshny,
Roshney, Roshnee, Roshnea

Ross (Gaelic) Woman from the headland
Rosse, Rossa, Rosslyn, Rosslynn, Rosslynne

Roux (French) A red-haired woman

Rowa (Arabic) A lovely vision
Rowah

Rowan (Gaelic) Of the red-berry tree
Rowann, Rowane, Rowanne, Rowana,
Rowanna

Rowdy (American) A spirited woman
Rowdey, Rowdi, Rowdie, Rowdee, Rowdea

Rowena (Welsh / German) One who is fair
and slender / having much fame and hap-
piness
Rhowena, Roweena, Roweina, Rowenna,
Rowina, Rowinna, Rhonwen, Rhonwyn,
Rowyna

Roxanne (Persian) Born with the morning's
first light
Roksanne, Roxana, Roxandra, Roxana,
Roxane, Roxann, Roxanna, Roxeena,
Roxene, Roxey, Roxi, Roxiane, Roxianne,
Roxie, Roxine, Roxy, Roxyanna, Ruksana,
Ruksane, Ruksanna

Roya (English) Feminine form of Roy; a
red-haired woman
Roiya, Royanna, Royleen, Roylene, Roia

Royale (French) A regal and elegant lady
Royalla, Royalene, Royalina, Royall, Royalle,
Royalyn, Royalynne, Roial, Roialle, Roiall,
Roiale

Ruana (Indian) One who is musically
inclined
Ruanah, Ruanna, Ruannah, Ruane, Ruann,
Ruanne

Rubaina (Indian) A bright woman
Rubaine, Rubain, Rubayne, Rubayn,
Rubayna, Rubana, Rubane, Rubaena,
Rubaen, Rubaene

Rubena (Hebrew) Feminine form of
Reuben; behold, a daughter!
Reubena, Reubina, Rubenia

Ruby (English) As precious as the red gem-
stone
Rubee, Rubetta, Rubey, Rubi, Rubia,
Rubianne, Rubie, Rubina, Rubinia, Rubyna,
Rubyne, Roobee, Rubea

Rudella (German) A well-known woman
Rudela, Rudelah, Rudell, Rudelle, Rudel,
Rudele, Rudy, Rudie, Rudey, Rudea, Rudee,
Rudi

Rudrani (Indian) Feminine form of Rudra,
the god of death
Rudranie, Rudranee, Rudrany, Rudraney,
Rudranea

Rue (Greek) From the medicinal herb
Ruta, Rou

Rufina (Latin) A red-haired woman
Rufeena, Rufeine, Ruffina, Rufine, Ruffine,
Rufyna, Ruffyna, Rufyne, Ruffyne, Rufeina,
Ruphina, Ruphyna, Rufa, Rufah, Ruffa,
Ruffah, Rufeana

Ruhamah (Hebrew) One who has been
given mercy
Ruhama, Ruhamma, Ruhammah, Ruhamia,
Ruhamea, Ruhamiah, Ruhameah

Ruhette (Latin) As precious as a small jewel
Ruhete, Ruhett, Ruhet, Ruhetta, Ruheta

Ruhi (Arabic) A spiritual woman
Roohee, Ruhee, Ruhie, Ruhy, Ruhey, Roohi,
Roohie, Ruhea, Roohea

Rui (Japanese) An affectionate woman

Ruihi (Maori) Form of Lucy, meaning "one
who is illuminated"
Ruihie, Ruihee, Ruihea, Ruihey, Ruihy

Rukan (Arabic) A confident and steadfast
woman
Rukann, Rukane, Rukanne, Rukanna,
Rukana, Rukanah

Rukmini (Hindi) Adorned with gold; in
Hinduism, the first wife of Krishna
Rukminie, Rukminy, Rukminey, Rukminee,
Rukminea, Rukminni, Rukminii

Rumah (Hebrew) One who has been exalted
Ruma, Rumia, Rumea, Rumiah, Rumeah,
Rumma, Rummah

Rumer (English) A gypsy

Rumina (Latin) In mythology, a protector goddess of mothers and babies
Ruminah, Rumeena, Rumeenah, Rumeina, Rumiena, Rumyna, Rumeinah, Rumienah, Rumynah, Rumeana, Rumeanah

Rumor (American) A falsity spread by word of mouth
Rumer, Rumora, Rumera, Rumoria, Rumeria

Runa (Scandinavian) Feminine form of Rune; of the secret lore
Runah, Roona, Roone

Runcina (Latin) In mythology, goddess of agriculture
Rucinah, Ruceena, Ruceina, Ruciena, Rucyna, Ruceana

Rupali (Indian) A beautiful woman
Rupalli, Rupalie, Rupalee, Rupallee, Rupal, Rupa, Rupaly, Rupaley, Rupalea

Ruqayyah (Arabic) A gentle woman; a daughter of Muhammad
Ruqayya, Ruqayah, Ruqaya

Rusalka (Slavic) A woodland sprite
Rusalke, Rusalk, Rusalkia, Rusalkea

Rusty (American) A red-haired woman; a fiery woman
Rusti, Rustie, Rustee, Rustey, Rustea

Ruth (Hebrew) A beloved companion
Ruthe, Ruthelle, Ruthellen, Ruthetta, Ruthi, Ruthie, Ruthina, Ruthine, Ruthy, Ruthey, Ruta, Rute, Rut, Ruthann, Ruthanne, Ruthane, Ruthana, Ruthanna

Ruwaydah (Arabic) One who walks softly
Ruwayda, Ruwaidah, Ruwaida, Ruwaeda, Ruwaedah

Ryba (Slavic) Resembling a fish
Rybah, Rybba, Rybbah

Ryder (American) An accomplished horse-woman
Rider

Ryo (Japanese) An excellent woman
Ryoko

S

Saada (African) One who aids others; a helper
Saadaa, Saadah

Saadiya (Arabic) One who brings good fortune
Sadiya, Sadiyah, Sa'diah, Sadia, Sadiah, Saadiyah

Saba (Greek / Arabic) Woman from Sheba / born in the morning
Sabah, Sabaa, Sabba, Sabbah, Sabaah

Sabana (Spanish) From the open plain
Sabanah, Sabanna, Sabann, Sabanne, Sabane, Saban

Sabi (Arabic) A lovely young lady
Sabie, Saby, Sabey, Sabee, Sabbi, Sabbee, Sabea

Sabiha (Arabic) One who is beautiful; attractive
Sabihah, Sabyha, Sabeeha, Sabeiha, Sabieha, Sabeyha, Sabeaha

Sabina (Italian) Of an ancient culture
Sabinah, Sabeena, Sabiena, Sabeina, Sabyna, Saveena, Savina, Sabenah, Sabiny, Saby, Sebina, Sebinah, Sebyna, Sebynah, Sabena, Sabeana

Sabine (Latin) Of a tribe in ancient Italy
Sabeen, Sabene, Sabienne, Sabyne, Sebine, Sebyn, Sebyne, Sabin, Sabyn, Sabeene, Sabean, Sabeane

Sabirah (Arabic) Having great patience
Sabira, Saabira, Sabeera, Sabiera, Sabeira, Sabyra, Sabirra, Sabyrra, Sabeerra, Sabeara

Sabiya (Arabic) Born in the morning / of an easterly wind
Sabaya, Sabayah, Sabea, Sabia, Sabiah, Sabiyah, Sabya, Sabyah

Sable (English) One who is sleek
Sabel, Sabela, Sabelah, Sabele, Sabella, Sabelle

Sabra (Hebrew) Resembling the cactus fruit; to rest
Sabrah, Sebra, Sebrah, Sabrette, Sabbra, Sabraa, Sabarah, Sabarra, Sabarrah, Sabera, Sabira, Sabre, Sabara

Sabria (Latin) Woman from Cyprus
Sabriah, Sabreea, Sabrea, Sabreah, Sabrya, Sabriya, Sabri, Sabree, Sabrie, Sabrea, Sabry, Sabrey

Sabriel (American) A hero of God
Sabrielle, Sabriell, Sabryel, Sabryelle, Sabriele, Sabryele, Sabryell, Sabriela, Sabriella, Sabryela, Sabryella

Sabrina (English) A legendary princess
Sabrinah, Sabrinna, Sabreena, Sabriena, Sabreina, Sabryna, Sabrine, Sabryne, Sabreene, Sabrynna, Sabreanah, Sabreenah, Sabreen, Sabreane, Sabrene, Sabrena, Sabrin, Sabrinas, Sabrinia, Sabriniah, Sebree, Subrina, Sabrynah, Sabreana

Sacha (Greek) Form of Alexandra, meaning "helper and defender of mankind"
Sachenka, Sachka, Sache, Sachia, Sachah, Sachea

Sachet (Hindi) Having consciousness
Sachett, Sachette

Sachi (Japanese) Child of bliss; one who is blessed
Sachie, Sachy, Sachey, Sachee, Sachiko, Saatchi, Sachea

Sada (Japanese) The pure one
Sadda, Sadaa, Sadako, Saddaa

Sadaf (Indian / Iranian) Resembling a pearl / resembling a seashell
Sadafa, Sadafah, Sadafia, Sadafea, Sadafiya, Sadafe

Sadah (Arabic) Form of Zada, meaning "fortunate one; lucky; prosperous"
Sada, Sayda, Saida, Sayeda, Saeda

Sadbh (Irish) One who is well-behaved
Sadb

Sade (Yoruban) One who is honorable
Sadea, Saedea, Shadae, Shadai, Shaday, Sharde

Sadella (American) A beautiful fairylike princess
Sadel, Sadela, Sadelah, Sadele, Sadell, Sadellah, Sadelle, Sydel, Sydell, Sydella, Sydelle

Sadhana (Hindi) A devoted woman
Sadhanah, Sadhanna, Sadhannah, Sadhane, Sadhanne, Sadhann, Sadhan

Sadhbba (Irish) A wise woman
Sadhbh, Sadhba

Sadie (English) Form of Sarah, meaning "princess; lady"
Sadi, Sady, Sadey, Sadee, Saddi, Saddee, Sadiey, Sadye, Saedee, Saedi, Saedie, Saedy, Saide, Saidea, Saidee, Saidey, Saidi, Saidia, Saidie, Saidy, Seidy, Saddie, Sadia, Sadea, Saedea

Sadiqa (Arabic) One who is sincere; truthful
Sadiqaa, Saadiqa, Sadyqa, Sadiqua, Sadiquah

Sadira (Persian) Of the lotus tree
Sadirah, Sadiera, Sadeira, Sadyra, Sadirra, Sadeera, Sadyrra, Sadra, Sadrah, Sadyrah, Sadyre, Sadire, Sadeara

Sadiya (Arabic) One who is fortunate; lucky
Sadiyah, Sadiyyah, Sadya, Sadyah

Sadzi (American) Having a sunny disposition
Sadzee, Sadzey, Sadzia, Sadziah, Sadzie, Sadzya, Sadzyah, Sadzy, Sadzea

Safa (Arabic) One who is innocent and pure
Safah, Saffa, Sapha, Saffah, Saphah

Safara (African) Her place in this world
Safarra, Safaria, Safarah, Safariya

Saffi (Danish) Having great wisdom
Saffie, Saffy, Saffee, Saffey, Saffye, Safee, Safey, Safie, Safy, Safi, Saffea, Safea

Saffron (English) Resembling the yellow flower
Saffrone, Saffronn, Saffronne, Safron, Safronn, Safronne, Saffronah, Safrona, Safronah, Safrone, Safronnu, Safronnah, Saffrona

Safia (Arabic / African) One who is pure / having the lion's share
Safiah, Saffia, Safya, Safyah, Safiya, Safiyeh, Safiyyah, Saffiya, Safeia, Safeya, Safiyah

Safiwah (Arabic) One who is tranquil; peaceful
Safiwa, Safywah, Safywa, Saphiwa, Saphiwah

Saga (Norse) Seeing one; in mythology, goddess of poetry and history
Sagah, Sagga

Sagara (Hindi) From the ocean
Sagarra, Sagarah, Saggara, Saggarra, Sagaria, Sagarea

Sage (English) Wise one; type of spice
Saige, Sayge, Saege, Sagia, Saig, Sayg, Saeg

Sagira (Egyptian) The little one
Sagirah, Sageera, Sagyra, Sagiera, Sageira, Saqhira, Sagirra, Sagyrra

Sagittarius (Latin) The ninth sign of the zodiac; the archer
Sagitarius, Saggitarius, Sagitarios, Sagittarios

Sahar (Arabic) Of the dawn; awakening
Saharr, Sahare, Saharre, Saheer, Saher

Sahara (Arabic) Of the desert
Saharah, Saharra, Sahra, Saharia, Sahariya, Saharrah, Sahira, Sahrah, Sahari

Saheli (Indian) A beloved friend
Sahelie, Sahely, Saheley, Sahelee, Saheleigh, Sahyli, Sahelea

Sahiba (Indian) A young lady; a maiden
Sahibah, Saheeba, Sahyba, Saheiba, Sahieba, Saheyba, Saheaba

Sahila (Indian) One who provides guidance
Sahilah, Saheela, Sahyla, Sahiela, Saheila, Sahela, Sahilla, Sahylla, Saheella, Saheala

Sahirah (Egyptian) One who is pristine; clean
Sahira, Saheera, Sahiera, Saheira, Sahyra, Sahera, Sahirra, Saheerra, Sahyrra, Saheara

Sahkyo (Native American) Resembling the mink
Sakyo

Sai (Egyptian / Japanese) In mythology, the personification of destiny / one who is talented
Sae, Say, Saye, Saiko

Saida (Arabic) Fortunate one; one who is happy
Saidah, Sa'ida, Sayida, Saeida, Saedah, Said, Sayide, Sayidea, Sayda, Saydah, Saeda

Saihah (Arabic) One who is useful; good
Saiha, Sayiha

Sailor (American) One who sails the seas
Sailer, Sailar, Saylor, Sayler, Saylar, Saelor, Saeler, Saelar, Saler, Salor, Salar, Salore

Saima (Arabic) A fasting woman
Saimah, Saimma, Sayima

Saira (Arabic) A woman who travels; a wanderer
Sairah, Sairra, Sayra, Sairi, Sairie, Sairy, Sairey, Sairee, Sairea

Sajili (Indian) One who is decorated; adorned
Sajilie, Sajily, Sajyly, Sajiley, Sajyley

Sajni (Indian) One who is dearly loved
Sajnie, Sajny, Sajney, Sajnee, Sajnea

Sakae (Japanese) One who is prosperous
Sakai, Sakaie, Sakay, Sakaye

Sakari (Native American) A sweet girl
Sakarie, Sakary, Sakarri, Sakarey, Sakaree, Sakarree, Sakarah, Sakarrie, Sakaria, Sakariah, Sakarya, Sakaryah, Sakkara, Sakkarah, Sakara, Sakarea, Sakarrea

Saki (Japanese) One who wears a cloak
Sakiko, Sakia, Sakiah, Sakie, Saky, Sakya, Sakyah, Sakee, Sakea

Sakina (Indian / Arabic) A beloved friend / having God-inspired peace of mind
Sakinah, Sakeena, Sakiena, Sakeina, Sakyna, Sakeyna, Sakinna, Sakeana

Sakti (Hindi) In Hinduism, the divine energy
Saktie, Sakty, Sakkti, Sackti, Saktee, Saktey, Saktia, Saktiah, Saktya, Saktyah, Saktea

Saku (Japanese) Remembrance of the Lord
Sakuko

Sakujna (Indian) A birdlike woman
Sakujnah, Sakoujna, Sakoujnah

Sakuna (Native American) Resembling a bird
Sakunah, Sakoona, Sakoonah, Sakouna, Sakounah

Sakura (Japanese) Resembling a cherry blossom
Sakurah, Sakurako, Sakurra

Sala (Hindi) From the sacred sala tree
Salah, Salla, Sallah

Salacia (Latin) In mythology, a sea goddess
Salaciah, Salacea, Sulasea, Salaciya, Salasia, Salasiya

Salal (English) An evergreen shrub with flowers and berries
Sallal, Salall, Sallall, Salalle, Salale, Sallale

Salali (Native American) Resembling a squirrel
Salalie, Salaly, Salaley, Salalee, Salaleigh, Salalli, Salallie, Sallalli, Salaleah, Salalei, Salalia, Salaliah, Salalya, Salalyah, Salalea

Salama (Egyptian) One who is peaceful and safe
Salamah, Salma, Salamma, Sallama

Salamanca (Spanish) A woman from a city in western Spain

Salamasina (Samoan) A princess; born to royalty
Salamaseena, Salamasyna, Salamaseana, Salumaseina, Salamasiena

Salem (Arabic) One who is at peace
Saleme, Saleem

Salette (English) Form of Sally, meaning "princess; lady"
Salet, Salcta, Saletuh, Salete, Salett, Saletta, Salettah, Sallet, Salletta, Sallettah, Sallette

Salihah (Arabic) One who is agreeable; correct
Saliha, Saaleha, Salyha, Saleeha, Saleaha

Salima (Arabic) One who is healthy and safe
Salimah, Saleema, Salyma, Saliema, Selima, Saleyma, Sileema, Salema, Salim, Salymah, Salma, Salmah, Saleama

Salina (French) One of a solemn, dignified character
Salin, Salinah, Salinda, Salinee, Sallin, Sallina, Sallinah, Salline, Sallyn, Sallyna, Sallynah, Sallyne, Sallynee, Salyn, Salyna, Salynah, Salyne, Salana, Salanah, Salane, Salean, Saleana, Saleanah, Saleane, Salen, Salenah, Salenna, Sallene, Salena

Salliann (English) A gracious princess
Saleann, Saleanna, Saleannah, Saleanne, Saleean, Saleeana, Saleeanah, Saleeane, Saleeann, Saleeanna, Saleeannah, Saleeanne, Salian, Saliana, Salianah, Saliane, Saliann, Salianna, Saliannah, Salianne, Salleeann, Salleeanna, Salleeannah, Salleeanne, Sallian, Salliana, Sallianah, Salliane, Sallianna, Salliannah, Sallianne, Sally-Ann, Sally-Anne, Sallyann, Sallyanna, Sallyannah, Sallyanne

Sally (English) Form of Sarah, meaning "princess; lady"
Salley, Salli, Sallie, Sallee, Salleigh, Salia, Saliah, Salie, Saliee, Sallia, Salliah, Sailee, Saileigh, Sailey, Saili, Sailia, Sailie, Saily, Sal, Salaid, Salea, Saleah, Salee, Salei, Saleigh, Saley, Sallea, Salleah, Sallei, Sallya, Sallyah, Sallye, Saly, Salya, Salyah, Salye, Sali

Saloma (Hebrew) One who offers peace and tranquility
Salomah, Salome, Salomia, Salomiah, Schlomit, Shulamit, Salomeaexl, Salomma, Salaome, Salomea, Salomee, Salomei, Salomey, Salomi, Salomya, Salomyah

Saloni (Hindi) A beautiful dear one
Salonie, Salony, Saloney, Salonee, Salonni, Salloni, Sallonee, Salonea

Salus (Latin) In mythology, goddess of health and prosperity; salvation
Saluus, Salusse, Saluss

Salva (Latin) A wise woman
Salvah, Salvia, Salvina, Salvinia, Salviya, Sallviah, Salviah, Salviana, Salvianah, Salviane, Salvianna, Salviannah, Salvianne, Salvinah, Salvine, Salvyna, Salvynah, Salvyne, Sallvia

Salvadora (Spanish) Feminine form of Salvador; savior
Salvadorah, Salvadoria, Salbatora, Salbatoria, Salvatora, Salvatoria

Salwa (Arabic) One who provides comfort; solace
Salwah

Samah (Arabic) A generous, forgiving woman
Sama, Samma, Sammah

Samala (Hebrew) One who is requested by God
Samalah, Samale, Sammala, Sammalah, Samalla, Samallah

Samanfa (Hebrew) Form of Samantha, meaning "one who listens well"
Samanffa, Sammanfa, Sammanffa, Semenfa, Semenfah, Samenffa, Semenffah

❂ **Samantha** (Aramaic) One who listens well
Samanthah, Samanthia, Samanthea, Samantheya, Samanath, Samanatha, Samana, Samanitha, Samanithia, Samanth, Samanthe, Samanthi, Samanthiah, Semantha, Sementha, Simantha, Smantha, Samantah, Smanta, Samanta, Sammatha, Samatha, Samea, Samee, Samey, Samie, Samy, Samye, Sami, Sammanth, Sammanthia, Sammanthiah, Sammanthya, Sammanthyah, Sammantha, Sammi, Sammie, Sammy, Samm, Samma, Sammah, Sammee, Sammey, Sammijo, Sammyjo

Samar (Arabic) One who provides evening conversation
Samarr, Samare, Samarre

Samara (Hebrew) Protected by God
Samarah, Samaria, Shemariah, Samarra, Samarie, Samariya, Samaira, Samar, Samary, Sammar, Sammara, Samora, Samarah, Samari, Samariah, Samarrea, Sameria, Saimara

Sameh (Arabic) One who forgives
Sammeh, Samaya, Samaiya

Samihah (Arabic) One who is generous; magnanimous
Samiha, Sameeha, Samyha, Sameaha, Sameyha, Samieha, Sameiha

Samina (Arabic) A healthy woman
Saminah, Samine, Sameena, Samyna, Sameana, Sameina, Samynah

Samira (Arabic) Feminine form of Samir; companion for evening conversation
Samirah, Samire, Sameera, Samyra, Sameira, Samera, Samiria, Samirra, Samyrah, Samyre, Samiriah, Sameara

Samone (Hebrew) Form of Simone, meaning "one who listens well"
Samoan, Samoane, Samon, Samona, Samonia

Sampada (Indian) A blessing from God
Sampadah, Sampadda, Sampadia, Sampadiya, Sampadea, Sampadya

Sampriti (Indian) An attachment
Sampritie, Samprity, Sampritey, Sampritee, Sampryti, Sampryty, Sampritti, Sampritea

Samuela (Hebrew) Feminine form of Samuel; asked of God
Samuelah, Samuella, Samuell, Samuelle, Sammila, Sammile, Samella, Samielle, Samilla, Samille, Samiella, Samelia

Samularia (Hebrew) Sweet one forever
Samulariah, Samulara, Samularra, Samulariya, Samularea, Samulareah

Samya (Arabic) One who is exalted
Samiyah, Samia, Samiha, Sammia, Sammiah, Sammya, Sammyah, Samyah, Samiah, Samiya

Sana (Persian / Arabic) One who emanates light / brilliance; splendor
Sanah, Sanna, Sanako, Sanaah, Sane, Saneh

Sanaa (Swahili) Beautiful work of art
Sanae, Sannaa

Sancha (Spanish) Feminine form of Sancho; saintly; holy
Sanchah, Sanchia, Sancia, Sancta, Sanchiya, Sanchiah, Sanchie, Sanchya, Sanchyah, Sanciah, Sancie, Sanctia, Sancya, Sancyah, Santsia, Sanzia, Sanziah, Sanzya, Sanzyah, Sancharia, Sanche, Sancheska, Sanceska

Sandeep (Punjabi) One who is enlightened
Sandeepe, Sandip, Sandipp, Sandippe, Sandeyp, Sandeype

Sandhya (Hindi) Born at twilight; name of the daughter of the god Brahma
Sandhiya, Sandhyah, Sandya, Sandyah

Sandia (Spanish) Resembling a watermelon
Sandiah, Sandea, Sandya, Sandeea, Sandiya

Sandra (Greek) Form of Alexandra, meaning "helper and defender of mankind"
Sandrah, Sandrine, Sandy, Sandi, Sandie, Sandey, Sandee, Sanda, Sondra, Shandra, Sandira, Sandah, Sandirah, Sandrica, Sanndra, Sahndra, Sandia, Sandiah, Sandley, Sandine, Sanndie, Sandea, Sandye

Sandrea (Greek) Form of Sandra, meaning "helper and defender of mankind"
Sandreah, Sandreea, Sandreia, Sandreiah, Sandrell, Sandrella, Sandrellah, Sandrelle, Sandria, Sandriah, Sanndria

Sandrica (Greek) Form of Sandra, meaning "helper and defender of mankind"
Sandricca, Sandricah, Sandricka, Sandrickah, Sandrika, Sandrikah, Sandryca, Sandrycah, Sandrycka, Sandryckah, Sandryka, Sandrykah

Sandrine (Greek) Form of Alexandra, meaning "helper and defender of mankind"
Sandrin, Sandreana, Sandreanah, Sandreane, Sandreen, Sandreena, Sandreenah, Sandreene, Sandrene, Sandrenna, Sandrennah, Sandrenne, Sandrianna, Sandrina, Sandrinah, Sandryna, Sandrynah, Sandryne

Sangita (Indian) One who is musical
Sangitah, Sangeeta, Sangeita, Sangyta, Sangieta, Sangeata

Sangrida (Norse) In mythology, a Valkyrie
Sangridah, Sangridda, Sangryda, Sangrydah

Saniya (Indian) A moment in time preserved
Saniyah, Sanya, Sanea, Sania

Sanjeet (Indian) One who is invincible
Sanjit, Sanjitte, Sanjeete, Sanjeat, Sanjeate

Sanjna (Indian) A conscientious woman

Sanjula (Indian) One who is beautiful; attractive
Sanjulah, Sanjulla, Sanjoula, Sanjoulah

Sanne (American) Form of Susanna, meaning "resembling a graceful white lily"

Santana (Spanish) A saintly woman
Santa, Santah, Santania, Santaniah, Santaniata, Santena, Santenah, Santenna, Shantana, Shantanna

Santuzza (Italian) One who is holy
Santuzzah, Santuza, Santuzah, Santuzzia, Santuzia, Santouza, Santouzza

Sanura (African) One who is kittenlike
Sanurah, Sanuria, Sanurea, Sanurru

Sany (Indian) Born on a Sunday
Saney, Sanie, Sani, Sanee, Sanni, Sannee, Sanea

Sanyu (Japanese) One who brings happiness

Saoirse (Gaelic) An independent woman; having freedom
Saoyrse

Sapna (Hindi) A dream come true
Sapnah, Sapnia, Sapniah, Sapnea, Sapneah, Sapniya, Sapniyah

Sapphire (Arabic / English) One who is beautiful / a precious gem
Sapphira, Sapphirah, Saffir, Saffira, Saffire, Safire, Safira, Sapphyre, Saffyre

Sarah (Hebrew) Princess; lady; in the Bible, wife of Abraham
Sara, Sari, Sariah, Sarika, Saaraa, Sarita, Sarina, Sarra, Saara, Saarah, Saaraah, Saarrah, Sharita, Sharie, Sharri, Sharrie, Sharry, Shary, Shari, Soraya

Sarai (Hebrew) One who is contentious and argumentative
Sarae, Saray, Saraye

Saraid (Irish) One who is excellent; superior
Saraide, Saraed, Saraede, Sarayd, Sarayde

Sarama (African / Hindi) A kind woman / in Hinduism, Indra's dog
Saramah, Saramma, Sarrama, Sarramma

Saran (African) One who brings joy to others
Sarane, Sarran, Saranne, Saranna, Sarana, Sarann

Sarasvati (Hindi) In Hinduism, goddess of learning and the arts
Sarasvatti, Sarasvatie, Sarasvaty, Sarasvatey, Sarasvatee, Sarasvatea

Saraswati (Hindi) Owning water; in Hinduism, a river goddess
Saraswatti, Saraswatie, Saraswaty, Saraswatey, Saraswatee, Saraswatea

Sarda (African) One who is hurried; quick
Sardah, Sardda, Sardia, Sardiya, Sardea

Sardinia (Italian) Woman from a mountainous island
Sardiniah, Sardinea, Sardineah, Sardynia, Sardyniah, Sardynea, Sardyneah

Saree (Arabic) Most noble woman
Sarri, Sarie, Sarey, Sary, Sarea

Sarff (Welsh) Resembling a snake; serpentine
Sarf, Sarffe, Sarph, Sarphe

Sarika (Indian / Hungarian) Resembling a parrot / form of Sarah, meaning "princess; lady"
Sarikah, Sareeka, Saryka, Saricka, Saricca, Saryca, Sarica, Sareaka

Sarisha (Hindi) One who is charming; pleasing
Sarysha, Sareesha, Sariesha, Sareysha, Sareasha

Sarki (African) Woman who has the rank of chief
Sarkie, Sarky, Sarkey, Sarkee, Sarkeigh, Sarkki, Sarcki, Sarckie, Sarkea

Sarohildi (German) An armored battle-maiden
Sarohildie, Sarohildy, Sarohildey, Sarohyldi, Sarohyldy, Sarohilde, Sarohilda, Serhild, Serhilda, Serihilde, Serilda, Serilde, Serohilda, Serohilde, Serohild, Serohildi

Sarsoureh (Arabic) A buglike woman
Sarsoure, Sasureh, Sasure

Saryu (Indian) From the river
Saryyu, Saryue

Sasa (Japanese) One who is helpful; gives aid
Sasah

Sasha (Russian) Form of Alexandra, meaning "helper and defender of mankind"
Sascha, Sashenka, Saskia

Sason (Hebrew) One who brings joy
Sasson, Sasone

Sati (Hindi) One who speaks the truth; in Hinduism, a goddess
Satti, Satie, Satty, Saty, Satey, Sattey, Satee, Sattee, Satea, Sattea

Satin (French) A glossy, smooth fabric
Satine, Sattin, Sattine, Satyn, Satyne, Satynne, Sateen, Sateene, Satean, Sateane

Satinka (Native American) A magical dancer
Satinkah, Satincka, Satynka, Satynka

Sato (Japanese) Of a sweet nature

Satu (Finnish) From a fairy tale
Sattu, Satue

Saturday (American) Born on a Saturday
Saturdaye, Saterday, Satarday, Satirday, Saturdai, Saturdae, Saterdai, Saterdae

Saturnina (Spanish) Gift of Saturn, the god of agriculture
Saturneena, Saturnyna, Saturninia, Saturniniya, Saturneana

Satya (Indian) The unchangeable truth
Satiya, Satyana

Satyavati (Hindi) In Hinduism, the mother of Vyasa
Satyavatti, Satyavatie, Satyavaty, Satyavatey, Satyavatee, Satyavatea

Sauda (Swahili) A dark beauty
Saudaa, Sawda, Saudda

Saura (Hindi) Of the heavens
Sawra

❂ **Savannah** (English) From the open, grassy
❂ plain
Savanna, Savana, Savanne, Savann, Savane, Savanneh

Savarna (Hindi) Daughter of the ocean
Savarnia, Savarnea, Savarniya, Savarneia

Saveage (English) In Arthurian legend, the sister of Lyones
Saveyage, Saviage, Savage

Saveria (Italian) Feminine form of Xavier; owner of a new house; one who is bright
Saveriah, Saverea, Saverya, Savereea, Saveriya

Savitri (Hindi) In Hinduism, the daughter of the god of the sun
Savitari, Savitrie, Savitry, Savitarri, Savitarie, Savitree, Savitrea, Savitrey

Savvy (American) Smart and perceptive woman
Savy, Savvi, Savvie, Savvey, Savee, Savvee, Savvea, Savea

Sawsan (Arabic) Form of Susannah, meaning "resembling the graceful white lily"
Sausan, Sawsann, Sawsanna, Sawsanne, Sausanne, Sausanna

Sawyer (English) A woodcutter
Sauyer

Saxona (English) Of the sword people
Saxonah, Saxonia, Saxen, Saxon, Saxons, Saxton, Saxonna, Saxonea, Saxoniya, Saxone

Sayo (Japanese) Born at night
Sayoko, Sayomi, Sayori, Sayyo

Sayyam (Arabic) A fasting woman
Sayyawm, Saaim, Sayam, Sayiam, Sayame

Sayyida (Arabic) A mistress
Sayyidah, Sayida, Sayyda, Seyyada, Seyyida, Seyada, Seyida

Scarlet (English) Vibrant red color; a vivacious woman
Scarlett, Scarlette, Skarlet, Skarlette, Skarlett

Scelflesh (English) From the meadow

Schaaph (Hebrew) One who is thoughtful
Schaph, Schaphe

Scholastica (Latin) Having knowledge; learned; a student
Scholastic, Scholastika, Skolastica, Skolastika, Scholastyca, Skolastyka

Scirocco (Arabic) Of a warm wind

Scorpio (Latin) The eighth sign of the zodiac; a scorpion
Scorpia, Scorpius, Scorpiya, Skorpio, Skorpia, Skorpya, Scorpya

Scota (Irish) Woman of Scotland
Scotta, Scotah, Skota, Skotta, Skotah

Scotia (Latin) A woman from Scotland
Skotia, Scosha, Skosha

Scout (American) An explorer
Scoutt, Scoutte, Skout

Scylla (Greek) In mythology, a sea monster
Scyla, Skylla, Skyla

Sea'iqa (Arabic) Thunder and lightning
Seaqa, Seaqua

Searlait (French) Petite and womanly
Searlaite

Season (Latin) A fertile woman; one who embraces change
Seazon, Seeson, Seezon, Seizon, Seasen, Seasan, Seizen, Seizan

Sebastiana (Italian) Feminine form of Sebastian; one who commands respect
Sebastianna, Sebastiane, Sebastienne, Sebastiene, Sebastene, Sebastina, Sebasteene, Sebastyne, Sebastyna

Sebille (English) In Arthurian legend, a fairy
Sebylle, Sebill, Sebile, Sebyle, Sebyl

Sebiya (Arabic) A lovely young girl
Sebiyah, Sebeeya, Sebeia, Sebeea, Sebeya, Sebeaya

Secunda (Latin) The second-born child
Secundah, Secuba, Secundus, Segunda, Sekunda

Seda (Armenian) Voices of the forest
Sedda, Sedah, Seddah

Sedona (American) Woman from a city in Arizona
Sedonah, Sedonna, Sedonnah, Sedonia, Sedonea

Seema (Greek) A symbol; a sign
Seyma, Syma, Seama, Seima, Siema

Sefarina (Greek) Of a gentle wind
Sefarinah, Sefareena, Sefareenah, Sefaryna, Sefarynah, Sefareana, Sefareanah

Seghen (African) An ostrichlike woman

Segovia (Spanish) From a city in central Spain
Segoviah, Segovea, Segoveah, Segoviya, Segoviyah, Segovya, Segovyah

Segulah (Hebrew) One who is precious
Segula, Segulla, Segullah, Segoula, Segoulla

Seiko (Japanese) The force of truth

Seina (Spanish) Innocent one; pure

Sekai (African) One who brings laughter and great joy

Sekhmet (Egyptian) The powerful one; in mythology, a goddess of war and vengeance
Sakhmet, Sekhmeta, Sakhmeta, Sekhmette, Sakhmette, Sekhmetta, Sakhmetta

Sela (Hebrew / African) As strong as a rock / a savior
Sella, Sele, Seleta, Selata, Selah

Selam (African) She is peaceful
Selamawit, Sellam

Selas (African) Refers to the Trinity
Sellas, Selass, Selasse, Selasa, Selassa

Selby (English) Of the manor of the farm
Selbey, Selbi, Selbie, Selbee, Selbye, Selbea

Selene (Greek) Of the moon; in mythology, the goddess of the moon
Selena, Seline, Salena, Saline, Saleen, Salina, Salena, Salena, Salene, Selina, Saleena, Saleenah, Saleene, Salleen, Salleena, Salleenah, Salleene, Seleane, Seleana, Saleane, Saleana

Selima (Hebrew) One who brings comfort and peace
Selimah, Seleema, Seliema, Seleima, Selyma, Selimma, Seleyma, Seleama

Selma (German) Form of Anselma, meaning "having divine protection"
Selmah

Sema (Arabic) A divine omen; a known symbol
Semah

Semadar (Hebrew) Resembling a berry
Semadarr, Semadarre, Semadara, Semadaria, Semadarea

Semele (Greek) In mythology, one of Zeus's lovers and the mother of Dionysus
Semelle, Semyle

Semine (Danish) In mythology, the goddess of the sun, moon, and stars
Semyne, Semeene, Semeane, Semeine, Semiene

Semira (African / Hebrew) One who is fulfilled / from heaven
Semirah, Semeera, Semyra, Semeira, Semeyra, Semeara

Semiramis (Hebrew) From the highest heaven
Semyramis, Semiramys, Semyramys

Sen (Vietnamese) Resembling the lotus flower

Sena (Latin) One who is blessed
Senna, Senah, Sennah

Senalda (Spanish) A sign; a symbol
Senaldah, Senaldia, Senaldiya, Senaldea, Senaldya

Seneca (Native American) A tribal name
Senecka, Senecca, Seneka

Senga (Greek) Form of Agnes, meaning "one who is pure; chaste"
Sengah, Sengya, Sengyah, Sengia, Sengiah, Sengea, Sengeah, Sengiya, Sengiyah

Sennett (French) One who is wise
Senett, Sennette, Senette, Senet, Senete, Sennetta, Senetta, Senneta, Seneta

Senona (Spanish) A lively woman
Senonah, Senonna, Senonia, Senoniya, Senonea

Senta (German) Acting as an assistant
Sentah, Sente

Sentia (Latin) In mythology, goddess of children's development
Sentiah, Sensia, Senzia

Seonaid (Gaelic) A gift from God
Seonaide, Seonayde, Seonayd, Seonaede, Seonaed, Seonade

Seosaimhin (Irish) A fertile woman
Seosaimhthin

Sephora (Hebrew) A beautiful bird
Sephorah, Sefora, Sephorra, Seforra, Sephoria

September (American) Born in the month of September
Septimber, Septymber, Septemberia, Septemberea

Septima (Latin) The seventh-born child
Septimah, Septeema, Septyma, Septeama

Sequoia (Native American) Of the giant redwood tree
Sequoya, Sequoiya, Sekoia, Sekoya

Serafina (Latin) A seraph; a heavenly winged angel
Serafinah, Serafine, Seraphina, Serefina, Seraphine, Sera

Seren (Welsh) From the starlight
Serin, Seran, Seron, Serun

Serena (Latin) Having a peaceful disposition
Serenah, Serene, Sereena, Seryna, Serenity, Serenitie, Serenitee, Serepta, Serina, Sereana

Serendipity (American) A fateful meeting; having good fortune
Serendipitey, Serendipitee, Serendipiti, Serendipitie, Serendypyty

○ **Serenity** (English) Serene, calm, peaceful
Serenitie, Serenitee, Serepta, Serina, Sereana, Serena, Serenah, Serene, Sereena, Seryna

Serilda (Greek) An armed woman of war
Serild, Serilde, Sarilda, Sarildah, Serildah, Serylda, Seryldah

Serpuhi (Armenian) One who is pious
Serpuhie, Serpuhy, Serpuhey, Serpuhee, Serpuhea

Serwa (African) As precious as a jewel
Serwah, Serwi, Serwy, Serwia, Serwiya, Serwie

Sesame (English) Resembling the flavorful seed
Sesami, Sesamie, Sesamy, Sesamey, Sesamee, Sesamea

Sesen (African) One who longs for more
Sesenn, Sesenne, Sesena, Sesenna

Sesha (Hindi) In Hinduism, a serpent who represents time
Seshia, Seshea, Seshiya

Sesheta (Egyptian) In mythology, goddess of the stars

Sevati (Indian) Resembling the white rose
Sevatie, Sevatti, Sevate, Sevatee, Sevatea, Sevaty, Sevatey, Sevti, Sevtie, Sevtee, Sevtea, Sevty, Sevtey

Sevda (Turkish) A parent's great love
Sevdah

Seven (American) The seventh-born child
Sevene, Seveen, Seveene, Sevyn, Sevyne, Sevin

Severa (Italian) Feminine form of Severo; one who is stern
Severra, Severah, Severia, Severea, Severiya, Severya, Severana, Severanna, Severeen, Severeene, Severine, Severyne

Sevilen (Turkish) One who loves and is loved
Sevilene, Sevilyn, Sevilynn, Sevilynne, Sevileen, Sevileene, Seviline, Sevilyne

Sevilla (Spanish) A woman from Seville
Sevil, Sevila, Sevilah, Sevile, Sevill, Sevillah, Seville, Sevyl, Sevyla, Sevylah, Sevyle, Sevyll, Sevylla, Sevyllah, Sevylle

Sevita (Indian) One who is cherished
Sevitta, Sevitah, Seveta, Seveeta, Sevyta, Sevieta, Seveita, Seveata

Sezja (Russian) A protector of mankind

Shabana (Arabic) A maiden belonging to the night
Shabanah, Shabanna, Shabaana, Shabanne, Shabane

Shabiba (Arabic) A godmother
Shabibah, Shabeebah, Shabeeba, Shabyba, Shabibba, Shabeba, Shabeaba, Shabeabah

Shabnam (Arabic) Of the morning's dew
Shabname, Shabnamn

Shabnan (Persian) A falling raindrop
Shabnane, Shabnann, Shabnanne

Shada (Native American) Resembling a pelican
Shadah, Shadda, Shaddah

Shadha (Arabic) An aromatic fragrance
Shadhah

Shadi (Persian) One who brings happiness and joy
Shadie, Shady, Shadey, Shadee, Shadea

Shadiyah (Arabic) A singer; one who is musical
Shadiya, Shadiyya, Shadiyaa, Shadeeya, Shadeya

Shadow (English) Shade from the sun
Shadowe, Shadoe

Shafiqa (Arabic) A compassionate woman
Shafiqah, Shafiqua, Shafeeqa, Shafeequa

Shagufa (Arabic) A flourishing woman; budding
Shagufah, Shagupha, Shagoofa, Shagoopha, Shagufta, Shagoufa, Shagoupha

Shahdi (Persian) One who is happy
Shahdie, Shahdy, Shahdey, Shahdee, Shahdea

Shahida (Arabic) A witness
Shahidah, Shahyda, Shaahida, Shaahyda

Shahina (Arabic) Resembling a falcon
Shahinah, Shaheenah, Shaheena, Shahyna, Shahinna, Shaheana, Shahynah, Shaheanah

Shahla (Arabic) Having bluish-black eyes
Shahlah, Shahlaa

Shahnaz (Arabic) A king's pride
Shanaz, Shahnaaz, Shahnazze, Shanazz, Shanazze

Shahzadi (Arabic) A princess; born into royalty
Shahzadie, Shahzaadee, Shahzadee, Shahzady, Shahzadey, Shahzadea

Shai (Gaelic) A gift of God
Shay, Shae, Shayla, Shea, Shaye

Shaibya (Indian) A faithful wife
Shaibyah, Shaybya, Shabya, Shaibia, Shaibiya, Shaebya

Shaila (Indian) Of the mountain stone
Shailah, Shayla, Shaylah, Shaela, Shailla

Sha'ira (Arabic) Poetess or singer
Shairah, Shaira, Shaa'ira, Shira, Sheera, Shiri

Sha'ista (Arabic) One who is polite and well-behaved
Shaistah, Shaista, Shaa'ista, Shayista, Shaysta

Shakila (Arabic) Feminine form of Shakil; beautiful one
Shakilah, Shakela, Shakeela, Shakeyla, Shakyla, Shakeila, Shakiela, Shakina, Shakilla, Shakeala

Shakira (Arabic) Feminine form of Shakir; grateful; thankful
Shakirah, Shakiera, Shaakira, Shakeira, Shakyra, Shakeyra, Shakura, Shakirra, Shakeara

Shakti (Indian) A divine woman; having power
Shaktie, Shakty, Shaktey, Shaktee, Shaktye, Shaktea

Shalimar (Indian) A Guerlain perfume; a famous garden in Pakistan
Shalimarr, Shalimare, Shalimarre, Shalimara, Shalimarra

Shalini (Indian) One who is modest
Shalinie, Shaliny, Shalyni, Shalinee, Shalyny, Shalinea, Shalynee

Shaliqa (Arabic) One who is sisterly
Shaliqah, Shaliqua, Shaleeqa, Shaleequa, Shalyqa, Shalyqua

Shalishah (Hebrew) Place name from the Bible
Shalesa, Shalesah, Shalese, Shalessa, Shalice, Shalicia, Shaliece, Shalisa, Shalisah, Shalise, Shalisha, Shalishea, Shalisia, Shalisiah, Shalissa, Shalissah, Shalisse, Shalyce, Shalys, Shalysa, Shalysah, Shalyse, Shalyss, Shalyssa, Shalyssah, Shalysse, Shaleashah, Shaleesha, Shaleashah, Shaleeshah

Shalom (Hebrew) One who is peaceful

Shama (Arabic) The lighted mark
Shamah, Shamma, Shammah

Shamara (Arabic) Woman who is ready for battle
Shamarah, Shamarra, Shamarrah, Shamaria, Shamarie

Shamima (Arabic) A woman full of flavor
Shamimah, Shameema, Shamiema, Shameima, Shamyma, Shameama

Shamira (Hebrew) A guardian; protector
Shamirah, Shameera, Shamiera, Shameira, Shamyra, Shameara

Shamita (Indian) A peacemaker
Shamitah, Shamyta, Shameeta, Shamitta, Shameata

Shana (Hebrew) God is gracious
Shanah, Shanna, Shania, Shanae, Shanaia, Shane, Shanessa, Shanelle, Shanell, Shandi, Shanice, Shaniece, Seana, Shaana, Shaanah, Shan, Shanda, Shandae, Shandah, Shannda

Shandy (English) One who is rambunctious; boisterous
Shandey, Shandee, Shandi, Shandie, Shandye, Shandea

Shani (African) A marvelous woman
Shanie, Shany, Shaney, Shanee, Shanni, Shanea, Shannie, Shanny, Shanney, Shannee, Shannea

Shanice (American) Form of Janice, meaning "God is gracious"
Shaneace, Shanease, Shaneece, Shaneese, Shaneise, Shanicea, Shannice, Sheneice, Shenyce

Shanika (American) A woman from a settlement in Africa
Shanica, Shanicah, Shanicca, Shanicka, Shanickah, Shanieka, Shanikah, Shanike, Shanikia, Shanikka, Shanikqua, Shanikwa, Shanyca, Shanycah, Shanycka, Shanyckah, Shanyka, Shanykah, Shineeca, Shonnika, Shaneeka, Shaneaka

Shanley (Gaelic) Small and ancient woman
Shanleigh, Shanlee, Shanly, Shanli, Shanlie, Shanlea

Shannelle (English) Form of Chanel, meaning "from the canal; a channel"
Shanele, Shanel, Shanell, Shanelle, Shannele, Shannelle, Shannell

Shannon (Gaelic) Having ancient wisdom; river name
Shanon, Shannen, Shannan, Shannin, Shanna, Shannae, Shannun, Shannyn

Shanta (Hindi) One who is calm
Shantah, Shantta, Shantia, Shantea, Shantiya

Shantelle (American) Form of Chantal, meaning "from a stony place; a beautiful singer"
Shantell, Shantel, Shantele, Shanton, Shantal, Shantale

Shanti (Indian) One who is peaceful; tranquil
Shantie, Shanty, Shantey, Shantee, Shantea, Shanata, Shante

Shaquana (American) Truth in life
Shaqana, Shaquanah, Shaquanna, Shaqanna, Shaqania

Sharara (Arabic) Born of lightning; a spark
Shararah, Sharaara, Shararra

Sharifah (Arabic) Feminine form of Sharif; noble; respected; virtuous
Sharifa, Shareefa, Sharufa, Sharufah, Sharyfa, Sharefa, Shareafa, Shariefa, Shareifa

Sharik (African) One who is a child of God
Shareek, Shareake, Sharicke, Sharick, Sharike, Shareak, Sharique, Sharyk, Sharyke, Sharyque

Sharikah (Arabic) One who is a good companion
Sharika, Shareeka, Sharyka, Shareka, Shariqua, Shareaka

Sharise (English) Form of Charis, meaning "having grace and kindness"
Shareace, Sharease, Shereece, Shareese, Sharese, Sharesse, Shariece, Sharis, Sharise, Sharish, Shariss, Sharisse, Sharyce, Sharyse

Sharlene (French) Feminine form of Charles; a small, strong woman
Sharleene, Sharleen, Sharla, Sharlyne, Sharline, Sharlyn, Sharlean, Sharleane

Sharmane (English) Form of Charmaine, meaning "charming and delightful woman"
Sharman, Sharmaine, Sharmain, Sharmayne, Sharmayn, Sharmaen, Sharmaene

Sharmila (Indian) One who provides comfort, joy, and protection
Sharmilah, Sharmyla, Sharmeela, Sharmilla, Sharmylla

Sharon (Hebrew) From the plains; a flowering shrub
Sharron, Sharone, Sharona, Shari, Sharis, Sharne, Sherine, Sharun, Sharin, Sharan, Sharen

Shashi (Hindi) Of the moonlight; a moonbeam
Shashie, Shashy, Shashey, Shashee, Shashea

Shasmecka (African) A princess; highborn girl
Shasmecca, Shasmeka, Shasmeckia, Shasmeckiya

Shasta (Native American) From the triple-peaked mountain
Shastah, Shastia, Shastiya, Shastea, Shasteya

Shasti (Hindi) In Hinduism, a protective goddess of children
Shastie, Shasty, Shastee, Shastey, Shastea

Shauna (Irish) Feminine form of Shaun; God is gracious
Shawna, Shaunna, Shawnna, Seana, Seanna, Shawnessa, Shawnnessy, Shona

Shavon (American) Variant of Siobhan, meaning "God is gracious"
Shavonne, Schavon, Schevon, Shavan, Shavaun, Shavone, Shavonia, Shavonn, Shavonni, Shavonnia, Shavonnie, Shavontae, Shavonte, Shavoun, Sheavon, Shivaun, Shivawn, Shivon, Shivonne, Shyvon, Shyvonne

Shawnee (Native American) A tribal name
Shawni, Shawnie, Shawnea, Shawny, Shawney, Shawnea

Shayla (Irish) Of the fairy palace
Shaylah, Shaylagh, Shaylain, Shaylan, Shaylea, Shayleah, Shaylla, Sheyla

Shaylee (Gaelic) From the fairy palace; a fairy princess
Shalee, Shayleigh, Shailee, Shaileigh, Shaelee, Shaeleigh, Shayli, Shaylie, Shayly, Shayley, Shaeli, Shaelie, Shaely, Shaeley, Shaili, Shailie, Shaily, Shailey

Shayna (Hebrew) A beautiful woman
Shaynah, Shaine, Shaina, Shaena, Shayndel, Shana, Shaynae, Shaynee, Shayney, Shayni, Shaynia, Shaynie, Shaynna, Shaynne, Shayny, Shayne

Shea (Gaelic / Irish) Of admirable character / from the fairy palace
Shearra, Sheah

Sheba (Hebrew) An oath; a biblical place
Shebah, Sheeba, Shyba, Sheyba, Sheaba

Sheehan (Celtic) Little peaceful one; peacemaker
Shehan, Sheyhan, Shihan, Shiehan, Shyhan, Sheahan

Sheela (Indian) One of cool conduct and character
Sheelah, Sheetal

Sheena (Gaelic) God's gracious gift
Sheenah, Shena, Shiena, Sheyna, Shyna, Sheana, Sheina

Sheherezade (Arabic) One who is a city dweller

Sheila (Irish) Form of Cecilia, meaning "one who is blind"
Sheilah, Sheelagh, Shelagh, Shiela, Shyla, Selia, Sighle, Sheiletta, Sheilette, Sheilett, Sheileta, Sheyla, Sheala

Sheiramoth (Hebrew) Musician of the temple
Sheiramothe, Sheramoth, Shyramoth, Shiramoth, Sheeramoth

Shelby (English) From the willow farm
Shelbi, Shelbey, Shelbie, Shelbee, Shelbye, Shelbea

Shelley (English) From the bank's meadow
Shelly, Shelli, Shellie, Shellee, Shelleigh, Shella, Shellaine, Shellana, Shellany, Shellea, Shelleah, Shellei, Shellene, Shellian, Shelliann, Shellina, Shell

Shepry (American) A mediator who is honest and friendly
Sheprey, Shepri, Sheprie, Shepree, Sheprye, Sheprea

Shera (Aramaic) A very bright light
Sheara, Shearah, Sheera, Sheerah, Sherae, Sherah, Sheralla, Sheralle, Sheray, Sheraya

Sheridan (Gaelic) One who is wild and untamed; a searcher
Sheridann, Sheridanne, Sherydan, Sherridan, Sheriden, Sheridon, Sherrerd, Sherida, Sheridane, Sherideen, Sheridian, Sheridin, Sheridyn, Sherridana, Sherridane, Sherridanne, Sherridon, Sherrydan, Sherrydana, Sherrydane, Sherrydin, Sherrydon, Sherrydyn, Sherydana, Sherydane

Sherise (Greek) Form of Charis, meaning "having grace and kindness"
Sherisse, Sherissa, Sheris, Sheriss, Sherys, Sheryse, Sherysse, Sherysa, Sherisa, Scherise, Sherece, Shereece, Sherees, Shereese, Sherese, Shericia, Sherrish, Sherryse, Sheryce

Sherry (English) Form of Cherie, meaning "one who is greatly loved; a darling"
Sherrey, Sherri, Sherrie, Sherie, Sheri, Sherree, Sherea, Sherrea

Sheryl (English) Form of Cheryl, meaning "one who is greatly loved; a darling"
Sheryll, Sherylle, Sherylyn, Sheryle, Sherile, Sherill, Sherille, Sharilyn, Sherilin, Sherilina, Sherilinah, Sheriline, Sherilyna, Sherilynah, Sherilyne, Sherilynn, Sherilynna, Sherilynnah, Sherilynne, Sherilyn

Sheshebens (Native American) Resembling a small duck

Shields (English) A loyal protector
Sheelds, Sheylds, Shylds, Shilds, Shealds

Shifra (Hebrew) A beautiful midwife
Shifrah, Shiphrah, Shiphra, Shifria, Shifriya, Shifrea

Shika (Japanese) A little, gentle deer
Shicka, Shicca, Sheka, Shecka, Shyka, Shycka, Sheeka

Shikha (Indian) Flame burning brightly
Shikhah, Shikkha, Shekha, Shykha

Shiloh (Hebrew) One who is peaceful; abundant
Shilo, Shyloh, Shylo

Shilpa (Indian) Strong as a rock
Shilpah, Shilpha, Shylpa, Shylpha

Shima (Native American) Little mother
Shimah, Shimma, Shyma, Shymah

Shin (Korean) One having faith and trust
Shinn, Shyn, Shynn

Shina (Japanese) A virtuous woman; having goodness
Shinah, Shinna, Shyna, Shynna

Shira (Hebrew) My joyous song
Shirah, Shiray, Shire, Shiree, Shiri, Shirit

Shirin (Persian) One who is sweet and pleasant
Sheerin, Sheereen, Shirina, Shirinia, Shiriniya, Shiryn, Shirynn, Shirynne

Shirley (English) From the bright clearing
Shirly, Shirlie, Shirli, Shirleigh, Shirlee, Shirl, Shirlyn, Shirlea, Sherle, Sherley, Sherly, Sherli, Sherlie, Sherlee, Sherlea, Sherleigh

Shobha (Indian) An attractive woman
Shobhah, Shobbha, Shoba, Shobhan, Shobhane

Shobhna (Indian) A shiny ornament
Shobhnah, Shobbhna, Shobna, Shobhnan, Shobhnane

Shona (Irish) Form of Joan, meaning "God is gracious"
Shiona, Shonagh, Shonah, Shonalee, Shone, Shonette

Shoney (Celtic) In mythology, a sea goddess
Shony, Shoni, Shonie, Shonee, Shonni, Shonea, Shonnie

Shoshana (Arabic) Form of Susan, meaning "resembling a graceful white lily"
Shosha, Shoshan, Shoshanah, Shoshane, Shoshanha, Shoshann, Shoshanna, Shoshannah, Shoshauna, Shoshaunah, Shoshaunah, Shoshawna, Shoshona, Shoushan, Shushana, Sosha, Soshana

Shoshone (Native American) A tribal name
Shoshoni, Shoshonie, Shoshonee, Shoshonea, Shoshony, Shoshoney

Shradhdha (Indian) One who is faithful; trusting
Shraddha, Shradha, Shradhan, Shradhane

Shreya (Indian) A lucky woman
Shreyah

Shriya (Indian) One who is wealthy; prosperous
Shriyah, Shreeya, Shreeyah

Shruti (Indian) Having good hearing
Shrutie, Shruty, Shrutey, Shrutee, Shrutye, Shrutea

Shu Fang (Chinese) One who is gentle and kind

Shulamit (Hebrew) One who is peaceful; tranquil
Shulamite, Schulamit, Scholamit, Shulamitte, Shulamith, Shulamithe, Shulamitha

Shuman (Native American) One who charms rattlesnakes
Shumane, Shumaine, Shumayne, Shumanne, Shumanna, Shumaene

Shunnareh (Arabic) Pleasing in manner and behavior
Shunnaraya, Shunareh, Shunarreh

Shura (Russian) Form of Alexandra, meaning "helper and defender of mankind"
Shurah, Shurra, Shurrah

Shyann (English) Form of Cheyenne, meaning "unintelligible speaker"
Shyanne, Shyane, Sheyann, Sheyanne, Sheyenne, Sheyene

Shyla (English) Form of Sheila, meaning "one who is blind"
Shya, Shyah, Shylah, Shylan, Shylana, Shylane, Shylayah, Shyle, Shyleah, Shylee, Shyley, Shyli, Shylia, Shylie, Shylyn

Shysie (Native American) A quiet child
Shysi, Shysy, Shysey, Shysee, Shycie, Shyci, Shysea, Shycy, Shycey, Shycee, Shycea

Sian (Welsh) Form of Jane, meaning "God is gracious"
Sianne, Siann, Siane, Sione, Siana, Siania, Sianya, Sianna

Siany (Irish) Having good health
Sianie, Sianey, Sianee, Siani, Sianea

Siara (Arabic) One who is holy and pure
Siaraa, Siarah, Syara, Siarra, Syarra

Sibeal (Irish) Form of Isabel, meaning "my God is bountiful"
Sibeall, Sibealle, Sibeale, Sybeal, Sybeale, Sybeall

Sibyl (English) A prophetess; a seer
Sybil, Sibyla, Sybella, Sibil, Sibella, Sibilla, Sibley, Sibylla, Sibly, Sibli, Siblie, Siblee, Siblea, Sibleigh

Sicily (Italian) A woman from the large island off Italy
Sicilie, Sicili, Siciley, Sicilee, Sicilea, Sicileigh

Siddhi (Hindi) Having spiritual power
Sidhi, Syddhi, Sydhi

Siddiqa (Arabic) A righteous friend
Siddiqua, Sidiqa, Siddeeqa, Siddyqa, Siddeequa, Siddyqua

Side (Anatolian) Resembling a pomegranate, symbolizing abundance

Sidera (Latin) A luminous woman
Siderra, Sydera, Syderra, Sideria, Sideriya, Siderea

Sidero (Greek) In mythology, stepmother of Pelias and Neleus
Siderro, Sydero, Sideriyo

Sidonie (French) Feminine form of Sidonius; woman of Sidon
Sidonia, Sidone, Sidoniya, Sidonea, Sidony, Sidoni, Sidoney, Sidonee

Sidra (Latin) Resembling a star
Sidrah, Sydra, Sidriya, Sydriya

Sieglinde (German) Winning a gentle victory

Sienna (Italian) Woman with reddish-brown hair
Siena, Siennya, Sienya, Syenna, Syinna, Syenya

❂ **Sierra** (Spanish) From the jagged mountain range
Siera, Syerra, Syera, Seyera, Seeara

Sigfreda (German) A woman who is victorious
Sigfreeda, Sigfrida, Sigfryda, Sigfreyda, Sigfrieda, Sigfriede, Sigfrede

Sigismonda (Teutonic) A victorious defender
Sigismunda

Signia (Latin) A distinguishing sign
Signiya, Signea, Signeia, Signeya, Signa

Signy (Scandinavian) A newly victorious woman
Signe, Signi, Signie, Signey, Signee, Signild, Signilde, Signilda, Signea

Sigourney (Scandinavian / French) A woman who conquers / a daring queen
Sigourny, Sigourni, Sigournie, Sigournee, Sigournye, Sigournea, Sigurney, Sigurny, Sigurni, Sigurnie, Sigurnea, Sigurnee

Sigrid (Scandinavian) A victorious advisor
Sigryd, Sigryde, Sigrith, Sigrath, Sigrathe, Siri

Sigrun (Scandinavian) Having won a secret victory

Sigyn (Norse) In mythology, the wife of Loki

Siham (Arabic) Resembling an arrow

Sihar (Arabic) An enchanting woman
Syhar, Sihara, Syhara, Sihari, Siharie,
Sihary, Siharey, Siharee, Siharea, Siharia

Slhu (Native American) As delicate as a
flower

Sika (African) A woman with money
Sikah, Sikka, Sicka, Syka, Sykka, Sicca

Sikina (Arabic) A devout and peaceful
woman
Sikinah, Sikyna, Sickina, Sickyna, Sikeena,
Sikena, Sikeyna, Sikeana

Sila (Indian) A well-behaved, chaste woman
Silah, Silla, Syla, Sylah, Sylla

Silana (French) One who is dignified; a lady
Silanah, Silanna, Sylana, Sylanna, Silane,
Silann, Silan, Silanne

Sileas (Scottish) A woman who remains
youthful
Silis, Silys, Syleas, Silias, Sile, Silyas

Silence (American) A quiet and well-
behaved child
Silince, Silense, Silinse, Sylence, Sylense,
Sylince, Sylinse

Silka (Latin) Form of Cecelia, meaning "one
who is blind"
Silke, Silkia, Silkea, Silkie, Silky, Silkee,
Sylka, Sylke, Silja, Silken, Silkan

Silvana (Latin) Feminine form of Silvanus;
a woodland dweller
Silvanna, Silvane, Silvanne, Silva, Silvia,
Silviya, Sylvia, Sylvya, Sylva, Sylvana,
Sylvanna, Sylvane, Sylvanne, Silvestra

Silver (English) A precious metal; white-
skinned
Sylver, Silvera, Sylvera, Silvere, Sylvere

Silwa (Arabic) Resembling a quail
Silwah, Sylwa, Sylwah

Sima (Arabic) One who is treasured; a prize
Simma, Syma, Simah, Simia, Simiya

Simcha (Hebrew) One who is joyous
Simchia, Simchea, Symcha, Symchia,
Symchea

Simin (Iranian) A silvery woman
Simeen, Seemeen, Symeen, Simyn

Simona (Italian) Feminine form of Simon;
one who listens well
Simonah, Simonna, Symona, Simone,
Symone, Simoni, Simony, Simonee, Simoney,
Simonie

Simran (Indian) One who meditates
Simrana, Simrania, Simrann, Simranne,
Simrane, Simranna

Sina (Samoan) In mythology, goddess of the
moon

Sine (Scottish) Form of Jane, meaning "God
is gracious"
Sinead, Sineidin, Sioned, Sionet, Sion,
Siubhan, Siwan, Sineh

Sinmore (Norse) In mythology, the wife of
Surt
Sinmorre, Sinmora, Sinmorra, Synmore,
Synmora

Sinobia (Greek) Form of Zenobia, meaning
"sign or symbol"
Sinobiah, Sinobya, Sinobe, Sinobie, Sinovia,
Senobia, Senobya, Senobe, Senobie, Senobey,
Senovia

Sinopa (Native American) Resembling a fox

Sinope (Greek) In mythology, one of the
daughters of Asopus

Sintra (Spanish) A woman from the town in
Portugal

Siobhan (Irish) Form of Joan, meaning
"God is gracious"
Shibahn, Shibani, Shibhan, Shioban,
Shobana, Shobhana, Siobahn, Siobhana,
Siobhann, Siobhon, Siovaun, Siovhan

Sippora (Hebrew) A birdlike woman
Sipporah, Sipora, Syppora, Sypora, Siporra,
Syporra

Siran (Armenian) An alluring and lovely
woman

Siren (Greek) A seductive and beautiful
woman; in mythology, a sea nymph whose
beautiful singing lured sailors to their
deaths
Sirene, Sirena, Siryne, Siryn, Syren, Syrena,
Sirine, Sirina, Sirinia, Sirenia

Siria (Spanish / Persian) Bright like the sun / a glowing woman
Siriah, Sirea, Sireah, Siriya, Siriyah, Sirya, Siryah

Siroun (Armenian) A lovely woman
Sirune

Sirpuhi (Armenian) One who is holy; pious
Sirpuhie, Sirpuhy, Sirpuhey, Sirpuhea, Sirpuhee

Sirvat (Armenian) Resembling a beautiful rose

Sisay (African) A blessing from God; an omen of good things to come
Sisaye, Sissay, Sissaye

Sisi (African) Born on a Sunday
Sisie, Sisea, Sisee, Sisy, Sisey

Sisika (Native American) Resembling a bird

Sissy (English) Form of Cecilia, meaning "one who is blind"
Sissey, Sissie, Sisley, Sisli, Sislee, Sissel, Sissle, Syssy, Syssi

Sita (Hindi) In Hinduism, goddess of the harvest and wife of Rama

Sitara (Indian) Of the morning star
Sitarah, Sitarra, Sitaara, Siteare

Sitembile (African) A woman worthy of trust
Sitembyle

Siti (African) A distinguished woman; a lady
Sitie, Sity, Sitey, Sitee, Sitea

Sitka (English) A woman from a city in western Alaska
Sytka

Siv (Norse) A beautiful bride; in mythology, the wife of Thor
Sif

Sive (Irish) A good and sweet girl
Sivney, Sivny, Sivni, Sivnie, Sivnee, Sivnea

Siyanda (African) The village is expanding

Skaoi (Norse) In mythology, a mountain giantess and goddess of skiers

Sky (American) From the heavens

Skye (Gaelic) Woman from the Isle of Skye

Skylar (English) One who is learned; a scholar
Skylare, Skylarr, Skyler, Skylor, Skylir, Skylur

Slaine (Irish) A woman of good health
Slain, Slayne, Slane, Slany, Slanee, Slania, Slainie, Slanie, Slaney, Siany, Slaen, Slaene

Sloane (Irish) A strong protector; a woman warrior
Sloan, Slone

Smita (Indian) One who smiles a lot

Snana (Native American) Having a sound like bells
Snanah, Snanna, Snannah

Snow (American) Frozen rain
Snowy, Snowie, Snowi, Snowey, Snowee, Snowea, Sno

Snowdrop (English) Resembling a small white flower

Socorro (Spanish) One who offers help and relief
Socoro, Sokorro, Sokoro, Sockorro, Sockoro

Sohalia (Indian) Of the moon's glow
Sohaliah, Sohalea, Sohaliya, Sohaleah, Sohalya

Sokanon (Native American) Born of the rain

Solace (Latin) One who gives comfort
Solase

Solada (Thai) One who listens well

Solaina (French) A dignified and respected woman
Solaine, Solayna, Solanya, Solaynya, Solainia, Solaena

Solana (Latin / Spanish) Wind from the East / of the sunshine
Solanah, Solanna, Solann, Solanne

Solange (French) One who is religious and dignified

Solaris (Greek) Of the sun
Solarise, Solariss, Solarisse, Solarys, Solaryss, Solarysse, Sol, Soleil, Solstice

Solita (Latin) One who is solitary
Solitah, Solida, Soledad, Soledada, Soledade

Solona (Greek) Feminine form of Solon; wisdom
Solonah, Solone, Solonie, Soloni, Solony, Soloney, Solonee, Solonea

Solveig (Norse) The strength of the house
Solvig, Solveige, Solvige

Soma (Indian) An exalted woman; one who gives praise

Somatra (Indian) Of the excellent moon

Sona (Arabic) The golden one
Sonika, Sonna

Sonora (Spanish) A pleasant-sounding woman
Sonorah, Sonoria, Sonorya, Sonoriya

Soo (Korean) Having an excellent, long life

Sooleawa (Native American) Resembling silver

⊕ **Sophia** (Greek) Form of Sophie, meaning "having great wisdom and foresight"
Sofia, Sofiya

⊕ **Sophie** (Greek) Having great wisdom and foresight
Sofie, Sofi, Sofiyko, Sofronia, Sophronia, Sophy, Sonia, Sonya, Sonja

Sora (Native American) Resembling a chirping songbird
Sorah, Sorra, Sorrah

Sorano (Japanese) Of the heavens

Sorcha (Gaelic) One who is bright; intelligent; form of Sarah, meaning "princess; lady"
Sorchah, Sorchia, Sorchiah, Sorchea, Sorcheah, Sorchiya, Sorchiyah, Sorchya, Sorchyah

Sorina (Romanian) Feminine form of Sorin; of the sun
Sorinah, Sorinna, Sorinia, Soriniya, Sorinya, Soryna, Sorynia, Sorine, Soreena, Soreana

Soroushi (Persian) A bringer of happiness
Soroushie, Soroushy, Soroushey, Soroushea, Sorushi, Sorushie, Sorushy, Sorushey, Sorushea, Sorushee

Sorrel (French) From the surele plant
Sorrell, Sorrelle, Sorrele, Sorrela, Sorrella

Soubrette (French) One who is coquettish
Soubrett, Soubret, Soubrete, Soubretta, Soubreta

Southern (American) Woman of the South

Sovann (Cambodian) The golden one
Sovane, Sovanne, Sovana, Sovanna, Sovania, Sovaniya

Soyala (Native American) Born during the winter solstice
Soyalah, Soyalla, Soyalia, Soyaliya, Soyalya

Sparrow (English) Resembling a small songbird
Sparro, Sparroe, Sparo, Sparow, Sparowe, Sparoe

Spencer (English) An administrator; dispenser of provisions
Spenser, Spincer, Spinser

Speranza (Italian) Form of Esperanza, meaning "filled with hope"
Speranzia, Speranzea, Speranziya, Speranzya

Spes (Latin) In mythology, goddess of hope

Spica (Latin) One of the brightest stars
Spicah, Spicka, Spika, Spicca, Spyca, Spycka, Spyka

Spring (English) Refers to the season; born in spring
Spryng

Sraddha (Hindi) One having faith and trust
Sraddhah, Sradha, Sradhah

Sroda (African) A respected woman
Srodah, Srodda, Sroddah

Sslama (Egyptian) One who is peaceful

Stacey (English) Form of Anastasia, meaning "one who shall rise again"
Stacy, Staci, Stacie, Stacee, Stacia, Stasia, Stasy, Stasey, Stasi, Stasie, Stasee, Steise, Stacea, Stasea

Stanislava (Slovene) Feminine form of Stanislav; government's glory
Stanislavah, Stanyslava, Stanislavia, Stanislaviya, Stanislavya, Stanyslavia

Stansie (Italian) One who is constant; stead-fast
Stansi, Stansey, Stansy, Stansee, Stansea, Stanzie, Stanzi, Stanzy, Stanzey, Stanzee, Stanzea

Star (American) A celestial body
Starr, Starre, Starry, Starrie, Starri, Starling, Starla

Starbuck (American) An astronaut

Stella (English) Star of the sea
Stela, Stelle, Stele, Stellah, Stelah

Stephanie (Greek) Feminine form of Stephen; crowned in victory
Stephani, Stephany, Stephaney, Stephanee, Stephene, Stephana, Stefanie, Stefani, Stefany, Stefaney, Stefanee, Steffani, Steffanie, Stephania, Stefania, Steffine, Stephenie, Stesha, Stephie, Stephi, Stephy, Stephia, Stefia

Stetson (English) Child of one who is crowned
Stetsun, Stetsan, Stetsin, Stetsyn, Stetsen

Stevonna (Greek) A crowned lady
Stevonnah, Stevona, Stevonah, Stevonia, Stevonea, Stevoniya

Stheno (Greek) A mighty woman; in mythology, one of the Gorgons

Stina (Danish) Form of Christina, meaning "follower of Christ"
Stinna, Stinne, Stine, Styna, Stynna, Styne, Stynne, Steena, Steana

Stockard (English) From the yard of tree stumps
Stockhard, Stockhard, Stokkard

Storm (American) Of the tempest; stormy weather; having an impetuous nature
Storme, Stormy, Stormi, Stormie, Stormey, Stormee, Stormia, Stormea

Strephon (Greek) One who turns
Strephone, Strephonn, Strephonne, Strep

Struana (Scottish) From the stream
Struanna, Struanah, Struanne, Struan, Struann, Struane

Styx (Greek) In mythology, the river of the underworld
Stixx, Styxx, Stix

Suadela (Latin) In mythology, goddess of persuasion
Suadelah, Suadell, Suadelle, Suadele, Suada

Suave (American) A smooth and courteous woman
Swave

Subha (Indian) One who is beautiful; attractive

Subhadra (Hindi) In Hinduism, the sister of Krishna

Subhaga (Indian) A fortunate person

Subhuja (Hindi) An auspicious Apsara (heavenly nymph)

Subira (African) One who is patient
Subirah, Subirra, Subyra, Subyrra, Subeera, Subeara, Subeira, Subiera

Suchin (Thai) A beautiful thought

Suchitra (Indian) A beautiful picture
Suchitrah, Suchytra, Suchitran, Suchitrane

Sugar (American) A sweetheart

Sughra (Arabic) A pure young woman
Sughraa, Sughrah

Suha (Arabic) The name of a star

Suhaila (Arabic) Feminine form of Suhail; a gentle woman; bright star
Suhayla, Suhaela, Suhala, Suhailah, Suhaylah, Suhaelah, Suhalah

Suhaymah (Arabic) The little arrow
Suhayma, Suhaimah, Suhaima, Suhaemah, Suhaema

Sujata (Indian) From a good social class
Sujatah, Sujatta, Sujatia, Sujatea, Sujatiya, Sujatya

Sukanya (Indian) A well-behaved young woman
Sukanyah, Sukania, Sukaniah, Sukaniya

Suki (Japanese) One who is dearly loved
Sukki, Sooki, Sookie, Suky, Sooky, Sukie, Sukey, Sukee, Sukea, Sookey, Sookee, Sookea

Suksma (Indian) A fine young lady
Suksmah

Sully (Gaelic / English) A dark-eyed woman / from the south meadow
Sulley, Sulli, Sullie, Sullee, Sullye, Sulleigh, Sullea

Sultana (Arabic) An empress; queen; ruler
Sultanah, Sultaana, Sultanna

Sulwyn (Welsh) One who shines as bright as the sun
Sulwynne, Sulwynn, Sulwinne, Sulwin, Sulwen, Sulwenn, Sulwenne

Suma (English / Egyptian) Born during the summer / to ask
Sumah, Summa, Summah

Sumana (Indian) A good-natured woman
Sumanah, Sumanna, Sumane, Sumanne, Sumann

Sumayah (Arabic) One with pride
Sumaya, Sumayyah, Sumayya, Sumaiya, Sumaiyah, Sumaiyya, Sumaeya, Sumaeyah

Sumehra (Arabic) Having a beautiful face
Sumehrah, Sumehraa, Sumehrae, Sumehrai

Sumey (Asian) Resembling a delicate flower
Sumy, Sumee, Sumea

Sumi (Japanese) One who is elegant and refined
Sumie

Sumiko (Japanese) Child of goodness

Sumitra (Indian) A beloved friend
Sumitrah, Sumita, Sumytra, Sumyta, Sumeetra, Sumeitra, Sumietra, Sumeatra

Summer (American) Refers to the season; born in summer
Sommer, Sumer, Somer, Somers

Sun (Korean) An obedient child

Suna (Turkish) A swanlike woman

Sunanda (Indian) Having a sweet character
Sunandah, Sunandia, Sunandiya, Sunandea, Sunandya

Sunbul (Arabic) Resembling an ear of grain
Sunbool, Sunbulle, Sunbull, Sunbule, Sunboole, Sunboul, Sunboule

Sunday (American) Born on a Sunday
Sundae, Sundai, Sundaye

Sundown (American) Born at dusk

Sunee (Thai) A good thing

Sunhilda (Teutonic) A sun battlemaiden
Sunhild, Sunhilde, Sonnehilde, Sonnehilda, Sonnehild

Sunila (Indian) Feminine form of Sunil; very blue
Sunilah, Sunilla, Sunilya, Suniliya

Sunita (Indian) One who is well-behaved; having good morals
Sunitah, Sunitra, Sunitrah, Sunitha, Suniti, Suneeta, Suneata

Sunki (Native American) To catch up with
Sunkie, Sunky, Sunkey, Sunkye, Sunkee, Sunkea

Sunniva (English) Gift of the sun
Synnove, Synne, Synnove, Sunn

Sunny (American) Of the sun; one who is brilliant and cheerful
Sunni, Sunney, Sunnie, Sunnea, Sunnye, Sonnenschein

Suparna (Indian) Resembling a beautiful leaf
Suparnah, Suparniya, Suparnia, Suparnya, Suparnea

Suprabha (Indian) A radiant woman; brilliant

Supriti (Indian) One's true love
Supritie, Supritye, Supryty, Supryti, Supritee, Suprytee, Supritea, Suprytea

Supriya (Indian) One who is dearly loved; beloved
Supriyya, Supriyaa, Supriyah

Surabhi (Indian) Having a lovely fragrance
Surbhii, Surabhie, Surabhy, Surabhey, Surabhee, Surabhea

Suravinda (Indian) A beautiful attendant
Suravindah, Suravynda, Suravindia, Suravindiya

Surotama (Indian) An auspicious Apsara (heavenly nymph)
Surotamma, Surotamah

Suri (Armenian / Sanskrit / Hebrew) Wealthy / mother of the sun / go away

Suruchi (Indian) Having good taste
Suruchie, Suruchy, Suruchey, Suruchee,
Suruchea

Surupa (Indian) One who is beautiful

Susannah (Hebrew) Resembling a graceful
white lily
Susanna, Susanne, Susana, Susane, Susan,
Suzanna, Suzannah, Suzanne, Suzane,
Suzan, Susette, Suzette, Sueanne, Suelita,
Suellen, Sukey, Susie, Suzie, Sue, Susy,
Susey, Susi, Suzy, Suzi, Suzey, Susa, Suza,
Suzetta, Shoshana, Shoshanah, Shoshanna,
Shoushan, Shousnan, Shushana, Shushanna,
Sonel, Sosanna, Sousan, Siusan, Souzan,
Soki

Sushanti (Indian) A peaceful woman;
tranquil
Sushantie, Sushanty, Sushantey, Sushantee,
Sushantea

Sushila (Indian) One who is well-behaved;
good conduct
Sushilah, Sushilla, Sushyla, Sushiela,
Susheila, Susheela, Susheala

Sushma (Indian) A beautiful woman
Sushmah

Sushmita (Indian) Having a beautiful smile
Sushmitah, Sushmeeta, Sushmeata,
Sushmyta

Suvarna (Indian) The golden one; having
good color
Suvarnah, Suvarniya, Suvarnya

Suzu (Japanese) One who is long-lived
Suzue, Suzuko

Suzuki (Japanese) Of the bell tree
Suzukie, Suzukey, Suzuky, Suzukee,
Suzukye, Suzukea

Svaha (Hindi) In Hinduism, a minor goddess

Svea (Swedish) From the motherland

Sveta (Slavic) A brilliant star's light
Svetta, Svetlana, Svetlanna, Svetlania,
Svetlaniya

Swagata (Indian) One who is welcome
Swagatah, Swagatta

Swanhilda (Norse) A woman warrior; in
mythology, the daughter of Sigurd
Swanhild, Swanhilde, Svanhilde, Svanhild,
Svenhilde, Svenhilda

Swann (Scandinavian) A swanlike woman
Swan, Swawn, Swaantje, Swantje, Swana,
Swanna

Swapnali (Indian) A dreamlike child
Swapnalie, Swapnalee, Swapna, Swapnaly,
Swapnaley, Swapnalea

Swarna (Indian) The golden one

Swarupa (Indian) One who is devoted to
the truth

Swati (Indian) The name of a star
Swatie, Swaty, Swatey, Swatee, Swatea

Sweta (Indian) A light-skinned woman; fair

Sydelle (Hebrew) A princess; born to royalty
Sydell, Sydele, Sydel, Sidelle, Sidell, Sidele,
Sidel

✿ **Sydney** (English) Of the wide meadow
Sydny, Sydni, Sydnie, Sydnea, Sydnee,
Sidney, Sidne, Sidnee, Sidnei, Sidneya, Sidni,
Sidnie, Sidny, Sidnye

Syna (Greek) Two together
Synah

Syrinx (Greek) In mythology, a nymph
transformed into reeds
Syrinks

Taariq (Swahili) Resembling the morning
star
Tariq, Taarique, Tarique

Taban (Gaelic) A genius; one of immeasur-
able intelligence
Tabban, Tabann, Tabanne, Tabana,
Tabanna

Tabia (African / Egyptian) One who makes
incantations / a talented woman
Tabiah, Tabya, Tabea, Tabeah, Tabiya

Tabina (Arabic) A follower of Muhammad
Tabinah, Tabyna, Tabeena, Tabeana

Tabita (African) A graceful woman
*Tabitah, Tabyta, Tabytah, Tabeeta, Tabeata,
Tabieta, Tabeita*

Tabitha (Greek) Resembling a gazelle;
known for beauty and grace
*Tabithah, Tabbitha, Tabetha, Tabbetha,
Tabatha, Tabbatha, Tabotha, Tabbotha,
Tabytha, Tabbytha, Tabiatha, Tabithia,
Tabtha, Tabathia, Tabathe, Tabby, Tabbey,
Tabbie, Tabbi, Tabbee*

Tablita (Native American) A woman wear-
ing a tiara
*Tablitah, Tableta, Tableeta, Tablyta, Tableyta,
Tableata*

Tabora (Spanish) One who plays a small drum
Taborah, Taborra, Taboria, Taborya

Taborri (Native American) Having a voice
that carries
*Taborrie, Taborry, Taborrey, Taborree, Tabori,
Taborie, Tabory, Taborey, Taboree, Taborea*

Tacincala (Native American) Resembling
a deer
*Tacincalah, Tacyncala, Tacyncalah,
Tacincalla, Tacyncalla*

Tacita (Latin) Feminine form of Tacitus;
mute; silenced
*Tacitah, Taceta, Tacyta, Taycita, Taycyta,
Tasita, Tacey, Taci, Tacie, Tacy, Tacee, Tacea,
Taicey, Taici, Taicie, Taicee, Taicy, Taicea,
Taycey, Taycy, Tayci, Taycie, Taycee, Taycea*

Tadita (Native American) Having great abil-
ity as a runner
*Taditah, Tadeta, Tadyta, Taditta, Tadetta,
Tadytta, Tadeeta, Tadeata*

Taffy (Welsh) One who is much loved
*Taffey, Taffi, Taffie, Taffee, Taffye, Tafy,
Tafey, Taffia, Tafia, Taffea, Tafea, Taffine*

Tafui (African) One who gives glory to God

Tahapenes (Hebrew) A secret temptation
Tahpenes

Tahirah (Arabic) One who is chaste; pure
*Tahira, Taheera, Taheira, Tahyra, Tahera,
Taahira, Tahiria, Tahiara, Taherri, Tahirra,
Taheara*

Tahiyya (Arabic) A greeting of cheer
Tahiyyah, Tahiya, Taheeyya, Taheeya

Tahki (Native American) From the cold
*Tahkie, Tahky, Tahkey, Tahkee, Tahkye,
Taki, Tahkea*

Tahsin (Arabic) Beautification; one who is
praised
*Tahseen, Tahsene, Tahsyne, Tasine, Tahseene,
Tahsean, Tahseane*

Tahupotiki (Maori) A beloved child
Tahupotikie, Tahupotikki, Tahupotyki

Tahzib (Arabic) One who is educated and
cultured
*Tahzeeb, Tahzebe, Tahzybe, Tazib, Tazyb,
Tazeeb, Tahzeab, Tazeab*

Tai (Chinese / Vietnamese) A very big
woman / one who is talented and prosperous

Taima (Native American) A loud crash of
thunder
*Taimah, Tayma, Taimi, Taimie, Taimy,
Taimey, Taimee, Taimma, Taymi, Taymie,
Taymmi, Taymmie, Taymy, Taymmy, Taimia,
Taema, Taemi, Taemie, Taemy, Taemey*

Taini (Native American) Born during the
returning moon
*Tainie, Tainy, Tainey, Tainee, Tainni, Tayni,
Taynie, Tayney, Tayny, Taynee, Tainia,
Tainn, Tainea, Taynea, Taeni, Taenie, Taeny,
Taeney, Taenea, Taenee*

Taipa (Native American) One who spreads
her wings
Taipah, Taypa, Taypah, Taippa, Taepa, Taepah

Taisa (Greek) One who is bound; the bond
*Taisah, Tais, Taysa, Tays, Thais, Thays,
Thaisa, Thaysa, Taiza*

Taite (English) One who is cheerful; pleas-
ant and bright
*Tait, Tayt, Tayte, Taita, Tayta, Tayten, Taet,
Taete, Taeta, Tate*

Taithleach (Gaelic) A quiet and calm young
lady

Taja (African / Hindi) One who is mentioned / wearing a crown
Tajah, Tajae, Teja, Tejah

Tajsa (Polish) A princess; born into royalty
*Tajsah, Tajsia, Tajsi, Tajsie, Tajsy, Tajsey,
Tajsee, Tajsea*

Taka (Japanese) Tall and honorable woman
Takah, Takka, Tacka

Takako (Japanese) A lofty child

Takala (Native American) Resembling a corn tassel
Takalah, Takalla, Takalya

Takara (Japanese) A treasured child; precious possession
Takarah, Takarra, Takarya, Takaria, Takra

Takoda (Native American) Friend to everyone
Takodah, Takodia, Takodya, Takota

Takouhi (Armenian) A queen
Takouhie, Takouhy, Takouhey, Takouhee, Takouhea

Tala (Native American) A stalking wolf
Talah, Talla

Talaith (Welsh) One who wears a royal crown
Talaithe, Talayth, Talaythe, Talaeth, Talaethe

Talasi (Native American) Resembling a cornflower
Talasie, Talasee, Talasea, Talasy, Talasey, Talasya, Talasia

Talia (Hebrew / Greek) Morning dew from heaven / blooming
Taliah, Talea, Taleah, Taleya, Tallia, Talieya, Taleea, Taleia, Taleiya, Tylea, Tyleah, Taleana, Tylia, Tahlia, Tahleah, Tahleea, Tahleia, Talaya, Talayia, Taliya, Taliyah, Taliatha, Talley, Taley, Tally, Taly, Talli, Tali, Tallie, Talie, Tallee, Talee, Talya

Talihah (Arabic) One who seeks knowledge
Taliha, Talibah, Taliba, Talyha, Taleehah, Taleahah

Taline (Armenian) Of the monastery
Talene, Taleen, Taleene, Talyne, Talinia, Talinya, Taliniya

Talisa (American) Consecrated to God
Talisah, Talysa, Taleesa, Talissa, Talise, Taleese, Talisia, Talisya, Talease, Taleasa

Talisha (American) A damsel; an innocent
Talesha, Taleisha, Talysha, Taleesha, Tylesha, Taleysha, Taleshia, Talishia, Tylesia, Talesia, Taliesha, Taleasha

Talitha (Arabic) A maiden; young girl
Talithah, Tulethu, Taleetha, Talytha, Talithia, Talethia, Tiletha, Talith, Talethe, Talythe, Talita, Taleatha

Tallis (French) Of the forest; woodland dweller
Talliss, Tallisse, Tallys, Tallyse, Taliss, Talis, Talise, Talyss, Talyse, Taleese, Taleyse, Taleise, Taliese, Talease, Taleece, Taleace, Taliece, Taleice, Talice, Taleyce, Talissa, Talisa, Tallysa, Talysa, Talisia, Talissa, Talysia

Tallulah (Native American) Running water; leaping water
Tallula, Talula, Talulah, Tallulla

Talon (French) Resembling a claw
Talen, Talan, Tallon, Talin, Tallin, Talyn, Taelyn, Taelon, Tallen

Talor (Hebrew) Touched by the morning's dew
Talore, Talora, Talori, Talorie, Talorey, Talory, Talorye, Taloria, Talorya, Talorra, Talorea

Tam (Vietnamese) Close to the heart

Tama (Japanese / Native American) As precious as a jewel / a thunderbolt
Tamah, Tamaa, Tamala, Tamaiah, Tamalia, Tamalya

Tamanna (Indian) One who is desired
Tamannah, Tamana, Tamanah, Tammana, Tammanna

Tamara (Hebrew / Sanskrit) From the palm tree / a spice
Tamarah, Tamarra, Tamarya, Tamaria, Tamaira, Tammara, Tamora, Temara, Tamari, Tamarie, Tamura, Tymara, Tomara, Tamary, Tamarey, Tamera, Tamerra, Timera, Tamarae, Tamaree, Tamar, Tamor, Tamour, Tamer, Tameria, Tammera, Tamerai, Tamoya, Tameran, Tamyra, Tamyria, Tamra, Tammra, Tamira, Tamirra, Tamiria, Tamarla, Tamarsha, Tamijo, Tammy, Tamy, Tami, Tamie, Tamee, Tamey, Tammey, Tammee, Tamlyn, Tamya, Tamia, Tameia, Tamiya, Tamilyn, Tamryn

Tamasha (African) Pageant winner
Tamasha, Tomosha, Tomasha, Tamashia, Tamashya

Tambre (English) One who brings great joy; music
Tamber, Tambreh, Tambrey, Tambry, Tambrie, Tambri, Tambree, Tambrea

Tameka (Aramaic) A twin
Tamekah, Tameeka, Tumieka, Tameika, Tamecka, Temeka, Tymeka, Tomeka, Tameca, Tameeca, Tamekia, Tamecia, Tameaka

Tamesis (Celtic) In mythology, the goddess of water; also the source of the name for the river Thames
Tamesiss, Tamesys, Tamesyss

Tamiko (Japanese) Child of the people; sweet
Tameko, Tamicko, Tammiko, Tamyko, Tameeko, Tamiyo, Tamika, Tamicka, Tamica, Tameeka, Tameiko, Tamieko, Tamikia, Tamycko, Tamyka, Tamycka, Timiko, Timika, Tomiko, Tomika, Tymiko, Tymika, Tamike, Tamiqua, Tameako, Tameaka

Tamma (Hebrew) One who is perfect; without flaw
Tammah, Teme, Temima

Tanaquil (Latin) Worshipped in the home
Tanaquille, Tanaquile, Tannaquil

Tanaya (Indian) Daughter of mine
Tanayah, Tannaya, Tanayya

Tandice (American) A team player
Tandyce, Tandise, Tandyse, Tandy, Tandey, Tandi, Tandie, Tandee, Tandea, Tandis, Tandia, Tandye, Tandya, Tanda, Tandalaya

Tandra (African) Having a beauty mark; a mole
Tandrah, Tandrea, Tandria, Tandrya, Tandriya

Tanesha (African) Born on a Monday
Taneshah, Tuneesha, Tanisha, Taniesha, Tanishia, Tanitia, Tannicia, Tanniece, Tannisha, Tenicia, Teneesha, Tinecia, Tiniesha, Tynisha, Tainesha, Taneshya, Taneasha, Taneisha, Tahniesha, Tanashia, Tanashea, Tanishea, Taneshea, Tanysha, Tanicha, Tanasha, Tanesia, Tanessa

Tangerina (English) From the city of Tangiers
Tangerinah, Tangereena, Tangeryna, Tangereana, Tangerine, Tangeryne

Tangia (American) The angel
Tangiah, Tangya, Tangiya, Tangeah

Tanginika (American) A lake goddess
Tanginikah, Tanginica, Tanginicka, Tangynika, Tanginyka

Tangwystl (Welsh) A pledge of peace

Tani (Japanese / Melanesian / Tonkinese) From the valley / a sweetheart / a young woman
Tanie, Tany, Taney, Tanee, Tanni, Tanye, Tannie, Tanny, Tanney, Tannee, Tanea, Tannea

Taniel (American) Feminine form of Daniel; God is my judge
Tanielle, Tanial, Tunialle, Taniele, Taniell, Taniela, Taniella

Tanika (American) Queen of the fairies
Tanikah, Taneeka, Tanyka, Tanica, Tanicka, Taniqua, Tanikka, Tannika, Tianika, Tannica, Tianeka, Taneka, Tanikqua, Taneaka

Tanith (Phoenician) In mythology, the goddess of love, fertility, moon, and stars
Tanithe, Tanyth, Tanythe, Tanitha, Tanytha, Tanithia

Tanner (English) One who tans hides
Taner, Tannar, Tannor, Tannis

Tansy (English / Greek) An aromatic yellow flower / having immortality
Tansey, Tansi, Tansie, Tansee, Tansye, Tansea, Tancy, Tanzy, Tansia, Tansya

Tanuja (Indian) My daughter
Tanujah, Tanujia, Tanujya, Tanujiya

Tanushri (Indian) One who is beautiful; attractive
Tanushrie, Tanushry, Tanushrey, Tanushree, Tanushrea

Tanvi (Indian) Slender and beautiful woman
Tanvie, Tanvy, Tanvey, Tanvee, Tanvye, Tannvi, Tanvea

Tao (Chinese) Resembling a peach; symbol of long life

Tapanga (African) One who is sweet and unpredictable
Tapangah

Tapati (Indian) In mythology, the daughter of the sun god
Tapatie, Tapaty, Tapatey, Tapatee, Tapatye, Tapatea

Taphath (Hebrew) In the Bible, Solomon's daughter
Tafath, Taphathe, Tafathe

Tapi (Indian) From the river
Tapie, Tapy, Tapey, Tapee, Tapti, Tapea, Taptie, Tapty, Taptey, Taptee, Taptea

Tappen (Welsh) Top of the rock
Tappan, Tappin, Tappon, Tapen, Tappene

Tara (Gaelic / Indian) Of the tower; rocky hill / star; in mythology, an astral goddess
Tarah, Tarra, Tayra, Taraea, Tarai, Taralee, Tarali, Taraya, Tarha, Tarasa, Tarasha, Taralynn, Tarrah

Tarachand (Indian) Silver star
Tarachande, Tarachanda, Tarachandia, Tarachandea, Tarachandiya, Tarachandya

Taraka (Indian) In mythology, a woman who was turned into a demon
Tarakah, Tarakia, Taracka, Tarackia, Tarakya, Tarakiya

Tarala (Indian) Resembling a honeybee
Taralah, Taralia, Taralla, Taralea, Taralya, Taraliya

Tarana (African) Born during daylight
Taranah, Tarania, Taranna

Taraneh (Persian) A beautiful melody; a song
Tarane, Taranne, Taranneh, Tarannum, Taranum

Taree (Japanese) A bending branch
Tarea, Tareya

Taregan (Native American) Resembling a crane
Tareganne, Taregann

Tareva-chine(shanay) (Native American) One with beautiful eyes

Tarian (Welsh) One acting as a shield; offering refuge
Tariane, Tarianne, Taryan, Taryanne

Tariana (American) From the holy hillside
Tariana, Tarianna, Taryana, Taryanna

Tarika (Indian) A starlet
Tarikah, Taryka, Tarykah, Taricka, Tarickah

Tarin (Irish) From the high, rocky hill
Tarine, Taryn, Tarynn, Tarryn, Taren, Tarene, Tareen, Tarrin, Tarren, Tarron, Tarryne, Taryne, Tarina, Tareena, Taryna, Tarrina, Tarrena, Tarryna

Tarisai (African) One to behold; to look at
Tarysai

Tarpeia (Latin) In mythology, a woman killed for an act of treason
Tarpeiah, Tarpia, Tarpya, Tarpiea

Tarub (Arabic) One who is merry; bringer of happiness
Tarube, Taroob, Tarrub, Taruh, Taroub, Taroube

Tasanee (Thai) A beautiful view
Tasane, Tasani, Tasanie, Tasany, Tasaney, Tasanye, Tasanea

Taskin (Arabic) One who provides peace; satisfaction
Taskine, Taskeen, Taskeene, Taskyne, Takseen, Taksin, Taksyn

Taslim (Arabic) One who offers salutation and submission
Taslime, Tasleem, Tasleeme, Taslyme, Taslym

Tasmine (American) A twin
Tasmin, Tazmine, Tasmeen, Tasmyne, Tasmynne, Tasmeene, Tazmeen, Tazmyne, Tasmina, Tazmina, Tasmyna, Tazmyna

Tasnim (Arabic) From the fountain of paradise
Tasnime, Tasneem, Tasneeme, Tasnyme, Tasnym, Tasneam, Tasneame

Tasya (Slavic) Form of Anastasia, meaning "one who shall rise again"
Tasia, Tasyah, Tazia, Tazya, Tasiya, Taziya

Tatiana (Slavic) Queen of the fairies
*Tatianah, Tatianna, Tatyana, Tatyanna,
Tiahna, Tiane, Tianna, Tiauna*

Tatum (English) Bringer of joy; spirited
Tatom, Tatim, Tatem, Tatam, Tatym

Taura (English) Feminine form of Taurus;
an astrological sign; the bull
*Taurah, Tauras, Taurae, Tauria, Taurina,
Taurinia, Taurya, Tauryna*

Tava (Swedish) Form of Gustava, meaning
"from the staff of the gods"
Tavah, Tave, Taveh

Tavi (Aramaic) One who is well-behaved
Tavie, Tavee, Tavy, Tavey, Tavea

Tavia (Latin) Form of Octavia, meaning "the
eighth-born child"
*Taviah, Tavya, Tavea, Taveah, Tavita,
Tavitah, Taviya*

Tawana (American) Form of Wanda, meaning "a wanderer"
Tawanah, Tawanna, Taiwana, Tawanda

Taweret (Egyptian) In mythology, the god-
dess of pregnant women and childbirth
*Tawerett, Tawerette, Tawerete, Tauret,
Taurett, Taurette, Taurete*

Tawia (African) First child born after twins
*Tawiah, Tawya, Tawyah, Tawiya, Tawiyah,
Tawea, Taweah*

Tawny (Irish / English) From the green field
/ light brown; a warm sandy color
*Tawney, Tawni, Tawnie, Tawnee, Tawnia,
Tawnya, Tawniya, Tawnea*

Tayanita (Native American) Resembling a
young beaver
*Tayanitah, Tayanitia, Tayanyta, Tayanytah,
Tayaneeta, Tayanieta, Tayaneita, Tayaneata*

Tayce (French) Silence; peace
*Taice, Tace, Taece, Taeyce, Taycia, Tayse,
Taise, Taese, Tase*

Tayen (Native American) Born during the
new moon
*Tayin, Tayon, Tayan, Tayene, Tayenne,
Tayine*

Taylor (English) Cutter of cloth; one who
alters garments
*Tailor, Taylore, Taylar, Tayler, Talour, Taylre,
Tailore, Tailar, Tailour, Taylour*

Tayten (American) Beautiful happiness
Taytan, Tayton, Taytin, Taytene

Tazanna (Native American) A princess;
born into royalty
*Tazannah, Tazana, Tazanah, Tazanne,
Tazane, Tazann*

Tazara (African) A railway line
Tazarah, Tazarra, Tazarrah

Teagan (Gaelic) One who is attractive; good-
looking
Tegan, Tegau, Teegan, Teygan

Teal (American) Resembling a bright-
colored duck; a greenish-blue color
Teale, Teala, Teela, Tealia, Tealiya

Teamhair (Irish) In mythology, a place
where kings met
Teamhaire, Teamhare, Teamharre

Teca (Hungarian) Form of Theresa, meaning "a harvester"

Tedra (Greek) A supreme gift
Tedrah, Tedre, Tedreh

Teenie (American) The small one
*Tynie, Teynie, Teeny, Teeney, Teenee, Teenye,
Teeni, Teenea*

Tefnut (Egyptian) In mythology, the goddess of water and fertility
Tefnutte, Tephnut, Tephnutte

Tehya (Native American) One who is precious
Tehyah, Tehiya, Tehiyah

Teige (American) A poet; one who is good-
looking

Teigra (Greek) Resembling a tiger
Teigre

Tekla (Greek) Glory of God
*Teklah, Tekli, Teckla, Tecla, Thecla, Theckla,
Thekla, Theclah, Theccla*

Telephassa (Latin) In mythology, the queen
of Tyre
Telephasa, Telefassa, Telefasa

Teleri (English) In Tolkien's works, those who came last; an elf clan
Telerie, Telery, Telerey, Teleree, Telleri, Telerea, Tellerie

Tellus (Latin) In mythology, the mother earth
Telus

Telyn (Welsh) Resembling a harp
Telynn, Telin, Telynne, Telinn, Telinne

Tema (Hebrew) One who is righteous; palm tree
Temah, Temma, Temmah

Temira (Hebrew) A tall woman
Temirah, Temeera, Temyra, Temiera, Temeira, Temeara

Temperance (English) Having self-restraint
Temperence, Temperince, Temperancia, Temperanse, Temperense, Temperinse

Tempest (French) One who is stormy; turbulent
Tempeste, Tempist, Tempiste, Tempesta, Tempress, Tempestt, Tempestta, Tempany, Tempani, Tempanie, Tempaney, Tempanee, Tempanea

Templa (Latin) Of the temple; sanctuary
Templah, Temple, Tempa, Tempy, Tempey, Tempi, Tempie, Tempee, Tempea

Tendai (African) Thankful to God
Tenday, Tendae, Tendaa, Tendaye

Tender (American) One who is sensitive; young and vulnerable
Tendere, Tendera, Tenderia, Tenderre, Tenderiya

Tenesea (American) Gathering place near water
Teneseah, Tenesia, Tennesea, Teness, Tenesse

Tenshi (Japanese) A messenger of God; an angel
Tenshie, Tenshy, Tenshey, Tenshee, Tenshea

Teranika (Gaelic) Victory of the earth
Teranikah, Teranieka, Teraneika, Teraneeka, Teranica, Teranicka, Teranicca, Teraneaka

Terehasa (African) The blessed one
Terehasah, Terehasia, Terehasea, Terehasiya, Terehasya

Terentia (Latin / Greek) One who is tender / a guardian
Terentiah

Terpsichore (Greek) In mythology, the muse of dancing and singing
Terpsichora, Terpsichoria, Terpsichoriya

Terra (Latin) From the earth; in mythology, an earth goddess
Terrah, Terah, Teralyn, Terran, Terena, Terenah, Terenna, Terrena, Terrenna, Terrene, Taran

Terrian (Greek) One who is innocent
Terriane, Terrianne, Terriana, Terianna, Terian, Terianne

Terrwyn (Welsh) A brave girl
Terrwyne, Terrwin, Terrwinne, Terwyn, Terwynne, Terrwynne, Terrwen, Terrwenn, Terrwenne

Tertia (Latin) The third-born child
Tertiah, Tertius, Tertullus, Terza, Terceira, Terceirah

Teryl (English) One who is vivacious and bright
Terryl, Teryll, Terylle, Terryll

Tesia (Polish) Loved by God
Tesiah, Tezia, Teziah

Tethys (Greek) In mythology, a sea goddess
Tethyss, Tethysse, Tethis, Tethiss, Tethisse

Tetsu (Japanese) A strong woman
Tetsue

Tetty (English) Form of Elizabeth, meaning "my God is bountiful"
Tettey, Tetti, Tettie, Tettee, Tettea

Teva (Hebrew / Scottish) Child of nature / a twin
Tevah, Tevva, Tevvah

Tevy (Cambodian) An angel
Tevey, Tevi, Tevie, Tevee, Tevea

Texas (Native American / English) A beloved friend / from the state of Texas
Texis, Texasia, Texus, Texa, Tex, Texcean, Texan, Texana, Texanna

Thaddea (Greek) Feminine form of Thaddeus; of the heart; courageous
Thaddeah, Thadea, Thaddia, Thadia, Thadina, Thadine, Thaddina, Thaddine, Thadyna, Thada, Thadda, Thadie, Thadya, Thadyne, Taddea, Thady

Thalassa (Greek) From the sea
Thalassah, Thalasa, Thalasse

Thalia (Greek) In mythology, the muse of comedy; joyful
Thaliah, Thaleia, Thalya, Thalie, Thali, Thaly, Thaley, Thalee, Thalea, Thaleigh

Thana (Arabic) One showing gratitude; thankfulness
Thanah, Thayna, Thaina, Thanna, Thane

Thandiwe (African) The loving one
Thandywe, Thandiewe, Thandeewe, Thandie, Thandi, Thandee, Thandy, Thandey

Thao (Vietnamese) One who is respectful of her parents

Thara (Arabic) One who is wealthy; prosperous
Tharah, Tharra, Tharrah, Tharwat

Theia (Greek) A goddess; in mythology, the mother of the sun, moon, and dawn
Thea, Thia, Thya

Thelma (Greek) One who is ambitious and willful
Thelmah, Telma, Thelmai, Thelmia, Thelmalina

Thelred (English) One who is well-advised
Thelrede, Thelread, Thelredia, Thelredina, Thelreid, Thelreed, Thelryd

Thelxepeia (Latin) In mythology, a siren
Thelxepia, Thelxiepeia

Thema (African) A queen
Themah, Theema, Thyma, Theyma, Theama

Themba (African) One who is trusted
Thembah, Thembia, Thembiya, Thembya

Themis (Greek) In mythology, the goddess of law and order
Themiss, Themisse, Themys, Themyss, Themysse

Thena (Greek) Form of Athena, meaning "wise"
Thina, Theena, Thyna, Theana

Thenoma (Greek) The name of God
Thenomah, Thenomia, Thenomea, Thenomiya, Thenomya

Theodora (Greek) Feminine form of Theodore; gift of God
Theodorah, Theodorra, Theadora, Teodora, Teodory, Teodozji, Theda, Thedya, Theodosia, Teddy, Teddey, Teddi, Teddie, Teddee, Teddea

Theola (Greek) One who is divine; godly
Theolah, Theona, Theone, Theolla, Theollah

Theophania (Greek) Manifestation of God
Theophaniah, Theophanie, Theophaneia, Theophane, Theofania, Theofaniya

Theophilia (Greek) Feminine form of Theophilus; loved by God
Theophiliah, Theophila, Theofilia, Theofiliya, Theofila

Theora (Greek) A watcher
Theorra, Theoria, Theoriya, Theorya

Theoris (Egyptian) One who is superior
Theoriss, Theorisse, Theorisa, Theorys, Theoryss, Theoyrsse, Theorysa

Thera (Greek) One who is untamed; wild
Thira, Therra

Theresa (Greek) A harvester
Teresa, Theresah, Theresia, Therese, Thera, Tresa, Tressa, Tressam, Treszka, Toireasa

Therona (Greek) Feminine form of Theron; huntress
Theronah, Theronia, Theroniya, Theronea, Theronya

Theta (Greek) Eighth letter of the Greek alphabet
Thetta

Thetis (Greek) In mythology, a sea nymph
Thetiss, Thetisse, Thetys, Thetyss, Thetysse

Thi (Vietnamese) One who inspires poetry

Thirza (Hebrew) A delightful lady
Thirsa, Therza, Thersa

Thisbe (Greek) In mythology, the lover of Pyramus who committed suicide
Thisby, Thisbey, Thisbi, Thisbie, Thisbee, Thizbe, Thizbie, Thisbea, Thizbi, Thizby, Thizbey, Thizbee, Thizbea

Thistle (English) Resembling the prickly, flowered plant
Thistel, Thissle, Thissel

Thomasina (Hebrew) Feminine form of Thomas; a twin
Thomasine, Thomsina, Thomasin, Tomasina, Tomasine, Thomasa, Thomaseena, Thomaseana, Thomaseina, Thomasiena, Thomasyna, Tomaseena, Tomaseana, Tomaseina, Tomasiena, Tomasyna

Thoosa (Greek) In mythology, a sea nymph
Thoosah, Thoosia, Thoosiah, Thusa, Thusah, Thusia, Thusiah, Thousa, Thousah, Thousia, Thousiah

Thorberta (Norse) Brilliance of Thor
Thorbiartr, Thorbertha

Thorbjorg (Norse) Protected by Thor
Thorborg, Thorgerd

Thordia (Norse) Spirit of Thor
Thordiah, Thordis, Tordis, Thordissa, Tordissa, Thoridyss

Thorgunna (Norse) Warrior for Thor
Thorgunn, Thorgun, Thorgunnah, Torgunna, Torgunn, Torguna

Thorhilda (Norse) Thor's maiden
Thorhilde, Thorhildah, Thorhild, Torhilda

Thu (Vietnamese) Born in autumn

Thuong (Vietnamese) One who is loved tenderly

Thurayya (Arabic) The seven stars in the constellation Taurus
Thuraya, Thurayaa, Thurayyaa

Thuy (Vietnamese) One who is gentle and pure
Thuye, Thuyy, Thuyye

Thwayya (Arabic) A starlet
Thwaya, Thwayaa, Thwayyaa

Thy (Vietnamese / Greek) A poet / one who is untamed
Thye

Thyra (Greek) The shield-bearer
Thyrah, Thira, Thirah

Tia (Spanish / Greek) An aunt / daughter born to royalty
Tiah, Tea, Teah, Tiana, Teea, Tya, Teeya, Tiia, Tiye, Tyah, Tyja, Tianda, Tiandria, Tiante, Tialeigh, Tiamarie

Tiara (Latin) One who is crowned
Tiarah, Tiarea, Tiari, Tiaria, Tyara, Teearia, Tiarra, Tiarie, Tiaree, Tiary, Tiarey

Tiaret (African) Resembling a lioness
Tiarett, Tiarette, Tiarret

Tiassale (African) It is forgotten
Tiasale

Tibelda (German) The boldest one
Tibeldah, Tybelda, Tibeldia, Tibeldina, Tibelde, Tibeldie, Tibeldi, Tibeldy, Tibeldey, Tibeldee, Tibeldea

Tiberia (Italian) Of the Tiber river
Tiberiah, Tiberiya, Tiberya, Tibeeria, Tibearia, Tibieria, Tibeiria

Tiegan (Aztec) A little princess in a big valley
Tiegann, Tieganne

Tien (Vietnamese) A fairy child; a spirit
Tienne, Tienn

Tienette (Greek) Crowned with laurel in victory
Tienett, Tienet, Tienete, Tieneta, Tienetta

Tierney (Gaelic) One who is regal; lordly
Tiernie, Tierni, Tiernee, Tierny, Tiernea

Tierra (Spanish) Of the earth
Tierrah, Tiera, Tierah

Tieve (Celtic) From the hillside

Tiffany (Greek) Form of Theophania, meaning "manifestation of God"
Tiffaney, Tiffani, Tiffanie, Tiffanee, Tifany, Tifaney, Tifanee, Tifani, Tifanie, Tiffeny, Tiffney, Tyfany, Tyffany, Tyfani, Tyfanni, Tyffani, Tifanny, Tiffanny, Tiphany, Tiphanie, Tiffanea, Tifanea

Tiger (American) A powerful cat; resembling a tiger
Tigyr, Tyger, Tygyr

Tigerlily (English) An orange flower with black spots
Tigerlilly, Tigerlili, Tigerlilli, Tigerlilie, Tigerlillie, Tygerlily, Tiger Lily

Tigris (Persian) The fast one; tiger
Tigrisa, Tigrisia, Tigriss, Tigrisse, Tigrys, Tigryss, Tigrysse

Tikva (Hebrew) One who has hope
Tikvah, Tickva, Ticva

Tilda (German) Form of Matilda, meaning "one who is mighty in battle"
Tildah, Tilde, Tildea

Timber (English) From the wood
Timbar, Tymber, Tymbar

Timberly (American) A tall ruling woman
Timberley, Timberli, Timberlie, Timberlee, Timberleigh, Timberlea

Timothea (English) Feminine form of Timothy; honoring God
Timotheah, Timothia, Timothya, Timothiya

Tina (English) From the river; also shortened form of names ending in -tina
Tinah, Teena, Tena, Teyna, Tyna, Tinna, Teana

Ting (Chinese) Graceful and slim woman

Tiombe (African) One who is shy
Tiombey, Tiomby, Tiombi, Tiombie, Tiombee, Tiombea

Tiponi (Native American) A child of importance
Tiponni, Tipponi, Tiponie, Tipony, Tiponey, Tiponee, Tiponeu

Tiponya (Native American) Resembling the great horned owl
Tiponiya, Tiponia

Tipper (Irish) One who pours water; a well
Tippar, Tippor, Tippur, Tippyr

Tira (Indian) Resembling an arrow

Tirza (Hebrew) One who is pleasant; a delight
Tirzah

Tisa (African) The ninth-born child
Tisah, Tiza

Tisha (English) Form of Letitia, meaning "one who brings joy to others"
Tishah, Tysha, Teisha, Tishia, Tyshia, Tishal, Tish, Tiesha

Tisiphone (Greek) In mythology, a Fury
Tisiphona, Tisiphonia, Tisiphonea, Tisiphonya, Tisiphoniya

Tita (Latin) Holding a title of honor
Titah, Teeta, Tyta, Teata

Titania (Latin / English) Of the giants / queen of the fairies
Titaniya, Titanea, Titaniah, Titaneah, Titaniyah, Titanya, Titanyah

Tiva (Native American) One who loves to dance
Tivah, Tivva, Tivvah

Tivona (Hebrew) Lover of nature
Tivonna, Tivone, Tivonia, Tivoniya

Toakase (Tonga) A woman of the sea
Toakasse, Toakasia, Toakasiya, Toakaseh

Toan (Vietnamese) Form of An-toan, meaning "safe and secure"
Toane, Toanne

Tobi (Hebrew) Feminine form of Tobias; God is good
Tobie, Toby, Tobey, Tobee, Toba, Tobit, Toibe, Tobea

Toinette (French) Form of Antoinette, meaning "priceless and highly praiseworthy; a flourishing flower"
Toinett, Toinete, Toinet, Toineta, Toinetta

Toki (Japanese / Korean) One who grasps opportunity; hopeful / resembling a rabbit
Tokie, Toky, Tokey, Tokye, Tokiko, Tokee, Tokea

Tola (Polish / Cambodian) Form of Toinette, meaning "priceless and highly praiseworthy; a flourishing flower" / born during October
Tolah, Tolla, Tollah

Tolinka (Native American) Having a coyote's hearing
Tolinkah, Tolynka, Tolinca, Tolincka, Toleenka, Toleanka

Tomiko (Japanese) Child of wealth
Tomyko

Tomoko (Japanese) One who is intelligent
Tomoyo

Toni (English) Form of Antoinette, meaning "priceless and highly praiseworthy; a flourishing flower"
Tonie, Tony, Toney, Tonee, Tonya, Tonia, Tonisha, Tonea, Tonny, Tonni, Tonnie, Tonnee, Tonney, Tonnea

Topanga (Native American) Where the mountain meets the sea
Topangah

Topaz (Latin) Resembling a yellow gemstone
Topazz, Topaza, Topazia, Topaziya, Topazya, Topazea

Topper (English) The most outstanding; excellent
Topsy, Toper, Topsi, Topsie, Topsee, Topsea, Topsey

Tora (Scandinavian) Feminine form of Thor; thunder
Thora, Thorah, Torah

Tordis (Norse) A goddess
Tordiss, Tordisse, Tordys, Tordyss, Tordysse

Toril (Scandinavian) Female warrior inspired by Thor
Torill, Torille, Torila, Torilla

Torny (Norse) New; just discovered
Torney, Tornie, Torni, Torne, Torn, Tornee, Tornea

Torra (Irish / Scottish) From the rocky top / from the castle

Torrin (Gaelic) From the craggy hills
Torin, Torrine, Torran, Toran, Torren, Toren, Torean, Torion, Torrian

Torunn (Norse) Thor's love
Torun, Torrun, Torrunn

Tory (American) Form of Victoria, meaning "victorious woman; winner; conqueror"
Torry, Torey, Tori, Torie, Torree, Tauri, Torye, Toya, Toyah, Torrey, Torri, Torrie, Toriana

Tosca (Latin) From the Tuscany region
Toscah, Toscka, Toska, Tosckah, Toskah

Tosha (English) Form of Natasha, meaning "born on Christmas Day"
Toshah, Toshiana, Tasha, Tashia, Tashi, Tassa

Toshi (Japanese) Mirror image
Toshie, Toshy, Toshey, Toshee, Toshea

Tosia (Latin) One who is inestimable
Tosiah, Tosya, Tosyah, Tosiya, Tozia, Tozea, Toziya

Totie (English) Form of Dorothy, meaning "a gift of God"
Toti, Tottie, Toty, Totey, Totee, Totea

Totsi (Native American) Wearing moccasins
Totsie, Totsy, Totsey, Totsee, Totsye, Totsea

Tourmaline (Singhalese) A stone of mixed colors
Tourmalyne, Tourmalina, Tourmalinia

Tova (Hebrew) One who is well-behaved
Tovah, Tove, Tovi, Toba, Toibe, Tovva

Toviel (Hebrew) God is good
Toviya, Tuviya, Tovielle, Toviell, Toviele, Toviela, Toviella

Tracey (Latin / English) A woman warrior / one who is brave
Tracy, Traci, Tracie, Tracee, Trace, Tracen, Tracea, Tracia, Traicey, Traicee, Traicy, Traisey, Traisee, Traisy, Tracie, Trasie, Traycie, Trayci, Traysie, Traysi, Tracilee, Tracilyn, Tracina, Tracell

Tranquilla (Spanish) One who is calm; tranquil
Tranquillah, Tranquila, Tranquille, Tranquile

Trapper (American) One who sets traps
Trappor, Trappur, Trappar, Trappir, Trappyr

Treasa (Irish) Having great strength
Treasah, Treesa, Treisa, Triesa, Treise, Treese, Toirease

Trella (Spanish) Form of Estelle, meaning "resembling a star"
Trellah, Trela, Trelah

Tress (English) A long lock of hair
Tresse, Trese, Tressa, Tressia, Tressiya, Tressya, Tressea

Treva (English / Celtic) From the homestead near the sea / one who is prudent
Trevah, Trevina, Trevva, Trevia, Treviya, Trevea, Trevya

Trilby (English / Italian) A soft felt hat / one who sings trills
Trillby, Trilbey, Trilbi, Trilbie, Trilbie, Trillare, Trillaire, Trilbee, Trilbea

Trina (Greek) Form of Catherina, meaning "one who is pure; virginal"
Trinah, Treena, Triena, Treina, Tryna, Triana, Trind, Trine, Trinh, Trinda, Treana

Trinetta (French) A little innocent
Trinettah, Trineta, Trinitta, Trenette, Trinette, Trinet, Trinete

❂ **Trinity** (Latin) The holy three
Trinitey, Triniti, Trinitie, Trinitee, Trynity, Trynitey, Tryniti, Trynitie, Trynitee, Trinyty, Trinytey, Trinyti, Trinytie, Trinytee, Trynyty, Trini

Trisha (Latin) Form of Patricia, meaning "of noble descent"
Trishah, Trishia, Tricia, Trish, Trissa, Trisa

Trishna (Polish) In mythology, the goddess of the deceased, and protector of graves
Trishnah, Trishnia, Trishniah, Trishnea, Trishneah, Trishniya, Trishniyah, Trishnya, Trishnyah

Trisna (Indian) The one desired
Trisnah, Trisnia, Trisniah, Trisnea, Trisneah, Trisniya, Trisniyah, Trisnya, Trisnyah

Trissie (Latin) Form of Beatrice, meaning "one who blesses others"
Trissi, Trissy, Trissey, Trissee, Trissia, Trissiya, Trissea

Trista (English) Feminine form of Tristan; one who is sorrowful
Tristah, Trysta, Tristia, Trystia, Tristana, Triste, Tristen, Tristessa, Tristina, Tristyn, Tristyne

Triveni (Hindi) Confluence of three sacred rivers
Trivenie, Triveney, Triveny, Trivenee, Tryveni, Tryvenie, Tryveney, Tryveny, Tryvenee, Tryvyny, Tryvyni, Trivyny, Trivyni, Trivenea

Trivia (Latin) Of the three ways; in mythology, the goddess of the crossroads
Triviah, Trivya, Tryvia, Tryvya

Trixie (English) Form of Beatrice, meaning "one who blesses others"
Trixi, Trixy, Trixey, Trixee, Trixye, Trix, Tryx, Tryxie, Tryxy, Trixea, Tryxea

Trudy (German) Form of Gertrude, meaning "one who is strong with a spear"
Trudey, Trudi, Trudie, Trude, Trudye, Trudee, Truda, Trudia, Trudel, Trudchen, Trudessa, Trudea

Truly (English) One who is genuine; sincere
Truleigh, Truley, Truli, Trulie, Trulee, Trulea, Trula, Trulah

Trupti (Indian) State of being satisfied
Truptie, Trupty, Truptey, Truptee, Trupte, Truptea

Trusha (Indian) Having great thirst
Trushah, Trushya, Trushia, Trushiya, Trushea

Tryamon (English) In Arthurian legend, a fairy princess
Tryamonn, Tryamonne, Tryamona, Tryamonna

Tryna (Greek) The third-born child
Trynah

Tryne (Greek) An innocent woman

Tryphena (Greek) One who is dainty; delicate
Tryphenah, Trypheena, Tryphiena, Tryphana, Tryphaena, Tryphyna, Tryfena, Tryfeena, Tryfenna, Trifena, Trifeena, Trifeyna, Trifiena, Trifyna, Tryfyna, Tryphaina, Trifine, Tryfeana, Trifeana

Tryphosa (Hebrew) Thrice shining; soft
Tryphosah, Tryphosia, Triphosa, Trifosa, Tryfosa

Tsifira (Hebrew) One who is crowned
Tsifirah, Tsifyra, Tsiphyra, Tsiphira, Tsipheera, Tsifeera

Tuccia (Latin) A vestal virgin

Tuesday (English) Born on Tuesday
Tuesdaye, Tewsday, Tuesdai, Tuesdae, Tewsdai, Tewsdaye, Tewsdae

Tugenda (German) One who is virtuous
Tugendah, Tugendia, Tugendiya, Tugendea, Tugendya

Tula (Hindi) Balance; a sign of the zodiac
Tulah, Tulla, Tullah

Tulasi (Indian) A sacred plant; basil plant
Tulasie, Tulasy, Tulasey, Tulasee, Tulsi, Tulasea, Tulsie, Tulsy, Tulsey, Tulsee, Tulsea

Tullia (Irish) One who is peaceful
Tulliah, Tullea, Tulleah, Tullya, Tulia, Tulea, Tuleah, Tulya, Tulliola, Tully, Tullie, Tulley, Tullye, Tulliya

Tusti (Hindi) One who brings happiness and peace
Tustie, Tusty, Tustey, Tustee, Tuste, Tustea

Tutilina (Latin) In mythology, the protector goddess of stored grain
Tutilinah, Tutileena, Tutileana, Tutilyna, Tutileina, Tutiliena, Tutilena, Tutylina, Tutylyna

Tuuli (Finnish) Of the wind
Tuulie, Tuulee, Tuula, Tuuly, Tuuley, Tuulea

Tuwa (Native American) Of the earth
Tuwah, Tuwia, Tuwiya, Tuwea, Tuwya, Tuwiah, Tuwiyah, Tuweah, Tuwyah

Tuyen (Vietnamese) An angel
Tuyenn, Tuyenne, Tuyena, Tuyenna

Tuyet (Vietnamese) Snow-white woman
Tuyett, Tuyete, Tuyette, Tuyeta, Tuyetta

Tvishi (Hindi) A ray of bright light; energy
Tvishie, Tvishee, Tvishye, Tvishey, Tvishy, Tvishea

Twyla (English) Woven with double thread
Twylah, Twila, Twilah, Twylla, Twilla

Tyler (English) Tiler of roofs

Tyme (English) The aromatic herb thyme
Time, Thyme, Thime

Tyne (English) Of the river
Tyna

Tyra (Scandinavian) Feminine form of Tyr, the god of war and justice
Tyrah, Tyrra, Tyrrah

Tyro (Greek) In mythology, a woman who bore twin sons to Poseidon

Tyronica (American) Goddess of battle
Tyronicah, Tyronyca, Tyronicka, Tyronika, Tyronycka, Tyronyka

Tzefanya (Hebrew) Protected by God
Tzefanyah, Tzephanya, Tzefaniya, Tzephaniya

Tzidkiya (Hebrew) Righteousness of the Lord
Tzidkiyah, Tzidkiyahu

Tzigane (Hungarian) A gypsy
Tzigan, Tzigain, Tzigaine, Tzigayne

Tzilla (Hebrew) A defender of her loved ones
Tzillah, Tzila, Tzilah, Tzilia, Tzillia

Tzivia (Hebrew) Resembling a doe
Tziviah, Tzivea, Tziveah, Tziveea, Tziviya

Tziyona (Hebrew) Woman of Zion
Tziyonah, Tziyonna, Tziyone, Tziyyona, Tziyyonah

Tzzipporah (Hebrew) Form of Zipporah, meaning "a beauty; little bird"
Tzzippora, Tzipporah, Tzippora, Tzzipora, Tzziporah, Tsipporah, Tsippora, Tsipora, Tzippa, Tzippah

U

U (Korean) One who is gentle and considerate

Uadjit (Egyptian) In mythology, a snake goddess
Ujadet, Uajit, Udjit, Ujadit

Ualani (Hawaiian) Of the heavenly rain
Ualanie, Ualany, Ualaney, Ualanee, Ualanea, Ualania, Ualana

Uald (Teutonic) A brave ruler
Ualda, Ualdah, Ualdia, Ualdaa, Ualdae, Ualdai

Uberta (Italian) A bright woman
Ubertah, Ubertha, Ubert, Uberte, Uberthe

Uchechi (African) Of God's will
Uchechie, Uchechy, Uchechey, Uchechee, Uchechea, Uchecheah

Uchenna (African) God's will
Uchennah, Uchena, Uchenah

Udavine (American) A thriving woman
*Udavyne, Udavina, Udavyna, Udevine,
Udevyne, Udevina, Udevyna*

Udele (English) One who is wealthy; prosperous
*Udelle, Udela, Udella, Udelah, Udellah, Uda,
Udah*

Uela (American) One who is devoted to God
Uelah, Uella, Uellah

Uganda (African) From the country in
Africa
*Ugandah, Ugaunda, Ugaundah, Ugawnda,
Ugawndah, Ugonda, Ugonduh*

Ugolina (German) Having a bright spirit;
bright mind
*Ugolinah, Ugoleena, Ugoliana, Ugolyna,
Ugoline, Ugolyn, Ugolyne*

Ujana (African) A young woman
Ujanah, Uyana, Uyanah, Ujanna

Ula (Irish) Jewel of the sea
Ulah, Ulaa, Ulai, Ulae

Ulalia (Greek) Form of Eulalia, meaning
"well-spoken"
Ulaliah, Ulalya, Ulalyah

Ulan (African) Firstborn of twins
Ulann, Ulanne

Ulanda (American) One who is confident
*Ulandah, Ulandia, Ulandiah, Ulandea,
Ulandeah, Ulandiya, Ulandiyah*

Ulani (Hawaiian) One who is cheerful
*Ulanie, Ulany, Ulaney, Ulanee, Ulana,
Ulanya, Ulania, Ulane*

Ulda (American) One who can foretell the
future
*Uldah, Uldia, Uldiah, Uldea, Uldeah, Uldiya,
Uldiyah*

Uldwyna (English) A special and beloved
friend
Uldwynah, Uldwina, Uldwaina, Uldweena

Ule (English) One who shoulders burdens
Ulle

Ulicia (Irish) Feminine form of Ulik; playful
heart
*Uliciah, Uliscia, Uleacia, Ulecea, Uleicia,
Uleisia, Uleisya, Uleighcia, Uleighsya,
Uleighsia, Ulicea, Ulicha, Ulichia, Ulician,
Ulicija, Uliecia, Ullicea, Ulisha, Ulishia,
Ulishya, Ulishaya, Ulishea, Uleesha*

Ulielmi (Polynesian) An intelligent lady
*Ulielmie, Ulielmee, Ulielmy, Ulielmey,
Ulielmea, Uleilmeah*

Ulima (Arabic) One who is wise and astute
*Ulimah, Ullima, Ulimma, Uleema, Uleama,
Ulyma, Uleima, Uliema*

Ulla (German) A willful woman
Ullah, Ullaa, Ullai, Ullae

Ulphi (American) A lovely woman
*Ulphie, Ulphy, Ulphey, Ulphee, Ulphea,
Ulpheah, Ulphia, Ulphiah, Ulphiya,
Ulphiyah*

Ulrica (German) Feminine form of Ulric;
wolf ruler; ruler of all
*Ulricah, Ulrika, Ulrikah, Ulrique, Ulrike,
Ulryca, Ulryka, Ulricka, Ulrycka, Ulryqua,
Ullrica, Ullrika, Ullricka, Ulka, Uli, Ulie,
Uly, Uley, Ulee, Uleigh, Ulli*

Ultima (Latin) One who is aloof; endmost
Ultimah, Ultyma, Ultymah

Ulu (African) Second-born child
Ullu

Ululani (Hawaiian) Born of heavenly inspiration
*Ululanie, Ululany, Ululaney, Ululanee,
Ululanya, Ululania*

Ulva (German) Resembling the wolf
Ulvah, Ulvia, Ulvya

Ulyssia (American) Feminine form of
Ulysses; one who wanders; an angry woman
*Ulyssiah, Ulyssea, Ulysseah, Ulissia, Ulissiah,
Ulissea, Ulisseah, Ulissya, Ulyssya, Ulyssi,
Ulissi, Ulyssie, Ulissie, Ulyssy, Ulissy, Ulyssey,
Ulissey, Ulyssee, Ulissee*

Uma (Hindi) Mother; in mythology, the
goddess of beauty and sunlight
Umah, Umma

Umay (Turkish) One who is hopeful
Umaa, Umui, Umae

Umayma (Arabic) Little mother
Umaymah, Umaema, Umaima

Umberla (French) Feminine form of
Umber; providing shade; of an earth color
*Umberlah, Umberly, Umberley, Umberlee,
Umberleigh, Umberli, Umberlea, Umberlie,
Umberleah, Umberlina, Umberlyna,
Umberleina, Umberliena, Umberleena,
Umberleana*

Umeko (Japanese) One who is patient; a
plum-blossom child
Umeeko, Umeiko, Umeyo, Ume

Ummi (African) Born of my mother
Ummie, Ummy, Ummey, Ummee, Umi

Umnia (Arabic) One who is desired
*Umniah, Umnea, Umneah, Umniya,
Umniyah*

Una (Irish / Latin / Native American) Form
of Agnes, meaning "one who is pure;
chaste" / unity; one / a fond memory
Unah, Unna, Unagh, Uny, Unnah

Undine (Latin) From the waves; in mythol-
ogy, a female water spirit
*Undene, Undeen, Undyn, Undyne, Undina,
Undinah, Undyna, Undinia, Undynia,
Undinya*

Undra (American) A long-suffering woman
*Undrah, Undria, Undriah, Undreah, Undrea,
Undriya, Undriyah*

Unelina (Latin) Woman who is bearlike
*Unelinah, Uneleena, Unelena, Unelyna,
Uneleana, Unelinia*

Unice (Greek) Form of Eunice, meaning
"one who conquers"
Unise, Unyce, Unyse

Unique (American) Unlike others; the only
one
*Unikue, Unik, Uniquia, Uniqia, Uniqua,
Unikqua, Unika, Unicka, Unica*

Unity (American) Woman who upholds
oneness; togetherness
*Unitey, Unitie, Uniti, Unitee, Unitea, Unyty,
Unytey, Unytie, Unyti, Unytee, Unytea,
Unite, Unita, Unyta*

Unn (Norwegian) She is loved

Unni (Norse / Hebrew) One who is modest /
a musician of the temple
Unnie, Unny, Unney, Unnee

Ura (Indian) Loved from the heart
Urah, Urra

Ural (Slavic) From the mountains
Urall, Urale, Uralle

Urania (Greek) From the heavens; in
mythology, the muse of astronomy
*Uraniah, Uraniya, Urainia, Urainiah,
Uraina, Uranya, Uranie*

Urbai (American) One who is gentle
Urbae, Urbay, Urbaye

Urbana (Latin) From the city; city dweller
*Urbanah, Urbanna, Urbane, Urbania,
Urbanya, Urbanne*

Urbi (Egyptian) Born to royalty; a princess
Urbie, Urby, Urbey, Urbea, Urbeah, Urbee

Urenna (African) A father's pride
*Urennah, Urena, Urenah, Urennia, Urennya,
Urenya*

Uri (Hebrew) My light; light of the Lord
Urie, Ury, Urey, Uree, Uria, Uriah

Uriana (Greek) From the unknown; heav-
enly
*Urianah, Urianna, Uryana, Uryanna,
Uriane, Uriann, Urianne, Uryan, Uryane,
Uryann, Uryanne*

Uriela (Hebrew) The angel of light
Uriella, Urielle, Uriel, Uriele, Uriell

Urika (Native American) One who is useful
to all
*Urikah, Urica, Uricka, Uryka, Uryca,
Urycka, Uriqua, Uryqua, Uricca, Urycca*

Urit (Hebrew) Emanating a bright light
*Uryt, Urita, Uritah, Uryta, Urytah, Urice,
Urith*

Ursula (Greek) Resembling a little bear
*Ursulla, Ursela, Ursella, Ursala, Ursalla,
Ursola, Ursolla, Ursila, Ursilla, Urzula,
Urzulla, Ursel, Ursule, Ursulina, Ursillane,
Ursulyna, Ursylyn, Urzuli, Ursule, Ursanne,
Ursa, Ursey, Ursy, Ursi, Ursie, Ursee, Ursea,
Uschi*

Urta (Latin) Resembling the spiny plant
Urtah

Urvasi (Hindi) In Hinduism, the most beautiful of the celestial maidens
Urvasie, Urvasy, Urvasee

Usagi (Japanese) Resembling a rabbit
Usagie, Usagy, Usagey, Usagee

Usha (Indian) Born at dawn; in mythology, the daughter of heaven, and the name of a demon princess
Ushah, Ushas, Ushai

Usher (Latin) From the mouth of the river
Ushar, Ushir, Ussher, Usshar, Usshir, Ushur, Usshur

Ushi (Chinese) Resembling an ox
Ushie, Ushy, Ushey, Ushee

Usoa (Basque) Woman who is dovelike
Usoah

Uta (German / Japanese) Fortunate maid of battle / poem
Utako, Ute

Utah (Native American) People of the mountains; from the state of Utah

Utas (Latin) A glorious woman

Utica (African) From the ancient city
Uticah, Utika, Utikah, Uticka, Utickah, Utyca, Utycah, Utyka, Utykah, Utycka, Utyckah, Uttica, Uttika, Uttyca, Uttyka, Utticka, Uttycka

Utopia (American) From the ideally perfect place
Utopiah, Utopea, Utopeah

Uttara (Indian) A royal daughter
Uttarae, Uttarai, Uttaray, Utara, Utarae, Utarai, Utaray

Uttasta (Arabic) From the homeland
Uttastah, Utasta, Utastah

Uzbek (Turkish) From Uzbekistan
Uzbeck, Uzbec, Uzbeka, Uzbecka, Uzbeca

Uzetta (American) One who is serious
Uzeta, Uzett, Uzet, Uzette, Uzete

Uzma (Spanish) A capable woman
Uzmah, Usma, Usmah

Uzoma (African) One who takes the right path
Uzomah, Uzomma, Uzommah

Uzuri (African) A known beauty
Uzurie, Uzury, Uzurey, Uzuree

Uzzi (Hebrew / Arabic) God is my strength / a strong woman
Uzzie, Uzzy, Uzzey, Uzzee, Uzi, Uzie, Uzy, Uzey, Uzee, Uzza, Uza, Uzzia, Uzia, Uzzya, Uzya, Uzziye

V

Vachya (Indian) One who is well-spoken
Vachyah, Vachia, Vach, Vac

Vacuna (Latin) A victorious woman
Vacunah, Vacunia, Vacunea

Vaetilda (Norse) Mother of the Skraeling children
Vaetild, Vaetilde, Vaetildha, Vaetildhe

Vafara (French) One who is brave
Vafarah, Vafarra, Vaphara, Vapharra, Vafaria, Vafarya

Vail (English) From the valley
Vaile, Vale, Vayl, Vayle, Valle

Vailea (Polynesian) From the talking waters
Vaileah, Vaileigh, Vailee, Vailey, Vaily, Vailie, Vailei, Vaili, Vailya, Vaylea, Vayleah, Vayleigh, Vaylee, Vayley, Vayly, Vaylie, Vaylei, Vayli, Vaylya

Vaisakhi (Indian) The beginning of spring

Vala (German) The chosen one; singled out
Valah, Valla

Valborga (Swedish / German) A powerful mountain / protecting ruler
Valborgah, Valborg

Valda (Teutonic / German) Spirited in battle / famous ruler
Valdah, Valida, Velda, Vada, Vaida, Vayda, Vaeda

Valdis (Norse) In mythology, the goddess of the dead
Valdiss, Valdys, Valdyss

Valeda (Latin) A brave and strong woman
Valedah, Valida, Valeeda, Valyda, Valeida, Valieda

Valencia (Spanish) One who is powerful; strong; from the city of Valencia
Valenciah, Valyncia, Valencya, Valenzia, Valancia, Valenica, Valanca, Valecia, Valence

Valene (Latin) Form of Valentina, meaning "one who is vigorous and healthy"
Valeen, Valeene, Valean, Valeane, Valine, Valien, Valyn, Valynn, Valain, Valaine, Valena, Valeena, Valeana, Valina, Valaina

Valentina (Latin) One who is vigorous and healthy
Valentinah, Valentine, Valenteena, Valenteana, Valentena, Valentyna, Valantina, Valentyne, Valentia, Valentya, Valtina, Valentijn, Valyn, Val, Valle

✪ **Valeria** (Latin) Form of Valerie, meaning
❶ "strong and valiant"
Valara, Valera, Valaria, Valeriana, Veleria, Valora

Valerie (Latin) Feminine form of Valerius; strong and valiant
Valeri, Valeree, Valerey, Valery, Valarie, Valari, Vallery, Valeraine, Valere, Valerye, Valaree, Vallerie, Valleri, Valka, Vairy, Valry, Vallirie, Valorie, Val, Valle

Valeska (Slavic) A glorious ruler
Valeskah, Valezka, Valesca, Valeshka, Valisha, Valeshia, Valdislava

Valiant (English) One who is brave
Valiante, Valeant, Valeante

Valkyrie (Scandinavian) In mythology, the handmaidens who led slain heroes to Valhalla
Valkry, Valkri, Valkrie, Valkree, Valkrea, Valkreah, Valki, Valkie, Valkee, Valkea, Valkey, Valky, Valkeah, Valkrey

Valley (American) Between the mountains
Valey, Valy, Vali, Valie, Valee, Vally, Valli, Vallie, Vallee, Valeigh, Valleigh, Valei, Vallei

Valma (Finnish) A dedicated protector
Valmah

Valmai (Welsh) Resembling a spring flower
Valmae, Valmay

Valonia (Latin) From the valley
Valoniah, Vallonia, Vallonya, Valonya, Vallonea, Valonea, Valione, Valionia, Valona, Valyona, Valyonia, Valyonya, Vallon

Valterra (American) Of the strong earth
Valterrah, Valtera, Valteira

Vamia (Spanish) An energetic woman
Vamiah, Vamea, Vameah, Vamie, Vami, Vamee, Vamea, Vameah, Vamey, Vamy

Vanda (German) Form of Wanda, meaning "a wanderer"
Vandah, Vande, Vandana, Vandi, Vandetta, Vandella, Vannda, Vanditta

Vandani (Hindi) One who is honorable and worthy
Vandany, Vandaney, Vandanie, Vandanee, Vandania, Vandanya

✪ **Vanessa** (Greek) Resembling a butterfly
❶ *Vanessah, Vanesa, Vannesa, Vannessa, Vanassa, Vanasa, Vanessia, Vanysa, Vanyssa, Varnessa, Vanessica, Vanesha, Vaniessa, Vanissa, Vanneza, Vaneza, Vannysa, Vanika, Vaneshia, Vanesia, Vanisa, Venessa*

Vanetta (Greek) Form of Vanessa, meaning "resembling a butterfly"
Vanettah, Vaneta, Vanette, Vanete, Vanett, Vanita, Vanitta, Vanneta, Vannita, Venetta

Vangie (Greek) Form of Evangelina, meaning "a bringer of good news"
Vangi, Vangy, Vangey, Vangee

Vania (Russian) Form of Anna, meaning "a woman graced with God's favor"
Vaniah, Vanea, Vanya, Vannya, Vanna, Vanija, Vanja, Vaniya, Vanka, Vannia, Vanina, Vannea

Vanity (English) Having excessive pride
Vanitey, Vanitee, Vaniti, Vanitie, Vanitty, Vanyti, Vanyty, Vanytie

Vanmra (Russian) A stranger; from a foreign place
Vanmrah

Vanna (Cambodian) Golden-haired woman
Vannah, Vana, Vanae, Vannie, Vanny, Vannalee, Vannaleigh, Vanelly, Vanelley

Vanora (Scottish) From the white wave
*Vanorah, Vannora, Vanorey, Vanory,
Vanorie, Vanori, Vanoree, Vanorea, Vanoria,
Vanorya*

Vanthe (Greek) Form of Xanthe, meaning
"yellow-haired woman; blonde"
Vanth, Vantha, Vanthia

Var (Scandinavian) In mythology, a goddess
who punishes those who break promises
Varr, Varre

Vara (Greek) The stranger; one who is careful
Varah, Varia, Varra

Varana (Hindi) Of the river
Varanah, Varanna, Varanne, Varann

Varda (Hebrew) Resembling a rose
*Vardah, Vardia, Vardina, Vardissa, Vardita,
Vardysa, Vardyta, Vardit, Vardis, Vardisse,
Vardice, Vardyce, Vardys, Vardyse, Vardina,
Varyna, Vardinia, Vardin, Vardine, Vardyn,
Vardyne, Vadit, Vared*

Varina (Slavic / English) Yet to be discovered / thorn
Varinah, Varyna, Vareena

Varouna (Hindi) Infinite
Varounah

Varsha (Hindi) Of the rain
Varshah

Vartouhi (Armenian) As beautiful as a rose
Vartoughi, Vartoughie, Vartouhie

Varuna (Hindi) Wife of the sea
Varunah, Varuna, Varun, Varunani, Varuni

Varvara (Slavic) Form of Barbara, meaning
"a traveler from a foreign land; a stranger"
*Varvarah, Varenka, Varinka, Varyusha,
Varushka, Vavka, Vava, Varya, Vavara,
Vavarah*

Vasanti (Hindi) Refers to the spring season
Vasantie, Vasanta, Vasantah, Vasant, Vasante

Vashti (Persian) A lovely woman
Vashtie, Vashty, Vashtey, Vashtee

Vasiliki (Greek) Feminine form of Basil; royalty
*Vasilikie, Vasiliky, Vasilikey, Vasilikee,
Vasilisa, Vasilisia, Vasilissa, Vassillissa*

Vassy (Persian) A beautiful young woman
*Vassey, Vassie, Vassi, Vassee, Vasy, Vasey,
Vasie, Vasi, Vasee*

Vasta (Persian) One who is pretty
Vastah

Vasteen (American) A capable woman
*Vasteene, Vastiene, Vastien, Vastein, Vasteine,
Vastean, Vasteane*

Vasuda (Hindi) Of the earth
*Vasudah, Vasudhara, Vasundhara,
Vasudhra, Vasundhra*

Vasumati (Hindi) Of unequaled splendor
*Vasumatie, Vasumatey, Vasumaty,
Vasumatee*

Vatusia (African) She leaves us behind
*Vatusiah, Vatutia, Vatushia, Vatuseah,
Vatuzia, Vatusya, Vatuzya*

Vaughn (English) The little beloved one
Vaughan, Vaun, Vawn, Vaunne

Vayu (Hindi) A vital life force; the air
Vayyu

Veata (Cambodian) Of the wind
Veatah

Veda (Sanskrit) Having sacred knowledge
Vedah, Veida, Vedad, Veleda

Vedas (Hindi) Eternal laws of Hinduism

Vedette (French) From the guard tower
Vedete, Vedett, Vedet, Vedetta, Vedeta

Vedi (Sanskrit) Filled with wisdom
Vedie, Vedy, Vedey, Vedee, Vedea, Vedeah

Vedis (German) Holy spirit of the forest
*Vediss, Vedisse, Vedys, Vedyse, Vedyss,
Vedysse, Vedissa, Vedyssa, Vidis, Vidisse,
Vidys, Vidyss, Vidyse, Videssa*

Vega (Latin) A falling star
Vegah

Velanie (American) Form of Melanie,
meaning "a dark-skinned beauty"
*Valaney, Valanie, Vel, Vela, Velaina, Velaine,
Velainey, Velana, Velanee, Velaney, Velani,
Velania, Velanney, Velannie, Velany, Vella,
Vellanie, Velli, Vellie, Velloney, Velly, Veloni,
Velonie, Velonnie, Velony, Velaena*

Veleda (Teutonic) Of inspired wisdom
Veledah

Velika (Slavic) A wondrous woman
Velikah, Velyka, Velicka, Velicca, Velycka, Velycca

Velinda (American) Form of Melinda, meaning "one who is sweet and gentle"
Valynda, Velinde, Vellinda, Velynda, Valinda, Valinde

Vellamo (Finnish) In mythology, the goddess of the sea
Velamo, Vellammo

Velma (German) Form of Wilhelmina, meaning "determined protector"
Velmah, Vellma, Valma, Vilma, Vylma, Vylna

Velvet (English) Wearing a soft fabric; velvety
Velvete, Velvette, Velvett, Velvit, Velvyt, Velveta, Velvetta, Velouette

Venda (African) Of the Bantu people
Vendah, Vendaa, Vendae, Vendai

Venecia (Latin) Woman of Venice
Veneciah, Venicia, Vanecia, Vanetia, Venesha, Venisha, Veniesa, Venishia, Veneece, Venise, Veniece, Veneise, Venyce, Vonysia, Vonizia, Vonizya, Vonysya, Venetia, Venitia, Vinetia, Vinita, Venita, Venetya, Veneta, Venetta, Vynita, Vynyta, Vonitia, Vonita, Venezia, Veniza, Venice, Venke

Veneranda (Spanish) One who is honored
Venerandah, Veneradah, Venerada

Ventana (Spanish) As transparent as a window
Ventanah, Ventanna, Ventane, Ventanne

Ventura (Spanish) Having good fortune
Venturah, Venturra

Venus (Greek) In mythology, the goddess of love and beauty
Venis, Venys, Vynys, Venusa, Venusina, Venusia

Venya (Hindi) One who is lovable
Venyah, Venyaa

Vera (Latin / Slavic) The truth / one with faith
Verah, Veera, Verra, Viera, Vira, Veira, Vyra, Vere, Vara, Verla, Verka, Verasha, Vjera

Veradis (Latin) One who is genuine; truthful
Veradise, Veradys, Veradisa, Verdissa, Veradysa, Veradyssa, Veradisia, Veraditia

Verbena (Latin) Sacred limb; sacred plants
Verbenae, Verbane, Verbenia, Verbeen, Verbeene, Verbeena, Verbene, Verbina, Verbine, Verbyna, Verbyne, Verbyn, Verben, Verbin

Verda (Latin) Springlike; one who is young and fresh
Verdah, Verdea, Virida, Verdy, Verdey, Verde, Verdi, Verdie, Verdee

Verdad (Spanish) An honest woman
Verdada, Verdadah

Verena (German) Protector and defender
Verenah, Verina, Vereena, Veryna, Vereana, Vereene, Verine, Verene, Veryn, Veryne, Vereane, Verean, Verin, Varyn, Varyna, Varyne, Verinka, Verunka, Verusya, Veroshka, Virna

Verenase (Swedish) One who is flourishing
Verenese, Verennase, Vyrenase, Vyrennase, Vyrenese, Verenace, Vyrenace

Verity (Latin) One who is truthful
Veritey, Veriti, Veritie, Veritee, Veritea, Verita, Veryty, Veryti, Verytie, Verytey, Verytee, Verytea, Veryta, Verochka

Verlee (American) Form of Verity, meaning "one who is truthful"
Verley, Verly, Verli, Verlie, Verlee, Verleigh, Verlea, Verlia

Verlene (Latin) A vivacious woman
Verleen, Verleene, Verlean, Verleane, Verlein, Verleine, Verlyn, Verlyne, Verlena, Verleena, Verleana, Verleina, Verlyna

Verlita (Spanish) One who is growing
Verlitah, Verlida, Verlidah, Verlyta, Verlytah, Verlyda, Verlydah

Vermekia (American) A natural beauty
Vermekiah, Vermekea, Vermekeah, Vermy, Vermey, Vermee, Vermea, Vermeah, Vermi, Vermie

Vermont (French) From the green mountain; from the state of Vermont
Vermonte

Verna (Latin / English) Born in the springtime / feminine form of Vernon; alder tree
Vernah, Vyrna, Virna, Verne, Verla, Vernia, Verasha, Verneta, Vernette, Vernetta, Vernita, Virida, Virnell, Vernetia

Verona (Italian) Woman from Verona
Veronah, Veronaa, Veronae, Veronia

Veronica (Latin) Displaying her true image
Veronicah, Veronic, Veronicca, Veronicka, Veronika, Veronicha, Veronique, Veranique, Veroniqua, Veronnica, Veronice, Varonica, Varonika, Verhonica, Verinica, Verohnica, Vironica, Vironiqua, Vironika, Vironique, Veronka, Veronkia, Veronne, Vyronica, Vronica, Vronika, Vroniqua, Vronique, Vyroniqua, Vyronique, Vyronika, Veruka, Veruszhka

Vertrelle (American) One who is organized
Vertrell, Vertrel, Vertrele, Vertrela, Vertrella

Veruca (Latin) A type of wart
Verucah, Verucka, Verucia, Verutia, Verusia

Vesna (Slavic) Messenger; in mythology, the goddess of spring
Vesnah, Vezna, Vesnia, Vesnaa

Vespera (Latin) Evening star; born in the evening
Vesperah, Vespira, Vespeera, Vesperia, Vesper

Vesta (Latin) In mythology, goddess of the hearth, home, and family
Vestah, Vestee, Vestea, Vesty, Vestey, Vestie, Vesti, Vessy, Vesteria, Vest

Vetaria (Slavic) A regal woman
Vetariah, Vetarea, Vetareah

Vevay (Welsh) Of the white wave
Vevae, Vevai

Vevila (Gaelic) Woman with a melodious voice
Vevilah, Veveela, Vevyla, Vevilla, Vevylla, Vevylle, Vevyle, Vevillia

Vevina (Irish) A sweet lady; pleasant
Vevinah, Vevyna, Veveena, Veveana, Vevine, Vevyne, Veveene, Vevean

Vian (English) One who is full of life; vivacious
Veean, Vean, Veane, Vyan, Vyanne, Vyane

Vianca (American) Form of Bianca, meaning "a shining, fair-skinned woman"
Viancah, Vianka, Viancka, Vyanca, Vyanka, Vyancka, Vianica, Vianeca, Vyaneca, Vyanica

Vibeke (Danish) A small woman
Vibekeh, Vibeek, Vibeeke, Vybeke, Viheke

Vibhuti (Hindi) Of the sacred ash; a symbol
Vibuti, Vibhutie, Vibhutee

✪ Victoria (Latin) Victorious woman; winner; conqueror
Victoriah, Victorea, Victoreah, Victorya, Victorria, Victoriya, Vyctoria, Victorine, Victoreana, Victoriana, Victorina, Victoryna, Victoreena, Viktoria, Vicktoria, Viktorina, Vyctoria, Vyktoria, Vyctorina, Vyktorina, Vyctoryna, Vyktoryna, Victoryn, Vyctorine, Vyctoryn, Vyktorine, Vyktoryn, Vyktoryne, Vitoria, Vicki, Vickie, Vicky, Vickey, Vikki, Vicka, Vika, Victriv, Victriva

Vida (Latin / Hebrew) Life / one who is dearly loved
Vidah, Veeda, Vieda, Vyda, Vidett, Vidette, Videtta, Videte, Videta, Videlle, Vidella, Videll, Videle, Videla

Vidonia (Latin) Of the vine branch
Vidoniah, Vidonya, Vydonia, Vydonya, Vedonia

Vidya (Indian) Having great wisdom
Vidyah

Vienna (Latin) From the wine country; from Vienna
Vienne, Vienette, Vienetta, Venia, Venna, Vena, Vennia

Viera (Spanish) A lively woman
Vierah, Vierra, Vierrah, Vyera, Vyerah, Vyerra, Vyerrah

Viet (Vietnamese) A woman from Vietnam
Vyet, Viett, Vyett, Viette, Vyette

Vigdis (Scandinavian) A goddess of war
Vigdiss, Vigdisse, Vigdys, Vigdyss

Vigilia (Latin) Wakefulness; watchfulness
Vigiliah, Vygilia, Vygylia, Vijilia, Vyjilia

Vignette (French) From the little vine
*Vignete, Vignet, Vignetta, Vignett, Vignetu,
Vygnette, Vygnete, Vygnet, Vygnett, Vygneta,
Vygnetta*

Vika (Scottish) From the creek
Vikah, Veeka, Veecka, Vicka, Vicca

Vilhelmina (Swedish) Form of Wilhemina,
meaning "determined protector"
*Vilhelminah, Vylhelmina, Vylhelmyna,
Vilhelmine, Villemina, Vilhelmine,
Vilhemine, Vilhemina, Villamena, Villene,
Villette, Villa, Vimene, Vimine, Vilhelmeena,
Villiamina, Vilma, Vilmetta, Vilmanie,
Vilmayra, Vylma, Villiemae, Vilmet, Vilna*

Vilina (Hindi) One who is dedicated
*Vilinah, Vileena, Vileana, Vylina, Vyleena,
Vyleana, Vylyna, Vilinia, Vilinya*

Villetta (French) From the country estate
*Villettah, Vileta, Villeta, Viletta, Vyleta,
Vylletta, Vylleta, Vyletta, Vileta*

Villette (French) From the small village
*Vilette, Villete, Vilete, Vilet, Vilett, Villet,
Villett, Vylet, Vylete, Vylett, Vylette, Vyllet,
Vyllete, Vyllette*

Vilmaris (Greek) Protector from the sea
*Vilmarise, Vilmarice, Vilmarisa, Vilmarissa,
Vilmarisia, Vilmariss, Vilmarys, Vilmaryss*

Vimala (Indian) Feminine form of Vamal;
clean and pure
Vimalah, Vimalia, Vimalla

Vina (Spanish / Hindi) From the vineyard
/ in mythology, the musical instrument of
the goddess of wisdom
*Vinah, Veena, Vinna, Vyna, Vynna, Vinesha,
Vinisha, Vinita, Viniece, Vinora, Vinique*

Vinata (Hindi) In Hinduism, the daughter
of Daksha, wife of Kasyapa, and mother of
Garuda
Vinatah

Vinaya (Hindi) One with discipline; good
behavior
Vinayah

Vincentia (Latin) Feminine form of
Vincent; conquerer; triumphant
*Vincentiah, Vincenta, Vincensia, Vincenzia,
Vyncentia, Vyncyntia, Vyncenzia, Vycenzya,
Vincenza, Vicenta, Vincensa, Vincentina,
Vincentena, Vicentah, Vicynta, Viecinta,
Vycenta, Viecynta, Visenta, Visynta, Vysenta*

Vincia (Spanish) One who is forthright
*Vinciah, Vyncia, Vynciah, Vincea, Vinceah,
Vyncea, Vynceah*

Vinia (Latin) Wine
Viniah, Vynia, Vynya

Viola (Italian) A stringed instrument; a
form of Violet, meaning "resembling the
purplish-blue flower"
*Violah, Viole, Vyola, Violanie, Violani,
Violaney, Violany, Violaine, Violaina,
Violanta, Violante, Violeine, Vyoila, Vyolani,
Vyolanie, Vyolania, Vyolanya, Violanth,
Violanthe, Violantha*

Violet (French) Resembling the purplish-
blue flower
*Violett, Violette, Violete, Vyolet, Vyolett,
Vyolette, Vyolete, Violeta, Violetta, Vyoleta,
Vyoletta, Violatta*

Virendra (Indian) One who is brave and
noble
Virendrah, Vyrendrah, Virindra, Virendria

Virgilia (Latin) A staff-bearer
*Virgiliah, Virgillia, Virgilya, Virgilea,
Virgileah, Virjilia, Virjillia, Virjilya, Virjilea,
Virjileah, Vyrgilia, Vyrgylya, Virgily, Virgiley,
Virgilie, Virgili, Virgilee, Virgileigh*

Virginia (Latin) One who is chaste; virginal;
from the state of Virginia
*Virginiah, Virginnia, Virgenya, Virgenia,
Virgeenia, Virgeena, Virgene, Virgena,
Virgine, Verginia, Verginya, Virjeana,
Virjinea, Virjinia, Vyrjinia, Vyrginia,
Vyrgynia, Vyrgynya, Virgenie*

Virgo (Latin) The virgin; a constellation; the
sixth sign of the zodiac

Viridis (Latin) Youthful and blooming;
green; innocent
*Viridiss, Viridys, Viridyss, Vyridis, Vyridys,
Vyrydys, Virdis, Viridissa, Viridia, Viridianai,
Viridiani, Viridiana*

Virika (Hindi) One who is brave
*Virikah, Viricka, Virica, Vyrika, Vyricka,
Vyrica, Vyryka, Viricca*

Virtue (Latin) Having moral excellence,
chastity, and goodness
Virtu, Vyrtue, Vyrtu, Vertue, Vertu

Visola (African) Longings are as waterfalls
Visolah, Visolaa, Visolae, Visolai, Visolia, Visolla

Vita (Latin) Feminine form of Vitus; life
Vitah, Vitta, Veeta, Veetta, Vyta, Vytta, Vitia, Vitella, Vitka, Vitalina, Vitaliana

Viveka (German) Little woman of the strong fortress
Vivekah, Vivecka, Vyveka, Viveca, Vyveca, Vivecca, Vivika, Vivieka, Vivyka

Vivian (Latin) One who is full of life; vibrant
Viviane, Vivianne, Viviann, Vivien, Viviene, Vivienne, Vivienn, Vivyan, Vivyann, Vivyanne, Vyvian, Vyviann, Vyvianne, Vyviane, Vyvyan, Vyvyann, Vyvyanne, Vyvyane, Viviana, Vivianna, Vivyana, Vyvyana, Vivina, Vivia, Viveca, Vivion, Viva, Vivan, Vyva, Vive, Vyv, Viv, Vivi, Vevey, Vevay, Vivie, Vivee

Vixen (American) A flirtatious woman
Vixin, Vixi, Vixie, Vixee, Vixea, Vixeah, Vixy, Vixey

Vlasta (Slavic) A friendly and likeable woman
Vlastah, Vlastia, Vlastea, Vlastiah, Vlasteah

Volante (Italian) One who is veiled
Volanta, Volantia, Volantea

Voleta (Greek) The veiled one
Voletah, Voletta, Volita, Volitta, Volyta, Volytta, Volet, Volett, Volette, Volit, Volitt, Volitte, Volyt, Volytt, Volytte

Volupia (Latin) Sensual pleasure; in mythology, the goddess of pleasure
Volupiah, Volupeah, Volupya, Volupyah

Volva (Scandinavian) In mythology, a female shaman
Volvah, Volvya, Volvaa, Volvae, Volvai, Volvay, Volvia

Vonda (Russian) Form of Wanda, meaning "a wanderer"
Vondah, Vonde, Vondana, Vondi, Vondetta, Vondella, Vonnda, Vonditta, Vondia

Vondila (African) Woman who lost a child
Vondilah, Vondilla, Vondilya, Vondilia, Vondyla, Vondylya

Vondra (Slavic) A woman's love; a loving woman
Vondrah, Vondria, Vondrea, Vondreah, Vondrya

Voni (Slavic) An affectionate woman
Vonie, Vony, Voney, Vonee, Vonea, Voneah

Vonna (French) Form of Yvonne, meaning "a young archer"
Vonnah, Vona, Vonah, Vonnia, Vonnya, Vonia, Vonya, Vonny, Vonney, Vonnie, Vonni

Vonnala (American) A sweetheart
Vonnalah, Vonnalla, Vonnallah, Vonala, Vonalah, Vonalla, Vonallah

Vonshae (American) One who is confident
Vonshay, Vonshaye, Vonshai

Vor (Norse) In mythology, an omniscient goddess
Vore, Vorr, Vorre

Voshkie (Armenian) The golden one
Voshki, Voshkey, Voshky, Voshkee, Voshckie, Voshcki, Voshckey, Voshcky, Voshcky, Voshckee

Voyage (American) One who enjoys travel

Vui (Vietnamese) One who is cheerful

Vulpine (English) A cunning woman; like a fox
Vulpyne, Vulpina, Vulpyna

Vyomini (Indian) A gift of the divine
Vyominie, Vyominy, Vyominey, Vyominee, Vyomyni, Vyomyny, Viomini, Viomyni, Viomyny, Vyomine

W

Wade (English) To cross the river ford
Wayde, Waid, Waide, Waddell, Wadell, Waydell, Waidell, Waed, Waede

Wafa (Arabic) One who is faithful; devoted
Wafah, Wafaa, Waffa, Wapha, Waffah, Waphah

Wafiqah (Arabic) A successful woman
Wafiqa, Wafiqaa, Wafeeqah, Wafeeqa, Wafyqa, Wafyqah, Wafieqa, Wafieqah, Wafeiqa, Wafeiqah

Wagaye (African) My sense of value; my price
Wagay, Wagai, Wagae

Wahibah (Arabic) The generous one; a giver
Wahiba, Waheeba, Wahyba, Waheebah, Wahybah, Wahieba, Wahiebah, Waheiba, Waheibah, Waheaba, Waheabah, Wabibah, Wabibah, Wabyba, Wabybah, Wabeeba, Wabeebah, Wabeiba, Wabeibah, Wabieba, Wabiebah, Wabeaba, Wabeabah

Wahidah (Arabic) Feminine form of Wahid; unique; one and only
Wahida, Waheeda, Wahyda, Waheedah, Waydah, Wahieda, Wahiedah, Waheida, Waheidah, Waheada, Waheadah

Wahifah (Arabic) Lady-in-waiting; servant
Wahifa, Waheefa, Wahyfa, Waheefah, Wahyfah, Waheifa, Waheifah, Wahiefa, Wahiefah, Waheafa, Waheafah

Wainani (Hawaiian) Of the beautiful waters
Wainanie, Wainany, Wainaney, Wainanee, Wainanea, Wainaneah

Wajihah (Arabic) One who is distinguished; eminent
Wajiha, Wajeeha, Wajyha, Wajeehah, Wajyhah, Wajieha, Wajiehah, Wajeiha, Wajeihah, Wajeaha, Wajeahah

Wakana (Japanese) A thriving woman
Wakanah, Wakanna, Wakannah

Wakanda (Native American) One who possesses magical powers
Wakandah, Wakenda, Wakinda, Wakynda

Wakeen (American) A feisty woman
Wakeene, Wakien, Wakiene, Wakein, Wakein, Wakean, Wakeane

Wakeishah (American) Filled with happiness
Wakeisha, Wakieshah, Wakiesha, Wakesha, Wakeshah, Wakeesha, Wakeeshah, Wakysha, Wakyshah, Wakeasha, Wakeashah

Waki (Native American) A place of protection
Wakie, Waky, Wakey, Wakee, Wakeah, Wakea

Walburga (German) Ruler of the fortress; protection
Walburgah, Walburgha, Walborgd, Waldhurga, Walba, Walda, Welda

Walda (German) One who has fame and power
Waldah, Wallda, Walida, Waldine, Waldina, Waldyne, Waldyna, Welda, Wellda, Waldeana

Waleria (Polish) A sweet woman
Waleriah, Wulerea, Walereah, Waleriya, Waleriyah

Walidah (Arabic) Newly born child
Walida, Walyda, Waleeda, Walada, Walad, Waleedah, Walydah, Waleida, Waleidah, Walieda, Waliedah, Waleada, Waleadah

Waliyya (Arabic) A holy lady; saint
Waliyyah, Waliya, Waliyah, Waliyyaa, Waliyaa

Walker (English) Walker of the forests
Wallker, Walkher

Wallis (English) Feminine form of Wallace; from Wales
Walis, Wallise, Walise, Wallys, Wallyse, Walliss, Walice, Wallisa, Wallysa, Waleis

Walta (African) One who acts as a shield
Waltah

Waltraud (Teutonic) Strong foreign ruler
Waltraude, Waltrawd, Waltrawde

Wambui (African) One who delivers a song; singer
Wamboi

Wan (Chinese) One who is gentle and gracious

Wanda (German) A wanderer
Wandah, Wannda, Wahnda, Wonda, Wonnda, Wohnda, Wande, Wandis, Wandy, Wandie, Wandey, Wandee, Wandely, Wandja, Wandzia, Wandea

Wandella (American) From the little tree
Wandellah, Wandela, Wandelah

Waneta (Native American) One who changes; a shapeshifter
Wanetah, Waneeta, Wanita, Wanneeta, Waneata, Waneita, Wanite, Wanete, Wanneta, Wannete, Waunita, Wonita, Wonyta, Wonnita, Wynita

Wanetta (English) A paleskinned woman
Wanettah, Wanette, Wannette, Wannetta, Wonetta, Wonette, Wonitta, Wonitte, Wonnyta, Wonnyte, Wann

Wangari (African) Resembling the leopard
Wangarie, Wangarri, Wangary, Wangarey, Wangaria, Wangaree

Wanyika (African) Of the bush
Wanyikka, Wanyicka, Wanyicca, Wanyica

Wapeka (Native American) One who is skillful; adroit
Wapekah

Waqi (Arabic) Falling; swooping
Waqqi

Warda (German / Arabic) A guardian / resembling a rose
Wardah, Wardia, Wardeh, Wardine, Wardena, Wardenia, Wordah

Warma (American) A caring woman
Warm, Warme, Warmia, Warmiah, Warmea, Warmeah

Warna (German) One who defends her loved ones
Warnah

Warner (German) Of the defending army
Werner, Wernher, Warnher, Worner, Wornher

Waseemah (Arabic) Feminine form of Waseem; beautiful
Waseema, Waseeme, Wasime, Waseme, Wasimah, Wasima, Wasyma

Washi (Japanese) Resembling an eagle
Washie, Washy, Washey, Washee, Washea, Washeah

Wattan (Japanese) From the homeland
Watan, Wattane

Wauna (Native American) A snow goose singing
Waunah, Waunakee

Wava (Slavic) Form of Barbara, meaning "a traveler from a foreign land; a stranger"
Wavah, Wavya, Wavia

Waverly (English) Of the trembling aspen
Waverley, Waverlie, Waverli, Waverlee, Waverleigh, Waverlea, Waverleah

Waynette (English) One who makes wagons
Waynett, Waynet, Waynete, Wayneta, Waynetta

Wednesday (American) Born on a Wednesday
Wensday, Winsday, Windnesday, Wednesdae, Wensdae, Winsdae, Windnesdae, Wednesdai, Wendsai, Winsdai, Wednesdaie

Weeko (Native American) A beautiful girl
Weyko, Wieko, Weiko

Wehilani (Hawaiian) A heavenly adornment
Wehilanie, Wehilany, Wehilaney, Wehilanee, Wehilanea, Wehilaneah

Wei (Chinese) One who is valuable and brilliant

Welcome (English) A welcome guest
Welcom, Welcomme

Welsie (English) From the West
Welsy, Welsi, Welsey, Welsee, Welss, Welssa, Welsia, Welsea, Welseah

Wende (Teutonic) A wanderer
Wendelin, Wendelina, Wendeline, Wendelle, Wendalla, Wendalle, Wendalina, Wendaline, Wendall, Wendella, Wendelly

Wendy (Welsh) Form of Gwendolyn, meaning "one who is fair; of the white ring"
Wendi, Wendie, Wendee, Wendey, Wenda, Wendia, Wendea, Wendya, Wendye, Wendaine, Wendayne, Wuendy

Weronikia (Polish) Form of Veronica, meaning "displaying her true image"
Weronicka, Weronykia, Weronikya, Weronika, Weronikka, Weronyka, Weronica, Weronicia

Wesley (English) From the western meadow
Wesly, Weslie, Wesli, Weslee, Weslia, Wesleigh, Weslea, Weslei, Weslene, Wesla, Weslya, Weslyn, Wesleah

Whisper (English) One who is soft-spoken
Whysper, Wisper, Wysper

Whitley (English) From the white meadow
Whitly, Whitlie, Whitli, Whitlee, Whitleigh, Whitlea, Whitlia, Whitlya, Whytley, Whytlie, Whytlea, Whytlee, Whytli, Whytly, Whytlya, Whitlei, Whittley, Whytlei

Whitney (English) From the white island
Whitny, Whitnie, Whitni, Whitnee, Whittney, Whitneigh, Whytny, Whytney, Whytnie, Whytni, Whytnee, Whytne, Witney, Whitne, Whiteney, Whitnei, Whitteny, Whitnye

Whitson (English) A white-haired lady
Whitsone, Whitsonne, Whytson, Whytsone, Whytsonne, Whitsona, Whytsona

Whoopi (English) One who is excited and happy
Whoopey, Whoopy, Whoopie, Whoopee, Whoopea, Whoopeah

Whynesha (American) A kindhearted woman
Whyneisha, Whyniesha, Whyneasha, Whynysha, Wynesha, Wyneisha, Wyniesha, Wyneasha, Whyneesha, Wyneesha, Whynesa, Whynessa, Wynesa, Wynessa

Wibeke (Scandinavian) A vibrant woman

Wicapi Wakan (Native American) A holy star

Widad (Arabic) One offering love and friendship
Widadd, Wydad, Wydadd

Wido (German) A warrior maiden
Wydo

Wijdan (Arabic) A sentiment
Widjan

Wijida (Arabic) An excited seeker
Wijidah, Weejida, Weejidah, Wijeeda, Wijeedah, Wijyda, Wijydah, Wijieda, Wijiedah, Wijeida, Wijeidah, Wijeada, Wijeadah

Wiktoria (Polish) Form of Victoria, meaning "victorious woman; winner; conqueror"
Wiktoriah, Wicktoria, Wyktoria, Wycktoria, Wikitoria, Wiktorja, Wicktorja, Wyktorja, Wycktorja, Wikta

Wilda (German) One who is untamed; wild; forest dweller
Wildah, Wylda, Willda, Wilde, Wylde, Whilda

Wileen (Teutonic) A firm defender
Wiline, Wilean, Wileane, Wilyn, Wileene, Wilene, Wyleen, Wyline, Wylean, Wyleane, Wylyn, Wylyne, Wyleen, Wyleene, Wylene, Wileena

Wiley (English) Of the willows
Wily, Wilie, Wili, Wilee, Wileigh, Wilea, Wileah

Wilfreda (English) Feminine form of Wilfred; determined peacemaker
Wilfredah, Wilfreeda, Wilfrida, Wilfreada, Wilfryda

Wilhelmina (German) Feminine form of Wilhelm; determined protector
Wilhelminah, Wylhelmina, Wylhelmyna, Wilhelmine, Willemina, Wilhelmine, Wilhemine, Wilhemina, Willamena, Willene, Willette, Willa, Wimene, Wimine, Vilhelmina, Williamina, Wilma, Wilmetta, Wilmanie, Wilmayra, Wylma, Williemae, Wilmet, Wilna, Wilmot

Willow (English) From the willow tree; symbol of healing and grace
Willo, Willough, Wyllow, Wylow, Wyllo

Wilona (English) One who is hoped for; desired
Wilonah, Willona, Wilone, Willone, Wylona, Wylone

Wilva (Teutonic) A determined woman; persistent
Wilvah, Wylva, Wylvah

Wind (American) Moving air; windy
Wynd, Windy, Windie, Windi, Windee, Windea, Windia, Wyndy, Wyndie, Wyndee, Wyndi, Wyndey, Wyndea, Wyndia

Winda (Swahili) A great huntress
Windah

Winema (Native American) A female chief
Winemah, Wynema, Wynemah

Winetta (American) One who is peaceful
Wineta, Wynetta, Wyneta, Winet, Winett, Winette, Wynet, Wynett, Wynette

Wing (Chinese) Woman of glory
Winge, Wyng

Winifred (German / Gaelic) Peaceful friend / fair; white-skinned
Winafred, Winifrid, Winefred, Winefrid, Winifride, Winifreda, Winfrieda, Winfreda, Winefride, Winifryd, Winnafred, Winifryda, Winnefred, Winnafred, Winniefred, Winnifrid, Wynifred, Wynafred, Wynifrid, Wynafrid, Wynefryd, Wynefred, Winnie, Wynnie

Winna (African) A beloved friend
Winnah, Wina, Wyna, Wynna, Winah, Wynah, Wynnah

Winnielle (African) A victorious woman
Winniell, Winniele, Winniel, Winniella, Winniela

Winola (German) Gracious and charming friend
Winolah, Wynola, Winolla, Wynolla, Wynolah, Winollah, Wynollah

Winona (Native American) Firstborn daughter
Winonah, Wynona, Wanona, Wenona, Wynonna, Winonna, Wynnona, Winnona

Winsome (English) A kind and beautiful lady
Wynsome, Winsom, Wynsom

Winta (African) One who is desired
Wintah, Whinta, Wynta, Whynta, Whintah, Wyntah, Whyntah

Winter (English) Born during the winter season
Wintr, Wynter, Winteria, Wynteria

Wira (Polish) Form of Elvira, meaning "a truthful woman; one who can be trusted"
Wirah, Wyra, Wiria, Wirke

Wisal (Arabic) Communion in love
Wisalle, Wisall

Wisconsin (French) Gathering of waters; from the state of Wisconsin
Wisconsyn, Wisconsen, Wisconson, Wysconsin, Wysconsen, Wysconson

Wisia (Polish) Form of Victoria, meaning "victorious woman; winner; conqueror"
Wisiah, Wysia, Wysya, Wicia, Wikta, Wiktoria, Wykta, Wyktoria

Wistar (German) One who is respected
Whistar, Wystar, Whystar, Wistarr, Wister, Wystarr, Wyster

Wisteria (English) Resembling the flowering vine
Whisteria, Wysteria, Whysteria, Wisterea, Whisterea, Wysterea, Whysterea

Woody (American) A woman of the forest
Woodey, Woodi, Woodie, Woodee, Woodea, Woodeah, Woods

Wova (American) A brassy woman
Wovah, Whova, Whovah

Wren (English) Resembling a small songbird
Wrenn, Wrene, Wrena, Wrenie, Wrenee, Wreney, Wrenny, Wrenna

Wub (African) One who is gorgeous
Wubb, Wubbe

Wyanet (Native American) A famously beautiful woman
Wyanete, Wyanette, Wyanett, Wyanetta, Wyaneta, Wynette, Wianet, Wianette, Wianete, Wianett, Wianetta, Wianeta

Wyetta (French) A feisty woman
Wyett, Wyeta, Wyette, Wyete

Wylie (American) A clever and coy woman
Wyli, Wylee, Wylea, Wyleah, Wyly, Wyley, Wiley, Wily, Wilee, Wileigh, Wilea, Wileah, Wili, Wilie, Wyleigh

Wyn (Welsh) Form of Guinevere, meaning "one who is fair; of the white wave"
Wynn, Wynne, Wyne, Wynnie, Wynie, Wynee, Wyny, Wyney, Wynea, Wyneah

Wynda (Scottish) From the narrow passage
Wyndah, Winda, Windah

Wynstelle (Latin) One who is chaste; pure
Wynstell, Wynstele, Wynstella, Wynstela, Winstelle, Winstell, Winstele, Winstel, Wynstel, Winstella, Winstela

Wyoming (Native American) Of the mountains and valleys; from the state of Wyoming
Wyoma, Wyomin, Wyomine, Wyomia, Wyomya, Wyome, Wyoh, Wyomie, Wyomi, Wyomee, Wyomey, Wyomy, Wyomea, Wyomeah

Wyss (Welsh) One who is fair
Wysse, Whyss, Whysse, Wyse, Whyse

X

Xabrina (Latin) Form of Sabrina, meaning "a legendary princess"
Xabrinah, Xabreena, Xabryna, Xabrienu, Xabreina

Xadrian (American) From the Adriatic
Xadrianne, Xadriane, Xadrien, Xadrienne, Xadriene, Xadrean, Xadreane

Xalvadora (Spanish) Form of Salvadora, meaning "savior"
Xalvadorah, Xalbadora, Xalbadorah, Xalvadoria, Xalbadoria

Xanadu (African) From the exotic paradise

Xandra (Greek) Form of Alexandra, meaning "helper and defender of mankind"
Xandrah, Xander, Xandria, Xandrea, Xandreia, Xandrya, Xandy, Xandie, Xandi, Xandey, Xandy, Xandee

Xannon (American) Ancient goddess
Xanon, Xannan, Xanan, Xannen, Xanen, Xannin, Xanin

Xantara (American) Protector of the Earth
Xantarah, Xanterra, Xantera, Xantarra, Xantarrah, Xanterah, Xanterrah

Xanthe (Greek) Yellow-haired woman; blonde
Xantha, Xanthia, Xana, Xanna, Xanne, Xanthippe, Xantippie

Xaquelina (Galician) Form of Jacqueline, meaning "the supplanter"
Xaqueline, Xaqueleena, Xaquelyna, Xaquelayna, Xaqueleana

Xara (Hebrew) Form of Sarah, meaning "princess; lady"
Xarah, Xarra, Xarya, Xarie, Xarri, Xarrie, Xarry, Xari, Xary, Xaria, Xarria

Xaviera (Basque / Arabic) Feminine form of Xavier; owner of a new house; one who is bright
Xaviere, Xavierra, Xavierre, Xavyera, Xavyere, Xiveria, Xavia, Xavaeir, Xaviar, Xaviara, Xavior, Xaviero, Xavian, Xavyer, Xavery, Xaver, Xavon, Xabier, Xzavier, Xxavier, Xizavier, Xevera, Xeveria

Xenia (Greek) One who is hospitable; welcoming
Xena, Xenea, Xenya, Xinia, Xeniah, Xeenia, Xenah, Xina, Xyna, Xene, Xeena, Xia

Xenobia (Greek) Form of Zenobia, meaning "sign or symbol"
Xenobiah, Xenobya, Xenobe, Xenobie, Xenobey, Xenovia, Xenobee, Xenoby, Xenobea, Xenobeah

Xerena (Latin) Form of Serena, meaning "sign or symbol"
Xerenah, Xerene, Xeren, Xereena, Xeryna, Xereene, Xerenna

Xetsa (African) A female twin
Xetsah, Xetse, Xetseh

Xexilia (American) Form of Celia, meaning "one who is blind"
Xexila, Xexilea, Xexileah, Xexilya

Xhosa (African) Leader of a nation
Xosa, Xhose, Xhosia, Xhosah, Xosah

Xiang (Chinese) Having a nice fragrance
Xyang, Xeang, Xhiang, Xhyang, Xheang

Xiao Hong (Chinese) Of the morning rainbow

Ximena (Spanish) Form of Simone, meaning "one who listens well"
Ximenah, Xymena, Ximono, Xymona

Xin Qian (Chinese) Happy and beautiful woman

Xinavane (African) A mother; to propagate
Xinavana, Xinavania, Xinavain, Xinavaine, Xinavaen, Xinavaene

Xing (Chinese) A star
Xhing

Xing Xing (Chinese) Twin stars
Xhing Xhing

Xiomara (Spanish / Teutonic) Famous in battle / from the glorious forest
Xiomarah, Xiomayra, Xiomaris, Xiomaria, Xiomarra, Xiomarrah

Xirena (Greek) Form of Sirena, meaning "a seductive and beautiful woman"
Xirenah, Xireena, Xirina, Xirene, Xyrena, Xyreena, Xyrina, Xyryna, Xyrine, Xyrene, Xyren

Xiu (Chinese) One who is elegant

Xiu Juan (Chinese) One who is elegant and graceful

Xiu Mei (Chinese) A beautiful plum

Xi-Wang (Chinese) One with hope

Xochiquetzal (Aztec) Resembling a flowery feather; in mythology, the goddess of love, flowers, and the earth

Xochitl (Native American) From the place of many flowers
Xochilt, Xochilth, Xochil, Xochiti

Xola (African) Stay in peace
Xolah, Xolia, Xolla, Xollah

Xolani (African) One who asks forgiveness
Xolanie, Xolaney, Xolany, Xolanee, Xolanea, Xolneah

Xuan (Vietnamese) Born in the spring
Xuana, Xuania, Xuanne, Xuane

Xue (Chinese) Woman of snow

Xue Fang (Chinese) Woman of fragrant snow

Xuxa (Portuguese) Form of Susanna, meaning "resembling a graceful white lily"
Xuxah, Xuxxa, Xuxia

Xyleena (Greek) One who lives in the forest
Xylina, Xyliana, Xylinia, Xylona, Xileana, Xileena, Xilina, Xilyna, Xyleana, Xylyna, Xilona, Xilonia, Xylonia, Xylonya, Xyleen, Xyleene, Xylin, Xyline, Xyleana, Xylyn, Xylyne, Xilean, Xileane, Xileen, Xileene, Xilin, Xiline, Xilyne, Xylean, Xilon, Xylone, Xilone, Xylon

Xylia (Greek) Form of Sylvia, meaning "a woodland dweller"
Xiliah, Xilya, Xilia

Xylophia (Greek) One who loves the forest
Xylophiah, Xylophila, Xilophia, Xilophila

Xyza (Gothic) Of the sea
Xyzah

y

Ya akove (Hebrew) One who replaces another (can also be hyphenated: Ya-akove)

Yabel (Latin) One who is lovable
Yabell, Yabele, Yabelle, Yabela, Yabella

Yachi (Japanese) Eight thousand
Yachie, Yachee, Yachey, Yachy, Yachea, Yacheah

Yachne (Hebrew) One who is gracious and hospitable
Yachnee, Yachney, Yachnie, Yachni, Yachnea, Yachneah

Yacquelin (Spanish) Form of Jacquelin, meaning "the supplanter"
Yacalin, Yacalyn, Yacalynn, Yackalin, Yackalinne, Yackelyn, Yacketta, Yackette, Yacki, Yackie, Yacklin, Yacklyn, Yacklynne, Yackqueline, Yacky, Yaclin, Yaclyn, Yacolyn, Yacqi, Yacqlyn, Yacqualine, Yacqualyn, Yacquel, Yacquelean, Yacqueleen, Yacquelin, Yacquelina, Yacquellu, Yacquelle, Yacquelyn, Yacquelyne, Yacquelynn, Yacquelynne, Yacquenetta, Yacquenette, Yacquetta, Yacquette, Yacqui, Yacquine, Yaculine, Yakleen, Yaklyn, Yaquelin, Yaqueline, Yaquelyn, Yaquelynn, Yaquith, Yaquenetta, Yaquetta

Yadira (Hebrew) A beloved friend
Yadirah, Yadyra, Yadirha, Yadeera, Yadeerah, Yadyrah, Yadeira, Yadeirah, Yadiera, Yadiera, Yadeara, Yadearah

Yadra (Spanish) Form of Madra, meaning "one who is motherly"
Yadre, Yadrah

Yael (Hebrew) Having the strength of God
Yaell, Yaelle, Yaella, Yaele, Yaela, Yaeli

Yaffa (Hebrew) A beautiful woman
Yaffah, Yaffit, Yafit, Yafeal

Yafiah (Arabic) Having a high standing
Yafia

Yair (Hebrew) God will teach
Yaire, Yayr, Yayre, Yaer, Yaere

Yaki (Japanese) A tenacious young woman
Yakie, Yaky, Yakey, Yakea, Yakeah, Yakee

Yakini (African) An honest woman
Yakinie, Yukiney, Yakiny, Yackini, Yackinie, Yackiney, Yackiny, Yakinee, Yakinea, Yakineah

Yakira (Hebrew) One who is precious; dear to the heart
Yakirah, Yakyra, Yakeera, Yakiera, Yakeira, Yahaira, Yahara, Yahira, Yahayra, Yajaira, Yajara, Yajira, Yajayra

Yakootah (Arabic) Resembling an emerald; precious stone
Yakoota, Yakuta, Yakutah

Yalena (Greek) Form of Helen, meaning "the shining light"
Yalenah, Yalina, Yaleena, Yalyna, Yalana, Yaleana, Yalane, Yaleene, Yaline, Yalyne, Yaleane, Yalenchka, Yalene, Yalens

Yaletha (American) Form of Oletha, meaning "one who is truthful"
Yalethia, Yalethea

Yalgonata (Polish) Form of Margaret, meaning "resembling a pearl / the child of light"
Yalgonatta

Yama (Japanese) From the mountain
Yamma, Yamah, Yammah

Yamha (Arabic) Resembling a dove
Yamhah

Yamileth (Spanish) A graceful young girl
Yamilethe, Yamyleth, Yamylethe

Yamilla (Arabic) A beautiful woman
Yamillah, Yamila, Yamilah, Yamylla, Yamyllah, Yamyla, Yamylah, Yamille, Yamill, Yamyl, Yamyll, Yamylle

Yamin (Hebrew) Right hand
Yamine, Yamyn, Yamyne, Yameen, Yameene, Yamein, Yameine, Yamien, Yamiene

Yaminah (Arabic) One who is right and proper
Yamina, Yameena, Yameenah, Yamyna, Yamini, Yemina, Yemini, Yesmina

Yamka (Native American) A budding flower; blossom
Yamkah, Yamcka, Yamckah

Yamuna (Indian) From the sacred Yamuna river
Yamunah, Yamoona, Yamoonah

Yana (Hebrew) He answers
Yanna, Yaan, Yanah, Yannah

Yanaba (Native American) One who is brave
Yanabah

Yanamai (Basque) Having bitter grace; refers to the Virgin Mary
Yanamaria, Yanamarie, Yanamay, Yanamaye, Yanamae

Yancy (Native American) A sassy woman; a Yankee
Yancey, Yanci, Yancie, Yancee, Yancea, Yanceah

Yanessa (American) Form of Vanessa, meaning "resembling a butterfly"
Yanessah, Yanesa, Yannesa, Yannessa, Yanassa, Yanasa, Yanessia, Yanysa, Yanyssa, Yarnessa, Yanessica, Yanesha, Yaniessa, Yanissa, Yanneza, Yaneza, Yannysa, Yanika, Yaneshia, Yanesia, Yanisa, Yenessa

Yang (Chinese) Of the sun

Yanisha (American) One with high hopes
Yanishah, Yaneesha, Yaneeshah, Yaniesha, Yanieshah, Yaneisha, Yaneishah, Yanysha, Yanyshah, Yaneasha, Yaneashah

Yanka (Slavic) God is good
Yancka, Yancca, Yankka

Yannis (Hebrew) A gift of God
Yanis, Yanys, Yannys, Yanni, Yani, Yanee, Yaney, Yanie, Yany, Yannee, Yanney, Yanny, Yannie

Yaqu' (Arabic) Resembling a hyacinth; a sapphire
Yaaqu', Yaaqoo'

Yara (Brazilian) In mythology, the goddess of the river; a mermaid
Yarah, Yarrah, Yarra

Yardenah (Hebrew) From the river Jordan
Yardena, Yardina, Yardeena, Yardyna, Yardenna, Yardennah

Yardley (English) From the fenced-in meadow
Yardly, Yardleigh, Yardli, Yardlie, Yardlee, Yardlea, Yarley, Yarly, Yeardly, Yeardley, Yeardleigh, Yeardlee, Yeardli, Yeardlie

Yareli (American) The Lord is my light
Yarelie, Yareley, Yarelee, Yarely, Yaresly, Yarelea, Yareleah

Yarina (Russian) Form of Irene, meaning "a peaceful woman"
Yarinah, Yaryna, Yarine, Yaryne, Yerina, Yerine, Yeryna, Yeryne

Yarkona (Hebrew) Having green eyes; innocent
Yarkonah, Yarkonna, Yarkonnah

Yarmilla (Slavic) A merchant; trader
Yarmillah, Yarmila, Yarmyla, Yarmylla, Yarmille, Yarmylle

Yaser (Arabic) One who is wealthy and prosperous
Yasera, Yaseria

Yashira (Japanese) Blessed with God's grace
Yashirah, Yasheera, Yashyra, Yashara, Yashieru, Yashierah, Yasheira, Yasheirah, Yasheara, Yashearah

Yashona (Hindi) A wealthy woman
Yashonah, Yashawna, Yashauna, Yaseana, Yashawnah, Yashaunah, Yaseanah

Yasirah (Arabic) One who is lenient
Yasira, Yaseera, Yasyra, Yasiera, Yaseira, Yaseeruh, Yasyrah, Yasierah, Yaseirah

Yasmine (Persian) Resembling the jasmine flower
Yasmin, Yasmene, Yasmeen, Yasmeene, Yasmen, Yasemin, Yasemeen, Yasmyn, Yasmyne, Yasiman, Yassmen, Yasmia, Yasmenne, Yassmeen, Yasmina, Yasmeena, Yasmyna, Yesmina, Yasminda, Yashmine, Yasmain, Yasmaine, Yasma, Yaasmeen, Yaasmin, Yasmon, Yasmeni, Yasiman, Yasimine, Yazmin, Yazmine, Yazmeen, Yazmyn, Yazmyne, Yazmen, Yazmene, Yazmina, Yazmyna, Yazzmine, Yuzzmyne, Yazzmeen, Yesmine, Yesmin, Yesmeen, Yesmean, Yesmyn, Yesmyne

Yasu (Japanese) One who is calm; tranquil
Yazoo, Yasuko, Yasuyo

Yatima (African) An orphan
Yatimah, Yateema, Yatyma, Yateemah, Yatymah, Yatiema, Yatiemah, Yateima, Yateimah

Yaura (American) One who is desired
Yara, Yaure, Yaur

Yauvani (Hindi) Full of youth
Yauvanie, Yauvaney, Yauvany, Yauvanee, Yauvanea, Yauvaneah

Yaxha (Spanish) Green-colored water; from the city of Yaxha
Yaxhah

Ydel (Hebrew) One who praises God
Ydele, Ydell, Ydelle

Yebenette (American) A small woman
Yebenett, Yebenet, Yebenete, Yebeneta, Yebenetta, Yebe, Yebey, Yeby, Yebee, Yebi, Yebie, Yebea, Yebeah

Yedda (English) Having a beautiful voice; a singer
Yeddah, Yeda, Yedah

Yedidah (Hebrew) A beloved friend
Yedida, Yedyda, Yedydah, Yedeeda, Yedeedah

Yehudit (Hebrew) Form of Judith, meaning "woman from Judea"
Yuta, Yuhudit

Yei (Japanese) A flourishing woman

Yeira (Hebrew) One who is illuminated
Yeirah, Yaira, Yeyra, Yairah, Yeyrah

Yejide (African) Image of her mother
Yejid

Yelena (Russian) Form of Helen, meaning "the shining light"
Yelenah, Yelina, Yeleena, Yelyna, Yelaina, Yelana, Yeleana, Yelenna, Yellayna, Yellena, Yilena, Yilina, Yileena, Yilyna, Yilaina, Yilana, Yileana, Yilenna, Yelane, Yelene, Yelenne, Yelain, Yeleane, Yelen, Yeline

Yelisabeta (Russian) Form of Elizabeth, meaning "my God is bountiful"
Yelizabeta, Yelisabeth, Yelizabeth, Yelisabet, Yelizabet

Yelizavetam (Hebrew) Form of Elizabeth, meaning "my God is bountiful"
Yelizaveta, Yelysaveta

Yemaya (African) An intelligent woman
Yemay, Yemaye, Yemai, Yemae, Yemye

Yen (Chinese) One who is desired
Yenic, Yeny, Yenny, Yeni

Yenene (Native American) A medicine man; wizard poisoning a person who is sleeping
Yenyne, Yenine, Yenena, Yenina, Yenyna

Yenge (African) A hardworking woman
Yenga, Yengeh, Yengah

Yepa (Native American) A winter princess; snow woman
Yepah, Yeppa, Yeppah

Yera (Basque) Having bitter grace; refers to the Virgin Mary
Yerah, Yerra, Yerrah

Yeriel (Hebrew) Founded by God
Yerial, Yeriele, Yerielle, Yerialle, Yeriale

Yesenia (Arabic) Resembling a flower
Yeseniah, Yesinia, Yesenya, Yecenia, Yasenya, Yesnia, Yessenia, Yessena, Yessenya, Yissenia

Yeshi (African) For a thousand
Yeshie, Yeshey, Yeshy, Yeshee, Yeshea, Yesheah

Yessica (Hebrew) Form of Jessica, meaning "the Lord sees all"
Yesica, Yessika, Yesika, Yesicka, Yessicka, Yesyka, Yesiko

Yestin (Welsh) One who is just
Yestine, Yestyn, Yestyne

Yetta (English) Form of Henrietta, meaning "ruler of the house"
Yettah, Yeta, Yette, Yitta, Yettie, Yetty

Yeva (Slavic) Form of Eve, meaning "giver of life; a lively woman"
Yevah, Yevunye, Yevon, Yetsye, Yevtsye

Yggsdrasil (Norse) The tree that binds Earth, heaven, and hell

Ygraine (English) Form of Igraine, the mother of Arthur in Arthurian legend
Ygrane, Ygrayne, Ygrain, Ygrayn, Ygraen, Ygraene

Yi (Chinese) One who brings happiness

Yi Min (Chinese) An intelligent woman

Yi Ze (Chinese) Happy and shiny as a pearl

Yihana (African) One deserving congratulations
Yihanah, Yhana, Yihanna, Yihannah, Yhanah, Yhanna, Yhannah

Yin (Chinese) A silvery woman

Yinah (Spanish) A victorious woman
Yina, Yinna, Yinnah

Yitta (Hebrew) One who emanates light
Yittah, Yita, Yitah

Ylwa (Scandinavian) Resembling a she-wolf
Ylwha

Ynes (French) Form of Agnes, meaning "one who is pure; chaste"
Ynez, Ynesita

Yoana (Hebrew) Form of Joana, meaning "God is gracious"
Yoanah, Yoanna, Yoannah, Yohana, Yohanna, Yohanka

Yobachi (African) One who prays to God
Yobachie, Yobachey, Yobachee, Yobachea, Yobacheah, Yobachy

Yocheved (Hebrew) Of God's glory

Yodelle (American) An old-fashioned woman
Yodell, Yodel, Yodele, Yodella, Yodela, Yodette, Yodete, Yodet, Yodetta, Yodeta, Yode, Yodey, Yody, Yodie, Yodi, Yodee, Yodea, Yodeah

Yoella (Hebrew) One who loves God
Yoellah, Yoelah, Yoela

Yogi (Hindi) One who practices yoga
Yogini, Yoginie, Yogie, Yogy, Yogey, Yogee, Yogea, Yogeah

Yohance (African) A gift from God
Yohanse

Yoki (Native American) Of the rain
Yokie, Yokee, Yoky, Yokey, Yokea, Yokeah

Yoko (Japanese) A positive child; good girl
Yo

Yolanda (Greek) Resembling the violet flower; modest
Yolande, Yoland, Yolana, Yolain, Yolaine, Yolane, Yolanna, Yorlanda, Yalanda, Yalando, Yalonda, Yolantha, Yolanthe, Yolette, Yulanda, Yulonda, Youlanda, Yolonda

Yolie (Greek) Resembling the violet flower
Yoli, Yolee, Yoley, Yoly, Yolea, Yoleah

Yomaris (Spanish) I am the sun
Yomariss, Yomarise, Yomarris

Yon (Korean) Resembling a lotus blossom

Yona (Hebrew) Feminine form of Jonah; dove
Yonah, Yonina, Yonita, Yonee, Yony, Yoney, Yonie, Yoni, Yoneena, Yonine, Yonyna, Yoneene, Yonati, Yonat, Yonit, Yonita, Yonyta

Yordana (Hebrew) Feminine form of Jordan; of the down-flowing river
Yordanah, Yordanna, Yordannah, Yordane, Yordain, Yordaine, Yordayn, Yordayne, Yordaen, Yordaene, Yordan

Yori (Japanese) One who is trustworthy; reliable
Yoriyo, Yoriko

York (English) From the yew settlement
Yorck, Yorc, Yorke, Yorki, Yorkie, Yorky, Yorkey, Yorkee, Yorkea, Yorkeah

Yoruba (African) Woman from Nigeria
Yorubah, Yorubba, Yorubbah

Yoseba (Hebrew) Form of Josephine, meaning "God will add"
Yosebah, Yosebe, Yosepha, Yosephina, Yosefa, Yosifa, Yosyfa, Yuseffa, Yosefina, Yosifina, Yosyfina, Yuseffina

Yoshe (Japanese) A beautiful girl

Yoshi (Japanese) One who is respectful and good
Yoshie, Yoshy, Yoshey, Yoshee, Yoshiyo, Yoshiko, Yoshino, Yoshea, Yosheah

Yovana (American) Form of Yvonne, meaning "a young archer"
Yovanah, Yovanna, Yovannah, Yovann, Yovane, Yovanne, Yoviana, Yovianna, Yovian, Yovianne, Yoviane, Yovhanna, Yovhannah, Yovhana, Yovhanah

Yovela (Hebrew) One who is full of joy; rejoicing
Yovelah, Yovella, Yovelle, Yovele

Ysabel (Spanish) Form of Isabel, meaning "my God is bountiful"
Ysabelle, Ysabela, Ysabele, Ysabell, Ysabella, Ysbel, Ysibel, Ysibela, Ysibele, Ysibell, Ysibelle, Ysibella, Ysobel, Ysobela, Ysobella, Ysobele, Ysobelle, Ysybel, Ysybelle, Ysyhell, Ysybele, Ysybela, Ysybella

Ysane (English) A graceful woman
Ysanne, Ysann, Ysana, Ysanna, Ysanah, Ysannah

Ysbail (Welsh) A spoiled girl
Ysbale, Ysbayle, Ysbaile, Ysbayl, Ysbael, Ysbaele

Yseult (Celtic / German / English) One who is fair / ruler of ice / in Arthurian legend, an Irish princess who married the king of Cornwall
Yseulte, Ysolt, Ysolte, Ysold, Ysolde

Yu (Asian) Resembling jade

Yu Jie (Chinese) Resembling a pure, beautiful jade

Yue (Chinese) Of the moonlight

Yue Yan (Chinese) One who is happy and beautiful

Yuette (American) A capable woman
Yuett, Yuete, Yuet, Yueta, Yuetta

Yuki (Japanese) Woman of the snow
Yukie, Yuky, Yukey, Yukee, Yukiko, Yukiyo, Yukea, Yukeah

Yulan (Spanish) A splendid woman
Yulann

Yule (English) Daughter of Christmastime
Yulle

Yulia (Russian) Form of Julia, meaning "one who is youthful; daughter of the sky"
Yulie, Yula, Yulka, Yulya, Yulene, Yuleen, Yuleene, Yuleena, Yulena, Yulean, Yuleane, Yuleana, Yulenia, Yulilya, Yulenke, Yulenka, Yulinke, Yulinka, Yuliana, Yuliani

Yumi (Japanese) A beautiful bow
Yumie, Yumy, Yumey, Yumee, Yumiko, Yumiyo, Yumako, Yumea, Yumeah

Yumn (Arabic) One with good fortune and success

Yuna (African) A gorgeous woman
Yunah, Yunna, Yunnah

Yuri (Japanese) Resembling a lily
Yurie, Yury, Yurey, Yuree, Yuriko, Yuriyo, Yurea, Yureah

Yuriana (American) A graceful lily
Yurianna, Yuriane, Yurianne, Yuriann

Yusra (Arabic) One who is most prosperous
Yusraa, Yusriyah

Yuta (Hebrew / Japanese) One who is awarded praise / one who is superior
Yutah, Yoota, Yootah

Yvana (Slavic) Form of Ivana, meaning "God is gracious"
Yvanna, Yvanya, Yvannya, Yvan, Yvania, Yvannia, Yvanah, Yvannah

Yvonne (French) A young archer; possibly a combination of Anna and Eve, meaning "a woman graced with God's favor" and "a giver of life; a lively woman"
Yvonna, Yvone, Yvon, Yvonnie, Yvonny, Yvonnia, Yavonne, Yavonna, Yavonda, Yavanda, Yavanna, Yavanne, Yveline, Yvette, Yvett, Yvet, Yvetta, Yveta, Yevette, Yevett, Yevetta, Yavette

Z

Zabel (Armenian) Form of Isabel, meaning "my God is bountiful"
Zabela, Zabelah, Zabella, Zabele, Zabelle, Zabele, Zabelia, Zabeliah, Zabelea, Zabeleah

Zabrina (American) Form of Sabrina, meaning "a legendary princess"
Zabreena, Zabrinah, Zabrinna, Zabryna, Zabryne, Zabrynya, Zabreana, Zabreane, Zabreenia, Zabrinia, Zabrinnia, Zabrynia, Zabrine

Zaccai (Hebrew) One who is pure and just
Zaccae, Zacae, Zacii, Zaccii, Zacai, Zackai, Zackae, Zakai, Zakae

Zachah (Hebrew) Form of Zacharie, meaning "God is remembered"
Zacha, Zachie, Zachi, Zachee, Zachea, Zacheah

Zacharie (Hebrew) God is remembered
Zacharee, Zacharey, Zacaree, Zaccaree, Zacari, Zaccari, Zecharie, Zecharee, Zecharey, Zacara, Zacceaus, Zacaria, Zachoia, Zackaria, Zakaria, Zakira, Zackeisha, Zackeria, Zacharea, Zachareah, Zakarea, Zakareah, Zacarea, Zacareah

Zada (Arabic) Fortunate one; lucky; prosperous
Zayda, Zaida, Zayeda, Zayedah, Zadda, Zaddah, Zadah, Zaeda, Zaedah

Zafara (Hebrew) One who sings
Zaphara, Zafarra, Zapharra, Zafarah, Zafarrah, Zapharah, Zapharrah

Zafirah (Arabic) She who is victorious; successful
Zafira, Zafyra, Zafyre, Zafire, Zafinah, Zafina, Zayfina, Zayfinah, Zafyna, Zafynah, Zafiera, Zafierah, Zafeira, Zafeirah, Zafiena, Zafienah, Zafeina, Zafeinah

Zagir (Armenian) Resembling a flower
Zagiri, Zagirie, Zagiree, Zagirea, Zagireah, Zagiry, Zagirey, Zagira, Zagirah

Zahar (Hebrew) Of the morning light; dawn
Zahir, Zahyr, Zaher

Zahavah (Hebrew) The golden one
Zahava, Zachava, Zahavya, Zechava, Zehavia, Zehava, Zehuva, Zehavit, Zehavi, Zehave, Zeheva

Zahia (Arabic) Feminine form of Zahi; brilliant and beautiful
Zahiah, Zaheea, Zaheeah

Zahida (Arabic) Feminine form of Zahid; one who is pious
Zaahida, Zahidah, Zaheeda, Zaheedah, Zaheida, Zaheidah, Zahieda, Zahiedah, Zahyda, Zahydah

Zahirah (Arabic) One who is shining, luminous; dazzling
Zahira, Zaheera, Zaheerah, Zahiera, Zahierah, Zaheira, Zaheirah, Zahyra, Zahyrah

Zahiya (Arabic) A brilliant woman; radiant
Zahiyah, Zehiya, Zehiyah, Zeheeya, Zaheeya, Zeheeyah, Zaheeyah, Zaheiya, Zaheiyah, Zahieya, Zahieyah

Zahra (Arabic / Swahili) White-skinned / flowerlike
Zahrah, Zahraa, Zahre, Zahreh, Zahara, Zaharra, Zahera, Zahira, Zahyra, Zeehera, Zahria, Zahirra, Zaherra

Zahvala (Serbo-Croatian) One who is grateful
Zahvalla, Zahvallah, Zahvalah, Zavala, Zavalah, Zavalla, Zavallah

Zaiba (Arabic) One who is beautiful and adorned
Zaibaa, Zaib, Zaibah, Zayba, Zaybah, Zaeba, Zaebah

Zaidee (Arabic) One who is rich; prosperous
Zaidie, Zaidi, Zaidey, Zaidy, Zaydee, Zaydie, Zaydi, Zaydey, Zaydy, Zaidea, Zaydea, Zayda, Zaedi, Zaedie, Zaedy, Zaedey, Zaedee, Zaedea, Zaedeah

Zaina (Arabic) A beautiful woman
Zainah, Zainna, Zeina, Zeinna, Zeinnah, Zainnah, Zinaida, Zinaidah, Zeinah, Zaynah, Zayna, Zaena, Zaenah

Zainab (Arabic) A fragrant flowering plant
Zaynab, Zaenab

Zainabu (Swahili) One who is known for her beauty
Zaynabu, Zaenabu

Zaira (Arabic / Irish) Resembling a rose / form of Sara, meaning "princess; lady"
Zairah, Zayra, Zayrah, Zaera, Zaerah

Zaire (African) A woman from Zaire; form of Zara, meaning "princess; lady / day's awakening; dawn"
Zair, Zaeire, Zaeir

Zaka (Swahili) One who is pure; chaste
Zaaka, Zacka, Zakka, Zacca, Zakah, Zackah, Zaccah

Zakelina (Russian) Form of Jacqueline, meaning "the supplanter"
Zakelinah, Zakelyna, Zakeleena, Zacelina, Zacelyna, Zackelina, Zackelyna, Zakeleana, Zakeline, Zakelyn, Zakelyne, Zaceline, Zacelyn, Zackelin, Zackelyn, Zakeleen, Zakelin

Zakia (Arabic / Swahili) One who is chaste; pure / an intelligent woman
Zakiah, Zakea, Zakeia, Zakiya, Zakiyah, Zakeya, Zakaya, Zakeyia, Zakiyyah, Zakiyya, Zakkiyya, Zakiyaa, Zakya, Zakeah

Zala (Slovene) One who is beautiful; from the river
Zalah, Zalla, Zallah

Zale (Greek) One who has the strength of the sea
Zail, Zaile, Zayle, Zayl, Zael, Zaele

Zalika (Swahili) Born into royalty; wellborn
Zalikah, Zalyka, Zalik, Zulika, Zuleika, Zaliki, Zalike, Zaleeka, Zaleekah, Zaleika, Zaleikah, Zalieka, Zaliekah

Zalina (French) Form of Selene, meaning "of the moon"
Zalinah, Zaleana, Zaleena, Zalena, Zalyna, Zaleen, Zaleene, Zalene, Zaline, Zalyne, Zaleane, Zaleina, Zaleinah, Zaliena, Zalienah

Zalisha (Swahili) To enrich; one who cultivates the land
Zalishah, Zaleesha, Zaleeshah, Zalysha, Zalyshah, Zaleisha, Zaleishah, Zaliesha, Zalieshah, Zaleasha, Zaleashah

Zaltana (Native American) From the high mountain
Zalantah, Zaltanah, Zalanta, Zaltanna, Zaltannah

Zama (Latin) One from the town of Zama
Zamah, Zamma, Zammah

Zamara (Hebrew) A songstress
Zemarah, Zamarah, Zamarra, Zamarrah, Zemara, Zemarra, Zemarrah, Zema, Zamirra, Zamirrah, Zamirah, Zumira

Zambda (Hebrew) One who meditates
Zambdah

Zambee (African) Woman from Zambia
Zambe, Zambi, Zambie, Zamby, Zambey, Zambea, Zambeah

Zamella (Zulu) One who strives to succeed
Zumellah, Zamy, Zamie, Zami, Zamey, Zamee, Zamea, Zameah

Zamilla (Greek) Having the strength of the sea
Zamillah, Zamila, Zamilah, Zamylla, Zamyllah, Zamyla, Zamylah

Zamir (Hebrew) An intelligent ruler
Zamire, Zameer, Zameere, Zamyr, Zamyre

Zamora (Spanish) From the city of Zamora
Zamorah, Zamorrah, Zamorra

Zamurrad (Arabic) Resembling an emerald; a precious stone
Zamurad, Zamurrada, Zamurada

Zamzummim (Hebrew) Of the race of giants
Zamzumim, Zumim

Zan (Chinese) One who offers support and praise

Zana (Romanian / Hebrew) In mythology, the three Graces / form of Susanna, meaning "resembling a graceful white lily"
Zanna, Zanah, Zannah

Zandra (Greek) Form of Alexandra, meaning "helper and defender of mankind"
Zandrah, Zanndra, Zahndra, Zandria, Zandrea, Zandrya, Zandry, Zandrie, Zondra, Zondria, Zondrya, Zohndra, Zohndria, Zohndrya, Zandree, Zandreah

Zane (Scandinavian) One who is bold
Zain, Zaine, Zayn, Zayne, Zaen, Zaene

Zaneta (Hebrew) A gracious gift from God
Zanetah, Zanita, Zaneeta, Zanetta, Zanyta, Zanete, Zanett, Zanette, Zanitra

Zannika (Native American) One who is healthy
Zannicka, Zanika, Zanicka, Zannyka, Zanyka

Zanoah (Hebrew) One who is prone to forgetfulness
Zanoa

Zanta (Swahili) A beautiful young woman
Zantah

Zanthe (Greek) Form of Xanthe, meaning "yellow-haired woman; blonde"
Zantha, Zanthia, Zanth, Zanthiya, Zanthea, Zantheah

Zara (Hebrew / Arabic) Form of Sarah, meaning "princess; lady" / day's awakening; dawn
Zarah, Zarra, Zareh, Zari, Zarie, Zaree, Zarri, Zarrie, Zarry, Zary, Zaria, Zareya, Zarea, Zariya, Zarya, Zarria, Zayra, Zareah, Zarreah, Zarree

Zarahlinda (Hebrew) Of the beautiful dawn
Zaralinda, Zaralynda, Zarahlindah, Zaralyndah, Zarahlynda, Zarahlyndah, Zaralenda, Zarahlenda

Zaria (Russian / Slavic) Born at sunrise / in mythology, the goddess of beauty; the heavenly bride
Zarya, Zariah, Zaryah

Zariel (American) The lion princess
Zariell, Zariele, Zarielle, Zariela, Zariella

Zarifa (Arabic) One who is successful; moves with grace
Zarifah, Zaryfa, Zaryfah, Zareefa, Zareefah, Zariefa, Zariefah, Zareifa, Zareifah, Zareafa, Zareafah

Zarina (African) The golden one; made of gold
Zarinah, Zareena, Zareenah, Zarena, Zarinna, Zaryna, Zarynna, Zareana, Zareane, Zarene, Zareene, Zarinne, Zaryne, Zarienah, Zariena, Zareina, Zareinah

Zarita (Spanish) Form of Sarah, meaning "princess; lady"
Zaritah, Zareeta, Zaritta, Zaryta, Zareata, Zarite, Zareete, Zaryte, Zareate, Zarieta, Zarietah, Zareita, Zareitah

Zarmina (Arabic) A bright woman
Zarminah, Zarmeena, Zarmeenah, Zarmiena, Zarmienah, Zarmeinah, Zarmeina, Zarmyna, Zarmynah, Zarmeana, Zarmeanah

Zarna (Hindi) Resembling a spring of water
Zarnah, Zarnia, Zarniah

Zarola (Arabic) A great huntress
Zarolla, Zarolia, Zarolya, Zarolea, Zarolah, Zarollah, Zaroleah, Zaroliah, Zarolyah

Zarqa (Arabic) Having bluish-green eyes; from the city of Zarqa
Zarqaa

Zasha (Russian) Form of Sasha, meaning "helper and defender of mankind"
Zascha, Zashka, Zasho, Zashenka, Zosha, Zoscha, Zoshka

Zashawna (American) A spontaneous young woman
Zashawne, Zashauna, Zashaune, Zashane, Zashayne, Zashaine, Zashaene, Zaseana, Zaseane, Zashona, Zashone

Zauditu (African) She is the crown
Zawditu, Zewditu, Zaudytu, Zawdytu, Zewdytu

Zaviera (Spanish) Form of Xaviera, meaning "owner of a new house; one who is bright "
Zavierah, Zavira, Zavera, Zavyera, Zavirah, Zaverah, Zavyerah

Zavrina (English) Form of Sabrina, meaning "a legendary princess"
Zavrinah, Zavreena, Zavreenah, Zavriena, Zavrienah, Zavryna, Zavrynah, Zavreina, Zavreinah, Zavreana, Zavreanah

Zawadi (Swahili) A gift; a present
Zawati, Zawadia, Zawatia, Zawady, Zawaty, Zawadie, Zawadee, Zawadea, Zawadeah, Zawadey, Zawatie, Zawatey, Zawatee, Zawatea, Zawateah

Zaya (Tibetan) A victorious woman
Zayah

Zayit (Hebrew) From the olive tree
Zayita, Zayitah

Zaylee (English) A heavenly woman
Zayleigh, Zayli, Zaylie, Zaylea, Zayleah, Zayley, Zayly, Zalee, Zaleigh, Zalie, Zali, Zaley, Zaly, Zalea, Zaleah

Zaypana (Tibetan) A beautiful woman
Zaypanah, Zaypo, Zaypanna, Zaypannah

Zaza (Hebrew / Arabic) Belonging to all / one who is flowery
Zazah, Zazu, Zazza, Zazzah, Zazzu

Zazula (Polish) An outstanding woman
Zazulah, Zazulla, Zazullah

Zdenka (Slovene) Feminine form of Zdenek; from Sidon
Zdena, Zdenuska, Zdenicka, Zdenika, Zdenyka, Zdeninka, Zdenynka

Zdeslava (Czech) Glory of the moment
Zdevsa, Zdysa, Zdisa, Zdyska, Zdiska, Zdislava, Zdyslava

Zea (Latin) Of the wheat field; grain
Zeah, Zia, Ziah

Zeahire (Arabic) One who is distinguished; outstanding

Zeal (American) One with passion; enthusiastic devotion
Zeale, Zeel, Zeele, Zeyl, Zeyle, Ziel, Ziele

Zebba (Persian) A known beauty
Zebbah, Zebara, Zebarah, Zebarra, Zebarrah

Zebina (Greek) One who is gifted
Zebinah, Zebeena, Zebeenah, Zebeana, Zebeanah, Zebyna, Zebynah, Zebiena, Zebienah, Zebeina, Zebeinah

Zehara (Hebrew) Surrounded by light
Zeharah, Zeharra, Zeharrah

Zehave (Hebrew) A golden child
Zehava, Zehavi, Zehavit, Zehuva, Zehavie, Zehavee, Zehavea, Zehaveah, Zehavy, Zehavey

Zehira (Hebrew) One who is protected
Zehirah, Zeheera, Zehyra, Zehiera, Zeheerah, Zehyrah, Zehierah, Zeheira, Zeheirah, Zeheara, Zehearah

Zeinab (Somali) One who is good and well-behaved

Zela (Greek) One who is blessed with happiness
Zelah

Zelda (German) Gray-haired battlemaiden
Zeldah, Zelde, Zellda

Zeleia (Greek) In mythology, a city that was home to Padarus
Zeleiah

Zelene (English) Of the sunshine
Zeline, Zeleen, Zeleene, Zelyn, Zelyne, Zelean, Zeleane, Zelen, Zelein, Zeleine

Zelfa (American) One who stays in control
Zelfah, Zelpha, Zelphah

Zelia (Greek / Spanish) Having great zeal / of the sunshine
Zeliah, Zelya, Zelie, Zele, Zelina, Zelinia

Zelinda (German) Shield of victory
Zelindah, Zelynda, Zalinda, Zalynda, Zelyndah, Zalindah, Zalyndah

Zella (German) One who resists
Zellah

Zelma (German) Form of Selma, meaning "having divine protection"
Zelmah, Zalma, Zalmah

Zemirah (Hebrew) A joyous melody
Zemira, Zemyra, Zimira, Zymira, Zymyra, Zemila, Zemilah, Zemeela, Zemyla, Zimyla, Zymyla

Zena (African) One having great fame
Zenah, Zina, Zeena, Zenna, Zana, Zeana, Zeina

Zenaida (Greek) White-winged dove; in mythology, a daughter of Zeus
Zenaidah, Zenayda, Zenaide, Zenayde, Zinaida, Zenina, Zenna, Zenaydah, Zenaeda, Zenaedah

Zenas (Greek) One who is generous

Zenda (Persian) A sacred woman
Zendah, Zinda, Zindah, Zynda, Zyndah

Zenechka (Russian) Form of Eugenia, meaning "a wellborn woman"

Zenevieva (Russian) Form of Genevieve, meaning "of the race of women; the white wave"
Zenavieve, Zeneve, Zeneveeve, Zenevie, Zenivee, Zenivieve, Zennie, Zenny, Zenovera, Zenoveva, Zenica, Zenna, Zenae, Zenaya, Zenowefa, Zinerva, Zinebra, Zinessa, Zinevra

Zenia (Greek) Form of Xenia, meaning "one who is hospitable; welcoming"
Zeniah, Zeenia, Zenya, Zennia, Zenea, Zeenya

Zenobia (Greek) Sign or symbol; in mythology, a child of Zeus
Zenobiah, Zenobya, Zenobe, Zenobie, Zenobey, Zenovia, Zenobee, Zenoby, Zenobea, Zenobeah

Zenochka (Russian) One who is born of Zeus

Zephyr (Greek) Of the West wind
Zephyra, Zephira, Zephria, Zephra, Zephyer, Zefiryn, Zefiryna, Zefyrin, Zefyrina, Zefyryn, Zefyryna, Zafirin, Zafirina, Zyphire, Zefuyn

Zeppelina (English) Born during a beautiful storm
Zepelina, Zeppeleana, Zepeleana, Zeppelyna, Zepelyna, Zeppeleina, Zepeleina, Zeppeliena, Zepeliena, Zeppeleena, Zepeleena

Zera (Hebrew) A sower of seeds
Zerah, Zeria, Zeriah, Zera'im, Zerra, Zerrah

Zeraldina (Polish) Form of Geraldina, meaning "one who rules with the spear"
Zeraldinah, Zeraldeena, Zeraldeenah, Zeraldiena, Zeraldienah, Zeraldeina, Zeraldeinah, Zeraldyna, Zeraldynah, Zeraldeana, Zeraldeanah

Zerdali (Turkish) Resembling the wild apricot
Zerdalie, Zerdaly, Zerdaley, Zerdalya, Zerdalia, Zerdalee, Zerdalea, Zerdalea

Zerelda (Teutonic) An armored battle-maiden
Zerelde, Zereld

Zerena (Turkish) The golden woman
Zerenah, Zereena, Zereenah, Zeriena, Zerienah, Zereina, Zereinah, Zeryna, Zerynah, Zereana, Zereanah

Zerlina (Latin) Of the beautiful dawn
Zerlinah, Zerleena, Zerlyna, Zerleen, Zerline, Zerlyn, Zerlyne, Zerlean, Zerleane, Zerleana, Zerlee, Zerla, Zerlinda, Zaralinda

Zerrin (Turkish) A golden woman
Zerren, Zerran, Zerryn, Zerron

Zesiro (African) The firstborn of twins
Zesyro, Zeseero, Zesiero, Zeseiro, Zesearo

Zesta (American) One with energy and gusto
Zestah, Zestie, Zestee, Zesti, Zesty, Zestey, Zestea, Zesteah

Zeta (Greek) Born last; the sixth letter of the Greek alphabet
Zetah

Zetta (Portuguese) Resembling the rose
Zettah

Zeuxippe (Greek) In mythology, the daughter of the river Eridanos

Zhen (Chinese) One who is precious and chaste
Zen, Zhena, Zenn, Zhenni

Zhenga (African) An African queen
Zhengah, Zenga, Zengah

Zhi (Chinese) A woman of high moral character

Zhong (Chinese) An honorable woman

Zhuo (Chinese) Having great intelligence

Zi (Chinese) A flourishing young woman

Zia (Arabic) One who emanates light; splendor
Ziah, Zea, Zeah, Zya, Zyah

Ziarre (American) Goddess of the sky
Ziarr, Zyarre, Zyarr

Ziazan (Armenian) Resembling a rainbow
Ziazann, Zyazan, Zyazann

Zigana (Hungarian) A Gypsy girl
Ziganah, Zygana, Zigane, Ziganna, Zigannah, Zyganna, Zygannah, Zyganah

Zihna (Native American) One who spins
Zihnah, Zyhna, Zyhnah

Zilias (Hebrew) A shady woman; a shadow
Zilyas, Zylias, Zylyas

Zillah (Hebrew) The shadowed one
Zilla, Zila, Zyla, Zylla, Zilah, Zylah, Zyllah

Zilpah (Hebrew) One who is frail but dignified; in the Bible, a concubine of Jacob
Zilpa, Zylpa, Zilpha, Zylpha, Zylpah, Zilphah, Zylphah

Zilya (Russian) Form of Theresa, meaning "a harvester"
Zilyah, Zylya, Zylyah

Zimbab (African) Woman from Zimbabwe
Zymbab, Zimbob, Zymbob

Zimra (Hebrew) Song of praise
Zimrah, Zimria, Zemira, Zemora, Zamora, Zamira, Zymria, Zamyra

Zimzi (Hebrew) My field, my vine
Zimzie, Zimzee, Zimzea, Zimzeah, Zimzey, Zimzy

Zina (African / English) A secret spirit / welcoming
Zinah, Zyna, Zynah, Zine, Zineh

Zinat (Arabic) A decoration; graceful beauty
Zeenat, Zynat, Zienat, Zeinat, Zeanat

Zinchita (Incan) One who is dearly loved
Zinchitah, Zinchyta, Zinchytah, Zincheeta, Zincheetah, Zinchieta, Zinchietah, Zincheita, Zincheitah, Zincheata, Zincheatah

Zinerva (Celtic / Russian) One who is fair; pale / one who is wise
Zinervah, Zynerva, Zynervah

Zinnia (Latin) A brilliant, showy, rayed flower
Zinia, Zinna, Zinya, Zeenia, Zynia, Zynya, Zinniah, Ziniah

Zintka Mani (Native American) Resembling a bird that walks

Zintkala (Native American) Resembling a bird
Zintkalah, Zintkalla, Zintkallah, Zyntkala, Zyntkalah, Zyntkallah, Zyntkalla

Zintkala Kinyan (Native American) Resembling a flying bird
Zintkalah Kinyan, Zintkalla Kinyan, Zintkallah Kinyan, Zyntkala Kinyan, Zyntkalah Kinyan, Zyntkallah Kinyan, Zyntkalla Kinyan

Zintkala Lowansa (Native American) Resembling a songbird
Zintkalah Lowansa, Zintkalla Lowansa, Zintkallah Lowansa, Zyntkala Lowansa, Zyntkalah Lowansa, Zyntkallah Lowansa, Zyntkalla Lowansa

Zintkato (Native American) Resembling a bluebird

Zinyeza (African) One who is aware
Zinyezah, Zynyeza, Zynyezah

Ziona (Hebrew) One who symbolizes goodness
Zionah, Zyona, Zyonah

Zipporah (Hebrew) A beauty; little bird; in the Bible, the wife of Moses
Zippora, Ziporah, Zipora, Zypora, Zyppora, Ziproh, Zipporia

Zira (African) The pathway
Zirah, Zirra, Zirrah, Zyra, Zyrah, Zyrra, Zyrrah

Ziracuny (Native American) From the water
Ziracuni, Ziracunie, Ziracuney, Ziracunee, Ziracunea, Ziracuneah, Zyracuny, Zyracuni, Zyracuni, Zyracunee, Zyracuney, Zyracunea, Zyracuneah

Zisel (Hebrew) One who is sweet
Zissel, Zisal, Zysel, Zysal, Zyssel, Zissal, Zyssal

Zita (Latin / Spanish) Patron of housewives and servants / little rose
Zitah, Zeeta, Zyta, Zeetah, Zytah, Zicta, Zietah, Zeita, Zeitah, Zeata, Zeatah

Zitomira (Slavic) To live famously
Zitomirah, Zytomira, Zitomeera, Zitomyra, Zytomyra, Zytomirah, Zitomeerah, Zytomeera, Zytomeerah

Ziva (Hebrew) One who is bright, radiant; splendor
Zivah, Zivia, Ziv, Zeeva, Zivi, Zyva, Zivanka

Ziwa (Swahili) Woman of the lake
Ziwah, Zywa, Zywah

Zizi (Hungarian) Dedicated to God
Zeezee, Zyzy, Ziezie, Zeazea, Zeyzey

Zizilia (Slavic) In mythology, the goddess of love and sexuality
Zezilia, Zizila, Zezila, Zyzilia, Zyzila

Zlata (Slavic) Feminine form of Zlatan; golden
Zlatta, Zlatah, Zlattah

Zlhna (Native American) To be spinning

Zoa (Greek) One who is full of life; vibrant

Zocha (Polish) Form of Sophie, meaning "having great wisdom and foresight"
Zochah, Zosia, Zotia, Zosiah, Zotiah

❂
❶ **Zoe** (Greek) A life-giving woman; alive
Zoë, Zoee, Zowey, Zowie, Zowe, Zoelie, Zoeline, Zoelle, Zoey, Zoelie, Zoel, Zooey, Zoie, Zoi, Zoye, Zoia, Zoya, Zoyara, Zoyya, Zoy, Zoyenka, Zoyechka

Zofia (Slavic) Form of Sophia, meaning "having great wisdom and foresight"
Zofiah, Zophia, Zophiah, Zophya, Zofie, Zofee, Zofey, Zofi, Zofy, Zophee, Zophy, Zophie, Zophi, Zophey

Zohar (Hebrew) Emanating a brilliant light; sparkle
Zohara, Zohera, Zoheret, Zohra, Zoharra, Zoharah, Zoharrah, Zoharr

Zohreh (Persian) One who brings happiness
Zohrah, Zahrah, Zehrah

Zola (Italian / African) A piece of earth / one who is quiet and tranquil
Zolah, Zoela, Zoila, Zolla, Zollah

Zona (Latin) A decorative sash; belt
Zonah, Zonia, Zonna, Zonnah

Zonta (Native American) An honest woman

Zoom (American) An energetic woman
Zoomi, Zoomie, Zoomy, Zoomey, Zoomee, Zoomea, Zoomeah

Zora (Slavic) Born at dawn; aurora
Zorah, Zorna, Zorra, Zorya, Zorane, Zory, Zorrah, Zorey, Zoree, Zorea, Zoreah, Zori, Zorie

Zoralle (Slavic) A heavenly and delicate woman
Zorale, Zorall, Zoral

Zorana (Sanskrit) A woman of power
Zordena, Zoranah, Zordenah, Zorrana, Zorranna

Zore (Slavic) Form of Zora, meaning "born at dawn; aurora"
Zorka, Zorcka, Zorkah, Zorckah, Zorke

Zoria (Basque) One who is lucky
Zoriah

Zorina (Slavic) Golden-haired woman
Zorinah, Zoryna, Zoreena, Zoreane, Zoreana, Zorean, Zoree, Zoreen, Zoreene, Zorie, Zori, Zorin, Zorine, Zoryne

Zoriona (Basque) One who is happy

Zosa (Greek) A lively and energetic woman
Zosah

Zsa Zsa (Hungarian) Form of Susan, meaning "resembling a graceful white lily"
Zhazha, Zsuka, Zsuzsa, Zsuzsanna, Zsuzsi, Zsuzsie, Zsuzsee

Zsofia (Greek) Form of Sophia, meaning "having great wisdom and foresight"
Zsofie, Zsofi, Zsofiah, Zsophia, Zsophie, Zsophi, Zsofika

Zuba (English) One who is musically talented
Zubah, Zubba, Zubbah

Zubaida (Arabic) A laborer; a hardworking woman
Zubaidah, Zubayda, Zubaydah, Zubaeda, Zubaedah

Zubeda (Swahili) The best one
Zubedah

Zudora (Arabic) A laborer; a hardworking woman
Zudorah, Zudorra, Zudorrah

Zula (African) One who is brilliant; from the town of Zula
Zul, Zulay, Zulae, Zulai, Zulah, Zulla, Zullah

Zuleika (Arabic) One who is brilliant and lovely; fair
Zuleikah, Zulaykha, Zeleeka, Zulekha, Zuleyka

Zulema (Arabic) Form of Salama, meaning "one who is peaceful and safe"
Zulima, Zuleima, Zulemah, Zulimah, Zalama, Zulyma, Zuleyma, Zuleyka

Zulma (Arabic) A vibrant woman
Zulmah

Zuni (Native American) One who is creative
Zunie, Zuny, Zuney, Zunee, Zunea, Zuneah

Zurafa (Arabic) A lovely woman
Zurafah, Zirafa, Zirafah, Ziraf, Zurufa, Zurufah, Zuruf, Zuraffa, Zuraffah

Zuri (Swahili / French) A beauty / lovely and white
Zurie, Zurey, Zuria, Zuriaa, Zury, Zuree, Zurya, Zurisha, Zurea, Zureah

Zuriel (Hebrew) The Lord is my rock
Zurielle, Zurial, Zuriella, Zuriela, Zuriele, Zuriale, Zurialle

Zurina (Spanish) One who is fair-skinned
Zurinah, Zurine, Zurinia, Zurinna, Zureena, Zureenah, Zurienah, Zuriena, Zureina, Zureinah, Zurynah, Zuryna

Zuwena (African) One who is pleasant and good
Zuwenah, Zwena, Zwenah, Zuwenna, Zuwennah, Zuwyna, Zuwynah

Zuyana (Sioux) One who has a brave heart
Zuyanah, Zuyanna, Zuyannah

Zuza (Polish) Form of Susan, meaning "resembling a graceful white lily"
Zuzah, Zusa, Zuzia, Zuzu, Zuzana, Zuzka, Zuzanka, Zuzanny

Zuzena (Basque) One who is correct
Zuzenah, Zuzenna, Zuzennah

Zweena (Arabic) A beautiful woman
Zweenah, Zwina, Zwinah, Zwyna, Zwynah, Zwiena, Zwienah, Zweina, Zweinah, Zweana, Zweanah

Zwi (Scandinavian) Resembling a gazelle
Zui, Zwie, Zwee, Zwey, Zwy, Zwea, Zweah

Zylia (Greek) Form of Xylia, meaning "a woodland dweller"
Zyliah, Zylea, Zyleah, Zilia, Zylina, Zyline, Zylin, Zylyn, Zylyna, Zilina, Ziline, Zilyna, Zilin

Zyta (Polish) Form of Theresa, meaning "a harvester"
Zytta, Zytah, Zyttah

Zytka (Polish) Resembling a rose; form of Zoe, meaning "a life-giving woman; alive"
Zytkah, Zytcka, Zytckah

Chapter 10

boys' names

a

Aabha (Indian) One who shines
Abha, Abbha

Aabharan (Hindu) One who is treasured; jewel
Abharan, Abharen, Aabharen, Aabharon, Abharon

Aabheer (Indian) One who herds cattle
Abheer, Aabher, Abher, Abhear, Aabhear, Abhyr, Aabhyr

Aadarsh (Indian) One who has principles
Adarsh, Aadersh, Adersh, Addarsh, Addersh

Aadesh (Indian) A message or command; to make a statement
Adesh, Adhesh, Addesh

Aadi (Hindi) Child of the beginning
Aadie, Aady, Aadey, Aadee, Aadea, Aadeah, Aadye, Aadhi, Aadhie, Aadhy, Aadhey, Aadhee

Aafreen (Indian) One who encourages others
Afreen, Aafrene, Aafrean, Afrene, Afrean

Aage (Norse) Representative of ancestors
Age, Ake, Aake

Aarif (Arabic) A learned man
Arif, Aareef, Areef, Aareaf, Areaf, Aareif, Areif, Aarief, Arief, Aaryf, Aryf

⊘ **Aaron** (Hebrew) One who is exalted; from the mountain of strength
Aaran, Aaren, Aarin, Aaro, Aaronas, Aaronn, Aarron, Aaryn, Aeron, Aeryn, Aharon, Ahran, Ahren, Ahron, Airen, Airyn, Aran, Arand, Arek, Aren, Arend, Arin, Arnie, Aron, Aronne, Arran, Arron, Arun, Auron, Ayren, Ayron

Abasi (Swahili) One who is stern
Abasie, Abasy, Abasey, Abasee, Abasea

Abayomi (African) A bringer of joy
Abayomie, Abayomy, Abayomey, Abayomee, Abayomea

Abba (Arabic) A father
Abbah, Aba, Abah

Abbas (Arabic) One who is stern; in Islam, Muhammad's uncle
Ab, Abba, Abas

Abbey (Hebrew) A father's joy
Abby, Abbi, Abbie, Abbee, Abbea, Abbye

Abbott (English) The leader of a monastery; a fatherly man
Abbot, Abot, Abott

Abda (Arabic) A servant
Abdah

Abdi (Hebrew) My servant
Abdie, Abdy, Abdey, Abdee, Abdea

Abdul (Arabic) A servant of God
Abdal, Abdall, Abdalla, Abdallah, Abdel, Abdell, Abdella, Abdellah, Abdoul, Abdoull, Abdoulla, Abdoullah, Abdull, Abdalah, Abdulla, Abdualla, Abdulah, Abdulla, Abedellah, Abdullah

Abe (Hebrew) Form of Abraham, meaning "father of a multitude; father of nations"
Ab, Abi, Abey, Abie, Abee, Abea, Aby

Abebe (African) One who is flourishing

Abedi (African) One who worships God
Abedie, Abedy, Abedey, Abedee, Abedea

Abednago (Aramaic) Servant of Nabu, the god of wisdom
Abednego

Abejundio (Spanish) Resembling a bee
Abejundo, Abejundeo, Abedjundiyo, Abedjundeyo

Abel (Hebrew) The life force; breath
Abele, Abell, Abelson, Able, Avel, Avele

Abelard (German) Of noble strength
Abelardo, Abelarde

Abena (African) Born on a Tuesday
Abenah, Abina, Abinah, Abyna, Abynah

Abida (Arabic / Hebrew) He who worships or adores / having knowledge
Abidah, Abeeda, Abyda, Abeedah, Abydah, Abeida, Abeidah, Abieda, Abiedah, Abeada, Abeadah, Abidan, Abiden, Abidin, Abidyn, Abidon, Abidun

Abiel (Hebrew) God is the father
Abiell, Ahbiell, Ahbiel, Abyel, Aybell, Abyell, Aybel

Abijah (Hebrew) The Lord is my father
Abia, Abbia, Abbiah, Abiam, Abija, Abbija, Abbijah

Abimelech (Hebrew) The Father is king
Abymelech, Abimeleck, Abimelek, Abymeleck, Ahymelek, Abimelcc, Abymelec

Abir (Arabic / Hebrew) Having a pleasant fragrance / one who is strong
Abeer, Abear, Abyr, Abier, Abeir, Abhir, Abhyr, Abheer, Abhear, Abheir, Abhier, Abeeri, Abeerie, Abiri, Abirie, Abirey, Abiry

Abisha (Hebrew) A gift from God
Ahidja, Abidjah, Abijah, Abishai

Abner (Hebrew) Father of the light
Abnor, Abnar, Abnur, Abnir, Abnyr

Abraham (Hebrew) Father of a multitude; father of nations
Abarran, Avraham, Aberham, Abrahamo, Abrahan, Abrahim, Abram, Abrami, Abramo, Abrams, Abran, Abramio, Abrian, Abriel

Absalom (Hebrew) The father of peace
Absalon, Abshalom, Absolem, Absolom, Absolon, Avshulom, Avsholom

Abu (African) A father
Abue, Aboo, Abou

Abundio (Spanish) A man of plenty
Abbondio, Abondio, Aboundio, Abundo, Abundeo, Aboundeo, Abondeo

Acacio (Greek) Of the thorny tree
Achazio, Accacio, Achacio, Acazio

Ace (English) One who excels; number one; the best
Acee, Acer, Acey, Acie, Ayce, Aci, Acy, Acea

Acelin (French) Born into nobility
Aceline, Acelene, Acelyn, Acelyne, Acel

Achav (Hebrew) An uncle
Achiav

Achidan (Hebrew) My brother judged
Abidan, Amidan, Avidan

Achilles (Greek) In mythology, a hero whose only vulnerability was his heel
Achill, Achille, Achillea, Achilleo, Achilleus, Achillios, Achillius, Akil, Akilles, Akillios, Akillius, Aquil, Aquiles, Aquilles

Achim (Hebrew) God will judge
Acim, Ahim, Achym, Acym, Ahym

Achiram (Hebrew) My brother has been exalted
Achyram, Achirem, Achyrem

Achishar (Hebrew) My brother lifts his voice in song
Achyshar, Amishar, Amyshar, Avishar, Avyshar

Aciano (Spanish) Resembling the blue-bottle flower
Acyano

Acilino (Spanish) Form of Aquila, meaning "resembling an eagle"
Acileeno, Acilyno, Acileino, Acilieno, Acileano

Ackerley (Old English) From the meadow of oak trees
Accerly, Acklea, Ackleigh, Ackley, Acklie, Ackerlea, Ackerleigh, Ackerly, Ackerleah

Acton (English) From the town of oak trees
Actun, Akton, Aktun

Adael (Hebrew) God witnesses
Adaele, Adayel, Adayele

Adahy (Native American) One who lives in the forest
Adahey, Adahi, Adahie, Adahee, Adahea

Adair (German) A wealthy spearman
Adaire, Adare, Adayre, Adayr, Adaer, Adaere

Adal (German) Possessing qualities of high moral character

Adalfieri (German) Of the noble oath
Adalfierie, Adalfiery, Adalfierey, Adalfieree, Adelfieri, Adelfierie, Adelfiery, Adelfierey, Adelfieree

Adalgiso (German) One who is noble
Adelgiso, Adalgyso, Adelgyso

Adalhard (German) Of noble strength
Adalard, Adelard, Adellard, Adelhard, Adallard

Adalrich (German) A noble ruler
Adalric, Adalrick, Adelric, Adelrich, Adelrick, Adalrik, Adalric

❀ **Adam** (Hebrew) Of the earth
*Ad, Adamo, Adams, Adan, Adao, Addam,
Addams, Addem, Addis, Ade, Adem, Adim,
Adnet, Adnon, Adnot, Adom, Atim, Atkins*

Adamson (English) The son of Adam
*Adamsson, Addamson, Adamsun, Adamssun,
Addamsun*

Adar (Hebrew) A noble man
Adarr, Adaar

Addison (English) The son of Adam
*Adison, Addisen, Addeson, Adisson, Adisen,
Adeson*

Addy (Teutonic) One who is awe-inspiring
*Addey, Addi, Addie, Addee, Addea, Adi, Ady,
Adie, Adey, Adee, Adea*

Adel (Hebrew / German) God is eternal / a
highborn man

Adelpho (Greek) A brotherly man
Aldelfo, Adelfus, Adelfio, Adelphe

Aden (Hebrew) One who is handsome and
adorned
Adan, Adin, Adon, Adun, Adyn

Adham (Arabic) Having dark features; a
black-haired man
Adhem, Adhom, Adhum, Adhim, Adhym

Adil (Arabic) A righteous man; one who is
fair and just
Adyl, Adiel, Adeil, Adeel, Adeal, Adyeel

Adir (Hebrew) A majestic and noble man
Adeer, Adear, Adier, Adeir, Adyr

Aditya (Hindi) Of the sun
*Adithya, Adithyan, Adityah, Aditeya,
Aditeyah*

Adiv (Hebrew) One who is considerate and
polite
*Adeev, Adeeve, Adeave, Adeav, Adiev, Adieve,
Adeiv, Adeive, Adyv, Adyve*

Adjatay (African) A prince; born to royalty
Adjataye, Adjatae, Adjatai

Adlai (Hebrew) My ornament
*Adlay, Adlaye, Adlae, Adley, Adly, Adlee,
Adleigh, Adlea, Adlie, Adli, Atley, Atly, Atlee,
Atlea, Atleigh, Atli, Atlie*

Adler (German) Resembling a soaring eagle
Adlar, Adlor, Adlir, Adlyr, Adlur

Admon (Hebrew) Of the red earth
Admen, Adman, Admun, Admin, Admyn

Adnah (Hebrew) An ornamented man
Adna

Adnan (Arabic) One who settles in a new
region
Adnen, Adnon, Adnun, Adnin, Adnyn

Adney (English) From the nobleman's
island
*Adny, Adni, Adnie, Adnee, Adnea, Addney,
Addny, Addni, Addnie, Addnee, Addnea*

Adolph (German) A noble, majestic wolf
*Adolf, Adolphe, Adolphus, Adolfus, Adolpho,
Adolfo, Adaulfo, Addolf, Addolph, Adulfus,
Adollf, Adalwolf*

Adonia (Greek) God is my lord
Adon, Adonias, Adonijah, Adoniya

Adonis (Greek) In mythology, a handsome
young man loved by Aphrodite
Addonia, Adohnes, Adonys, Adones

❀
❂ **Adrian** (Latin) A man from Hadria
*Ade, Adiran, Adrain, Adrean, Adreean,
Adreyan, Adreeyan, Adriaan, Adriano,
Adrien, Adrin, Adrino, Adrion, Adron,
Adryan, Adya, Arjen, Aydrean, Aydreean,
Aydrian, Aydrien*

Adriel (Hebrew) From God's flock
Adriell, Adriele, Adryel, Adryell, Adryele

Adwin (African) A great thinker; one who
is creative
*Adwinn, Adwinne, Adwen, Adwenne,
Adwenn, Adwyn, Adwynn, Adwynne*

Aegeus (Greek) Resembling a young goat;
in mythology, a king and father of Theseus
Aigeos, Aigeus

Aekley (English) From the oak-tree meadow
*Aekly, Aekleigh, Aeklee, Aeklea, Aekleah,
Aekli, Aeklie*

Aelfhere (English) An elf or divine warrior
Aelfhare, Aelvhere, Aelvhar, Aelvhare

Aelfric (English) An elf ruler
Aelfryc, Aelfrick, Aelfryck, Aelfrik, Aelfryk

Aelfwine (English) A friend of the elves
Aelfwynne, Aelfwin, Aelfwinn, Aelfwyn, Aelfwynn, Aelfwen, Aelfwenn, Aelfwenne

Aeneas (Greek) To be worthy of praise
Aenneas, Aineas, Aineias, Aineis, Ainneas

Aeolus (Greek) One who changes quickly; in mythology, god of the winds
Aeolos, Aiolos, Aiolus

Aeson (Greek) In mythology, the father of Jason
Aesun, Aison, Aisun, Ayson, Aysun

Afi (Norse) One who is grandfatherly
Afie, Afee, Afea, Afey, Afy

Afif (Arabic) One who is chaste; pure
Afeef, Afief, Afeif, Affeef, Affif, Afyf, Afeaf

Africa (English) One who is pleasant; from Africa
Afrika, Affreeca, Affrica, Africah, Afrycka, Afrycah, Afric, Affryka, Afrikah, Afryka, Afrykah, Africano, Afrikano, Afrycano, Afrykano, Afro

Agamemnon (Greek) One who works slowly; in mythology, the leader of the Greeks at Troy
Agamemno, Agamenon

Agapito (Spanish) A kind and loving person
Agapeto, Agapetus, Agapios, Agapitus

Agathias (Greek) One who is good and honorable
Agathios, Agathius, Agatha, Agathos

Aghy (Irish) A friend of the horse
Aghey, Aghi, Aghie, Aghee, Aghea, Aghe

Agnolo (Italian) A heavenly messenger; an angel
Agnolio, Agnoleo

Ahab (Hebrew) An uncle

Ahearn (Celtic) Lord of the horses
Ahern, Ahearne, Aherne, Aherin

Ahiga (Native American) One who fights
Ahyga

Ahmed (Arabic) One who always thanks God; a name of Muhammad
Achmad, Achmed, Ahmaad, Ahmad, Ahmet, Ahmod, Amad, Amadi, Amahd, Amed

Ahsan (Arabic) One who is merciful
Ahson, Ahsun, Ahsen, Ahsin, Ahsyn

♂
♉ **Aidan** (Irish) A fiery young man
*Aiden, Aedan, Aeden, Aidano, Aidyn, **Ayden**, Aydin, Aydan, Aidin, Aedin, Aedyn, Aideyn, Aidenn, Aedenn, Aidann, Aedann, Aydann, Aydenn, Aideynn*

Aiken (English) Constructed of oak; sturdy
Aikin, Aicken, Aickin, Ayken, Aykin, Aycken, Ayckin

Ailesh (Hindi) The lord of everything
Aylesh, Aileshe, Ayleshe

Aime (French) One who is loved

Aimery (Teutonic) Ruler of work
Aimory, Aimerey, Aimeric, Amerey, Aymeric, Aymery, Aymerey, Aimeri, Aimerie, Aimeree, Aimerea, Aimorey, Aimori, Aimorie, Aimoree, Amery, Ameri, Amerie, Ameree

Aimon (Teutonic) Ruler of the house; a protector
Aimond, Aymon, Aimund, Aimun, Aymun, Aymond, Aymund

Ainsley (Scottish) One's own meadow
Ainslie, Ainslea, Ainslee, Ainsleigh, Ainsly, Ainslei, Aynslie, Aynslea, Aynslee, Aynsleigh, Aynsley, Aynslie, Aynsly, Ainsleah, Aynsleah, Ainslye

Ainsworth (English) From Ann's estate
Answorth, Annsworth, Ainsworthe, Answorthe, Annsworthe

Aisley (English) From the ash-tree meadow
Aisly, Aisli, Aislie, Aislee, Aisleigh, Aislye, Aysley, Aysli, Ayslie, Aysly, Ayslye, Ayslee, Aysleigh, Aislea, Ayslea, Aisleah, Aysleah

Ajax (Greek) In mythology, a hero of the Trojan war
Aias, Aiastes, Ajaxx, Ajaxe

Ajayi (African) One who is born facedown
Ajayie, Ajaye, Ajayee, Ajayea, Ajayey

Ajit (Indian) One who is invincible
Ajeet, Ajeat, Ajeit, Ajiet, Ajyt

Akbar (Arabic) All-powerful and great
Acbar, Ackbar, Akbarr, Acbarr, Ackbarr

Akeno (Japanese) From the shining field
Akeeno, Akeano, Akyno, Akeyno, Akino

Akiko (Japanese) Surrounded by bright light
Akyko

Akili (Arabic) One who is wise
Akilie, Akily, Akiley, Akilee, Akilea, Akil, Akyl

Akim (Russian) God will judge
Akeem, Akeam, Akiem, Akeim, Akym, Akeym

Akin (African) A brave man; a hero
Akeen, Akean, Akein, Akien, Akyn

Akiva (Hebrew) One who protects or provides shelter
Akyva, Akeeva, Akeava, Akieva, Akeiva, Akeyva

Akmal (Arabic) A perfect man
Aqmal, Akmall, Aqmall, Acmal, Acmall, Ackmal, Ackmall

Akram (Arabic) A generous man
Akrem, Akrim, Akrym, Akrom, Akrum

Aladdin (Arabic) One who is noble in his faith
Aladin, Aladdyn, Aladyn

Alaire (French) Filled with joy
Alair, Alaer, Alaere, Alare, Alayr, Alayre

Alake (African) One who is honored
Alaik, Alaike, Alayk, Alayke, Alaek, Alaeke

Alamar (Arabic) Covered with gold
Alamarr, Alemar, Alemarr, Alomar, Alomarr

Alan (German / Gaelic) One who is precious / resembling a little rock
Ailean, Ailin, Al, Alain, Alun, Aland, Alann, Alano, Alanson, Alen, Alin, Allain, Allan, Allayne, Allen, Alley, Alleyn, Alleyne, Allie, Allin, Allon, Allyn, Alaen, Allaen

Alard (German) Of noble strength
Aliard, Allard, Alliard

Alaric (German) A noble ruler
Alric, Alrick, Alarick, Alarico, Aleric, Alerick, Allaric, Allarick, Alleric, Allerick, Alrick

Alastair (Scottish) Form of Alexander, meaning "helper and defender of mankind"
Alasdair, Alasteir, Alaster, Alastor, Alaisdair, Alaistair, Alaister, Aleister, Alester, Alistair, Alistar, Alister, Allaistar, Allaster, Allastir, Allistair, Allister, Allistir, Allysdair, Allystair, Allyster, Alysdair, Alysdare, Alystair, Alyster, Alli, Allie, Ally, Alley, Allee, Allea

Alban (Latin) One who is white or fair; a man from Alba
Albain, Alban, Albano, Albany, Albie, Albin, Albinet, Albis, Alby, Albys, Albey, Auban, Auben, Aubin, Albi, Albee, Albaney, Albani, Albanie, Albanee

Albany (Latin) From the white hill; white-skinned
Albaney, Albani, Albanie, Albanee, Albanye, Albin, Alban, Albhda, Aubine, Albanea, Albaneah

Albaric (French) A blonde-haired ruler
Albarik, Albarick, Albaryc, Albaryk, Albaryck

Alberich (Teutonic) A skillful ruler
Alberic, Alberik, Alberick, Alberyk, Alberyck, Alberyc

Albert (German) One who is noble and bright
Alberto, Albertus, Alburt, Albirt, Aubert, Albyrt, Albertos, Albertino

Albion (Latin / Celtic) One who is white or fair / from the rocks or crag
Albyon, Albeon

Alcander (Greek) Having strength and power
Alcindor, Alcandor, Alcinder, Alkander, Alkender, Alcender, Alkindor, Alkandor, Alkendor

Alcott (English) From the old cottage
Alcot, Allcot, Allcott, Alkott, Alkot, Allkot, Allkott

Alden (English) An old friend
Aldan, Aldin, Aldyn, Aldon, Aldun

Aldo (German) Old or wise one; elder
Aldous, Aldis, Aldus, Alldo, Aldys

Aldred (English) An old advisor
Alldred, Aldraed, Alldraed, Aldread, Alldread

Aldrich (English) An old king
Aldric, Aldridge, Aldrige, Aldrin, Aldritch, Alldrich, Alldridge, Aldrick, Aldrik, Aldryc, Aldryck, Aldryk, Aldrych, Audric, Audrick, Audrik

Aldwin (English) A wise old friend
Aldwinn, Aldwinne, Aldwyn, Aldwynne, Aldwine, Aldwynn, Aldwen, Aldwenn, Aldwenne

Alec (Greek) Form of Alexander, meaning "helper and defender of mankind"
Alek, Aleck, Alic, Alik, Alick, Alyc, Alyck, Alyk, Aleco, Alecko, Aleko, Alecos, Alekos, Aleckos

Aled (Welsh) A child; offspring

Alejandro (Spanish) Form of Alexander, meaning "helper and defender of mankind"
Alejandrino, Alejo

Alem (Arabic) A wise man
Alerio

Aleron (Latin) A winged one
Aileron, Alerun, Ailerun

○ **Alex** (English) Form of Alexander, meaning "helper and defender of mankind"
Aleks, Alecks, Alecs, Allex, Alleks, Allecks, Allecs

○ **Alexander** (Greek) Helper and defender of
○ mankind
Alaxander, Aleksandar, Aleksander, Aleksandr, Aleksanteri, Alesandro, Alessandre, Alessandri, Alessandro, Alexan, Alexandre, Alexandro, Alexandros, Alisander, Alissander, Alissandre, Alixandre, Alsandare, Alyksandr

○ **Alexis** (Greek) Form of Alexander, meaning "helper and defender of mankind"
Aleksei, Aleksi, Aleksio, Aleksios, Aleksius, Alexei, Alexey, Alexi, Alexio, Alexios, Alexius, Alexus, Alexy, Alexie, Alexee

Alfio (Italian) A white-skinned man
Alfeo, Alfiyo, Alfeyo

Alfonso (Italian) Prepared for battle; eager and ready
Alphonse, Affonso, Alfons, Alfonse, Alfonsin, Alfonsino, Alfonz, Alfonzo, Alphons, Alphonse, Alphonso, Alphonsus, Alphonz

Alfred (English) One who counsels the elves
Ahlfred, Ailfred, Ailfrid, Ailfryd, Alf, Alfey, Alfie, Alfre, Alfredas, Alfrey, Alfredo, Alfredos, Alfy, Alfee, Alfea, Alford, Alferd

Alger (English) One who is noble; an elf spear
Alga, Algar, Allgar, Allger, Algor, Allgor, Algur, Allgur, Algir, Allgir, Algyr, Allgyr

Algernon (French) One who has a mustache
Algernone, Algey, Algie, Algy, Aljernon, Allgernon, Algi, Algee, Algea

Algis (German) One who wields a spear
Algiss, Algisse, Algys, Algyss, Algysse

Ali (Arabic) The great one; one who is exalted
Aliyy, Alie, Aly, Aley, Alee, Aleigh, Alea

Alison (English) The son of a noble
Alisson, Allcen, Allison, Allisoun, Allson, Allyson

Almanzo (German) One who is highly esteemed; precious
Alma, Alman, Allmanzo, Almenzo, Allmenzo

Almarine (German) A work ruler
Almarin, Almarino, Almareen, Almereen, Almerene, Almerine, Almarene

Aloiki (Hawaiian) Form of Aloysius, meaning "a famous warrior"
Aloikie, Aloiky, Aloikey, Aloikee, Aloikea, Aloyki, Aloykie, Aloykey, Aloyky, Aloykee, Aloykea

Alon (Hebrew) Of the oak tree
Allona, Allon, Alonn

Alonzo (Spanish) Form of Alfonso, meaning "prepared for battle; eager and ready"
Alonso, Alanso, Alanzo, Allonso, Allonzo, Allohnso, Allohnzo, Alohnso, Alohnzo

Aloysius (German) A famous warrior
Ahlois, Aloess, Alois, Aloisio, Aloisius, Aloisio, Aloj, Alojzy, Aloys

Alpha (Greek) The firstborn child; the first letter of the Greek alphabet
Alphah, Alfa, Alfah

Alpheus (Hebrew) One who succeeds another
Alfaeus, Alfeos, Alfeus, Alpheaus, Alphoeus, Alphius, Alphyus

Alpin (Scottish) One who is fair-skinned
Alpine, Ailpein, Ailpin, Alpyn, Ailpyn, Alpyne

Alston (English) Of the elf stone
Alsdon, Alsten, Alstin, Allston, Allstonn, Alstun, Alstyn, Alstan

Alta (Latin) To be elevated
Alto, Altus, Allta, Alltus, Altos, Alltos

Altair (Greek) Resembling a bird
Alltair, Altaer, Altayr, Alltayr, Alltaer, Altare, Alltare, Alltayre

Alter (Hebrew) One who is old
Allter, Altar, Alltar

Altman (German) One who is prudent; an old man
Altmann, Alterman, Altermann, Altmann

Alton (English) From the old town
Aldon, Aldun, Altun, Alten, Allton, Alltun, Allten

Alucio (Spanish) One who is bright and shining
Allucio, Alucido, Aluxio, Aluzio

Aluf (Hebrew) One who is in charge
Alouf, Aluph, Alouph

Alured (Latin) Form of Alfred, meaning "one who counsels the elves"
Ailured

Alva (Hebrew) A bright man
Alvah

Alvar (English) Of the army of elves
Allvar, Allvarso, Alvarso, Allvaro

Alvaro (Spanish) Guardian of all
Alavaro, Alavero, Alvero, Alverio, Alvareo, Alvario

Alvern (Latin) Of the spring's growth
Alverne, Alvarn, Alvarne, Alvurn, Alvurne, Alvirn, Alvirne

Alvin (English) Friend of the elves
Alven, Alvan, Alvon, Alvyn, Alvun, Alvi, Alvie, Alvy, Alvey, Alvee, Alvea

Alvis (Norse) In mythology, a dwarf who fell in love with Thor's daughter
Alvise, Alvisse, Alviss, Alvys, Alvyss, Alvysse

Amadeus (Latin) Loved by God
Amadee, Amadei, Amadeo, Amado, Amadeusz, Amadi, Amadieu, Amadis, Amado, Amando, Amati, Amato, Amatus, Amedeo, Amyot

Amadour (French) A lovable man
Amador, Amadore, Amadoure

Amal (Hebrew / Hindi / Arabic) A hardworking man / one who is pure / filled with hope
Amahl, Amali, Amel, Amalie, Amaly, Amaley, Amalee, Amalea, Amaleigh

Amalio (Spanish) An industrious man
Amelio, Amallio, Amellio, Ameleo, Amaleo

Amani (African / Arabic) One who is peaceful / one with wishes and dreams
Amanie, Amany, Amaney, Amanee, Amanye, Amanea, Amaneah

Amari (African) Having great strength; a builder
Amarie, Amaree, Amarea, Amary, Amarey

Amarillo (Spanish) The color yellow
Amarilo, Amaryllo, Amarylo

Amasa (Hebrew) A burden
Amasah, Ammasa, Amahsa, Ammahsa

Amaury (French) A ruler
Amauri, Amaurie, Amaurey, Amauree, Amaurea

Ambrose (Greek) Immortal; in mythology, ambrosia was the food of the gods
Ambrosia, Ambrosius, Ambrosios, Ambroeus, Ambroise, Ambros, Ambrosi, Ambrosio, Ambrossij, Ambroz, Ambrus, Ambe, Ambroggio, Ambrogio, Ambi, Ambie, Amby, Ambey

Amerigo (Italian) Ruler of the home
America, Americo, Americus, Amerika, Ameriko, Amerikus, Arrigo

Ames (French) A beloved friend
Amos, Aimes, Aymes

Amid (Arabic) A general
Ameed, Amead, Amied, Ameid, Amyd

Amiel (Hebrew) The God of my people
Amyel, Amiell, Amyell

Amil (Hindi) One who is invaluable
Ameel, Ameal, Ameil, Amiel, Amyl

Amin (Arabic) One who faithful and trustworthy
Ameen, Amean, Amein, Amien, Amyn

Amir (Arabic /Hebrew) A prince / from the treetop
Ameer, Ameir, Amer, Amiran, Amiri, Amear, Amyr, Amier

Amit (Hindi) Without limit; endless
Ameet, Ameat, Ameit, Amiet, Amyt

Amitai (Hebrew) One who is truthful
Amiti, Amitay, Amitaye, Amitae, Amitie, Amity, Amitey, Amitee, Amitea

Amjad (Arabic) Having glory and honor
Amjaad, Amjed

Ammar (Arabic) A long and prosperous life
Ammer, Amr

Ammon (Hebrew) One who teaches or builds
Amon, Amnon, Ammnon

Amor (French) One who is loves and is loved
Amore

Amory (German) Ruler and lover of one's home
Aimory, Amery, Amorey, Amry, Amori, Amorie, Amoree, Amorea

Amos (Hebrew) To carry; hardworking
Amoss, Aymoss, Aymos

Amram (Hebrew) Of the mighty nation

Amyas (Latin) One who is loved
Amias, Amyes, Amyees

Anael (Hebrew) The name of an archangel
Anaele

Analu (Hawaiian) Form of Andrew, meaning "manly; a warrior"
Analue, Analoo, Analou

Anastasios (Greek) One who is resurrected
Anastas, Anastase, Anastagio, Anastasio, Anastasius, Anastatius, Anastice, Anastius, Anasto, Anstas, Anstasios, Anstasius, Anstice, Anstis, Anstiss

Anatole (Greek) Born with the break of day
Anatolius, Anatol, Anatolio, Antal, Antol, Antole, Antolle, Anatoli, Anatolie, Anatolee, Anatolea, Anatoly, Anatoley

Anchor (English) One who is reliable and stable
Ancher, Anker, Ankor

Anderson (English) The son of Andrew
Andersun, Andersson, Anderssun, Anders

Andino (Italian) Form of Andrew, meaning "manly; a warrior"
Andyno, Andeeno, Andeano, Andieno, Andeino

André (French) Form of Andrew, meaning "manly; a warrior"
Andrae, Andras, Andreas, Andrei, Andrej, Andres, Andreus, Andrey, Andris, Andrius, Aundray

● **Andrew** (Greek) Manly; a warrior
Adem, Aindrea, Aindreas, Andie, Andonia, Andor, Andresj, Andrewes, Andrews, Andrey, Andrezj, Andrian, Andriel, Andries, Andrij, Andrija, Andrius, Andro, Andros, Andru, Andruw, Andrzej, Andy, Antero

Andrik (Slavic) Form of Andrew, meaning "manly; a warrior"
Andric, Andrick, Andryk, Andryck, Andryc

Androcles (Greek) A glorious man
Androclus, Androclos, Androclas

Aneirin (Welsh) One who is noble
Aneiryn, Anierin, Anieryn, Aneurin, Aneuryn

Aneislis (Gaelic) A careful and thoughtful person
Anieslis, Aneislys, Anieslys

● **Angel** (Greek) A messenger of God
Andjelko, Ange, Angelino, Angell, Angelmo, Angelo, Angie, Angy, Aniol, Anjel, Anjelo, Anyoli

Angus (Scottish) One force; one strength; one choice
Aengus, Anngus, Aonghus

Anicho (German) An ancestor
Anico, Anecho, Aneco, Anycho, Anyco

Aniketos (Greek) One who remains unconquered
Anicetus, Aniceto, Anisio, Aniseto, Anicetos, Anisetos, Anicio

Ankur (Indian) One who is blossoming; a sapling

Annan (Celtic) From the brook
Anan

Anscom (English) From the valley of the majestic one
Anscomb, Anscombe, Anscoomb, Anscoombe

Ansel (French) One who follows nobility; protection from God
Ancell, Ansell, Anselm, Anselme, Anselmi, Anselmo, Anselmie, Anselmy, Anselmey

Ansley (English) From the noble's pastureland
Ansly, Anslie, Ansli, Anslee, Ansleigh, Anslea, Ansleah, Anslye

Anson (English) The son of Ann or Agnes
Annson, Annsen, Annsonia, Ansson, Ansen, Ansonia

Antaeus (Greek) Son of the Earth; in mythology, an invincible giant wrestler
Antaios, Antaius, Antaeos, Anteo, Anteus

Antares (Greek) A giant red star; the brightest star in the constellation Scorpio

Antenor (Spanish) One who antagonizes
Antener, Antenar, Antenir, Antenyr, Antenur

❂
❂ **Anthony** (Latin) A flourishing man; from an ancient Roman family
Antal, Anthone, Anthoney, Anntoin, Antin, Anton, Antone, Antonello, Antoney, Antoni, Antonije, Antons, Antony, Antun, Anthany

Antioco (Italian) A stubborn man
Antioch, Antio, Antiochos, Antiochus, Antioko, Antiocko, Antiocho

Antoine (French) Form of Anthony, meaning "a flourishing man; from an ancient Roman family"
Antione, Antjuan, Antuan, Antuwain, Antuwaine, Antuwayne, Antuwon, Antwahn, Antwain, Antwaine, Antwan, Antwaun, Antwohn, Antwoin, Antwoine, Antwon, Antwone

Antonio (Italian / Spanish) Form of Anthony, meaning "a flourishing man, from an ancient Roman family"
Antonin, Antonino, Antonius, Antonyo

Anwar (Arabic) Surrounded by light
Anwarr, Annwar, Annwarr

Anwell (Welsh) One who is loved dearly
Anwel, Anwil, Anwill, Anwyl, Anwyll

Aodh (Celtic) A fiery man; in mythology, the sun god
Aed, Aodhagan, Aoden, Aodhan, Aodan

Apache (Native American) A tribal name
Apachi, Apachie, Apachee, Apachea, Apachy, Apachey

Apollo (Greek) In mythology, the god of archery, music, and poetry
Apollon, Apollos, Apolo

Apollonio (Greek) A follower of Apollo
Apolonio, Apollonios, Apolonios, Apollonius, Apolonius, Apolloneo, Apoloneo

Apostolos (Greek) An apostle; a messenger of God
Apostolo, Apostolio, Apostolios, Apostoleo, Apostoleos

Aquarius (Latin) The water bearer; a constellation

Aquila (Latin) Resembling an eagle; also the name of a constellation
Acquila, Acquilino, Acquilla, Akila, Akilino, Akilla, Aquilina, Aquilino, Aquilla

Aquilo (Latin) Of the north wind
Aquillo, Aquilino, Aquillino

Ara (Armenian / Latin) A legendary king / of the altar; the name of a constellation
Araa, Aira, Arah, Arae, Ahraya

Aram (Assyrian) One who is exalted
Arram

Aramis (French) A swordsman
Arramis, Aramys, Aramiss, Aramyss, Arramys

Arcadio (Greek) From an ideal country paradise
Alcadio, Alcado, Alcedio, Arcadios, Arcadius, Arkadi, Arkadios, Arkadius, Arkady, Arkadie, Arkadey, Arkadee, Arkadea

Arcelio (Spanish) From the altar of heaven
Arcelios, Arcelius, Aricelio, Aricelios, Aricelius

Archard (German) A powerful holy man
Archerd, Archird, Archyrd

Archelaus (Greek) The ruler of the people
Archelaios, Arkelaos, Arkelaus, Arkelaios,
Archelaos

Archer (Latin) A skilled bowman
Archar, Archor, Archur, Archir, Archyr,
Archere

Archibald (French) One who is bold, brave,
and genuine
Archaimbaud, Archambault, Archibaldo,
Archibold, Archimbald, Archimbaldo,
Arquihaldo, Arquimbaldo, Archi, Archie,
Archy, Archey, Archee

Archimedes (Greek) A master of thought
Arkimedes, Arquimedes, Archimeedes,
Arkimeedes, Arquimeedes

Ardal (Gaelic) Having the valor of a bear
Ardghal

Ardell (Latin) One who is eager
Ardel, Ardelle, Ardele

Arden (Latin / English) One who is passionate
and enthusiastic / from the valley of the eagles
Ardan, Arrden, Arrdan, Ardin, Arrdin, Ard,
Ardyn, Arrdyn, Ardy, Ardi, Ardie, Ardee, Ardey

Ardley (English) Of the home-lover's
meadow
Ardly, Ardleigh, Ardlee, Ardli, Ardlie, Ardlea,
Ardleah, Ardsleigh, Ardslee, Ardslea, Ardsleah,
Ardsli, Ardslie, Ardsly, Ardsley

Ardmore (Latin) One who is zealous
Ardmorre, Ardmorr, Ardmor

Ardon (Hebrew) The color bronze
Arrdon, Ardun, Arrdun

Arduino (German) A valued friend
Ardwino, Arrduino, Ardueno

Ares (Greek) In mythology, god of war
Areis, Areys, Arees, Areas

Argento (Latin) Resembling silver
Argentio, Argentino

Argus (Greek) One who is vigilant and
watchful
Argos

Argyle (Scottish) A diamond pattern
Argyll, Argile

Ari (Hebrew) Resembling a lion or an eagle
Aree, Arie, Aristide, Aristides, Arri, Ary, Arye,
Arrie, Arry, Arrye

Aric (Scandinavian) Form of Eric, meaning
"ever the ruler"
Aaric, Arick, Aarick, Arik, Aarik, Arric,
Arrick, Arrik, Arrict, Arict

Ariel (Hebrew) A lion of God
Arielle, Ariele, Ariell, Arriel, Ahriel, Airial,
Areal, Arial, Areille, Ariellel

Aries (Latin) Resembling a ram; the first
sign of the zodiac; a constellation
Arese, Ariese

Arion (Greek) A poet or musician
Arian, Arien, Aryon

Aris (American) Form of Aristeo, meaning
"the best"
Arris, Arys, Aryss

Aristeo (Spanish) The best
Aristio, Aristo, Aristeyo, Aristos, Aristiyo,
Aristeides, Aristides, Aristide

Aristotle (Greek) Of high quality
Aristotelis, Aristotellis

Arius (Greek) Enduring life; everlasting;
immortal
Areos, Areus, Arios

Arizona (Native American) From the little
spring; from the state of Arizona

Arjuna (Hindi) The white one
Arjun, Arjune

Arkansas (Native American) Of the down-
river people; from the state of Arkansas

Arledge (English) From the hare's lake
Arlidge, Arlledge, Arllidge, Arrledge, Arrlidge

Arlen (Gaelic) A solemn, binding promise
Arlan, Arland, Arlend, Arlando, Arlendo,
Arlenn, Arlann, Arles, Arlas, Arlin, Arlind,
Arlindo, Arlinn, Arlyn, Arllen, Arlleno,
Arllend

Arley (English) From the hare's meadow
Arlea, Arleigh, Arlie, Arly, Arleah, Arli, Arlee

Arliss (Hebrew) Of the pledge
Arlyss, Aryls, Arlis, Arlisse, Arlysse

Arlo (Spanish) From the barberry tree
Arlow, Arlowe, Arrlo, Arrlow, Arrlowe

Armand (French) Of the army; a soldier
Arman, Armande, Armando, Armani, Armond, Armonde, Armondo, Armanie, Armany, Armaney, Armanee, Armante, Armaan, Armanno, Arminlo, Arminius, Armin

Armon (Hebrew) Resembling a chestnut
Armoni, Armonie, Armonno, Armony, Armoney, Armonee

Armstrong (Scottish) A strong warrior
Armstrang

Arnan (Hebrew) One who is quick; filled with joy

Arne (Norse) Resembling an eagle
Arni, Arnie, Arney, Arny, Arnee, Arnea, Arn

Arnett (French) Resembling a little eagle
Arnat, Arnet, Arnot, Arnott, Arnatt

Arno (German) An eagle-wolf
Arnoe, Arnou, Arnoux, Arnow, Arnowe

Arnold (German) The eagle ruler
Arnaldo, Arnaud, Arnauld, Arnault, Arnd, Arndt, Arnel, Arnell, Arnoldo, Arnoud, Arnout

Arnon (Hebrew) From the torrent river

Arrio (Spanish) A belligerent man
Aryo, Ario, Arryo

Arsenio (Greek) A manly man
Arcenio, Arcinio, Arsanio, Arseenio, Arseinio, Arsemio, Arsen, Arsene, Arseni, Arsenios, Arsenius, Arseno, Arsenyo, Arsinio, Arsino

Artemas (Greek) A follower of the goddess Artemis
Artemio, Artemis, Artemus, Artimas, Artimis, Artimus

Arthur (Celtic) As strong as a bear; a hero
Aart, Arrt, Art, Artair, Arte, Arther, Arthor, Arthuro, Artie, Arto, Artor, Artro, Artturi, Artur, Arturo, Artus, Arty, Arthel, Arthus

Arundel (English) From the eagle's valley
Arundell, Arundele, Arondel, Arondell, Arundale, Arundayl, Arundayle, Arundael, Arundaele, Arundail, Arundaile

Arvad (Hebrew) A wanderer; voyager
Arpad

Arvid (Norse) From the eagle's tree
Arvyd, Arved, Arvod, Arvud

Arvin (English) A friend to everyone
Arvinn, Arvinne, Arven, Arvenn, Arvenne, Arvyn, Arvynn, Arvynne, Arvis, Arviss, Arvys, Arvyss, Arwen, Arwenn, Arwenne, Arwyn, Arwynn, Arwynne, Arwin, Arwine, Arwinn, Arwinne

Arvind (Indian) Resembling a lotus
Arvynd, Arvinde, Aryvnde

Asa (Hebrew) One who heals others
Asah, Ase, Aseh

Asad (Arabic) A fortunate man
Assad, Asaad

Asael (Hebrew) God has created
Asaya, Asayel, Asahel, Asiel, Asiell, Asaell

Asaph (Hebrew) One who gathers or collects
Asaf, Asaphe, Asafe, Asiph, Asiphe, Asif, Asife

Ascanius (Latin) In mythology, the son of Aeneas
Ascanios, Ascanious

Ascott (English) One who lives in the eastern cottage
Ascot

Asgard (Norse) From the courtyard of the gods; in mythology, the dwelling place of the gods
Asgarde

Ash (English) From the ash tree
Ashe

Ashby (English) From the ash-tree farm
Ashbi, Ashbie, Ashbee, Ashbea, Ashbey

Asher (Hebrew) Filled with happiness
Ashar, Ashor, Ashir, Ashyr, Ashur

Ashford (English) From the ash-tree ford
Asheford, Ashenford

Ashley (English) From the meadow of ash trees
Ashely, Asheley, Ashelie, Ashlan, Ashleigh, Ashlen, Ashli, Ashlie, Ashlin, Ashling, Ashlinn, Ashly, Ashlyn, Ashlynn

Ashraf (Arabic) A distinguished man
Asheraf, Ashraph, Asheraph

● **Ashton** (English) From the ash-tree town
Asheton, Ashtun, Ashetun, Ashtin, Ashetin, Ashtyn, Ashetyn, Aston, Astun

Asim (Arabic) A protector or guardian
Aseem, Aseam, Aseim, Asiem, Asym, Azim, Azeem, Azeam, Azeim, Aziem, Azym

Aslan (Turkish) Resembling a lion
Aslen, Azlan, Azlen

Aspen (American) From the aspen tree
Aspin, Aspyn, Aspon, Aspun, Aspan

Astraeus (Greek) In mythology, one of the Titans
Astraios

Aswin (English) A spear friend
Aswinn, Aswinne, Aswyn, Aswynn, Aswynne, Aswen, Aswenn, Aswenne, Aswine

Athanasois (Greek) Having eternal life
Atanasio, Atanasios, Atanasius, Athan, Athanasius

Athelstan (English) Of the noble stone
Athelston, Athelsten, Athelstin, Athelstyn, Athelstun

Athens (Greek) From the capital of Greece
Athenios, Athenius, Atheneos, Atheneus

Atherton (English) From the town near the spring
Athertun

Athol (Gaelic) From the new Ireland
Atholl

Atif (Arabic) A kind man
Ateef, Ateaf, Atief, Ateif, Atyf, Atiph, Ateeph, Ateaph, Atieph, Ateiph, Atyph

Atlas (Greek) In mythology, a Titan who carried the world on his shoulders
Attlas, Atlass, Attlass

Atley (English) From the meadow
Atlea, Atlee, Atleigh, Attlee, Attleigh, Atleah, Atly, Atli, Atlie, Attlea, Attleah, Attli, Attlie, Attly, Attley

Atsushi (Japanese) A compassionate warrior
Atsushie, Atsushy, Atsushey, Atsushee, Atsushea

Atticus (Latin) A man from Athens
Attikus, Attickus, Aticus, Atickus, Atikus

Attila (Hungarian) One who is fatherly
Atila, Atilano, Atilo, Attilia, Attilio, Attileo

Atwater (English) One who lives at the water
Attwater

Atwell (English) One who lives at the spring
Attwell, Atwel, Attwel

Atwood (English) One who lives at the forest
Attwood, Atwode, Attwode

Atworth (English) One who lives at the farmstead
Attworth, Atworthe, Attworthe

Auberon (French) A royal bear
Auberron, Auberun, Auberrun

Aubrey (English) One who rules with elf-wisdom
Aubary, Aube, Aubery, Aubry, Aubury, Aubrian, Aubrien, Aubrion, Aubri, Aubrie, Aubree, Aubrea

Auburn (Latin) Having a reddish-brown color
Aubirn, Auburne, Aubyrn, Abern, Abirn, Aburn, Abyrn, Aubern

Auden (English) An old friend
Audin, Audyn, Audan, Audon, Audun

Audey (English) Of noble strength
Audi, Audie, Audee, Audea, Audy

Audley (English) From the old meadow
Audly, Audleigh, Audlee, Audlea, Audleah, Audli, Audlie

Audrey (English) Of noble strength
Audry, Audree, Audri, Audrie, Audrea

August (Latin) One who is venerable; majestic
Auguste, Agosto, Augusto, Augi, Augie, Augy, Augey, Augee, Augea

Augustine (Irish) Form of August, meaning "one who is venerable; majestic"
Agoston, Aguistin, Agustin, Augustin, Augustyn, Avgustin, Augusteen, Agosteen, Agostino, Agustino

Augustus (Latin) Form of August, meaning "one who is venerable; majestic"
Augostos, Augustos, Agostos, Agostos, Agustus

Aurelio (Latin) The golden one
Aurelius, Aurilius, Aurilio, Aurelian, Aureliano, Aureli, Aurelie, Aurely, Aureley, Aurelee, Aureleigh, Aurelo

♥ **Austin** (English) Form of August, meaning "one who is venerable; majestic"
Austen, Austyn, Austan, Auston, Austun

Autrey (English) Form of Audrey, meaning "of noble strength"
Autry, Autri, Autrie, Autree, Autrea

Avenall (French) From the oat field
Avenal, Aveneil, Aveneill, Avenel, Avenell, Avenil, Avenill, Avenelle

Avery (English) One who is a wise ruler; of the nobility
Avrie, Averey, Averie, Averi, Averee, Averea, Avereah, Avri, Avry, Avrey, Avree, Avrea

Aviel (Hebrew) My father is Lord
Aviell, Avyel, Avyell

Aviram (Hebrew) My Father is mighty
Avyram, Avirem, Avyrem

Avishae (Hebrew) The gift of my Father
Avyshae, Avishay, Avyshay, Avishaye, Avyshaye, Avishai, Avyshai

Avital (Hebrew) The father of the morning's dew
Avitall, Avytal, Avytall

Avner (Hebrew) My Father is the light
Avnar, Avnor, Avnur, Avnir, Avnyr

Avon (Celtic) Of the river
Avun, Aven, Avan, Avin, Avyn

Avram (Hebrew) My Father is exalted
Avrem, Avrim, Avrym, Avrom, Avrum

Avshalom (Hebrew) My Father is peace
Avsalom

Axel (German / Latin / Hebrew) Source of life; small oak / axe / peace
Aksel, Ax, Axe, Axell, Axil, Axill, Axl

Aya (Hebrew) Resembling a bird
Ayah

Ayawamat (Native American) An obedient man

Ayers (English) The heir to a fortune
Ayer, Aires, Aire

Aylmer (English) A renowned and noble man
Aillmer, Ailmer, Allmer, Ayllmer

Aylward (English) A noble guardian
Ailward, Aylwerd, Ailwerd

Aylwen (English) A noble friend
Aylwenn, Aylwenne, Aylwin, Aylwine, Aylwinn, Aylwinne, Aylwyn, Aylwynn, Aylwynne

Ayman (Arabic) One who is fortunate; lucky
Aymen, Aymeen, Aymean, Aymin, Aymein, Aymien, Aymyn

Ayo (African) Filled with happiness
Ayoe, Ayow, Ayowe

Ayubu (African) One who perseveres

Az (Hebrew) Having great strength

Aza (Arabic) One who provides comfort

Azad (Arabic) One who is free

Azamat (Arabic) A proud man; one who is majestic

Azariah (Hebrew) One who is helped by God
Azaria, Azarya, Azria, Azriah, Azuria, Azuriah, Azarious, Azaryah, Azaryahu

Azarni (Japanese) Resembling the thistle flower
Azarnie, Azarny, Azarney, Azarnee, Azarnea

Azekel (African) One who praises the lord
Azekell, Azekil, Azekill, Azekyl, Azekyll

Azhar (Arabic) A famous and shining man
Azhare, Azhair, Azhaire, Azhayr, Azhayre, Azhaer, Azhaere

Azi (African) One who is youthful
Azie, Azy, Azey, Azee, Azea

Azibo (African) Of the earth
Azybo

Azikiwe (African) One who is full of life
Azikiwi, Azikiwie, Azikiwy, Azikiwey, Azikiwee, Azikiwea

Aziz (Arabic) The all-powerful
Azeez, Aziez, Azeiz, Azeaz, Azyz, Azize

Azizi (African) The precious one
Azizie, Azizy, Azizey, Azizee, Azizea

Azmer (Islamic) Resembling a lion
Azmar, Azmir, Azmyr, Azmor, Azmur

Azmera (African) The harvester

Azra (Hebrew) One who is pure; chaste
Azrah, Azraa

Azrael (Hebrew) One who is helped by God
Azraeil, Azrial, Azriel, Azreel, Azreil, Azreal, Azryl, Azril

Azraff (Arabian) An elegant man
Azraf

Azure (French / Persian) Sky blue / resembling a blue semiprecious stone
Azzure, Azuree, Azurine, Azore, Azurah, Azureen, Azuryn, Azuryne, Azuri, Azurie, Azury, Azurey

Azzam (Arabic) One who is determined
Azam

b

Baahi (Arabic) One who is magnificent
Baahie, Baahy, Baahey, Baahee, Baahea

Baakir (African) The eldest child
Baakeer, Baakyr, Baakear, Baakier, Baakeir

Baback (Persian) A loving father
Babak, Babac

Babar (Turkish) Resembling a tiger
Baber, Babir, Babyr, Babor, Babur, Babr

Babatunde (African) One who resembles his grandfather
Babatund, Babatundi, Babatundie, Babatundy, Babatundey, Babatundee

Babson (English) The son of Barbara
Babsun, Babsen, Babsan, Babsin, Babsyn

Babu (African / Hindi) One who is grandfatherly / a fierce man
Babue, Baboo, Babou

Baby (English) A beloved child; a spoiled son
Babi, Babie, Babey, Babe, Bebe, Babea, Babe

Bacchus (Latin) In mythology, the god of wine
Baccus, Baakus, Baackus, Backus, Bach, Bache

Bachelor (French) An unmarried man
Bachellor, Batcheler, Batcheller, Batchelor, Batchellor, Bachelar, Bachellar, Batchelar, Batchellar, Bachelur, Bachellur, Batchelur, Batchelur, Bachelir, Bachellir, Batchelir, Batchelir, Bachelyr, Bachellyr, Batchelyr, Batchelyr, Bacheler, Bacheller, Batch

Bachir (Hebrew) The oldest son
Bacheer, Bachear, Bachier, Bacheir, Bachyr

Bacon (American) One who is outspoken
Bakon, Bacun, Bakun

Badar (Arabic) Born beneath the full moon
Badarr, Bade, Bader, Badr, Badrani, Badranie, Badruny, Badraney, Badranee, Badranea

Badawi (Arabian) A nomad
Badawie, Badawy, Badawey, Badawee, Badawea

Baden (German) One who bathes
Badin, Badyn, Badan, Badon, Badun

Badger (American) A difficult man
Badgar, Badgyr, Badgir, Badgor, Badgur, Badgent, Badgeant, Bagent, Bageant

Badi (Arabic) A wonderful man
Badie, Bady, Badey, Badee, Badea

Badru (African) Born beneath the full moon
Badrue, Badrou, Badroo

Badu (African) The tenth-born child
Badue, Badoo, Badou

Baethan (Irish) The foolish one
Bathan, Baethen, Baythan, Baythen, Bathen, Baithan, Baithen

Baghel (Arabic) Resembling an ox
Baghell, Baghele, Baghelle

Baha (Arabic) A glorious and splendid man
Bahah

Bahadur (Arabic) A courageous man

Bahari (African) A man of the sea
Baharie, Bahary, Baharey, Baharee, Baharea

Bahij (Arabic) A delightful man
Baheej, Baheaj, Baheij, Bahiej, Bahyj

Bahir (Arabic) A shining man
Baheer, Bahear, Bahier, Baheir, Bahyr

Bahjat (Arabic) One who brings joy to others
Bahgat

Bailey (English) From the courtyard within castle walls; a public official
Bailee, Bayley, Baylee, Baylie, Baili, Bailie, Baileigh, Bayleigh, Baileah, Bailea, Baylea, Bayleah, Baylee, Bayli

Bailintin (Irish) A valiant man
Bailinten, Bailentin, Bailenten, Bailintyn, Bailentyn

Bain (Irish) A fair-haired man
Baine, Bayn, Bayne, Baen, Baene, Bane, Baines, Baynes, Baenes, Banes

Bainbridge (English) From the bridge over the pale water
Baynbridge, Baenbridge, Banebridge, Bainbrige, Baynbrige, Baenbrige, Banebrige

Baird (Gaelic) A minstrel; a poet
Bairde, Bayrd, Bayrde, Bayerd, Baerd, Baerde

Bairn (Gaelic) A child
Bairne, Bayrn, Bayrne, Baern, Baerne

Bajnok (Hungarian) A victorious man
Bajnock, Bajnoc

Bakari (Swahili) One who is promised
Bakarie, Bakary, Bakarey, Bakaree, Bakarea

Baker (English) One who bakes
Bakar, Bakor, Bakur, Bakir, Bakyr

Bakhit (Arabic) A lucky man
Bakheet, Bukheut, Bukheil, Bakhiet, Bakhyt, Bakht

Bal (Hindi) Having great strength

Bala (Hindi) One who is youthful
Balu, Balue, Balou

Balamani (Indian) A young jewel
Balamanie, Balamany, Balamaney, Balamanee, Balamanea

Balark (Hindi) Born with the rising sun

Balasi (Basque) One who is flat-footed
Balasie, Balasy, Balasey, Balasee, Balasea

Balbir (Indian) A strong man
Balbeer, Balbear, Balbier, Balbeir, Balbyr

Balbo (Latin) One who mutters
Balboe, Balbow, Balbowe, Ballbo, Balbino, Balbi, Balbie, Balby, Balbey, Balbee, Balbea

Baldemar (German) A famous and bold man
Baldemarr, Baldomar, Baldomero, Baumar, Baldomarr, Baldemero, Baumer, Baumor, Baumir, Baumur, Baumyr

Balder (English / Norse) Of the brave army / in mythology, the god of light
Baldar, Baldur, Baldor, Baldir, Baldyr

Baldev (Indian) Having great strength

Baldric (German) A brave ruler
Baldrik, Baldrick, Baldryc, Baldryk, Baldryck, Balderic, Balderik, Balderick, Balderyc, Balderyk, Balderyck, Baudric, Baudrik, Baudrick, Baudryc, Baudryk, Baudryck

Baldwin (German) A brave friend
Baldwine, Baldwinn, Baldwinne, Baldwen, Baldwenn, Baldwenne, Baldwyn, Baldwynn, Baldwynne, Baldewin, Baldovino, Balduin, Balduino, Balldwin, Balldwyn, Balldwen, Baudoin, Baldi, Baldie, Baldy, Baldey, Baldee

Balendin (Basque) A strong and brave man
Balendyn, Balendon, Balendun, Balendan, Balenden

Balfour (Gaelic) From the grazing land
Balfer, Balfor, Balfore, Ballfour, Ballfer, Ballfor, Ballfore

Balfre (Spanish) A courageous man
Balfri, Balfrie, Balfrey, Balfry, Balfree, Balfrea

Balgair (Scottish) Resembling a fox
Balgaire, Balgayr, Balgayre, Balgaer, Balgaecre, Balgare

Baliff (French) A steward
Balyff, Balif, Balyf

Balint (Latin) A healthy and strong man
Balent, Balin, Balen, Balynt, Balyn

Ballard (German) A strong and brave man
Balard, Ballhard, Bulhard, Ballardt, Balardt, Ballhardt, Balhardt

Balloch (Scottish) From the grazing land

Balraj (Hindi) A strong ruler

Balthasar (Babylonian) Baal protect the king; in the Bible, Baltazar was one of the three wise men
Baldassare, Baltasar, Baltazar, Balthasaar, Balthazaar, Balthazar, Balto, Belshazzar, Baldasarre, Baldassario, Baltsaros

Balwin (English) Form of Baldwin, meaning "a brave friend"
Balwinn, Balwinne, Balwine, Balwen, Balwenn, Balwenne, Balwyn, Balwynn, Balwynne

Banan (Irish) A white-skinned man
Banen, Banon, Banin, Banyn, Banun

Bancroft (English) From the bean field
Bancrofte, Banfield, Banfeld, Bankroft, Bankrofte

Bandana (Spanish) A brightly colored head-wrap
Bandanah, Bandanna, Bandannah

Bandele (African) One who is born away from home
Bandel, Bandelle, Bandell

Bandy (American) A feisty man
Bandey, Bandi, Bandie, Bandee, Bandea

Banji (African) The second born of twins
Banjie, Banjy, Banjey, Banjee, Banjea

Banjo (English) One who plays the musical instrument
Banjoe, Banjow, Banjowe

Banner (French) One who holds the flag; an ensign bearer
Baner, Bannor, Bannur, Bannir, Bannyr, Bannar, Bannerman, Banerman, Bannermann, Banermann

Banning (Gaelic) A blonde-haired child
Bannyng, Baning, Banyng

Bannock (Gaelic) Oat bread that is unleavened
Bannok, Bannoc, Bannoch

Bansi (Indian) One who plays the flute
Bansie, Bansy, Bansey, Bansee, Bansea

Bao (Vietnamese / Chinese) To order / one who is prized

Baptist (Latin) One who is baptized
Baptiste, Battista, Battiste, Bautiste, Bautista

Baqir (Arabic) A learned man
Baqeer, Baqear, Baqier, Baqeir, Baqyr, Baqer

Barack (Swahili) Blessed, a blessing
Barrack, Barak

Barak (Hebrew) Of the lightning flash
Barrak, Barac, Barrac, Barrack

Baram (Hebrew) The son of the nation
Barem, Barum, Barom, Barim, Barym

Barber (French) One who trims or shaves beards
Barbour, Barbar, Barbor, Barbir, Barbyr, Barbur

Barbod (Persian) A hero

Barclay (English) From the meadow of birch trees
Barcley, Barklay, Barkley, Barklie, Barrclay, Barrklay, Barklea, Barkleah, Barkli, Barkly

Bard (English) A minstrel; a poet
Barde, Bardo

Barden (English) From the barley valley; from the boar's valley
Bardon, Bardun, Bardin, Bardyn, Bardan, Bardene

Bardol (Basque) A farmer
Bardo, Bartol

Bardolf (English) An axe-wolf
Bardolph, Bardalf, Bardalph, Bardulf,
Bardulph, Bardawulf, Bardawulph,
Bardawolf, Bardawolph

Bardrick (Teutonic) An axe ruler
Bardric, Bardrik, Bardryck, Bardryc,
Bardarick, Bardaric, Bardarik, Bardaryck,
Bardaryk, Bardaryc, Bardarich, Bardrich

Barek (Arabic) One who is noble
Barec, Bareck

Barend (German) The hard bear
Barende, Barind, Barinde, Barynd, Barynde

Baris (Turkish) A peaceful man
Bariss, Barys, Baryss, Barris, Barrys, Barriss,
Barryss

Barker (English) A shepherd
Barkar, Barkir, Barkyr, Barkor, Barkur, Bark,
Barke

Barksdale (English) From the valley of
birch trees
Barksdayl, Barksdayle, Barksdail, Barksdaile,
Barksdael, Barksdaele, Barksdell, Barksdel

Barlaam (Hebrew) The name of a hermit
Barlam

Barlow (English) From the bare hill
Barlowe, Barlo, Barloe, Barrlow, Barrlowe,
Barrlo, Barrloe

Barnabas (Hebrew) The son of the prophet;
the son of encouragement
Barna, Barnaba, Barnabé, Barnabee,
Barnabey, Barnabie, Barnabus, Barnaby,
Barnebas, Barnebus, Barnebi, Barnabea

Barnes (English) One who lives near the
barns
Barns, Barn, Barne

Barnett (English) Of honorable birth
Barnet, Baronet, Baronett

Barney (English) Form of Barnabas, meaning "the son of the prophet; the son of
encouragement"
Barny, Barni, Barnie, Barnee, Barnea, Barner

Barnum (English) From the baron's estate
Barnam, Barnem, Barnom, Barnham,
Barnhum, Barnhem

Baron (English) A title of nobility
Barron, Barun, Barrun, Barin, Barrin,
Baren, Barren, Baryn, Barryn, Baran, Barran

Barr (English) A lawyer
Barre, Bar

Barra (Gaelic) A fair-haired man

Barram (Irish) A handsome man
Barrem, Barrim, Barrym, Barrom, Barrum

Barrett (German / English) Having the
strength of a bear / one who argues
Baret, Barrat, Barratt, Barret, Barrette

Barric (English) From the grain farm
Barrick, Barrik, Barryc, Barryk, Barryck,
Beric, Beryc, Berik, Beryk, Berick, Beryck

Barry (Gaelic) A fair-haired man
Barrey, Barri, Barrie, Barree, Barrea,
Barrington, Barryngton, Barringtun,
Barryngtun, Barringten, Barryngten

Bartholomew (Aramaic) The son of the
farmer
Bart, Bartel, Barth, Barthelemy, Bartho,
Barthold, Bartholoma, Bartholomaus,
Bartholomé, Barthlomeo, Barthol, Barthold,
Bartholomeus, Bartin, Bartle, Bartolome,
Bartolomeo, Bartolommeo, Bartome, Bartow,
Bartt, Bartholemew, Bartholomaios, Barto,
Bartalan, Barta, Bates, Bartholemus

Bartlett (French) Form of Bartholomew,
meaning "the son of the farmer"
Bartlet, Bartlitt, Bartlit, Bartlytt, Bartlyt

Bartley (English) From the meadow of birch
trees
Bartly, Bartli, Bartlie, Bartlee, Bartlea,
Bartleah, Bartleigh

Bartoli (Spanish) Form of Bartholomew,
meaning "the son of the farmer"
Bartolie, Bartoly, Bartoley, Bartolee,
Bartoleigh, Bartolea, Bartolo, Bartolio

Barton (English) From the barley town
Bartun, Barten, Bartan, Bartin, Bartyn

Bartram (Scandinavian) The glorious raven
Bartrem, Barthram, Barthrem

Baruch (Hebrew) One who is blessed
Boruch, Baruchi, Baruchie, Baruchey,
Baruchy, Baruchee, Baruchea, Baruj

Baruti (African) One who teaches others
Barutie, Baruty, Barutey, Barutea, Barutee

Barwolf (English) The axe-wolf
Barrwolf, Barwulf, Barrwulf

Bary (Celtic) A marksman
Bari, Barie, Barey, Baree, Barea

Basant (Arabic) One who smiles often
Basante

Base (English) A short man

Bash (African / American) The forerunner / one who likes to party
Bashe, Bashi, Bashie, Bashy, Bashey, Bashee, Bashea

Bashir (Arabic) A bringer of good news
Basheer, Bashear, Bashier, Basheir, Bashyr

Bashiri (African) A prophet
Bashirie, Bashiry, Bashirey, Bashiree, Bashirea

Basil (Greek) Of the royal family; a kingly man
Basile, Basilic, Basilides, Basileios, Basilie, Basilio, Basilius, Bazeel, Bazeelius, Bazil, Bazyli

Basim (Arabic) A smiling man
Baseem, Baseam, Basiem, Baseim, Basym, Bahsim, Bahseem, Bahseam, Bahseim, Bahsiem, Bahsym, Bassam

Basir (Turkish) An intelligent man
Baseer, Basear, Basier, Baseir, Basyr

Bass (English) Resembling the fish
Bassy, Bassey, Bassi, Bassie, Bassee, Bassea

Bassett (English) A little person
Baset, Basset, Basett

Bastian (French) Form of Sebastian, meaning "the revered one"
Bastien, Bastiaan

Basy (American) A homebody
Basey, Basi, Basie, Basee, Basea, Basye

Batal (Arabic) A hero

Baul (English) Resembling a snail
Baule, Bawl, Bawle

Baurice (American) Form of Maurice, meaning "a dark-skinned man; Moorish"
Baurell, Baureo, Bauricio, Baurids, Baurie, Baurin, Baurio, Baurise, Baurits, Bauritius, Bauritz, Baurizio, Bauro, Baurus, Baury, Baurycy

Bavol (English) Of the wind
Bavoll, Bavole, Bavolle

Baxley (English) From the baker's meadow
Baxly, Baxlea, Baxleah, Baxlee, Baxleigh, Baxli, Baxlie

Baxter (English) A baker
Baxtor, Baxtar, Baxtir, Baxtyr, Baxtur, Bax, Baxe

Bay (Vietnamese / English) The seventh-born child; born during the month of July / from the bay
Baye, Bae, Bai

Bayard (French) An auburn-haired man
Baiardo, Bajardo, Bayhard, Baylen, Baylon, Baylan, Baylun, Baylin, Baylyn

Bayless (French) One who leases a bay
Bayles, Baylless, Baylles

Bayode (African) One who brings joy

Bayou (French) From the slow-moving river
Bayu, Bayue

Bazi (Arabic) One who is generous
Bazie, Bazy, Bazey, Bazee, Bazea

Beacher (English) One who lives near the beech trees
Beache, Beech, Beeche, Beach, Beecher, Beachy, Beachey, Beachi, Beachie, Beachee, Beachea, Beechy, Beechey, Beechi, Beechie, Beechee, Beechea

Beacon (English) A signalling light
Beacan, Beacun, Beacen, Beackon, Beackan, Beacken, Beacken, Beecon, Beeckon, Beecun, Beeckun, Beecan, Beeckan, Beecen, Beecken, Beakon, Beakun, Beaken, Beakan, Beekon, Beekun, Beekan, Beeken

Beagan (Gaelic) The small one
Beagen, Beagun, Beagon, Beagin, Beagyn, Beegan, Beegen, Beegin, Beegyn, Beegon, Beegun

Beal (French) A handsome man
Beals, Beale, Beall, Bealle

Beaman (English) A beekeeper
Beeman, Beamon, Beemon, Beamen, Beemen, Beamun, Beemun, Beamin, Beemin, Beamyn, Beemyn

Beamer (English) One who plays the trumpet
Beamor, Beamir, Beamyr, Beamur, Beamar, Beemer, Beemar, Beemir, Beemyr, Beemor, Beemur

Bean (Scottish) One who is lively
Beann, Beane

Beanon (Irish) A well-behaved boy
Beanan, Beanin, Beanyn, Beanun, Beanen, Beinean, Beineon, Binean

Beasley (English) From the pea meadow
Beasly, Beasli, Beaslie, Beaslee, Beaslea, Beasleah, Beasleigh

Beate (German) One who is serious
Beatte, Beahta, Beahtae, Bayahtah

Beattie (Gaelic) One who brings joy
Beatty, Beattey, Beatti, Beattee, Beattea, Beaty, Beatey, Beati, Beatie, Beatee, Beatea

Beau (French) A handsome man; an admirer
Beaudan, Beaudine, Beauden, Beaudin, Beaudyn, Beauregard

Beauchamp (French) From the beautiful field
Beecham, Beachem, Beechem, Beachem

Beauford (French) From the beautiful ford
Beauforde, Beauferd, Beauferde, Beaufurd, Beaufurde

Beaufort (French) From the beautiful fortress

Beaumont (French) From the beautiful mountain
Beaumonte, Belmont, Bellmont, Belmonte, Bellmonte

Beaver (American) Resembling the animal
Beever, Beiver, Biever

Becher (Hebrew) The firstborn son

Beck (English) From the small stream; from the brook
Becker, Becke, Beckar, Beckor, Beckur, Beckir, Beckyr, Beckett, Becket

Bedar (Arabic) One who is attentive
Beder, Bedor, Bedur, Bedyr, Bedir

Bede (English) One who prays; the name of a saint
Beda

Bedell (French) A messenger
Bedel, Bedelle, Bedele, Bedall, Bedal, Bedalle, Bedale

Bedrich (Czech) A peaceful ruler
Bedrych, Bedrick, Bedryck, Bedrik, Bedryk, Bedric, Bedryc

Beebe (English) One who farms bees
Beeson, Beesun, Beesin, Beesyn, Beesen, Beesan

Behrouz (Persian) A lucky man
Behrooz, Behrouze, Behrooze, Behruze

Beige (American) One who is tranquil
Bayge, Baige, Beyge, Baege

Beircheart (Anglo-Saxon) Of the intelligent army

Bekele (African) He has grown
Bekel, Bekelle, Bekell, Bekeel, Bekeal, Bekeil, Bekiel

Bela (Slavic) A white-skinned man
Belah, Bella, Bellah

Belay (African) A superior man
Belaye, Belai, Belae

Beldane (English) From the beautiful glen
Beldayn, Beldayne, Beldaen, Beldaene, Beldain, Beldaine

Belden (English) From the beautiful valley
Beldan, Beldon, Beldun, Beldin, Beldyn, Bellden, Belldan, Belldon, Belldun, Belldin, Belldyn, Beldene, Belldene

Belen (Greek) Of an arrow
Belin, Belyn, Belan, Belon, Belun

Belindo (English) A handsome and tender man
Belyndo, Belindio, Belyndio, Belindeo, Belyndeo, Belindiyo, Belyndiyo, Belindeyo, Belyndeyo

Belisario (Spanish) One who wields a sword
Belisareo, Belisarios, Belisarius, Belisareos, Belisareus

Bellamy (French) A handsome friend
Bellamey, Bellami, Bellamie, Bellamee, Bellumea, Bell, Belamy, Belamey, Belami, Belamie, Belamee, Belamea

Bellarmine (Italian) One who is hand-somely armed
Bellarmin, Bellarmeen, Bellarmeene, Bellarmean, Bellarmeane, Bellarmyn, Bellarmyne

Bello (African) One who helps others

Belton (English) From the beautiful town
Bellton, Beltun, Belltun, Belten, Bellten

Beluchi (African) God's approval
Beluchie, Beluchy, Beluchey, Beluchee, Beluchea

Belvedere (Italian) One who is beautiful to see
Bellveder, Bellvedere, Bellvidere, Belveder, Belvider, Belvidere

Belvin (American) Form of Melvin, meaning "a friend who offers counsel"
Belven, Belvyn, Belvon, Belvun, Belvan

Bem (African) A peaceful man

Bemossed (Native American) A walker

Bemus (Greek) The foundation
Beemus, Beamus, Bemis, Beemis, Beamis, Bemys, Beemys, Beamys

Ben (English) Form of Benjamin, meaning "son of the south; son of the right hand"
Benn, Benni, Bennie, Bennee, Benney, Benny, Bennea, Benno, Benji, Benjie, Benjy, Benjey, Benjee, Benjea

Benaiah (Hebrew) God has established
Benaia, Benaya, Benayah, Benayahu, Beniah

Benci (Hungarian) One who is blessed
Bencie, Bency, Bencey, Bencee, Bencea

Benedict (Latin) One who is blessed
Bendick, Bendict, Benedetto, Benedick, Benedicto, Benedictos, Benedictus, Benedikt, Benedikte, Bengt, Benicio, Benito, Bennedict, Bennedikt, Bennett, Benet, Benett, Bennet, Benoit, Bennito, Bennt, Bent, Bendek, Bendyk, Benes, Benneit

Benigno (Italian) One who is wellborn and kind
Benygno, Benignio, Benigneo, Benygnio, Benygneo

❍ Benjamin (Hebrew) Son of the south; son of the right hand
Benejamen, Beniamino, Benjaman, Benjamen, Benjamino, Benjamon, Benjiman, Benjimen, Benyamin, Benyamino, Binyamin, Binyamino

Benjiro (Japanese) One who enjoys peace
Benjyro

Benoni (Hebrew) The son of my sorrow
Benonie, Benony, Benoney, Benonee, Benonea

Benson (English) The son of Ben
Bensen, Bensun, Bensan, Bensin, Bensyn, Bensonand, Bense, Bence, Binse, Bince

Bentley (English) From the meadow of bent grass
Bently, Bentleigh, Bentlea, Bentleah, Bentlee, Bentli, Bentlie

Benton (English) From the town in the grassy place
Bentun, Benten, Bentan, Bentin, Bentyn

Benvenuto (Italian) One who is welcome

Beowulf (Anglo-Saxon) An intelligent wolf
Beowolf, Beowulfe, Beowolfe

Berdy (German) Having a brilliant mind
Berdey, Berdee, Berdea, Berdi, Berdie

Berend (German) As brave as a bear
Berand, Berind, Berynd, Berond, Berund, Behrend, Behrind, Behrynd, Behrand, Behrond, Behrund

Beresford (English) From the barley ford
Beresforde, Beresfurd, Beresfurde, Beresferd, Beresferde, Berford, Berforde, Berfurd, Berfurde, Berferd, Berferde

Berg (German) From the mountain
Bergh, Burg, Burgh

Bergen (Scandinavian) One who lives on the mountain; one who lives on the hill
Bergan, Bergin, Bergyn, Bergon, Bergun, Birgen, Birgan, Birgon, Birgun, Birgin, Birgyn

Berger (French) A shepherd
*Bergar, Bergor, Bergur, Bergir, Bergyr,
Bergeron, Bergeren, Bergeran, Bergerun,
Bergerin, Bergeryn*

Berilo (Spanish) Resembling a pale-green gem
Berillo, Berylo, Beryllo

Berkeley (English) From the meadow of birch trees
*Berkely, Berkeli, Berkelie, Berkelea, Berkeleah,
Berkelee, Berkeleigh, Berkley, Berkly,
Berkleigh, Berklee, Berklea, Berkleah, Berkli,
Berklie, Berk, Berke*

Berlin (German) From the borderline

Berlyn (German) The son of Berl
Burlyn

Bern (Scandinavian) Resembling a bear
*Berne, Berni, Bernie, Berny, Berney, Bernee,
Bernea, Bernis, Bernys*

Bernal (German) Having the strength of a bear
Bernald, Bernhald, Bernhold, Bernold, Bernol

Bernard (German) As strong and brave as a bear
*Barnard, Barnardo, Barnhard, Barnhardo,
Bearnard, Bernardo, Bernarr, Bernd, Berndt,
Bernhardo, Burnard, Bernadyn, Bernadin,
Bernaden, Benard, Benat*

Berry (English) Resembling a berry fruit
Berrey, Berri, Berrie, Berree, Berrea

Bert (English) One who is illustrious
*Berte, Berti, Bertie, Bertee, Bertea, Berty,
Bertey*

Berthold (German) Having bright strength
*Berthoud, Bertol, Bertoll, Bertold, Bertolde,
Bertell, Bertel, Bertill, Bertil, Bertyll, Bertyl,
Bertolt*

Berton (English) From the bright town
Bertan, Berten, Bertin, Bertyn, Bertun

Bertram (German) The renowned bright raven
*Beltran, Beltrano, Bertran, Bertrand,
Bertrando, Bertranno*

Berwin (English) A friend of the bear; a bright friend
*Berwine, Berwinn, Berwinne, Berwen,
Berwenn, Berwenne, Berwyn, Berwynn,
Berwynne*

Bethel (Hebrew) The house of God
*Bethell, Bethele, Bethelle, Betuel, Betuell,
Betuele, Betuelle*

Bevan (Welsh) The son of Evan
*Beavan, Beaven, Bev, Beven, Bevin, Bevon,
Bevvan, Bevvin, Bevvon, Bevun, Beavon,
Beavun, Bevvun, Beavin*

Beverly (English) From the beaver's stream
*Beverlee, Beverley, Beverlie, Beverli, Beverlee,
Beverleigh, Beverlea, Beverleah*

Bevis (Teutonic) An archer
*Beviss, Bevys, Bevyss, Beavis, Beaviss, Beavys,
Beavyss*

Biagio (Italian) One who has a stutter
Biaggio

Bickford (English) From the axman's ford
*Bickforde, Bickfurd, Bickfurde, Bickferd,
Bickferde, Biecaford*

Bienvenido (Spanish) One who is welcome
Beinvenido

Biff (American) A bully
Biffe, Bif, Byff, Byffe, Byf

Bill (English) Form of William, meaning "the determined protector"
*Byll, Billi, Billie, Billy, Billey, Billee, Billea,
Billeigh*

Birch (English) From the birch tree
Birche, Burche, Burch, Birk, Birke

Birchall (English) From the birch manor
Burchall, Birchell, Burchell

Birkett (English) From the birch headland
*Birket, Birkit, Birkitt, Burket, Burkett, Burkit,
Burkitt, Birkhead, Birkhed*

Birkey (English) From the island of birch trees
Birky, Birkee, Birkea, Birki, Birkie

Birney (English) From the island with the brook
Birny, Birnee, Birnea, Birni, Birnie

Birtle (English) From the bird hill
Bertle, Byrtle, Byrtel, Birtel

Bishop (English) A religious overseer
Byshop, Bishopp, Byshopp

Bjorn (Scandinavian) Resembling a bear
Björn, Bjorne, Bjarn, Bjarne

Black (English) A dark-skinned man
Blak, Blac, Blacke

Blackburn (English) From the dark brook
*Blackburne, Blackborn, Blackborne,
Blackbourn, Blackbourne*

Blackstone (English) Of the dark stone

Blackwell (English) From the dark spring
Blackwel, Blackwelle, Blackwele

Blade (English) One who wields a sword or
knife
Blayd, Blayde, Blaid, Blaide, Blaed, Blaede

Bladen (English) A hero
Bladan, Bladon, Bladun, Bladin, Bladyn

Blagden (English) From the dark valley
Blagdon, Blagdan, Blagdun, Blagdin, Blagdyn

Blaine (Scottish / Irish) A saint's servant /
a thin man
*Blayne, Blane, Blain, Blayn, Blaen, Blaene,
Blainy, Blainey, Blaini, Blainie, Blainee,
Blayni, Blaynie, Blaynee, Blayney, Blayny,
Blaeni, Blaenie, Blaeny, Blaeney, Blaenee*

Blair (Scottish) From the field of battle
Blaire, Blare, Blayre, Blaer, Blaere, Blayr

Blaise (French) One with a lisp or a stammer
*Blais, Blaisdell, Blaese, Blase, Blayse, Blaes,
Blays, Blasien, Blasius*

❍ **Blake** (English) A dark, handsome man
Blayk, Blayke, Blaik, Blaike, Blaek, Blaeke

Blakely (English) From the dark meadow
*Blakeley, Blakeli, Blakelie, Blakeleigh,
Blakelea, Blakeleah, Blakelee*

Blakeney (English) From the dark island
*Blakeny, Blakeni, Blakenie, Blakenee,
Blakenea*

Blanco (Spanish) A blonde-haired man; a
fair-skinned man
Bianco

Blandon (Latin) A gentle man; one who is
mild-tempered
*Blanden, Blandan, Blandin, Blandyn,
Blandun, Blantun, Blanton, Blantin, Blantyn,
Blanten, Blantan*

Blanford (English) From the gray-haired
man's ford
*Blanforde, Blanferd, Blanferde, Blanfurd,
Blanfurde, Blandford, Blandforde, Blandferd,
Blandferde, Blandfurd, Blandfurde*

Blaze (Latin / American) Form of Blaise,
meaning "one with a lisp or a stammer" /
a fiery man
Blaize, Blaiz, Blayze, Blayz, Blaez, Blaeze

Bliss (English) Filled with happiness
Blis, Blyss, Blys

Blondell (English) A fair-haired boy
Blondel, Blondele, Blondelle

Blythe (English) One who is cheerful and
carefree
*Blyth, Blith, Blithe, Bligh, Blighthe, Blighth,
Bly*

Bo (Chinese / Swedish) A precious son / a
lively man
Boe

Boaz (Hebrew) One who is swift
Boaze, Boas, Boase

Bob (English) Form of Robert, meaning
"one who is bright with fame"
Bobbi, Bobbie, Bobby, Bobbey, Bobbee, Bobbea

Boden (French / Scandinavian) One who
brings news; a herald / one who provides
shelter or is sheltered
*Beaudean, Bodie, Bodin, Bodine, Bowden,
Bowdin, Bowdyn, Bodyn, Bodi, Body, Bodey,
Bodee, Bodea*

Bogart (French) One who is strong with the
bow
*Bogaard, Bogaart, Bogaerd, Bogey, Bogie,
Bogi, Bogy, Bogee, Bogea, Boghart, Boghard*

Bolivar (Spanish) A mighty warrior
*Bolevar, Bolivarr, Bolevarr, Bollivar, Bollivarr,
Bollevar, Bollevarr*

Bolton (English) From the town with many
bends
*Boltin, Boltyn, Boltun, Boltan, Bolten,
Boulton, Boultan, Boulten, Boultun, Boultin,
Boultyn, Boalton, Boaltun, Boalten, Boaltin,
Boaltyn, Boaltan*

Bonamy (French) A good friend
*Bonamey, Bonami, Bonamie, Bonamee,
Bonamea*

Bonar (French) A gentleman; one who is mannerly
Bonnar, Bonor, Bonnor, Boner, Bonner, Bonur, Bonnur, Bonir, Bonnir, Bonyr, Bonnyr

Bonaventure (Latin) One who undertakes a blessed venture
Bonaventura, Buenaventure, Buenaventura, Bueaventure, Bueaventura

Bond (English) A peasant farmer
Bonde

Boniface (Latin) Having good fortune; one who is benevolent
Bonifacio, Bonifaceo, Bonifacius, Bonifacios, Bonifaco

Booker (English) One who binds books; a scribe
Bookar, Bookir, Bookyr, Bookur, Bookor

Boone (Latin) A good man
Boon

Booth (English) One who lives in a small hut
Boothe, Boot, Boote, Bothi, Bothe, Bothie, Bothy, Bothey, Bothee, Bothea

Borak (Arabic) Of the lightning
Borack, Borac

Bordan (English) From the boar's valley
Borden, Bordin, Bordyn, Bordon, Bordun

Borg (Scandinavian) From the castle
Borge, Borj, Borje

Boris (Slavic) A warrior; having battle glory
Boriss, Borys, Boryss, Borris, Borrys

Bosley (English) From the meadow near the forest
Bosly, Boslee, Boslea, Bosleah, Bosleigh, Bosli, Boslie, Bozley, Bozly, Bozlea, Bozleah, Bozleigh, Bozlee, Bozli, Bozlie

Boston (English) From the town near the forest; from the city of Boston
Bostun, Bostin, Bostyn, Bosten, Bostan

Boswell (English) From the spring near the forest
Boswel, Boswelle, Boswele

Bosworth (English) From the enclosure near the forest
Bosworthe

Botolf (English) The messenger wolf
Botolff, Botolph, Botulf, Botulff, Botulph

Bourbon (French) Resembling the liquor
Borbon, Bourban, Borban, Bourben, Borben, Bourbin, Borbin, Bourbyn, Borbyn, Bourbun, Borbun

Bourne (English) From the brook
Bourn, Born, Borne

Bouvier (Latin) Resembling an ox

Bowen (Welsh) The son of Owen
Bowon, Bowan, Bowun, Bowin, Bowyn

Bowie (Gaelic) A blonde-haired man
Bowi, Bowy, Bowey, Bowee, Bowea

Boyce (French) One who lives near the forest
Boice, Boyse, Boise

Boyd (Celtic) A blonde-haired man
Boyde, Boid, Boide, Boyden, Boydan, Boydin, Boydyn, Boydon, Boydun, Boiden, Boidan, Boidon, Boidun, Boidin, Boidyn

Boyne (Irish) Resembling a white cow
Boyn, Boin, Boine

Boynton (Irish) From the town near the river Boyne
Boyntun, Boynten, Boyntin, Boyntan, Boyntyn

Bracken (English) Resembling the large fern
Braken, Brackan, Brakan, Brackin, Brakin, Brackyn, Brakyn, Brackon, Brakon, Brackun, Brakun

Brad (English) One who has broad shoulders
Bradd

Bradburn (English) From the wide brook
Bradburne, Bradborn, Bradborne, Bradbourn, Bradbourne

Braddock (English) From the broadly spread oak
Bradock, Braddoc, Bradoc, Braddok, Bradok

Braden (Gaelic / English) Resembling salmon / from the wide valley
Bradan, Bradon, Braden, Bradin, Bradyn, Braddon, Braddan, Braddin, Braddyn, Bradden, Braedon, Braeden, Braedan, Braedin, Braedyn, Braidon, Braiden, Braidan, Braidin, Braidyn, Bradene

Bradford (English) From the wide ford
Bradforde, Bradferd, Bradferde, Bradfurd, Bradfurde

Bradley (English) From the wide meadow
Bradly, Bradlea, Bradleah, Bradlee, Bradleigh, Bradli, Bradlie

Brady (Irish) The son of a large-chested man
Bradey, Bradee, Bradea, Bradi, Bradie, Braidy, Braidey, Braidee, Braidea, Braidi, Braidie, Braydee, Braydea, Braydy, Braydey, Braydi, Braydie, Braedi, Braedie, Braedee, Braedea, Braedy, Braedey

Brainard (English) A brave raven
Braynard, Branard, Braenard, Brainerd, Braynerd, Braenerd, Branerd

Bram (Gaelic / Irish) Resembling a raven / a thicket of wild gorse
Brahm, Bramm, Brahmm, Brom, Brohm

Bramley (English) From the wild gorse meadow; from the raven's meadow
Bramly, Bramlee, Bramlea, Bramleah, Bramleigh, Bramli, Bramlie

Bramwell (English) From the bramble bush spring; from the raven's spring
Brammell, Bramwel, Bramwyll, Branwell, Branwill, Branwyll, Bramwill

Branch (Latin) An extension
Branche

Brand (English / Norse) A fiery torch / one who wields a sword
Brande, Brandell, Brander, Brando, Brant, Brandt, Brannt, Brantt, Brantli, Brantlie, Brantlea, Brantlee, Brantleigh, Brantly, Brantley

⊙
⊙ **Brandon** (English) From the broom or gorse hill
Brandun, Brandin, Brandyn, Brandan, Branden, Brannon, Brannun, Brannen, Brannan, Brannin, Brannyn

Branley (English) From the raven's meadow
Branly, Branli, Branlie, Branlee, Branleigh, Branlea, Branleah

Branson (English) The son of Brand or Brandon
Bransun, Bransen, Bransan, Bransin, Bransyn

Branton (English) From the broom or gorse town
Brantun, Brantin, Branten, Brantyn, Brantan, Branston, Branstun, Bransten, Branstin, Branstyn, Branstan

Braulio (Spanish) One who is glowing
Braulo, Brauleo, Brauliyo, Brauleyo, Bravilio, Braviliyo, Bravileo, Bravileyo, Bravlio, Bravleo

Braun (German) Having great strength
Braune, Brawn, Brawne, Brauni, Braunie, Brauny, Brauney, Braunee, Braunea, Brawni, Brawnie, Brawnee, Brawnea, Brawney, Brawny

Bravo (Italian) An excellent man
Brahvo, Bravoe, Bravow, Bravowe, Brahvoe, Bravvo

Brawley (English) From the meadow at the hillslope
Brawly, Brawli, Brawlie, Brawlea, Brawleah, Brawleigh, Brawlee, Brauly, Brauley, Brauli, Braulie, Braulea, Brauleah, Brauleigh, Braulee

Braxton (English) From Brock's town
Braxtun, Braxten, Braxtan, Braxtin, Braxtyn

Bray (English) One who cries out
Braye, Brai, Brae

⊙ **Brayden** (Gaelic / English) Form of Braden, meaning "resembling salmon / from the wide valley"
Braydon, Braydan, Braydin, Braydyn

Brazier (English) One who works with brass
Braiser, Bruser, Brayser, Braizer, Brazer, Braezer, Braeser, Brayzer

Brazil (English) From the country of Brazil
Brasil, Brazyl, Brasyl

Breck (Gaelic) One who has freckles
Brek, Brec, Brecken, Breckan, Breckin, Breckyn, Breckon, Breckun, Brexton, Brextun, Brextin, Brextyn, Brextan, Brexten

Bredon (Celtic) One who wields a sword
Bredan, Bredin, Bredyn, Breden, Bredun

Breen (Irish) From the fairy place
Breene, Brean, Breane, Brein, Breine

Breezy (American) A lighthearted man
Breeze, Breezey, Breezi, Breezie, Breezee, Breezea

Brendan (Irish) Born to royalty; a prince
Brendano, Brenden, Brendin, Brendon, Brendyn, Brendun

Brennan (Gaelic) A sorrowful man; a tear-drop
Brenan, Brenn, Brennen, Brennin, Brennon, Brennun, Brennyn, Brenin, Brenyn, Brenon, Brenun, Brenen

Brent (English) From the hill
Brendt, Brennt, Brentan, Brenten, Brentin, Brenton, Brentun, Brentyn, Brentt

Brentley (English) From the meadow near the hill
Brently, Brentlea, Brentleah, Brentleigh, Brentlee, Brentli, Brentlie

Brett (Latin) A man from Britain or Brittany
Bret, Breton, Brette, Bretton, Brit, Briton, Britt, Brittain, Brittan, Britte, Britton

Brewster (English) One who brews
Brewer, Brewstere

✿
ⓣ **Brian** (Gaelic / Celtic) Of noble birth / having great strength
*Briano, Briant, Brien, Brion, **Bryan**, Bryant, Bryen, Bryent, Bryon*

Briar (English) Resembling a thorny plant
Brier, Bryar, Bryer

Brice (Scottish / Anglo-Saxon) One who is speckled / the son of a nobleman
Bryce, Bricio, Brizio, Brycio, Bryzio

Brick (English) From the bridge
Bryck, Bric, Bryc, Brik, Bryk, Brickman, Brikman, Bricman, Bryckman, Brykman, Brycman, Bridger, Brydger, Briger, Bryger

Brigham (English) From the homestead near the bridge
Brigg, Briggham, Briggs

Brighton (English) From the town near the bridge
Brightun, Brighten, Brightin, Brightyn, Brightan

Brinley (English) From the burnt meadow
Brinly, Brinli, Brinlie, Brinleigh, Brinleu, Brinleah, Brinlee, Brindley, Brindly, Brindli, Brindlie, Brindleigh, Brindlea, Brindleah, Brindlee, Brynley, Brynly, Brynli, Brynlie, Brynleigh, Brynlea, Brynleah, Brynlee, Bryndley, Bryndly, Bryndli, Bryndlie, Bryndleigh, Bryndlea, Bryndleah, Bryndlee

Bristol (English) From the city in England
Brystol, Bristow, Brystow

Brock (English) Resembling a badger
Broc, Brok, Brocke, Brockman, Brokman, Brocman

Brockhoist (English) From the badger's den
Brokhoist, Brochoist

Brockley (English) From the badger meadow
Brockly, Brockli, Brocklie, Brocklea, Brockleah, Brocklee, Brockleigh

Brockton (English) From the badger town
Brokton, Brocton, Brocktun, Broktun, Broctun, Brockten, Brokten, Brocten, Brocktin, Broktin, Broctin, Brocktyn, Broktyn, Broctyn

Broderick (English) From the wide ridge
Broderik, Broderic, Brodrick, Brodryk, Brodryc, Brodrik, Brodric, Broderyck, Broderyc, Broderyk, Brodrig, Broderig

Brodie (Scottish) From the castle Brodie
Broden, Brodan, Brodin, Brodyn, Brodon, Brodun

✿ **Brody** (Gaelic) From the ditch
Brodey, Brodi, Brodie, Brodee, Brodea

Brogan (Gaelic) One who is sturdy; reliable
Broggan, Brogen, Broggen, Brogon, Broggon, Brogun, Broggun, Brogin, Broggin, Brogyn, Broggyn

Broin (Celtic) Resembling a raven
Broine, Broyn, Broyne

Bromley (English) From the broom meadow
Bromly, Bromli, Bromlie, Bromlee, Bromlea, Bromleah, Bromleigh, Broomli, Broomlie, Broomly, Broomley, Broomleigh, Broomlea, Broomleah, Broomlee

Bromwell (English) From the spring where the broom grows
Bromwel, Bromwill, Bromwil, Bromwyll, Bromwyl

Bronco (Spanish) Resembling an unbroken horse
Bronko, Broncko

Bronson (English) The son of Brown
Bronnson, Bronsen, Bronsin, Bronsonn, Bronsson, Bronsun, Bronnsun, Bronssun, Bronsenn, Bronssen, Bronsinn, Bronssin

Brooks (English) From the running stream
Brookes, Brook, Brooke

Brookson (English) The son of Brooks
Brooksen, Brooksun, Brooksone, Brooksan, Brooksin, Brooksyn

Broughton (English) From the fortress town
Broughtun, Broughten, Broughtin, Broughtyn, Broughtan

Brown (English) One who has a russet complexion
Browne, Broun, Broune, Brun, Bron, Brune, Brone

Bruce (Scottish) A man from Brieuse; one who is wellborn; from an influential family
Brouce, Brooce, Bruci, Brucie, Brucey, Brucy, Brucee, Brucea

Bruno (German) A brown-haired man
Brunoh, Brunoe, Brunow, Brunowe, Bruin, Bruine, Brunon, Brunun, Brunen, Brunan, Brunin, Brunyn, Bruino

Brunswick (German) From Bruno's village
Brunswic, Brunswik, Brunswyck, Brunswyc, Brunswyk

Brutus (Latin) A dull-witted man
Bruto

Bryn (Welsh) From the hill
Brinn, Brin, Brynn

Brynmor (Welsh) From the large hill
Brynmore, Brinmor, Brinmore, Brynnmor, Brynnmore, Brinnmor, Brinnmore

Bryson (Welsh) The son of Brice
Brysen, Brysin, Brysun, Brysyn, Brycen, Brycin, Brycyn, Brycun

Buagh (Irish) A victorious man
Buach

Bubba (German) A boy
Buba, Bubbah, Bubah

Buck (English) Resembling a male deer
Buk, Buc, Bucki, Buckie, Bucky, Buckey, Buckee, Buckea

Buckley (English) From the deer meadow
Buckly, Buckli, Bucklie, Bucklea, Buckleah, Bucklee, Buckleigh

Buckminster (English) From the monastery where deer live
Buckmynster

Bud (English) One who is brotherly
Budd, Buddi, Buddie, Buddee, Buddea, Buddey, Buddy

Buddha (Sanskrit) One who has achieved spiritual enlightenment

Budha (Hindi) Another name for the planet Mercury
Budhan, Budhwar

Budhil (Indian) A learned man
Budheel, Budheal, Budheil, Budhiel, Budhyl

Buell (German) One who lives on a hill
Buel, Bueller, Buhl, Buhler, Buehl, Buehler

Bulat (Russian) Having great strength
Bulatt

Bundar (Arabic) One who is smart and wealthy
Bunder, Bundor, Bundur, Bundir, Bundyr

Bundy (English) A free man
Bundey, Bundi, Bundie, Bundee, Bundea

Bunmi (African) My gift
Bunmie, Bunmy, Bunmey, Bunmee, Bunmea

Burbank (English) From the riverbank of burrs
Burrbank, Burhbank

Burchard (English) As strong as a castle
Bucardo, Burckhardt, Burgard, Burgaud, Burkhart, Burckhart, Burkhardt

Burdett (English) Resembling a bird
Burdet, Burdette, Burdete

Burdon (English) One who lives at the castle
Burdun, Burdan, Burden, Burdin, Burdyn,
Burhdon, Burhdun, Burhden, Burhdan,
Burhdin, Burhdyn

Burford (English) From the castle near the
ford
Burforde, Burfurd, Burfurde, Burferd,
Burferde, Buford, Buforde, Bufurd, Bufurde,
Buferd, Buferde

Burgess (German) A free citizen of the
town
Burges, Burgiss, Burgis, Burgyss, Burgys,
Burgeis

Burke (French) From the fortress on the hill
Berk, Berke, Birk, Bourke, Burk, Birke, Bourk,
Byrk, Byrke

Burl (English) From the knotted wood
Burle, Burrel, Burrell, Burell, Burel

Burleigh (English) From the meadow of
knotted wood
Burlea, Burleah, Burlee, Burli, Burlie, Burley,
Burly, Byrleigh, Byrlea, Byrleah, Byrli, Byrlie,
Byrly, Byrley, Byrlee

Burnaby (Norse) From the warrior's estate
Burnabey, Burnabi, Burnabie, Burnabee,
Burnabea

Burne (English) Resembling a bear; from
the brook; the brown-haired one
Burn, Beirne, Burnis, Byrn, Byrne, Burns,
Byrnes

Burnell (French) The small brown-haired
one
Burnel, Burnelle, Burnele, Brunell, Brunel,
Brunele, Brunelle

Burnet (French) Having brown hair
Burnett, Burnete, Burnette, Bernet, Bernett,
Bernete, Bernette

Burney (English) From the island with the
brook
Burny, Burnee, Burnea, Burni, Burnie,
Beirney, Beirnie, Beirny, Beirni, Beirnee,
Beirnea, Burneig, Beirnig

Burr (English) A bristle

Burt (English) From the fortress
Burte, Burtt

Burton (English) From the fortified town
Burtun, Burten, Burtin, Burtyn, Burtan

Busby (Scottish) From the village near the
thicket
Busbey, Busbee, Busbea, Busbi, Busbie, Bussby,
Bussbey, Bussbi, Bussbie, Bussbee, Bussbea

Butch (American) A manly man
Butcher

Butler (English) The keeper of the bottles
(wine, liquor)
Buttler, Butlar, Buttlar, Butlor, Buttlor,
Butlir, Buttlir, Butlyr, Buttlyr

Buzz (Scottish) A popular young man
Buzze, Buzzi, Buzzy, Buzzee, Buzzea,
Buzzy, Buzzey

Bwana (Swahili) A gentleman
Bwanah

Byford (English) One who lives near the ford
Byforde, Byferd, Byferde, Byfurd, Byfurde

Byrd (English) Resembling a bird
Byrde, Bird, Birde, Byrdi, Byrdie, Byrdee,
Byrdea, Byrdy, Byrdey, Birdi, Birdie, Birdee,
Birdea, Birdey, Birdy

Byron (English) One who lives near the cow
sheds
Byrom, Beyren, Beyron, Biren, Biron, Buiron,
Byram, Byran, Byren, Byrem, Byrun, Byrum

C

Cabalero (Spanish) A horseman or a knight
Caballero, Cabaliero, Caballiero, Cabalerio,
Caballerio, Cabalereo, Caballareo

Cable (French) One who makes rope
Cabel, Caibel, Caible, Caybel, Cayble, Caebel,
Caeble, Cabe

Cabot (French) One who sails
Cabbot

Cabrera (Spanish) An able-bodied man
Cabrere, Cabrero, Cabrerio, Cabreriyo,
Cabrereo, Cabrereyo

Cack (American) Full of laughter
*Cak, Cac, Cackie, Cacki, Cacky, Cackey,
Cackee, Cackea*

Cactus (American) Resembling the prickly
plant
Caktus, Cucklus

Cadarn (Welsh) Having great strength
Cadern, Cadorn, Cadurn, Cadirn, Cadyrn

Cadby (English) From the warrior's settlement
Cadbey, Cadbee, Cadbea, Cadbi, Cadbie

Cadda (English) A warring man
Cada, Caddah, Cadah

Caddarik (English) A leader during battle
*Caddarick, Caddaric, Caddaryk, Caddaryck,
Caddaryc, Cadarik, Cadarick, Cadaric,
Cadaryk, Cadaryck, Cadaryc*

Caddis (English) Resembling a worsted fabric
Caddys, Caddiss, Caddice, Caddyss

Caddock (Welsh) One who is eager for war
Caddoc, Caddok, Caddog

Cade (English / French) One who is round /
of the cask
*Caid, Caide, Cayd, Cayde, Caed, Caede,
Caden, Cayden, Caiden, Caeden, Cadon,
Caydon, Caedon, Caidon, Cadan, Caydan,
Caedan, Caidan, Cadin, Caedin, Caydin,
Caidin, Cadyn, Caedyn, Caydyn, Caidyn*

Cadell (Welsh) Having the spirit of battle
Cadel, Caddell, Caddel

Caden (Welsh) Spirt of battle

Cadence (Latin) Rhythmic and melodious; a
musical man
*Cadenze, Cadense, Cadian, Cadienne,
Cadince, Cadiene, Caydence, Cadinse,
Caidence, Caidense, Caidenze, Caydense,
Caydenze, Caedence, Caedense, Caedenze*

Cadman (Welsh) A wise warrior
*Cadmon, Cadmun, Cadmin, Cadmyn,
Cadmen, Caedman, Caedmon, Caedmun,
Caedmin, Caedmyn, Caedmen, Caydman,
Caydmon, Caydmun, Caydmen, Caydmin,
Caydmyn, Caidmun, Caidmon, Caidmun,
Caidmen, Caidmin, Caidmyn*

Cadmus (Greek) A man from the East; in
mythology, the man who founded Thebes
Cadmar, Cadmo, Cadmos, Cadmuss

Cadogan (Welsh) Having glory and honor
during battle
*Cadogawn, Cadwgan, Cadwgawn, Cadogaun,
Cadwgaun*

Caduceus (Greek) The symbol of the medical
profession; in mythology, Hermes's insignia
*Caduseus, Caducius, Cadusius, Caducios,
Cadusios*

Caelan (Gaelic) A slender warrior; one who
is slender and fair
*Cailan, Caylan, Calan, Caelen, Cailen,
Caylen, Calen, Cailon, Caylon, Caelon,
Calon, Cailin, Caylin, Caelin, Calin, Cailyn,
Caelyn, Caylyn, Calyn*

Caellum (Celtic) A brave warrior
Caellom, Caillum, Caillom, Cayllom, Cayllum

Caesar (Latin) An emperor; having a full
head of hair
*Caezar, Casar, César, Cesar, Cesare, Cesaro,
Cesario, Cezar, Chezare, Caesarius, Ceasar,
Ceazer, Ceasario*

Caflice (Anglo-Saxon) A brave man
Caflyce, Caflise, Caflyse

Cahal (Celtic) One who is strong in battle
Cahall, Cahale, Cahalle

Cahil (Turkish) A young boy
Cahyl, Caheel, Caheal, Caheil, Cahiel

Cahir (Irish) A mighty warrior
Caheer, Cahear, Cahier, Caheir, Cahyr

Cain (Hebrew) One who wields a spear;
something acquired; in the Bible, Adam
and Eve's first son, who killed his brother
Abel
Cayn, Caen, Cane, Caine, Cayne, Caene

Caindale (English) From the valley with the
clear river
*Caindail, Caindayl, Caindaile, Caindayle,
Caindell, Cayndale, Cayndail, Cayndaile,
Cayndayl, Cayndayle, Cayndell, Caendail,
Caendaile, Caendale, Caendayl, Caendayle,
Caendell, Canedell, Canedail, Canedaile,
Canedayl, Canedayle, Canedale*

Caird (Scottish) A traveling metal worker
Cairde, Cayrd, Cayrde, Caerd, Caerde

Cairn (Gaelic) From the mound of rocks
Cairne, Cairns, Caern, Caerne, Caernes

Cairo (Arabic) One who is victorious; from the capital of Egypt

Cais (Vietnamese) One who rejoices

Caith (Irish) Of the battlefield
Caithe, Cayth, Caythe, Cathe, Caeth, Caethe

Caius (Latin) One who rejoices
Cai, Caio

Cajetan (English) A man from Gaeta
Cajetano, Cajetanio, Cajetaneo

Calbert (English) A cowboy
Calberte, Calburt, Calburte, Calbirt, Calbirte, Calbyrt, Calbyrte

Calder (Scottish) Of the rough waters or stream
Caldar, Caldor, Caldur, Caldir, Caldyr, Caldre

Caldwell (English) From the cold spring
Cadwell, Caldwel, Cadwel

Cale (English) Form of Charles, meaning "one who is manly and strong / a free man"
Cail, Caile, Cayl, Cayle, Cael, Caele

❂
❂ **Caleb** (Hebrew) Resembling a dog
Cayleb, Caileb, Caeleb, Calob, Cailob, Caylob, Caelob

Caley (Gaelic) One who is lean
Caly, Cali, Calie, Caleigh, Calee, Calea, Cailey, Caily, Cailee, Cailea, Caileigh, Caili, Cailie, Cayley, Cayly, Caylee, Cayleigh, Caylea, Cayli, Caylie, Caeley, Caely, Caelee, Caeleigh, Caelea, Caeli, Caelie

Calhoun (Gaelic) From the narrow forest
Callhoun, Colhoun, Colquhoun, Coillcumhann

Calian (Native American) A warrior of life
Calien, Calyan, Calyen

Calibur (English) Form of Excalibur, in mythology, King Arthur's sword
Calibor, Caliborn, Caliborne, Calibourn, Calibourne, Caliburn, Caliburne

Calix (Greek) A handsome man
Calyx, Calex, Calax, Calox, Calux

Callis (Latin) Resembling a chalice
Callys, Callice, Callyce, Callyx

Calogero (Italian) Of fair old age
Calogeros, Calogerus, Calogerio, Calogereo

Calum (Gaelic) Resembling a dove
Callum, Calom, Callom

Calumet (French) Resembling a reed
Callumet

Calvagh (Irish) One who is bald
Calvaugh, Callough

Calvert (English) One who herds cows; a cowboy
Calbert, Calvirt, Calbirt, Calvurt, Calburt, Calvex

Calvin (French) The little bald one
Calvyn, Calvon, Calven, Calvan, Calvun, Calvino, Calvinio, Calvineo, Cal

Camara (African) One who teaches others

Camden (Gaelic) From the winding valley
Camdene, Camdin, Camdyn, Camdan, Camdon, Camdun

Cameo (English) A small, perfect child
Cammeo

❂
❂ **Cameron** (Scottish) Having a crooked nose
Cameren, Cameran, Camerin, Cameryn, Camerun, Camron, Camren, Camran, Camrin, Camryn, Camrun, Cameroon, Camero, Camaeron, Camri, Camrie, Camry, Camrey, Camree, Camrea, Cam, Camy, Camey, Camee, Camea, Cami, Camie

Camilo (Latin) One who is born free; one who is noble
Camillo, Camylo, Camyllo, Camillus, Camyllus

Campbell (Scottish) Having a crooked mouth
Campbel, Cambell, Cambel, Camp, Campe, Cambeul, Cambeull, Campbeul, Campbeull

Campion (English) The champion
Campian, Campien, Campiun

Can (Turkish) One who is dearly loved

Canby (English) From the farm near the reeds
Canbey, Canbi, Canbie, Canbee, Canbea

Candan (Turkish) A sincere man
Canden, Candin, Candyn, Candon, Candun

Candelario (Spanish) Refers to the feast of Candlemas
Candelareo, Candelaro, Candelerio, Candelero, Candelariyo, Candelareyo

Candido (Latin) One who is white; pure; chaste
Candide, Candidio, Candideo, Candydo, Candyde, Candydio, Candydeo

Canfield (English) From the field of reeds
Canfeld, Cannfield, Cannfeld

Canh (Vietnamese) Of the endless environment

Canice (Irish) A handsome man
Canyce, Canis, Caniss, Cunys, Canyss, Canicius, Cainneach

Cannon (French) An official of the church
Canon, Canning, Caning, Cannyng, Canyng, Cannan, Canan, Cannun, Canun

Canute (Scandinavian) A knot
Cnute, Cnut

Canyon (Spanish / English) From the footpath / from the deep ravine
Cuniyon, Canyun, Caniyun

Caolan (Irish) A lean man
Caolen, Caolin, Caolyn, Caolun, Caolon

Capek (Czech) Resembling a small stork
Capec, Capeck

Capp (French) A chaplain
Cap, Capps, Caps

Capricorn (Latin) The tenth sign of the zodiac; the goat

Car (Celtic) A warrior

Caradoc (Welsh) One who is much loved
Caradok, Caradock, Caradog, Caradawc, Caradawk, Caradawck, Caradawg

Carbry (Celtic) One who drives a chariot
Carbrey, Carbri, Carbrie, Carbree, Carbrea

Carden (English) One who cards wool
Cardan, Cardin, Cardyn, Cardon, Cardun, Card, Carde

Cardew (Celtic) From the dark fortress
Cardou, Cardu, Cardoo

Carew (Latin) Of the chariot
Carewe, Crew, Crewe

Cargan (Gaelic) From the small rock
Cargen, Cargon, Cargun, Cargin, Cargyn

Carl (German) Form of Karl, meaning "a free man"
Carel, Carlan, Carle, Carlens, Carlitis, Carlin, Carlo, Carrel, Carol, Caroly, Carlen, Caarl, Caarlo, Carlis, Carlys, Carroll, Carolus, Carrol, Caroll, Caryl, Caryll

Carley (English) From the farmer's meadow
Carly, Carli, Carlie, Carleigh, Carlea, Carleah

Carlomagno (Spanish) Charles the great
Carlmagno, Carlemagno

❷ **Carlos** (Spanish) Form of Karl, meaning "a free man"
Carolos, Carolo, Carlito

Carlow (Ireland) From a town in Ireland
Carlowe, Carloe

Carlsen (Scandinavian) The son of Carl
Carlssen, Carlson, Carlsson, Carlsun, Carllsun, Carlsin, Carllsin, Carlsyn, Carllsyn

Carlton (English) From the free man's town
Carltun, Carltown, Carston, Carstun, Carstown, Carleton, Carletun, Carlten, Carsten, Carleten

Carlyle (English) From the fort at Luguvalium
Carlile, Carlisle

Carmelo (Hebrew) From the fruitful orchard
Carmello, Carmel, Carmeli, Carmelie, Carmely, Carmeley, Carmelee, Carmelea, Carmeleigh, Carmi, Carmie, Carmee, Carmea, Carmy, Carmey

Carmichael (Scottish) A follower of Michael

Carmine (Latin / Aramaic) A beautiful song / the color crimson
Carman, Carmen, Carmin, Carmino, Carmyne, Carmon, Carmun, Carmyn

Carnell (English) The defender of the castle
Carnel, Carnele, Carnelle, Carne, Carn

Carney (Irish) The victor
Cearnach, Carny, Carni, Carnie, Carnee, Carnea

Carnig (Armenian) Resembling a lamb
Carnigg, Carnyg, Carnygg

Carollan (Irish) The little champion
*Carolan, Carollen, Carolen, Carollin, Carolin,
Carollyn, Carolyn*

Carpenter (Latin) One who makes carriages
*Carpentar, Carpentor, Carpentur, Carpentir,
Carpentyr, Charpentier*

Carr (Scandinavian) From the swampy place
Carre

Carrick (Irish) From the rocks
*Carrik, Carric, Carryck, Carryk, Carryc,
Carick, Carik, Caric, Caryc, Caryk, Caryck*

Carrington (English) From the rocky town
*Carryngton, Carringtun, Carryngtun,
Carringten, Carryngten*

❂ **Carson** (Scottish) The son of a marsh dweller
Carsen, Carsun, Carsan, Carsin, Carsyn

Carswell (English) From the watercress spring
*Carswel, Caswell, Caswel, Cresswell, Creswell,
Creswel, Cresswel*

❂ **Carter** (English) One who transports goods;
one who drives a cart
*Cartar, Cartir, Cartyr, Cartor, Cartur,
Cartere, Cartier, Cartrell, Cartrel*

Cartland (English) From Carter's land
Carteland, Cartlan, Cartlend, Cartelend, Cartlen

Carvell (French) From the village near the
swamp
*Carvelle, Carvel, Carvele, Carvil, Carvile,
Carville, Carvill*

Carver (English) One who carves wood
Carvar, Carvor, Carvir, Carvyr, Carvur

Cary (Celtic / Welsh / Gaelic) From the river /
from the fort on the hill / having dark features
*Carey, Cari, Carie, Caree, Carea, Carry,
Carrey, Carri, Carrie, Carree, Carrea*

Case (French) Refers to a chest or box
Cace

Casey (Gaelic) One who is alert; watchful
*Casy, Casi, Casie, Casee, Cacey, Cacy, Caci,
Cacie, Cacee, Caycey, Caycy, Cayci, Caycie,
Caycee, Caicey, Caicy, Caici, Caicie, Caicee,
Caysey, Caysy, Caysi, Caysie, Caysee, Caisey,
Caisy, Caisi, Caisie, Caisee*

Casimir (Slavic) One who demands peace
*Casimeer, Casmire, Casimiro, Casmir,
Casimear, Casimyr, Casimeir, Casimier*

Caspar (Persian) The keeper of the treasure
Casper, Caspur, Caspor, Caspir, Caspyr

Caspian (English) From the sea
Caspien, Caspion, Caspiun

Cassander (Spanish) A brother of heroes
*Casander, Casandro, Cassandro, Casandero,
Cassandero*

Cassidy (Gaelic / Irish / Welsh) A clever man /
a curly-haired man / one who is ingenious
*Cassidey, Cassidi, Cassidie, Cassidee, Cassady,
Cassadey, Cassadi, Cassadie, Cassadee,
Cassedy, Cassedey, Cassedi, Cassedie, Cassedee,
Cass*

Cassiel (Hebrew) The name of an archangel
Cassiell, Casiel, Casiell

Cassius (Latin) One who is empty; hollow;
vain
*Cassios, Cassio, Cach, Cache, Cashus, Cashos,
Cassian, Cassien, Cassianus*

Castel (Spanish) From the castle
*Castell, Castal, Castall, Castol, Castoll,
Castul, Castull, Castil, Castill, Castyl, Castyll*

Castor (Greek) Resembling a beaver; in
mythology, one of the Dioscuri
*Castur, Caster, Castar, Castir, Castyr,
Castorio, Castoreo, Castoro, Castro*

Cat (American) Resembling the animal
Catt, Chait, Chaite

Cathair (Celtic) A fighter
*Cathaire, Cathayr, Cathayre, Cathaer,
Cathaere, Cathare, Cathaoir*

Cathal (Gaelic) The ruler of the battle
Cathel, Cathol, Cathul, Cathil, Cathyl

Cathan (American) Form of Nathan, mean-
ing "a gift from God"
*Caithan, Cathun, Cathon, Cathen, Caithun,
Caithon, Caithen, Caethan, Caethun,
Caethon, Caethen, Caythan, Caythun,
Caython, Caythen*

Cathmore (Irish) A renowned fighter
Cathmor, Cathemore, Cathemor

Catlin (Irish) One who is pure; chaste
*Catlon, Catlyn, Catlun, Catalin, Catalyn,
Catalen, Catalan, Catlen, Catlan, Catalon,
Catalun*

Cato (Latin) One who is all-knowing
Cayto, Caito, Caeto

Caton (Spanish) One who is knowledgable
Caten, Catun, Catan, Catin, Catyn

Catori (Native American) A spiritual man
Catorie, Catory, Catorey, Catoree, Catorea

Cauley (Scottish) A righteous man; a relic
*Cauly, Caulee, Cauleigh, Caulea, Cauli,
Caulie, Cawley, Cawly, Cawleigh, Cawlee,
Cawlea, Cawli, Cawlie*

Cavan (Gaelic) A handsome man
Caven, Cavin, Cavyn, Cavon, Cavun

Cavanagh (Irish) A follower of Kevin
Cavanaugh, Cavanaw, Cavanawe

Cavell (Teutonic) One who is bold
Cavel, Cavele, Cavelle

Caxton (English) From the lump settlement
Caxtun, Caxten

Ceallach (Irish) A bright-headed man
Ceallachan

Ceard (Scottish) A smith
Ceardach

Ceastun (English) From the army camp
*Ceaston, Ceasten, Ceastan, Ceastin, Ceastyn,
Ceaster, Ceastar, Ceastor, Ceastir, Ceastyr,
Ceastur*

Cecil (Latin / Welsh) One who is blind / the
sixth-born child
Cecilio, Cecilius, Celio

Cedric (Welsh) One who is kind and loved;
of the spectacular bounty
*Caddaric, Ced, Cedrick, Cedrik, Cedryc,
Cedryk, Cedryck*

Cedro (Spanish) Form of Isadoro, meaning
"a gift of Isis"
*Cedroe, Cedrow, Cedrowe, Cidro, Cidroe,
Cidrow, Cidrowe*

Celesto (Latin) From heaven
*Célestine, Celestino, Celindo, Celestyne,
Celestyno*

Celso (Italian) One who is lofty
Celsius, Celsus

Cendrick (English / Gaelic) A royal ruler /
the champion
*Cendric, Cendricks, Cendrik, Cendrix, Cendryck,
Cenrick, Cenrik, Cenricks, Cendryk, Cendryc,
Cenric, Cendriek, Cendryek, Cenrich, Cendrich,
Cenriek, Cenryk, Cynric, Cynrick, Cynrik,
Cynrich, Cyneric, Cynerik, Cynerick, Cynerich*

Cenehard (English) A bold guardian
Cenhard, Cynhard, Cynehard

Cenewig (English) A bold warrior
Cenwig, Cenwyg, Cenewyg

Cephas (Hebrew) As solid as a rock

Cerdic (Anglo-Saxon) A king
Cerdick, Cerdik, Cerdyc, Cerdyck

Cermak (Czech) Resembling a robin
Cermac, Cermack

Cerny (Czech) A black-haired man
Cerney, Cerni, Cernie, Cernee, Cernea

Cerys (Welsh) One who is dearly loved
Ceris, Ceryss, Ceriss

Cestmir (Slavic) From the fortress
*Cestmeer, Cestmear, Cestmeir, Cestmier,
Cestmyr*

Chacha (African) Having great strength

Chad (English) One who is warlike
*Chaddie, Chadd, Chadric, Chadrick, Chadrik,
Chadryck, Chadryc, Chadryk*

Chadburn (English) From the warrior's
stream
*Chadburne, Chadborn, Chadborne,
Chadbourn, Chadbourne, Chadbyrn,
Chadbyrne*

Chadwick (English) From Chad's dairy farm
*Chadwik, Chadwic, Chadwyck, Chadwyk,
Chadwyc*

Chael (Latin) A heavenly messenger; an
angel
Chaele

Chagai (Hebrew) One who meditates

Chai (Hebrew) A giver of life
Chaika, Chaim, Cahyim, Cahyyam

Chairo (Spanish) Having a sacred name
Chiro

Chaka (African) A great king
Chakah

Chakra (Arabic) A center of spiritual energy

Chale (Spanish) A strong man
Chail, Chaile, Chael, Chaele, Chayl, Chayle

Chalkley (English) From the chalk meadow
Chalkly, Chalkleigh, Chalklee, Chalkleah, Chalkli, Chalklie, Chalklea

Chalmers (French) A chamber servant
Chalmer, Chamber, Chambers, Chalmar, Chalmars

Chamberlain (English) The chief officer of the noble's household
Chambellan, Chamberlin, Chamberlyn, Chamberlen

Champion (English) A warrior; the victor
Champeon, Champiun, Champeun, Champ

Chan (Spanish / Sanskrit) Form of John, meaning "God is gracious" / a shining man
Chayo, Chano, Chawn, Chaun

Chanan (Hebrew) God is compassionate
Chanen, Chanin, Chanyn, Chanun, Chanon

Chance (English) Having good fortune
Chanse, Chantz, Chanze, Chaunce, Chancey, Chancy, Chanci, Chancie, Chancee, Chancea

Chancellor (French) The office holder; the keeper of the records
Chancelor, Chansellor, Chanselor, Chauncellor, Chauncelor, Chaunsellor, Chaunselor, Chanceller, Chanceler, Chanseller, Chanseler, Chaunceller, Chaunceler, Chaunsellor, Chaunseler

Chand (Hindi) Born beneath the moon's light
Chande, Chandak, Chandan

Chandler (English) One who makes candles
Chandlar, Chandlor, Chandlur, Chandlir, Chandlyr

Chaney (French) From the oak tree
Chany, Chani, Chanie, Chanee, Chanea, Chalney, Chalny, Chalni, Chalnie, Chalnee, Cheney, Cheny, Cheni, Chenie, Chenee

Chang (Chinese) One who is unhindered

Chaniel (Hebrew) The grace of God
Chanyel, Chaniell, Chanyell

Chann (English) Resembling a young wolf
Channe, Channon, Channun, Channen, Channan, Channin, Channyn, Channer, Channar, Channir, Channor, Channur, Channyr

Channing (French / English) An official of the church / resembling a young wolf
Channyng, Canning, Cannyng

Chanoch (Hebrew) A dedicated man
Channoch, Chanok, Chanoc, Chanock, Channok, Channoc, Channock

Chansomps (Native American) Resembling a locust

Chantry (French) One who sings
Chantrey, Chantri, Chantrie, Chantree, Chantrea

Chao (Chinese) The great one

Chapal (Indian) One who is quick

Chaparral (Spanish) From the dwarf oak
Chaparrall, Chaparal, Chaparall

Chaplin (English) A secretary; a spiritual guide
Chaplain, Chaplinn, Chaplyn, Chappelin, Chappelyn

Chapman (English) A merchant; a peddler
Chapmann, Chap, Chappy, Chappi, Chappey, Chappie, Chappee

Chappel (English) One who works in the chapel
Capel, Capell, Capello, Cappel, Chappell

❂ **Charles** (English / German) One who is manly and strong / a free man
Charls, Chas, Charli, Charlie, Charley, Charly, Charlee, Charleigh, Charlea, Chaz, Chazz, Chars

Charleson (English) The son of Charles
Charlesen, Charlesin, Charlesyn, Charlesan,
Charlesun

Charlot (French) The son of Charlemagne

Charlton (English) From the free man's town
Churleton, Charltun, Charletun, Charleston,
Charlestun

Charro (Spanish) A cowboy
Charo

❍ **Chase** (English) A huntsman
❶ *Chace, Chasen, Chayce, Chayse, Chaise,*
Chaice, Chaece, Chaese, Chacen, Chaycen,
Chaysen, Chaisen, Chaicen, Chaecen,
Chaesen, Chaseyn, Chayson, Chaison,
Chaeson, Chason

Chatwin (English) A warring friend
Chatwine, Chatwinn, Chatwinne, Chatwen,
Chatwenn, Chatwenne, Chatwyn, Chatwynn,
Chatwynne

Chauncey (French / English) An office
holder; keeper of records / having good
fortune
Chauncy, Chaunci, Chauncie, Chauncee,
Chaunsey, Chaunsy, Chaunsie, Chaunsi,
Chaunsee, Chawncey, Chawncy, Chawnci,
Chawncie, Chawncee, Chawnsey, Chawnsy,
Chawnsi, Chawnsie, Chawnsee

Chavez (Spanish) A dream maker
Chaves

Chaviv (Hebrew) One who is dearly loved
Chaveev, Chaveav, Chaviev, Chaveiv, Chavyv,
Chavivi, Chavivie, Chavivy, Chavivey,
Chavivee

Chay (Gaelic) From the fairy place
Chaye, Chae

Chayim (Hebrew) A giver of life
Chayem

Chayton (Native American) Resembling a
falcon
Chaiton, Chaeton, Chaton, Chayten, Chaiten,
Chaeten, Chaten

Che (Spanish) Form of José, meaning "God
will add"
Chepe, Chepito

Cheikh (African) A learned man

Chelsey (English) From the landing place
for chalk
Chelsee, Chelseigh, Chelsea, Chelsi, Chelsie,
Chelsy, Chelcey, Chelcy, Chelci, Chelcie,
Chelcee, Chelcea

Chen (Hebrew / Chinese) Having grace or
favor / of the dawn

Cherokee (Native American) A tribal name
Cheroki, Cherokie, Cherokey, Cheroky,
Cherokeigh, Cherokea, Cherokeah

Cherut (Hebrew) One who is free
Cheroot, Cherout, Cherute, Cheroote,
Cheroute

Cheslav (Russian) From the fortified camp
Cheslaw

Chesley (English) From the meadow
Chesli, Cheslie, Chesly, Chesleigh, Cheslea,
Chesleah, Cheslee

Chesmu (Native American) A gritty man
Chesmue, Chesmew, Chesmoo

Chesney (English) One who promotes
peace
Chesny, Chesni, Chesnie, Chesnea, Chesneah,
Chesnee

Chester (Latin) From the camp of the sol-
diers
Chet, Chess, Cheston, Chestar, Chestor,
Chestur, Chestir, Chestyr

Chetwin (English) From the cottage on the
winding lane
Chetwen, Chetwyn, Chetwynd, Chetwynn,
Chetwenn, Chetwinn

Cheung (Chinese) Having good fortune

Chevalier (French) A knight or horseman
Cheval, Chevall, Chevy, Chevi, Chevey,
Chevie, Chevce, Chevea, Chevel, Chevell

Cheveyo (Native American) A spirit warrior

Cheyenne (Native American) Of the tribe of
the Great Plains; of the unintelligible speakers
Cheyann, Cheyen, Cheyan, Chian, Chiann,
Chayan, Chayann

Cheyne (French) An oak-hearted man
Chane, Cheyn, Chain, Chaine, Chayn,
Chayne, Chaen, Chaene

Chi (Chinese) Life energy

Chiamaka (African) The splendor of God

Chibale (African) A kinship
Chibail, Chibaile, Chibael, Chibaele, Chibayl, Chibayle, Chybale, Chybail, Chybaile, Chybael, Chybaele, Chybayl, Chybayle

Chicahua (Nahuatl) Having great strength

Chicha (African) One who is dearly loved
Chicah, Chyca, Chycah

Chick (English) Form of Charles, meaning "one who is manly and strong / a free man"
Chik, Chicki, Chickie, Chicky, Chickey, Chickee, Chickea, Chic

Chico (Spanish) A boy; a lad

Chidi (African) God exists
Chidie, Chidy, Chidey, Chidee, Chidea, Chydi, Chydie, Chydee, Chydea, Chydy, Chydey

Chieko (Japanese) One who has grace and wisdom

Chien (Vietnamese) A combative man

Chike (African) God is powerful
Chyke

Chiko (Japanese) Of the pledge

Chilly (American) One who is cold
Chilley, Chilli, Chillie, Chillee, Chillea

Chilton (English) From the farm near the spring
Chiltun, Chylton, Chyltun, Chelton, Cheltun, Chilten, Chylten, Chill, Chyll

Chimalli (Nahuatl) One who is shielded
Chimallie, Chimalley, Chimally, Chimallee, Chimallea

Chimalsi (African) A proud man
Chimalsie, Chimalsy, Chimalsey, Chimalsee, Chimalsea

Chimelu (African) One who is made of God
Chimelue, Chimeloo, Chimelou

Chin (Korean) One who is precious
Chyn

Chinh (Vietnamese) A righteous man

Chinja (Indian) Our son
Chynja

Chino (Spanish) A man from China
Chyno

Chintak (Hindi) A great thinker
Chintac, Chintack, Chyntak, Chyntac, Chyntack

Chinua (African) One who is blessed by God

Chip (English) Form of Charles, meaning "one who is manly and strong / a free man"
Chyp, Chipp, Chypp, Chipper, Chypper

Chiram (Hebrew) One who is noble
Chirem, Chyram, Chyrem

Chiron (Greek) A wise tutor
Chyron, Chirun, Chyrun

Chochmo (Native American) From the mud mound

Chogan (Native American) Resembling a blackbird
Chogen, Chogon, Chogun, Chogin, Chogyn

Choni (Hebrew) A gracious man
Chonie, Chony, Choney, Chonee, Chonea

Choovio (Native American) Resembling an antelope
Chooveo

Choviohoya (Native American) Resembling a young deer

❁ **Christian** (Greek) A follower of Christ
Chrestien, Chretien, Chris, Christan, Christer, Christiano, Christie, Christo, Christos, Christy, Cristian, Cristen, Crystian, Cristiano, Cristino, Criston, Cristos, Cristy, Christiaan, Chrystian, Cretien, Christien

Christiansen (Danish) The son of Christian
Christianson, Christiansun, Christiansan

Christmas (English) Born during the festival of Christ

❁ **Christopher** (Greek) One who bears Christ inside
Christof, Christofer, Christoffer, Christoforo, Christoforus, Christoph, Christophe, Christophoros, Cristobal, Cristofer, Cristoforo, Cristovano, Cristoval, Christofor

Chuchip (Native American) A deer spirit

Chuck (English) Form of Charles, meaning "one who is manly and strong / a free man"
Chucke, Chucki, Chuckie, Chucky, Chuckey, Chuckee, Chuckea

Chul (Korean) One who stands firm

Chun (Chinese) Born during the spring

Churchill (English) From the hill near the church
Churchil, Churchyll, Churchyl

Cian (Irish) From an ancient family
Cein, Cianan, Ceinan

Ciaran (Gaelic) A black-haired man; having dark features
Ciaren, Ciaron, Ciarun, Ciarin, Ciaryn, Cerin, Ceran, Ceron, Cerun, Cerin, Ceryn

Cicero (Latin) Resembling a chickpea
Ciceron

Cid (Spanish) A lord
Cyd

Cillian (Gaelic) One who suffers strife

Cinco (Spanish) The fifth-born child
Cynco

Cipriano (Spanish) A man from Cyprus
Cypriano, Cyprian, Ciprian, Cyprianus, Ciprianus, Cyprianos, Ciprianos

Ciqala (Native American) The little one

Ciriaco (Greek) A lord

Cirilo (Spanish) One who is noble

Cirrus (Latin) A lock of hair; resembling the cloud
Cyrrus

Cisco (Spanish) Form of Francisco, meaning "a man from France; one who is free"
Cysco, Cisko, Cysko, Ciscko, Cyscko

Citlali (Nahuatl) Resembling a star
Citlalie, Citlaly, Citlaley, Citlalee, Citlalea

Claiborne (English) Born of the earth's clay
Claiborn, Claibourn, Claibourne, Clayborn, Clayborne, Claybourn, Claybourne, Claeborn, Claeborne, Claebourn, Claebourne

Clair (Latin) One who is bright
Clare, Clayr, Claer, Clairo, Claro, Claero

Clancy (Celtic) Son of the red-haired warrior
Clancey, Clanci, Clancie, Clancee, Clancea, Clansey, Clansy, Clansi, Clansie, Clansee, Clansea

Clarence (Irish) From the Clare river
Claran, Clarance, Clarens, Claron, Clarons, Claronz, Clarrance, Clarrence, Clarri, Clarrie, Clarry, Clarrey, Clarree, Clarrea, Clarendon

Clark (English) A cleric; a clerk
Clarke, Clerk, Clerke, Clerc

Claude (English) One who is lame
Claud, Claudan, Claudell, Claidianus, Claudicio, Claudien, Claudino, Claudio, Claudius, Claudon, Clodito, Clodo, Clodomiro, Claudus, Claudios

Clay (English) Of the earth's clay

Clayland (English) From the land of clay
Claland

Clayton (English) From the town settled on clay
Claytun, Clayten, Claytin, Claytyn, Claytan, Cleyton, Cleytun, Cleytan, Cleyten, Cleytin, Cleytyn

Cleander (English) Form of Leander, meaning "a lion of a man"
Cliander, Cleandre, Cliandre, Cleandro, Cliandro, Cleandrew, Cleandros, Cleanther, Cleiandros, Cleand, Cleande

Cleanth (Greek) A philosopher
Cleanthes, Cleante, Cleanto, Cleneth, Clianth, Clianthes, Cleanthe

Cleary (Irish) A learned man; a scholar
Cleari, Clearie, Clearey, Clearee, Clearea

Cleavant (English) From the cliffs
Cleavon, Cleevant, Cleeve, Cleevont, Cleavont, Cleevon, Cleave

Clement (Latin) A merciful man
Clem, Clemencio, Clemens, Clemente, Clementino, Clementius, Clemmie, Clemmons, Clemmy, Clemmi, Clemmee, Clemmey, Clementios

Cleon (Greek) A well-known man
Cleone, Clion, Clione, Clyon, Clyone

Cleophas (Greek) Having a vision of glory
Cleofas, Cleofaso, Cleophus, Cleophos, Cleofus, Cleofos

Cletus (Greek) One who has been summoned
Clete, Cletis, Cletos, Cleytus, Cleetus, Cleatus, Cleetos, Cleatos

Cleveland (English) From the land of cliffs
Cleaveland, Cleavland, Cleeveland, Cleevland

Clever (American) One who is smart
Clevar, Clevor, Clevur, Clevir, Clevyr

Clevon (English) From the cliff
Clevun, Clevin, Clevyn, Cleven, Clevan

Cliff (English) Form of Cliffton, meaning "from the town near the cliff"
Cliffe, Clyff, Clyffe, Clifft, Clift, Clyfft, Clyft

Clifford (English) From the ford near the cliff
Clyfford, Cliford, Clyford

Cliffton (English) From the town near the cliff
Clifftun, Clyffton, Clyfftun, Cliffeton, Clyffeton, Cliffetun, Clyffetun

Clifland (English) From the land of the cliffs
Cliffland, Clyfland, Clyffland

Clinton (English) From the town on the hill
Clynton, Clintun, Clyntun, Clint, Clynt, Clinte, Clynte

Cliry (English) A beloved friend
Clirey, Cliree, Clirea, Cliri, Clirie

Clive (English) One who lives near the cliff
Clyve, Cleve

Clove (French) Resembling the spice; a nail

Clovis (French) A renowned warrior
Clovys, Clodoveo, Clovisito, Clovio, Clovito

Cloy (French) One who works with nails
Cloye, Cloi, Cloyce, Cloyd, Cloice, Cloid

Clud (Welsh) One who is lame

Cluny (Irish) From the meadow
Cluney, Cluni, Clunie, Clunee, Clunea, Cluneah

Clyde (Scottish) From the river Clyde
Clide, Clywd, Clydel, Clydell

Coakley (English) From the charcoal meadow
Coakly, Coakli, Coaklie, Coakleigh, Coaklee, Coaklea, Coakleah, Cokeley, Cokelie, Cokeli, Cokely, Cokeleigh, Cokelee, Cokelea, Cokeleah

Cobb (English) From the cottage
Cob, Cobbet, Cobbett, Cobett, Cobet

Cobden (English) From the cottage in the valley
Cobdenn, Cobdale, Cobdail, Cobdaile, Cobdell, Cobdel, Cobdayl, Cobdayle, Cobdael, Cobdaele

Cobham (English) From the cottage in the village
Cobbham, Cobam, Cobbam

Coby (English) Form of Jacob, meaning "he who supplants"
Cobey, Cobee, Cobea, Cobi, Cobie

Cochise (Native American) A renowned warrior
Cocheece, Cochiece, Cocheice, Cocheace, Cochyce

Cochlain (Irish) One who is hooded
Cochlaine, Cochlayn, Cochlayne, Cochlaen, Cochlaene, Cochlane

Cockburn (Scottish) From the rooster's stream
Cockbern, Cockbirn, Coburn, Cobern, Cobirn, Cockburne, Cockberne, Cockbirne, Coburne, Coberne, Cobirne

Cockrell (French) Resembling a young rooster
Cockrel, Cokrell, Cokrel, Cockrill, Cockril, Cockerel, Cockerell

Cody (Irish / English) One who is helpful; a wealthy man / acting as a cushion
Codi, Codie, Codey, Codee, Codeah, Codea, Codier, Codyr

Coffin (English) A container; one who makes coffins
Coffyn, Coffen, Coffan, Coffon, Coffun

Colbert (French) A famous and bright man
Colvert, Culbert, Colburt, Colbirt, Colbyrt, Colbart, Culburt, Culbirt, Culbyrt, Culbart, Colvirt, Colvyrt, Colvart

Colby (English) From the coal town
*Colbey, Colbi, Colbie, Colbee, Collby, Coalby,
Colbea, Colbeah, Coalbee, Coalbie, Coalbi,
Coalbey, Coalbea, Coalbeah*

Colden (English) From the dark valley
*Coldun, Coldon, Coldun, Coldin, Coldyn,
Coldell, Coldale, Coldail, Coldael, Coldayl,
Coldayle, Codaile, Coldaele*

☘ **Cole** (English) Having dark features; having
coal-black hair
*Coley, Coli, Coly, Colie, Colee, Coleigh, Colea,
Colson, Colsun, Colsen, Colsan, Colsin, Colsyn*

Coleman (English) One who burns charcoal; resembling a dove
Colemann, Colman, Colmann, Colm, Colme

Coleridge (English) From the dark ridge
Colerige, Colridge, Colrige

Colgate (English) From the dark gate
*Colegate, Colgait, Colegait, Colgayt, Colegayt,
Colgaet, Colegaet*

Colin (Scottish) A young man; form of
Nicholas, meaning "of the victorious
people"
*Cailean, Colan, Colyn, Colon, Colun, Colen,
Collin, Collan, Collen, Collyn, Collun, Collon,
Collins*

Coll (Irish) Form of Nicholas, meaning "of
the victorious people"
Colla, Colle

Colley (English) A dark-haired man
Colly, Colli, Collie, Collee, Colleigh, Collea

Collier (English) A coal miner
Collyer, Colier, Colis, Collayer, Collis, Colyer

Colorado (Spanish) From the red river;
from the state of Colorado

Colt (English) A young horse; from the coal
town
Colte

Colter (English) A horse herdsman
*Coltere, Coltar, Coltor, Coltir, Coltyr, Coulter,
Coultar, Coultir, Coultyr, Coultor, Coultur*

☘ **Colton** (English) From the coal town
*Colten, Coltun, Coltan, Coltin, Coltyn,
Coltrain, Coltrane, Coleton, Collton, Colston*

Columba (Latin) Resembling a dove; the
name of a saint
*Collumbano, Colombain, Colum, Columbano,
Columbanus, Columcille, Colombe, Columbia,
Colam, Columbine., Columbo, Columbus,
Colombo, Colombus*

Colwyn (Welsh) From the river in Wales
*Colwynn, Colwynne, Colwin, Colwinn,
Colwinne, Colwen, Colwenn, Colwenne*

Coman (Arabic) One who is noble
Comen, Comin, Comyn, Comon, Comun

Comanche (Native American) A tribal name
*Comanchi, Comanchie, Comanchee,
Comanchea, Comanchy, Comanchey*

Comhghall (Irish) A fellow hostage
Cowall, Cowal

Como (Latin) From the province

Comus (Latin) In mythology, the god of
mirth and revelry
Comos, Comes, Comas, Comis, Comys

Conaire (Irish) One who is wise
Conair, Conaer, Conaere, Conayr, Conayre

Conall (Celtic) Resembling a wolf; having
strength and wisdom
Conal

Conan (English / Gaelic) Resembling a wolf /
one who is high and mighty
Conant

Concord (Latin) Of peace and harmony
Concorde

Condon (Celtic) A dark, wise man
Condun, Condan, Conden, Condin, Condyn

Coney (English) Resembling a rabbit
Cony, Coni, Conie, Conee, Conea

Cong (Chinese) A clever man

Conlan (Gaelic) A hero
Conlen, Conlon, Conlun, Conlin, Conlyn

Conleth (Irish) One who is wise
Conlethe

Conley (Gaelic) One who is pure; chaste
*Conly, Conlie, Conli, Conleigh, Conlee,
Conlea*

Conn (Irish) The chief
Con

Connal (Celtic) One who is high and mighty
Connall, Connell, Connel

Connecticut (Native American) From the place beside the long river; from the state of Connecticut

Connery (Scottish) A daring man
Connary, Connerie, Conneri, Connerey, Connarie, Connari, Connarey, Conary, Conery, Conarie, Conari, Conarey, Coneri, Conerie, Conerey

Connie (Irish) Form of Constantine, meaning "one who is steadfast; firm"
Conni, Conny, Conney, Connee, Connea

❂ **Connor** (Gaelic) A wolf-lover
ⓣ *Conor, Conner, Coner, Connar, Conar, Connur, Conur, Connir, Conir, Connyr, Conyr*

Conrad (German) A brave and bold ruler; a bold advisor
Conrade, Conrado, Corrado, Conradin

Conroy (Irish) A wise advisor
Conroye, Conroi

Constantine (Latin) One who is steadfast; firm
Constans, Constanz, Constant, Constantin, Constantino, Constantius, Costa, Constantio, Constanze, Constanty

Consuelo (Spanish) One who offers consolation
Consuel, Consuelio, Consueleo, Consueliyo, Consueleyo

Conway (Gaelic) The hound of the plain; from the sacred river
Conwaye, Conwai, Conwae, Conwy

Cook (English) One who prepares meals for others
Cooke

Cooney (Irish) A handsome man
Coony, Cooni, Coonie, Coonee, Coonea

❂ **Cooper** (English) One who makes barrels
Coop, Coopar, Coopir, Coopyr, Coopor, Coopur, Coopersmith, Cupere

Corbett (French) Resembling a young raven
Corbet, Corbete, Corbette, Corbit, Corbitt, Corbite, Corbitte

Corbin (English) Resembling a raven
Corben, Corban, Corbyn, Corbon, Corbun, Corbe, Corbi, Corbie, Corby, Corbey, Corbee, Corbea, Corbinian, Corvin, Corvan, Corven, Corvon, Corvun, Corvyn

Corcoran (Gaelic) Having a ruddy complexion
Cochran

Cordell (English) One who makes cord
Cord, Cordale, Cordas, Corday, Cordelle, Cordel, Cordaye, Cordai, Cordae

Cordero (Spanish) Resembling a lamb
Corderio, Corderiyo, Cordereo, Cordereyo

Corey (Irish) From the hollow; of the churning waters
Cory, Cori, Corie, Coree, Corea, Correy, Corry, Corri, Corrie, Corree, Correa

Coriander (Greek) A romantic man; resembling the spice
Coryander, Coriender, Coryender

Cork (Gaelic) From the swampland
Corki, Corkie, Corke, Corkee, Corkea, Corkey, Corky

Corlan (Irish) One who wields a spear
Corlen, Corlin, Corlyn, Corlon, Corlun

Corliss (English) A benevolent man
Corlis, Corlyss, Corlys, Corless, Corles, Corley, Corly, Corlee, Corleigh, Corli, Corlea, Corlie

Cormick (Irish) A charioteer
Cormyck, Cormik, Cormyk, Cormic, Cormyc, Cormac, Cormack, Cormak, Cormag

Cornelius (Latin) Refers to a horn
Cornall, Cornel, Corneille, Cornelio, Cornelious, Cornell, Cornelus, Corney, Cornilius, Corny, Corni, Cornie, Cornee, Cornea

Cornwallis (English) A man from Cornwall
Cornwalis, Cornwallace, Cornwalace

Corrado (German) A bold counselor
Corrade, Corradeo, Corradio

Corrick (English) A benevolent ruler
Corryck, Corrik, Corryk, Corric, Corryc, Corick, Coryck, Corik, Coryk, Coric, Coryc

Corridon (Irish) One who wields a spear
Corridan, Corridun, Corriden, Corridin, Corridyn

Corrin (Irish) One who wields a spear
Corryn, Corran, Corren, Corron, Corrun, Corin, Coryn, Coren, Coran, Coron, Corun

Cort (English) A court attendant; a courtier
Cortland, Corty, Court, Courtland, Cortey, Corti, Cortie, Cortee, Courty, Courtey, Courti, Courtie, Courtee

Cortez (Spanish) A courteous man
Cortes

Corwin (English) A friend of the heart
Corwinn, Corwinne, Corwyn, Corwynn, Corwynne, Corwen, Corwenn, Corwenne, Corwine

Corydon (Greek) One who is ready for battle
Coridon, Corydun, Coridun, Corydan, Coridan, Coryden, Coriden, Corydin, Coridin, Corydyn, Coridyn

Cosgrove (Gaelic) The champion
Cozgrove, Cosgrave, Cozgrave

Cosmo (Greek) The order of the universe
Cosimo, Cosmé, Cosmos, Cosmas, Cozmo, Cozmos, Cozmas

Coster (English) A peddler
Costar, Costor, Costir, Costyr, Costur

Cotton (American) Resembling or farmer of the plant
Cottin, Cotten, Cottyn, Cottun, Cottan

Coty (French) From the riverbank
Cotey, Coti, Cotie, Cotee, Cotea

Cougar (American) Resembling the wild animal
Couger, Cougor, Cougir, Cougyr, Cougur

Coulson (French) Form of Nicholas, meaning "of the victorious people"
Colson, Coulsun, Colsun

Courtney (English) A courteous man; courtly
Cordney, Cordni, Cortenay, Corteney, Cortni, Cortnee, Cortneigh, Cortney, Cortnie, Cortny, Courtenay, Courteneigh, Courteney, Courtnay, Courtnee, Courtnie, Courtny, Courtnea, Cortnea, Courtni, Court, Courte

Covell (English) From the cave on the slope
Covel, Covyll, Covyl

Covert (English) One who provides shelter
Couvert

Covey (English) A brood of birds
Covy, Covi, Covie, Covee, Covea, Covvey, Covvy, Covvi, Covvie, Covvee, Covvea

Covington (English) From the town near the cave
Covyngton, Covingtun, Covyngtun

Cowan (Irish) From the hollow near the hill; one of twins
Cowen, Cowin, Cowyn, Cowon, Cowun

Cowrie (African) Resembling the shell
Cowry, Cowrey, Cowri, Cowree, Cowrea, Courey, Coury, Couri, Courie, Couree, Courea

Cox (English) A coxswain
Coxe, Coxi, Coxie, Coxey, Coxy, Coxee, Coxea

Coy (English) From the woods
Coye, Coi

Coyan (French) A modest man
Coyen, Coyon, Coyun, Coyin, Coyne, Coyn

Coyle (Irish) A leader during battle
Coyl, Coil, Coile

Craddock (Welsh) One who is much loved
Craddoc, Craddok, Cradock, Cradoc, Cradok

Craig (Gaelic) From the rocks; from the crag
Crayg, Craeg, Craige, Crayge, Craege, Cruge, Crag

Cramer (German) A peddler
Craymer, Craimer, Craemer, Cramar, Craymar, Craimar, Craemar, Cramor, Craimor, Craymor, Craemor, Cramir, Craymir, Craimir, Craemir

Crandell (English) From the valley of cranes
Crandel, Crandale, Crandail, Crandaile, Crandayl, Crandayle, Crandael, Crandaele, Crandal, Crandall

Crane (English) Resembling the long-legged bird
Crain, Craine, Crayn, Crayne, Craen, Craene

Cranford (English) From the crane's ford
Cranforde, Cranferd, Cranferde, Cranfurd, Cranfurde

Cranley (English) From the meadow of cranes
Cranly, Cranleigh, Cranli, Cranlie, Cranlee, Cranlea, Cranleah

Cranston (English) From the crane town
Cranstun, Cranton, Crantun

Craven (English) A cowardly man
Cravin, Cravyn, Cravan, Cravon, Cravun

Crawford (English) From the crow's ford
Crawforde, Crawferd, Crawferde, Crawfurd, Crawfurde

Cree (Native American) A tribal name
Crei, Crey, Crea, Creigh

Creed (Latin) A guiding principle; a belief
Creede, Cread, Creade, Creedon, Creadon, Creedun, Creadun, Creedin, Creadin, Creedyn, Creadyn, Creeden, Creaden, Creedan, Creadan

Creek (English) From the small stream
Creeke, Creak, Creake, Creik, Creike

Creighton (Scottish) From the border town
Creightun, Crayton, Craytun, Craiton, Craitun, Craeton, Craetun, Crichton, Crichtun

Creketun (English) From the town near the creek
Creketon, Creketen, Creekton, Creektun, Creekten

Crescent (French) One who creates; increasing; growing
Creissant, Crescence, Cressant, Cressent, Crescant

Crevan (Gaelic) Resembling a fox
Creven, Crevin, Crevyn, Crevon, Crevun

Cricket (American) Resembling a chirping insect of the night
Crycket, Criket, Cryket, Crickit, Cryckit

Crisanto (Spanish) Resembling the gold flower
Cresento, Crisento, Crizant, Crizanto, Crisantio, Crizantio, Crisanteo, Crizanteo

Crispin (Latin) A curly-haired man
Crisspin, Crepin, Crespin, Crispian, Crispino, Crispo, Crispus, Crispos, Crispyn, Crespyn, Crispen, Crespen

Crockett (English) A crook; a shepherd
Crock, Crocket, Croquet, Croquett, Crooke, Crookes, Crooks

Crofton (English) From the town of cottages
Croftun, Croften, Croffton, Crofftun, Crofften, Croft, Crofte

Crogher (Irish) One who loves hounds
Crohoore, Crohoor

Cromwell (English) One who lives near the winding stream
Cromwel, Cromwill, Cromwil, Cromwyll, Cromwyl, Crom

Cronan (Irish) The small, dark one
Cronen, Cronyn, Cronin, Cronon, Cronun

Cronus (Greek) In mythology, the youngest Titan
Cronos, Cronas, Crones, Cronis, Cronys

Crosby (English) From the farm near the cross
Crosbey, Crosbi, Crosbie, Crosbee, Crosbea

Crosley (English) From the meadow near the cross
Crosleigh, Croslee, Croslea, Crosleah, Crosly, Crosli, Croslie

Crowell (English) From the spring near the cross
Crowel

Crowther (English) A fiddler
Crowthir, Crowthyr, Crowthar, Crowthor, Crowthur, Crother, Crothir, Crothyr, Crothur, Crothor, Crothar

Cruz (Spanish) Of the cross
Cruzito, Cruze, Cruiz, Cruize

Cualli (Nahuatl) A good man
Cuallie, Cually, Cualley, Cuallee, Cualleigh, Cuallea

Cuarto (Spanish) The fourth-born child
Cuartio, Cuartiyo, Cuarteo, Cuarteyo

Cuetzpalli (Nahuatl) Resembling a lizard
*Cuetzpallie, Cuetzpally, Cuetzpalley,
Cuetzpallee, Cuetzpallea*

Cuinn (Celtic) An intelligent man
Cuin, Cuinne, Cuine

Cullen (Gaelic) A good-looking young man
Cullin, Cullyn, Cullan, Cullon, Cullun

Culum (Gaelic) Resembling a dove

Culver (English) Resembling a dove
*Culvar, Culvir, Culvyr, Culvor, Culvur,
Colver, Colvar, Colvir, Colvyr, Colvor, Colvur*

Cunningham (Gaelic) From the village of milk
*Conyngham, Cuningham, Cunnyngham,
Cunyngham*

Cuong (Vietnamese) One who is healthy and prosperous

Curcio (French) One who is courteous
Curceo

Curley (English) Having great strength
Curly, Curlie, Curli, Curleigh, Curlee, Curlea

Curragh (Gaelic) From the moor

Curran (Gaelic) One who wields a dagger; a hero
Curry, Currey, Curri, Currie, Curree, Currea

Curro (Spanish) One who is free
Currito

Curt (English) A brave counselor
Curte

Curtis (English) One who is courteous; polite
*Curtiss, Curtys, Curtyss, Curtice, Curcio,
Curtell*

Custodio (Spanish) A guardian
Custodeo, Custodiyo, Custodeyo

Cuthbert (English) One who is bright and famous
Cuthbeorht, Cuthburt, Cuthbirt, Cuthbyrt

Cutler (English) One who makes knives
Cutlar, Cutlor, Cutlir, Cutlyr, Cutlur

Cyan (English) Having blue-green eyes
Cyen, Cyin, Cyon, Cyun

Cydney (English) Form of Sydney, meaning "of the wide meadow"
*Cydny, Cydni, Cydnie, Cydnee, Cidney,
Cidnee, Cidnie, Cidni, Cidny, Cyd, Cydnea,
Cydneah, Cidnea, Cidneah, Cid*

Cynbel (Welsh) A warrior chief
Cynbal, Cynbell, Cynball, Cynbil, Cynbill

Cyneley (English) From the royal meadow
*Cynely, Cyneli, Cynelie, Cynelee, Cynelea,
Cyneleah, Cyneleigh*

Cyrano (French) A man from Cyrene
Cyran, Cyranno, Cirano, Ciranno, Ciran

Cyril (Greek) A master or lord
*Ciril, Cirilio, Cirillo, Cirilo, Cy, Cyrill, Cyrille,
Cyrillus*

Cyrus (Persian) A king
Cirus, Ciro, Cyro, Cyris, Ciris

Czar (Russian) An emperor

Dabeet (Indian) A warrior
Dabeat, Dabeit, Dabiet, Dabyt, Dabit

Dabi (Hebrew) One who is dearly loved
Dabie, Daby, Dabey, Dabee, Dabea

Dabir (Arabic) One who teaches others
Dabeer, Dabear, Dabeir, Dabier, Dabyr

Dabney (French) One who is from Aubigny
*Dabnie, Dabny, Dabni, Dabnee, Dabnea,
Dabneah*

Dace (French) Born to the nobility
*Daice, Dayce, Daece, Dacian, Dacien, Dacio,
Dacius, Dacios, Dacias, Daceas*

Dacey (Gaelic / Latin) A man from the south / a man from Dacia
*Dacy, Dacee, Dacea, Daci, Dacie, Daicey,
Daicy, Daicee, Daicea, Daici, Daicie, Daecey,
Daecey, Daecee, Daecea, Daeci, Daecie,
Daycey, Daycy, Daycee, Daycea, Dayci,
Daycie*

Dack (English) From the French town of Dax
Dacks

Dada (African) A curly-haired man
Dadah

Dadrian (English) Form of Adrian, meaning "a man from Hadria"
Dade, Dadiran, Dadrain, Dadrean, Dadreean, Dadreyan, Dadreeyan, Dadriaan, Dadriano, Dadrien, Dadrin, Dadrino, Dadrion, Dadron, Dadryan, Dadya, Darjen, Daydrean, Daydreean, Daydrian, Daydrien

Daedalus (Greek) A craftsman
Daldalos, Dedalus

Daelan (American) Form of Waylon, meaning "from the roadside land"
Daelin, Daelyn, Daelon, Daelen, Daylan, Daylin, Daylyn, Daylon, Daylen, Dailan, Dailen, Dailin, Dailyn, Dailon, Dalan, Dalen, Dalon, Dalin, Dalyn

Dag (Scandinavian) Born during the daylight
Dagney, Dagny, Dagnee, Dagnea, Dagni, Dagnie, Daeg, Dagget, Daggett, Daggan, Daggen, Daggon, Daggun, Daggin, Daggyn

Dagan (Hebrew) Of the grain; of the earth
Daigan, Daygan, Daegan

Dagen (Irish) A black-haired man
Dagon, Dagun, Dagin, Dagyn, Deegen, Deegon, Deegun, Deegin, Deegyn, Daegan, Daegon, Daegun, Daegin, Daegyn

Dagobert (German) Born on a bright and shining day
Dagoberto, Dagbert, Dagoburt, Dagoburto, Dagburt, Dagobirt, Dagobirto, Dagbirt

Dagwood (English) From the shining forest
Dagwode

Dahy (Irish) One who is quick
Dahey, Dahi, Dahie, Dahee, Dahea

Dai (Japanese / Welsh) One who is large / a shining man

Daijon (American) A gift of hope
Dayjon, Daejon, Dajon

Dailey (Gaelic) Of the assembly
Daily, Dailee, Dailea, Daileigh, Daili, Dailie, Daly, Daley, Dalee, Dalea, Daleigh, Dali, Dalie, Dawley, Dawly, Dawlee, Dawleigh, Dawlea, Dawli, Dawlie, Daeley, Daely, Daelee, Daelea, Daeleigh, Daeli, Daelie

Dainan (Australian) A kindhearted man
Dainen, Dainon, Dainun, Dainyn, Dainin, Daynan, Daynen, Daynon, Daynun, Daynin, Daynyn, Daenan, Daenen, Daenin, Daenyn, Daenon, Daenun

Dainard (English) A bold and courageous Dane
Danehard, Danehardt, Daneard, Daneardt, Dainehard, Dainhard, Daynard, Daynhard, Daynhardt, Dainhardt

Daire (Irish) A wealthy man
Dair, Daere, Daer, Dayr, Dayre, Dare, Dari, Darie, Dary, Darey, Daree, Darea

Daithi (Irish) The beloved; one who is quick
Daithie, Daithy, Daithey, Daithee, Daithea, Daythi, Daythie, Daythey, Daythy, Daythee, Daythea, Daethi, Daethie, Daethy, Daethey, Daethee, Daethea

Daivat (Hindi) A powerful man

Dakarai (African) Filled with happiness

Dakota (Native American) A friend to all
Daccota, Dakoda, Dakodah, Dakotah, Dakoeta, Dekota, Dekohta, Dekowta, Dakoeta, Dakoetah

Daksha (Indian) A brilliant man
Dakshah

Daktari (African) One who heals others
Daktarie, Daktary, Daktarey, Daktaree, Daktarea

Dalai (Indian) A peaceful man

Dalbert (English) The bright and shining one
Dalburt, Dalbirt, Dalbyrt

Dale (English) From the valley
Dail, Daile, Dael, Daele, Dayl, Dayle

Dalgus (American) An outdoorsy man
Dalgas, Dalgos, Dalges, Dalgis, Dalgys

Dalil (Arabic) One who acts as a guide
Daleel, Daleal, Daleil, Daliel, Dalyl

Dallan (Irish) One who is blind
Dalan, Dallen, Dalen, Dallon, Dalon, Dallun, Dalun

Dallas (Scottish) From the dales; from the city in Texas
Dalles, Dallis, Dallys, Dallos, Dallus

Dallin (English) From the valley
Dalin, Dallyn, Dalyn

Dalmar (African) One who is versatile

Dalston (English) An intelligent man
Dalsten, Dalstin, Dalstyn, Dalstun, Dalstan

Dalton (English) From the town in the valley
Daltun, Dalten, Daltan, Daltin, Daltyn, Daleton, Daletun, Daletin, Daletyn, Daleten, Daletan, Daulton, Daultun, Daulten, Daultan, Daultin, Daultyn, Dallton, Dalltun, Dallten, Dalltan, Dalltin, Dalltyn, Dalt, Dalte

Dalziel (Scottish) From the little field

Damacio (Spanish) One who is calm
Damasio, Damazio, Damaceo, Damaseo, Damazeo, Damaso, Damazo

Damario (Greek / Spanish) Resembling a calf / one who is gentle
Damarios, Damarius, Dumaro, Damero, Damerio, Damereo, Damareo, Damerios, Damerius

Damaris (Greek) One who is gentle
Damariss, Damarys, Damaryss

Damary (Greek) One who is tamed
Damarey, Damari, Dumarie, Damaree, Damarea

Damaskenos (Greek) A man from Damascus
Damaskinos, Damaskus, Damascus, Damuskeno, Damaskino, Damasco, Damasko

Damek (Slavic) Of the red earth
Damec, Dameck, Damik, Damic, Damick, Damyk, Damyc, Damyck

Damel (American) A strong-willed man
Damell, Damele, Damelle

Damerae (Jamaican) A joyous boy
Dameray, Dameraye, Damerai, Damarae, Damaray, Damaraye, Damarai

Damian (Greek) One who tames or subdues others
Daemon, Daimen, Daimon, Daman, Damen, Dameon, Damiano, Damianos, Damianus, Damien, Damion, Damon, Damyan, Damyen, Damyon, Dayman, Daymian, Daymon, Daeman, Daemen, Damean, Damyean, Damyun, Damyn, Damiean

Damir (Slavic) One who promotes peace
Dameer, Damear, Damier, Dameir, Damyr

Damis (Arabic) A dark-skinned man
Damiss, Damys, Damyss

Damisi (African) A cheerful man
Damisie, Damisy, Damisey, Damisee, Damisea

Dan (English) Form of Daniel, meaning "God is my judge"
Dann, Danny, Danni, Dannie, Dannee, Dannea, Dani, Danie, Dany, Daney, Danee, Danea

Danawi (Arabic) A worldly man
Danawie, Danawy, Danawey, Danawee, Danawea

Dandre (American) A lighthearted man
Dandray, Dandraye, Dandrae, Dandree

Dane (English) A man from Denmark
Dain, Daine, Dayn, Dayne, Daen, Daene, Dana, Danon, Danin, Danun, Danan, Danen, Danyn

Daneil (American) The champion
Daneile, Daneel, Daneele, Daneal, Daneale

Danely (Scandinavian) A man from Denmark
Daneley, Daneli, Danelie, Danelee, Daneleigh, Danelea, Daineley, Dainely, Dainelee, Daineleigh, Dainelea, Daineli, Dainelie, Daynely, Dayneley, Daynelee, Daynelea, Dayneli, Daynelie

Dang (Vietnamese) One who is praiseworthy

Danger (American) One who takes great risks
Dainger, Daynger, Daenger, Dangery, Dangerey, Dangeree, Dangerea, Dangeri, Dangerie

Danh (Vietnamese) A famous man

Daniachew (African) A mediator

Danick (American) One who is friendly and well-liked
Danyck, Danik, Danyk, Danic, Danyc, Dannick, Dannyck, Dannik, Dannyk, Dannic, Dannyc

❂ **Daniel** (Hebrew) God is my judge
⊕ *Danal, Daneal, Danek, Danell, Danial, Daniele, Danil, Danilo, Danko, Dannel, Dantrell, Danyal, Danyel*

Danno (Japanese) From the gathering in the field

Dannon (Hebrew) Form of Daniel, meaning "God is my judge"
Dannun, Dannan, Dannen, Dannin, Dannyn

Danso (African) A reliable man
Dansoe, Dansow, Dansowe

Dante (Latin) An enduring man; everlasting
Dantae, Dantay, Dantel, Daunte, Dontae, Dontay, Donte, Dontae, Dawnte, Dauntay, Dawntay, Dauntae, Dawntae, Dontrell, Dohntay, Dohntaye, Dohntae, Dontell

Danton (English) From Dan's town
Danten, Dantin, Dantyn, Dantun, Dantan

Dantre (American) A faithful man
Dantray, Dantraye, Dantrae, Dantrey, Dantri, Dantrie, Dantry, Dantrey, Dantree, Dantrea, Dontre, Dontray, Dontraye, Dontrae, Dontrai, Dontrey, Dontri, Dontrie, Dontree, Dontry, Dontrea, Dontrey

Danuta (Polish) A gift from God

Daoud (Arabian) Form of David, meaning "the beloved one"
Daoude, Dawud, Doud, Daud, Da'ud

Daphnis (Greek) In mythology, the son of Hermes
Daphnys

Daquan (American) A high-spirited man
Dakwan, Daquann, Dakwann, Dequan, Dequann, Dekwan, Dekwann

Dar (Hebrew) Resembling a pearl
Darr

Daray (Gaelic) A dark-skinned man
Daraye, Darai, Darae

Darbrey (Irish) A lighthearted man; a free man
Darbry, Darbri, Darbrie, Darbree, Darbrea

Darby (English) Of the deer park
Darb, Darbee, Darbey, Darbie, Darrbey, Darrbie, Darrby, Derby, Derbie, Derbey, Derbee, Darbea, Darbeah

Darcel (French) Having dark features
Darcell, Darcele, Darcelle, Darcio, Darceo

Darcy (Gaelic) Having dark features
Darcey, Darcee, Darcea, Darci, Darcie, D'Arcy, Darsy, Darsey, Darsee, Darsea, Darsi, Darsie, Darce, Darse

Dardanus (Greek) In mythology, the founder of Troy
Dardanio, Dardanios, Dardanos, Dard, Darde

Dareh (Armenian) A wealthy man

Darek (English) Form of Derek, meaning "the ruler of the tribe"
Darrek, Darec, Darrec, Darreck, Dareck

Daren (African) One who is born at night

Darence (American) Form of Clarence, meaning "from the Clare river"
Darense, Darance, Darens, Daron, Darons, Daronz, Darrance, Darrence

Darion (Greek) A gift
Darian, Darien, Dariun, Darrion, Darrian, Darrien, Daryon, Daryan, Daryen, Darryon, Darryen, Darryan

Darius (Greek) A kingly man; one who is wealthy
Darias, Dariess, Dario, Darious, Darrius, Derrius, Derrious, Derrias

Darko (Slavic) A manly man
Darkoe, Darkow, Darkowe, Dark, Darke

Darlen (American) A sweet man; a darling
Darlon, Darlun, Darlan, Darlin, Darlyn

Darnell (English) From the hidden place
Darnall, Darneil, Darnel, Darnele, Darnelle

Darnley (English) From the grassy meadow
Darnly, Darnleigh, Darnlee, Darnlea, Darnleah, Darnli, Darnlie

Darold (English) Form of Harold, meaning "the ruler of an army"
Darrold, Derald, Derrald, Derold, Derrold

Darrah (Gaelic) From the dark oak tree
Darra, Darach, Darrach, Daragh, Darragh

Darrel (English) One who is dearly loved
Darel, Dariel, Dariell, Darral, Darrell, Darrill, Darrol, Durroll, Darry, Darryl, Darryll, Daryl, Derell, Derrall, Derrel, Derrell, Derril, Derrill, Deryl, Deryll, Dareau, Derryl, Derryll

Darren (Gaelic / English) A great man / a gift from God
Darran, Darrin, Darryn, Darron, Darrun, Daren, Darin, Daran, Daryn, Daron, Darun, Derron, Derrun, Derrin, Derryn, Derran, Derren, Deron, Derun, Derin, Deryn, Deran, Deren

Darrett (American) Form of Garrett, meaning "one who is mighty with a spear"
Darett, Darret, Darretson, Darritt, Darrot, Darrott, Derrit, Derritt, Derrity, Darrity, Daret

Darroch (Irish) An oak-hearted man; one who is strong
Darrick, Darryck, Darrik, Darryk, Darric, Darryc, Darick, Daryck, Darik, Daryk, Daric, Daryc, Darrock, Darock, Daroch, Darri, Darrie, Darry, Darrey, Darree

Darrow (English) One who wields a spear
Darrowe, Darro, Darow, Darowe, Daro, Darroe, Daroe, Darroh, Daroh

Darshan (Hindi) Of a vision
Darshon

Dart (English) From the river
Darte

Dart (American) One who is fast
Darte, Darrt, Darrte, Darti, Dartie, Dartee, Dartea, Darty, Dartey

Dartagnan (French) A leader
D'Artagnan

Darton (English) From the deer town
Dartun, Darten, Dartan, Dartin, Dartyn, Deortun

Darvell (French) From the eagle town
Darvel, Darvele, Darvelle

Darvin (English) Form of Darwin, meaning "a beloved friend"
Darvinn, Darvinne, Darvyn, Darvynn, Darvynne, Darven, Darvenn, Darvenne

Darwin (English) A beloved friend
Darwine, Darwinn, Darwinne, Darwen, Darwenn, Darwenne, Darwyn, Darwynn, Darwynne, Darwon

Das (Indian) A slave; a servant
Dasa

Dasan (Native American) A great ruler

Dash (American) A charming man; one who is fast
Dashe, Dashy, Dashey, Dashee, Dashea, Dashi, Dashie, Dashell, Dashel, Dashele, Dashelle, Dasher

Dasras (Indian) A handsome man

Dasya (Indian) A servant

Dat (Vietnamese) One who is accomplished

Dathan (Hebrew) From the spring
Dathen, Dathin, Dathyn, Dathon, Dathun

Daudi (African) One who is dearly loved
Daudie, Daudy, Daudey, Daudee, Daudea

Davian (English) Form of David, meaning "the beloved one"
Davien, Davion, Daviun, Davyen, Davyan, Davyon, Davyun, Daveon, Davean, Daveun

● **David** (Hebrew) The beloved one
Dave, Davey, Davi, Davidde, Davide, Davie, Daviel, Davin, Daven, Davon, Davy, Davyd, Davydd, Davan

Davidson (English) The son of David
Davydson, Davidsun, Davydsun, Davidsen, Davydsen, Davidsin, Davydsin, Davidsyn, Davydsyn, Davidsone, Davison, Davisen, Duvisun, Davysen, Davyson, Davysun

Davis (English) The son of David
Davies, Daviss, Davys, Davyss

Davonte (American) One who is energetic
Devontay, Devontaye, Devontae, Devontai, Devonte, Devontay, Devontaye, Devontae, Devontai

Davu (African) Of the beginning
Davue, Davoo, Davou, Davugh

Dawar (Arabian) A wanderer
Duwarr

Dawber (English) A humorous man
Dawbar, Dawbor, Dawbir, Dawbyr, Dawbur, Dawbi, Dawbie, Dawbee, Dawbea, Dawby, Dawbey

Dawk (American) A spirited man
Dawke, Dauk, Dauke, Dawkin, Daukin, Dawkins, Daukins

Dawson (English) The son of David
Dawsan, Dawsen, Dawsin, Dawsyn, Dawsun, Daw, Dawe, Dawes

Dax (French) From the French town Dax
Daxton, Daxtun, Daxten, Daxtan, Daxtin, Daxtyn, Daxi, Daxie, Daxee, Daxea, Daxy, Daxey

Day (American) Born during the daylight
Daye, Dai, Dae

Dayakar (Indian) A kind man

Dayanand (Hindi) A compassionate man
Dayanande, Dayan

Dayo (African) Our joy has arrived
Dayoe, Dayow, Dayowe

Dayton (English) From the sunny town
Dayten, Daytan, Daytin, Daytyn, Daytun, Daiton, Daitun, Daiten, Daitan, Daitin, Daityn, Daeton, Daetun, Daetin, Daetyn, Daeten, Daetan

De (Vietnamese) Born to royalty

Deacon (Greek) The dusty one; a servant
Deecon, Deakon, Deekon, Deacun, Deecun, Deakun, Deekun, Deacan, Deecan, Deakan, Deekan, Deacen, Deecen, Deaken, Deeken, Deacin, Deecin, Deakin, Deekin, Deak, Deek, Deke

Dean (English) From the valley; a church official
Deane, Deen, Deene, Dene, Deans, Deens, Deani, Deanie, Deany, Deaney, Deanee, Deanea

DeAndre (American) A manly man
D'André, DeAndrae, DeAndray, DeAndre, Diandray, Diondrae, Diondray

Deangelo (Italian) A messenger from God
Deangelo, De'Angelo, Diangelo, DiAngelo, D'Angelo, Deanjelo, De'Anjelo, D'Anjelo

Deanza (Spanish) A smooth man
Denza

Dearborn (English) From the deer brook
Dearborne, Dearbourn, Dearbourne, Dearburn, Dearburne, Deerborn, Deerborne, Deerbourn, Deerbourne, Deerburn, Deerburne, Derebourne, Derebourn, Dereborn, Dereborne, Dereburn, Dereburne

Dearon (American) One who is much loved
Dearan, Dearen, Dearin, Dearyn, Dearun

Debonair (French) One who is nonchalant
Debonnair, Debonnair, Debonaire, Debonnaire, Debonnaire

Debythis (American) An unusual man
Debiathes, Debithis, Debiathis, Debythys, Debithys, Debiathys

December (American) Winter's child; born in December
Decimber, Decymber, Decembar, Decimbar, Decymbar

Decimus (Latin) The tenth-born child
Decimos, Decimo, Decimu, Decio

Decker (German / Hebrew) One who prays / a piercing man
Deker, Decer, Dekker, Deccer, Deck, Decke

Declan (Irish) The name of a saint

Dedrick (English) Form of Dietrich, meaning "the ruler of the tribe"
Dedryck, Dedrik, Dedryk, Dedric, Dedryc

Deegan (Irish) A black-haired man
Deagan, Degan, Deegen, Deagen, Degen, Deegon, Deagon, Degon, Deegun, Deagun, Degun, Deegin, Deagin, Degin, Deegyn, Deagyn, Degyn

Deems (English) The son of the judge
Deams, Deims, Diems, Deyms

Deepak (Indian) One who carries the little lamp
Dipak, Deipak, Diepak, Deapak, Dypak

Deeter (American) A friendly woman
Deater, Deter, Deetar, Deatar, Detar, Deetor, Deator, Detor, Deetur, Deatur, Detur

DeForest (English) One who lives near the forest
Deforest, DeForrest, Deforrest

Deinorus (American) A lively man
Denorius, Denorus, Denorios, Deinorius, Deinorios

Deiondre (American) From the valley
Deiondray, Deiondraye, Deiondrae

Dejuan (American) A talkative man
Dejuane, Dewon, Dewonn, Dewan, Dewann, Dwon, Dwonn, Dajuan, Dajuane, Dawon, Dawonn, Dawan, Dawann

Dekel (Hebrew) From the palm tree
Dekell, Dekele, Dekelle, Dekle

Delancy (Irish) From the elder tree grove
Delancey, Delancee, Delancea, Delanci, Delancie

Delaney (Irish / French) The dark challenger / from the elder-tree grove
Delany, Delanee, Delanea, Delani, Delanie, Delainey, Delainy, Delaini, Delainie, Delainee, Delainea, Delaeney, Delaeny, Delaenee, Delaenea, Delaeni, Delaenie, Delayney, Delayny, Delaynee, Delaynea, Delayni, Delaynie, Delane, Delaine, Delaene, Delayne, Delano, Delayno, Delaeno, Delaino

Delaware (English) From the state of Delaware
Delawair, Delaweir, Delwayr, Delawayre, Delawaire, Delawaer, Delawaere

Delbert (English) One who is noble; a bright man
Delburt, Delbirt, Delbyrt, Dilbert, Dilburt, Dilbirt, Dilbyrt, Dealbeorht, Dealbert

Delgado (Spanish) A slim man
Delgadio, Delgadeo

Delius (Greek) A man from Delos
Delios, Delos, Delus, Delo

Dell (English) From the small valley
Delle, Del

Delling (Norse) A scintillating man
Dellyng, Deling, Delyng, Dellinger, Dellynger, Delinger, Delynger

Delman (English) A man from the valley
Dellman, Delmann, Dellmann

Delmar (French) A man of the sea
Delmarr, Delmor, Delmorr, Delmore, Delmare, Delmer, Delmere, Delmoor

Delmis (Spanish) A beloved friend
Delmiss, Delmisse, Delmys, Delmyss, Delmysse

Delmon (English) A man of the mountain
Delmun, Delmen, Delmin, Delmyn, Delmont, Delmonte, Delmond, Delmonde

Delmy (American) Form of Delmar, meaning "a man of the sea"
Delmey, Delmee, Delmea, Delmi, Delmie

Delphin (Greek) Resembling a dolphin
Delfin, Delfino, Delfinos, Delfinus, Delphino, Delphinos, Delphinus

Delroy (French) The king
Delray, Delrick, Delrico, Delroi, Delron, Delren, Delran, Delrin, Delryn, Delrun, Delryck, Delrik, Delryk, Delric, Delryc

Delsi (American) An easygoing guy
Delsie, Delsy, Delsey, Delsee, Delsea, Delci, Delcie, Delcee, Delcea, Delcy, Delcey

Delton (English) From the town in the valley
Deltun, Deltin, Deltyn, Deltan, Delten

Delvin (English) A godly friend
Delvinn, Delvinne, Delvyn, Delvynn, Delvynne, Delven, Delvenn, Delvenne, Delvon, Delvonn, Delvonne, Delevin, Delevinn, Delevinne, Delevyn, Delevynn, Delevynne

Delwin (English) A friend from the valley
Delwine, Delwinn, Delwinne, Delwen, Delwenn, Delwenne, Delwyn, Delwynn, Delwynne

Demarcus (American) The son of Marcus
DeMarcus, DaMarkiss, DeMarco, Demarkess, DeMarko, Demarkus, DeMarquess, DeMarquez, DeMarquiss, Damarcus, Damarkus

Demario (American) The son of Mario
Demarrio, DeMario, D'Mario, Dimario, DiMario

Dembe (African) A peaceful man
Dembi, Dembie, Dembee, Dembea, Dembey, Demby

Demetrick (American) Of the earth
Demetryck, Demetric, Demetryc, Demetrik, Demetryk

Demetrius (Greek) A follower of the goddess Demeter
Dametrius, Demetri, Demetrice, Demetrio, Demetris, Demitri, Demitrios, Demitrius, Dhimitrios, Dimetre, Dimitri, Dimitrios, Dimitrious, Dimitry, Dmitri, Dmitrios, Dmitry, Dimas, Demas

Demissie (African) The destroyer
Demissi, Demissy, Demissey, Demissee, Demissea

Demont (French) Man of the mountain
Demonte, Demond, Demonde, Demunt, Demunte, Demund, Demunde

Demos (Greek) Of the people
Demus, Demmos, Demmus

Demothi (Native American) A talker
Demothie, Demothy, Demothey, Demothee, Demothea

Dempsey (Irish) A proud man
Dempsy, Dempsi, Dempsie, Dempsee, Dempsea

Dempster (English) One who judges
Dempstar, Dempstor, Dempstur, Dempstir, Dempstyr

Denali (American) From the national park
Denalie, Denaly, Denaley, Denalee, Denalea, Denaleigh

Denby (Scandinavian) From the Danes village
Denbey, Denbi, Denbie, Denbee, Denbea, Danbey, Danby, Danbee, Danbea, Danbi, Danbie

Denham (English) From the village in the valley

Denholm (Scandinavian) From the home of the Danes

Denim (American) Made of a strong cloth
Denym, Denem, Denam

Denley (English) From the meadow near the valley
Denly, Denlea, Denleah, Denlee, Denleigh, Denli, Denlie

Denman (English) One who lives in the valley
Denmann, Denmin, Denmyn, Denmen, Denmon, Denmun

Denmark (Scandinavian) From the country of Denmark
Denmarck, Denmarc, Denmarq

Dennis (French) A follower of Dionysus
Den, Denies, Denis, Dennes, Dennet, Denney, Dennie, Denys, Denny, Dennys, Denni, Dennee, Dennea, Deni, Denie, Denee, Denea, Deny, Deney

Dennison (English) The son of Dennis
Denison, Dennisun, Denisun, Dennisen, Denisen, Dennisan, Denisan, Dennisin, Denisin, Dennisyn, Denisyn, Dennyson, Denyson

Denton (English) From the town in the valley
Dentun, Dentin, Dentyn, Dentan, Denten, Denti, Dentie, Denty, Dentey, Dentee, Dentea

Denver (English) From the green valley
Denvar, Denvor, Denvir, Denvyr, Denvur

Denzel (English) From a place in Cornwall
Denzell, Denziel, Denzil, Denzill, Denzyl, Denzyll

Deo (Greek) A godly man

Deodar (Sanskrit) From the divine wood
Deodarr

Deogol (Anglo-Saxon) A secretive man

Deonte (French) An outgoing man
Deontay, Deontaye, Deontae, Dionte, Diontay, Diontaye, Diontae

Deorsa (Gaelic) Form of George, meaning "one who works the earth; a farmer"

Deotis (American) A learned man; a scholar
Deotiss, Deotys, Deotyss, Deotus, Deotuss

Derek (English) The ruler of the tribe
Dereck, Deric, Derick, Derik, Deriq, Derk, Derreck, Derrek, Derrick, Derrik, Derryck, Derryk, Deryck, Deryk, Deryke, Dirk, Dirke, Dyrk, Dyrke, Dirck, Dierck, Dieric, Dierick

Derland (English) From the deer's land
Derlande, Durland, Durlande, Derlen, Derlin, Derlyn, Durlin, Durlyn, Durlen

Dermot (Irish) A free man
Dermott, Dermod, Dermud, Dermut, Dermutt

Derry (Gaelic) From the grove of oak trees
Derrey, Derree, Derrea, Derri, Derrie

Dervin (English) A gifted friend
Dervinn, Dervinne, Dervyn, Dervynn, Dervynne, Dervon, Dervan, Dervun, Derven, Dervenn, Dervenne

Derward (English) A guardian of the deer
Derwerd, Deerward, Deerwerd, Deorward, Deorwerd, Derwent

Derwin (English) A friend of the deer; a gifted friend
Derwine, Derwinn, Derwinne, Derwen, Derwenn, Derwenne, Derwyn, Derwynn, Derwynne, Deorwine

Deshae (American) A confident man
Deshuy, Deshaye, Deshai, Deshi, Deshie, Deshy, Deshey, Deshee, Deshea

Deshan (Hindi) Of the nation
Deshal, Deshad

Deshawn (African American) God is gracious
Dashaun, Dashawn, Desean, Deshane, DeShaun, D'Shawn, Deshon, DeShawn

Desiderio (Latin) One who is desired; hoped for
Derito, Desi, Desideratus, Desiderios, Desiderius, Desiderus, Dezi, Diderot, Desie, Dezie, Desy, Dezy, Desey, Dezey, Desee, Dezee, Desea, Dezea, Didier, Dizier, Deseo, Des, Dez

Desmond (Gaelic) A man from South Munster
Desmonde, Desmund, Desmunde, Dezmond, Dezmonde, Dezmund, Dezmunde, Desmee, Dezmee, Desmea, Dezmea, Desmi, Dezmi, Desmie, Dezmie, Desmy, Dezmy, Desmey, Dezmey, Desmon, Dezmon, Desmun, Dezmun

Desperado (Spanish) A renegade

Destin (French) Recognizing one's certain fortune; fate
Destyn, Deston, Destun, Desten, Destan

Destrey (American) A cowboy
Destry, Destree, Destrea, Destri, Destrie

Detlef (German) One who is decisive
Detleff, Detlev

Deuce (American) A gambling man
Deuse, Dewce, Dewse

Deutsch (German) A German

Dev (Indian) A kingly man

Deval (Hindi) A divine man
Dev, Devak

Devanshi (Hindi) A divine messenger
Devanshie, Devanshy, Devanshey, Devanshee, Devanshea

Devante (Spanish) One who fights wrong-doing

Deverell (French) From the riverbank
Deverel, Deveral, Deverall, Devereau, Devereaux, Devere, Deverill, Deveril, Deverick, Deveryck, Deverik, Deveryk, Deveric, Deveryc, Devery, Deverey, Deveree, Deverea, Deveri, Deverie, Devry, Devrey, Devree, Devrea, Devri, Devrie

Devine (Gaelic / French) Resembling an ox / of the divine

Devisser (Dutch) A fisherman
Deviser, Devysser, Devyser

Devland (Irish) A courageous man
Devlande, Devlind, Devlinde, Devlend, Devlende

Devlin (Gaelic) Having fierce bravery; a misfortunate man
Devlyn, Devlon, Devlen, Devlan, Devlun

Devon (English) From the beautiful farmland; of the divine
*Devan, Deven, Devenn, **Devin**, Devonn, Devone, Deveon, Devonne, Devvon, Devyn, Devynn, Deheune, Devun, Devunn, Devion, Deavon, Deavun, Deavin, Deavyn, Devron, Devren, Devrin, Devryn*

Devoss (Dutch) Resembling a fox

Dewey (Welsh) A highly valued man
Dewy, Dewee, Dewea, Dewi, Dewie, Duey

Dewitt (Flemish) A blonde-haired man
DeWitt, Dewytt, DeWytt, Dewit, DeWit, Dewyt, DeWyt

Dexter (Latin) A right-handed man; one who is skillful
Dextor, Dextar, Dextur, Dextir, Dextyr, Dexton, Dextun, Dexten, Dextan, Dextin, Dextyn, Dex, Dexe

Dhyanesh (Indian) One who meditates
Dhianesh, Dhyaneshe, Dhianeshe

Dia (African) The champion

Diallo (African) One who is bold

Diamond (English) A highly valued man; resembling the gem; a bright protector
Diamont, Diamonde, Diamonte, Diamund, Diamunde, Diamunt, Diamunte, Diamon

Diarmid (Irish) A free man
Diarmaid, Diarmait, Diarmi, Diarmie, Diarmee, Diarmea, Diarmy, Diarmey

Dice (American) A gambling man
Dyce

Dichali (Native American) One who talks a lot
Dichalie, Dichaly, Dichaley, Dichalee, Dichalea, Dichaleigh

Dick (English) Form of Richard, meaning "a powerful ruler"
Dik, Dic, Dyck, Dyc, Dyk

Dickinson (English) The son of Dick
Dicken, Dickens, Dickson, Dickenson

Dickran (Armenian) The name of a king
Dikran, Dicran, Dyckran, Dykran, Dycran

✿ **Diego** (Spanish) Form of James, meaning "he who supplants"
Dyego, Dago

Dien (Vietnamese) A farmer

Diesel (American) Having great strength
Deisel, Diezel, Deizel, Dezsel

Dietmar (German) One who is famous
Dietmarr, Deitmar, Deitmarr

Dietrich (German) The ruler of the tribe
Dietrick, Dietryck, Dietrik, Dietryk, Dietric, Dietryc, Dieter, Dietar, Dietor, Dietur, Dietir, Dietyr, Deidrich, Deidrick, Deidryck, Deidrik, Deidryk, Deidric, Deidryc

Digby (Norse) From the town near the ditch
Digbey, Digbee, Digbea, Digbi, Digbie

Diggory (English) From the dyke
Diggorey, Diggori, Diggorie, Diggoree, Diggorea, Digory, Digorey, Digoree, Digorea, Digori, Digorie, Diggery, Diggerey, Diggeree, Diggerea, Diggeri, Diggerie, Digery, Digerey, Digeree, Digerea, Digeri, Digerie

Diji (African) A farmer
Dijie, Dijee, Dijea, Dijy, Dijey

Dilip (Indian) Of the royalty
Deleep, Dileap, Dilyp

Dillon (Gaelic) Resembling a lion; a faithful man
Dillun, Dillen, Dillan, Dillin, Dillyn, Dilon, Dilan, Dilin, Dilyn, Dilen, Dilun, Dillion, Dillian, Dillien, Dill

Dima (Slavic) A mighty warrior
Dyma, Dimah, Dymah

Din (African) A great man
Dyn

Dinesh (Hindi) Of the sun
Dineshe, Dynesh, Dyneshe

Dingo (Australian) Resembling the wild dog
Dyngo

Dinh (Vietnamese) One who is peaceful; calm

Dino (Italian) One who wields a little sword
Dyno, Dinoh, Dynoh, Deano, Deanoh, Deeno, Deenoh, Deino, Deinoh

Dinos (Greek) Form of Constantine, meaning "one who is steadfast; firm"
Dynos, Deanos, Deenos, Deinos, Dinose, Dinoz, Dinoze

Dins (American) One who climbs to the top
Dinz, Dyns, Dynz

Dinsmore (Celtic) From the fortress on the hill
Dinsmor, Dinnsmore, Dinnsmor, Dynsmore, Dynsmor, Dynnsmore, Dynnsmor, Dinny, Dinni, Dinney, Dinnie, Dinnee, Dinnea

Diogenes (Greek) An honest man
Dyogenes

Dion (Greek) Form of Dionysus, in mythology, the god of wine and revelry
Deion, Deon, Deonn, Deonys, Deyon, Diandre, Diondre, Dionte, Dondre, Diondray, Diandray, Diondrae, Diandrae

Dionizy (Polish) Form of Dionysus, in mythology, the god of wine and revelry
Dionizey, Dionizi, Dionizie, Dionizee, Dionizea

Dionysus (Greek) In mythology, the god of wine and revelry
Dionio, Dionisio, Dioniso, Dionysios, Dionysos, Dionysius, Dionysio, Dionyso, Deonysis, Deonysus, Deonisis, Deonisus, Dionis

Dior (French) The golden one
D'Or, Diorr, Diorre, Dyor, Deor, Dyorre, Deorre

Diron (American) Form of Darren, meaning "a great man / a gift from God"
Dirun, Diren, Diran, Dirin, Diryn, Dyron, Dyren, Dyran, Dyrin, Dyryn, Dyrun

Dix (English) The tenth-born child
Dixe, Dixx, Dyx, Dyxe, Dyxx, Dixo, Dyxo

Dixon (English) The son of Dick
Dixen, Dixin, Dixyn, Dixan, Dixun

Doane (English) From the rolling hills
Doan

Dobber (American) An independent man
Dobbar, Dobbor, Dobbur, Dobbir, Dobbyr

Dobbs (English) A fiery man
Dobbes, Dobes, Dobs

Dobi (African) One who does laundry
Dobie, Doby, Dobey, Dobee, Dobea

Dobromir (Polish) A good man
Dobromeer, Dobromear, Dobromier, Dobromeir, Dobromere, Dobromyr, Dobrey, Dobree, Dobrea, Dobri, Dobrie, Dobry

Doctor (American) A physician; one who heals others
Docter, Doctur, Doctar, Doktor, Doktur, Dokter, Doktar, Dock, Doc, Dok

Dodek (Polish) A hero
Dodeck, Dodec

Dodge (English) Form of Roger, meaning "a famous spearman"
Dodger, Doge, Dodgson, Dodds, Dodd, Dod, Dods

Dog (American) Resembling the animal; one who is loyal
Dawg, Daug, Dogg, Doggie, Doggi, Doggy, Doggey, Doggee, Doggea

Doherty (Irish) One who is harmful
Dohertey, Doherti, Dohertie, Dohertee, Dohertea, Dougherty, Doughertey, Dougherti, Doughertie, Doughertee, Doughertea, Douherty, Douhertey, Douherti, Douhertie, Douhertee, Douhertea

Dohosan (Native American) From the bluff
Dohosen, Dohoson, Dohosun, Dohosin, Dohosyn

Doire (Scottish) From the grove
Doyre, Dhoire, Dhoyre

Dolan (Gaelic) A dark-haired man; one who is bold
Dolen, Dolon, Dolun, Dolin, Dolyn

Dolgen (American) A tenacious man
Dolgan, Dolgin, Dolgyn, Dolgun, Dolgon, Dolge, Dolg

Dolph (German) A noble wolf
Dolf, Dollfus, Dollfuss, Dollphus, Dolphus, Dolfus

Domani (Italian) Man of tomorrow
Domanie, Domany, Domaney, Domanee, Domanea

Domevlo (African) One who doesn't judge others
Domivlo, Domyvlo

Domingo (Spanish) Born on a Sunday
Domyngo, Demingo, Demyngo

❷ **Dominic** (Latin) A lord
Demenico, Dom, Domenic, Domenico, Domenique, Domini, Dominick, Dominico, Dominie, Dominik, Dominique, Domenik, Domenick, Dominie, Dominy, Dominey, Dominee, Dominea, Domino

Domnall (Gaelic) A world ruler
Domhnall, Domnull, Domhnull

Domokos (Hungarian) One who belongs to God
Domokus, Domonkos, Domonkus, Domos

Don (Scottish) From of Donald, meaning "ruler of the world"
Donn, Donny, Donney, Donnie, Donni, Donnee, Donnea, Donne, Donnan, Donnen, Donnon, Donnun, Donnin, Donnyn

Donaciano (Spanish) Having dark features
Donace, Donase, Donasiano

Donagh (Celtic) A brown-haired warrior
*Donaghie, Donaghy, Donaghey, Donaghi,
Donaghee, Donaghea*

Donahue (Irish) A dark warrior
*Donahoe, Donohoe, Donohue, Donahugh,
Donohugh*

Donald (Scottish) Ruler of the world
Donold, Donuld, Doneld, Donild, Donyld

Donar (Teutonic) In mythology, the god of
thunder
Doner, Donor, Donur, Donir, Donyr

Donatello (Spanish) A gift from God
*Donato, Donatien, Donatus, Donatelo,
Donatio, Donateo, Donat, Donzel, Donzell,
Donzele, Donzelle*

Donder (Dutch) Resembling thunder
Dondar, Dondor, Dondur, Dondir, Dondyr

Dong (Vietnamese) Born during the winter

Donis (English) Form of Adonis, in mythol-
ogy, a handsome young man loved by
Aphrodite
Donys, Donnis, Donys, Dones, Donnes

Donkor (African) A humble man
Donkur, Donkir, Donkyr, Donker, Donkar

Donnan (Irish) A brown-haired man
Donnen, Donnon, Donnun, Donnin, Donnyn

Donnell (Scottish) Ruler of the world; a
brown-haired warrior
*Donnel, Donell, Donel, Donnall, Donal,
Donnal, Donall, Donnelly, Donnelley, Donnelli,
Donnellie, Donnellee, Donally, Donalley,
Donalli, Donallie, Donallee, Donaly, Donaley,
Donali, Donalie, Donalee, Donnally, Donnalley,
Donnallee, Donnallea, Donnalli, Donnallie*

Donovan (Irish) A brown-haired chief
*Donavan, Donavon, Donevin, Donevon,
Donoven, Donovon, Donovin, Donovyn,
Donaven, Donavin, Donavyn, Donevyn,
Donevan, Doneven*

Dontavius (English) Form of Dante, mean-
ing "an enduring man; everlasting"
*Dantavius, Dawntavius, Dewontavius,
Dontavious, Dontav, Dontave*

Donton (American) One who is confident
*Dontun, Daunton, Dauntun, Donti, Dontie,
Donty, Dontey, Daunti, Dauntie, Dauntey,
Daunty*

Donyale (American) One who is regal
*Donyail, Donyaile, Donyael, Donyaele,
Donyayl, Donyayle*

Donyell (American) A faithful man
*Donyel, Donyele, Donyelle, Danyel, Danyell,
Danyele, Danyelle*

Doocey (American) A quick-witted man
Doocy, Doocee, Doocea, Dooci, Doocie

Dooley (Irish) A dark hero
Dooly, Doolee, Doolea, Dooleigh, Dooli, Doolie

Dor (Hebrew) Of this generation
*Doram, Doriel, Dorli, Dorlie, Dorlee, Dorlea,
Dorleigh, Dorly, Dorley*

Doran (Irish) A stranger; one who has been
exiled
Doren, Dorin, Doryn

Dorek (Polish) A gift from God
Dorec, Doreck

Dorian (Greek) Of the ancient Greek tribe,
the Dorians
*Dorrian, Dorien, Dorrien, Dorion, Dorrion,
Doriun, Dorriun, Dori, Dorri, Dorie, Dorrie,
Dorry, Dory, Dorey, Dorrey, Doree, Dorree,
Dorrea, Dorea*

Dorjan (Hungarian) A dark man
Dorjen, Dorjin, Dorjyn, Dorjon, Dorjun

Doron (Hebrew) A gift; the dweller
*Dorron, Dorun, Dorrun, Doroni, Doronie,
Doronee, Dorone, Doronea, Dorony, Doroney,
Dorroni, Dorronie, Dorronee, Dorronea,
Dorrone, Dorrony, Dorroney*

Dorran (Irish) A dark-haired man
*Dorren, Dorrin, Dorryn, Dorrell, Dorrel,
Dorrance, Dorrence*

Dorset (English) Of the people who live
near the sea
*Dorsett, Dorsete, Dorsette, Dorzet, Dorzete,
Dorzett, Dorzette*

Dorsey (Gaelic) From the fortress near the sea
Dorsy, Dorsee, Dorsea, Dorsi, Dorsie

Dosne (Celtic) From the sand hill
Dosni, Dosnie, Dosney, Dosny, Dosnee, Dosnea

Dost (Arabic) A beloved friend
Doste, Daust, Dauste, Dawst, Dawste

Dotan (African) A hardworking man
Doten, Dotin, Dotyn, Doton, Dotun

Dotson (English) The son of Dot
Dotsen, Dotsan, Dotsin, Dotsyn, Dotsun, Dottson, Dottsun, Dottsin, Dottsyn, Dottsan, Dottsen

Dougal (Celtic) A dark stranger
Dougall, Dugal, Duguld, Dugall, Dougald, Doughal, Doughald, Doughall, Dughall

Douglas (Scottish) From the black river
Douglass, Dugaid, Doug, Doughlas, Dougy, Dougey, Dougi, Dougie, Dougee, Dougea, Duglass, Dughlass, Duglas, Dughlas

Dour (Scottish) A man from the water
Doure

Dov (Hebrew) Resembling a bear
Dohv, Dahv

Dove (American) A peaceful man
Dovi, Dovie, Dovy, Dovey, Dovee, Dovea

Dover (Welsh) From the water
Dovor, Dovar, Dovur, Dovir, Dovyr

Dovev (Hebrew) One who speaks softly
Doviv, Dovyv

Dow (Irish) A dark-haired man
Dowe, Dowson, Dowsun, Dowsen, Dowsan, Dowsin, Dowsyn, Dowan, Dowen, Dowon, Dowyn, Dowin, Dowun

Dowd (American) A serious-minded man
Dowde, Dowed, Dowdi, Dowdie, Dowdy, Dowdey, Dowdee, Dowdea

Doyle (Gaelic) A dark stranger
Doile, Doyl, Doil, Doy, Doye, Dowle, Dowl, Doyal

Doylton (English) From Doyle's town
Doyltun, Doylten, Doyltan, Doyltin, Doyltyn

Drade (American) A serious-minded man
Draid, Draide, Drayd, Drayde, Draed, Draede, Dradell, Dradel

Dragon (American) Resembling the fire-breathing creature
Dragan, Dragen, Dragun, Dragin, Dragyn

Drake (English) Resembling a dragon
Draik, Draike, Draek, Draeke, Drayk, Drayke, Draco, Dracko, Drako, Dracon, Drackon, Drakon, Drago, Draico, Draicko, Draiko, Drayco, Draycko, Drayko, Draeco, Draecko, Draeko, Draicon, Draickon, Draikon, Draycon, Drayckon, Draykon, Draecon, Draeckon, Draekon, Draygo, Draigo, Draego, Dracul, Drakul

Draper (English) One who sells cloth
Drapar, Drapor, Drapur, Drapir, Drapyr

Drayce (American) Form of Drake, meaning "resembling a dragon"
Drayse, Draice, Draise, Draece, Draese, Drace, Drase, Dracie, Draci, Dracey, Dracy, Dracee, Dracea, Drasy, Drasey, Drasee, Drasea, Drasi, Drasie

Drefan (Anglo-Saxon) A troublemaker
Drefon, Drefun, Drefen, Drefin, Drefyn

Dreng (Anglo-Saxon) A mighty warrior; one who is brave
Drenge, Dring, Dringe, Dryng, Drynge

Dreogan (Anglo-Saxon) A suffering man
Dreogen, Dreogon, Dreogun, Dreogin, Dreogyn

Drew (Welsh) One who is wise
Drue, Dru, Droo, Drou, Dryw, Druw

Drexel (American) A thoughtful man
Drexell, Drexele, Drexelle, Drex, Drexe

Driscoll (Celtic) A mediator; one who is sorrowful; a messenger
Dryscoll, Driscol, Dryscol, Driskoll, Dryskoll, Driskol, Dryskol, Driskell, Dryskell, Driskel, Dryskel

Druce (Gaelic / English) A wise man; a druid / the son of Drew
Drews, Drewce, Druece, Druse, Druson, Drusen, Drusin, Drusyn, Drusan, Drusun, Drywson, Drywsen, Drywsan, Drywsun, Drywsin, Drywson, Drewson, Drewsun, Drewsan, Drewsen, Drewsin, Drewsyn

Drugi (German) Having great strength
Drugie, Drugy, Drugey, Drugee, Drugea

Drummond (Scottish) One who lives on the ridge
Drummon, Drumond, Drumon, Drummund, Drumund, Drummun, Drumun, Drummand, Drumand, Drumman, Druman

Drury (French) One who is dearly loved
Drurey, Druri, Drurie, Druree, Drurea, Drewry, Drewrey, Drewri, Drewrie, Drewree, Drewrea

Dryden (English) From the dry valley
Driden, Drydan, Dridan, Drydon, Dridon, Drydun, Dridun, Drydin, Dridin, Drydyn, Dridyn, Drygedene

Drystan (Welsh) Form of Tristan, meaning "a sorrowful man"
Drystan, Dris, Dristam, Dristen, Dristian, Dristin, Driston, Dristram, Dristyn, Driste, Drysten, Dryston, Drystyn

Duane (Gaelic) A dark or swarthy man
Dewain, Dewayne, Duante, Duayne, Duwain, Duwaine, Duwayne, Dwain, Dwaine, Dwayne, Dawayne, Dwane

Duarte (Spanish) A wealthy guardian
Duartay, Duartaye, Duartai, Duartae, Duardo, Duard, Duarde, Dueart, Duearte, Duart, Duartee, Duartea, Duarti, Duartie, Duarty, Duartey

Dubh (Scottish) A black-haired man
Dub, Dubg, Dubb, Dubv

Dublin (Irish) From the capital of Ireland
Dublyn, Dublen, Dublan, Dublon, Dublun

Duc (Vietnamese) One who has upstanding morals

Dude (American) A cowboy

Dudley (English) From the people's meadow
Dudly, Dudlee, Dudlea, Dudleah, Dudleigh, Dudli, Dudlie

Due (Vietnamese) A virtuous man

Duer (Celtic) A heroic man

Duff (Gaelic) A swarthy man
Duffe, Duffi, Duffie, Duffee, Duffea

Dugan (Gaelic) A dark and swarthy man
Doogan, Dougan, Douggan, Duggan

Duke (English) A title of nobility; a leader
Dooke, Dook, Duki, Dukie, Dukey, Duky, Dukee, Dukea

Dulal (Indian) One who is dearly loved
Dulall, Dullal, Dullall

Dume (African) Resembling a bull

Dumi (African) One who inspires others
Dumie, Dumy, Dumey, Dumee, Dumea

Dumisani (African) A great leader
Dumisanie, Dumisany, Dumisaney, Dumisanee, Dumisanea

Dumont (French) Man of the mountain
Dumonte, Dumount, Dumounte

Dunbar (Gaelic) From the castle at the headland
Dunbarr, Dunbaron, Dunbaran, Dunbarin, Dunbaryn, Dunbaren, Dunbarun

Duncan (Scottish) A dark warrior
Dunkan, Dunckan, Dunc, Dunk, Dunck

Dundee (Scottish) From the town on the Firth of Tay
Dundea, Dundi, Dundie, Dundy, Dundey

Dung (Vietnamese) A brave man; a heroic man

Dunham (Celtic) A brown-haired man

Dunia (American) Having dark features
Duniah, Dunya, Dunyah, Duniya, Duniyah

Dunley (English) From the hilly meadow
Dunly, Dunli, Dunlie, Dunleigh, Dunlea, Dunleah, Dunnley, Dunnly, Dunnleigh, Dunnlee, Dunnlea, Dunnleah, Dunnli, Dunnlie

Dunlop (Scottish) From the muddy hill

Dunmore (Scottish) From the fortress on the hill
Dunmor

Dunn (Gaelic) A brown-haired man
Dun, Dunne, Dune

Dunphy (American) A dark and serious man
Dunphey, Dunphi, Dunphie, Dunphee, Dunphea, Dunphe

Dunstan (English) From the hill of brown stones
Dunsten, Dunstin, Dunstyn, Dunston, Dunstun

Dunton (English) From the town on the hill
Duntun, Dunten, Duntan, Duntin, Duntyn

Durand (Latin / French) An enduring man / one who stands firm
Duran, Durant, Durante, Durrant, Durrand, Durande, Durrande, Durandt

Durango (French) Having great strength
Durengo, Duringo, Duryngo

Durbin (Latin) One who lives in the city
Durbyn, Durban, Durben, Durbon, Durbun

Dureau (French) Having great strength
Dureaux, Dureax, Durell, Durel, Durelle, Durele

Durga (Hindi) The unreachable

Durin (Norse) In mythology, one of the fathers of the dwarves
Duryn, Duren, Duran, Duron, Durun

Durjaya (Hindi) One who is difficult to defeat

Durrell (English) One who is strong and protective
Durrel, Durell, Durel

Durward (English) A gatekeeper
Durwerd, Durwald, Durwarden, Durwerden, Derward, Derwerd, Derwarden, Derwerden

Durwin (English) A friend of the deer
Durwinn, Durwinne, Durwine, Durwen, Durwenn, Durwenne, Durwyn, Durwynn, Durwynne

Duryea (Gaelic) An enduring man

Dusan (Slavic) God is my judge
Dusen, Duson, Dusun, Dusin, Dusyn

Duscha (Slavic) Filled with the divine spirit

Dustin (English / German) From the dusty area / a courageous warrior
Dustyn, Dusten, Dustan, Duston, Dustun, Dusty, Dusley, Dusti, Dustie, Dustee, Dustea, Duster

Dutch (German) From the Netherlands

Duvall (French) From the valley
Duval, Duvale

Dwade (English) A dark traveler
Dwaid, Dwaide, Dwayd, Dwayde, Dwaed, Dwaede

Dwan (American) A fresh-faced man
Dwawn, Dwaun, Dewan, Dewawn, Dewaun

Dweezel (American) A creative man
Dweezell, Dweeze, Dweezil, Dweezill, Dweezyl, Dweezyll, Dweezi, Dweezie, Dweezy, Dweezey, Dweezee, Dweezea

Dwight (Flemish) A white- or blonde-haired man
Dwite, Dwhite, Dwyght, Dwighte

Dwyer (Gaelic) A dark and wise man
Dwire

Dyami (Native American) Resembling an eagle
Dyamie, Dyamy, Dyamey, Dyamee, Dyamea, Dyame

Dyer (English) A creative man
Dier, Dyar, Diar, Dy, Dye, Di, Die

❂
❂ **Dylan** (Welsh) Son of the sea
Dyllan, Dylon, Dyllon, Dylen, Dyllen, Dylun, Dyllun, Dylin, Dyllin, Dylyn, Dyllyn

Dymas (Greek) In mythology, the father of Hecabe
Dimas

Dynell (American) A man of the sea
Dynel, Dynele, Dynelle, Dinell, Dinel, Dinele, Dinelle

Dyre (Scandinavian) A dear and precious man
Dyr, Dyri, Dyrie, Dyry, Dyrey, Dyree, Dyrea

Dyson (American) Form of Tyson, meaning "one who is high-spirited; fiery"
Dysen, Dysan, Dysun, Dysin, Dysyn, Dison, Disan, Disen, Disun, Disin, Disyn

Dyumani (Indian) Of the sun
Dyumanie, Dyumany, Dyumaney, Dyumanee, Dyumanea

Dzigbode (African) One who is patient

e

Eachan (Irish) A horseman
Eachann, Echan, Echann

Eadburt (English) A wealthy man
Eadbert, Eadbirt, Eadbyrt, Eadbeorht

Eagan (Irish) A fiery man
Eegan, Eagen, Eegen, Eagon, Eegon, Eagun, Eegun, Ea

Eagle (Native American) Resembling the bird
Eegle, Eagel, Eegel

Eamon (Irish) Form of Edmond, meaning "a wealthy protector"
Eaman, Eamen, Eamin, Eamyn, Eamun, Eamonn, Eames, Eemon, Eeman, Eemen, Eemin, Eemyn, Eemun, Eemes

Ean (Gaelic) Form of John, meaning "God is gracious"
Eion, Eyan, Eyon, Eian

Earl (English) A nobleman
Earle, Erle, Erl, Eorl

Earlham (English) From the earl's village
Erlham

Earlston (English) From the earl's town
Earlstun, Erlston, Erlstun, Earlton, Earltun, Erlton, Erltun

Early (American / English) One who is punctual / from Earl's meadow
Earley, Earli, Earlie, Earleigh, Earlee, Earlea, Earleah, Erly, Erley, Erleigh, Erlee, Erlea, Erleah, Erli, Erlie

Earm (Anglo-Saxon) A wretched man
Erm, Eerm, Eirm

Earnan (Irish) A knowing man
Earnen, Earnin, Earnyn, Earnon, Earnun, Ernan, Ernen, Ernon, Ernun, Ernin, Ernyn

Earvin (English) Friend of the sea
Earven, Earvan, Earvyn, Earvon, Earvun, Ervin, Ervyn, Erven, Ervan, Ervon, Ervun, Ervine

Easey (American) An easygoing man
Easy, Easi, Easie, Easee, Easea, Eazey, Eazy, Eazi, Eazie, Eazee, Eazea, Ezy, Ezey, Ezee, Ezea, Ezi, Ezie

Eastman (English) A man from the east
Eestman, East, Easte, Eest, Eeste

Easton (English) From the eastern town
Eeston, Eastun, Eestun

Eaton (English) From the island village
Eatton, Eton, Etton, Eyton, Eytton, Eatun, Etun, Eytun, Etawn, Etaun, Eatawn, Eataun

Eben (Hebrew) As solid as a rock
Eban, Ebon, Ebin, Ebyn, Ebun, Eb, Ebbe

Ebenezer (Hebrew) The rock of help
Ebbaneza, Ebeneezer, Ebeneser, Ebenezar, Eveneser, Evenezer, Ebenzer, Ebby, Ebbey, Ebbea, Ebbee, Ebbi, Ebbie

Eberhard (German) As strong as a boar; as brave as a boar
Eberado, Eberhardt, Eberdt, Ebert, Eberte, Eberhart, Eburhard, Eburhart, Eburhardt, Eburt, Eburdt

Eberlein (German) Resembling a small boar
Eberleen, Eberlean, Eberlien, Eberlin, Eberlyn, Eberle, Eberley, Eberly, Eberlee, Eberleigh, Eberlea, Eberli, Eberlie

Ebisu (Japanese) In mythology, the patron god of fishermen
Ebysu, Ebisue, Ebysue, Ebisoo, Ebysoo, Ebisou, Ebysou

Eblis (Arabic) A devilish man
Ebliss, Eblisse, Eblys, Eblyss, Eblysse

Ebo (African) Born on a Tuesday
Eboe, Ebow, Ebowe

Ebrahim (Arabic) Form of Abraham, meaning "father of a multitude; father of nations"
Ebraheem, Ebraheim, Ebrahiem, Ebraheam, Ebrahym

Echo (Greek) Sound returned
Ekko, Ekho, Eko, Ecco, Ekow, Ecko

Eckerd (German) One who is sacred
Ekerd, Ecerd, Eckherd, Eckhert, Ekherd

Eckhard (German) Of the brave sword point
Eckurd, Eckardt, Eckhardt, Ekkehard,
Ekkehardt, Ekhard, Ekhardt

Ed (English) Form of Edward, meaning "a
wealthy protector"
Edd, Eddi, Eddie, Eddy, Eddey, Eddee, Eddea,
Edi, Edie, Edy, Edey, Edee, Edea

Edan (Celtic) One who is full of fire
Edon, Edun

Edbert (English) One who is prosperous
and bright
Edberte, Edburt, Edburte, Edbirt, Edbirte,
Edbyrt, Edbyrte

Edel (German) One who is noble
Edelin, Edlin, Edell, Edlen, Edelen, Edelyn,
Edlyn

Edelmar (English) One who is noble
Edelmarr

Eden (Hebrew) Place of pleasure; in the
Bible, the first home of Adam and Eve
Eaden, Eadin, Edin, Ednan, Edyn

Edenson (English) Son of Eden
Eadenson, Edensun, Eadensun, Edinson,
Edinsun, Edensen, Eadensen

Eder (Hebrew) Of the flock
Edar, Edir, Edyr, Edor, Edur

Edet (African) Born on the market day
Edett, Edete

Edgar (English) A powerful and wealthy
spearman
Eadgar, Eadger, Edgard, Edgardo, Edghur,
Edgur, Edger, Edgor, Eadgur, Eadgor, Eadgir,
Edgir, Eadgyr, Edgyr, Eadgard

Edge (American) A trendsetter
Edgi, Edgie, Edgey, Edgy, Edgee, Edgea

Edilberto (Spanish) One who is noble
Edylberto, Edilbert, Edylbert, Edilburt,
Edylburt, Edilbirt, Edylbirt, Edilberto,
Edilburto, Edylburto, Edilbirto, Edylbirto

Edison (English) Son of Edward
Eddison, Edisun, Eddisun, Edisen, Eddisen,
Edisyn, Eddisyn, Edyson, Eddyson, Edysun,
Eddysun, Edysen, Eddysen, Edson, Edsun,
Edsen, Eddis, Eddys, Eddiss, Eddyss

Edlin (Anglo-Saxon) A wealthy friend
Edlinn, Edlinne, Edlyn, Edlynn, Edlynne,
Eadlyn, Eadlin, Edlen, Edlenn, Edlenne,
Eadlinn, Eadlinne, Eadlynne, Eadlynn

Edmar (English) Of the wealthy sea
Edmarr, Eddmar, Eddmarr, Eadmar,
Eadmarr

Edmond (English) A wealthy protector
Edmon, Edmund, Edmonde, Edmundo,
Edmondo, Edmun, Edmunde, Eadmund,
Eadmunde, Eadmond, Eadmonde, Ede

Edom (Hebrew) A red-haired man
Edum, Edam, Edem, Edim, Edym

Edred (Anglo-Saxon) A king
Edread, Edrid, Edryd

Edrian (Latin) A man from Hadria
Ede, Ediran, Edrain, Edrean, Edreean,
Edreyan, Edreeyan, Edriaan, Edriano, Edrien,
Edrin, Edrino, Edrion, Edron, Edryan, Edya,
Erjen, Eydrean, Eydreean, Eydrian, Eydrien

Edric (English) A prosperous and lucky ruler
Edrik, Eddrick, Ederic, Ederick, Edrich,
Edrick, Edryc, Edryk, Edryck, Edri, Edrie,
Edry, Edrey, Edree, Eadric, Eadrick, Eadrik,
Eadryc, Eadryck, Eadryk

Edrigu (Basque) A famous ruler
Edrygu, Edrigue, Edrygue, Edrigou, Edrygou,
Edingu, Edyngu, Edingu, Edingue, Edyngue,
Edingou, Edyngou

Edsel (German / English) One who is noble
and bright / from the wealthy man's house
Edsil, Edsyl, Edsal, Edsol, Edsul, Edsell, Edcell,
Edcel, Edcil, Edcyl

Edwald (English) A wealthy ruler
Edwaldo, Edwalde, Edwaldio, Edwaldeo

Edward (English) A wealthy protector
Eadward, Edik, Edouard, Eduard, Eduardo,
Edvard, Edvardas, Edwardo, Ewart, Edoardo,
Edorta

Edwardson (English) The son of Edward
Edwardsun, Eadwardsone, Eadwardsun

Edwin (English) A wealthy friend
Edwinn, Edwinne, Edwine, Edwyn, Edwynn,
Edwynne, Edwen, Edwenn, Edwenne, Eadwin,
Eadwyn, Eadwen, Easwine, Edwy, Edwey,
Edwee, Edwea, Edwi, Edwie

Effiom (African) Resembling a crocodile
Efiom, Effyom, Efyom, Effeom, Efeom

Efigenio (Greek) Form of Eugene, meaning
"a wellborn man"
*Ephigenio, Ephigenios, Ephigenius, Efigenios,
Efigenius*

Efisio (Italian) A man from Ephesus

Efrain (Spanish) Form of Ephraim, mean-
ing "one who is fertile; productive"
*Efraine, Efrayn, Efrayne, Efraen, Efraene,
Efrane, Efren, Efran, Efrun, Efrin, Efryn*

Efrat (Hebrew) One who is honored
Efratt, Ephrat, Ephratt

Efron (Hebrew) Resembling a songbird
*Ephron, Efroni, Ephroni, Efronie, Ephronie,
Efrony, Ephrony, Efroney, Ephroney, Efronee,
Ephronee*

Efton (American) Form of Ephraim, meaning "one who is fertile; productive"
Eftun, Eften, Eftan, Eftin, Eftyn

Egan (Gaelic) A little flame; one who is fiery
Egen, Egin, Egyn, Egann, Eghan, Eghann

Egbert (English) One who wields a brilliant
sword
*Egberte, Egburt, Egburte, Egbirt, Egbirte,
Egbyrt, Egbyrte*

Egborn (English) One who is ready
*Egborne, Egbourn, Egbourne, Egbern, Egberne,
Egburn, Egburne*

Egerton (English) From the town on the
edge; from Edgar's town
*Egertun, Edgerton, Edgertun, Egarton,
Egartun, Edgarton, Edgartun*

Egesa (Anglo-Saxon) One who creates ter-
ror
Egessa, Egeslic, Egeslick, Egeslik

Egeus (American) A protective man
Egius, Eges, Egis

Eghert (German) An intelligent man
*Egherte, Eghurt, Eghurte, Eghirt, Eghirte,
Eghyrt, Eghyrte*

Egidio (Italian) Resembling a young goat
*Egydio, Egideo, Egydeo, Egidiyo, Egydiyo,
Egidius, Egydius, Egidios, Egydios*

Egil (Scandinavian) Of the sword's point or
cdge
Egyl, Eigil, Eigyl

Eginhard (German) One who is strong with
a sword
*Eginard, Eginhardt, Einhard, Einhardt,
Einard*

Egmont (French) A fierce defender
*Egmonte, Egmunt, Egmunte, Egmond,
Egmonde, Egmund, Egmunde, Egmon, Egmun*

Egon (German) Of the sword's point
Egun

Egor (Russian) One who works the earth; a
farmer
Eigor, Eygor

Egyed (Hungarian) A shield-bearer
Egied

Ehren (German) An honorable man
Ehran, Ehrin, Ehryn, Ehron, Ehrun

Ehud (Hebrew) One who loves and is loved

Eikki (Finnish) A powerful man
*Eikkie, Eikky, Eikkey, Eikkee, Eikkea, Eiki,
Eikie, Eiky, Eikey, Eikee, Eikea*

Eilad (Hebrew) God is eternal

Eilam (Hebrew) One who is eternal
*Elam, Eilem, Elem, Eilim, Elim, Eilym, Elym,
Eilom, Elom, Eilum, Elum*

Eilert (Scandinavian) Of the hard point
*Elert, Eilart, Elart, Eilort, Elort, Eilurt, Elurt,
Eilirt, Elirt, Eilyrt, Elyrt*

Eilif (Norse) One who is immortal
Elif, Eilyf, Elyf

Eilon (Hebrew) From the oak tree
Eilan, Eilin, Eilyn, Eilen, Eilun

Eimhin (Irish) One who is swift
Eimhyn, Eimarr, Eimar

Einar (Scandinavian) A leading warrior
*Einer, Ejnar, Einir, Einyr, Einor, Einur, Ejnir,
Ejnyr, Ejnor, Ejnur, Ejner*

Einion (Welsh) An anvil
Einyon, Enion, Enyon, Einian, Enian

Einri (Teutonic) An intelligent man
Einrie, Einry, Einrey, Einree, Einrea

Eisa (Arabic) Form of Jesus, meaning "God is my salvation"
Eisah, Eissa, Eissah

Eisig (Hebrew) One who laughs often
Eisyg

Ejnar (Danish) A warrior
Ejnarr

Eknath (Hindi) A poet
Ecknath, Ecnath, Eknathe, Ecknathe, Ecnathe

Ekon (African) Having great strength
Ekun, Ekan, Eken, Ekin, Ekyn

Ekram (Hindi) One who is honored
Eckram, Ecram

Eladio (Spanish) A man from Greece
Eladeo, Eladiyo, Eladeyo

Elbert (English / German) A wellborn man / a bright man
Elberte, Elburt, Elburte, Elhirt, Elbirte, Ethelbert, Ethelburt, Ethelbirt, Elber, Elbur, Elbir

Elbis (American) One who is exalted
Elbys, Elbiss, Elbyss, Elbase, Elbace, Elbus, Elbuss

Elbridge (English) From the old bridge
Ellbridge, Elbrige, Ellbrige, Elbrydge, Elbryge, Ellbrydge, Ellbryge

Elchanan (Hebrew) God is gracious
Elchana, Elhanan, Elhannan, Elchannan, Elhana

Eldan (English) From the valley of the elves

Elden (English) An old friend
Eldin, Eldyn, Eldwin, Eldwinn, Eldwinne, Eldwen, Eldwenn, Eldwenne, Eldwyn, Eldwynn, Eldwynne, Eldwine

Elder (English) From the elder tree
Eldir, Eldyr, Eldor, Eldur, Eldar

Eldon (English) From the sacred hill
Eldun

Eldorado (Spanish) The golden man

Eldred (English) An old, wise advisor
Eldrid, Eldryd, Eldrad, Eldrod, Edlrud, Ethelred, Ethelread, Eldread

Eldrian (English) An old, wise ruler
Eldryan, Eldriann, Eldryann, Eldrien, Eldryen, Eldrienn, Eldryenn

Eldrick (English) An old, wise ruler
Eldrik, Eldric, Eldryck, Eldryk, Eldryc, Eldrich, Eldrych

Eldridge (German) A wise ruler
Eldredge, Eldrege, Eldrige, Eldrydge, Eldryge

Eleazar (Hebrew) God will help
Elazar, Eleasar, Eleazaro, Eliazar, Eliezer, Elazaro, Eleazaro, Elazer

Elegy (Spanish) One who is memorable
Elegey, Elegi, Elegie, Elegee, Elegea

Elek (Hungarian) Form of Alexander, meaning "helper and defender of mankind"
Elec, Eleck

Eleodoro (Spanish) A gift from the sun

Elford (English) From the old ford
Ellford, Elforde, Ellforde, Elfurd, Ellfurd

Elgan (Welsh) Of the bright circle
Elgen, Elgann, Elgenn

Elger (English) One who wields an elf spear
Ellger, Elgar, Ellgar, Elgir, Ellgir, Elgyr, Ellgyr, Elgor, Ellgor, Elgur, Ellgur, Elga

Elgin (English) A noble man; one who is white-skinned
Elgyn, Elgine, Elgyne, Eljin, Eljine, Eljyn, Eljyne

❂ **Eli** (Hebrew) One who has ascended; my God on high
Ely, Elie, Eliy, Elye

Eliachim (Hebrew) God will establish
Eliakim, Elyachim, Elyakim, Eliachym, Eliakym

Eliam (Hebrew) The God of my nation
Elami, Elamie, Elamy, Elamey, Elamee, Elamea, Elyam

Elian (Spanish) A spirited man
Elyan, Elien, Elyen, Elion, Elyon, Eliun, Elyun

Elias (Hebrew) Form of Elijah, meaning "Jehovah is my God"
Elia, Elice, Ellice, Elyas, Ellyce

Elihu (Hebrew) My God is He
Elyhu, Elihue, Elyhue, Elihugh, Elyhugh

● **Elijah** (Hebrew) Jehovah is my God
⊤
Elija, Eliyahu, Eljah, Elja, Elyjah, Elyja, Elijuah, Elyjuah

Elim (Hebrew) From the oasis
Elym, Eleem, Eleam, Eleim, Eliem

Elimelech (Hebrew) God is kind
Elymelech, Elimelek, Elimeleck, Elymelek, Elymeleck

Elimu (African) Having knowledge of science
Elymu, Elimue, Elymue, Elimoo, Elymoo

Eliphalet (Hebrew) God is my deliverance
Elifalet, Elifelet, Eliphelet, Elyphalet, Elyfalet, Elyfelet, Elyphelet

Eliron (Hebrew) My God is song
Elyron, Elirun, Elyrun, Eliran, Elyran, Eliren, Elyren, Elirin, Elyrin, Eliryn, Elyryn

Elisha (Hebrew) God is my salvation
Elisee, Eliseo, Elisher, Eliso, Elisio, Elysha, Elysee, Elyseo, Elysio, Elysher, Elyso, Elizeo, Elishah, Elyshah, Elishua, Ellsha, Elsha

Elkanah (Hebrew) One who belongs to God
Elkana, Elkannah, Elkanna, Elkan, Elken, Elkon, Elkun, Elkin, Elkyn, Ellkan, Ellken, Ellkon, Elkon, Ellkin, Ellkyn, Ellkanna

Ellard (German) A noble and brave man
Ellerd, Ellird, Ellyrd, Ellord, Ellurd, Eallard, Ealhhard

Ellery (English) From the alder tree
Ellerey, Elleri, Ellerie, Elleree, Ellerea, Ellary, Ellarey, Ellari, Ellarie, Ellaree, Ellarea, Ellar, Eller

Ellesmere (English) From Ellis's pond
Ellesmeer, Ellesmir, Ellesmyr, Elesmere, Elesmeer, Elesmir, Elesmyr

Elliott (English) Form of Elijah, meaning "Jehovah is my God"
Eliot, Eliott, Elliot, Elyot, Elyott, Ellyott, Ellyot

Ellis (English) Form of Elias, meaning "Jehovah is my God"
Elliss, Ellyss, Ellys, Elliston, Ellyston, Ellice, Ellise

Ellison (English) The son of Elias
Elison, Ellyson, Elyson, Ellisun, Elisun, Ellysun, Elysun, Eallison, Ealison

Ellory (Cornish) Resembling a swan
Ellorey, Elloree, Ellorea, Ellori, Ellorie, Elory, Elorey, Elorea, Eloree, Elori, Elorie

Ellsworth (English) From the nobleman's estate
Elsworth, Ellswerth, Elswerth, Ellswirth, Elswirth

Ellwood (English) From the nobleman's forest; from the old forest
Elwood, Ellwode, Elwode, Ealdwode, Ealdwood

Elman (English) A nobleman
Elmann, Ellman, Ellmann

Elmer (English) A famous nobleman
Ellmer, Elmar, Ellmar, Elmir, Ellmir, Elmyr, Ellmyr, Ellmor, Elmor, Elmur, Ellmur

Elmo (English / Latin) A protector / an amiable man
Elmoe, Elmow, Elmowe

Elmore (English) From the moor of the elm trees
Ellmore, Elmoor, Ellmoor

Elmot (American) A lovable man
Elmott, Ellmot, Ellmott

Elne (Anglo-Saxon) A courageous man
Elni, Elnie, Elny, Elney, Elnee, Elnea

Elof (Swedish) The only heir
Eluf, Eloff, Eluff, Elov, Ellov, Eluv, Elluv

Eloi (French) The chosen one
Eloy, Eligio, Eligius

Elois (German) A famous warrior
Eloys, Eloyis, Elouis

Elon (Hebrew) From the oak tree
Elan, Elin, Elen, Elyn, Elun

Elonzo (Spanish) Filled with happiness
Elonso

Elpidio (Spanish) A fearless man; having heart
Elpydio, Elpideo, Elpydeo, Elpidios, Elpydios, Elpidius, Elpydius

Elpidos (Greek) Filled with hope
Elpydos, Elpido, Elpydo

Elrad (English) One who provides noble counsel
Ellrad, Elred, Ellred, Elrod, Ellrod, Elrud, Ellrud, Elrid, Ellrid, Elryd, Ellryd

Elroy (Irish / English) A red-haired young man / a king
Elroi, Elroye, Elric, Elryc, Elrik, Elryk, Elrick, Elryck

Elsdon (English) From the nobleman's hill
Elsdun, Elsden, Elsdin, Elsdyn, Elsdan

Elston (English) From the nobleman's town
Ellston, Elstun, Ellstun, Elson, Ellson, Elsun, Ellsun

Elsu (Native American) Resembling a flying falcon
Elsue, Elsoo, Elsou

Elton (English) From the old town
Ellton, Eltun, Elltun, Elten, Ellten, Eltin, Elltin, Eltyn, Elltyn, Eltan, Elltan

Elu (Native American) One who is full of grace
Elue, Eloo, Elou

Eluwilussit (Native American) A holy man

Elvey (English) An elf warrior
Elvy, Elvee, Elvea, Elvi, Elvie

Elvin (English) A friend of the elves
Elvinn, Elvyn, Elvynn, Elvinne, Elvynne, Elwin, Elwinn, Elwinne, Elwen, Elwenn, Elwenne, Elwyn, Elwynn, Elwynne, Elwine, Elven, Elvenn, Elvenne, Elvine, Elvern, Elvirn, Elvyrn, Elvind, Elvynd, Elvend

Elvio (Spanish) A blonde-haired man
Elviyo, Elveo, Elveyo, Elvo, Evoy

Elvis (Scandinavian) One who is wise
Elviss, Elvys, Elvyss

Elwell (English) From the old spring
Elwel, Ellwell, Ellwel, Elwill, Ellwill, Elwil, Ellwill

Elwold (English) An old Welshman
Elwald, Ellwold, Ellwald

Elzie (English) Form of Ellsworth, meaning "from the nobleman's estate"
Elzi, Elzy, Elzey, Elzee, Elzea, Ellzi, Ellzie, Ellzee, Ellzea, Ellzy, Ellzey

Emberto (Italian) One who is assertive
Embert, Emburto, Emburt, Embirto, Embirt, Embyrto, Embyrt

Emeric (German) The work ruler
Emerick, Emerik, Emric, Emrick, Emrik, Emeryc, Emeryck, Emeryck, Emryc, Emryk, Emryck, Emmerich

Emerson (German) The son of Emery
Emersun

Emery (German) The work ruler; the strength of home
Emerey, Emeri, Emerie, Emeree, Emerea, Emmery, Emmerey, Emmeri, Emmerie, Emmeree, Emmerea, Emory, Emmory, Emorey, Emmorey, Emori, Emmori, Emorie, Emmorie, Emoree, Emmoree, Emorea, Emmorea

Emest (German) One who is serious
Emeste, Emesto, Emestio, Emestiyo, Emesteo, Emesteyo, Emo, Emst, Emste

Emeth (Hebrew) A faithful man
Emethe

Emil (Latin) One who is eager; an industrious man
Emelen, Emelio, Emile, Emilian, Emiliano, Emilianus, Emilio, Emilion, Emilyan, Emlen, Emlin, Emlyn, Emlynn, Emyl, Emyle

Emir (Arabic) A prince; a ruler
Emeer, Emire, Emeere, Emear, Emeare, Emyr, Emyre

Emmanuel (Hebrew) God is with us
Eman, Emanual, Emanuel, Emanuele, Emmanual, Emmonual, Emmonuel, Emonual, Emonuel, Emuel

Emmett (German) A universal man
Emmet, Emmit, Emmitt, Emmot, Emmott

Emre (Turkish) One who is brotherly
Emreh, Emra, Emrah, Emreson, Emrason

Emrys (Welsh) An immortal man

Emsley (English) A gift from God
Emsly, Emslee, Emslea, Emsleigh, Emsli, Emslie

Enando (German) A bold man
Enandio, Enandiyo, Enandeo, Enandeyo

Enapay (Native American) A brave man
Enapaye, Enapai, Enapae

Enar (Swedish) A great warrior
Ener, Enir, Enyr, Enor, Enur

Endicott (English) From the cottage at the end of the lane
Endicot, Endycott, Endycot, Endecott, Endecot

Endre (Hungarian) Form of Andre, meaning "manly; a warrior"
Endray, Endraye, Endrai, Endrae, Endree

Endymion (Greek) In mythology, a handsome young man whose youth was preserved in eternal sleep
Endymyon, Endimion, Endimyon, Endymeon, Endimeon

Enea (Italian) The ninth-born child

Eneas (Spanish) One who is praised
Enneas

Engel (German) A messenger from heaven; an angel
Engle, Engelo, Engjell, Enjell, Engell, Enjel, Enjelo

Engelbert (German) As bright as an angel
Englebert, Englbert, Engelburt, Engleburt, Englburt, Englebirt, Engelbirt, Englbirt, Englebyrt, Engelbyrt, Englbyrt, Englbehrt

Enkoodabooaoo (Native American) One who lives alone
Enkoodabaoo

Enlai (Chinese) One who is thankful

Ennis (Gaelic) From the island; the only choice
Ennys, Enniss, Ennyss, Enis, Enys

Enno (German) One who is strong with a sword
Ennoh, Eno, Enoh, Ennoe, Enoe

Enoch (Hebrew) One who is dedicated to God
Enoc, Enok, Enock

Enos (Hebrew) A man
Enoes, Enows

Enrique (Spanish) The ruler of the estate
Enrico, Enriko, Enricko, Enriquez, Enrikay, Enreekay, Enrik, Enric, Enrick, Enrike, Enryco, Enryko, Enrycko, Enryk, Enryc, Enryck

Ensign (Latin) A badge or symbol

Enver (Turkish) A bright child
Envar, Envir, Envyr, Envor, Envur

Enyeto (Native American) One who walks like a bear

Enzi (African) A strong young boy
Enzie, Enzee, Enzea, Enzy, Enzey

Enzo (Italian) The ruler of the estate
Enzio, Enzeo, Enziyo, Enzeyo

Eoin Baiste (Irish) Refers to John the Baptist

Ephah (Hebrew) Of the darkness
Epha

Ephraim (Hebrew) One who is fertile; productive
Efraim, Efrayim, Efrem, Efrim, Ephraem, Ephream, Ephrem, Ephrim, Ephrym, Ephram, Ephron

Epicurus (Greek) One who enjoys the pleasures of life
Epycurus, Epicuros, Epycuros, Epicurius, Epycurius, Epicurios, Epycurios

Epifanio (Spanish) One who brings light
Epefano, Epefanio, Epephanio, Epifan, Epifano, Epiphany, Epifany, Epiphani, Epifani, Epiphanie, Epifanie, Epiphaney, Epifaney, Epiphafanee, Epifanee, Epiphaneo, Epifaneo

Eran (Hebrew) One who has been awakened

Erasmus (Greek) One who is dearly loved
Erasme, Erasmios, Erasmo, Erazmo

Erasto (African) A peaceful man
Erastio, Erastiyo, Erasteo, Erasteyo

Erastus (Greek) A loving man
Eraste, Erastos

Erc (Irish) A red-haired young man
Erk, Earc, Eark, Earck, Erck

Ercole (Italian) A splendid gift
Ercolo, Ercolio, Ercoleo, Ercoliyo, Ercoleyo

Erhard (German) A man of strong resolve
Erhardt, Erhart

Erian (Anglo-Saxon) One who ploughs
Eriann, Eryan, Eryann

○ **Eric** (Scandinavian) Ever the ruler
Erek, Erich, Erick, Erik, Eriq, Erix, Errick, Eryk, Eryck, Eryc, Ericas, Erickas, Erikas, Erec, Ereck

Ericson (Scandinavian) The son of Eric
Ericsun, Erickson, Ericksun, Erikson, Eriksun, Erycson, Erycsun, Eryckson, Erycksun, Erykson, Eryksun, Ericsen, Ericksen, Eriksen, Erycsen, Erycksen, Eryksen

Erin (Gaelic) A man from Ireland
Erienne, Erine, Erinn, Erinne, Eryne, Eryn, Erynne, Erynn, Erryn, Errin, Eri, Erie, Ery, Erey, Eree, Erea

Erland (English / Norse) From the nobleman's land / a foreigner; stranger
Erlande, Erlend, Erlende, Eorland, Erlan, Earland, Earlan, Erlin, Erlyn, Earlin, Earlyn, Erlen, Earlen

Erling (English) The son of a nobleman
Erlyng

Ermin (German) A man of the army; a soldier
Ermyn, Erman, Ermano, Erminio, Ermino, Ermen, Ermon, Ermun, Ermanno

Ernest (English) One who is sincere and determined; serious
Earnest, Ernesto, Ernestus, Ernst, Erno, Ernie, Erni, Erney, Erny, Ernee, Ernea, Earnesto, Earni, Earnie, Earnee, Earnea, Earny, Earney

Eron (Spanish) Form of Aaron, meaning "one who is exalted"
Erun, Erin, Eran, Eren, Eryn

Eros (Greek) In mythology, the god of love
Erose, Eroce

Errapel (Basque) A divine healer
Errapal, Erapel, Erapal, Errapol, Erapol, Errapul, Erapul, Errapil, Erapil, Errapyl, Erapyl

Errigal (Gaelic) From the small church
Errigel, Errigol, Errigul, Errigil, Errigyl, Erigal, Erigel, Erigol, Erigul, Erigil, Erigyl

Erroll (English) A wanderer
Errol, Erryl, Erryle, Eryle, Eroll, Eryl

Erskine (Gaelic) From the high cliff
Erskin, Erskyne, Erskyn, Erskein, Erskeine, Erskien, Erskiene

Erving (English) A friend of the sea
Ervyng, Ervine, Ervyne, Erv, Erve

Erwin (English) A friend of the wild boar
Erwine, Erwinn, Erwinne, Erwen, Erwenn, Erwenne, Erwyn, Erwynn, Erwynne, Earwine, Earwin, Earwinn, Earwinne, Earwen, Earwenn, Earwenne, Earwyn, Earwynn, Earwynne

Esam (Arabic) A safeguard
Essam

Esau (Hebrew) A hairy man; in the Bible, Jacob's older twin brother
Esaw, Eesau, Eesaw, Easau, Easaw

Esben (Scandinavian) Of God
Esbin, Esbyn, Esban, Esbon, Esbun

Esbjorn (Norse) A bear of the gods
Esbern, Esborn, Esburn, Esbirn, Esbyrn, Esbjorne, Esberne, Esburne, Esbirne, Esbyrne

Escott (English) From the cottage near the stream
Escot

Eshkol (Hebrew) A cluster of grapes
Eshkoll, Eshkole, Eshckol

Esias (Hebrew) God is my salvation
Esyas, Esaias, Esiason, Esiasson

Eskel (Norse) From the cauldron of the gods
Eskell, Eskil, Eskill, Eskyl, Eskyll

Esmé (French) One who is esteemed
Esmay, Esmaye, Esmai, Esmae, Esmeling, Esmelyng

Esmond (English) One who is protected by God's grace
Esmonde, Esmund, Esmunde, Esmont, Esmonte, Esmunt, Esmunte

Esmun (American) A kind man
Esmon, Esman, Esmen, Esmin, Esmyn

Espen (Scandinavian) Form of Esbjorn, meaning "a bear of the gods"
Espan, Espin, Espyn, Espon, Espun, Espn

Esperanze (Spanish) Filled with hope
Esperance, Esperence, Esperenze, Esperanzo, Esperenzo

Essex (English) From the eastern place
Esex

Essien (African) The sixth-born son
Esien, Essyen, Esyen

Estcott (English) From the eastern cottage
Estcot

Este (Italian) A man from the east

Esteban (Spanish) One who is crowned in victory
Estebon, Estevan, Estevon, Estefan, Estefon, Estebe, Estyban, Estyvan

Estes (Latin) One who lives near the estuary
Estas, Estis, Estys

Eston (English) From the eastern town
Estun, Estown, Esten, Estin, Estan, Estyn

Etchemin (Native American) A canoe man

Etereo (Spanish) A spiritual man
Eterio, Etero, Etereyo, Eteriyo, Eteryo

Eth (Irish) Born of fire
Ethe

✪
✝ **Ethan** (Hebrew) One who is firm and stead-fast
Ethen, Ethin, Ethyn, Ethon, Ethun, Eitan, Etan, Eithan, Eithen, Eithin, Eithyn, Eithon, Eithun, Eythan, Eytan

Ethanael (American) God has given me strength
Ethaniel, Ethaneal, Ethanail, Ethanale

Ethel (Hebrew) One who is noble
Ethal, Etheal

Ethelwin (Anglo-Saxon) A wellborn friend
Ethelwinn, Ethelwinne, Ethelwine, Ethelwen, Ethelwenn, Ethelwenne, Ethelwyn, Ethelwynn, Ethelwynne

Ethelwulf (Anglo-Saxon) A noble wolf
Ethelwolf

Etienne (French) One who is crowned
Estienne, Ettie, Etta

Etlelooaat (Native American) One who shouts

Ettore (Italian) One who is loyal
Etore, Ettoer, Etoer, Etor, Ettor

Etu (Native American) Of the sun
Etue, Etow, Etowe, Etou

Euan (Gaelic) The little swift one
Ewan, Euen, Ewen, Eoghan, Eoghann

Euclid (Greek) An intelligent man
Euclyd, Euclide, Euclyde, Euclides, Euclydes

Eudocio (Greek) One who is respected
Eudoceo, Eudociyo, Eudoceyo, Eudoco

Eudor (Greek) A good gift
Eudore

Eugene (Greek) A wellborn man
Eugen, Eugenio, Eugenios, Eugenius, Evgeny, Evgeni, Evgenie, Evgeney

Eulogio (Greek) A reasonable man
Eulogiyo, Eulogo, Eulogeo, Eulogeyo

Euodias (Greek) Having good fortune
Euodeas, Euodyas

Euphemios (Greek) One who is well-spoken
Eufemio, Eufemius, Euphemio, Eufemios, Euphemius, Eufemius

Euphrates (Turkish) From the great river
Eufrates, Euphraites, Eufraites, Euphraytes, Eufraytes

Eural (American) From the mountains
Eurel, Eurol, Eurul, Euril, Euryl

Eusebius (Greek) One who is devout
Esabio, Esavio, Esavius, Esebio, Eusabio, Eusaio, Eusebio, Eusebios, Eusavio, Eusevio, Eusevios

Eustace (Greek) Having an abundance of grapes
Eustache, Eustachios, Eustachius, Eustachy, Eustaquio, Eustashe, Eustasius, Eustatius, Eustazio, Eustis, Eustiss, Eustys, Eustyss, Eustacio, Eustasio

❶❷ **Evan** (Welsh) Form of John, meaning "God is gracious"
Evann, Evans, Even, Evin, Evon, Evyn, Evian, Evien, Evion, Eviun, Evanus, Evaristo, Evariso, Evaro

Evander (Greek) A benevolent man
Evandor, Evandar, Evandir, Evandur, Evandyr

Evangel (Greek) A bringer of good news
Evangelin, Evangelino, Evangelo, Evangelio, Evangeliyo, Evangeleo, Evangeleyo, Evagelo, Evagelos

Evelyn (German) A birdlike man
Evelean, Eveleen, Evaline, Evalyn, Evelin, Eveline, Evelyne, Evelynn, Evelynne, Evie, Evlynn

Everest (American) From the highest mountain peak
Evrest

Everett (English) Form of Everhard, meaning "as strong as a boar; as brave as a boar"
Everet, Everrett, Everret, Everitt, Everit, Everritt, Everrit

Everhard (English) As strong as a boar; as brave as a boar
Evarado, Everado, Everardo, Evered, Everhart, Evrard, Evraud, Everard

Everild (English) As battle-ready as a boar
Evuld, Evaldo, Everald, Everhild, Everildo, Everyld, Everyldo

Everley (English) From the boar's meadow
Everly, Everli, Everlie, Everleigh, Everlee, Everlea, Everleah

Evers (English) Resembling a wild boar
Ever, Evert, Everte

Everton (English) From the boar town
Evertun

Evett (American) A bright man
Evet, Evatt, Evat, Evitt, Evit, Evytt, Evyt

Evgenii (Russian) A wellborn man; a nobleman

Evo (German) Of the yew wood
Evoh, Evoe, Evoeh, Evow, Evowe

Evzen (Czech) Of noble birth
Evzin, Evzyn, Evzan, Evzon, Evzun

Ewald (English) A powerful man
Ewalde

Ewert (English) A shepherd
Ewart, Ewerd, Eward, Eweheorde, Eawart, Eawert, Eaward, Eawerd

Ewing (English) A lawyer; a friend of the law
Ewine, Ewyng, Ewinn, Ewin, Ewinne, Ewyn, Ewynn, Ewynne

Excalibur (English) In Arthurian legend, King Arthur's sword
Escalibur, Excaliber, Escaliber, Excalibor, Escalibor, Excalibar, Escalibar

Excell (American) A competitive man
Excel, Exsell, Exsel

Extany (English) One who is not like others
Extaney, Extani, Extanie, Extanee, Extanea

Eyab (Arabian) One who has returned

Eyad (Arabic) A powerful man

Eyal (Hebrew) Having great strength

Eyolf (Norwegian) A lucky wolf
Eyulf

Eystein (Norse) A lucky man
Eistein, Eysteinn, Eisteinn

Eze (African) A king

Ezeji (African) The king of yams
Ezejie, Ezejy, Ezejey, Ezejee, Ezejea

Ezekiel (Hebrew) Strengthened by God
Esequiel, Ezechiel, Eziechiele, Eziequel, Ezequiel, Ezekial, Ezekyel, Esquevelle

Ezer (Hebrew) One who offers help
Eizer, Ezar, Eizar, Ezzy, Ezzey, Ezzi, Ezzie, Ezzee, Ezzea, Ezy, Ezey, Ezi, Ezie, Ezea, Ezee

Ezhno (Native American) One who walks alone
Ezno, Ezhnoe, Eznoe

Ezio (Italian) Resembling an eagle
Eziyo, Ezeo, Ezeyo

Ezra (Hebrew) A helper
Ezrah, Esdras, Esra, Ezri, Ezrie, Ezree, Ezreu, Ezry, Ezrey, Eza, Ezira, Ezyra, Ezirah, Ezyrah

f

Fabian (Latin) One who grows beans
Fabe, Fabek, Faber, Fabert, Fabianno, Fabiano, Fabianus, Fabien, Fabio, Fabion, Fabius, Fabiyus, Fabyan, Fabyen, Faebian, Faebien, Faybian, Faybien, Faybion, Faybionn, Faberto

Fable (American) One who tells stories
Fabel, Fabal, Fabol, Fabul, Fabyl, Fabil

Fabrice (French) One who works with his hands
Fabriano, Fabricius, Fabritius, Fabrizio, Fabrizius, Fabryce, Fabreece, Fabreace, Fabriece, Fabreice

Fabron (French) A young blacksmith
Fabre, Fabroni, Fabronie, Fabrony, Fabroney, Fabronee, Fabronea

Fabulous (American) One who is vain
Fabulus, Fab, Fabby, Fabbi, Fabbey, Fabbie, Fabbee

Fabunni (African) Whom God has given
Fabunny, Fabuni, Fabuny, Fabunney, Fabuney, Fabunnee, Fabunee, Fabunnie, Fabunie

Fachnan (Irish) The name of a saint
Fachnen, Fachnin, Fachnyn, Fachnon, Fachnun

Factor (English) A businessman
Facter, Factur, Factir, Factyr, Factar

Faddis (American) One who keeps to himself
Faddys, Fadis, Fadys, Faddiss, Faddyss, Fadiss, Fadyss, Fadice, Fadyce, Fadise, Fadyse

Fadi (Arabic / Slavic) A savior / a courageous man
Fadie, Fady, Fadey, Fadee, Fadea, Fadeyka

Fadil (Arabic) A generous man
Fadeel, Fadeal, Fadiel, Fadeil, Fadyl, Fadl

Fafnir (Norse) In mythology, a dragon
Fafner, Fafnyr, Fafnor, Fafnur

Fagan (Gaelic) The little ardent one
Fegan, Feggan, Fagin, Fagen, Fagon, Fagun, Fagyn, Faegan, Faigan, Faygan

Fahd (Arabic) Resembling a leopard or a panther
Fahad

Fahesh (Arabic) Excessive
Faheshe

Fahey (Irish) From the green field
Fahy, Fahi, Fahie, Fahee

Fahim (African) A learned man
Faheem, Faheim, Fahiem, Faheam, Fahym

Fai (Chinese) Of the beginning; a bright light

Fairbairn (Scottish) A fair-haired boy
Fayrbairn, Faerbairn, Fairbaern, Fayrbaern, Faerbaern, Fairbayrn, Fayrbayrn, Faerbayrn

Fairbanks (English) From the bank along the path
Fayrbanks, Faerbanks, Farebanks

Fairchild (English) A fair-haired child
Faerchild, Fayrchild, Farechild, Fairchyld, Faerchyld, Fayrchyld, Farechyld

Fairfax (English) A blonde-haired man
Fayrfax, Faerfax, Farefax

Faisal (Arabic) One who is decisive; resolute
Faysal, Faesal, Fasal, Feisal, Faizal, Fasel, Fayzal, Faezal, Fazel

Faiyaz (Indian) An artistic man
Fayyaz, Faeyza, Fayaz

Faizon (Arabic) An understanding man
Fayzon, Faezon, Fazon, Faizun, Fayzun, Faezun, Fazun, Faizan, Fayzan, Faezan, Fazan

Fakhir (Arabic) A proud man
Fakheer, Fakhear, Fakheir, Fakhier, Fakhyr, Faakhir, Faakhyr, Fakhr, Fakhri, Fakhrie, Fakhry, Fakhrey, Fakhree

Fakih (Arabic) A legal expert
Fakeeh, Fakeah, Fakieh, Fakeih, Fakyh

Falak (Indian) Of the sky
Falac, Falach, Falack

Falakee (Arabic) An astronomer
*Falake, Falaki, Falakie, Falaky, Falakey,
Falakea*

Falco (Latin) Resembling a falcon; one who
works with falcons
*Falcon, Falconer, Falconner, Falk, Falke,
Falken, Falkner, Faulconer, Faulconner,
Faulkner*

Falgun (Hindi) A Hindu month
Falgon, Falgen, Falgan, Falgin, Falgyn

Falguni (Hindi) Born during the month of
Falgun
*Falgunie, Falguny, Falguney, Falgunee,
Falgunea*

Faline (Hindi) A fertile man
*Faleene, Faleane, Faleine, Faliene, Falyne,
Falin, Faleen, Falean, Falien, Falein, Falyn*

Fallon (Irish) A ruler
*Fallun, Fallen, Fallan, Fallin, Fallyn,
Fallamhain*

Fallows (English) From the unplanted field
Fallow, Fallos, Fallo, Fallowe, Fallowes

Fam (American) A family-oriented man

Famous (American) One who is well-known
Fame

Fane (English) Filled with joy
*Fain, Faine, Fayn, Fayne, Faen, Faene,
Fannin, Fannon, Fannen, Fannun, Fannan,
Fannyn*

Fang (Scottish) From the sheep pen
Faing, Fayng, Faeng

Faolan (Gaelic) Resembling a little wolf
*Felan, Faelan, Faolen, Fuelen, Felen, Faolin,
Faelin, Felin, Faolyn, Faelyn, Felyn*

Faraj (Arabian) One who offers remedies
Farag

Faraji (African) One who provides consolation
Farajie, Farajy, Farajey, Farajee, Farajea

Faramond (English) A protected traveler
*Faramund, Farrimond, Farrimund,
Farimond, Farimund*

Faran (Anglo-Saxon / American) One who
advances / a sincere man
*Faren, Faron, Farin, Faryn, Farun, Fahran,
Feran, Feren*

Fardoragh (Irish) Having dark features

Fares (Arabic) A knight or horseman
Farees, Fareas, Faries, Fareis, Farys

Fargo (American) One who is jaunty
Fargoh, Fargoe, Fargouh

Farha (Arabic) Filled with happiness
*Farhah, Farhad, Farhan, Farhat, Farhani,
Farhanie, Farhany, Farhaney, Farhanee*

Farid (Arabic) One who is unequaled
*Fareed, Faread, Faryd, Faried, Fareid, Faride,
Farideh*

Fariq (Arabic) One who holds rank as lieu-
tenant general
*Fareeq, Fareaq, Fareiq, Farieq, Faryq, Farik,
Fareek, Fareak, Fariek, Fareik, Faryk*

Farkas (Hungarian) Resembling a wolf
*Farckas, Farcas, Farkes, Farckes, Farces,
Farkus, Farckus, Farcus*

Farlan (Scottish) A son of the furrows
*Farlane, Farlain, Farlaine, Farlayn, Farlayne,
Farlaen, Farlaene*

Farley (English) From the bull pasture
*Farly, Farleigh, Farlee, Farlea, Farleah, Farle,
Farli, Farlie, Fairlay, Fairlee, Fairleigh,
Farlay, Fairlea, Fairleah, Fairli, Fairlie,
Farlow, Farlowe, Farlo*

Farmer (English) One who works the earth
Farmar, Farmor, Farmur, Farmir, Farmyr

Farmon (Anglo-Saxon) A traveler
Farmun, Farmen, Farman, Farmin, Farmyn

Farnell (English) From the fern hill
*Farnel, Farnall, Farnal, Fernauld, Farnauld,
Fernald, Farnald*

Farnham (English) From the fern field
Farnam, Farnum, Fernham, Farnam, Fernam

Farnley (English) From the fern meadow
*Farnly, Farnli, Farnlie, Farnlee, Farnleigh,
Farnlea, Farnleah*

Farold (English) A mighty traveler
Farould, Farald, Farauld, Fareld

Faron (Spanish) A pharoah
Faro, Farun, Faren, Faran

Farouk (Arabic) One who knows the truth
Farouke, Faruk, Faruke, Faruq, Farouq

Farquhar (Scottish) One who is very dear
Farquar, Farquharson, Farquarson, Fearchar

Farr (English) A traveler; a voyager
Faer, Farrs, Faers, Far, Fars, Farrson, Farson

Farran (Irish / Arabic / English) Of the land /
a baker / one who is adventurous
*Fairran, Fayrran, Faerran, Farren, Farrin,
Farron, Ferrin, Ferron*

Farrar (English) A blacksmith
*Farar, Farrer, Farrier, Ferrar, Ferrars, Ferrer,
Ferrier, Farer, Farier, Ferar, Ferars, Ferer,
Ferier*

Farrell (Irish) A courageous man
Farrel, Farel, Farell, Farryl, Faryl, Faryll

Farris (English) One who is as strong as iron
*Farrys, Faris, Farys, Farice, Ferris, Ferrys,
Feris, Ferys*

Farro (Italian) Of the grain
Farroe, Faro, Faroe, Farrow, Farow

Farry (Irish) One who is manly and strong
Farrey, Farri, Farrie, Farree, Farrea

Fasta (Spanish) One who makes an offering
Fastah

Faste (Norse) One who is firm
Fasti, Fastie, Fastee, Fastea, Fasty, Fastey

Fateh (Arabic) A victorious man
*Fath, Fathe, Fathi, Fathie, Fathy, Fathey,
Fathee, Fathea*

Fatik (Indian) Resembling a crystal
Fateek, Fateak, Fatyk, Fatiek, Fateik

Fatin (Arabic) An intelligent man
Fateen, Fatean, Fatien, Fatein, Fatyn

Faunus (Latin) In mythology, the god of
nature and the forests
Fawnus, Faunos, Fawnos

Faust (Latin) Having good luck
*Fauste, Faustino, Fausto, Faustos, Faustus,
Fauston, Faustin, Fausten, Faustun, Faustan*

Favian (Latin) Full of wisdom
Favien, Favyan, Favyen

Fawcett (American) An audacious man
*Fawcet, Fawcette, Fawcete, Fawce, Fawci,
Fawcie, Fawcy, Fawcey, Fawcee, Fawcea*

Fawwaz (Arabic) A successful man
Fawaz, Fawwad, Fawad

Fawzi (Arabic) The winner
Fawzie, Fawzy, Fawzey, Fawzee, Fawzea

Faxon (Latin) One who has thick, long hair
Faxen, Faxan, Faxin, Faxyn, Faxun

Fay (Irish) Resembling a raven
Faye, Fai, Fae, Feich

Faysal (Arabic) A judge
Faisal, Faesal, Fasal

Fazil (Arabic) A virtuous man
*Fazill, Fazyl, Fazyll, Fazeel, Fazeal, Fazeil,
Faziel*

Febronio (Spanish) A bright man
Febroneo, Febrono, Febroniyo, Febroneyo

February (American) Born in the month of
February
*Februari, Februarie, Februarey, Februaree,
Februarea*

Februus (Latin) A pagan god

Fedde (Italian) One who is true

Fedor (Russian) A gift from God
*Faydor, Feodor, Fyodor, Fedyenka, Fyodr,
Fydor, Fjodor*

Fedrick (American) Form of Cedric, meaning "one who is kind and loved; of the spectacular bounty"
Fedrik, Fedric, Fedryck, Fedryk, Fedryc

Feechi (African) One who worships God
*Feechie, Feechy, Feechey, Feechee, Feachi,
Feachie, Feachy, Feachey, Feachee*

Feige (Hebrew) Resembling a bird

Feivel (Hebrew) The brilliant one
*Feival, Feivol, Feivil, Feivyl, Feivul, Feiwel,
Feiwal, Feiwol, Feiwul, Feiwil, Feiwyl*

Fela (African) A warlike man
Felah, Fella, Fellah

Felding (English) From the field
Feldyng, Felman, Felmann

Feldon (English) From the town near the field
Feldun, Felton, Feltun

Feleti (Italian) A peaceful man
Feletie, Felety, Feletey, Feletee, Feletea

Felim (Gaelic) One who is always good
Felym, Feidhlim, Felimy, Felimey, Felimee, Felimea, Felimi, Felimie

Felipe (Spanish) Form of Phillip, meaning "one who loves horses"
Felippe, Filip, Filippo, Fillip, Flip, Fulop, Fullop, Fulip, Fullip, Filib, Fillib

Felix (Latin) One who is happy and prosperous
Felyx, Fee, Felic, Felice, Feliciano, Felicio, Felike, Feliks, Felizio

Fell (English) From the field
Fel, Felle, Fele

Felton (English) From the town near the field
Feltun, Felten, Feltan, Feltyn, Feltin

Fenn (English) From the marsh
Fen

Fenner (English) An able-bodied man
Fennar, Fennir, Fennyr, Fennor, Fennur

Fenris (Norse) In mythology, a giant wolf
Fenrys

Fenton (English) From the town near the marsh
Fentun, Fenten, Fentan, Fentyn, Fentin

Fentress (English) One who is natural
Fentres, Fentriss, Fentris, Fentryss, Fentrys

Fenwick (English) From the village near the marsh
Fenwyck, Fenwik, Fenwyk, Fenwic, Fenwyc

Feo (Native American / Spanish) A confident man / an ugly man
Feeo, Feyo

Feoras (Gaelic) Resembling a smooth rock
Feores, Feoris, Feorys, Feoros, Feorus

Ferda (Czech) A brave man
Ferdah, Firda, Firdah, Furda, Furdah

Ferdinand (German) A courageous voyager
Ferd, Ferdie, Ferdinando, Ferdo, Ferdynand, Fernand, Fernandas, Fernando, Fernande

Ferenc (Hungarian) An independent man; one who is free
Ferenck, Ferenk, Ferko

Fergall (Gaelic) A strong and brave man
Fergal, Fearghall, Ferghall, Ferghal, Forgael

Fergus (Gaelic) The first and supreme choice
Fearghas, Fearghus, Feargus, Fergie, Ferguson, Fergusson, Furgus, Fergy, Fergi, Fergee, Fergea

Ferhan (Arabic) One who rejoices
Ferhen, Ferhon, Ferhun, Ferhin, Ferhyn

Ferlin (American) A man from the country
Ferlyn, Ferlen, Ferlan, Ferlon, Ferlun

Fermin (Spanish) Having great strength
Firmin, Fermyn, Firmyn, Fermen, Firmen, Ferman, Firman, Fermon, Firmon, Fermun, Firmun

Fernley (English) From the fern meadow
Fernly, Fernli, Fernlie, Fernlee, Fernleigh, Fernlea, Fernleah, Fearnleah, Fearnlea, Fearnli, Fearnlie, Fearnlee, Fearnleigh, Fearnly, Fearnley

Ferran (Arabic) A baker
Ferren, Ferron, Ferrun, Ferrin, Ferryn

Ferrand (French) A gray-haired man
Farand, Farrand, Farrant, Ferand, Ferrant, Ferant, Farant

Ferrell (Irish) A brave man; a hero
Ferell, Ferel, Ferrel

Ferreres (Spanish) A blacksmith
Ferares, Fereres

Festus (Latin) A joyous man
Festis, Festys, Festos, Festas, Festes

Fews (Celtic) From the woods

Fiacre (Celtic) Resembling a raven
Fyacre, Fiacra, Fyacra, Fiachra, Fyachra, Fiachre, Fyachre

Fidel (Latin) A faithful man
Fadelio, Fedele, Fidele, Fedelio, Fidal, Fidalio, Fidelio, Fidelis, Fidelix, Fidello, Fidelo, Fido, Fidelity

Fielding (English) From the field
Fieldyng, Fielder, Field, Fielde, Felding, Feldyng, Fields

Fien (American) An elegant man
Fiene, Fine

Fiero (Spanish) A fiery man
Fyero

Fikri (Arabic) A strong and intelligent man
Fikrie, Fikry, Fikrey, Fikree, Fikrea, Fykri, Fykrie, Fykree, Fykrea, Fykry, Fykrey

Filbert (German) A brilliant man
Filberte, Filberto, Filbertos, Filbertus

Filmore (English) One who is famous
Filmor, Fillmor, Fillmore, Fylmore, Fylmor, Fyllmore, Fyllmor, Filmer, Fylmer, Filmar, Fylmar, Filmarr, Fylmarr

Filomelo (Spanish) A beloved friend
Fylomelo, Filo, Fylo

Finbar (Irish) A fair-haired man
Finnbar, Finnbarr, Fionn, Fionnbharr, Fionnbar, Fionnbarr, Fynbar, Fynnbar, Fynbarr, Fynnbarr, Finnobarr, Finobarr, Finnobar, Finobar

Finch (English) Resembling the small bird
Fynch, Finche, Fynche, Finchi, Finchie, Finchy, Finchey, Finchee

Fineas (Egyptian) A dark-skinned man
Fyneas, Finius, Fynius

Finian (Irish) A handsome man; fair
Finan, Finnian, Fionan, Finien, Finnien, Finghin, Finneen, Fineen, Finnean, Finean, Finnin, Finnine

Finlay (Gaelic) A fair-haired hero
Findlay, Findley, Finlea, Finlee, Finley, Finly, Finli, Finlie, Findly, Findlee, Findlea, Findli, Findlie, Finnly, Finnley, Finnlee, Finnli, Finnlie

Finn (Gaelic) A fair-haired man
Fin, Fynn, Fyn, Fingal, Fingall

Finnegan (Irish) A fair-haired man
Finegan, Finnegen, Finegen, Finnigan, Finigan

Fintan (Irish) The little fair-haired one
Finten, Finton, Fintun, Fintyn, Fintin, Fyntan, Fynten, Fynton, Fyntun, Fyntin, Fyntyn

Fiorello (Italian) Resembling a little flower
Fiorelo, Fiorelio, Fioreleo, Fiorellio, Fiorelleo

Firdus (Indian) From paradise
Fyrdus, Firdos, Fyrdos

Firman (French) A loyal man
Firmin, Firmen, Firmon, Firmun, Firmyn

Firoze (Indian) Resembling turquoise
Fyroze, Firoz, Fyroz, Feroze, Feroz

Firth (Scottish) From an inlet of the sea
Firthe, Fyrth, Fyrthe

Fishel (Hebrew) Resembling a fish
Fyshel, Fishell, Fyshell, Fishele, Fyshele, Fishelle, Fyshelle

Fisher (English) A fisherman
Fysher, Fischer, Fisscher, Fyscher, Fysscher, Fish, Fyshe, Fysh, Fishe

Fisk (English) Resembling a fish
Fiske, Fysk, Fyske

Fitch (English) Resembling an ermine
Fytch, Fich, Fych, Fitche, Fytche

Fitz (French) The son of ...
Fytz

Fitzadam (English) The son of Adam
Fytzadam

Fitzgerald (English) The son of Gerald
Fytzgerald

Fitzgibbon (English) The son of Gibson
Fytzgibbon, Fitzgibon, Fytzgibon

Fitzgilbert (English) The son of Gilbert
Fytzgilbert

Fitzhugh (English) The son of Hugh
Fytzhugh

Fitzjames (English) The son of James
Fytzjames

Fitzpatrick (English) The son of Patrick
Fytzpatrick

Fitzroy (English) The son of Roy
Fytzroy

Fitzsimon (English) The son of Simon
Fytzsimon, Fitzsymon, Fytzsymon, Fitzsimmons, Fytzsimmons, Fitzsimons, Fytzsimons

Fitzwalter (English) The son of Walter
Fytzwalter

Fitzwilliam (English) The son of William
Fytzwilliam

Fiyas (Indian) An artistic man

Flag (American) A patriotic man
Flagg

Flaminio (Spanish) A Roman priest
Flamino, Flamineo, Flaminiyo, Flamineyo

Flann (Irish) One who has a ruddy complexion
Flan, Flainn, Flannan, Flannery, Flanneri, Flannerie, Flannerey, Flanneree, Flannerea, Flanagan, Flannagain, Flannagan

Flash (American) A shining man; one who is fast
Flashy, Flashey, Flashee, Flashea, Flashi, Flashie, Flashe

Flavian (Latin) Having yellow hair
Flavel, Flavelle, Flaviano, Flavien, Flavio, Flavius, Flawiusz, Flaviu, Flavean, Flabio, Flubien, Flabian

Fleada (American) One who keeps to himself
Flayda, Flaida, Flaeda, Fleade, Flayde, Flaide, Flaede

Fleetwood (English) From the forest with the stream
Fleetwode

Fleming (English) A man from Flanders
Flemyng, Flemming, Flemmyng

Fletcher (English) One who makes arrows
Fletch, Fletche, Flecher

Flint (English) Resembling the hard quartz; from the stream
Flynt, Flintt, Flyntt

Florent (French) Resembling a flower; one who is flourishing
Fiorentino, Florentin, Florentino, Florentz, Florenz, Florinio, Florino, Floris, Florys, Florus, Florentius, Florian, Florien, Floryan, Florrian, Florrien

Floyd (Welsh) A gray-haired man
Floyde, Floid, Floide

Flux (English) One who is constantly moving
Fluxx

Flynn (Irish) One who has a ruddy complexion
Flyn, Flinn, Flin, Flen, Flenn, Floinn

Fodjour (African) The fourth-born child
Fodjur, Fodjure, Fodjoure

Fodor (Hungarian) A curly-haired man
Fodur, Fodir, Fodyr, Fodar, Foder

Fogarty (Irish) One who has been exiled
Fogartey, Fogartee, Fogartea, Fogarti, Fogartie, Fogerty, Fogertey, Fogerti, Fogertie, Fogertee, Fogertea, Fogartaigh, Fogertaigh

Foley (English) A creative man
Foly, Folee, Foleigh, Folea, Foli, Folie

Folker (German) A guardian of the people
Folkar, Folkor, Folkur, Folkir, Folkyr, Folke, Folko, Folkus, Folkos, Floke, Floker, Flokar, Flokur, Flokir, Flokyr, Flokor

Foma (Hebrew) One of twins
Fomah

Fonda (Spanish) One who is profound

Fonso (German) Form of Alfonso, meaning "prepared for battle; eager and ready"
Fonzo, Fonsie, Fonzell, Fonzie, Fonsi, Fonsy, Fonsey, Fonsee, Fonsea, Fonzi, Fonzey, Fonzy, Fonzee, Fonzea

Fontaine (French) From the water source
Fontayne, Fontaene, Fontane, Fonteyne, Fontana, Fountain

Forbes (Gaelic) From the field
Forbs, Forba, Forb, Forbe

Ford (English) From the river crossing
Forde, Forden, Fordan, Fordon, Fordun, Fordin, Fordyn, Forday, Fordaye, Fordai, Fordae

Forend (American) One who is bold
Foren, Forind, Forin, Forynd, Foryn

Forest (English) From the woodland
Forester, Forrest, Forrester, Forestor, Forrestor, Forster, Forstor

Fortney (Latin) Having great strength
Fortny, Fortni, Fortnie, Fortnee, Fortnea, Fourtney, Fourtny, Fourtni, Fourtnie, Fourtnea, Fourtnea, Fortenay, Forteney, Forteney, Forteni, Fortenie, Fortenee, Fortenea

Fortune (French) A lucky man
Fortino, Fortunato, Fortunatus, Fortunio, Fortuny, Fortuney, Fortuni, Fortunie, Fortunee, Fortunea

Foster (English) A forest ranger
Fost, Foste, Fosti, Fostie, Fostee, Fostea

Fouad (Arabic) One who has heart
Fuad

Fowler (English) One who traps birds
Fowlor, Fowlar, Fowlir, Fowlyr, Fowlur

Fox (English) Resembling the animal
Foxe, Foxx, Foxen, Foxan, Foxon, Foxun, Foxin, Foxyn

Foy (Celtic) An adventurous man; a journey
Foye, Foi

Fraco (Spanish) One who is weak
Fracko, Frako

Fraley (English) A friar
Fraly, Frali, Fralie, Fralee, Fraleigh, Fralea, Frayley, Frayly, Frayli, Fraylie, Frayleigh, Fraylea, Fraylee, Fraeley, Fraely, Fraeli, Fraelie, Fraelee, Fraeleigh, Frailey, Fraily, Frailee, Frailea, Fraileigh, Fraili, Frailie

Francis (Latin) A man from France; one who is free
Fran, Frances, Francesco, Franche, Franchesco, Franchesko, Franchot, Francisco, Franciscus, Franciskus, Francois, Franio, Frann, Frannie, Frans, Fransisco, Frants, Frantz, Franz, Franzel, Franzen, Franzin, Frasco, Frascuelo, Frasquito, Frisco, Frisko, Frascuelo, Frang

Franciszek (Polish) Form of Francis, meaning "a man from France; one who is free"
Frantisek, Franciszec, Frantisec

Frank (Latin) Form of Francis, meaning "a man from France; one who is free"
Franc, Franco, Franck, Francke, Frankie, Franky, Franki, Frankey, Frankee, Frankea

Franklin (English) A free man; a landholder
Franklinn, Franklyn, Franklynn, Francklin, Francklyn

Fraomar (Anglo-Saxon) The name of a king
Fraomarr, Fraomare, Fraomarre

Fraser (Scottish) Of the forest men
Fraiser, Frayser, Fraeser, Frazer, Frayzer, Fraezer, Fraizer, Frasier, Frazier

Frayne (English) A foreigner
Frayn, Frain, Fraine, Fraen, Fraene, Frane, Freyne, Freyn, Frayme, Fraym, Fraime, Fraim, Frame, Fraem, Fraeme, Freyme, Freym

Fred (German) Form of Frederick, meaning "a peaceful ruler"
Freddi, Freddie, Freddy, Freddey, Freddee, Freddea, Freddis, Fredis, Freddys, Fredys

Frederick (German) A peaceful ruler
Federico, Federigo, Fredek, Frederic, Frederich, Frederico, Frederik, Fredric, Fredrick, Fredrik, Frido, Friedel, Friedrich, Friedrick, Fridrich, Fridrick, Fryderky, Frederyck, Fredryck, Fredryc, Fredryk, Frederyc, Frederyk, Fryderyk, Fico

Freeborn (English) One who was born a free man
Freeborne, Freebourn, Freebourne, Freeburn, Freeburne, Free

Freed (English) A peaceful man; one who is free
Freid, Fried, Fread

Freedom (American) An independent man

Freeman (English) One who is free
Freemen, Freemon, Freemin, Freemyn, Freemun, Freman, Fremen, Fremon, Fremun, Fremin, Fremyn

Fremont (French) The protector of freedom
Freemont, Fremonte, Freemonte, Fremond, Freemond, Fremonde, Freemonde, Frimunt, Frimont, Frimond, Frimund, Frimunte, Frimonte, Frimunde, Frimonde

French (English) A man from France

Fresco (Spanish) A fresh-faced man
Frescko, Fresko, Frescoe, Fresckoe, Freskoe

Frewin (English) A noble or free friend
Frewine, Frewinn, Frewinne, Frewen, Frewenn, Frewenne, Frewyn, Frewynn, Frewynne, Freowine

Frey (Scandinavian) One who is exalted; in mythology, the god of peace, prosperity, and good weather

Frick (English) A courageous man
Fryck, Frik, Fric, Fryc, Fryk

Fridolf (English) The peaceful wolf
Freydolf, Freydulf, Friedolf, Fridulf, Friedulf, Fridolph, Freydolph, Fridulph, Freydulph, Friedolph, Friedulph, Friduwulf, Friduwolf, Fridwolf, Fridwulf, Friedwolf, Friedwulf, Frieduwolf, Frieduwulf

Fridolin (German) A free man
Frydolin, Fridolinn, Frydolinn, Fridolyn, Frydolyn, Fridolynn, Frydolynn

Friedhelm (German) One who wears the helmet of peace
Friedelm, Fridhelm, Fridelm

Frigyes (Hungarian) A mighty and peaceful ruler

Frika (English) One who is bold
Fryka, Fricka, Frycka, Frica, Fryca, Freca, Frecka, Freka

Friso (English) A curly-haired man
Fryso

Fritz (German) Form of Frederick, meaning "a peaceful ruler"
Frits, Fritzchen, Fritzi, Fritzl, Fritzie, Fritzy, Fritzey, Fritzee, Fritzea

Frode (Norse) A wise man
Froad, Froade

Fromel (Hebrew) An outgoing man
Fromell, Fromele, Fromelle

Frost (English) One who is cold
Frosty, Frostey, Frosti, Frostie, Frostee, Frostea

Froyim (Hebrew) A kind man
Froiim

Fructuoso (Spanish) One who is fruitful
Fructo, Fructoso, Fructuso

Fry (English) A father's offspring
Frye, Fryer

Fu (Chinese) A wealthy man

Fudail (Arabic) Of high moral character
Fudaile, Fudayl, Fudayle, Fudale, Fudael, Fudaele

Fugol (Anglo-Saxon) Resembling a bird
Fugul, Fugel, Fugal, Fugil, Fugyl

Fukuda (Japanese) From the field

Fulbright (English) A brilliant man
Fullbright, Fulbrite, Fullbrite, Fulbryte, Fullbryte, Fulbert, Fullbert

Fulgentius (Latin) A shining man
Fulgentios, Fulgentio, Fulgento, Fulgencio, Fulgenteos, Fulgenteus, Fulgenteo

Fulke (English) Of the people
Fulk, Folke, Folk, Fawk, Fawke, Fowk, Fowke

Fulki (Indian) A spark
Fulkie, Fulkey, Fulky, Fulkee, Fulkea

Fuller (English) One who presses, shrinks, and thickens cloth
Fullar, Fullor, Fullur, Fullir, Fullyr, Fullere, Fuler

Fullerton (English) From Fuller's town
Fullertun, Fullertin, Fullertyn, Fullertan, Fullerten

Fulton (English) From the people's town
Fultun, Fulten, Fultan, Fultin, Fultyn, Fulaton, Fulatun, Fulatin, Fulaten, Fulatyn, Fulatan, Fugeltun, Fugelton, Fugeltan, Fugeltin, Fugeltyn, Fugelten

Furlo (American) A manly man
Furlow, Furlowe, Furloe, Furl, Furle, Furlio, Furleo

Furman (German) A ferryman
Furmen, Furmin, Furmyn, Furmon, Furmun, Furmann, Fuhrman, Fuhrmen, Fuhrmon, Fuhrmun, Fuhrmin, Fuhrmyn

Fursey (Gaelic) The name of a missionary saint
Fursy, Fursi, Fursie, Fursee, Fursea

Fyfe (Scottish) A man from Fifeshire
Fife, Fyffe, Fiffe, Fibh

Fyren (Anglo-Saxon) A wicked man
Fyrin, Fyryn, Fyran, Fyron, Fyrun

Fyrsil (Welsh) Form of Virgil, meaning "the staff-bearer"
Fyrsyl, Fyrsill, Fyrsyll

Gaagii (Native American) Resembling a raven
Gaagi, Gagii, Gagi

Gabai (Hebrew) A delightful man

Gabal (Arabian) From the mountain
Gaball

Gabbana (Italian) A creative man
Gabbanah, Gabana, Gabanah, Gabbanna, Gabanna

Gabbar (Arabian) A proud and strong man
Gabber, Gabbor, Gabbur, Gabbir, Gabbyr

Gabbay (Hebrew) A tax collector
Gabbaye, Gabbai, Gabbae

Gabbo (English) To joke or scoff
Gabboe, Gabbow, Gabbowe

Gabor (Hebrew) God is my strength
Gabur, Gabar, Gaber, Gabir, Gabyr

Gabra (African) An offering
Gabre

✿
❂ **Gabriel** (Hebrew) A hero of God
Gabrian, Gabriele, Gabrielli, Gabriello, Gaby, Gab, Gabbi, Gabbie, Gabby, Gabe, Gabi, Gabie, Gabey, Gabee, Gabbey, Gabbee, Gable, Gabrio, Gabino, Gabrielo

Gace (French) Of the pledge
Gayce, Gayse, Gaese, Gaece, Gaice, Gaise

Gad (Hebrew / Native American) Having good fortune / from the juniper tree
Gadi, Gadie, Gady, Gadey, Gadee, Gadea

Gaddis (American) A high-maintenance man
Gaddys, Gadis, Gadys, Gaddiss, Gaddyss,

Gadiss, Gadyss, Gaddes

Gaderian (Anglo-Saxon) A gatherer
Gaderean, Gadrian, Gadrean, Gaderyan, Gadryan

Gadiel (Arabic) God is my fortune
Gadiell, Gadiele, Gadielle, Gaddiel, Gaddiell, Gadil, Gadeel, Gadeal, Gadeil, Gadyl

Gadish (Arabic) A shock of corn
Gadysh, Gadishe, Gadyshe

Gael (English) One who is or speaks Gaelic
Gaele, Gaell, Gaelle, Gall

Gaerwn (Welsh) From the white fort

Gaetan (Italian) A man from Gaeta
Gaeten, Gaeton, Gaetun, Gaetin, Gaetyn, Gaetano, Gaetanio, Gaetaneo, Gaetaniyo, Gaetaneyo

Gaffney (Irish) Resembling a calf
Gaffny, Gaffni, Gaffnie, Gaffnee, Gaffnea

Gagan (French) A dedicated man
Gagen, Gagon, Gagun, Gagin, Gagyn

Gage (French) Of the pledge
Gaige, Gaege, Gayge

Gahan (Scottish) Form of John, meaning "God is gracious"
Gahen, Gahon, Gahun, Gahin, Gahyn, Gehan, Gehen, Gehon, Gehun, Gehin, Gehyn

Gahuj (African) A hunter

Gaillard (English) A brave and spirited man
Gailliard, Gaillhard, Gaillardet, Gaillhardt, Gaillart

Gaines (English) One who acquires
Gaynes, Gaenes, Ganes, Gaine, Gayne, Gaene, Gane

Gair (Gaelic) A man of short stature
Gayr, Gaer, Gaire, Gayre, Gaere, Gare

Gaius (Latin) One who rejoices
Gaeus

Gaizka (Basque) A savior
Gayzka, Gaezka

Gajendra (Indian) The king of elephants

Gal (Hebrew) From the rolling wave

Galahad (English) One who is pure and selfless

Galal (Arabic) A majestic man
Galall, Gallal, Gallall

Galanos (Greek) Having blue eyes
Galanios, Galanus, Galanius

Galav (Hindi) The name of a sage

Galbraith (Irish) A foreigner; a Scot
Galbrait, Galbreath, Gallbraith, Gallbreath, Galbraithe, Gallbraithe, Galbreathe, Gallbreathe

Gale (Irish / English) A foreigner / one who is cheerful
Gail, Gaill, Gaille, Gaile, Gayl, Gayle, Gaylle, Gayll

Galegina (Native American) Resembling a deer
Galagina, Galegyna, Galagyna, Galegena, Galagena

Galen (Greek) A healer; one who is calm
Gaelan, Gaillen, Galan, Galin, Galyn, Gaylen, Gaylin, Gaylinn, Gaylan, Gaelen, Gaelin, Gailen, Gailan, Gailin, Gaylon, Galon, Gaelon, Gailon

Galeno (Spanish) A bright child
Galenio, Galeneo, Galeniyo, Galeneyo, Galenios, Galeneos

Gali (Hebrew) From the fountain
Galie, Galy, Galey, Galee, Galea, Galeigh

Galil (Hebrew) From the hilly place
Galeel, Galeal, Galeil, Galiel, Galyl

Galileo (Italian) A man from Galilee
Galilio, Galyleo, Galylio, Galiliyo, Galileyo, Galeleo, Galelio, Galeleyo, Galeliyo

Galip (Turkish) A victorious man
Galyp, Galup, Galep, Galap, Galop

Gallagher (Gaelic) An eager helper
Gallaghor, Gallaghar, Gallaghur, Gallaghir, Gallaghyr, Gallager, Gallagar, Gallagor, Gallagur, Gallagir, Gallagyr

Gallatin (American) From the river
Gallatyn, Gallaten, Gallatan, Gallaton, Gallatun

Galloway (Latin) A man from Gaul
Galoway, Gallowaye, Galowaye, Galo, Gallo, Galway, Gallway, Gallman, Galman, Gallmann, Galmann

Galt (English) From the high wooded land
Galte, Gallt, Gallte

Galtero (Spanish) Form of Walter, meaning "the commander of the army"
Galterio, Galteriyo, Galtereo, Galtereyo, Galter, Galteros, Galterus, Gualterio, Gualtier, Gualtiero, Gutierre

Galton (English) From the town on the high wooded land
Galtun, Galten, Galtan, Galtin, Galtyn, Gallton, Galltun, Gallten, Galltin, Galltyn, Galltan

Galvin (Irish) Resembling a sparrow
Galvyn, Galven, Galvan, Galvon, Galvun, Gallvin, Gallvyn, Gallvon, Gallvun, Gallven, Gallvan

Gamal (Arabic) Resembling a camel
Gamul, Gemal, Gemali, Gemul, Gamali, Gamalie, Gamalee, Gamaleigh, Gumalea, Gamaly, Gamaley, Gemalie, Gemaly, Gemaley, Gemalea, Gemalee, Gemaleigh

Gamaliel (Hebrew) God's reward
Gamliel, Gamalyel, Gamlyel, Gamli, Gamlie, Gamly, Gamley, Gamlee, Gamlea, Gamleigh

Gamba (African) A warrior
Gambah

Gamble (Norse) An old man; of an old family
Gamblen, Gambling, Gamel, Gammel, Gamlin, Gamlen, Gamblin, Gamblyn, Gamlyn

Gameel (Arabic) A handsome man
Gameal, Gamil, Gamiel, Gameil, Gamyl

Gamon (American) One who enjoys playing games
Gamun, Gamen, Gaman, Gamin, Gamyn, Gammon, Gammun, Gamman, Gammin, Gammyn, Gammen

Gan (Chinese) A wanderer

Gandy (American) An adventurer
Gandey, Gandi, Gandie, Gandee, Gandea

Ganesh (Hindi) In Hinduism, the god of wisdom
Ganeshe, Ganesha, Ganeshah

Ganit (Hebrew) The defender
Ganyt, Ganot, Ganut

Gann (English) One who defends with a spear
Gan

Gannet (German) Resembling a goose
Gannett, Ganet, Ganett

Gannon (Gaelic) A fair-skinned man
Gannun, Gannen, Gannan, Gannin, Gannyn, Ganon, Ganun, Ganin, Ganyn, Ganen, Ganan

Ganso (Spanish) Resembling a goose
Gansio, Ganseo, Gansos, Gansios, Gansius, Ganzo, Ganzio, Ganzeo, Ganz, Gans

Ganya (Russian) Having great strength
Ganyah, Ganiya, Ganiyah

Garaden (English) From the triangle-shaped hill
Garadin, Garadan, Garadon, Garadun, Garadyn

Garafeld (English) From the triangle-shaped field
Garafield

Garai (Basque) A conqueror

Garan (Welsh / German) Resembling a stork / a guardian
Garen, Garin, Garyn, Garon, Garun

Garbhan (Irish) One who is rough
Garbhen, Garbhon, Garbhun, Garbhin, Garbhyn, Garban, Garben, Garbin, Garbyn, Garbon, Garbun

Garcia (Spanish) One who is brave in battle
Garce, Garcy, Garcey, Garci, Garcie, Garcee, Garcea

Gardner (English) The keeper of the garden
Gardener, Gardenner, Gardie, Gardiner, Gardnar, Gardnard, Gard, Gardell, Gardi, Gardy, Gardey, Gardee, Gardea, Gardenor, Gardnor, Gardenir, Gardnir, Gardenyr, Gardnyr

Gared (English) Form of Gerard, meaning "one who is mighty with a spear"
Garad, Garid, Garyd, Garod, Garud

Gareth (Welsh) One who is gentle
Garith, Garreth, Garrith, Garyth, Garryth, Garath, Garrath

Garfield (English) From the spear field
Garfeld

Garland (French / English) One who is crowned / from the spear land
Garlan, Garlen, Garlend, Garlin, Garlind, Garllan, Garlland, Garlyn, Garlynd, Garlon, Garlond, Garlun, Garlund, Gariland, Garilend

Garman (English) A spearman
Garmann, Garmen, Garmin, Garmon, Garmun, Garmyn, Gar, Garr, Garrman, Garrmen, Garrmon, Garrmun, Garrmin, Garrmyn

Garn (American) One who is prepared
Garne, Garni, Garnie, Garny, Garney, Garnee, Garnea

Garner (English) One who gathers or keeps grain
Garnar, Garnor, Garnur, Garnir, Garnyr, Garnier, Garnell, Garnel

Garnett (English / French) Resembling the dark-red gem / one who wields a spear
Garnet, Garnette, Garnete

Garnock (Welsh) From the river of alder trees
Garnoc, Garnok, Gwernach, Garnoch

Garrad (English) Form of Gerard, meaning "one who is mighty with a spear"
Garred, Garrod, Garrud, Garrid, Garryd

Garrett (English) Form of Gerard, meaning "one who is mighty with a spear"
Garett, Garret, Garretson, Garritt, Garrot, Garrott, Gerrit, Gerritt, Gerrity, Garrity, Garet

Garrick (English) One who rules by the spear
Garek, Garreck, Garrik, Garryck, Garryk, Garick, Garik, Garic, Garyck, Garyk, Garyc, Garric, Garryc

Garridan (English) One who is quiet
Garriden, Garridin, Garridyn, Garridon, Garridun

Garrison (English) From the spear-fortified town
Garrisun, Garrisen, Garison, Garisun, Garisen, Garris, Garrys, Garryson, Garrysun, Garrysen, Garrysan, Garrysin, Garrysyn

Garron (Gaelic) Resembling a gelding; workhorse
Garrion, Garran, Garren, Garrin, Garrun, Garryn

Garroway (English) One who fights with a spear
Garoway, Garrowaye, Garowaye, Garrowae, Garowae, Garrowai, Garowai, Garwig, Garwyg, Garrwig, Garrwyg

Garson (English) The son of Gar (Garrett, Garrison, Gareth, etc.)
Garrson, Garsen, Garrsen, Garsun, Garrsun, Garsone, Garrsone

Garth (Scandinavian) The keeper of the garden
Garthe, Gart, Garte

Garthay (Irish) Form of Gareth, meaning "one who is gentle"
Garthaye, Garthai, Garthae

Garton (English) From the triangle-shaped town
Gartun, Garrton, Garrtun, Garten, Garrten, Garaton, Garatun, Garatin, Garatyn, Garaten, Garatan

Garvey (Gaelic) A rough but peaceful man
Garvy, Garvee, Garvea, Garvi, Garvie, Garrvey, Garrvy, Garrvee, Garrvea, Garrvi, Garrvie, Garve

Garvin (English) A friend with a spear
Garvyn, Garven, Garvan, Garvon, Garvun

Garwin (English) Form of Garvin, meaning "a friend with a spear"
Garwine, Garwinn, Garwinne, Garwen, Garwenn, Garwenne, Garwyn, Garwynn, Garwynne, Gaarwine

Garwood (English) From the triangle-shaped forest; from the spear forest
Garrwood, Garwode, Garrwode

Gary (English) One who wields a spear
Garey, Gari, Garie, Garea, Garee, Garry, Garrey, Garree, Garrea, Garri, Garrie

Gaspar (Persian) The keeper of the treasure
Gasper, Gaspir, Gaspyr, Gaspor, Gaspur, Gaspare, Gaspard, Gasparo

Gassur (Arabic) A courageous man
Gassor, Gassir, Gassyr, Gassar, Gasser

Gaston (French) A man from Gascony
Gastun, Gastan, Gasten, Gascon, Gascone, Gasconey, Gasconi, Gasconie, Gasconee, Gasconea, Gascony

Gate (American) One who is close-minded
Gates, Gait, Gaite, Gaits, Gaites, Gayt, Gayte, Gayts, Gaytes, Gaet, Gaete, Gaets, Gaetes

Gaudy (American) One who is colorful
Gaudey, Gaudi, Gaudie, Gaudee, Gaudea, Gauden, Gaudan, Gaudin, Gaudyn, Gaudon, Gaudun

Gaurav (Hindi) A proud man

Gaute (Norse) A great man
Gauti, Gautie, Gauty, Gautey, Gautee, Gautea

Gauthier (Teutonic) A strong ruler
Gaultier, Gautier, Gualterio, Gualtiero, Gualtereo, Gaulterio, Gaultereo, Gaultiero, Gauther

● **Gavin** (Welsh) A little white falcon
Gavan, Gaven, Gavino, Gavyn, Gavynn, Gavon, Gavun, Gavyno, Gaveno, Gawain, Gawaine, Gawayn, Gawayne, Gawaine, Gwayne, Gwayn, Gawen, Gawath, Gawin

Gavriel (Hebrew) God is my strength
Gavriell, Gavril, Gavrilo, Gavryel, Gavryell, Gavryl, Gavrill, Gavryll, Gavrylo, Gavi, Gavie, Gavy, Gavey, Gavee, Gavea, Gavri, Gavrie, Gavry, Gavrey, Gavree, Gavrea

Gaylord (French) One who is high-spirited
Gay, Gayelord, Gayler, Gaylor, Gaylur, Gaylar, Gaylir, Gaylyr, Gaylard

Gaynor (Gaelic) The son of a fair-haired man
Gaynur, Gayner, Gaynir, Gaynar, Gaynyr, Gainor, Gainur, Gainer, Gainar, Gainir, Gainyr, Gaenor, Gaenur, Gaenar, Gaener, Guenir, Gaenyr

Gazali (African) A mystic
Gazalie, Gazaly, Gazaley, Gazalee, Gazalea, Gazaleigh

Gazsi (Hungarian) One who protects the treasure
Gazsie, Gazsy, Gazsey, Gazsee, Gazsea

Geary (English) One who is flexible
Geari, Gearie, Gearey, Gearee, Gearea, Gery, Gerey, Geri, Gerie, Geree, Gerea

Gedaliah (Hebrew) God is great
Gedalia, Gedaliahu, Gedalio, Gedulya,
Gedalyah

Geedar (Arabian) From the enclosure
Geeder, Geedor, Geedur, Geedir, Geedyr

Geert (German) One who is brave and
strong
Geart, Geerte, Gearte

Gefen (Hebrew) Of the vine
Gafni, Gefania, Gefaniah, Gefanya,
Gefanyah, Gefanyahu, Geffen, Gephania,
Gephaniah, Gefni, Gefnie, Gefney, Gefny,
Gefnea, Gefnee

Geir (Scandinavian) One who wields a spear
Geire, Geer, Geere, Gear, Geare

Geirleif (Norse) A descendant of the spear
Geirleaf, Geerleif, Geerleaf

Geirolf (Norse) The wolf spear
Geirulf, Geerolf, Geerulf

Geirstein (Norse) One who wields a rock-
hard spear
Geerstein, Gerstein

Geldersman (Dutch) A man from Guelders
Geldersmann, Geldersmen, Geldersmon

Gellert (Hungarian) A mighty soldier
Gellart, Gellirt, Gellyrt, Gellort, Gellurt

Gemini (Latin) The twins; the third sign of
the zodiac
Gemineye, Gemyni, Geminie, Gemynie

Genaro (Latin) A dedicated man
Genaroh, Genaroe, Genarow, Genarowe

Gene (English) Form of Eugene, meaning
"a wellborn man"
Genio, Geno, Geneo, Gino, Ginio, Gineo

General (American) A military leader
Generel, Generol, Generil, Generyl, Generul

Genero (Latin) One who is generic
Generoe, Generoh, Generow, Generowe

Generoso (Spanish) One who is generous
Generosio, Generoseo, Generos

Genesis (Hebrew) Of the beginning
Genesys, Gennesis, Ginesis, Ginesys, Gennesys

Genet (African) From Eden
Genat, Genit, Genyt, Genot, Genut

Gennaro (Italian) Born of Janus
Gennarius, Gennaros, Gennarios, Gennarus,
Gennareo, Gennario

Genoah (Italian) From the city of Genoa
Genoa, Genovise, Genovize

Gent (English) A gentleman
Gente, Gynt, Gynte

Gentian (Latin) Resembling the blue flower
Genshian

Gentile (Latin) A foreigner or heathen
Gentyle, Gentilo, Gentylo, Gentilio, Gentylio,
Gentileo, Gentyleo, Gentil

Gentry (English) Of good breeding; holding
a high social standing
Gentrey, Gentree, Gentrea, Gentri, Gentrie

Gentza (Basque) A peaceful man
Gentzah

Geoffrey (English) Form of Jeffrey, mean-
ing "a man of peace"
Geffrey, Geoff, Geoffery, Geoffroy, Geoffry,
Geofrey, Geofferi, Geofferie, Geofferee, Geoffri,
Geoffrie, Geoffree, Geffry, Geffri, Geffrie,
Geffree

Geol (English) Born at Christmastime
Geoll, Geole, Geolle

Geomar (German) One who is famous in
battle
Geomarr, Geomare, Geomarre, Giomar,
Giomarr, Giomare, Giomarre

George (Greek) One who works the earth;
a farmer
Georas, Geordi, Geordie, Georg, Georges,
Georgi, Georgie, Georgio, Georgios, Georgiy,
Georgy, Gheorghe, Giorgi, Giorgio, Giorgios,
Giorgius, Goran, Gyorgy, Gyuri, Georgii

Geraghty (Irish) From the court
Geraghtey, Geraghti, Geraghtie, Geraghtee,
Geraghtea

Geraint (Latin) An old man
Gerainte, Gerant, Geraynt, Geraynte,
Geraent, Geraente

Gerald (German) One who rules with the spear
Garald, Garold, Gearalt, Geralde, Geraldo, Geraud, Gere, Gerek, Gerik, Gerold, Gerolld, Gerolt, Gerollt, Gerrald, Gerrell, Gerri, Gerrild, Gerrold, Geryld, Giraldo, Giraud, Girauld, Girault, Geralt, Gerred

Gerard (English) One who is mighty with a spear
Garrard, Gearard, Gerardo, Geraud, Gerrard, Girard, Girault, Giraud, Gherardo, Gerhard, Gerard, Gerd, Gerod

Gerbold (German) One who is bold with a spear
Gerbolde

Geremia (Italian) Form of Jeremiah, meaning "one who is exalted by the Lord"
Geremiah, Geremias, Geremija, Geremiya, Geremyah, Geramiah, Geramia

Gerlach (Scandinavian) A spear thrower
Gerlaich

Germain (French / Latin) A man from Germany / one who is brotherly
Germaine, German, Germane, Germanicus, Germano, Germanus, Germayn, Germayne, Germin, Germaen, Germaene

Gerodi (Italian) A hero
Gerodie, Gerody, Gerodey, Gerodee, Gerodea

Geron (French) A guardian
Gerun, Geren, Geran, Gerin, Geryn

Geronimo (Spanish) Form of Jerome, meaning "of the sacred name"; a great Native American chief
Geronimus, Geronimos, Geronymo

Gerontius (Latin) An old man
Gerontios, Gerontio, Geronteo

Gerry (German) Short form of names beginning with Ger-, such as Gerald or Gerard
Gerrey, Gerri, Gerrie, Gerrea, Gerree

Gershom (Hebrew) One who has been exiled
Gersham, Gershon, Gershoom, Gershem, Gershim, Gershym, Gershum, Gersh, Gershe, Gerzson

Gervase (German) One who is honored; one who serves the spear
Gervais, Gervaise, Gervasio, Gervasius, Gervaso, Gervayse, Gerwazy, Gerwazey, Gerwazi, Gerwazie, Gerwazee, Gerwazea, Gervis, Gervys

Getachew (African) Their master

Geteye (African) My master

Gethin (Welsh) A dark-skinned man
Gethyn, Gethan, Gethen, Gethon, Gethun

Gevariah (Hebrew) The strength of God
Gevaria, Gevarya, Gevaryah, Gevarayahu, Gevariya, Gevariyah

Ghalib (Arabic) A victorious man
Ghaleeb, Ghaleab, Ghaleib, Ghalieb, Ghalyb

Ghassan (Arabic) One who is in the prime of his youth
Ghasan, Ghassen, Ghasen, Ghasson, Ghason, Ghassun, Ghasun, Ghassin, Ghasin, Ghassyn, Ghasyn

Ghayth (Arabic) The winner
Ghaith, Ghaeth, Ghathe, Ghaythe, Ghaithe, Ghaethe

Ghazal (Arabian) Resembling a deer
Ghazall, Ghazale

Ghazi (Arabic) An invader; a conqueror
Ghazie, Ghazy, Ghazey, Ghazee, Ghazea

Ghedi (African) A traveler
Ghedie, Ghedy, Ghedey, Ghedee, Ghedea

Ghislain (German) Of the oath
Ghislaine, Ghislayn, Ghislayne, Ghislaen, Ghislaene, Ghislane

Ghoshal (Hindi) A speaker
Ghoshil, Ghoshyl

Ghoukas (Armenian) Form of Lucas, meaning "a man from Lucania"
Ghukas

Giacomo (Italian) Form of James, meaning "he who supplants"
Gyacomo

Gian (Italian) Form of John, meaning "God is gracious"
Gyan, Gianney, Gianni, Gianny, Giannie, Giannee, Giannea, Gyanney, Gyanny, Gyanni, Gyannie, Gyannee, Gyannea, Gi, Gy, Giann, Gyann

Giancarlo (Italian) One who is gracious and mighty
Gyancarlo

Gibor (Hebrew) Having great strength
Gybor, Gibbor, Gybbor

Gibson (English) The son of Gilbert
Gibb, Gibbes, Gibby, Gibbons, Gibbs, Gibsen, Gibsun, Gilson, Gilsun, Gilsen, Gillson, Gillsun, Gillsen, Gibbon, Gibbens, Gibben, Gibbesone

Gideon (Hebrew) A mighty warrior; one who fells trees
Gideone, Gidi, Gidon, Gidion, Gid, Gidie, Gidy, Gidey, Gidee, Gidea, Gedeon, Gedion, Gedon

Gidney (English) Having great strength
Gidny, Gidni, Gidnie, Gidnee, Gidnea, Gydney, Gydny, Gydni, Gydnie, Gydnee, Gydnea

Giffin (English) A giving man
Giffen, Giffyn, Giffon, Giffun, Giffan, Giff, Gyf, Gyff, Giffe, Gyffe

Gifford (English) One who gives bravery
Gyfford, Gifforde, Gyfforde, Giffurd, Gyffurd, Gifferd, Gyfferd, Giffurde, Gyffurde, Gifferde, Gyfferde, Giffard, Giffarde, Gyffard, Gyffarde, Gifuhard

Gifre (Anglo-Saxon) A greedy man
Gifri, Gifrie, Gifree, Gifrea, Gifry, Gifrey

Gijs (English) An intelligent man

Gilad (Hebrew / Arabic) From the monument / a camel's hump
Gylad, Gilead, Giladi, Giladie, Gilady, Giladey, Giladee, Giladea, Gyladi, Gyladie, Gylady, Gyladey, Gyladee, Gyladea

Gilam (Hebrew) The joy of the people
Gylam, Gilem, Gylem, Gilim, Gylim, Gilym, Gylym, Gilom, Gylom, Gilum, Gylum, Gil, Gyl

Gilamu (Basque) A determined soldier
Gilamue, Gilamou, Gylamu, Gylamue, Gylamou

Gilbert (French / English) Of the bright promise / one who is trustworthy
Gib, Gibb, Gil, Gilberto, Gilburt, Giselbert, Giselberto, Giselbertus, Guilbert, Gilbirt, Gilbyrt, Gilbart, Gilibeirt, Giliburt, Gilibert, Gilibirt, Gilleabart, Guilbert, Guilbirt, Guilburt

Gilby (Norse / Gaelic) From the hostage's estate / a blonde-haired man
Gilbey, Gilbee, Gilbea, Gilbi, Gilbie, Gillbey, Gillbie, Gillby, Gillbi, Gillbee, Gillbea

Gilchrist (Irish) A servant of Christ
Gylchrist, Gillchrist, Gyllchrist, Gikhrist, Gilkhrist, Gilkrist

Gildas (Irish / English) One who serves God / the golden one
Gyldas, Gilda, Gylda, Gilde, Gylde, Gildea, Gyldea, Gildes, Gyldes

Giles (Greek) Resembling a young goat
Gyles, Gile, Gil, Gilles, Gillis, Gilliss, Gyle, Gyl, Gylles, Gylliss, Gyllis

Gilfred (Teutonic) One who has taken an oath of peace
Gilfrid, Gilfryd, Gilfried, Gilfreid, Gylfred, Gylfrid, Gylfryd, Gylfried, Gylfreid

Gill (Gaelic) A servant
Gyll, Gilly, Gilley, Gillee, Gillea, Gilli, Gillie, Ghill, Ghyll, Ghilli, Ghillie, Ghilly, Ghilley, Ghillee, Ghillea

Gillanders (Scottish) A servant of St. Andrew
Gyllanders, Gilanders, Gylanders

Gillean (Irish) A servant of St. John
Gyllean, Gillian, Gyllian, Gilean, Gilian, Gillan, Gillen, Gilleon, Gillion, Gillon

Gilleasbuig (German) One who is bold

Gillespie (Gaelic) A servant of the bishop; the son of the bishop's servant
Gillespi, Gillespy, Gillespey, Gillespee, Gillespea, Gillaspi, Gillaspie, Gillaspee, Gillaspea, Gillaspy, Gillaspey

Gillett (Spanish) A little or young Gilbert
Gilet, Gilett, Gillet, Gylet, Gylett, Gyllet, Gyllett

Gillies (Scottish) A servant of Jesus
Ghilles, Ghillies, Gillees, Ghillees

Gillivray (Scottish) A servant of God
Gillivraye, Gillivrae, Gillivrai

Gilman (Gaelic) A manservant
Gillman, Gilmann, Gillmann, Gylman, Gylmann, Gyllman, Gyllmann

Gilmat (Scottish) One who wields a sword
Gylmat, Gilmet, Gylmet

Gilmer (English) A famous hostage
Gilmar, Gilmor, Gilmur, Gilmir, Gilmyr, Gillmer, Gillmar, Gillmor, Gillmur, Gillmir, Gillmyr

Gilmore (Gaelic) A servant of the Virgin Mary
Gillmore, Gillmour, Gilmour

Gilon (Hebrew) Filled with joy
Gilun, Gilen, Gilan, Gilin, Gilyn, Gilo

Gilpin (English) A trustworthy man
Gilpen, Gilpyn, Gilpan, Gilpon, Gilpun

Gilroy (Gaelic) The son of a red-haired man
Gilderoy, Gildray, Gildroy, Gillroy, Gillray, Gilray

Gimm (Anglo-Saxon) As precious as a gem
Gim, Gymm, Gym

Ginton (Arabic) From the garden
Gintun, Gintan, Ginten, Gintin, Gintyn

Giona (Italian) Form of John, meaning "God is gracious"
Gion, Gione

Giovanni (Italian) Form of John, meaning "God is gracious"
Geovani, Geovanney, Geovanni, Geovanny, Geovany, Giannino, Giovan, Giovani, Giovanno, Giovanny, Giovel, Giovell, Giovonni

Giri (Indian) From the mountain
Girie, Giry, Girey, Giree, Girea

Girioel (Welsh) A lord

Girvan (Gaelic) The small, rough one
Gyrvan, Girven, Gyrven, Girvin, Gyrvin, Girvyn, Gyrvyn, Girvon, Gyrvon, Girvun, Gyrvun

Gitano (Italian) A gypsy
Gytano, Gitanos, Gytanos, Gitanio, Gitaneo

Gitel (Hebrew) A good man
Gitell, Gitele, Gitelle, Gytel, Gytell, Gytele, Gytelle

Giulio (Italian) One who is youthful
Giuliano, Giuleo

Giuseppe (Italian) Form of Joseph, meaning "God will add"
Giuseppi, Giuseppie, Giuseppy, Giuseppee, Giuseppea, Giuseppey, Guiseppe, Guiseppi, Guiseppie, Guiseppey, Guiseppy, Guiseppea, Guiseppee

Giustino (Italian) Form of Justin, meaning "one who is just and upright"
Giusto, Giustio, Giusteo, Giustinian, Giustiniano

Givon (Arabic) From the heights
Givun, Given, Givan, Givin, Givyn

Gizmo (American) One who is playful
Gismo, Gyzmo, Gysmo, Gizmoe, Gismoe, Gyzmoe, Gysmoe

Gjest (Norse) A stranger

Gjord (Norse) Form of Godfried, meaning "God is peace"
Gjurd, Gjorn, Gjurn

Glad (American) One who is lighthearted and happy
Gladd, Gladdi, Gladdie, Gladdy, Gladdey, Gladdee, Gladdea

Glade (English) From the clearing in the woods
Glayd, Glayde, Glaid, Glaide, Glaed, Glaede

Gladstone (English) From the kite-shaped stone
Gladston

Gladus (Welsh) One who is lame
Glados, Glades, Gladas, Gladis, Gladys

Gladwin (English) A lighthearted and happy friend
Gladwine, Gladwinn, Gladwinne, Gladwen, Gladwenn, Gladwenne, Gladwyn, Gladwynn, Gladwynne

Glaisne (Irish) One who is calm; serene
Glaisny, Glaisney, Glaisni, Glaisnie, Glaisnee, Glasny, Glasney, Glasni, Glasnie, Glasnee

Glancy (American) Form of Clancy, meaning "son of the red-haired warrior"
Glancey, Glanci, Glancie, Glancee, Glancea, Glansey, Glansy, Glansi, Glansie, Glansee, Glansea

Glanville (French) From the village of oak trees
Glanvil, Glanvill, Glanvylle, Glanvyl, Glanvyll

Glasgow (Scottish) From the city in Scotland
Glasgo

Glen (Gaelic) From the secluded narrow valley
Glenn, Glennard, Glennie, Glennon, Glenny, Glin, Glinn, Glyn, Glynn, Glean, Glendale, Glendayle, Glendail, Glendael, Glenney, Glenni, Glenard, Glennerd, Glenerd

Glenavon (English) From the valley near the river Avon
Glennavon, Glenavin, Glennavin, Glenavyn, Glennavyn, Glenaven, Glennaven, Glenavan, Glennavan, Glenavun, Glennavun

Glendon (Gaelic) From the town in the glen
Glendun, Glendan, Glenden, Glendin, Glendyn

Glendower (Welsh) From the valley near the water
Glyndwer, Glyndwr, Glendwer, Glendwr, Glyndower

Glenville (Gaelic) From the village in the glen
Glenvil, Glenvill, Glenvyll, Glenvyl, Glenvylle, Glinville, Glinvill, Glinvil, Glinvylle, Glinvyll, Glinvyl

Glenwood (English) From the forest near the glen
Glenwode

Glover (English) One who makes gloves
Glovar, Glovir, Glovyr, Glovur, Glovor

Gobha (Scottish) A smith
Gobhah

Gobind (Sanskrit) The cow finder
Gobinde, Gobinda, Govind, Govinda, Govinde

Goby (American) An audacious man
Gobi, Gobie, Gobey, Gobee, Gobea

Godana (African) A male child
Godanah, Godanna, Godannah

Goddard (German) One who is divinely firm
Godard, Godart, Goddart, Godhart, Godhardt, Gothart, Gotthard, Gotthardt, Gotthart

Godfrey (German) God is peace
Giotto, Godefroi, Godfry, Godofredo, Goffredo, Gottfrid, Gottfried, Godfried, Godfreid, Godfrid, Godfred, Godfryd, Gofraidh, Gofried, Gofreid, Gofryd, Gofred, Gofrid, Gothfraidh

Godric (English) One who rules with God
Godrick, Godrik, Godryc, Godryk, Godryck, Goderick, Goderyck, Goderic, Goderyc, Goderik, Goderyk

Godwin (English) A friend of God
Godwine, Godwinn, Godwinne, Godwen, Godwenn, Godwenne, Godwyn, Godwynn, Godwynne, Godewin, Godewen, Godewyn

Goel (Hebrew) One who has been redeemed
Goell, Goele, Goelle

Gogarty (Irish) One who has been banished
Gogartey, Gogarti, Gogartie, Gogartee, Gogartea

Gogo (African) A grandfatherly man

Gohn (American) A spirited man
Gon

Goku (Japanese) From the sky

Golding (English) The golden one
Goldyng, Golden, Goldan, Goldin, Goldyn, Goldon, Goldun, Goldman, Goldmann, Gold, Golde, Goldo

Goldsmith (English) One who works with gold
Goldschmidt, Goldshmidt

Goldwin (English) A golden friend
Goldwine, Goldwinn, Goldwinne, Goldwen, Goldwenn, Goldwenne, Goldwyn, Goldwynn, Goldwynne, Goldewin, Goldewen, Goldewyn

Goliath (Hebrew) One who has been exiled; in the Bible, the giant killed by David
Goliathe, Golliath, Golliathe, Golyath, Golyathe, Gollyath, Gollyathe

Gomda (Native American) Of the wind
Gomdah

Gomer (English) Of the good fight
Gomar, Gomor, Gomur, Gomir, Gomyr

Gong (American) A forceful man

Gonzalo (Spanish) Of the battle; resembling a wolf
Gonsalve, Gonzales, Gonsalo, Gonsales, Gonzalez, Gonze, Gonz

Goode (English) An upstanding man
Good, Goodi, Goodie, Goody, Goodey, Goodee, Goodea

Goodman (English) An upstanding man
Goodmann, Guttman, Guttmann

Goodrich (English) A good ruler
Goodriche

Goodwin (English) A beloved friend
Goodwine, Goodwinn, Goodwinne, Goodwen, Goodwenn, Goodwenne, Goodwyn, Goodwynn, Goodwynne

Gordain (Scottish) Form of Gordan, meaning "from the great hill; a hero"
Gordaine, Gordayn, Gordayne, Gordaen, Gordaene, Gordane

Gordon (Gaelic) From the great hill; a hero
Gorden, Gordin, Gordyn, Gordun, Gordan, Gordi, Gordie, Gordee, Gordea, Gordy, Gordey, Gordo

Gore (English) From the triangle-shaped land
Goring, Gor, Gorre, Gorr

Goren (Hebrew) From the granary
Gorin, Goryn, Goran, Gorun, Goron, Gorren, Gorrin, Gorryn, Gorran, Gorrun, Gorron

Gorham (English) From the village in the triangle-shaped land

Gorka (Basque) A farmer
Gorko, Gorke, Gorki, Gorkey, Gorky, Gorkie, Gorkee, Gorkea, Gyurka

Gorman (Irish) Having blue eyes
Gormain, Gormaine, Gormayn, Gormayne, Gormaen, Gormaene

Gormley (Irish) The blue spearman
Gormly, Gormlee, Gormlea, Gormleah, Gormleigh, Gormli, Gormlie, Gormaly, Gormaley, Gormalee, Gormaleigh, Gormalea, Gormaleah, Gormali, Gormalie, Gormilly, Gormilley, Gormillee, Gormilleigh, Gormillea, Gormilleah, Gormilli, Gormillie

Goro (Japanese) The fifth-born child

Gorrell (English) From the marsh thicket
Gorell, Gorrel

Gorry (Irish) One who achieves peace through God
Gorrey, Gorri, Gorrie, Gorrea, Gorree

Gorton (English) From the town in the triangle-shaped land
Gortun, Gorten, Gortan, Gortin, Gortyn

Gosheven (Native American) One who leaps
Goshevin, Goshevyn, Goshevan, Goshevon, Goshevun

Gotam (Indian) The best ox
Gotem, Gautam, Gautem, Gautom, Gotom

Gotzon (Basque) A heavenly messenger; an angel

Govannon (Irish) In mythology, the god of the forge
Govannen, Govannan, Govannun, Govannin, Govannyn, Govan, Govane

Govind (Indian) The one who finds and owns cows
Govinde, Govynd, Govynde, Govend, Govende

Gow (Scottish) A smith
Gowe, Gowan

Gower (Welsh) One who is pure; chaste
Gwyr, Gowyr, Gowir, Gowar, Gowor, Gowur

Gowon (African) A rainmaker
Gowun

Gowyn (English) A friend of God
Gowynn, Gowynne, Gowen, Gowenn, Gowenne, Gowin, Gowinn, Gowinne, Gowine

Gozal (Hebrew) Resembling a baby bird
Gozall, Gozel, Gozell, Gozale, Gozele

Graceland (American) From the land of grace
Graiceland, Grayceland, Graeceland, Gracelan, Graycelan, Graicelan, Graecelan

Grady (Gaelic) One who is famous; noble
Gradey, Gradee, Gradea, Gradi, Gradie, Graidy, Graidey, Graidee, Graidea, Graidi, Graidie, Graydy, Graydey, Graydee, Graydea, Graydi, Graydie, Graedy, Graedey, Graedee, Graedea, Graedi, Graedie, Graden, Gradan, Gradon, Gradun, Gradin, Gradyn

Graham (English) From the gravelled area; from the gray home
Grahame, Graeham, Graeme, Graehame, Graeghamm, Graem, Grahem, Gram

Grail (English) One who is greatly desired
Graile, Grayl, Grayle, Grael, Graele, Grale

Grand (English) A superior man
Grande, Grandy, Grandey, Grandi, Grandie, Grandee, Grandea, Grander

Granderson (English) The son of Grand
Grandersun, Grandersen, Grandersin, Grandersyn, Grandersan, Granders

Granger (English) A farmer
Grainger, Graynger, Graenger, Grange, Graynge, Graenge, Grainge, Grangere

Granite (American) One who is steadfast; unyeilding
Granit, Granyte, Granyt, Granete, Granet

Grant (English) A tall man; a great man
Grante, Graent

Grantham (English) From the large estate

Grantland (English) From the land of large fields
Grantlande, Granteland, Grantelande

Grantley (English) From the large meadow
Grantly, Grantleah, Grantlee, Grantlea, Grantleigh, Grantli, Grantlie

Granville (French) From the large village
Granvylle, Granvil, Granvyl, Granvill, Granvyll, Granvile, Granvyle, Grenvill, Grenville, Grenvyll, Grenvylle, Grenvil, Grenvile, Grenvyl, Grenvyle

Graves (English) From the burial ground
Graives, Grayves, Graeves, Grave, Graive, Grayve, Graeve

Gray (English) A gray-haired man
Graye, Grai, Grae, Greye, Grey, Graylon, Graylen, Graylin, Graylyn, Graylun, Graylan

Grayson (English) The son of a gray-haired man
Graysen, Graysun, Graysin, Graysyn, Graysan, Graison, Graisun, Graisen, Graisin, Graisyn, Graisan, Graeson, Graesun, Graesan, Graesen, Graesin, Graesyn, Greyson, Greysun, Greysin, Greysyn, Greysen, Greysan

Grayton (English) From the gray town
Graytun, Graiton, Graytun, Graeton, Graetun, Graydon, Graydun, Graidon, Graidun, Graedon, Graedun, Greytun, Greyton, Greydon, Greydun

Graziano (Italian) One who is dearly loved
Gracian, Graciano, Grazian

Greeley (English) From the gray meadow
Greely, Greeli, Greelie, Greeleigh, Greelee, Greelea, Greeleah

Greenley (English) From the green meadow
Greenly, Greenleigh, Greenlea, Greenleah, Greenli, Greenlie, Greenlee

Greenwood (English) From the green forest
Greenwode

Gregory (Greek) One who is vigilant; watchful
Graig, Greer, Greg, Greger, Gregg, Greggory, Gregoire, Gregoor, Gregor, Gregori, Gregorio, Gregorius, Gregos, Grygor, Grzegorz, Gregorie, Gregorey, Gregorios, Gergo, Greguska, Griogair, Grioghar, Griorgair

Gregson (English) The son of Greg
Gregsun, Gregsen, Gregsan, Gregsin, Gregsyn

Gremian (Anglo-Saxon) One who enrages others
Gremien, Gremean, Gremyan

Gresham (English) From the grazing land
Greshem, Greshim, Greshym, Greshom, Greshum, Grisham, Grishem, Grishim, Grishym, Grishom, Grishum

Greyley (English) From the gray meadow
Greyly, Greyli, Greylie, Greylea, Greyleah, Greyleigh, Greylee, Grayley, Grayly, Graylee, Grayleigh, Graylea, Grayleah, Grayli, Graylie, Graeley, Graely, Graelee, Graelea, Graeleah, Graeleigh, Graeli, Graelie

Gridley (English) From the flat meadow
Gridly, Gridlee, Gridlea, Gridleah, Gridleigh, Gridli, Gridlie

Griffin (Latin) Having a hooked nose
Griff, Griffen, Griffon, Gryffen, Gryffin, Gryphon, Gryphen, Gryphin, Gryphyn, Griffyn

Griffith (Welsh) A mighty chief
Griffyth, Gryffith, Gryffyth, Griphith, Gryphith, Gryphyth

Grigori (Russian) Form of Gregory, meaning "one who is vigilant; watchful"
Grigor, Grigorios, Grigory, Grigorie, Grigorey, Grigoree, Grigorea, Grig, Grigg, Grigorii, Grisha

Grimaldo (German) A mighty protector
Grymaldo, Grimaldi, Grymaldi, Grimaldie, Grymaldie, Grimaldy, Grymaldy, Grimaldey, Grymaldey, Grimaldee, Grymaldee, Grimaldea, Grymaldea

Grimbold (Anglo-Saxon) One who is fierce and bold
Grymbold, Grimbald, Grymbald

Grimm (Anglo-Saxon) One who is fierce; dark
Grimme, Grymm, Grymme

Grimshaw (English) From the dark woods
Grymshaw, Grimshawe, Grymshawe

Grimsley (English) From the dark meadow
Grimsly, Grimslee, Grimslea, Grimsleah, Grimsleigh, Grimsli, Grimslie

Grindan (Anglo-Saxon) A sharp man
Grinden, Grindon, Grindun, Grindin, Grindyn, Gryndan, Grynden, Gryndon, Gryndun, Gryndin, Gryndyn

Gris (German) A gray-haired man
Griz, Grys, Gryz

Griswold (German) From the gray forest
Griswald, Gryswold, Gryswald, Greswold, Greswald

Grosvenor (French) A great hunter
Grosveneur

Grover (English) From the grove of trees
Grovar, Grovor, Grovur, Grovir, Grovyr, Grafere

Gruffydd (Welsh) A fierce lord
Gruffyd, Gruffud, Gruffudd, Gruffen, Gruffin, Gruffyn, Gruffan

Guadalupe (Spanish) From the river of the wolf
Guadaloupe, Guadaloope

Guang (Chinese) Of the light

Guard (American) One who protects others
Guarde, Guarder, Guardor, Guardar, Guardur

Guban (African) One who has been burnt
Guben, Gubin, Gubyn, Gubon, Gubun

Guedado (African) One who is unwanted

Guerdon (English) A warring man
Guerdun, Guerdan, Guerden, Guerdin, Guerdyn

Guerrant (French) One who is at war

Guido (Italian) One who acts as a guide
Guidoh, Gwedo, Gwido, Gwydo, Gweedo

Guildford (English) From the flowered ford
Guildforde, Guildferd, Guildferde, Guildfurd, Guildfurde, Gilford, Gilferd, Gilfurd, Gilforde, Gilfurde, Gilferde, Guilford, Guilforde, Guilferd, Guilferde, Guilfurd, Guilfurde

Guillaume (French) Form of William, meaning "the determined protector"
Gillermo, Guglielmo, Guilherme, Guillermo, Gwillyn, Gwilym, Guglilmo

Gulshan (Hindi) From the gardens

Gulzar (Arabic) One who is flourishing
Gulzarr, Gulzaar

Gundy (American) A friendly man
Gundey, Gundee, Gundea, Gundi, Gundie

Gunn (Scottish) A white-skinned man; a white-haired man
Gunne, Gun

Gunnar (Scandinavian) A bold warrior
Gunner, Gunnor, Gunnur, Gunnir, Gunnyr

Gunnbjorn (Norse) A warrior bear
Gunbjorn

Gunnolf (Norse) A warrior wolf
Gunolf, Gunnulf, Gunulf

Gunther (German) A warrior
*Guntur, Guenter, Guenther, Gunthir,
Gunthyr, Gunth, Gunthe, Gunterson,
Guntar, Gunter, Guntero, Gunthar, Gunthor,
Gunthur, Guntersen*

Gunyon (American) A tough man
Gunyan, Gunyen, Gunyin, Gunyun

Gur (Hebrew) Resembling a lion cub
*Guryon, Gurion, Guriel, Guriell, Guryel,
Guryell, Guri, Gurie, Guree, Gurea, Gury,
Gurey*

Gure (African) A left-handed man

Gurpreet (Indian) A devoted follower
*Gurpreat, Gurpriet, Gurpreit, Gurprit,
Gurpryt*

Guru (Indian) A teacher; a religious head

Gurutz (Basque) Of the holy cross
Guruts

Gus (German) A respected man; one who
is exalted
Guss

Gustave (Scandinavian) Of the staff of the
gods
*Gustaaf, Gustaf, Gustaff, Gustaof, Gustav,
Gustavo, Gustavus, Gustaw, Gustovo, Gustus,
Gusztav*

Gusty (American) Of the wind; a revered
man
Gustey, Gustee, Gustea, Gusti, Gustie, Gusto

Guthrie (Gaelic) From the windy spot
*Guthri, Guthry, Guthrey, Guthree, Guthrea,
Guth, Guthe*

Guwayne (American) Form of Wayne,
meaning "one who builds wagons"
*Guwayn, Guwain, Guwaine, Guwaen,
Guwaene, Guwane*

Guy (German / Welsh / French) A warrior;
from the wood / a lively man / one who
acts as a guide
Gui, Guido, Guydo, Gye

Guyapi (Native American) One who is
frank; candid
*Guyapie, Guyapy, Guyapey, Guyapee,
Guyapea*

Guyon (English) A lively man
Guyen, Guyun, Guyan, Guyin

Guzet (American) One who puts on a show
of courage
*Guzzet, Guzett, Guzzett, Guzzi, Guzzie,
Guzzy, Guzzey, Guzzee, Guzzea*

Gwalchmai (Welsh) A battle hawk

Gwandoya (African) Suffering a miserable
fate

Gwern (Welsh) An old man
Gwerne, Gwirn, Gwirne, Gwyrn, Gwyrne

Gwill (American) Having dark eyes
*Gwil, Gwyll, Gwyl, Gewill, Guwill, Gewyll,
Guwyll*

Gwri (Celtic) The golden-haired boy
Gwrie, Gwree, Gwrea, Gwry, Gwrey

Gwydion (Welsh) In mythology, a magician
Gwydeon, Gwydionne, Gwydeonne

Gwynn (Welsh) A handsome man; one who
is fair
*Gwynne, Gwyn, Gwen, Gwenn, Gwenne,
Gwin, Gwinn, Gwinne, Gwynedd, Gwyned,
Gwenedd, Gwened, Gwinedd, Gwined,
Gwynfor, Gwenfor, Gwinfor*

Gyala (Hungarian) A youth

Gyan (Hindi) Having knowledge or wisdom
Gyandev

Gyasi (African) A superior man
Gyasie, Gyasy, Gyasey, Gyasee, Gyasea

Gylfi (Scandinavian) A king
*Gylfie, Gylfee, Gylfea, Gylfi, Gylfie, Gylphi,
Gylphie, Gylphey, Gylphy, Gylphee, Gylphea*

Gypsy (English) A wanderer; a nomad
*Gipsee, Gipsey, Gipsy, Gypsi, Gypsie, Gypsey,
Gypsee, Gipsi, Gipsie, Gipsea, Gypsea*

Gyth (American) An able-bodied man
Gythe, Gith, Githe

Gyula (Hungarian) One who is honored
Gyulah, Gyulla, Gyullah

Gyuszi (Hungarian) One who is youthful
Gyuszie, Gyuszy, Gyuszey, Gyuszee, Gyuszea

h

Haas (Scandinavian) A good man

Habakkuk (Hebrew) One who embraces others
Habakuk, Habacuk, Habaccuk, Habacuc, Habackuc, Habacuck, Habaccuc

Haben (African) A proud man
Haban, Habin, Habyn, Habon, Habun

Habib (Arabic) One who is dearly loved
Habeeb, Habeab, Habieb, Habeib, Habyb, Habeyb

Habimama (African) One who believes in God
Habymama

Hache-Hi (Native American) Resembling a wolf

Hachiro (Japanese) The eighth-born son
Hachyro

Hackett (German) A little woodsman
Hacket, Hackitt, Hackit, Hakett, Haket

Hackman (French) A woodsman; a hewer of wood
Hackmann, Hakman, Hakmann, Hacman, Hacmann

Hadar (Hebrew) Glory and splendor; one who is respected
Hadur, Hader, Hador, Hadaram

Haddad (Arabic) A smith
Hadad

Hadden (English) From the heather-covered hill
Haddan, Haddon, Haddin, Haddyn, Haddun

Hadeon (Ukrainian) A destroyer
Hadion, Hadeyon, Hadiyon

Hades (Greek) In mythology, the god of the underworld
Hadies, Hadees, Hadiez, Hadeez

Hadi (Arabic) One who guides others along the right path
Hadie, Hady, Hadey, Hadee, Hadea

Hadley (English) From the heather meadow
Hadly, Hadleigh, Hadlee, Hadlea, Hadleah, Hadli, Hadlie, Haddy, Haddey, Haddee, Haddea, Haddi, Haddie

Hadrian (English) Form of Adrian, meaning "a man from Hadria"
Hade, Hadiran, Hadrain, Hadrean, Hadreean, Hudreyan, Hadreeyan, Hadriaan, Hadriano, Hadrien, Hadrin, Hadrino, Hadrion, Hadron, Hadryan, Hadya, Harjen, Haydrean, Haydreean, Haydrian, Haydrien, Hadrianus, Hadrianos

Hadriel (Hebrew) The splendor of God
Hadryel, Hadriell, Hadryell

Hadwin (English) A friend in war
Hadwinn, Hadwinne, Hadwen, Hadwenn, Hadwenne, Hadwyn, Hadwynn, Hadwynne, Hadwine, Hedwin, Hedwine, Hedwinn, Hedwinne, Hedwen, Hedwenn, Hedwenne, Hedwyn, Hedwynn, Hedwynne, Haethowine, Haethowin, Haethowen, Haethowyn

Hafiz (Arabic) A protector
Haafiz, Hafeez, Hafeaz, Hafiez, Hafeiz, Hafyz, Haphiz, Haaphiz, Hapheez, Hapheaz, Haphiez, Hapheiz, Haphyz

Hagar (Hebrew) A wanderer

Hagaward (English) The guardian of the hedged enclosure
Hagawerd

Hagen (Gaelic) One who is youthful
Haggen, Hagan, Haggan, Hagin, Haggin, Hagyn, Haggyn, Hagon, Haggon, Hagun, Haggun

Hagley (English) From the enclosed meadow
Hagly, Haglee, Haglea, Hagleah, Hagleigh, Hagli, Haglie, Hagaleah, Hagalea, Hagalee, Hagaleigh, Hagali, Hagalie, Hagaly, Hagaley

Hagop (Armenian) Form of James, meaning "he who supplants"
Hagup, Hagap, Hagep, Hagip, Hagyp

Hagos (African) Filled with happiness

Hahn (German) Resembling a rooster

Hahnee (Native American) A beggar
Hahnea, Hahni, Hahnie, Hahny, Hahney

Hai (Vietnamese) Of the river

Haiba (African) One who is charming
Haibah, Hayba, Haybah, Haeba, Haebah, Haba, Habah

Haidar (Arabic) Resembling a lion
Haider, Haydar, Hayder, Haedar, Haeder, Haidor, Haydor, Haedor, Haidur, Haydur, Haedur, Haidir, Haydir, Haedir, Haidyr, Haydyr, Haedyr

Haig (English) From the hedged enclosure
Haeg, Hayg

Haike (Asian) From the water

Haim (Hebrew) A giver of live
Hayim, Hayyim

Haines (English) From the vined cottage;
from the hedged enclosure
Haynes, Haenes, Hanes, Haine, Hayne, Haene, Hane

Hajari (African) One who takes flight
Hajarie, Hajary, Hajarey, Hajaree, Hajarea

Haji (African) Born during the hajj
Hajie, Hajy, Hajey, Hajee, Hajea

Hajime (Japanese) Of the beginning

Hakan (Norse / Native American) One who
is noble / a fiery man

Hakim(Arabic) One who is wise; intelligent
Hakeem, Hakeam, Hakeim, Hakiem, Hakym

Hako (Japanese) An honorable man

Hakon (Scandinavian) Of the chosen race;
one who is exalted
Haaken, Haakin, Haakon, Hacon, Hackon, Haken, Hakin, Hakyn, Haakyn

Hal (English) Form of Henry, meaning "the
ruler of the house"

Haland (English) From the island
Halande, Halland, Hallande

Halbert (English) A shining hero
Halberte, Halburt, Halburte, Halbirt, Halbirte, Halbyrt, Halbyrte, Halbart, Halbarte

Haldas (Greek) A dependable man

Halden (Scandinavian) A man who is half-
Dane
Haldan, Haldane, Halfdan, Halfdane, Halvdan, Halfden, Halvden, Haldayne, Haldaene, Haldayn, Haldaen

Haldor (Scandinavian) Of the thunderous
rock
Haldur, Halder, Haldar, Haldir, Haldyr

Hale (English) From the hall; a hero
Hail, Haile, Hayl, Hayle, Hael, Haele

Halen (Swedish) From the hall of light
Hallen, Hailen, Haylen, Haelen, Halan, Hailan, Haylan, Haelan, Halin, Haylin, Haelin, Hailin, Halyn, Haylyn, Hailyn, Haelyn, Halon, Haylon, Hailon, Haelon, Halun, Haylun, Hailun, Haelun

Haley (English) From the field of hay
Haly, Halee, Haleigh, Haleah, Halea, Hali, Halie, Hayley, Hayly, Haylee, Hayleigh, Hayleah, Haylea, Hayli, Haylie, Haeley, Haely, Haeleigh, Haeleah, Haelea, Haeli, Haelie, Hailey, Haily, Haileigh, Haileah, Hailea, Haili, Hailie

Halford (English) From the hall by the ford
Hallford, Halfurd, Hallfurd, Halferd, Hallferd

Halian (Native American) One who is
youthful
Haliann, Halyan, Halyann, Halien, Halyen, Halienn, Halyenn

Halig (Anglo-Saxon) A holy man
Halyg

Haligwell (English) Form of Halliwell,
meaning "from the holy spring"
Haygwell, Haligwel, Halygwel, Haligwiella

Halil (Turkish) A beloved friend
Haleel, Haleal, Haleil, Haliel, Halyl

Halim (Arabic) One who is gentle
Haleem, Haleam, Haleim, Haliem, Halym

Hall (English) From the manor
Heall

Halla (African) An unexpected gift
Hallah, Hala, Halah

Hallam (English) From the hills; from the
rocks
Hallem, Hallim, Hallum, Hallom, Hallym

Hallberg (Norse) From the rocky mountain
Halberg, Hallburg, Halburg

Halle (Norse) As solid as a rock

Halley (English) From the hall near the meadow
Hally, Halli, Hallie, Halleigh, Hallee, Halleah, Hallea

Halliwell (English) From the holy spring
Hallewell, Hallowell, Helliwell, Halliwel, Hallewel, Hallowel, Helliwel, Hallwell, Haliwell, Haliwel, Halewell, Halewel, Halowell, Halowel, Heliwel, Heliwell, Hallwell, Halwell, Hallwel, Hulwel, Holwell, Hollwell, Holwel, Hollwel

Hallward (English) The guardian of the hall
Halward, Hallwerd, Halwerd, Hallwarden, Halwarden, Hawarden, Haward, Hawerd

Halmer (English) A robust man
Halmar, Halmir, Halmyr, Halmor, Halmur

Halsey (English) From Hal's island
Halsy, Halsi, Halsie, Halsee, Halsea, Hallsey, Hallsy, Hallsi, Hallsie, Hallsee, Hallsea, Halcey, Halcy, Halcee, Halcea, Halci, Halcie, Hallcey, Hallcy, Hallcee, Hallcea, Hallci, Hallcie, Halsig, Halsyg

Halstead (English) From the manor grounds
Hallstead, Hallsted, Halsted

Halton (English) From the manor on the hill
Hallton, Haltun, Halltun, Halten, Hallten, Halston, Halstun, Halsten, Hallston, Hallstun, Hallsten

Halvard (Norse) The guardian of the rock
Hallvard, Hallverd, Hallvor, Halvar, Halver, Halverd, Halvor

Halwende (Anglo-Saxon) One who is lonely
Hallwende, Halwendi, Hallwendi, Halwendie, Hallwendie, Halwendy, Hallwendy, Halwendey, Hallwendey, Halwendee, Hallwendee

Ham (Hebrew) One who produces heat
Hamaker, Hamu, Hamue, Hamou, Hamm, Hammu, Hammue, Hammou

Hamal (Arabic) Resembling a lamb
Hamahl, Hamall, Hamaal, Hamaahl

Hamar (Norse) One who wields a hammer
Hamer, Hamor, Hamur, Hamir, Hamyr

Hamden (Arabic) One who is praised
Hamdan, Hamdin, Hamdyn, Hamdon, Hamdun

Hamid (Arabic / Indian) A praiseworthy man / a beloved friend
Hameed, Hamead, Hameid, Hamied, Hamyd, Haamid

Hamidi (Swahili) One who is commendable
Hamidie, Hamidy, Hamidey, Hamidee, Hamidea, Hamydi, Hamydie, Hamydee, Hamydea, Hamydy, Hamydey, Hamedi, Hamedie, Hamedy, Hamedey, Hamedee, Hamedea, Hammad

Hamill (English) One who is scarred
Hamil, Hamel, Hamell, Hamyll, Hamyl, Hammill, Hammil

Hamilton (English) From the flat-topped hill
Hamylton, Hamiltun, Hamyltun, Hamilten, Hamylten, Hamelton, Hameltun, Hamelten, Hamilston, Hamilstun, Hamelston, Hamelstun

Hamish (Scottish) Form of James, meaning "he who supplants"
Haymish, Haemish, Haimish, Hamesh, Haymesh, Haemesh, Haimesh

Hamlet (German) From the little home
Hamlett, Hammet, Hammett, Hamnet, Hamnett, Hamlit, Hamlitt, Hamoelet

Hamlin (German) The little home-lover
Hamlyn, Humblin, Hamelin, Hamlen, Hamlan, Hamlon, Hamlun, Hamelen, Hamelan, Hamelyn, Hamelon, Hamelun

Hammer (German) One who makes hammers; a carpenter
Hammar, Hammor, Hammur, Hammir, Hammyr

Hammond (German) The protector of the home
Hammund, Hammend, Hammand, Hammind, Hammynd, Hamond, Hamund, Hamend, Hamand, Hamind, Hamynd

Hamon (Scandinavian) A great leader
Hamun, Hamen, Haman, Hamin, Hamyn

Hampden (English) From the home in the valley
Hampdon, Hampdan, Hampdun, Hampdyn, Hampdin

Hampton (English) From the home town
Hamptun, Hampten, Hamptan, Hamptin, Hamptyn, Hamp, Hampe

Hamza (Arabic) Having great strength
Hamzah, Hammza, Hammzah

Han (German) A gift from God
Hann, Hano, Hanno

Hanan (Hebrew) Of God's grace
Hananel, Hanenel, Hananell, Hanenell, Hanania, Hananiah

Hanani (Arabic) One who is merciful
Hananie, Hanany, Hananey, Hananee, Hananea

Hancock (English) One who owns a farm
Hancok, Hancoc

Hand (English) A hardworking man
Hande, Handy, Handey, Handi, Handie, Handea, Handee

Ha-Neul (Korean) Of the sky

Hanford (English) From the high ford
Hanferd, Hanfurd, Hanforde, Hanferde, Hanfurde

Hani (Arabic) Filled with joy
Hanie, Hany, Haney, Hanee, Hanea

Hania (Native American) A spirit warrior
Haniah, Hanya, Hanyah, Haniya, Haniyah

Hanif (Arabic) A true believer of Islam
Haneef, Haneaf, Haneif, Hanief, Hanyf

Hanisi (Swahili) Born on a Thursday
Hanisie, Hanisy, Hanisey, Hanisee, Hanisea, Hanysi, Hanysie, Hanysy, Hanysey, Hanysee, Hanysea

Hank (English) Form of Henry, meaning "the ruler of the house"
Hanke, Hanks, Hanki, Hankie, Hankee, Hankea, Hanky, Hankey

Hanley (English) From the high meadow
Hanly, Hanleigh, Hanleah, Hanlea, Hanlie, Hanli, Handlea, Handleigh, Handley, Handleah, Handly, Handlie, Handli

Hanna (Arabic) Form of John, meaning "God is gracious"
Hannah, Hana, Hanah

Hannan (Arabic) Having warm feelings
Hannen, Hannon, Hannun, Hannin, Hannyn

Hannibal (Hebrew) Having the grace of Baal
Hanibal, Hanniball, Haniball, Hannybal, Hanybal, Hannyball, Hanyball

Hanoch (Hebrew) One who is dedicated
Hanock, Hanok, Hanoc

Hanraoi (Irish) Form of Henry, meaning "the ruler of the house"

Hans (Scandinavian) Form of John, meaning "God is gracious"
Hanz, Hannes, Hanns, Hansel, Hanss, Hanzel, Hons, Hansa, Hanza

Hanson (Scandinavian) The son of Hans
Hansen, Hanssen, Hansson, Hansun, Hanssun

Hansraj (Hindi) The swan king

Hanuman (Indian) The monkey god
Hanumant, Hanumanth, Hanumane, Hanumante, Hanumanthe

Hao (Vietnamese) A good man

Happy (American) Filled with joy
Happey, Happi, Happie, Happee, Happea

Haqq (Arabic) A truthful man
Haq

Harac (English) From the ancient oak tree
Harak, Harack

Harailt (Scottish) Form of Harold, meaning "the ruler of an army"
Haraylt, Haraelt, Haralt, Haraild, Harayld, Haraeld

Harb (Arabic) A war
Harbe

Harbin (French) A bright warrior
Harben, Harbyn, Harbon, Harbun, Harban, Harbi, Harbie, Harbee, Harbea, Harby, Harbey

Harcourt (French) From the fortified farm
Harcourte, Harcort, Harcorte

Harden (English) From the hare's valley
Hardan, Hardin, Hardyn, Hardon, Hardun

Hardik (Indian) One who has heart
Hardyk, Hardick, Hardyck, Hardic, Hardyc

Harding (English) The son of the courageous one
Hardyng, Hardinge, Hardynge

Hardwick (English) From the courageous man's settlement
Harwick, Hardwyck, Harwyck, Hardwik, Harwik, Hardwyk, Harwyk

Hardwin (English) A courageous friend
Hardwinn, Hardwinne, Hardwen, Hardwenn, Hardwenne, Hardwine, Hardwyn, Hardwynn, Hardwynne

Hardy (German) One who is bold and courageous
Hardey, Hardi, Hardie, Hardee, Hardea

Hare (English) Resembling a rabbit

Harean (African) One who is aware; alert
Hareane, Harian, Hariane, Haryan, Haryane

Harel (Hebrew) From the mountain of God
Haral, Haril, Haryl, Harol, Harul, Harell, Harrell, Harall, Harrall, Haroll, Harroll, Harull, Harrull, Harill, Harrill, Haryll, Harryll

Harelache (English) From the hare's lake
Harlache, Harelach, Harlach, Harelock, Harlock, Harelocke, Harlocke, Harlak, Harelak, Harlake, Harelake

Harence (English) One who is swift
Harince, Harense, Harinse, Harynce, Harynse

Harford (English) From the hare's ford
Harforde, Harrford, Harrforde, Harfurd, Harfurde, Harrfurd, Harrfurde, Harferd, Harferde, Harrferd, Harrferde, Haraford, Haraferd, Harafurd

Hargrove (English) From the hare's grove
Hargrave, Hargreaves

Hari (Indian) Resembling a lion
Harie, Hary, Harey, Haree, Harea

Harim (Arabic) A superior man
Hareem, Haream, Hariem, Hareim, Harym

Hariman (German) One who is protective
Harimann, Haryman, Harymann

Harith (African) A cultivator; a provider
Harithe, Haryth, Harythe, Hareth, Harethe

Harkin (Irish) Having dark red hair
Harkyn, Harken, Harkan, Harkon, Harkun

Harlan (English) From the army
Harlen, Harlon, Harlun, Harlin, Harlyn, Harlenn, Harlinn, Harlynn, Harlann, Harlonn, Harlunn, Harland

Harlemm (American) A soulful man
Harlam, Harlom, Harlim, Harlym, Harlem

Harley (English) From the meadow of the hares
Harlea, Harlee, Harleen, Harleigh, Harlene, Harlie, Harli, Harly, Harleah, Harlean, Haraleigh, Haralee, Haralea, Haraleah, Harali, Haralie, Haraly, Haraley

Harlow (English) From the army on the hill
Harlowe, Harlo, Harloe

Harman (French) A soldier
Harmann, Harmen, Harmon, Harmonn, Harmenn

Harmony (English) Unity; musically in tune
Harmonie, Harmoni, Harmonee, Harmonia, Harmoney, Harmonea, Harmonio

Harod (Hebrew) A heroic man; in the Bible, a king
Harrod, Herod, Herrod

Harold (Scandinavian) The ruler of an army
Haruld, Haralds, Harolda, Haroldo, Heraldo, Herald, Herold, Herrold

Harper (English) One who plays or makes harps
Harpur, Harpar, Harpir, Harpyr, Harpor, Hearpere

Harpo (American) A cheerful man
Harpoe, Harpow, Harpowe, Harpoh

Harrington (English) From of Harry's town; from the herring town
Harringtun, Harryngton, Harryngtun, Harington, Haringtun, Haryngton, Haryntun

Harrison (English) The son of Harry
Harrisson, Harris, Harriss, Harrisun, Harryson, Harrysun, Harrys, Harryss

Harry (English) Form of Harold, meaning "the ruler of an army"; form of Henry, meaning "the ruler of the house"
Harri, Harrie, Harrey, Harree, Harrea

Harshad (Indian) A bringer of joy
Harsh, Harshe, Harsho, Harshil, Harshyl, Harshit, Harshyt

Hart (English) Resembling a stag
Harte, Heort, Heorot

Hartford (English) From the stag's ford
Harteford, Hartferd, Harteferd, Hartfurd, Hartefurd, Hartforde, Harteforde, Hartferde, Harteferde, Hartfurde, Hartefurde

Harti (German) One who is daring
Hartie, Harty, Hartey, Hartee, Hartea

Hartley (English) From the stag's meadow
Hartly, Hartli, Hartlie, Hartleigh, Hartlea, Hartleah, Hartlee

Hartman (German) A hard and strong man
Hartmann, Hartmen, Hartmon, Hartmun, Hartmin, Hartmyn

Hartun (English) From the gray estate
Harton, Harten, Hartan, Hartin, Hartyn

Hartwell (English) From the stag's spring
Hartewell, Hartwel, Hartewel, Hartwill, Hartewill, Hartwil, Hartewil, Harwell, Harwel, Harwill, Harwil, Heortwiella, Heortweill

Hartwig (German) One who is brave during battle

Hartwood (English) From the stag's forest
Hartwode, Hartewood, Hartewode, Heortwode, Heortwood

Haru (Japanese) Born during the spring

Haruki (Japanese) One who shines brightly
Harukie, Haruky, Harukey, Harukee, Harukea

Haruko (Japanese) The firstborn child

Harun (Arabic) A superior man; one who is exalted
Haroun, Harune, Haroune, Haroon, Haroone

Haruni (African) A mountaineer
Harunie, Haruny, Haruney, Harunee, Harunea

Harvard (English) The guardian of the home
Harverd, Hurvord, Harvurd, Harvird, Harvyrd, Havard, Haverd, Havord, Havurd, Havird, Havyrd

Harvey (English / French) One who is ready for battle / a strong man
Harvy, Harvi, Harvie, Harvee, Harvea, Harv, Harve, Hervey, Hervy, Hervi, Hervie, Hervee, Hervea, Harvae, Herve

Harwin (English) A friend of the hare
Harwinn, Harwinne, Harwen, Harwenn, Harwenne, Harwyn, Harwynn, Harwynne

Harwood (English) From the hare's forest
Harewood, Harwode, Harewode

Hasad (Turkish) The harvester

Hasdai (Aramaic) A good man
Hasday, Hasdaye, Hasdae

Hashim (Arabic) The destroyer of evil
Hasheem, Hasheam, Hashiem, Hasheim, Hashym

Hasim (Arabic) One who is decisive
Haseem, Haseam, Hasiem, Haseim, Hasym

Hasin (Arabic) A handsome man
Haseen, Hasean, Hasein, Hasien, Hasyn

Haskel (Hebrew) An intelligent man
Haskle, Haskell, Haskil, Haskill, Haske, Hask

Haslett (English) From the hazel-tree headland
Haslet, Haslit, Haslitt, Hazel, Hazlett, Hazlet, Hazlitt, Hazlit, Haslyt, Haslytt, Hazlyt, Hazlytt

Hassan (Arabic) A handsome man
Hassaun, Hassawn, Hasan, Hasani, Hasanie, Hasany, Hasaney, Hasanee, Hasanea, Hassain

Hasso (German) Of the sun
Hassoe, Hassow, Hassowe

Hassun (Native American) As solid as a stone

Hastiin (Native American) A man

Hastin (Hindi) Resembling an elephant
Hasteen, Hastean, Hastien, Hastein, Hastyn

Hastings (English) Son of the stern and grave man
Hasting, Hastyngs, Hastyng, Hasti, Hastie, Hasty, Hastey, Hastee, Hastea

Hatim (Arabic) A judge; one who is determined
Hateem, Hateam, Hateim, Hatiem, Hatym

Hattan (American) From Manhattan; a sophisticated man
Hatten, Hattin, Hattyn, Hatton, Hattun

Hau (Vietnamese) One who is bold

Havelock (Scandinavian) One who takes part in a sea battle
Havlock, Havelocke, Havlocke

Haven (English) One who provides sanctuary; shelter
Havan, Havin, Havyn, Havon, Havun, Haeven, Haevon, Haevin, Haevyn, Haevan, Haevun, Haiven, Haivan, Haivin, Haivyn, Haivon, Haivun, Haefen, Hayven, Hayvan, Hayvon, Hayvun, Hayvin, Hayvyn

Hawaii (Hawaiian) From the homeland; from the state of Hawaii

Hawes (English) From the hedged place
Haws, Hayes, Hays, Hazin, Hazen, Hazyn, Hazon, Hazan, Hazun

Hawiovi (Native American) One who descends on a ladder
Hawiovie, Hawiovy, Hawiovey, Hawiovee, Hawiovea

Hawk (English) Resembling the bird of prey
Hawke, Hauk, Hauke

Hawkins (English) Resembling a small hawk
Haukins, Hawkyns, Haukyn

Hawley (English) From the hedged meadow
Hawly, Hawleigh, Hawlea, Hawleah, Hawli, Hawlie, Hawlee

Hawthorne (English) From the hawthorn tree
Hawthorn

⊕ **Hayden** (English) From the hedged valley
⊕ *Haydan, Haydon, Haydun, Haydin, Haydyn, Haden, Hadan, Hadon, Hadun, Hadin, Hadyn, Haiden, Haidan, Haidin, Haidyn, Haidon, Haidun, Haeden, Haedan, Haedin, Haedyn, Haedon, Haedun, Haydn, Haidn, Haedn, Hadn*

Haye (Scottish) From the stockade
Hay, Hae, Hai

Haytham (Arabic) Resembling a young hawk
Haythem, Haitham, Haithem, Haetham, Haethem, Hatham, Hathem

Hayward (English) The guardian of the hedged area
Haywerd, Haiward, Haiwerd, Haeward, Haewerd, Hayword, Haiword, Haeword

Haywood (English) From the hedged forest
Haywode, Haiwood, Haiwode, Haewood, Haewode

Hazaiah (Hebrew) God will decide
Hazaia, Haziah, Hazia

Hazard (French) One who takes chances; having luck
Hazzard, Hazerd, Hazzerd

Hazleton (English) From the hazel-tree town
Hazelton, Hazletun, Hazelton, Hazleten, Hazelten

Hazlewood (English) From the hazel-tree forest
Hazelwood, Hazlewode, Hazelwode

Heath (English) From the untended land of flowering shrubs
Heathe, Heeth, Heethe

Heathcliff (English) From the cliff near the heath
Heathecliff, Heathclyff, Heatheclyff, Heathclif, Heathclyf, Heatheclif, Heatheclyf, Hetheclif, Hethecliff, Hetheclyf, Hetheclyff

Heathden (English) From the heath
Heathdan, Heathdon, Heathdin, Heathdyn, Heathdun

Heathley (English) From the heath meadow
Heathly, Heathleigh, Heathlea, Heathleah, Heathli, Heathlie, Heathlee

Heaton (English) From the town on high ground
Heatun, Heeton, Heetun, Heaten, Heeten

Heber (Hebrew) A partner or companion
Heeber, Hebar, Heebar, Hebor, Heebor, Hebur, Heebur, Hebir, Heebir, Hebyr, Heebyr

Hector (Greek) One who is steadfast; in mythology, the prince of Troy
Hecter, Hectur, Hectar, Hectir, Hectyr, Hektor, Hekter, Hektar, Hektir, Hektyr, Hektur, Hecktor, Hecktar, Heckter, Hecktur, Hecktir, Hecktyr, Heitor

Heddwyn (Welsh) One who is peaceful and fair
Heddwynn, Hedwyn, Hedwynn, Heddwen, Heddwenn, Hedwen, Hedwenn, Heddwin, Heddwinn, Hedwin, Hedwinn

Hedeon (Russian) One who fells trees
Hedion, Hedyon, Hedeyon, Hediyon

Hedley (English) From the meadow of heather
Hedly, Hedlie, Hedli, Hedleigh, Hedlea, Hedleah, Hedlee, Headleigh, Headley, Headly, Headlea, Headleah, Headli, Headlie, Headlee

Heer (Indian) Resembling a diamond

Hegarty (Irish) One who is unjust
Hegartey, Hegartee, Hegartea, Hegarti, Hegartie

Hei (Korean) Of grace

Heikki (Finnish) Form of Henry, meaning "the ruler of the house"
Heiki, Heicki, Heicci, Heici

Heimdall (Norse) The white god; in mythology, one of the founders of the human race
Heimdal, Heiman, Heimann

Heinrich (German) Form of Henry, meaning "the ruler of the house"
Heinrick, Heinric, Heinrik, Heine, Heini, Heinie, Heiny, Heiney, Heinee, Heinea, Heimrich, Heimrick, Heimric, Heimrik

Heinz (German) Form of Hans, meaning "God is gracious"
Heins, Hines, Hein, Hine, Heiner, Heinlich, Hynes, Hynz

Heladio (Spanish) A man who was born in Greece
Heladeo, Heladiyo, Heladeyo, Helado

Helaku (Native American) Born on a sunny day
Helakue, Helakou

Helgi (Norse) One who is productive and happy
Helgie, Helgy, Helgey, Helgee, Helgea, Helge, Helje, Helji, Heljie, Heljy, Heljey, Heljee, Heljea

Helio (Greek) Son of the sun
Heleo, Helios, Heleos

Helki (Native American) To touch
Helkie, Helky, Helkey, Helkee, Helkea, Hekli, Heklie, Hekly, Hekley, Heklee, Heklea, Hekleigh

Heller (German) Of the sun; one who is bright or brilliant
Hellar, Hellor, Hellur, Hellir, Hellyr, Helly, Helley, Helli, Hellie, Hellee, Hellea, Helleigh

Helmer (Teutonic) A warrior's wrath
Helmar, Helmor, Helmir, Helmyr, Helmur

Helmut (French) One who is protected
Helmot, Helmet, Helmat, Helmit, Helmyt, Helmuth, Helmuthe, Helmutt, Helmett, Helmatt, Helmitt, Helmytt, Helmott, Hellmut, Hellmat, Hellmet, Hellmit, Hellmyt, Hellmot, Helmond, Hellmond, Helmund, Hellmund, Helmand, Hellmand

Hem (Indian) The golden son

Hemadri (Indian) Of the Himalaya
Hemadrie, Hemadree, Hemadrea, Hemadry, Hemadrey

Heman (Hebrew) A faithful man
Hemann, Hemen, Hemenn

Hemendra (Indian) A wealthy man
Hemindra, Hemyndra

Hemendu (Indian) Born beneath the golden moon
Hemendue, Hemendoo, Hemendou

Hemi (Maori) Form of James, meaning "he who supplants"
Hemie, Hemy, Hemee, Hemea, Hemey

Henderson (Scottish) The son of Henry
Hendrie, Hendries, Hendron, Hendri, Hendry, Hendrey, Hendree, Hendrea, Henryson, Hendersun, Henrysun, Hendrun, Henson, Hensun, Hender, Hend, Hensen

Hendrick (English) Form of Henry, meaning "the ruler of the house"
Hendryck, Hendrik, Hendryk, Hendric, Hendryc

Henley (English) From the high meadow
Henly, Henleigh, Henlea, Henleah, Henlee, Henli, Henlie

Henning (Scandinavian) Form of Henry, meaning "the ruler of the house"
Hening, Hennyng, Henyng, Hemming, Heming, Hemmyng, Hemyng

❂ **Henry** (German) The ruler of the house
Henri, Henrie, Henrey, Henree, Henrea, Henrick, Henrik, Henrique, Henryk, Henryck, Henryc, Henric, Henning, Hening, Hennyng, Henyng

Heolstor (Anglo-Saxon) Of the darkness
Heolster, Heolstir, Heolstur, Heolstyr, Heolstar

Heorhiy (Ukrainian) A farmer; one who works the earth

Heraldo (Spanish) Of the divine

Herbert (German) An illustrious warrior
Herbirt, Herburt, Harbert, Harbirt, Harburt, Heribert, Heriberto, Herb, Herbi, Herbie, Herbee, Herbea, Herby, Herbey, Herbst

Hercules (Greek) In mythology, a son of Zeus who possessed superhuman strength
Herakles, Hercule, Herculi, Herculie, Herculy, Herculey, Herculee, Herculea, Herculeigh, Herkules, Herckules, Herkuel, Hercuel

Heremon (Gaelic) Form of Irving, meaning "a friend of the sea"
Hereman, Heremen, Heremun, Heremin, Heremyn

Hererinc (Anglo-Saxon) A hero
Hererink, Hererinck, Hererync, Hererynk, Hererynck

Heretoga (Anglo-Saxon) A commander or ruler

Herman (German) A soldier
Hermon, Hermen, Hermun, Hermin, Hermyn, Hermann, Hermie, Herminio, Hermi, Hermy, Hermey, Hermee, Hermea

Hermes (Greek) In mythology, the messenger of the gods
Hermus, Hermos, Hermis, Hermys, Hermilo, Hermite, Hermez

Hermod (Scandinavian) One who welcomes others

Hernando (Spanish) A bold adventurer
Hernandez, Hernan

Herndon (English) From the heron's valley
Hernden, Herndan, Herndin, Herndyn, Herndun

Herne (English) Resembling a heron
Hern, Hearn, Hearne

Hernley (English) From the heron's meadow
Hernly, Hernleigh, Hernlee, Hernlea, Hernleah, Hernli, Hernlie

Hero (Greek) The brave defender
Heroe, Herow, Herowe

Herodotus (Greek) The father of history
Herodotos, Herodotius, Herodotios

Herrick (German) A war leader or ruler
Herric, Herrik, Herryck, Herryc, Herryk

Hershel (Hebrew) Resembling a deer
Hersch, Herschel, Herschell, Hersh, Hertzel, Herzel, Herzl, Heschel, Heshel, Hirsch, Hirschel, Hirschl, Hirsh, Hirsche, Hirshe, Hershey, Hershy, Hershi, Hershie, Hershee, Hershea, Herzon, Herzun, Herzan, Herzin, Herzyn, Herzen

Hertz (German) My strife

Herwin (Teutonic) A friend of war
Herwinn, Herwinne, Herwen, Herwenn, Herwenne, Herwyn, Herwynn, Herwynne

Hesed (Hebrew) A kind man

Hesperos (Greek) Born beneath the evening star
Hesperus, Hesperios, Hespero, Hesperius

Hessel (Dutch) One who is bold
Hessle, Hess, Hes

Hesutu (Native American) A rising yellow-jacket nest
Hesutou, Hesoutou

Hevataneo (Native American) A hairy rope
Hevatanio, Hevataneyo, Hevataniyo

Hevel (Hebrew) A life source; breath
Hevell, Hevle

Hewett (French) The small intelligent one
Hewet, Hewie, Hewitt, Hewlett, Hewit, Hewlet, Hewlitt, Hewlit, Hewi, Hewy, Hewey, Hewee, Hewea

Hewney (Irish) Refers to the color green; one who is innocent
Hewny, Hewni, Hewnie, Hewnea, Hewnee

Hewson (English) The son of Hugh
Hewsun

Heywood (English) Form of Haywood, meaning "from the hedged forest"
Heywode

Hezekiah (Hebrew) God is my strength
Hezekia, Hezekyah, Hezekya, Hezeki, Hezekie, Hezekea, Hezekee, Hezeky, Hezekey

Hiamovi (Native American) The high chief
Hiamovie, Hiamovy, Hiamovey, Hiamovee, Hiamovea

Hiawatha (Native American) He who makes rivers
Hiawathah, Hyawatha, Hiwatha, Hywatha

Hickey (Irish) One who heals others
Hicky, Hickee, Hickea, Hicki, Hickie

Hickok (American) A famous frontier marshal
Hickock, Hickoc, Hikock, Hikoc, Hikok, Hyckok, Hyckock, Hyckoc, Hykoc, Hykok, Hykock

Hidalgo (Spanish) The noble one
Hydalgo

Hideaki (Japanese) A clever man; having wisdom
Hideakie, Hideaky, Hideakey, Hideakee, Hideakea

Hideo (Japanese) A superior man
Hideyo, Hydeo

Hien (Vietnamese) A gentle and kind man

Hieremias (Hebrew) God will uplift
Hieremeas, Hyeremias, Hyeremeas

Hiero (Irish) The name of a sain
Hyero

Hieronim (Polish) Form of Jerome, meaning "of the sacred name"
Hieronym, Hieronymos, Hieronimos, Heronim, Heronym, Heronymos, Heronimos

Hietamaki (Finnish) From the sand hill
Hietamakie, Hietamaky, Hietamakey, Hietamakee, Hietamakea

Hieu (Vietnamese) A pious man

Hifz (Arabic) One who is memorable
Hyfz

Higgins (Irish) An intelligent man
Hyggins, Higins, Hygins, Higgyns, Hyggyns, Higyns, Hygyns

Higinio (Spanish) A forceful man
Higineo, Higiniyo, Higineyo

Hikmat (Islamic) Filled with wisdom
Hykmat

Hilary (Greek) A cheerful woman; bringer of joy
Hillary, Hilaree, Hilarie, Hilarey, Hilari, Hillari, Hillarie, Hillaree, Hillarey, Hillory, Hilaire, Hilorio, Hilery, Hillery, Hiliary, Hiliarie, Hylary, Hylarie, Hylari, Hylarey, Hylaree, Hyllari, Hyllary, Hilaeiro, Hiolair, Hillarea, Hylarea, Hyllarea, Hilarea, Helario, Hilaire, Hilar, Hilarid, Hilarius, Hilario, Hilarion

Hildebrand (German) One who wields a battle sword
Hyldebrand, Hildbrand, Hyldbrand, Hildehrand, Hildhrand, Hyldehrand, Hyldhrand, Hildebrant, Hyldebrant, Hildbrant, Hyldbrant

Hildefuns (German) One who is ready for battle
Hildfuns, Hyldefuns, Hyldfuns

Hilderinc (Anglo-Saxon) A warrior
Hilderink, Hilderinch, Hilderinck, Hilderync, Hilderynck, Hilderynch, Hilderynk

Hillel (Hebrew) One who is praised
Hyllel, Hillell, Hyllell, Hilel, Hylel, Hilell, Hylell

Hilliard (German) A defender or guardian during war
Hillyard, Hillierd, Hillyerd, Hillier, Hillyer, Hylliard, Hyllierd, Hyllyard, Hyllyerd, Hillard, Hillerd

Hillock (English) From the small hill
Hillok, Hilloc, Hillocke, Hilloke, Hill, Hille, Hilli, Hillie, Hilly, Hilley, Hillee, Hillea, Hilleigh

Hilton (English) From the town on the hill
Hillton, Hiltun, Hilltun, Helton, Hellton, Heltun, Helltun, Hilten, Hillten, Helten, Hellten

Himesh (Indian) The snow king
Himeshe, Hymesh, Hymeshe

Hinto (Native American) Refers to the color blue
Hintoe, Hynto, Hyntoe

Hippocrates (Greek) A great philosopher
Hyppocrates, Hipocrates, Hypocrates

Hippolyte (Greek) Of the stampeding horses
Hippolytos, Hippolit, Hippolitos, Hippolytus, Hyppolytos, Hyppolyte, Hyppolit, Hippolitus

Hiram (Hebrew) My brother has been exalted
Hirom, Hirum, Hirem, Hyram, Hyrom, Hyrum, Hyrem

Hiramatsu (Japanese) One who is exalted

Hiranmay (Indian) The golden one
Hiranmaye, Hiranmai, Hiranmae, Hyranmay, Hyranmaye, Hyranmai, Hyranmae

Hiro (Japanese) A giving man
Hyro

Hiromasa (Japanese) One who is open-minded and just
Hyromasa

Hiroshi (Japanese) A generous man
Hiroshie, Hiroshy, Hiroshey, Hiroshee, Hiroshea, Hyroshi, Hyroshie, Hyroshey, Hyroshy, Hyroshee, Hyroshea

Hirsi (African) An amulet
Hirsie, Hirsy, Hirsey, Hirsee, Hirsea

Hirza (Hebrew) Resembling a deer
Hyrza, Hirzah, Hyrzah

Hisham (Arabic) A generous man
Hysham, Hishem, Hyshem

Hisoka (Japanese) One who is secretive
Hysoka, Hisokie, Hysokie, Hisoki, Hysoki, Hisokey, Hysokey, Hisoky, Hysoky, Hisokee, Hysokee, Hisokea, Hysokea

Hitakar (Indian) One who wishes others well
Hitakarin, Hitakrit

Hitesh (Indian) A good man
Hiteshe, Hytesh, Hyteshe

Hjalmar (Norse) One who wears an army helmet
Hjalmarr, Hjalamar, Hjallmar, Hjalamarr, Hjalmer, Hjalamer, Hjalmerr, Hjalamerr, Hjallmer

Ho (Chinese) A good man

Hoai (Vietnamese) For eternity; always

Hoang (Vietnamese) The phoenix

Hoashis (Japanese) Of God
Hoashys

Hobart (American) Form of Hubert, meaning "having a shining intellect"
Hobarte, Hoebart, Hoebarte, Hobert, Hoberte, Hoburt, Hoburte, Hobirt, Hobirte, Hobyrt, Hobyrte, Hobard, Hobi, Hobie, Hoby, Hobey, Hobee, Hobea, Hobbard

Hobbes (English) Form of Robert, meaning "one who is bright with fame"
Hobbs, Hob, Hobs, Hobbi, Hobbie, Hobby, Hobbey, Hobbee, Hobbea

Hobson (English) The son of Robert
Hobsen, Hobsun, Hobsin, Hobsyn, Hobsan, Hobbson, Hobbsun, Hobbsen, Hobbsan, Hobbsin, Hobbsyn

Hoc (Vietnamese) A studious man

Hockley (English) From the high meadow
Hockly, Hocklee, Hockleigh, Hocklea, Hockleah, Hockli, Hocklie

Hockney (English) From the high island
Hockny, Hocknee, Hockneigh, Hocknea, Hockni, Hocknie

Hodge (English) Form of Roger, meaning "a famous spearman"
Hoge, Hodges, Hoges, Hodger, Hoger, Hodgi, Hodgie, Hodgey, Hodgy, Hodgee, Hodgea

Hodgson (English) The son of Roger
Hodgsen, Hodgsin, Hodgsyn, Hodgsan, Hodgsun

Hodson (English) The son of the hooded man
Hodsun, Hodsen, Hodsan, Hodsin, Hodsyn, Hodeson

Hoffman (German) A courtier
Hoffmann, Hofman, Hofmann, Hoffmen, Hofmen

Hogan (Gaelic) One who is youthful
Hogen, Hogin, Hogyn, Hogun, Hogon

Hohberht (German) One who is high and
bright
Hohbert, Hohburt, Hohbirt, Hohbyrt, Hoh

Hoireabard (Irish) A soldier

Hojar (American) Having a wild spirit
Hogar, Hobar, Hodar

Hok'ee (Native American) One who has
been abandoned

Holbrook (English) From the hollow near
the stream
Holbrooke

Holcomb (English) From the deep valley
Holcom, Holcombe

Holden (English) From the hollow in the
valley
Holdan, Holdin, Holdyn, Holdon, Holdun

Holder (English) One who is muscially
talented
Holdar, Holdor, Holdur, Holdir, Holdyr

Holic (Czech) A barber
Holyc, Holick, Holyck, Holik, Holyk

Holiday (American) Born on a festive day
*Holliday, Holidaye, Hollidaye, Holidai,
Hollidai, Holidae, Hollidae*

Holland (American) From the Netherlands
*Hollend, Hollind, Hollynd, Hollande,
Hollende, Hollinde, Hollynde*

Holleb (Polish) Resembling a dove
Hollab, Hollob, Hollub, Hollib, Hollyb

Hollis (English) From the holly tree
*Hollys, Holliss, Hollyss, Hollace, Hollice,
Holli, Hollie, Holly, Holley, Hollee, Hollea,
Holleigh, Hollyce, Hollister, Hollistar,
Hollistir, Hollistyr, Hollistur, Hollistor*

Hollywood (American) One who is cocky;
one who is flashy
Holliwood, Holliewood

Holman (English) A man from the valley
*Holmann, Holmen, Holmin, Holmyn,
Holmon, Holmun*

Holmes (English) From the river island
*Holmmes, Holm, Holme, Holms, Hulmes,
Hulmmes, Hulm, Hulme, Hulms*

Holt (English) From the forest
*Holte, Holyt, Holyte, Holter, Holtar, Holtor,
Holtur, Holtir, Holtyr*

Homain (American) A homebody
*Homaine, Homayn, Homayne, Homaen,
Homaene, Homane*

Homer (Greek) Of the pledge; an epic poet
*Homar, Homere, Homero, Homeros,
Homerus, Hohmer, Hohmar*

Honani (Native American) Resembling a
badger
*Honanie, Honany, Honaney, Honanee,
Honanea*

Honaw (Native American) Resembling a
bear
Honawe, Honau

Honcho (American) A leader
*Honchi, Honchey, Honchee, Honchea,
Honchie, Honchy, Honche, Honch*

Hondo (African) A warring man
Hondoh, Honda, Hondah

Honesto (Spanish) One who is honest
*Honestio, Honestiyo, Honesteo, Honesteyo,
Honestoh*

Hong (Vietnamese) Refers to the color red

Honi (Hebrew) A gracious man
Honie, Honey, Hony, Honee, Honea

Honiahaka (Native American) Resembling
a little wolf

Honnesh (Indian) A wealthy man
Honneshe, Honesh, Honeshe

Honon (Native American) Resembling a
bear
Honun, Honen, Honan, Honin, Honyn

Honoré (Latin) One who is honored
*Honord, Honorius, Honorios, Honoratus,
Honoratos, Honore, Honorato, Honoray,
Honoraye, Honorae, Honorai*

Honovi (Native American) Having great
strength
Honovie, Honovy, Honovey, Honovee, Honovea

Hont (Hungarian) One who breeds dogs
Honte

Honza (Czech) A gift from God

Hooker (English) A shepherd
Hookar, Hookor, Hookur, Hookir, Hookyr

Hooper (English) One who makes hoops
for barrels
Hoopar, Hoopor, Hoopur, Hoopir, Hoopyr

Hopkins (Welsh) The son of Robert
*Hopkin, Hopkinson, Hopkyns, Hopper,
Hoppner, Hopkyn, Hopkynson, Hopkinsen,
Hopkynsen*

Horace (Latin) The keeper of time
*Horacio, Horatio, Horatius, Horaz, Horase,
Horice, Horise, Horate, Horaysho, Horashio,
Horasheo, Horado, Horatiu*

Horsley (English) From the horse meadow
*Horsly, Horslea, Horsleah, Horslee, Horsleigh,
Horsli, Horslie*

Horst (German) From the thicket
*Horste, Horsten, Horstan, Horstin, Horstyn,
Horston, Horstun, Horstman, Horstmen,
Horstmon, Horstmun, Horstmin, Horstmyn*

Hortense (Latin) A gardener
Hortence, Hortus, Hortensius, Hortensios

Horton (English) From the gray town
Hortun, Horten, Hortan, Hortin, Hortyn

Horus (Egyptian) In mythology, the god of
light

Hosaam (Arabic) A handsome man
Hosam

Hosea (Hebrew) One who reaches salvation
*Hoshea, Hoseia, Hosheia, Hosi, Hosie, Hosy,
Hosey, Hosee, Hosaya*

Hoshi (Japanese) Resembling a star
*Hoshiko, Hoshyko, Hoshie, Hoshee, Hoshea,
Hoshy, Hoshey*

Hosni (Arabic) A superior man
Hosnie, Hosney, Hosny, Hosnee, Hosnea

Hotah (Native American) A white-skinned
man; a white-haired man

Hototo (Native American) One who whistles; a warrior spirit that sings

Houerv (English) A bitter man

Houghton (English) From the town on the
headland
*Houghtun, Houghtin, Houghtyn, Houghten,
Houghtan, Hough*

Houston (Gaelic / English) From Hugh's
town / from the town on the hill
*Hughston, Housten, Hughsten, Houstin,
Hughstin, Houstyn, Hughstyn, Huston,
Husten, Hustin, Hustyn, Houstun,
Hughstun, Houstan, Hughstan, Hustan*

Hovannes (Armenian) Form of John,
meaning "God is gracious"
*Hovennes, Hovann, Hovenn, Hovane,
Hovene, Hovan, Hoven*

Hovsep (Armenian) Form of Joseph, meaning "God will add"
Hovsepp

How (German) One who is lofty
Howe

Howahkan (Native American) Having a
mysterious voice

Howard (English) The guardian of the home
*Howerd, Howord, Howurd, Howird, Howyrd,
Howi, Howie, Howy, Howey, Howee, Howea*

Howell (Welsh) A distinguished or eminent
man
*Howel, Howill, Howil, Howyll, Howyl,
Hywell, Hywel*

Howi (Native American) Resembling a
turtledove

Howland (English) From the highlands;
from the hilly land
*Howlande, Howlend, Howlende, Howlan,
Howlen, Howlin, Howlyn, Howlon, Howlun,
Howlond, Howlonde, Howlind, Howlinde,
Howlynd, Howlynde, Howlund, Howlunde*

Hoyte (Norse) A soulful man
Hoyt, Hoit, Hoite, Hoyce, Hoice

Hriday (Indian) Of the heart and mind
*Hridaye, Hridae, Hridai, Hryday, Hrydaye,
Hrydai, Hrydae*

Hroc (English) Resembling a crow

Hrocby (English) From the crow's farm
Hrocbey, Hrocbee, Hrocbea, Hrocbi, Hrocbie

Hrocley (English) From the crow's meadow
Hrocly, Hroclee, Hroclea, Hrocleah, Hrocleigh, Hrocli, Hroclie

Hrocton (English) From the crow's town
Hroctun, Hrocten, Hroctin, Hroctyn, Hroctan

Hrothgar (Anglo-Saxon) A king
Hrothgarr, Hrothegar, Hrothegarr, Hrothgare, Hrothegare

Huang (Chinese) A wealthy man

Hubert (German) Having a shining intellect
Huberte, Huburt, Huburte, Hubirt, Hubirte, Hubyrt, Hubyrte, Hubie, Hubi, Hubey, Huby, Hubee, Hubea, Hube, Huberto, Humberto, Hubbard

Huckleberry (English) Resembling the fruit
Hucklebery, Hukleberry, Huklebery, Huckleberri, Hukleberri, Huckleberi, Hukleberi, Huckleberrie, Hukleberrie, Huckleberie, Hukleberie, Huck, Hucke, Hucks, Huk, Huc

Hud (English) A hooded man
Hudd, Houd, Houdd, Hudde, Hood, Hoodi, Hoodie, Hoodee, Hoodea, Hoody, Hoodey, Hod, Hodd, Hodde

Hudak (Czech) A blonde-haired man
Hudack, Hudac

Hudson (English) The son of Hugh; from the river
Hudsun, Hudsen, Hudsan, Hudsin, Hudsyn

Hudya (Arabic) One who follows the correct path
Hudyah, Hudiya, Hudiyah

Huelett (English) A young Hugh
Hughlett, Huelet, Hughlet

Hugh (German) Having a bright mind
Hew, Hewe, Huey, Hughes, Hughie, Hugues, Huw, Hugo, Hughi, Hughy, Hughey, Hughee, Hughea, Hu, Hue

Hugi (English) An intelligent man
Hugie, Hugy, Hugey, Hugee, Hugea

Hugin (Norse) A thoughtful man
Hugyn, Hugen, Hugan, Hugon, Hugun

Huland (English) A bright man
Hulande, Hulend, Hulende, Hulind, Hulinde, Hulynd, Hulynde

Hulbert (German) A bright and graceful man
Hulburt, Hulbirt, Hulbyrt, Hulbart, Hulberd, Hulburd, Hulbird, Hulbyrd, Hulbard, Huldiberaht

Hull (American) A spirited man
Hulle

Humam (Arabic) A generous and brave man

Humayd (Arabic) One who is praised
Humayde, Humaid, Humaide, Humaed, Humaede, Humade

Humbert (German) A famous warrior
Humberto, Humberte, Humbirt, Humbirte, Humbirto, Humburt, Humburte, Humburto, Humbyrt, Humbyrte, Humbyrto, Humbart, Humbarte, Humbarto

Hume (Scottish / English) From the cave / one who promotes peace
Home

Humility (English) One who is modest
Humilitey, Humiliti, Humilitie, Humilitee, Humilitea

Humphrey (German) A peaceful warrior
Humphry, Humphri, Humphrie, Humphree, Humphrea, Humfrey, Humfry, Humfri, Humfrie, Humfree, Humfrea, Humfrid, Humfryd, Humfried, Humfreid, Humph, Humphredo, Humfredo

Humvee (American) Resembling the vehicle; a macho man
Humvi, Humvie, Humvey, Humvy, Humvea, Hummer

Hunfrid (German) A peaceful Hun
Hunfryd, Hunfried, Hunfreid

Hung (Vietnamese) A hero

Hungan (Haitian) A spirit master or priest
Hungen, Hungon, Hungun, Hungin, Hungyn

Hungas (Irish) A vigorous man

Hunn (German) A warring man
Hun

❂
❶ **Hunter** (English) A great huntsman and provider
Huntar, Huntor, Huntur, Huntir, Huntyr, Hunte, Hunt, Hunting, Huntyng, Huntler, Huntlar, Huntlor, Huntlur, Huntlir, Huntlyr

Huntington (English) From the hunter's town
Huntingtun, Huntingten, Huntingtan, Huntingtin, Huntingtyn, Huntingdon, Huntingdan, Huntingden, Huntingdun, Huntingdin, Huntingdyn

Huntley (English) From the hunter's meadow
Huntly, Huntlee, Huntlea, Huntleah, Huntleigh, Huntli, Huntlie, Huntle

Huon (Hebrew) Form of John, meaning "God is gracious"

Huritt (Native American) A handsome man
Hurit, Hurytt, Huryt, Hurett, Huret

Hurlbert (English) Of the shining army
Hurlberte, Hurlburt, Hurlburte, Hurlbirt, Hurlbirte, Hurlbyrt, Hurlbyrte, Hurlbutt, Hurlbart, Hurlbarte

Hurley (Irish) Of the sea tide
Hurly, Hurleigh, Hurlea, Hurleah, Hurlee, Hurli, Hurlie

Hurst (English) From the tree thicket
Hurste, Hearst, Hearste, Hirst, Hirste, Hyrst, Hyrste

Husam (Arabic) One who wields a sword

Husani (African) Form of Hussein, meaning "the small handsome one; a good man"
Husanie, Husany, Husaney, Husanee, Husanea, Hussani, Hussanie, Hussany, Hussaney, Hussanee, Hussanea

Husky (American) A big man; a manly man
Huski, Huskie, Huskey, Huskee, Huskea, Husk, Huske

Huslu (Native American) Resembling a hairy bear
Huslue, Huslou

Hussein (Arabic) The small handsome one; a good man
Hussain, Husain, Husayn, Husein, Hussayn, Hussaen, Husaen, Husane, Hussane

Husto (Spanish) A righteous man
Hustio, Husteo, Hustiyo, Husteyo

Hutch (American) A unique man
Hutche, Hutchi, Hutchie, Hutchey, Hutchy, Hutchee, Hutchea

Hutter (English) One who lives near the bluff
Huttar, Huttor, Huttir, Huttyr, Huttur, Hutti, Huttie, Hutty, Huttee, Huttea, Huttey, Hutte, Hutt

Hutton (English) From the town on the bluff
Huttun, Hutten, Huttan, Huttin, Huttyn

Huw (Welsh) Of great intellect
Huwe

Huxford (English) From Hugh's ford
Huxeford, Huxforde, Huxeforde, Huxferd, Huxferde, Huxeferd, Huxeferde, Huxfurd, Huxfurde, Huxefurd, Huxefurde

Huxley (English) From Hugh's meadow
Huxly, Huxlea, Huxleah, Huxleigh, Huxlee, Huxli, Huxlie, Huxle

Huy (Vietnamese) A bright or glorious man

Huynh (Vietnamese) An older brother

Hwang (Japanese) Refers to the color yellow
Hwange

Hwitby (English) From the white farm
Hwitbey, Hwitbee, Hwitbea, Hwitbi, Hwitbie

Hwitcomb (English) From the white hollow
Hwitcom, Hwitcombe, Hwitcum, Hwitcumb, Hwitcumbe

Hwitely (English) From the white meadow
Hwiteley, Hwitelee, Hwitelea, Hwiteleah, Hwiteleigh, Hwiteli, Hwitelie

Hwitford (English) From the white ford
Hwitforde, Hwitferd, Hwitferde, Hwitfurd, Hwitfurde

Hyacinthe (French) Resembling the hyacinth flower
Hyacinthos, Hyacinthus, Hyakinthos, Hyakinthus

Hyatt (English) From the high gate
Hyat, Hiatt, Hiat, Hyett, Hyet, Hyutt, Hyut, Hiett, Hiet, Hiut, Hiutt

Hydd (Welsh) Resembling a deer
Hydde

Hyde (English) From the hide
Hyd, Hide, Hid

Hyman (Hebrew) A giver of life
Hymann, Hayim, Hayyim, Hymie, Hymi,
Hymy, Hymey, Hymee, Hymea, Hyam, Hy

Hyroniemus (Latin) A holy man
Hyroneimus, Hyronemus, Hyronimus,
Hyroniemos, Hyroneimos, Hyronemos,
Hyronimos

i

Iagan (Scottish) A fiery man
Iagen, Iagin, Iagyn, Iagon, Iagun

Iago (Spanish) Form of James, meaning "he
who supplants"
Iyago, Iagoh, Iyagoh

Iakovos (Hebrew) Form of Jacob, meaning
"he who supplants"
Iakovus, Iakoves, Iakovas, Iakovis, Iakovys

◉ **Ian** (Gaelic) Form of John, meaning "God is
gracious"
Iain, Iaine, Iayn, Iayne, Iaen, Iaene, Iahn

Iassen (Bulgarian) From the ash tree
Iassan, Iassin, Iassyn, Iasson, Iassun

Iau (Welsh) Form of Zeus, meaning "ruler
of the gods"
Iaue

Iavor (Bulgarian) From the sycamore tree
Iaver, Iavur, Iavar, Iavir, Iavyr

Ib (Danish) Of the pledge
Ibb

Ibaad (Arabic) One who believes in God
Ibad

Ibrahim (Arabic) Form of Abraham, mean-
ing "father of a multitude; father of nations"
Ibraheem, Ibraheim, Ibrahiem, Ibraheam,
Ibrahym

Ibu (Japanese) One who is creative
Ibue, Iboo, Ibou

Icarus (Greek) In mythology, the man who
attached wings with wax which melted off
when he flew too close to the sun
Ikarus, Ickarus, Icaros, Ikaros, Ickaros

Ich (Hebrew) Form of Ichabod, meaning
"the glory has gone"
Iche, Ichi, Ichie, Ichy, Ichey, Ichee, Ichea

Ichabod (Hebrew) The glory has gone
Ikabod, Ickabod, Icabod, Ichavod, Ikavod,
Icavod, Ickavod, Icha

Ichiro (Japanese) The firstborn son
Ichyro, Ichirio, Ichyrio, Ichireo, Ichyreo

Ichtaca (Nahuatl) A secretive man
Ichtaka, Ichtacka

Icnoyotl (Nahuatl) A beloved friend

Ida (Anglo-Saxon) A king
Idah

Idal (English) From the yew-tree valley
Idall, Idale, Idail, Idaile, Idayl, Idayle, Idael,
Idaele

Idan (Hebrew) Of the time; of the era

Iden (English) One who is prosperous;
wealthy
Idin, Idyn, Idon, Idun

Idi (African) Born during the holiday of Idd
Idie, Idy, Idey, Idee, Idea

Ido (Arabic / Hebrew) A mighty man / to
evaporate
Iddo, Idoh, Iddoh

Idona (Teutonic) A hardworking man
Idonah

Idowu (Welsh) A dark-haired man
Idowue, Idowoo, Idowou

Idris (Welsh) An eager lord
Idrys, Idriss, Idrisse, Idryss, Idrysse

Idwal (Welsh) A well-known man
Idwall, Idwale, Idwalle

Iefan (Welsh) Form of John, meaning "God
is gracious"
Iefon, Iefen, Iefin, Iefyn, Iefun, Ifan, Ifon,
Ifen, Ifin, Ifyn, Ifun

Ieuan (Welsh) Form of Ivan, meaning "God is gracious"
Iuan, Ieuane, Iuane

Ife (African) One who is widely loved
Iffe, Ifi, Ifie, Ifee, Ifea, Ify, Ifey

Ifor (Welsh) An archer
Ifore, Ifour, Ifoure

Iftikhar (Arabic) One who brings honor
Iftichar, Iftickhar, Iftikar, Ifticar, Iftickar, Iftykhar, Iftykar, Iftychar, Iftycar, Iftyckhar, Iftyckar

Igasho (Native American) A wanderer
Igashoe, Igashow, Igashowe

Ige (African) One who is delivered breech
Igi, Igie, Igy, Igey, Igee, Igea

Iggi (African/Latin) The only son/form of Ignatius, meaning "a fiery man; one who is ardent"
Iggie, Iggy, Iggey, Iggee, Iggea

Ignatius (Latin) A fiery man; one who is ardent
Ignac, Ignace, Ignacio, Ignacius, Ignatious, Ignatz, Ignaz, Ignazio, Inacio, Ignatia, Ignado, Ignatios, Ignaci, Ignacy, Ignacie, Ignacey, Ignacee, Ignacea

Igon (Basque) The ascension
Igun

Igor (Scandinavian/Russian) A hero/Ing's soldier
Igoryok

Ihab (Arabic) A gift

Ihaka (Maori) Form of Isaac, meaning "full of laughter"
Ihaca, Ihacka, Ihakah, Ihackah, Ihacah, Ihacca, Ihakka

Iham (Indian) One who is expected

Ihit (Indian) One who is honored
Ihyt, Ihitt, Ihytt

Ihsan (Arabic) A charitable man
Ihsann, Ihsen, Ihsin, Ihsyn, Ihson, Ihsun

Iiari (Basque) A cheerful man
Iiarie, Iiary, Iiarey, Iiaree, Iiarea

Ikaika (Hawaiian) Having great strength
Ikaica, Ikayka, Ikayca, Ikaeka, Ikaeca, Ikaka, Ikaca

Ike (Hebrew) Form of Isaac, meaning "full of laughter"
Iki, Ikie, Iky, Ikey, Ikee, Ikea

Iker (Basque) A visitor
Ikar, Ikir, Ikyr, Ikor, Ikur

Ilan (Hebrew) Of the tree
Illan, Ilen, Illen, Ilin, Illin, Ilyn, Illyn, Ilon, Illon, Ilun, Illun

Ilario (Italian) A cheerful man
Ilareo, Ilariyo, Ilareyo, Ilar, Ilarr, Ilari, Ilarie, Ilary, Ilarey, Ilaree, Ilarea

Ilhuitl (Nahuatl) Born during the daytime

Ilias (Hebrew) Form of Elijah, meaning "Jehovah is my God"
Ileas, Ili, Ilie, Ily, Iley, Ilee, Ileigh, Ilea, Illias, Illeas, Ilyas, Illyas

Illanipi (Native American) An amazing man
Illanipie, Illanipy, Illanipey, Illanipee, Illanipea

Illinois (Native American) From the tribe of warriors; from the state of Illinois

Illtyd (Welsh) The land of the populas
Illtud, Illtid, Illted, Illtad, Illted

Ilo (African) Of the sunshine; filled with joy
Iloe, Ilow, Ilowe

Ilom (African / Welsh) Having many enemies / filled with happiness
Ilum, Ilem, Ilam, Ilim, Ilym

Iluminado (Spanish) One who shines brightly
Illuminado, Iluminato, Illuminato, Iluminados, Iluminatos, Illuminados, Illuminatos

Ilya (Russian) Form of Elijah, meaning "Jehovah is my God"
Ilyah, Ilia, Iliah, Iliya, Iliyah

Im (Norse) In mythology, a giant

Imad (Arabic) One who offers support

Imaran (Indian) Having great strength
Imaren, Imaron, Imarun, Imarin, Imaryn

Immanuel (German) Form of Emmanuel, meaning "God is with us"
Imanuel, Iman, Imani, Imanoel, Immannuel, Imanie, Imany, Imaney, Imanee, Imanea, Imanol, Imanole

Imran (Arabic) One who acts as a host
Imren, Imrin, Imron, Imrun, Imryn

Imre (Hungarian / German / Hebrew) One who is innocent / ruler of the home / of my words
Imray, Imri, Imrie, Imry, Imrey, Imree, Imrea, Imraye, Imrai, Imrae

Ina (African) An illuminated man
Inah, Inna, Innah

Inaki (Basque) An ardent man
Inakie, Inaky, Inakey, Inakee, Inakea, Inacki, Inackie, Inackee, Inackea, Inacky, Inackey

Inapo (Chamoru) Of the waves
Inapoe, Inapow, Inapowe

Inazin (Native American) Resembling a standing elk
Inazen, Inazyn, Inazon, Inazun, Inazan

Ince (Hungarian) One who is innocent
Inse

Incendio (Spanish) Of the fire
Incendeo, Incendiyo, Incendeyo

Independence (American) One who has freedom
Independance, Indepindence, Indipindince, Indypyndynce

Indiana (English) From the land of the Indians; from the state of Indiana
Indianna, Indyana, Indyanna

Indivar (Indian) Resembling a blue lotus
Indyvar, Indivarr, Indyvarr

Indore (Indian) From the city in India
Indor, Indoor, Indoore

Indra (Hindi) In Hinduism, the god of the sky and weather
Indrah, Inder, Inderjeet, Inderjit, Inderjyt, Indervir, Indrajit, Indrajeet, Indrajyt

Ine (Anglo-Saxon) A king

Inerney (Irish) The church's steward
Inerny, Inernee, Inernea, Inerni, Inernie

Infinity (American) A man unbounded by space or time
Infinitey, Infiniti, Infinitie, Infinitee, Infinitye, Infinitea

Ing (Norse) In mythology, god of fertility

Ingall (German) A messenger of God; an angel
Ingal, Ingalls, Ingals, Ingel, Ingell, Ingels, Ingells

Ingemar (Scandinavian) The son of Ing
Ingamar, Ingemur, Ingmar, Ingmur, Ingar, Ingemer, Ingmer

Inger (Scandinavian) One who is fertile
Inghar, Ingher

Inglebert (German) As bright as an angel
Ingbert, Ingelbert, Ingelburt, Ingburt, Ingleburt, Ingelbirt, Ingbirt, Ingelbyrt, Inglebirt, Inglebyrt, Ingbyrt

Ingo (Scandinavian / Danish) A lord / from the meadow
Ingoe, Ingow, Ingowe

Ingolf (Norse) Ing's wolf
Ingulf, Ingolfe, Ingulfe

Ingra (English) Form of Ingram, meaning "a raven of peace"
Ingrah, Ingri, Ingrie, Ingree, Ingrea

Ingram (Scandinavian) A raven of peace
Ingrem, Ingrim, Ingrym, Ingrum, Ingrom, Ingraham, Ingrahame, Ingrams, Inghram

Ingvar (Scandinavian) A soldier of Ing's army
Ingevar, Ingevur, Ingvur

Inigo (Portuguese) An ardent man
Inygo, Inigoe, Inygo, Inigow, Inygow, Inigowe, Inygowe

Iniko (African) Born during troubled times
Inicko, Inico, Inyko, Inycko, Inyco

Inman (English) An innkeeper
Innman, Inmann, Innmann

Innis (Scottish) From the island
Innes, Inness, Inniss, Inis, Iniss, Ines, Iness

Innocenzio (Italian) One who is innocent
Incencio, Innocencio, Innocenzeo, Inocenzeo, Inocenzio, Innocent, Innocenty, Innocente, Innocenti, Innocentie, Innocentee, Innocentey

Intekhab (Indian) The chosen one
Intechab, Inteckhab

Inteus (Native American) One who has no shame
Intius, Intyus

Inver (Gaelic) From the estuary
Invar, Invir, Invyr, Invor, Invur

Ioakim (Russian) Form of Joachim, meaning "one who is established by God; God will judge"
Ioachim, Iakim, Ioacheim, Ioaquim, Ioaquin, Iosquin, Ioakim, Ioakeen, Iokim, Iokin, Ioachime, Iaokim

Ioanis (Russian) Form of John, meaning "God is gracious"
Ioanys, Ioaniss, Ioanyss, Ioan, Ioane, Iohanis, Iohanys, Iohaniss, Iohanyss, Ioanes, Ioaness

Iomhair (Gaelic) An archer
Iomhaire

Ion (Greek) In mythology, the son of Apollo
Ionn, Ione, Ionne, Ionnes

Ior (Welsh) An attractive man
Iore

Iorgos (Greek) An outgoing man
Iorgas, Iorges, Iorgis, Iorgys, Iorgus

Iorwerth (Welsh) A handsome lord
Ioworth, Iowerthe, Ioworthe, Iowirth, Iowirthe, Iowyrth, Iowyrthe

Ioseph (Gaelic) Form of Joseph, meaning "God will add"
Iosef, Iosep, Iosip, Iosyp

Iov (Hebrew) God will establish
Iove

Ira (Hebrew) One who is vigilant; watchful
Irah, Irra, Irrah

Iram (Hebrew) A shining man
Irham, Irem, Irhem, Irim, Irhim, Irym, Irhym, Irom, Irhom, Irum, Irhum

Iranga (Sri Lankan) One who is special

Iravath (Scandinavian) Indra's elephant
Iravathe, Iravat, Iravate

Ireland (American) One who pays homage to Ireland

Irenbend (Anglo-Saxon) From the iron bend
Ironbend

Irenio (Spanish) A peaceful man
Ireniyo, Ireneo, Ireneyo, Irenaeus, Ireneus, Irenious, Irenius, Irenios

Irfan (Indian / Arabic) One who is knowledgeable / one who is thankful
Irfen, Irfin, Irfyn, Irfon, Irfun

Irish (American) Man from Ireland
Irysh, Irishe, Iryshe

Irshad (Indian) A sign or signal
Irshaad

Irving (English) A friend of the sea
Irv, Irven, Irvin, Irvine, Irvyn, Irvyne, Irvene

Irwin (English) A friend of the wild boar
Irwinn, Irwinne, Irwyn, Irwynne, Irwine, Irwen, Irwenn, Irwenne

❂ Isaac (Hebrew) Full of laughter
Isaack, Isaak, Isac, Isacco, Isak, Issac, Itzak, Itzhak, Izaac, Izaak, Izak, Izik, Izsak, Isaakios

❂ Isaiah (Hebrew) God is my salvation
Isa, Isaia, Isais, Isia, Isiah, Issiah, Izaiah, Iziah, Isaias, Isai

Isam (Arabic) One who is protected
Issam

Isandro (Spanish) The liberator of man
Isander, Isandero, Isandoro, Isanderio, Isandorio, Isandereo, Isandoreo

Isas (Japanese) One who is worthwhile

Iseabail (Hebrew) One who is devoted to God
Iseabaile, Iseabayl, Iseabyle, Iseabael, Iseabaele

Isen (Anglo-Saxon) Of iron
Isin, Isyn, Ison, Isun, Isan

Isha (Hindi) One who is protective
Ishah

Ishaan (Hindi) Of the sun
Ishan

Isham (English) From the iron one's estate
Ishem, Ishom, Ishum, Ishim, Ishym, Isenham, Isenhem, Isenhim, Isenhym, Isenhom, Isehum

Ishaq (Arabic) A laughing child
Ishak, Ishack, Ishac

Ishi (Japanese) As solid as a rock
Ishie, Ishy, Ishey, Ishee, Ishea

Ishmael (Hebrew) God will listen
Ismail, Ismaal, Ismael, Ismal, Ismayl, Izmail, Ishmaal, Ishmal, Ishmayl, Ishmail

Isidore (Greek) A gift of Isis
Isador, Isadore, Isidor, Isidoro, Isidorus, Isidro, Issy, Izidor, Izydor, Izzy, Issey, Issi, Issie, Issee, Izzey, Izzi, Izzie, Izzee, Isidoros, Izidro, Izydro, Isydro

Iskander (Arabic) Form of Alexander, meaning "helper and defender of mankind"
Iskinder, Iskandar, Iskindar, Iskynder, Iskyndar, Iskender, Iskendar

Ismat (Arabic) One who is protective

Ismet (Turkish) One who is honored
Ismit, Ismyt

Isra (Turkish) An independent man; one who is free
Israh

Israel (Hebrew) God perseveres
Israeli, Israelie, Israely, Israeley, Israelee, Israeleigh, Israelea, Isreal, Izreal, Izrael

Israj (Hindi) The king of gods

Issa (Hebrew) A gift of God
Issah

Issachar (Hebrew) He will be rewarded
Isachar

Issay (African) One who is hairy
Issaye, Issai, Issae

Isser (Slavic) One who is creative
Issar, Issir, Issyr, Issor, Issur

Istaqa (Native American) A coyote man
Istaka, Istaca, Istacka

Istu (Native American) As sweet as sugar
Istue, Istoo, Istou

Istvan (Hungarian) One who is crowned
Istven, Istvin, Istvyn, Istvon, Istvun

Itai (Hebrew) God is beside me
Ittai, Itiel, Itiell, Ittiel

Italo (Italian) A man from Italy
Itallo, Italio, Italeo, Italiyo, Italeyo

Itamar (Hebrew) From the island of palms
Ittamar, Itamarr, Ittamarr, Ithamar, Ithamarr

Iulian (Romanian) A youthful man
Iulien, Iulio, Iuleo

Iuwine (Anglo-Saxon) A beloved friend
Iuwin, Iuwinn, Iuwinne, Iuwyn, Iuwynn, Iuwynne, Iuwen, Iuwenn, Iuwenne

Iva (Japanese) Of the yew tree
Ivah

Ivan (Slavic) Form of John, meaning "God is gracious"
Ivann, Ivanhoe, Ivano, Iwan, Iban, Ibano, Ivanti, Ivantie, Ivante, Ivant, Ivanty, Ivantey, Ivantee, Ivantea

Ives (Scandinavian) The archer's bow; of the yew wood
Ivair, Ivar, Iven, Iver, Ivo, Ivon, Ivor, Ivaire, Ivayr, Ivayre, Ivaer, Ivaere, Ivare, Ibon, Ive

Ivo (German / English) Of cut wood / an archer's bow
Ivoe, Ivow, Ivowe, Ivoh, Ivon, Ivor

Ivory (English) Having a creamy-white complexion; as precious as elephant tusks
Ivorie, Ivorine, Ivoreen, Ivorey, Ivoree, Ivori, Ivoryne, Ivorea, Ivoreah, Ivoreane

Ivrit (Hebrew) The Hebrew language
Ivryt

Ivy (English) Resembling the evergreen vining plant
Ivee, Ivey, Ivie, Ivi, Ivea, Iveah

Ixaka (Basque) Laughter
Ixaca, Ixacka

Iyar (Hebrew) Surrounded by light
Iyyar, Iyer, Iyyer

Iye (Native American) Of the smoke

Izaan (Arabic) One who is obedient
Izan, Izane, Izain, Izaine, Izaen, Izaene, Izayn, Izayne

j

Ja (Korean / African) A handsome man / one who is magnetic

Jabal (Indian) An attractive man
Jaball

Jabari (African) A valiant man
Jabarie, Jabary, Jabarey, Jabaree, Jabarea

Jabbar (Indian) One who consoles others
Jabar

Jabez (Hebrew) One who is delivered in pain
Jabes, Jabesh, Jabeshe, Jabezz

Jabilo (African) A medicine man
Jabylo, Jabeilo, Jabielo, Jabeelo, Jabealo

Jabin (Hebrew) God has built; one who is perceptive

Jabir (Arabic) One who provides comfort
Jabeer, Jabier, Jabeir, Jabear, Jabyr, Jaber

Jabon (American) A feisty man
Jabun, Jabin, Jabyn, Jaben, Jaban

Jabulani (African) Filled with happiness
Jabulanie, Jabulany, Jabulaney, Jabulanee, Jabulanea

Jacan (Hebrew) A troublemaker
Jachin, Jachan, Jacen, Jachen, Jacin

Jace (Hebrew) God is my salvation
Jacen, Jacey, Jacian, Jacy, Jaice, Jayce, Juece, Jaycen, Jaecen, Jaicen, Jacie, Jaci, Jaicey, Jaicy, Jaici, Jaicie, Jaycey, Jaycy, Jayci, Jaycie, Jaecey, Jaecy, Jaeci, Jaecie, Jaycee

Jacinto (Spanish) Resembling a hyacinth
Jacynto, Jacindo, Jacyndo, Jacento, Jacendo, Jacenty, Jacentey, Jacentee, Jacentea, Jacenti, Jacentie, Jacek, Jacent, Jacint

○ **Jack** (English) Form of John, meaning "God
○ is gracious"
Jackie, Jackman, Jacko, Jacky, Jacq, Jacqin, Jak, Jaq, Jacki, Jackee

Jackal (Sanskrit) Resembling a wild dog
Jackel

○ **Jackson** (English) The son of Jack or John
Jacksen, Jacksun, Jacson, Jakson, Jaxen, Jaxon, Jaxun, Jaxson, Jaxsen, Jaxsun, Jaksen, Jacsen, Jax

○ **Jacob** (Hebrew) He who supplants
○ *Jaco, Jacobo, Jacobi, Jacoby, Jacobie, Jacobey, Jacobo, Jacobus, Jakob, Jakov, Jakub, Jacobe, Jachym, Jacobs, Jakobs, Jaykob, Jaycob*

Jacquard (French) A distinguished man
Jaquard, Jaquarde, Jaqard, Jacquarde, Jackard, Jackarde, Jakard, Jakarde

Jacques (French) Form of Jacob, meaning "he who supplants"
Jacot, Jacque, Jaques, Jock, Jocke, Jok, Jacue

Jadal (American) One who is punctual
Jadall, Jadel, Jadell

Jade (Spanish) Resembling the green gemstone
Jaide, Jaid, Jayd, Jayde, Jaed, Jaede, Jada

○ **Jaden** (Hebrew / English) One who is thankful to God; God has heard / form of Jade, meaning "resembling the green gemstone"
*Jadine, Jadyn, Jadon, **Jayden**, Jadyne, Jaydyn, Jaydon, Jaydine, Jadin, Jaydin, Jaidyn, Jaedan, Jaeden, Jaedin, Jaedon, Jaedyn, Jaidan, Jaidin, Jaidon, Jaidyn, Jaydan, Jader*

Jadrien (American) One who is bold
Jadrian, Jadrienn, Jadriann, Jadrienne, Jadrianne, Jadrion, Jadriun

Jaegar (German) A mighty hunter
Jaygar, Jaiger, Jagar, Jaeger, Juyger, Jaiger, Jager, Jaecar, Jaycar, Jaicar, Jacar, Jaecer, Jaycer, Jaicer, Jacer

Jaegel (English) A salesman
Jaygel, Jagel, Jaigel

Jael (Hebrew) Resembling a mountain goat
Jaele

Jaequon (American) An outgoing young man
Jaquon, Jaiquon, Jayquon, Jaequan, Jaquan, Jaiquan, Jayquan

Jafar (Arabic) From the small stream
Jaffar, Jafaar, Jaffaar, Jaafar, Jaaffar, Jafari, Jafarie, Jafary, Jafarey, Jafaree, Jafaru, Jafarue, Jafaroo, Jafarou

Jagan (English) One who is self-confident
Jagen, Jagin, Jagyn, Jagon, Jagun, Jago

Jagger (English) One who carts provisions
Jaggar, Jaggor, Jaggir, Jaggur, Juggyr

Jago (English) Form of Jacob, meaning "he who supplants"
Jagoe, Jagow, Jagowe

Jaguar (English) Resembling the animal; one who is fast
Jagwar, Jaghuar, Jagwhar

Jahan (Indian) Man of the world
Jehan, Jihan, Jag, Jagat, Jagath

Jahi (African) A dignified man
Jah, Jahie, Jahy, Jahey, Jahee, Jahea

Jaichand (Indian) The victory of the moon
Jaychand, Jachand, Jaechand, Jaichande, Jaychande, Jachande, Jaechande

Jaidayal (Indian) The victory of kindness
Jadayal, Jaydayal, Jaedayal

Jaidev (Indian) The victory of God
Jaydev, Jadev, Jaidev, Jaedev

Jaime (Spanish) Form of James, meaning "he who supplants"
Jamie, Jaime, Jaimee, Jaimey, Jaimi, Jaimie, Jaimy, Jamee, Jamei, Jamey, Jami, Jaymey, Jayme, Jaymi, Jaymy, Jaymie, Jaymee, Jammie

Jaimin (French) One who is loved
Jaimyn, Jamin, Jamyn, Jaymin, Jaymyn, Jaemin, Jaemyn

Jaimini (Indian) A victorious man
Jaymini, Jaemini, Jaiminie, Jayminie, Jaeminie, Jaiminy, Jayminy, Jaeminy

Jairdan (American) One who enlightens others
Jardan, Jayrdan, Jaerdan, Jairden, Jarden, Jayrden, Jaerden

Jairus (Hebrew) God enlightens
Jairo, Jair, Jaire

Jaiwant (Indian) A victorious man
Jaywant, Jaewant, Jawant

Jaja (African) A gift from God

Jajuan (American) One who loves God

Jakar (English) A man from Jakarta
Jakart, Jakarte

Jake (English) Form of Jacob, meaning "he who supplants"
Jaik, Jaike, Jayk, Jayke, Jakey, Jaky

Jakeem (Arabic) One who is exalted
Jakeim, Jakiem, Jakeam, Jakim, Jakym

Jakhi (American) Having great strength
Jakhie, Jakhy, Jakhey, Jakhee, Jakhea

Jakome (Basque) Form of James, meaning "he who supplants"
Jackome, Jakom, Jackom, Jacome

Jal (English) A traveler; wanderer
Jall

Jaladhi (Hindi) Of the ocean
Jaladhie, Jaladhy, Jaladhey, Jaladhee, Jaladi, Jaladie, Jalady, Jaladey, Jaladee, Jeladi, Jeladie, Jelady, Jeladey, Jeladee

Jalal (Arabic) A superior man
Jalall, Jallal, Jalil, Jaliyl, Jelal, Jellal

Jaleel (Arabic) A majestic man
Jaleal, Jalil, Jalyl, Jaleil, Jaliel

❂ **Jalen** (American) One who heals others; one who is tranquil
*Jaelan, Jaelin, Jaelon, Jailin, Jaillen, Jaillin, Jailon, Jalan, Jalin, Jalon, Jayelan, Jayelen, Jaylan, Jaylon, Jaylonn, Jaylin, **Jaylen***

Jam (American) As sweet as the condiment

Jamaine (Arabic) An attractive man
Jamain, Jamayn, Jamayne, Jamaen, Jamaene, Jamane

Jamal (Arabic) A handsome man
Jahmal, Jamaal, Jamael, Jamahl, Jamall, Jamaul, Jameel, Jamel, Jamell, Jamiel, Jamil, Jamile, Jamill, Jammal, Jemaal, Jemahl, Jemall, Jimal, Jimahl, Jomal, Jomahl, Jomall, Jemal, Jamaal

Jamar (American) Form of Jamal, meaning "a handsome man"
Jamarr, Jemar, Jemarr, Jimar, Jimarr, Jamaar, Jamari, Jamarie, Jamary, Jamarey, Jamaree

Jamarion (American) A strong-willed man
Jamareon, Jamarrion, Jamarreon, Jamarien, Jamarrien

❂
❂ **James** (Hebrew) Form of Jacob, meaning "he who supplants"
Jaimes, Jaymes, Jame, Jaym, Jaim, Jaem, Jaemes, Jamese, Jascha

Jameson (English) The son of James
Jaimison, Jamieson, Jaymeson, Jamison, Jaimeson, Jaymison, Jaemeson, Jaemison, Jamisen, Jaimesen, Jaymesen

Jamin (Hebrew) The right hand of favor
Jamian, Jamiel, Jamon, Jaymin, Jaemin, Jaymon, Jaemon, Jaimin, Jaimon

Jan (Slavic) Form of John, meaning "God is gracious"
Janek, Jano, Janos, Jonam, Jens, Janak

Janaan (Arabic) Having heart and soul
Janan, Janen, Janin, Janyn, Janon, Janun

Janesh (Hindi) A leader of the people
Janeshe

Jani (Finnish) Form of John, meaning "God is gracious"
Janie, Jannes, Janes, Jancsi, Jancsie, Janne, Janeth, Janneth, Janko, Janco, Jankya, Jussi, Jussie, Janksi, Janksie, Jantje

Janson (Scandinavian) The son of Jan
Janse, Jansen, Janssen, Jansson, Jantzen, Janzen, Jensen, Jenson, Jansahn, Jantz, Janzon

Jantis (German) One who wields a sharp spear
Jantys, Jantiss, Jantyss, Janyd, Janid

Janus (Latin) From the archway; in mythology, the god of gateways and beginnings
Januus, Janiusz, Januarius, Janusz, Jenaro, Jenarius, Jennaro

Japa (Indian) One who chants
Japeth, Japesh, Japendra

Japheth (Hebrew) May he expand; in the Bible, one of Noah's sons
Jaypheth, Jaepheth, Jaipheth, Jafeth, Jayfeth, Jaefeth, Jaifeth, Japhet, Jafet

Jarah (Hebrew) One who is as sweet as honey
Jarrah, Jara, Jarra

Jard (American) One who is long-lived
Jarrd, Jord, Jorrd, Jerd, Jerrd

Jardine (French) Of the gardens
Jardyne, Jardeen, Jardean, Jardeene, Jardeane

Jareb (Hebrew) He will struggle

Jared (Hebrew) Of the descent; descending
Jarad, Jarid, Jarod, Jarrad, Jarryd, Jarred, Jarrid, Jarrod, Jaryd, Jerad, Jerod, Jerrad, Jerred, Jerrod, Jerryd, Jered

Jarek (Slavic) Born during the spring
Jareck, Jarec

Jareth (American) One who is gentle
Jarethe, Jarreth, Jarrethe, Jereth, Jerreth, Jerethe, Jerrethe

Jarlath (Irish) A tributary lord
Jarleath, Jarlaith, Jarlaeth, Jarlayth, Jarleeth, Jariath, Jaryath

Jarman (German) A man from Germany
Jarmann, Jerman, Jermann

Jaromil (Czech) Born during the spring
Jaromyl, Jaromeel, Jaromeal, Jaromiel, Jaromeil, Jarmil, Jarmyl

Jaromir (Slavic) From the famous spring
Jaromeer, Jaromear, Jaromeir, Jaromier, Jaromyr

Jaron (Israeli) A song of rejoicing
Jaran, Jaren, Jarin, Jarran, Jarren, Jarrin, Jarron, Jaryn, Jeran, Jeren, Jerren, Jerrin, Jerron

Jaroslav (Slavic) Born with the beauty of spring
Jaroslaw

Jarrell (English) One who rules with the spear
Jarel, Jarrel, Jarell, Jarrall, Jarall, Jarral, Jerall, Jeryl, Jerel, Jeriel, Jeril, Jeroll, Jerrall, Jerrel, Jerrill, Jerroll, Jerryl, Jaryl, Jerrell, Jerriel, Jerriell

Jarrett (English) One who is strong with the spear
Jarett, Jarret, Jarrot, Jarrott, Jerett, Jerrett, Jerrot, Jerrott, Jarrit, Jarritt, Jaret, Jarot, Jeret, Jerot, Jarit, Jerit

Jarvis (French) One who wields a spear
Jarvee, Jarvell, Jarvey, Jary, Jervey, Jervis,
Jarvys, Jervys, Jarvi, Jarvie, Jarvy

Jasbeer (Indian) A victorious hero
Jasbir, Jasbear, Jasbier, Jasbeir, Jasbyr

Jase (American) Form of Jason, meaning
"God is my salvation / a healer"
Jaise, Jayse, Jaese

Jaser (Arabic) One who is fearless
Jasir, Jasyr, Jasar, Jasor, Jasur

Jaskirit (Indian) One who praises the lord
Jaskiryt, Jaskyryt, Jaskyrit

❂ **Jason** (Hebrew / Greek) God is my salvation /
a healer; in mythology, the leader of the
Argonauts
Jacen, Jaisen, Jaison, Jasen, Jasin, Jasun,
Jayson, Jaysen, Jaeson, Jaesen

Jaspal (Indian) One who is pure; chaste

Jasper (Persian) One who holds the treasure
Jaspar, Jaspir, Jaspyr, Jesper, Jespar, Jespir,
Jespyr

Jatan (Indian) One who is nurturing

Jathan (American) An attractive young man
Jaithan, Jaethan, Jaythan, Jathen, Jaithen,
Jaethen, Jaythen, Jathun, Jaithun, Jaethun,
Jaythun, Jathe, Jath

Jatin (Hindi) A saintly man
Jatyn, Jateen, Jatean, Jatien, Jatein

Javan (Hebrew) Man from Greece; in the
Bible, Noah's grandson
Jayvan, Jayven, Jayvern, Jayvon, Javon,
Javern, Javen

Javaris (American) One who is ever-ready
Javarys, Javares, Javarez, Javariz, Javy, Javey,
Javi, Javie, Javee

Javas (Indian) One who is quick; having
bright eyes

Javed (Persian) One who is immortal
Javid, Javyd

Javier (Spanish) The owner of a new house
Javiero

Javonte (American) A cheerful man
Javontay, Javontuye, Javontai, Javontae,
Javawnte, Javawntay, Javawntaye, Javawntai,
Javawntae, Jevonte, Jevontay, Jevontaye,
Jevontai, Jevontae

Jawad (Arabic) A generous man
Jawaid, Jawayd, Jawaide, Jawayde, Jawaed,
Jawaede, Jawade

Jawara (African) One who loves peace
Jawarra, Jawarah, Jawarrah

Jawdat (Arabic) One who is superior
Jaudat

Jawhar (Arabic) As precious as a jewel
Jawahar

Jawon (American) One who is shy
Jawan, Jawaun, Jawawn, Jawaughn

Jay (Latin / Sanskrit) Resembling a jaybird /
one who is victorious
Jae, Jai, Jaye, Jayron, Jayronn, Jey

Jayant (Indian) One who is victorious
Jayante, Jayanti, Jayantie, Jayantee, Jayantea,
Jayantey, Jayanty

Jayvyn (African) Having a light spirit
Jayvin, Jaivyn, Jaivin, Javyn, Javin, Jaevyn,
Jaevin

Jazon (Polish) One who heals others
Jazen, Jazin, Jazyn, Jazun

Jazz (American) Refers to the style of music
Jaz, Jaze, Jazzy, Jazzey, Jazzee, Jazzi, Jazzie

Jean (French) Form of John, meaning "God
is gracious"
Jeanne, Jeane, Jene, Jeannot, Jeanot

Jebediah (Hebrew) A friend of God
Jebedia, Jebadiah, Jebadia, Jebidia, Jebidiah,
Jeb, Jebb, Jebbe, Jebby, Jebbey, Jebbi, Jebbie

Jecori (American) An exuberant man
Jecorie, Jecory, Jecorey, Jecoree, Jekori, Jekorie,
Jekory, Jekorey, Jekoree

Jediah (Hebrew) God knows all
Jedia, Jedaiah, Jediya, Jediyah, Jedya, Jedyah,
Jedi, Jedie, Jedy, Jedey, Jedee

Jedidiah (Hebrew) One who is loved by God
Jedadiah, Jedediah, Jed, Jedd, Jedidiya,
Jedidiyah, Jedadia, Jedadiya, Jedadiyah,
Jededia, Jedediya, Jedediyah

Jedrek (Polish) Having great strength
Jedrec, Jedreck, Jedrik, Jedrick, Jedric, Jedrus

Jeevan (Hindi) Full of life
Jeeven, Jeevon, Jeevin, Jeevyn

Jefferson (English) The son of Jeffrey
Jeferson, Jeffersun, Jefersun, Jeffersen, Jefersen

Jeffrey (German) A man of peace
Jefery, Jeff, Jefferey, Jefferies, Jeffery, Jeffree,
Jeffries, Jeffry, Jeffy, Jefry, Jeoffroi, Joffre,
Joffrey

Jehoiakim (Hebrew) God will judge
Jehoioachim, Jehoiakin, Jehoiachim,
Jehoiachin

Jehu (Hebrew) He is God
Jayhu, Jahu, Jehue, Jeyhu, Jeyhue, Jayhue,
Jahue, Jehew, Jayhew, Jeyhew, Jahew

Jela (Swahili) During birth, the father suffered
Jelah, Jella, Jellah

Jelani (African) One who is mighty; strong
Jelanie, Jelany, Jelaney, Jelanee, Jelanea

Jem (English) Form of Jacob, meaning "he who supplants"
Jemm, Jemme, Jemmi, Jemmie, Jemmy,
Jemmey, Jemmee

Jemonde (French) A man of the world
Jemond, Jemont, Jemonte

Jenci (Hungarian) A wellborn man
Jencie, Jency, Jencey, Jencee, Jencea, Jensi,
Jensie, Jensy, Jensey, Jensee, Jensea

Jenda (Czech) Form of John, meaning "God is gracious"
Jendah, Jinda, Jindah, Jynda, Jyndah

Jengo (African) One who has a ruddy complexion
Jengoe, Jengow, Jengowe

Jenkin (Flemish) Little John; son of John
Jenkins, Jenkyn, Jenkyns

Jennett (Hindi) One who is heaven-sent
Jenett, Jennet, Jenet, Jennitt, Jenitt, Jennit,
Jenit

Jennings (English) A descendant of John
Jenning, Jennyngs, Jennyng

Jens (Scandinavian) Form of John, meaning "God is gracious"
Jensen, Jenson, Jensin, Jennsen, Jennson,
Jennsin, Jenns

Jenski (English) One who has come home
Jenskie, Jensky, Jenskey, Jenskee, Jenskea

Jep (American) An easygoing man
Jepp, Jeppe

Jephthah (Hebrew) God will judge
Jephtha, Jephtah, Jephta

Jerald (English) Form of Gerald, meaning "one who rules with the spear"
Jeraldo, Jerold, Jerrald, Jerrold

Jerard (English) Form of Gerard, meaning "one who is mighty with a spear"
Jerrard, Jerardo, Jerrardo

⊙ **Jeremiah** (Hebrew) One who is exalted by
● the Lord
Jeremia, Jeremias, Jeremija, Jeremiya,
Jeremyah, Jeramiah, Jeramia

Jeremy (Hebrew) Form of Jeremiah, meaning "one who is exalted by the Lord"
Jemmie, Jemmy, Jeramee, Jeramey, Jeramie,
Jeramy, Jerami, Jereme, Jeremie, Jeromy,
Jeremey, Jeremi, Jeremee, Jeromey, Jeromi,
Jeromie, Jeromee

Jeriah (Hebrew) God has seen
Jeria, Jera, Jerah, Jerra, Jerrah

Jericho (Arabic) From the city of the moon
Jericko, Jeriko, Jerikko, Jerico, Jericco, Jerycho,
Jeryko, Jeryco, Jerychko, Jerrico, Jerricho,
Jerriko, Jerricko

Jermaine (French / Latin) A man from Germany / one who is brotherly
Jermain, Jermane, Jermayne, Jermin, Jermyn,
Jermayn, Jermaen, Jermaene, Jerma, Jermi,
Jermie, Jermy, Jermey

Jermon (American) One who is dependable
Jermonn, Jermun, Jermunn

Jerncy (Slavic) A humorous man
Jerny, Jerne, Jerni, Jernie, Jernee, Jernea

Jero (American) One who is cheerful
Jeroh, Jerro, Jerroh

Jeroen (Arabic) A holy man

Jerome (Greek) Of the sacred name
Jairome, Jeroen, Jeromo, Jeronimo, Jerrome, Jerom, Jerolyn, Jerolin

Jerone (English) Filled with hope
Jerohn, Jeron, Jerrone

Jerram (Hebrew) Form of Jeremiah, meaning "one who is exalted by the Lord"
Jeram, Jerrem, Jerem, Jerrym, Jerym

Jerrick (English) A strong and gifted ruler
Jerack, Jereck, Jerek, Jeric, Jerick, Jerric, Jerrik, Jerriq

Jerry (Greek) A holy man; having great strength
Jerri, Jerrie, Jerrey, Jerree, Jerre, Jerrye, Jere

Jersey (English) From a section of England; one who is calm
Jersy, Jersi, Jersie, Jersee, Jersea

Jerzy (Polish) One who works the earth; a farmer
Jerzey, Jerzi, Jerzie, Jerzee, Jerzea

Jeshurun (Hebrew) A righteous man

Jesimiel (Hebrew) The Lord establishes
Jessimiel

Jesse (Hebrew) God exists; a gift from God; God sees all
Jess, Jessey, Jesiah, Jessie, Jessy, Jese, Jessi, Jessee, Jessamine, Jessamyne, Jesmar, Jessmar, Jesmarr, Jessmarr

Jesuan (Spanish) One who is devout

❂ **Jesus** (Hebrew) God is my salvation
Jesous, Jesues, Jesús

Jethro (Hebrew) Man of abundance
Jethroe, Jethrow, Jethrowe, Jeth, Jethe

Jeton (French) A feisty man
Jetan, Jetun, Jetaun, Jetawn

Jett (English) Resembling the jet-black lustrous gemstone
Jet, Jette, Jete, Jettie, Jetty, Jetti, Jettey, Jettee, Jettea, Jettal, Jetal, Jetahl, Jettale

Jevon (American) A spirited man
Jeavan, Jeaven, Jeavin, Jevan, Jeven, Jevin, Jevvan, Jevven, Jevvin, Jevvyn

Ji (Chinese) One who is organized

Jibben (American) A lively man
Jiben, Jybben, Jyben

Jibril (Arabic) Refers to the archangel Gabriel
Jibryl, Jibri, Jibrie, Jibry, Jibrey, Jibree

Jie (Chinese) One who is pure; chaste

Jignesh (Indian) A curious man
Jigneshe, Jygnesh, Jygneshe

Jiles (American) The shield bearer
Jyles

Jilt (Dutch) One who has money
Jylt, Jilte, Jylte

Jim (English) Form of James, meaning "he who supplants"
Jimi, Jimmee, Jimmey, Jimmie, Jimmy, Jimmi, Jimbo

Jimiyu (African) One who is born during a dry period
Jimiyue, Jimiyoo, Jimiyou

Jimoh (African) Born on a Friday
Jymoh, Jimo, Jymo

Jin (Chinese / Korean) The golden one / one who is treasured
Jyn

Jinan (Arabic) From the garden of paradise
Jynan

Jindrich (Czech) A great ruler
Jindrick, Jindrik, Jindric, Jindrisek, Jindrousek, Jindra

Jing (Chinese) One who is flawless
Jyng

Jirair (Armenian) A hardworking man
Jiraire, Jirayr, Jirayre, Jiraer, Jiraere, Jirare

Jiri (African / Czech) From the fruitful forest / one who works the earth; a farmer
Jirie, Jiry, Jirey, Jiree, Jirea, Jirka, Jira, Jirisek, Jiricek

Jiro (Japanese) The second-born son
Jyro, Jeero, Jearo

Jivan (Hindi) A giver of life
Jivin, Jiven, Jivyn, Jivon

Joab (Hebrew) To praise God
Joabe

Joachim (Hebrew) One who is established by God; God will judge
Jachim, Jakim, Joacheim, Joaquim, Joaquin, Josquin, Joakim, Joakeen, Jokim, Jokin

Joash (Hebrew) God has given
Joashe

Job (Hebrew) One who is persecuted; afflicted
Johb, Jobe, Joby, Jobey, Jobi, Jobee, Jobie, Jobson, Jobsun

Joben (Japanese) One who enjoys being clean
Joban, Jobin, Jobyn, Jobun, Jobon

Jocheved (Hebrew) The glory of God

Jody (English) Form of Joseph, meaning "God will add"
Jodey, Jodi, Jodie, Jodee, Jodea

Joe (English) Form of Joseph, meaning "God will add"
Jo, Joemar, Jomur, Joey, Joie, Joee, Joeye

Joed (Hebrew) God is witness

Joel (Hebrew) Jehovah is God; God is willing
Joell

Johar (Hindi) As precious as a jewel
Joharr, Jahar, Jahara

❶❶ John (Hebrew) God is gracious; in the Bible, one of the Apostles
Jian, Jianni, Joannes, Joao, Jahn, Johan, Johanan, Johann, Johannes, Johnn, Johon, Johnie, Johnnie, Johnny, Jon, Jona, Jonn, Jonnie, Jonny, Jonte, Johntay, Johnte, Jontae, Jontell, Jontez, Jaan, Joen, Jonni

Johnavon (American) From God's river
Jonavon, Johnaven, Jonaven

Johnson (English) The son of John
Jonson, Johnsun, Jonsun, Johston, Johnstun, Jonstun, Jonston

Joji (Japanese) Form of George, meaning "one who works the earth; a farmer"
Jojie, Jojy, Jojey, Jojee

Jokull (Scandinavian) From the glacier
Jokule, Jokulle, Jokul

Jolon (Native American) From the valley of dead oak trees
Jolun, Jolin, Jolyn, Jolen, Jolan

Jomei (Japanese) One who spreads light
Jomay, Jomaye, Jomai, Jomae

Jomo (African) One who works the earth; a farmer
Jomoe, Jomow, Jomowe

Jonah (Hebrew) Resembling a dove; in the Bible, the man swallowed by a whale
Joenah, Jonas, Jonasco, Joah

❶ Jonathan (Hebrew) A gift of God
Johnathan, Johnathon, Jonathon, Jonatan, Jonaton, Jonathen, Johnathen, Jonaten, Jonathyn, Johnathyn, Jonatyn

Jonco (Slavic) Form of John, meaning "God is gracious"
Jonko, Joncko, Joncco, Jonkko

Jones (English) From the family of John

Joo-chan (Korean) One who praises the lord

Jorah (Hebrew) God has reproached
Jora

Joram (Hebrew) Jehovah is exalted
Jorim, Jorem, Jorom, Jorum, Jorym

❶❶ Jordan (Hebrew) Of the down-flowing river; in the Bible, the river where Jesus was baptized
Johrdan, Jordain, Jordaine, Jordane, Jordanke, Jordann, Jorden, Jordaen, Jordaene, Jordayn, Jordayne, Jourdayne, Jordenn, Jordie, Jordin, Jordyn, Jordynn, Jorey, Jori, Jorie, Jorrdan, Jorry, Jourdan, Jourdain, Jourdayn, Jourdaen, Jourdaene, Jordell, Jordel, Jordy, Jordey, Jordi, Jory, Jordon, Jourdano, Jourdon

Jordison (American) The son of Jordan
Jordyson, Jordisun, Jordysun, Jordisen, Jordysen

Joren (Scandinavian) Form of George, meaning "one who works the earth; a farmer"
Joran, Jorian, Jorien, Joron, Jorun, Joryn, Jorin, Jorn, Jorne, Joergen, Joris, Jorma

Jorge (Spanish) Form of George, meaning "one who works the earth; a farmer"
Jorje

Jorn (German) A vigilant watchman
Jorne

Jorryn (American) Loved by God
Jorrin, Jorren, Jorran, Jorron, Jorrun

⊙ **Jose** (Spanish) Form of Joseph, meaning "God will add"
José, Joseito, Joselito

⊙ **Joseph** (Hebrew) God will add
Jessop, Jessup, Joop, Joos, Josef, Josep, Josip, Josif, Josephe, Josephus, Joss, Josslin, Joslin, Joszef, Jozef, Joseba, Joosef, Joosep, Jooseppi, Joosepe, Joosepi, Jopie, Jopi, Josu, Joza, Jozka

⊙ **Joshua** (Hebrew) God is salvation
Josh, Joshuah, Josua, Josue, Joushua, Jozua, Joshwa, Joshuwa, Joshuam, Joshyam, Joshka, Josha

⊙ **Josiah** (Hebrew) God will help
Josia, Josias, Joziah, Jozia, Jozias

Jotham (Hebrew) God is perfect

Journey (American) One who likes to travel
Journy, Journi, Journie, Journee, Journye, Journea

Jovan (Latin) One who is majestic; in mythology, another name for Jupiter, the supreme god
Jeovani, Jeovanni, Jeovany, Jovani, Jovann, Jovanni, Jovanny, Jovany, Jove, Jovi, Jovin, Jovito, Jovon, Jov

Joyner (English) One who works with wood; a carpenter
Joiner

⊙ **Juan** (Spanish) Form of John, meaning "God is gracious"
Juanito, Juwan, Jwan

Jubal (Hebrew) Resembling a ram
Juball, Joubal, Jouball, Joobal, Jooball

Jubilo (Spanish) One who is rejoicing
Jubylo, Jubilio, Jubylio, Jubileo, Jubyleo

Judah (Hebrew) One who praises God
Juda, Jude, Judas, Judsen, Judson, Judd, Jud, Judule

Judge (English) One who sits in judgment of others
Judg, Juge

Juha (Hebrew) A gift from God
Juhah, Juka, Jukah, Jukka, Jukkah, Juca, Jucah, Jucca, Juccah

⊙ **Julian** (Greek) The child of Jove; one who is youthful
Juliano, Julianus, Julien, Julyan, Julio, Jolyon, Jullien, Julen, Julean, Jilliann, Jillian, Jilian

Julius (Greek) The child of Jove; one who is youthful
Julis, Jule, Jules, Julious, Julios, 38899, Juli, Julee, Juley, Juleus, Junius

Juma (African) Born on a Friday
Jumah

Jumaane (African) Born on a Tuesday

Jumbe (African) Having great strength
Jumbi, Jumbie, Jumby, Jumbey, Jumbee

Jumoke (African) One who is dearly loved
Jumok, Jumoak

Jun (Japanese) One who is obedient

Junaid (Arabic) A warrior
Junaide, Junayd, Junayde, Junade, Junaed, Junaede

June (Latin) One who is youthful; born during the month of June
Junae, Junel, Junell, Juin

Jung (Korean) A righteous man

Junior (English) The younger one
Junyor, Junyer, Junier

Juniper (Latin) Resembling the evergreen shrub with berries
Junyper, Junipyre, Junypyre

Jupiter (Latin) In mythology, the supreme god
Jupyter, Juppiter, Juppyter

Jurass (American) Resembling a dinosaur
Juras, Jurassic, Jurassik, Jurasic, Jurasik

Jurgen (German) Form of George, meaning "one who works the earth; a farmer"
Jorgen, Jurgin, Jorgin, Jurgyn, Jorgyn

Juri (Slavic) Form of George, meaning "one who works the earth; a farmer"
Jurie, Jurey, Juree, Jurea, Jury, Jurg, Jeirgif, Jaris

Justice (English) One who upholds moral rightness and fairness
Justyce, Justiss, Justyss, Justis, Justus, Justise

○ **Justin** (Latin) One who is just and upright
○ *Joost, Justain, Justan, Just, Juste, Justen, Justino, Justo, Justyn*

Justinian (Latin) An upright ruler
Justinien, Justinious, Justinius, Justinios, Justinas, Justinus

Juvenal (Latin) A young boy
Juvinal, Juvenel, Juvinel, Juventino, Juvy, Juvey, Juvee, Juvi, Juvie

k

Kaaria (African) A wise, soft-spoken man
Karia, Kaarya, Karya, Kaariya, Kariya

Kabaka (African) A king
Kabakka, Kabaaka

Kabili (African) A possession
Kabilie, Kabily, Kabiley, Kabilee, Kabileigh, Kabilea

Kabir (Indian) A spiritual leader
Kabeer, Kabear, Kabier, Kabeir, Kabyr, Kabar

Kabonero (African) A sign or symbol
Kabonerio, Kabonereo

Kabonesa (African) One who is born during difficult times

Kabos (Hebrew) A swindler
Kaboes

Kacancu (African) The firstborn child
Kacancue, Kakancu, Kakancue, Kacanku, Kacankue

Kacey (Irish) A vigilant man; one who is alert
Kacy, Kacee, Kacea, Kaci, Kacie, Kasey, Kasy, Kasi, Kasie, Kasee, Kasea, Kaycey, Kaycy, Kayci, Kaycie, Kaycee, Kaicey, Kaicy, Kaici, Kaicie, Kaicee, Kaysey, Kaysy, Kaysi, Kaysie, Kaysee, Kaisey, Kaisy, Kaisi, Kaisie, Kaisee

Kachada (Native American) A white-skinned man

Kade (Scottish) From the wetlands
Kaid, Kaide, Kayd, Kayde, Kaed, Kaede, Kady, Kadey, Kadee, Kadea, Kadi, Kadie

○ **Kaden** (Arabic) A beloved companion
*Kadan, Kadin, Kadon, Kaidan, Kaiden, Kaidin, Kaidon, Kaydan, **Kayden**, Kaydin, Kaydon, Kaeden, Kaedan, Kaedin, Kaedon*

Kadir (Arabic) One who is capable; one who is competent
Kadeer, Kadear, Kadier, Kadeir, Kadyr

Kadmiel (Hebrew) One who stands before God
Kamiell

Kado (Japanese) From the gateway
Kadoe, Kadow, Kadowe

Kaelan (Gaelic) A mighty warrior
Kaelen, Kaelin, Kaelyn, Kalan, Kalen, Kalin, Kalyn, Kaylan, Kaylin, Kaylen, Kaylin, Kailan, Kailen, Kailin, Kailyn, Kaele, Kael, Kail, Kaile, Kale, Kayl, Kayle

Kaelem (American) An honest man
Kalem, Kaylem, Kailem

Kaemon (Japanese) Full of joy; one who is right-handed
Kamon, Kaymon, Kaimon

Kafele (Egyptian) A son to die for
Kafel, Kafell, Kafelle

Kafi (African) A quiet and well-behaved boy
Kafie, Kafy, Kafey, Kafee, Kafea

Kafka (Czech) Resembling a bird
Kofka

Kaga (Native American) One who chronicles
Kagah, Kagga, Kaggah

Kagen (Irish) A fiery man; a thinker
Kaigen, Kagan, Kaigan, Kaygen, Kaygan, Kaegen, Kaegan

Kahale (Hawaiian) A homebody
Kahail, Kahaile, Kahayl, Kahayle, Kahael, Kahaele

Kaherdin (English) In Arthurian legend, the brother of Isolde
Kaherden, Kaherdan, Kaherdyn

Kahlil (Arabic) A beloved friend
Kahleil, Kahlyl, Kahleel, Kalil, Kaleil, Kalyl, Kaleel, Khalil, Khaleil, Khalyl, Khaleel, Kahil, Kaheil, Kahyl, Kaheel

Kahn (Hebrew) A priest
Kan, Khan

Kahoku (Hawaiian) Resembling a star
Kahokue, Kahokoo, Kahokou

Kaholo (Hawaiian) A running boy

Kai (Hawaiian / Welsh / Greek) Of the sea / the keeper of the keys / of the earth
Kye, Keh

Kaihe (Hawaiian) One who wields a spear
Kayhe, Kaehe, Kaihi, Kayhi, Kaehi, Kaihie, Kayhie, Kaehie

Kaikara (African) God

Kaikura (African) Resembling a ground squirrel

Kaila (Hawaiian) A stylish man
Kayla, Kaela

Kailas (Hindi) The home of Lord Shiva

Kaili (Hawaiian) A god
Kailie, Kaily, Kailey, Kailee, Kaileigh, Kailea

Kaimi (Hawaiian) The seeker
Kaimie, Kaimy, Kaimey, Kaimee, Kaimea

Kain (Hebrew) The acquirer

Kaipo (Hawaiian) One who embraces others; a sweetheart
Kaypo, Kaepo, Kapo

Kairo (African) From the city of Cairo

Kaiser (German) An imperial ruler
Keyser, Kaizer, Keyzer, Kyser, Kyzer, Kiser, Kizer

Kaj (Scandinavian) Of the earth

Kajika (Native American) One who walks silently
Kajica, Kajicka, Kajyka, Kajyca, Kajycka, Kijika, Kyjika

Kala (Hawaiian) Son of the sun
Kalah, Kalla, Kallah

Kalama (Hawaiian) A source of light
Kalam, Kalame

Kalani (Hawaiian) From the heavens
Kalanie, Kalany, Kalaney, Kalanee, Kaloni, Kalonie, Kalonee, Kalony, Kaloney, Kalonea, Keilani, Kalanea

Kaleb (Hebrew) Resembling an aggressive dog
Kaileb, Kaeleb, Kayleb, Kalob, Kailob, Kaelob, Kaylob, Kalb

Kalei (Hawaiian) An attendant of the king

Kalevi (Finnish) A hero
Kalevie, Kalevy, Kalevey, Kalevea, Kalevee

Kali (Polynesian) One who provides comfort
Kalie, Kaly, Kaley, Kalee, Kaleigh, Kalea

Kalidas (Hindi) A poet or musician; a servant of Kali
Kalydas

Kaliq (Arabic) One who is creative
Kaleeq, Kaleaq, Kalieq, Kaleiq, Kalyq, Kaleek, Kaleak, Kaliek, Kaleik, Kalik, Kalyk

Kalki (Indian) Resembling a white horse
Kalkie, Kalky, Kalkey, Kalkee, Kalkea

Kalkin (Hindi) The tenth-born child
Kalkyn, Kalken, Kalkan, Kalkon, Kalkun

Kallen (Greek) A handsome man
Kallin, Kallyn, Kallon, Kallun, Kallan

Kalman (French) Having great strength
Kalmann, Kalle, Kalli, Kallie, Kally, Kalley, Kallee, Kallea

Kalogeros (Greek) One who ages well

Kaloosh (Armenian) A blessed birth
Kalooshe, Kaloush, Kaloushe

Kalunga (African) One who is alert and watchful

Kalvin (English) The little bald one
Kalvyn, Kalvon, Kalvan, Kalven, Kalvun

Kalyan (Indian) One who is happy and prosperous

Kamaka (Hawaiian) Having a handsome face

Kamal (Arabic) The perfect man
Kamall, Kamaal, Kamil, Kameel, Kameal, Kameil, Kamiel, Kamyl

Kamau (African) A quiet warrior

Kamden (English) From the winding valley
Kamdun, Kamdon, Kamdan, Kamdin, Kamdyn

Kame (African) From a desolate land
Kaim, Kaime, Kaym, Kayme, Kaem, Kaeme

Kameron (English) Having a crooked nose
Kamerin, Kameryn, Kamrin, Kamron, Kamryn, Kamren, Kameren, Kamran, Kameran, Kam

Kami (Hindi) A loving man
Kamie, Kamy, Kamey, Kamee, Kamea, Kamilyn, Kamilin

Kamon (American) Resembling an alligator
Kaman, Kaymon, Kayman, Kaimon, Kaiman, Kaemon, Kaeman

Kamuzu (African) One who heals others
Kamuzue, Kamuezue, Kamouzu, Kamouzou

Kamwimbile (African) One who praises God

Kana (Hawaiian) In mythology, a demigod who could transform into rope

Kanad (Indian) An ancient
Kaned, Kanid, Kanyd

Kanak (Indian) The golden one
Kanac, Kanack, Kanek, Kanec, Kaneck

Kanan (Indian) From the garden
Kanen, Kanin, Kanyn, Kanon, Kanun

Kanaye (Japanese) A zealous man
Kanay, Kanui, Kanae

Kance (American) An attractive man
Kanse, Kaince, Kainse, Kaynce, Kaynse, Kaence, Kaense

Kane (Gaelic) The little warrior
Kayn, Kayne, Kaen, Kaene, Kahan, Kahane

Kanelo (African) Enough
Kaneloh, Kanello, Kanelloh

Kang (Korean) A healthy man

Kanga (Native American) Resembling a raven
Kange, Kangee, Kangea, Kangy, Kangey, Kangi, Kangie

Kaniel (Hebrew) Supported by the Lord
Kaniell, Kanielle, Kanyel, Kanyell, Kanyelle

Kannon (Japanese) The Buddhist deity of mercy
Kannun, Kannen, Kannan, Kannin, Kannyn

Kano (Japanese) A powerful man
Kanoe, Kanoh

Kanoa (Hawaiian) One who is free

Kansas (Native American) Of the south wind people; from the state of Kansas

Kant (German) A philosopher
Kante

Kantrava (Indian) Resembling a roaring animal

Kantu (Indian) Filled with joy
Kantue, Kantou, Kantoo

Kanva (Indian) From the river; a sage

Kanvar (Indian) A young prince
Kanvarr

Kaori (Japanese) Having a pleasant scent
Kaorie, Kaory, Kaorey, Kaoree, Kaorea

Kaper (American) One who is capricious
Kahper, Kapar, Kahpar

Kapila (Hindi) A prophet
Kapyla, Kapil, Kapyl

Kaplony (Hungarian) Resembling a tiger
Kaploney, Kaploni, Kaplonie, Kaplonee, Kaplonea

Kapono (Hawaiian) A righteous man

Karan (Greek) One who is pure; chaste

Karcher (German) A handsome blonde-haired man
Karchar, Karchir, Karchyr, Karchor, Karchur

Karcsi (French) A strong manly man
Karcsie, Karcsy, Karcsey, Karcsee, Karcsea

Kardal (Arabic) Of the mustard seed
Kardall

Kardos (Hungarian) One who wields a sword

Kare (Scandinavian) An enormous man
Kair, Kaire, Kayr, Kayre, Kaer, Kaere

Kareem (Arabic) A generous man
Kaream, Karim, Karym, Kariem, Kareim, Karam, Kharim, Khareem, Khaream, Khariem, Khareim, Kharym

Kari (Norse) Of the wind/one with curly hair
Karie, Kary, Karey, Karee, Karea

Karif (Arabic) Born during autumn
Kareef, Kareaf, Karief, Kareif, Karyf

Karl (German) A free man
Karel, Karlan, Karle, Karlens, Karli, Karlin, Karlo, Karlos, Karlton, Karrel, Karol, Karoly, Karson, Kaarl, Kaarlo, Karlis, Karlys, Karlitis

Karman (Gaelic) The lord of the manor
Karmen, Karmin, Karmyn, Karmon, Karmun

Karmel (Hebrew) From the garden or vineyard
Karmeli, Karmelli, Karmelo, Karmello, Karmi, Karmie, Karmee, Karmy, Karmey, Karmelie, Karmellie, Karmely, Karmelly, Karmeley, Karmelley

Karolek (Russian) A small strong man
Karolec, Karoleck

Karr (Scandinavian) From the marshland
Kerr, Kiarr

Karsa (Hungarian) Resembling a falcon
Karsah

Karsten (Greek) The anointed one
Karstan, Karstin, Karstyn, Karston, Karstun

Kartal (Hungarian) Resembling an eagle
Kartall

Kartar (Indian) A master

Karu (Indian) One who shows compassion
Karue, Karun, Karuen, Karune, Karunal, Karunakar

Karunamay (Indian) Surrounded by light
Karunamaye, Karunamai, Karunamae

Kasar (Indian) Resembling a lion
Kasarr

Kasch (German) Resembling a blackbird
Kasche, Kass, Kas, Kasse

Kaseko (African) One who is mocked

Kasem (Asian) Filled with joy

Kasen (Basque) Protected by a helmet
Kasin, Kasyn, Kason, Kasun, Kasan

Kashka (African) A friendly man
Kashkah

Kashvi (Indian) A shining man
Kashvie, Kashvy, Kashvey, Kashvee, Kashvea

Kasib (Arabic) One who is fertile
Kaseeb, Kaseab, Kasieb, Kaseib, Kasyb

Kasim (Arabic) One who is divided
Kassim, Kaseem, Kasseem, Kaseam, Kasseam, Kasym, Kassym

Kasimir (Slavic) One who demands peace
Kasimeer, Kasimear, Kasimier, Kasimeir, Kasimyr, Kaz, Kazimierz, Kazimir, Kazmer, Kazimeirz, Kazimeerz, Kazimearz, Kazimyrz

Kaspar (Persian) The keeper of the treasure
Kasper, Kaspir, Kaspyr, Kaspor, Kaspur, Kasbar, Kasber, Kansbar, Kansber

Kassa (African) One who has been compensated

Kassidy (English) A curly-haired man
Kassidey, Kassidi, Kassidie, Kassidee, Kasidy, Kasidey, Kasidi, Kasidie, Kasidee, Kassidea, Kasidea

Kasumi (Japanese) From the mist
Kasumie, Kasume, Kasumy, Kasumey, Kasumee, Kasumea

Kateb (Arabic) A writer

Kathan (American) Form of Nathan, meaning "a gift from God"
Kaithan, Kathun, Kathon, Kathen, Kaithun, Kaithon, Kaithen, Kaethan, Kaethun, Kaethon, Kaethen, Kaythan, Kaythun, Kaython, Kaythen

Kato (Latin / African) A man of good judgment / the second born of twins
Kaeto, Kaito, Kayto

Katungi (African) A wealthy man
Katungie, Katungy, Katungey, Katungee, Katungea

Katura (African) To ease the burden

Katzir (Hebrew) The harvester
Katzyr, Katzeer, Katzear, Katzier, Katzeir

Kauai (Hawaiian) From the garden island
Kawai

Kaufman (German) A merchant
Kauffman, Kaufmann, Kauffmann, Kofman, Koffman, Kofmann, Koffmann

Kaushal (Indian) One who is skilled
Kaushall, Koshal, Koshall

Kavan (Irish) A handsome man
Kavin, Kaven, Kavyn, Kavon, Kavun, Kayvan, Kayven, Kayvon, Kayvun, Kayvin, Kayvyn

Kavanagh (Gaelic) A follower of Kevin
Kavanau, Kavanaugh, Kavana

Kavi (Hindi) A poetic man
Kavie, Kavy, Kavey, Kavee, Kavea, Kavindra, Kavian, Kavien, Kaviraj, Kavyanand

Kawaii (Hawaiian) Of the water

Kay (Welsh) Filled with happiness; rejoicing
Kaye, Kae

Kayin (African) A long-awaited child
Kayen, Kayan, Kayon, Kayun

Kayonga (African) Of the ash
Kayunga

Kazan (Greek) A creative man
Kazen, Kazin, Kazyn, Kazon, Kazun

Kazi (African) A hardworking man
Kazie, Kazy, Kazey, Kazee, Kazea

Kazim (Arabic) An even-tempered man
Kazeem, Kazeam, Kaziem, Kazeim, Kazym

Kazuo (Japanese) A peaceful man

Keahi (Hawaiian) Of the flames
Keahie, Keahy, Keahey, Keahee, Keahea

Kealoha (Hawaiian) From the bright path
Keeloha, Kieloha

Kean (Gaelic / English) A warrior / one who is sharp
Keane, Keen, Keene, Kein, Keine, Keyn, Keyne, Kien, Kiene

Keandre (American) One who is thankful
Kiandre, Keandray, Kiandray, Keandrae, Kiandrae, Keandrai, Kiandrai

Keanu (Hawaiian) Of the mountain breeze
Keanue, Kianu, Kianue, Keanoo, Kianoo, Keanou, Kianou

Kearn (Irish) Having dark features
Kearne, Kern, Kerne

Kearney (Irish) The victor
Kearny, Kearni, Kearnie, Kearnee, Kearnea, Karney, Karny, Karni, Karnie, Karnee, Karnea

Keaton (English) From the town of hawks
Keatun, Keeton, Keetun, Keyton, Keytun

Keawe (Hawaiian) A lovable young man

Keb (African) Of the earth
Kebb

Kecalf (American) One who is inventive
Keecalf, Keacalf, Keicalf, Kiecalf, Keycalf

Kedar (Arabic) A powerful man
Keder, Kedir, Kedyr, Kadar, Kader, Kadir, Kadyr

Kedem (Hebrew) An old soul
Kedam, Kedim, Kedym, Kedom, Kedum

Kedrick (English) A gift of splendor
Kedryck, Kedrik, Kedryk, Kedric, Kedryc, Keddrick, Keddrik, Keddric

Keefe (Gaelic) A handsome and beloved man
Keef, Keafe, Keaf, Keif, Keife, Kief, Kiefe

Keegan (Gaelic) A small and fiery man
Kegan, Keigan, Kiegan, Keagan, Keagen, Keegen, Keeghan, Keaghan

Keelan (Gaelic) A slender man
Kelan, Kealan, Keallan, Keallin, Keilan, Keillan, Keelin, Keellan, Keellin, Keeland, Kealand, Keiland

Keely (Irish) A handsome man
Keeley, Keeli, Keelie, Keelee, Keeleigh, Kealey, Kealy, Keali, Kealie, Kealee, Kealeigh

Keenan (Gaelic) Of an ancient family
Keenen, Keenon, Kennan, Kennon, Kienan, Kienen, Keanan, Keanen, Keanon, Kienon, Keandre

Keeney (American) Having a clear and sharp mind
Keeny, Keeni, Keenie, Keenee, Keaney, Keany, Keani, Keanie, Keanee

Keerthi (Indian) Having fame and glory
Kearthi, Keerthie, Kearthie, Keerthy, Kearthy, Keerthey, Kearthey

Kefir (Hebrew) Resembling a young lion
Kefyr, Kefeer, Kefear, Kefier, Kefeir

Keiji (Japanese) A cautious ruler
Keijie, Keijy, Keijey, Keijee, Kayji, Kayjie, Kayjee, Kayjy, Kayjey

Keir (Gaelic) Having dark features
Keer, Kear, Keire, Keere, Keare, Keirer, Kearer, Keirer, Kerer

Keita (African) A worshiper

Keitaro (Japanese) One who is blessed
Kaytaro

Keith (Scottish) Man from the forest
Keithe, Keath, Keathe, Kieth, Kiethe, Keyth, Keythe, Keithen, Keethan, Keathen, Keythen

Kekipi (Hawaiian) A rebel
Kekipie, Kekipy, Kekipey, Kekipee, Kekipea

Kekoa (Hawaiian) A warrior
Kekowa

Kelby (Gaelic) From the farm near the spring
Kelbey, Kelbe, Kelbee, Kelbea, Kelbi, Kelbie

Kele (Native American) Resembling a sparrow hawk

Keleman (Hungarian) One who is kind and gentle
Kelemen, Kelemin, Kelemyn, Kelemon, Kelemun, Kellman, Kellmen, Kellmin, Kellmyn, Kellmon, Kellmun, Kelman, Kelmen, Kelmin, Kelmyn, Kelmon, Kelmun

Kelii (Hawaiian) The chief

Kelile (African) My protector
Kelyle

Kell (Norse) From the spring
Kelle, Kel

Kellach (Irish) One who suffers strife during battle
Kelach, Kellagh, Kelagh, Keallach

Kelleher (Irish) A loving husband
Keleher, Kellehar, Kelehar, Kellehir, Kelehir, Kellehyr, Kelehyr

Kellen (Gaelic / German) One who is slender / from the swamp
Kelle, Kellan, Kellon, Kellun, Kellin, Kellyn

Keller (German / Celtic) From the cellar / a beloved friend
Kellar, Kellor, Kellur, Kellir, Kellyr

Kelley (Celtic / Gaelic) A warrior / one who defends
Kelly, Kelleigh, Kellee, Kellea, Kelleah, Kelli, Kellie

Kellicka (Latin / Irish) One who is strong-willed / a charming man
Kelicka, Kellika, Kelika, Kellica, Kelica

Kelsey (English) From the island of ships; of the ship's victory
Kelsie, Kelcey, Kelcie, Kelcy, Kellsie, Kelsa, Kelsea, Kelsee, Kelsi, Kelsy, Kellsey, Kelcea, Kelcee

Kelton (English) From the town of keels
Keldon, Kelltin, Kellton, Kelten, Keltin, Keltun, Kelltun, Keltyn, Kelltyn

Kelvin (English) A friend of ships; a man of the river
Kellven, Kelvan, Kelven, Kelvon, Kelvyn, Kelwin, Kelwinn, Kelwinne, Kelwyn, Kelwynn, Kelwynne, Kelwen, Kelwine, Kelwenn, Kelwenne

Kelvis (American) One who is ambitious
Kelviss, Kelvys, Kelvyss, Kellvis, Kellvys

Kemal (Turkish) One who receives the highest honor
Kemall

Keme (Native American) A secretive man

Kemen (Spanish) Having great strength
Keman, Kemin, Kemyn, Kemon, Kemun

Kemenes (Hungarian) One who makes furnaces

Kemp (English) The champion
Kempe, Kempi, Kempie, Kempy, Kempey, Kempee

Kemper (American) One who is noble
Kempar, Kempir, Kempyr, Kempor, Kempur

Kempton (English) From the champion's town
Kemptun

Kemuel (Hebrew) God's helper

Ken (English / Japanese) Form of Kenneth, meaning "born of the fire; an attractive man" / one who is strong and healthy
Kenny, Kenney, Kenni, Kennie, Kennee

Kenan (Hebrew) One who acquires
Kenen, Kenin, Kenyn, Kenon, Kenun

Kenaz (Hebrew) A bright man
Kenez, Kenaaz

Kendall (Welsh) From the royal valley
Kendal, Kendale, Kendel, Kendell, Kendill, Kendle, Kendyl, Kendyll, Kendhal, Kendhall

Kendan (English) Having great strength
Kenden, Kendin, Kendyn, Kendon, Kendun

Kende (Hungarian) One who is honored

Kendi (African) One who is much loved
Kendie, Kendy, Kendey, Kendee, Kendea

Kendis (American) One who is pure; chaste
Kendiss, Kendys, Kendyss

Kendrew (Scottish) A warrior
Kendru, Kendrue

Kendrick (English / Gaelic) A royal ruler / the champion
Kendric, Kendricks, Kendrik, Kendrix, Kendryck, Kenrick, Kenrik, Kenricks, Kendryk, Kendryc, Kenric, Kendriek, Kendryek, Kenrich, Kendrich, Kenriek, Kenryk

Kenelm (English) Of the brave helmet
Kenhelm

Kenji (Japanese) A smart second son; one who is vigorous
Kenjie, Kenjy, Kenjey, Kenjee, Kenjiro

Kenley (English) From the king's meadow
Kenly, Kenlee, Kenleigh, Kenleu, Kenleah, Kenli, Kenlie

Kenn (Welsh) Of the bright waters

Kennard (English) Of the brave or royal guard
Kennerd, Kennaird, Kennward, Kenard, Kenerd, Kenward

Kennedy (Gaelic) A helmeted chief
Kennedi, Kennedie, Kennedey, Kennedee, Kennedeu, Kenudie, Kenadi, Kenady, Kenadey, Kenadee, Kenadea, Kennady, Kennadey, Kennadee, Kennadi, Kennadie

Kenner (English) An able-bodied man
Kennar, Kennir, Kennor, Kennur, Kennyr

Kenneth (Irish) Born of the fire; an attractive man
Kennet, Kennett, Kennith, Kennit, Kennitt

Kent (English) From the edge or border
Kentt, Kennt, Kentrell

Kentaro (Japanese) One who is sharp/a big boy

Kentigem (Celtic) A chief
Kentygem, Kentigim, Kentygim

Kentley (English) From the meadow's edge
Kentleigh, Kentlea, Kentleah, Kentlee, Kently, Kentli, Kentlie

Kenton (English) From the king's town
Kentun, Kentan, Kentin, Kenten, Kentyn

Kentucky (Native American) From the land of tomorrow; from the state of Kentucky
Kentucki, Kentuckie, Kentuckey, Kentuckee, Kentuckea

Kenway (English) A brave or royal warrior
Kennway, Kenwaye, Kennwaye

Kenyatta (African) One who is musically talented
Kenyata, Kenyatt, Kenyat

Kenyi (African) A son born after daughters
Kenyie, Kenyee, Kenyea, Kenyey

Kenyon (Gaelic) A blonde-haired man
Kenyun, Kenyan, Kenyen, Kenyin

Kenzie (Gaelic) One who is fair; light-skinned
Kenzi, Kenzy, Kenzey, Kenzee, Kenzea

Keoki (Hawaiian) Form of George, meaning "one who works the earth; a farmer"
Keokie, Keoky, Keokey, Keokee, Keokea

Keola (Hawaiian) Full of life; one who is vibrant

Keon (Irish) Form of John, meaning "God is gracious"
Keyon, Kion, Kiyon, Keoni, Keonie, Keony, Keoney, Keonee, Keonea

Keontay (American) An outrageous man
Keontaye, Keontai, Keontae, Kiontay, Kiontaye, Kiontai, Kiontae

Kepler (German) One who makes hats
Keppler, Kappler, Keppel, Keppeler

Keran (Armenian) A wooden post
Keren, Keron, Kerun, Kerin, Keryn

Kerbasi (Basque) A warrior
Kerbasie, Kerbasee, Kerbasea, Kerbasy, Kerbasey

Kerecsen (Hungarian) Resembling a falcon
Kereksen, Kerecsan, Kereksan, Kerecsin, Kereksin

Kerel (African) One who is forever young
Keral, Keril, Keryl, Kerol, Kerul

Kerem (Turkish / Hebrew) A kind and noble man / from the vineyard

Kerman (French) A man from Germany
Kermen, Kermin, Kermyn, Kermon, Kermun

Kermit (Gaelic) One who is free of envy
Kermyt, Kermot, Kermet, Kermat, Kermut, Kerme, Kerm, Kermi, Kermie, Kermy, Kermey, Kermee

Kernaghan (Gaelic) A victorious man
Kernohan, Kernahan, Kernoghan

Kerrick (English) Under the king's rule
Kerryck, Kerrik, Kerryk, Kerric, Kerryc

Kerry (Gaelic) Having black hair
Kerrey, Kerri, Kerrie, Kerree, Keary, Kearey, Kearee, Keari, Kearie, Keri, Kerie, Kery, Kerey, Keree, Kerrigan, Kerigan

Kers (Indian) Resembling the plant

Kersen (Indonesian) Resembling a cherry
Kersan, Kersin, Kersyn, Kerson, Kersun

Kershet (Hebrew) Of the rainbow

Kert (American) One who enjoys the simple pleasures of life
Kerte

Kerwin (Irish / English) Little dark one / a friend from the swamp
Kerwinn, Kerwinne, Kerwyn, Kerwynn, Kerwynne, Kerwen, Kerwenn, Kerwenne, Kervin, Kervyn, Kirwin, Kirvin, Kirwyn, Kirvyn, Kirwinn, Kirwinne, Kirwynn, Kirwynne, Kirwen, Kirwenn, Kirwenne

Kesegowaase (Native American) One who is swift

Keshawn (American) A friendly man
Keshaun, Keshon, Keyshawn, Keyshaun, Keyshon

Keshi (Indian) A long-haired man
Keshie, Keshey, Keshy, Keshee, Keshea

Kesler (American) An energetic man; one who is independent
Keslar, Keslir, Keslyr, Keslor, Keslur

Keslie (American) Form of Leslie, meaning "from the holly garden; of the gray fortress"
Keslea, Keslee, Kesleigh, Kesley, Kesli, Kesly, Kezlee, Kezley, Kezlie, Kezleigh, Kezli, Kezlea

Kesse (American) An attractive man
Kessee, Kessea, Kessi, Kessie, Kessy, Kessey

Kestejoo (Native American) A slave
Kesteju, Kestejue

Kester (Latin / Gaelic) From the Roman army's camp / a follower of Christ
Kestar, Kestir, Kestyr, Kestor, Kestur

Kestrel (English) One who soars
Kestral, Kestril, Kestryl, Kestrol, Kestrul

Kettil (Swedish) Of the cauldron
Ketil, Keld, Kjeld, Ketti, Kettie, Ketty, Kettey, Kettee, Ketill

Keung (Chinese) A universal spirit

Keval (Indian) One who is pure; chaste
Kevel, Kevil, Kevyl, Kevol, Kevul

Keve (Hungarian) Resembling a pebble

♻ **Kevin** (Gaelic) A beloved and handsome man
Kevyn, Kevan, Keven, Keveon, Kevinn, Kevion, Kevis, Kevon, Kevron, Kevren, Kevran, Kevrun, Kevryn, Kevrin

Kevork (Armenian) One who works the earth; a farmer
Kevorke, Kevorc, Kevorkk, Kevorcc, Kevorck

Khadim (Arabic) A servant of God
Khadeem, Khadym, Khadiem, Khadeim, Khadeam, Kadeem, Kadim, Kadeam, Kadiem, Kadeim

Khairi (Swahili) A kingly man
Khairie, Khairy, Khairey, Khairee, Khairea

Khaldun (Arabic) An eternal soul
Khaldon, Khaldoon, Khaldoun, Khaldune

Khalid (Arabic) One who is immortal
Khaleed, Khalead, Khaleid, Khalied, Khalyd, Khaled

Khalon (American) A strong warrior
Khalun, Khalen, Khalan, Khalin, Khalyn

Khambrel (American) One who is well-spoken
Kambrel, Khambrell, Kambrell

Khamisi (Swahili) Born on a Thursday
Khamisie, Khamisy, Khamisey, Khamisee, Khamisea

Khan (Turkish) Born to royalty; a prince
Khanh

Kharouf (Arabic) Resembling a lamb
Karouf, Kharoufe, Karoufe

Khayri (Arabic) One who is charitable
Khayrie, Khayry, Khayrey, Khayree, Khayrea

Khayyat (Arabic) A tailor
Khayat, Kayyat, Kayat

Khorshed (Persian) Of the sun

Khortdad (Persian) A man of perfection
Khourtdad, Kortdad, Kourtdad

Khouri (Arabic) A spiritual man; a priest
Khourie, Khoury, Khourey, Khouree, Kouri, Kourie, Koury, Kourey, Kouree

Khushi (Indian) Filled with happiness
Khushie, Khushey, Khushy, Khushee

Khuyen (Vietnamese) One who offers advice

Kian (Irish) From an ancient family
Kiann, Kyan, Kyann, Kiyan, Keyan, Kianni, Kiannie, Kianny, Kianney, Kiannee, Kiani, Kianie, Kianey, Kiany, Kianee

Kibbe (Native American) A nocturnal bird
Kybbe

Kibo (African) From the highest moutain peak
Keybo, Keebo, Keabo, Keibo, Kiebo

Kibou (Japanese) Filled with hope
Kybou

Kidd (English) Resembling a young goat
Kid, Kydd, Kyd

Kiefer (German) One who makes barrels
Keefer, Keifer, Kieffer, Kiefner, Kieffner, Kiefert, Kuefer, Kueffner

Kieran (Gaelic) Having dark features; the little dark one
Keiran, Keiron, Kernan, Kieren, Kiernan, Kieron, Kierren, Kierrin, Kierron, Keeran, Keeron, Keernan, Keeren, Kearan, Kearen, Kearon, Kearnan

Kiet (Thai) One who is honored; respected
Kyet, Kiete, Kyete

Kifle (African) My due
Kyfle, Kifel, Kyfel

Kiho (African) Of the fog
Kihoe, Kyho, Kyhoe

Kijana (African) A youthful man
Kyjana

Kildaire (Irish) From county of Kildare
*Kyldaire, Kildare, Kyldare, Kildair, Kyldair,
Killdaire, Kylldaire, Kildayr, Kyldayr,
Kildayre, Kyldayre, Kildaer, Kildaere, Kyldaer,
Kyldaere*

Killian (Gaelic) One who is small and fierce
*Killean, Kilean, Kilian, Killyan, Kilyan,
Kyllian, Kylian*

Kim (Vietnamese) As precious as gold
Kym

Kimane (African) Resembling a large bean
*Kymane, Kimain, Kimaine, Kymain,
Kymaine, Kimaen, Kimaene, Kymaen,
Kymaene, Kimayn, Kimayne, Kymayn,
Kymayne*

Kimathi (African) A determined provider
*Kimathie, Kimathy, Kimathey, Kimathee,
Kymathi, Kymathie, Kymathy, Kymathey,
Kymathee*

Kimball (English) One who leads warriors
Kimbal, Kimbel, Kimbell, Kimble

Kimberly (English) Of the royal fortress
*Kimberley, Kimberli, Kimberlee, Kimberleigh,
Kimberlin, Kimberlyn, Kymberlie, Kymberly,
Kymberlee, Kim, Kimmy, Kimmie, Kimmi,
Kym, Kimber, Kymber, Kimberlie, Kimbra,
Kimbro, Kimbrough, Kinborough, Kimberlea,
Kimberleah, Kymberlea, Kymberleah*

Kimn (English) A great ruler

Kimo (Hawaiian) Form of James, meaning
"he who supplants"
Kymo

Kimoni (African) A great man
*Kimonie, Kimony, Kimoney, Kimonee,
Kymoni, Kymonie, Kymony, Kymoney,
Kymonee*

Kin (Japanese) The golden one
Kyn

Kincaid (Celtic) The leader during battle
*Kincade, Kincayd, Kincayde, Kincaide, Kincaed,
Kincaede, Kinkaid, Kinkaide, Kinkayd,
Kinkayde, Kinkaed, Kinkaede, Kinkade*

Kindin (Basque) The fifth-born child
Kinden, Kindan, Kindyn, Kindon, Kindun

Kindle (American) To set aflame
Kindel, Kyndle, Kyndel

Kinfe (African) Having wings
Kynfe

King (English) The royal ruler
Kyng

Kingman (English) The king's man
Kingmann, Kyngman, Kyngmann

Kingsley (English) From the king's meadow
*Kingsly, Kingsleigh, Kingslea, Kingsleah,
Kingsli, Kingslie, Kingslee, Kinsley, Kinsly,
Kinsleigh, Kinslee, Kinslea, Kinsleah, Kinsli,
Kinslie*

Kingston (English) From the king's town
*Kingstun, Kinston, Kinstun, Kingdon, Kindon,
Kingdun, Kindun*

Kingswell (English) From the king's spring
Kinswell, Kyngswell, Kynswell

Kinion (English) Of the family
Kinyon

Kinnard (Irish) From the tall hill
*Kinard, Kinnaird, Kinaird, Kynnard, Kynard,
Kynnaird, Kynaird*

Kinnell (Gaelic) From the top of the cliff
*Kinel, Kinnel, Kinell, Kynnell, Kynel, Kynnel,
Kynell*

Kinnon (Scottish) One who is fair-born
Kinnun, Kinnen, Kinnan, Kinnin, Kinnyn

Kinsey (English) The victorious prince
*Kynsey, Kinsi, Kynsi, Kinsie, Kynsie, Kinsee,
Kynsee, Kinsea, Kynsea, Kensey, Kensy, Kensi,
Kensie, Kensee, Kensea*

Kintan (Hindi) One who is crowned
Kinten, Kinton, Kintun, Kintin, Kintyn

Kione (African) One who has come from
nowhere

Kioshi (Japanese) One who is quiet
*Kioshe, Kioshie, Kioshy, Kioshey, Kioshee,
Kyoshi, Kyoshe, Kyoshie, Kyoshy, Kyoshey,
Kyoshee, Kiyoshi, Kiyoshie, Kiyoshey, Kiyoshy,
Kiyoshee*

Kipp (English) From the small pointed hill
Kip, Kipling, Kippling, Kypp, Kyp, Kiplyng, Kipplyng, Kippi, Kippie, Kippar, Kipper, Kippor, Kippur, Kippyr

Kirabo (African) A gift from God
Kiraboe, Kirubow, Kyrabo, Kyraboe, Kyrabow

Kiral (Turkish) The supreme chief; a lord
Kyral, Kirall, Kyrall

Kiran (Hindi) A ray of light
Kyran, Kiren, Kyren, Kiron, Kyron, Kirun, Kyrun, Kirin, Kyrin, Kiryn, Kyryn

Kirby (German) From the village with the church
Kirbey, Kirbi, Kirbie, Kirbee, Kerby, Kerbey, Kerbi, Kerbie, Kerbee

Kiri (Vietnamese) Resembling the mountains
Kirie, Kiry, Kirey, Kiree, Kirea

Kiril (Greek) Of the Lord
Kirill, Kirillos, Kyril, Kyrill

Kirit (Hindi) One who is crowned
Kiryt, Kireet, Kireat, Kiriet, Kireit

Kirk (Norse) A man of the church
Kyrk, Kerk, Kirklin, Kirklyn

Kirkan (Armenian) One who is vigilant
Kirken, Kirkin, Kirkyn, Kirkon, Kirkun, Kirkor, Kirkur, Kirkar, Kirker, Kirkir, Kirkyr

Kirkland (English) From the church's land
Kirklan, Kirklande, Kyrkland, Kyrklan, Kyrklande

Kirkley (English) From the church's meadow
Kirkly, Kirkleigh, Kirklea, Kirkleah, Kirklee, Kirkli, Kirklie

Kirkwell (English) From the church's spring
Kyrkwell, Kirkwel, Kyrkwel

Kirkwood (English) From the church's forest
Kirkwode, Kyrkwood, Kyrkwode

Kishi (Native American) Born at night
Kishie, Kishy, Kishey, Kishee, Kishea, Kyshi, Kyshie, Kyshy, Kyshey, Kyshee, Kyshea

Kisho (Japanese) A self-assured man
Kysho

Kit (English) Form of Christopher, meaning "one who bears Christ inside"
Kitt, Kyt, Kytt

Kitchi (Native American) A brave young man
Kitchie, Kitchy, Kitchey, Kitchee, Kitchea

Kito (African) One who is precious
Kyto

Kitoko (African) A handsome man
Kytoko

Kivi (Finnish) As solid as stone
Kivie, Kivy, Kivey, Kivee, Kivea

Kizza (African) One who is born after twins
Kyzza, Kiza, Kyzza

Kizzy (Hebrew) Resembling cinnamon
Kizzi, Kizzey, Kizzie, Kizzee, Kizzea

Klaus (German) Of the victorious people
Klaas, Klaes

Klay (English) A reliable and trustworthy man
Klaye, Klai, Klae, Klaie

Kleef (Dutch) From the cliff
Kleefe, Kleaf, Kleafe, Kleif, Kleife, Klief, Kliefe, Kleyf, Klyf

Klein (German) A man of small stature
Kline, Kleiner, Kleinert, Kleine

Klemens (Latin) A merciful man
Klemenis, Klement, Kliment, Klimens

Kleng (Norse) Having claws

Knight (English) A noble solidier
Knights

Knightley (English) From the knight's meadow
Knightly, Knightli, Knightlie, Knightleigh, Knightlee, Knightlea, Knightleah

Knoll (English) From the little hill
Knolles, Knollys, Knowles

Knoton (Native American) Of the wind
Knotun, Knotan, Knoten, Knotin, Knotyn

Knox (English) From the rounded hill
Knoxx, Knoks, Knocks

Knud (Danish) A kind man
Knude

Knut (Norse) A knot
Knute

Koa (Hawaiian) A fearless man
Koah

Kobi (Hungarian) Form of Jacob, meaning
"he who supplants"
Kobie, Koby, Kobey, Kobee, Kobea, Kobe

Kodiak (American) Resembling a bear
Kodyak

Kody (English) One who is helpful
Kodey, Kodee, Kodea, Kodi, Kodie

Koen (German) An honest advisor
Koenz, Kunz, Kuno

Kofi (African) Born on a Friday
Kofie, Kofee, Kofea, Kofy, Kofey

Kohana (Native American/Hawaiian) One
who is swift/the best

Kohler (German) One who mines coal
Koler

Koi (Hawaiian) One who implores

Kojo (African) Born on a Monday
Kojoe, Koejo, Koejoe

Koka (Hawaiian) A man from Scotland

Kokil (Indian) Resembling a nightingale
Kokyl, Kokill, Kokyll

Kolbjorn (Swedish) Resembling a black bear
Kolbjorne, Kolbjourn, Kolbjourne

Kolby (German) A dark-haired man
Kolbey, Kolbee, Kolbea, Kolbie, Kolbi

Koldobika (Basque) One who is famous in
battle
Koldobyka

Kole (English) The keeper of the keys
Koal, Koale

Kolichiyaw (Native American) Resembling
a skunk

Kolinkar (Danish) Of the conquering people
Kolynkar, Kolin, Kollin, Kolyn, Kollyn

Koll (Norse) Having dark features
Kolli, Kollie, Kolly, Kolley, Kollee, Kolleigh

Kolos (Hungarian) A scholar

Kolton (English) From the coal town
*Koltun, Koltan, Kolten, Koltin, Koltyn, Kolt,
Kolte*

Kolya (Slavic) The victorious warrior
Koliya, Kolenka

Konala (Hawaiian) A world ruler
Konalla

Konane (Hawaiian) Born beneath the bright
moon
*Konain, Konaine, Konayn, Konayne, Konaen,
Konaene*

Kondo (African) A fighter
Kondoe, Kondow, Kondowe

Kong (Chinese) A bright man; from heaven

Konnor (English) A wolf-lover; one who is
strong-willed
Konnur, Konner, Konnar, Konnir, Konnyr

Kono (African) An industrious man

Konrad (Polish) A bold advisor

Konstantine (English) One who is stead-
fast; firm
*Konstant, Konstantio, Konstanty, Konstanz,
Kostas, Konstantinos, Konstance, Kostantin,
Kostenka, Kostya*

Kontar (Ghanese) An only child
Kontarr

Koofrey (African) Remember me
Koofry, Koofri, Koofrie, Koofree

Korbin (Latin) A raven-haired man
Korbyn, Korben, Korban, Korbon, Korbun

Kordell (English) One who makes cord
Kordel, Kord, Kordale

Koren (Hebrew) One who is gleaming
Korin, Koryn

Koresh (Hebrew) One who digs in the
earth; a farmer
Koreshe

Korneli (Basque) Resembling a horn
Kornelie, Kornely, Korneley, Kornelee,
Korneleigh, Kornell, Kornel, Kornelisz,
Kornelius

Korrigan (English) One who wields a spear
Korigan, Korregan, Koregan, Korrighan,
Korighan, Korreghan, Koreghan

Kort (Danish) One who provides counsel
Korte

Korvin (Latin) Resembling a crow
Korvyn, Korvan, Korven, Korvon, Korvun

Kory (Irish) From the hollow; of the churning waters
Korey, Kori, Korie, Koree, Korea, Korry,
Korrey, Korree, Korrea, Korri, Korrie

Kosey (African) Resembling a lion
Kosy, Kosi, Kosie, Kosee, Kosea

Koshy (American) A lighthearted man
Koshey, Koshi, Koshe, Koshie, Koshee

Kosmo (Greek) A universal man
Kozmo, Kasmo, Kazmo, Kosmos, Kozmos,
Kasmos, Kazmos

Koster (American) A spiritual man
Kostar, Kostor, Kostur, Kostir, Kostyr

Kosumi (Native American) One who uses a spear to fish
Kosumie, Kosume, Kosumee, Kosumy,
Kosumey

Kotori (Native American) A screech-owl spirit
Kotorie, Kotory, Kotorey, Kotoree

Kourtney (American) One who is polite; courteous
Kourtny, Kordney, Kortney, Kortni,
Kourtenay, Kourtneigh, Kourtni, Kourtnee,
Kourtnie, Kortnie, Kortnea, Kourtnea,
Kortnee, Kourtnee

Kovit (Scandinavian) An expert; a learned man
Kovyt

Kozel (Czech) Resembling a goat
Kozell, Kozele, Kozelle

Kozma (Greek) One who is decorated
Kozmah

Kozue (Japanese) Of the tree branches
Kozu, Kozoo, Kozou

Kraig (Gaelic) From the rocky place; as solid as a rock
Kraige, Krayg, Krayge, Kraeg, Kraege, Krage

Kral (Czech) A king
Krall

Kramer (German) A shopkeeper
Kramar, Kramor, Kramir, Kramur, Kramyr,
Kraymer, Kraimer, Kraemer, Kraymar,
Kraimar, Kraemar

Kramoris (Czech) A merchant
Kramorris, Kramorys, Kramorrys

Krany (Czech) A man of short stature
Kraney, Kranee, Kranea, Krani, Kranie

Krikor (Armenian) A vigilant watchman
Krykor, Krikur, Krykur

Kripal (Indian) One who is merciful
Krypal, Kripa, Krypa

Krishna (Hindi) In Hiniduism, an avatar of Vishnu, portrayed as a handsome man playing the flute
Kryshna, Krishnadeva, Krishnachundra,
Krishnakanta, Krishnakumar, Krishnala,
Krishnamurari, Krishnamurthy, Krishnendu

Krispin (English) A curly-haired man
Kryspin, Krispyn, Krispen, Kryspen, Krisoijn

Kristian (Scandinavian) An anointed Christian
Kristan, Kristien, Krist, Kriste, Krister, Kristar,
Khristian, Khrist, Khriste, Khristan

Kristopher (Scandinavian) A follower of Christ
Khristopher, Kristof, Kristofer, Kristoff,
Kristoffer, Kristofor, Kristophor, Krystof,
Krystopher, Krzysztof, Kristophoros, Kristos,
Khristos, Khristopher, Khristo, Kris, Krys,
Krystos, Krysto

Kruz (Spanish) Of the cross
Kruze, Kruiz, Kruize, Kruzito

Kuba (Polish) Form of Jacob, meaning "he who supplants"
Kubas

Kuckunniwi (Native American) Resembling a little wolf
Kukuniwi

Kueng (Chinese) Of the universe

Kugonza (African) One who loves and is loved

Kulbert (German) One who is calm; a bright man
Kulberte, Kuhlbert, Kuhlberte, Kulbart, Kulbarte, Kuhlbart, Kuhlbarte

Kuleen (Indian) A highborn man
Kulin, Kulein, Kulien, Kulean, Kulyn

Kuma (Japanese) Resembling a bear

Kumar (Indian) A prince; a male child

Kumi (African) A forceful man
Kumie, Kumy, Kumey, Kumee, Kumea

Kunsgnos (Celtic) A wise man

Kupakwashe (African) A gift from God
Kupakwashi, Kupakwashie, Kupakwashy, Kupakwashey, Kupakwashee, Kupak, Kupakwash

Kuper (Hebrew) Resembling copper
Kupar, Kupir, Kupyr, Kupor, Kupur

Kuri (Japanese) Resembling a chestnut
Kurie, Kury, Kurey, Kuree, Kurea

Kuron (African) One who gives thanks
Kurun, Kuren, Kuran, Kurin, Kuryn

Kurt (German) A brave counselor
Kurte

Kurtis (French) A courtier
Kurtiss, Kurtys, Kurtyss

Kuruk (Native American) Resembling a bear
Kuruck, Kuruc

Kushal (Indian) A talented man; adroit
Kushall

Kutty (American) One who wields a knife
Kutti, Kuttey, Kuttie, Kuttee, Kuttea

Kwabena (African) Born on a Tuesday
Kwabina, Kwabyna, Kwabana

Kwahu (Native American) Resembling an eagle
Kwahue, Kwahoo, Kwahu

Kwaku (African) Born on a Wednesday
Kwakue, Kwakou, Kwako, Kwakoe

Kwame (African) Born on a Saturday
Kwam, Kwami, Kwamie, Kwamy, Kwamey, Kwamee

Kwan (Korean) Of a bold character
Kwon

Kwasi (African) Born on a Sunday
Kwasie, Kwasy, Kwasey, Kwasee, Kwase, Kwesi, Kwesie, Kwesey, Kwesy, Kwesee, Kwese

Kwatoko (Native American) Resembling a bird with a large beak

Kwesi (African) Born on a Sunday
Kwesie, Kwesy, Kwesey, Kwesee, Kwasi, Kwasie, Kwasy, Kwasey, Kwasee

Kwintyn (Polish) The fifth-born child
Kwentyn, Kwinton, Kwenton, Kwintun, Kwentun, Kwintan, Kwentan, Kwinten, Kwenten, Kwint, Kwynt

Kyan (American) The little king
Kyann

✪
Ⓣ **Kyle** (Gaelic) From the narrow channel
Kile, Kiley, Kye, Kylan, Kyrell, Kylen, Kily, Kili, Kilie, Kileigh, Kilee, Kyley, Kyly, Kyleigh, Kylee, Kyli, Kylie

Kylemore (Gaelic) From the great wood
Kylmore, Kylemor, Kylmor

Kyler (Danish) An archer
Kylar, Kylir, Kylyr, Kylor, Kylur

Kynan (Welsh) The chief; a leader
Kynen, Kynon, Kynun, Kynin, Kynyn

Kynaston (English) From the peaceful royal town
Kynastun, Kinaston, Kinastun

Kyne (English) Of the royalty
Kine, Kyn

Kyran (Persian / Irish) A lord / having dark features
Kyren, Kyrin, Kyryn, Kyron, Kyrun, Kyri, Kyrie, Kyree, Kyrea, Kyrey, Kyry

Kyrone (English) Form of Tyrone, meaning "from Owen's land"
Kyron, Keirohn, Keiron, Keirone, Keirown, Kirone

Kyros (Greek) A leader or master
Kiros

L

Laban (Hebrew) A white-haired or white-skinned man
Laben, Labon, Labin, Labyn, Labun, Lavin, Lavan, Lavyn, Laven, Lavon, Lavun, Labarn, Labarne

Labaron (French) The baron
LaBaron

Label (Hebrew) Resembling a lion
Labell, Labal, Laball

Labhras (Irish) Form of Lawrence, meaning "man from Laurentum; crowned with laurel"
Lubhras, Labhrus, Lubhrus, Labhros, Lubhros, Labhrainn, Labhrain

Labib (Arabic) One who is sensible
Labeeb, Labeab, Labieb, Labeib, Labyb

Laborc (Hungarian) As brave as a panther
Labork, Laborck

Labryan (American) One who is brash
Labrian, Labrien, Labryant, Labrion

Lacey (French) Man from Normandy; as delicate as lace
Lacy, Laci, Lacie, Lucee, Lacea

Lachie (Scottish) A boy from the lake
Lachi, Lachy, Lachey, Lachee, Lachea

Lachlan (Gaelic) From the land of lakes
Lachlen, Lachlin, Lachlyn, Locklan, Locklen, Locklin, Locklyn, Loklan, Laklan, Laklin, Laklen, Lakleyn, Laochailan, Lochlan, Lochlen, Lochlin, Lochlyn, Loche, Loch, Lach, Lache, Lakeland, Lochlann, Lochlain

Lachman (Gaelic) A man from the lake
Lachmann, Lockman, Lockmann, Lokman, Lokmann, Lakman, Lakmann

Lachtna (Irish) One who ages with grace

Lacrosse (French) Of the cross; a player of the game
Lacross, Lacros, Lacrose

Ladan (Hebrew) One who is alert and aware
Laden, Ladin, Ladyn, Ladon, Ladun

Ladd (English) A servant; a young man
Lad, Laddey, Laddie, Laddy, Laddi, Laddee, Laddea, Ladde

Ladden (American) An athletic man
Laddan, Laddin, Laddyn, Laddon, Laddun

Ladisiao (Spanish) One who offers help
Ladysiao, Ladiseao, Ladyseao, Ladisio, Ladiseo

Ladislas (Slavic) A glorious ruler
Lacko, Ladislaus, Laslo, Laszlo, Lazlo, Ladislav, Ladislauv, Ladislao, Ladislaw, Laco, Lako, Lado, Lazuli, Lazulie, Lazuly, Lazuley, Lazulee

Ladomér (Hungarian) One who traps animals
Ladomir, Ladomeer, Ladomear, Ladomyr

Lae (Laos) A dark-skinned man
Lai, Lay, Laye

Lael (Hebrew) One who belongs to God
Lale, Lail, Laile, Laele, Layl, Layle

Laertes (English) One who is adventurous
Lairtes, Layrtes, Lartes

Lafay (American) A lighthearted man
Lafaye, Lafai, Lafae, Lafayye, Laphay, Laphai, Laphae, Laphaye, Lafee, Laphee

Lafayette (French) Man of the faith
Lafeyette, Lafayet, Lafeyet, Lafayett, Lafeyett

Lafe (American) One who is on time
Laif, Laife, Layf, Layfe, Laef, Laefe

Lafi (Polynesian) A shy young man
Lafie, Lafy, Lafey

Lagan (Indian) One who arrives at the appropriate time
Lagen, Lagon, Lagin, Lagyn, Lagun

Lagrand (American) A majestic man
Lagrande

Lahib (Arabic) A fiery man
Laheeb, Laheab, Lahieb, Laheib, Luhyb

Lahthan (Arabic) A thirsty man
Lahthen, Lahthin, Lahthyn, Lahthon, Lahthun

Laibrook (English) One who lives on the road near the brook
Laebrook, Laybrook, Laibroc, Laebroc, Laybroc, Laibrok, Laebrok, Laybrok

Laidley (English) From the meadow with the creek
Laidly, Laidleigh, Laidlee, Laidlea, Laidleah, Laidli, Laidlie, Laedley, Laedly, Laedleigh, Laedlea, Laedleah, Laedli, Laedlee, Laedlie, Laydley, Laydly, Laydleigh, Laydlea, Laydleah, Laydli, Laydlie, Laydlee

Laionela (Hawaiian) As bold as a lion
Laionele, Laionel, Laionell

Laird (Scottish) The lord of the manor
Layrd, Laerd, Lairde, Layrde, Laerde

Laith (Arabic) Resembling a lion
Laithe, Layth, Laythe, Laeth, Laethe, Lath, Lathe, Lais

Lajos (Hungarian) A well-known holy man
Lajus, Lajcsi, Lali, Lalie, Laly, Laley, Lalee

Laken (American) Man from the lake
Laike, Laiken, Laikin, Lakin, Lakyn, Lakan, Laikyn, Laeken, Laekin, Laekyn, Layke, Laeke, Lake, Layken, Laykin, Laykyn, Laykan, Laikan, Laekan, Laec

Lakista (American) One who is bold
Lakeista, Lakiesta, Lakeesta, Lakeasta, Lakysta

Lakota (Native American) A beloved friend
Lakoda, Lacota, Lacoda, Lackota, Lackoda

Lakshman (Hindi) A man of good fortune
Lakshmann, Lakshmana, Lakshan

Lakshya (Indian) A target; a mark
Lakshiya, Lakshyah, Lakshiyah

Lal (Sanskrit / Slavic) One who is dearly loved / resembling a tulip
Lall, Lalle

Lalam (Indian) The best
Lallam, Lalaam, Lallaam

Lalit (Indian) One who is simple and handsome
Laleet, Laleat, Laleit, Laliet, Lalyt, Lalitmohan

Lalo (Latin) One who sings a lullaby
Lallo, Laloh, Lalloh

Lalor (Irish) A leper
Lalur, Laler, Lalir, Lalyr, Lalar, Leathlobhair

Lam (Vietnamese) Having a full understanding

Laman (Arabic) A bright and happy man
Lamaan, Lamann, Lamaann

Lamar (German / French) From the renowned land / of the sea
Lamarr, Lamarre, Lemar, Lemarr

Lambert (Scandinavian) The light of the land
Lambart, Lamberto, Lambirt, Landbert, Lambirto, Lambrecht, Lambret, Lambrett, Lamber, Lambur, Lambar

Lambi (Norse) In mythology, the son of Thorbjorn
Lambie, Lamby, Lambey, Lambe, Lambee

Lamech (Hebrew) One who is strong and powerful
Lameche, Lameck, Lamecke

Lameh (Arabic) A shining man

Lamont (Norse) A man of the law
Lamonte, Lamond, Lamonde, Lammond

Lamorak (English) In Arthurian legend, the brother of Percival
Lamerak, Lamurak, Lamorac, Lamerac, Lamurac, Lamorack, Lamerack, Lamurack, Lamorat

Lancelot (French) An attendant; in Arthurian legend, a knight of the Round Table
Launcelot, Lance, Lancelin, Lancelyn, Lanse, Lancelott, Launcelott, Launci, Launcie, Launcey, Launcy, Launcee

Lander (English) One who owns land
Land, Landers, Landis, Landiss, Landor, Lande, Landry, Landri, Landrie, Landrey, Landree, Landrea, Landise, Landice, Landus

Landmari (German) From the renowned land
Landmarie, Landmaree, Landmare, Landmary, Landmarey, Landmarea

Lando (American) A manly man
Landoe, Landow, Landowe

Landon (English) From the long hill
Landyn, Landan, Lunden, Landin, Lando, Langdon, Langden, Langdan, Langdyn, Langdin, Lancdon, Lancden, Lancdin

Lane (English) One who takes the narrow path
Laine, Lain, Laen, Laene, Layne, Layn

Lang (Norse) A tall man
Lange, Leng, Lenge, Longe, Long, Langer, Lenger, Langham

Langford (English) From the long ford
Langforde, Langferd, Langferde, Langfurd, Langfurde, Lanford, Lanforde, Lanferd, Lanferde, Lanfurd, Lanfurde

Langhorn (English) Of the long horn
Langhorne, Lanhorn, Lanhorne

Langilea (Polynesian) Having a booming voice, like thunder
Langileah, Langilia, Langiliah

Langiloa (Polynesian) Resembling a tempest; one who is moody
Langiloah

Langley (English) From the long meadow
Langleigh, Langly, Langlea, Langleah, Langlee, Langli, Langlie

Langston (English) From the tall man's town
Langsten, Langstun, Langstown, Langstin, Langstyn, Langstan, Langton, Langtun, Langtin, Langtyn, Langten, Langtan, Lankston, Lankstun, Lanston, Lanstun

Langundo (Native American / Polynesian) A peaceful man / one who is graceful

Langward (Native American) A tall guardian
Lanward, Langwerd, Lanwerd, Langwurd, Lanwurd

Langworth (English) One who lives near the long paddock
Langworthe, Lanworth, Lanworthe

Lanh (Vietnamese) One who is quick-witted

Lani (Hawaiian / Irish) From the sky; one who is heavenly / a servant
Lanie, Lany, Laney, Lanee, Lanea

Lanier (French) One who works with wool

Lann (Celtic) Man of the sword
Lan

Lanny (English) Form of Roland, meaning "from the renowned land"
Lanney, Lanni, Lannie, Lannee, Lunnea

Lansa (Native American) Man of the spear

Lantos (Hungarian) One who plays the lute
Lantus

Lanty (Irish) Full of life
Lantey, Lantee, Lantea, Lanti, Lantie

Lanzo (German) From the homeland
Lanzio, Lanziyo, Lanzeo, Lanzeyo

Laochailan (Scottish) One who is waning

Laoidhigh (Irish) One who is poetic

Lap (Vietnamese) An independent man
Lapp

Laphonso (American) One who is centered
Lafonso, Laphonzo, Lafonzo

Lapidos (Hebrew) One who carries a torch
Lapydos, Lapidot, Lapydot, Lapidoth, Lapydoth, Lapidus, Lapydus

Lapu (Native American) Of the cedar's bark
Lapue, Lapoo, Lapou

Laquinton (American) Form of Quinton, meaning "from the queen's town or settlement"
Laquinntan, Laquinnten, Laquinntin, Laquinnton, Laquintain, Laquintan, Laquintyn, Laquintynn, Laquintin, Laquinten, Laquintann, Laquint, Laquinte, Laquynt, Laquynte, Laquinneton, Laquienton, Laquientin, Laquiten, Laquitin, Laquiton

Lar (Anglo-Saxon) One who teaches others

Laramie (French) One who is pensive
Larami, Laramee, Laramea, Laramy, Laramey

Larch (Latin) Resembling the evergreen tree
Larche

Larcwide (Anglo-Saxon) One who provides counsel
Larkwide, Larcwyde, Larkwyde

Lare (American) A wealthy man
Larre, Layr, Layre, Lair, Laire, Laer, Laere

Largo (Spanish) A tall man

Lariat (American) A cowboy
Lariatt, Laryat, Laryatt

Lark (English) Resembling the songbird
Larke

Larkin (Gaelic) One who is fierce
Larkyn, Larken, Larkan, Larkon, Larkun

Larmine (American) One who is boisterous
*Larmyne, Larrmine, Larrmyne, Larmen,
Larrmen*

Larnell (American) A generous man
*Larnel, Larndell, Larndel, Larndi, Larndie,
Larndy, Larndey, Larne, Larn*

Laron (American) An outgoing young man
Larron, Larone, Larrone

Larson (Scandinavian) The son of Lawrence
Larsan, Larsen, Larsun, Larsin, Larsyn

Lasalle (French) From the hall
Lasall, Lasal, Lasale

Lashaun (American) An enthusiastic man
Lashawn, Lasean, Lashon, Lashond

Laskey (English) A lighthearted man
Lasky, Laskie, Laski, Laskee, Laskea, Laske, Lask

Lassen (English) From the mountain's peak
*Lassan, Lassin, Lassyn, Lasson, Lassun, Lasen,
Lasan, Lasin, Lasyn, Lason, Lasun*

Lassit (American) One who is open-minded
Lassyt, Lasset

Lassiter (American) One who is quick-witted
Lassyter, Lasseter, Lassater

Latafat (Indian) One who is elegant
Lataphat

Latham (Scandinavian) One who lives near
the barn
Lathom, Lathum, Lathem, Lathim, Lathym

Lathan (American) Form of Nathan,
meaning "a gift from God"
*Lathen, Lathun, Lathon, Lathin, Lathyn,
Latan, Laten, Latun, Laton*

Lathrop (English) From the farm with the
barn
Lathrup

Latif (Arabic) One who is kind and gentle
Lateef, Lateaf, Latief, Lateif, Latyf

Latimer (English) One who serves as an
interpreter
*Latymer, Latimor, Latymor, Latimore,
Latymore, Lattemore, Lattimore*

Latorris (American) A notorious man
Latoris, Latorrys, Latorys

Latravious (American) A healthy and
strong man
*Latraveus, Latravius, Latravios, Latraveos,
Latrave*

Latty (English) A generous man
Lattey, Latti, Lattie, Lattee, Lattea

Laud (Latin) One who is praised
Laude, Lawd, Lawde

Laughlin (Irish) From the land of the fjord;
a servant
Loughlin, Laughlyn, Loughlyn

Launder (English) From the grassy plains
Lawnder

Launfal (English) In Arthurian legend, a
knight
*Lawnfal, Launfall, Lawnfall, Launphal,
Lawnphal*

Laurian (English) One who lives near the
laurel trees
*Laurien, Lauriano, Laurieno, Lawrian,
Lawrien, Lawriano, Lawrieno*

Lavaughn (American) A spirited man
*Lavon, Lavawn, Lavan, Lavonn, Levaughn,
Levon, Levone*

Lave (Italian) Of the burning rock
Lava

Lavesh (Hindi) One who is calm
Laveshe

Lavi (Hebrew) Form of Levi, meaning "we
are united as one"
Lavie, Lavy, Lavey, Lavee, Lavea

Law (English) From the hill
Lawe

Lawford (English) From the ford near the hill
*Lawforde, Lawferd, Lawferde, Lawfurd,
Lawfurde*

Lawler (Gaelic) A soft-spoken man; one who mutters
Lauler, Lawlor, Loller, Lawlar, Lollar, Loller, Laular, Laulor

Lawley (English) From the meadow near the hill
Lawly, Lawli, Lawlie, Lawleigh, Lawlee, Lawlea, Lawleah

Lawrence (Latin) Man from Laurentum; crowned with laurel
Larance, Laranz, Larenz, Larrance, Larrence, Larrens, Larrey, Larry, Lars, Laurance, Lauren, Laurence, Laurens, Laurent, Laurentios, Laurentius, Laurenz, Laurie, Laurits, Lauritz, Lavrans, Lavrens, Lawrance, Lawrey, Lawrie, Lawry, Lenci, Lon, Lonny, Lorance, Lorant, Loren, Lorenc, Lorence, Lorencz, Lorens, Lorentz, Lorenz, Lorenzen, Lorenzo, Lorin, Loritz, Lorrence, Lorrenz, Lorry, Larri, Larrie, Lowrance, Laureano, Larz, Larenzo, Loron, Lorren, Lorrin, Laren, Laurin, Laurins, Laurentij, Laurenty, Laurentzi, Laurentiu, Lorand, Loran, Lirinc

Lawson (English) The son of Lawrence

Lawton (English) From the town on the hill
Lawtun, Lawtown, Laughton, Loughton, Laughtun, Loughtun, Litton, Littun, Lytton, Lyttun, Lanton, Lantun, Lifton, Liftun

Lawyer (American) An attorney; one who defends or prosecutes others
Lauyer, Lawyor, Lauyor

Layt (American) A fascinating young man
Layte, Lait, Laite, Laet, Laete, Late

Lazarus (Hebrew) Helped by God; in the Bible, the man raised from the dead by Jesus
Lazar, Lazare, Lazarillo, Lazaro, Lazear, Lazer, Lazzaro, Lazre

Laziz (Arabic) One who is pleasant
Lazeez, Lazeaz, Laziez, Lazeiz, Lazyz

Le (Chinese) Filled with joy

Leal (French) A faithful man
Leale, Leel, Leele, Liel, Liele, Lele

Leaman (American) A powerful man
Leeman, Leamon, Leemon, Leamond, Leamand

Leander (Greek) A lion of a man; in mythology, Hero's lover who swam across the Hellespont to meet her
Liander, Leandre, Liandre, Leandro, Liandro, Leandrew, Leandros, Leanther, Leiandros, Leand, Leande

Leanian (Anglo-Saxon) One who has been rewarded
Leanien, Leanion, Leaniun

Lear (Greek) Of the royalty
Leare, Leer, Leere

Learly (English) A majestic man
Learly, Learli, Learlie, Learlee, Learle, Learlea, Learleigh

Leary (Irish) A cattle herder
Learey, Learee, Learea, Leari, Learie, Laoghaire

Leathan (Scottish) Of the river
Leethan, Leathen, Leethen

Leather (American) As tough as hide
Lether

Leavery (American) A generous man
Leaverey, Leaveri, Leaverie, Leaveree, Leavry, Leavrey, Leavri, Leavrie, Leavree

Leavitt (English) A baker
Leavit, Leavytt, Leavyt, Leavett, Leavet

Leax (Anglo-Saxon) Resembling salmon

Leben (English) Filled with hope

Lebna (African) A soulful man
Lebnah, Leb

Lebrun (French) A brown-haired man
Lebrune, Labron, Labrun, Lebron, Lebrone, Labrone, Labrune

Lech (Slavic) In mythology, the founder of the Polish people
Leche

Lector (American) One who is disturbed
Lictor, Lektor, Liktor

Ledyard (Teutonic) The protector of the nation
Ledyarde, Ledyerd, Ledyerde

Lee (English) From the meadow
Leigh, Lea, Leah, Ley

Leeto (African) One who embarks on a journey
Leato, Leito, Lieto

Lefty (American) A left-handed man
Leftey, Lefti, Leftie, Leftee, Leftea

Legend (American) One who is memorable
Legende, Legund, Legunde

Leggett (French) A delegate
Leget, Legget, Legett, Legate, Leggitt, Legit, Legitt, Leggit, Liggett, Liget, Ligget, Ligett

Lehman (German) One who rents; a tenant
Lehmann

Lei (Hawaiian / Chinese) Adorned with flowers / resembling thunder

Leibel (Hebrew) Resembling a lion
Leib, Leibe

Leidolf (Norse) A descendant of the wolf
Leidulf, Leidolfe, Leidulfe

Leif (Scandinavian) A beloved heir
Lief, Leef, Leaf, Leyf, Life, Layf, Laif, Laef, Lyf, Leof

Leighton (English) From the town near the meadow
Leightun, Layton, Laytun, Leyton, Leytun

Leil (Arabic) Born at night
Leile, Leel, Leele, Leal, Leale

Leilani (Hawaiian) Child of heaven; adorned with heavenly flowers
Lalani, Leilanie, Leilanee, Leilaney, Leilany, Lalanie, Lalaney, Lalanee, Lalany, Leilanea, Lalanea

Leith (Gaelic) From the broad river
Leithe, Leath, Leathe, Leeth, Leethe, Lieth, Liethe, Leithan, Liethan, Leathan, Leethan

Lekhak (Hindi) An author
Lekhan

Lel (Slavic) A taker
Lél

Leland (English) From the meadow land
Leeland, Leighland, Lealand, Leyland

Leldon (American) A bookworm
Leldun, Leldan, Lelden, Leldin, Leldyn

Lema (African) One who is cultivated
Lemah, Lemma, Lemmah

Lemon (American) Resembling the fruit
Lemun, Lemin, Lemyn, Limon, Limun, Limin, Limyn, Limen, Lemen

Lemuel (Hebrew) One who belongs to God
Lemyouel, Lemyuel, Lemuell, Lemmi, Lemmie, Lemmy, Lemmey, Lemmee, Lem

Len (Native American) One who plays the flute

Lencho (African) Resembling a lion
Lenchos, Lenchio, Lenchiyo, Lencheo, Lencheyo

Lennart (Scandinavian) One who is brave
Lennert

Lenno (Native American) A brave man
Lennoe, Leno, Lenoe

Lennon (English) Son of love
Lennan, Lennin, Lenon, Lenan, Lenin

Lennor (English) A courageous man

Lennox (Scottish) One who owns many elm trees
Lenox, Lenoxe, Lennix, Lenix, Lenixe

Lenoris (American) A respected man
Leenoris, Lenorris, Leanoris

Lensar (English) One who stays with his parents
Lenser, Lensor, Lensur

Lenton (American) A pious man
Lentin, Lentyn, Lentun, Lentan, Lenten, Lent, Lente

Leo (Latin) Resembling a lion
Lio, Lyo

Leocadie (French) Having the heart of a lion
Leocadi, Leocady, Leocadey, Leocadee, Leocado, Leocadio, Leocadeo

Leod (Scottish) An ugly man
Leode

Leolin (Polynesian) One who is alert; watchful
Leolyn, Leoline, Leolyne

Leomaris (Latin) The lion of the sea
Liomaris, Leomariss, Liomariss, Leomarys, Liomarys, Leomaryss, Liomaryss

Leon (Greek) Form of Leo, meaning "resembling a lion"
Leoncio, Leone, Lioni, Lionisio, Lionni, Lionie, Lionnie, Liony, Lionny, Lioney, Lionney, Lionee, Lionnee, Leonce, Leonel, Leonell

Leonard (German) Having the strength of a lion
Len, Lenard, Lenn, Lennard, Lennart, Lennerd, Lennie, Lenny, Leonardo, Leondaus, Leonerd, Leonhard, Leonid, Leonidas, Leonides, Leonis, Lonnard, Lenni, Lonni, Lonnie, Lonny, Lenya, Lyonechka, Lennell, Lennel, Lenel, Lenell, Leovardo, Leovard

Leonidus (Latin) Having great strength
Leonydus, Leonidos, Leonydos, Leonidas, Leonydas

Leopaul (American) One who exhibits calm bravery
Leopaule

Leopold (German) A bold ruler of the people
Leopoldo, Leupold, Leupoldo, Leopolde, Leupolde, Luitpold, Luitpolde, Lepold, Lepolde, Lepoldo, Lopold, Lopolde, Lopoldi

Leor (Latin) One who listens well
Leore

Leoti (American) An outdoorsy man
Leotie, Leoty, Leotey, Leotee, Leotea

Leotis (American) One who is carefree
Leodis, Leotys, Leodys, Leeotis, Leeodis

Lepolo (Polynesian) A handsome man
Lepoloh, Lepollo, Lepolloh

Lerato (Latin) The song of my soul
Leratio, Lerateo

Leron (French / Arabic) The circle / my song
Lerun, Leran, Leren, Lerin, Leryn

Leroux (French) The red-haired man
Larue, Lerue, Laroux

Leroy (French) The king
Leroi, Leeroy, Leeroi, Learoy, Learoi

Lesharo (Native American) The chief
Leshario, Leshareo

Leshem (Hebrew) Resembling a precious stone

Leslie (Gaelic) From the holly garden; of the gray fortress
Leslea, Leslee, Lesleigh, Lesley, Lesli, Lesly, Lezlee, Lezley, Lezlie, Lezleigh, Lezli, Lioslaith, Lezlea, Les, Lez

Lesner (American) A serious-minded man
Lezner

Lester (English) A man from Leicester
Lestor, Lestir, Lestyr, Lestar, Lestur

Lev (Hebrew / Russian) Of the heart / form of Leo, meaning "resembling a lion"
Levka, Levushka

Levant (French) One who rises above
Levante, Levent, Levente

Levar (American) One who is soft-spoken
Levarr, Levare

Leverett (French) Resembling a young rabbit
Leveret, Leveritt, Leverit

Leverton (English) From the rush town
Levertun, Levertown

❍ **Levi** (Hebrew) We are united as one; in the Bible, one of Jacob's sons
Levie, Levin, Levyn, Levy, Levey, Levee

Leviticus (Greek) Of the Levites
Levyticus, Levitikus, Levytikus

Lew (German / Slavic / English) A famous warrior / resembling a lion / one who provides shelter
Leu, Lewe

Lex (English) Form of Alexander, meaning "helper and defender of mankind"
Lexer, Lexis, Lexys, Lexus, Lexo, Lexiss, Lexyss

Leyati (Native American) Having a smooth and round head
Leyatie, Leyatee, Leyatea, Leyaty, Leyatey, Leyti, Leytie, Leytee, Leytea, Leyty, Leytey

Leyman (English) Man of the meadow
Leighman, Leman, Leaman, Leahman, Lyman

Lezane (American) One who is dearly loved
Lezain, Lezaine, Lezayn, Lezayne, Lezaen, Lezaene

Li (Chinese) Having great strength

❂ **Liam** (Gaelic) Form of William, meaning "the determined protector"
Lyam

Lian (Chinese) Of the willow

Liang (Chinese) A good man
Lyang

Liberio (Latin) One who is independent; free
Liberato, Liberatus, Liberto, Libero

Liberty (English) An independent man; having freedom
Libertey, Libertee, Libertea, Liberti, Libertie, Libertas, Libyr, Liber, Libor

Lidio (Portugese) A man from Lydia
Lydio, Lidiyo, Lydiyo, Lideo, Lydeo, Lideyo, Lydeyo

Lidmann (Anglo-Saxon) A man of the sea; a sailor
Lidman, Lydmann, Lydman

Lidon (Hebrew) Judgment is mine
Lydon, Leedon, Leadon, Liedon, Leidon, Ledon

Liem (Vietnamese) An honest man

Lif (Scandinavian) An energetic man; lively

Lihau (Hawaiian) A spirited man

Like (Asian) A soft-spoken man
Lyke

Liko (Hawaiian) A flourishing young man
Lyko

Lilo (Hawaiian) One who is generous
Lylo, Leelo, Lealo, Leylo, Lielo, Leilo

Limu (Polynesian) Resembling seaweed
Lymu, Limue, Lymue

Lincoln (English) From the village near the lake
Lincon, Lyncoln, Lyncon, Linken, Lynken, Linkoln, Link, Linc, Lynk, Lync

Lindberg (German) From the linden tree hill
Lindbergh, Lindburg, Lindburgh, Lindi, Lindie, Lindee, Lindy, Lindey, Lindeberg, Lindebergh, Lindeburg, Lindeburgh

Lindell (English) From the valley of linden trees
Lendell, Lendall, Lindall, Lyndall, Lindel, Lendel, Lendal, Lindal, Lyndal, Lyndell, Lyndel, Lindael, Lindale, Lindayle, Lindayl, Lindaele

Linden (English) From the lime tree
Lindenn, Lindon, Lindynn, Lynden, Lyndon, Lyndyn, Lyndin, Lindin, Lind, Linde, Lin, Linddun, Lindun

Lindford (English) From the linden-tree ford
Linford, Lindforde, Linforde, Lyndford, Lynford, Lyndforde, Lynforde

Lindhurst (English) From the village by the linden trees
Lyndhurst, Lindenhurst, Lyndenhurst, Lindhirst, Lindherst, Lyndhirst, Lyndherst, Lindenhirst, Lyndenhirst, Lindenherst, Lyndenherst

Lindley (English) From the meadow of linden trees
Lindly, Lindleigh, Lindlea, Lindleah, Lindlee, Lindli, Lindlie, Lyndley, Lyndly, Lyndleigh, Lyndlea, Lyndleah, Lyndlee, Lyndli, Lyndlie

Lindman (English) One who lives near the linden trees
Lindmann, Lindmon, Lindmonn

Lindo (American) One who is sturdy
Lindoh, Lyndo, Lyndoh

Lindsay (English) From the island of linden trees; from Lincoln's wetland
Lind, Lindsea, Lindsee, Lindseigh, Lindsey, Lindsy, Linsay, Linsey, Linsie, Linzi, Linzee, Linzy, Lyndsay, Lyndsey, Lyndsie, Lynnsey, Lynnzey, Lynsey, Lynzey, Lynzi, Lynzy, Lynzee, Lynzie, Lindse

Line (English) From the bank

Linley (English) From the flax field
*Linly, Linleigh, Linlee, Linlea, Linleah,
Linli, Linlie, Lynley, Lynly, Lynleigh, Lynlea,
Lynleah, Lynli, Lynlie*

Linton (English) From the flax town
Lynton, Lintun, Lyntun

Linus (Greek) One who has flaxen-colored
hair; in mythology, the musician son of
Apollo
Lynus, Lino, Linos, Lynos, Lyno

Linwood (English) From the forest of linden trees
Linwode, Lynwood, Lynwode

Lion (English) Resembling the animal
Lyon, Lions, Lyons

Lionel (Latin) Resembling a young lion
*Leonel, Leonello, Lionell, Lionelo, Lionello,
Lionnel, Lionnell, Lionnello, Lonell, Lonnell,
Lyonel, Lyinell, Lyonelo, Lyonnel, Lyonnell,
Lyonnello*

Lipot (Hungarian) A brave young man

Lirit (Hebrew) Having musical grace

Liron (Hebrew) My song
Leeron, Learon, Lieron, Leiron, Lyron

Lise (Native American) Resembling a rising
salmon

Lisiate (Polynesian) A courageous man

Lisimba (African) One who has been
attacked by a lion
Lisymba, Lysimba, Lysymbu

List (Anglo-Saxon) One who is cunning
Liste, Lyst, Lyste, Lister, Lyster

Liu (Asian) One who is quiet; peaceful

Liuz (Polish) Surrounded by light

Livingston (English) From the town of a
beloved friend
Livingstun, Livingsten, Livingstin, Livingstone

Liviu (Romanian) Of the olive tree

Liwanu (Native American) Having the
growl of a bear
Lywanu, Liwanue, Lywanue, Liwanou, Lywanou

Lleu (Welsh) A shining man
Lugh, Lugus

Llewellyn (Welsh) Resembling a lion
*Lewellen, Lewellyn, Llewellen, Llewelyn,
Llwewellin, Llew, Llewe, Llyweilun*

Lloyd (Welsh) A gray-haired man; one who
is sacred
Lloid, Loyd, Loid, Llwyd

Llyr (Celtic) In mythology, a king; of the sea

Loba (African) One who talks a lot

Lobo (Spanish) Resembling a wolf
Loboe, Lobow, Lobowe

Lochan (Hindi / Irish) The eyes / one who
is lively

Locke (English / German) Man of the forest /
from the fortress
Lock

Lockhart (English) Resembling a deer from
the forest
Lokhart, Lockharte, Lokharte

Lockwood (English) From the fortress near
the forest
Lokwood, Lockwode, Lokwode

Lodewuk (Scandinavian) A famous warrior
Ladewijk, Lodovic, Lodovico, Lojza

Lodge (English) One who provides shelter

Lodur (Norse) In mythology, one who par-
ticipated in animating humans
Lodor, Loder, Lodir, Lodyr

Loeb (German) Resembling a lion
Loebe, Loeber, Loew, Loewe

Loefel (English) One who is dearly loved

Loey (American) A daring man; one who is
adventurous
Loeey, Lowee, Lowi, Lowie, Loie

❂ **Logan** (Gaelic) From the little hollow
*Logann, Logen, Login, Logyn, Logenn, Loginn,
Logynn*

Lohengrin (English) In Arthurian legend,
the son of Percival
Lohengren, Lohengryn

Lokela (Hawaiian) One who is known for throwing spears
Lokelah, Lokella, Lokellah

Lokene (Hawaiian) One who is open-minded
Lokeen, Lokeene, Lokean, Lokeane, Lokein, Lokeine, Lokien, Lokiene, Lokyn, Lokyne

Loki (Norse) In mythology, a trickster god
Lokie, Loky, Lokey, Lokee, Lokea

Lokni (Hawaiian) As dashing as a red rose
Loknie, Lokny, Lokney, Loknea, Loknee

Lolonyo (African) The beauty of love
Lolonyio, Lolonyeo, Lolonio, Lolonea

Lolovivi (African) The sweetness of love
Lolovyvy, Lolovivie, Lolovievie, Lolovivee

Loman (Gaelic) One who is small and bare
Lomann, Loeman, Loemann

Lomar (English) The son of Omar
Lomarr

Lomas (Spanish) A good man

Lombard (Latin) One who has a long beard
Lombardi, Lombardo, Lombardie, Lombardy, Lombardey, Lombardee

Lonan (Native American) Resembling a cloud
Lonann

Lonato (Native American) Possessing a flint stone

London (English) From the capital of England
Lundon, Londen, Lunden

Long (Chinese) Resembling a dragon
Longe

Longfellow (English) A tall man
Longfello, Longfelow, Longfelo

Lonzo (Spanish) One who is ready for battle
Lonzio, Lonzeo

Lootah (Native American) Refers to the color red
Loota, Loutah, Louta, Lutah, Luta

Lorcan (Irish) The small, fierce one
Lorcen, Lorcin, Lorcyn, Lorcon, Lorcun, Lorkan, Lorken, Lorkin, Lorkyn, Lorkon, Lorkun

Lord (English) One who has authority and power
Lorde, Lordly, Lordley, Lordlee, Lordlea, Lordleigh, Lordli, Lordlie

Lore (Basque / English) Resembling a flower / form of Lawrence, meaning "man from Laurentum; crowned with laurel"
Lorea

Loredo (Spanish) A cowboy; one who is intelligent
Lorado, Loraydo, Loraido, Loraedo, Larado, Laredo

Lorimer (Latin) One who makes harnesses
Lorrimer, Lorimar, Lorrimar, Lorymar, Lorrymar, Lorymer, Lorrymer

Loring (German) One who is famous in battle
Loryng, Lorring, Lorryng

Lorne (English) Form of Lawrence, meaning "a man from Laurentum; crowned with laurel"
Lorn, Lornel, Lornell, Lornele, Lornelle

Lot (Hebrew) One who is veiled; hidden; in the Bible, the man who fled God's destruction of Sodom and Gomorrah

Lothar (German) A famous warrior
Lathair, Lother, Lothair, Lothario, Lothur, Lotharing

Louden (American) One who is enthusiastic
Loudon, Loudan, Lowden, Lowdon, Lowdan, Loudun, Lowdun

Louis (German) A famous warrior
Lew, Lewes, Lewis, Lodewick, Lodovico, Lou, Louie, Lucho, Ludovic, Ludovicus, Ludvig, Ludvik, Ludwig, Luigi, Lewi, Lewie, Lewy, Ludweg, Ludwik, Luduvico

Loundis (American) A visionary
Loundys, Loundas, Loundes, Loundos, Loundus, Lowndis, Lowndys, Lowndas, Lowndes, Lowndos, Lowndus

Louvain (English) From the city in Belgium
Louvaine, Louvayn, Louvayne, Louvane, Louvaen, Louvaene

Lovett (English) One who is full of love
Lovet, Lovatt, Lovat, Lovitt, Lovit, Lovytt, Lovyt

Lowell (French) Resembling a young wolf
Lowel, Louvel, Lovel, Lovell, Lowe

Lowman (English) A dearly loved man
Loweman, Lowmann, Lowemann

Lowry (English) A great leader
Lowrey, Lowri, Lowrie, Lowree, Lowrea

Loyal (English) One who is faithful and true
*Loyalty, Loyalti, Loyaltie, Loyaltee, Loyaltea,
Loyaltey, Loys, Loyse, Loyce*

Luba (Yugoslavian) One who loves and is loved
Lubah

Lubomir (Polish) A great love
Lubomeer, Lubomear, Lubomyr

Lucan (Latin) A man from Lucania
Lukan, Loucan, Louccan, Luckan, Louckan

❂ **Lucas** (English) A man from Lucania
*Lukas, Loucas, Loukas, Luckas, Louckas,
Lucus, Lukus*

Lucho (Spanish) Surrounded by light; a
lucky man
Luchio, Luchiyo, Lucheo, Lucheyo

Lucian (Latin) Surrounded by light
*Luciano, Lucianus, Lucien, Lucio, Lucjan,
Lukianos, Lukyan, Luce, Lucero, Lucius, Luca,
Lucca, Luka, Lukka, Lucious, Luceous, Lushus*

Lucky (English) A fortunate man
Luckey, Luckee, Luckea, Lucki, Luckie

Lucretius (Latin) A successful or wealthy man
Lucretious

Ludlow (English) The ruler of the hill
Ludlowe

Ludoslaw (Polish) Of the glorious people
Ludoslav, Luboslaw, Luboslav

Lufian (Anglo-Saxon) One who is full of love
Lufyan, Lufyann, Lufiann

Lufti (Arabic) A kind man
Luftie, Luftee, Luftea, Lufty, Luftey

❂ **Luis** (Spanish) Form of Louis, meaning "a
famous warrior"
Luiz

❂ **Luke** (Greek) A man from Lucania
Luc, Luken

Luki (German) A renowned fighter
Lukie, Luky, Lukey, Lukee, Lukea

Lulani (Polynesian) Sent from heaven
Lulanie, Lulaney, Lulany, Lulanee, Lulanea

Lumumba (African) A talented or gifted man
Lumomba

Lundy (French / Gaelic) Born on a Monday /
from the marshland
*Lundey, Lundi, Lundie, Lundee, Lundea,
Lunde, Lund*

Lunn (Gaelic) Having great strength; one
who is warlike
Lun, Lon, Lonn

Lunt (Scandinavian) From the grove
Lunte

Luong (Vietnamese) From the bamboo land

Lusk (American) An energetic man
*Luske, Luski, Luskie, Lusky, Luskey, Luskee,
Luskea*

Lutalo (African) A bold warrior

Luthando (Latin) One who is dearly loved

Luther (German) A soldier of the people
*Louther, Luter, Luthero, Lutero, Louthero,
Luthus, Luthas, Luthos*

Lutz (German) A famous warrior

Lux (Latin) A man of the light
Luxe, Luxi, Luxie, Luxee, Luxea, Luxy, Luxey

Ly (Vietnamese) A reasonable man

Lyall (Gaelic / Norse) A faithful man /
resembling a wolf
Lyell, Lyal, Lyel

Lydell (English) From the open valley
Lydel, Ledell, Ledel

Lyle (English) From the island
Lisle, Lysle, Lile, Lyell

Lynn (English) A man of the lake
Linn, Lyn, Lynne, Linne

Lyric (French) Of the lyre; the words of a song
Lyrik, Lyrick

Lysander (Greek) The liberator
Lesandro, Lisandro, Lizandro, Lysandros

m

Maahes (Egyptian) Resembling a lion

Mablevi (African) Do not deceive
Mablevie, Mablevy, Mablevey, Mablevee, Mablevea

Mabon (Welsh) Our son
Mabun, Maban, Mabin, Mabyn, Maben

Mac (Gaelic) The son of ...
Mack, Mak, Macky, Macky, Macki, Mackie, Mackee, Mackea, Macken, Mackan, Mackon, Mackin, Mackyn, Mackun

Macadam (Gaelic) The son of Adam
Macadhamh, MacAdam, McAdam, MacAdhamh

Macallister (Gaelic) The son of Alistair
MacAlister, McAlister, McAllister, Macalister

Macalpin (Gaelic) The son of Alpine
MacAlpin, Macalpine, MacAlpine, McAlpine, MacAlpyn, Macalpyn, MacAplyne, Macalpyne, MacAlpyne, McAlpyne, McAlpin, McAlpyn

Macandrew (Gaelic) The son of Andrew
MacAndrew, McAndrew

Macardle (Gaelic) The son of great courage
MacArdle, McCardle, Macardell, MacArdell, McCardell

Macario (Spanish) Filled with happiness
Macareo, Makario, Makareo

Macartan (Gaelic) The son of Artan
MacArtan, McArtan, Macarten, MacArten, McArten

Macarthur (Gaelic) The son of Arthur
MacArthur, McArthur, Macarther, MacArther, McArther

Macauley (Gaelic) The son of righteousness
Macaulay, McCauley, McCaulay, MacCauley, MacCaulay

Macauliffe (Gaelic) The son of Olaf
MacAuliffe, Macaulife, MacAulife, Macaulif, MacAulif, McAuliffe, McAulife, McAulif

Macauslan (Gaelic) The son of Absalon
MacAuslan, McAuslan, Macauslen, MacAuslen, McAuslen

Macbain (Gaelic) The son of Beathan
MacBaine, McBain, McBaine, MacBayn, MacBayne, McBayne, McBayne, MacBean, McBean, MacBeane, McBeane, MacBain

Macbeth (Gaelic) The son of Beth
McBeth, MacBethe, McBethe, MacBeth, Macbethe

Macbride (Gaelic) The son of a follower of St. Brigid
Macbryde, MacBride, MacBryde, McBride, McBryde

Maccabee (Hebrew) A hammer
Macabee, Mackabee, Makabee, Maccabea, Macabea, Mackabea, Makabea, Maccus

Maccallum (Gaelic) The son of Callum
MacCallum, MacCalum, Macalum, McCallum, McCalum

Macclennan (Gaelic) The son of Finnian's servant
Maclennan, MacClennan, McClennan, MacClenan, McClenan, Macclenan

Maccoll (Gaelic) The son of Coll
McColl, Maccoll, MacColl

Maccormack (Gaelic) The son of Cormac
McCormack, MacCormack, Maccormak, MacCormak, Maccormac, MacCormac, McCormak, McCormak

Maccoy (Gaelic) The son of Hugh
MacCoy, McCoy, Mccoy

Maccrea (Gaelic) The son of grace
McCrea, Macrae, MacCrae, MacCray, MacCrea

Macdonald (Gaelic) The son of Donald
McDonald, MacDonald, Macdonell, Macdonel, MacDonell, MacDonel, McDonell, McDonel, MacDomhnall, McDomhnall

Macdougal (Gaelic) The son of Dougal
MacDougal, MacDowell, McDougal, Macdowell, McDowell, MacDubhgall, McDubhgall, Macdubhgall

Macduff (Gaelic) The son of the black-skinned man
McDuff, MacDuff, Macduf, MacDuf, McDuf

Mace (English) One who wields the medieval weapon
Mayce, Maice, Muece, Maceo, Macio, Maci, Macey, Macie, Macy, Macee, Macea, Macerio, Macereo

Macedonio (Greek) A man from Macedonia
Macedoneo, Macedoniyo, Macedoneyo

Macegan (Gaelic) The son of Egan
MacEgan, McEgun, Macegen, MacEgen, McEgen

Macelroy (Gaelic) The son of Elroy
MacElroy, McElroy

Macewen (Gaelic) The son of Ewen
McEwen, MacEwen

Macfarlane (Gaelic) The son of Farlan
MacFarlane, McFarlane, Macfarlan, MacFarlan, McFarlan, Macfarlin, MacFarlin, McFarlin

Macgill (Gaelic) The son of Gill
MacGill, Macgyll, MacGyll, McGill, McGyll

Macgowan (Gaelic) The son of a blacksmith
MacGowan, Magowan, McGowan, McGowen, McGown, MacCowan, MacCowen

Macgregor (Gaelic) The son of Gregor
McGregor, MacGregor

Machakw (Native American) Resembling a horny toad

Machar (Scottish) Plain
Machair, Machaire, Machare, Machayr, Machayre, Machaer, Machaere

Machau (Hebrew) A gift from God

Machenry (Gaelic) The son of Henry
MacHenry, McHenry

Machk (Native American) Resembling a bear

Machupa (African) One who likes to drink
Machupah, Machoupa, Machoupah, Machoopa, Machoopah

Macintosh (Gaelic) The son of the thane
MacIntosh, McIntosh, Macintoshe, MacIntoshe, McIntoshe, Mackintosh, MacKintosh

Macintyre (Gaelic) The son of the carpenter
MacIntyre, McIntyre, Macintire, MacIntire, McIntire

Maciver (Gaelic) The son of an archer
MacIver, McIver

Mackay (Gaelic) The son of fire
MacKay, McKay, Mackaye, MacKaye, McKaye

Mackendrick (Gaelic) The son of Henry
MacKendrick, Mackendrik, MacKendrik, Mackendric, MacKendric, Mackendryck, Mackendryk, Mackendryc, MacKendryck, MacKendryk, MacKendryc, McKendrick, McKendrik, McKendric, McKendryck, McKendryk, McKendryc

Mackenzie (Gaelic) The son of a wise leader; a fiery man; one who is fair
Mackenzey, Makensie, Makenzie, M'Kenzie, McKenzie, Meckenzie, Mackenzee, Mackenzy, Mackenzi, Mackenzea, MacKenzie, MacKensie, McKensie

Mackinley (Gaelic) The son of the white warrior
MacKinley, McKinley, MacKinlay, McKinlay, Mackinlay, Mackinlie, MacKinlie

Mackinnon (Gaelic) The son of the fair one
MacKinnon, Mackennon, MacKennon, Mackinon, MacKinon, Mackenon, MacKenon

Macklin (Gaelic) The son of Flann
Macklinn, Macklyn, Macklynn, Macklen, Macklenn

Maclachlan (Gaelic) The son of Lachlan
MacLachlan, Maclachlen, MacLachlen, Maclachlin, MacLachlin, McLachlan, McLachlen, McLachlin

Maclaine (Gaelic) The son of John's servant
MacLaine, Maclain, MacLain, Maclayn, McLaine, McLain, Maclane, MacLane, McLane, Maclean, MacLean, McLean

Maclaren (Gaelic) The son of Laren
MacLaren, McLaren

Macleod (Gaelic) The son of the ugly one
MacLeod, McLeod, McCloud, MacCloud

Macmahon (Gaelic) The son of the bear
MacMahon, McMahon

Macmillan (Gaelic) The son of the bald one
MacMillan, McMillan, Macmillen, MacMillen, McMillen

Macmurray (Gaelic) The son of Murray
MacMurray, McMurray, Macmurra, MacMurra

Macnab (Gaelic) The son of the abbot
MacNab, McNab

Macnachtan (Gaelic) The son of the chaste or pure one
MacNachtan, McNachtan, Macnaughton, MacNaughton, McNaughton

Macnair (Gaelic) The son of the heir
MacNair, McNair, Macnaire, MacNaire, McNaire

Macneill (Gaelic) The son of Neil
MacNeill, Macneil, MacNeil, Macneal, MacNeal, Macniel, MacNiel, McNeill, McNeil, McNeal, McNiel, Macniall, MacNiall, McNiall

Macon (English / French) To make / from the city in France
Macun, Makon, Makun, Maken, Mackon, Mackun

Macpherson (Gaelic) The son of the parson
MacPherson, McPherson, Macphersen, MacPhersen, McPhersen, Macphersan, MacPhersan, McPhersan

Macquaid (Gaelic) The son of Quaid
MacQuaid, McQuaid, Macquaide, MacQuaide, McQuaide

Macquarrie (Gaelic) The son of the proud one
MacQuarrie, McQuarrie, Macquarie, MacQuarie, McQuarie, Macquarry, MacQuarry, McQuarry, Macquarrey, MacQuarrey, McQuarrey

Macqueen (Gaelic) The son of the good man
MacQueen, McQueen

Macrae (Gaelic) The son of Ray
MacRae, McRae, Macray, MacRay, McRay, Macraye, MacRaye, McRaye

Macsen (Welsh) Form of Maximilian, meaning "the greatest"
Macsan, Macsin, Macsyn, Macson, Macsun, Maksen, Maksan, Makson, Maksun, Maksin, Maksyn, Macksen, Macksan, Macksin, Macksyn, Mackson, Macksun

Madan (Indian) The god of love

Madden (Pakistani) One who is organized; a planner
Maddon, Maddan, Maddin, Maddyn, Maddun, Maden, Madon, Madun, Madin, Madyn

Maddock (Welsh) A generous and benevolent man
Madock, Maddok, Madok, Maddoc, Madoc, Madog

Maddox (Welsh) The son of the benefactor
Madox, Madocks, Maddocks

Madelhari (German) A battle counselor
Madelharie, Madelhary, Madelharey, Madelharee, Madelharea

Madhav (Indian) A kind or sweet man

Madhu (Indian) As sweet as honey
Madhue, Madhou

Madhuk (Indian) Resembling a honeybee

Madhur (Indian) A sweet man

Madison (English) Son of a mighty warrior
Maddison, Madisen, Madisson, Madisyn, Madyson, Madysen, Madisan, Maddisan, Maddi, Maddie, Maddy, Maddey, Maddee, Maddea

Madu (African) A manly man
Madue, Madou

Madzimoyo (African) One who is nourished with water
Madzymoyo

Maemi (Japanese) An honest child
Maemie, Maemy, Maemey, Maemee, Maemea

Maeron (Gaelic) One who is bitter
Maeren, Maerun, Maerin, Maeryn, Maeran

Magaidi (African) The last-born child
Magaidie, Magaidy, Magaidee,
Magaydey, Magaydy, Magaydi, Magaydie,
Magaydee, Magaedey, Magaedy, Magaedi,
Magaedie, Magaedee, Magadey, Magady,
Magadi, Magadie, Magadee

Magal (Hebrew) One who uses a scythe
Magel, Magol, Magul, Magil, Magyl

Magan (Anglo-Saxon) One who is competent
Magen, Magin, Magyn, Magon, Magun

Magar (Armenian) An attendant
Magarr, Mager, Magor, Magur, Magir,
Magyr

Magee (Gaelic) The son of Hugh
MacGee, McGee, MacGhee, Maghee

Magglio (Hispanic) One who is healthy and
strong; athletic
Maggleo, Maggliyo, Maggleyo

Magic (American) One who is full of wonder and surprise
Majic, Magyc, Magik, Magick, Majik, Majick

Magnar (Polish) A strong warrior
Magnarr, Magnor, Magnorr

Magne (Norse / Latin) A fierce warrior / a
great man
Magni, Magnie, Magnee, Magnea, Magney,
Magny

Magnus (Latin) A great man; one who is
large
Magnos, Magnes, Magnusson, Magno, Mago

Maguire (Gaelic) The son of the beige one
Magwire, MacGuire, McGuire, MacGwire,
McGwire

Magus (Latin) A sorcerer
Magis, Magys, Magos, Magas, Mages

Mahabala (Indian) Having great strength
Mahabahu

Mahan (American) A cowboy
Mahahn, Mahen, Mayhan, Maihan,
Maehan, Mayhen, Maihen, Maehen

Mahanidhi (Indian) One who is treasured

Mahaniya (Indian) One who is worthy of
honor

Mahant (Indian) Having a great soul
Mahante

Mahari (African) A forgiving man
Maharie, Mahary, Maharey, Maharee,
Maharea

Mahatma (Hindi) Of great spiritual development

Mahavira (Hindi) A great hero
Mahaveera, Mahaveara, Mahaveira,
Mahaviera, Mahavyra, Mahavir, Mahaveer,
Mahavear, Mahaveir, Mahavier, Mahavyr

Mahdi (African) One who is expected
Mahdie, Mahdee, Mahdea, Mahdey, Mahdy

Maher (Irish) A generous man

Mahesh (Hindi) A great ruler
Maheshe

Mahfouz (Arabic) One who is protected
Mafouz, Mahfooz, Mafooz, Mahfuz, Mafuz

Mahieu (French) A gift from God

Mahin (Indian) Of the earth
Mahen, Mahyn

Mahir (Arabic) One who is skilled
Maheer, Mahear, Mahier, Maheir, Mahyr

Mahkah (Native American) Of the earth
Mahka, Makah, Maka

Mahlon (Hebrew) One who is sick
Mahlun, Mahlin, Mahlyn, Mahlan, Mahlen

Mahluli (African) A conqueror
Mahlulie, Mahluly, Mahluley, Mahlulee,
Mahlulea

Mahmud (Arabic) One who is praiseworthy
Mahmood, Mahmoud, Mehmood, Mehmud,
Mehmoud

Mahogany (English) Resembling the rich,
dark wood
Mahogani, Mahoganey, Mahoganie,
Mahogane, Mahogonee, Mahogonea

Mahomet (Arabic) One who is much
praised
Mahomat, Mahomit, Mahomyt, Mahomot,
Mahomut

Mahon (Gaelic) Resembling a bear
*Mahone, Mahoni, Mahonie, Muhoney,
Mahony, Mahonee, Mahonea*

Mahpee (Native American) Of the sky
Mahpea, Mahpi, Mahpie, Mahpy, Mahpey

Mahuizoh (Nahuatl) A glorious man
Mahuizo

Maiele (Hawaiian) One who is well-spoken
*Mayele, Maielle, Mayelle, Maiel, Mayel,
Maiell, Mayell*

Mailhairer (French) An ill-fated man

Maimon (Arabic) One who is dependable;
having good fortune
*Maymon, Maemon, Maimun, Maymun,
Maemun, Mamon, Mamun*

Maine (French) From the mainland; from
the state of Maine

Maisel (Persian) A warrior
Maysel, Maesel, Meisel, Meysel

Maitland (English) From the meadow land
*Maytland, Maetland, Maitlande, Maytlande,
Maetlande*

Majdy (Arabic) A glorious man
Majdey, Majdi, Majdie, Majdee, Majdea

Majid (Arabic) Of noble glory
Majeed, Majead, Majied, Majeid, Majyd, Majed

Major (Latin) The greater
Majur, Majer, Majar, Majir, Majyr, Majeur

Makaio (Hawaiian) A gift from God

Makani (Hawaiian) Of the wind
*Makanie, Makany, Makaney, Makanee,
Makanea, Makan*

Makarios (Greek) One who is blessed
*Makkarios, Macaire, Macario, Macarios,
Macarius, Maccario, Maccarios, Mackario,
Mackarios, Makar, Makari, Makario,
Makary, Makarie, Makarey, Makaree*

Makena (Hawaiian) Man of abundance
Makenah

Makepeace (English) One who promotes
peace
*Maekpeace, Maykpeace, Maikpeace,
Makepeece, Maikpeece, Maykpeece, Maekpeece*

Maki (Finnish) From the hill
Makie, Maky, Makey, Makee, Makea

Makin (Arabic) Having great strength
Makeen, Makean, Makein, Makien, Makyn

Makis (Hebrew) A gift from God
Madys, Makiss, Makyss, Makisse, Madysse

Makkapitew (Native American) One who
has big teeth

Makonnen (African) A king
*Makonnan, Makonnon, Makonnun,
Makonnin, Makonnyn, Makonen, Makonan,
Makonin, Makonyn, Makonun, Makonon*

Makoto (Japanese) A good and sincere man

Makram (Arabic) A noble and generous man
*Makrem, Makrim, Makrym, Makrom,
Makrum*

Makya (Native American) An eagle hunter
Makyah

Mal (Irish / Hindi / Hebrew) A chief / of
the gardens / a messenger of God

Malachi (Hebrew) A messenger of God
*Malachie, Malachy, Malaki, Malakia,
Malakie, Malaquias, Malechy, Maleki,
Malequi, Malakai, Malak, Maeleachlainn*

Malajit (Indian) A victorious man
*Malajeet, Malajeit, Malajiet, Malajyt,
Malajeat*

Malawa (African) A flourishing man

Malay (Indian) From the mountain
Malaye, Malae, Malai

Malcolm (Gaelic) Follower of St. Columbus
*Malcom, Malcolum, Malkolm, Malkom,
Malkolum*

Malden (English) From the valley of the
strong warrior
Maldan, Maldin, Maldyn, Maldon, Maldun

Malfred (German) A peaceful ruler
Malfried, Malfreid, Malfryd, Malfrid

Mali (Indian) A ruler; the firstborn son
Malie, Maly, Maley, Malee, Malea

Malik (Arabic) The sovereign
*Maleek, Maleak, Maleik, Maliek, Mulyk,
Maleeq, Malek, Maliq, Malique, Malyq,
Maleaq, Malieq, Maleiq, Malic, Malyc,
Maleec, Maleac, Maleic, Maliec, Maalik*

Malin (English) The little warrior
*Malyn, Malen, Malon, Malun, Malan, Mallin,
Mallyn, Mallon, Mallun, Mallan, Mallen*

Malise (French) One who is masterful
Malyse

Malki (Hebrew) My king
*Malkie, Malky, Malkey, Malkee, Malkea,
Malcam, Malkam, Malkiel, Malkior,
Malkiya, Malqui*

Mallory (French) An unlucky young man;
ill-fated
*Mallary, Mallerey, Mallery, Malloreigh,
Mallorey, Mallori, Mallorie, Malorey,
Malori, Malorie, Malory, Malloree, Mallorea,
Malorea, Maloree*

Mallow (Gaelic) From the river Allo
Mallowe, Malow, Malowe

Malo (Hawaiian) A victorious man
Maloh, Maloe, Mallo, Malloh

Malone (Irish) A follower of St. John
*Malon, Maloney, Malony, Maloni, Malonie,
Malonee, Malonea*

Malvin (Celtic / English) A leader / a friend
who offers counsel
*Malvinn, Malvinne, Malvyn, Malvynn,
Malvynne, Malven, Malvenn, Malvenne*

Mamduh (Arabic) One who is praised
Mamdouh, Mamdu, Mamdou

Mamo (African) A little boy
Mamoe, Mamow, Mamowe

Mamoru (Japanese) Of the earth
Mamorou, Mamorue, Mamorew, Mamoroo

Mamun (Arabic) A trustworthy man
Ma'mun, Mamoun, Mamoon, Mamune

Manasseh (Hebrew) One who is forgetful
*Manassas, Manases, Manasio, Menashe,
Menashi, Menashi, Menashy, Menashey,
Menashee, Menashea, Manasses, Manasas*

Manchester (English) From the city in
England
*Manchestar, Manchestor, Manchestir,
Manchestyr, Manchestur*

Manchu (Chinese) One who is pure;
unflawed
Manchue, Manchew, Manchou, Manchoo

Manco (Peruvian) A king
Mancko, Manko, Mancoe, Mancoh

Mandan (Native American) A tribal name
Manden, Mandon, Mandun, Mandin, Mandyn

Mandar (Indian) Of the sacred tree
Mundarr, Mandare

Mandeep (Indian) One who has a bright
mind
*Mandip, Mandeap, Mandeip, Mandiep,
Mandyp*

Mandek (Polish) A soldier
Mandeck, Mandec

Mandel (German) Resembling an almond;
having almond-shaped eyes
Mandell, Mandelle, Mandele

Mander (English) My son
Mandir, Mandyr, Mandur, Mandor

Mandhatri (Indian) A prince; born to royalty
*Mandhatrie, Mandhatry, Mandhatrey,
Mandhatree, Mandhatrea*

Mandy (English) One who is much loved
Mandee, Mandea, Mandi, Mandie, Mandey

Manelin (Persian) The prince of all princes
*Manelen, Manelyn, Manelan, Manelon,
Manelun*

Manfred (German) A man of peace
*Manfreid, Manfried, Manfrid, Manfryd,
Mannfred, Mannfreid, Mannfried, Mannfrid,
Mannfryd, Manfredo, Manfrit, Mannfrit,
Manfryt, Mannfryt*

Mani (African) From the mountain
Manie, Many, Maney, Manee, Manea

Maninder (Hindi) A manly man

Manipi (Native American) An amazing
man; a wonder
Manipie, Manipy, Manipey, Manipee, Manipea

Manjit (Indian) A conqueror of the mind; having great knowledge
Manjeet, Manjeat, Manjeit, Manjiet, Manjyt

Mankato (Native American) Of the blue earth

Manley (English) From the man's meadow; from the hero's meadow
Manly, Manli, Manlie, Manlea, Manleah, Manlee, Manleigh

Manmohan (Indian) A handsome and pleasing man
Manmohen, Manmohin, Manmohyn

Mann (English) A man; a hero
Man

Manneville (English) From the hero's estate; from the man's estate
Mannevylle, Mannevile, Mannevyle, Mannevill, Mannevyll, Mannevil, Mannevyl, Mannville, Mannvylle, Mannvile, Mannvyle, Mannvill, Mannvyll, Mannvil, Mannvyl, Manville, Manvylle, Manvile, Manvyle, Manvill, Manvyll, Manvil, Manvyl

Mannheim (German) From the hamlet in the swamp
Manheim

Manning (English) The son of the man; the son of the hero
Mannyng, Maning, Manyng

Mannis (Irish) A great man
Mannys, Manniss, Mannyss, Mannes, Mannus, Manis, Manys, Manes, Manus, Mannuss, Manness, Mannas, Mannass, Manas

Mannix (Irish) A little monk
Manix, Mannicks, Manicks, Manniks, Maniks, Mannyx, Manyx, Mannyks, Manyks, Mannycks, Manycks

Mannley (English) From the hero's meadow; from the man's meadow
Mannly, Mannli, Mannlie, Mannleigh, Mannlee, Mannlea, Mannleah

Mano (Hawaiian) Resembling a shark
Manoe, Manow, Manowe

Manoach (Hebrew) A restful place
Manoah, Manoa, Manoache

Manohar (Indian) A delightful and captivating man
Manoharr, Manohare

Mansa (African) A king
Mansah

Manse (English) A victorious man

Mansel (English) From the clergyman's house
Mansle, Mansell, Mansele, Manselle, Manshel, Manshele, Manshell, Manshelle

Mansfield (English) From the field near the small river
Mansfeld, Maunfield, Maunfeld

Mansur (Arabic) One who is victorious with God's help
Mansour, Mansure, Mansoor

Mantel (French) One who makes clothing
Mantell, Mantele, Mantelle, Mantle

Manton (English) From the man's town; from the hero's town
Mantun, Manten, Mannton, Manntun, Mannten

Mantotohpa (Native American) Of the four bears

Manu (African) The second-born child
Manue, Manou, Manoo

Manuel (Spanish) Form of Emmanuel, meaning "God is with us"
Manuelo, Manuello, Manolito, Manolo, Manollo, Manny, Manni, Manney, Mannie, Mannee, Mannea

Manville (French) From the great town
Manvil, Manvile, Manvylle, Manvyl, Manvyle, Mandeville, Mandevil, Mandevill, Mandevile, Mandevylle, Mandevyll, Mandevyl, Mandevyle, Manvill, Manvyll

Manya (Indian) A respected man
Manyah

Manzo (Japanese) The third son with ten-thousand-fold strength

Maolmuire (Scottish) A dark-skinned man

Maponus (Anglo-Saxon) In mythology, the god of music and youth

Mar (Spanish) Of the sea
Marr, Mare, Marre

Maram (Arabic) One who is desired

Marcel (French) The little warrior
Marceau, Marcelin, Marcellin, Marcellino, Marcell, Marcello, Marcellus, Marcelo, Marcely, Marciano, Marceley, Marceli, Marcelie, Marcelee, Marceleigh, Marcelino, Marcelus, Marcial

March (French) From the borderland; born during the month of March
Marche, Marzo, Marcio

Marconi (Italian) One who is inventive
Marconie, Marcony, Marconey, Marconee, Marconea

Marcus (Latin) Form of Mark, meaning "dedicated to Mars, the god of war"
Markus, Marcas, Marco, Markos, Marcos, Marko, Marqus, Marqos, Marcoux

Marden (Old English) From the valley with the pool
Mardin, Mardyn, Mardon, Mardun, Mardan

Mareechi (Indian) A sage
Mareechie, Mareechy, Mareechey, Mareechee, Mareechea

Marek (Polish) Form of Mark, meaning "dedicated to Mars, the god of war"
Marik, Maryk, Mareck, Maryck, Marick

Mareo (Japanese) One who is rare; unlike others
Marayo, Maraeo, Maraio

Margarito (Spanish) Resembling a pearl

Mariano (Spanish) A manly man
Marianos, Marianus, Meirion, Marion

Mariatu (African) One who is pure; chaste
Mariatue, Mariatou, Mariatoo

Marid (Arabic) A rebellious man
Maryd

Marino (Latin) Of the sea
Marinos, Marinus, Mareno, Marenos, Marenus

Mario (Latin) A manly man
Marius, Marios, Mariano, Marion, Mariun, Mareon

Marjuan (Spanish) A contentious man
Marwon, Marhjuan, Marhwon

❶ **Mark** (Latin) Dedicated to Mars, the god of war
Marc, Markey, Marky, Marki, Markie, Markee, Markea, Markov, Marq, Marque, Markell, Markel, Marx

Markham (English) From Mark's village
Markam

Markku (Scandinavian) A rebel
Markkue, Marku, Markue, Markkou, Markou

Marland (English) From the land near the lake
Marlond, Marlande, Marlonde, Marlando, Marlondo

Marlas (Greek) From the high tower
Marles, Marlos, Marlis, Marlys, Marlus

Marley (English) From the meadow near the lake
Marly, Marlea, Marleah, Marlee, Marleigh, Marli, Marlie, Marl, Marle

Marlon (English) Resembling a little hawk
Marlan, Marlen, Marlin, Marlyn, Marlun, Marlonn, Marlinn, Marlynn, Marlann, Marlenn, Marlunn

Marlow (English) Resembling driftwood
Marlowe, Marlo, Marloe

Marmaduke (Irish) An upper-class man; a follower of St. Maedoc
Marmeduke

Marmion (French) Our little one
Marmyon, Marmeon

Marnin (Hebrew) One who brings joy to others
Marnyn, Marnon, Marnun, Marnen, Marnan

Maro (Japanese) Myself

Marom (Hebrew) From the peak
Merom, Marum, Merum

Marquis (French) A lord of the borderlands; a nobleman
Markeece, Markeese, Markese, Markess, Markise, Markiss, Markize, Markwees, Markwess, Marques, Marquess, Marquez, Marqui, Marquise, Marquiz, Marquel, Marqes

Marr (German) From the marshland
Mar

Marriner (English) Of the sea; a seaman; a
sailor
*Mariner, Marrinor, Marinor, Marrinur,
Marinur, Marrinar, Marinar, Marrinir,
Marinir, Marrinyr, Marinyr, Marrinel,
Marinel, Marrin, Marin, Marryn, Maryn,
Maren*

Mars (Latin) The god of war

Marsden (English) From the valley near the
marshland
*Marsdon, Marsdun, Marsdan, Marsdin,
Marsdyn*

Marsh (English) From the marshland
Marshe

Marshall (French / English) A caretaker of
horses / a steward
*Marchall, Marischal, Marischall, Marschal,
Marshal, Marshell, Marshel, Marschall*

Marshawn (American) An outgoing young
man
*Marshon, Marsean, Marshown, Mashawn,
Masean, Mashon, Mashaun, Marshaun*

Marston (English) From the town near the
marsh
*Marstun, Marsten, Marstin, Marstyn,
Marstan*

Martin (Latin) Dedicated to Mars, the god
of war
*Martyn, Mart, Martel, Martell, Marten,
Martenn, Marti, Martie, Martijn, Martinien,
Martino, Martinos, Martinus, Marton, Marty,
Martey, Martee, Martea, Martainn, Maarten,
Marcin, Martial, Martinez, Martiniano*

Martinek (Czech) Form of Martin, meaning
"dedicated to Mars, the god of war"
*Martineck, Martinec, Martynek, Martyneck,
Martynec*

Marut (Indian) Of the wind
*Marout, Marute, Maruti, Marutie, Marutee,
Marutea, Maruty, Marutey*

Marvell (Latin) An extraordinary man
Marvel, Marvele, Marvelle, Marveille

Marvin (Welsh) A friend of the sea
*Marvinn, Marvinne, Marven, Marvenn,
Marvenne, Marvyn, Marvynn, Marvynne,
Marwen, Marwenn, Marwenne, Marwin,
Marwinn, Marwinne, Marwine, Marwyn,
Marwynn, Marwynne, Murvyn, Murvynn,
Murvynne, Murvin, Murvinn, Murvinne,
Murven, Murvenn, Murvenne, Marv, Marve*

Marwood (English) From the forest near
the lake
Marwode

Maryland (English) Honoring Queen Mary;
from the state of Maryland
*Mariland, Maralynd, Marylind, Marilind,
Marylend, Marilend*

Masa (African) One who is centered
Masah, Massa, Massah

Masaaki (African) An unfortunate man
*Masaki, Masakie, Masakee, Masakea,
Masaky, Masakey*

Masajiro (Japanese) Having integrity
*Masajyro, Masaji, Masajie, Masajy, Masajey,
Masajee, Masajea*

Masamba (African) One who leaves

Masamitsu (Japanese) A sensitive man

Masanao (Japanese) A good man

Masao (Japanese) A righteous man

Masato (Japanese) One who is just
Masatoe, Masatow, Masatowe

Masayuki (Japanese) One who causes
trouble
*Masayukie, Masayuky, Masayukey,
Masayukee, Masayukea*

Masefield (English) From the cornfield
Masefeld, Maisefield, Maisefeld

Mashaka (African) One who causes trouble

Mashiro (Japanese) One who is open-
minded
Mashyro

Masichuvio (Native American) Resembling
a gray deer

Maska (Native American) Having great
strength

Maskini (African) A poor man
Maskinie, Maskiny, Maskiney, Maskinee, Maskinea

Maslin (French) Little Thomas
Maslyn, Maslen, Maslan, Maslon, Maslun, Masling, Masslin, Masslyn, Masslon, Masslun, Masslan, Masslen

● **Mason** (English) One who works with stone
● *Masun, Masen, Masan, Masin, Masyn, Masson, Massun, Massen, Massan, Massin, Massyn*

Masos (Hebrew) Filled with happiness

Massachusetts (Native American) From the big hill; from the state of Massachusetts
Massachusets, Massachusette, Massachusetta, Massa, Massachute, Massachusta

Masselin (French) A young Thomas
Masselyn, Masselen, Masselan, Masselon, Masselun, Maselin, Maselyn, Maselon, Maselun, Maselan, Maselen

Massey (English) A superior man
Massy, Massee, Massea, Massi, Massie, Masey, Masy, Masi, Masie, Masee, Masea

Masud (African) A fortunate man
Masood, Masoode, Masoud, Masoude, Masude, Mas'ud

Masura (Japanese) A good destiny
Masoura

Mataniah (Hebrew) A gift from God
Matania, Matanya, Matanyahu, Mattania, Mattaniah, Matanyah

Matata (African) One who causes trouble

Matchitehew (Native American) One who has an evil heart

Matchitisiw (Native American) One who has a bad character

Math (Scottish) Resembling a bear
Mathe

Mathani (African) Of the commandments
Mathanie, Mathany, Mathaney, Mathanee, Mathanea

Mathau (American) A lively man
Mathow, Mathowe, Mathou, Mathoy

Mather (English) Of the powerful army
Matther, Maither, Mayther, Maether

Matherson (English) The son of Mather
Mathersun, Mathersin, Mathersyn, Mathersen, Mathers

Matheson (English) The son of Matthew
Mathesun, Mathesen, Mathesin, Mathesyn, Mathison, Mathisun, Mathisen, Mathisin, Mathisyn, Mathyson, Mathysen, Mathysin, Mathysyn, Mathysun, Matthews, Mathews, Matson, Matsen, Matsun, Matsin, Matsyn, Matteson, Mattesun, Mattesin, Mattesyn, Mattesen, Mattison, Mattisun, Mattisen, Mattisin, Mattisyn, Matthewson, Matthewsun, Matthewsen, Matthewsin, Matthewsyn, Mathewson, Mathewsun, Mathewsin, Mathewsyn, Mathewsen

Matin (Arabic) Having great strength
Maten, Matan, Matyn, Maton, Matun

Matisse (French) One who is gifted
Matiss, Matysse, Matyss, Matise, Matyse

Matland (English) From Matthew's land
Matlande, Mattland, Mattlande

Matlock (American) A rancher
Matlok, Matloc

Matoskah (Native American) Resembling a white bear
Matoska

Matsu (Japanese) From the pine
Matsue, Matsoo, Matsou

Matsya (Indian) Resembling a fish
Matsyuh

● **Matthew** (Hebrew) A gift from God
● *Madteo, Madteos, Madtheos, Mat, Mata, Mateo, Mateus, Mateusz, Mathé, Matheu, Mathew, Mathian, Mathias, Mathieu, Matias, Matico, Mats, Matt, Mattaeus, Mattaus, Matteo, Matthaus, Mattheus, Matthias, Matthieu, Matthiew, Mattias, Mattie, Mattieu, Matty, Matvey, Matyas, Matz, Matai, Mate, Matei, Matfei, Matro, Matteus, Mattithyahu, Mattox*

Matunde (African) One who is fruitful
Matundi, Matundie, Matundy, Matundey, Matundee, Matundea

Matvey (Russian) Form of Matthew, meaning "a gift from God"
Matvy, Matvee, Matvea, Matvi, Matvie, Motka, Matviyko

Matwau (Native American) The enemy

Mauli (Hawaiian) A black-haired man; a giver of life
Maulie, Mauly, Mauley, Maulee, Mauleigh, Maulea

Maurice (Latin) A dark-skinned man; Moorish
Maurell, Maureo, Mauricio, Maurids, Maurie, Maurin, Maurio, Maurise, Maurits, Mauritius, Mauritz, Maurizio, Mauro, Maurus, Maury, Maurycy, Mauri, Maurey, Mauree, Maurea, Maurilio

Maverick (English) An independent man; a nonconformist
Maveric, Maverik, Mavrick, Mavric, Mavrik

Mavi (Turkish) Refers to the color blue
Mavie, Mavy, Mavey, Mavee, Mavea

Mavis (English) Resembling a small bird
Mavys, Maviss, Mavyss, Mavisse, Mavysse, Mavas, Mavus, Mavasse, Mavass, Mavuss, Mavusse

Mawali (African) A lively man; one who is vibrant
Mawalie, Mawaly, Mawaley, Mawalee, Mawalea, Mawaleigh

Mawulol (African) One who gives thanks to God

Max (Latin) Form of Maximilian, meaning "the greatest"
Macks, Maxi, Maxie, Maxy, Maxey, Maxee, Maxea, Maxx, Maxen, Maxon, Maxan, Maxin, Maxyn, Maks

Maxfield (English) From Mack's field
Mackfield, Maxfeld, Macksfeld

Maximilian (Latin) The greatest
Maksim, Maksym, Maksymilian, Massimiliano, Massimo, Maxemillian, Maxemilion, Maxie, Maxim, Maxime, Maxemilian, Maximiliano, Maximilianus, Maximilien, Maximillien, Maximino, Maximo, Maximos, Maxymillian, Maxymilian, Maximous, Maximus, Maksimilian, Maxinen, Maxanen

Maxwell (English) From Mack's spring
Maxwelle, Mackswell, Maxwel, Mackswel, Mackwelle, Maxwill, Maxwille, Mackswill, Maxwil, Mackswil

Mayer (Latin / German / Hebrew) A large man / a farmer / one who is shining bright
Maier, Mayar, Mayor, Mayir, Mayur, Meyer, Meir, Myer, Mayeer, Meier

Mayes (English) From the field
Mays

Mayfield (English) From the strong one's field
Mayfeld, Maifield, Maifeld, Maefield, Maefeld

Mayhew (French) Form of Matthew, meaning "a gift from God"
Maihew, Maehew, Mayhugh, Maihugh, Maehugh, Mayhue, Maehue, Maihue

Maynard (German) One who is brave and strong
Maynhard, Maynor, Meinhard, Meinhardt, Menard, Mainard, Maenard, Maynar, Mainor, Maenor, Mainar, Maenar, Maynerd

Mayne (German) A powerful and great man
Mayn, Main, Maine, Maen, Maene, Mane

Mayo (Gaelic) From the yew-tree plain
Mayoe, Maiyo, Maeyo, Maiyoe, Maeyoe, Mayoh, Maioh

Maz (Hewbrew) One who provides aid
Maiz, Maze, Maiz, Maez, Maeze, Mazi, Mazie, Mazee, Mazea, Mazy, Mazey, Mazin, Mazyn, Mazon, Mazun, Mazen, Mazan

Mazal (Arabic) One who is calm; tranquil
Mazall

Mazor (Hebrew) One who is bandaged
Mazur, Mazar, Mazer, Mazir, Mazyr

Mccoy (Gaelic) The son of Coy
McCoy

McKenna (Gaelic) The son of Kenna; to ascend
McKennon, McKennun, McKennen, McKennan

Mckile (Gaelic) The son of Kyle
McKile, Mckyle, McKyle, Mackile, Mackyle, MacKile, MacKyle

Mead (English) From the meadow
Meade, Meed, Meede, Maed, Maede

Meallan (Irish) A kind man
Meallen, Meallon, Meallun, Meallin, Meallyn

Meara (Irish) Filled with joy
*Meare, Mearie, Meari, Meary, Mearey,
Mearee, Mearea, Meadhra*

Medad (Hebrew) A beloved friend
Meydad

Medford (English) From the meadow near
the ford
*Medforde, Medfurd, Medfurde, Medferd,
Medferde, Meadford, Meadforde, Meadfurd,
Meadfurde, Meadferd, Meadferde*

Medgar (German) Having great strength
Medgarr, Medgare, Medgard, Medard

Medwin (German) A strong friend
*Medwine, Medwinn, Medwinne, Medwen,
Medwenn, Medwenne, Medwyn, Medwynn,
Medwynne, Medvin, Medvinn, Medvinne,
Medven, Medvenn, Medvenne, Medvyn,
Medvynn, Medvynne*

Meged (Hebrew) One who has been blessed
with goodness

Megedagik (Native American) One who has
conquered many

Mehdi (Arabian) One who is guided
Mehdie, Mehdy, Mehdey, Mehdee, Mehdea

Mehetabel (Hebrew) One who is favored
by God
*Mehetabell, Mehitabel, Mehitabell, Mehytabel,
Mehytabell*

Mehrdad (Persian) Gift of the sun
*Mehrded, Mehrdod, Mehrdid, Mehrdyd,
Mehrdud*

Meilyr (Welsh) A regal ruler

Meino (German) One who stands firm
Meinke

Meinrad (German) A strong counselor
*Meinred, Meinrod, Meinrud, Meinrid,
Meinryd*

Meka (Hawaiian) Of the eyes
Mekah

Mekledoodum (Native American) A conceited man

Mekonnen (African) The angel
*Mekonnin, Mekonnyn, Mekonnan,
Mekonnon, Mekonnun*

Mel (Gaelic / English) A mill worker / form
of Melvin, meaning "a friend who offers
counsel"
Mell

Melancton (Greek) Resembling a black
flower
*Melankton, Melanctun, Melanktun,
Melancten, Melankten, Melanchton,
Melanchten, Melanchthon, Melanchthen*

Melanio (Spanish) Born into royalty
Melaniyo, Melaneo, Melaneyo

Melbourne (English) From the mill stream
*Melborn, Melburn, Milbourn, Milbourne,
Milburn, Millburn, Millburne, Melburne,
Melborne, Milborne, Melbyrne, Millbyrne,
Milbyrne, Millborn, Millbourne, Millborne*

Melchior (Polish) The king of the city
*Malchior, Malkior, Melker, Melkior, Melchoir,
Melchor, Melcher*

Melchisedek (Hebrew) My God is
righteousness
Melchisadak, Melchisadeck, Melchizadek

Meldon (English) From the mill on the hill
Meldun, Melden, Meldan, Meldin, Meldyn

Meldrick (English) The ruler of the mill
*Meldrik, Meldric, Melderick, Melderik,
Melderic, Meldryck, Meldryc, Meldryk,
Melderyck, Melderyk, Melderyc*

Mele (Hawaiian) One who is happy

Melesio (Spanish) An attentive man; one
who is careful
*Melacio, Melasio, Melecio, Melicio, Meliseo,
Milesio*

Melesse (African) He has returned
Melisse, Melysse

Meletius (Greek) A cautious man
Meletios, Meletious, Meletus, Meletos

Meli (Native American) One who is bitter
Melie, Mely, Meley, Melee, Melea, Meleigh

Melito (Spanish) A calm boy
Melyto

Melker (Swedish) A king
Melkar, Melkor, Melkur, Melkir, Melkyr

Mellen (Gaelic) The little pleasant one
Mellin, Mellyn, Mellan, Mellon, Mellun

Melos (Greek) The favorite
Milos, Mylos

Melroy (American) Form of Elroy, meaning
"a red-haired young man / a king"
Melroye, Melroi

Melton (English) From the mill town
Meltun, Meltin, Meltyn, Melten, Meltan

Melville (English) From the mill town
*Melvill, Melvil, Melvile, Melvylle, Melvyll,
Melvyl, Melvyle*

Melvin (English) A friend who offers counsel
*Melvinn, Melvinne, Melven, Melvenn,
Melvenne, Melvyn, Melvynn, Melvynne,
Melwin, Melwinn, Melwinne, Melwine,
Melwen, Melwenn, Melwenne, Melwyn,
Melwynn, Melwynne, Melvon, Melvun,
Melvan, Maelwine*

Melvis (American) Form of Elvis, meaning
"one who is wise"
Melviss, Melvisse, Melvys, Melvyss, Melvysse

Memphis (American) From the city in
Tennessee
*Memfis, Memphys, Memfys, Memphus,
Memfus*

Menachem (Hebrew) One who provides
comfort
*Menaheim, Menahem, Menachim,
Menachym, Menahim, Menahym, Machum,
Machem, Mechum, Mechem*

Menassah (Hebrew) A forgetful man
Menassa, Menass, Menas, Menasse, Menasseh

Mendel (Farsi) A learned man
*Mendell, Mendle, Mendeley, Mendely,
Mendeli, Mendelie, Mendelee, Mendelea,
Mendeleigh*

Menefer (Egyptian) Of the beautiful city
Menefar, Menefir, Menefyr, Menefor, Menefur

Menelik (African) The son of a wise man
*Menelick, Menelic, Menelyk, Menelyck,
Menelyc*

Mensah (African) The third-born child
Mensa

Mentor (Greek) A wise guide
Mentur, Menter, Mentar, Mentir, Mentyr

Menyhért (Hungarian) Of the royal light

Mercator (Latin) A merchant
*Mercatur, Mercater, Mercatar, Mercatir,
Mercatyr*

Mercer (English) A storekeeper
*Merce, Mercar, Mercor, Mercur, Mercir,
Mercyr, Murcer, Murcar, Murcir, Murcyr,
Murcor, Murcur*

Mercury (Latin) In mythology, the god of
commerce and a messenger god
*Mercuri, Mercurie, Mercuree, Mercurea,
Mercurey, Mercure, Mercher, Mercutio,
Mercurius*

Mercy (English) One who shows compas-
sion and pity
*Mercey, Merci, Mercie, Mercee, Mercea, Mirci,
Mircee, Mircea, Mircey, Mircy, Mircie, Mersy,
Mersie, Mersi, Mersey, Mersee, Mersea*

Meredith (Welsh) A great ruler; protector
of the sea
*Meredyth, Merideth, Meridith, Meridyth,
Meredeth*

Mereston (English) From the town near
the lake
*Merestun, Meresten, Merston, Merstun,
Mersten*

Merewood (English) From the forest with
the lake
Merwood, Merewode, Merwode

Meris (Latin) Of the sea
Meriss, Merisse, Merys, Meryss, Merysse

Merle (French) Resembling a blackbird
Merl, Meryle, Meryl, Myrle, Myrl

Merlin (Welsh) Of the sea fortress; in Arthurian legend, the wizard and mentor of King Arthur
Merlyn, Merlan, Merlon, Merlun, Merlen, Merlinn, Merlynn, Merlonn, Merlunn, Merlann, Merlenn

Merlow (English) From the hill near the lake
Merelow, Merlowe, Merelowe

Merrick (English) Form of Maurice, meaning "a dark-skinned man; Moorish"
Merric, Merrik, Merryck, Merryc, Merryk, Merick, Meric, Merik, Meryck, Merik, Meric, Meyrick, Meyrik, Meyric, Meyryck, Meyryc, Meyryk, Myrick, Myric, Myrik, Myryck, Myryc, Myryk

Merrill (English) Of the shining sea
Meril, Merill, Merrel, Merrell, Merril, Meryl, Merryll, Meryll, Merryl, Merel, Merell

Merritt (English / Latin) From the boundary's gate / one who deserves good fortune
Merit, Meritt, Merrit, Merrett, Meret, Merett, Merret, Merrytt, Meryt, Merryt, Merytt

Merry (English) Filled with joy
Merri, Merrie, Merrey, Merree, Merrea

Mersey (English) From the river
Mersy, Mersi, Mersie, Mersee, Mersea

Merton (English) From the town near the lake
Mertun, Mertan, Merten, Mertin, Mertyn, Murton, Murtun, Murten, Murtan, Murtin, Murtyn

Mervin (Welsh) Form of Marvin, meaning "a friend of the sea"
Mervinn, Mervinne, Mervyn, Mervynn, Mervynne, Merven, Mervenn, Mervenne, Merwin, Merwinn, Merwinne, Merwine, Merwyn, Merwynn, Merwynne, Merwen, Merwenn, Merwenne, Merv, Merve

Meshach (Hebrew) An enduring man
Meshack, Meshac, Meshak, Meeshach, Meeshack, Meeshak, Meeshac

Mesquite (American) A spicy man
Meskeet, Mesqueet, Mesqeet

Methodios (Greek) A traveling companion
Methodius, Methodious

Methuselah (Hebrew) He who was sent; in the Bible, the longest-living man
Methusela, Methusella, Methusellah, Mathusela, Mathuselah, Mathusella, Mathusellah

Mhina (African) One who is delightful
Mhinah, Mheena, Mheenah, Mheina, Mheinah, Mhienah, Mhienah, Mhyna, Mhynah

Miach (Gaelic) A medic
Myach, Miack, Myack, Miak, Myak, Miac, Myac

Micah (Hebrew) Form of Michael, meaning "who is like God?"
Mica, Mycah, Myca, Micaiah, Mycaiah, Maacah, Mika, Mikah, Myka, Mykah

❷ **Michael** (Hebrew) Who is like God?
Makai, Micael, Mical, Micha, Michaelangelo, Michail, Michal, Micheal, Michel, Michelangelo, Michele, Michiel, Mihail, Mihaly, Mikael, Mike, Mikel, Mikell, Mikey, Mikkel, Mikhail, Mikhalis, Mikhos, Miko, Mikol, Miky, Miquel, Mischa, Misha, Mychael, Mychal, Mykal, Mykel, Mykell, Micheil, Maichail, Mckale, McKale, Mihangel, Mikeal, Mikhael, Mikko, Miksa, Mysha, Myscha

Michigan (Native American) From the great waters; from the state of Michigan
Mishigan, Michegen, Mishegen

Michio (Japanese) One who has the strength of three thousand
Mychio

Michon (Hebrew) Form of Michael, meaning "who is like God?"
Mychon, Michonn, Mychonn, Mishon, Myshon, Mishonn, Myshonn, Micheon

Mick (English) Form of Michael, meaning "who is like God?"
Micke, Mickey, Micky, Micki, Mickie, Mickee, Mickea, Mickel

Middleton (English) From the central town
Midleton, Middletun, Midletun, Middleten, Midleten

Mieko (Japanese) A bright man

Migdal (Hebrew) From the tower
Migdall, Migdahl, Migdol, Migdoll

❂ **Miguel** (Portuguese / Spanish) Form of Michael, meaning "Who is like God?"
Migel, Myguel

Mihir (Indian) Of the sun
Miheer, Mihear, Miheir, Mihier, Mihyr

Mikaili (African) Form of Michael, meaning "who is like God?"
Mikailie, Mikailee, Mikailey, Mikaily, Mikailea, Mikaley, Mikaly, Mikalee, Mikalea, Mikaleigh, Mikali, Mikalie

Mikasi (Native American) Resembling a coyote
Mikasie, Mikasy, Mikasey, Mikasee, Mikasea

Miki (Japanese) From the trees
Mikie, Miky, Mikey, Mikee, Mikea

Mikio (Japanese) From the three trees standing together
Mikeo, Mikeyo, Mikiyo

Mikolas (Basque) Form of Nicholas, meaning "of the victorious people"
Mikolaus, Miklas, Mickolas, Mickolaus, Micklas, Mikolus, Mickolus, Mikolaj, Mikolai, Milek, Mileck, Milec

Milagro (Spanish) A miracle child
Milagros, Milagrio, Milagreo, Milagrios, Mylagro, Mylagros, Mylagrio, Mylagreo, Mylagrios

Milan (Latin) An eager and hardworking man
Mylan

Miland (Indian) Resembling a bee
Myland, Milande, Mylande, Milind, Milinde, Mylinde, Mylind, Milend, Milende, Mylend, Mylende

Milap (Native American) A charitable man
Mylap

Milbank (English) From the mill on the riverbank
Millbank, Mylbank, Myllbank

Miles (German / Latin) One who is merciful / a soldier
Myles, Milo, Mylo, Miley, Mily, Mili, Milie, Milee, Milea, Milos, Mylos, Milosh, Mylosh

Milford (English) From the mill's ford
Millford, Milfurd, Millfurd, Milferd, Millferd, Milforde, Millforde, Milfurde, Millfurde, Milferde, Millferde

Millard (English) The guardian of the mill
Milurd, Millerd, Milerd, Millward, Milward, Millwerd, Milwerd

Miller (English) One who works at the mill
Millar, Millor, Millur, Millir, Millyr, Myller, Millen, Millan, Millon, Millun, Millin, Millyn, Millman, Millmann, Milman, Milmann, Muller, Mueller, Melar, Mellar, Meler, Meller

Mills (English) One who lives near the mill
Mylls

Miloslav (Czech) One who is honored; one who loves glory
Myloslav, Miloslaw, Myloslaw

Milson (English) The son of Miles
Milsun, Milsen, Milsin, Milsyn, Milsan

Milton (English) From the mill town
Miltun, Milten, Millton, Milltun, Millten, Mylton, Myllton, Mylten, Myllten, Myltun, Mylltun, Milt, Mylt, Milte, Mylte, Milty, Miltee, Miltea, Milti, Miltie, Miltey

Mimir (Norse) In mythology, a giant who guarded the well of wisdom
Mymir, Mimeer, Mimyr, Mymeer, Mymyr, Meemir, Meemeer, Meemyr

Miner (Latin / English) One who works in the mines / a youth
Minor, Minar, Minur, Minir, Minyr

Mingan (Native American) Resembling a gray wolf
Mingen, Mingin, Mingon, Mingun, Mingyn

Mingo (American) A flirtatious man
Mingoe, Myngo, Myngoe

Minh (Vietnamese) A clever man

Minnesota (Native American) From the sky-tinted waters
Minesota, Minnesoda, Minesoda, Minisota, Minisoda

Minninnewah (Native American) Of the whirlwind

Minnow (American) A beachcomber
Mynnow, Minno, Mynno, Minnoe, Mynnoe

Minoru (Japanese) To bear fruit
Minorue, Minoroo, Minorou, Mynoru, Mynorue, Mynoroo, Mynorou

Minos (Greek) In mythology, the king of Crete who constructed the labyrinth
Mynos

Minster (English) Of the church
Mynster, Minstar, Mynstar, Minstor, Mynstor, Minstur, Mynstur, Minstir, Mynstir, Minstyr, Mynstyr

Minty (English) One who collects his thoughts
Mintey, Mintee, Mintea, Minti, Mintie, Minte, Mint

Mio (Spanish) He is mine
Myo

Miracle (American) An act of God's hand
Mirakle, Mirakel, Myracle, Myrakle

Mirage (French) An illusion
Myrage

Mirek (Czech) A peaceful ruler
Myrek, Mireck, Myreck, Mirec, Myrec

Mirit (Hebrew) A bitter man
Miryt, Myrit, Myryt

Miroslav (Russian) Of peaceful glory
Miroslaw, Mircea, Myroslav, Myroslaw, Myrcea

Mirsab (Arabic) One who is judicious
Myrsab

Mirumbi (African) Born during a period of rain
Mirumbie, Mirumby, Mirumbey, Mirumbee, Mirumbea

Miruts (African) The chosen one
Mirut, Myruts, Myrut

Mirza (Turkey) A well-behaved child
Myrza, Myrzah, Mirzah

Misae (Native American) Born beneath the white-hot sun
Misay, Misaye, Mysae, Mysay, Mysaye

Mishal (Arabic) One who holds the torch
Myshal, Mishall, Myshall, Mishaal, Myshaal

Mississippi (Native American) Of the great river; from the state of Mississippi
Misisipi, Missisippi, Mississipi, Misissipi, Misisippi

Missouri (Native American) From the town of large canoes; from the state of Missouri
Missourie, Mizouri, Mizourie, Missoury, Mizoury, Missuri, Mizuri, Mizury, Missury

Mistico (Italian) A mystical man
Misticko, Mystico, Mysticko, Mistiko, Mystiko

Misu (Native American) From the rippling water
Mysu, Misue, Mysue, Misou, Mysou

Mitali (Indian) A beloved friend
Mitalie, Mitaly, Mitaley, Mitalee, Mitaleigh, Mitalea

Mitchell (English) Form of Michael, meaning "who is like God?"
Mitch, Mitchel, Mitchill, Mytchell, Mytch, Mytchel, Mytchill, Mitchil, Mytchil, Mitchem, Mitcham, Mitchum, Mitchom, Mitchim, Mitchym

Mithra (Persian) In mythology, the god of light
Mitra, Mythra, Mytra

Mitsu (Japanese) Of the light
Mytsu, Mitsue, Mytsue

Mizell (English) Resembling a tiny gnat
Myzell, Mizel, Myzel, Mizele, Myzele, Mizelle, Myzelle

Mladen (Slavic) One who is eternally young
Mladan, Mladon, Mladun, Mladin, Mladyn

Mochni (Native American) Resembling a talking bird
Mochnie, Mochny, Mochney, Mochnee, Mochneu

Modesty (Latin) One who is without conceit
Modesti, Modestie, Modestee, Modestus, Modestey, Modesto, Modestio, Modestine, Modestin, Modestea

Modig (Anglo-Saxon) A courageous man
Modyg, Modigg, Modygg

Moe (American) A dark-skinned man
Mo, Moey, Moeye

Mogens (Dutch) A powerful man
Mogen, Mogins, Mogin, Mogyns, Mogyn, Mogan, Mogans

Mogue (Irish) The name of a saint

Mohajit (Indian) A charming man
Mohajeet, Mohajeat, Mohajeit, Mohajiet, Mohajyt

Mohammed (Arabic) One who is greatly praised; the name of the prophet and founder of Islam
Mahomet, Mohamad, Mohamed, Mohamet, Mohammad, Muhammad, Muhammed, Mehmet, Mihammed, Mihammad, Muhamed, Muhamad, Muhamet, Mehemet, Muhameed

Mohan (Hindi) A charming and alluring man; in Hinduism, one of the names of Krishna
Mohann, Mohana, Mohanna

Mohandas (Hindi) A servant of Mohan
Mohandes, Mohandos, Mohandus

Mohave (Native American) A tribal name
Mohav, Mojave

Mohawk (Native American) A tribal name
Mohauk, Mohawke, Mohauke

Mohegan (Native American) A tribal name
Moheegan, Mohican, Mahican, Mohikan, Mahikan, Moheagan

Mojag (Native American) One who is never quiet

Moki (Native American) Resembling a deer
Mokie, Moky, Mokey, Mokee, Mokea

Molan (Irish) The servant of the storm
Molen

Molimo (Native American) Resembling a bear seeking shade
Molymo, Moleemo, Moliemo, Moleimo, Moleamo

Moline (American) A narrow-minded man
Moleen, Moleene, Molean, Moleane, Molyn, Molyne, Molein, Moleine, Molien, Moliene

Molloy (Irish) A noble chief
Molloi, Malloy, Malloi, Molloye, Molloye

Momo (American) A warring man

Mona (African) A jealous man
Monah

Monahan (Gaelic) A monk; a religious man
Monahen, Monahon, Monahun, Monahin, Monahyn, Monohan, Monohen, Monohon, Monohun, Monohin, Monohyn

Monckton (English) From the monk's settlement
Moncktun, Monckten, Monkton, Monktun, Monkten

Monet (French) A solitary man; one who advises others
Monay, Monaye, Monai, Monae

Money (American) A wealthy man
Moni, Monie, Mony, Monee, Monea, Muney, Muny, Muni, Munie, Munee, Munea

Mongo (African) A well-known man
Mongoe, Mongow, Mongowe

Mongwau (Native American) Resembling an owl

Monroe (Gaelic) From the mouth of the river Roe
Monro, Monrow, Monrowe, Munro, Munroe, Munrow, Munrowe

Montague (French) From the pointed mountain
Montagew, Montagu, Montaigu, Montaigue, Montaigew

Montaine (French) From the mountain
Montain, Montayn, Montayne, Montaen, Montaene, Montane

Montana (Spanish) From the mountainous region; from the state of Montana
Montanna, Montanus

Montaro (Japanese) A big boy

Monte (English) Form of Montague, meaning "from the pointed mountain"
Montae, Montay, Montel, Montes, Montez, Montaye, Montrel, Montrell, Montrele, Montrelle

Montego (Spanish) From the mountains
Montaygo, Montayego, Montaego, Monteego, Monteigo, Montiego, Monteygo, Monteago

Montenegro (Spanish) From the black mountain

Montgomery (French) From Gomeric's mountain
Montgomerey, Montgomeri, Montgomerie, Montgomeree, Montgomerea

Montrae (American) A high-maintenance man
Montraie, Montray, Montraye, Montrey

Montrose (French) A high and mighty man
Montroce, Montros

Monty (English) Form of Montgomery, meaning "from Gomeric's mountain"
Montey, Monti, Montie, Montee, Montea, Montes, Montez

Monyyak (African) Born during a drought

Moody (American) A tempermental man
Moodi, Moodie, Moodee, Moodea, Moodey

Moon (American) Born beneath the moon; a dreamer

Mooney (Irish) A wealthy man
Moony, Mooni, Moonie, Maonaigh, Moonee, Moonea, Moone

Moore (French) A dark-skinned man; one who is noble
More, Moor, Mör, Möric, Mooring, Mooryng

Moose (American) Resembling the animal; a big, strong man
Moos, Mooze, Mooz

Moral (American) An upstanding man

Moran (Irish) A great man
Morane, Morain, Moraine, Morayn, Morayne, Moraen, Moraene

Morathi (African) A wise man
Morathie, Morathy, Morathey, Morathee, Morathea

Mordecai (Hebrew) A servant of Marduk, a Babylonian god
Mordechai, Mordekai, Mordeckai, Morducai, Morduchai, Mordukai, Morduckai

Mordred (English) A brave counselor; in Arthurian legend, Arthur's illegitimate son
Modraed, Modrad, Moordred, Moordrad, Moordraed, Modred, Mordraed, Mordread, Mordrad

Moreland (English) From the moors
Moorland, Morland

Morell (French) A dark-skinned man; Moorish
Morel, Morelle, Morele, Morrell, Morrelle, Morrel, Morrele

Morenike (African) Having good luck
Moreniky, Morenikey, Morenikie, Moreniki, Morenikee, Morenikea

Morgan (Welsh) Circling the bright sea; a sea dweller
Morgaine, Morgann, Morgance, Morgane, Morgunne, Morgayne, Morgen, Morgin, Morgaen, Morgaene, Morgaena, Morgon, Morgun

Moriarty (Irish) A warrior of the sea
Moriarti, Moriartey, Moriartie, Moriartee, Moriartea

Moriel (Hebrew) God is my teacher
Moryel, Moriell, Moryell, Moriah, Moria

Morio (Japanese) A boy from the forest

Morlen (English) From the moor
Morlan, Morlin, Morlyn, Morlon, Morlun

Morley (English) From the meadow on the moor
Morly, Morleigh, Morlee, Morlea, Morleah, Morli, Morlie, Moorley, Moorly, Moorlea, Moorleah, Moorlee, Moorleigh, Moorli, Moorlie, Moreley, Morely, Morelee, Morelea, Moreleah, Moreleigh, Moreli, Morelie

Morpheus (Greek) In mythology, the god of dreams
Morfeus, Morphius, Mofius

Morris (Latin) Form of Maurice, meaning "a dark-skinned man; Moorish"
Morriss, Morey, Morice, Moricz, Morino, Moris, Moritz, Moriz, Morrel, Morrey, Morrice, Morrill, Moriss, Mori, Morie, Moree, Mory, Morri, Morrie, Morree, Morry

Morrison (English) The son of Morris
Morison, Morrisun, Morisun, Morrisen, Morisen, Morse

Morrissey (Irish) The sea's choice
Morrissy, Morrissi, Morrissie, Morrissee, Morrissea, Morrisey, Morrisy, Morisey, Morrisi, Morrisie, Morrisee, Morisy, Morisey, Morisi, Morisie, Morisee, Morrisea, Morisea

Mortimer (French) Of the still water; of the dead sea
Mortimar, Mortimor, Mortimur, Mortimir, Mortimyr, Mortymer, Mortymar, Mortymir, Mortymyr, Mortymor, Mortymur

Morton (English) From the town near the moor
Mortun, Morten, Mortan, Mortin, Mortyn

Morty (French) Form of Mortimer, meaning "of the still water; of the dead sea"
Mortey, Morti, Mortie, Mortee, Mortea, Mort, Morte

Morven (Gaelic) From the large mountain gap
Morvin, Morvyn, Morvan, Morvun, Morfin, Morfen, Morfyn, Morfun, Morfan

Mosaed (Arabic) A samaritan; a good man

Moses (Hebrew) A savior; in the Bible, the leader of the Israelites; drawn from the water
Mioshe, Mioshye, Mohsen, Moke, Moise, Moises, Mose, Moshe, Mosheh, Mosiah, Mosie, Mosie, Mozes, Moyses, Moss, Moesen, Moeshe

Mosi (African) The firstborn child
Mosie, Mosy, Mosey, Mosee, Mosea

Mostyn (Welsh) From the mossy settlement
Mostin, Mosten, Moston, Mostun, Mostan

Moswen (African) A light-skinned man
Moswenn, Moswenne, Moswin, Moswinn, Moswinne, Moswyn, Moswynn, Moswynne

Motavato (Native American) Of the black kettle
Motavatoe, Motavatow, Motavatowe, Mokovaoto, Mokovato, Meturato, Mokatavatah, Moketavato, Moketaveto

Motega (Native American) A new arrow
Motayga, Motaega, Motaiga, Motaga

Motor (American) One who is fast
Motar, Moter, Motir, Motyr, Motur

Mottel (Hebrew) A warrior
Mottell, Mottle

Moubarak (Arabian) One who is blessed
Mubarak, Moobarak

Moukib (Arabic) The last of the prophets
Moukeeb, Moukeab, Moukeib, Moukieb, Moukyb

Moulik (Indian) A valuable man
Moulyk

Moulton (English) From the mule town
Moultun, Moulten, Moultan, Moultin, Moultyn

Mounafes (Arabic) A rival

Mountakaber (Arabic) A conceited man

Moyo (African) Of the heart

Moyolehuani (Aztec) The enamored one

Mozam (African) A man from Mozambique
Mozambi, Mozambe, Mozambie, Mozamby, Mozambey, Mozambee, Mozambea

Muata (Native American) Of the yellow-jackets' nest

Mudawar (Arabic) One who has a round head
Mudawarr, Mudewar, Mudewarr

Muenda (African) A caring man

Mufid (Arabic) One who is useful
Mufeed, Mufeid, Mufied, Mufead, Mufyd

Mufidy (Scottish) A man of the sea
Mufidey, Mufidee, Mufidea, Mufidi, Mufidie

Muhannad (Arabic) One who wields a sword
Muhanned, Muhanad, Muhaned, Muhunnad, Muhunad, Muhanned, Muhaned

Muhsin (Arabic) A charitable man
Muhsyn, Muhseen, Muhsean, Muhsein, Muhsien

Muhtadi (Arabic) One who is guided along the right path
Muhtadie, Muhtady, Muhtadey, Muhtadee, Muhtadea

Muir (Gaelic) From the moor
Muire

Mujahid (Arabic) A warrior
Mujaheed, Mujaheid, Mujahied, Mujahead, Mujahyd

Mukasa (Ugandan) An adminstrator of God

Mukhtar (Arabic) The chosen one
Muktar

Mukisa (Ugandan) Having good fortune
Mukysa

Mukki (Native American) Our child
Mukkie, Mukky, Mukkey, Mukkee, Mukkea

Mukonry (Irish) From the prosperous house
Mukonrey, Mukonree, Mukonrea, Mukonri, Mukonrie

Mukti (Sanskrit) One who is born free
Muktie, Mukty, Muktey, Muktee, Muktea

Mukul (Indian) One who is flourishing
Mukoul, Mukule, Mehul, Mehule

Mulcahy (Irish) A war chief
Mulcahey, Mulcahi, Mulcahie, Mulcahee, Mulcahea

Mulder (American) Of the darkness
Muldar, Muldor, Muldur, Muldir, Muldyr

Munachiso (African) God is with me
Munachyso

Munchin (Gaelic) A little monk
Munchyn, Munchen, Munchan, Munchon, Munchun, Mainchin, Mainchen, Mainchyn, Mainchon, Mainchun, Mainchan

Mundhir (Arabic) One who cautions others
Mundheer, Mundhear, Mundheir, Mundhier, Mundhyr

Mundo (Spanish) Form of Edmundo, meaning "a wealthy protector"
Mundoe, Mundowe, Mundow, Mondo, Mondow, Mondowe, Mondoe

Mungo (Gaelic) One who is very dear
Mungoe, Mungow, Mungowe

Munir (Arabic) A luminous man
Muneer, Munear, Muneir, Munier, Munyr, Mouneer, Mouneir, Mounir, Mounier, Mounear, Mounyr

Muraco (Native American) Born beneath the white moon
Murako, Muracko

Murali (Indian) One who plays the flute
Muralie, Muraly, Muraley, Muraleigh, Muralee, Muralea

Murdock (Scottish) From the sea
Murdok, Murdoc, Murdo, Murdoch, Murtagh, Murtaugh, Murtogh, Murtough

Mureithi (African) A shepherd
Mureithie, Mureithy, Mureithey, Mureithee, Mureithea

Murfain (American) Having a warrior spirit
Murfaine, Murfayn, Murfayne, Murfaen, Murfaene, Murfane

Muriel (Gaelic) Of the shining sea
Muryel, Muriell, Muryell, Murial, Muriall, Muryal, Muryall, Murell, Murel, Murrell, Murrel

Murphy (Gaelic) A warrior of the sea
Murphey, Murphee, Murphea, Murphi, Murphie, Murfey, Murfy, Murfee, Murfea, Murfi, Murfie, Murf, Murph

Murray (Gaelic) The lord of the sea
Murrey, Murry, Murri, Murrie, Murree, Murrea, Murry

Murron (Celtic) A bitter man
Murrun, Murren, Murran, Murrin, Murryn

Murrow (Celtic) A warrior of the sea
Murow, Murough, Murrough, Morrow, Morow, Morrowe, Murrowe, Morowe, Murowe, Morogh, Morrough

Murtadi (Arabic) One who is content
Murtadie, Murtady, Murtadey, Murtadee, Murtadea

Musa (Arabic) Form of Moses, meaning "a savior"
Musah, Mousa, Mousah, Moosa, Moosah

Musad (Arabic) One who is lucky
Musaad, Mus'ad

Musawenkosi (African) The Lord is generous

Mushin (Arabic) A charitable man
Musheen, Mushean, Mushein, Mushien, Mushyn

Muskan (Arabic) One who smiles often
Musken, Muskon, Muskun, Muskin, Muskyn

Muslim (Arabic) An adherent of Islam
Muslym, Muslem, Moslem, Moslim, Muslym

Musoke (African) Born beneath a rainbow
Musoki, Musokie, Musoky, Musokey, Musokee, Musokea

Mustapha (Arabic) The chosen one
Mustafa, Mostapha, Mostafa, Moustaphu, Moustafa

Mutazz (Arabic) A powerful man
Mutaz, Mu'tazz, Mu'taz

Muti (Arabic) One who is obedient
Mutie, Muty, Mutey, Mutee, Mutea, Muta

Mutka (African) Born on New Year's Day
Mutkah

Muwaffaq (Arabic) A successful man

Mwaka (African) Born on New Year's Eve

Mwinyi (African) The lord or master
Mwinyie, Mwinyey, Mwinyee, Mwinyea

Mwita (African) One who calls
Mwitah, Mwyta, Mwytah

Mykelti (American) Form of Michael, meaning "who is like God?"
Mykeltie, Mykelty, Mykeltey, Mykeltee, Mykeltea

Myron (Greek) Refers to myrrh, a fragrant oil
Myrun, Myran, Myren, Myrin, Myryn, Miron, Mirun, Miran, Miren, Mirin, Miryn

Myrzon (American) A humorous man
Mirzon, Merzon, Myrzun, Mirzun, Merzun, Myrzen, Mirzen, Merzen, Merz, Myrz, Mirz

Mystery (American) A man of the unknown
Mysteri, Mysterie, Mysterey, Mysteree, Mistery, Misteri, Misterie, Misteree, Misterey, Mysterea, Misterea

Mystique (French) A man with an air of mystery
Mystic, Mistique, Mysteek, Misteek, Mystiek, Mistiek, Mysteeque, Misteeque, Mystik, Mystikal, Mistikal

Naal (Gaelic) A celebrated birth; the name of a saint

Naalnish (Native American) A hardworking man
Nalnish, Naalnysh, Nalnysh

Naaman (Hebrew) A pleasant man

Naaz (Indian) A proud man
Naz

Nabarun (Indian) Born beneath the morning sun
Nabaron

Nabendu (Indian) Born beneath the new moon
Nabendue, Nabendoo, Nabendou

Nabha (Indian) Of the sky
Nabhah

Nabhan (Arabic) An outstanding man; a noble man
Nabhann

Nabhi (Indian) The best
Nabhie, Nabhy, Nabhey, Nabhee, Nabhea

Nabhomani (Indian) Of the sun
Nabhomanie, Nabhomany, Nabhomaney, Nabhomanee, Nabhomanea

Nabil (Arabic) A highborn man
Nabeel, Nabeal, Nabeil, Nabiel, Nabyl

Nabu (Babylonian) In mythology, the god of writing and wisdom
Nabue, Naboo, Nabo, Nebo, Nebu, Nebue, Neboo

Nachman (Hebrew) One who comforts others
Nacham, Nachmann, Nahum, Nachmanke, Nechum, Nachum, Nehum

Nachshon (Hebrew) An adventurous man; one who is daring
Nachson

Nachton (Scottish) One who is pure; chaste
Nachtun, Nachten, Nachtin, Nachtyn, Nachtan, Naughton, Naughtun, Naughten, Naughtin, Naughtyn, Nechtan, Nechton, Nechtun, Nechtin, Nechtyn, Nechten

Nada (Arabic) Covered with the morning's dew
Nadah

Nadav (Hebrew) A generous man
Nadaav

Nadif (African) One who is born between seasons
Nadeef, Nadief, Nadeif, Nadyf, Nadeaf

Nadim (Arabic) A beloved friend
Nadeem, Nadeam, Nadiem, Nadeim, Nadym

Nadir (Arabic) One who is precious and rare
Nadeer, Nadear, Nadier, Nadeir, Nadyr, Nader

Nadish (Indian) Of the sea
Nadysh, Nadeesh, Nadeash, Nadiesh, Nadeish

Nadiv (Hebrew) One who is noble
Nadeev, Nadeav, Nadiev, Nadeiv, Nadyv

Naftali (Hebrew) A struggling man; in the Bible, one of Jacob's sons
Naphtali, Naphthali, Neftali, Nefthali, Nephtali, Nephthali, Naftalie, Naphtalie, Naphthalie, Neftalie, Nefthalie, Nephtalie, Nephthalie, Nafis, Naphis, Nafys, Naphys

Nagel (German) One who makes nails
Nagle, Nagler, Naegel, Nageler, Nagelle, Nagele, Nagell

Nagid (Hebrew) A great leader; ruler
Nageed, Naged, Nagead, Nagyd, Nageid, Nagied

Nahele (Native American) A man of the forest
Naheel, Naheal, Nahiel, Naheil, Naheyl, Nahyl

Nahiossi (Native American) Having three fingers
Nahiossie, Nahiossy, Nahiossey, Nahiossee, Nahiossea

Nahir (Hebrew) A clearheaded and bright man
Naheer, Nahear, Naheir, Nahier, Nahyr, Naher

Nahum (Hebrew) A compassionate man
Nahom, Nahoum, Nahoom, Nahuem

Naim (Arabic) One who is content
Naeem, Naeam, Naiym, Naym, Naeim, Naeym

Nairit (Indian) From the southwest
Nayrit, Nairyt, Nayryt, Naerit, Naeryt, Narit, Naryt

Nairn (Scottish) From the alder-tree river
Nairne, Nayrn, Nayrne, Naern, Naerne

Nairobi (African) From the capital of Kenya
Nairobie, Nayrobi, Nayrobie, Naerobi, Naerobie, Nairoby, Nuirobey, Nairobee

Naiser (African) A founder of the clans
Nayser, Naeser, Naizer, Nayzer, Naezer

Naji (Arabic) One who is safe
Najea, Naje, Najee, Najie, Najy, Najey, Nanji, Nanjie, Nanjee, Nanjea, Nanjy, Nanjey

Najib (Arabic) Of noble descent; a highborn man
Najeeb, Najeab, Najeib, Najieb, Najyb, Nageeb, Nageab, Nagyb, Nageib, Nagieb, Nagib

Najjar (Arabic) One who works with wood; a carpenter
Najjer, Najjor, Najjur

Nakos (American) A sage
Nakus, Nakes, Nakis, Nakys, Nakas

Nalani (Hawaiian) A calmness of the skies; heaven's calm
Nalanie, Nalany, Nalaney, Nalany, Nalanee, Nalaneigh, Nalanea, Nalanya

Naldo (Spanish) Form of Reginald, meaning "the king's advisor"
Naldio, Naldiyo

Nalin (Hindi) Resembling the lotus flower
Naleen, Nalean, Nalein, Nalien, Nalyn

Nally (Irish) A poor man
Nalley, Nalli, Nallie, Nallee, Nallea, Nalleigh

Nalo (African) One who is lovable
Naloh, Nallo, Nalloh

Nam (Vietnamese) A man from the south

Naman (Indian) A friendly man; salutations
Namann, Namaan

Namdev (Indian) A poet or saint

Nami (Japanese) Of the waves
Namie, Namy, Namey, Namee, Namea

Namid (Native American) The star dancer
Nameed, Namead, Namied, Nameid, Namyd

Namir (Israeli) Resembling a leopard
Nameer, Namear, Namier, Nameir, Namyr

Nand (Indian) Filled with joy
Nande, Nandi, Nandie, Nandy, Nandey, Nandee, Nandea

Nandan (Indian) One who is pleasing
Nanden, Nandin, Nandyn, Nandon, Nandun

Nansen (Scandinavian) The son of Nancy
Nansan, Nansyn, Nansin, Nanson, Nansun

Nantai (Native American) The chief
Nantae, Nantay, Nantaye

Nantan (Native American) A spokesman
Nanten, Nantun, Nanton, Nantyn, Nantin

Naois (Celtic) In mythology, a great warrior
Naoys, Nayois, Nayoys, Naoise, Naoyse

Naoko (Japanese) One who is straightforward; honest

Naolin (Spanish) The Aztec sun god
Naolyn, Naolinn, Naolynn

Naotau (Indian) Our new son
Naotou

Napayshni (Native American) Having great strength; a courageous man
Napayshnie, Napayshnee, Napayshnea, Napayshny, Napayshney, Napaishni, Napaishnie, Napaishny, Napaishney, Napaishnee, Napaishnea

Napier (French / English) A mover / one who takes care of the royal linens
Neper

Napoleon (Italian / German) A man from Naples / son of the mists
Napolean, Napolion, Napoleone, Napoleane, Napolione

Narcissus (Greek) Resembling a daffodil; self-love; in mythology, a youth who fell in love with his reflection
Narciso, Narcisse, Narkissos, Narses, Narcisus, Narcis, Narciss

Nardo (Italian) A strong and hardy man
Nardio, Nardiyo, Nardoe

Naren (Hindi) The best among all men
Narin, Naryn, Naran, Naron, Narun

Naresh (Indian) A king
Nareshe, Natesh, Nateshe

Narsi (Hindi) A poet; a saint
Narsie, Narsy, Narsey, Narsee, Narsea

Narve (Dutch) Having great strength

Nasario (Spanish) One who is devoted to God
Nasareo, Nassario, Nassareo, Nazario, Nazareo, Nasaro, Nazaro

Nash (English) From the cliffs
Nashe

Nashashuk (Native American) As loud as thunder
Nashua

Nashoba (Native American) Resembling a wolf

Nasih (Arabic) One who advises others
Nasyh

Nasim (Arabic) As refreshing as a breeze
Nasym, Naseem, Naseam, Nasiem, Naseim

Nasir (Arabic) One who offers his support
Naseer, Nasear, Nasier, Naseir, Nasyr, Naser, Nasr, Naasir

Nasser (Arabic) One who is triumphant
Nassar, Nassor, Nassur, Nassyr, Nassir

Nastas (Native American) Curved like fox-tail
Nastis, Nastys, Nastes, Nastus, Nastos

Natal (Spanish) Born at Christmastime
Natale, Natalino, Natalio, Natall, Natalle, Nataleo, Natica

Nathair (Scottish) Resembling a snake
Nathaer, Nathayr, Nathaire, Nathaere, Nathayre, Nathrach, Nathraichean

❀ **Nathan** (Hebrew) Form of Nathaniel, meaning "a gift from God"
Nat, Natan, Nate, Nathen, Nathon, Nathin, Nathyn, Nathun, Natty, Natti, Nattie, Nattee, Nattey, Nayan

❀ **Nathaniel** (Hebrew) A gift from God
Natanael, Nataniel, Nathanael, Nathaneal, Nathanial, Nathanyal, Nathanyel, Nethanel, Nethaniel, Nethanyel

Natine (African) A tribal name
Naleen, Nateene, Natean, Nateane, Natien, Natiene, Natein, Nateine, Natyn, Natyne, Natin

Nation (American) A patriotic man

Natividad (Spanish) Refers to the Nativity
Natividade, Natyvydad, Nativydad, Natyvidad

Nato (American) One who is gentle
Natoe, Natow, Natowe

Natsu (Japanese) Born during the summer
Natsue, Natsoo, Natsou

Nature (American) An outdoorsy man
Natural

Naufal (Arabic) A handsome man
Naufall, Nawfal, Nawfall

Naval (Indian) A wonder

Navarro (Spanish) From the plains
Navaro, Navarrio, Navario, Navarre, Navare, Nabaro, Nabarro

Naveed (Persian) Our best wishes
Navead, Navid, Navied, Naveid, Navyd

Naveen (Gaelic / Indian) A pleasant, handsome man / one who is strong-willed
Naveene, Navine, Navyne, Navin, Navyn, Navean, Naveane

Navon (Hebrew) A wise man
Navun

Nawat (Native American) A left-handed man
Nawatt, Nawate, Nawatte

Nawkaw (Native American) From the woods
Nawkah, Nawka, Naukaw, Naukau, Naukah, Nauka

Nay (Arabic) His grace
Naye, Nai, Nae, Nayef, Naief

Nayati (Native American) One who wrestles
Nayatie, Nayate, Nayatee, Nayatea, Nayaty, Nayatey

Naylor (English) Of the sea / one who makes nails
Nayler, Nailor, Nailer, Naelor, Naeler, Nalor, Naler

Nazaire (Latin) A man from Nazareth
Nazaere, Nazayre, Nazare, Nazor, Nasareo, Nasarrio, Nazario, Nazarius, Nazaro

Nazih (Arabic) One who is pure; chaste
Nazeeh, Nazieh, Nazeih, Nazeah, Nazyh

Nazim (Arabian) Of a soft breeze
Nazeem, Nuzeam, Naziem, Nazeim, Nazym

Nazir (Arabic) One who is observant
Nazeer, Nazear, Nazier, Nazeir, Nazyr

Ndulu (African) Resembling a dove
Ndooloo, Ndulou, Ndoulou

Neander (Greek) A new man
Neandar, Neandor, Neandur, Neandir, Neandyr

Neason (Irish) The name of a saint
Neeson, Nessan, Neasan

Nebraska (Native American) From the flat water land; from the state of Nebraska

Neci (Hungarian) A fiery man
Necie, Necy, Necey, Necee, Necea

Neckarios (Greek) Of the nectar; one who is immortal
Nectaire, Nectarios, Nectarius, Nektario, Nektarius, Nektarios, Nektaire

Ned (English) Form of Edward, meaning "a wealthy protector"
Nedd, Neddi, Neddie, Neddy, Neddey, Neddee, Neddea

Nedrun (American) One who is difficult
Nedron, Nedren, Nedran, Nedrin, Nedryn

Neelmani (Indian) Resembling a sapphire
Nealmani, Neelmanie, Nealmanie, Neelmany, Nealmany, Neelmaney, Nealmaney, Neelmanee, Nealmanee

Neelotpal (Indian) Resembling the blue lotus
Nealotpal, Nielotpal, Neilotpal, Nilothpal, Neelothpal

Neely (Gaelic) Form of Neil, meaning "the champion"
Neeley, Neeli, Neelie, Neeleigh, Neelea, Neelee

Neeraj (Indian) Resembling a lotus
Nearaj, Neiraj, Nieraj, Niraj

Neese (Celtic) Our choice
Nease, Neise, Niese, Neyse, Neece, Neace, Neice, Niece, Nyce, Nyse, Neyce

Nefin (German) A nephew
Nefen, Nefyn, Neffin, Neffyn, Neffen, Neff, Nef

Negasi (African) He will become the king
Negassi, Negasie, Negassie, Negasy, Negassy, Negasey, Negassey, Negasee, Negassee, Negashe, Negash

Negm (Arabian) Resembling a star

Negus (African) Of the royalty; a king; an emperor
Negos, Negous

Nehal (Indian) Born during a period of rain
Nehall, Nehale, Nehalle

Nehemiah (Hebrew) God provides comfort
Nehemia, Nechemia, Nechemiah, Nehemya, Nehemyah, Nechemya, Nechemyah

Nehru (Indian) From the canal
Nehrue, Nehroo, Nehrou

Neil (Gaelic) The champion
Neal, Neale, Neall, Nealle, Nealon, Neel, Neilan, Neile, Neill, Neille, Neils, Niel, Niles, Nyles, Neele, Niels

Neirin (Irish) Surrounded by light
Neiryn, Neiren, Neerin, Neeryn, Neeren

Neka (Native American) Resembling a wild goose
Nekah, Nekka, Nekkah

Nelek (Polish) Resembling a horn
Nelec, Neleck

Nels (Scandinavian) Of the victorious people
Nells, Nils, Nills, Nyls, Nylls

Nelson (English) The son of Neil; the son of a champion
Nealson, Neilson, Neillson, Nelsen, Nilson, Nilsson, Nelli, Nellie, Nellee, Nellea, Nelleigh, Nelly, Nelley, Nell, Nelle

Nemesio (Spanish) A man of justice and vengeance
Nemeseo, Nemeses, Nemesies, Nemesiyo

Nemo (Latin) A nobody; a no-name
Nemoe, Nemow, Nemowe

Nen (Arabic) From the ancient waters
Nenn

Neo (Greek) Brand-new
Neyo, Nio, Niyo

Neptune (Latin) In mythology, god of the sea
Neptun, Neptoon, Neptoone, Neptoun, Neptoune

Ner (Hebrew) Born during Hanukkah

Nereus (Greek) In mythology, the father of the Nereids, the sea nymphs
Nereos, Nereo, Nerius, Nerios, Nerio

Nerian (Anglo-Saxon) One who protects others
Nerien, Neriun

Nero (Latin) A powerful and unyielding man
Neroh

Neroli (Italian) Resembling an orange blossom
Nerolie, Neroly, Neroley, Neroleigh, Nerolea, Nerolee

Neron (Spanish) One who is strong and firm
Nerun, Neren, Nerin, Neryn, Neran

Nery (Spanish) One who is daring
Nerey, Neri, Nerie, Neree, Nerea, Nerry, Nerrey, Nerri, Nerrie, Nerree, Nerrea

Nesbit (English) One who lives near the bend in the road
Nezbit, Naisbit, Naisbitt, Nesbitt, Nisbet, Nisbett

Ness (Scottish) From the headland
Nesse, Nessi, Nessie, Nessy, Nessey, Nessee, Nessea

Nesto (Spanish / Greek) A serious man / one who is adventurous
Nestoh, Nestoro, Nestio, Nestorio, Neto

Nestor (Greek) A traveler; in mythology, a wise man who counseled the Greeks at Troy
Nester, Nesterio, Nestore, Nestorio, Netzer, Netzor

Netar (American) A bright man
Netardas, Netardos

Nevada (Spanish) From the place covered
in snow; from the state of Nevada

Nevan (Irish) The little saint
Naomhan

Neville (French) From the new village
*Nev, Nevil, Nevile, Nevill, Nevylle, Nevyl,
Nevyle, Nevyll, Neuveville, Neuville,
Neuvevylle, Neuvylle*

Nevin (Latin) One who is sacred; little bone
*Neven, Nevins, Nevon, Nevun, Niven, Nevyn,
Nivon, Nivun*

Newbie (American) A novice
*Newbi, Newby, Newbey, Newbee, Newbea,
Neubie, Neubi, Neuby, Neubey, Neubee,
Neubea*

Newbury (English) From the new settlement
*Newbery, Newburry, Newberry, Neubury,
Neubery, Neuburry, Neuberry*

Newcomb (English) From the new valley
*Newcom, Newcome, Newcombe, Neucomb,
Neucombe, Neucom, Neucome*

Newell (English) From the new manor
*Newel, Newelle, Newele, Newhall, Newhal,
Neuwell, Neuwel, Neuwele, Neuwelle,
Niewheall, Nuell*

Newland (English) From the new land
Newlande, Neuland, Neulande

Newlin (Welsh) From the new pond
*Newlinn, Newlyn, Newlynn, Neulin, Neulinn,
Neulyn, Neulynn*

Newman (English) A newcomer
Newmann, Neuman, Neumann

Newport (English) From the new port
Neuport

Newton (English) From the new town
*Newtun, Newtown, Neuton, Neutun,
Neutown, Newt, Newte*

Neylan (Turkish) Our wish has been granted
Neylen, Neylin, Neylyn, Neylon, Neylun

Neyman (American) A bookworm
Neymann

Nezer (Hebrew) One who is crowned
Nezar, Nezor, Nezur, Nezir, Nezyr

Nhat (Vietnamese) Having a long life
Nhatt, Nhate, Nhatte

Niabi (Native American) Resembling a fawn
*Niabie, Niaby, Niabey, Niabee, Niabea,
Nyabi, Nyabie, Nyaby, Nyabey, Nyabee,
Nyabea*

Niall (Celtic) Form of Neil, meaning "the
champion"
*Nial, Niallan, Nyall, Nyal, Nyallan, Niallen,
Nyallen*

Niamh (Gaelic) A bright man

Niaz (Persian) A gift
Nyaz

Nibal (Arabic) Man of the arrows
Nybal, Niball, Nyball

Nibaw (Native American) One who stands
tall
Nybaw, Nibau, Nybau

Nicandro (Spanish) A victorious man
*Nicandreo, Nicandrios, Nicandros, Nikander,
Nikandreo, Nikandrios*

❍
❶ **Nicholas** (Greek) Of the victorious people
*Nicanor, Niccolo, Nichol, Nicholai, Nicholaus,
Nichole, Nicholl, Nichols, Nicklas, Nickolas,
Nickolaus, Nicol, Nicola, Nicolaas, Nicolai,
Nicolao, Nicolas, Nicolaus, Nicolay, Nicolet,
Nicoli, Nicolis, Nicoll, Nicollet, Nicolls, Nicolo,
Nikita, Nikkolas, Nikkolay, Niklaas, Niklas,
Niklos, Nikolai, Nikolas, Nikolaus, Nikolay,
Nikolos, Nikos, Nilos, Neacal, Neakail,
Nickson, Nico, Nikalus, Nikkos, Niko*

Nick (English) Form of Nicholas, meaning
"of the victorious people"
*Nik, Nicki, Nickie, Nickey, Nicky, Nickee,
Nickea, Niki, Nikki, Nikie, Nikkie, Niky,
Nikky, Nikey, Nikkey, Nikee, Nikkee, Nic*

Nickleby (English) From Nicholas's farm
*Nicklebey, Nicklebee, Nicklebea, Nicklebi,
Nicklebie, Nikelby, Nikelbey, Nikelbe,
Nikelbee, Nikelbea, Nikelbi, Nikelbie, Nikleby,
Niklebey, Niklebee, Niklebea, Niklebi, Niklebie*

Nickler (American) One who is swift
Nikler, Nicler, Nyckler, Nykler, Nycler

Nicodemus (Greek) The victory of the people
Nicodemo, Nikodema, Nikodemus, Nikodim, Nikodemos, Nikodem, Nicodem

Nicomedes (Greek) One who thinks of victory
Nikomedes, Nicomedo, Nikomedo

Nida (Native American) Resembling an elf
Nyda, Nidah, Nydah

Nigan (Native American) One who surpasses others
Nygan, Nighan, Nyghan

Nigarvi (Indian) A humble man
Nigarvie, Nigarvy, Nigarvey, Nigarvee, Nigarvea

Nigel (English) Form of Niall, meaning "the champion"
Nigellus, Niguel, Nijel, Njal, Nygel, Nigell, Nygell

Night (American) Born during the evening
Nite

Nihal (Indian) One who is content
Neehal, Neihal, Niehal, Neahal, Neyhal, Nyhal

Nihar (Indian) Covered with the morning's dew
Neehar, Niehar, Neihar, Neahar, Nyhar

Niichaad (Native American) One who is swollen
Nichad, Niichad, Nichaad

Nikan (Persian) One who brings good things
Niken, Nikin, Nikyn, Nikon, Nikun

Nike (Greek) One who brings victory
Nyke, Nykko, Nikko

Nikeese (African) One who is greatly loved
Nikease, Nikeise, Nikiese, Nikeyse, Nikyse, Nikeece, Nikeace, Nikeice, Nikiece, Nikeyce, Nikyce

Nikhil (Indian) One who is complete
Nikhel, Nykhil, Nykhel, Nykhyl, Nikhyl

Nikiti (Native American) Having a smooth and round head
Nikitie, Nikity, Nikitey, Nikitee, Nikitea

Nikostratos (Greek) Of the victorious army
Nicostrato, Nicostratos, Nicostratus, Nikstrato, Nikstratus

Nikshep (Indian) One who is treasured
Nykshep

Nikunja (Indian) From the grove of trees

Nilalochan (Indian) Having blue eyes

Nili (Hebrew) Of the pea plant
Nilie, Nily, Niley, Nilee, Nilea, Nileigh

Nimbus (Latin) Resembling a rain cloud
Nymbus, Nimbos, Nymbos

Nimrod (Hebrew) A mighty hunter

Ninian (Armenian) A studious man
Ninien, Ninyan, Ninyen

Nino (Italian / Spanish) God is gracious / a young boy
Ninoshka

Ninyun (American) A high-spirited man
Ninion, Ninyan, Nynyn, Nynion, Nynyan

Nipun (Indian) A clever man
Nypun, Nipon, Nypon

Nirad (Indian) Of the clouds
Nyrad

Nirajit (Indian) An illuminated man
Nirajeet, Nirajyt, Nirajeat

Niran (Thai) The eternal one
Nyran, Niren, Nirin, Niryn, Niron, Nirun, Nyren, Nyrin, Nyryn, Nyron, Nyrun

Nirav (Indian) One who is quiet
Nyrav

Nirbheet (Indian) A fearless man
Nirbhit, Nirbhyt, Nirbhay, Nirbhaye, Nirbhai, Nirbhae

Nirel (Hebrew) From God's field
Niriel, Nirle, Nirell, Nirele, Nirelle

Niremaan (Arabic) One who shines as brightly as fire
Nyremaan, Nireman, Nyreman

Nirmal (Indian) One who is peaceful; pure
Nirmall, Nyrmal, Nyrmall, Nischal, Nyschal

Nirmohi (Indian) One who is unattached
Nirmohie, Nirmohy, Nirmohey, Nirmohee,
Nirmohea

Niru (Persian) Having great strength and
power
Nirue, Niroo, Nirou

Nishan (Armenian) A sign or symbol

Nishant (Indian) Born with the dawn; one
who is peaceful
Nyshant, Nishante, Nyshante, Nishanth,
Nishanthe, Nyshanth, Nyshanthe

Nishok (Indian) Filled with happiness
Nyshok, Nishock, Nyshock

Nissan (Hebrew) A miracle child
Nisan

Nissim (Hebrew) A believer; a wondrous
boy
Nissym, Nyssim, Nyssym

Nitis (Native American) A beloved friend
Nitiss, Nitisse, Nitys, Nityss, Nitysse, Nytis,
Nytys

Nixkamich (Native American) A grandfatherly man

Nixon (English) Form of Nicholas, meaning
"of the victorious people"
Nixen, Nixun, Nixin, Nixyn, Nixan, Nix,
Nixs

Niyol (Native American) Of the wind

Njau (African) Resembling a young bull

Njord (Scandinavian) A man from the north
Njorde, Njorth, Njorthe

Nkrumah (African) The ninth-born child
Nkruma

Noach (Hebrew) One who provides comfort

Noadiah (Hebrew) God has assembled
Noadia, Noadya, Noadyah, Noadiya,
Noadiyah

✚ **Noah** (Hebrew) A peaceful wanderer
❶ *Noa*

Noam (Hebrew) A beloved friend
Noame

Noble (Latin) A wellborn man
Nobel, Nobile, Nobe, Nobie, Nobie, Nobee,
Nobea

Nodin (Native American) Of the wind
Nodyn, Noden, Nodan, Nodon, Nodun

Noe (Spanish) One who is peaceful; resting;
quiet
Noeh

Noel (French) Born at Christmastime
Noele, Noell, Noelle, Noél

Noi (Laos) A man of small stature
Noy, Noye

Nolan (Gaelic) A famous and noble man; a
champion of the people
Nolen, Nolin, Nolon, Nolun, Nolyn, Noland,
Nolande

Nolden (American) One who is noble
Noldan, Noldin, Noldyn, Noldon, Noldun

Nolly (Scandinavian) Filled with hope
Nolley, Nolli, Nollie, Nollee, Nollea, Nolleigh,
Noll, Nolle

Nonnie (Latin) The ninth-born child
Nonni, Nonny, Nonney, Nonnee, Nonnea,
Noni, Nonie, Nony, Noney, Nonee, Nonea

Noor (Arabic) Surrounded by light
Nour, Nur

Nootau (Native American) A fiery man
Noutau, Nutau, Nuetau

Norbert (English) One who shines from the
north
Norberte, Norberth, Norberthe, Norberto,
Norbie, Norbi, Norby, Norbey, Norbee,
Norbea, Norb, Norbe

Norcross (English) From the northern
crossroads
Norcros, Northcross, Northcros, Norcrosse,
Northcrosse

Nordin (Norse) A handsome man
Norden, Nordyn, Nordon, Nordun, Nordan

Norice (French) One who takes care of others
Noryce, Norise, Noryse, Noriece, Noreice,
Noreece, Noreace, Noriese, Noreise, Noreese,
Norease

Noriyuki (Japanese) Filled with happiness

Norman (English) A man from the north
Normand, Normano, Normando, Normi, Normie, Normee, Normea, Normy, Normey, Normun, Normon, Normen, Normin, Normyn, Norm, Norme

Norris (English) A man from the north
Noris, Noriss, Norriss, Norrys, Norryss, Norys

Norshell (American) One who is brash
Norshel, Norshelle, Norshele

North (English) A man from the north
Northe

Northcliff (English) From the northern cliff
Northcliffe, Northclyf, Northclyff, Northclyffe

Northrop (English) From the northern farm
Northrup

Norton (English) From the northern town
Nortun, Nortown, Norten, Nortin, Nortyn, Nortan, Northtun, Northton, Northten, Northtin, Northtyn, Northtan

Norval (Scottish) From the northern valley
Norvall, Norvale, Norvail, Norvaile, Norvayl, Norvayle, Norvael, Norvaele

Norvel (English) From the northern state

Norville (English) From the northern settlement
Norvil, Norvill, Norvile, Norvylle, Norvyl, Norvyll, Norvyle

Norward (English) A guardian of the north
Norwarde, Norwerd, Norwerde, Norwurd, Norwurde

Norwell (English) From the northern spring
Norwel, Norwele, Norwelle

Norwin (English) A friend from the north
Norwinn, Norwinne, Norwyn, Norwynn, Norwynne, Norwen, Norwenn, Norwenne, Norwine, Norvin, Norvinn, Norvinne, Norvyn, Norvynn, Norvynne, Norven, Norvenn, Norvenne

Norwood (English) From the northern forest
Norwoode, Northwood, Norwode, Northwode

Noshi (Native American) A fatherly man
Noshie, Noshy, Noshey, Noshee, Noshea, Nosh, Noshe

Notaku (Native American) Resembling a growling bear
Notakou, Notakue, Notakoo

Nova (Latin) New
Novah, Novva, Novvah

Novak (Czech) A newcomer
Novac, Novack

November (American) Born in the month of November
Novimber, Novymber

Now (Arabic) Born of the light
Nowe

Nowey (American) One who knows all
Nowy, Nowi, Nowie, Nowee, Nowea

Nowles (English) From the forest cove
Nowels, Nowel, Nowle

Nripa (Indian) The king
Nrypa, Nripah, Nrypah

Nripesh (Indian) The kings of all kings
Nrypesh, Nripeshe, Nrypeshe

Nuhad (Arabic) A brave young man
Nuehad, Nouhad, Neuhad

Nukpana (Native American) An evil man
Nukpanah, Nukpanna, Nukpannah, Nuckpana, Nucpana

Nulte (Irish) A man from Ulster
Nulti, Nultie, Nulty, Nultey, Nultee, Nultea

Numair (Arabic) Resembling a panther
Numaire, Numayr, Numayre, Numaer, Numaere

Nuncio (Spanish) A messenger
Nunzio

Nunri (American) A generous man
Nunrie, Nunry, Nunrey, Nunree, Nunrea

Nuri (Arabic) Surrounded by light
Nurie, Nury, Nurey, Nuree, Nurea, Nuriya, Nuriyah, Nuris

Nuriel (Hebrew) God's light
Nuriell, Nuriele, Nurielle, Nuryel, Nuryell, Nuryele, Nuryelle, Nooriel, Nooriell

Nuru (African) My light
Nurue, Nuroo, Nurou, Nourou, Nooroo

Nyack (African) One who is persistent
Niack, Nyak, Niak, Nyac, Niac

Nyasore (African) A thin man
Niasore, Nyasoar, Niasoar

Nye (English) One who lives on the island
Nyle, Nie, Nile

Nyék (Hungarian) From the borderlands

Nyoka (African) Resembling a snake
Nyokah, Nioku, Niokah

Nyoko (Japanese) Resembling a gem
Nioko

Oakes (English) From the oak-tree grove
*Oaks, Oak, Oake, Ochs, Oachs, Oaki, Oaki,
Oaky, Oakey, Oakee, Oakea, Okes*

Oakley (English) From the meadow of oak trees
*Oakly, Oakleigh, Oaklee, Oaklea, Oakleah,
Oakli, Oaklie*

Oba (African) A king
Obah, Obba, Obbah

Obadiah (Hebrew) A servant of God
*Obadias, Obadya, Obed, Obediah, Obbi,
Ovadiah, Ovadiach, Obbie, Obbee, Obbea, Obby,
Obbey, Ovediah, Ovedia, Ovadya, Ovedya*

Obasi (African) One who honors God
Obasie, Obasy, Obasey, Obasee, Obasea

Obayana (African) The king of fire

Obedience (American) A well-behaved man
Obediance, Obedyence, Obedeynce

Obelix (Greek) A pillar of strength
Obelex, Obelux, Obelius, Obelias

Oberon (German) A royal bear; having the
heart of a bear
Oberron

Obert (German) A wealthy and bright man
*Oberte, Oberth, Oberthe, Odbart, Odbarte,
Odbarth, Odbarthe, Odhert, Odherte,
Odherth, Odherthe, Orbart, Orbarte, Orbarth,
Orbarthe, Orbert, Orberte, Orberth, Orberthe*

Obi (Nigerian) Having a big heart
Obie, Oby, Obey, Obee, Obea

Obiajulu (African) One whose heart has
been consoled
Obyajulu, Obiajulue, Obiajuloo, Obiajooloo

Obike (African) One who is dearly loved;
from a strong household
Obyke

Oceanus (Greek) Of the ocean; deity of the
sea; in mythology, a Titan
*Oceanos, Oceane, Ocean, Ocie, Oci, Ocee,
Ocea, Ocy, Ocey*

Ocelfa (English) From the elevated plains
*Ocelfah, Ocelpha, Ocelphah, Ocelfus,
Ocelphus, Ocelfos, Ocelphos*

Ochen (African) One of twins
*Ochein, Ochin, Ochyn, Ochan, Ochon,
Ochun*

Ochi (African) Filled with laughter
Ochie, Ochee, Ochea, Ochy, Ochey

Ociel (Latin) From the sky
*Ociell, Ociele, Ocielle, Ocyel, Ocyele, Ocyelle,
Ocyell*

Octavio (Latin) The eighth-born child
*Octave, Octavius, Octavian, Octovien,
Octavious, Octavo, Octavus, Ottavio*

October (American) Born during autumn;
born in the month of October
Oktober, Octobar, Oktobar

Ocumwhowurst (Native American)
Resembling a yellow wolf
*Ocumwhowerst, Ocumwhowirst,
Ocunnowhurst, Ocunnowherst, Ocunnowhirst*

Ocvran (English) In Arthurian legend, the
father of Guinevere
Ocvrann, Okvran, Okvrann

Odakota (Native American) A friendly man
Odacota, Odakoda, Odacoda

Odale (English) From the valley
Odayl, Odayle, Odail, Odaile, Odael, Odaele

Odam (English) A son-in-law
Odom, Odem, Odum

Odanodan (Irish) Of the red earth
Odanoden, Odanodin, Odanodyn, Odanodon, Odanodun

Oddvar (Norse) The point of the spear
Oddvarr, Odvarr, Odvar

Ode (Egyptian / Greek) Traveler of the road / a lyric poem

Oded (Hebrew) One who is supportive and encouraging

Odell (Greek / German) A sweet melody / one who is wealthy
Odall, Odelle, Odel, Odele, Odie, Ody, Odi, Odey, Odee, Odea, Odyll, Odylle

Oder (English) From the river
Odar, Odir, Odyr, Odur

Odhran (Gaelic) Refers to a pale-green color
Odran, Odhrann, Odrann

Odilo (German) One who is fortunate in battle
Odile, Odilio, Odilon, Otildo, Ottild, Ottildo

Odin (Norse) In mythology, the supreme deity
Odyn, Odon, Oden, Odun

Odinan (Hungarian) One who is wealthy and powerful
Odynan, Odinann, Odynann

Odion (African) The firstborn of twins
Odiyon, Odiun, Odiyun

Odissan (African) A wanderer; traveler
Odyssan, Odisan, Odysan, Odissann, Odyssann, Odisann, Odysann

Odolf (German) A prosperous wolf
Odolfe, Odolff, Odolffe, Odulf, Odulff, Odulffe, Odulfe, Odwolf, Odwolfe, Odwulf, Odwulfe

Odongo (African) The second-born of twins
Odongyo, Odongio, Ondgiyo

Odysseus (Greek) One who roams; an angry man; in mythology, a hero who spends ten years trying to return home from war
Odysse, Odisoose, Odysseos, Odyseus, Odyseos

Oengus (Irish) A vigorous man
Oenguss

Offa (Anglo-Saxon) A king
Offah

Ofir (Hebrew) The golden son
Ofeer, Ofear, Ofyr, Ofier, Ofeir, Ofer

Og (Aramaic) A king

Ogaleesha (Native American) A man wearing a red shirt
Ogaleasha, Ogaleisha, Ogaleysha, Ogalesha, Ogaliesha, Ogalisha

Ogano (Japenese) A wise man

Ogden (English) From the valley of oak trees
Ogdin, Ogdyn, Ogdan, Ogdon, Ogdun, Oakden, Oakdin, Oakdyn, Oakdan, Oakdon, Oakdun

Ogelsvy (English) A fearsome warrior
Ogelsvey, Ogelsvi, Ogelsvie, Ogelsvee, Ogelsvea, Ogelsby, Ogelsbey, Ogelsbee, Ogelsbea, Ogelsbi, Ogelsbie

Oghe (Irish) One who rides horses
Oghi, Oghie, Oghee, Oghea, Oghy, Oghey

Ogilvy (Scottish) From the high peak
Ogilvey, Ogilvi, Ogilvie, Ogilvee, Ogilvea, Ogilhinn, Ogylvy, Ogylvey, Ogylvi, Ogylvie, Ogylvee, Ogylvea

Ogima (American) Holding the rank of chief
Ogyma, Ogimo, Ogymo

Ogun (Japanese) One who is undaunted
Ogin, Ogyn, Ogen, Ogan, Ogon

Oguz (Hungarian) An arrow
Oguze, Oguzz, Oguzze

Ohad (Hebrew) One who is dearly loved
Ohed

Ohanko (Native American) A reckless man
Ohankio, Ohankiyo

Ohanzee (Native American) A shadow
Ohanzea, Ohanzi, Ohanzie, Ohanzy, Ohanzey

Ohcumgache (Native American) Resembling a little wolf
Ohkumgache, Ohcumgachi, Ohkumgachi, Ohcumgachie, Ohkumgachie, Ohcumgachy, Ohkumgachy, Ohcumgachey, Ohkumgachey, Ohcumgachee, Ohkumgachee, Okhmhaka, Okhmhuca, Okmhaka, Okmhaca

Ohin (African) A chief
Ohine, Ohini, Ohinie, Ohiny, Ohiney, Ohinee, Ohinea, Ohene, Oheen, Oheene, Ohean, Oheane

Ohio (Native American) Of the good river; from the state of Ohio

Ohitekah (Native American) A courageous man
Ohiteka, Ohytekah, Ohyteka

Oidhche (Scottish) Born at night
Oidche, Oidhchi, Oidchi, Oidhchie, Oidchie, Oidhchy, Oidchy, Oidhchey, Oidchey, Oidhchee, Oidchee

Oisin (Irish) Resembling a little deer; in mythology, a warrior and poet
Ossian, Ossin, Oissine, Oissene, Oisseen, Oisene, Oiseen, Oisean

Ojaswit (Indian) A powerful and radiant man
Ojaswyt, Ojaswin, Ojaswen, Ojaswyn, Ojas

Ojay (American) One who is brash
Ojaye, Ojai, Ojae, O.J.

Oji (African) One who brings gifts
Ojie, Ojy, Ojey, Ojee, Ojea

Ojo (African) Of a difficult birth
Ojoe

Okal (African) To cross
Okall

Okan (Turkish) Resembling a horse
Oken, Okin, Okyn

Okapi (African) Resembling an animal with a long neck
Okapie, Okapy, Okapey, Okapee, Okapea, Okape

Oke (Hawaiian) Form of Oscar, meaning "a spear of the gods / a friend of deer"

Okechuku (African) Blessed by God

Okello (African) One who is born following twins
Okelo

Okemos (African) One who provides counsel

Oki (Japanese) From the center of the ocean
Okie, Oky, Okey, Okee, Okea

Oklahoma (Native American) Of the red people; from the state of Oklahoma

Oko (African / Japanese) One of twins / a charming man

Okon (Japanese) Born of the darkness
Okun

Okoth (African) Born during a period of rain
Okothe

Okpara (African) The firstborn son
Okparra, Okparo, Okparro

Oktawian (African) The eighth-born child
Oktawyan, Oktawean, Octawian, Octawyan, Octawean

Ola (African) A wealthy man; an honored child
Olah, Olla, Ollah

Oladele (African) One who is honored at home
Oladel, Oladell, Oladelle

Olaf (Norse) The last of the ancestors
Olaff, Olav, Olave, Olle, Olof, Olov, Olef, Oluf, Olan, Oleif

Olafemi (African) A lucky young man
Olafemie, Olafemy, Olafemey, Olafemee, Olafemea

Olajuwon (Arabic) An honorable man
Olajuwun, Olajouwon, Olajouwun, Olajuwan, Olujuwon, Olujuwun, Olujuwan

Olakeakua (Hawaiian) One who lives for God
Olakeekua, Olakeykua, Olakiekua, Olakeikua, Olakekua, Olakikua, Olakykua

Olamide (African) Our son is our prosperity
Olamyde, Olamidi, Olamydi, Olamidie, Olamydie, Olamidy, Olamydy, Olamidey, Olamydey, Olamidee, Olamydee

Olamina (African) A spirited man
Olameena, Olamine, Olameene, Olameana, Olameane, Olameina, Olameine, Olamiena, Olamiene, Olamyna, Olamyne

Olaniyan (African) Honored by all
Olaniyen, Olaniyon, Olaniyin, Olaniyun

Oldrich (Czech) A strong and wealthy leader
Oldriche, Oldrisk, Oldriske, Oldrisek, Oldra, Olda, Olecek, Olouvsek

Ole (Scandinavian) One who is alert; watchful
Olaye, Olay, Olai, Olae

Oleg (Russian) One who is holy
Olezka

Oleos (Spanish) A sacred oil

Olexei (Slavic) Form of Alexander, meaning "helper and defender of mankind"
Oleksei, Oleksey, Oleksi, Oleksiy, Olexey, Olexi, Olexiy, Oles

Olimpio (Greek) From Mount Olympus
Olimpo, Olympio, Olympios, Olympus

Olin (English) Filled with happiness
Olyn, Olen

Olindo (Latin) Having a pleasant scent
Olyndo, Olendo

Oliphant (Scottish) Having great strength
Olyphant, Oliphent, Olyphent, Oliphont, Olyphont

Olis (German) A powerful man
Olys, Oliss, Olyss, Olisse, Olysse

✿ **Oliver** (Latin) From the olive tree
Oliverio, Olivero, Olivier, Oliviero, Olivio, Olivor, Olley, Ollie, Olliver, Ollivor, Oilbhries, Oliveer, Oliverios, Oliveros, Oluvor, Olghar

Oliwa (Hawaiian) Of the army of elves
Olywa, Oliwah, Olywah

Olney (English) From the loner's field
Olny, Olnee, Olnea, Olni, Olnie, Ollaneg, Olaneg

Olorun (African) One who counsels others
Oloron, Oloroun, Oloroon

Olubayo (African) Filled with happiness

Olufemi (African) Loved by God
Olufemie, Olufemy, Olufemey, Olufemee, Olufemea

Olugbala (African) The God of all
Olugbalah, Olugballa, Olugballah

Olujimi (African) One who is close to God
Olujimie, Olujimy, Olujimey, Olujimee, Olujimea

Olumide (African) God has arrived
Olumidi, Olumidie, Olumidy, Olumidey, Olumidee, Olumidea, Olumyde, Olumydi, Olumydie, Olumydy, Olumydey, Olumydee, Olumydea

Olumoi (African) One who has been blessed by God
Olumoy

Olushegun (African) One who walks with God
Olushigun, Olushygun, Olushagun, Olushegon, Olushigon, Olushygon, Olushygan

Olushola (African) Blessed by God
Olusholah, Olusholla, Olushollah

Oluwa (African) One who believes in God
Oluwah

Oluwatosin (African) A servant of God
Oluwatosyn, Oluwatosen

Oluyemi (African) Full of God; a pious man
Oluyemie, Oluyemy, Oluyemey, Oluyemee, Oluyemea

Olvery (English) One who draws others
Olverey, Olveri, Olverie, Olveree, Olverea

Olviemi (African) Loved by God
Olviemie, Olviemy, Olviemey, Olviemee, Olviemea

Oma (Arabic) A commanding man
Omah, Omma, Ommah

Omanand (Hindi) A happy and thoughtful man
Omamande, Omanando

Omar (Arabic) A flourishing man; one who is well-spoken
Omarr, Omer, Omerr, Ommar, Ommer

Omari (Arabic / African) One who is full of life / from God the highest
Omarie, Omary, Omarey, Omaree, Omarea

Omeet (Hebrew) My light
Omeete, Omeit, Omeite, Omeyt, Omeyte, Omit, Omeat, Omeate, Omite, Omyt, Omyte, Omet, Omete

Omega (Greek) The last great one; the last letter of the Greek alphabet
Omegah

Omie (Italian) A homebody
Omi, Omee, Omea, Omey, Omy, Omye

Omkar (Hindi) A sacred letter and sound

Omprakash (Indian) Surrounded by a divine light
Omparkash, Omprakashe, Omparkashe

Omri (Hebrew) A sheaf of grain; a servant of God
Omrie, Omry, Omrey, Omree, Omrea

On (Chinese / African) A peaceful man / one who is desirable

Onacona (Native American) Resembling a white owl
Onakona, Onaconah, Onakonah

Onan (Turkish) A wealthy man
Onann

Onani (Asian) A sweet man
Onanie, Onuny, Onaney, Onanee, Onanea

Onaona (Hawaiian) Having a pleasant scent

Ond (Hungarian) The tenth-born child
Onde

Ondré (Greek) Form of André, meaning "manly; a warrior"
Onndre, Ohndrae, Ohndray, Ohndre, Ohndrei, Ohndrey, Ondrae, Ondray, Ondrei, Onndrae, Onndrai, Onndray

Ondrej (Czech) A manly man
Ondrejek, Ondrejec, Ondrousek, Ondravsek

Onesimo (Spanish) The firstborn son
Onesymo, Onesimio, Onesimiyo, Onesymio, Onesymiyo

Onkar (Indian) The purest one
Onckar, Oncar, Onkarr, Onckarr, Oncarr

Onofrio (Italain) A defender of peace
Onofre, Onofrius, Onophrio, Onophre, Onfrio, Onfroi

Onslow (Arabic) From the hill of the enthusiast
Onslowe, Ounslow, Ounslowe

Onur (Turkish) One who shows promise
Onurr, Onure, Onurre

Onwaochi (African) A pious man
Onwaochie, Onwaochy, Onwaochey, Onwaochee, Onwaochea

Onyebuchi (African) God is in everything
Onyebuchie, Onyebuchy, Onyebuchey, Onyebuchee, Onyebuchea

Oqwapi (Native American) Resembling a red cloud
Oqwapie, Oqwapy, Oqwapey, Oqwapee, Oqwapea

Or (Hebrew) Surrounded by light

Oracle (Greek) One who provides divine messages
Orakle, Orackle, Oracel, Orakel, Orackel

Oral (Latin) An eloquent speaker

Oram (English) From the enclosure near the riverbank
Oramm, Oraham, Orahamm, Orham, Orhamm

Oran (Aramaic / Gaelic) Surrounded by light / a pale-skinned man
Orann

Orane (Greek) A flourishing man
Oraine, Orain, Orayn, Orayne, Oraen, Oraene

Orazio (Italian) One who prays to God
Oratio

Orbon (Hungarian) One who lives in the city
Orbo

Ord (Anglo-Saxon) A spear
Orde

Ordell (Latin) Of the beginning
Ordel, Ordele, Ordelle, Orde

Ordland (English) From the pointed hill
Ordlande

Ordway (Anglo-Saxon) A fighter armed
with a spear
Ordwaye, Ordwai, Ordwae

Orel (Latin) The golden one
*Oral, Oriel, Orrel, Orry, Orrey, Orri, Orrie,
Orree, Orrea*

Oren (Hebrew / Gaelic) From the pine tree /
a pale-skinned man
*Orenthiel, Orenthiell, Orenthiele, Orenthielle,
Orenthiem, Orenthium, Orin*

Orestes (Greek) From the mountain; in
mythology, the son of Agamemnon who
murdered his mother for being unfaithful
Oreste

Orev (Hebrew) Resembling a raven

Orford (English) From the cattle ford
Orforde

Ori (Hebrew) Surrounded by the light of
truth
Orie, Ory, Orey, Oree, Orea

Oringo (African) One who enjoys hunting
Oryngo

Oriole (Latin) Resembling the gold-speckled
bird
Oreolle, Oriolle, Oreole, Oriol, Orioll, Oriolle

Orion (Greek) In mythology, a great hunter;
a constellation
Oryon, Orian, Oryan, Orien, Oryen, Oreon

Oris (Hebrew) Of the trees
Oriss, Orisse, Orys, Oryss, Orysse

Orji (African) Of the majestic tree
Orjie, Orjy, Orjey, Orjee, Orjea

Orkeny (Hungarian) A frightening man
Orkeney, Orkenee, Orkenea, Orkeni, Orkenie

Orlando (Spanish) From the renowned land
*Orlan, Orland, Orlondo, Orlond, Orlon,
Orlande, Orlonde, Olo*

Orleans (Latin) The golden child
*Orlean, Orleane, Orleens, Orleen, Orleene,
Orlins, Olryns, Orlin, Orline, Orlyn, Orlyne*

Orlege (Anglo-Saxon) Suffering strife during war

Orly (Hebrew) Surrounded by light
Orley, Orli, Orlie, Orlee, Orleigh, Orlea

Orman (English / German) One who wields
a spear / a man of the sea
*Ormand, Ormande, Ormeman, Ormemand,
Ormemande, Ordman, Ordmand, Ordmande*

Orme (English) A kind man
Orm

Ormod (Anglo-Saxon) A sorrowful man

Ormond (English) One who defends with a
spear; from the mountain of bears
*Ormonde, Ormund, Ormunde, Ormemund,
Ormemond, Ordmund, Ordmunde, Ordmond,
Ordmonde*

Ormos (Hungarian) From the cliff

Orn (Scandinavian) Resembling an eagle
Orne

Ornice (Irish / Hebrew) A pale-skinned
man / from the cedar tree
*Ornyce, Ornise, Orynse, Orneice, Orneise,
Orniece, Orniese, Orneece, Orneese, Orneace,
Ornease*

Oro (Spanish) The golden one

Oron (Hebrew) Having a light spirit

Orpheus (Greek) Having a beautiful voice;
in mythology, a talented musician, trained
by the Muses
*Orphius, Orphyus, Orfeus, Orfius, Orfyus,
Orphi, Orphie, Orphy, Orphey, Orphee,
Orphea, Orpheo, Orfeo*

Orrick (English) From the old oak tree
Orick, Orrik, Orik, Orric, Oric

Orrin (English) From the river
Orran, Orren, Orryn

Orris (Latin) One who is inventive
Orriss, Orrisse, Orrys, Orryss, Orrysse

Ors (Hungarian) A heroic man

Orson (Latin) Resembling a bear; raised by a bear
Orsen, Orsin, Orsini, Orsino, Orsis, Orsonio, Orsinie, Orsiny, Orsiney, Orsinee, Orsinea

Orth (English) An honest man
Orthe

Orton (English) From the settlement by the shore
Ortun, Oraton, Oratun

Orunjan (African) Born beneath the noon sun
Orunjun, Orunjon, Orunjen, Orunjin, Orunjyn

Orval (English) Having the strength of a spear
Orvall, Orvalle, Orvald, Orwald, Ordval, Ordwald, Ordvald

Orville (French) From the gold town
Orvell, Orvelle, Orvil, Orvill, Orvele, Orvyll, Orvylle, Orvyl, Orvyle

Orvin (English) A courageous friend; a spear friend
Orvyn, Orwen, Orwenn, Orwenne, Orwyn, Orwynn, Orwynne, Orwin, Orwinn, Orwinne, Ordwen, Ordwenn, Ordwenne, Ordwin, Ordwinn, Ordwinne, Ordwyn, Ordwynn, Ordwynne, Ordwine

Orway (American) A kind man
Orwaye, Orwai, Orwae

Orwel (Welsh) Of the horizon
Orwell, Orwele, Orwelle

Os (English) The divine

Osage (Native American) A tribal name

Osakwe (Japanese) Having a favorable destiny
Osakwi, Osakwie, Osakwy, Osakwey, Osakwee, Osakwea

Osama (Arabic) Resembling a lion
Osamah, Osamma, Osammah

Osayaba (Japanese) A great thinker

Osaze (Hebrew) One who is favored by God
Osazi, Osazie, Osazee, Osazea, Osazy, Osazey

Osbert (English) One who is divinely brilliant
Osberte, Osberth, Osberthe, Osbart, Osbarte, Osbarth, Osbarthe, Osbeorht, Osburt, Osburte, Osburth, Osburthe

Osborn (Norse) A bear of God
Osborne, Osbourn, Osbourne, Osburn, Osburne

Oscar (English / Gaelic) A spear of the gods / a friend of deer
Oskar, Osker, Oscer, Osckar, Oscker, Oszkar, Oszcar

Oscard (Greek) A warrior
Oscarde, Oskard, Oskarde, Osckard, Osckarde

Osei (African) An honorable man

Osgood (English) A Goth god
Osgoode, Ozgood, Ozgoode

Oshea (Hebrew) A kind spirit
Oshey, Oshay, Osheye, Oshaye, Oshae, Oshai

Osher (Hebrew) A man of good fortune

Osias (Greek) Salvation
Osyas

Osier (English) One who lives near the willows
Osyer, Osiar, Osyar, Osior, Osyor, Osiur, Osyur

Osileani (Polynesian) One who talks a lot
Osileanie, Osileany, Osileaney, Osileanee, Osileanea

Osip (Ukrainian) Form of Joseph, meaning "God will add"
Osyp, Osipp, Osypp

Osman (Scandinavian) Protected by God
Osment, Osmin, Osmond, Osmonde, Osmont, Osmund, Osmunde, Osmonte

Osmar (English) The glory of God
Osmarr

Osred (English) One who receives counsel from God
Osraed, Osread, Osrad, Osrade, Osrid, Osryd

Osric (English) One who follows God's rule
Osrick, Osrik, Osryc, Osryck, Osryk, Osrec, Osreck, Osrek

Ossie (English) Form of Oswald, meaning "the power of God"
Ossi, Ossy, Ossey, Ossee, Ossea

Osten (Latin) One who is worthy of respect; a magnificent man
Ostan, Ostin, Ostyn, Ostun, Oistin, Oisten, Oistan

Oswald (English) The power of God
Oswalde, Osvald, Osvaldo, Oswaldo, Oswell, Osvalde, Oswallt, Osweald, Osweld, Oswalt

Oswin (English) A friend of God
Oswinn, Oswinne, Oswen, Oswenn, Oswenne, Oswyn, Oswynn, Oswynne, Oswine

Oswiu (Anglo-Saxon) A king
Oswy, Oswey, Oswi, Oswie, Oswee, Oswea

Ota (Czech) A wealthy man

Otadan (Native American) A man of plenty

Otaktay (Native American) One who kills many
Otaktaye, Otaktai, Otaktae

Othman (German) A wealthy man
Otheman, Othmann, Othemann, Othoman, Othomann

Othniel (Hebrew) God's lion
Othniell, Othnielle, Othniele, Othnyel, Othnyell, Othnyele, Othnyelle

Otieno (African) Born at night
Othieno, Otyeno, Othyeno

Otik (German) One who is lucky
Otick, Otic, Otyk, Otyck, Otyc

Otis (German / Greek) A wealthy man / one who is acute
Otys, Otess, Ottis

Otmar (Teutonic) A famous warrior
Otmarr, Othmar, Othmarr, Otomar, Ottomar, Otomarr, Ottomarr

Otoahhastis (Native American) Resembling a tall bull

Otoahnacto (Native American) Resembling a bull bear

Otoniel (Spanish) A stylish man
Otoniell, Otoniele, Otonielle, Otonel, Otonell, Otonele, Otonelle

Otskai (Native American) One who leaves

Ottah (African) A slender boy
Otta

Ottar (Norse) A warrior

Ottfried (German) A wealthy and peaceful man
Ottfrid, Ottfryde, Ottfryd, Ottfred, Ottfrede

Otto (German) A wealthy man
Otess, Ottis, Othello, Ottone, Oto, Odo, Oddo, Otho

Ottokar (German) A spirited warrior
Otokar, Otokarr, Ottokarr, Ottokars, Otokars, Ottocar, Otocar, Ottocars, Otocars

Ottway (Teutonic) One who is fortunate in battle
Otway, Ottoway, Otoway, Ottwae, Otwae, Ottwai, Otwai

Otu (Native American) An industrious man
Otoo, Otue, Otou

Oukounaka (Asian) From the surf
Oukoonaka, Oukunaka, Okounaka, Okoonaka, Okunaka, Okonaka, Oukonaka

Ouray (Native American) The arrow
Ouraye, Ourae, Ourai

Ourson (French) Resembling a little bear
Oursun, Oursoun, Oursen, Oursan, Oursin, Oursyn

Oved (Hebrew) One who worships God
Ove

Overton (English) From the upper town
Overtun, Overtown

Ovid (Latin) A shepherd; an egg
Ovyd, Ovidio, Ovido, Ovydio, Ovydo, Ovidiu, Ovydiu, Ofydd, Ofyd, Ofid, Ofidd

❂
❂ **Owen** (Welsh / Gaelic) Form of Eugene, meaning "a wellborn man" / a youthful man
Owenn, Owenne, Owin, Owinn, Owinne, Owyn, Owynn, Owynne, Owain, Owaine, Owayn, Owayne, Owaen, Owaene, Owane, Owein, Oweine

Owney (Irish) An elderly man
Owny, Owni, Ownie, Ownee, Ownea, Oney, Ony, Oni, Onie, Onee, Onea

Ox (American) Resembling the animal; having great strength
Oxe, Oxy, Oxey, Oxee, Oxea, Oxi, Oxie

Oxford (English) From the oxen's crossing
Oxforde, Oxxford, Oxxforde, Oxferd, Oxferde, Oxfurd, Oxfurde, Oxnaford, Oxnaferd, Oxnafurd

Oxley (English) From the meadow of oxen
Oxly, Oxleigh, Oxlea, Oxleah, Oxlee, Oxli, Oxlie, Oxnaley, Oxnaly, Oxnaleigh, Oxnalea, Oxnaleah, Oxnali, Oxnalie, Oxnalee

Oxton (English) From the oxen town
Oxtun, Oxtown, Oxnuton, Oxnatun, Oxnatown

Oysten (Norse) Filled with happiness
Oystein, Oystin, Oystyn

Oz (Hebrew) Having great strength
Ozz, Ozzi, Ozzie, Ozzy, Ozzey, Ozzee, Ozzea, Ozi, Ozie, Ozy, Ozey, Ozee, Ozea

Oziel (Spanish) Having great strength
Oziell, Ozielle, Oziele, Ozell, Ozel, Ozele, Ozelle

Ozni (Hebrew) One who knows God
Oznie, Ozny, Ozney, Oznee, Oznea

Ozséb (Hungarian) A pious man

Ozturk (Turkish) One who is pure; chaste

Ozuru (Japanese) Resembling a stork
Ozurou, Ozourou, Ozuroo, Ozooroo

p

Paavo (Finnish) Form of Paul, meaning "a small or humble man"
Paaveli

Pablo (Spanish) Form of Paul, meaning "a small or humble man"

Pace (Hebrew / English) Refers to Passover / a peaceful man
Paice, Payce, Paece, Pacey, Pacy, Pacee, Paci, Pacie, Paicey, Paicy, Paicee, Paici, Paicie, Paycey, Paycy, Paycee, Payci, Paycie, Paecey, Paecy, Paecee, Paeci, Paecie, Pacian, Pacien

Pacho (Spanish) An independent man; one who is free

Pachu'a (Native American) Resembling a water snake

Paciano (Spanish) A man of peace
Pacyano

Pacifico (Spanish) One who is calm; tranquil
Pacificus, Pacificos, Pacificas

Packard (German) From the brook; a peddler's pack
Packarde, Pakard, Pakarde, Pacard, Pacarde, Packer, Packert, Packe, Pack, Pac, Pak

Paco (Spanish) A man from France
Pacorro, Pacoro, Paquito

Paddy (Irish) Form of Patrick, meaning "a nobleman; patrician"
Paddey, Paddee, Paddea, Paddi, Paddie, Padraic, Padraig, Padhraig

Padgett (French) One who strives to better himself
Padget, Padgette, Padgete, Padgeta, Padgetta, Padge, Paget, Pagett

Padman (Indian) Resembling the lotus
Padmann

Padre (Spanish) A father
Padray, Padraye, Padrai, Padrae

Padruig (Scottish) Of the royal family

Pagan (Latin) A man from the country
Paige

Page (English) A young assistant
Paige, Payge, Paege

Pagiel (Hebrew) God disposes
Pagiell, Pagiele, Pagielle

Pahana (Native American) A lost white brother
Pahanah, Pahanna, Pahannah

Paine (Latin) Man from the country; a peasant
Pain, Payn, Payne, Paen, Paene, Pane, Paien

Paisley (English) Man of the church
Paisly, Paisli, Paislie, Paislee, Paysley, Paysly,
Paysli, Payslie, Payslee, Pasley, Pasly, Pasli,
Paslie, Paslee, Paizley, Payzley, Pazley,
Paislea, Paizlea, Paslea, Payslea

Pajackok (Native American) Resembling
thunder
Pajakok, Pajacok, Pajackock, Pajakock,
Pajakoc, Pajackoc, Pajacoc, Pajakoc

Paki (African) One who sees the truth
Pakie, Paky, Pakey, Pakee, Pakea

Paladio (Spanish) A follower of the goddess
Athena
Palladius, Palladio, Paladius, Paladios,
Palladios

Palamedes (English) In Arthurian legend,
a knight
Palomydes, Palomedes, Palamydes, Palsmedes,
Palsmydes, Pslomydes

Palani (Hawaiian) A free man; one who is
independent
Palanie, Palanee, Palanea, Palany, Palaney

Palash (Indian) Resembling a flowering
tree
Palashe

Palban (Spanish) A blonde-haired man
Palben, Palbin, Palbyn, Palbon, Palbun

Paley (English) Form of Paul, meaning "a
small or humble man"
Paly, Pali, Palie, Palee, Palea

Palila (Hawaiian) A birdlike man
Palilla, Palilah, Pallila, Pallilla, Palyla, Palylla

Palladin (Greek) Filled with wisdom
Palladyn, Palladen, Palladan, Paladin,
Paladyn, Paladen, Paladan

Pallaton (Native American) A tough warrior
Pallatin, Pallatyn, Pallaten, Pallatun

Palma (Latin) A successful man

Palmer (English) A pilgrim bearing a palm
branch
Pallmer, Palmar, Pallmar, Palmerston,
Palmiro, Palmeero, Palmeer, Palmire,
Palmere

Palomo (Spanish) Resembling a dove; a
peaceful man
Palomio, Palomiyo

Paltiel (Hebrew) God is my deliverance
Paltiell, Paltiele, Paltielle, Palti, Paltie, Palty,
Paltey, Paltee, Paltea, Platya, Platyahu

Pan (Greek) In mythology, god of the shepherds
Pann

Panama (Spanish) From the canal

Pananjay (Hindi) Resembling a cloud
Pananjaye, Pananjae, Pananjai

Pancho (Spanish) A man from France

Pancrazio (Italian) One who is all-powerful
Pankrazio, Pancraz, Pankraz, Pancrazie,
Pancrazi, Pancrazy, Pancrazey, Pancrazee,
Pankrazi, Pankrazie, Pankrazy, Pankrazey,
Pankrazee

Pandu (Indian) A pale-skinned man

Panfilo (Spanish) One who loves nature
Panphilo, Panfilio, Panphilio

Pankaj (Indian) Resembling the lotus
flower

Panos (Greek) As solid as a rock

Pantias (Greek) A philosophical man
Pantyas

Panya (African) Resembling a mouse
Panyah

Panyin (African) The firstborn of twins
Panyen

Parakram (Indian) A strong and brave man

Paras (Hindi) A touchstone
Parasmani, Parasmanie, Parasmany,
Parasmaney, Parasmanee

Parfait (French) The perfect man

Paris (English / Greek) Man from the city
in France / in mythology, the prince of
Troy who abducted Helen
Pariss, Parisse, Parys, Paryss, Parysse, Peris,
Perris, Perys, Perrys

Park (English / Chinese) Of the forest / from the cypress tree
Parke, Parkey, Parky, Parki, Parkie, Parkee, Parkea

❂ **Parker** (English) The keeper of the park
Parkar, Parkes, Parkman, Parks

Parkins (English) As solid as a rock; son of Peter
Parkens, Parken, Parkin, Parkyns, Parkyn, Parkinson

Parley (Scottish) A reluctant man
Parly, Parli, Parlie, Parlee, Parlea, Parle

Parmenio (Spanish) A studious man; one who is intelligent
Parmenios, Parmenius

Parnell (Latin) From the country
Parnel, Parnelle, Parnele, Parrnel, Parrnell, Parrnele, Parrnelle, Pernell, Pernel, Pernele, Pernelle

Paros (Greek) From the island
Paro

Parounag (Armenian) One who is thankful

Parr (English) From the castle's park
Parre

Parrish (Latin) Man of the church
Parish, Parrishe, Parishe, Parrysh, Parysh, Paryshe, Parryshe, Parisch, Parrisch

Parry (Welsh) The son of Harry
Parrey, Parri, Parrie, Parree, Parrea

Parryth (American) An up-and-coming man
Parrythe, Parrith, Parrithe, Paryth, Parythe, Parith, Parithe, Parreth, Parrethe, Pareth, Parethe

Parsons (English) A man of the clergy
Parson, Person, Persons, Pherson, Pharson, Phersons, Pharsons

Parthenios (Greek) One who is pure; chaste
Parthenius

Parthik (Greek) One who is pure; chaste
Parthyk, Parthick, Parthyck, Parthic, Parthyc

Partholon (Irish) Man of the earth; a farmer
Partholun, Partholan, Partholen, Partholyn, Parlan, Parlon, Parlann, Parlonn

Parton (English) From the town near the castle's park; from Peter's town
Partun, Parten, Partan, Partin, Partyn

Parvaiz (Persian) A commendable man
Parvez, Parviz, Parvayz, Parvaz, Parvaez, Parwiz, Parwez, Parwaiz, Parwaez, Parwayz, Parwaz

Parvath (Indian) From the mountain
Parvathe

Parveneh (Persian) Resembling a butterfly
Parvene

Pascal (Latin) Born during Easter
Pascale, Pascalle, Paschal, Paschalis, Pascoe, Pascual, Pascuale, Pasqual, Pasquale

Pastor (English) Man of the church
Pastur, Paster, Pastar, Pastir, Pastyr

Patakin (Indian) One who holds the banner
Patakyn, Patackin, Patackyn

Patamon (Native American) Resembling a tempest
Patamun, Patumen, Pataman, Patamyn, Patamin

Patch (American) Form of Peter, meaning "as solid and strong as a rock"
Pach, Patche, Patchi, Patchie, Patchy, Patchey, Patchee

Patli (Aztec) A medicine man
Patlie, Patly, Patley, Patlee, Patleigh, Patlea

Patrick (Latin) A nobleman; patrician
Packey, Padric, Pat, Patrece, Patric, Patrice, Patrece, Putricio, Patrik, Patrizio, Patrizius, Patryk, Pats, Patsy, Patty, Padrig, Patek, Patec, Pateck, Patricius, Patrido

Patriot (American) One who is devoted to his country
Patryot, Patriotic, Patryotic, Patriotik, Patryotik

Patterson (English) The son of Peter
Paterson, Pattison, Patison

Patton (English) From the town of warriors
Paten, Patin, Paton, Patten, Pattin, Paddon, Padden, Paddin, Paddyn, Paegastun, Payden

Patwin (Native American) A manly man
Patwinn, Patwinne, Patwyn, Patwynne,
Patwynn, Patwen, Patwenn, Patwenne

Paul (Latin) A small or humble man
Pal, Paolo, Pasha, Pauel, Pauli, Paulie, Paulin,
Paulino, Paulinus, Paulo, Paulos, Paulsen,
Paulson, Paulus, Pauly, Pavel, Pavle, Pavlik,
Pavlo, Pawel, Pol, Poll, Poul, Pascha, Pashenka,
Pavlushka, Paulis, Paulys, Pavlof, Pawl

Paurush (Indian) A courageous man
Paurushe, Paurushi, Paurushie, Paurushy,
Paurushey, Paurushee

Pavan (Indian) Resembling a breeze
Pavann

Pavanjit (Indian) Resembling the wind
Pavanjyt, Pavanjeet, Pavanjeat, Pavanjete

Pavit (Indian) A pious man
Pavyt

Pavithra (Indian) One who is holy
Pavythra

Pawnee (Native American) A tribal name
Pawnea, Pawni, Pawnie, Pawny, Pawney

Pax (Latin) A peaceful man
Paxx, Paxi, Paxie, Paxy, Paxey, Paxee,
Paxea

Paxton (English) From the peaceful town
Packston, Paxon, Paxten, Paxtun, Packstun,
Packsten

Payat (Native American) He is coming
Payatt, Pay, Paye

Payod (Indian) Resembling a cloud
Paiod, Paeod, Paod

Payoj (Indian) Resembling a lotus
Paioj, Paeoj, Paoj

Paytah (Native American) A fiery man
Payta, Paetah, Paeta, Paitah, Paita, Patah,
Pata

Paz (Spanish) A peaceful man
Pazz

Pazel (Hebrew) God's gold; treasured by
God
Pazell, Pazele, Pazelle

Pazman (Hungarian) One who is right

Peabo (Irish) As solid as a rock
Peebo, Peybo, Peibo

Peak (English) From the mountain's top;
one who surpasses others
Peake, Peek, Peeke, Peke, Pico

Peale (English) One who rings the bell
Peal, Peall, Pealle

Pearroc (English) Man of the forest
Pearoc, Pearrok, Pearok, Pearrock, Pearock

Pecos (American) From the river; a cowboy
Pekos, Peckos

Pedahel (Hebrew) One who has been
redeemed by God
Pedael, Pedayel

Pedaias (Hebrew) Loved by God
Pedias

Pedro (Spanish) Form of Peter, meaning
"as solid and strong as a rock"
Pedrio, Pepe, Petrolino, Piero, Pietro

Peel (English) From the fortified tower
Peele

Pegasus (Greek) In mythology, a winged
horse

Pekar (Czech) A baker
Pecar, Peckar

Pekelo (Hawaiian) Form of Peter, meaning
"as solid and strong as a rock"
Pekeloh, Pekello, Pekelloh

Pelagios (Greek) Man of the sea
Pelagius, Pelayo, Pelagos, Pelagus

Peleh (Hebrew) A miracle child
Pele

Pelham (English) From the house of furs;
from Peola's home
Pellham, Pelam, Pellam

Pell (English) A clerk or one who works
with skins
Pelle, Pall, Palle

Pellegrin (Hungarian) A traveler; a pilgram
Pellegrine, Pelegrin, Pelegrine, Pellegryn, Pelegryn

Pelly (English) Filled with happiness
Pelley, Pelli, Pellie, Pellee, Pellea

Pelon (Spanish) Filled with joy
Pellon

Pelton (English) From the town by the lake
Pellton, Peltun, Pelltun, Peltan, Pelltan, Pelten, Pellten, Peltin, Pelltin, Peltyn, Pelltyn

Pembroke (Celtic) From the headland
Pembrook, Pembrooke

Penda (African) One who is dearly loved
Pendah, Penha, Penhah

Pendragon (Anglo-Saxon) From the enclosed land of the dragon

Penley (English) From the enclosed meadow
Penly, Penleigh, Penli, Penlie, Penlee, Penlea, Penleah, Pennley, Pennly, Pennleigh, Pennli, Pennlie, Pennlee, Pennlea, Pennleah

Penn (English) From the enclosure
Pen, Pyn, Pynn

Pennsylvania (English) The land of Penn; from the state of Pennsylvania

Penrod (German) A respected commander

Pentele (Hungarian) A merciful man
Pentelle, Pentel, Pentell

Penton (English) From the enclosed town
Pentun, Pentin, Pentyn, Penten, Pentan

Penuel (Hebrew) The face of God
Penuell, Penuele, Penuelle

Pepin (German) A determined man; a petitioner
Peppin, Pepyn, Peppyn, Pepun, Peppun, Pepen, Peppen, Peppi, Peppie, Peppey, Peppy, Peppee, Peppea

Pepper (American) Resembling the pepper plant; flavorful
Peper

Percival (French) One who can pierce the vale; in Arthurian legend, the only one who could retrieve the Holy Grail
Parsafal, Parsefal, Parsifal, Perce, Perceval, Percevall, Purcell, Percivall, Percyvelle, Percyval, Percyvel

Percy (Latin) Form of Percival, meaning "one who can pierce the vale"
Percey, Perci, Percie, Percee, Percea, Persy, Persey, Persi, Persie, Persee, Persea

Perdido (Latin) One who is lost
Perdydo, Perdedo

Peregrine (Latin) One who travels; a wanderer
Peregrin, Peregrino, Peregryn, Peregreen, Peregrein, Peregreyn, Peregrien, Peregrinus

Perez (Hebrew) To break through
Peretz

Perfecto (Spanish) One who is flawless
Perfectio, Perfectiyo, Perfection, Perfecte

Pericles (Greek) One who is in excess of glory
Perricles, Perycles, Perrycles, Periclees, Perriclees, Peryclees, Perryclees, Periclez, Perriclez, Peryclez, Perryclez

Peril (Latin) One who undergoes a trial or test
Perill, Perile, Perille, Peryl, Peryll, Perylle, Peryle

Perine (Latin) An adventurer
Perrin, Perrine, Perin, Peryne, Perryne

Perk (American) One who is cheerful and jaunty
Perke, Perky, Perkey, Perki, Perkie, Perkee, Perkea

Perkin (English) Form of Peter, meaning "as solid and strong as a rock"
Perkins, Perkyn, Perkyns

Perkinson (English) The son of Perkin; the son of Peter
Perkynson

Perry (Latin) Form of Peregrine, meaning "one who travels; a wanderer"
Perrey, Perree, Perrea, Perri, Perrie

Perseus (Greek) In mythology, son of Zeus who slew Medusa
Persius, Persyus, Persies, Persyes

Perth (Celtic) From the thorny thicket
Perthe, Pert, Perte

Perye (English) From the pear tree

Pesach (Hebrew) One who has been spared
Pessach, Pesache, Pessache

Peter (Greek) As solid and strong as a rock
Peder, Pekka, Per, Petar, Pete, Peterson, Petr, Petre, Petros, Petrov, Piotr, Piet, Pieter, Pyotr, Peader, Peat, Peate, Petenka, Pytor, Peterka, Peterke, Petrus, Petruso, Petur, Petter, Petya

Pethuel (Aramaic) God's vision
Pethuell, Pethuele, Pethuelle

Petuel (Hindi) The Lord's vision
Petuell, Petuele, Petuelle

Peverell (French) A piper
Peverel, Peverelle, Peverele, Peverall, Peveral, Peverale, Peveralle, Peveril, Peverill, Peverile, Peverille

Peyton (English) From the village of warriors
Payton, Peytun, Paytun, Peyten, Payten, Paiton, Paitun, Paiten, Paton, Patun, Paten, Paeton, Paetun, Paeten

Phallon (Irish) The ruler's grandson
Phallen, Phallun, Phallin, Phallyn, Phallan

Pharis (Irish) A heroic man
Pharys, Pharris, Pharrys

Phelan (Gaelic) Resembling a wolf
Phelim, Phelym, Phelam, Phelin, Phelyn

Phelipe (Spanish) Filled with hope

Phelps (English) The son of Phillip
Phelpes

Phex (American) A kind man
Phexx

Philander (Greek) One who loves mankind
Phylander

Philemon (Hebrew) A loving man
Phylemon, Philimon, Phylimon, Philomon, Phylomon, Philamon, Phylamon

Philetus (Greek) A collector
Phyletus, Philetos, Phyletos

Phillip (Greek) One who loves horses
Phil, Philipp, Philippe, Philippos, Philippus, Philips, Philip, Phillips, Philly, Phyllip, Pilipo, Pip, Pippo, Phipps, Phips, Phillipe

Philo (Greek) One who loves and is loved

Phineas (Hebrew) From the serpent's mouth; an oracle
Phinehas, Pincas, Pinchas, Pinchos, Pincus, Pinhas, Pinkus, Pyncus, Pynkus, Pinckus, Pynckus, Pinkas, Pinckas, Pinchus

Phoebus (Greek) A radiant man
Phoibos

Phoenix (Greek) A dark-red color; in mythology, an immortal bird
Phoenyx

Phomello (African) A successful man
Phomelo

Phong (Vietnamese) Of the wind

Photius (Greek) A scholarly man
Photeus, Photyus, Photias, Photyas, Photeas

Phuc (Vietnamese) One who is blessed
Phuoc

Phuong (Vietnamese) One who recognizes his destiny

Phyre (Armenian) One who burns brightly
Phyr, Phire, Phir

Picardus (Hispanic) An adventurous man
Pycardus, Picardos, Pycardos, Picardas, Pycardas, Picardis, Pycardis, Picardys, Pycardys

Pickford (English) From the woodcutter's ford
Pickforde, Picford, Picforde, Pikford, Pikforde

Pickworth (English) From the woodcutter's estate
Pikworth, Picworth, Pickworthe, Pikworthe, Picworthe

Pierce (English) Form of Peter, meaning "as solid and strong as a rock"
Pearce, Pears, Pearson, Pearsson, Peerce, Peirce, Pierson, Piersson, Piers, Pyrs, Pyrse, Pyrce

Pierpont (French) A social man
Pierrepont, Pierponte, Pierrponte

Pierre (French) Form of Peter, meaning "as solid and strong as a rock"
Pyerre, Piere, Pyere, Pierrel, Pierrell, Pierel, Pierell, Pierelle, Pierrelle, Pierele, Pierrele

Pike (English) One who wields a spear
Pyke

Pilan (Native American) Of the supreme essence
Pilann, Pylan, Pylann

Pilgrim (English) A traveler; wanderer
Pylgrim, Pilgrym, Pylgrym

Pili (African) The second-born child
Pilie, Pily, Piley, Pilee, Pilea

Pillan (Native American) The god of storms
Pyllan, Pillann, Pyllann

Pillar (American) One who provides a good foundation
Pyllar, Pilar, Pylar

Pillion (French) An excellent man
Pyllion, Pillyon, Pilion, Pylion, Pilyon, Pilot

Pim (Dutch) One who is precise
Pym

Pin (Vietnamese) Filled with joy
Pyn

Piney (American) From the pine trees
Piny, Pinee, Pinea, Pini, Pinie

Ping (Chinese) One who is peaceful
Pyng

Pinya (Hebrew) A faithful man
Pinyah, Pynya, Pynyah

Pio (Latin) A pious man
Pyo, Pios, Pius, Pyos, Pyus

Piper (English) One who plays the flute
Pipere, Pyper, Pypere, Piperel, Pyperel, Piperell, Pyperell, Piperele, Pyperele, Piperelle, Pyperelle, Pepperell

Pippin (English) One who is shy
Pippen, Pippyn, Pyppin, Pyppen, Pyppyn

Pippino (Italian) Form of Joseph, meaning "God will add"
Peppino

Pirney (Scottish) From the island
Pirny, Pirnee, Pirnea, Pirni, Pirnie, Pyrney, Pyrny, Pyrnee, Pyrnea, Pyrni, Pyrnie

Pirro (Greek) A red-haired man
Pyrro

Pisces (Latin) The twelfth sign of the zodiac; the fishes
Pysces, Piscees, Pyscees, Piscez, Pisceez

Pitney (English) From the island of the stubborn man
Pitny, Pitni, Pitnie, Pitnee, Pitnea, Pytney, Pytny, Pytni, Pytnie, Pytnee, Pytnea

Pitt (English) From the ditch
Pit, Pytt, Pyt

Pittman (English) A laborer
Pyttman, Pitman, Pytman

Pivane (Native American) Resembling a weasel
Pyvane, Pivaen, Pivaene, Pyvaen, Pyvaene, Pivain, Pivaine, Pyvain, Pyvaine, Pivayn, Pivayne, Pyvayn, Pyvayne

Placido (Spanish) One who is calm
Plasedo, Placedo, Placidus, Placijo, Placyd, Placydo, Plasido, Placid, Plasid

Plaise (Irish) Having great strength
Playse, Plase, Plaese, Plaize, Playze, Plaze, Plaeze

Plan (American) An organized man
Planner, Plannar, Plannor, Plannir, Plannyr, Plann

Plantagenet (French) Resembling the broom flower

Platinum (English) As precious as the metal
Platynum, Platnum, Platie, Plati, Platee, Platy, Platey, Platea

Plato (Greek) One who has broad shoulders
Platon, Playto, Plaito, Plaeto

Platt (French) From the flat land
Plat

Plutarco (Greek) A wicked man

Pluto (Greek) In mythology, god of the underworld

Podi (Teutonic) One who is bold
Podie, Pody, Podey, Podee, Podea

Poe (English) A mysterious man
Po

Poetry (American) A romantic man
Poetrey, Poetri, Poetrie, Poetree, Poetrea, Poet, Poete

Pollard (English) A small man
Pollerd, Pollyrd

Pollux (Greek) One who is crowned
Pollock, Pollok, Polloc, Pollack, Polloch

Polo (African) Resembling an alligator
Poloe, Poloh

Polygnotos (Greek) One who loves many
Polygnotus

Pomeroy (French) From the apple orchard
Pommeroy, Pomeroi, Pommeroi, Pomeray, Pommeray, Pommelraie

Pompeo (Italian / Greek) The fifth-born child / the one in charge
Pompey, Pompeyo, Pompi, Pompilio, Pomponio

Pomposo (Spanish) A pompous man
Pomposio, Pomposiyo

Ponce (Spanish) The fifth-born child
Ponse

Pongor (Hungarian) A mighty man
Pongorr, Pongoro, Pongorro

Poni (African) The second-born son
Ponni, Ponie, Ponnie, Pony, Ponny, Poney, Ponney, Ponee, Ponnee, Ponea, Ponnea

Ponipake (Hawaiian) One who has good luck
Ponipaki, Ponipakie, Ponipaky, Ponipakey, Ponipakee, Ponipakea

Pons (Latin) From the bridge
Pontius, Ponthos, Ponthus

Pontius (Latin) The fifth-born child
Pontias, Pontios, Pontyus, Ponteas, Ponteus, Pontus

Poogie (American) A snuggly little boy
Poogi, Poogy, Poogey, Poogee, Poogea

Pooky (American) A cute little boy
Pookey, Pooki, Pookie, Pookee, Pookea

Poorna (Indian) One who is complete
Pourna

Poornachandra (Indian) Born beneath the full moon
Pournachandra, Poornachandre, Pournachandre

Poornamruth (Indian) Full of sweetness
Pournamruth

Poornayu (Indian) Full of life; blessed with a full life
Pournayu, Poornayou, Pournayou, Poornayue, Pournayue

Pope (Greek) The father

Porat (Hebrew) A productive man

Porfirio (Greek) Refers to a purple coloring
Porphirios, Prophyrios, Porfiro, Porphyrios

Poriel (Hebrew) The fruit of God
Poriell, Poriele, Porielle

Porter (English) The gatekeeper
Porteur, Portier, Port, Porte, Poart, Portur, Portor, Portar, Portir, Portyr

Portland (English) From the land near the port

Poseidon (Greek) In mythology, the god of the waters
Posidon, Posydon, Posiydon

Potter (English) One who makes pots
Pottir, Pottor, Pottar, Pottur, Pottyr

Powa (Native American) A wealthy man
Powah

Powder (American) A lighthearted man
Powdar, Powdir, Powdur, Powdor, Powdi, Powdie, Powdy, Powdey, Powdee, Powdea

Powell (English) Form of Paul, meaning "a small or humble man"
Powel

Powhatan (Native American) From the chief's hill

Powwaw (Native American) A priest

Prabal (Indian) Resembling coral
Praball, Prabale, Prabulle

Prabhakar (Hindu) Of the sun

Prabhat (Indian) Born during the morning

Pradeep (Hindi) One who is surrounded by light
Pradip, Pradyp, Pradeepe, Pradype, Pradipe, Pradeap, Pradeape

Pragun (Indian) One who is straightforward; honest

Prahlad (Indian) Filled with joy

Prairie (American) From the flatlands
Prairi, Prairy, Prairey, Prairee, Prairea, Prair, Praire

Prajit (Indian) A kind man
Prajeet, Prajeat, Prajyt, Prajin, Prajeen, Prajean, Prajyn

Prakash (Indian) Surrounded by light
Parkash, Prakashe, Parkashe

Pramod (Indian) A delightful young man

Pramsu (Indian) A scholar
Pramsue, Pramsou, Pramsoo

Pran (Indian) A giver of life
Prann

Pranav (Indian) The sacred syllable Om

Pranay (Indian) One who is dearly loved
Pranaye, Pranai, Pranae

Pranit (Indian) One who is humble; modest
Pranyt, Praneet, Praneat

Prasad (Indian) A gift from God

Prashant (Indian) One who is peaceful; calm
Prashante, Prashanth, Prashanthe

Pratap (Hindi) A majestic man

Pratik (Indian) A sign or symbol
Pratyk, Prateek, Prateak, Pratim, Pratym, Prateem, Prateam

Pravat (Thai) History

Praveen (Hindi) One who is proficient
Pravean, Pravein, Pravyn, Pravin

Prem (Indian) An affectionate man

Prembhari (Indian) One who is full of love
Prembharie, Prembhary, Prembharey, Prembharee, Prembharea

Prentice (English) A student; an apprentice
Prentyce, Prentise, Prentyse, Prentiss, Prentis

Prerak (Indian) One who encourages others

Preruet (French) A brave man

Prescott (English) From the priest's cottage
Prescot, Prestcot, Prestcott, Preostcot

Presley (English) From the priest's meadow
Presly, Presle, Presli, Preslie, Preslee, Presleigh, Preslea, Prezley, Prezly, Prezli, Prezlie, Prezlee, Prezleigh, Prezlea, Prestley, Priestley, Prestly, Priestly

Preston (English) From the priest's town
Prestin, Prestyn, Prestan, Prestun, Presten, Pfeostun

Preto (Latin) An important man
Prito, Preyto, Pryto, Preeto, Preato

Prewitt (French) A brave young one
Prewet, Prewett, Prewit, Pruitt, Pruit, Pruet, Pruett

Price (French) One who is very dear; prized
Pryce, Prise, Pryse, Prys

Primerica (American) A patriotic man
Primericus, Primerico, Primerika, Primerikus, Primeriko

Primitivo (Spanish) A primitive man

Primo (Italian) The firstborn child
Preemo, Premo, Priemo, Preimo, Preamo, Prymo, Prime, Primeiro

Prince (Latin) The royal son
Printz, Printze, Prinz, Prinze, Princeton

Prine (English) One who surpasses others
Pryne

Prisciliano (Spanish) A wise and elderly man

Priyavrat (Indian) An older brother

Probert (American) A ray of sunshine
Proberte, Proberth, Proberthe

Procopio (Spanish) One who is progressive
Procopius, Prokopios

Proctor (Latin) A steward
Procter, Procktor, Prockter

Prometheus (Greek) In mythology, he stole fire from the heavens and gave it to man
Promitheus, Promethius, Promithius

Prop (American) A fun-loving man
Propp, Proppe

Prosper (Latin) A fortunate man
Prospero, Prosperus

Proteus (Greek) In mythology, a sea deity with the gift of prophecy
Protius, Protyus, Proteas, Protyas, Protias

Proverb (English) A wise saying

Prudencio (Spanish) A cautious man
Prudentius

Pryderi (Celtic) Son of the sea
Pryderie, Prydery, Pryderey, Pryderee, Pryderea

Prydwen (Welsh) A handsome man
Prydwenn, Prydwenne, Prydwin, Prydwinne, Prydwinn, Prydwyn, Prydwynn, Prydwynne

Pryor (Latin) Head of the monastery
Prior

Publias (Greek) A great thinker
Publios, Publius, Publyas, Publyos, Publyus

Pueblo (Spanish) From the city

Pullman (English) One who works on a train
Pulman, Pullmann, Pulmann

Puma (Latin) Resembling a mountain lion
Pumah, Pouma, Pooma

Pumeet (Indian) An innocent man
Pumit, Pumyt, Pumeat

Pundarik (Indian) A white-skinned man
Pundaric, Pundarick, Pundaryk, Pundaryc, Pundaryck

Purujit (Indian) One who has defeated many
Purujyt, Purujeet, Purujeat

Purvin (English) One who helps others
Purvyn, Purvon, Purven, Purvan, Purvun, Pervin, Pervyn, Pervon, Pervun, Pervan, Perven

Purvis (English) One who provides provisions
Purviss, Purvisse, Purvys, Purvyss, Purvysse

Pusan (Hindi) A wise man; a sage
Pusann, Pousan, Pousann, Poosan, Poosann

Putnam (English) One who lives by the water
Putni, Putnie, Putny, Putney, Putnee, Putnea

Pygmalion (Greek) In mythology, a king of Cyprus and talented sculptor
Pigmalion, Pymalien, Pigmalien, Pygmalian, Pigmalian

Pyralis (Greek) Born of fire
Pyraliss, Pyralisse, Pyralys, Pyralyss, Pyralysse, Pyre

q

Qabil (Arabic) An able-bodied man
Qabyl, Qabeel, Qabeal, Qabeil, Qabiel

Qadim (Arabic) From an ancient family
Qadeem, Qadiem, Qadeim, Qadym, Qadeam

Qadir (Arabic) A capable man; one who is competent
Qadyr, Qadeer, Qadeir, Qadear, Qadeir, Qadar, Qadry, Quadir, Quadeer

Qaiser (Arabic) A king; a ruler
Qeyser

Qaletaqa (Native American) The people's guardian

Qamar (Arabic) Born beneath the moon
Qamarr, Quamar, Quamarr

Qasim (Arabic) One who is charitable; generous
Qasym, Qaseem, Qaseim, Qasiem, Qaseam, Quasim, Quaseem, Quasym

Qays (Arabic) One who is firm
Qais, Qayse, Qaise, Qaes, Qaese, Qase

Qiao (Chinese) A handsome man

Qimat (Hindi) A highly valued man
Qymat

Qing (Chinese) Of the deep water
Qyng

Qochata (Native American) A white-skinned man
Qochatah, Qochatta, Qochattah

Qssim (Arabic) He divides
Qssym

Quaashie (American) An ambitious man
Quashie, Quashi, Quashy, Quashey, Quashee, Quashea, Quaashi, Quaashy, Quaashey, Quaashee, Quaashea

Quacey (Scottish) Of the moonlight
Quacy, Quaci, Quacie, Quacee, Quacea

Quaddus (American) A bright man
Quadus, Quaddos, Quados

Quade (Latin) The fourth-born child
Quadrees, Quadres, Quadrys, Quadries, Quadreis, Quadreys, Quadreas, Quadrhys

Quaid (Irish) Form of Walter, meaning "the commander of the army"
Quaide, Quayd, Quayde, Quaed, Quaede

Quan (Vietnamese) A dignified man; a soldier

Quanah (Native American) One who has a pleasant scent
Quana, Quanna, Quunnah

Quang (Vietnamese) A clear-headed man

Quant (Latin) Our son's worth
Quante, Quantai, Quantay, Quantaye, Quantae, Quantey, Quanty, Quanti, Quantie, Quantee, Quantea, Quantez, Quantal

Quaronne (American) One who is haughty
Quarone, Quaron, Quaronn

Quarrie (Scottish) A proud man
Quarri, Quarry, Quarrey, Quarree, Quarrea, Quany, Quaney, Quanee, Quanea, Quani, Quanie

Quashawn (American) A tenacious man
Quashaun, Quasean, Quashon, Quashi, Quashie, Quashee, Quashea, Quashy, Quashey

Quauhtli (Aztec) Resembling an eagle

Qubilah (Arabic) An agreeable man
Qubila, Qubeelah, Qubeela, Qubeilah, Qubeila, Qubielah, Qubiela, Qubealah, Qubeala, Qubylah, Qubyla

Qudamah (Arabic) A courageous man
Qudama

Qued (Native American) Wearing a decorated robe

Quelatikan (Native American) One who has a blue horn
Quelatykan, Quelatican, Quelatycan, Quelatickan, Quelatyckan

Quenby (English) From the queen's estate; a giving man
Quenbey, Quenbi, Quenbie, Quenbee, Quenbea, Quinby, Quinbey, Quinbee, Quinbea, Quinbi, Quinbie

Quennell (French) From the small oak
Quennelle, Quenell, Quennel, Quenelle, Quennele, Quenel, Quentrell, Quentrelle, Quentrel, Quentrele, Quesnel, Quesnell, Quesnele, Quesnelle

Quentin (Latin) The fifth-born child
Quent, Quenten, Quenton, Quentun, Quentan, Quentyn, Quente, Qwentin, Qwenton, Qwenten

Queran (Irish) A dark and handsome man
Queron, Queren, Querin, Queryn, Querun

Quick (American) One who is fast; a witty man
Quik, Quicke, Quic

Quico (Spanish) A beloved friend
Quiko, Quicko, Quyco, Quyko, Quycko, Quiqui

Quiessence (Spanish) An essential; the essence
Quiessince, Quiessense, Quiessinse, Quiesence, Quiesense, Quiess, Quiesse, Quiese, Quies

Quigley (Irish) One with messy or unruly hair
Quigly, Quigleigh, Quiglee, Quiglea, Quigli, Quiglie

Quillan (Gaelic) Resembling a cub
Quilan, Quillen, Quilen, Quillon, Quilon

Quiller (English) A scriber
Quillar, Quillor, Quillir, Quillyr, Quillur

Quilliam (Gaelic) Form of William, meaning "the determined protector"
Quilhelm, Quilhelmus, Quilliams, Quilliamson, Quilliamon, Quillem, Quillhelmus, Quilmot, Quilmott, Quilmod, Quilmodd

Quimby (Norse) From the woman's estate
Quimbey, Quimbee, Quimbea, Quimbi, Quimbie

Quincy (English) The fifth-born child; from the fifth son's estate
Quincey, Quinci, Quincie, Quincee, Quinncy, Quinnci, Quyncy, Quyncey, Quynci, Quyncie, Quyncee, Quynncy, Quince, Quinnsy, Quinsey

Quinlan (Gaelic) A strong and healthy man
Quindlan, Quinlen, Quindlen, Quinian, Quinlin, Quindlin, Quinlyn, Quindlyn, Quinnlan

Quinn (Gaelic) One who provides counsel; an intelligent man
Quin, Quinne, Qwinn, Quynn, Qwin, Quiyn, Quyn, Qwinne, Quinnell

Quintavius (American) The fifth-born child
Quintavios, Quintavus, Quintavies

Quinto (Spanish) The fifth-born child
Quynto, Quintus, Quintos, Quinty, Quinti, Quintie, Quintey, Quintee, Quintea

Quinton (English) From the queen's town or settlement
Quinntan, Quinnten, Quinntin, Quinnton, Quintain, Quintan, Quintyn, Quintynn, Quintin, Quinten, Quintann, Quint, Quinte, Quynt, Quynte, Quinneton, Quienton, Quientin, Quiten, Quitin, Quiton

Quintrell (English) An elegant and dashing man
Quintrel, Quintrelle, Quyntrell, Quyntrelle, Quyntrel, Quyntrele, Quintrele

Quirin (American) One who is magical
Quiryn, Quiran, Quiren, Quiron, Quirun

Quirinus (Latin) One who wields a spear
Quirinos, Quirynus, Quirynos, Quirinius, Quirynius

Quito (Spanish) A lively man
Quyto, Quitos, Quytos

Qunnoune (Native American) One who is tall
Qunnoun, Qunnoone, Qunnoon

Quoc (Vietnamese) A patriot
Quok, Quock

Quoitrel (American) A mediator
Quoytrel, Quoitrell, Quoytrell, Quoitrele, Quoytrele, Quoitrelle, Quoytrelle

Quon (Chinese) A luminous man
Quonn, Quone, Quonne

Qusay (Arabic) One who is distant
Qusaye, Qusai, Qusae, Qussay, Qussaye, Qussai, Qussae

Qutaybah (Arabic) An impatient man
Qutayba, Qutaibah, Qutaiba, Qutabah, Qutaba, Qutaebah, Qutaeba

Qutub (Indian) One who is tall

Raanan (Hebrew) A fresh-faced man

Rabbaanee (African) An easygoing man

Rabbani (Arabic) Of the divine
Rabbanie, Rabbany, Rabbaney, Rabbanee, Rabbanea

Rabbi (Hebrew) The master

Rabbit (English) Resembling the animal
Rabbyt

Rabi (Arabic) Of the gentle wind
Rabie, Rabee, Raby, Rahea, Rabey

Rabia (African) Born during the spring
Rabiah, Rabiya, Rabiyah

Rabul (Hispanic) A wealthy man
Rabule, Rabool, Raboole, Raboul, Raboule

Race (American) One who is fast; a competitor
Racer, Raci, Racie, Racy, Racey, Racee, Racea

Rach (African) Resembling a frog

Racham (Hebrew) One who shows mercy
Rachim, Rachem, Rachym, Rachaam, Rachan, Rachin

Racqueab (Arabic) A homebody

Rad (English) One who provides counsel
Radd, Raad, Raadd

Radames (Egyptian) A hero
Radamays, Radamayes, Radamais, Radamaise, Radamaes, Radamaese

Radbert (English) A red-haired advisor
Radberte, Radberth, Radberthe, Radburt, Radburth, Radburte, Radburthe

Radburn (English) From the red brook
Radburne, Radbern, Radberne, Radborn, Radborne, Radbourn, Radbourne, Radbyrne, Raedburne, Raedburn, Raedborn, Raedborne, Raedbourn, Raedbourne

Radcliff (English) From the red cliff
Radcliffe, Radclyff, Radclyffe, Ratcliff, Ratcliffe, Ratclyff, Ratclyffe, Radclyf, Ratclyf, Radeliffe, Raedclif, Raedclyf, Raedcliff, Raedclyff

Raddy (Slavic) A cheerful person
Raddey, Raddi, Raddie, Raddee, Raddea, Radde, Radman, Radi, Radie, Rady, Radey, Radee, Radea

Radek (Slavic) A famous ruler
Radec, Radeck

Radford (English) From the red ford
Radforde, Radferd, Radfurd, Radferde, Radfurde, Redford, Redforde, Raedford, Raedforde, Raedfurd, Raedfurde, Raedferd, Raedferde

Radimir (Slavic) A well-known joyful person
Radimeer, Radimyr, Radymir, Radymyr, Radymeer, Radimear, Radymear, Radomir, Radomyr, Radomeer, Radomear

Radley (English) From the red meadow
Radly, Radli, Radlie, Radlee, Radleigh, Radlea, Radleah, Redley, Redly, Redli, Redlie, Redleigh, Redlee, Redlea, Redleah, Raedleah, Raedlea, Raedleigh, Raedlee, Raedli, Raedlie, Raedley, Raedly

Radnor (English) From the red shore
Radnur, Radner, Radnar, Radnir, Radnyr, Raedanoran, Raedanor

Radolf (English) Resembling a red wolf
Radolph, Radulf, Radulph, Raedwolf, Raedwulf

Radoslaw (Polish) One who loves peace
Radoslav

Radwan (Arabic) A delightful man

Raedan (Anglo-Saxon) One who provides counsel
Raydan, Raidan, Radan, Raedbora

Raekwon (American) A proud man
Raekwonn, Raykwon, Raykwonn, Rakwon, Rakwonn, Raikwon, Raikwonn

Rael (African) As innocent as a lamb
Raele, Rayl, Rayle, Rail, Raile, Rale

Rafe (Irish) A tough man
Raffe, Raff, Raf, Raif, Rayfe, Raife, Raef, Raefe

Rafer (Gaelic) A wealthy man
Raffer

Rafferty (Gaelic) One who wields prosperity
Raffertey, Rafferti, Raffertie, Raffertea, Raffertee, Raffarty, Raffartey, Raffarti, Raffartie, Raffartea, Raffartee, Raferty, Rafertey, Raferti, Rafertie, Rafertea, Rafertee, Rafarty, Rafartey, Rafarti, Rafartie, Rafartea, Rafartee

Rafi (Arabic) One who is exalted
Rafie, Rafy, Rafey, Rafea, Rafee, Raffi, Raffie, Raffy, Raffey, Raffea, Raffee, Rafat

Rafiki (African) A gentle friend
Rafikie, Rafikea, Rafikee, Rafiky, Rafikey

Rafiq (Arabic) A beloved friend
Rafeeq, Rafeaq, Rafyq, Rafik, Rafeek, Rafeak, Rafyk

Rafiya (African) A dignified man
Rafeeya, Rafeaya, Rafeiya, Rafieya

Raghib (Arabic) One who is desired
Ragheb, Ragheeb, Ragheab, Raghyb, Ragheib, Raghieb

Raghid (Arabic) One who is carefree
Ragheed, Raghead, Raghied, Ragheid, Raghyd

Ragnar (Norse) A warrior who places judgment
Ragnor, Ragner, Ragnir, Ragnyr, Ragnur, Regnar, Regner, Regnir, Regnyr, Regnor, Regnur, Ragnal, Ragnall, Raghnal, Raghnall

Rahim (Arabic) A compassionate man
Rahym, Raheim, Rahiem, Raheem, Raheam

Rahimat (Arabic) Full of grace
Rahymat

Rahman (Arabic) One who is full of compassion
Rahmann, Rahmahn, Raman

Rai (Japanese) A trustworthy man; of lightning and thunder

Ra'id (Arabic) A great leader

Raiden (Japanese) In mythology, the god of thunder and lightning
Raidon, Rayden, Raydon, Raeden, Raedon, Raden, Radon, Raijin, Rayjin, Raejin, Rajin, Raidyn, Raydyn, Raedyn, Radyn

Raighne (Irish) A strong man

Raimi (African) A compassionate man
Raimie, Raimy, Raimey, Raimee, Raimea

Rainart (German) One who provides brave counsel
Rainhard, Rainhardt, Reinart, Reinhard, Reinhardt, Reinhart, Renke

Rainer (German) A decisive warrior
Rainier, Ranier, Rainor, Rayner, Raynor, Raner

Raines (English) A wise ruler; a lord
Rain, Raine, Rains, Rayne, Raynes, Raene, Raenes

Rainey (German) One who is helpful; generous
Rainy, Raini, Rainie, Ruinee, Rainea, Rayney, Rayny, Rayni, Raynie, Raynee, Raynea

Rajab (African) A glorified man

Rajan (Indian) A king
Raj, Raja, Rajah

Rajarshi (Indian) The king's sage
Rajarshie, Rajarshy, Rajarshey, Rajarshee, Rajarshea

Rajas (Indian) A famous and proud man

Rajat (Indian) As precious as silver

Rajdeep (Indian) The light of the king
Rajdip, Rajdyp, Rajdeip, Rajdiep, Rajdeap

Rajendra (Hindi) A powerful king
Rajindra, Rajyndra

Rajesh (Hindi) The king's rule

Rajit (Indian) One who is decorated
Rajeet, Rajeit, Rajiet, Rajyt, Rajeat

Rajiv (Hindi) To be striped
Rajyv, Rajeev, Rajeav

Raka (Indian) Born beneath the full moon
Rakah, Rakka, Rakkah

Rakesh (Hindi) A king

Rakin (Arabic) A respectful young man
Rakeen, Rakean, Rakyn, Rakein, Rakien

Rakshak (Indian) One who protects others

Rald (German) A famous ruler
Ralde, Rauld, Raulde

Raleigh (English) From the clearing of roe deer
Ralee, Raley, Raly, Rali, Ralie, Rawley, Rawly, Rawleigh, Rawli, Rawlie, Rawlea, Ralea, Raleah, Rawleah, Raleich, Ralegh

Ralik (Hindi) One who has been purified
Raleek, Raleak, Ralyk, Raleik, Raliek

Ralis (Latin) A thin man
Raliss, Ralisse, Ralys, Ralyss, Ralysse, Ralus, Rallis, Rallus

Ralph (English) Wolf counsel
Ralf, Ralphe, Ralfe, Ralphi, Ralphie, Ralphee, Ralphea, Ralphy, Ralphey

Ralston (English) From Ralph's town
Ralstun, Ralsten, Ralstan, Ralstin, Ralstyn

Ram (Hebrew / Sanskrit) A superior man / one who is pleasing
Rahm, Rama, Rahma, Ramos, Rahmos, Ram, Ramm

Rambert (German) Having great strength; an intelligent man
Ramberte, Ramberth, Ramberthe, Ramburt, Ramburte, Ramburth, Ramburthe, Ramhart, Ramharte

Ramel (Hindi) A godly man
Ramell, Ramele, Ramelle, Raymel, Raymell, Raymele, Raymelle

Rami (Arabic) A loving man
Ramee, Ramea, Ramie, Ramy, Ramey

Ramin (Persian) A great warrior
Ramen, Ramyn

Ramiro (Portuguese) A famous counselor; a great judge
Ramyro, Rameero, Rameyro, Ramirez, Ramyrez, Rameerez

Ramsden (English) From the ram's valley
Ramsdin, Ramsdyn, Ramsdan, Ramsdon, Ramsdun

Ramses (Egyptian) Born of the sun god
Rameses, Ramesses, Ramzes, Ramzees, Ramsees, Ramzan, Ramsies, Ramzies

Ramsey (English) From the raven island; from the island of wild garlic
Ramsay, Ramsie, Ramsi, Ramsee, Ramsy, Ramsea, Ramzy, Ramzey, Ramzi, Ramzie, Ramzee, Ramzea, Rams, Ramz

Ranajit (Indian) A victorious man
Ranajeet, Ranajyt, Ranajeat, Ranajay, Ranajaye, Ranajae, Ranajai

Rance (French / African) A type of marble / borrowed
Rencei, Rancell, Ransel, Ransell, Rancy, Rancey, Runcye, Ranci, Rancie, Rancee, Rancea

Rand (German) One who shields others
Rande

Randall (German) The wolf shield
Randal, Randale, Randel, Randell, Randl, Randle, Randon, Rendall, Rendell

Randolph (German) The wolf shield
Randolf, Ranolf, Ranolph, Ranulfo, Rundulfo, Randwulf, Ranwulf, Randwolf, Ranwolf, Ranulf

Randy (English) Form of Randall or Randolph, meaning "the wolf shield"
Randey, Randi, Randie, Randee, Randea

Ranen (Hebrew) Filled with joy
Rainen, Raynen, Raenen, Ranon, Rainon, Raynon, Raenon

Rang (English) Resembling a raven
Range

Rangarajan (Hindi) A charming man

Ranger (French) The guardian of the forest
Rainger, Raynger, Raenger

Rangey (English) From raven's island
Rangy, Rangi, Rangie, Rangee, Rangea

Rangle (American) A cowboy
Rangel

Ranit (Hebrew) One who raises his voice in song
Rani, Ranie, Rany, Raney, Ranee, Ranea, Ronit

Ranjan (Indian) A delightful boy

Ranjit (Hindi) One who is charmed
Ranjeet, Ranjeat, Ranjyt

Rankin (English) The little shield
Rankinn, Rankine, Rankyn, Rankynn, Rankyne, Randkin, Randkyn, Rank

Ransford (English) From the raven's ford
Ransforde, Ransferd, Ransferde, Ransfurd, Ransfurde, Rangford, Rangforde, Rangfurd, Rangferd

Ransley (English) From the raven's meadow
Ransly, Ransli, Ranslie, Ranslee, Ransleigh, Ranslea, Ransleah, Rangley, Rangly, Ranglee, Rangleigh, Rangli, Ranglie, Ranglea, Rangleah

Ransom (English) The warrior's shield
*Ransum, Ransem, Ransam, Ransim,
Ransym, Ransome*

Rante (American) An amorous man
Ranti, Rantie, Ranty, Rantey, Rantea, Rantee

Raoul (French) Form of Ralph, meaning
"wolf counsel"
Raoule, Raul, Roul, Rowl, Raule, Roule, Rowle

Raphael (Hebrew) One who is healed by
God
*Rafal, Rafael, Rafaelle, Rafaelo, Rafaello,
Rafel, Rafello, Raffael, Raffaello, Raphaello,
Raphello*

Raqib (Arabic) A glorified man
*Raqyb, Raqeeb, Raqeab, Rakib, Rakeeb,
Rakeab, Rakyb*

Rashad (Arabic) One who has good judgment
Rashaad, Rashod

Rashard (American) A good-hearted man
Rasherd, Rashird, Rashurd, Rashyrd

Rashaun (American) Form of Roshan,
meaning "born during the daylight"
*Rashae, Rashane, Rashawn, Rayshaun,
Rayshawn, Raishaun, Raishawn, Raeshaun,
Raeshawn*

Rashid (Arabic) One who is guided along
the right path
*Rasheed, Rasheid, Rashied, Rashead, Rashyd,
Rasheyd, Raashid, Rascheed, Raschid,
Raschyd*

Rashne (Persian) A judge
*Rashni, Rashnie, Rashnea, Rashnee, Rashney,
Rashny*

Rasmus (Greek) Form of Erasmus, meaning "one who is dearly loved"
Rasmos, Rasmes, Rasmis, Rasmys, Rasmas

Rasool (Arabic) A messenger; a herald
Rasule, Rasoole, Rasul, Rasoul, Rasoule

Rasputin (Russian) A mystic
*Rasputyn, Rasputen, Rasputan, Rasputon,
Rasputun*

Rastus (Greek) Form of Erastus, meaning
"a loving man"
Rastos, Rastes, Rastis, Rastys, Rastas

Ratri (Indian) Born at night
Ratrie, Ratry, Ratrey, Ratrea, Ratree

Ratul (Indian) A sweet man
Ratule, Ratoul, Ratoule, Ratool, Ratoole

Raudel (American) One who is rowdy
Raudell, Raudele, Raudelle

Rauf (Arabic) A compassionate man
Rauff, Raufe, Rauffe

Raulo (Spanish) One who is wise
Rawlo

Raven (English) Resembling the blackbird;
a dark and mysterious man
*Raiven, Rayvenne, Rayven, Rayvinn, Ravyn,
Raevin, Raeven, Ravenne, Ravinn, Ravin*

Ravi (Hindi) From the sun
Ravie, Ravy, Ravey, Ravee, Ravea

Ravid (Hebrew) A wanderer; one who
searches
Ravyd, Raveed, Ravead, Raviyd, Ravied, Raveid

Ravindra (Indian) The strength of the sun
Ravyndra

Ravinger (English) One who lives near the
ravine
Ravynger

Raviv (Hebrew) Resembling a raindrop
*Ravyv, Ravive, Ravyve, Raveev, Raveeve,
Raveav, Raveave, Raviev, Ravieve, Raveiv,
Raveive*

Rawdon (Teutonic) From the hill
Rawden, Rawdun, Rawdan, Rawdin, Rawdyn

Rawlins (French) From the renowned land
*Rawlin, Rawson, Rawlinson, Rawlings,
Rawling, Rawls, Rawl, Rawle*

Ray (English) Form of Raymond, meaning
"a wise protector"
*Rae, Rai, Rayce, Rayder, Rayse, Raye,
Rayford, Raylen, Raynell, Reigh*

Rayburn (English) From the brook of the
roe deer
*Raeborn, Raeborne, Raebourn, Raeburn,
Rayborn, Raybourne, Raybourn, Rayborne,
Rayburne, Raeburne, Raiborn, Raiborne,
Raibourn, Raibourne, Raiburn, Raiburne,
Reyhurn, Reyhern, Reyburn, Reyborn*

Rayfield (English) From the field of roe deer
Rayfeld

Rayford (French) From the roe deer crossing
Rayforde, Rayferd, Rayferde, Rayfurd, Rayfurde

Rayhan (Arabic) One who is favored by God
Ruihan, Raehan, Rahan

Rayhurn (English) From the roe deer's stream
Rayhurne, Rayhorn, Rayhorne, Rayhourn, Rayhourne

Raymond (German) A wise protector
Raemond, Raemondo, Raimond, Raimondo, Raimund, Raimundo, Rajmund, Ramon, Ramond, Ramonde, Ramone, Rayment, Raymondo, Raymund, Raymunde, Raymundo, Reymond, Reymundo, Raymon, Raemon, Rayman, Raeman, Raimon, Raiman

Raymont (American) A distinguised gentleman
Raymonte, Raimont, Raimonte, Raemont, Raemonte, Ramont, Ramonte

Raynor (German) The decisive warrior
Raynar, Rayne, Raynell, Rayner, Raynord, Reinier, Renier, Ranell, Ranieri, Raniero, Raynard, Rane

Raza (Arabic) Filled with hope
Razah, Razza, Razzah

Razak (Arabic) A devoted man
Razac, Razack, Razach

Raziel (Aramaic) The Lord is my secret
Raziell, Raziele, Razielle, Razyel, Razyell, Razyele, Razyelle, Razi, Razie, Razea, Razee, Razy, Razey

Reading (English) Son of a red-haired man
Reeding, Reyding, Redding, Reiding

Reaner (American) An even-tempered man
Reener, Riener, Rener

Rebel (American) An outlaw
Rebell, Rebele, Rebelle, Rebe, Rebbe, Rebbi, Rebbie, Rebbea, Rebbee, Rebby, Rebbey

Recene (Anglo-Saxon) One who is quick
Receen, Receene, Recean, Receane, Recein, Receine, Recien, Reciene, Recyn, Recyne, Recin, Recine

Red (American) A red-haired man
Redd, Redde, Reddi, Reddie, Reddy, Reddey, Reddea, Reddee, Reod

Reda (Arabic) One who is satisfied; content
Redah, Rida, Ridah, Ridha, Ridhah, Ridhaa

Redell (English) From the red valley
Redel, Redelle, Redele, Redale, Redayl, Redayle, Redail, Redaile, Redael, Redaele

Redman (English) A red-haired advisor
Redmann, Raedmann, Raedman, Readman, Readmann, Redaman, Redamann

Redmond (English) Form of Raymond, meaning "a wise protector"
Redmonde, Radmond, Radmund, Radmonde, Radmunde, Redmund, Redmunde, Raedmund, Raedmunde, Raedmond, Raedmonde, Redmon, Redmun

Redwald (English) Strong counsel
Redwalde, Raedwalde, Raedwald

Reece (Welsh) Having great enthusiasm for life
Rees, Reese, Reice, Reise, Reace, Rease, Riece, Riese, Rhys, Rhyss, Rhyse, Rice, Ryce

Reem (Hebrew) Resembling a horned animal
Reeme, Ream, Reame

Reeve (English) A bailiff
Reve, Reuve, Reeford, Reeves, Reaves, Reves, Reaford

Refugio (Spanish) One who provides shelter
Refuge, Resugio, Resuge

Regal (American) Born into royalty
Regall

Regan (Gaelic) Born into royalty; the little ruler
Raegan, Ragan, Raygan, Reganne, Regann, Regane, Reghan, Reugan, Reaghan, Reegan, Rayghun, Raygen, Regen, Riagan

Regenfrithu (English) A peaceful raven

Regent (Latin) A regal man; born into royalty
Regant, Regint, Regynt

Regenweald (English) Having great strength

Reggie (Latin) Form of Reginald, meaning "the king's advisor"
Reggi, Reggy, Reggey, Reggea, Reggee, Reg

Reginald (Latin) The king's advisor
Raghnall, Rainault, Rainhold, Raonull, Raynald, Rayniero, Regin, Reginaldo, Reginalt, Reginauld, Reginault, Regino, Reginvald, Reginvalt, Regnauld, Regnault, Reinald, Reinaldo, Reinaldos, Reinhold, Reinold, Reinwald, Renaud, Renault, Rene, Rheinallt, Rinaldo, Reginaldus, Raynaldo, Regulo

Regine (French) One who is artistic
Regeen, Regeene, Regean, Regeane, Regein, Regeine, Regien, Regiene, Regyn, Regyne

Reginhard (German) Having great strength; an intelligent man
Reginhart, Regynhard, Regynhart, Reginheraht, Regynheraht, Regenhard, Regenhart, Regenheraht, Reinhard, Reinhart

Regis (Latin) A kingly or regal man
Regiss, Reegis, Reagis, Regys, Regyss, Reegys, Reagys, Riegis, Riegys

Rehman (Indian) One who is merciful
Rehmat

Rei (Japanese) One who strives to uphold the law

Reid (English) A red-haired man; one who lives near the reeds
Read, Reade, Reed, Reede, Reide, Raed

Reidar (Scandinavian) A warrior or soldier
Reider, Reidor, Reidur, Reidir, Reidyr

Reilly (Gaelic) An outgoing man
Reilley, Reilli, Reillie, Reillee, Reilleigh, Reillea

Reiner (German) One who provides counsel
Reinir, Reinar, Reinor, Reinur, Reinyr

Reith (American) One who is shy
Reyth, Reeth, Reath, Rieth

Reizo (Japanese) One who is calm and well-kept

Remedios (Spanish) One who is assisted by God
Remedy, Remedi, Remedie, Remedee, Remedey, Remedea, Remedio, Remediyo

Remington (English) From the town of the raven's family
Remyngton, Remingtun, Remyngtun

Remuda (Spanish) A herd of horses
Remooda, Remouda

Remus (Latin) One who is swift; in mythology, along with his brother Romulus, one of the founders of Rome
Reemus, Remos, Reemos, Reamus, Reamos

Remy (French) Man from the town of Rheims
Remi, Remie, Remmy, Remmi, Remmie, Remy, Remmey, Remey, Rhemy, Rhemmy, Remee, Remmee, Remo, Remmo, Remigio

Rendor (Hungarian) One who keeps the peace
Rendur, Rendir, Rendyr, Render, Rendar

René (French) One who has been reborn
Ranae, Ranay, Rané, Renae, Renat, Renay, Renaye, Renee, Rene, Renato, Renell, Renelle, Renie, Reni, Renne, Rennie, Renny, Rrenae, Rennee, Renne, Rennay, Renate, Renatus, Ren, Renn

Renferd (English) One who loves peace
Renferde, Renfurd, Renfurde, Renfred

Renfield (English) From the raven's field
Renfeld, Ranfield, Ranfeld, Rangfield, Rangfeld

Renfred (English) A powerful and peaceful man
Renfreid, Renfrid, Renfryd, Renfried

Renfrew (Welsh) From the calm waters
Rhinfrew

Renfro (Welsh) One who is calm
Renfroe, Renfrow, Renfrowe, Renphro, Renphroe, Renphrow, Renphrowe

Renjiro (Japanese) An honest and upright man
Renjyro, Renjeero, Renjeryo

Renshaw (English) From the raven's forest
Renshawe, Renishaw, Renishawe

Renton (English) From the town of the roe deer
Rentun, Rentin, Rentyn, Rentan, Renten

Renweard (Anglo-Saxon) The guardian of the house
Renward, Renwarden, Renwerd

Renwick (English) From the village of the roe deer; from the village of the ravens
Renwik, Renwic, Renwyck, Renwyk, Renwyc

Renzo (Japanese) The third-born son

Reth (African) A king
Rethe

Retta (African) He has triumphed
Rettah, Reta, Retah

Reuben (Hebrew) Behold, a son!
Reuban, Reubin, Reuven, Rouvin, Rube, Ruben, Rubin, Rubino, Ruby, Rubi, Rubie, Rubey, Rubee, Rubea, Reuhen, Rueban, Re'uven

Reuel (Hebrew) A friend of God
Ruel, Reuell, Ruell, Reuelle, Ruelle, Reuele, Ruele

Rev (American) One who is distinct
Revv, Revin, Reven, Revan, Revyn, Revon, Revun

Revelin (Celtic, Gaelic) Form of Roland, meaning "from the renowned land"
Revelyn, Revelen, Revelan, Revelon, Revelun

Rex (Latin) A king
Reks, Recks, Rexs

Rexford (English) From the king's ford
Rexforde, Rexferd, Rexferde, Rexfurd, Rexfurde

Rexley (English) From the king's meadow
Rexly, Rexleigh, Rexlee, Rexlea, Rexleah, Rexli, Rexlie

Rexton (English) From the king's town
Rextun, Rextown, Royalton, Royaltun

Rey (Spanish) Of the kings
Reyes, Reyni, Reynie, Reyney, Reyny, Reynee, Reynea

Reynard (French / German) Resembling a fox / a strong counselor
Reynardo, Raynard, Reinhard, Reinhardt, Renard, Renardo, Rennard, Reinhart, Reynaud

Reynold (English) Form of Reginald, meaning "the king's advisor"
Reynald, Reynaldo, Reynolds, Reynalde, Reynolde

Reza (Iranian) One who is content
Rezah, Rezza, Rezzah

Reznik (Czech) A butcher
Reznick, Reznic, Reznyk, Reznyck, Reznyc

Rhene (American) One who smiles a lot
Rheen, Rheene, Rhean, Rheane

Rhett (Latin) A well-spoken man
Rett, Rhet, Ret

Rhinebeck (German) From the stream of the Rhine
Rheinbeck, Rhinebek, Rheinbek, Rinebeck, Reinbeck, Rinebek, Reinbek

Rhodes (Greek) From the place where the roses grow
Rhoads, Rhodas, Rodas, Rodes, Roads

Rhodree (Welsh) A strong ruler
Rhodrea, Rhodri, Rhodrie, Rhodry, Rhodrey, Rodree, Rodrea, Rodri, Rodrie, Rodry, Rodrey

Rhydderch (Welsh) Having reddish-brown hair

Rich (English) Form of Richard, meaning "a powerful ruler"
Richi, Richie, Richy, Richey, Richee, Richea, Richer, Ritch, Ritchy, Ritchey, Ritchi, Ritchie, Ritchee, Ritchea

Richard (English) A powerful ruler
Ricard, Ricardo, Riccardo, Richardo, Richart, Richerd, Rickard, Rickert, Rikard, Riocard, Ritchard, Ritcherd, Ritchyrd, Ritshard, Ritsherd, Ryszard, Richman

Richmond (French / German) From the wealthy hill / a powerful protector
Richmonde, Richmund, Richmunde

Richter (English) One who is hopeful
Rickter, Rikter, Ricter

Rick (English) Form of Richard, meaning "a powerful ruler"
Ric, Ricci, Ricco, Rickie, Ricki, Ricky, Rico, Rik, Rikk, Rikke, Rikki, Rikky, Rique, Rickman, Ricman, Rikman, Ricker

Rickward (English) A strong protector
Rickwerd, Rickwood, Rikward, Ricward, Rickweard, Rikweard, Ricweard

Riddhiman (Indian) One who possesses good fortune

Riddock (Irish) From the smooth field
Ridock, Riddoc, Ridoc, Ryddock, Rydock, Ryddoc, Rydoc, Ryddok, Rydok, Riddok, Ridok, Reidhachadh

Ridgeley (English) One who lives at the meadow's ridge
Ridgely, Ridgeli, Ridgelie, Ridgeleigh, Ridgelea, Ridgeleah, Ridgelee, Ridgley, Ridgly, Ridgli, Ridglie, Ridglea, Ridgleah, Ridgleigh, Ridglee, Ridgeiey

Ridgeway (English) One who lives on the road near the ridge
Rydgeway, Rigeway, Rygeway

Ridley (English) From the meadow of reeds
Ridly, Ridli, Ridlie, Ridleigh, Ridlee, Ridlea, Ridleah, Riddley, Riddly, Riddli, Riddlie, Riddlea, Riddleah, Riddlee, Riddleigh

Ridpath (English) One who lives near the red path
Rydpath, Ridpathe, Rydpathe, Raedpath, Raedpathe

Ridvik (Indian) A priest
Ridvic, Ridvick, Rydvik, Rydvic, Rydvick, Ritvik, Ritvic, Ritvick, Rytvik, Rytvic, Rytvick

Ridwan (Arabic) One who is accepting
Rydwan, Ridwann, Rydwann

Rigby (English) From the valley of the ruler
Rigbey, Rigbi, Rigbie, Rigbee, Rigbea

Rigel (Arabic) One who travels on foot; a blue star in the constellation Orion

Rigg (English) One who lives near the ridge
Rig, Ridge, Rygg, Ryg, Rydge, Rige, Ryge, Riggs, Ryggs

Rigoberto (Spanish) A shining warrior
Rigoberte, Rybgobert, Rygoberte, Rigoberth, Rigoberthe, Rygoberth, Rygoberthe, Rigobert, Rygoberto

Rijul (Indian) An innocent man
Rijule, Rijool, Rijoole, Rijoul, Rijoule

Rike (American) A high-spirited man
Ryke, Rikee, Rykee, Rikea, Rykea, Ryki, Rykie

Rimon (Arabic) Resembling a pomegranate
Rymon

Rin (Japanese) From the park; a good companion

Rinan (Anglo-Saxon) Born during a period of rain
Rynan, Rinen, Rinin, Rinyn, Rinon, Rinun, Rynen, Rynin, Rynyn, Rynon, Rynun

Rinc (Anglo-Saxon) A mighty warrior
Rync, Rink, Rynk, Rinck, Rynck

Ring (English) Resembling a ring
Ryng, Ringo, Ryngo, Ringling, Ryngling

Rinji (Japanese) Of the peaceful forest
Rinjie, Rinjy, Rinjey, Rinjee, Rinjea

Rio (Spanish) From the river
Reo, Riyo, Reyo, Riao, Ryo

Riobard (Irish) A bard of the royal court
Reobard, Ryobard

Riocard (German) A powerful ruler
Ryocard, Reocard

Riordain (Irish) A bright man
Riordane, Riordayn, Riordaen, Reardain, Reardane, Reardayn, Reardaen

Riordan (Gaelic) A royal poet; a bard or minstrel
Riorden, Rearden, Reardan, Riordon, Reardon

Ripley (English) From the noisy meadow
Riply, Ripleigh, Ripli, Riplie, Riplea, Ripleah, Riplee, Rip

Ripudaman (Indian) One who defeats his enemies

Ris (English) One who loves the outdoors
Riz

Rishab (Indian) One who is musically talented
Ryshab, Rishaub, Ryshaub, Rishawb, Ryshawb

Rishley (English) From the untamed meadow
Rishly, Rishli, Rishlie, Rishlee, Rishlea, Rishleah, Rishleigh

Rishon (Hebrew) The firstborn son
Ryshon, Rishi, Rishie, Rishea, Rishee, Rishy, Rishey

Risley (English) From the brushwood meadow
Risly, Risli, Rislie, Risleigh, Rislea, Risleah, Rislee, Rizley, Rizly, Rizli, Rizlie, Rizleigh, Rizlea, Rizleah, Rizlee

Risto (Finnish) Form of Christopher, meaning "one who bears Christ inside"
Rhisto, Rysto, Rhysto

Riston (English) From the brushwood settlement
Ryston, Ristun, Rystun

Ritter (German) A knight
Rytter, Ritt, Rytt

River (American) From the river
Ryver, Rivers, Ryvers

Rives (French) One who lives by the riverbank
Ryves

Riyad (Arabic) From the gardens
Riyadh, Riyaz

Ro (Anglo-Saxon / English) A red-haired man / resembling a roe deer
Roe, Row, Rowe

Roald (Norse) A famous ruler
Roal

Roam (American) One who wanders, searches
Roami, Roamie, Roamy, Roamey, Roamea, Roamee

Roark (Gaelic) A champion
Roarke, Rorke, Rourke, Rork, Rourk, Ruark, Ruarke

Rob (English) Form of Robert, meaning "one who is bright with fame"
Robb, Robbi, Robbie, Robby, Robbey, Robbea, Robbee, Robi, Robie, Roby, Robey, Robea, Robee

❂ Robert (German) One who is bright with fame
Riobard, Roban, Robers, Roberto, Robertson, Robartach, Rubert

Robin (English) Form of Robert, meaning "one who is bright with fame"; resembling the red-breasted songbird
Robbin, Robben, Roben, Robinson, Robbinson, Robins, Robbins, Robson, Robyn, Robbyn, Robynson, Robbynson, Roibin, Roiben

Roble (African) Born during a period of rain
Robel

Rocco (Italian) One who is calm; restful
Roch, Roche, Rochus, Rock, Rocko, Rocky, Roque, Rocki, Rockie, Rockee, Rockea, Rocke

Rochester (English) From the stone fortress

Rocio (Spanish) Covered with dew

Rocket (American) One who is fast
Roket, Rocet, Rokket, Roccet

Rockford (English) From the rocky ford
Rockforde, Rokford, Rokforde, Rockferd, Rokferd, Rockfurd, Rokfurd

Rockland (English) From the rocky land
Rocklande, Rokland, Roklande

Rockley (English) From the rocky meadow
Rockly, Rockli, Rocklie, Rocklea, Rockleah, Rocklee, Rockleigh

Rockney (American) One who is brash
Rockny, Rockni, Rocknie, Rocknee, Rocknea

Rockwell (English) From the rocky spring
Rockwel, Rokwell, Rokwel

Rod (English) Form of Roderick, meaning "a famous ruler"
Rodd, Roddi, Roddie, Roddy, Roddee, Roddea, Roddey

Rodel (French) Form of Roderick, meaning "a famous ruler"
Rodell, Rodele, Rodelle, Roedel, Roedell, Roedele, Roedelle

Rodeo (French / American) One who takes part in the roundup / a cowboy
Rodio, Rodeyo, Rodiyo

Roderick (German) A famous ruler
Rhoderick, Rhodric, Rodderick, Roddric, Roddrick, Roderic, Roderich, Roderigo, Roderik, Roderyck, Rodric, Rodrick, Rodrik, Rodrigo, Rodrigue, Rodrigues, Rodriguez, Rodrique, Rodriquez, Rodryck, Rodryk, Rurek, Rurik

Rodman (German) One who is famous
Roddman, Rodmann, Roddmann

Rodney (German / English) From the famous one's island / from the island's clearing
Rodny, Rodni, Rodnie, Rodnea, Rodnee

Rodor (Anglo-Saxon) Of the sky
Rodur, Rodir, Rodyr, Roder, Rodar

Rodwell (English) One who lives on the road near the spring
Roddwell, Rodwel, Roddwel

Roe (English) One who hunts deer
Row, Rowe

Roel (French) As solid as a rock
Roele, Roell, Roelle

Rogan (Gaelic) A red-haired man
Rogann, Roegan, Roegann, Ruadhagan

Rogelio (Spanish) A famous soldier
Rogelo, Rogeliyo, Rogeleo, Rogeleyo, Rojelio, Rojeleo

Roger (German) A famous spearman
Rodge, Rodger, Rog, Rogelio, Rogerio, Rogers, Rogiero, Rojay, Rufiger, Ruggero, Ruggiero, Rutger, Ruttger, Rudiger

Rohan (Irish / Sanskrit) A red-haired man / one who ascends
Rohann, Rohaan, Royan, Royann, Royaan

Rohit (Indian) Refers to the color red
Rohyt, Roheet, Roheat, Roheit, Rohiet

Roho (African) A soulful man
Roehoe, Rohoe, Roeho

Rohon (American) From the horse country
Rohun

Roland (German) From the renowned land
Roeland, Rolando, Roldan, Roley, Rollan, Rolland, Rollie, Rollin, Rollins, Rollo, Rolly, Rowland

Rolf (Scandinavian) Form of Rudolph, meaning "a famous wolf"
Rolfe, Rolph, Rolphe, Rolt, Rolte

Roman (Latin) A citizen of Rome
Romain, Romaine, Romanes, Romano, Romanos, Romanus, Romayn, Romayne, Romaen, Romaene, Rome, Romeo, Romi, Romie, Romee, Romea, Romy, Romey

Romney (Welsh) From the winding river
Romny, Romni, Romnie, Romnee, Romnea

Romulus (Latin) In mythology, along with his twin brother Remus, one of the founders of Rome
Romolo, Roemello, Romulo

Ron (English) Form of Ronald, meaning "the king's advisor"
Ronn, Ronnie, Ronni, Ronny, Ronney, Ronnee, Ronnea, Roni, Ronie, Rony, Roney, Ronea, Ronee, Rohn, Rahn

Ronak (Scandinavian) A powerful man
Ronack, Ronac

Ronald (Norse) The king's advisor
Ranald, Renaldo, Ronal, Ronaldo, Rondale, Roneld, Ronell, Ronello, Ronson

Ronan (Gaelic) Resembling a little seal

Ronel (Israeli) The song of God
Ronele, Ronen, Ronnel, Ronnen

Rong (Chinese) Having glory

Ronin (Japanese) A Samurai who doesn't have a master
Ronyn

Ronith (Hindi) A charming man
Ronithe, Ronyth, Ronythe

Rook (English) Resembling a raven
Rooke, Rouk, Rouke, Ruck, Ruk

Rooney (Gaelic) A red-haired man
Roony, Rooni, Roonie, Roonea, Roonee, Roon, Roone

Roopesh (Hindi) A handsome man
Roupesh, Rupesh, Rupad, Roopad, Roupad

Roosevelt (Danish) From the field of roses
Rosevelt

Roper (English) One who makes rope
Rapere

Rory (Gaelic) A red-haired man
*Rori, Rorey, Rorie, Rorea, Roree, Rorry,
Rorrey, Rorri, Rorrie, Rorrea, Rorree, Rorik,
Rorric, Rorrik, Roric*

Rosario (Spanish) Refers to the rosary
*Rasario, Rasareo, Rosareo, Rosalio, Rosaleo,
Rasulio, Rasaleo*

Roscoe (German) From the forest of deer
*Rosco, Rosscoe, Rossco, Rosko, Rossko, Roskoe,
Rosskoe*

Roser (American) A red-haired man
Rozer

Roshan (Persian) Born during the daylight
*Roshaun, Roshawn, Roeshan, Roeshaun,
Roeshawn*

Rosk (American) One who is swift
Roske, Rosck, Roscke, Rosc, Rosce

Roslin (Gaelic) A little red-haired boy
*Roslyn, Rosselin, Rosslyn, Rozlin, Rozlyn,
Rosling, Rozling*

Ross (Gaelic) From the headland
Rosse, Rossell, Rossiter, Rosston, Ros, Rossano

Rossain (American) Filled with hope
*Rossaine, Rossaen, Rossaenc, Rossayn,
Rossayne, Rossane*

Roswald (German) Of the mighty horses
Rosswald, Roswalt, Rosswalt

Roswell (English) A fascinating man
Rosswell, Rozwell, Roswel, Rozwel

Roth (German) A red-haired man
Rothe

Rothwell (Norse) From the red spring
Rothwel, Rothewell, Rothewel

Roupen (American) A quiet little boy
Roupan, Roupin, Roupyn, Roupon, Roupun

Rousseau (French) A little red-haired boy
*Roussell, Russo, Rousse, Roussel, Rousset,
Rousskin*

Rover (English) A traveler; wanderer
Rovor, Rovir, Rovyr, Rovar, Rovur, Rovere

Rovonte (French) A roving man
Rovontay, Rovontaye, Rovontae, Rovontai

Rowan (Gaelic) From the tree with red ber-
ries; a little red-haired boy
*Rowen, Rowin, Rowyn, Rowon, Rowun,
Roan, Roane*

Rowdon (English) From the rough hill
Rowdun, Rowden, Rowdan, Rowdin, Rowdyn

Rowdy (English) A boisterous man
Rowdey, Rowdi, Rowdie, Rowdee, Rowdea

Rowell (English) From the spring of the roe
deer
Rowel, Roewel, Roewell

Rowley (English) From the rough meadow
*Rowly, Rowli, Rowlie, Rowlea, Rowleah,
Rowlee, Rowleigh*

Rowtag (Native American) Born of fire
Roetag, Rotag

Roxbert (English) A bright raven
*Roxberte, Roxberth, Roxberthe, Roxburt,
Roxburte, Roxburth, Roxburthe*

Roxbury (English) From the raven's fortress
Roxburry, Roxbery, Roxberry, Roxburghe

Roy (Gaelic / French) A red-haired man /
a king
Roye, Roi, Royer, Ruy

Royal (English) Of the king; a regal man
Royale, Royall, Royle

Royce (German / French) A famous man /
son of the king
Roice, Royse, Roise

Royd (English) A good-humored man
Roid, Royde, Roide

Royden (English) From the rye hill
Roydon, Roydan, Roydin, Roydyn, Roydun

Royston (English) From Royce's town
Roystun, Roystown

Rozen (Hebrew) A great ruler
Rozin, Rozyn, Rozon, Rozun

Ruadhan (Irish) A red-haired man; the name of a saint
Ruadan, Ruadhagan, Ruadagan

Ruarc (Irish) A famous ruler
Ruarck, Ruarcc, Ruark, Ruarkk, Ruaidhri, Ruaidri

Rubio (Spanish) Resembling a ruby

Rudd (English) One who has a ruddy complexion
Ruddy, Ruddey, Ruddee, Ruddea, Ruddi, Ruddie

Rudeger (German) A friendly man
Rudegar, Rudger, Rudgar, Rudiger, Rudigar

Rudo (African) A loving man
Rudoe, Rudow, Rudowe

Rudolph (German) A famous wolf
Rodolfo, Rodolph, Rodolphe, Rodolpho, Rudy, Rudey, Rudi, Rudie, Rudolf, Rudolfo, Rudolpho, Rudolphus, Rudee

Rudyard (English) From the red paddock

Rufaro (African) Filled with happiness
Ruffaro

Ruff (French) A red-haired man
Ruffe, Ruffin, Rufin, Rufio, Ruffio, Rufeo, Ruffeo, Rufo, Ruffo

Ruford (English) From the red ford; from the rough ford
Ruforde, Rufford, Rufforde

Rufus (Latin) A red-haired man
Ruffus, Rufous, Ruffous, Rufino, Ruffino

Rugby (English) From the rock fortress
Rugbey, Rugbi, Rugbie, Rugbee, Rugbea

Rui (French) A regal man

Ruiz (Spanish) A good friend

Rujul (Indian) An honest man
Rujool, Rujoole, Rujule, Rujoul, Rujoule

Rulon (Native American) A spirited man
Rullon, Rulonn, Rullonn

Rumford (English) From the broad ford
Rumforde, Rumferd, Rumferde, Rumfurd, Rumfurde

Rumford (English) From the broad river crossing
Rumforde

Rumor (American) A falsity spread by word of mouth
Rumer, Rumur, Rumir, Rumyr, Rumar

Runako (African) A handsome man
Runacko, Runaco, Runacco, Runakko

Rune (Norse) A secret

Rupert (English) Form of Robert, meaning "one who is bright with fame"
Ruprecht

Rush (English) One who lives near the marsh plants
Rushe, Rusch, Rusche, Rysc

Rushford (English) From the ford with rushes
Rusheford, Rushforde, Rusheforde, Ryscford

Rushkin (French) A little red-haired boy
Ruskin

Rusk (Spanish) An innovator
Rusck, Rusc, Ruske, Ruskk, Ruscc

Russell (French) A little red-haired boy
Russel, Roussell, Russ, Rusel, Rusell

Russom (African) The chief; the boss
Rusom, Russome, Rusome

Ruston (English) From the red-haired man's estate
Rustun, Rustown, Rusten, Rustin, Rustyn, Rustan

Rusty (English) One who has red hair or a ruddy complexion
Rustey, Rusti, Rustie, Rustee, Rustea, Rust, Ruste, Rustice

Rutherford (English) From the cattle's ford
Rutherfurd, Rutherferd, Rutherforde, Rutherfurde, Rutherferde

Rutland (Norse) From the root land; from the red land
Rotland, Rootland, Routland

Rutledge (Norse / English) From the red ledge / from the root ledge
Routledge, Rotledge, Rootledge

Rutley (English) From the root meadow
Rutly, Rutli, Rutlie, Rutlee, Rutleigh, Rutlea, Rutleah

Ruvim (Hebrew) One who is meaningful
Roovim, Rouvim, Ruvym, Roovym, Rouvym

⚢ **Ryan** (Gaelic) The little ruler; little king
Rian, Rien, Rion, Ryen, Ryon, Ryun, Rhyan, Rhyen, Rhyon, Rhyun, Rhian, Rhien, Ryne, Ryn, Rynn

Rycroft (English) From the rye field
Ryecroft, Rygecroft

Ryder (English) An accomplished horseman
Rider, Ridder, Ryden, Rydell, Rydder

Rye (English / Irish) Resembling the grain / from the island's meadow
Ry

Ryker (Danish) Form of Richard, meaning "a powerful ruler"
Riker

Ryland (English) From the place where rye is grown
Ryeland, Rylan, Ryelan, Ryle, Rygeland

Ryley (English) From the rye clearing
Ryly, Ryli, Rylie, Rylee, Ryleigh, Rylea, Ryleah, Riley, Rily, Rili, Rilie, Rilee, Rilea, Rileah, Rileigh

Ryman (English) A rye merchant
Ryeman, Rymann, Ryemann, Rygeman, Rygemann

Rypan (Anglo-Saxon) One who plunders

Ryton (English) From the rye town
Ryeton, Rytown, Ryetown, Rytun, Ryetun

Ryu (Japanese) A dragon

Ryuichi (Japanese) First son of the dragon
Ryuichie, Ryuichy, Ryuichey, Ryuichee, Ryuichea

Ryuji (Japanese) The dragon man
Ryujie, Ryujy, Ryujey, Ryujea, Ryujee

S

Saad (Aramaic) One who offers help; the Lord's helper
Saada, Saadya, Saadiya, Saudyo, Saadiyo, Saahdia, Saahdya, Saahdiya, Seadya, Seadiya

Saarik (Hindi) Resembling a small songbird
Saarick, Saaric, Sarik, Sarick, Saric, Saariq, Sareek, Sareeq, Sariq

Sabah (Arabic) Born during the morning hours
Saba, Sabbah, Sabba

Saber (French) Man of the sword
Sabere, Sabr, Sabre

Sabih (Arabic) A handsome man
Sabeeh, Sabeih, Sabieh, Sabeah, Sabyh

Sabino (Latin) Of a tribe of ancient Italy
Sabeeno, Sabeino, Sabieno, Sabeano, Sabin, Savin, Savino, Saveeno, Savieno, Saveino, Saveano, Sabian, Sabien

Sabir (Arabic) One who is patient
Subyr, Sabeer, Sabear, Sabeir, Sabier, Sabri, Sabrie, Sabree, Sabry, Sabrey

Sable (English) One who is sleek
Sabel

Saburo (Japanese) The third-born son
Saburio, Saburiyo

Sacha (Russian) Form of Alexander, meaning "helper and defender of mankind"
Sascha, Sasha, Socha, Soscha, Sosha, Sashenka, Shura, Schura, Shoura, Schoura

Sachairi (Gaelic) Form of Zachary, meaning "the Lord remembers"
Sachary, Sachari, Sacharie, Sakary, Sakari, Sakarie, Sakarey, Sachery, Sacheri, Sacherie, Sackery, Sackerey, Sackeri, Sackerie

Sachar (Hebrew) One who is rewarded
Sacar

Sachchit (Indian) One who is conscious of the truth
Sachchyt, Sachchite, Sachchyte, Sachet, Sachyt, Sachit

Sachetan (Indian) One who is animated
Sacheten, Sacheton, Sachetyn, Sachetin, Sachetun

Sacheverell (French) Resembling a leaping buck
Sacheverel, Sacheverele, Sachie, Sachy, Sachi, Sachey, Sachee, Sachea

Sachiel (Hebrew) An archangel
Sachiele, Sachiell, Sachielle

Sachio (Japanese) One who is fortunately born
Sachiyo

Sackville (English) From the Saxton's town
Sakville, Sacville

Sadaka (African) A religious offering
Sadakah, Sadakka, Sadakkah

Saddam (Arabic) A powerful ruler; the crusher
Saddum, Saddim, Saddym

Sadiki (African) One who is faithful
Sadikie, Sadiky, Sadikey, Sadikee, Sadikea, Sadyki, Sadykie, Sadyky, Sadykey, Sadykee, Sadykea

Sadiq (Arabic) A beloved friend
Sadeeq, Sadyq, Sadeaq, Sadeek, Sadeak, Sadyk, Sadik

Sadler (English) One who makes harnesses
Saddler, Sadlar, Saddlar, Sadlor, Saddlor

Sadwrn (Welsh) Form of Saturn, in mythology, god of agriculture

Sae (American) A talkative man
Saye, Say, Sai

Saehrimnir (Norse) In mythology, a magical boar

Safar (Arabic) A devout man

Safford (English) From the willow ford
Safforde, Saford, Saforde, Salford, Salforde, Salhford, Salhforde

Saffron (English) Resembling the yellow flower
Saffrone, Saffronn, Saffronne, Safron, Safronn, Safronne, Saffran, Saffren, Saphron, Saphran, Saphren

Saga (American) A storyteller
Sago

Sagar (Indian / English) A king / one who is wise
Saagar, Sagarr, Saagarr

Sagaz (Spanish) One who is clever
Sagazz

Sage (English) Wise one; type of spice
Saige, Sayge, Saege, Saje, Saije, Sayje, Saeje

Saghir (Arabic) One who is short in stature
Sagheer, Saghyr, Saghier, Sagheir, Saghear, Sager

Saginaw (Native American) A bold and courageous man
Sagynaw, Saginau, Sagynau

Sagiv (Hebrew) Having great strength
Sagev, Segiv, Segev

Sagramour (English) In Arthurian legend, a knight
Sagremour, Sagramor, Sagramore, Sagremor, Sagremore

Saguaro (American) Resembling the cactus
Seguaro, Saguariyo, Seguariyo

Sagwau (Chinese) A silly young man
Sagwaw

Sahadev (Hindi) The son of a king
Sahadiv, Sahadyv, Sahdev, Sahdiv, Sahdyv

Sahaj (Indian) One who is natural

Sahale (Native American) Resembling a falcon
Sahail, Sahaile, Sahayl, Sahayle, Sahan, Sahane, Sahain, Sahaine, Sahayn, Sahayne, Sahaen, Sahaene, Sahael, Sahaele, Sahen

Sahansan (African) One who travels with caution

Sahas (Indian) One who shows bravery

Sahib (Indian) Lord of the house
Sahyb, Sahibe, Sahybe, Saheeb, Saheebe, Saheab, Saheabe, Sahieb, Sahiebe, Saheib, Saheibe

Sahil (Indian) A great leader
Suhile, Saheel, Saheele, Saheal, Saheale, Sahel, Sahele, Saheil, Saheile, Sahiel, Sahiele, Sahyl, Sahyle

Sahir (Arabic) One who is alert and aware
Sahire, Saheer, Sahear, Sahyr, Saheir, Sahier, Saher, Sahran

Sahyadri (Indian) From the mountain range
Suhyadrie, Sahyadry, Sahyadrey, Sahyadree, Sahyadrea

Said (Arabic) Filled with happiness
Saeed, Saiyid, Sayeed, Sayid, Syed, Sa'id, Sa'eed, Saied

Saidi (African) One who helps others
Saidie, Saidee, Saidey, Saidy, Saedi, Saedie, Saedy, Saedey, Saedee, Saydi, Saydie, Saydy, Saydey, Saydee

Saieshwar (Hindi) A well-known saint
Saishwar

Sailor (American) Man who sails the seas
Sailer, Sailar, Saylor, Sayler, Saylar, Saelor, Saeler, Saelar, Sail, Saile, Sayle, Saele

Sainsbury (English) From the saint's settlement
Sansbury, Saynsbury, Saensbury, Sainsberry, Saynsberry, Saensberry, Sansberry

Saint (Latin) A holy man
Sainte, Saent, Saente, Saynt, Saynte

Sairam (Hindi) A well-known saint
Sayram, Saeram

Saith (English) One who is well-spoken
Saithe, Sayth, Saythe, Saeth, Saethe, Sath, Sathe

Sajal (Indian) Resembling a cloud
Sajall, Sajjal, Sajjall

Sajan (Indian) One who is dearly loved
Sajann, Sajjan, Sajjann

Sajid (Arabic) One who worships God
Sajeed, Sajyd, Sajead, Sajeid, Sajied

Sakeri (Hebrew) The Lord has remembered
Sakerie, Sakery, Sakerey, Sakeree, Sakerea

Saki (Japanese) One who is cloaked
Sakie, Saky, Sakey, Sakee, Sakea

Sakima (Native American) A king
Sakeema, Sakyma, Sakema, Sakeima, Sakiema, Sakeama

Saku (Japanese) The remembrance of the Lord
Sakue, Sakoo

Salaam (African) Resembling a peach

Saladin (Arabic) One who is righteous in his faith
Saladen

Salado (Spanish) A humorous man
Saladio, Saladiyo

Salah (Arabic) A righteous man
Sala, Salla, Sallah

Salehe (African) A good man
Saleh, Salih

Salil (Indian) Of the water
Saleel, Saleil, Saliel, Salyl, Saleal

Salim (Arabic) One who is peaceful
Saleem, Salem, Selim

Salisbury (English) From the willow settlement
Sallsbury, Salisbery, Salisberry, Saulsberry, Saulsbery, Saulsbury, Saulisbury

Salman (Arabic) One who provides security
Salmann, Saman, Samann

Saloman (Hebrew) One who is peaceful
Salomon, Salamon, Salaman

Saltiel (Hebrew) Asked of God
Shaltiel, Saltiele, Shaltiele, Saltielle, Shaltielle

Salton (English) One who lives near the willow settlement
Salten, Saltan, Saltun, Salhton, Salhtun

Salus (Greek) In mythology, goddess of health
Salas, Sales, Salos

Salute (American) A patriotic man
Saloot, Saloote, Salout, Saloute

Salvador (Latin) A savior
*Sal, Salvator, Salvatore, Salvidor, Salvino,
Sauveur, Salvadore, Salvatorio, Salbatore,
Soterios*

Salvio (Latin) One who has been saved
Salvian, Salviano, Salviatus, Salviyo

Samadarshi (Indian) One who is unbiased
*Samadarshie, Samadarshy, Samadarshey,
Samadarshee, Samadarshea*

Samanjas (Indian) One who is proper

Samantaka (Indian) A destroyer of peace

Samarth (Indian) A powerful man; one who
is efficient
Samarthe

Sambaran (Indian) An ancient king

Sambhddha (Indian) Having great wisdom

Sameen (Indian) One who is treasured
*Samine, Sameene, Samean, Sameane,
Samyn, Samyne*

Sameh (Arabic) A forgiving man
Samih

Sami (Arabic) One who has been exalted
Samie, Samy, Samey, Samee, Samea

Samir (Arabic) A special man
*Sameer, Samyr, Samier, Sameir, Samear,
Samere*

Samiran (Indian) As gentle as a breeze
Samyran, Sameeran, Samearan, Sameran

Samman (Arabic) One who sells groceries
Sammen, Sammon

Sammohan (Indian) An attractive man
Sammohane

Sampath (Indian) A wealthy man
Sampathe, Sampat

Sampooran (Indian) One who is blissful
Sampoornanand

Sampreet (Indian) One who is content
*Sampreyt, Sampryt, Sampriet, Sampreit,
Sampreat*

Samrakshan (Indian) One who is protected

Samson (Hebrew) As bright as the sun;
in the Bible, a man with extraordinary
strength
Sampson, Sansom, Sanson, Sansone

Samudra (Indian) The lord of the ocean
Samudrasen, Samudras

❀ **Samuel** (Hebrew) God has heard
*Sam, Sammie, Sammy, Samuele, Samuello,
Samwell, Samuelo, Sammey, Sammi,
Sammee, Sammea, Samoel, Sammoel,
Samuka, Schmuel*

Samuru (Japanese) The name of God

Samvel (Hebrew) One who knows the
name of God
Samvell, Samvele, Samvelle

Sanam (Indian) One who is dearly loved

Sanborn (English) From the sandy brook
*Sanborne, Sanbourn, Sanburn, Sanburne,
Sandborn, Sandbourne*

Sancho (Spanish) One who is sacred
Sanche, Sanctio, Sancos, Sanzio, Sauncho

Sandaidh (Gaelic) Form of Alexander,
meaning "helper and defender of mankind"

Sandburg (English) From the sandy village
Sandbergh, Sandberg, Sandburgh

Sandeepen (Indian) A wise man; a sage
Sandepen, Sandeapen, Sandypen, Sandipen

Sander (German) Form of Alexander,
meaning "helper and defender of mankind"
*Sandino, Sandor, Sender, Sandy, Sandi,
Sandie, Sandee, Sandea, Sandro, Sandu*

Sanderson (English) Son of Alexander
*Sanders, Saunders, Saunderson, Sandros,
Sanersone*

Sandhurst (English) From the sandy thicket
*Sanhurst, Sandherst, Sanherst, Sandhirst,
Sanhirst*

Sanditon (English) From the sandy town
Sandton, Santon

Sandon (English) From the sandy hill
Sanden, Sandan, Sandun, Sandyn, Sandin

Sanford (English) From the sandy crossing
Sandford, Sanforde, Sandforde, Sanfurd,
Sanfurde, Sandfurd, Sandfurde

Sang (Vietnamese) A bright man
Sange

Sani (Native American) The old one
Sanie, Sany, Saney, Sanee, Sanea

Sanjay (Indian) One who is victorious
Sanjaye, Sanjae, Sanjai

Sanjeet (Indian) One who is invincible
Sanjyt, Sanjit, Sanjeat, Sanjeit, Sanjiet

Sanjiro (Japanese) An admirable man
Sanjyro

Sanjiv (Indian) One who lives a long life
Sanjeev, Sanjyv, Sanjeiv, Sanjiev, Sanjeav,
Sanjivan

Sanketh (Indian) A sign or symbol
Sankethe, Sanket

Sanobar (Indian) From the palm tree

Sanorelle (American) An honest man
Sanorell, Sanorel, Sanorele

Sansone (Italian) Having great strength

Santana (Spanish) A saintly man
Santanna, Santanah, Santannah, Santa

Santiago (Spanish) Refers to Saint James
Sandiago, Sandiego, Santeago, Santiaco,
Santigo

Santo (Italian) A holy man
Sante, Santino, Santos, Santee, Santi, Santie,
Santea, Santy, Santey

Santob (Hebrew) One who has a good
name
Shemtob

Santosh (Indian) One who is content
Santoshe

Sanyu (Japanese) Filled with happiness
Sanyoo, Sanyue

Sapan (Indian) A dream or vision
Sapann

Sapir (Hebrew) Resembling a sapphire
Safir, Saphir, Saphiros, Safiros, Sapyr,
Saphyr, Sapfyr, Sapyre, Saphyre, Safyre

Saquib (Indian) A bright man
Saquyb

Sar (Anglo-Saxon) One who inflicts pain
Sarlic, Sarlik

Sarat (Indian) A wise man; a sage
Saratt, Sarrat, Sharad

Sarbajit (Indian) The conquerer
Sarbujeet, Sarbajyt, Sarbajeat, Sarbajet,
Sarvajit, Sarvajeet, Sarvajyt, Sarvajeat

Sarda (African) One who is in a hurry
Sardah

Sarday (American) A sociable man
Sardaye, Sardai, Sardae

Sarfaraz (Indian) One who walks with his
head held high
Safarez

Sargent (French) Officer of the army
Sarge, Sergeant, Sergent, Serjeant, Sargeant

Sarki (African) A chief
Sarkie, Sarky, Sarkey, Sarkee, Sarkea

Sarkis (Armenian) Born to royalty
Sarkiss, Sarkisse, Sarkys, Sarkyss, Sarkysse

Sarojin (Hindu) Resembling a lotus
Saroj

Sarosh (Persian) One who prays
Saroshe

Sarsour (Arabic) Resembling a bug

Sartaj (Indian) One who is crowned

Sarthak (Indian) One who is fulfilled
Sarthac, Sarthack

Sarvagya (Indian) One who is all-knowing
Sarvagiya

Sashreek (Indian) One who is prosperous
Sashrik, Sashreak, Sashryk

Sassacus (Native American) A wild man
Sasacus, Sassakus, Sasakus

Sasson (Hebrew) Filled with joy
Sassen, Sassun, Sassin, Sassyn

Satayu (Hindi) In Hinduism, the brother of
Amavasu and Vivasu
Satayoo, Satayou, Satayue

Satchel (Latin) A small bag
Satchell, Sachel, Sachell

Satordi (French) Form of Saturn, in mythology, god of agriculture
Satordie, Satordy, Satordey, Satordee, Satordea

Satoshi (Japanese) Born from the ashes
Satoshie, Satoshy, Satoshey, Satoshee, Satoshea

Satparayan (Indian) A good-natured man

Satu (Japanese) From a fairy tale
Satue, Satoo, Satou

Saturday (American) Born on a Saturday
Saterday, Saturdai, Saterdai, Saturdae, Saterdae, Saturdaye, Saterdaye

Saturn (Latin) In mythology, the god of agriculture
Saturnin, Saturno, Saturnino

Satyanand (Indian) One who has found true happiness
Satyanande

Satyankar (Indian) One who speaks the truth
Satyancar, Satyancker

Satyaprakash (Indian) Glowing with the light of truth

Satyavanth (Indian) One who is honest
Satyavanthe, Satyavant, Satyavante, Satyavan

Saud (Arabic) A fortunate man

Saul (Hebrew) One who was prayed for
Saulo, Shaul, Sol, Sollie, Solli, Sollee, Sollea, Solly, Solley

Saunak (Indian) A child sage
Saunac, Saunack, Sawnak, Sawnac, Sawnack

Savage (American) A wild man
Savag, Savaje, Savaj

Saviero (Spanish) Form of Xavier, meaning "owner of a new house / one who is bright"
Savyero, Saverio, Saveriyo

Saville (French) From the willow town
Savil, Savile, Savill, Savyile, Savylle, Savyle, Sauville, Sauvile, Sauvil

Savir (Indian) A great leader
Savire, Saveer, Saveere, Savear, Saveare, Savyr, Savyre

Savoy (French) From the kingdom in France
Savoye, Savoi

Savyon (Hebrew) Resembling the yellow weed
Savion, Savionn

Sawyer (English) One who works with wood
Sawyere, Sayer, Sawyers, Sayers, Sayres, Saer

Saxe (Swedish) Man from Saxonny
Sachs, Sachsen

Saxon (English) A swordsman
Saxen, Saxan, Saxton, Saxten, Saxtan

Sayad (Arabic) An accomplished hunter

Sayam (Indian) Born in the evening

Sayed (Indian) A great leader

Sayyid (Arabic) The master

Scadwielle (English) From the shed near the spring
Scadwyelle, Scadwiell, Scadwyell, Scadwiel, Scadwyel, Scadwiele, Scadwyele

Scafell (English) From the mountain

Scand (Anglo-Saxon) One who is disgraced
Scande, Scandi, Scandie, Scandee, Scandea

Scandleah (English) From the noisy meadow
Scandlea, Scandlee, Scandlie, Scandli, Scandly, Scandley, Scandleigh, Shandley, Shandly, Shandlee, Shandli, Shandlie, Shandleigh, Shandlea, Shandleah

Scanlon (Irish) A devious young man
Scanlun, Scanlin, Scanlyn, Scanlen, Scanlan

Scanlon (Irish) A little trapper
Scanlan, Scanlen, Scanlun, Scanlin, Scanlyn, Scannalan, Scannalon, Scannalen

Scant (American) A man of small stature
Scante, Scanti, Scantie, Scanty, Scantey, Scantee, Scantea

Scead (Anglo-Saxon) One who provides shade
Sceadu, Sceadue, Sceadou

Sceotend (Anglo-Saxon) An archer

Schae (American) One who is cautious
Schay, Schaye, Schai

Schaeffer (German) A steward
Schaffer, Shaeffer, Shaffer, Schaeffur, Schaffur, Shaeffur, Shaffur

Schelde (English) From the river
Shelde

Schmidt (German) A blacksmith
Schmit, Schmitt

Schneider (German) A tailor
Shneider, Sneider, Snider, Snyder

Schubert (German) One who makes shoes
Shubert, Schuberte, Shuberte, Schubirt, Shubirt, Schuburt, Shuburt

Schultz (German) The town's magistrate

Schuyler (Danish) A scholarly man
Schuylar, Schylar, Schyler, Skuyler

Scipio (Latin) A legendary general

Scipio (Greek) A great leader
Scipiyo, Scypio, Scypyo, Scypiyo

Scirloc (English) A blonde-haired man
Scirlok, Scirlock, Scyrloc, Scyrlok, Scyrlock

Scirocco (Italian) Of the warm wind
Sirocco, Scyrocco, Syrocco

Scorpio (Latin) The scorpion; the eighth sign of the zodiac
Skorpio, Scorpios, Skorpios

Scott (English) A man from Scotland
Scot, Scottie, Scotto, Scotty, Scotti, Scottey, Scottee, Scottea, Scottas

Scout (American) An explorer
Scoutt, Scoutte, Skout, Skoutt, Skoutte

Scowyrhta (Anglo-Saxon) One who makes shoes

Scribner (English) A scribe
Skribner, Scribnar, Skribnar

Scully (Irish) A herald; the town crier
Sculley, Sculli, Scullie, Scullee, Scullea, Sculleigh, Scolaighe

Scur (Anglo-Saxon) Born during a storm
Scurr

Seabert (English) Of the shining sea
Seabright, Sebert, Seibert, Seebert, Seybert, Siebert, Seaburt, Seburt, Seiburt, Seeburt, Seyburt, Sieburt, Saebeorht

Seabrook (English) From the stream by the sea
Seabrooke, Seabroc, Seabrok, Seabrock

Seabury (English) From the village by the sea
Seaburry, Sebury, Seburry, Seaberry, Seabery, Seberry, Sebery

Seadon (English) From the hill by the sea

Seafraid (Irish) One who receives peace from God
Seafrayd, Seafraed, Seafra, Seafrah

Seaghda (Irish) A majestic man

Seal (English) Resembling the animal
Seale, Seel, Seele

Seaman (English) A mariner

Seamere (Anglo-Saxon) A tailor

Seamus (Irish) Form of James, meaning "he who supplants"
Seumas, Seumus, Shamus, Shemus, Sekove, Sheamus

❍ **Sean** (Irish) Form of John, meaning "God is gracious"
Shaughn, Shawn, Shaun, Shon, Shohn, Shonn, Shaundre, Shuwnel, Shawnell, Shawnn, Shandon, Shaunden

Seanachan (Irish) One who is wise

Seanan (Hebrew / Irish) A gift from God / an old, wise man
Sinon, Senen, Siobhan

Seanlaoch (Irish) An elderly hero

Searbhreathach (Irish) One who is judicious

Searle (English) An armored man
Serle, Searl, Serl, Searlas, Searlus, Searles, Searcy, Searci, Searcey, Searcie, Searcee, Searcea

Seaton (English) From the town by the sea
Seeton, Seton, Seatown, Seetown, Setown

Seaver (Anglo-Saxon) From the fierce stronghold
Seever, Seiver, Siever, Seyver, Sener, Sever

Sebag (Arabic) One who dyes cloth
Sabag

⚙ **Sebastian** (Greek) The revered one
Sabastian, Seb, Sebastiano, Sebastien, Sebestyen, Sebo, Sebastyn, Sebestyen

Sebes (Hungarian) One who is swift

Secundo (Italian) The second-born son
Segundo

Sedge (English) A swordsman
Secg, Sege

Sedgley (English) From the meadow of the swordsman
Sedgly, Sedgli, Sedglie, Sedglee, Sedgleigh, Sedglea, Sedgeley, Sedgelee, Sedgeleigh, Sedgeli, Sedgelie, Sedgely, Sedgelea

Sedgwick (English) From the place of sword grass
Sedgewick, Sedgewyck, Sedgwyck, Sedgewic, Sedgewik, Sedgwic, Sedgwik, Sedgewyc, Sedgewyk, Sedgwyc, Sedgwyk, Secgwic

Seeley (French) One who is blessed
Seely, Seelee, Seelea, Seeli, Seelie, Sealey, Sealy, Seali, Sealie, Sealee, Sealea

Seerath (Indian) A great man
Seerathe, Searath, Searathe

Sef (Egyptian) Son of yesterday
Sefe

Seferino (Greek) Of the west wind
Seferio, Sepherino, Sepherio, Seferyno, Sepheryno

Seff (Hebrew) Resembling a wolf
Seffe

Sefton (English) From the village in the rushes

Sefu (African) One who wields a sword
Sefue, Sefoo, Sefou

Segenam (Native American) One who is lazy

Seger (English) Warrior of the sea
Seager, Segar, Seagar, Saeger

Seghen (African) Resembling an ostrich
Seghan, Seghin, Seghyn

Seif (Arabic) Wielding a sword of faith
Sayf, Saef, Saif

Seignour (French) Lord of the house

Seiji (Japanese) One who manages the affairs of the state
Seijie, Seijy, Seijey, Seijee, Seijea

Seiko (Japanese) The force of truth

Sein (Spanish) One who is innocent
Seine

Sekai (African) One who laughs often
Sekani, Sekanie, Sekany, Sekaney, Sekanee, Sekanee

Sekou (African) A learned man

Sela (Hebrew) Man from the cliff
Selah

Selas (African) Refers to the Trinity
Selassi, Selassie, Selassy, Selassey, Selassee, Selassea

Selby (English) Of the manor of the farm
Selbey, Selbi, Selbie, Selbee, Selbye, Selbea, Seleby, Selebey, Selebi, Selebie, Selebee, Selebea

Seldon (English) From the valley of willows
Selldon, Selden, Sellden, Seldan, Selldan, Seldun, Selldun, Salhdene, Saldene

Selestino (Spanish) One who is heaven-sent
Selestyno, Selesteeno, Selesteano

Selig (German) One who is blessed
Seligman, Seligmann, Selyg, Selygman, Selygmann, Selik, Selyk, Selick, Selyck, Selic, Selyc, Saelac, Saelig

Selkirk (Scottish) Man of the church
Selkyrk, Selkirck, Selkyrck

Sellers (English) One who dwells in the marshland
Sellars, Sellurs, Sellirs, Sellyrs

Selvon (American) A gregarious man
Selvonn, Selvonne, Selvawn, Selvaun, Selvaughn

Selwyn (English) A friend of the manor
Selwynn, Selwynne, Selwin, Selwinn, Selwinne, Selwen, Selwenn, Selwenn, Selwenne

Seminole (Native American) A tribal name
Semynole

Sen (Japanese) A wood sprite

Senan (Irish) The people's hero

Seneca (Native American) A tribal name
Senecka, Seneka

Senghor (African) A descendant of the gods
Sengor

Senior (French) The lord of the manor
Senor

Sennet (French) One who is elderly and wise
Sennett, Senet, Senett

Senon (Spanish) Born of Zeus; one who is lively
Sennon

Seoc (Gaelic) God is gracious
Seocan, Seok, Seokan

Seoras (Gaelic) One who works the earth; a farmer
Seorass, Seorasse

Seosaph (Hebrew) Form of Joseph, meaning "God will add"
Seosamh, Sepp

Seppanen (Finnish) A blacksmith
Sepanen, Seppenen, Sepenen, Seppanan, Sepanan

September (American) Born in the month of September
Septimber, Septymber, Septemberia, Septemberea

Septimus (Latin) The seventh-born child
Septymus

Sequoia (Native American) Of the giant redwood tree
Sequoya, Sequoiya, Sekoia, Sekoya, Sequoyah

Seraphim (Hebrew) The burning ones; heavenly winged angels
Sarafino, Saraph, Serafin, Serafino, Seraph, Seraphimus, Serafim

Sereno (Latin) One who is calm; tranquil

Serfati (Hebrew) A man from France
Sarfati, Serfatie, Sarfatie, Serfaty, Sarfaty, Serfatey, Sarfatey, Serfatee, Sarfatee

Sergio (Latin) An attendant; a servant
Seargeoh, Serge, Sergei, Sergeo, Sergey, Sergi, Sergios, Sergiu, Sergius, Sergiusz, Serguei, Serjio, Sirgio, Sirgios, Seriozha, Seriozhenka

Seriannu (Welsh) A sparkling man
Serian, Serianu

Servas (Latin) One who is redeemed
Servaas, Servacio, Servatus

Sesame (English) Resembling the flavorful seed
Sesami, Sesamie, Sesamy, Sesamey, Sesamee, Sesamea

Set (Hebrew) One who has been compensated
Sett, Shet, Shett

Seth (Hebrew) One who has been appointed
Sethe, Seath, Seathe

Seung (Korean) A victorious successor

Seven (American) Refers to the number; the seventh-born child
Sevin, Sevyn

Severin (Latin) One who is strict; stern
Severino, Severinus, Severo, Sevrin, Sevryn, Severyn, Severn, Severne, Seweryn, Severus, Severius, Severince, Severence, Severynce

Sevilin (Turkish) One who is dearly loved
Sevilen, Sevylin, Sevylen

Sevillano (Spanish) Man from Sevilla
Sevilano, Sevyllano, Sevylano, Sevillanio, Sevilanio

Sewall (English) Having the strength of the sea
Sewal, Sewald, Sewalde, Sewell, Saewald, Seawell

Seward (English) A guardian of the sea
Siward, Sewerd, Siwerd, Saeweard, Seaward

Sewati (Native American) Resembling a bear claw
Sewatie, Sewaty, Sewatey, Sewatee, Sewatea

Sexton (English) The church's custodian
Sextun, Sextan, Sextin, Sextyn

Sextus (Latin) The sixth-born child
Sesto, Sixto, Sixtus

Seymour (French) From the French town of Saint Maur
Seamore, Seamor, Seamour, Seymore

Shaan (Hebrew) A peaceful man

Shabab (Arabian) One who is youthful
Shaabab

Shabat (Hebrew) The last child
Shabbat, Shabatt, Shabbatt

Shabnam (Persian) Covered with the morning's dew

Shachar (Hebrew) Born with the morning's first light
Shachare, Shacharr

Shade (English) A secretive man
Shaid, Shaide, Shayd, Shayde, Shaed, Shaede

Shadi (Persian / Arabic) One who brings happiness and joy / a singer
Shadie, Shady, Shadey, Shadee, Shadea

Shadow (English) A mysterious man
Shadoe, Shado

Shadrach (Hebrew) Under the command of the moon god Aku
Shadrack, Shadrick, Shad, Shadd

Shadwell (English) From the shed near the spring
Shadwel

Shafiq (Arabic) One who is compassionate
Shafeeq, Shafik, Shafyq, Shafyk, Shafeek

Shafir (Hebrew) A handsome man
Shafeer, Shafier, Shafeir, Shafear, Shafyr, Shafar, Shefer

Shah (Persian) The king

Shahid (Indian) A patriot
Shaheed, Shahead, Shahyd, Shahide, Shaheede, Shaheade, Shahyde

Shahzad (Persian) Son of the king

Shai (Hebrew) A gift from God

Shail (Indian) A mountain rock
Shaile, Shayl, Shayle, Shael, Shaele, Shale

Shaiming (Chinese) Of the sunshine
Shaeming, Shayming, Shaimyng, Shaemyng, Shaymyng

Shaka (African) A tribal leader
Shakah

Shakib (Indian) One who is patient
Shakeeb, Shakeab, Shakyb

Shakil (Arabic) A handsome man
Shakeel, Shakhil, Shakyl, Shakill, Shakille, Shaquille, Shaq, Shaqeell, Shaque, Shaqueel, Shaquil, Shaquile

Shakir (Arabic) One who is grateful
Shakeer, Shaqueer, Shakier, Shakeir, Shakear, Shakar, Shaker, Shakyr

Shakti (Indian) A powerful man
Shaktie, Shakty, Shaktey, Shaktee, Shaktea

Shakur (Arabic) One who is thankful
Shakurr, Shaku

Shalom (Hebrew) A peaceful man
Sholom, Sholem, Shelomo, Shelomi, Shlomi, Shulamith, Shlomo

Shaman (Native American) A holy man
Shawman, Shamon, Shayman, Shaeman, Shaiman, Schamane, Shamain, Shamaen, Shamane, Shamayn

Shamir (Hebrew) A material that can cut stone
Shameer, Shamyr, Shameir, Shamier, Shamear

Shamshu (Indian) A handsome man
Shamshad, Shamshue

Shan (Chinese / Gaelic) Resembling coral / one who is wise and elderly
Shann, Shandon

Shanahan (Irish) One who is clever; wise
Seanachan, Shanahen, Seanachen, Shanihan, Shanyhan

Shance (American) Form of Chance, meaning having good fortune
Shancy, Shancey, Shanci, Shancie, Shancee, Shancea

Shandar (Indian) One who is proud
Shandarr

Shandy (English) A high-spirited man
Shandey, Shandee, Shandea, Shandi, Shandie

Shane (English) Form of John, meaning "God is gracious"
Shayn, Shayne, Shaen, Shaene, Shain, Shaine, Seaghan

Shani (Hebrew) A crimson-red color
Shanie, Shany, Shaney, Shanee, Shanea

Shanley (Gaelic) An ancient hero
Shanly, Shanle, Shanlee, Shanlea, Shanli, Shanlie, Shannly, Shannley, Shannlee, Shannle, Shannli, Shannlea, Shannlie

Shannon (Gaelic) Having ancient wisdom
Shanan, Shanen, Shannan, Shannen, Shanon

Shante (American) One who is poised
Shantae, Shantai, Shantay, Shantaye

Sharang (Indian) Resembling a deer
Sharange

Shardul (Indian) Resembling a tiger
Shardule, Shardull, Shardulle

Sharif (Arabic) One who is honored
Shareef, Sharyf, Sharief, Shareif, Shareaf, Sherif, Sheryf, Shereef, Shereaf, Sherief, Shereif

Shariq (Indian) An intelligent man
Shareeq, Shareaq, Shareq, Shareek, Sharik, Shareak, Sharyk, Sharyq

Shashi (Indian) Of the moonbeam
Shashie, Shashy, Shashey, Shashee, Shashea, Shashhi

Shashwat (Hindi) One who has a long life
Shashwatt, Shashwate, Shashwatte

Shasta (Native American) From the triple-peaked mountain
Shastah

Shatrujit (Indian) One who conquers his enemies
Shatrujeet, Shatrujyt

Shaunak (Indian) A well-known sage
Shawnak, Shanak, Shaunack, Shawnack, Shanack

Shavon (American) One who is open-minded
Shavaughn, Shavonne, Shavaun, Shovon, Shovonne, Shovaun, Shovaughn

Shaw (English) From the woodland
Shawe

Shawnee (Native American) A tribal name
Shawney, Shawny, Shawnea, Shawni, Shawnie

Shawon (American) One who is optimistic
Shawan, Shawaun, Shawaughn, Shawonne

Shayan (American) Form of Cheyenne, meaning "of the tribe of the Great Plains; of the unintelligible speakers"
Shayann, Sheyan, Sheyann, Shyane, Shyanne

Shaykeen (American) A successful man
Shaykean, Shaykein, Shakeyn, Shakine

Shea (Gaelic) An admirable man/from the fairy fortress
Shae, Shai, Shay, Shaye, Shaylon, Shays

Sheehan (Gaelic) A small and peaceful man
Sheyhan, Sheahan, Sheihan, Shiehan, Shyhan, Siodhachan

Sheen (English) A shining man
Sheene, Shean, Sheane

Sheffield (English) From the crooked field
Sheffeld

Sheiling (Scottish) From the summer pasture
Sheilyng, Sheeling, Shealing, Sheelyng, Shealyng

Shel (Hebrew) Our son

Shelby (English) From the willow farm
Shelbi, Shelbey, Shelbie, Shelbee, Shelbye, Shelbea

Sheldon (English) From the steep valley
Shelden, Sheldan, Sheldun, Sheldin, Sheldyn, Shel

Shelley (English) From the meadow's ledge
Shelly, Shelli, Shellie, Shellee, Shellea, Shelleigh, Shelleah

Shelton (English) From the farm on the ledge
Shellton, Sheltown, Sheltun, Shelten, Shelny, Shelney, Shelni, Shelnie, Shelnee, Shelnea, Skelton, Skeltun

Shem (Hebrew) Having a well-known name

Shen (Chinese) A spiritual man; one who is introspective

Sheng (Chinese) One who is victorious

Shepherd (English) One who herds sheep
Shepperd, Shep, Shepard, Shephard, Shepp, Sheppard

Shepley (English) From the meadow of sheep
Sheply, Shepli, Sheplie, Sheplea, Shepleah, Sheplee, Shepleigh, Sceapleigh

Sherborne (English) From the shining brook
Sherborn, Sherbourn, Sherburn, Sherburne, Sherbourne

Sheridan (Gaelic) A seeker
Sheredan, Sheridon, Sherridan, Seireadan, Sheriden, Sheridun, Sherard, Sherrard, Sherrerd, Shererd, Sherrod, Sherod

Sherill (English) From the bright hill
Sherrill, Sheryll, Sherryll

Sherlock (English) A fair-haired man
Sherlocke, Shurlock, Shurlocke

Sherman (English) One who cuts wool cloth
Shermon, Scherman, Schermann, Shearman, Shermann, Sherm, Sherme

Shermarke (African) One who brings good luck
Shermark

Sherrerd (English) From the open field
Shererd, Sherrard, Sherard

Sherrick (English) One who has already left
Sherryck, Sherrik, Sherick, Sherik, Sheryck

Sherwin (English) A bright friend
Sherwen, Sherwind, Sherwinn, Sherwyn, Sherwynn, Sherwynne, Sherwinne, Sherwenn, Sherwenne

Sherwood (English) From the bright forest
Sherwoode, Shurwood, Shurwoode

Shevon (American) A humorous man
Shevonne, Shevaun, Shevaughn

Shields (Gaelic) A faithful protector
Sheelds, Shealds

Shikha (Indian) A fiery man
Shykha

Shilah (Native American) One who is brotherly
Shylah, Shila, Shyla

Shiloh (Hebrew) He who was sent
Shilo, Shyloh, Shylo

Shing (Chinese) A victorious man
Shyng

Shino (Japanese) A bamboo stem
Shyno

Shipley (English) From the meadow of ships; from the meadow of sheep
Shiply, Shiplee, Shiplea, Shipleah, Shipli, Shiplie, Shipleigh

Shipton (English) From the ship town; from the sheep town

Shire (English) From the country
Shyre

Shiriki (Native American) Resembling a coyote
Shirikie, Shiriky, Shirikey, Shirikee, Shirikea, Shyriki, Shyryki, Shyryky

Shiro (Japanese) The fourth-born son
Shyro

Shishir (Indian) Born during the winter
Shyshir, Shyshyr, Shishyr, Shisheer, Shysheer

Shiva (Hindi) One who is good; lucky; in Hinduism, the god of destruction and restoration
Shivah, Sheeva, Sheevah, Siva, Sivah, Shiv

Shiye (Native American) Our son

Shoda (Japanese) From the level field

Shomer (Hebrew) The watchman

Shoney(Celtic) In mythology, god of the sea
Shony, Shoni, Shonie, Shonee, Shonea

Shontae (American) Filled with hope
Shontay, Shontaye, Shontai, Shauntae, Shauntay, Shauntaye, Shauntai, Shawntae, Shawntay, Shawntaye, Shawntae, Shonti, Shontie, Shonty, Shontey, Shontee, Shontea

Shoorsen (Indian) One who is brave
Shoursen, Shorsen

Shorty (American) A man who is small in stature
Shortey, Shorti, Shortie, Shortee, Shortea

Shoshone (Native American) A tribal name
Shoshoni, Shoshonie, Shoshonee, Shoshonea, Shoshony, Shoshoney

Shoval (Hebrew) One who walks the path
Shovall, Shovalle, Shovale

Shoval (Hebrew) One who is on the right path
Shovall, Shovalle

Shrenik (Indian) One who is organized
Shrenyk, Shrenick, Shrenyck, Shrenic, Shrenyc

Shreshta (Indian) The best; one who is superior

Shuang (Chinese) A bright man

Shubha (Indian) A lucky man
Shubhah, Shubham

Shubhang (Indian) A handsome man

Shunnar (Arabic) Resembling a bird; a pleasant man

Shuo (Chinese) One who achieves greatness

Shuraqui (Arabic) A man from the east

Shuu (Japanese) A responsible man

Si (Vietnamese) A gentleman
Sigh

Siamak (Persian) A bringer of joy
Syamak, Siamack, Syamack, Siamac, Syamac

Sicheii (Native American) One who is grandfatherly

Sicily (Italian) From the island
Sicilly, Sicili, Sicilie, Sicilee, Sicilea, Sicilley, Sicilli, Sicillie, Sicillee, Sicillea

Sidell (English) From the wide valley
Sidel, Sidelle, Sydel, Sydell, Siddel, Siddell, Syddel, Syddell, Siddael, Sidael, Siddayl, Sidayl

Sidney (English) From the wide meadow
Sydney, Sidni, Sidnie, Sidny, Sidnee, Sidnea, Sydny, Sydni, Sydnie, Sydnee, Sydnea, Sid, Syd

Sidonio (Latin) Man from Sidon
Sidono, Sidoniyo, Sydonio, Sydono, Sydoniyo

Sidor (Russian) One who is talented
Sydor

Sidus (Latin) Resembling a star
Sydus, Sidos, Sydos

Sidwell (English) From the wide spring
Sydwell, Sidwel, Sydwel

Siegfried (German) One who enjoys the peace of victory
Sygfried, Sigfred, Sigfrid, Sigfried, Sigfryd, Sigvard, Sygfred, Sigfreid, Sigifrid, Sigifryd, Sigifrith, Sigfrith, Sygfrith, Sygifrith

Sierra (Spanish) From the jagged mountain range
Siera, Syerra, Syera, Seyera, Seeara

Sigbjorn (Norse) The victorious bear
Siegbjorn

Sigehere (English) One who is victorious
Sygehere, Sigihere, Sygihere

Sigenert (Anglo-Saxon) A king
Sygenert, Siginert, Syginert

Sigmund (German) The victorious protector
*Seigmond, Segismond, Siegmund, Sigismond,
Sigismondo, Sigismund, Sigismundo,
Sigismundus, Sigmond, Szymond, Sigurd,
Sigvard*

Signe (Scandinavian) A victorious man
Signy, Signey, Signi, Signie, Signee, Signea

Sigourney (Scandinavian / French) One
who conquers / a daring king
*Sigourny, Sigourni, Sigournie, Sigournee,
Sigournye, Sigournea, Sigurney, Sigurny,
Sigurni, Sigurnie, Sigurnea, Sigurnee*

Sigurd (Norse) The protector of victory
Sigerd, Sigurde, Sigerde, Seigurd, Siegurd

Sigwald (German) A victorious leader
*Siegwald, Seigwald, Sigwalt, Siegwalt,
Seigwalt, Sigiwald, Sygwald, Sigiwalt, Sygwalt*

Sihtric (Anglo-Saxon) A king
*Sihtrik, Sihtrick, Syhtric, Syhtrik, Syhtrick,
Sihtryc, Sihtryk, Sihtryck*

Sike (Native American) A homebody
Syke

Sik'is (Native American) A friendly man

Sikyahonaw (Native American) Resembling
a yellow bear
Sikyahonau, Sykyahonaw, Sykyahonau

Sikyatavo (Native American) Resembling a
yellow rabbit

Silas (Latin) Form of Silvanus, meaning "a
woodland dweller"
Sylas, Siles, Silus, Syles, Sylus, Silous, Sylous

Silko (African) A king
Sylko

Sill (English) A bright as a beam of light
Sills, Syll, Sylls

Silny (Czech) Having great strength
Silney, Silni, Silnie, Silnee, Silnea

Silsby (English) From Sill's farm
*Sillsby, Silsbey, Sillsbey, Silsbi, Sillsbi, Silsbie,
Sillsbie, Silsbee, Sillsbee*

Silvanus (Latin) A woodland dweller
*Silvain, Silvano, Silverio, Silvino, Silvio,
Sylvanus, Sylvio, Silvaine, Silvaen, Silvaene,
Silvayn, Silvayne, Silvius, Silviu, Silvan,
Sylvan*

Silver (English) A precious metal; a white-
skinned man
Sylver

Silverman (German) One who works with
silver
*Sylverman, Silberman, Sylberman,
Silvermann, Sylvermann, Silbermann,
Sylbermann*

Silverton (English) From the silver town
Sylverton, Silvertown, Sylvertown

Simba (African) Resembling a lion
Simbah, Symba, Symbah

Simbarashe (African) The power of God
*Simbarashi, Simbarashie, Simbarashy,
Simbarashey, Simbarashee*

Simcha (Hebrew) Filled with joy
Symcha, Simha, Symha

Simmons (Hebrew) The son of Simon
*Semmes, Simms, Syms, Simmonds, Symonds,
Simpson, Symms, Simson*

Simon (Hebrew) God has heard
*Shimon, Si, Sim, Samien, Semyon, Simen,
Simeon, Simone, Symon, Szymon, Siman,
Simu, Siomon, Simao, Symeon*

Sinai (Hebrew) From the clay desert

Sinbad (Arabic) A wealthy adventurer
Synbad, Sindbah, Syndbah

Sinclair (English) Man from Saint Clair
*Sinclaire, Sinclare, Synclair, Synclaire,
Synclare*

Sindile (African) The survivor
Syndile, Sindyle, Syndyle

Singer (American) A vocalist
Synger

Singh (Indian) Resembling a lion
Syngh

Sinh (Vietnamese) A flourishing boy

Sinjin (English) Refers to Saint John
Sinjon, Synjin, Synjon

Sinley (Anglo-Saxon) A friendly man
Sinly, Sinlee, Sinleigh, Sinlea, Sinli, Sinlie

Sion (Armenian) From the fortified hill
Sionne, Syon, Syonne

Siraj (Arabic) One who holds the torch
Syraj

Sirius (Greek) Resembling the brightest star
Syrius

Sisto (American) A cowboy
Systo

Sitanshu (Indian) Born beneath the moon
Sytanshu, Sitanshue, Sytanshue, Sitanshoo, Sytanshoo, Sitanshou, Sytanshou

Sivan (Hebrew) Born during the ninth month
Syvan

Sivney (Gaelic) A good and sweet boy
Sivny, Sivni, Sivnie, Sivnee, Sivnea, Syvney, Syvny, Syvni, Syvnie, Syvnee, Syvnea, Sivneigh, Syvneigh

Siwili (Native American) The fox's tail
Siwilie, Siwile, Siwiley, Siwily, Siwilee, Siwileigh, Siwileu

Six (American) Refers to the number; the sixth-born child

Siyamak (Persian) A man who has dark eyes
Siyamac, Siyamack

Siyavash (Persian) One who owns black horses
Siyavashe

Skah (Native American) A white-skinned man

Skeet (English / Norse) One who is swift / one who shoots
Skeets, Skeete, Skeat, Skeate, Skeit, Skeite, Skete, Sketes, Skeeter, Skeetz

Skelly (Gaelic) A storyteller; a bard
Skelli, Skellie, Skelley, Skellee, Skellea

Skerry (Norse) From the rocky island
Skereye, Skerrey, Skerri, Skerrie, Skerree, Skerrea

Skilling (American) One who is masterful
Skillings, Skylling, Skyllings

Skinner (English) One who skins hides
Skinnor, Skinnar, Skinnur, Skinnir, Skinnyr

Skipper (English) The master of a ship
Skippere, Skip, Skipp

Skye (Gaelic) Man from the Isle of Skye
Sky, Skie

Skyler (English / Danish) One who is learned; a scholar / a fugitive
Skylare, Skylar, Skielar, Skylor, Skylir, Skylur, Skielor, Skyelar, Skylen, Skyller, Skylarr

Slade (English) Son of the valley
Slaid, Slaide, Slaed, Slaede, Slayd, Slayde

Sladkey (Slavic) A glorious man
Sladky, Sladki, Sladkie, Sladkee, Sladkea

Slater (English) One who installs slate roofs
Slator, Slatar, Slatur, Slatir, Slatyr

Slavek (Polish) One who is intelligent
Slavek, Slaveck, Slavyk, Slavyc, Slavyck, Slavik, Slavick

Slavin (Gaelic) Man from the mountains
Slavyn, Slaven, Slawin, Slawon, Slawyn, Sleven, Slevan, Slevyn, Slevin

Slavomir (Czech) Of renowned glory
Slavomeer, Slavomyr, Slavomere, Slawomir, Slawomeer, Slawomyr, Slawomere

Slean (Anglo-Saxon) One who strikes
Sleane, Slene, Sleen, Sleene

Slim (English) A slender man
Slym

Sloan (Gaelic) A high-ranking warrior
Sloane, Slown, Slowne, Slone

Slobodan (Croatian) Having a strong intellect

Slocum (English) Filled with happiness
Slocom, Slocumb, Slocomb

Smedley (English) From the flat meadow
Smedly, Smedli, Smedlie, Smedlee, Smedleigh, Smedlea, Smedleah, Smetheleah

Smith (English) A blacksmith
Smyth, Smithe, Smythe, Smedt, Smid, Smitty, Smittee, Smittea, Smittey, Smitti, Smittie

Smithson (English) The son of a black-smith
Smythson, Smitheson, Smytheson, Smithesone, Smythesone

Smokey (American) One with a raspy voice; a rebel
Smoky, Smoki, Smokie, Smokee, Smokea

Snell (Anglo-Saxon) One who is bold
Snel, Snelle, Snele

Snowden (English) From the snowy peak
Snoden, Snowdon, Snodon, Snowdun, Snodun

So (Vietnamese) A smart man

Soberano (Spanish) A sovereign

Socorro (Spanish) One who offers help
Socorrio, Socoro, Socorio

Socrates (Greek) An ancient philosopher
Sokrates, Socratees, Sokratees

Sofian (Arabic) A devoted man

Sofronio (Greek) A self-controlled man
Sofrono, Sophronio, Sophrono

Sofus (Greek) Having great wisdom
Sophus

Sohan (Indian) A handsome man
Sohil, Sohail

Solange (French) An angel of the sun

Solaris (Greek) Of the sun
Solarise, Solariss, Solarisse, Solarys, Solaryss, Solarysse, Solstice, Soleil

Solomon (Hebrew) A peaceful man
Salmon, Salomo, Salomon, Salomone, Shalmon, Sol, Solaman, Sollie, Soloman

Solt (Hungarian) One who is honored
Solte

Solyom (Hungarian) Resembling a falcon

Somansh (Indian) Born beneath the half moon
Somanshe, Somanshi, Somanshie, Somanshy, Somanshey, Somanshee, Somanshea

Somer (French) Born during the summer
Somers, Sommer, Sommers, Sommar, Somar

Somerby (English) From the summer vil-lage
Somersby, Sommersby, Somerbey, Somerbi, Somerbie, Somerbee, Somerbea

Somerley (Gaelic) Of the summer sailors; from the summer meadow
Somerly, Somerli, Somerlie, Somerlee, Somerleigh, Somerlea, Somerleah, Somerled

Somerset (English) From the summer settlement
Sommerset, Sumerset, Summerset

Somerton (English) From the summer town
Somertown, Somerville, Somervile, Somervil, Sumarville, Sumarton, Sumerton, Sumertun, Sumerville

Sondo (African) Born on a Sunday

Songaa (Native American) Having great strength
Songan

Sonny (English) Our son
Sonney, Sonni, Sonnie, Sonnee, Sonnea

Sophocles (Greek) An ancient playwright
Sofocles

Soren (Scandinavian) Form of Severin, meaning "one who is strict; stern"
Soran, Soron, Sorun, Sorin, Soryn

Sorley (Irish) Of the summer vikings
Sorly, Sorlee, Sorlea, Sorli, Sorlie

Sorrell (French) Having reddish-brown hair
Sorel, Sorelle, Sorrelle, Sorrel

Soto (Spanish) From the marshland

Soumil (Indian) A beloved friend
Soumyl, Soumille, Soumylle, Soumill, Soumyll

Southern (English) Man from the south
Sothern, Suthern

Southwell (English) From the south spring
Sothwell

Sovann (Cambodian) The golden son
Sovan, Sovane

Sowi'ngwa (Native American) Resembling a black-tailed deer

Spalding (English) From the split field
Spaulding, Spelding

Spanky (American) One who is outspoken or stubborn
Spanki, Spankie, Spankey, Spankee, Spankea

Spark (English / Latin) A gallant man / to scatter
Sparke, Sparki, Sparkie, Sparky, Sparkey, Sparkee, Sparkea

Spear (English) One who wields a spear
Speare, Spears, Speer, Speers, Speir, Speirs, Spier, Spiers, Spere

Speed (English) Having good fortune
Speede, Sped, Spede, Spead, Speade

Spencer (English) One who dispenses provisions
Spenser, Spence, Spensar, Spincer, Spince

Spengler (German) One who works with tin
Spangler

Spider (English) Resembling the arachnid
Spyder

Spike (English) A large, heavy nail
Spyke, Spiker, Spyker

Spiridon (Greek) One who transports goods; a basket
Speero, Spero, Spiridion, Spiro, Spiros, Spyridon, Spyro, Spyros

Sprague (German) A lively man; full of energy

Springer (English) A fresh-faced man
Sprynger

Sproul (English) An active man
Sproule, Sprowl, Sprowle

Spud (American) A little boy; a potato
Spudd

Spunk (American) A lively man
Spunky, Spunkey, Spunkee, Spunkea, Spunki, Spunkie

Spurs (American) A cowboy
Spur, Spurr, Spurrs

Squire (English) A knight's companion; the shield-bearer
Squier, Squiers, Squires, Squyre, Squyres

Stacey (English) Form of Eustace, meaning "having an abundance of grapes"
Stacy, Staci, Stacie, Stacee, Stacea, Stace, Stayce, Staice, Staece

Stafford (English) From the landing ford
Stafforde, Staford, Staforde, Steathford

Stamos (Greek) A reasonable man
Stammos, Stamohs, Staymos, Staimos, Staemos

Stanbury (English) From the stone fortress
Stanberry, Stanbery, Stanburghe, Stansberry, Stansburghe, Stansbury, Stanburh, Stanbeny

Stancliff (English) From the stone cliff
Stancliffe, Stanclyffe, Stanscliff, Stanscliffe, StancIyf

Standish (English) From the stony park
Standysh, Standishe, Standyshe

Stanfield (English) From the stony field
Stansfield, Stanfeld, Stansfeld

Stanford (English) From the stony ford
Standford, Standforde, Standforde, Stamford, Stamforde

Stanhope (English) From the stony hollow
Stanhop

Stanislaus (Slavic) The glory of the camp
Stana, Stanek, Stanicek, Stanislas, Stanislav, Stanislav, Stanislaw, Stannes, Stanousek, Stanislov

Stanley (English) From the stony meadow
*Stanly, Stanli, Stanlie, Stanlee, Stanleigh,
Stanlea, Stanleah, Stan*

Stanmore (English) From the stony lake
Stanmere, Stanmor

Stanton (English) From the stone town
*Stantown, Stanten, Staunton, Stantan,
Stantun*

Stanway (English) From the stone road
*Stanwaye, Stanwae, Stanwai, Stanaway,
Stannaway, Stannway, Stanweg, Stannweg*

Stanwick (English) One who lives in the
stone village
*Stanwic, Stanwik, Stanwicke, Stanwyck,
Stanwyc, Stanwyk*

Stanwood (English) From the stony forest
Stanwode, Stannwood, Stanwoode

Star (American) A celestial body; as bright
as a star
*Starr, Starre, Starry, Starrie, Starri, Starrey,
Starree*

Starbuck (American) An astronaut
*Starrbuck, Starbuk, Starrbuk, Starbuc,
Starrbuc*

Stark (German) Having great strength
Starke, Starck, Starcke

Starling (English) Resembling the bird
Starrling, Starlyng, Starrlyng, Staerling

Stash (American) Of the sun's rays
Stashe

Stavros (Greek) One who is crowned

Steadman (English) One who lives at the
farm
Stedman, Steadmann, Stedmann, Stedeman

Steed (English) Resembling a stallion
Steede, Stead, Steade

Steele (English) As strong as steel
Steel

Stein (German) As solid as a stone
*Steen, Sten, Steno, Stensen, Steene, Stenssen,
Steiner, Stine*

Steinar (Norse) A rock-hard warrior
Steinard, Steinart, Steinhardt

Stennis (Scottish) From the place of the
standing stones
Stennys, Stinnis, Stinnys

Stephen (Greek) Crowned with garland
*Staffan, Steba, Steben, Stefan, Stefano,
Steffan, Steffen, Steffon, Stefon, Stephan,
Stephano, Stephanos, Stephanus, Stephens,
Stephenson, Stephon, Stevan, Steve, Steven,
Stevenson, Stevie, Stevey, Stevy, Stéphane,
Stevon, Stevyn, Stefanas, Stefanos, Stefanus,
Stephanas, Step*

Stepney (English) From Stephen's island
Stepny, Stepni, Stepnie, Stepnee, Stepnea

Sterling (English) One who is highly valued
Sterlyng, Stirling, Sterlyn

Sterne (English) A serious-minded man;
one who is strict
Stern, Stearn, Stearne, Stearns

Stetson (American) A cowboy
Stettson, Stetcyn, Stetsen, Stetsan

Stian (Norse) A voyager; one who is swift
*Stig, Styg, Stygge, Stieran, Steeran, Steeren,
Steeryn, Stieren, Stieryn*

Stillman (English) A fisherman; one who
is quiet
Stilleman, Styllman, Stylleman, Stillmann

Stilwell (Anglo-Saxon) From the quiet
spring
*Stillwell, Stilwel, Stylwell, Styllwell, Stylwel,
Stillwel*

Stobart (German) A harsh man
Stobarte, Stobarth, Stobarthe

Stock (English) From the tree stump
Stok, Stoc, Stocke, Stoke

Stockard (English) From the yard of tree
stumps
Stockhard, Stockhard, Stokkard, Stocker

Stockley (English) From the meadow of tree
stumps
*Stockly, Stockli, Stocklie, Stocklee, Stockleigh,
Stocklea, Stockleah, Stocleah, Stoclea*

Stockton (English) From the town of tree stumps
Stocktown, Stocktun, Stocktan, Stockten

Stockwell (English) From the spring near the tree stumps
Stocwielle, Stockwiell

Stod (English) Resembling a horse
Stodd

Stoddard (English) The guardian or keeper of horses
Stodard, Stoddart, Stodart

Stonewall (English) From the stone fortress
Stonwall, Stanwall, Stannwall

Stoney (English) As solid as a stone
Stony, Stoni, Stonie, Stonee, Stonea, Stoner, Stone, Stones

Storm (American) Of the tempest; stormy weather; having an impetuous nature
Storme, Stormy, Stormi, Stormie, Stormey, Stormee, Stormea

Stowe (English) A secretive man
Stow, Stowey, Stowy, Stowee, Stowea, Stowi, Stowie

Strahan (Gaelic) A poet; a minstrel
Sruthan, Strachan

Stratford (English) From the street near the river ford
Strafford, Stratforde, Straford, Strafforde, Straforde

Stratton (Scottish) A homebody
Straton, Stratten, Straten, Strattan, Stratan, Strattun, Stratun

Straus (German) Resembling an ostrich
Strauss, Strause, Strausse

Stretch (American) An easygoing man
Stretcher, Strech, Strecher

Strickland (English) From the flax field
Stryckland, Strikland, Strykland

Strider (English) A great warrior
Stryder

Striker (American) An aggressive man
Strike, Stryker, Stryke

Strom (German) From the brook
Stromm, Strome, Stromme

Strong (English) A powerful man
Stronge, Strang

Stroud (Old English) from the thicket
Strod, Strode, Stroude

Struthers (Irish) One who lives near the brook
Struther, Sruthair, Strother, Strothers

Stuart (English) A steward; the keeper of the estate
Steward, Stewart, Stewert, Stuert, Stu, Stew

Studs (English / American) From the homestead / a cocky man
Studds, Stud, Studd

Sture (Scandinavian) A difficult man

Styles (English) From the stairway
Stiles, Stigols

Stylianos (Greek) A stylish man
Styli, Stylie, Style, Stylee, Stylea, Styleigh

Suave (American) A smooth and sophisticated man
Swave

Subhash (Indian) One who speaks well
Subhashe

Subhi (Arabic) Born during the early morning hours
Subhie, Subhy, Subhey, Subhee, Subhea

Sudbury (English) From the southern settlement
Sudbery, Sudberry, Sudborough

Sudi (African) A successful or lucky man
Sudie, Sudee, Sudea, Sudy, Sudey

Suffield (English) From the southern field
Suffeld, Suthfeld, Suthfield

Suffolk (English) Of the southern people

Suhail (Arabic) A gentle man; bright star
Suhaile, Suhayl, Suhayle, Suhael, Suhaele, Suhale

Sujay (Indian) Winning a good victory
Sujaye, Sujai, Sujae, Sujit

Sukarno (African) The chosen one

Sukumar (Indian) A tender man

Sulayman (Arabic) Form of Solomon, meaning "a peaceful man"
Sulaiman, Suleiman, Suleyman, Sulaymaan

Sule (African) An adventurous man

Sullivan (Gaelic) Having dark eyes
Sullavan, Sullevan, Sullyvan

Sully (English) From the southern meadow
Sulley, Sulli, Sullie, Sulleigh, Sullee, Sullea, Sulleah, Suthley, Suthly, Suthleigh, Suthlee, Suthli, Suthlie, Suthlea, Suthleah

Sultan (African / American) A ruler / one who is bold
Sultane, Sulten, Sultun, Sulton, Sultin, Sultyn

Suman (Hindi) A wise man

Sumner (English) A legal official; one who serves summons
Sumenor, Sumernor

Sunday (American) Born on a Sunday
Sundae, Sundai, Sundaye

Sundiata (African) Resembling a hungry lion
Sundyata, Soundiata, Soundyata, Sunjata

Sundown (American) Born at dusk
Sundowne

Sunil (Indian) A deep dark-blue gem
Suneel, Sunyl, Suneil, Suniel, Suneal

Sunny (American) Of the sun; one who is brilliant and cheerful
Sunni, Sunney, Sunnie, Sunnea, Sunnye, Sonnenschein

Sunukkuhkau (Native American) He who crushes

Suraj (Indian) Of the sun
Sooraj, Souraj

Surur (Arabic) Filled with joy

Sutcliff (English) From the southern cliff
Sutcliffe, Sutclyff, Sutclyf, Suthclif, Suthcliff, Suthclyf, Suthclyff, Suttecliff, Sutteclyff

Sutherland (Norse) From the southern island
Suthrland, Southerland

Sutton (English) From the southern town
Suttun, Sutter

Su'ud (Arabic) One who has good luck
Suoud

Svan (Norse) Resembling a swan
Svann

Svatomir (Slavic) Of sacred glory
Svatomeer, Svatomear, Svatomyr

Svatoslav (Slavic) One who celebrates sacredness

Sven (Norse) A youthful man; a lad
Svein, Sveinn, Svend, Swain, Swen, Swensen, Swenson

Svenbjorn (Swedish) Resembling a young bear

Swahili (Arabic) Of the coastal people
Swahily, Swahiley, Swahilee, Swahiley, Swaheeli, Swaheelie, Swaheely, Swaheeley, Swaheelee

Swain (English) A country boy; one who herds swine; a knight's attendant
Swain, Swayn, Swayne, Swane, Swaen, Swaene

Swanton (English) From the swan town
Swantun, Swantown

Sweeney (Gaelic) Little hero; a brave young boy
Sweeny, Sweeni, Sweenie, Sweenee, Sweenea, Suidhne

Swift (Anglo-Saxon) One who is fast
Swifte, Swyft, Swyfte, Swifty, Swiftey, Swifti, Swiftie, Swiftee, Swiftea

Swinburne (English) From the swine stream
Swinborn, Swinbourne, Swinburn, Swinbyrn, Swynborne, Swynburne

Swinford (English) From the swine ford
Swynford, Swinforde, Swynforde

Swinton (English) From the swine town
Swynton, Swintun, Swyntun

Swithin (English) One who is quick and strong
Swithinn, Swithun

Sydney (English) Of the wide meadow
Sydny, Sydni, Sydnie, Sydnea, Sydnee, Sidney, Sidne, Sidnee, Sidnei, Sidni, Sidnie, Sidny, Sidnye

Sylvester (Latin) Man from the forest
Silvester, Silvestre, Silvestro, Sylvestre, Sylvestro, Sly, Sevester, Seveste

Symotris (African) A fortunate man
Symetris, Symotrise, Symotrice, Symotrys, Symotryce, Symotryse

Syon (Indian) One who is followed by good fortune

Szemere (Hungarian) A man of small stature
Szemir, Szemeer, Szemear, Szemyr

Szervac (Hungarian) One who has been freed

t

Taaveti (Hebrew) One who is dearly loved
Taavetie, Taavety, Taavetey, Taavetee, Taavetea, Taveti, Tavetie, Tavetee, Tavetea, Tavety, Tavetey, Taavi, Taavetti, Tavetti

Tab (German / English) A brilliant man / a drummer
Tabb

Taban (Gaelic) A genius
Taben, Tabon, Tabin, Tabyn, Tabun

Tabansi (African) An enduring man
Tabansie, Tabansy, Tabansey, Tabansee, Tabansea

Tabari (Arabic) A famous historian
Tabarie, Tabary, Tabarey, Tabaree, Tabarea

Tabasco (American) Resembling the spicey pepper
Tabasko, Tabascko

Tabbai (Hebrew) A well-behaved boy
Tabbae, Tabbay, Tabbaye

Tabbart (German) A brilliant man
Tabbert, Tabart, Tabert, Tahbert, Tahberte

Tabbebo (Native American) Son of the sun
Tabebo, Tabbebio, Tabebio

Tabib (Turkish) One who heals others; a doctor
Tabibe, Tabeeb, Tabeebe, Tabeab, Tabeabe

Tabor (Hungarian / Hebrew) From the trenches / having bad luck
Taber, Tuibor, Tavor, Taybor, Tayber, Taiber, Taebor, Taeber

Tacari (African) As strong as a warrior
Tacarie, Tacary, Tacarey, Tacaree, Tacarea

Tacitus (Latin) A well-known historian
Tacitas, Tacites

Tadao (Japanese) One who is satisfied

Tadashi (Japanese) One who is accurate
Tadashie, Tadashy, Tadashey, Tadashee, Tadashea

Tadelesh (African) A lucky man
Tadelesho, Tadeleshio, Tadeleshiyo

Tadeo (Spanish) Form of Thaddeus, meaning "having heart"
Taddeo, Tadzio, Tadzo

Tadeusuz (Polish) One who is worthy of praise
Tadesuz

Tadi (Native American) Of the wind
Tadie, Tady, Tadey, Tadee, Tadea

Tadzi (American / Polish) Resembling the loon / one who is praised
Tadzie, Tadzy, Tadzey, Tadzee, Tadzea

Taff (American) A sweet man
Taffy, Taffey, Taffi, Taffie, Taffee, Taffea

Taft (French / English) From the homestead / from the marshes
Tafte

Tage (Danish) Born during the daytime

Taggart (Gaelic) Son of a priest
Taggert, Taggort, Taggirt, Taggyrt

Taghee (Native American) A chief
Taghea, Taghy, Taghey, Taghi, Taghie

Taha (Polynesian) The firstborn child
Tahatan

Taheton (Native American) Resembling a hawk

Tahi (Polynesian) One who lives by the sea
Tahie, Tahy, Tahey, Tahee, Tahea

Tahir (Arabic) One who is pure; chaste
Tahire, Taheer, Taheere, Tahier, Tahiere, Taheir, Taheire, Tahear, Taheare, Tahyr, Tahyre, Taher, Tahu

Tahkeome (Native American) The little robe
Tahkiome, Tahkyome, Takeome, Takiome, Takyome

Tahmelapachme (Native American) Wielding a dull knife

Tahmores (Persian) Resembling a strong wild dog

Tahoe (Native American) From the big water
Taho

Tahoma (Native American) From the snowy mountain peak
Tehoma, Tacoma, Takoma, Tohoma, Tocoma, Tokoma, Tekoma, Tecoma

Tahurer (English) A drummer
Tahurar, Tahurir, Tahuryr, Tahuror, Tahurur

Tai (Vietnamese) One who is talented

Taicligh (Irish) One who is peaceful

Taima (Native American) Of the thunder
Tayma, Taema

Taine (Gaelic) Of the river
Tain, Tayn, Tayne, Taen, Taene, Tane

Taishi (Japanese) An ambitious man
Taishie, Taishy, Taishey, Taishee, Taishea

Taiwo (African) The firstborn of twins
Tawo, Taewo, Taywo

Taizeen (Indian) One who offers encouragement
Tazeen, Taezeen, Tayzeen, Taizean, Tazean, Taezean, Tayzean

Taizo (Japanese) The third-born son
Tayzo, Tazo, Taezo

Taj (Indian) One who is crowned
Tahj, Tajdar

Taji (Japanese) A yellow and silver color
Tajie, Tajy, Tajey, Tajee, Tajea

Tajo (Spanish) Born during the daytime

Takeo (Japanese) As strong as bamboo
Takio, Takyo, Takeshi, Takeshie, Takeshee, Takeshea, Takeshy, Takeshey

Taklishim (Native American) A gray-haired man
Taklishym, Taklisheem, Taklisheam, Taklyshim, Taklyshym, Taklysheem, Taklysheam

Takoda (Native American) One who is a friend to everyone
Tacoda, Tackoda

Taksa (Hindi) In Hinduism, a son of Bharata
Taksha

Takshaka (Indian) One who works with wood

Taksony (Hungarian) One who is content; well-fed
Taksoney, Taksoni, Taksonie, Taksonee, Taksonea, Tas

Tal (Hebrew) Covered with the morning's dew
Tahl

Talak (Indian) One who is superior
Talac, Talack

Talasi (Native American) Resembling a cornflower
Talasie, Talasy, Talasey, Talasee, Talasea

Talat (Indian) One who prays
Talatt, Tallat, Tallatt

Talbert (English) Born to the nobility
Talbet, Talbot, Talbott, Tallbot, Tallbott, Talbort, Tallbet, Talbett, Tallbett, Tolbert, Tollbert, Tolbart, Tollbart, Tolburt, Tollburt

Talcot (English) One who lives in a cottage by the lake
Talcott, Talcote, Talcotte

Talehot (French) Resembling a bloodhound

Talford (English) From the high ford
Talforde, Tallford, Tallforde

Talfryn (Welsh) From the high hill
Talfrynn, Talfrin, Talfrinn, Talfren, Talfrenn, Tallfryn, Tallfrin, Tallfren

Talib (Arabic) One who seeks knowledge
Talibe, Taleeb, Taleebe, Taleib, Taleibe, Talieb, Taliebe, Taleab, Taleabe, Talyb, Talybe, Taleb, Talebe

Taliesin (Welsh) Having a shiny forehead
Taliesyn, Taliesen, Talieson, Talyessin, Talessin

Talleen (Hindi) One who is engrossed
Tallein, Tallean, Talleyn, Tallien, Tallene, Talline, Tallen

Talli (Native American / Hebrew) A legendary hero / of the morning dew
Tallie, Tally, Talley, Tallee, Tallea

Tallis (English) A composer of religious music
Talles, Tallas, Tallys, Talis, Talys, Tales, Talas

Talmadge (English) One who loves nature
Tallmadge, Talmidge, Tallmidge

Talmai (Hebrew) From the furrows
Talmae, Talmay, Talmaye

Talmon (Hebrew) One who is oppressed
Talman, Talmin, Talmyn, Talmen

Talo (Finnish) From the homestead

Talon (English) Resembling a bird's claw
Tallon, Talen, Talin, Tallan, Tallen, Tallin

Talos (Greek) In mythology, the protector of Minos island; a giant

Tam (Vietnamese / Hebrew) Having heart / one who is truthful

Tamal (Hindi) Of the dark tree
Tamall, Tamalle

Tamam (Arabic) One who is generous

Taman (Hindi) One who is needed

Tamar (Hebrew) From the palm tree
Tamare, Tamarr, Tamarre

Tamarack (Latin) From the tree
Tamarak, Tamarac

Tamarisk (Latin) Resembling the shrublike tree
Tamarysk, Tamaresk

Tamarius (American) A stubborn man
Tamarias, Tamarios, Tamerius, Tamerias, Tamerios

Tamerlane (English) One who is lame
Tamarlain, Tamarlayn, Tamberlain, Tumberlaine, Tamberlane, Tamburlaine, Tamburlane, Tamurlaine, Tamurlayn

Tameron (American) Form of Cameron, meaning "having a crooked nose"
Tameryn, Tamryn, Tamerin, Tamren, Tamrin, Bamron

Tamir (Arabic / Hebrew) A wealthy man / one who stands tall
Tamire, Tameer, Tameere, Tamear, Tameare, Tamyr, Tamyre, Tamier, Tamiere, Tameir, Tameire

Tamirat (African) A miracle child
Tamyrat, Tamiratt, Tamyratt

Tammany (Native American) A friendly chief
Tammani, Tammanie, Tammaney, Tammanee, Tammanea

Tamson (English) Son of Thomas
Tamsen, Tamsin, Tamsyn, Tamsun

Tan (Japanese) A high achiever

Tanafa (Polynesian) A drumbeat

Tanaki (Polynesian) One who counts
Tanakie, Tanaky, Tanakey, Tanakee, Tanakea

Tanay (Hindi) Our beloved son
Tanaye, Tanai, Tanae, Tanuj

Tancred (German) One who gives thoughtful counsel
Tancreid, Tancried, Tancrid, Tancryd, Tancredo, Tancreed, Tancread, Tancredi, Tancredie, Tancredy, Tancredey, Tancredee, Tancredea

Tandy (Scottish) Form of Andrew, meaning "a warrior"
Tandi, Tandey, Tandie, Tandee, Tandea

Tanek (Polish) One who is immortal

Taneli (Hebrew) He will be judged by God
Tanelie, Tanely, Taneley, Tanelee, Tanelea

Tangakwunu (Native American) Resembling a rainbow
Tangakwunoo, Tangakwunou

Tangaloa (Polynesian) A courageous man
Tangalo

Tanguy (Celtic) A warrior

Tanh (Vietnamese) One who gets his way

Tanish (Indian) An ambitious man
Tanishe, Taneesh, Taneeshe, Taneash, Taneashe, Tanysh, Tanyshe

Tanjiro (Japanese) The prized second-born son
Tanjyro

Tank (American) A man who is big and strong
Tankie, Tanki, Tanky, Tankey, Tankee, Tankea

Tanmay (Indian) One who is absorbed
Tanmaye, Tanmae, Tanmai

Tanner (English) One who makes leather
Tannere, Tannor, Tannar, Tannir, Tannyr, Tannur, Tannis

Tannon (German) From the fir tree
Tannan, Tannen, Tannin, Tansen, Tanson, Tannun, Tannyn

Tano (Ghanese) From the river
Tanu

Tansy (Greek / Native American) Having immortality / resembling the flower
Tansey, Tansi, Tansie, Tansee, Tansea

Tanton (English) From the town near the quiet river
Tanten, Tantan, Tantown, Tantun, Tantin, Tantyn, Tamtun, Tamton, Tamten, Tamtan, Tamtyn, Tamtin

Tanvir (Indian) An enlightened man
Tanvire, Tanveer, Tanveere, Tanvyr, Tanvyre, Tanvear, Tanveare

Tao (Chinese) One who will have a long life

Taos (Spanish) From the city in New Mexico

Tapani (Hebrew) A victorious man
Tapanie, Tapany, Tapaney, Tapanee, Tapanea

Tapko (American) Resembling an antelope

Tapomay (Indian) A virtuous man
Tapomaye, Tapomai, Tapomae

Tappen (Welsh) From the top of the cliff
Tappan, Tappon, Tappin, Tappyn, Tappun

Tarachand (Indian) Of the silver star
Tarachande

Tarafah (Arabic) From the trees
Tarafa, Taraphah, Tarapha

Tarak (Indian) One who protects others
Tarac, Tarack

Taral (Indian) Resembling the honeybee
Tarall, Taralle

Taramandal (Indian) Of the Milky Way

Taran (Gaelic) Of the thunder
Taren, Taron, Tarin, Taryn, Tarun

Taranga (Indian) Of the waves

Tarasios (Greek) Man of Tarentum
Taraseos, Tarasio, Taraseo

Tardos (Hungarian) One who is bald
Tardus, Tardis, Tardys, Tardas

Taregan (Native American) Resembling a crane
Taregen, Taregon, Taregin, Taregyn

Tarhe (Native American) Having the strength of a tree
Tarhi, Tarhie, Tarhy, Tarhey, Tarhee, Tarhea

Tarif (Arabic) Unlike the others; one who is unique
Tarife, Taryf, Taryfe, Tareef, Tareefe, Tareif, Tareife, Tarief, Tariefe, Tareaf, Tareafe

Tarin (Gaelic) From the rocky hill
Taren, Taron, Taran, Taryn, Tarun

Tariq (Arabic) One who demands entry; of the morning star
Tarique, Tareek, Tarek, Tareq, Tarick, Tarik, Tareak, Tureeq, Tareaq, Taryq, Taryque

Tarit (Indian) Resembling lightning
Tarite, Tareet, Tareete, Tareat, Tareate, Taryt, Taryte

Tarjan (Hungarian) One who is honored

Tarleton (English) From the thunder town
Tarlton, Tarletown, Tarltown

Tarmon (Gaelic) From the church's land
Tarman, Tarmen, Tarmun, Tarmin, Tarmyn

Tarn (Norse) From the mountain pool

Taro (Japanese) The firstborn son; a big boy
Taroe

Tarquin (Latin) One who is impulsive
Tarquinn, Tarquinne, Tarquen, Tarquenn, Tarquenne, Tarquyn, Tarquynn, Tarquynne

Tarquin (Latin) A king
Tarquen, Tarquinn, Tarquinne, Tarquyn, Tarquynn, Tarquynne, Tarquenn, Tarquenne, Tarquinius, Tarquino, Tarquinus

Tarrant (Welsh) Son of thunder
Tarrent, Tarrint, Tarrynt, Tarront, Tarrunt

Tarrant (American) One who upholds the law
Tarrent, Tarrint, Tarrynt, Tarront, Tarrunt

Tarso (Italian) A dashing young man
Tarsio, Tarsiyo

Tarun (Indian) A youthful man
Taroun, Taroon, Tarune, Taroune, Taroone

Taruntapan (Indian) Born beneath the morning sun

Tashi (Tibetan) One who is prosperous
Tashie, Tashy, Tashey, Tashee, Tashea

Tashunka (Native American) One who loves horses
Tashunko, Tashunke, Tasunka, Tasunko, Tasunke

Tassilo (Scandinavian) A fearless defender
Tassillo, Tasilo, Tasillo

Tassos (Greek) A harvester
Tasso, Tassus, Tassu, Tasses

Tatankamimi (Native American) Resembling a walking buffalo

Tate (English) A cheerful man; one who brings happiness to others
Tayt, Tayte, Tait, Taite, Taet, Taete

Tatonga (Native American) Resembling a deer

Tatry (English) From the mountain in Poland
Tatrey, Tatri, Tatrie, Tatree, Tatrea

Tau (African) Resembling a lion

Taurus (Latin) The bull; the second sign of the zodiac
Taurean, Taurino, Tauro, Toro, Taurinus, Taurin

Tausiq (Indian) One who provides strong backing
Tauseeq, Tauseaq, Tausik, Tauseek, Tauseak

Tavaris (American) Of misfortune; a hermit
Tavarius, Tavaress, Tavarious, Tavariss, Tavarous, Tevarus, Tavorian, Tavarian, Tavorien, Tavarien

Tavas (Hebrew) Resembling a peacock

Taverner (English) One who keeps a tavern
Tavener, Tavenner, Tavernier, Tavernar, Tavenar

Tavi (Aramaic) A good man
Tavie, Tavy, Tavey, Tavee, Tavea

Tavin (German) Form of Gustav, meaning "of the staff of the gods"
Tavyn, Taven, Tavan, Tavon, Tavun, Tava, Tave

Tavio (Spanish) Form of Octavio, meaning "the eighth-born child"
Taviyo, Taveo, Taveyo

Tavish (Scottish / Irish) A twin / from the hillside
Tavishe, Tavysh, Tavyshe, Tavis, Tevis, Tavi, Tavie, Tavee, Tavea, Tavy, Tavey

Tavon (American) An outdoorsy man; lover of nature
Tavion, Taveon

Tawa (Native American) Born beneath the sun
Tawah

Tawagahe (Native American) One who builds
Tawagahi, Tawagahie, Tawagahy, Tawagahey, Tawagahee, Tawagahea

Tawanima (Native American) One who tries to measure the sun
Tawaneema, Tawaneama, Tawanyma, Tawanema

Taweel (Arabic) A tall man
Taweil, Taweal, Taweyl, Tawil, Tawl

Tawfiq (Arabic) One who is successful
Tawfeeq, Tawfeaq, Tawfyq

Tawno (American) A man of small stature
Tawnio, Tawniyo

Tay (Scottish) From the river
Taye, Tae, Tai

Tayib (Arabic) A good man
Tayeeb, Tayibe, Tayeebe, Tayeib, Tayeibe, Tayieb, Tayiebe, Tayeab, Tayeabe, Tayyib

❀ **Taylor** (English) One who alters garments
Tailer, Tailor, Tayler, Taelor, Taeler, Taylan, Taylon, Tayson

Taymullah (Arabic) A servant of God
Taemullah, Taimullah, Taymulla, Taemulla, Taimulla

Taysir (Arabic) One who helps others
Taysire, Taesir, Taesire, Taisir, Taisire, Taysyr, Taesyr, Taisyr

Tayton (American) A bringer of happiness
Tayten, Taytin, Teytan, Teyten, Teytin, Teyton

Taz (American) Man from Tasmania
Tazz, Tazze, Tazman, Tazzman, Tasman

Teagan (Gaelic) A handsome man
Teegan, Teygan, Tegan, Teigan

Teague (Gaelic) A wise poet
Tadhg, Teagam, Tegan, Teger, Teigan, Teige, Teigen, Teigue, Teeg, Teege, Teag, Teage, Teaghue, Tighe, Tadleigh, Taidghin, Tag

Teal (American) Having greenish-blue eyes
Teale, Teel, Teele

Tearlach (Scottish) Having great strength
Tearloch

Techoslav (Native American) One who provides comfort to others

Tecumseh (Native American) A traveler; resembling a shooting star
Tekumseh, Tecumse, Tekumse

Ted (English) Form of Theodore, meaning "a gift from God"
Tedd, Teddy, Teddi, Teddie, Teddee, Teddea, Teddey, Tedric, Tedrick, Tedric

Tedmund (English) A protector of the land
Tedmunde, Tedmond, Tedmonde, Tedman, Theomund, Theomond, Theomunde, Theomonde

Teetonka (Native American) One who talks too much
Teitonka, Tietonka, Teatonka, Teytonka

Teferi (African) A ferocious man; feared by his enemies
Teferie, Tefery, Teferey, Teferee, Teferea

Tefo (African) One who pays his debts

Tegene (African) My protector
Tegeen, Tegeene, Tegean, Tegeane

Teiji (Japanese) One who is righteous
Teijo

Teilo (Welsh) A saintly man

Teithi (Celtic) In mythology, the son of Gwynham
Teethi, Teithie, Teethie, Teithy, Teethy, Teithey, Teethey, Teithee, Teethee

Tejano (Spanish) Man from Texas
Tejanio, Tejaniyo

Tejas (Indian) A lustrous man; brilliance; splendor
Tejus, Tejes

Tejomay (Hindi) A glorious woman
Tejomaye, Tejomae, Tejomai

Teka (African) He has replaced

Tekeshi (Japanese) Formidable and brave man
Tekeshie, Tekeshy, Tekeshey, Tekeshee, Tekeshea

Tekle (African) The fruit of my seed
Tekli, Teklie, Tekly, Tekley, Teklee, Teklea

Tekonsha (Native American) Resembling a caribou
Tekonsho

Telamon (Greek) In mythology, the father of Ajax
Telemon, Telimon, Telomon, Telumon

Telemachus (Greek) In mythology, the son of Penelope and Odysseus
Telamachus, Telemakus, Telamakus, Telemechus, Telamechus, Telemekus, Telamekus

Telford (French) One who works with iron
Telforde, Telfer, Telfor, Telfour, Tellfer, Tellfour, Tellford, Tellforde, Taillefer, Telek

Tellan (Anglo-Saxon) One who considers his decisions
Tellen, Tellun, Tellon, Tellin, Tellyn

Teller (English) One who tells stories
Tellar, Tellor, Tellir, Tellur, Tellyr

Telly (Greek) The wisest man
Telley, Tellee, Tellea, Telli, Tellie

Tem (English) A man from the country

Temani (Hebrew) Man from the south
Temanie, Temany, Temaney, Temanee, Temanea, Teman, Temeni, Temenie, Temeny, Temeney, Temenee, Temenea

Temman (Anglo-Saxon) One who has been tamed

Tempest (French) One who is stormy; turbulent
Tempesto, Tempeste, Tempestio, Tempestt, Tempist, Tempiste, Tempisto

Temple (Latin) From the sacred place
Tempel, Templar, Templer, Templo

Templeton (English) From the town near the temple
Templetown, Templeten, Tempeltun, Tempelton, Tempelten

Tempo (Italian) A keeper of time

Tenchi (Japanese) Of heaven and earth
Tenchie, Tenchy, Tenchey, Tenchee, Tenchea

Tendoy (Native American) One who climbs higher
Tendoye, Tendoi

Tene (African) One who is much loved

Teneangopte (Native American) Resembling a high-flying bird

Teneil (American) Form of Neil, meaning "the champion"
Teneile, Teneal, Teneale, Teneel, Teneele

Tenen (African) Born on a Monday

Teng (Greek) A well-known warrior
Tenge

Tennant (English) One who rents
Tennent, Tenant, Tenent

Tennessee (Native American) From the state of Tennessee
Tenese, Tenesee, Tenessee, Tennese, Tennesee, Tennesse

Tennyson (English) Son of Dennis
Tennison, Tenneson, Tenny, Tenni, Tennie, Tennee, Tennea, Tenney

Teo (Spanish) A godly man
Teyo

Teom (African) One of twins

Teon (Anglo-Saxon) One who harms others

Teoxihuitl (Aztec) As precious as turquoise

Tepiltzin (Aztec) Born to privelege

Teppo (Hebrew) A victorious man

Terach (Hebrew) Resembling a wild goat
Terah, Terrah

Terciero (Spanish) The third-born child
Terceiro, Tercyero, Terceyero

Terence (Latin) From an ancient Roman clan
Tarrants, Tarrance, Tarrence, Tarrenz, Terencio, Terrance, Terrence, Terrey, Terri, Terris, Terrious, Terrius, Terry, Terrey, Terree, Terrea, Terronce, Terenge

Teris (Irish) The son of Terence
Terys, Teriss, Teryss, Terris, Terrys, Terriss, Terryss

Tern (Latin) Resembling a marine bird
Terne

Terran (English) Man of the earth
Terrin, Terren, Terryn, Terrun

Terrell (French / German) One who is stubborn / a powerful man
Tarrall, Terell, Terrall, Terrel, Terrelle, Terrill, Terryal, Terryl, Terryll, Tirrell, Tyrell, Tyrel, Tyrelle, Tyrrel, Tyrrell

Terrian (American) One who is strong and ambitious
Terrien, Terriun, Terriyn

Terron (English) Form of Terence, meaning "from an ancient Roman clan"
Tarran, Tarren, Tarrin, Tarron, Tarryn, Teron, Teran

Terryal (American) One who harvests
Terrial, Terryall, Terriall

Tertius (Greek) The third-born child

Teryysone (English) The son of Terrell
Terryysone, Terrysone, Terysone

Tesar (Czech) One who works with wood

Tesfaye (African) Our hope
Tesfay, Tesfai, Tesfae

Tesher (Hebrew) A gift from God

Teshi (African) One who is full of laughter
Teshie, Teshy, Teshey, Teshee, Teshea

Teshombe (American) An able-bodied man
Teshomb

Tessema (African) One to whom people listen

Tet (Vietnamese) Born on New Year's

Teteny (Hungarian) A chieftain

Teva (Hebrew) A natural man
Tevah

Tevaughn (American) Resembling a tiger
Tevan, Tevaughan, Tivaughn, Tivaughan, Tevaun, Tevawn

Tevel (Hebrew) One who is dearly loved
Tevell, Tevele, Tevelle

Tevey (Hebrew) A good man
Tevy, Tevi, Tevie, Tevee, Tevea

Tevin (American) Son of Kevin
Tevyn, Tevan, Teven, Tevinn, Tevonn

Tevis (American) One who is flamboyant
Tevas, Teviss, Tevys, Tevyss

Tewodros (African) Form of Theodore, meaning "a gift from God"

Tex (American) Man from Texas
Texx, Texan, Texon, Texun, Texen

Texas (Native American) One of many friends; from the state of Texas
Texus, Texis, Texes, Texos, Texys

Teyrnon (Celtic) A regal man
Teirnon, Tayrnon, Tairnon, Taernon, Tiarchnach, Tiarnach

Thabiti (African) A real man
Thabitie, Thabity, Thabitey, Thabitee, Thabitea, Thabit, Thabyt

Thabo (African) Filled with happiness

Thackary (English) Form of Zachary, meaning "the Lord remembers"
Thackery, Thakary, Thakery, Thackari, Thackarie, Thackarey, Thackaree, Thackarea, Thackerey, Thackeree, Thackerea, Thackeri, Thackerie

Thaddeus (Aramaic) Having heart
Tad, Tadd, Taddeo, Taddeusz, Thad, Thadd, Thaddaios, Thaddaos, Thaddaeus, Thaddaus, Thaddius, Thadeus, Thady, Thaddy, Thaddeaus

Thai (Vietnamese) Man from Thailand

Thakur (Indian) A godly leader
Thackur

Than (Vietnamese) A brilliant man
Thann

Thandiwe (African) One who is dearly loved
Thandie, Thandi, Thandy, Thandey, Thandee, Thandea

Thane (English) One who owns land
Thayn, Thayne, Thain, Thaine, Thaen, Thaene, Theyn, Theyn

Thang (Vietnamese) One who is victorious

Thanh (Vietnamese) One who is accomplished

Thanos (Greek) One who is noble and praiseworthy
Thanasis, Thanasos

Thanus (American) One who owns land

Thao (Vietnamese) One who is courteous

Thaqib (Arabic) Resembling a shooting star
Thaqeeb, Thaqeab, Thaqyb, Thaqieb, Thaqeib

Thatcher (English) One who fixes roofs
Thacher, Thatch, Thatche, Thaxter, Thacker, Thaker, Thackere, Thakere

Thaw (English) The process of melting
Thawe, Thawain, Thawayne, Thawaine, Thawaen, Thawaene, Thawayn

Thayer (Teutonic) Of the nation's army

Thelred (English) One who receives good counsel
Thelread, Thellred, Thellread

Themba (African) One who is trustworthy
Thembah

Thembalwethu (African) Our hope

Theobald (German) Of the courageous and bold people
Teobaldo, Thebault, Thibaud, Thibault, Thibaut, Tibold, Tiebold, Tiebout, Tybald, Tybalt, Tybault, Theobold, Thieny, Tibbot, Tibalt, Tibault, Tihalt, Tihault, Tyhalt, Tyhault

Theodore (Greek) A gift from God
Teador, Teodoor, Teodor, Teodoro, Theo, Theodon, Theodor, Theodorus, Theodosios, Theodosius, Todo, Tedor, Theodis, Tudor, Tedros, Teyo

Theodoric (German) The power of the people
Teodorico, Thedric, Thedrick, Theodorik, Theodric, Theodrik, Thedrik, Thierry, Thierri, Thierrey, Thierree, Thierrea

Theon (French) An untamed man
Theone

Theophilus (Greek) One who is loved by God
Teofil, Teofilo, Theofil, Theofilo, Théophile, Theophil, Theophilos

Theron (Greek) A great hunter
Therron, Tharon, Theon, Tharron

Theseus (Greek) In mythology, hero who slew the Minotaur
Thesius, Thesyus

Thialfi (Norse) In mythology, a servant of Thor
Thialfie, Thialfy, Thialfey, Thialfee, Thialfea

Thiassi (Scandinavian) A crafty man
Thiassie, Thiassy, Thiassey, Thiassee, Thiassea

Thierry (French) A ruler of the people
Thierrey, Thierree, Thierrea, Thierri, Thierrie, Thiery, Thierey, Thieri, Thierie, Thieree, Thierea

Thimba (African) One who hunts lions
Thymba, Thimbah, Thymbah

Thinh (Vietnamese) A prosperous man

Tho (Vietnamese) Having a long life

❂ **Thomas** (Aramaic) One of twins
Tam, Tamas, Tamhas, Thom, Thoma, Thomason, Thomson, Thompson, Tomas, Tomaso, Tomasso, Tomasz, Tome, Tomek, Tommie, Tommey, Tomislaw, Tommaso, Thomkins, Tom, Tommy, Tuomas, Tomik, Tomo, Tomos, Tamasine, Tamnais

Thor (Norse) In mythology, god of thunder
Thorian, Thorin, Thorsson, Thorvald, Tor, Tore, Turo, Thorrin, Thors, Thour

Thorald (Norse) Follower of Thor
Thorualdr, Torald, Thorauld, Torauld, Thorold, Torold, Thoreau, Thoraux, Thorer, Thorvald, Thorvauld, Thorvid

Thoraldtun (English) From Thor's esate
Thoraldton, Thoraldten, Thoraldtan

Thorbert (Norse) Shining with the glory of Thor
Thorbiartr, Thorberte, Thorbierte, Torbert

Thorburn (Norse) Thor's bear
Thorburne, Thorbern, Thorberne, Thorbjorn, Thorbjorne, Torbjorn, Torborg, Torben, Torbern, Torburn

Thorer (Scandinavian) A great warrior

Thorley (English) From Thor's meadow
Thorly, Thorlee, Thorli, Thorlie, Thorleigh, Thorlea, Thurley, Thurly, Thurleigh, Thurlee, Thurlea, Thurleah, Thurli, Thurlie, Torley, Torly, Torli, Torlie, Torlee, Torlea, Torleigh

Thormond (Norse) Protected by Thor
Thormonde, Thormund, Thormunde, Thurmond, Thurmonde, Thurmund, Thurmunde, Thormun, Thurmun, Thorman, Thurman, Thormon, Thurmon, Therman

Thorndike (English) From the thorny embankment
Thorndyke, Thorndik, Thorndyk, Thorndic, Thorndyc, Thomdic, Thomdik, Thomdike, Thomdyke

Thorne (English) From the thorn bush
Thorn

Thornley (English) From the thorny meadow
Thornly, Thornlee, Thornleigh, Thornli, Thornlie, Thornlea

Thornton (English) From the town of thorn bushes
Thorntown, Thorntun, Thornten, Thorntan

Thornycroft (English) From the field of thorn bushes
Thornicroft, Thorneycroft, Thorniecroft, Thorneecroft, Thorneacroft

Thorolf (Norse) Thor's wolf
Thorulf, Thorolfe, Thorulfe, Torolf, Torulf, Torolfe, Torulfe

Thorpe (English) From the village
Thorp

Thrythwig (English) A warrior of great strength
Thrythwyg, Thrythweg

Thu (Vietnamese) Born during the autumn

Thuan (Vietnamese) One who is tamed
Thuann

Thuc (Vietnamese) One who is alert and aware
Tinh

Thunder (English) One with a temper

Thuong (Vietnamese) One who loves tenderly

Thurgood (English) An upstanding man
Thurgoode, Thergood, Thergoode

Thurl (Irish) From the strong fortress
Thurle, Therl, Therle

Thurlow (English) From Thor's hill
Thurlowe, Thurlo, Thurloe, Thurhloew, Thurloew

Thurston (English) From Thor's town; Thor's stone
Thorston, Thorstan, Thorstein, Thorsten, Thurstain, Thurstan, Thursten, Torsten, Torston, Thurstun, Thurstin

Thuy (Vietnamese) One who is kind

Thwaite (Scandinavian) From the fenced-in pasture
Thwait, Thwayt, Thwayte, Thwate, Thwaet, Thwaete

Tiago (Spanish) A courageous man
Tyago

Tiassale (African) It has been forgotten

Tiberio (Italian) From the Tiber river
Tibero, Tyberio, Tybero, Tiberius, Tiberios, Tyberius, Tyberios

Tibor (Slavic) From the sacred place

Tiburon (Spanish) Resembling a shark

Tien (Vietnamese) The first and foremost

Tiernan (Gaelic) Lord of the manor
Tiarnan, Tiarney, Tierney, Tierny, Tiernee, Tiernea, Tierni, Tiernie, Tiarny, Tiarnee, Tiarnea, Tiarni, Tiarnie, Tyernan, Tyrnan, Tier, Tighearnach

Tiger (American) As powerful as the animal
Tyger, Tigre, Tygre, Tige, Tigris, Tigur, Tygur

Tihamér (Hungarian) A quiet boy; one who enjoys silence

Tihkoosue (Native American) A man of short stature
Tikoosue, Tihkousue, Tikousue

T'iis (Native American) Of the cottonwood
Tiis

Tilak (Hindi) A great leader
Tylak, Tilac, Tylac, Tilack, Tylack

Tilden (English) From the fertile valley
Tillden, Tildon, Tilldon, Tildan, Tilldan, Tildin, Tilldin, Tildun, Tilldun, Tiladene

Tilford (English) From the fertile ford
Tilforde, Tillford, Tillforde

Tilian (Anglo-Saxon) One who strives to better himself
Tilien, Tiliun, Tilion

Till (German) Form of Theodoric, meaning "the power of the people"
Tille, Tilly, Tilley, Tilli, Tillie, Tillee, Tillea

Tillery (German) A great leader
Tillerey, Tilleri, Tillerie, Tilleree, Tillerea

Tilman (English) One who plows the earth
Tillman, Tilmann, Tilghman

Tilon (Hebrew) A generous man
Tilen, Tilan, Tilun, Tilin, Tilyn

Tilton (English) From the fertile estate
Tillton, Tilten, Tillten, Tiltan, Tilltan, Tiltin, Tilltin, Tiltun, Tilltun

Timeus (Greek) The perfect man

Timir (Indian) Born in the darkness
Timirbaran

Timon (Greek) A respected man
Tymon

Timothy (Greek) One who honors God
Tim, Timmo, Timmy, Timmothy, Timmy, Timo, Timofei, Timofeo, Timofey, Timoteo, Timothé, Timotheo, Timothey, Timotheus, Tymmothy, Tymoteusz, Tymothy, Timin, Timotheos, Timoleon

Timur (African) One who is timid

Tin (Vietnamese) A great thinker

Tinashe (African) One who is with the Lord
Tinashi, Tinashie, Tinashee, Tinashea, Tinashy, Tinashey

Tinks (American) One who is coy
Tynks, Tincks, Tyncks, Tink, Tinke, Tinki, Tinkie, Tinkee, Tinkea, Tinkey, Tinky

Tino (Italian) A man of small stature
Teeno, Tieno, Teino, Teano, Tyno

Tinotenda (African) One who is thankful

Tinsley (English) A sociable man
Tinsly, Tinsli, Tinslie, Tinslee, Tinslea

Tintagel (English) In Arthurian legend, the birthplace of Arthur
Tentagel, Tintagil, Tentagil

Tip (American) Form of Thomas, meaning "one of twins"
Tipp, Tipper, Tippy, Tippee, Tippea, Tippey, Tippi, Tippie

Tipu (Indian) Resembling a tiger
Tipoo, Tipou, Tippu, Tippoo, Tippou

Tiru (Hindi) A pious man
Tyru, Tirue, Tyrue

Tirumala (Hindi) From the sacred hills

Tisa (African) The ninth-born child
Tisah, Tysa, Tysah

Titus (Greek / Latin) Of the giants / a great defender
Tito, Titos, Tytus, Tytos, Titan, Tytan, Tyto

Titusz (Hungarian) Resembling a dove
Tytusz

Tivadar (Hungarian) A gift from God
Tivadarr, Tyvadar, Tyvadarr

Tivon (Hebrew) One who loves nature
Tyvon

Tjasse (Norse) In mythology, a giant

Toa (Polynesian) A brave-hearted woman

Toafo (Polynesian) One who is spontaneous

Toai (Vietnamese) One who is content

Toal (Irish) One who is deeply rooted
Toale

Toan (Vietnamese) One who is safe
Toane

Tobbar (American) An active man

Tobechukwu (African) One who praises God

Tobias (Hebrew) The Lord is good
Thobey, Thobie, Thoby, Tobe, Tobee, Tobey, Tobi, Tobia, Tobiah, Tobie, Tobin, Tobit, Toby, Tobyn, Tobyas, Tohias, Tohy, Tohey, Tohee, Tohea, Tohi, Tohie, Tobes

Tobikuma (Japanese) Resembling a cloud

Tobrecan (Anglo-Saxon) A destroyer
Tolucan, Tobrucan, Tolecan

Tocho (Native American) Resembling a mountain lion
Tochio, Tochiyo

Tochtli (Aztec) Resembling a rabbit
Tochtlie, Tochtly, Tochtley, Tochtlee, Tochtlea

Todd (English) Resembling a fox
Tod

Todhunter (English) One who hunts foxes
Toddhunter

Todor (Bulgarian) A gift from God
Todos, Todros

Toft (English) From the small farm
Tofte

Togquos (Native American) One of twins

Tohon (Native American) One who loves the water

Tohopka (Native American) Resembling a wild beast

Tokala (Native American) Resembling a fox
Tokalo

Toki (Japanese) Filled with hope
Tokie, Toky, Tokey, Tokee, Tokea

Toks (American) A carefree man

Tokutaro (Japanese) A virtuous son

Tolan (Anglo-Saxon / American) From the taxed land / one who is studious
Tolen, Toland, Tolande, Tolend, Tolende, Tollan, Tolland

Tolek (Polish) A gift from God
Toleck, Tolec

Tolfe (American) An outgoing man

Toli (Spanish) One who ploughs the earth
Tolie, Toly, Toley, Tolee, Tolea

Tolman (English) One who collects taxes
Tollman, Toleman, Tolmann

Tolomey (French) One who plans
Tolomy, Tolomee, Tolomea, Tolomi, Tolomie

Toltecatl (Aztec) An artist

Tomaj (Hungarian) Of an ancient clan

Tomeo (Japanese) One who is cautious
Tomeyo

Tomer (Hebrew) A man of tall stature
Tomar, Tomur, Tomir, Tomor, Tomyr

Tomi (Japanese / African) A wealthy man / of the people
Tomie, Tomee, Tomea, Tomy, Tomey

Tomlin (English) Little Tom; son of Tom; the smaller of twins
Tomalin, Tomlinson, Tomkin, Tompkin, Tompkins, Tompkinson, Tomkinson

Tomochichi (Hawaiian) One who seeks the truth
Tomocheechee, Tomochychy

Tonauac (Aztec) One who possesses the light

Tong (Vietnamese) Having a pleasant fragrance
Tonge

Tony (English) Form of Anthony, meaning "a flourishing man; from an ancient Roman family"
Toney, Tonee, Tonea, Toni, Tonie, Tonio, Tonye, Tonion

Tooantuh (Native American) Resembling a spring frog
Tooantu, Touantuh, Touantu

Toopweets (Native American) Having great strength
Toupweets, Toopwets, Toupwets

Topher (Greek) Form of Christopher, meaning "one who bears Christ inside"
Toffer, Tofer

Topper (English) From the hill

Topwe (American) A jovial man
Topweh

Torao (Japanese) Resembling a tiger

Torcall (Norse) One who has been summoned by Thor
Thorcall, Torcalle, Thorcalle, Torcal, Thorcal

Tord (Dutch) One who is peaceful
Torde

Torger (Norse) The power of Thor's spear
Thorger, Torgar, Thorgar, Terje, Therje

Torgny (Scandinavian) The sound of weaponry
Torgnie, Torgni, Torgney, Torgnee, Torgnea

Torht (Anglo-Saxon) A bright man
Torhte

Toribio (Spanish) Having great strength
Toribo, Toribiyo

Toril (Hindi) One who has a temper
Torill, Torril, Torrill, Torile, Torille, Torrille

Torin (Celtic) One who acts as chief
Toran, Torean, Toren, Torion, Torran, Torrian, Toryn

Torio (Japanese) Resembling a bird's tail
Toriyo, Torrio, Torriyo

Tormaigh (Irish) Having the spirit of Thor
Tormey, Tormay, Tormaye, Tormai, Tormae

Tormod (Gaelic) A man from the north

Toro (Spanish) Resembling a bull

Torquil (Gaelic) Thor's helmet
Thirkell, Thorkel, Torkel, Torkill, Torquill, Thorquil, Thorquill, Thorkill

Torr (English) From the tower
Torre

Torrence (Gaelic) From the little hills
Torence, Torrance, Torrens, Torrans, Toran, Torran, Torrin, Torn, Torne

Torry (Norse / Gaelic) Refers to Thor / form of Torrence, meaning "from the little hills"
Torrey, Torree, Torrea, Torri, Torrie, Tory, Torey, Tori, Torie, Toree, Torea

Toru (Japanese) Man of the sea

Toshan (Indian) One who is satisfied
Toshann

Toshi (Japanese) One who sees his true image
Toshie, Toshy, Toshey, Toshee, Toshea

Toshiro (Japanese) One who is talented and intelligent
Toshihiro

Toshith (Indian) Filled with happiness
Toshithe, Toshyth, Toshythe

Tostig (English) A well-known earl
Tostyg

Tosya (Russian) One who exceeds expectations
Tosiya, Tusya, Tusiya

Tototl (Aztec) Resembling a bird

Toussaint (French) All saints
Toussnint, Toussaent, Toussanynt, Toussant

Toviel (Hebrew) The Lord is good
Toviell, Toviele, Tovielle, Tovi, Tovie, Tovee, Tovea, Tovy, Tovey, Tov, Tova, Tove

Towley (English) From the town near the meadow
Towly, Towleigh, Towlee, Towlea, Towleah, Towli, Towlie, Townly, Townley, Townlee, Townleigh, Townlea, Townleah, Townli, Townlie

Townsend (English) From the end of town
Townsand, Tonsend, Tonsand

Toyo (Japanese) A man of plenty

Tracy (Gaelic) One who is warlike
Tracey, Traci, Tracie, Tracee, Tracea, Treacy, Trace, Tracen, Treacey, Treaci, Treacie, Treacee, Treacea

Trahan (English) A handsome man
Trahahn, Trahain, Trahaine, Trahaen, Trahaene, Trahane, Trahen

Trahern (Welsh) As strong as iron
Trahayarn, Trahearn, Trahearne, Traherne, Trahaearn

Traigh (Irish) A strand

Trail (English) A lover of nature
Traill, Traile, Trayl, Trayle, Trael, Traele, Trale

Trailokva (Indian) Of the three worlds
Trailokvya, Traelokva, Traelokvya, Traylokva, Traylokvya

Trang (Vietnamese) One who is honored

Tranter (English) A wagoneer
Trantir, Trantar, Trantor, Trantur, Trantyr

Trapper (American) One who traps animals
Trappar, Trappor, Trappir, Trappyr, Trappur

Traugott (German) One who has faith in God
Trawgott, Traugot, Trawgot

Travis (French) To cross over
Travys, Traver, Travers, Traviss, Trevis, Trevys, Travus, Traves

Travon (American) At the crossroads; a traveler
Travaughn, Traveon, Travion, Trayvon, Travoun, Travawn

Treadway (English) Having the strength of a warrior
Treadwai, Treadwaye, Treadwae, Tredway, Tredwaye, Tredwai, Tredwae

Treasach (Irish) A mighty fighter
Treasaigh, Treasigh

Tredan (Anglo-Saxon) One who tramples others
Treden, Tredin, Tredon, Tredun, Tredyn

Treddian (Anglo-Saxon) One who leaves
Treddien, Treddion, Treddiun

Treffen (German) One who socializes
Treffan, Treffin, Treffon, Treffyn, Treffun

Tremain (Celtic) From the town built of stone
Tramain, Tramaine, Tramayne, Tremaine, Tremayne, Tremaen, Tremaene, Tramaen, Tramaene, Tremane, Tramane

Tremont (French) From the three mountains
Tremonte, Tremount, Tremounte

Trennen (German) Of the divided people
Trennon, Trennan, Trennin, Trennun, Trennyn

Trent (Latin) From the rushing waters
Trente, Trint, Trinte, Trynt, Trynte

Trenton (English) From the town near the rapids; from Trent's town
Trenten, Trentin, Trentyn

Treoweman (English) A loyal man
Treowe

Tretan (German) One who walks
Treten, Tretun, Treton, Tretyn, Tretin

Trevelian (Welsh) From the house of Elian
Trevelien, Trevelyan, Trevelyen

Trevet (Gaelic) From the three hills
Trevett, Trevete, Trevette

Trevin (English) From the fair town
Trevan, Treven, Trevian, Trevion, Trevon, Trevyn, Trevonn

Trevor (Welsh) From the large village
Trefor, Trevar, Trever, Treabhar, Treveur, Trevir, Trevur

Trevrizent (English) In Arthurian legend, Percival's uncle

Trey (English) The third-born child
Tre, Trai, Trae, Tray, Traye, Trayton, Treyton, Trayson, Treyson

Triage (French) One who handles emergencies

Trigg (Norse) One who is truthful
Trygg

Tripp (English) A traveler
Trip, Trypp, Tryp, Tripper, Trypper

Tripsy (American) One who enjoys dancing
Tripsey, Tripsee, Tripsea, Tripsi, Tripsie

● **Tristan** (Celtic) A sorrowful man; in Arthurian legend, a knight of the Round Table
Trystan, Tris, Tristam, Tristen, Tristian, Tristin, Triston, Tristram, Tristyn, Triste

Trocky (American) A manly man
Trockey, Trocki, Trockie, Trockee, Trockea

Trond (Norse) A growing man
Tronde

Trong (Vietnamese) One who is respected

Trory (American) The red one
Trorey, Troree, Trorea, Trori, Trorie

Trowbridge (English) From the bridge near the tree
Trowbrydge, Trowhridge, Treowbrycg

Troy (Gaelic) Son of a footsoldier
Troye, Troi

Troyes (French) A man with curly hair

True (American) One who is honest
Tru, Trew, Truit, Truitt, Truitte

Truesdale (English) From the valley of the honest man
Trusdale, Truesdayle, Trusdayle, Truesdail, Trusdail, Truesdaele, Trusdaele, Truesdayl, Trusdayl, Truesdaile, Trusdaile, Truesdael, Trusdael, Truesdell, Trusdell, Truitestall, Trudell, Trudel, Trudelle

Truman (English) One who is loyal
Trueman, Trumann, Trumain, Trumaine, Trumaen, Trumaene, Trumayn, Trumayne, Trumen

Trumbald (English) A bold man
Trumbold, Trumbalde, Trumbolde

Trumble (English) One who is powerful
Trumball, Trumbell, Trumbo, Trumbull

Trumhall (English) Having great strength
Trumhal, Trumhale, Trumhail, Trumhaile, Trumhayl, Trumhayle, Trumhael, Trumhaele

Trung (Vietnamese) One who is centrally located

Truong (Turkish) From the field near the school

Trygg (Scandinavian) One who speaks the truth

Trygve (Norse) One who wins with bravery

Trymian (Anglo-Saxon) One who encourages others
Trymyan, Trymien, Trymyen

Trymman (Anglo-Saxon) One who strengthens others

Tsalani (African) One who leaves
Tsalanie, Tsalany, Tsalaney, Tsalanee, Tsalanea

Tsatoke (Native American) One who hunts on horseback

Tse (Native American) As solid as a rock

Tsela (Native American) Resembling a star

Tsidhqiyah (Hebrew) The Lord is just
Tsidqiyah, Tsidhqiya, Tsdqiya

Tsiishch'ili (Native American) One who has curly hair

Tsin (Native American) One who rides a horse
Tsen, Tsyn

Tsoai (Native American) As big as a tree

Tsubasa (Japanese) A winged being
Tsubasah, Tsubase, Tsubaseh

Tsvetan (Bulgarian) Refers to Palm Sunday

Tu (Vietnamese) One who is quick-minded

Tuan (Vietnamese) A gentleman

Tuari (Native American) Resembling a young eagle
Tuarie, Tuary, Tuarey, Tuaree, Tuarea

Tucker (English) One who makes garments
Tuker, Tuckerman, Tukerman, Tuck, Tuckman, Tukman, Tuckere, Toukere

Tucson (Native American) From the city in Arizona
Tooson, Touson

Tuesday (English) Born on a Tuesday
Tewsday, Tuesdai, Tewsdai, Tuesdae, Tewsdae, Tuesdaye, Tewsdaye

Tufan (Indian) Resembling a tempest
Tufann, Tuphan, Tuphann

Tuhin (Indian) Of the snow
Tuhine, Tuhyn, Tuhyne

Tuhinsurra (Indian) As white as snow
Tuhinsura, Tuhynsurra, Tuhynsura

Tuketu (Native American) Resembling a running bear
Tuketue, Tuketoo, Tuketou, Telutci, Telutcie, Telutcy, Telutcey, Telutcee, Telutki, Telutkie, Telutky, Telutkey, Telukee

Tukuli (American) Resembling a caterpillar
Tukulie, Tukuly, Tukuley, Tukulee, Tukulea

Tulasidas (Hindi) One who is devoted to Tulasi

Tulio (Spanish) A lively man
Tuliyo, Tullio, Tulliyo

Tully (Gaelic) Of the mighty people
Tulley, Tulli, Tullie, Tullee, Tullea, Tulleigh, Tullis

Tulsi (Indian) A holy man
Tulsie, Tulsy, Tulsey, Tulsee, Tulsea

Tumaini (African) An optimist
Tumainie, Tumainee, Tumainy, Tumainey, Tumayni, Tumaynie, Tumaynee, Tumayney, Tumayny, Tumaeni, Tumaenie, Tumaenee, Tumaeny, Tumaeney

Tumbura (Indian) Resembling a celestial being
Tumburra

Tumo (African) A famous man
Tummo

Tumu (American) Resembling a deer
Tummu

Tunde (African) One who returns
Tundi, Tundie, Tundee, Tundea, Tundy, Tundey

Tune (English) One who plays melodies
Toon, Toone, Toun, Toune

Tung (Vietnamese) Resembling the coniferous tree
Tunge

Tunleah (English) From the town near the meadow
Tunlea, Tunleigh, Tunly, Tunley, Tunlee, Tunli, Tunlie

Tupac (African) A messenger warrior
Tupack, Tupoc, Tupock

Tupi (Native American) To pull up
Tupie, Tupee, Tupea, Tupy, Tupey

Tupper (English) One who herds rams
Tuper, Tuppere, Tupere

Turbo (Latin) Resembling a spinning object

Turfeinar (Norse) In mythology, the son of Rognvald
Turfaynar, Turfaenar, Turfanar, Turfenar, Turfainar

Turi (Spanish) Resembling a bear
Turie, Turee, Turea, Tury, Turey, Turio

Turk (English) A man from Turkey
Turck, Turc

Turner (English) One who works with wood
Turnar, Turnir, Turnyr, Turnor, Turnur, Tournour

Tushar (Indian) Of the snow
Tusharr, Tushare

Tusharsuvra (Indian) As white as snow

Tusita (Chinese) One who is heaven-sent

Tut (Egyptian) A courageous man

Tutu (African) Man from the cliffs

Tuvya (Hebrew) The Lord is good
Tuvyah, Tov, Toviach, Tovyah, Toviah, Tuviyahu, Tutyahu

Tuwa (Native American) One who loves nature
Tuwah

Tuxford (Norse) From the spearman's ford
Tuxforde

Tuyen (Vietnamese) A heavenly messenger

Twain (English) One who is divided in two
Twaine, Twayn, Twayne, Twaen, Twaene, Twane, Twein, Tweine

Twitchel (English) One who lives on a narrow lane
Twitchele, Twitchell, Twitchelle

Twrgadarn (Welsh) From the strong tower

Twyford (English) From the double river crossing
Twiford, Twyforde, Twiforde

Txanton (Basque) Form of Anthony, meaning "a flourishing man; from an ancient Roman family"
Txantony, Txantoney, Txantonee, Txantoni, Txantonie, Txantonea

Txomin (Basque) A godly man

Tybalt (Latin) He who sees the truth
Tybault, Tybalte, Tybaulte

Tychon (Greek) One who is accurate
Tycho

Tye (English) From the fenced-in pasture
Tyg, Tyge, Tie, Tigh, Teyen

Tyee (Native American) A great chief
Tyea, Tyey, Tyi, Tyie

Tyeis (French) The son of a German

Tyfiell (English) Follower of the god Tyr
Tyfiel, Tyfielle, Tyfiele

Tygie (American) Full of energy
Tygi, Tygey, Tygy, Tygee, Tygea

Tyjah (African) One who is intelligent
Tyja

Tyke (Scandinavian) One who is determined
Tike

❍
❶ **Tyler** (English) A tiler of roofs
Tilar, Tylar, Tylor, Tiler, Tilor, Ty, Tyc, Tylere, Tylore

Tyme (English) The aromatic herb thyme
Time, Thyme, Thime

Tynan (Gaelic) One who is dark and dusty
Tienan, Tynell, Tynen, Tynin, Tynnen, Tynnin, Tynon

Tyne (English) From the river
Tyn, Tine

Typhoon (Chinese) Of the great wind
Tiphoon, Tyfoon, Tifoon, Typhoun, Tiphoun, Tyfoun, Tifoun

Tyr (Norse) In mythology, an ancient god

Tyree (American) One who is courteous
Tyry, Tyrey, Tyrea, Tyri, Tyrie, Tyrae

Tyreece (American) One who is combative
Tyreace, Tyriece, Tyreice, Tyrece, Tyreese, Tyrease, Tyriese, Tyreise, Tyrese, Tyryce, Tyryse

Tyrique (American) A defender of the people
Tyreeque, Tyreek, Tyreaque, Tyreak, Tyreeke, Tyreake, Tyriq, Tyreeq, Tyreaq, Tyreq, Tyreque

Tyrone (Gaelic) From Owen's land
Tirone, Tirohn, Tirown, Tyron, Tyronne, Turone

Tyrus (Latin) Man from the ancient city of Tyre
Tyris, Tyres, Tyros, Tyras, Tyrys

Tyson (French) One who is high-spirited; fiery
Thyssen, Tiesen, Tyce, Tycen, Tyeson, Tyssen, Tysen, Tysan, Tysun, Tysin, Tyesone

Tywysog (Welsh) Born to royalty; a prince

Tzadok (Hebrew) One who is just and fair
Tzadock, Tzadoc, Tzadoke, Tzadocke

Tzefanyahu (Hebrew) One who is treasured by God
Tzefanyahue, Tzefanyah, Tzefanya

Tzion (Hebrew) From the mountain
Tzionn, Tzionne

Tziyon (Hebrew) The son of Zion

Tzuriel (Hebrew) God is my strength
Tzuriell, Tzuriele, Tzurielle

Tzvi (Hebrew) Resembling a deer
Tzvie, Tzvy, Tzvey, Tzvee, Tzvea

u

U (Korean) A kind and gentle man

Uaid (Irish) Form of Walter, meaning "the commander of the army"
Uaide, Uayd, Uayde, Uade, Uaed, Uaede

Uaithne (Gaelic) One who is innocent; green
Uaithn, Uaythne, Uaythn, Uathne, Uathn, Uaethne, Uaethn

Ualan (Scottish) Form of Valentine, meaning "one who is strong and healthy"
Ualane, Ualayn, Ualayne, Ualen, Ualon

Ualtar (Irish) A strong warrior
Ualtarr, Ualter, Ualterr

Uba (African) One who is wealthy; lord of the house
Ubah, Ubba, Ubbah

Ubadah (Arabic) One who serves God
Ubada, Ubaidah, Ubaida, Ubaydah, Ubayda, Ubaeda, Ubaedah

Ubaid (Arabic) One who is faithful
Ubaide, Ubade, Ubayde, Ubayd, Ubaed, Ubaede

Ubel (German) An evil man
Ubell, Ubele, Ubul, Ubull, Ubule

Uberto (Italian) Form of Hubert, meaning "having a shining intellect"
Ulberto, Umberto

Uchdryd (Welsh) In mythology, the son of Erim
Uchdrid, Uchdred, Uchdried, Uchdreid, Uchdread

Uchechi (African) God's will be done
Uchechie, Uchechy, Uchechey, Uchechee, Uchechea, Uchi, Uchie, Uchee, Uchea, Uchy, Uchey

Udadhi (Indian) Man of the sea
Udadhie, Udadhy, Udadhey, Udadhea, Udadhee

Udank (Indian) In mythology, a sage
Udanke

Udar (Indian) A generous man
Udarr, Udarre, Udari, Udarie, Udary, Udarey, Udaree, Udarea

Udath (Indian) One who is noble
Udathe

Uday (Indian) Our son has arrived
Udaye, Udai, Udae

Udayachal (Indian) From the eastern hill
Udayachall, Udaiachal, Udaiachall

Udayachandra (Indian) Born with the rising moon
Udayachande

Udayan (Indian) One who is thriving
Udayen

Udayaravi (Indian) Born with the rising sun
Udayarvie, Udayarvy, Udayarvey, Udayarvee, Udayarvea

Udbhuddah (Indian) One who is blossoming
Udbhudda

Uddam (Indian) An exceptional man

Uddeepath (Indian) An illuminated man
Uddeepth, Uddeepthe, Udeepath, Udeepathe, Uddepath, Uddepathe

Uddhar (Indian) One who is free; an independent man
Uddharr, Udhar, Udharr

Uddhav (Hindi) In Hinduism, Krishna's friend
Uddhaav, Udhav, Udhaav

Udeh (Hebrew) One who praises God
Ude

Udell (English) From the valley of yew trees
Udale, Udel, Udall, Udayle, Udayl, Udail, Udaile, Udele, Udelle, Udael, Udaele

Udi (Hebrew) One who carries a torch
Udie, Udy, Udey, Udee, Udea

Udit (Indian) One who is thriving
Udite, Udyt, Udyte

Udo (German / African) One who is prosperous / one who is peaceful

Udolf (English) A prosperous wolf
Udolfo, Udulf, Udulfo, Udolph, Udolpho,
Udulph, Udulpho

Udup (Indian) Born beneath the moon's
light
Udupp, Uddup, Uddupp

Udyam (Indian) One who puts forth an
effort
Udiam, Udeam

Udyan (Indian) Of the garden
Uddyan, Udyann, Uddyann

Ueli (Swedish) Form of Ulrich, meaning
"having wealth and power"
Uelie, Uely, Ueley, Uelee, Uelea

Ufuk (Turkish) Of the horizon

Ugo (Italian) A great thinker

Ugutz (Basque) Refers to John the Baptist

Uigbiorn (Norse) A warrior bear
Ugbjorn, Ugbiorn, Ugbyorn, Uigbyorn,
Uigbjorn

Uilleag (Irish) Having a playful heart
Uileag, Uilleage, Uileage, Uylleag, Uyleag,
Uylleage, Uyleage

Uilleam (Scottish) Form of William, mean-
ing "the determined protector"
Uileam, Uilleame, Uileame, Uylleam,
Uylleame, Uyleam, Uyleame, Uilliam,
Uylliam

Uinseann (Irish) Form of Vincent, meaning
"one who prevails; the conquerer"
Uinsean, Uyseann, Uysean, Uinseane,
Uynseane, Uinseanne, Uynseanne

Uisdean (Scottish) From the stone island
Uisdeann, Uysdean, Uysdeann, Uisdeane,
Uysdeane, Uysdeanne, Uisdeanne

Uistean (Teutonic) An intelligent man
Uisteane, Ustean, Usteane, Uystean, Uysteane

Ujwal (Indian) One who is bright
Ujjal, Ujal, Ujual

Ukiah (Native American) From the deep
valley
Ukia, Ukyah, Ukya

Ukko (Finnish) In mythology, god of the sky
and thunder
Uko, Ucco, Ucko, Uco

Ulan (African) The firstborn of twins
Ullan, Ulann, Ullann

Uland (English) From the noble country
Ulande, Ulland, Ullande, Ulandus, Ullandus

Ulani (Hawaiian) One who is cheerful
Ulanie, Ulany, Ulaney, Ulanee, Ulana,
Ulanya, Ulania, Ulane, Ulanea

Ulbrecht (German) The bright wolf
Ulbrekt, Ulbreckt, Ulbrech, Ulbrek, Ulbreck

Ulderico (Italian) A merciful ruler
Uldericco, Uldericko, Ulderiko, Ulderyco,
Ulderycco, Ulderycko, Ulderyko

Ulf (German) Resembling a wolf
Ulfe, Ulff, Ulffe, Ulph, Ulphe, Ulv, Ulve

Ulfred (English) Wolf of peace
Ulfrid, Ulfryd, Ulfried, Ulfreid

Ulger (English) Rules with a wolf spear
Ulgar, Ulgerr, Ulgarr

Ulhas (Indian) Filled with happiness
Ulhass, Ullhas, Ullhass

Uli (German) A noble ruler
Ulie, Uly, Uley, Ulee, Ulea

Ulick (Gaelic) Little William; son of William
Ulik, Ulic, Ulyck, Ulyk, Ulyc

Ull (Norse) Having glory; in mythology, god
of justice and patron of agriculture
Ulle, Ul, Ule

Ullok (English) The wolf sport
Ullock, Ulloc, Ulok, Ulock, Uloc, Ulvelaik,
Ulvelayk, Ulvelake

Ulloriaq (Native American) Resembling a
star
Uloriaq, Ulloryaq, Uloryaq

Ulmer (German) Having the fame of the
wolf
Ullmer, Ullmar, Ulmarr, Ullmarr, Ulfmer,
Ulfmar, Ulfmaer

Ulric (German) Having the power of the wolf; the wolf ruler
Ulryc, Ulrik, Ulryk, Ulrick, Ulryck

Ulrich (German) Having wealth and power
Ulyrich, Utz

Ultan (Gaelic) A man from Ulster
Ulltan, Ulttan, Ullttan, Ultann, Ulltann, Ullttann

Ultman (Indian) A godly man
Ultmann, Ultmane

Ulysses (Latin) Form of Odysseus, meaning "one who roams; an angry man"
Ulises, Ulisse, Ulyses, Ulysse, Ulisses

Ulz (German) A noble ruler
Ulze

Umar (Arabic) One who is thriving; prosperous
Umer, Umarr, Umare, Umerr

Umber (French) Providing shade; of an earth color
Umbar, Umbro

Umed (Hindi) Filled with desire, hope

Umi (African) A giver of life
Umee, Umy, Umey, Umea, Umie

Ummi (African) His mother's son
Ummie, Ummy, Ummey, Ummee, Ummea

Umrao (Indian) One who is noble

Umut (Turkish) Filled with hope
Umit, Umutt, Umitt, Umyt, Umytt

Unai (Basque) A shepherd
Unay, Unaye, Unae

Unathi (African) God is with us
Unathie, Unathy, Unathey, Unathee, Unathea

Uncas (Native American) Resembling a fox
Unkas, Unckas

Uner (Turkish) One who is famous
Unerr, Unar, Unarr

Ungus (Irish) A vigorous man
Unguss

Unique (American) Unlike others; the only one
Unikue, Unik, Uniqui, Uniqi, Uniqe, Unikque, Unike, Unicke, Unick

Unnat (Indian) An energized or elevated man
Unnatt, Unatt, Unat

Unni (Norse) One who is modest
Unnie, Unny, Unney, Unnee, Unnea

Unnikrishnan (Indian) A young Krishna
Unikrishnan, Unnikrishna, Unikrishna

Unwin (English) One who is unfriendly
Unwinn, Unwinne, Unwyn, Unwynn, Unwynne, Unwine, Unwyne, Unwen, Unwenn, Unwenne

Uny (Latin / Irish) United as one / one who is pure
Uni, Unie, Uney, Unee, Unea, Uno

Uolevi (Finnish) Form of Olaf, meaning "the last of the ancestors"
Uolevie, Uolevee, Uolevy, Uolevey, Uolevea

Upchurch (English) From the upper church
Upchurche

Updike (English) From the upper bank
Updyk, Updyke

Upen (Hindi) In Hinduism, Indra's younger brother
Uppen, Upenn, Uppenn

Upendo (African) One who loves and is loved
Upendio

Upshaw (English) From the upper thicket
Upshawe

Upton (English) From the upper town
Uptun, Uptown

Upwode (English) From the upper forest
Upwood, Upwoode

Uranus (Greek) In mythology, the father of the Titans
Urainus, Uraynus, Uranas, Uraynas, Urainas, Uranos, Uraynos, Urainos

Urban (Latin) From the city
Urbain, Urbaine, Urbane, Urbano, Urbanus, Urbayn, Urbayne

Urho (Finnish) A brave man

Uri (Hebrew) Form of Uriah, meaning "the Lord is my light"
Urie, Ury, Urey, Uree, Urea

Uriah (Hebrew) The Lord is my light
Uria, Urias, Urija, Urijah, Uriyah, Urjasz, Uriya

Urian (Greek) Sent from heaven
Urian, Uriann, Urianne, Uryan, Uryann, Uryanne

Uriel (Hebrew) The angel of light
Uriell, Urielle, Uryel, Uryell, Uryelle

Urien (Welsh) Of a priveleged birth
Urienn, Urienne, Uryen, Uryenn, Uryenne, Uriens

Urjavaha (Hindu) Of the Nimi dynasty

Uros (Hungarian) The little lord

Urquhart (Scottish) From the knoll with the fountain

Ursus (Latin) Resembling a bear
Urs, Urso, Ursel, Ursino, Ursins, Ursinus

Urtzi (Basque) From the sky
Urtzie, Urtzy, Urtzey, Urtzee, Urtzea

Urvakhsha (Persian) One who is filled with joy
Urvakhshah, Urvaksha, Urvakshah

Usamah (Arabic) Resembling a lion
Usama, Usamma, Usammah

Usbeorn (English) A divine warrior

Ushakanta (Indian) Born beneath the sun

Usher (Latin) From the mouth of the river
Ushar, Ushir, Ussher, Usshar, Usshir

Ushi (Chinese) As strong as an ox
Ushie, Ushy, Ushey, Ushee, Ushea

Usko (Finnish) Having much faith
Uskko, Uscco, Uscko

Utah (Native American) People of the mountains; from the state of Utah

Utathya (Indian) In mythology, a sage
Utathiya, Utathyah, Utathiyah

Utgardloki (Norse) In mythology, a giant and ruler of the city Utgard
Utgardlokie, Utgardloky, Utgardlokey, Utgardlokee, Utgardlokea, Utgardlokki

Uther (English) In Arthurian legend, Arthur's father
Uthar, Uthir, Uthyr

Uthman (Arabic) Resembling a young bustard
Uthemun, Uthmann, Usman, Useman, Usmann

Utkarsh (Indian) One who achieves advancement
Utkarshe, Utkarse, Utkars, Utckars, Utckarsh, Utckarshe, Uthkarsh, Uthkarshe

Utpal (Indian) Resembling the lotus
Utpall, Utpale, Utphal, Utphall, Utphale

Utsav (Indian) Born during a celebration
Utsavi, Utsave, Utsava, Utsavie, Utsavy, Utsavey, Utsavee, Utsavea

Utt (Arabic) One who is kind and wise
Utte

Uwe (German) Of the blade

Uxio (Galician) Form of Eugene, meaning "a wellborn man"
Uxo, Uxyo

Uzi (Hebrew) Having great power
Uzie, Uzy, Uzey, Uzee, Uzea, Uzzi, Uzzie, Uzzy, Uzzey, Uzzee, Uzzea

Uzima (African) One who is full of life
Uzimah, Uzimma, Uzimmah, Uzyma, Uzymma, Uyziema, Uzeima, Uzeema, Uzeemah, Uzeama

Uzoma (African) Born during the course of a journey
Uzomah, Uzomma, Uzommah

Uzumati (Native American) Resembling a grizzly bear
Uzumatie, Uzumatee, Uzumaty, Uzumatey, Uzumatea

Uzziah (Hebrew) The Lord is my strength
Uzzia, Uziah, Uzia, Uzzya, Uzzyah,
Uzyah, Uzya, Uzziel, Uziel, Uzziell, Uziell,
Uzzyel, Uzyel, Uzzyell, Uzyell

V

Vachaspati (Indian) A learned man; the
lord of speech
Vachaspatie, Vachaspaty, Vachaspatey,
Vachaspatee

Vachel (French) Resembling a small cow
Vachele, Vachell

Vachlan (English) One who lives near water

Vaclav (Czech) Form of Wenceslas, meaning "one who receives more glory"
Venceslav, Vaclar, Vaclovas

Vada (Hebrew) Resembling a rose
Vadah, Vadda, Vaddah, Vardis, Vardys,
Vardiss, Vardyss, Vered

Vadar (Dutch) A fatherly man
Vader, Vadyr

Vaddon (Welsh) Man from Bath
Vadden, Vaddan

Vadhir (Spanish) Resembling a rose
Vadhyr, Vadheer

Vadim (Russian) A good-looking man
Vadime, Vadym, Vadyme, Vadeem, Vadeeme

Vadin (Hindi) A known speaker
Vadine, Vadeen, Vadeene, Vadyn, Vadyne,
Vachan

Vagas (Spanish) From the meadow

Vagish (Hindi) In Hinduism, another name
for Brahma
Vagishe, Vagysh, Vagyshe

Vahan (Armenian) One who shields others
Vahane, Vahann

Vahe (Armenian) One who is strong
Vahi, Vahee, Vahey, Vahy, Vahea, Vahie

Vahid (Persian) The only one
Vahide, Vahyd, Vahyde, Vaheed, Vaheede

Vahu (Persian) One who is well-behaved
Vahue, Vahoo

Vai (Teutonic) A mighty ruler
Vae

Vaibhav (Indian) One who is wealthy
Vabhav, Vaybhav

Vaijnath (Hindi) Refers to Lord Shiva
Vaejnath, Vaijnathe, Vaejnathe

Vail (English) From the valley
Vaile, Vayl, Vayle, Vale, Vaill, Vayll

Vainamoinen (Finnish) From the wide,
slow river; in mythology, a wise magician
Vaino

Vaiveahtoish (Native American) One who
lands on the cloud
Vaiveatoish, Vaive Atoish, Vaive Ahtoish

Valazquez (Spanish) Resembling a crow

Valborg (Swedish) From the powerful
mountain
Valborge

Valdemar (German) A well-known ruler
Valdemarr, Valdemare, Valto, Valdmar,
Valdmarr, Valdimar, Valdimarr

Valdis (Teutonic) One who is spirited in
battle
Valdiss, Valdys, Valdyss

Valente (Italian) One who is valiant
Valient, Valiente

Valentine (Latin) One who is strong and
healthy
Val, Valen, Valentijn, Valentin, Valentinian,
Valentino, Valentinus, Valentyn, Vallen

Valerian (Latin) One who is strong and
healthy
Valerien, Valerio, Valerius, Valery, Valeryan,
Valere, Valeri, Valerii, Valeray, Valeriy,
Valero, Valeriu, Vali, Valerik, Vallen

Valfrid (Swedish) Form of Walfried, meaning "a peaceful ruler"
Valfried, Valfred, Vallfried, Vallfrid, Vallfred, Valfryd, Vallfryd

Vali (Norse) In mythology, a son of Odin

Valin (Hindi) The monkey king

Vallabh (Indian) One who is dearly loved
Valbh, Vallab, Valab

Valle (French) From the glen
Vallejo

Vallis (French) A man from Wales
Vallois

Valo (Finnish) Man of the light
Vallo

Valri (French) One who is strong
Valrie, Valry, Valrey, Valree

Valter (Swedish) Form of Walter, meaning "the commander of the army"
Valther, Valtteri

Van (Vietnamese / Slavic) Of the clouds / form of Ivan, meaning "God is gracious"
Vann

Van Aken (Dutch) Man from Aachen

Van Eych (Dutch) From the oak tree

Van Ness (Dutch) From the headland

Vanajit (Indian) King of the forest
Vanajyt, Vanajeet

Vance (English) From the marshland
Vanse

Vandal (Latin) One who destroys

Vander (Greek) Form of Evander, meaning "a benevolent man"

Vanderbilt (Dutch) From the hill
Vanderbylt, Vanderbelt, Vanderbalt

Vanderpool (Dutch) From the pool
Vanderpol, Vanderpul, Vanderpull

Vanderveer (Dutch) From the ferry
Vandervere, Vandervir, Vandervire, Vandervyr, Vandervyre

Vandy (Dutch) One who travels; a wanderer
Vandey, Vandi, Vandie, Vandee

Vandyke (Danish) From the dike
Vandike

Vane (English) A banner; a symbol

Vanek (English) Form of John, meaning "God is gracious"
Vanko, Vanechka

Vangelo (English) Form of Evangel, meaning "a bringer of good news"
Vangelios, Vangelis

Vanig (Armenian) From a small town
Vaneg, Vanyg

Vanir (Norse) Of the ancient gods

Vannes (English) Of the grain fans
Vanness, Vannese, Vannesse

Vanya (Russian) Form of John, meaning "God is gracious"
Vanyah

Varad (Hungarian) From the fortress

Varante (Arabic) From the river

Vardon (French) From the green hill
Varden, Verdon, Verdun, Verden, Vardun, Vardan, Verddun, Varddun, Varddon, Verddon

Varen (Hindi) One who is superior
Varren, Varan, Varran, Varon, Varron, Varun, Varrun

Varfolomey (Russian) Form of Bartholomew, meaning "the son of the farmer"
Varfolomei, Varfolomew, Varfolom

Varg (Norse) Resembling a wolf

Varick (German) A protective ruler
Varrick, Varyck, Varryck, Varik, Varyk, Varek, Vareck

Varij (Indian) Resembling the lotus

Varindra (Indian) Lord of the sea
Varyndra, Varindrah, Varyndrah

Varius (Latin) A versatile man
Varian, Varinius

Variya (Hindu) The excellent one

Varlaam (Russian) Form of Barlaam, meaning "the name of a hermit"
Varlam

Varnava (Russian) Form of Barnabas, meaning "the son of the prophet; the son of encouragement"
Varnavas, Varnavus, Varnavee, Varnavey, Varnavie, Varnavus, Varnavy, Varnevas, Varnevus

Varney (Celtic) From the alder tree grove
Varny, Varni, Varnie, Varnea, Varneah, Varnee

Varten (Persian) One who gives roses
Vartan, Vartin

Varun (Hindi) The lord of the waters
Varoun, Varune, Varoune, Varoon, Varoone

Vasant (Indian) Born during the spring
Vasante, Vasanth, Vasanthe

Vasava (Hindi) Refers to Indra

Vaschel (Hebrew) From the small ash tree

Vasco (Basque) Resembling a crow

Vashon (American) The Lord is gracious
Vashan, Vashawn, Vashaun, Vashone, Vashane, Vashayn, Vashayne

Vasilis (Greek) One who is kingly; born to royalty
Vasileios, Vasilij, Vasily, Vaso, Vasos, Vassilij, Vassily, Vasya, Vasilios, Vasilii, Vasile, Vasil, Vasili, Vasilica, Vasilije, Vasek, Vaseck, Vasska, Vassil, Vassi, Vasyl, Vasylko

Vasin (Indian) A great ruler
Vasine, Vaseen, Vaseene, Vasyn, Vasyne

Vasistha (Indian) Name of a sage
Vasisstha, Vasystha, Vasysstha, Vasosta, Vasoshta

Vasu (Indian) One who is bright; an excellent man
Vasue, Vasoo

Vasudev (Indian) Refers to Lord Krishna

Vasuki (Hindi) In Hinduism, a serpent king
Vasukie, Vasuky, Vasukey, Vasukee, Vasukea

Vasuman (Indian) Son born of fire

Vatsa (Indian) Our beloved son
Vathsa

Vatsal (Indian) One who is affectionate

Vaughn (Welsh) One who is small
Vaughan

Vavrinec (Czech) Form of Lawrence, meaning "man from laurentum; crowned with laurel"
Vavrinek, Vavrynec, Vavrynek, Vavrineck, Vavryneck, Vavrin, Vavryn

Vayk (Hungarian) One who is wealthy

Ve (Norse) In mythology, brother of Odin

Veasna (Cambodian) One who has good fortune

Veda (Sanskrit) Refers to the sacred texts; having great knowledge
Vaada, Vaida, Vaeda, Ved, Vyda, Vedas

Vegard (Norse) One who offers protection
Vegarde, Vagard, Vagarde

Veli (Finnish) One who is brotherly
Veikko, Veiko

Velimir (Croatian) One who wishes for great peace
Velimeer, Velimyr, Velimire, Velimeere, Velimyre

Velvel (Hebrew) Resembling a wolf

Velyo (Bulgarian) A great man
Velcho, Veliko, Velin, Velko

Vencel (Hungarian) Form of Wenceslas, meaning "one who receives more glory"
Venzel, Vencele, Venzele

Venceslao (Italian) Form of Wenceslas, meaning "one who receives more glory"
Venceslas

Venedict (American) Form of Benedict, meaning "one who is blessed"
Vendick, Vendict, Venedick, Venedicto, Venedictos, Venedictus, Venedikt, Venedikte, Vennedict, Vennedikt

Venezio (Italian) Man from Venice
Venetziano, Veneziano

Venjamin (Hebrew) Form of Benjamin, meaning "son of the south; son of the right hand"
Yamin, Yamino, Venejamen, Veniamino, Venjaman, Venjamen, Venjiman, Venjimen, Veniamin, Venamin

Venkat (Indian) From the sacred hill

Venturo (Spanish) A fortunate man; one who is lucky
Venturio

Verbrugge (Dutch) From the bridge

Vercingetorix (Celtic) The king of warriors

Verdell (French) One who is flourishing
Verdel, Verdele, Vernell, Vernel, Vernele

Vere (French) From the alder tree

Verge (Anglo-Saxon) One who owns four acres

Verissimo (Portuguese) One who is very truthful

Verlyn (American) Form of Vernon, meaning "from the alder-tree grove"
Verlynn, Verlin, Verllin, Verlon, Vyrlyn, Virlyn, Vyrlin, Vyrlon, Virlon

Vermont (French) From the green mountains; from the state of Vermont

Vernados (Greek) Having the bravery of a bear
Vemados

Verner (Scandinavian) Form of Werner, meaning "of the defending army"
Verneri, Vernery, Vernerey, Verneree, Vernerie

Vernon (French) From the alder-tree grove
Vern, Vernal, Vernard, Verne, Vernee, Vernen, Verney, Vernin, Vernay, Vernus, Vernas

Verrier (French) A glassblower
Verier, Verriere, Veriere

Verrill (French) One who is faithful
Verill, Verrall, Verrell, Verroll, Veryl, Veryll, Verol, Verall, Verle, Vyrle, Verel, Verell

Vesa (Finnish) Resembling a young tree; a sprout

Vespasian (Latin) Born in the evening; resembling a wasp
Vespasiano, Vespasianus, Vespasien, Vespasieno, Vespasienus

Vester (Latin) Form of Sylvester, meaning "from the wooded place"
Vestar, Vestir, Vestor

Vesuvio (Italian) From the volcano
Vesuvo

Veto (Spanish) An intelligent man

Vibol (Cambodian) A man of plenty
Viboll, Vibole, Vybol, Vyboll, Vybole

Victor (Latin) One who is victorious; the champion
Vic, Vick, Victoriano, Victorien, Victorin, Victorino, Victorio, Vidor, Viktor, Vitorio, Vittorio, Vittorios, Victoir, Vicq, Victoro, Vico, Viko, Victorius, Viktorus, Vitor, Vittore, Vittorino

Vid (Hungarian) Form of Vito, meaning "one who gives life"
Vida, Vidas, Vidal

Vidal (Spanish) A giver of life
Videl, Videlio, Videlo, Vidalo, Vidalio, Vidas

Vidar (Norse) Warrior of the forest; in mythology, a son of Odin
Vidarr

Vidur (Indian) Having great wisdom
Vidhur, Vydur, Vydhur

Vidvan (Indian) A learned man

Vien (Vietnamese) One who is complete; satisfied

Vieno (Finnish) One who is gentle

Viet (Vietnamese) Of Vietnamese descent

Viho (Native American) One who ranks as chief

Vijay (Hindi) One who is victorious; the conquerer
Vijaye, Veejay, Veejaye, Vijun

Vikas (Indian) One who makes progress in life

Viking (Norse) Of the seafaring people
Vikyng, Vyking, Vykyng

Vikram (Hindi) One who keeps pace; in
Hinduism, another name for the god
Vishnu
Vicram, Vickram

Vilfred (Danish) Form of Wilfred, meaning
"one who wishes for peace"
*Vilfredo, Vilfrid, Vilfried, Vilfryd, Vill, Villfred,
Villfredo, Villfrid, Villfried, Villfryd*

Vilhelm (Danish) Form of William, mean-
ing "the determined protector"
*Villem, Vilho, Viljo, Vilchjo, Vilem,
Vilhelmus, Vilhemas, Vilhelmi, Vilhelmo,
Vilhelmio, Vilhelms, Vilhjalmur, Vili, Viliam,
Vilis, Viljami, Viljem, Vilko, Ville, Vilmos*

Villiers (French) One who lives in town

Vilmar (English) Form of Wilmer, meaning
"a strong-willed and well-known man"
*Vilmer, Vilmore, Villmar, Villmer, Vylmer,
Vylmar, Vyllmer, Vyllmar, Villmarr, Viljalmr*

Vilppu (Finnish) Form of Phillip, meaning
"one who loves horses"
Vilpu, Vilppue, Vilpue

Vimal (Indian) One who is clean, pure
Vimall, Vymal, Vymall

Vinal (English) From the vine hall
*Vinale, Vynal, Vynale, Vinall, Vynall, Vinay,
Vinaye*

Vincent (Latin) One who prevails; the con-
querer
*Vicente, Vicenzio, Vicenzo, Vin, Vince,
Vincens, Vincente, Vincentius, Vincents,
Vincenty, Vincenz, Vincenzio, Vincenzo,
Vincien, Vinicent, Vinnie, Vinny, Vinzenz,
Vikenti, Vincenc, Vincentas, Vinko*

Vindhya (Indian) From the range of hills
Vyndhya, Vindya, Vyndya

Vineet (Indian) A modest man
Vineete, Vinyt, Vinyte, Vynyt, Vynyte

Vinh (Vietnamese) From the bay

Vinicio (Italian) Man of the vine; wine
Vinicius, Vinicios

Vinod (Indian) One who is a pleasure

Vinson (English) The son of Vincent
Vinsin, Vinsen, Vinsan, Vinsone

Vinton (English) From the vine settlement

Viorel (Romanian) Resembling the bluebell
Viorell, Vyorel, Vyorell

Vipin (Indian) From the forest
*Vippin, Vypin, Vypyn, Vyppin, Vyppyn,
Vipyn, Vippyn*

Vipponah (Native American) Having a slen-
der face
*Vippona, Viponah, Vipona, Vypponah,
Vyppona, Vyponah, Vypona*

Vipul (Indian) A man of plenty
Vypul, Vipull, Vypull, Vipool, Vypool

Virag (Hungarian) Resembling a flower

Viraj (Hindi) A magnificent man; in
Hinduism, a primeval being

Viral (Indian) Our precious son

Virat (Hindi) A supreme ruler

Virendra (Hindi) One who is brave and
noble
Vyrendra, Virindra, Vyrindra

Virgil (Latin) The staff-bearer
*Verge, Vergil, Vergilio, Virgilio, Vergilo,
Virgilo, Virgilijus*

Virginius (Latin) One who is pure; chaste
Virginio, Virgino

Virgo (Latin) The virgin; the sixth sign of
the zodiac

Viriato (Portuguese) One who wears the ruling bracelets

Virote (Thai) A powerful man

Vischer (German) A fisherman
Visscher, Vyscher, Vysscher

Vishal (Indian) A large man; one with broad
shoulders
Vyshal, Vishall, Vyshall

Vishap (Armenian) In mythology, an evil
spirit of thunder

Vishnu (Hindi) In Hinduism, the supreme
god

Visvajit (Indian) Conquerer of the universe

Vitéz (Hungarian) A courageous warrior

Vito (Latin) One who gives life
Vital, Vitale, Vitalis, Vitaly, Vitas, Vitus, Vitali, Vitaliy

Vivatma (Hindu) Of a universal soul

Vivek (Hindi) One who is judicious; filled with wisdom
Vyvek, Viveck, Vyveck

Vivian (Latin) One who is full of life
Viviani, Vivien, Vivyan, Vyvian, Vyvyan, Vivianus, Vian, Viau

Vjekoslav (Croatian) Of the glorious age
Vjek, Vjeko

Vladimir (Slavic) A famous prince
Vladamir, Vladimeer, Vladimyr, Vladimyre, Vladamyr, Vladamyre, Vladameer, Vladimer, Vladamer, Vlad, Vadim, Vladalen, Vladalin, Vlatko, Vladko, Volodya, Volodymyr, Volya, Vova

Vladislav (Slavic) One who rules with glory

Vlassis (Greek) Form of Blaise, meaning "one with a lisp or a stammer"
Vlasis, Vlassys, Vlasys, Vlasi, Vlaho

Vlastimil (Czech) One who has power and favor of the people
Vlastmil, Vlastimyl, Vlastmyl

Vlastislav (Czech) One who has power and glory

Vogel (Dutch) Resembling a bird
Vogle, Vogal, Vogol, Vogil

Vohkinne (Native American) Having a Roman nose

Voistitoevitz (Native American) Resembling a white cow
Voisttitoevetz

Voitto (Finnish) One who is victorious

Vokivocummast (Native American) Resembling a white antelope

Volga (Russian) From the river

Volkan (Turkish) From the volcano

Volker (German) A defender of the people

Volney (German) The spirit of the people
Volny, Volnee, Volni, Volnie, Volnea, Vollney, Vollny, Vollni, Vollnie, Vollnee, Vollnea

Volos (Slavic) Resembling an ox; in mythology, god of cattle

Von (Norse) Filled with hope
Vonne, Vonn, Vondell, Vondel, Vondele, Vontell, Vontel, Vontele

Vortigern (English) The supreme king

Vortimer (English) A legendary king; Vortigem's son

Vromme (Dutch) Having great wisdom
Vromm, Vrom, Vrome

Vruyk (English) From the fortress

Vsevolod (Russian) The ruler of all

Vuk (Servian) Resembling a wolf
Vukasin

Vulcan (Latin) In mythology, the god of fire
Vulkan, Vulckan

Vyacheslav (Russian) Form of Wenceslas, meaning "one who receives more glory"

W

Waail (Arabic) One who goes back to God
Waaile, Waeil, Waeile

Waban (Native American) Of the east wind
Wabann, Wabane

Wachiru (African) The son of the lawmaker
Wachirue, Wachyru, Wachyrue

Wacian (Anglo-Saxon) One who is watchful; alert
Wacien, Wacion

Waclaw (Polish) Form of Wenceslas, meaning "one who receives more glory"
Waclawe

Wade (English) To cross the river ford
Wayde, Waid, Waide, Waddell, Wadell, Waydell, Waidell, Waed, Waede

Wadham (English) From the village near the ford

Wadley (English) From the meadow near the ford
Wadly, Wadlee, Wadli, Wadlie, Wadleigh

Wadron (German) A might raven; a ruling raven
Waldrone, Waldrom, Waldrome, Waldrum, Waldrume, Waldhramm, Waldhram

Wadsworth (English) From the estate near the ford
Waddsworth, Wadsworthe, Waddsworthe

Wafai (Arabic) One who is faithful
Wafae, Wafay, Wafa

Wafi (Arabic) One who is trustworthy
Wafie, Wafy, Wafey, Wafee, Wafiy, Wafiyy

Wafiq (Arabic) One who is successful
Wafiq, Wafeeq, Wafieq, Wafeiq

Wagner (German) One who builds wagons
Wagoner, Waggner, Waggoner

Wahab (Indian) A big-hearted man

Wahanassatta (Native American) One who walks pigeon-toed
Wahanasata, Wahansata, Wahanasat

Wahchinksapa (Native American) Having great wisdom
Wachinksapa, Wahchinksap, Wachinksap

Wahchintonka (Native American) One who practices often
Wachintonka

Wahib (Arabic) A giving man; one who donates
Wahibe, Waheeb, Waheebe, Wahieb, Wahiebe, Waheib, Waheibe, Wahyb, Wahybe

Wahid (Arabic) One who is unequaled; unique
Wahide, Waheed, Waheede, Wahied, Wahiede, Waheid, Waheide, Wahyd, Wahyde

Wahkan (Native American) One who is sacred
Wakan, Wahkhan, Wakhan

Wail (Arabic) One who seeks shelter
Waile, Wayl, Wayle, Wale, Wael, Waele

Wainwright (English) One who builds wagons
Wainright, Wainewright, Wayneright, Waynewright, Waynwright

Waite (English) A guardsman
Waites, Waight, Waights, Wayt, Wayte, Waytes, Wate, Wates

Waitimu (African) Born for the spear
Waytimu, Watimu

Wajih (Arabic) A noble man; one who is distinguished
Wajeeh, Wajieh, Wajyh

Wakefield (English) From the damp field
Wakfield, Wakefeld, Waikfield, Waikfeld, Waykfield, Waykfeld, Wacfeld, Waycfeld, Wacfield, Waycfield

Wakeley (English) From the damp meadow
Wakely, Wakeleigh, Wakelee, Wakeli, Wakelie, Wakelea, Wakeleah, Wacleah, Waklea, Wakleah, Wakley, Wakly, Wacly, Waclea

Wakeman (English) A watchman
Wakemann, Wake, Wacuman, Wakuman

Wakil (Arabic) A lawyer; a trustee
Wakill, Wakyl, Wakyle, Wakeel, Wakeele

Wakiza (Native American) A desperate fighter
Wakyza, Wakeza, Wakieza, Wakeiza

Wakler (English) One who thickens cloth
Wackler, Waklar, Wacklar, Waklor, Wacklor, Waklir, Wacklir

Walbridge (English) From the Welshman's bridge
Wallbridge, Walbrydge, Wallbrydge

Walby (English) From the Welshman's farm
Walbey, Walbi, Walbie, Walbee, Walbea, Wallby, Wallbey, Wallbi, Wallbie, Wallbee, Wallbea

Walcott (English) From the cottage near the wall
Wallcot, Wallcott, Wolcott, Wollcot, Wollcott, Welcott, Wellcot, Wellcott, Walcot, Welcot, Wolcot

Wald (German) Man of the forest
Walde

Waldemar (German) A famous ruler
*Waldemarr, Waldemare, Waldmar,
Waldmar, Weldemar, Weldemarr, Weldemar,
Weldmar, Weldmarr*

Walden (English) From the wooded valley
Waldan, Waldon, Waldin, Waldyn

Waldmunt (German) Mighty protector
*Waldmunte, Waldmont, Waldmonte,
Walmunt, Walmunte, Walmont, Walmonte,
Waldmund, Waldmunde, Waldmond,
Waldmonde, Walmund, Walmunde,
Walmond, Walmonde*

Waldo (English) A powerful ruler

Walenty (Polish) Form of Valentine, meaning "one who is strong and healthy"
*Walenti, Walentie, Walentey, Walentee,
Walentine, Walentyne, Walentyn*

Walerian (Polish) Form of Valerian, meaning "one who is strong and healthy"
*Waleran, Walerion, Waleron, Waleryan,
Waleryon*

Walford (English) From the Welshman's ford
Wallford, Walforde, Wallforde

Walfried (German) A peaceful ruler
*Walfrid, Walfred, Wallfried, Wallfrid,
Wallfred, Walfryd, Wallfryd*

Walid (Arabic) Our newborn son
*Walide, Waleed, Waleede, Waleid, Waleide,
Walied, Waliede, Walyd, Walyde*

Waljan (Welsh) The chosen one
Walljan, Waljen, Walljen, Waljon, Walljon

Walker (English) One who trods the cloth
Walkar, Walkir, Walkor

Wallace (Scottish) A Welshman; a man from the south
*Wallach, Wallas, Wallie, Wallis, Wally,
Walsh, Welch, Walli, Walley, Wallee, Walshe,
Welche, Wallase, Wallache, Waleis*

Walter (German) The commander of the army
*Walther, Walt, Walte, Walder, Wat, Wouter,
Wolter, Woulter, Walthar*

Walton (English) From the walled town; from the stream town
*Walten, Waltan, Waltin, Waltun, Waller,
Walworth, Walworthe*

Walwyn (English) A Welsh friend
*Walwynn, Walwin, Walwinn, Wallwyn,
Wallwynn, Wallwin, Wallwinn*

Wamblee (Native American) Resembling an eagle
*Wambli, Wamblie, Wambly, Wambley,
Wambleigh, Wamblea*

Wambleeska (Native American) Resembling the white eagle
*Wambleesha, Wambliska, Wamblisha,
Wamblieska, Wambliesha, Wambleiska,
Wambleisha, Wamblyska, Wamblysha*

Wambua (African) Born during a period of rain
Wambooa, Wambuah, Wambooah

Wamocha (African) One who is never satisfied
Wamocka, Wamocho, Wumocko

Wanageeska (Native American) Of the white spirit
*Wanageska, Wanagiska, Wanagyska,
Wanagieska, Wanageiska*

Wanikiy (Native American) A savior
*Wanikiya, Wanikie, Wanikey, Waniki,
Wanikee*

Wanjala (African) Born during a famine
Wanjalla, Wanjal, Wanjall

Wapasha (Native American) Resembling the red leaf
Wapashah, Waposha, Waposhah

Wapi (Native American) One who is fortunate; lucky
Wapie, Wapy, Wapey, Wapee

Waquini (Native American) Having a hooked nose
Waquinie, Waquiny, Waquiney, Waquinee

Ward (English) A guardian
Warde, Warden, Worden, Weard

Wardell (English) From the guardian's hill
*Wardel, Wardele, Weardhyll, Weardhill,
Weardell*

Wardley (English) From the guardian's meadow
Wardly, Wardleigh, Wardli, Wardlie, Wardlee, Wardlea, Weardleigh, Weardlee, Weardli, Weardlie, Weardly, Weardley, Weardlea, Weardleah

Warfield (English) From the field near the weir
Warfeld, Weirfeild, Weirfeld, Weifield, Weifeld

Warford (English) From the ford near the weir
Warforde, Weirford, Weirforde, Weiford, Weiforde

Warley (English) From the meadow near the weir
Warly, Warleigh, Warlee, Warlea, Warleah, Warli, Warlie, Weirley, Weirly, Weirli, Weirlie, Weirlea, Weirleah, Weirleigh, Weirlee

Warner (German) Of the defending army
Werner, Wernher, Warnher, Worner, Wornher

Warra (Aboriginal) Man of the water
Warrah, Wara, Warah

Warrain (Aboriginal) One who belongs to the sea
Warraine, Warrayne, Warrayn, Warraen, Warraene, Warain, Waraine, Warayn, Warayne, Waraen, Waraene

Warren (English / German) From the fortress; from the enclosure / a gamekeeper
Warrane, Waran, Warane, Warrin, Warin, Waren, Waren

Warrick (English) Form of Varick, meaning "a protective ruler"
Warrik, Warric, Warick, Warik, Waric, Warryck, Warryk, Warryc, Waryck, Waryk, Waryc, Warwick, Warwik, Warwic, Warrwick, Warrwik, Warrwic

Warrigal (Aboriginal) One who is wild
Warrigall, Warigall, Warigal, Warygal, Warygall

Warrun (Aboriginal) Of the sky
Warun

Warwick (English) From the farm near the weir
Warwik, Warwyck, Warwyk

Washburn (English) From the flooding stream
Washbourn, Washburne, Washbourne, Washborn, Washborne, Waescburne, Waescburn

Washi (Japanese) Resembling an eagle
Washie, Washy, Washey, Washee

Washington (English) From the intelligent one's town
Washyngton, Washingtown, Washyngtown

Wasi (Arabic) An open-minded and learned man
Wasie, Wasy, Wasey, Wasee

Wasim (Arabic) A handsome man
Wasime, Waseem, Waseeme, Waseim, Waseime, Wasiem, Wasieme, Wasym, Wasyme, Wassim, Wassym, Wasseem

Wasswa (African) The firstborn of twins
Waswa, Wasswah, Waswah

Watson (English) The son of Walter
Watsin, Watsen, Watsan, Watkins, Watckins, Watkin, Watckin, Wattekinson, Wattikinson, Wattkins, Wattkin, Wattson, Wattsen, Wattsan, Wattesone, Watts, Watt, Watte

Waverly (English) Of the trembling aspen
Waverley, Waverli, Waverlie, Waverleigh, Waverlea, Waverlee, Waefreleah, Waefrelea, Waefreley, Wafrely, Wafrelee

Waylon (English) From the roadside land
Way, Waylan, Wayland, Waylen, Waylin, Weylin, Wylan, Wyland, Wylen, Wylin, Wegland, Weyland, Weylyn

Wayne (English) One who builds wagons
Wayn, Wain, Waine, Wane, Waen, Waene

Wayra (Native American) Born of the wind
Wayrah, Waira, Wairah, Waera, Waerah

Weayaya (Native American) Born with the setting sun

Webley (English) From the weaver's meadow
Webbley, Webly, Webbly, Webleigh, Webbleigh, Weblea, Webblea, Webleah, Webbleah, Webli, Webbli, Weblie, Webblie

Webster (English) A weaver
Weeb, Web, Webb, Webber, Weber, Webbestre, Webestre, Webbe, Wevers, Wever

Wednesday (American) Born on a Wednesday
Wensday, Winsday, Windnesday, Wydnesday, Wynsday, Wednesdai, Wednesdae, Wensdai, Winsdai, Windnesdai, Wydnesdai, Wynsdai, Wensdae, Winsdae, Windnesdae, Wydnesdae, Wynsdae

Wei (Chinese) A brilliant man; having great strength

Wekesa (African) Born during the harvest time

Welborne (English) From the spring brook
Welborn, Welburn, Welburne, Wellborne, Wellborn, Wellburn, Wellburne

Welby (English) From the farm near the spring
Welbey, Wellby, Wellbey, Welbi, Wellbi, Welbie, Wellbie, Welbee, Wellbee, Welbea, Wellbea

Welcome (English) A welcome guest
Welcom, Welcomme

Weldon (English) From the hill near a spring
Welldon, Welden, Wellden, Wieldun, Weildun

Wells (English) From the springs
Welles

Welton (English) From the town near the well
Wellton, Weltun, Welltun, Weltin, Welltin

Wematin (Native American) One who is brotherly
Wematen, Wematyn, Wemetin, Wemeten, Wemetyn

Wemilat (Native American) Born into prosperity
Wemilatt, Wemylat, Wemylatt

Wenceslas (Slavic) One who receives more glory
Wenzeslas, Wenceslaus, Wenzeslaus

Wendell (German) One who travels; a wanderer
Wendel, Wendale, Wendall, Wendele, Wendal, Windell, Windel, Windal, Wyndell, Wyndel, Wyndal, Windall, Wyndall

Wenzel (German) Form of Wenceslas, meaning "one who receives more glory"
Wenzell, Wenzle, Winzel, Winzell, Winzle, Wynzel, Wynzell, Wynzle

Werther (German) A soldier worthy of the army

Wesley (English) From the western meadow
Wes, Wesly, Wessley, Westleigh, Westley, Wesli, Weslie, Wesleigh, Westli, Westlie, Wess, Weslee, Westlee, Wessel, Wessle, Wesleah, Westleah

Westbrook (English) From the western stream
Wesbrook, Westbrok, Wesbrok, Westbroc, Wesbroc, Westbrock, Wesbrock

Westby (English) From the western farm
Westbey, Wesby, Wesbey, Westbi, Wesbi, Westbie, Wesbie, Westbee, Wesbee, Westbea, Wesbea

Westcott (English) From the western cottage
Wescott, Westcot, Wescot, Westkott, Weskott, Westkot, Weskot

Weston (English) From the western town
West, Westan, Westen, Westun, Westin, Weste

Wetherby (English) From the ram farm
Wetherbey, Wetherbee, Wetherbi, Wetherbie, Whetherby, Whetherbey, Whetherbee, Whetherbi, Whetherbie, Weatherby, Weatherbey, Weatherbee, Weatherbi, Weatherbie

Wetherly (English) From the ram's meadow
Wetherley, Wetherlee, Wetherli, Wetherlie, Whetherly, Whetherley, Whetherlee, Whetherli, Whetherlie, Weatherly, Weatherley, Weatherlee, Weatherli, Weatherlie, Wetherlea, Wetherleah, Whetherlea, Whetherleah, Weatherlea, Weatherleah

Wharton (English) From the settlement near the weir
Warton, Wharten, Warten, Whartun, Wartun

Wheatley (English) From the wheat meadow
Wheatly, Wheatli, Wheatlie, Wheatleigh, Wheatlea, Wheatleah, Wheatlee, Weatley, Weatly, Weatli, Weatleigh, Weatlea, Weatleah, Weatlee, Weatlie

Wheaton (English) From the town of wheat
Wheatown, Wheeton, Wheyton, Weaton, Weeton, Weyton

Wheeler (English) A driver; one who makes wheels

Whistler (English) One who whistles

Whit (English) A white-skinned man
White, Whitey, Whitt, Whitte, Whyt, Whytt, Whytte, Whytey

Whitaker (English) From the white acre
Witaker, Whittaker, Wittaker

Whitby (English) From the white farm
Whitbey, Whitbi, Whitbie, Whitbee, Whytbey, Whytby, Whytbi, Whytbie, Whytbee, Witby, Witbey, Witbi, Witbie, Witbee, Wytby, Wytbey, Wytbi, Wytbie, Wytbee

Whitcomb (English) From the white valley
Whitcom, Whitcome, Whytcomb, Whytcome, Whytcom, Witcomb, Witcom, Witcome, Wytcomb, Wytcom, Wytcome

Whitfield (English) From the white field
Whitfeld, Whytfield, Whytfeld, Witfield, Witfeld, Wytfield, Wytfeld

Whitford (English) From the white ford
Whitforde, Whytford, Whytforde, Witford, Witforde, Wytford, Wytforde

Whitlaw (English) From the white hill
Whitelaw, Whitlawe, Whytlaw, Whytlawe, Witlaw, Witlawe, Wytlaw, Wytlawe

Whitley (English) From the white meadow
Whitly, Whitli, Whitlie, Whitlee, Whitleigh, Whytley, Whytly, Whytli, Whytlie, Whytlee, Whytleigh, Witley, Witly, Witli, Witlie, Witleigh, Witlee, Wytley, Wytly, Wytli, Wytlie, Wytleigh, Wytlee

Whitlock (English) A white-haired man
Whitlok, Whytlock, Whytlok, Witlock, Witlok, Wytlock, Wytlok

Whitman (English) A white-haired man
Whitmann, Witman, Witmann, Whitmane, Witmane, Whytman, Whytmane, Wytman, Wytmane

Whitney (English) From the white island
Whitny, Whitni, Whitnie, Whitnee, Witney, Witni, Witny, Witnie, Witnee, Whytney, Whytny, Whytni, Whytnie, Whytnee

Wicasa (Native American) One who is wise; a sage
Wickasa, Wikasa, Wicassa, Wickassa, Wikassa

Wickham (English) From the village paddocks
Wyckham, Wikham, Wykham, Wickam, Wyckam, Wykam, Wiccum, Wichamm

Wickley (English) From the village meadow
Wickly, Wickli, Wicklie, Wicklee, Wicklea, Wyckley, Wyckly, Wyckli, Wycklie, Wycklee, Wycklea, Wykley, Wykly, Wykli, Wyklie, Wyklee, Wyklea, Wikley, Wikly, Wikli, Wiklie, Wiklee, Wiklea, Wikleigh, Wickleigh, Wyckleigh, Wykleigh, Wicleah, Wicleigh, Wiclea

Wielislaw (Polish) Form of Wieslav, meaning "one who receives great glory"
Wieslaw, Wislaw

Wieslav (Slavic) One who receives great glory

Wiktor (Polish) Form of Victor, meaning "one who is victorious; the champion"
Wikter, Wiktar

Wikvaya (Native American) A bringer

Wilbert (German) One who is willful; a bright man
Wilber, Wilbur, Wilburn, Wilburt, Wilbar, Wilbart, Wilbern, Wilbarn, Wilburh, Wilperht, Wilpert

Wildon (English) From the wooded hill
Willdon, Wilden, Willden

Wiley (English) One who is crafty; from the meadow by the water
Wily, Wileigh, Wili, Wilie, Wilee, Wylie, Wyly, Wyley, Wylee, Wyleigh, Wyli

Wilford (English) From the willow ford
Willford, Wilferd, Willferd, Wilf, Wielford, Weilford, Wilingford, Wylingford

Wilfred (English) One who wishes for peace
Wilfredo, Wilfrid, Wilfried, Wilfryd, Will, Willfred, Willfredo, Willfrid, Willfried, Willfryd

Willard (German) A resolute and brave man
Wilard, Willerd, Wilerd, Willhard, Wilhard, Willherd, Wilherd, Wilheard, Willet, Willett, Wilet, Wilett

William (German) The determined protector
Wilek, Wileck, Wilhelm, Wilhelmus, Wilkes, Wilkie, Wilkinson, Will, Willem, Willhelmus, Willi, Williams, Williamson, Willie, Willis, Willkie, Wills, Williamon, Willy, Wilmot, Wilmott, Wim, Wilmod, Wilmodd

Willoughby (English) From the willow farm
Wiloughby, Willoughbey, Wiloughhey, Willoughbi, Wiloughbi, Willoughbee, Wiloughbee, Willoby, Wiloby, Willobey, Wilobey, Willobee, Wilobee, Wiligby, Wyligby

Willow (English) Of the willow tree
Willowe, Willo, Willoe

Wilmer (German) A strong-willed and well-known man
Wilmar, Wilmore, Willmar, Willmer, Wylmer, Wylmar, Wyllmer, Wyllmar, Willmarr

Wilson (German) The son of William
Willson, Willsn, Wilsen, Wilsin, Willsen, Willsin, Willesone, Wilesone

Wilton (English) From the town on the river
Willton, Wylton, Wyllton, Wiltan, Willtan, Wilten, Willten, Wilt, Wilte, Wylton, Wyllton

Wincenty (Polish) Form of Vincent, meaning "one who prevails; the conquerer"
Wincentey, Wincenti, Wincentie, Wincentee

Winchell (English) One who draws water
Winnchell, Wynchell, Wynnchell

Windsor (English) From the river that has a winch
Winsor, Windser, Winser, Wyndsor, Wynsor, Wyndser, Wynser, Wendsor, Wensor, Wenser

Winfield (German) From a friend's field
Winnfield, Wynfield, Wynnfield, Wynsfield, Wynnsfield, Winefield, Winefeld

Winford (English) From a friend's ford
Winnford, Winforde, Winnforde, Wynford, Wynforde, Wynnford, Wynnforde

Winfred (English) A friend of peace
Wynfred, Winfrid, Wynfrid, Winfryd, Wynfryd, Winfrith, Wynfrith, Winfried, Wynfried, Winefrith, Wynefrith, Wylfrid, Wylfred

Winslow (English) From a friend's hill
Winslowe, Wynslow, Wynslowe, Winslo, Wynslo

Winston (English) Of the joy stone; from the friendly town
Win, Winn, Winsten, Winstonn, Wynstan, Wynsten, Wynston, Winstan

Winthrop (English) From the friendly village
Winthrope, Wynthrop, Wynthrope, Winthorp, Wynthorp

Winton (English) From the enclosed pastureland
Wintan, Wintin, Winten, Wynton, Wyntan, Wyntin, Wynten

Wirt (Anglo-Saxon) One who is worthy
Wirte, Wyrt, Wyrte, Wurt, Wurte

Wisconsin (Native American) From the grassy place; from the state of Wisconsin
Wisconsen, Wisconson, Wysconsin, Wysconsen, Wysconson

Wise (English) Filled with wisdom
Wyse, Wyze, Wize

Wissian (Anglo-Saxon) One who guides others

Wit (Polish) Form of Vitus, meaning "giver of life"
Witt

Witold (German) Ruler of the wide land

Wladyslaw (Polish) To rule with glory
Wladislaw, Wlodzislaw, Wlodzyslaw

Wlodzimierz (Polish) To rule with peace
Wlodzimir, Wlodzimerz

Woden (Anglo-Saxon) Form of Odin, meaning "king of the gods"
Wodin, Wotan, Woten, Wotin, Wodan

Wohehiv (Native American) One who wields a dull knife
Wohehev, Wohehive, Woheheev, Woheheeve, Wohehieve, Woheheive, Wohehyve, Wohehiev, Woheheiv, Wohehyv

Wokaihwokomas (Native American) Resembling the white antelope

Wolcott (English) One who lives in Wolf's cottage
Wolcot, Wolfcott, Wolfcot, Woolcot, Woolcott, Wulfcot, Wulfcott

Wolfe (English) Resembling the wolf
Wolf, Wolff, Wolffe, Wulf, Wulfe, Wulff, Wulffe

Wolfgang (German) One who takes the wolf's path

Wolfgar (German) Wielding a wolf spear
Wolfgarr, Wolfgare, Wulfgar, Wulfgarr, Wulfgare

Wolfram (German) Resembling a black wolf; a raven-wolf
Wolframe, Wolfrem, Wolfrim

Wolfric (German) A wolf ruler
Wolfrick, Wolfrik, Wulfric, Wulfrick, Wulfrik, Wolfryk, Wolfryck, Wolfryc, Wulfryc, Wulfryck, Wulfryk

Woodley (English) From the wooded meadow
Woodleigh, Woodly, Woodlee, Woodlea, Woodleah, Woodli, Woodlie, Wodolea, Wodoleah, Wodoleigh, Wodolee, Wodoli, Wodolie, Wodoly, Wodoley

Woodrow (English) From the row of houses near the forest
Woodrowe, Woodro, Woodroe

Woody (American) A man of the forest
Woodey, Woodi, Woodie, Woodee, Woodward, Woods, Woodruff, Woodman, Woudman, Woudruff, Woudward, Woudy, Woudman, Wood, Woud

Woorak (Aboriginal) From the plains
Woorack, Woorac

Wright (English) A wood carver; a carpenter

Wu (Chinese) Of the army; a sorcerer

Wulfhere (Anglo-Saxon) The name of a king
Wulfhear, Wulfheer, Wolfhere, Wolfhear, Wolfheer

Wuyi (Native American) Resembling a soaring turkey vulture
Wuyie, Wuyey, Wuyee, Wuyea

❂ **Wyatt** (English) Having the strength of a warrior
Wyat, Wyatte, Wyate, Wiatt, Wiatte, Wiat, Wiate, Wyeth, Wyath, Wyathe, Wyethe, Wye

Wybert (Anglo-Saxon) One who is smart during battle
Wyberth, Wyberte, Wyberthe, Wibert, Wiberte, Wiberth, Wiberthe

Wyborn (Norse) A warrior bear
Wybjorn

Wycliff (English) From the white cliff
Wyclif, Wyclyf, Wyclyff, Wycliffe, Wyclyffe, Wyclef, Wycleffe

Wyler (English) One who makes wheels
Wylar, Wylor, Wiler, Wilar, Wilor

Wyman (English) A fair-haired warrior
Wymann, Wymane

Wymond (English) A defender during battle
Wymonde, Wymund, Wymunde, Wimond, Wimonde, Wimund, Wimunde

Wyndam (English) From the winding path in the field
Windam

Wyndham (English) From the windy village
Windham

Wynn (Welsh / English) One who is fair-skinned/a beloved friend
Wyn, Winn, Win, Winne, Wynne, Wenn, Wen, Wenne, Wine, Wyne

Wynono (Native American) The firstborn child

Wynter (English) Born during the winter
Wynters, Winter, Winters

Wynwode (English) From the friendly forest
Wynswode, Winwode, Winswode, Wynwood, Winwood, Winward, Wynwodem, Wynward, Wynwodem

Wyoming (Native American) From the large prairie; from the state of Wyoming
Wyomen, Wyom, Wyome

Wystan (English) As solid as a stone during battle
Wysten, Wistan, Wisten

Wythe (English) From the willow tree
Wyth

X

Xadrian (American) Form of Adrian, meaning "man from Hadria"
Xade, Xadiran, Xadrain, Xadrean, Xadreean, Xadreyan, Xadreeyan, Xadriaan, Xadriano, Xadrien, Xadrin, Xadrino, Xadrion, Xadron, Xadryan, Xadya, Xarjen, Xaydrean, Xaydreean, Xaydrian, Xaydrien

Xakery (American) Form of Zachary, meaning "the Lord remembers"
Xaccary, Xaccery, Xach, Xacharie, Xachery, Xack, Xackarey, Xackary, Xackery, Xak, Xakari, Xakary

Xalvador (Spanish) Form of Salvador, meaning "a savior"
Xalvadore, Xalvadoro, Xalvadorio, Xalbador, Xalbadore, Xalbadorio, Xalbadoro, Xabat, Xabatt, Xabate, Xabatio, Xabato

Xan (Hebrew) One who is well-fed
Xian, Xoan, Xann

Xander (Greek) Form of Alexander, meaning "helper and defender of mankind"
Xandro, Xandrio, Xandy, Xandie, Xanderlee, Xanderr, Xanderre, Xandere

Xannon (American) From an ancient family
Xanon, Xannen, Xanen, Xannun, Xanun

Xanthus (Greek) A blonde-haired man
Xanthos, Xanthe, Xanth

Xanti (Basque) Honoring St. James
Xantie, Xanty, Xantey, Xantee, Xantis, Xantys

Xanto (Greek) A blonde-haired man
Xantio, Xantow, Xantowe, Xantoe

Xarles (French) Form of Charles, meaning "one who is manly and strong / a free man"
Xarel, Xarl, Xarlo, Xarlos, Xarrol, Xarroll, Xary, Xaryl, Xhad, Xarleson, Xarley, Xarlie, Xarlot, Xarls, Xarlton, Xarly

❂ **Xavier** (Basque / Arabic) Owner of a new house / one who is bright
Xaver, Xever, Xabier, Xaviere, Xabiere, Xaviar, Xaviare, Xavior, Xaviore, Xzavier, Xzabier, Xzaviar, Xzavior

Xenocrates (Greek) A foreign ruler

Xenon (Greek) From a foreign land; a stranger
Xenonn, Xenos, Xenus

Xenophon (Greek) One who speaks with a foreign voice
Xeno, Xenophone, Xenofon, Xenofone

Xerxes (Persian) A monarch; a ruler of heroes
Xerxus, Xerxos, Xerxas

Xesus (Galician) Form of Jesus, meaning "God is my salvation"

Xiang (Chinese) One who soars above others

Ximon (Hebrew) Form of Simon, meaning "God has heard"
Ximun, Ximen

Xiomar (Spanish) One who is famous in battle
Xiomarr, Xiomarre, Xiomare

Xiuhcoatl (Aztec) Wielding a weapon of destruction

Xi-wang (Chinese) One who is filled with hope

Xoan (Galician) Form of John, meaning "God is gracious"
Xoane, Xohn, Xon

Xochipilli (Aztec) In mythology, god of love and flowers

Xose (Galician) Form of Joseph, meaning "God will add"

Xuan (Vietnamese) Born during the spring

Xue (Chinese) A studious young man

Xun (Chinese) One who is swift

Xurxo (Galician) Form of George, meaning "one who works the earth; a farmer"
Xurxio

Xylon (Greek) A forest dweller
Xylun, Xylonio, Xylan, Xylanio, Xylunio, Xylono, Xyluno, Xylano

y

Yaakov (Hebrew) Form of Jacob, meaning "he who supplants"
Yaacob, Yachov, Yacov, Yago, Yakob, Yakov, Yaakob, Yaacov, Yaachov, Yacoub, Yakoub

Yabiss (Arabian) From the dry land
Yabyss, Yabis, Yabys

Yadid (Hebrew) One who is dearly loved
Yadide, Yadyd, Yadyde, Yadeed, Yadeede, Yadiel, Yadial

Yadon (Hebrew) The Lord will judge
Yadone, Yadun, Yadune, Yaadon

Yael (Israeli) Strength of God
Yaele

Yafeu (African) One who is bold
Yafeuh, Yafeo, Yafeoh

Yagil (Hebrew) One who rejoices, celebrates
Yagill, Yagyl, Yagylle

Yago (Hebrew) Form of Iago, meaning "he who supplants"
Yagoh, Yaggo, Yaggoh

Yaholo (Native American) One who shouts
Yaholoh, Yahollo, Yaholloh, Yaholio

Yahto (Native American) Having blue eyes; refers to the color blue
Yahtoe, Yahtow, Yahtowe

Yahweh (Hebrew) Refers to God
Yahveh, Yaweh, Yaveh, Yehowah, Yehweh, Yehoveh

Yahya (Arabic) Form of John, meaning "God is gracious"
Yahyah, Yahia, Yahiah, Yahea, Yaheah, Yahyaa

Yakar (Hebrew) One who is precious
Yakarr, Yakare, Yackar, Yaccar, Yackare

Yakecan (Native American) One who sings to the sky
Yakecann, Yakecen, Yackecan, Yakacan, Yackacan, Yakacen

Yakim (Hebrew) Form of Joachim, meaning "one who is established by God; God will judge"
Yachim, Yackim, Yakeem, Yacheem, Yackeem

Yakiv (Ukranian) Form of Jacob, meaning "he who supplants"
Yakive, Yakeev, Yakeeve, Yackiv, Yackeev, Yakieve, Yakiev, Yakeive, Yakeiv

Yakout (Arabian) As precious as a ruby

Yale (Welsh) From the fertile upland
Yayle, Yayl, Yail, Yaile

Yamal (Hindi) One of twins
Yamall, Yamale, Yamalo, Yamalio

Yamin (English) Form of Benjamin, meaning "son of the south; son of the right hand"
Yemin, Yamino, Yemino, Yameen, Yemeen, Yaman, Yamen

Yaminichandra (Hindi) Born beneath the night moon
Yaminichandro

Yan Tao (Chinese) A handsome man

Yan (Hebrew) Form of John, meaning "God is gracious"
Yann, Yannic, Yanni, Yanne, Yanny, Yannick, Yannik, Yannis, Yannakis, Yanakis, Yannig, Yanig, Yanis, Yianni, Yiannie, Yianne, Yianny, Yianney, Yiannee, Yiannis

Yanai (Aramaic) God will answer
Yanae, Yana, Yani

Yancy (Indian) An Englishman
Yancey, Yanci, Yancie, Yancee, Yantsey, Yance, Yank, Yankee, Yanky, Yankey

Yanisin (Native American) One who is ashamed
Yanisen, Yanysin, Yanysen, Yanisan, Yanysan, Yanisyn, Yanysyn

Yaniv (Hebrew) One who is prosperous
Yanive, Yaneeve, Yaneev, Yaneiv, Yaneive, Yanieve, Yaniev

Yankel (Hebrew) Form of Jacob, meaning "he who supplants"
Yankell, Yanckel, Yanckell, Yankle, Yanckle

Yanko (Bulgarian) Form of Yan, meaning "God is gracious"
Yankoh, Yancko, Yanckoh

Yaotl (Aztec) A great warrior
Yaotyl, Yaotle, Yaotel, Yaotyle

Yaphet (Hebrew) A handsome man
Yaphett, Yapheth, Yaphethe

Yaqub (Arabic) Form of Jacob, meaning "he who supplants"
Ya'qub, Yaqob, Yaqoub

Yardan (Arabic) Form of Jordan, meaning "of the down-flowing river"
Yarden, Yardin, Yardann, Yardane, Yardene, Yardine

Yardley (English) From the fenced-in meadow
Yardly, Yardleigh, Yardli, Yardlie, Yardlee, Yardlea, Yarley, Yarly, Yeardly, Yeardley, Yeardleigh, Yeardlee, Yeardli, Yeardlie

Yarema (Hebrew) One who has been appointed by God
Yaryma, Yarima, Yaremo, Yarymo, Yarem, Yaremka

Yarin (Hebrew) One who is understanding
Yaryn, Yarine, Yaryne, Yavin, Yavine, Yavyn, Yavyne

Yaromir (Russian) Form of Jaromir, meaning "from the famous spring"
Yaromire, Yaromeer, Yaromeere, Yaromyr, Yaromyre

Yaron (Hebrew) To lift one's voice in praise
Yarron, Yaronn, Yarone

Yaroslav (Russian) Form of Jaroslav, meaning "born with the beauty of spring"

Yarrow (English) Resembling the fragrant herb
Yurro, Yarroe, Yarrowe, Yarow, Yarowe, Yaro, Yaroe

Yas (Native American) Child of the snow

Yasahiro (Japanese) One who is peaceful and calm

Yasashiku (Japanese) One who is polite and gentle
Yasashiko

Yash (Indian) A famous man; one who is glorious
Yashe, Yashi, Yashie, Yashee, Yashy, Yashey, Yashas

Yashpal (Indian) One who is successful
Yashpall, Yashpali, Yashpalie, Yashpaley, Yashpaly, Yashpalee, Yaspal

Yashwant (Indian) A glorious man
Yaswant

Yasin (Arabic) A wealthy man
Yasine, Yaseen, Yaseene, Yasyn, Yasyne, Yasien, Yasiene, Yasein, Yaseine

Yasir (Arabic) One who is well-off financially
Yassir, Yasser, Yaseer, Yasr, Yasyr, Yassyr, Yasar, Yassar, Yaser

Yasuo (Japanese) One who is peaceful
Yasuzo

Yateem (Arabian) An orphaned boy
Yateeme, Yatim, Yatime, Yatym, Yatyme, Yatiem, Yatieme, Yateim, Yateime

Yates (English) Keeper of the gates
Yayts, Yaytes, Yaits, Yaites, Yeats

Yavuz (Turkish) A stern man

Yaw (African) Born on a Thursday
Yawo, Yao

Yazid (Arabic) One who strives to better himself
Yazide, Yazeed, Yazeede, Yazeid, Yazeide, Yazied, Yaziede, Yazyd, Yazyde

Yazid (Arabic) God will add
Yazide, Yazeed, Yazeede, Yazyd, Yazyde, Yazied, Yaziede, Yazeid, Yazeide

Yebadiah (Hebrew) A gift from God
Yebadia, Yebadiya, Yebadiyah, Yeb, Yebe, Yebediah, Yebedia, Yebediya, Yebediyah, Yebedee, Yebedi, Yebedie, Yevadiah, Yevadia, Yevadiya, Yevadiyah

Yechezkel (Hebrew) Form of Ezekiel, meaning "strengthened by God"
Yechezkiel, Yechezekiel, Yekezekiel, Yekezkel

Yedidiah (Hebrew) One who is beloved by God
Yedidia, Yedediah, Yedediah, Yedidyah, Yedidya, Yededyah, Yededya

Yefim (Russian) One who speaks well
Yeffim, Yephim, Yefem, Yephem, Yeffem

Yefrem (Russian) Form of Ephraim, meaning "one who is fertile; productive"
Yefram, Yefraim, Yefreme, Yeframe, Yefraym, Yefrayme

Yegor (Russian) Form of George, meaning "one who works the earth; a farmer"
Yegore, Yegorr, Yegeor, Yeorges, Yeorge, Yeorgis

Yehonadov (Hebrew) A gift from God
Yehonadav, Yehonedov, Yehonedav, Yehoash, Yehoashe, Yeeshai, Yeeshae, Yishai, Yishae

Yehudi (Hebrew) Form of Judah, meaning "one who praises God"
Yehudie, Yehudy, Yehudey, Yehudee, Yehuda, Yehudah, Yechudi, Yechudit, Yehudit

Yemelyan (Russian) Form of Emil, meaning "one who is eager; an industrious man"
Yemalyan, Yemalyen, Yemelyen, Yemel, Yemele, Yemil, Yemile

Yenge (African) A hardworking man
Yengi, Yengie, Yengy, Yengey, Yengee

Yentl (Hebrew) A kindhearted man
Yentle, Yentel, Yentele, Yentil, Yentile, Yentyl, Yentyle

Yeoman (English) A manservant
Youman, Yoman

Yerachmiel (Hebrew) One who loves the Lord
Yerachmiele, Yerachmiell, Yerachmyel, Yerachmial, Yerachmyal

Yered (Hebrew) Form of Jared, meaning "of the descent; descending"
Yarad, Yarid, Yarod, Yarrad, Yarrard, Yarred, Yarrid, Yarrod, Yaryd, Yerad, Yerod, Yerrad, Yerred, Yerrod

Yeriel (Hebrew) Founded by God
Yeriell, Yerial, Yeriall, Yeriele, Yeriale

Yerik (Russian) One who has been appointed by God
Yerick, Yeric, Yeryk, Yeryck, Yeryc

Yermolai (Russian) Follower of Hermes, the messenger god
Yermolah, Yermolae, Yermolay, Yermolaye, Yermolaa

Yerodin (African) One who is studious
Yerodine, Yerodyn, Yerodyne, Yerodeen, Yerodeene

Yerucham (Hebrew) One who is beloved by God
Yeruchame, Yerukam, Yerukame

Yervant (Armenian) A king; born to royalty
Yervante

Yeshaya (Hebrew) To whom God lends
Yeshayah, Yeshaia, Yeshaiah, Yeshaea, Yeshaeah

Yestin (Welsh) One who is just and fair
Yestine, Yestyn, Yestyne

Yesuto (African) This child belongs to Jesus

Yevgeny (Russian) Form of Eugene, meaning "a wellborn man"
Yevgeney, Yevgenee, Yevgeni, Yevgenie, Yevgeniy, Yevheniy, Yevheny, Yevheni, Yevhenie, Yevhenee, Yevheney

Ygor (English) Form of Igor, meaning "warrior of the bow"
Yegor, Ygorr, Ygore, Yegore, Yegorr

Yigil (Hebrew) He shall be redeemed
Yigile, Yigyl, Yigyle, Yigol, Yigole, Yigit, Yigat

Yiorgos (Greek) Form of George, meaning "one who works the earth; a farmer"
Yiorges, Yirgos, Yirges, Yorgos, Yorges

Yishachar (Hebrew) He will be rewarded
Yishacharr, Yishachare, Yissachar, Yissachare, Yisachar, Yisachare

Yiska (Native American) The night has gone

Yitro (Hebrew) A man of plenty

Yitzhak (Hebrew) Form of Isaac, meaning "full of laughter"
Yitchak, Yitzhack, Yitzchack

Ymir (Norse) In mythology, a giant from whom the earth was created
Ymire, Ymeer, Ymeere, Ymyr

Yngram (English) Form of Ingram, meaning "a raven of peace"
Yngraham, Yngrahame, Yngrams, Yngrim

Yngvar (Norse) Form of Ingvar, meaning "a soldier in Ing's army"
Yngevar, Yngvarr, Yngevarr, Yngevare, Yngevare

Yngve (Scandinavian) Refers to the god Ing

Yo (Cambodian) One who is honest

Yoan (Bulgarian) Form of John, meaning "God is gracious"
Yoane, Yohn, Yon, Yoano

Yoav (Hebrew) Form of Joab, meaning "to praise God"
Yoave, Yoavo, Yoavio

Yobachi (African) One who prays to God
Yobachie, Yobachy, Yobachee, Yobachey

Yochanan (Hebrew) Form of John, meaning "God is gracious"
Yochan, Yohannan, Yohanan, Yochannan

Yoel (Hebrew) Form of Joel, meaning "Jehovah is God; God is willing"
Yoell, Yoele

Yoelvis (English) Form of Elvis, meaning "one who is wise"
Yoelviss, Yoelvys, Yoelvyss

Yogi (Hindi) One who practices yoga
Yogie, Yogee, Yogy, Yogey, Yoganand, Yoganande

Yohan (German) Form of Johan, meaning "God is gracious"
Yohanan, Yohann, Yohannes, Yohon, Yohonn, Yohonan

Yohance (African) A gift from God

Yonah (Hebrew) Form of Jonah, meaning "resembling a dove"
Yona, Yonas

Yonatan (Hebrew) Form of Jonathan, meaning "a gift of God"
Yonaton, Yohnatan, Yohnaton, Yonathan, Yonathon, Yoni, Yonie, Yony, Yoney, Yonee

Yong (Korean) One who is courageous

Yorath (Welsh) A handsome lord
Yorathe

Yordan (Hebrew) Form of Jordan, meaning "of the down-flowing river"
Yourdan, Yorden, Yourden, Yordun, Yourdun

Yori (Japanese) One who is dependent
Yorie, Yory, Yorey, Yoree

Yorick (English) Form of George, meaning "one who works the earth; a farmer"
Yorik, Yoric, Yorrick, Yorrik, Yorric, Yurick, Yurik, Yuric, Yurrick, Yurric, Yurrik

York (English) From the yew settlement
Yorck, Yorc, Yorke

Yosemite (Native American) Resembling a grizzly bear
Yosemete, Yosemiti, Yosemity, Yosemitey, Yosemetee, Yosemitee

Yoshi (Japanese) A good-hearted man; one who is free
Yoshie, Yoshy, Yoshey, Yoshee, Yoshio

Yoshiro (Japanese) The good son; a free son
Yoshyro

Yosyp (Ukranian) Form of Joseph, meaning "God will add"
Yosip, Yosype, Yosipe

Young (Korean) One who is prosperous
Yung

Yovanny (English) Form of Giovanni, meaning "God is gracious"
Yovanni, Yovannie, Yovannee, Yovany, Yovani, Yovanie, Yovanee

Yrjo (Finnish) Form of George, meaning "one who works the earth; a farmer"
Yrjos, Yrjon, Yrjan, Yrjas

Yrre (Anglo-Saxon) An angry man

Ysandro (English) Form of Isandro, meaning "the liberator of man"
Ysander, Ysandre, Ysandrow, Ysandroe, Ysandero

Ysbaddaden (Welsh) In mythology, a giant and the father of Olwen
Ysbadaden, Ysbadda, Yspaddaden, Yspadaden, Yspadda, Ysbaddadin, Ysbadadin, Yspaddadin, Yspadadin

Ysmael (English) Form of Ishmael, meaning "God will listen"
Yshmael, Ysmaele, Ysmail, Ysmaile, Yshmaile, Yshmail, Yishmael, Yismael

Yu (Chinese) One who is honored; born during a rainfall

Yudel (Hebrew) Form of Judah, meaning "one who praises God"
Yudele, Yudell

Yue (Chinese) Born beneath the moon

Yuki (Japanese) Man of the snow; one who is lucky
Yukie, Yuky, Yukey, Yukee, Yukio, Yukiko, Yokio, Yoki, Yokiko

Yukon (English) From the settlement of gold
Youkon, Yucon, Youcon, Yuckon, Youckon

Yukta (Indian) One who is attentive and adroit
Yuktah, Yuckta, Yucktah, Yucta, Yuctah

Yule (English) Born during the winter solstice
Yuell, Yuel, Yuwell, Yuwel, Yool, Yul, Yoole

Yuliy (Russian) Form of Julius, meaning "the child of love; one who is youthful"
Yuli, Yulie, Yulee, Yuleigh, Yuly, Yuley, Yulika, Yulian, Yulien

Yuma (Native American) The son of a chief
Yumah, Yumma, Yummah, Yooma, Yoomah

Yunus (Turkish) Resembling a dolphin
Yoonus, Yunes, Yoones, Yunas, Yoonas, Yunis, Yoonis

Yuriy (Russian) Form of George, meaning "one who works the earth; a farmer"
Yuri, Yurii, Yury, Yurochka, Yurey, Yuree, Yure

Yushua (Arabic) Form of Joshua, meaning "God is salvation"
Yushuah, Yoshua, Yoshuah, Yosh, Yoshe, Yusua, Yusuah, Yosua, Yosuah, Yehoshua, Yehoshuah

Yussel (Hebrew) Form of Joseph, meaning "God will add"
Yusel, Yussell, Yusell, Yusele

Yusuf (Arabic) Form of Joseph, meaning "God will add"
Yosef, Yoseff, Yusef, Yuseff, Yusuff, Yosif, Yosiff, Yusif, Yusiff, Yousef, Yousuf, Youseff, Yousuff, Youssof, Yosefu

Yuu (Japanese) A superior man
Yuuta, Yuuto

Yuudai (Japanese) A great hero
Yudai, Yuudae, Yudae, Yuuday, Yuday

Yuval (Hebrew) Form of Jubal, meaning "resembling a ram"
Yuvale, Yuvall, Yubal, Yubale, Yuball

Yves (French) A young archer
Yve, Yvo, Yvon, Yvan, Yvet, Yvete

Z

Zabian (Arabic) One who worships celestial bodies
Zabion, Zabien, Zaabian

Zabulon (Hebrew) One who is exalted
Zabulun, Zabulen

Zacchaeus (Hebrew) Form of Zachariah, meaning "The Lord remembers"
Zachaeus, Zachaios, Zaccheus, Zackaeus, Zacheus, Zackaios, Zaccheo

Zachariah (Hebrew) The Lord remembers
Zacaria, Zacarias, Zaccaria, Zaccariah, Zachaios, Zacharia, Zacharias, Zacherish, Zackariah, Zackerias, Zakarias, Zakariyyah, Zechariah, Zecheriah, Zekariah, Zekeriah, Zackaria, Zakariyya, Zecharya, Zakhar

⊕ ⊕ **Zachary** (Hebrew) Form of Zachariah, meaning "The Lord remembers"
Zaccary, Zaccery, Zach, Zacharie, Zachery, Zack, Zackarey, Zackary, Zackery, Zak, Zakari, Zakary, Zakarie, Zakery

Zaci (African) In mythology, the god of fatherhood

Zadeer (Arabic) Our new son
Zadir, Zadier, Zadeir, Zadyr, Zadear

Zaden (Dutch) A sower of seeds
Zadin, Zadan, Zadon, Zadun, Zede, Zeden, Zedan

Zadok (Hebrew) One who is righteous; just
Zadoc, Zaydok, Zadock, Zaydock, Zaydoc, Zaidok, Zaidock, Zaidoc, Zaedok, Zaedoc, Zaedock, Zadoq

Zador (Hungarian) An ill-tempered man
Zadoro, Zadorio

Zadornin (Basque) A follower of Saturn, god of agriculture
Zadorin, Zadornan, Zadoran, Zadornen, Zadoren

Zadrian (American) Form of Adrian, meaning "a man from Hadria"
Zade, Zadiran, Zadrain, Zadrean, Zadreean, Zadreyan, Zadreeyan, Zadriaan, Zadriano, Zadrien, Zadrin, Zadrino, Zadrion, Zadron, Zadryan, Zadya, Zarjen, Zaydrean, Zaydreean, Zaydrian, Zaydrien

Zafar (Arabic) The conquerer; a victorious man
Zafarr, Zaffar, Zhafar, Zhaffar, Zufer, Zuffer, Zaferr, Zaafar, Zaafer, Zafir, Zhafir, Zaffir, Zafirr, Zafeer, Zaffeer, Zhafeer

Zahi (Arabic) A brilliant man
Zahie, Zahey, Zahy, Zahee

Zahid (Arabic) A pious man
Zahide, Zahyd, Zahyde, Zaheed, Zaheede, Zaheide, Zahiede, Zaheid, Zahied

Zahir (Arabic) A radiant and flourishing man
Zahire, Zahireh, Zahyr, Zahyre, Zaheer, Zaheere, Zaheir, Zuhier, Zaheire, Zahiere, Zhahir

Zahur (Arabic) Resembling a flower
Zahure, Zahureh, Zhahur, Zaahur

Zaim (Arabic) An intelligent leader
Zaime, Zaym, Zayme, Zame, Zaam, Zaem, Zaeme

Zaire (African) A man from Zaire
Zair, Ziare, Ziar, Zyair, Zyaire

Zakar (Babylonian) In mythology, the god of dreams
Zakarr, Zakarre, Zakare, Zakkar, Zaakar, Zaakkar

Zaki (Arabic) One who is pure; innocent
Zakie, Zakee, Zakki, Zhaki, Zakae, Zakkai, Zakkae, Zakai, Zakiy, Zakey

Zale (Greek) Having the strength of the sea
Zail, Zaile, Zayl, Zayle, Zuel, Zaele

Zalman (Hebrew) Form of Solomon, meaning "a peaceful man"
Zalaman, Zaloman, Zolomon, Zallman, Zaleman, Zalomon, Zolemon, Zalemon, Zulema, Zuloma

Zalmon (Hebrew) One who is shady
Zallmon, Zolmon, Zollmon

Zaman (Arabic) The keeper of time
Zamaan, Zaaman, Zamane, Zhaman

Zameel (Arabic) A beloved friend
Zameele, Zamil, Zamile, Zamyl, Zamyle, Zameil, Zameile, Zamiel, Zamiele

Zamir (Hebrew) Resembling a songbird
Zamire, Zameer, Zameere, Zamyr, Zamyre, Zameir, Zameire, Zamier, Zamiere

Zamor (Hungarian) One who plows the land
Zamoro, Zamorio, Zamore, Zamorr, Zaamor, Zamori

Zan (Hebrew) A well-fed man
Zann, Zaan

Zander (Slavic) Form of Alexander, meaning "helper and defender of mankind"
Zandros, Zandro, Zandar, Zandur, Zandre

Zane (English) Form of John, meaning "God is gracious"
Zaan, Zayne, Zayn, Zain, Zaine, Zaen, Zaene

Zanebono (Italian) The good son
Zanbono, Zaynebono, Zaynbono, Zainebono, Zainbono, Zaenebono, Zaenbono

Zani (Hebrew) A gift from God
Zanie, Zaney, Zany, Zanee, Zanipolo, Zanipollo

Zaniel (English) Form of Daniel, meaning "God is my judge"
Zaneal, Zanek, Zanell, Zanial, Zaniele, Zanil, Zanilo, Zanko, Zannel, Zannie, Zanny, Zantrell, Zanyal, Zanyel

Zapotocky (Slavic) From just beyond the stream
Zapotocki, Zapotockey, Zapotoky, Zapotokey, Zapotoki

Zarand (Hungarian) The golden son
Zarande

Zarathustra (Persian) The golden star
Zarathustrah, Zarathust, Zarathurst, Zarathursta, Zoroaster, Zoroester

Zareb (African) The protector; guardian
Zarebb, Zaareb, Zarebe, Zarreb, Zareh, Zaareh

Zared (Hebrew) One who has been trapped
Zarede, Zarad, Zarade, Zaared, Zaarad

Zarek (Greek) God protect the king
Zareke, Zareck, Zaarek

Zasha (Russian) A defender of the people
Zashah, Zosha, Zoshah, Zashiya, Zoshiya

Zavad (Hebrew) A gift from God
Zavade, Zavaad, Zaavad, Zavadi, Zawad, Zawadi, Zaawad, Zawade

Zavier (Arabic) Form of Xavier, meaning "owner of a new house / one who is bright"
Zaver, Zever, Zabier, Zaviere, Zabiere, Zaviar, Zaviare, Zavior, Zaviore, Zavion, Zavian, Zavien

Zayd (Arabic) To become greater; to grow
Zayde, Zaid, Zaide, Zade, Zaad, Zaade, Zayden, Zaydan

Zayit (Hebrew) From the olive tree
Zayat

Zazu (Hebrew) An active man
Zazoo, Zaazu, Zaazoo

Zbigniew (Polish) One who lets go of anger

Zdenek (Slavic) A man from Sidon
Zdeneck, Zdeneke, Zdenecke, Zdenco, Zdenko, Zdencko

Zdravko (Croatian) One who is healthy
Zdravcko

Zdzislaw (Polish) Glorious in the moment
Zdzislav, Zdislaw, Zdeslav, Zdislav, Zdzeslaw, Zdzeslav

Ze (Portugese) Form of Joseph, meaning "God will add"

Zeal (American) A passionate man
Zeale, Zeel, Zeele, Zeyl, Zeyle

Zebadiah (Hebrew) A gift from God
Zebadia, Zebadiya, Zebadiyah, Zeb, Zebe, Zebediah, Zebedia, Zebediya, Zebediyah, Zebedee, Zebedi, Zebedie, Zevadiah, Zevadia, Zevadiya, Zevadiyah

Zebedeo (Aramaic) A servant of God
Zebedio, Zebadeo, Zebadio

Zebenjo (African) One who strives to avoid sinning
Zebinjo, Zebenjoe, Zebinjoe

Zebulon (Hebrew) One who has been exalted
Zebulone, Zebulun, Zebulune, Zevulon, Zevulone, Zevulun, Zevulune

Zedekiah (Hebrew) The Lord is just
Zedekia, Zedakiah, Zedakia, Zedekiya, Zedakiya, Zed

Zeeman (Dutch) Man of the sea; a sailor
Zeyman, Zeiman, Zieman, Zeaman

Ze'ev (Hebrew) Resembling a wolf
Ze'eve, Zeev, Zeeve, Zev, Zeve, Z'ev

Zef (Dutch) Form of Joseph, meaning "God will add"
Zefe, Zeff, Zeffe

Zefirino (Greek) Form of Zephyr, meaning "of the west wind"
Zeffirino, Zeferino, Zefferino, Zefiro, Zeffiro

Zeheb (Turkish) Covered with gold
Zehebb, Zehebe, Zeeheb, Zyheb

Zeke (English) Form of Ezekiel, meaning "strengthened by God"
Zekiel, Zeek, Zeeke, Zeeq

Zeki (Turkish) Having great intelligence
Zekie, Zekee, Zekey, Zeky

Zelen (Croatian) Green; one who is innocent
Zeleny, Zeleney, Zeleni, Zelenie, Zelenee, Zeleno, Zelenio

Zelig (German) Form of Selig, meaning "one who is blessed"
Zeligg, Zelyg, Zelygg

Zelimir (Slavic) One who advocates for peace
Zelimirr, Zelemir, Zelamir, Zelameer, Zelimeer, Zelemeer, Zelimyr, Zelamyr, Zelemyr

Zen (Japanese) One who is enlightened
Zenn

Zenas (Greek) One who is generous
Zenaas, Zenias, Zenase

Zene (African) A handsome man
Zeene, Zeen, Zein, Zeine

Zenith (English) From the highest point
Zenyth, Zenithe, Zenythe

Zeno (Greek) A gift of Zeus
Zenon, Zino, Zinon, Zenos, Zenobio, Zenobo, Zenobios, Zinoviy, Zenoviy

Zentavious (American) A thoughtful man
Zentavios, Zentavio, Zentavo

Zephaniah (Hebrew) God has hidden
Zephania, Zefaniah, Zefania, Zephan, Zephane, Zefan, Zefane, Zephaniya, Zefaniya, Zeph

Zephyr (Greek) Of the west wind
Zephirin, Zephryn, Zephiren, Zepherin, Zephren, Zephrin, Zephyrus, Zephros

Zerachiel (Hebrew) God has commanded
Zerachial, Zerecheil, Zerechial, Zerachiol, Zerechiol, Zerichiel, Zerichial, Zer, Zerr

Zereen (Arabic) The golden one
Zereene, Zeryn, Zeryne, Zerein, Zereine, Zerrin, Zerren, Zerran

Zerind (Hungarian) Man from Serbia
Zerinde, Zerynd, Zerynde, Zerend, Zerende

Zero (English) Having no value
Zeroe, Zerow, Zerowe, Zerro, Zeroh

Zeroun (Armenian) One who is respected for his wisdom
Zeroune, Zeroon, Zeroone

Zeru (Basque) Of the sky
Zeruh, Zeroo, Zerooh

Zeshawn (American) God is merciful
Zeshaun, Zeshan, Zeshane, Zeshayne, Zeshayn

Zesiro (African) The firstborn of twins
Zesirio, Zesero, Zeserio, Zesyro, Zesyrio

Zeth (English) Form of Seth, meaning "one who has been appointed"
Zethe

Zeus (Greek) In mythology, the ruler of the gods
Zeuse, Zeuc, Zeuce, Zews, Zewse, Zoos, Zoose

Zhenechka (Russian) A noble man
Zhenya, Zenechka

Zhi (Chinese) One who has good intentions

Zhivko (Bulgarian) A lively man
Zhivcko, Zhyvko, Zhyvcko, Zivko, Zivcko, Zyvko, Zyvcko

Zhorah (Russian) One who works the earth; a farmer
Zhora, Zorah, Zora, Zorya, Zhorya, Zoryah, Zhoryah

Zhou (Chinese) One who helps others

Zia (Arabic) A brilliant, glowing man
Ziah, Ziya, Ziyah

Ziemowit (Polish) Lord of the household
Ziemowitt, Ziemowitte, Ziemowite, Ziemowyt, Ziemowytt, Ziemowytte

Ziff (Hebrew) Resembling a wolf
Ziffe, Zif, Zife, Zyf, Zyff, Zyfe, Zyffe

Ziga (Sloven) Form of Sigmund, meaning "the victorious protector"
Zigah, Zigga, Ziggah, Ziggy, Ziggi, Ziggie, Ziggey

Zigor (Basque) The punished
Zigore, Zigorr, Zigar, Zigarr, Zigare

Zikomo (African) One who is thankful
Zikom, Zikome, Zykomo, Zykom, Zykome, Zikomio, Zykomio

Zimraan (Arabic) A song of praise
Zimran, Zymraan, Zymran, Zimri, Zimrie, Zimry, Zimrey, Zimree, Zimra, Zimrah, Zimre, Zimreh

Zinan (Japanese) The second-born son
Zinann, Zynan, Zynann, Zinen, Zynen

Zindel (Hebrew) Defender of mankind
Zyndel, Zindele, Zyndele, Zindell, Zyndell

Zion (Hebrew) From the citadel
Zionn, Zione, Zionne, Zionia, Zioniah, Ziona, Zionah

Ziv (Hebrew) A radiant man
Zive, Ziiv, Zivi, Zivie, Zivee, Zivy, Zivey

Ziven (Slavic) One who is vigorous; full of life
Zivon, Zivan

Ziyad (Arabic) One who betters himself; growth
Ziad

Zlatan (Croatian) The golden son
Zlattan, Zlatane, Zlatann, Zlatain, Zlatayn, Zlaten, Zlaton, Zlatin, Zlatko, Zlatcko

Zo (African) A spiritual counselor
Zoe, Zow, Zowe

Zoan (African) One who takes leave
Zoane

Zobor (Hungarian) Of the congregation
Zoborr, Zobore, Zoboro, Zoborro, Zoborio

Zody (American) Form of Cody, meaning "one who is helpful; a wealthy man / acting as a cushion"
Zodey, Zodi, Zodie, Zodee, Zodell, Zodel

Zohar (Hebrew) Surrounded by light
Zohare, Zoharr, Zohair, Zohaer, Zohayr, Zuhair, Zuhar, Zuharr, Zuhayr

Zoilo (Greek) One who is active
Zoylo, Zoiloh, Zoyloh, Zoilow, Zoylow

Zoltan (Hungarian) A kingly man; a sultan
Zoltann, Zoltane, Zoltanne, Zsolt, Zsoltan

Zoltin (Hungarian) A lively man
Zoltinn, Zoltine, Zoltyn, Zoltynn, Zoltyne

Zombor (Hungarian) Resembling a buffalo
Zsombor, Zomboro, Zsomboro, Zomborio, Zsomborio

Zopyros (Greek) A glowing man

Zoraavar (Arabic) Having great courage
Zoravar, Zoraavarr, Zoravarr, Zoravare

Zoran (Slavic) Born with the morning's first light
Zorann, Zorane, Zoranne

Zorba (Greek) One who lives life to the fullest
Zorbah, Zorbiya, Zorbiyah

Zorion (Basque) Filled with happiness
Zorian, Zorien

Zorro (Slavic) Hero of the golden dawn
Zoro, Zorio, Zorrio, Zorriyo, Zoriyo

Zosimo (Greek) One who is able to survive
Zosimio, Zosimos, Zosimus

Zosio (Polish) One who is wise

Zoticus (Greek) Full of life
Zoticos, Zoticas

Zsigmond (Hungairan) Form of Sigmund, meaning "the victorious protector"
Zsigmund, Zsigmonde, Zsigmunde, Zsig, Zsiga

Zsolt (Hungarian) One who is honored
Zsolte, Zolt, Zolte

Zubair (Arabic) One who is pure
Zubaire, Zubayr, Zubayre, Zubar, Zubarr, Zubare, Zubaer

Zuberi (African) Having great strength
Zuberie, Zubery, Zuberey, Zuberee, Zubari, Zubarie, Zubary, Zubarey, Zubaree

Zubin (English) One with a toothy grin
Zubine, Zuben, Zuban, Zubun, Zubbin

Zulekha (African) Our precious son
Zuleka, Zulecka, Zulekah, Zuleckah, Zuleckha

Zulfaqar (Arabic) One who is clever; the name of Muhammad's sword
Zulphaqar, Zulfaquar, Zulphaquar, Zulfiqar, Zulphiqar, Zulfikar, Zulficar, Zulphikar, Zulphicar

Zulu (African) Man from Africa
Zuluh, Zullu, Zulluh, Zoolu, Zooluh, Zooloo

Zuriel (Hebrew) The Lord is my rock
Zurial

Zurley (English) Form of Hurley, meaning "of the sea tide"
Zurly, Zurl, Zurlee, Zurleigh, Zurli, Zurlie

Zusman (Hebrew) One with a sweet disposition
Zusmann, Zusmane, Zoosman, Zoosmann, Zhusman

Zuzen (Basque) One who is just and fair
Zuzenn, Zuzan, Zuzin

Zvi (Hebrew) Resembling a deer
Zvie, Zvee, Zvy, Zvey, Zevi, Zevie, Zevy,
Zevey, Zevee

Zvonimir (Croatian) The sound of peace
Zvonimirr, Zvonimeer, Zvonimire,
Zvonmeere, Zvonimer, Zvonko, Zvoncko

Zwi (Scandinavian) Resembling a gazelle
Zwie, Zwee, Zwy, Zwey

Zygfryd (Polish) Form of Siegfried, mean-
ing "one who enjoys the peace of victory"
Zygfried, Zygfreed, Zigfryd, Zigfreed, Zigfried,
Zygfrid, Zygfred, Zigfrid, Zigfred

Zygmunt (Polish) Form of Sigmund, mean-
ing "the victorious protector"
Zygmund, Zygmont, Zygmond, Zygmunte,
Zygmonde, Zygmunde, Zygmonte

my favorite names:

_____

_____

_____

_____

_____

_____

_____

_____

Visit us at
www.mostbabynames.com

my favorite names:

_____

_____

_____

_____

_____

_____

_____

_____

Visit us at
www.mostbabynames.com

my favorite names:

_____

_____

_____

_____

_____

_____

_____

_____

_____

Visit us at
www.mostbabynames.com